Microeconomic Theory

(7th *Edition*)

Microeconomic Theory

(7th *Edition*)

Dr. H.S. Agarwal

Professor of Economics (Retd.)
Agra College, AGRA

Ane Books Pvt. Ltd.

New Delhi ♦ Chennai

Microeconomic Theory
H. S. Agarwal

Published by

Ane Books Pvt. Ltd.

4821, Parwana Bhawan, 1st Floor, 24 Ansari Road, Darya Ganj,
New Delhi - 110 002, Tel.: +91(011) 23276843-44, Fax: +91(011) 23276863
e-mail: kapoor@anebooks.com, Website: www.anebooks.com

Branch Office:

- Avantika Niwas, 1st Floor, 19 Doraiswamy Road, T. Nagar,
  Chennai - 600 017, Tel.: +91(044) 28141554, 28141209
  e-mail: anebookschennai@gmail.com, rathinam@anebooks.com

ISBN : 978-81-8052-218-5

Printed at : Sagar Colorscan, New Delhi.

Preface to the Seventh Edition

In this present edition, almost every chapter has been revised and the text contains some significant alterations and additions. Besides a number of new chapters added to the existing six parts, two new parts have also been added. All diagrams have been redrawn and recast. *Part One* of the book now includes the new chapters on Methods, Laws and Models in Economics; The Production Possibility Curve and Circular Flow of Economic Activity; Economic Systems; Role of Price Mechanism; National Income; and Objectives of the Firm. *Part Two* on Consumption Theory has been recasted. *Part Three* includes new chapters on Factors of Production; Characteristics of Land and Labour; Division of Labour; Localisation of Industries; Organisation; Types of Business Units; Capital and Capital Formation; etc. *Part Four* incorporates new chapters on Monopsony and Bilateral Monopoly; Full Cost Pricing and Sales Maximisation; and Linear Programming. *Part Five* on Factor Pricing has been fully amended. *Part Six* on Welfare Analysis has been reduced and simplified. *Part Seven* on Theory of International Trade is a new part. It includes six chapters on The Principle of Comparative Advantage; Modern Theory of International Trade; The Gains from Trade; The Terms of Trade; International Trade and Factor Prices; and The Optimum Tariff. *Part Eight* on Taxation is also a new part. It contains three chapters on Tax-A Source of Public Revenue; Direct and Indirect Taxes; and Incidence and Effects of Taxes. In the end of the book select bibliography has been added for further reading.

Besides the above alterations and additions, several new diagrams and illustrations have been added to improve the exposition of the complicated problems of microeconomic theory. Each chapter contains exercises and multiple choice questions to refurbish the memory of the students.

I am confident that this revised edition will not only help maintaining its popularity but will enhance it still further.

The book is primarily meant for B.A. and B.Com. (Pass and Hons.) courses and will be equally useful for the students appearing for various competitive examinations and management courses.

Finally, I thank my hank my wife Dr. (Mrs.) Shobha wife Dr. (Mrs.) Shobha Agarwal and my son Pankaj Agarwal who rendered a lot of help in revising the book. The author also expresses his deep debt of gratitude to Ane Books India for taking pains in bringing out the book in time. The author craves the indulgence of the reader for any errors of omission which he may come across in the course of his study of the book. The ultimate responsibility for the final product is that of the author.

Further suggestions from the teachers and the students for the improvement of the book shall be most welcome.

H.S. Agarwal

Preface to the First Edition

There are many excellent textbooks on microeconomics written by well-known English and American writers. However, none of these can claim to cover the entire courses of study prescribed by Indian universities. Moreover, most of these books are above the understanding of an average Indian student. The present book is an humble effort in this direction.

This book is designed to provide a comprehensive introduction to the subject matter of Microeconomic Theory. It should prove a useful to any student embarking upon a course of study in this subject. It covers the syllabi prescribed by all the Indian universities in microeconomic theory for B.A. and B.Com. (Pass and Hons.) classes.

During the post-war period, countless monographs and technical articles in the various journals have extended the bounds of the economic any Indian science. This vast fund of research has not been included in textbook. The usual textbooks deal only with the orthodox economic principles. Throughout this book, my purpose has been to incorporate these extensions into the main body of the text, merging the newer with the older doctrines. Such a task bristles with difficulties. But I have always tried to avoid the highly controversial issues. Further, I have not attempted to advocate or attack any particular school of economics. My aim has always been to discuss, in impartial terms, the main principles of economics and to make the science of economics comprehensive, and at the same time understandable. Simplicity of language and lucidity of treatment have been followed throughout the book. Further, the explanation of various economic theories has been supported by appropriate tables and diagrams. Diagrammatic treatment often stimulates interest and facilitates understanding, particularly where the student is meeting economic valuations and quantities for the first time.

I do not claim to have provided any new theory in this book. I feel deeply indebted to all economists who have written on the subject, and wherever possible, I have acknowledged my debt to them throughout in the footnotes. I must, however, take full responsibility for the shortcomings of this book.

I also express my grateful thanks to the publishers, Shiva Lal Agarwal & Company and the artist Shri B. D. Seth for their magnificent co- operation in the production of this book.

In the end, I shall appeal to my learned friends and colleagues to favour me with their comments and valuable suggestions for improving upon this book.

H.S. Agarwal

Contents

Part One

BASIC CONCEPTS

Part Two

CONSUMPTION THEORY

Part Three
PRODUCTION THEORY

Part Four

PRODUCT PRICING

Part Five

FACTOR PRICING

Part Eight

TAXATION

PART 1
BASIC CONCEPTS

Chapter 1

NATURE AND SCOPE OF ECONOMICS

1. INTRODUCTION

One of the most controversial topics in economics is the definition of economics. The science of economics is sometimes called political economy or social economy, because it deals with the process by which people as a political group or society attempt to make economical use of the scarce resources of nature. The words *economics* and *economy* both come from the two Greek terms—*oikos* and *nemo*—meaning "household management", the management of the household being one of the most familiar fields for the practice for economy. Just as the family in the household must economise if it is to get the most out of its income, so society at large must utilize its resources wisely, if the production process is to contribute the most that it can, towards meeting the needs and desires of the people. Therefore, it was so since the time of Aristotle who described economics as a household management and stated how it was useful in acquiring, guarding and making proper use of wealth. In the 16th and 17th centuries, mercantilists, who were the leaders of economic thought since the time of Renaissance upto the time of Adam Smith, understood that wealth was useful for the state or the society and, therefore, economics was defined as the study of wealth. Like other social sciences, Economics developed out of the necessity to explain certain aspects of man's social and industrial environment. With the appearance of *Wealth of Nations* in 1776, 'Economics' saw the light of the day. In the early days it was called Political Economy and regarded as a branch of statecraft. Between 1760 and 1840, tremendous development of large scale production due to the Industrial Revolution changed the content of the subject.

At present, there are number of definitions of economics. A critical study of these definitions will make it clear that the growth of economics as a science has been most irregular and hapazard. For simplicity, the various definitions of Economics can be studied under the following four categories:

(1) 'Wealth' Definitions, (2) 'Welfare' Definitions, (3) 'Scarcity' Definitions and (4) 'Growth' Definitions.

2. 'WEALTH' DEFINITIONS

The classical school of economists defined economics as the science of wealth. Adam Smith, the father of modern economic theory, defined economics as ***"an enquiry into the nature and causes of wealth"***. J.B. Say, the follower of Adam Smith, regarded economics as "the practical science of the production and distribution of wealth". In other words, he looked upon economics as the study of the laws that govern wealth. It was an art which enabled people to provide themselves with a revenue sufficient for themselves and the public services. According to the classical economists, self-interest was the only motive which actuated men in all their economic activities. Some of the followers of Adam Smith went further and gave rise to the idea that what economics was concerned with was not the ordinary man, but some sort of "economic man", who was extremely selfish, and who subordinated every other motive to that of earning money. Hence, the classical economists interpreted the term "wealth" in a very narrow sense to mean riches or abundance of money. The science of economics was made to suggest ways and means of increasing wealth of the state.

The "wealth" definition of economics came to be vigorously criticised, especially at the hands of Carlyle, Ruskin, and other literary writers (the German Historical School) of the 19th century. The English classical economists understood that self-interest was the only economic motive in the society. It has long been discarded by the later writers on the subject. According to the Historical School, economics is concerned, not with the activities of an imaginary "economic man," but with those of ordinary man. It does not study only selfish motives. It is not at all concerned with the motives which actuate men in their economic activities. The motives may be selfish, or honest, or altruistic. The economist simply takes them as given data. Further, Adam Smith firmly believed in the harmony between individual and social interests; while the Historical School believed that individual interests were subordinate to social and national interests.

If the term "wealth" is rightly understood, the definition of wealth is more or less correct. As we shall see in the following discussion of the definition of economics, the word "wealth" is used in economics in a special sense. It does not mean riches or abundance of money as is understood in "wealth" definition. In a broad sense, it refers to those scarce goods and services which are used to satisfy the human wants. In other words, wealth is a means and the end is human welfare. Therefore, in economics we study the human activities which centre round wealth. Wants of man lead him to activity. Thus, economics is the study of these activities of man. As such, in economics, we study one of the most important aspects of human life, i.e., activities which lead to his welfare.

3. 'WELFARE' DEFINITIONS

As the 'wealth' definition has given rise to some misunderstandings, the emphasis has now been shifted from 'wealth' to 'welfare'. Marshall was the first economist who gave this idea. According to him, economics is still regarded as a study of wealth; but it is "on the other and more important side a part of the study of man."[1] He states that economics is no longer concerned with motives, but it is concerned with human activities. It does not study the activities of an economic man, but of ordinary man. Thus, Marshall defined economics as follows:

"Political economy or economics is a study of mankind in the ordinary business of life; it examines that part of individual and social action which is most closely connected with the attainment and with the use of the material requisites of well-being. Thus, on the one side, it is a study of wealth and on the other and more important side, a part of the study of man."[2]

The important features of Marshall's definition are explained in the following manner:

1. ***Human welfare.*** Marshall used the term "economics" for "political economy" to make it similar to physics. He assumed that economics must be a science though it dealt with the ever changing forces of human nature.

2. ***Ordinary business of life.*** The classical economists emphasized

1. Marshall A., *Principles of Economics,* p. 1.
2. *Ibid.*

wealth in their definition of economics, but Marshall emphasized both mankind and wealth. As he puts it, economics is "a study of mankind in the ordinary business of life". It is a study of human beings, not of animals or plants. Further, it deals with the economic aspect of the life of human beings. There are number of activities of man, viz., political, social, religious and economic. Economics is not concerned with the social, political and religious activities of man. It is concerned purely with the economic activities of man. The term 'ordinary business of life' relates to how a person earns his income and how he spends it. More specifically, it relates to whether to produce this or that, whether to sell more or less at a certain price, whether to buy more or less, this or that, whether to accept work on a certain wage or not—all these are the problems which the economists fruitfully studies.

3. ***Wealth is a means.*** In Marshall's definition, wealth is not considered as an end in itself but as a means to welfare, as a source of the betterment of the human life. Further, it does not study the whole of human welfare but only apart of it, i.e., *economic* or *material welfare.*

After Marshall, Pigou also clearly defined economics as a study of economic welfare. His definition runs as follows:

"The range of our enquiry becomes restricted to that part of social welfare that can be brought directly or indirectly into relation with the measuring rod of money."[3]

This definition increases the scope of economics. It included all goods, material or non-material, which take a money price.

Edwin Cannan also defined economics in the following way:

"The aim of Political Economy is the explanation of the general causes on which the material welfare of human beings depends."

Criticisms of Welfare Definitions

The 'welfare' definition of Marshall and Pigou has in recent years been criticised on several grounds. The main critic of the 'material welfare' definitions is Prof. Lionel Robbins.[4]

1. ***Economics is only a social science.*** Marshall assumes economics as a social science rather than as a human science. A social science studies the activities of those individuals who are the members of the society; while a human science studies all human beings, whether they live in an organised community or live outside the society. Although, Marshall used

3. Pigou, A.C., *Economics of Welfare,* p. 1.
4. L. Robbins, *An Essay on the Nature and Significance of Economic Science,* 1932.

the word 'individual and social action' but by relating their activities to the measuring rod of money, he narrowed the subject matter of economics to the study of persons living in the society using some type of currency. Broadly speaking, the fundamental laws of economics apply to all human beings and, therefore, economics should be treated as a human science and not as a social science.

2. ***Classificatory.*** Marshall's definition is assumed to be classificatory. He stated that economics dealt with only those activities which are not closely connected with the attainment and with the use of the material requisites of well-being. It means that there are two types of human activities—economic and non-economic: Activities which are related to wealth, are economic activities and those which are not related to wealth, such as, political, social and religious are non-economic activities. Prof. Robbins objected to this type of distinction. He points out that in actual life, the distinction between the material and the non-material things is not so clear-cut as is assumed by Marshall. There are several things in our daily life which satisfy our basic needs, but they are not material in any sense of the term. According to Prof. Robbins, an economic problem will arise wherever scarce means are involved in the satisfaction of certain wants. Such a problem will arise even in the case of a person who lives outside the society and may not perform any economic activity in the sense of Marshall. Therefore, economics should study the economic problem wherever and whenever it is found.

3. ***Material welfare.*** According to Marshall, only those activities connected with the production and consumption of goods and services which aim at increasing material welfare can come under the scope of economics. In other words, Marshall's definition gave emphasis to economic welfare, while Prof. Robbins would have nothing to do with welfare at all. He points out that there are several activities which come under the purview of economics, but are hardly conducive to welfare. For example, activities relating to alcoholic drinks satisfy human wants and are studied in economics, but they are not conducive to human welfare. Prof. Robbins, therefore, states that "whatever economics is concerned with, it is not concerned with the causes of material welfare as such".

4. ***Impossibility of quantitative measurement.*** Further, the critics point out that welfare cannot be quantitatively measured. Even if money price is used as an instrument for the measurement of welfare, it is only a rough and not a satisfactory measure of welfare. When two persons pay the same price for a commodity, it would not mean that both are getting

an equal amount of utility or welfare. The welfare (utility) of a relatively poor person will be more than the other.

On the above grounds Prof. Robbins criticised the 'welfare' definition and developed a new definition of economics. His definition is also known as 'scarcity' definition. We shall discuss this definition in the following section.

4. 'SCARCITY' DEFINITIONS

Until the beginning of 20th century, the 'welfare' definition of Marshall and Pigou was undoubtedly accepted by all the economists. But the publication of Prof. Robbins' book, ***An Essay on the Nature and Significance of Economic Science*** in 1932 created doubts in the minds of some economists regarding the welfare definition of Marshall, Pigou and others. In his book, Prof. Lionel Robbins defined economics in the following way:

"Economics is the science which studies human behaviour as a relationship between ends and scarce means which have alternative uses."

The main features of this definition may be analysed as below:

1. ***Human wants (ends) are unlimited.*** In our daily life we perform a number of wants. The fulfillment of one want gives rise to a number of new wants. Hence, wants are numerous and it is very difficult, rather impossible, to satisfy all the wants of a person. Therefore, a few urgent wants are made to be satisfied.

2. ***Means are scarce.*** The means of a person by which his wants may be satisfied are limited. It leads to an economic problem as to which wants are to be satisfied by these limited means—time and money at his disposal. No economic problem will arise if means are also unlimited.

3. ***Alternative uses of scarce means.*** According to Robbins, for an economic problem the limited means should have alternative uses. If there are specific uses of these limited means, i.e., each may be put to only a single use and to none else, then there will be no economic problem as such. Therefore, means should have their alternative uses.

4. ***Problem of choice.*** Further, the alternative uses of the limited means should possess varying degrees of importance, so that a fair selection among the different uses is possible. According to Milton Friedman, an economic problem exists whenever scarce means are used to satisfy alternative ends. If the means are not scarce, there is no problem at all; there is *Nirvana.* If the means are scarce but there is only a single

end, the problem of how to use the means is a technological problem. No value judgements enter into its solution; only knowledge of physical and technical relationships.[5]

Hence modern economics is said to be based upon a theory of scarcity and choice. We should look at some of the reasons for this particular view of the subject. We know that to an economist, all economic goods (i.e., goods which command a price) are scarce goods. The word "scarce" is used in a relative sense; economic goods are scarce in relation to the desire for them. Since wants are many but the resources available for their satisfaction are limited in supply, we are faced with a problem of choice. We cannot have more of everything. At any given moment of time the economic resources (raw materials, machines, factories, land and labour) are limited and so, therefore, is the quantity of goods and services which these resources can produce. The economic problem is how best to use the resources available at any given time to satisfy human wants; how to achieve the highest level of economic welfare with the means available.

An individual is constantly confronted with this problem of choice. He has a limited income and must, therefore, choose between alternatives when he spends his income. He must decide whether to buy cigarettes or spend the money on books; to spend more on clothes or more on entertainment. Just as a person or a family has to make these choices in disposing of their earnings, so as a society has to choose between alternative uses for the means it has available.

The above economic problem developed the concept of *opportunity cost.* The true cost of using economic resources in any given project (or industry) is the loss of the alternative output which they might have produced. If we use a certain amount of land, labour and capital to build a factory, the economic cost (or opportunity cost) of the factory might be the houses which these resources could have produced. Hence, the *opportunity cost* represents the loss of the next most desired alternative. The purchase of a cinema ticket could be viewed in terms of the alternatives forgone—the opportunity cost might well have been a new fountain pen or a textbook of economics.

Again, the problem of choice which we find in Robbins' definition is universal. It is found everywhere and in all times. For, under the Robbins' definition, rich and poor, the businessman and the administrator of the nation, all are reduced to a common denominator. In other words,

5. Milton Friedman, *Price Theory,* 1962, p. 6.

economics is not so much concerned with the theories of production and distribution of wealth, rather it is concerned with certain aspects of human behaviour. According to Eric Roll, "The laws which shall be derived from this definition shall be applicable to all the societies. The laws of choice, like the laws of gravitation, will be independent of the legal and political framework in which they work."[6] Similarly, Wickstead puts it, "Its laws are the laws of life and are applicable to fields that have no connection whatever with business or production of wealth." Hence the problem of choice has to be solved in dictatorships and democracies, in planned and unplanned economies, although different methods are applied in different economies.

Criticisms of 'Scarcity' Definitions

This definition is also not free from criticisms. According to the critics this definition of economics does not attach due importance to the social character of economics. An economist is not concerned with individual behaviour of individual ends unless and until the individual activities have consequences on other persons' behaviour or ends. For example, the problems of Robinson Crusoe are of no importance to the people of the modern society. The main criticisms of these definitions are the following:

1. ***Human welfare is ignored.*** According to Boulding,[7] Robbins' definition makes the jurisdiction of economics too narrow. Economics is not only a study of "scarce means", but also of human welfare, for welfare is an end in itself.

2. ***Social character.*** Prof. Chaircross suggests that to emphasis the social character of economics, the definition given by Robbins should be modified as follows: "Economics is a social science studying how people attempt to accommodate scarcity to their wants and how these attempts interact through exchange."[8] It means that according to Chaircross the 'scarcity' definition converts economics into a pure science, a science that is concerned with the formulation of economic laws. It has nothing to do with the practicability of these economic generalisations. Most of the modern economists accept the Chaircross' modification of Robbins' definition.

3. ***Absence of practical aspect.*** According to critics, the definitions of Robbins' is based on theoretical analysis of human conduct. In this

6. Eric Roll, *The Elements of Economic Theory,* p. 17.
7. Boulding, *Economic Analysis,* Chap. 1.
8. Chaircross, *Introduction to Economics,* Chap. 1.

definition there is no place for morality and human welfare. There is complete absence of practical aspect in the Robbins' definition. This definition is purely theoretical.

4. ***No difference between ends and means.*** Another criticism of Robbins' definition is that this definition does not distinguish between 'ends' and 'means'; because means are mere sources of enjoyment and the 'end' is nothing but satisfaction. Hence, enjoyment and satisfaction are one and the same thing.

5. ***Widended the scope of economics.*** According to critics, Robbins has unnecessarily widened the scope of economic science. He did not agree with Marshall on the point of limiting the scope of economics merely to the human activities which can be measured with the aid of money. If this concept of Robbins is accepted, then in the absence of money, economics would become barren.

6. ***Welfare aspect ignored.*** The end of human activities is human welfare. Robbins did not appreciate the end of human activities. He accepted that the end of human behaviour was to get maximum satisfaction by the use of limited resources at his disposal.

7. ***Non-economic aspect.*** In Robbins' definition, a number of non-economic problems have been included under economic aspect. For example, when a person chooses to divide his time between work and leisure, it becomes a problem of economics. But in case the person spends his leisure for reading, writing and sleeping, economic problem does not arise.

In spite of the criticism, the Robbins' definition presents the true picture of an economic problem. This is the reason why Prof. Robbins' definition is known as the best definition of economics.

Comparison between Robbins' Definition and Marshall's Definition

The definitions of economics as given by Marshall and Robbins have similarities as well as dissimilarities. The main points of similarity and difference can be discussed in the following manner.

Similarities. We find the following similarities in the two definitions:

(1) Both Marshall's and Robbins' definitions emphasise on the point that under economics we study man and his actions.

(2) Both the definitions have ignored the importance of wealth and have laid emphasis on the study of man and his activities.

(3) Robbins' and Marshall's definitions are similar in the sense that there is no fundamental difference between scarcity and welfare. What early economists called as 'wealth', Marshall called it as

'requisite of well being' and Robbins called it as 'scarce means'. Thus, 'wealth', 'requisite of well being' and 'scarce means' indicate one and the same thing in different terminology.

Dissimilarities. The main points of differences between the two definitions are the following:

(1) According to Marshall, economics is a social science under which we study the actions of those persons who live in the society. While according to Marshall, economics is a human science under which we study the conduct of all human beings whether they live in the society or not.

(2) According to Marshall, the scope of economics is limited, while according to Robbins, the scope of economics is sufficiently wide.

(3) Marshall's definition is based on materialistic conception and is, therefore, classificatory. Further, Marshall has distinguished between material and non-material, economic activities. While, on the other hand, Robbins' definition is analytical. He analyses human behaviour and states that human behaviour is the subject matter of the science of economics.

(4) Marshall, in his definition, states that human behaviour is the ultimate 'end' of the science of economics. According to Robbins, the science of economics is 'neutral' between' 'ends' . He states that there is no relationship between welfare and economics.

5. 'GROWTH' DEFINITIONS

The 'growth' definition of economics has been given by a number of modem economists. This definition is very similar to that of Robbins' definition. It has 'modified the static view of 'scarcity' definition. According to Prof. Boulding, there are three types of human activity which may be described as "economic", viz., production, consumption and exchange. Study of these activities involves enquiry into certain "quantities", e.g., output of goods, the amount of accumulated stocks prices, wages, interest and rent. These things are called "economic quantities". ***Economics is a scientific study of economic quantities.*** The collection of figures relating to economic quantities is the task of economic statistics and economic history and their interpretation is the task of economic analysis.[9]

Here, the views of Prof. Samuelson are also of great importance. According to him, ". . . . **logically there is nothing fundamental about**

9. Boulding, *Economic Analysis,* Chap. 1.

the traditional boundaries of economic science. In fact, a system may be as broad and as narrow as we please depending upon the purpose at hand; and the data of one system may be the variables of a wider system depending upon expediency. The fruitfulness of any theory will hinge upon the degree to which factors relevant to the particular investigation at hand are brought into sharp focus."[10] Further, he puts economics as "the study of how men and society choose, with or without the use of money, to employ scarce productive resources which could have alternative uses, to produce various commodities over time and distribute them for consumption now and in the future among various people and groups of society."

The most important implication of his 'growth' oriented definition is that it is not only dynamic in its scope but it is applicable even in a barter economy where money measurement is absent. The problem of choice may take place in a barter economy as well as in a money economy. The inclusion of time element makes the scope of economics dynamic. Human wants are not fixed or static. They change over time. Therefore, Samuelson's definition presents the choice problem in its dynamic setting. This definition also possesses universality in its applicability. Hence, it is an improvement over and above the 'scarcity' definition of Prof. Robbins.

6. SCOPE OF ECONOMICS

In order to know the scope of any particular science, it is necessary to know the nature of the subject-matter, its peculiarities and the objectives of its study. We have already known something about the subject-matter of economics from its definitions.

On the basis of definitions, we can say that economics studies man's life and work, not all aspects of it, but only a part of it. Economics is not concerned with how a person is born, how he grows up and dies. Economics also does not study how a human body is made up and how it functions. This is the task of Physiology. Similarly, economics is not concerned with the organisation of State and its functions. This is the job of political science.

There are different views regarding the scope of economics. According to Prof. Pigou, **"Economics is a positive science of what is and what tends to be; it is not a normative science of what ought to be."** This type of view narrows the scope of economics too much.

10. Paul A. Samuelson, *Foundations of Economic Analysis,* p. 9.

Sometimes, it is not possible to discuss "what is" without the knowledge of "what ought to be". On the other hand, Prof. Viner states that **"economics is what the economists do".** This type of view widens the scope of economics too much. The economist performs many things which are entirely different from scientific discussion. Now to determine the scope of economics, we must understand the aim of economic studies. According to Prof. Marshall, the scope of economics includes the study of physical facts and human activities relating to production, consumption, exchange and distribution of wealth. Naturally, the study is concerned primarily with those activities which can be measured in terms of money. This part of economics can be called a positive science. It includes such rules of practical guidance in social and economic affairs as may be formulated by economists. Further, it includes a normative part, i.e., a discussion of how existing facts may be altered for the betterment of mankind. Hence, it is possible to state the scope of economics in more specific terms. Economics deals with problems relating to the consumption, production, exchange and distribution of wealth. Economists find out the ways by which the efficiency in production can be increased; they investigate the causes of low productivity, depression, unemployment and poverty. Again, the economists suggest the steps which can be taken for the removal of these evils from the economic system. According to Keynes,[11] the scope of economics should include the following:

(1) Subject-matter of economics,
(2) Nature of economics,
(3) Relation of economics with other subjects.

I. Subject Matter of Economics

Since the time of Adam Smith uptill now economists have given different opinions regarding the subject matter of economics. With the change and development of social conditions, the subject matter of economics has also changed. If we look at the history of economic science, we may find that at first the main subject matter of economics was "Wealth." Adam Smith and other classical economists considered economics as a science of wealth. The neo-classical economists added welfare in the subject matter of economics. Thus, in the time of Marshall it was considered as the science of both wealth and welfare. Marshall confined the subject matter of economics to the consumption, production, exchange and distribution of wealth by men engaged in the ordinary business of life.

11. J. M. Keynes, *Scope and Method o/Political Economy.*

Men who are rational and act under the existing social, legal and institutional set-up. It excludes the behaviour and activities of socially undesirable people like drunkards, misers, etc. According to Robbins and other modern economists, economics studies man and its behaviour. According to them, we are all aware of those matters 'which may be described as "economic"— production and productivity, unemployment, the location of industry, the size off firms, monopolies, wages, profits, rent, interest, taxation, exports, imports, etc. He cites numerous examples to show that certain human activities possess a definite economic significance but have little or no connection with material welfare. The same commodity or service may promote material welfare at one time and under one set of circumstances and not at another time under different circumstances. Robbins is, therefore, of the opinion that for a commodity or service to have economic importance, it must be related to price; and for a commodity or service to command a price, it is not essential that it must definitely promote material welfare, rather it must be scarce and capable of being put to alternative uses. Thus economics is not related so much with the analysis of the consumption, production, exchange and distribution of wealth as with a special aspect of human behaviour; that of allocating scarce means among competing ends. Thus the subject matter of economics is mainly concerned with the economic problem of the household, firms, and the administrative bodies.

But it is not possible to say exactly whether economics is related to wealth or human behaviour or scarce resources.

According to Boulding,[12] there are three types of human activity which may be described as economic: (*i*) Production, (*ii*) Consumption, and (*iii*) Exchange.

Production is the process whereby man transforms the resources available to him (land, labour and capital) into the products which people want, making them available where they are wanted. It, therefore, includes all the operations which are required to provide the suit in the tailor's shop; operations which began no doubt on an Australian sheep farm, etc.

Consumption is the process of using up the products of man's labour; the wearing of clothes, the use of transportation, the use of a television set, the use of a house, etc.

The acts of ***Exchange*** make up by far the greater part of the subject matter of economics. According to Boulding the 90 per cent part of economic analysis comes under exchange. In general, goods are exchanged for money and this money is subsequently exchanged for other goods and exchange. Prof. Boulding states that exchange not only includes the money exchange of goods and services, but it also includes the determination of prices of factors of production (land, labour and capital) as well as the price determination of commodities in the market. Since the exchange of factors of production and their price determination are separately studied, the study related to factors of production is named as distribution.

We all recognise the purchase and sale of a commodity as an act of exchange. For instance, the acts of exchange are the renting of houses, the hiring of labour, and the lending of money. When a house is rented, the use of the house is exchanged for a money payment. When money is borrowed, the use of "present" money is exchanged for "future" money. The amount repaid in the future is greater than the amount borrowed by a sum of money known as interest. The interest is the payment made for the use of money during the period of the loan. Similarly, when labour is hired, the person exchanges hours of labour for a money payment known as wages.

But if the subject matter of economics is viewed on micro basis, then it is clear that the entire micro economics is the analysis of the theories of price determination based on demand and supply of commodities. On demand side we study the laws of consumer behaviour, while on supply side we study the laws of production. The situation of market equilibrium is studied under exchange. Hence, economics is concerned with the production, consumption and exchange of goods and service. But it is not sufficient merely to see that these activities are carried on. We must also see the *quantities* which are involved in these activities. The economist is interested in the factors which determine the output of cloth, the number of persons unemployed, the wages of workers, the tariff on imports and the price of steel, etc. All these are economic quantities.

A further part of the subject matter of economics is devoted to the organisations which control and direct a large part of economic activity of our country. The acts of production, consumption and exchange are performed by individuals, but the individual usually carries out his economic activities as part of some organisation. In the case of the one-man business, the individual is acting on his own behalf, but most people work for a limited company, a local institution, a public corporation or a government department. It is within and through such institutions that the greater part of economic activity takes place. Further, ***Public Finance***

12. K.E. Boulding, *Economic Analysis,* Vol. I., *Microeconomics,* IVth Edition, pp. 3-4.

is that part of the subject matter of economics which is concerned with the income and expenditure of Public Authorities (the Government and local authorities). There has been a great expansion in those services provided by the state which are required for the enforcement of regulations designed to protect the community as a whole or certain groups within the community. Life in a civilized society is extremely complex and calls for a vast range of regulations which impose and enforce certain standards of conduct on the industrial, commercial and civilian communities. The state now intervenes extremely in economic life in order to achieve specific social and economic ends. Economic laws which govern the government (or state) activities are studied under Public Finance.

Thus economics is a social science concerned with the proper use and allocation of scarce resources for the achievement and maintenance of growth and stability.

2. Nature of Economics

In order to understand the nature of economic laws, we have to indicate whether economics is a science or art? If it is a science, then is it a positive science or a normative science? In order to answer these questions, it is essential to know what science is and to what extent the characteristics of science are applicable to economics.

(1) ***Is Economics a Science?*** The systematized body of knowledge regarding a subject is commonly defined as "science". A science is not a mere collection off acts, but it indicates a relationship between cause and effect. In other words, it studies uniformities pervading a subject and tries to find out generalizations which we call laws. In this sense, physics is a science because it studies certain uniformities regarding the external universe. Also psychology is a science that studies the uniformities of the mental world. In the same sense, economics can also be regarded as a full-fledged science, because it studies the uniformities of human conduct in the ordinary business relations. It investigates the possibility of deducing generalizations as regards the behaviour of human beings and their economic motives. Hence, economics is a science, because it tries to discover the universal out of the chaotic facts. According to Prof. Marshall, "The economist seeks to discover the many in the one, the one in the many."

Some writers point out that the phenomena of science must be easily amenable to measurement. Here the claim of economics to be regarded as a science is based upon the fact that it deals with that part of man's actions which can be measured by the measuring rod of money. Like the chemist's balance, economics has an external measure for measuring human motives, and the measure is furnished by dollars or rupees, etc. Thus, of all social sciences, economics is the most exact; because none of the social sciences has got any external measure to make possible a definite quantitative measurement.

Here, one should remember that human motives cannot be accurately measured and that the moving forces of economic action can only be measured roughly and imperfectly. Therefore, economics which is the most perfect of all social sciences, is not exact as the physical science, because it deals with human motives which are very complex. Although man is a rational being having the capacity of reasoning logically about the consequences of particular actions. In the large majority of cases human actions in response to a particular set of circumstances will follow a particular pattern. Marshall observed that, "Uniformity of reason implies some uniformity in human affairs." Therefore, it is possible to formulate economic laws. But there are always exceptional individuals who may behave in an irrational manner. The economist assumes that such persons form only a small minority. But since they exist, we must accept that the laws of economics are true only in "general", i.e., they are statements which are true in the majority of cases and not universally. The physical sciences have developed a large body of laws possessing universal validity; and capable of quantitative measurement. But economics cannot claim to have discovered such laws of universal validity, because of the nature of the subject matter of economics the behaviour of mankind.

Again, the existence of "free-will" in men prevents economics from being a science. Economists cannot claim precision for their laws. As men have free will, what guarantee is there that men will behave similarly under similar circumstances, so that there might be a homogeneous group of human actions for our study of economic science? But even admitting that men have free will, it is possible to build up an economic science on the following grounds: (*i*) There are certain experiences which do riot come within the purview of man's choice. Man cannot decide to feel pleased or sorry. These uncontrollable experiences help the economists to for in general laws. (*ii*) Some economic experiences of man are governed by laws of external nature beyond his control, e.g., the law of diminishing returns. (*iii*) Free will does not mean that men act unreasonably. Even if they do so, we are in a position to foretell the course of their activities by means of the mathematical law of probability. But, on the whole, men behave reasonably. People usually buy a thing where it is cheap. A producer will sell more if the price of product increases. Because of this fact, we can predict the future course of human activities, and frame general laws.

Further, some writers say that "economics is not a science because economist disagree". According to Mrs. Barbara Wootton, "Whenever six economists are gathered, there are seven opinions."[13] This criticism is not true, because doctors frequently disagree but none contends that the study of medicine is not a science. Economists will not disagree so far as the facts are concerned; they may disagree on questions of policy. Moreover, the policy recommendations depend on the ethical ideas and political views. In a developing science, there are always differences of opinion.

It is, no doubt, true that economic prophecies are often found to be false by subsequent events. The reason for this must be sought, not in the unscientific nature of economic studies but in our ignorance of the causes at work. The laws of biology are not always borne out by subsequent events; but no one would, on that ground, deny that biology was not a science. The onset of a trade depression (economic forecast) can often be predicted a much longer time in advance than the coming of a cyclone (meteorological forecast). It means that sometimes economic forecasts are more reliable than meteorological forecasts. Therefore, the task of the economist is the same as that of the natural scientist—to apply the processess of sustained and unbiased argument to the data of observation and to determine the general laws of all events. Hence, the claim of economics to be regarded as a science cannot be denied on the ground that it lacks precision and prophetic power.

Now we can say that economic science is ordinarily regarded as a dry collection of abstract formulas having only a remote relation to the realities of human existence. The interests of all men are fundamentally compatible, that there is and can be no antagonism between the welfare of one and the welfare of all, that all mankind can live in peace and prosperity, provided that violence or threat of violence is reserved exclusively for the maintenance, by the State, of a tree market in which goods and services are voluntarily exchanged without coercion from any quarter.

(2) ***Nature of Economic Laws.*** There are various meanings of the term 'law'. It may mean a rule established in a community, permitting or prohibiting a course of action; it may mean a rule of procedure as the

13. Barbara Wootton, *Lamentfor Economics* (1938), p. 14.

laws of games; it may mean an Act passed by the legislature; and it may mean a statement of causal relationship between two groups of phenomena. An economic law is a statement of tendencies, i.e., a statement that under certain conditions, we may assume a definite course of action from human beings in the aggregate. An economic law affirms that if certain causes exist, certain results are bound to ensue. All natural laws are laws in the same sense. Things fall on the ground as a result of the pull of the gravity, if nothing interferes to prevent them from falling. So also in economics, economic laws represent certain economic tendencies or principles expressing what is likely to happen, other things being equal. For example, the law of demand states that, *ceteris paribus,* demand for a commodity, will increase if its price falls and vice versa. According to Prof. Marshall, **"A law of social science is a statement of social tendencies; that is, a statement that a certain course of action may be expected under certain conditions from members of a social group. Economic laws, or statements of economic tendencies, are those social laws which relate to branches of conduct in which the strength of the motives chiefly concerned can be measured by a money price."**

Here it is important to note that economic laws deal with human behaviour. Human nature is not constant, and at times inconsistent; hence, economic laws can predict what men usually will do, but not with certainty what they actually will do. The laws of natural sciences are precise and exact. The law of gravitation is an exact statement and it is used for many mathematical calculations regarding the movement of the heavenly bodies. Therefore, the laws of economic science are not exact as those of the natural sciences. Economic facts can be modified by human effort, but a law of physics cannot be modified by human effort. According to Seligman, "An economic law is a natural law so far as it states that given conditions will lead to given results. An economic law is not a natural law so far as it implies that human effort is important in modifying the conditions which lead to the results." Marshall has also pointed out that "the laws of economics are to be compared with the laws of tides rather than with the simple and exact law of gravitation." This means that economic laws as statement of tendencies, are only approximate. The laws of tides state how there is a rise and fall of tides twice a day under the influence of the sun and the moon, how there are strong tides at new and full moon, etc. Thus, these laws predict at what time the tide will probably be the highest on any day. Here the word 'probability' is used, because tides may not come at the expected hour owing to many unforeseen circumstances. Similarly, there are many unforeseen circumstances in human activities, as a result of which the expected course of action may not occur. It is why Prof. Seligman states that "economic laws are essentially. Hypothetical". It means that economic laws are conclusions drawn from certain assumptions or hypotheses. The economic relationship between cause and effect is subject to the condition that other things are equal. The proviso "other things being equal" is contained in all economic laws. But other things are not always equal and consequently in economics, definite conclusions cannot be predicted from definite" facts. Economic laws are, therefore, described as hypothetical.

But in this sense, economic laws do not differ from other scientific laws. The laws of all other sciences are also hypothetical, i.e., they start from certain hypotheses and deduce certain consequences. As Prof. Marshall has pointed out, every scientific law will always contain conditions or the proviso "other things being equal". Then, what is the difference between the physical and economic law? The only difference is that the hypothetical element is specially prominent in economics. In physics, though there may be a complexity of forces at work, they can be definitely measured, and the results predicted. In economics, many of the forces cannot be measured; hence, no definite result can be predicted.

To conclude, economic laws, like scientific laws, would be correct if the assumptions are not inconsistent with one another and if the reasoning process is logical. If unpracticable or contradictory assumptions are made, the conclusions are not relevant or of value.

(3) ***Economics as a Positive or a Normative Science.*** There are two types of science a positive science and a normative science. According to Keynes, "A positive science may be defined as a body of systematized knowledge concerning what is; a normative science or regulative science is a body of systematized knowledge relating to the object of what ought to be, and concerned with the ideal as distinguished from the actual. The object of a positive science is the establishment of uniformities; of a normative science the determination of ideals." These two conflicting views regarding the nature of economic science have been prevalent from the earliest days. Keynes also states that "The theory of economics does not furnish a body of settled conclusions immediately applicable to policy. It is a method rather than a doctrine, an apparatus of the mind, a technique of thinking which helps its processors to draw correct conclusions." According to this view, the object of economic science is to point out why certain effects follow from certain given causes. This means that the economist deals with facts and figures. He is to explore and explain, but not to point a moral or adorn a tale.

The positive character of economics has also been explained by Robbins in the following words: "It enables us to describe the distribution of resources which, given the valuations of individuals concerned, satisfies demand most fully. But it does not by itself provide any ethical sanctions. To show that, under certain conditions demand is satisfied more adequately than under any alternative set of conditions does not prove that the set of consideration is desirable. There is not a penumbra of approbation round the theory of equilibrium." Therefore, economics is not concerned with the rightness or wrongness of the existing social structure. For example, the economist cannot condemn the drink-trade, though as a social reformer he might oppose it; but as an economist, he is bound to consider the economics of the drink-trade. Further, economist cannot give any final judgement on any matter. For example, if in a society adopting a policy of living wage it is generally assumed that the gain by the absence of wage payments below the standard of living more than compensates for the unemployment and that losses it involves, such a policy cannot be condemned off-hand as undesirable. Policy is always based on a compromise between the economic, ethical and political aspects. The role of economist is to analyse the facts arid to supply the results to the statesmen. Now, it is the task of the statesmen and the reformers to apply the results for increasing the welfare of the society.

Hence the old English Classical School was of the opinion that economics was purely a positive science which had no right to comment upon the rightness or wrongness of economic policy. The 20th century economist, Prof. Robbins gave similar views regarding the nature of economics. It is on this ground that Robbins and his followers are assumed to be as the Neo-classical School. The Historical School of Germany gave just the contrary view. These economists emphasise the normative functions of economics, According to Hawtrey, "Economics cannot be dissociated from ethics." This means that a strict neutrality on the ethical aspect of economic analysis cannot be maintained, for every step in economics carries an ethical import. Even Prof. Marshall states that "the ethical assumption which must always be present before the economist is that both the productive and monetary systems should be organized so as to open up to all the material means of a refined and noble life." According to Pigou, "Economic science is chiefly valuable neither as an intellectual gymnastics, nor even as a means of writing truth for its own sake, but as a handmaid of ethics and the end of all economic activities is to promote human welfare. In other words, it is difficult to have an exclusively positive science even if we desire to do so. The economist cannot be as objective in his investigations as the physical or the chemist can. As Friedman puts it, economics is sometimes divided into two parts: positive economics and normative economics. The former deals with how the economic problem is solved; the latter deals with how the economic problem should be solved. For example, the effects of price or rent control on the distribution of income are problems of positive economics. On the other hand, the desirability of these effects on income distribution is a problem of normative economics. Therefore, economics is a positive science as well as a normative science.

(4) ***Economics as an Art.*** The use of systematic knowledge is an 'art'. According to Prof. Keynes, "An art is a system of rules for the settlement of a given end." In this sense economics is an art. The economist presents the ways based on his theoretical knowledge and experience which help in reaching the optimum situation. For example, the law of equimarginal utility tells a consumer how to maximise his total utility or satisfaction.

More specifically, in order to make the decision, three kinds of information are required: (*i*) a knowledge of the alternatives open to the decision-maker; (*ii*) a knowledge of the consequences of choosing each of the alternatives, and (*iii*) a criterion or rule that tells the decision-maker which of the sets of consequences is the most valuable to him. For example, a producer is trying to decide how much of a commodity to produce. His range of alternatives then consists of each of the possible quantities his industry is capable of producing. The consequences of choosing each alternative can be summarised by means of two numbers for each: the cost of producing that amount and the revenue which can be obtained from selling it. Now the objective of the producer is to make his profits as high as possible. This is his criterion; therefore, he searches the alternatives for the one which provides the greatest difference between Total Revenue (*TR*) and Total Cost (*TC*). The economic law that marginal cost equals marginal revenue will provide this situation.

Therefore, economics is both a science and an art simultaneously.

3. Relation of Economics with Other Subjects

The human behaviour is very complex. It is impossible to categorize it. Economics is a study of human activities which are affected by the circumstances and traditions of the *society—(i)* legal, (*ii*) political, (*iii*) religious, (*iv*) moral, etc. These activities of human behaviour are so intermixed that it is impossible to separate them in watertight compartments. In other words, human nature is indivisible. We study it in many social and human sciences, namely, history, psychology, sociology, politics, statistics, ethics, etc. In each social science we study some particular aspect of human behaviour. Thus, all social sciences are related and it is not possible to separate them. Economics is also a social science. Therefore, economics is closely related to all social sciences which deal with human behaviour.

Economics and Sociology. Sociology deals with the fundamental facts of all social life—economic, political and historical, etc. and, therefore, it is the general social science. Since economics is also one of the sciences, it is not possible to separate it from sociology. According to Comte, "Economics cannot claim to be a separate science, but must be included within sociology." It means that sociology is an all-comprehensive social science. It takes into consideration all the conclusions arrived at by different social sciences to make further conclusions. In other words, sociology is the fundamental social science of which other social sciences are but differentiations. On the other hand, economics is a branch of sociology. It studies a particular aspect of human behaviour, not the whole of it.

Economics and Politics. Both Economics and Politics deal with human activities and are therefore, closely related. It is why the earlier writers used to regard Economics as a branch of Politics. The Greeks regarded Political Economy as the art of providing revenue for the state. Modern writers regarded economics as an art to be employed for farthering the purposes of the state.

Economics is the science of wealth in relation to man. Economic welfare of a country depends upon the system of government. Every modern government is closely connected with economic matters.

Further, the political organization of a country is often a reflex of its economic organization. Political movements are profoundly influenced by economic causes. State-socialism, Syndicalism, Fascism, and many other movements are not merely economic movements, but are political movements as well. Hence, the two are closely related.

Economics and Ethics. Economics and Ethics are also closely related. Ethics deals with principles of morality while economics deals with actually existing facts and the human welfare. But human behaviour is always influenced by moral considerations. Men's actions are usually guided by their ideas of what is proper. In other words, the normative aspect of economic science is economic ethics. The discussion of the relation of wealth to welfare shows the essentially ethical bent of the science. As we have already mentioned, economics is the handmaid of ethics and the end of all economic activities is to promote human welfare.

Further economic conclusions give certain data for the study of ethics and nom these data ethics draws further conclusions. According to Seligman, "Economics, like ethics, is primarily a social science, the true economic action must in the long run be an ethical action."

Economics and History. History is a record of past events which also include economic events. The economist learns much by a study of past experiences. Historical facts can be used to formulate new economic theories. Their correctness may also be tested by the historical facts. Hence, the study of history is of a great help to the economist. Sir John Secley has summed up the mutual relationship between History and Economics in the following words: "Economics without History has no root. History without Economics has no fruit." History is a record of human behaviour and it is also a part of society. Thus, under both Economics and History, we study the human behaviour. It is, therefore, obvious that History and Economics are mutually related. A knowledge of history is important for correct appreciation of economics. Similarly, a knowledge of economics is essential for correct appreciation of history.

Economics is the foundation of History. According to Karl Marx, "History can be explained only through economic events. In order to have a correct knowledge about any system of Government, it is always necessary to have knowledge about the contemporary economic conditions and events of the country."

Economics and Statistics. Today, various methods of mathematical statistics are applied to the problems of economics. The economist, therefore, must have a fairly good grounding in the fundamentals of mathematical statistics. Since much of what is written in the field of economics and in other social sciences involves statistical analysis, any serious student of economics must know these fundamentals. Statistics, specially modern statistical theory, is of great importance to economists. Statistical methods of sampling are already useful for collecting the data which are the raw material of economic studies. Statistics has the additional advantage of giving an idea about the reality of the data. The use of probabilistic models is particularly suitable in the measurement of economic relationships that are difficult to measure exactly because of number of sources of error. Errors arise in economic data and relationships for a number of reasons. Firstly, there are errors of measurement. For example, a country's exports or imports are unlikely to be measured with complete accuracy as mistakes will be made on invoices, customs officials will often incorrectly record prices and quantities of goods moving into or out of customs houses and mistakes will be made in adding up individual items to get an export or import total. Secondly, errors are introduced when economic data are compiled on sampling basis. Thirdly, errors may arise because of random shocks such as war, natural disaster or variations in the weather. The economist makes use of various statistical methods to remove these errors as far as possible. Hence, the techniques of statistical inference enable the economist to make probabilistic statements concerning the parameters of theoretical models of economic processes.

Economics and Geography. Economics and Geography are also intimately related. Under Geography, we study man and the physical conditions around which he lives. Under Economics, we study the physical conditions which affect human behaviour. Thus it is clear that Economic and Geography are closely related.

Again, there are certain topics which are studied under both the subjects, e.g., climate, mineral resources, forests, animals, natural resources, etc.

Further, the economic conditions and development of a country is greatly Influenced by its natural conditions. Therefore, Economics and Geography are closely related.

Economics and Psychology. As we know, Psychology is the science of mind. Under Psychology, we study the mental state of man and actions of his mind. The economic behaviour of man is purely the result of this mental behaviour. Since behaviour is conditioned by mind, economics is related to Psychology. The economic laws such as the Law of Diminishing Marginal Utility, the Law of Demand and the Law of Supply, etc. are based on Psychology. Hence, Psychology has always helped economic development. According to Robbins, "An economist should be a Psychologist also." The economic laws and facts can be tested through Psychology. Similarly, Economics also influences the Psychological laws.

Economics and Natural Sciences. Economics is related to natural sciences like Physics and Chemistry. Natural sciences deal with natural objects. Economics and Natural Sciences are to great extent complementary to each other. The laws of economics are influenced by natural factors. Various discoveries made in the field of natural sciences affect economics. Economics creates a number of problems which the scientists have to tackle and solve. This has led to a number of researches in the field of natural sciences. Thus economics and technology go together. According to Prof. Stigler, "Whereas the economist is concerned only with the best allocation of scarce means among the competing ends, the technologist studies the best means to attain a specific end."

EXERCISES

1. Explain the nature and scope of economics.
2. "Economics is a study of man's actions in the ordinary business of life." Discuss.
3. Analyse different definitions of economics. Which of these definitions explain the correct nature of economics? Give reasons.
4. "Economics studies human behaviour as a relationship between unlimited ends and scarce resources having alternative uses." Do you agree with this statement?
5. "The science of economics has both positive and normative aspects." Explain.
6. Explain the nature of economics as a positive science and normative science. Is it a social science?
7. "Whatever economics is concerned with, it is not concerned with the causes of material welfare as such." (Robbins) Discuss.
8. "Economics is a social science studying how people attempt to accommodate security to their wants and how these attempts interact through exchange." Explain the statement.
9. "Economics is neutral between ends." (Robbins). How far is this statement valid in a welfare state?
10. "Economics may be defined as the study of the allocation of scarce resources among competing ends." Examine the statement.

Multiple Choice Questions

11. (*i*) "The meaning of the word 'economic' is most closely associated with the word
    (*a*) free (*c*) unlimited
    (*b*) scarce (*d*) unrestricted [*Ans.* (*b*)]

    (*ii*) Wealth definition is given by
    (*a*) classical economists (*c*) modern economists
    (*b*) neo-classical economists (*d*) all of the above [*Ans.* (*a*)]

    (*iii*) Welfare Definition of Economics is mostly associated with the name of
    (*a*) Adam Smith (*c*) Robbins'
    (*b*) Marshall (*d*) Samuelson [*Ans.* (*b*)]

Chapter 2

ECONOMIC THEORY AND PRACTICE

1. MEANING OF ECONOMIC THEORY

Economics is a science which, like any other science, depends on an organised body of theoretical knowledge. Theoretical knowledge is based on facts. Such facts based on verified hypothesis are converted into the status of a theory.

According to Boulding, **"Theories without facts may be barren, but facts without theories are meaningless."**[1] A theory, in fact, expresses a causal relationship between two sets of phenomena, one as cause and the other as effect. Marshall defined a scientific theory as "a general proposition or statement of tendencies, more or less certain, more or less definite." Every cause has a tendency to produce some definite result, if nothing happens to prevent it. Things fall on earth as a result of the pull of gravity, if nothing interferes to prevent them from falling.

Economic theories or economic laws represent certain economic tendencies or principles expressing what is likely to happen, other things being equal. For instance, the law of market demand states that *ceteris paribus,* consumers increase their purchases of the community when its price falls and vice versa. The phrase, "other things being equal"indicates the limitations within which many, if not all, economic laws operate. Human nature is changing and at times inconsistent; hence economics can predict what men usually will do, but' not with certainty what they actually will do.

Prof. Ernest Nagel defines an economic theory as a set of statements, organised in a characteristic way and designed to serve as partial premises for explaining as well as predicting an indeterminately large (and usually varied) class of economic phenomena.

1. K.E. Boulding, *Economic Analysis* (3rd ed.), p. 2.

2. THE NATURE OF ECONOMIC THEORY

The aim of economics, like all other sciences, is to obtain generalisation or laws which would help us to understand the past and offer trustworthy guidance for the future. The task of a scientist is the discovery of laws. Every science uses terms such as hypothesis, theory and laws. We have a tentative hypothesis of facts. If the hypothesis can explain new facts and is not contradicted by new discoveries, it may be called as a theory. If a theory continues to stand test of time and experience, a law may be formulated.

The following steps are required to formulate an economic theory:

(1) ***Selection of the Problem.*** The first step is to clearly define the problem, because the following steps will depend upon the problem which is to be solved. The problem may be related to an individual unit (i.e., a consumer or a producer or a firm) which will be a problem of microeconomics, or it may be related to the entire society (i.e., the problem of unemployment, poverty or inflation, etc.) which will be a problem of macroeconomics.

(2) ***Collection of Data.*** Once the problem is cleared, the second step is to collect the necessary data or facts pertaining to the problem to be explored. If the problem is related to micro units, then the data can be easily collected. But if the problem is related to macro units, then it may require many months or even years to collect the necessary data.

(3) ***Classification of Data.*** After data collection, the next step is to arrange the data according to the aspects of the problem. For example, if the problem is to study the changes in the composition of population, then the census data may be collected and classified by sex, age groups, literacy, marital status, occupational distribution, etc.

(4) ***Formulation of Hypothesis.*** After data classification, the researcher has to formulate the hypothesis. A hypothesis is a suggested answer to a problem by the nelp of which the cause and effect relationship is to be explained. The hypothesis is formed on the basis of the observed facts, experience or previous knowledge of the researcher. Here the researcher has to make certain underlying assumptions and conditions under which the hypothesis is to be tested. For example, the assumption may be that a consumer wants to maximise his satisfaction or total utility, i.e., on the basis of this assumption the theory of consumer behaviour can be developed.

(5) ***Testing of Hypothesis.*** After the formulation of hypothesis, the researcher has to test it. He has to see whether the formulated hypothesis

explains the facts considered or not. The hypothesis should be tested by well established statistical techniques. Here the hypothesis should provide the answer to the problem which led to the inquiry. A successful tested hypothesis becomes a theory, otherwise it is to be rejected.

(6) ***Verification of Theory.*** The tested hypothesis i.e., the theory may be verified by observation or by checking the consistency of the theory with related facts. When the theory is verified and proved true, possible solutions to the problem are formulated. Thus in the final stage, it becomes a law which can be established in the economy.

3. APPLICATIONS AND USES OF ECONOMIC THEORIES

(1) ***To Provide Tools of Economic Analysis.*** Economic theories provide economic tools to the economists by which they analyse the economic problems of microeconomics and macroeconomics. They are applicable to all economic systems and all the countries of the world.

(2) ***Interpretation of Economic Phenomena.*** With the help of economic theories, the economists may interpret and explain the economic phenomena of the real world. They can also suggest the possible solutions to the prevailing problems in various countries.

(3) ***Basis for Predicting Unobserved Economic Events.*** Economic theories may explore the economic problems of the real world. For example, if we find that with the increase in the supply of sugar, the prices do not fall, given the demand for sugar, we can predict that there is likely to be shortage of sugar in the near future. The reason may be some natural calamity or expectation of some emergency in the economy.

(4) ***Formulation of Economic Policies.*** The government has to seek the advice of the economists to formulate various public policies such as tax policy, export-import policy or policy of public expenditure. Here on the basis of various relevant economic theories, the economists are able to suggest the policy measures to the government related to various economic problems.

(5) ***Judging the Performance of the Economy.*** Economic theories help in judging the performance of various sectors of the economy.

4. LIMITATIONS OF ECONOMIC THEORIES

(1) ***Lack of Reliable Data.*** All economic theories are based on available data related to the problem. If the data are not accurate or sufficient, then the theories will become unrealistic.

(2) ***Lack of Correct Predictions.*** Economic theories are not able to make correct predictions regarding various issues, as they are based on human behaviour. The probability of accurate predictions in economics is much less than in physical sciences.

(3) ***Unrealistic Assumptions.*** The assumptions, on which the economic theories are based, are not realistic. For example, we assume that consumers and producers beliave rationally. But we fmd that they never behave rationally. According to Boulding, "Economic analysis is not a perfect picture of economic life; it is a map of it. Just we do not expect a map to show every tree, every house, and every blade of grass in a landscape, so we should not expect economic analysis to take into account every detail and quirk of real economic behaviour."[2]

(4) ***Not Applicable to Economic Policies.*** Economic theories are not fully applicable to formulate economic policies, because the assumptions on which these theories are based become unrealistic in the context of the subject undertaken. They are different to actual economic situation. For example, most economic theories are based on the assumption of perfect competition and full employment. Now such situations are rarely in existence and therefore, the theories based on such assumptions can not be applied to form the economic policies for that particular area or field.

5. ECONOMIC POLICY (PRACTICE) AND ECONOMIC THEORY

Economic policy (practice) or applied economics provides a practical picture of an economic theory. In practice, we make use of several economic theories and principles for analying the actual conditions of the economy. In fact economic policy and economic theory are closely related to each other. One can not exist without the other. For economic policy to be successful, it has to be framed on the basis of economic theories. For example, if the society aims at maximing its advantage then the social budget should be prepared with the help of the economic principle of maximum social advantage. Thus it is the knowledge of economic theories and principles that leads to the formulation of economic policies. According to Richard G. Lipsey, "The role of the economist is not only to analyse the consequences of a proposed policy (or to compare

2. K.E. Boulding, *op. cit.,* p. 11.

two or more policies), but also to suggest policies applicable for certain specific issues."[3]

EXERCISES

1. Explain the nature and limitations of economic theory. How is economic theory related to policy?
2. What do you mean by an economic theory? How is it formulated?

Multiple Choice Questions

3. (*i*) "Theories witbout facts may be barran, but facts without theories are meaningless." This statement is given by
    - (*a*) K.E. Boulding
    - (*b*) Richard G. Lipsey
    - (*c*) Musgrave
    - (*d*) John F. Due

   (*ii*) A theory expresses
    - (*a*) the behaviour of people
    - (*b*) a causal relationship between cause and effect
    - (*c*) a positive relationship between dependent and independent variables
    - (d) all of the above. [*Ans.* (*b*)]

   (*iii*) A theory is
    - (*a*) an assumption
    - (*b*) a hypothesis
    - (*c*) a validated hypothesis
    - (d) an if-then proposition [Ans. (*c*)]

---

3. Please also go through the matter given under positive and normative science in 'chapter 1.

Chapter 3

METHODS AND MODELS IN ECONOMICS

1. INTRODUCTION

Every science has its own methods of investigation. Broadly speaking, there are two methods of scientific studies available to the economist: (*i*) Deductive or Abstract Method, and (*ii*) Inductive or Historical Method. The deductive method involves reasoning from a few fundamental propositions, the truth of which is assumed. In other words, here first the principal factors in operation in any field of investigation are determined and then the consequences that will ensue from the operation of these factors under given conditions, are deduced by a process of reasoning. Therefore, deductive method descends from the general to the particular. The inductive method, on the other hand, involves collection offacts, drawing conclusions from them and testing the conclusion by other facts founded on experience. Therefore, 'under inductive method, we go from the particular to the general. Here economic theorems (laws) are based on observed facts.

During the 19th century, there was a bitter controversy between the Classical School of Britain and the Historical School of Germany on the relative uses of deductive and inductive methods. The classical economists of the 19th century (J.S. Mill and others) used the deductive method, while the Historical School (notably Hildebrand and Frederick List) and Statistical School of modern times, uses the inductive method to formulate economic laws and theorems. It was first Schmollar and then Alfred Marshall who attempted to resolve the controversy between the deductive and inductive methods of economics. In the words of Alfred Marshall,

"... induction and deduction are both needed for scientific thought as the left and right foot are both needed for walking."[1]

Now we will explain the merits and demerits of the methods in the following section..

2. DEDUCTIVE METHOD

This method is also known as the abstract, hypothetical or the "a priori" method of economic analysis. The classical and neo-classical economists applied the deductive method in their investigations. They tried to deduce the whole of economic science from certain generalisations about human motives and habits. This method is called "hypothetical," because some of the assumptions or axioms may not correspond to the facts, but they are so near to the facts that they may be used as generalisatioins for drawing inferences. This method is also known as "abstract" method because the phenomenon is simplified after removing all the irrelevant facts. Therefore, under this method, economics provides certain analytical tools and principles which are assumed to be logically consistent and universally held and hence, no historical or empirical evidence is warranted to test them. For example, every consumer wants to achieve maximum satisfaction from his given limited income. Any evidence is hardly required to support it. It is a self-evident truth. Similarly, it is also self-evident truth that every firm tries to maximise its profits. For drawing further conclusions, we also assume that there is perfect competition in the market. In such a situation the price of a comm odity is given for a firm. Therefore, to attain maximum profit, a firm will continue her production until the marginal cost equals the price of the product or marginal revenue. In other words, we conclude that for profit maximisation a firm should produce at a point where marginal cost equals marginal revenue. In brief, deductive method may be described as the technique of an abstract or 'a priori' approach to the problems of economic science. From this, it is clear that under deductive process of study, we move to "general" from "particulars". When a general truth is found, which itself proves, then there cannot be any doubt about this truth. Once we are able to know the truth, it is taken to be fundamentally right and there does not arise any controversy about its truth and definiteness.

However, according to Adam Smith, the founder of classical school, the deductive method is not an exclusive method. It is aided by inductive method in the formulation of economic laws and theorems. As Prof.

1. Alfred Marshall, *Principles of Economics,* p. 24.

Keynes pointed out, "Smith first raised political economy to the dignity of a deductive science, but he has also been regarded as the founder of the historical method (inductive method) in political economy."[2] Thus, Adam Smith used every method of economics that helped him in his investigations.

After Adam Smith, Malthus emphasized inductive reasoning in support of his population theory. But the later English School regarded Ricardo rather than Malthus for popularisation of the deductive method of reasoning. Later on, Senior, Mill and Walter developed the abstract method or deductive method of economics. According to Nassau William Senior, "The subject treated by the political economist is not happiness but wealth; his premises consist of a few general prepositions, the result of observation or consciousness and scarcely requiring proof or even formal statement which almost every man, as soon as he hears them, admits as familiar to his thoughts or at least as included in his previous knowledge and his inferences are nearly as general and, if he has reasoned correctly, as certain as his premises."[3] Thus, in the views of Prof. Senior, economics was a positive science where the conclusions were deduced 'a priori' from general considerations.

J.S. Mill and others also expressed similar views. According to them, the problem should be stated in the simplest form and then it should be gradually made complicated, because the actual world is very complex and complicated. If we deal with the complicated problems directly, then we will not be able to draw any final conclusion. For example, J.S. Mill stated that the subject of international trade is very complicated in itself. For this, Mill starts with very simple assumptions and then gradually introduces more and more complicated issues in his analysis till he derives a complete theory of international trade. Hence, the classical economists held the view that political economy was an abstract science where the conclusions were based upon few fundamental assumptions.

The deductive method, as used by modern economists can also be described as the method of *Intellectual Experiment.*[4] Here, Boulding argues that economic analysis includes price, wages and other various economic quantities. The real world of economic quantities and their relationships is very complicated. It is very difficult, rather impossible to understand the various economic effects of even a simple economic

2. Keynes, J.M., *The Scope and Method of Political Economy.*
3. Senior, N.W., *An Outline of the Science of Political Economy.*
4. K.E. Boulding, *Economic Analysis,* Chapter 1.

activity. In such situations, conditions and postulates which are simpler than reality are first assumed and the consequences are worked out. Gradually, more and more complex assumptions are introduced until reality is approached.[5]

This method is very similar to the method of pure mathematics. As Prof. Jevons argues, economics is essentially mathematical in character, taking the term math ematical to mean all enquiries that deal with quantitative relations. Economics is concerned with those phenomena whose quantitative aspect is of fundamental importance, and in those phenomena this method may be used gainfully.

Therefore, the deductive method may be classified into two types: (*i*) *non‑mathematical deductive method,* and (*ii*) *mathematical deductive method.* The former was used by the classical and neo-classical economists while the latter was used by the modern economists. Edgeworth (1845-1926) was the only economist who applied mathematics to a considerable extent in the economic analysis in the 19th century. Later on, in France and Italy, the mathematical method occupied an important place in the development of economic analysis. In the words of Heinrich Von Stackelberg, "Wherever quantitative analysis is necessary, there mathematics is employed ... for the latter is only another name for quantitative analysis ... All that mathematics can do is to produce precise thinking even about imprecise data.' The modern writers are of the opinion that the mistake ofthe classical writers is their starting with insufficient data. According to Gide and Rist, "Even when the premises were correct, they were too ready to think and not careful enough to prove that their conclusions were always borne out by facts. No one can defend their incomplete analysis, their hasty generalisations or their ambiguous formulae."[6] The mistake of the classical school was not that they adopted the deductive method, but that they had too often mistaken the abstraction for the reality. The fault does not lie in the method, but in the doctrinal theory of some of the writers. Thus, Stiglar points out the profitability of mathematics in economics by saying that "mathematics can exhaust the implications of known quantitative relationships and it can often wring (squeeze) much information from only generally defined relationships. Mathematics is indeed the queen of sciences. Without mathematics one can give only an intuitive proof of complicated relationships; such as

5. *Ibid.,* p. 11.
6. Gide and Rist, *A History of Economic Doctrines,* p. 396.

those expressed by Euler's theorem, Slutsky's equation, the theory of general equilibrium and certain theorems in the theory of games." Today, diagrammatical and mathematical methods occupy an important place in economic theory.

The chief advantage of such method is that it leads to higher standards of precision in abstract economic reasoning. Chances of mistake are few. Another advantage of this mathematical deductive method is that it explains the relation of mutual dependence which may exist between different economic variables such as supply, demand and price. But the chief defect of this method is to attach too much importance to the method itself. It leads to intellectual toys and the real end disappears in the intellectual gymnastics of mathematical treatment. It is why Alfred Marshall opposed too frequent and avoidable use of mathematics. He stated. "The chief use of pure mathematics in economic questions seems to be in helping a person to write quickly, shortly and exactly, some of his thoughts for his own use; and to make sure that he has enough, and only enough, premises for his conclusion. But when a great many symbols have to be used, they become very laborious to anyone but the writer himself."[7]

Advantages of Deductive Method

The following are the main advantages of the deductive method of economics:

(1) ***Simplicity.*** Deductive method was not only used intensively by the classical economists, but it is also used in modem times. It is admitted that the use of deductive method is a very simple task. We start from a few assumptions and derive a number of conclusions. Therefore, it helps us to get results without any botheration of collecting facts and studying them.

(2) ***Limited Use of Experimentation.*** The use of experimentation is very limited in economics and that increases the importance of this method of economics. As we know that experimentation can be made to a greater extent in the physical and chemical science, but the method of experimentation is not available in economic science and therefore, the best alternative is to adopt the method of deductive reasoning. The deductive method does not assume the necessity of experimentation in economic analysis.

---

7. A. Marshall, *op. cit.*, p. 9.

(3) ***Use of Logic and Mathematics.*** As we have noted above, the deductive method is today known as mathematical method. It makes use of logic and mathematics which results in accurate conclusions or generalisations. Due to enough application of mathematical formulae, there remain very few chances of mistakes or inaccuracies in drawing inferences.

(4) ***Certainty and Clarity.*** Deductive method of analysis leads to exactness and certainty. This method is based on logic which is said to be an unfailing companion. If the reasoning is correctly used and assumptions are rightly taken, we always get correct conclusions. This method can easily correct the mistakes and results become quite clear.

(5) ***Effectiveness.*** This method is very effective, if its assumptions are true. With the help of this method, we may forecast about the future. We can easily say that under certain given conditions how the individuals will react. For example, if the price of a commodity goes up, we can easily forecast that the demand for that commodity will fall, while the supply of the same will rise.

(6) ***Universality.*** The theories derived under the deductive method of reasoning are found to be universally true. They hold good in every country and in every period of history. For example, the law of diminishing utility states that if a number of units of a commodity are given to one person, he must feel after a certain stage that the utility of additional units will diminish.

(7) ***Impartiality.*** The results deduced from this method are impartial. They are not affected by any favour or prejudice.

(8) ***Suitability.*** This method is most suitable in the study of economic science. Since man is a rational being, he cannot be put to much experiment. It is with the help of reason alone that we can rightly interpret the human behaviour.

(9) ***Complementary.*** According to Prof. Cairnes, "The method of deduction is incomparable when conducted under perfect checks, the most powerful instrument of discovery ever wielded by human intelligence." It is clear that where inductive method fails, it is the deductive method of analysis that comes to our rescue.

Limitations of Deductive Method

In spite of its advantages, the deductive method suffers from a number of limitations also. The main critics of the deductive methods are economists of the Historical School, which flourished mainly in Germany. They argued that theories must emerge if only adequate statistical or historical evidence is available to support them. According to their view, theories developed without facts are baseless. In the context of rapid changing circumstances no hypotheses may be assumed universally true. If the entire economic analysis is based on such axioms then the conclusions deduced from them will not be reliable. In brief, we find.the following important limitations of the deductive method.

(1) ***Lack of Reliability.*** Since classical theories are based on the aforementioned universally held axioms, they are true only when the axioms hold good. In other words, the condition of *ceteris paribus* is assumed throughout the process of reasoning. But most of these assumptions are not true in the changing world and therefore the conclusions drawn from them lack reliability.

(2) ***Lack of Empirical Evidence.*** The followers of deductive method do not think it necessary to test their theories on the basis of facts or empirical evidence. Therefore in deductive process, there is danger of being too much abstract.

(3) ***Lack of Personal Experience.*** This method ignores the importance of personal and historical experiences. It leads to conclusions having little or no connection with reality. If such results are applied in the formulation of government policies, then it will be followed by disastrous consequences.

Due to the above limitations of the deductive method, the economists belonging to the Historical School of Germany (notably Schmoller, Knies, Hildebrand, Roscher, etc.) developed a new method known as induction method of studying economic phenomena.

3. INDUCTIVE METHOD

This method is also known as historical, empirical or 'a posteriori' method of economics analysis. The German School of economists advocated this method. They develop the economic science from economic history. They study particular instances from economic history and draw general conclusions from them. These conclusions are further verified by reference to subsequent economic facts. Thus, under this method *we go from particular to general.* The followers of this method believe that economic theory and economic laws have only a relative value. It is not possible to uniformally apply an economic law to all the countries and in all periods of history. The economists verify their conclusions from observation and analysis by subsequent economic facts. Observation and experiments are the chief instruments of this method. In this method, we make an attempt to connect the economic laws with reality and practical facts.

The rapid development in the science of statistics during recent years and the collection of data by governments and private individuals have enhanced the value of this method. From the data thus collected, valuable and scientific conclusions have been drawn. In this way the theorems and theories developed by this inductive method are more accurate and perfect than the abstract or deductive method.

According to Prof. Boulding, the inductive method may be classified into two types:[8] (1) Experimental Method, and (2) Statistical Method. Now we explain these forms in the following manner:

(1) ***Experimental Method.*** Prof. Boulding states that the experimental method has been very popular in chemistry, biology and other physical sciences; but it cannot be applied in economics except in narrow limited fields. This method tests the validity of the generalisations (arrived at as a result of deductive reasoning) by resorting to the study of actual facts.

Since the economist lacks the laboratory facilities, he is unable to make necessary experiments. Moreover, economics is concerned with the behaviour of human beings where the experiments are not possible. As Prof. Albert L. Meyers states, "Human beings have wills of their own and resent being treated as guinea pigs for the purpose of social experimentation."[9] The economist, therefore, uses the statistical method.

(2) ***Statistical Method.*** This method consists in collecting figures regarding economic phenomena. The figures may be used to prove or disprove propositions derived theoretically or to correlate different phenomena and draw conclusions.

In economics, the statistical method is used as substitute for the controlled experimental method. Therefore, it fulfills the requirement. The statistical method is applied in the collection, classification and tabulation offacts and also applied to draw conclusions. Its results are based on sampling method and therefore covers the entire population (or region). For example, if we want to study the consumption pattern of one thousand labourers. Now we will apply the sampling technique where the family budgets of a sample of labourers (may be one hundred) will do the needful. The sampling method is a scientific procedure. Its results are reliable and we may also investigate the errors.

Advantages of Inductive Method

The inductive method of economics possesses the following main

8. K.E. Boulding, *op. cit.*, pp. 10-12.
9. Albert L. Meyers, *Elements of Modern Economics,* p. 2.

advantages:

(1) ***Reliability of Economic Analysis.*** The economic generalisations derived by this method are more reliable than the same under deductive method. Such generalisations are made on the basis of collected facts of the real world.

(2) ***Formulation of Sound Policy.*** The conclusions arrived at by the process of induction may be tested on the basis of facts. They may be revised according to the changes in statistics. Such results are very well used .in the formulation of government policies.

(3) ***Based on Scientific Procedure.*** Under statistical method, we draw inferences on the basis of a representative sample. If we increase the size of the sample, then we may get more accurate results.

(4) ***Universality.*** Since inductive reasoning is based on empirical facts, it may explain clearly the problem of any class, region or country. Such generalisations or theorems are based on very sure and realistic facts, and as such, their validity cannot be challenged.

(5) ***Complimentary.*** The inductive method of reasoning is of positive advantages where the deductive method fails to interpret the results. Thus this method possesses the advantage of being complementary. We can easily testify the results drawn through deductive method by putting the results under experiments.

(6) ***Development of Mental Capacity.*** With the help of this method, we can develop our mental capacity and increase our knowledge. It is possible because under this method, we clarify and verify the historical events by analysing the facts under which causes and effects are involved.

Limitations of Inductive Method

The inductive method is also not free from criticisms. It has been criticised on the following grounds:

(1) ***Faulty Statistics.*** The statistical method or induction should be used with caution because statistics are in many cases faulty and co-relation is not causation. If two facts appear together, we cannot conclude that one causes the other; all that we can say is that there is a possibility that they may be so connected.

Moreover, the statistics related to human behaviour should not be assumed unbiased. Therefore, statistical results are accurate only on approximation.

(2) ***Limited Scope.*** Generally, we may not be able to collect data regarding all the economic units, of the phenomena in all circumstances. It is very difficult to say whether the sample represents the entire

population. This is the reason why theories based on induction lack the predictive power so profoundly embedded in the deductive method. Theories related to the pricing of products and productive services and macroeconomic theories of employment, interest and national income, are all deduced from certain widely accepted principles. Likewise, modern welfare propositions have also been deduced from the general, ethical principles of humnn behaviour.

(3) ***Imperfection.*** The inductive method alone is unable to draw accurate economic generalisations unless it is supplemented by a process of deductive reasoning. Of course, it is true that we must establish and know the facts first of all. No science can develop without data or with incomplete data. The conclusions formed by general reasoning must also be verified by facts. To admit that is not to admit the uselessness of the deductive method. As Prof. Durbin states, "Facts do not speak for themselves. It is only by analysis, comparison, hypothesis and prophecy that they can be made to speak at all."[10] No science can develop without the aid of reason and hypothesis. Without the use of deductive reasoning, the historical or inductive method runs the risk of remaining purely descriptive. It can serve only to accumulate a mass of unconnected and unserviceable facts.

(4) ***Costly Method.*** The inductive method is very costly. Collection of facts and data involve a number of experiments and require much investment. It is also necessary to provide sufficient training to the persons who are put for collection of data and conducting experiments.

(5) ***Biased Results.*** The conclusions drawn with the help of this method are often not impartial. They are generally found prejudiced on account of individual likes and dislikes.

Complementarity of the Two Methods

As we have noted that neither the inductive method alone nor the deductive method alone can serve the purpose of economic analysis and investigation. Different methods are appropriate to different branches of economics. The mathematical method or the deductive method is very suitable for the theory of value while in trade cycles and monetary theory, inductive or statistical method is appropriate. Thus, both deduction and induction are useful in economic analysis. Hence, the two methods seem to be really complementary rather than rival methods. According to Pareto,

10. Durbin, "Methods of Research" in the *Economic Journal,* June 1938, p. 187.

"Discussion of method is a pure waste of time. The aim of the science is to discover economic uniformities, and it is always right to follow any path or to pursue any method that is likely to lead to that end." Marshall also observed, "Induction and deduction are both needed for scientific thought as the left and right foot are both needed for walking."[11] Adolf Wanger, a leading economist of the historical school also felt that "the true solution of the contest about method is not to be found in the selection of deduction or induction, but in the acceptance of deduction and induction. Each must be employed in the cases where it is specially adapted to the particular nature of the problem to be solved, and, as far as possible—for it is not always possible—there must be a combination of both, although in concrete cases one or the other will take precedence." It means that both the methods maybe profitably employed by economists but in different propositions for different purposes.

Today, the modern economists find it more appropriate to blend the two approaches. According to Lipsey and Steiner, "Both induction and deduction are used in the scientific method which is applied in economic analysis."[12] Prof. Samuelson also remarks, "Properly understood, theory and observation, deduction and induction cannot be in conflict."[13]

4. CONCEPT IN MODEL BUILDING

Meaning of Economic Models

Economic theory is mainly concerned with relationships among economic variables. Demand function, consumption function, cost function, production function are some of the examples of the relations which are to be faced by all economists. In fact, the entire body of economic theory can be regarded as a collection of relations among variables. The universe of the study is very complex. Many factors affect one economic variable at one time. The main task of an investigator is to sort out the economic variables which are most closely linked with the phenomena we are going to analyse. The projected goal of a researcher is to reduce the economic analysis, as far as possible, to directly linked factors. It would be a happy state of affairs if important relationships could be reduced to simple mathematical formulas manipulated in mechanical ways. It is also very important to understand a theory well. Thus a concrete and well defined-

11. 'Alfred Marshall, *op. cit.,* p. 24.
12. Lipsey and Steiner, *Economics.* p. 22.
13. Samuelson, P.A., *Economics,* 7th ed, 1967, p. 8.

mathematical model is essential for testing the hypothesis and for economic policy formation. That is why the word 'model' occurs with increasing frequency in modern economic research.

In layman language, model is a simplification of reality. A model is an abstract representation of reality which clears what is relevant to a particular question at a particular time and neglects all other aspects. They are usually elaborated in terms of well defined variables and functions. Prof. C.F. Christ wrote, "A model can be described by a list of endogenous variables, a list of exogenous variables and a list, of specifications as to which variables are present in each equation."[14]

According to Prof. Edward J. Kane, "An economic model is a logical (usually mathematical) representation of whatever a priori or a theoretical knowledge economic analysis suggests is most relevant for treating a particular problem. Usually, a model takes the form of a system of equations embodying certain assumed inter dependencies among more or less operationally defmed variables.[15]

The information contained in a model is often referred to as a priori information or a priori restrictions or assumptions or the maintained hypothesis. A model establishes the main variables involved and connects them by means of mathematical statements. Thus a model simplifies the reality, points out the basic features of the problem and denotes a set of hypothesis.

Models are generally set out in the form of equations using mathematical, symbols. Some models can be summed up in a single equation while others may consist of an impressive array of relations. The number of equations included in a model depends upon the objectives for which the model is constructed. Prof. C.F. Christ suggested some desirable properties that we would like our equations to have.

These properties are relevance, simplicity, theoretical plausibility, explanatory ability and forecasting ability.

Nature of Economic Models

Nowadays most of the sciences use models. But economic models are different from models of physical sciences. We study the human being made of flesh and bones. Thus to think of a rigid and exact model is a myth. Economic models study economic phenomena.

A statistical model denotes a set of hypothesis that permits statistical

14. C.F. Christ, *Econometrics,* pp. 21-22.
15. Edward J. Kane, *Economic Statistics and Econometrics,* p. 12.

inference from the particular data under review. An economic model is usually adapted to yield a definite' and precise formulation of the economic processes at work. The statistical model must specify the stochastic elements that are supposed to enter into the determination of the observations. Thus an economic model needs exact and precise knowledge while for statistical model the understanding of what is relevant to the particular observations at hand is far more important than a wide knowledge of economic theory.

Economic models are based upon abstract economic theory. Therefore their models are insufficient to permit an empirical application.

Economic models contain only established facts and theory, while new relation can be introduced into the initial statistical model. In the process of analysis, first, we construct a statistical model. It becomes economic model only after testing with data. Most of the economic models explain the phenomena as a whole. Statistical models on the other hand often include partial analysis all that can be achieved on available data. These are the models of special aspects of an economic phenomena. Economic models are concerned with the explanation of economic laws. While statistical models are designed to forecast about economic phenomena and to serve as aids to policy formation. These models are often called policy-models. Most of the economic models are prepared after the formulation of economic laws while construction of a statistical model is the starting point of any statistical investigation. Statistical models are classified according to the types of data involved, *i.e.*, time series and cross section studies. Most of the time series analysis are concerned with the national aggregates like national income, employment, consumption, etc. Usually cross-section studies are based upon surveys which yield direct information about economic conditions from micro-economic units like households, firms, etc.

Statistical methods used in economics are similar to those developed for other branches of study, but the nature of the data is quite different. The distinguishing feature of economic data is that they are non-experimental. A physical scientist concerned with some aspect of Bowyl's Law can control the external conditions (temperature, etc.) within the four walls of a laboratory and can study that volume of gas at varying amounts of pressure. He can minimise the error of observations in a controlled atmosphere. In economic science we are not so fortunate with our raw materials. Here we cannot set up laboratory type situations, thus controlled experiments are not possible.

In economics, experiment is seldom possible. Nature does experiment with the economy by the cycle of day and night, winter and summer and good and bad harvest years. Here we deal with data pertaining to observations made about men. The numerous influences under which he lives and works, defy any attempt at controlled experiments. In the absence of controlled conditions, we simply record the consumer's behaviour, e.g., the purchases made by consumer at different price levels. Thus we get only associated set of prices and purchases which are made by different consumers under different conditions. The variations between observations are not subject to experimental control. Thus in physical sciences we have sound theoretical reasons for postulating a specific model, while in economics neither theoretical nor empirical reasons are available to justify the analysis. Economic behaviour is less predictable than physical sciences phenomena. All this results in unstable and unsupported laws. That is why economic laws are called mere statements of tendencies. No economic law can be so exact and stable as a physical science law.

Tools of Economic Model

When we have to work on an economic problem, we first frame a mathematical model which describes the events that we want to incorporate and the assumptions that are related to it. Thus a mathematical model contains three elements: (*i*) A dependent variable, i.e., the event to be explained; (*ii*) one or more independent variables, i.e., the factors by which the dependent variable is influenced; and (*iii*) the behavioural assumptions which explain the nature of causal relationships between explanatory and dependent variables.

An economic model consists of a set of behavioural relations and a set of equilibrium conditions. Thus we should specify the variables and the parameters that we want to include in the model. We may explain the various toncepts used in model building as under:

1. Variables. A variable can be defined as something whose magnitude can change over a period of time. For example we may represent price by *P,* tlemand by *D* and supply by S.

Further a model may have dependent variable and a number of independent variables. A dependent variable is one whose magnitude will change as a result of a change in some other (independent) variable. An independent variable is one whose change is not influenced by the dependent variable. For example, when we define a demand functions as

$D = f(P)$. It means that quantity demand is a function of price. Thus demand is a dependent variable and price is an independent variable.

Further, a model may have endogenous variables and exogenous variables. Endogenous variables are those whose values are determined within the model. On the other hand, exogenous variables are those values are determined outside the model. It must be remembered that a variable may be endogenous to one model and exogenous to another model.

Again, there may be flow variables and stock variables in the model. A flow variable is a quantity that can be measured in terms of specific time period while a stock variable is a quantity which can be measured in a point of time.

2. Constants. A constant is something whose magnitude does not change. Thus it is opposite to a variable. When a constant is joined to a variable, it is known as the coefficient of that variable.

3. Parameters. A parameter is a symbol which is constant for the purpose of any particular problem but may assume different values in different problems.

4. Functional Relationships. A functional relationship between two variables exists when a change in the value of one variable uniquely determines the change in the value of the other variables.

5. Equations. In economic models, three types of equations are used: (*i*) Definitional Equations, (*ii*) Behavioural Equations, and (*iii*) Equilibrium Equations.

(*i*) *Definitional Equations.* It specifies a relation between two alternative expressions having the same meaning. The sign = (identically equal to) is used for such an equation.

(*ii*) *Behavioural Equation.* It specifies how a variable behaves in response to changes in other variables. A behavioural equation is always based on some defmite assumptions on which the particular behaviour of the variable under study is based.

(*iii*) *Equilibrium Equation.* It explains the attainment of equilibrium. The equilibrium condition can be derived on the basis of be havioural equations.

Building A Micro Static Model

Let us construct a micro static model of an industry under perfect competition. The model can be framed by explaining a functional relationship among three variables: quantity demanded for the commodity (D), quantity supplied of the commodity (S) and the price of the commodity

(P). Here D and S are the dependent variables while P is an independent variable.

Now the fundamental relationships can be established as under:

$$D = f(P) \quad .... (1)$$

$$S = f(P) \quad .... (2)$$

and

$$D = S \quad .... (3)$$

The important assumptions of the model are as under:

(*i*) Quantity demanded (D) is inversely related with price (P).

(*ii*) Quantity supplied (S) is positively related with price (P) but only after a certain minimum positive price.

(*iii*) D and S are stock variables.

(iv) The equilibrium condition is $D = S$

The Model

In this static market model, there are two behavioural equations and one equilibrium condition:

$$D = \alpha - \beta P$$

$$S = \delta - \gamma P \text{ (Behavioural Equations)}$$

and

$$D = S \text{ Equilibrium condition}$$

where α, β, δ, and γ are constants.

Suppose we have the following values for the above equations:

$$D = 400 - 100P \quad .... (4)$$

$$S = -50 + 50P \quad .... (5)$$

$$D = S \quad .... (6)$$

Now substituting equation (4) and equation (5) into equation (6) we have

$$400 - 100P = -50 + 50P$$

or

$$-100P - 50P = -50 - 400$$

or

$$150P = 450$$

or

$$P = 3$$

Putting the value of $P = 3$ in equation (4) and equation (5) we have

$$D = 400 - 100 \times 3 = 100$$

$$S = -50 + 50 \times 3 = 100$$

$$\therefore \quad D = S = 100$$

Thus the industry will be in equilibrium at price Rs. 3 when quantity demanded and supplied is equal to 100 units.

EXERCISES

1. "Induction and dedution are both needed for scientific thought as the left and right foot are both needed for walking"—(Schmoller). Discuss and explain the uses and limitations of the two methods of economic analysis.

2. Explain the merits and demerits of inductive and deductive methods of economtic analysis.
3. Discuss whether deduction or induction should be used as a method of study in economics.
4. Discuss the methods for the derivation of economic laws. Are these methods complementary?
5. Distinguish between deductive and inductive methods of reasoning and evaluate their usefulness in economic analysis.
6. Discuss the various concepts used in model building in economics.
7. Write notes on: (*a*) Variables, (*b*) Constants, (*c*) Parameters, (*d*) Functional Relationships, (*e*) Behavioural and Equilibrium Equations.

Multiple Choice Questions

8. (*i*) A function refers to
    - (*a*) the demand for a commodity
    - (*b*) the supply of a commodity
    - (*c*) the demand and supply of a commodity, service or resource
    - (*d*) the relationship between dependent variable and one or more independent variables. [*Ans.* (*d*)]

   (*ii*) In an economic model

   $$D = f(P)$$

   an independent variable is
    - (*a*) P
    - (*b*) D
    - (*c*) D and P
    - (*d*) none of the above [*Ans.* (*a*)]

   (*iii*) Induction is the process of reasoning from
    - (*a*) a part to the whole
    - (*b*) particulars to general
    - (*c*) individual to universal
    - (*d*) all of the above [*Ans.* (*d*)]

Chapter 4

THE PRODUCTION POSSIBILITY CURVE AND CIRCULAR FLOW OF ECONOMIC ACTIVITY

1. PRODUCTION POSSIBILITY CURVE

Meaning of Production Possibility Curve

The production possibility curve (PPC) is an analytical tool which is used to illustrate and explain the problem of choice or economising process in a hypothetical economy or society. In every economic society, the economising problem arises on account of the limited resources in relation to multiple (unlimited) ends. Prof. Samuelson[1] has used production possibility curve to clear the problem of scarcity and choice. Here the idea is that a full employment, full-production economy cannot have an unlimited output of goods and services in view of its limited resources. Thus to clear this idea, we make certain specific assumptions as under:

1. We assume that the economy is operating at full employment level of output.
2. We assume that the available supply of factors of production is fixed, although it can be reallocated within limits among various uses.
3. We assume that during the course of time the state of technology remains constant.
4. Only two goods *X* (consumer goods) and *Y* (capital goods) are produced in different proportions in the economy.
5. The same resources can be used to produce either or both of the two goods and can be shifted freely between them.

---

1. Paul A. Samuelson, *Economics,* 1961, pp. 19-24.

To simplify the problem, let us further assume that the economy is producing just two products—steel and wheat, or say, two types of goods—the capital goods and the consumer goods. Here steel is symbolic of capital goods and wheat is symbolic of consumer goods. Now, since the resources available in the economy are fixed; the maximum production of steel or wheat is also limited. It means that limited resources always mean limited output. Here more of steel can be produced only at the cost of less of wheat and vice versa. Thus the economy cannot increase the supply of both from its scarce resources. This is in fact the economic problems that the society has to face.

We may also clear this problem with the help of a simple imaginary example as shown in Table 4.1.

Table 4.1: *Production Possibilities of Steel and Wheat with Full Employment*

Products	*Production Alternatives*					
	A	*B*	C	*D*	*E*	*F*
Steel (units)	0	1	2	3	4	5
Wheat (units)	50	40	25	5	2	0

As is clear from the above table, at alternative *A* the economy may produce 50 units of wheat with zero steel from its (limited) available resources. Similarly, at alternative *F* it can produce 5 units of steel with zero wheat. Both these alternatives are extreme and unrealistic as the society needs both steel and wheat. Thus as we move from *A* to *F,* the economy can produce steel and more of it only at lower levels of wheat. This is done by transfering resources away from the production of wheat (consumer goods) to the production of steel. If consumer goods are the current satisfaction (consumption) and capital goods are the future satisfaction (consumption) then we may say that in moving from *A* to *F,* the society is sacrificing current satisfaction (consumer goods) in the interest of future satisfaction (capital goods). Similarly in moving from *F* to *A,* the society is, in effect, choosing 'more now' (consumer goods) at the cost of 'much more later' (capital goods). It clearly means that the society can produce more of any goods only at the cost of the other product.

We may also represent the above illustration with the help of a production possibility curve or a transformation curve. In Fig 4.1, we represent steel along *X* axis and wheat along *Y* axis.

In Fig. 4.1 points *A, B,* C, *D, E* and *F* show the combinations of the two products that the society may produce from its limited resources. When we join these various points, we obtain a curve which is known as the Production Possibility Curve. This curve is also known as the Transformation Curve, because when we move from one point to another, say from *C* to *D,* we will be transforming wheat into steel by shifting resources from the production of wheat to the production of steel. Any point inside this curve, say point *R* indi-cates that resources are not being fully utilized. The society cannot go outside this curve (as point *K* in Fig 4.1) as its resources do not permit it to do so. This is the reason that the curve is also known as the frontier.

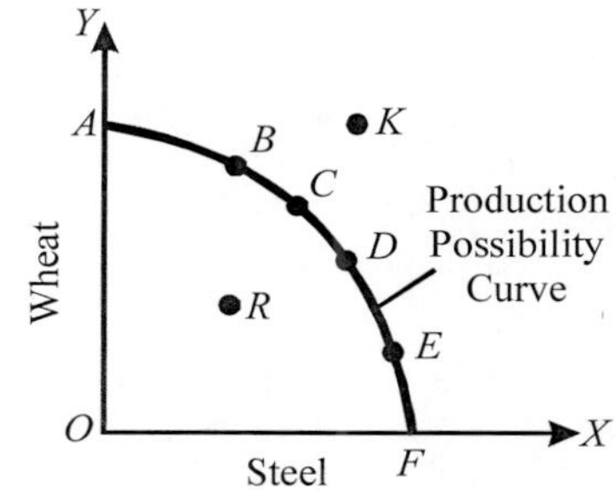

Fig. 4.1

Uses or Applications of Production Possibility Curve

With the help of production possibility curve we can explain the basic problems of an economy such as the problem of unemployment, technological progress, economic growth and economic efficiency.

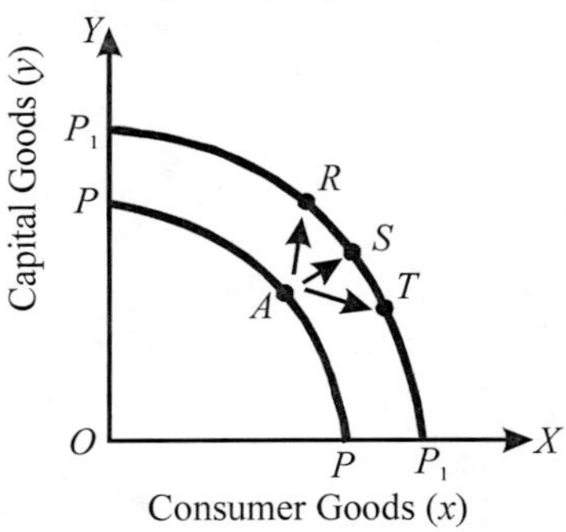

Fig. 4.2

(1) ***Unemployment.*** According to Keynes, there is always unemployment in an economy. It is because of lack of effective demand or because of inequality between savings and investment in an economy. Thus if we relax the assumption of full employment of resources, we can find out the level of unemployment prevailing in the economy with the help of *PP* curve. It has been shown in Fig. 4.2. According to Lipsey, "The higher the proportion of resources unemployed, the closer will be the production possibility curve to the origin. In Fig. 4.2, the original production possibility curve of the economy is *PP* which depicts substantial unemployment in the economy. The economy can attain the level of full employment if it is able to go to any point on a higher production possibility curve P_1P_1. The economy can do so by employing its idle resources either producing more of capital goods, i.e., on point *R* on P_1P_1 curve, or more of consumer goods, i.e.,

point *T on* P_1P_1 curve or more of both the goods, i.e., at point S on P_1P_1 *curve.*

(2) ***Technological Progress.*** Under this, the economy is not able to get maximum returns of the available resources because of lack of technical progress. Technical progress enables an economy to get more output from the same quantities of factors of production. It is shown in Fig. 4.3. Initially, the economy is enjoying production possibility curve *PP* from its available resources. Now if the productive efficiency of the economy improves by technical progress, its *PP* curve will shift outward throughout to P_1. The new P_1P_1 curve shows a higher level of both the consumer goods as well as the capital goods and the economy may enjoy say point *S* on P_1P_1 curve.

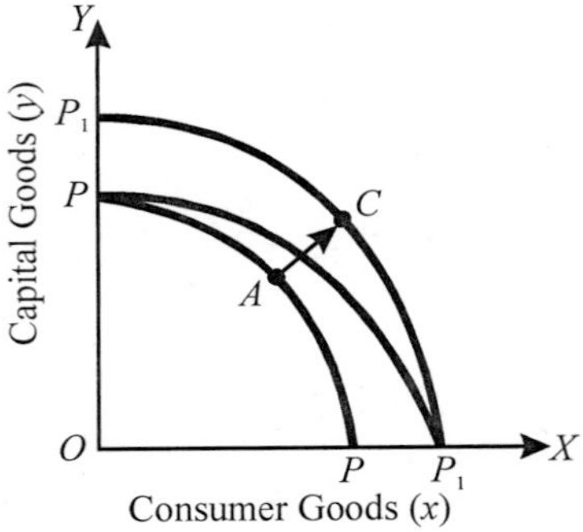

Fig. 4.3

Now suppose, the economy makes the technical progress in the production of only consumer goods, then it may shift to any point on P_1P_1 curve. This curve may also enable the economy to produce more of both the goods although the technical progress has taken place only in the production of consumer goods.

(3) ***Economic Growth.*** Under this we may say that the quantities of factors of production like land, capital, labour and enterprise are fixed only in the short period. Development is a continuous and long-period process. Thus these resources may change over time and shift the *PP* curve upwards as shown in Fig. 4.4. Now, if the economy is stagnant at point *R,* then economic growth will shift it to point S on production possibility curve *PP* and a further increase in factor quantities may shift the *PP* curve towards the right to P_1P_1 and the economy may go to any point on this higher production possibility curve, i.e. either point A or B or C as suits to the economy.

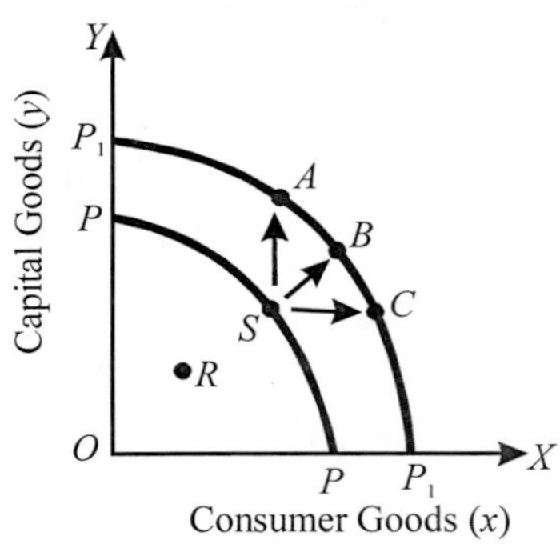

Fig. 4.4

(4) ***Present goods vs Future goods.*** Here we may say that if an economy allocates more of its resources in the present to produce capital

goods than to consumer goods, it will have more of both kinds of goods in the future. It will thus acquire a higher rate of growth in the future. This is because of the fact that consumer goods satisfy the present wants while capital goods satisfy future wants. Figure 4.5 indicates the fact that the outward shift of the economy's future production possibility curve P_1P_1 from point R of the present curve PP is greater when more capital goods are produced in the future. Further, Fig. 4.6 shows lesser outward shift of the present curve PP from point T to the future curve P_1P_1 when less capital goods are produced in the future.

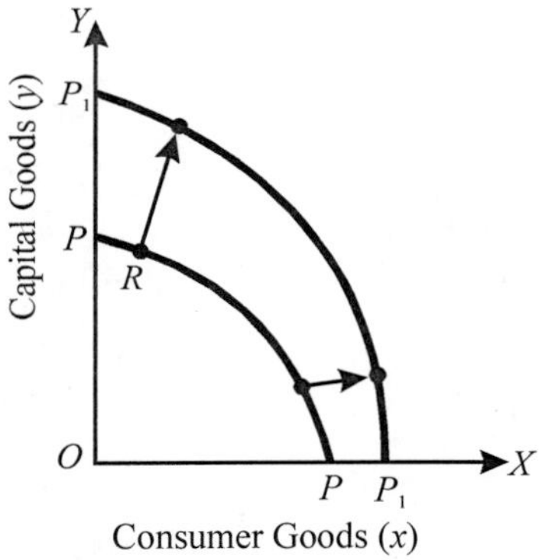

Fig. 4.5

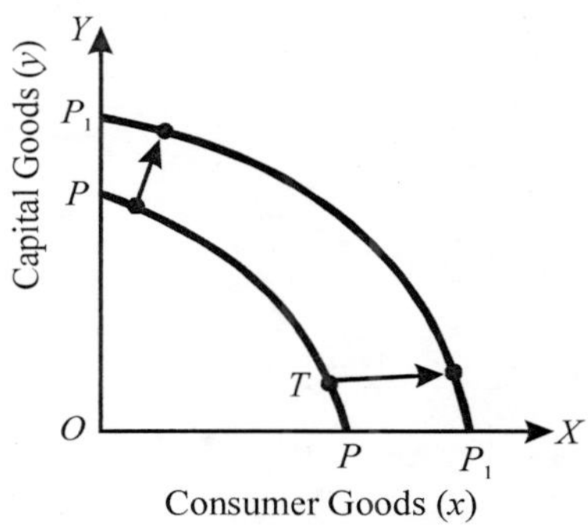

Fig. 4.6

Similar to the above interpretation, we may also predict any number of different pairs of goods or services on the production possibility curves, such as public goods *vs* private goods; agricultural goods *vs* industrial goods or consumption *vs* investment (or saving), etc.

2. CIRCULAR FLOW OF ECONOMIC ACTIVITY

The above stated economic problem is solved by the three institutions (i.e., decision making agents) of an economy; namely, the households (or individuals), business firms and government. These decision making agents are actively engaged in three economic activities of consumption, production and exchange of goods and services in the society. They act and react in such a manner that all economic activities move in a circular flow and lead to full employment in the economy. First of all, we shall explain the nature of these agents and their role in decision making.

Households. The households perform two economic activities simultaneously. As agents of the factors of production, they supply productive inputs to the business firms and receive incomes in return in the form of rent, wages, interests and profits. At the same time, the households act as consumers as well and spend their incomes on consumer goods produced by the business firms.

Business Firms. The business firms are the producers and they take the decisions to manufacture goods and services. For this purpose, they procure different factors of production and make payments to them in the form of wages, rent, and interest, etc.

Government. In modern times, the government plays an important role in all types of economic systems, i.e., capitalist, socialist, and mixed economy.

All the above decision making agents take economic decisions to produce goods and to exchange them in order to consume them for satisfying the wants of the whole economy. Production, consumption and exchange are the three main activities of the economy. Consumption and production are to be performed simultaneously. They are interrelated and interdependent. Production leads to consumption and consumption necessitates production. These two activities are related to each other through the mechanism of exchange.

The Circular Flow in a Two-Sector Economy

Here we assume that there are only two sectors of the economy, i.e., the households and the business firms. Figure 4.7 presents a graphic analysis of the mode in which income flows between the households and the business firms. For simplicity, the economy has been divided into two markets, i.e., the product market and the factor market. The households (consumers) supply factors of production (such as land, labour, capital and enterprise) to business firms (producers), and receive money (income) for their services in different forms. Such receipts, in fact, constitute the total cost of production of goods and services produced in the economy. On the contrary, business firms sell consumer goods to households and receive money in return. In a simplified economy, the households are assumed to spend their entire income on the purchase of consumer goods and services. At the same time, the entire business receipts are paid out for the purchase of productive inputs from the households. Since there are no taxes, no savings and no foreign trade, the upper half of the circle would obviously be equal to the lower half. In other words, the flows of income between the factor and the product markets will not only be equal, but their size will also remain constant.

In Fig. 4.7, the upper half of the circle constitutes the market for consumer goods and shows the interaction between households, as buyers of such goods and the business firms, as sellers. By definition, prices of goods and services in this market form the connecting link between the flow of goods and the money payments.

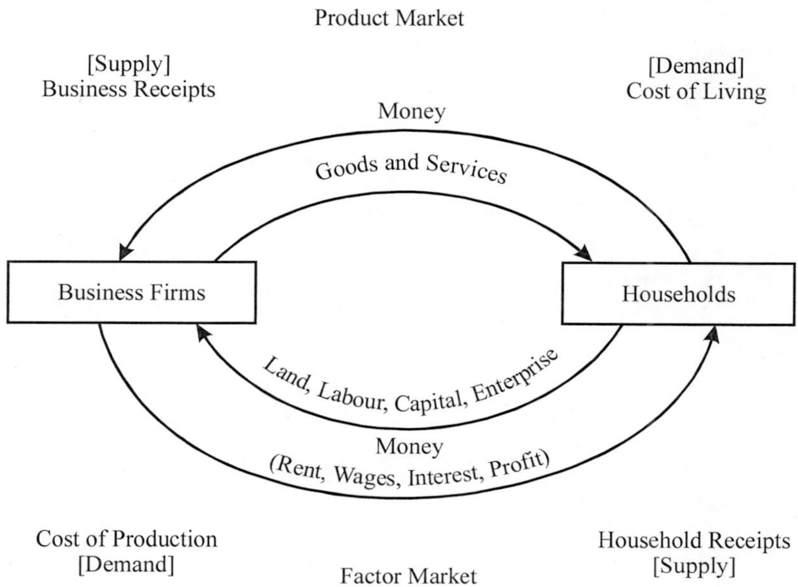

Fig. 4.7

In Fig. 4.7, the lower half of the circle shows the interaction between households and business firms in the factor market. In this case, the input prices constitute a link between the flow of inputs and money. In a simplified economy, the household receipts are equal to total cost of production. At the same time, cost of production is equal to the business receipts, which in turn are equal to total money spent on the purchase of goods and services.

Thus the two money flows are equal.

The Circular Flow in a Three-Sector Economy

The above analysis of a simplified economy was based upon two-sector model. Now we add the government sector so as to make it a three-sector closed model of circular flow of economic activity. Now we will see that even if the govt. sector is added, the fundamental principles governing the circular 'flow of income would not show a significant difference. For the third sector, we add taxes and government purchases (or expenditure) in our presentation. Taxes are outflows from the circular flow and government purchases are inflows into the circular flow. The three-sector model of the circular flow of economic activity is shown in Fig. 4.8.

In Fig. 4.8, the government increases aggregate expenditure in the economy through purchases of services of the households, making transfer payments in the form of old age pensions, unemployment relief, sickness benefit, etc. and also through providing services like education, health, housing, water supply and other facilities. All such expenditures by the government are inflows into the circular flow. Contrarily taxes in the form of personal income taxes and commodity taxes paid by the households are outflows from the circular flow.

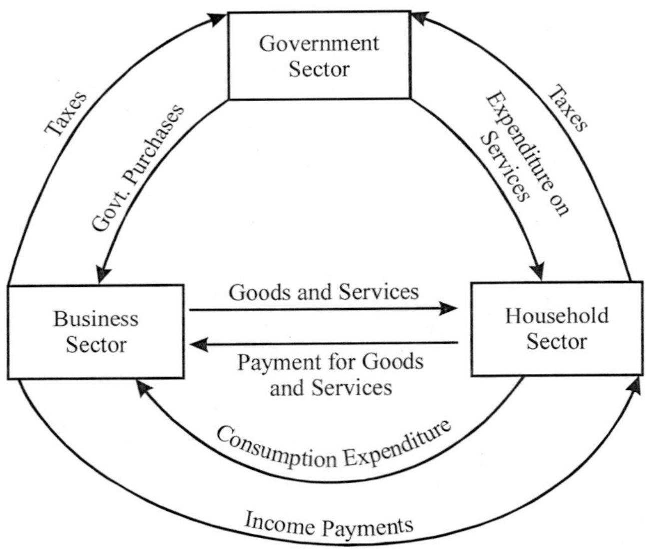

Fig. 4.8

Further, we may also see the circular flow between the business firms and the government. The government buy all its requirements of goods from the business sector, gives subsidies and makes transfer payments to business firms in order to encourage their production. All these expenditures are inflows into the circular flow. Contrarily, all types of taxes paid by the business firms to the government are outflows from the circular flow.

Now we may discuss the combined effects between the three sectors together. As we know, taxes are a leakage from the circular flow. They tend to decrease consumption and saving of the household sector. Decreased consumption, in turn, reduces the sales and incomes of the firms. On the other hand, taxes on business firms tend to decrease their investment and production. The government fills this gap by making purchases from the business firms and buying services of the households exactly equal to the amount of taxes. Thus inflows equal outflows in the circular flow.

EXERCISES

1. Write a brief note on production possibility curve.
2. Define a production possibility curve (PPC). Explain its uses in economic analysis.
3. Explain circular flow of income in an economy.
4. Describe the role of households, firms and the government in economic activity. Also describe their interrelationships.
5. Describe the circular flow of economic activity in an economy.

Multiple Choice Questions

6. (*i*) Production Possibility Curve under increasing cost condition is
   (*a*) convex to the origin (*c*) straight line curve
   (*b*) concave to the origin (*d*) none of the above [*Ans.* (*b*)]

(*ii*) Which of the following problem can be explained with the help of production possibility curve?
   (*a*) Unemployment (*c*) Economic Growth
   (*b*) Technological Progress (*d*) All of the above [*Ans.* (*d*)]

(*iii*) Production is an economic activity which means
   (*a*) creation of utility
   (*b*) additional utility
   (*c*) transformation of inputs through form, place, time, service, possession or knowledge into outputs for consumption.
   (*d*) all of the above [*Ans.* (*d*)]

Chapter 5

MICRO-AND MACROECONOMICS

1. INTRODUCTION

Microeconomics and macroeconomics are the two approaches to economic prob-lems and economic analysis. These terms were first coined and used by Ragnar Frisch in 1933 and have now been adopted by the economists all the world over. *Microeconomics* studies the economic actions of a particular individual and a well-defined group of individuals, i.e., households, firms, industries, etc. and *macroeconomics* studies the broad aggregates, such as, total employment, the total consumption, and the aggregate national income. Microeconomics is also known as *partial analysis* and macroeconomics as *aggregate analysis.* It is because that microeconomics is the partial differentiation of the total (macro). This type of distinction is, in a sense, artificial, since aggregates are merely sums of individual' figures. However, the distinction is justified by the basic differences in the objectives and methods of the two branches.

Before the distinction between microeconomics and macroeconomics came into vogue, the fundamental dichotomy was between price and income analysis. This dichotomy can be applied over into the micro and macro branches of economic. theory Normally, prices play it major role in the microeconomic analysis and its objective is to define price determination and the allocation of specific resources to particular uses. Macroeconomics, on the other hand, is the study of the economy as a whole, i.e., the determination of the levels of national income and aggregate resource employment. Here, one should not understand that income concepts are non-existent in microeconomics or that prices are ignored in macroeconomics. However, in the theories of microeconomics, the determination of incomes of individuals is encompassed within the general pricing process: people earn their incomes by selling factors of production, the prices of which are determined in the same manner as all other prices. On the other hand, prices are relevant in macro-economic theories, but macro theorists usually abstract from the problems of determining individual prices and their relations to one another and deal with aggregate price indices as determined by the level of aggregate spending. In simple words, microeconomics is related to particular individuals or particular business units, i.e., it includes the income of a particular individual, the output of a particular firm, etc., while macro economies is related to the economy as a whole, i.e., it includes the total income, total output and other aggregates relating to the whole economy.

Some economists prefer to begin their analysis of economic problems from the variables concerning individuals, individual firms and individual industries, i.e., microeconomics. Other economists prefer to begin their analysis from the broad aggregates or the national totals, i.e., macro-economics. The greater part of Marshallian economics is concerned with microeconomics. The later works of Keynes *General. Theory of Employment. Interest and Money* relate to macro-economics. These two branches of economics are complementary and for a thorough discussion of economic problems, the micro and macro views of economic life are both necessary.

2. MICROECONOMICS

Meaning of Microeconomics

According to Boulding, "Microeconomics is the study of particular firms, particular households, individual prices, wages, incomes, individual industries, particular commodities."[1] From this definition, it is clear that under microeconomics we study particular economic organism; for instance, individual prices, wages or incomes; economic behaviour of individual consumers and producers, etc.

According to Prof. Gardner Ackley, "Microeconomics deals with the division of total output among industries, products and firms and the allocation of resources among competing groups. It considers problems of income distribution. Its interest is in relative prices of particular goods and services."[2]

According to Prof. Lerner, "Microeconomics consists of looking at the economy through a microscope, as it were, to see how the millions of cells in the body economic—the individuals or households as

1. K.E. Boulding, *Economic Analysis,* 3rd ed., p. 237.
2. G. Ackley, *Macroeconomic Theory,* p. 4.

consumers, and the individuals or firms as producers—play their part in the working of the whole economic organism." For example, in micro economic analysis, we study the demand of individual consumer for a good and from there go on to derive the group demand for the good.

The study of microeconomics clears the economic status of the individual units. It helps us in determining the remuneration of individual units.

Types of Microeconomics

Microeconomics has been divided into following three types:

(1) ***Simple Micro-statics.*** It studies different microeconomic variables and their relationships at a given point of time under the conditions of equilibrium. It, therefore, assumes that the values of microeconomic variables will remain unchanged and for this reason a simple micro-static model does not involve time period.

For example, the equilibrium price of a commodity in the market is established at a point where the demand is equal to the supply. Now, as long as the demand function *DD* and supply function SS, as shown in Fig. 5.1, remain unchanged, the price of the commodity will stick to *OP*. Micro-statics discusses the question of how an equilibrium price is arrived at in a market where demand and supply functions are known and remain unchanged.

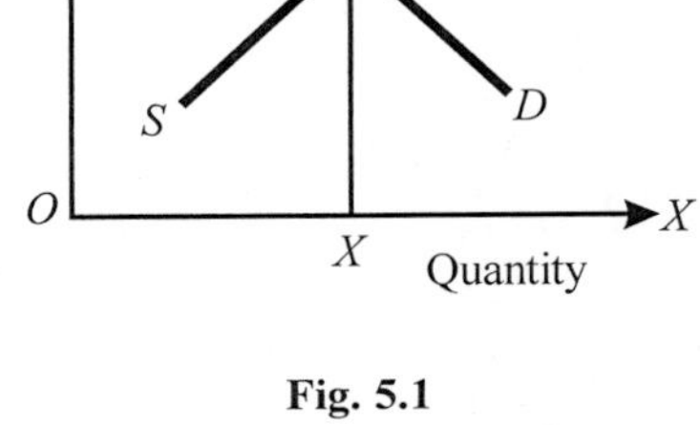

Fig. 5.1

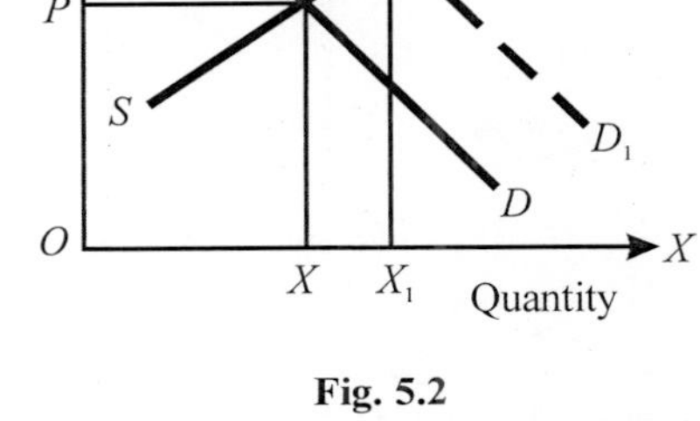

Fig. 5.2

(2) ***Comparative Micro-statics.*** It compares the equilibrium positions at different points of time. In micro-statics, we assume that there is no change in the demand and supply functions. But due to a change in the independent variable, the demand function or the supply function or both

will shift and the market will reach a new state of equilibrium giving a new price. This new equilibrium position will also be studied under micro-statics. But in comparative micro-statics, we compare the two equilibrium positions and will throw no light on the process by which the new equilibrium has been arrived at.

It has been shown in Fig. 5.2. The old equilibrium point is *E*. Due to a change in some independent variable, the demand function shifts upward from *DD* to D_1D_1. It results in a new equilibrium position at *E*, where the price is *OP* and quantity demanded and supplied is *OX*. These two equilibrium positions are compared by the comparative micro-statics.

(3) ***Microdynamics (The Cobweb Model):*** It explains lagged relationship between the microeconomic variables. Microdynamics throws full light on the happenings in the market during the period of transition from one static equilibrium to another. It is a study of disequilibrium. More specifically, it studies the process through which the new equilibrium in the market is established. The Cobweb Model is used to explain the dynamics of demand, supply and price over long periods of time. As prices move up and down in cycles, quantities produced also seem to move lip and down in a counter cycle manner.

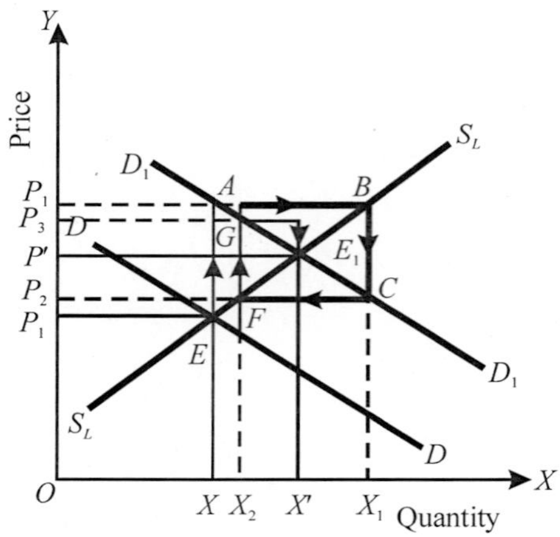

Fig. 5.3.

For example, in Fig. 5.3 the initial price of a commodity is fixed at *OP* where the quantity demanded and supplied is *OX*. Now, due to a change in some independent variable, the demand curve *DD* shifts upward to D_1D_1. As a result, a disequilibrium will occur in the market. This will be followed by a series of disequilibria before the final equilibrium is arrived at and a new equilibrium price takes place. As soon as demand increases, supply cannot be increased at the same moment. Therefore, the immediate effect of the upward shift in the demand curve is that the suppliers enjoy a higher price *XA*. It is due to the fact that the supply is perfectly inelastic at a given point of time. This sharp increase in price in the market period will attract the suppliers to increase their supply in the short run. This leads to increase in the supply at the level OX_1. It will result in a decrease in price by *BC*. But at this price the demand decreases to OX_2. This level of output again leads to an increase in price to the level OP_3.

This process will continue until the new equilibrium is established at point E_1 where the price is OP' and quantity supplied and demand is OX'. This entire process is studied under microdynamics.

Uses of Microeconomics

According to Prof. Bilas, the main uses of microeconomics are the following:

(1) ***Price Determination and Allocation of Resources.*** Microeconomics is useful in the determination of price and for the allocation of resources between alternative uses. We shall see that demand-supply model is used in price-theory. The model states that price is determined by the forces of demand and supply, and at equilibrium price, the quantity demanded equals quantity supplied. If price increases then the quantity demanded will be less than quantity supplied.

Further, microeconomics studies the behaviour of an individual consumer, family, firm and industry. Suppose we want to study steel industry. For this, we will study the cost situations of various steel producing units. Their element of competition will also be studied. The demand and supply for their products will be studied. The price of steel will be determined by the aggregate demand and aggregate supply of steel. This price will be given to all steel producing units in the industry. The firms in the industry will determine individually their level of outputs of steel. In microeconomics, we will also study the factor-employment by these various firms in the industry.

(2) ***Determination of Economic Policy.*** Microeconomics, to some extent, states the relevance of economic policies of the government. The effect of direct and indirect tax on consumption and production of a commodity can easily be found by the analysis of microeconomics. Not only this, but the rationale of price policy and wage policy of the government can also be determined by the analysis of the allocation of

resources by a firm under microeconomics. Microeconomics will also state whether the rationing is justified or not in the interest of citizens of a country.

(3) ***Optimum Utilisation of Factors of Production.*** We may also find the situation of optimum utilisation of resources for a consumer and a producer by the help of microeconomics. Microeconomics provides the law of substitution by which a consumer will maximise his satisfaction when the ratio of marginal utilities equals the ratio of various commodities. Similarly, a producer will maximise his profit when the ratio of marginal product off actors of production equals the ratio of their prices. This situation will be the situation of maximum welfare on micro level.

Mathematically, a consumer maximises satisfaction when,

$$\frac{MU_1}{P_1} = \frac{MU_2}{P_2} = ... = \frac{MUn}{Pn}$$

where MU is marginal utility and P is price. The subscripts 1, 2 ... n indicate the respective commodities.

Also a producer maximises profit or minimizes costs when,

$$\frac{MP_1}{P_1} = \frac{MP_2}{P_2} = ... = \frac{MPn}{Pn}$$

where MP is marginal product and P is price. Subscripts 1, 2, ... n indicate the respective factors of production.

(4) ***Linear Programming.*** Microeconomics provides the technique of linear programming by which a producer takes a number of important decisions. He can know which factor is available in abundance and whose supply is scarce in quantity. This knowledge helps a farmer or an entrepreneur to mix the factors of production in an optimum manner and can increase his income. Linear programming also investigates the best possible production process among the alternative production processes to attain maximum income.

Hence, we can say that microeconomics provides such important tools which are helpful in determining the optimum mix of commodities and optimum distribution of income among the factors of production. Therefore, microeconomics is an important branch of economic analysis.

Limitations of Microeconomics

As we have seen that microeconomics is very useful in economic analysis, yet it has its own limitations. The important limitations are the following:

(1) It does not throw light on the collective activity of the national

economy. Today the policies which affect the entire economy such as tax-policy and expenditure policy of the government, monetary policy, fiscal policy, etc. are assumed to be of greater importance. These policies do not come within the purview of microeconomics, but are studied under macroeconomics.

(2) Microeconomics assumes other things remaining the same and has based its results on the assumption of full employment in the society. These assumptions do not hold in real life. Lord Keynes criticised this assumption and stated that "To assume full employment is to assume our difficulties away." It is why the reliability of microeconomic results becomes doubtful.

In spite of these two limitations, microeconomics possesses its own importance. It is widely used in the problems of macroeconomic analysis.

3. MACROECONOMICS

Meaning of Macroeconomics

According to Boulding, "Macroeconomics deals not with individual quantities, as such, but with aggregates of these quantities; not with individual incomes, but with national income; not with individual prices, but with price level; not with individual outputs, but with national output."

He further states that "Macroeconomics is that part of the subject which deals with the great aggregates and averages of the system rather than a particular item in it, and attempts to define these aggregates in a useful manner and to examine their relationship."

According to Prof. Ackley, "Macroeconomics also uses aggregates smaller than for the whole economy, but only in a context which makes them sub-divisions of an economy wide total. Macroeconomics also uses aggregates, but not in a context which relates them to an economy wide total."

From the above definitions, it is evident that macroeconomics concerns itself with those aggregates which-relate to the whole economy. Macroeconomics also discusses the sub-aggregates of the large aggregates relating to the whole economy, but these sub-aggregates, unlike the aggregates of microeconomics which examine aggregates relating to a particular product, a particular industry or a particular market, cut across various products and industry.

Types of Macroeconomics

Macroeconomics has been divided into following three types:

(1) *Simple macrostatics.* It studies relationships between macro-economic variables in a stationary situation. It is concerned with equilibrium points and not the process through which it is attained. Hence, macrostatics deals with the final equilibrium of the economy at a particular point of time. For example, the position of final equilibrium can be shown by the following Keynesian equation:

$$Y = C + I$$

where Y = Total Income, C =Total Consumption, I = Total Investment

The above equation explains the relationship between three macro-economic variables Y, C and I. The equality between Y and $C + I$ indicates the equilibrium position. It does not involve the study of time analysis. The above macrostatic model can also be shown diagramma-tically. In Fig. 5.4, a 45° line indicates that at all points on this line the equality between Y and $C + I$ exists. The consumption schedule is shown by C and .the combined consumption and investment schedule is shown by $C + I$. The equilibrium point will be attained at E where the equilibrium national income is OY. This equilibrium position E will be studied under macroeconomics.

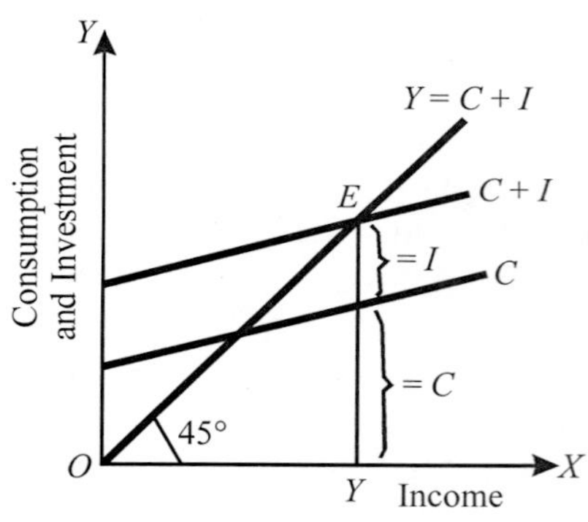

Fig. 5.4.

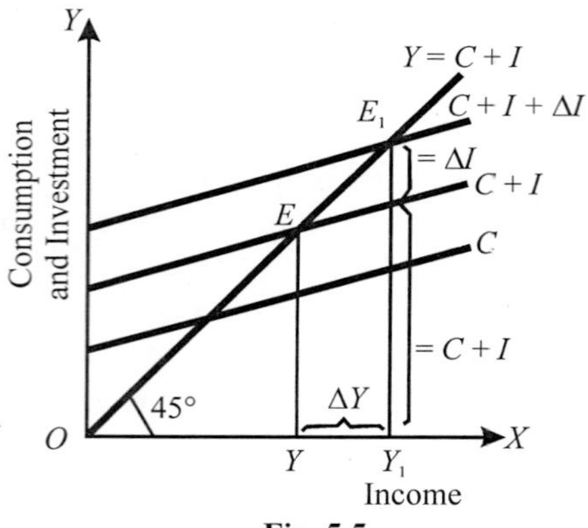

Fig. 5.5

(2) *Comparative macrostatics.* It involves a comparative study of different macro static equilibrium positions which are attained by the economy. But it does not study the process of adjustment by which the economy shifts from one equilibrium position to another equilibrium position.

For example, if there is an increase in investment (ΔI), then the initial level of income (OY) will be disturbed. In Fig. 5.5, the equilibrium is attained at point E_1, where the new level of equilibrium income is OY_1.

Comparative macrostatics studies these two equilibrium positions E and E_1 and does not talk about the process through which the equilibrium takes place. It states that when aggregate investment increases by ΔI, the aggregate increase in income will be ΔY.

(3) *Macrodynamics.* This concept has recently been developed by some eminent economists like D.H. Robertson, J.R. Hicks, M. Kalecki, J. Timbergen, R.F. Harrod, E.D. Domar and P.A. Samuelson. It studies the process through which a new equilibrium is established after a change in independent macroeconomic variables. According to Prof. Kurihara, "Macroeconomics enables to separate the process of trial and error into a series of continuously changing reactions and indicates the cause and effect. It analyses the discrete or continuous changes of aggregates, the sequence of cause and effect events arising from some initial change and the time paths (roots) of macroeconomic variables."[3] In other words, it studies fluctuations of income at various points of time, and, therefore, involves period analysis.

For example, initially the economy is in equilibrium at point E in Fig. 5.6. At point E the equilibrium income is OY. Now there is an increase in investment (ΔI) which leads to an increase in the aggregate expenditure.

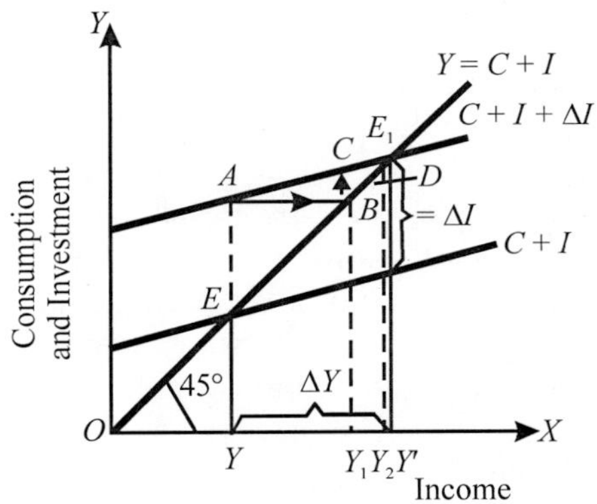

Fig. 5.6

The community would increase its expenditure from YE to YA at OY level of national income. This increase in community's expenditure increases the level of aggregate income is the next period to a level of OY_1. At this increased new level of income people will spend more on consumption goods (C) and therefore the next period's total expenditure

3. Kenneth K. Kurihara, *Introduction to Keynesian Dynamics.*

$(C + I)$ increases to Y_1C. Further, this increase in expenditure raises the level of aggregate income and consequently the consumption expenditure. This process continues until the find (long-run) equilibrium point E is attained where the new level of equilibrium national income is OY'. Hence, the entire process is studied under the macrodynamics.

Uses of Macroeconomics

The old economists emphasised particularly the problems of microeconomics. They were not interested in the concepts of total national income, total national employment and total investment. But, during the last 40-45 years macroeconomics has gained much popularity. The 1930s worldwide depression compelled the world economists to think over the macroeconomic policies. Since the publication of Keynes' famous book, *General Theory of Employment. Interest and Money* in 1936, macroeconomics has been growing fast. In this context, the following points are important:

(1) ***Determination of Economic Policies of the Government.*** The study of macroeconomics becomes indispensable for formulation and successful execution of economic policies of the government. The main objective of the government is to attain maximum social benefit. It is not concerned with the benefit of an individual, but it is concerned with the collective benefits (welfare) of the individuals. Therefore, it is concerned with the regulation of aggregates of the economic system, the general price-leve1, the general level of production, consumption and investment, the general volume of trade, etc. This means that accurate and reliable data of the aggregative variables are the first prerequisite for the formulation of sound public policies. For example, population is rapidly increasing in India and, therefore, necessary macro decisions must be taken for creating the situation of more employment in the economy. Further, a lack of effective demand creates unemployment in more developed countries. For this, necessary monetary and fiscal policies are adopted.

In this way, macroeconomics contributes a lot in the determination of government economic policies which affect the level of national income, price and employment. Future targets of saving and investment may also be determined with the help of macro quantities. .

(2) ***Economic Planning.*** The developed and developing countries of the world are making use of economic planning for their economic development. Economic planning is concerned with aggregative variables and therefore, it comes under macroeconomic analysis. The rates of saving

and investment are determined and efforts are made to increase them. The annual rate of economic growth this also determined and efforts are made to achieve it. In this way, a number of aggregative variables are used in economic planning.

(3) ***Development of Microeconomic Theories.*** The study of macroeconomics is useful even for the purpose of building and developing microeconomic theories. The determination of wage in an industry will be influenced by the general wage rate of the economy. Similarly, the price of a commodity will also be influenced by the prevailing general price level in the economy. In the situations of inflation, generally the prices will increase, while in the years of depression the prices will go down. Thus, no microeconomic law can be formulated without a pre-study of macroeconomics.

(4) ***International Comparisons.*** Macroeconomics provides necessary information for international comparisons. For example, a comparative study of average national income, consumption and saving between different countries requires macroeconomic information.

(5) ***The Necessity of Separate Knowledge of the Aggregates.*** The aggregates are not merely sums of individual units. They possess their own peculiarities. According to Prof. Boulding,[4] it is not possible to discover the behaviour pattern of the aggregates simply by generalising from the behaviour of the individual units. As he points, out that the forest is an aggregation of trees, but it does not possess the characteristics and behaviour-patterns of individual trees. The forest has its own characteristic and behaviour pattern which is to be distinguished. As we know that an individual tree grows and decays, while a forest goes on for ever with exactly the same internal composition in regard to the behaviour of the trees that constitute it. The reason is very clear as individual trees grow, mature and decay, new trees spring up to take their places and the forest goes on for ever.

Similarly, an economy is not merely a sum of independent economic units. As old industries are destroyed and new industries are created, the economy moves on for ever. Thus, the knowledge of total economy possesses its own importance.

Macroeconomic reasoning can take account of many relationships which are not applicable to individual parts. For example, for any individual or group of individuals, income and expenditure on currently produced output obviously can and usually will be different magnitudes; but for a whole society, income and expenditure (properly defined) can

4. Boulding, K.E., *A Reconstruction of Economics,* p. 173.

always be shown to be equal. Any individual can save without investing or invest without having previously saved, but carefully defined saving and investment must be identical for the whole economy. One country's imports may well exceed its exports, but for all countries combined, total imports and exports must obviously be equal. Similarly, one firm (or industry) can increase its output and employment by binding workers away from other firms; when there is full employment, industry as a whole cannot increase total labour input so as output (because full employment exists).

Hence the study of macroeconomics is useful in both theory and practice.

Limitations of Macroeconomics

In spite of the growing popularity macroeconomics is not free from its limitations. The important limitations are as follows:

(1) It is a complicated task to find out total national income by the help of the estimates of prices of different goods and services. Wholesale price index numbers are made to find out general price level. These index numbers involve the problems of weighing, averaging and a number of other difficulties.

(2) The aggregates which are homogeneous in nature can lead to accurate results. But sometimes we may have to take into our account aggregates which are homogeneous in character. Results based on these heterogeneous aggregates are not accurate and we should always avoid such problems.

(3) Due to imperfect knowledge of statistical techniques, some persons may predict the aggregates in a false way. For example, the agricultural prices decrease by 50 per cent while industrial prices increase by 50 per cent, the general price level remains the same, because the two types of price changes neutralise each other. In such a situation one may advise the government to make no change in its policy, because general price level remains the same. But actually the government needs to implement a policy which helps the farmers who get a loss due to fall in their product prices. Thus, sometimes the aggregative results may be misleading. It requires special ability to predict the results in such a situation.

(4) An aggregative change may not influence all the sectors of the economy in the same manner. For instance, a general rise in prices does not mean that the prices of all the commodities have increased and have increased in the same proportion. It is quite possible that the prices of a

few commodities may rather decrease. Further, due to. this aggregative change, some sectors may be affected more adversely than others. On the other hand, some individuals may be benefited more than the others.

4. INTERDEPENDENCE OF MICRO-AND MACROECONOMICS

Microeconomics deals with the division of total output among industries, products, and firms and the allocation of resources among competing uses, i.e., it deals with the behaviour of individual units. On the other hand, macroeconomics deals with economic affairs in "the large", i.e., with the aggregates of individual decision-making units. Therefore, the two branches seem to be independent of each other. As we know that the size of an individual unit is assumed to be so small that it has no bearing on the aggregate demand, supply or prices. Similarly, an increase in macroeconomic units, such as, the GNP of a country or the level of employment will make no effect on an individual unit.

In spite of these differences, the two branches are not assumed to be mutually exclusive. Actually, the line between microeconomic and macroeconomic theory cannot be precisely drawn. A truly "general" theory of the economy would clearly embrace both; it would explain individual behaviour, individual outputs, incomes, and prices; and the sums or averages of the individual results would constitute the aggregates with which macroeconomics is concerned. Such a general theory exists, but its very generality leaves it with little substantive content. Rather, to reach meaningful results, we find that we must approach macroeconomic problems with macroeconomic variables and microeconomic problems with microeconomic variables. Prof. Samuelson has rightly expressed this relationship in 'the following words: "There is really no opposition between micro and macroeconomics. Both are absolutely vital. And you are only half educated if you understand the one while being ignorant of the other."

EXERCISES

1. Distinguish between microeconomics and macroeconomics. Explain the uses and limitations of macroeconomic analysis.
2. Explain and distinguish between macro and microeconomic analysis. Can we use both these methods of economic analysis together?
3. Distinguish between microeconomics and macroeconomics. "To have proper appreciation of the working of economic forces it will be necessary to supplement the study of one by the study of the other." Do you agree with this statement?

4. What is the difference between static, comparative static and dynamic microeconomic analysis? Discuss their principal characteristics and the areas of their use.
5. Define macroeconomics. What are the various types of macroeconomics? Discuss their usefulness in economic analysis.

Multiple Choice Questions

6. (*i*) Microeconomic theory studies how a free enterprise economy determines
   (*a*) the price of goods
   (*b*) the price of services
   (*c*) the price of economic resources
   (*d*) all of the above [*Ans*. (*d*)]

(*ii*) Microeconomics deals primarily with
   (*a*) comparative statics, partial equilibrium and positive economics
   (*b*) comparative statics, general equilibrium and positive economics
   (*c*) comparative dynamics and ormative economics.
   (*d*) all of the above [*Ans*. (*a*)]

(*iii*) Macroeconomics is the study of
   (*a*) individual economic units
   (b) economy as a whole
   (*c*) price theory
   (*d*) all of the above [*Ans*. (*b*)]

(*iv*) Microeconomics is primarilly concerned with comparative statics rather than, dynamics
   (*a*) True
   (*b*) False
   (*c*) Uncertain [*Ans*. (*a*)]

Chapter 6

ECONOMIC STATICS AND DYNAMICS

1. INTRODUCTION

The distinction between statics and dynamics is of vital importance for the proper understanding of modern economic theory. These words are also used in physical sciences, but in economics the meaning of the two terms is different from the meaning given to them in physical sciences. According to the dictionary meaning the word 'static' means 'causing to rest or stand' and the word 'dynamic' means 'causing to move'. These dictionary meanings clearly indicate the basic distinction between the two terms. The analysis of both these types is designed for different purposes. According to Stonier and Hague, "Static analysis mainly discusses the question of how, for example, an equilibrium price is arrived at in a market where the demand and supply curves are known and remain unchanged. Static analysis, therefore, shows us how consumers, firms, industries and whole economies can remain instable, or static equilibrium at certain levels of prices, output, income and employment."[1] On the other hand, economic dynamics refers to a state where the rates of output, income and employment are changing. Most economists do not agree about what actual economic statics and dynamics mean. Yet, many of them have explained the distinctive features of the two methods.

It was first Auguste Comte (1798-1857), a French sociologist who introduced the two concepts of Statics and Dynamics in the domain of social science. But these two terms were first employed in economics by John Stuart Mill who was influenced by Comte. Today, these terms have been developed and popularised by modern economists.

The most important thesis on economic statics and dynamics has been developed by J.R. Hicks. According to him, "We call economic statics

1. Stonier and Hague, *A Textbook of Economic Theory,* 1964, p. 499.

those parts of economic theory where we do not trouble about dating: economic, dynamics those parts where every quantity must be dated. For example, in economic statics we think of an entrepreneur employing; such quantities of factors and producing by their aid such and such quantities of products but we do not ask when the factors are employed and when the products come to be ready. In economic dynamics, we do ask such Questions and we pay special attention to the way changes in these dates affect the relations between factors and prices."[2] Thus, economic dynamics are those parts of economic theory where the question of dates comes in and is not only important but also inevitable. Statics studies stationary situations in which there are no changes and, therefore, they do not require any comparison with past or future.

In a stationary state, the factor analysis of the present may be employed to predict the future. In the views of Prof. Hicks, it is only a change in the system which causes the analysis to be dynamic. He states that changes will cause things to be different at different dates and, therefore, they make the analysis dynamic.

Many economists nave criticised Hicks' definition. They expressed the view that the dynamic theory of Hicks includes many problems where methods of static analysis are called for. Prof. Hicks has not appreciated that dynamics is not something which should be applied to have a comparative study of the two phenomena. Such a study could be called comparative statics. Hicks only emphasises that dynamic economics or economic dynamics includes an element of change which is, according to subsequent economists, not valid.

Harrod, in this context, states, "Hicks appears to be analysing the effects of once-over change in fundamental conditions. There is no recognition that a different technique may be required for analysing the effects of continuing changes." Harrod thus wants to base the definition of dynamic economics on continuing changes as against those which take place once for all. Harrod further states, "One change over is the same thing as a once-over change in taste." In a dynamic system, the determinant will not be the existence of a certain expectation or once-over change in that expectation. This may itself be determined by a rate of change in some other' fundamental condition. The effects of a once-over change in expectation are likely to continue to be handled by the method of economic statics.[3]

---

2. J.R. Hicks: *Value and Capital,* p. 115.
3. Harrod, R.F., *Towards a Dynamic Economics.* 1949.

According to Ragnar Frisch the most important basis of dynamics is the analysis of the *process of change and not the non-stationarity* of the system analysed. He argues, "By static analysis is meant a method of dealing with economic phenomena that tries to establish relations between the elements of the economic system, prices and quantities of commodities—all of which have the same point of time." "Dynamic economic analysis is one in which we consider the magnitudes of certain variables on different points of time and introduce certain equations which embrace at the same time several of those magnitudes at different instants."[4] Thus, dynamic study analyses the influences of relative factors in relation to a change in some particular economic variable.

Further, William Baumol, an American economist, believes that economic dynamics is prediction, i.e., it enables us to answer many questions about the present and the future on the basis of the historical facts of the past. Baumol, also believes that the purpose of economic dynamics is not only forecasting market trends, but also relating these trends to different events, past and present. As he puts it, "Economic dynamics is a study of economic phenomena in relation to preceding and succeeding events."

The main difference between the definitions of William Baumol and Ragnar Frisch lies in the fact that while Prof. Baumol believes that the basis of economic dynamics is the predictability, Prof. Frisch considers it to be the analysis of a process. There are a number of other economists who define economic dynamics as the study of the processes through which 'the final position of equilibrium is reached via a series of adjustments over time. Prof. Hicks and Prof. Harrod, on their part, confine themselves to the definition of the contents of economic dynamics. According to Prof. Hicks, the concept of economic dynamics is economic statics involving time, and not dynamic as such.

2. ECONOMIC STATICS

In economic statics, we study the laws of equilibrium. Here we assume certain factors to be constant and then study their results. Prof. Marshall observed, "The forces to be dealt with are, however, so numerous that it is best to take a few at a time and to work out a number of partial solutions as auxiliaries to our main study. Thus, we begin by isolating the primary

4. R. Frisch, "Propagation Problems and Impulse Problems in Dynamic Economics," *Economic Essays in Honour of Gustav Cassel.*

relations of supply, demand and price in regard to a particular commodity. We reduce to inaction all other forces by the phrase, *other things being equal.* We do not suppose that they are inert, but for the time being, we ignore their activity. This scientific device is a great deal older than science; it is the method by which consciously or unconsciously sensible men deal from time immemorial with every difficult problem of ordinary life. In the second stage, more forces are released from the hypothetical slumber than had been imposed on them. Gradually, the area of dynamical problem becomes larger; the area covered by provisional statical assumptions becomes smaller."[5]

The basic idea in economic statics is clearly a notion of equilibrium and hence of forces in equilibrium. As compared with mechanics, the notion of forces is much more or less troublesome in economics. However, a majority of economists use the terms like equilibrium and tendency in the sense of statical modes and mathematical limits. While in a physical set-up of mechanical equilibrium, the forces unavoidably act through things having mass—weights or springs—and hence act upon these mass as well as upon each other. If friction (disagreement) could be eliminated from such a system, it would never actually come from any other position to a stationary equilibrium and would perpetually oscillate or move around the same circuit which could be represented by an equation. It is rather crude in economics to attribute any continuing divergence of conditions from those of theoretical equilibrium to a friction as sometimes economists do, since the theory of a frictionless system calls not for equilibrium but for perpetual oscillation. It seems that the analogy in the minds of economists for discussing the tendency toward equilibrium is that of movement against a viscious friction, with inertia absent or negligible.

The method of economic statics is generally associated with the concept of a stationary state which is only a methodological fiction (or imaginary method); more specifically, a simplifying device or a tool of analysis. As Prof. Walter Eucken puts it, "The static state has never been realised historically. Large changes in data have been constantly occurring, occasionally only small changes but never no changes at all."[6] In the basic economic law of uniform prices in a market, the assumption of perfect competition is common. Only the time dimension seems to carry over directly and be available for use in the field of economics. We cannot reduce the economic process of quantitative terms unless we can give

5. Alfred Marshall, *op. cit.,* Preface, pp. 14-15.
6. Walter Eucken, *The Foundation of Economics.* 1950, p. 204.

workable meaning to space and to mass. We constantly speak of frictions in economic changes and even of degrees of position or identity, yet, it is not always possible to use the notion (idea) of social forces and processes in a definite sense which might be represented by perfect coordinates. It may be added that the problems in economic statics are those problems connected with equilibrium conditions which do not involve any variations in the time element. An equilibrium for a specified model is characterised by a lack of tendency to change. For this reason the analysis of equilibrium is known as statics.

As already stated, statics analysis discusses the question of how, for example, an equilibrium price is arrived at in a market where demand and supply functions are known and remain unchanged. In economic statics the equilibrium value of a dependent variable will remain unchanged so long as the independent variable remains constant. For this reason, such a static model involves no dating of economic variables. The theory of product pricing is a good example of economic statics. Here we presume that the price of the commodity will be determined by the forces of supply and demand existing at a particular time.

Similarly, if saving and investment functions are known, we may find the equilibrium national income where savings are equal to investment. The equilibrium level of income will remain unchanged, so long as the saving and investment functions remain unchanged.

Scope of Static Economics

The classical economists in the past have made an extensive use of the methods of economic statics. Today, the various assumptions associated with the static analysis have narrowed down the scope of static economics in the study of real world problems. The important assumptions of economic statics are perfect knowledge, absence of uncertainty, given consumer tastes, given population, perfect fact or mobility, etc. Some of these assumptions are quite unrealistic and for this reason the static analysis is rendered incapable of any application in the real world. Butin spite of this fact, Prof. Harrod remarks, "I am sure that statics will remain an important part of the whole." The method of economic statics is the only device to make the treatment of complex problems easier and clearer.

Even today economic statics covers the following problems of the economic statics:

(1) The problem of free trade will be studied under the method of economic statics.

(2) Monopoly price-determination may also be regarded as the part of economic statics; because it is based on the assumption that the behaviour pattern of the buyers and sellers remains the same with the passage of time. Here, it is the marginal cost and not the average cost of production which governs price of the product.

(3) Since the law of diminishing marginal utility assumes no time interval in the consumption of a commodity, it comes within the purview of economic statics.

(4) The economic behaviour of a man or the law of equi-marginal utility is also studied under static economics, because it is based on a timeless consideration.

(5) The comparative costs theory of international trade is studied under economic statics so far as it assumes perfect mobility between factors of production within the country and absence of change, etc.

(6) The marginal analysis comes under economic statics.

(7) Economic statics can study those problems arising out of the once-over changes. When the once-over changes take place in any of the assumptions of economic statics, the relevant static equations may define the position of the new static equilibrium.

Under relatively more stable conditions, that is, conditions undergoing slower processes of change, the static analysis serves as theoretical analysis as a framework or setting of given conditions with reference to shorter period adjustments. These short-run adjustments have the character of tending to establish equilibrium with reference to their respective given conditions at any given time. According to Prof. Hicks, economic statics includes the theories of traditional economics which are studied without reference to time element. According to Prof. Tinbergen, static economics can be used to study the long-run tendencies of certain cases, i.e., the determination of the final results.

Advantages of Economic Statics

The main advantages of economic statics are given below:

(1) We can understand the working of the complex economic system with the help of this method.

(2) We can understand the nature of the functioning of the economic system only when we study economic statics, i.e., the position of static equilibrium.

(3) The study of dynamic economics requires a pre-study of static economics. In order to understand the various implications of dynamic

analysis, we must know the contents of economic statics, as the study of the laws of rest is necessary to understand the laws of motion.

(4) Economic statics is a simple method because it assumes several things remaining the same while studying an economic law.

Limitations of Economic Statics

The limitations of this method are mostly based upon its unrealistic assumptions. The main weaknesses of this device are given below:

(1) Static analysis is largely unrealistic and unsuitable for many purposes. The problems which involve dating are not studied by this method.

(2) It assumes no change in both the dependent variable and the independent variable under consideration and, therefore, ignores a comparative study of the economic phenomena.

(3) If we make a change in any of the variables (independent variables), it affects our final conclusions.

(4) In the real world where rapid changes take place, the economic statics cannot provide accurate results. Its results are misleading.

3. COMPARATIVE STATICS

In a static analysis, we are concerned with the stationary state or the non-evolutionary process. In other words, in a static economic model, the values of both the dependent variables as well as the independent variables are assumed to be constant and they explain the economic phenomena at a given point of time. More specifically, the process of the adjustment of such variables towards equilibrium does not cause any shift in any of the independent variables, and consequently the equilibrium position remains unchanged. But in a comparative static analysis, there may be a change in the independent variable, and here, we analyse its impact on the dependent variable. In other words, a shift will take place due to a change in independent variable and it will lead to a new equilibrium position. A method which compares these two equilibrium positions is referred to as the method of comparative statics.

It must be borne in mind that comparative statics oblivates the path which has been followed while moving from one static equilibrium to another. In this method, we, however, study the evolutionary process in a series of equilibria, and often compare the new position of equilibrium to the old one. In the words of Prof. Lipsey, "Comparative statics involves a comparison of the new equilibrium position (E_1) with the original equilibrium position (*E*) .... We wish to form an hypothesis about the effect of some change in data; for example, the introduction of a tax or a change in the conditions of demand. We start from a position of equilibrium and then introduce the change to be studied. The new equilibrium position is determined and it is compared with the original one. The differences in the two positions of equilibrium must be due to changes in the data that were introduced. This analysis, which is based on a comparison of two positions of equilibrium, is called comparative static equilibrium analysis."[7]

Therefore, the method of comparative statics deals only with the final equilibrium positions. Suppose, in our previous static model of demand and supply, the demand function shifts upward due to an increase in the value of α caused by a change in some independent variable, say, income and with the values of α, b and β remaining unchanged, price will increase. In other words, in period (t_{+1}), due to an increase (upward shift) in the demand function, the price level (P_{t+1}) will be higher than P_t.

Comparative statics, therefore, compares the two equilibrium prices. Comparative statics also occupies an important place in economic analysis, particularly in the theories of monopolies and competition. But it is unable to study the path which the market follows when it shifts from one position of equilibrium to another. This would call for economic dynamics which explains how one situation emerges out of the preceding situation.

4. ECONOMIC DYNAMICS

Various economists have defined economic dynamics in different ways. According to Prof. J.R. Hicks, dynamic economics includes only those parts of economic theory where every quantity must be dated.[8] According to Prof. R.F. Harrod, economic dynamics is the study of an economy in which the rates of output are changmg.[9] Harrod has observed, "Dynamics will specially be concerned with the effects of continuing changes and with the rates of change in the values that have to be determined." In the words of Prof. William J. Baumol, "Economic dynamics is the study of economic phenomena in relation to preceding and succeeding events." According to Prof. Lipsey, "Dynamic analysis may be defined as the study of the behaviour of systems, single markets or whole economics, in disequilibrium conditions." According to Hicks, "Economic dynamics refers to those parts of economic theory where the problem of dating is

7. Richard G. Lipsey, *An Introduction to Positive Economics* (1964), p. 118.
8. J.R. Hicks, *op. cit.*, p. 115.
9. R.F. Harrod, *op. cit.*, p. 5.

conspicuously important." Similarly, Prof. Ragnar Frisch has defined dynamic economics as "one whose behaviour over a time is determined by functional equations at which variables at different points of time are involved in an essential way." Thus, the main concern of all these definitions of economic dynamics is with the dates. This implies that unlike the static analysis economic dynamics explains lagged relationship between the dependent and the independent variables.

There are economists who define dynamic economics in relation to equilibrium. According to these economists dynamic economics studies the process through which the final position of equilibrium is reached through a series of adjustments over a series of time. Baumol states that dynamic economics has the power of forecasting future.

Economic growth and fluctuations are studied with the help of dynamic analysis. During 1930s and 1940s many theories regarding dynamic analysis have been developed. Frisch, Kelecki and Samuelson developed mathematical analysis in relation to economic fluctuations. They are helpful to understand the causes of economic fluctuations. On the other hand, Harrod in England and Domar in America developed the theories of economic growth. In the field of national income analysis, economists like Robertson, Haberler, Hansen, Machlup and others have emphasised the use of dynamic processes. The Swedish economists (notably, Gunnar Myrdal, Bertil Ohlin, Lindall and Lundberg) have made use of dynamic models to discuss national income analysis. Today, the theories of interest and profit are also studied under dynamic analysis.

In simple words, complex problems in economics, especially when they involve movements towards a constantly changing equilibrium, may be analysed by economic dynamics. Several examples of this type from both microeconomics and macroeconomics can be given. If we assume that consumption expenditure (C) in period t is determined by the income (Y) received in the preceding time period, i.e., $t - 1$, then such type of relationship will be studied under economic dynamics. Mathematically,

$$Ct = f(Y_{t-1})$$

or

$$Ct + 1 = f(Y_t)...$$

Similarly, we may also define such a relationship from microeconomics. Here it may be assumed that the supply of a commodity in period t may be a function of its price prevailing in previous period, i.e., $t - 1$. Mathematically,

$$St = f(P_{t-1})$$

or $$S_{t+1} = f(P_t)$$
or $$S_{t+2} = f(P_{t+1})$$
or $$S_{t-1} = f(P_{t-2})$$
or $$S_{t-2} = f(P_{t-3})...$$

Thus, economic dynamics defines lagged relationships between the dependent and the independent variables; *Cobwebs theorem* is the simplest model of these dynamics of demand, supply and price. The essential features of the model are:

$$D_t = f(P_t) \qquad ...(1)$$

and $$S_t = f(P_{t-1}) \qquad ...(2)$$

Hence, supply of lagged one period behind price. Agricultural commodities provide good examples of lagged supply functions. Suppose, this year's price of wheat (*Pt*) is high. Now farmers make their plans for next year ($t + 1$); each assuming that next year's price will be high too. But in the following year the price actually falls because in the time period, $t + 1$, the supply of wheat is greater than the demand. Here, the main assumption of the theorem is that nothing is stored and entire production is in the market. It clears that quantity demanded in any period depends upon the price in that period, but quantity supplied depends upon the price in the previous year. In other words, equations (1) and (2) hold in the real world.

Hence, the analysis of the path travelled between the new and the initial equilibrium position is economic dynamics. Hicks also agrees that the presence of expectations is sufficient to characterise an economy as dynamic. He says, "Once the missing element of the anticipations is added, equilibrium analysis can be used, not only in the remote stationary conditions to which many economists have found themselves driven back, but even in the real world in disequilibrium."[10]

Advantages of Economic Dynamics

As we have already discussed, the importance of economic dynamics has always been realised. Even in the development of classical theories, economic dynamics was assumed to be equally important with economic statics. Later on, more emphasis has been given to economic dynamics. The main advantages of economic dynamics are the following:

(1) As we know, economic statics can study only the final result of a change from one equilibrium position to another equilibrium position. It cannot study the process of the change or the problems of transitional

---

10. J.R. Hicks, *op. cit.*, p. 115.

period. For this, economic dynamics is used.

(2) The complex economic phenomena, such as, cyclical fluctuations and secular growth are reasonably studied under dynamic economics.

(3) Moreover, it is used to correct the unrealistic nature of economic statics. As we know, economic statics is based on unrealistic assumptions, such as, perfect knowledge, absence of uncertainty, given consumer tastes, given population, perfect factor mobility, etc. It further assumes a stationary state to exist. All this leads to unrealistic conclusions. Economic dynamics is free from these unrealistic assumptions and, therefore, is much nearer to reality than economic statistics.

(4) This method is highly flexible. It can develop a number of models to explore all the possibilities concerning a particular problem. Most of the modern theories of trade cycles are based on the dynamic models of Ragnar Frisch and Paul A. Samuelson.

Limitations of Economic Dynamics

The method of economic dynamics possesses the following weaknesses:

(1) Although economic dynamics is more realistic than economic statics, yet it is essentially very complex and only a highly trained mathematician and economist could make full use of it.

(2) The method of economic dynamics is not yet fully developed and therefore, possesses a limited scope in present-day economic analysis.

From the above, one can conclude that both economic statics and economic dynamics are complementary to each other. Economic analysis can neither do without dynamics nor can it do without statics. Some of the problems of economic analysis can only be solved by the help of economic dynamics while many others can be better tackled by the simple static economics. A few problems are there which can be solved with the collective application of both the methods. Thus, economic statics and economic-dynamics are both needed for the study of economic analysis.

EXERCISES

1. What are the differences between economic statics and economic dynamics? Discuss their principal characteristics and the areas of their use.
2. "I call economic statics those parts of economic theory where we do not trouble about dating; economic dynamics are those parts where every quantity must be dated"—(J.R. Hicks). How far do you agree with the above statement?
3. Distinguish between economic statics and economic dynamics. Explain the impor-tance and shortcomings of statics as a methodological device.
4. Write a lucid note on the concept of economic dynamics.
5. What do you understand by economic dynamics? Discuss in brief the main

methods by which economists have sought to cope with dynamic problems.

6. Describe the Cobweb Model with the help of micro and macro variables.

Multiple Choice Questions

7. (*i*) In micro-static model, supply and demand relationships determine price at
   (*a*) point of time
   (*b*) period of time
   (*c*) constant range of time
   (*d*) none of the above [*Ans.* (*a*)]

   (*ii*) micro-dynamic analysis is
   (*a*) the demand-supply model at a point of time
   (*b*) the Cobweb model
   (*c*) the income-consumption model
   (*d*) all of the above [*Ans.* (*b*)]

Chapter 7

ECONOMY AND ITS VITAL PROCESSES

1. WHAT IS AN ECONOMY?

An economy is a system or a set-up which provides people with the means of livelihood. It is the organisation of the process of production and distribution where, in co-operation with others, people produce and acquire goods and services for the satisfaction of their wants. According to A.J. Brown, "It is a system by which people get a living."[1] According to J.R. Hicks, "An economy consists of nothing else but an immense cooperation of workers or producers to make things which consumer wants."[2] The Indian economy, for example, is the collection of all the farms, factories, workshops, mines, roads, railways, banks, schools, cinema-houses and hospitals, looked at, as a huge workshop, which provides Indian people with the goods which either they consume, or use for further production or export to the foreign countries. Not only goods, are produced but services are also rendered by professional people, like doctors, teachers, lawyers, musicians etc. These services are directly consumed by the members of the society. Each one of these individuals who renders services, is as important a production unit as are the big farms and factories that constitute the economy.

The simplest type of economy is one where every one has to provide for himself all the goods that he requires. The famous example given by the textbooks on economics is that of Robinson Crusoe, who being lonely on the island had to produce everything for himself. But today the economies are much more complex, based upon high degree of specialisation. The number of occupations in which people are engaged today runs into thousands. Consequently the number of goods produced are also very large.

---

1. A.J. Brown, *Introduction to the World Economy,* 1965, p. 11.
2. I.R. Hicks, *The Social Framework—An Introduction to Economics,* 1972, pp. 17-18.

An economy, today is a system of parts, all of which depend upon each other in a complicated way. A retail shopkeeper, selling ready-made shirts, for example, is one of the thousands and thousands of people engaged in the business of manufacturing and selling clothes. The retailer may have purchased this shirt from a wholesaler, who in turn got it from sole distributor. The distributor got it from the manufacturer. The manufacturer in turn got the cloth manufactured and stitched in various departments of his factory where probably thousands of people are employed. Then the raw material for cloth came from cotton field, the machinery for manufacturing must have been made somewhere in huge factories. If we include all those people who are making agricultural tools, weaving and sewing machines, those engaged in transport, packing and marketing, the number would become enormously large. In simple terms, the farmers, the weavers and spinners, the tailors, employers and workers and many more people have co-operated and come together in the process of making a shirt for the consumer. What is true of the shirt is also true of all other commodities.

Economies of the world differ from one another in many respects. The differences may sometimes arise because of the coverage of geographical area. We often talk about village economy, the economy of a region or of a nation, according to the area or territory which we are considering. These days we find a considerable economic independence among the various economies. Developments in transport and trade have bought the various economies close to each other. Events in one part of the world have their repercussion upon the other. Hence we find a growing trend among economists to think of the whole world as one economy.

Simple and Complex Economy

A simple economy is one in which every person provides for himself all the goods and services that he uses. No one has any economic relation with others. There is no exchange and hence no trade with any individual or community. It is a state of complete self-sufficiency. The famous illustration of this type of economy is provided by Robinson Crusoe, who being alone on the island, had to provide himself with all his requirements. In actual world this type of economy can be said to have existed in the primitive times, when wants were few and limited. Even now, instances of such an economy may be found in some isolated village communities where every family produces all its requirements by itself. Self-sufficient manorial villages of feudal England, and the self contained rural communities of India are good examples of simple economy.

As wants multiply and diversify, the simple economies give way to the complex ones. It is no more possible for any individual and family to produce all the things which they use. Specialisation and exchange become essential. Self-sufficiency of village communities is broken. Highly specialised firms crop-up to produce goods and services. Specialised markets evolve for the purchase and sale of the continuous stream of a large variety of goods that flow from the productive units. Larger the number of wants greater is the specialisation and interdependence. Higher the degree of interdependence, greater is the complexity of an economy. Every individual and family, farm and factory, plant and company, depends upon many others for the purchase of materials, and production or sale of goods. Thus the essence of complex economy is a very high degree of specialisation and extreme interdependence.

Market and Subsistence Economy

A classification is also made between a market and subsistence economy. A market economy is one, where the production is carried on mainly with the purpose of sale in the market. Only a small portion of produce is retained for personal consumption. But in a subsistence economy, the things are produced mainly for self consumption. Only a small fraction of produce is sold in the market, and that too only occasionally. Indian agriculture is said to be of a subsistence nature. We very well know that the Indian farmer, having a very small amount of land and other resources, generally produces only those things which he requires for this own consumption. Only a few rich farmers produce goods for the market. But in countries like New Zealand, Australia and Canada where agriculture is well developed, production is meant to be sold, not only in the local market, but is also exported to the rest of the world. Generally a subsistence economy is found in simple and primitive forms. A market economy is essentially a complex economy, because here things are bought and sold in the market. This leads to a considerable inter dependence.

Closed and Open Economy

A closed economy is one, which is self-sufficient and hence does not have any external economic relationship. It neither imports anything, nor does it export. Those economies, on the other hand, which have trade relationship with other economies are called open economies. They export and import things as a normal part of their economic activity. Most of the economies today are open; because they depend to a considerable extent upon the other countries for the goods which they import or export.

Examples of closed economies could be only found in the self-contained village communities or in certain communist countries which may be completely cut-off from the rest of the world in matters of foreign trade.

2. BROAD FEATURES OF MODERN ECONOMIES

The world, as we find it today, consists of a large number of economies, small and big which have widely divergent economic systems. Some of these are capitalist or free enterprise economies while others are completely controlled. Some economies have adopted planning as an integral part of their economic policy, while the others are still largely unplanned. Further a few of these economies are rich, developed and industrialised, whereas a large number of them in Asia, Africa and Southern America are poor, backward or underdeveloped. But one thing common in all these economies whether rich or poor, free or controlled, planned or unplanned, is that all of them are complex economies. Of course the advance industrialised countries of the West have a greater degree of complexity than the underdeveloped agricultural countries. Yet all of them, taken together are more complex today when compared with the simple economies of the primitive ages. At that time people were mostly self sufficient. Every one produced almost all those things which he required. But with the advance of time and dawn of civilisation, the wants multiplied, and therefore, it has become impossible for anyone to make all those goods which he needs. The self-sufficiency of old times has been completely broken. Today we are, to a great degree, dependent upon others for the goods we require for our consumption. In fact, each one of us works in cooperation with the others to acquire what we want, and at the same time, giving to others what they want. In essence the fundamental principle upon which the modern economy works is "you do this for me and I do that for you". Some of the broad features, which are common to all the economies today, are given below:

1. Division of Labour and Specialisation

Since our wants are unlimited, it is not possible for us to make all the things we require to satisfy them. Therefore we produce only those things for the production of which we are best suited. Every body takes up a job for which he is supposed to nave the interest, aptitude, training and capability. This process of picking up a particular job and doing it repeatedly, is known as specialisation. For example, some people specialise in agriculture. Their job is to work on land and produce food etc. At the same time others specialise in the production of industrial goods. Some may specialise in services like those of doctors, teachers, lawyers etc. All these people produce things for which they are best suited and after keeping a part of them for their own use they exchange their surplus with the others. The specialisation, in other words, is a division of labour among various people, to satisfy each others needs. Agriculturists produce to satisfy their own needs as well as of those who are outside agriculture. Similarly the producers in industry make their goods also for those who are outside the field of industrial production.

Specialisation and division of labour have become very complex today. People, now, do not produce the complete commodities. In most of the cases, they make only a part of them. For example, in the modern cloth mills people working in the spinning department, may know nothing about weaving and those working in weaving may be absolutely ignorant about the dying and designing of the cloth. This means, that an ordinary worker performs only a small operation in the production of the whole commodity. The finished commodity is the result of the joint effort of a large number of workers.

This complex division of labour has made the process of production quick and efficient by facilitating the introduction of machinery. The modem economies, with the help of latest machinery and highly advanced technical knowledge, produce more goods and better goods than the earlier simple type of economies.

2. Capitalistic Production

Another important feature of modern economies is the use of capitalistic methods of production. By capitalistic method we mean those methods of production in which capital is extensively used. Capital goods like machines, factories, tools and implements are indispensable to the process of production these days. With the use of machinery the volume of production has enormously increased. The quality of production has also improved because the machines take note of even those details which human being cannot. Of course even the primitive man in the simplest economy, used capital in the form of bows and arrows for hunting for some simple tools for cultivation of land. But the technological advancement of the past two centuries have made the use of capital wider and deeper. Today we use huge, complicated, automatic type of goods. As a result the production has become round about. We do not produce the things directly. For production of consumer goods, first of all we have to produce the machinery to be used for production. Every economy today invests a large part of its resources for the making of capital goods (machinery). The countries, which produce the large amount of capital goods, are in fact the richest countries of the world. This is so, because the machines add to the productive capacity of the nation. The larger the number of machines, factories or plants in a country, the greater is the flow of goods out of them, making the economy richer.

3. Excess Use of Money

A necessary consequence of specialisation and division of labour in the modern economy, is the growth of exchange. When the individuals specialise in the production of few commodities, they must exchange them for others. In the simple economy, exchange was done in terms of barter. Barter exchange means giving one thing and getting another for it. If the farmer gives wheat and gets cloth from the weaver, this is a barter exchange. But this process of exchange being full of difficulties, could not continue in modern times. Nowadays we exchange goods with the help of money. The farmer sells his wheat for money and with that money he purchases the cloth. The weaver sells cloth for money and purchases wheat with it. In fact the farmer has given wheat and got cloth while the weaver has given cloth and got wheat. But all this happened with the help of money. Thus money performs today the important function of being the medium of exchange. It has greatly facilitated and developed the exchange system. The large scale production, based upon specialisation and division of labour in the modern economies, would have been absolutely impossible in the absence of money. In fact money plays a very important role in the field of production, exchange and distribution in the modern economy.

4. Expansion of World Trade

It is well known that most of the economies today are specialised, to some degree in certain lines of production. They produce more of some goods than what they need for their domestic consumption and exchange the surplus with other countries. Thus specialisation among the various economies has given rise to international trade. No economy of the world can be said to be completely self-sufficient. Every one depends upon others to some extent. Of course the degree of dependence differs from one economy to the other. Soviet Union, for example, produces almost all that it requires; the amount of its transactions with the rest of the world amounts to 2 to 3 per cent of its national income. USA produces all except 4 to 5 per cent of what it requires. On the other hand Great Britain,

Canada, Switzerland etc. have a comparatively much larger volume of foreign trade.

The expansion of world trade have brought the various countries economically close to each other. What happens in one part of the world has its effect, through trade, upon the other countries. With the existing high degree of interdependence and interrelationship among the various countries, the interest of the economists has shifted from national economy to the world economy. The economic problems are today seen in context with the world as a whole and the various international agencies like UNO, IMF, IBRD, WTO, UNCTAD, etc. are busy in finding solutions of the world economic problems.

5. Dominant Role of the Government

The government, these days, is playing an increasingly important role in the working of modern economies. In old times, functions of the government were limited only to the maintenance of law and order within the country, the defence of country from foreign aggression and providing administrative services. The interference in economic activity by the government was not only thought to be undesirable, but regarded as positively harmful for the working of the economy. In modern times the governments of advanced countries have taken upon themselves the responsibility of assuring economic stability and maintaining output, employ-ment and incomes at a high level. Economic policy in these countries is framed so as to avoid the trade cycles—recurrance of booms and depressions. In the backward economies, the government undertakes direct investment with a view to raise the levels of output, income and employment.

3. VITAL PROCESSES OF AN ECONOMY

An economy, being an organisation of activities which enables the people to get livelihood, has certain vital processes, which keep on going in it simultaneously and continuously. These processes are: (*a*) production, (*b*) consumption, and (*c*) investment. The health of the economy depends upon how vigorously and regularly these processes are going on. Slowing down of anyone of these processes will affect the others and this might result in bringing the economy to a lower level of activity. Therefore, the economy has to see that these are maintained at a reasonable high level so as to utilise to the maximum the stock of available resources, and to further add to the level of economic activity.

1. Production

Production to a layman means producing goods as making of cloth, or growing of food. In economics, however production has a much wider meaning. It implies the creation or addition of utility. Man cannot produce matter. Everything in the world is given and fixed. We can neither add to it nor destroy it. Therefore the job of man is to work upon this given matter and make it more useful for human beings. When a carpenter makes a table out a log of wood, he does not create matter. He merely changes the shape of wood and transforms it into a table. The wood was already there in the form of a tree in jungle or log lying somewhere. By changing the shape the same wood now becomes more serviceable. Similarly a potter who makes pots of clay or the goldsmith making the ornaments and the tailor making a shirt, all create utilities. They create those qualities in commodities by which they can satisfy human wants. Production then, we may conclude, means creation or addition of economic utilities.

Not only the material goods, like the examples we have taken above are being produced, but services are also rendered in the economy. The services like those of the doctors, teachers, lawyers and household servants are as important a part of production, as the output of material things. If we regard the radio set as being produced by some one, then the mechanic, who sets it right whensoever it goes out of order, must also be regarded as an equally important producer, in this case he is producing the services of radio repairs. The same is true for all other services.

Thus all goods and services which originate in an economy during a given period of time are to be included in the production of an economy. The only exceptions are the non-economic activities, i.e., those activities which are done without expecting any corresponding monetary return. For example, the activities of the housewife like looking after the children or house-keeping, which are very important for smooth living, and which have a considerable influence on a person's ability and willingness to work are not to be treated as a part of production. This is so, because these services are being done not for any monetary reward. And further, there is no method of evaluating them.

2. Consumption

The second process which is vital for an economy is consumption. It is a process of taking out satisfaction from the commodities. When we wear a shirt, we are said to consume it. The use of the shirt gives us some satisfaction. Even when we are not wearing it, it may be kept at home. Yet the fact that we possess a shirt gives us the desired satisfaction. The consumption of the shirt, therefore, may be said to go on as long as it is in one's possession, whether he wears it right now, or might wear it in future.

Sometimes, consumption is used in sense of destruction. When we say the house has been consumed by fire, we mean that house has been destroyed. But such destruction, which does not satisfy anybody's wants will not be treated as consumption in economics. Consumption does not mean destruction of matter for the science tells us that matter cannot be destroyed. We only take out utility from the matter during the process of consumption. Therefore any process whereby utility is taken out of a commodity for the satisfaction of human wants, is known as consumption.

The process of consumption may be slow or rapid. When we consume perishable goods like food, fruit and vegetables, the process is rapid because utility is destroyed immediately. On the other hand in case of the durable goods like houses, furniture, clothes etc. the consumption goes on for a very long period of time. The utility of these commodities diminishes gradually and not at once. Services, which we regard as having been produced are also consumed. For the satisfaction of our wants we require services of many kinds. The services of domestic servants, the sweepers and washermen, the doctors and teachers, waiters and bus drivers are perhaps very important for our daily life. These services are consumed instantaneously, i.e., their consumption takes place at the same time at which they are produced. But there is always some time lag between the production and consumption of material goods. From factories, the goods may have to pass on to consumers through the long chain of middlemen, wholesales, and retailers, lying for sometime in go downs, before they pass out from each stage. In fact there is a sort of pipeline connecting the products, and the producers of finished products, with the final consumers. The goods flow regularly in these pipelines, and unless these pipelines have something in them at every stage, production at the next stage is likey to be held up.

3. Investment

If production is going on faster than consumption, goods in the pipeline will increase. Conversely, if the consumption is going on faster than production, the goods in pipeline decrease. This accumulation of stocks through an excess of production over consumption is called inventory investment. If the stocks are running down, the process is called negative investment or disinvestment.

There is another way in which the amount of goods produced may differ from amount of goods consumed. There are goods like machinery, factories, transport equipment, etc., which are produced not for direct consumption, but for indirectly satisfying our wants through further production of goods or services. Such goods are known as capital goods, and the amount of resources spent upon their production is called fixed capital. Some of the capital goods wear out during the process of production, and therefore have to be replaced. The part of community's production which is used for maintenance of existing machinery through repairs, and replacing the worn out machines, is also fixed investment.

The above analysis, gives a fair insight into the processes which keep going on in the economy. First there is a stream of goods flowing from the productive resources. A part of these goods is consumed, and the rest goes to add to productive resources in the form of capital goods and inventories (stocks). These three processes, production, consumption and investment, are compared to the three vital processes of human body viz., feeding, digestion and growth. As the strength of the man depends upon the vital processes which go on in his body, similarly the strength of economy depends upon the vital processes, which operate in it.

4. WORKING OF PRODUCTION PROCESS

Production is the result of the combination of different factors of production viz., land, labour, capital and organisation. The production of goods and services in an economy goes on continuously and indefinitely; it has been there since the origin of mankind and will continue till the man lives on in the world. To study the working of this production process we have to fix our mind on a particular period, say one year. At the beginning of the year there exists a certain stock of goods—consumers' goods as well as producers' goods. The goods are inherited from the previous year and are the result of productive activity during that year.

This is the position at the beginning of the year. Now the time moves on and the wheels of economy begin to revolve. The consumer goods are purchased by the consumers for consumption. The shopkeepers place more orders on the firms and factories for the further supplies. The firms arrange for raw material and put them into the processes of production. The labour starts working on the capital (machines etc.) to turn out finished goods. Thus the process goes on, a continuous stream of consumer's goods is passing into final consumption, raw material and semi-finished goods are being pressed into the production of final goods and thus, the wheels of production move forward and onward.

Those producers' goods (semi-finished products) which are produced during the year and used up in the production of finished goods during that year are not counted as a part of the annual output since they have been included in the value of final goods. However those semi-finished goods which are not used up in the production of final goods within the year and will be used only during the next year wilt-have to be taken into account while calculating annual output. Thus we find:

(1) A large quantity of consumer goods being produced and consumed repre-senting the community's consumption during the period of one year.

(2) Those consumer's goods which have been produced but have not been able to reach the final consumers during the year will add to the stock of consumer's goods. From this stock of consumer goods at the end of the year we deduct the stock of these goods, at the beginning of the year and find out the increase or decrease in the stock of consumer goods over the year. This would represent net inventory investment or disinvestment as the case may be.

(3) During the year a large amount of producers' goods (both single-use producer goods like unfinished and semi-finished products and durable-use producers' goods like machines etc.) have been produced. The single-use producers goods have changed into final products and hence they are not to be calculated. Only that quantity of single-use producers' goods which have remained unused is to be taken into account. The excess of the stock of such goods at the end of the year over the stock at the beginning of the year would represent the production during the year and would add to the stock of working capital. The production of durable-use producers goods add to the stock of fixed capital available in the economy. If from the value of durable-use producers goods produced during the year, we deduct the amount of depreciation for the use of capital, its wear and tear etc., we get the net addition to the stock of fixed capital. If the quantities of goods turned out is greater at the end of the year than at the beginning, the economy may be said to have grown during the year.

The same process would be repeated in the coming years. Economy, every year, would start with a certain stock of goods. During the year the production and consumption would take place. At the end of the year the economy may be left with a greater or smaller amount of goods re-presenting growth or decay. If the amount of goods at the end is the same as at the beginning of the year, the economy may be said to be stagnating.

This process of production can be summarised in the following way. At the beginning of the year the economy has a stock of goods of all kinds. This we call initial equipment. During the year, labour works upon this equipment and produces goods. A part of it consists of consumer goods which are consumed during the year. The rest adds to productive equipment in the form of durable producers goods. The stock of equipment in the beginning of next year would be equal to the initial equipment plus equipment produced during the year minus using up of equipment during this year.

The scheme of production can be summarised as follows:

Factors of production	:	Labour + Initial Equipments
Production or output	:	Consumption + New Equipment
Initial equipment (at the beginning of the next year)	:	Initial equipment (at the beginning of this year) + New equipments produced during this year – Using up of the equipments during this year.

So far we have excluded from our analysis the direct services rendered by labour. We have also excluded the durable-use consumer goods like houses and buildings etc. The houses that exist at the beginning of the year, go on rendering services over the year. The rental value of the houses may be taken as the indicator of their consumption during the year. With the introduction of these two, we can summarise the productive process in all completeness in the following diagram:

WORKING OF THE PRODUCTIVE PROCESS

(A diagrammatic presentation)

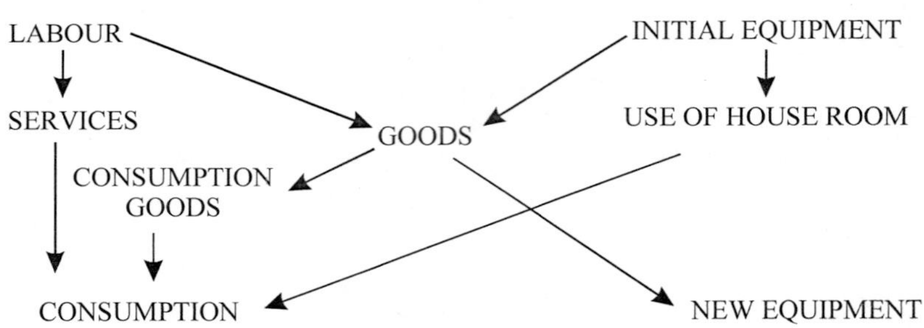

Fig. 7.1

Figure 7.1 shows that labour alone produces services which are immediately consumed. Labour with equipment produces goods, a part of these goods are single-use consumer's goods and are consumed during the year. Some of them are durable-use consumers' goods and hence are consumed slowly, only a small part of these goods being consumed during, the year. However an important category of goods produced during the year refers to the producers' goods which add to the initial equipment and hence during the coming year the available equipment will be greater than what it was at the beginning of the present year. The above picture of the productive process is however the simple to take account of the various intricate relationships. We know that present day organisation of production and exchange are extremely complex and therefore require a deep probing for its understanding. However the above analysis gives a sufficiently clear picture of the over-all working of an economy in a simplified manner.

EXERCISES

1. What is an economy? Discuss in brief the various types of economies.
2. Discuss the broad features of modern economies.
3. Explain the vital processes of an economy indicating in particular the relationship between production, consumption and investment.
4. Explain the working of productive process and account for its continuity.

Multiple Choice Questions

5. (*i*) A closed economy is one where
   (*a*) we don't find any export or import of commodities
   (*b*) all the required goods and services are produced by itself
   (*c*) the country does not have any external economic relationship
   (*d*) all the above [*Ans.* (*d*)]

   (*ii*) An open economy is one which
   (*a*) has trade relationship with other economies
   (*b*) imposes no taxes on exports and imports
   (*c*) produces surplus of goods and services
   (*d*) none of the above [*Ans.* (*a*)]

   (*iii*) Which of the following equation is correct for a continuous production process in an economy?
   (*a*) Factors of Production = Labour + Initial Equipment
   (*b*) Production or Output = Consumption + New Equipment
   (*c*) Initial Equipment (at the beginning of the next year) = Initial equipment (at the beginning of this year) + New equipments produced during this year – Using up of the equipments during this year
   (*d*) All the above [*Ans.* (*d*)]

Chapter 8

ECONOMIC SYSTEMS

1. MEANING OF ECONOMIC SYSTEM

The term 'economic system' refers to the mode of production and the distribution of goods and services within which economic activity takes place in the country. According to Leonard S. Silk, "Economic system refers to the way different economic elements, i.e., individual workers and managers, productive organisations such as factories or firms and government agencies etc., are linked together to form an organic whole."

The main economic systems prevailing in the world are capitalism, socialism and mixed economy. We shall discuss below the main features and the merits and demerits of these prevailing systems in the world.

2. CAPITALISM OR FREE ENTERPRISE ECONOMY

Capitalism or the free market economy is perhaps the oldest among all the economic systems which exist in the present day world. This type of economic system existed in some of the most advanced countries of Western Europe and America in the earlier days but with the advance of time it was considerably modified and diluted. Although it has been bitterly criticised from time to time, it still retains its existence in some of the most prosperous nations of the world. The United States of America is the largest capitalist country existing to day, although even here, capitalism has lost much of its purety and vigour.

In the words of MacWright, "Capitalism is a system in which on average, much of the greater portion of economic life, and particularly of new investment, is carried on by private units under conditions of active and substantially free competition and avowedly, at least, under the incentive of a hope for profit." According to Loucks and Hoots, "Capitalism is a system of economic organisation featured by the private ownership and the use for private profit of man-made and nature-made capital."

Features of Capitalism

The principle features of capitalism are discussed below:

1. ***Freedom to keep Private Property.*** Under capitalist system of economy, every individual is free to keep private property. This is, in fact, a fundamental right which every one enjoys under capitalism. Individuals have the freedom to own and enjoy private property in any manner they like. They have also the right to dispose off their property whenever, or to whomsoever they decide to give it.

2. ***The Right of Inheritance.*** In a capitalist economy, not only the people have the right to own private property, but they also have the legal right to inherit the property of their, predecessors. In fact the right to keep private property and the right of inheritance are so intimately connected, that they are sometimes taken to mean the same thing.

3. ***Profit Motive.*** The motive to earn and maximise the private profits is the guiding force for the working of a capitalist economy. It is sometimes referred to as the heart of a capitalist economy. Capitalism without the motive to earn private profits, is in fact unthinkable. On the other hand, the profit motive does not play much role in the socialist economies. It has little or no significance there. But under capitalism, every entrepreneur, producer or businessman is guided by the profit motive in pursuing his economic activities.

4. ***Freedom of Occupation.*** Freedom of occupation is another important feature of capitalism. It means that every individual under capitalism is free to choose whatsoever occupation or enterprise he wants to join. Labour is free to choose and change the masters, subject to the condition of agreement between them. An entrepreneur is free to start any type of business or production, provided, it is not against the law of the land.

5. ***Freedom of Choice to the Consumers.*** In the capitalist economy, consumer is free to choose whatever he wants to consume. He is free to spend his income in any manner he likes. There is no control of regulation of the goods which he wants to consume. In fact it is the consumer who directs the production in accordance with his own preference. Under capitalism, the consumer is said to be a king. It is his choice which determines what should be produced. The consumer directs the production through the price mechanism. When he wants more of a thing, the price goes up, indicating to the producers that more of this commodity should be produced. Thus the consumer's sovereignty prevails under capitalism.

6. ***Competition.*** Freedom of occupation and the freedom of consumption lead to the emergence of competition, both in the product

and the factor market. The labourers compete with each other to get jobs in different lines of production. Consumers compete with each other to purchase goods from those producers who sell the cheapest. There is very large number of buyers and sellers in the market. Thus a situation of perfect competition arises in the market.

The above discussion of capitalist economy focuses our attention on the leading features of pure capitalism or *laissez faire* capitalism. It describes that system of economic organization which is absolutely free from the government interference and control. The market forces operate freely and without the least obstruction from the state. But the description of capitalism may not tally with the capitalist societies found in the modern world. In all the capitalist countries, the free market economy is regulated by the state in order to promote the social interest. Capitalism, in fact, is a dynamic system. It has been changing according to the needs of time. Thus even in the leading capitalist countries, we find it only in a modified form, its important features being still retained.

Merits of Capitalism

1. ***Capitalism works Automatically.*** One of the chief merits of capitalist system of economic organisation is that it works automatically. Capitalism is described as a self-acting machine. It has not to be manipulated or directed by some outside authority like Planning Commission or the Central Government. It works with the help of price-mechanism which acts as an invisible hand and regulates the working of this system. Resources get allocated automatically into various lines of production. Prices of goods are decided by the automatic forces of demand and supply. Factor payments are also determined by the free play of the market forces. Every thing moves smoothly, because the forces are constantly operating to keep the economy on the path of equilibrium. Even if there are some deviations from the path of equilibrium these forces would immediately restore it. Maladjustments get corrected automatically by the free and unhampered operation of the price- mechanism. Thus the capitalist system of sociaty works automatically without any external aid or regulation.

2. ***Sprit of Enterprise.*** Another good thing about capitalism is the spirit of experimentation and adventure that is found ill the producers in a capitalist society. In the hope to maximise their profits, the producers would always be busy in trying to find out new and better methods of selling the things. At the same time they would try out new and better methods of production, that may reduce the cost of production, and thus raise the level of profits. In doing so, they are generally successful, in

finding out some new technique of production, which is after some time adopted by all the producers. This reduces the cost of product ion and, therefore, the price of goods in the market also becomes low. The consumers benefit from such inventions and innovations which reduce the cost of production because in the long run they are required to pay lower prices for commodities they consume. Thus the lure to maximise the private profits improves the technology on one hand and sales organisation on the other. As a result more output is produced and sold, while the cost of production declines. This is in the interest of the general people.

3. ***Technological Progress.*** As has already been pointed out the capitalist system of society provides a great encouragement to the inventions and innovations. Because under capitalist organisation each producer is facing a keen competition from others, he would be constantly trying to introduce new inventions which reduce the cost of production and thus maximise the profits of that man who has incorporated this change first. Of course later every one would come to know about this new method of production and adopt it.

4. ***Optimum Allocation of Resources.*** Under capitalist system the productive resources are automatically allocated in the different lines of production in an optimum way. This is because individual producer, in order to maximise his profits, would see to it that no part of the resources are wrongly used or wasted. Thus the wastage of men and materials is kept at the minimum level through the personal supervision of private producers.

5. ***Rising Levels of Living.*** Working of the capitalist system, by leading to a tremendous improvement in production and technology, has led to the availability of larger output at lower cost. This has made large amounts of goods available to the poor masses, thus leading to a rise in the standard of living of the common people. One has merely to look at the level of livings in USA to realise this fact. The Americans enjoy a level of prosperity, which perhaps the richest of the people could not afford to enjoy in the past. Of course, all this prosperity cannot be assigned to the institution of capitalism only. Much of it is due to the natural resources which are found in abundance in America. But it must not be forgotten that capitalist form of organisation has played a vital role in the exploitation and development of these resources.

Demerits of Capitalism

As against these advantages the working of a capitalist society suffers from some of the very grave defects. The main drawback and shortcomings of a capitalist society are given below:

1. ***Lack of Coordination.*** In a capitalist economy, there is no machinery to coordinate the decisions of a large number of producers and business-men who are carrying on production and distribution in the economy. Millions of businessmen take their own decisions guided by their own profit motive. Since these decisions are made by the individual businessmen without taking into consideration the decision made by the others, serious errors of judgement are likely to occur. This may result in an utter confusion in the market. In the words of Maurice Dobb, "how could order emerge from the conflict of a myriad of independent and autonomous wills." Lerner has compared an unplanned economy to an automobile without a driver.

2. ***Trade Cycles.*** The recurrence of trade cycles is the major drawback of a capitalist economy. Alternative periods of prosperity and depression continuously disturb the smooth functioning of the capitalist economy. During the period of depression, large scale unemployment spreads in the economy. The firms operate at a low level of their productive capacity. This leads to the tremendous waste" of the economic resources on one hand arid creates social unrest on the other.

3. ***Economic Inequality.*** One of the, most perturbing features of capitalist economy is the existence of sharp inequalities of income distribution. A few of the people are rich and prosperous while a very large number of them are leading life of misery and degradation. The inequality in the distribution of income increases as the capitalism proceeds. The rich go on becoming richer while the poverty of the masses goes on increasing rather rapidly. This is because the rich people who own the means of production, run the process of production to maximise their private profits.

4. ***Social Parasitism.*** In the capitalist economy there exists the evil of 'Social Parasitism'. This means that certain sections of community do not make any physical or mental effort towards earning for their own living. They live on the labour done by others. For example, under zamindari system, the landlords used to lead a life of luxury on the efforts done by the tenants. Incomes derived from inherited property and wealth is another example of living without doing any productive work.

5. ***Waste of Competition.*** Competition, which is a distinguishing feature of a capitalist economy, leads to the wastage of much of the precious resources. Lot of resources are spent on publicity, propaganda and advertisements by the individual producers to attract more and more

customers. Much of money may be wasted in the effort to drive out other producers from the market.

6. ***Human Welfare Ignored.*** Under the capitalist system of economic organisation, the motive for production being private profits, the productive resources of the community are not utilised for the maximisation of social benefit. Every producer tries to maximise his profits with devoting much attention to social welfare.

7. ***Artificial Scarcity.*** In order to maximise the profits, the producers under capitalism, sometimes, create artificial scarcity. They hold back the supplies to create a scarcity in the market and thus earn more when the prices rise. To achieve their motive, the producers enter into agreement with each other. This leads to the formation of trusts, cartels and other such monopolistic organisations. Those who possess sufficient financial resources manage to control the market. Big monopolies are formed, which restrict the output, sell it at high price and thus exploit the consumers.

8. ***Class Conflict.*** Under capitalism the society gets divided into two classes, the rich and the poor. The rich people, in order to maximise their private profits, keep on constantly exploiting the poor. The employers try to get the maximum work from the workers and pay them the least. The workers, on the other hand, try to work less and get more. Thus there is a clash of interest between these two classes viz., the workers and the masters. This clash of interest, often results in industrial disputes, which take the form of strikes and lock-outs. Gradually, this leads to a greater division of society between the haves (those who have wealth) and the have nots (those who are poor). This sort of a division is dangerous to the stability of the capitalist society, and if it proceeds fast enough, it may lead to its overthrow and replacement by the socialist system.

3. SOCIALISM

According to Prof. Dickinson, "Socialism is an economic organisation of society in which the material means of production are owned by the whole community and operated by organs representative of and responsible to the community according to a general plan, all members of the community being entitled to benefit from the results of such socialised planned production on the basis of equal rights."[1] This definition emphasises three fundamental features of socialism, namely: (*i*) an ownership of means of production by the state, (*ii*) general planning of

1. H.D. Dickinson, *Economics of Socialism,* 1939, p. 10.

economic activity, and (*iii*) an equitable distribution of national income. According to Maurice Dobb, "The fundamental character of socialism consists in its abolition of the class relations which form the basis of capitalist production through the expropriation of the propertied class and the socialisation of land and capital."

Forms of Socialism

Socialism has many brands, most of which can be broadly covered under two headings: (*i*) Evolutionary socialism, and (*ii*) Revolutionary socialism. The followers of the evolutionary philosophy advocate the gradual socialisation of the means of production by paying compensation to those who own them. They do not want any revolution or blood-shed, because it results in tremendous waste of national resources. The followers of revolutionary philosophy, on the other hand, advocate a sudden take-over of all means of production by the state, without payment of any compensation. The use of violence, according to them, is necessary for any such socialisation.

Apart from these two types, there are certain other varieties of socialism. Some of the important ones are given below:

1. ***Guild Socialism.*** According to the advocates of guild socialism, the state cannot run and manage industrial enterprises economically and efficiently. Management of industries by the government suffers from over-centralisation, red-tapism and corruption. Therefore, the guild socialists advocate that the state should own the industries, but for their actual management, they should be handed over to worker guilds or the organisations of the workers, who can run them more efficiently and economically. Guild socialists, thus, want to eliminate the evils of over-concentration and mismanagement of enterprises managed by the government.

2. ***Fabian Socialism.*** Fabian socialism is a variant of evolutionary socialism. The followers of the philosophy believe that socialism should not be forced upon the unwilling people. The people should be convinced and persuaded to adopt socialism as an economic system. Violence and bloodshed are completely ruled out for the achievement of socialism. Rahter, the propaganda for socialism is to be conducted on a literary level through books, magazines, novels and dramas.

3. ***Syndicalism.*** The syndicalists advocate the use of violence in the achievement of socialism. According to them the ownership and management of industrial enterprises should be vested with the local syndicates or trade unions. The workers should paralyse the working of industries

by violent strikes and sabotage the whole economic organisation to bring about a downfall of capitalism.

4. ***Communism.*** Communism is considered to be an extreme form of socialism. The communists advocate the use of violent methods for the achievement of a class-less society. They do not have any faith in the parliamentary democracy as a method of achieving state ownership of factors of production. The fundamental principle of communism is to get work from every one according to his ability and to make him payment according to his needs.

Merits of Socialism

1. ***Secures Co-ordinated Development.*** Socialist economy being essentially a planned economy, secures balanced and co-ordinated development of the various sectors of national economy. The central planning authority has a complete control over the various aspects of economic life and has a thorough knowledge of position regarding demand and supply as against the sketchy knowledge possessed by millions of isolated entrepreneurs under capitalism. Therefore, through the process of economic planning a socialist economy can secure a co-ordinated and more rapid economic development.

2. ***Eliminates Cyclical Fluctuations.*** Trade cycles, as we know, are an inherent feature of capitalism. Cyclical fluctuations in economic activity are a direct outcome of the uncoordinated nature of the capitalist economy. Under socialist system of economy the trade cycles are completely absent. This is because a socialist economy is a planned economy where every economic activity is properly co-ordinated and balanced with each other.

3. ***Secures Equitable Distribution of National Income.*** A socialist society by definition is a classless society. Therefore, there is no place for richness or poverty in such a society. A socialist society does not permit the existence of any class distinctions. Since the means of production are owned by the state, there is no question of private profits which increases and perpetuate the inequalities in the distribution of income.

4. ***Eliminates Social Parasitism.*** Under capitalism, as is well known, the richer sections of the people exploit the poor labourers. The privileged and influential sections exploit the economically weaker sections. A class of social parasites grows up which lives on the efforts and labour put in by the others. There is no place for such social parasites under socialism. A socialist economy makes full use of the services of all kind of people. It does not permit the existence of parasite people.

5. ***Prevents Unemployment.*** A socialist economy assures a job to each one of the able bodied citizens. The economic resources of the community are being fully utilised and each person is provided with a job according to his capacity, taste and suitability. This is made possible by planning the whole economic activity before hand and, thus, preventing the possibility of any maladjustment or waste of economic resources.

6. ***Provides Social Security.*** A socialist society makes proper arrangement for giving social security benefits to all the citizens. Immediate aid is provided to the people at times of sickness or accidents. Excellent medical care is promised to those who are subjected to such evils. Old-age pensions are given to all who become unfit for work due to old age. In case of premature death, the state bears the full expenses of the dependents of the deceased workers.

7. ***Eliminates Labour Disputes.*** A capitalist economy is marked by constant dispute between labour and capital. Strikes and lockouts keep on occurring every now and then. This results in a tremendous wastage of man-hours which is a loss not only to the labour or capitalists but also to the society as a whole, in the form of lower production and consequent higher prices. Such disputes do not occur in a socialist society because there is no clash of interest between those who work in the factories and those who manage them.

Demerits of Socialism

1. ***Concentration of Power.*** The entire economic life of the people in a socialist economy is controlled by the central planning authority. Thus, on one side the power keeps on concentrating in the hands of the government while on the other the human liberties are drastically curtailed. Generally, under such conditions, the democratic set up of the government is replaced by a dictatorship. Complete regimentation of the economic and social life of people reduces them to the state of mere wage earners, devoid of any individual initiative and enterprise.

2. ***Evils of Bureaucracy.*** Certain evils arise out of the bureaucratic management of the socialist economy. A lot of people are engaged in task of drawing elaborate schemes for economic development. This leads to a wastage of financial and human resources. Further, the government officials who manage the public enterprises are generally not competent to do so. This leads to the growth of inefficiency in the management of industries.

3. ***Leads to Labour Inefficiency.*** Under socialism, there is no incentive (or the labour to improve its efficiency. Since all workers are

employees of the state with fixed grades of salary, promotions to the higher jobs depend more on seniority than on merit. Therefore, there is no incentive for labour to bring about any improvement in its performance. However, this problem has been solved in Russia by giving special lifts and better grades to the people who are more efficient.

4. ***Loss of Consumer's Sovereignty.*** Under capitalism the production is directed according to the choice of consumers. When the consumers want more of certain goods, then prices rise and this induces the producers to produce more of those goods. But, under socialism, since the prices of goods are fixed by the state planning authority, the price mechanism does not operate freely. Under the system of controls and rationing, which are essential features of socialism, there is no method of expressing the will and choice of the consumers.

5. ***No Freedom of Occupational Choice.*** It is said that under socialism people are not free to change or choose jobs according to their own will. The man-power and other resources of the community are controlled by a central planning authority which directs them into various channels of production according to a certain general plan of the economy. Of course, as far as possible, the workers are put into different occupations according to their capacity, fitness and suitability.

4. MIXED ECONOMY

A mixed economy is that form of economic organisation where elements of a capitalist economy and those of a socialist economy are found mixed up together. Capitalism or a free enterprise system, as it is also called, refers to that type of economic organisation where there is freedom of enterprise, freedom of occupation and freedom to keep private property. It implies a competitive market where producers are guided by the profit motive and where the maximisation of private profits is the sole objective of production, exchange and distribution. A socialist or a controlled economy on the other hand is one where there is a central authority or the government which directs the entire economic activity. Means of product ion are no longer a private property. They are owned by the government which decides about what to produce, and how to produce. There is no freedom of occupation. It is the government which decides about the occupations of various people, which job is to be allocated to a particular group of workers and where factories or workshops are to be located. Thus, a purely socialist economy implies the complete control of economic activities like consumption, production, exchange and distribution.

In between these two systems, we find a third type of economic organisation, which is neither a completely free economy nor a completely controlled one. This is the mixed capitalist economy or popularly known as mixed economy. It is that type of economy which is free to a considerable extent but where freedom is moderated by the government interference, regulation and control of certain spheres of economic activity. Here the government either directly controls certain fields of economy or it exerts pressure on the private enterprise by starting public enterprise i.e., industrial units owned and managed by the government. These public enterprises compete with the private enterprises and hence keep a check on their activities. Most of the economies existing in the world today conform to this type of economic system. In the most of the countries which belonged to the category of free enterprise economies in the 17th and 18th centuries, there has been a steady increase in the government functions since the beginning of the 19th century. The increase in the functions of the state and the increasing interference of the government in the field of economic activity has led to the emergence of 'mixed economy', a new form of economic organisation which has come to be accepted in many countries of the world. India is an example of a country which has adopted mixed economy as its economic system.

Features of Mixed Economy

1. ***Coexistence of Private and Public Sectors.*** An important feature of a mixed economy is the coexistence of two sectors, the private and the public sector. The private sector consists of all those business units, firms and industries, which are owned, managed and controlled by the private people. Public sector, on the other hand, consists of the industrial units and business enterprises which are owned and managed by the government, may be the central government, state government or local authorities. There is no hard and fast rule regarding the size of the private and public sectors in a mixed economy. But normally it has been found that private sector, in such economies, is considerably larger than the public sector. However, there is a gradual expansion of the public sector as the government decides to enter into new lines of production or to nationalise the existing industries in national interest.

2. ***Freedom of Consumption.*** In the mixed economy, the consumer enjoys the freedom of consumption. Generally people are free to consume whatever they like and in how much quantity they like. But restrictions are imposed on the consumption of some commodities which are injurious to a person or harmful to the society. Similarly, when supply of some

commodity is expected to fall short of its demand the government may adopt price controls and rationing to see that the consumers are not being exploited or to ensure that every one gets a minimum amount of that commodity.

3. ***Labour Protection.*** For the protection of working classes, comprehensive and well conceived legislation regarding the terms and conditions of work is formulated and implemented in a mixed economy. Factory legislation fixing minimum wages, maximum hours of work, over time payments, compensation for accidents etc., is passed and strictly enforced in a mixed economy. This reduces the capitalist exploitation of the labour class and is regarded necessary for their welfare.

4. ***Less Inequalities of Income Distribution.*** An allout effort is made in a mixed economy to minimise the existing inequalities in the distribution of income and wealth. Measures are also adopted to see that these inequalities do not perpetuate. Progressive taxation, which hits the rich more than the poor, is a device which is very popular with the government for the purpose of minimising the gulf between the rich and the poor. Public expenditure providing free education, health and medical facilities to the poor people, adds to the real income of those who enjoy these facilities. Thus the effort is made to raise the income of the poor and at the same time to reduce the income of the rich thus narrowing down the difference between them.

5. ***Price Mechanism.*** Price mechanism plays an important part under capitalism, in the allocation of productive resources. Under socialism, the resource allocation takes place with the direction of the government or the planning commission. In a mixed economy the allocation of resources between different lines of production is done partly through price mechanism and partly through the government action. In the public sector all decisions regarding what to produce, and how to produce are taken by the government without much reference to the profits emerging out of that line of production. In the private sector, the decisions regarding production are taken by the private people in accordance with the relative profitability of that type of production. Thus, the price mechanism regulates the working of the private sector. But, here again, the price mechanism does not operate unhindered. In fact, the government regulates the working of the price mechanism through its laws, rules and regulations and permits it to operate within the framework of such regulations.

Conclusion

It may be concluded that a mixed economy is an attempt to reconcile the two extreme economic systems of capitalism and socialism. The motive to pursue the middle path provided by the mixed economy is to have the advantages of both the systems while at the same time leaving out those things which make those extreme systems rigid, unpopular and unacceptable.

EXERCISES

1. Define capitalism and discuss its main features.
2. Explain the relative merits and demerits of the free capitalist enterprise system.
3. Define socialism and discuss its various forms.
4. Give the main arguments for and against the socialist system of economic organisation.
5. What is a mixed economy? Discuss its main features.
6. Do you favour a socialist economy to a capitalist economy? If so, give arguments in support of your view.

Multiple Choice Questions

7. (*i*) Which of the following is not a feature of capitalist economy?
    (*a*) freedom of private property
    (*b*) profit motive
    (*c*) price mechanism
    (*d*) none of the above [*Ans.* (*d*)]

    (*ii*) Which of the follwoing is the feature of socialism?
    (*a*) public ownership of means of production
    (*b*) central planning
    (*c*) restricted consumers' sovereignty
    (*d*) all of the above [*Ans.* (*d*)]

    (*iii*) Mixed economy consists of
    (*a*) public sector
    (*b*) private sector
    (*c*) joint sector
    (*d*) all the above sectors [*Ans.* (*d*)]

    (*iv*) Indian economy is an example of
    (*a*) capitalist economy
    (*b*) socialist economy
    (*c*) mixed economy
    (*d*) free enterprise economy [*Ans.* (*c*)]

Chapter 9

THE ROLE OF PRICE MECHANISM

1. INTRODUCTION

In every economy, some fundamental problems arise and the economy has to face them. Since these problems are common for all economies whether they are rich or poor, capitalist or socialist, they are known as the central problems of an economy. This must be remembered that the root of all these problems is the 'law of scarcity'. Had the resoures been unlimited like sunshine and air, there would have been no problem whatsoever. In different economies these problems are attempted to be solved differently.

These problems are:

(1) *What to produce?* That is what commodity is to be produced and in what quantity?

(2) *How to produce?* That is what methods and techniques of production are to be used?

(3) *For whom to produce?* That is what are the people for whom the economy has to produce? This also means how the national income or national output is distributed?

Besides the above problems, every economy has to face two more problems. But they can be included in the above three central problems. However, they can be put up as below:

(4) *What should be the rate of growth of an economy?* That is what measures should be adopted by an economy to acquire an accelerated rate of growth? This problem is more important in an underdeveloped economy.

(5) *How to secure smooth working of an economy?* That is what measures should be adopted by an economy for its smooth growth? This problem is more relevant to a developed economy.

All the above problems are solved by the price mechanism. In fact, mechanism is a system of economic organisation in which each individual in his capacity as a consumer, producer and factor-owner is engaged in economic activity with a large measure of freedom. In every society there are legal and social institutions which govern it. The individual economic actions must confirm the system prevailing in an economy. Now we shall see how does the price mechanism play its role in solving the above central problems in various types of economies.

2. ROLE OF PRICE MECHANISM IN A FREE ENTERPRISE ECONOMY

Under a free enterprise economy, the price mechanism works through the demand and supply of goods and services in a competitive market. These in turn are determined by their prices. Prices determine the level of production of different goods and services. They also organise production and distribute it among the people of the society. We shall discuss all these problems in the following manner:

(1) ***What and how much to produce?*** In a free enterprise or capitalist state the choices are made by the people through the *price mechanism.* In such a system everything has a price. All the goods produced have a market price as do the factors (land, labour and capital) which produce them. Everyone receives money for what the sells (e.g., the worker sells his services) and uses this money to buy the goods he desires. If more of any particular product is desired there will be an increased demand for that commodity. This increase in demand will tend to raise its price and cause more of it to be produced. If more of any particular commodity is being produced than people desire, then the excess supply will cause its price to fall and producers will supply less of that commodity. We can say, therefore, that the manner in which people spend their income decides *what goods shall be produced and in what quantities.* It is the money votes of the people, votes which they place in the market, which decide the pattern of production. Buying a commodity is equivalent to voting for its production.

According to Friedman, "The votes of the members of a free enterprise exchange economy are manifested through prices which, in turn, reveal the standards of the society. Given these standards, there must be some machinery to translate these values or choices into productive activity. Productions must be organised both among and within industries. This is accomplished by the price system through the interaction of two sets of prices: prices of products and prices of resources. Prices of products in relation to the costs of producing them determine the distribution of resources among industries; the relative prices of factors, in turn, determine the coordination of factors within industries."[1]

The problem can also be explained with the help of Fig. 9.1. Here we assume that the economy produces consumer goods (*X*) and capital goods (*Y*). In deciding the level of output of the economy it has to choose that combination of goods *X* and Y which is possible within the available resources of the economy. The PP_1 curve is the production possibility curve of the economy. Thus it can not choose point *R* which lies below the production possibility curve as it indicates the economic inefficiency of the system in the form of unemployment of resources. It is also not possible for the economy to choose any point outside the production possibility curve, say, point *T* which is not allowed by its available resources. It will, therefore, choose any point among *A, B,* or *C* which lies on the production possibility curve. Since the total factor-endowment (or total cost) is fixed, the slope of production possibility curve will depict the change in the relative costs only, or the ratio of marginal cost of consumer goods (*X*) and capital goods (*Y*).

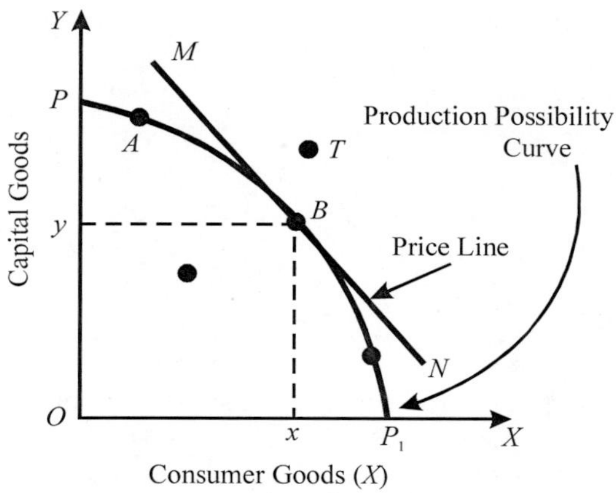

Fig. 9.1

The straight line *MN* shows the relative prices or $\frac{Px}{Py}$. The optimum allocation of resources (in a free economy) will be done at that level

1. Milton Friedman, *Price Theory: A Provisional Text*, 1970, p. 9.

where the slope of price line equals the slope of production possibility curve.

Thus in the present situation *Ox* quantity of consumer goods and *Oy* quantity of capital goods will be produced. If the relative prices change, the optimum level of factor used and the corresponding composition of output will also change.

(2) ***How to produce?*** The problem 'how to produce' means the problem of choosing the technique or method of production. There are various alternative methods of production and the economy has to choose those techniques of production which would maximise production but minimise costs. This is possible only when the production resources are utilised in the best possible manner. The utilisation of resources in turn depends, upon the various factors and conditions which govern the productivity and efficiency of factors of production.

First of all, the choice is between the labour-intensive technique or capital-intensive technique. Labour-intensive technique of production means the use of more labour and less capital. In underdeveloped economies where labour is plenty and capital is relatively scarce, labour-intensive technique of production will be better. On the other hand, capital-intensive technique refers to the use of more capital and less labour. In economies where labour is relatively scarce, capital-intensive methods of production are more suitable.

Secondly, there is the question of specialisation or division of labour. To produce more goods at less cost of production specialisation is essential. Under specialisation right man is placed at the right place. Specialisation brings about : (*a*) the use of modern and uptodate capital, (*b*) the use of each capital asset up *to* its full capacity, (*c*) inventions and innovation, and (*d*) economical use of raw material.

Thirdly, comes the question of organisation. Production is the result of the joint efforts of the factors of production. Better organisation will, therefore, increase the magnitude of output and lower the cost of production. The factors of production should be so employed as to equalise their marginal utilities. This means that the allocation of the various factors should be according to the principle of substitution.

Lastly, the economy has to decide regarding the localisation of the various firms. Since the factors of production are not equally distributed over all parts of the economy, different places are to be chosen for different firms. In the matter of localisation, the economy should take the following factors into consideration: (*i*) Natural advantages to the firms, viz., facilities to raw material, power, transport, suitable climate, etc.; (*ii*) economic advantages of the firms, viz., nearness to the market, availability of cheap labour, capital, etc.; (*iii*) other advantages, viz., political patronage, regional reputation, etc. Through localisation of industries or firms both internal and external economies are obtained. These economies reduce the cost of production. Here again, the problem is solved differently in different economies. In a capitalist economy the problem is solved by price mechanism.

As we know wages, rent, interest and profits are the prices paid by the entrepreneur (producer) for the services of the factors of production which make up the cost of production. Every producer aims at using the most efficient production process. An economically efficient production process is one which produces goods with the minimum costs. The choice of a production process will depend upon the relative prices of the factor services and the quantity of goods to be produced.

All this will be decided by competition between different producers. The more efficient producers will be able to supply a commodity at a lower price than less efficient producers. Price competition will decide the methods of production which the society uses. Those producers who are best able to meet the demands of the consumers will succeed and make profits; the efficient will make losses and go out of business. The large farm will tend to replace the small farm if this leads to lower production costs. Electricity will be generated from oil rather than coal if this means cheaper electricity. Motor cars will be manufactured by large-scale mass production methods if consumers demand cheap standardised models rather than expensive specially designed cars.

(3) ***For whom to produce?*** The problem 'for whom to produce' is relative to the problem of 'what to produce'. We cannot decide the problem of what to produce unless we first know the people for whom the economy has to produce. We must make sure whether we have to produce for rich or poor; young or old; men or women; civil people or military people and so on. This is clearly the problem of the distribution of national income. People with different incomes will, demand different goods and services. The producers will take into account the demand for those goods and services and produce accordingly. The solution of the problem depends upon the type of the economy. In a capitalist economy or free capitalist enterprise system, price plays a vital role and settles the problem of allocation of productive resources. In such an economy capitalists produce those goods which are used by rich people since they have more purchasing power. They pay huge prices for these goods and producers

earn huge profits. Thus goods like motor cars, refrigerators, air conditio-ners, etc. will be produced more. The result is that poor people do not get even their bare necessities.

According to Friedman, every society must provide some means of dividing the total wealth among individuals of the society. In a free enterprise exchange economy this task is accomplished by the price system. Individuals in such a society separately own the resources used in production. They get claim on the product by selling their services in the market for a price. The total claim of any individual is determined by the quantity of resources he owns and the prices at which he is able to sell all the services of these resources. Factor prices or the return per unit of time per unit of resource in conjunction with the distribution of ownership of resources thus determine the distribution of total wealth or product among the individuals in the society.[2]

In other words, the share of the national wealth which any individual enjoys depends on the level of his income. Incomes are paid in the form of money, but money is merely a claim to goods and services. The higher a person's income, the greater is his purchasing power and the share of the nation's wealth available to him. The manner in which the wealth of a society is distributed depends, therefore, on the way in which personal incomes are determined.

Now, income is derived in two ways, either in return for some kind of labour, or from the ownership of property. The income which people receive as a reward for labour is known as wages. Income derived from the ownership of property takes the form of rent, dividends and interest, and is paid to the owners of land and capital. The levels of these incomes are governed by conditions of supply and demand in the markets for the factors of production (land, labour and capital). Rent, wages and interest are prices, and whether these prices are high or low depends upon their supply and the society's demand for the products which they help to make.

Hence, under a free enterprise or capitalist economy, the goods which are produced, the methods of production used, and the incomes of the factors of production, are all determined by the price mechanism operating in free markets. It is a system of profits and losses.

Limitations of Price Mechanism in a Free Market Economy

(1) ***Production is guided by the demand of the elite and not by the need***

---

2. *Ibid.*, pp. 9-10.

of the poor. It is pointed out that even if the system worker perfectly in the manner described above, many persons would not consider it perfect. Commodities would obviously tend to go to those with most money. The system produces those goods which people demand, but demand implies the ability to pay. Hence, in this system, we may find the rich enjoying luxuries while the poor lack necessities. Only those goods would be produced which appear to offer the prospect of profit. It is, therefore, doubtful whether the system would provide such things as public parks, a universal system of education, or a national health service, etc.

(2) ***Non-existence of perfect competition.*** In actual life, competition is not perfect, but it is found to be imperfect. There is not a single country in the world today which adheres to the principles of *laissez faire.* Most of capitalist economies nave converted themselves into mixed economies—whatever objectives they may have before them.

(3) ***Price mechanism leads to unemployment and stagnation.*** Economists, businessmen and government officials in rich countries increasingly recognize that their country must maintain a sufficiently high rate of development if deep depression is to be avoided and the possibility of stagnation averted. Unless the rate of development is sufficiently high, a rich country may suffer from general over-production and face a long-run problem of unemployment.

(4) ***Nationalisation of social services.*** Measures aimed at nationalisation of social services also tend to modify the price system in favour of mixed economy.

3. ROLE OF PRICE MECHANISM IN A MIXED ECONOMY

The system we have described above is commonly known as a system of *private enterprise.* This particular type of organization allows private individuals to own the means of production. Private persons are allowed to buy and own land, buildings, machines, etc., to hire labour, and to produce and sell goods and services. But the competitive conditions required of a free market which never existed in actual fact. Furthermore, the doctrines of the *laissez faire* philosophers were neither completely accepted by all nor left unchallenged. The alternative to this is a system of *public enterprise.* In this case the means of production are owned and controlled by public authorties (i.e., the state or local councils). In our own country and in most western countries there are mixed systems where both private and public enterprises operate side by side.

Our economic structure is based on the system of private enterprise. Property can be privately owned and people are economically free, subject to the obedience to the laws, to use their time and means as they like. The state protects the right of the individual to control his property and his goods. Economic freedom means that the individual is free to do as he likes with his own property and with his own time and energy. Economic freedom and private enterprise do not preclude the possibility of State enterprise or "public" enterprise. Our economic system is one of comparative freedom: the freedom of the individual, whether acting alone or in conjunction with others, is restricted by the standards set up by society to ensure the welfare of the the community as a whole.

The economy of the US is still primarily a free enterprise economy, but it is more accurately described as a "mixed economy", a "dual economy" or as "mixed capitalism"; all these phrases indicating that both private enterprise and government play important roles. The extent of intervention by the government in the economy is indicated by the following: regulation of banks, the establishment of a strong Federal Reserve System; anti-trust regulation; a broad social security programme; the equalisation of bargaining power between capital and labour; controls on farm production; subsidies to many different types of businesses; protection of consumer interests from false and misleading advertising and business practices; the regulation of public utilities engaged in inter-state commerce; the regulation of monetary system, the redistribution of income, production of some products, specially during World War II; and governmental assumption of the responsibility to use the means at its disposal to help maintain full employment.

Similarly in Great Britain, a considerable part of the economy is under the direct control of public authorities. The coal industry, the electricity and gas industries, the railways, a part of road haulage, and most civil aviation, are some of the industries which are controlled by the state. Many local authorities in UK operate local omnibus services, build houses, build and control schools, and provide public baths and public parks, etc. In addition to this form of public enterprise which provides goods, and services directly, the state controls, in a variety of ways, the operations of private enterprise. The Factory Acts govern the conditions under which people are allowed to work in factories. The Companies Acts lay down the methods by which companies are allowed to conduct their financial affairs. The Monopolies and Restrictive Practices Acts supervise and control the procedures of businessmen in fixing their prices and the manner which they supply their goods to the public. The Distribution of Industry

Acts are designed to influence the decisions of businessmen in the location of their factories. The various Public Health Acts and Weights and Measures Acts also affect the manner in which business is carried on in Great Britain.

Many countries have adopted economic planning as a national policy. Not only the socialist and communist, but even some of the capitalist, countries have introduced and adopted the concept of planned economy. Great Britain has made tentative move towards national planning, although it has not set up any central planning body to direct the operations of the British economy in detail. But it did inaugurate the broad programme of planning designed to achieve full employment, agricultural development, restoration of foreign trade, housing, construction and increased social security through measures of control.

In present time, some economists feel that it could be possible to adopt the idea of central planning in a capitalist economy. They hold the opinion that planning could be worked out without too much encroachment on the rights of the private sector. They have worked out a system of planning that allows the price system to function as much as it now does but to achieve a better balance between demand and supply than is possible in an unplanned system, through an intelligent manipulation of the monetary system.

Let us now study as to how the central economic problems are attempted to be solved in a mixed capitalist enterprise system. We take these problems one by one.

(1) ***What to produce and in what quantity?*** In a capitalist economy profit motive or price mechanism decides as to what commodity and in what quantity is to be produced. Generally, the producers are induced to produce those commodities which can be sold for higher prices and which promise them high profits. In a mixed capitalist economy also price mechanism solves this problem. But in such an economy, the government keeps on interfering for general welfare of the people. In these economies, the government undertakes the production and distribution of essential goods and services. The private enterprise is also allowed to exist for all other non-essential goods and services. But this sector also functions under the supervision and control of the government. The government adjusts demand and supply of goods. To remove the scarcity of certain goods, the government gives to the producers of these goods incentives like bounties, tax rebates, etc., and to discourage the production of certain goods, the government provides disincentives like imposing of higher taxes on those commodities.

(2) ***How to produce?*** The problem 'how to produce' means the problem of choosing the method or technique of production. In a free market economy or capitalist economy this problem is solved automatically. In order to maximise his profits, each producer tries to reduce his cost of production. He would choose that method or technique of production which is the cheapest and which minimises the cost of production. The factors of production are available in the market at different prices. The producers also come to the market to purchase them. In order to maximise their profits, the producers would purchase more of those factors whose price is low and less of those whose price is relatively high. In this way the problem of the choice of method of production is solved by the price mechanism. Thus, under free market economy or capitalist economy, price mechanism allocates the productive resources. But in a mixed capitalist economy, the allocation of productive resources between different uses is done partly through the government direction and partly through price mechanism. In the public sector, all decisions as to 'how to produce' are taken by the government whereas in the private sector price mechanism decides the allocation of the resources among different lines of production. This decision is done on the basis of profit motive. But even in private sector the working of price mechanism is regulated by the government rules and regulations.

(3) ***For whom to produce?*** In a mixed capitalist economy need of the poor people are kept in mind by the government. The government undertakes the production and distribution of certain essential goods and services for the best interests of the society. Through price control and rationing the government ensures the supply of goods to both the rich and the poor classes of the society. The government imposes high direct taxes and reduces the purchasing power of the rich. Also the government levies high duties on the production of luxury goods and reduces their production. On the other hand, the government provides many social securities to the poor people.

4. ROLE OF PRICE MECHANISM IN A SOCIALIST ECONOMY

The price mechanism is regarded as a distinguishing feature of a free market economy. It has little relevance in a socialist economy. Economic planning under socialism plays the same role as is played by the price mechanism in a capitalist economy. Here the Planning Commission is required to solve the basic central problems of what to produce, how to produce and for whom to produce. It makes an estimate of the entire economic, human and natural resources at its command. The commission has to decide upon the various commodities which the economy should produce with the available resources. It takes the social welfare aspect and the development related goals of the nation while choosing the technique of production to be used. The price mechanism in a capitalist economy operates in such a way that production takes place only to meet the demands of all these people who have considerable amount of disposable income. Production of those commodities is neglected which belong to the poor man's basket in a socialist economy. But in a socialist economy income inequalities are dramatically reduced so that everyone has an adequate amount of disposable income. While determining the pattern and size of output the Planning Commission has to see to it that its decisions in this regard are such that they ensure the availability of commodities for all in the market. Every economic plan of the nation which determines the economy's pace and pattern of development should necessarily incorporate the elements-—

1. the way in which national income is to be distributed between consumption and accumulation, and

2. the manner in which investment is to be allocated among the different sectors of the economy.

The major characteristics of economic planning are as follows:

1. Economic planning is conscious and deliberate process which aims at attaining certain specific objectives and target within specified time limit.

2. It implies within the national economy of a single and undivided authority invested with the power of taking all the decisions on the basis of the comprehensive survey of existing and potential resources in the country.

3. Planning is comprehensive in nature, it covers in an integrated manner all the important sectors of the national economy.

4. Economic planning is characterised by the use of limited resources on the basis of pre-determined priorities with a view to attain maximum welfare of the commodity.

5. Economic planning covers not only planning of production of goods and services but also covers patterns of distribution of income and wealth as conceived by the planning authority.

The central planning authority is vested with the responsibility of preparing blue print for the allocation of resources among the different sectors of the economy and among the different uses within the different sectors. Different functions of the central planning authority are:

(*a*) to fix prices of goods,

(*b*) to fix prices of factor services,

(*c*) to determine the rate of capital accumulation, and

(*d*) to decide the resource allocation.

It would be seen that the central planning decision regarding what, how and for whom to produce can not be disputed. Thus in a socialistic economy the freely functioning price mechanism and consumer choices no longer decide what goods and services are to be produced. Those decisions invariably have to be taken by the central planning authority.

EXERCISES

1. Describe how resources are allocated in a free market economy.
2. Explain how resources are allocated in a socialist economy.
3. What do you understand by price mechanism? Discuss its role in an economy.
4. Explain the role of price mechanism in a mixed capitalist economy.
5. Describe how the price system solves the fundamental problems of an economy through the forces of demand and supply.
6. Explain in brief the central economic problems of an economy.
7. Discuss how the central problems of an economy are solved in a free enterprise economy?

Multiple Choice Questions

8. (*i*) In which type of system the role of price mechanism is assumed to be significant?

(*a*) Free Enterprise Economy

(*b*) Controlled Economy

(*c*) Planned Economy

(*d*) All of the above [*Ans.* (*a*)]

(*ii*) The central problem of an economy consists of

(*a*) What and how much to produce?

(*b*) How to produce?

(*c*) For whom to produce?

(*d*) All of the above [*Ans.* (*d*)]

(*iii*) In a free enterprise economy the problem of what, how and for whom are solved by

(*a*) A planned committee

(*b*) The price mechanism

(*c*) The elected representatives of the people

(*d*) None of the above [*Ans.* (*b*)]

Chapter 10

THE CONCEPT OF EQUILIBRIUM

1. MEANING OF EQUILIBRIUM

The modern economics is known as equilibrium economics.[1] The term "equilibrium" means a position from which there is no tendency to move. Economists sometimes regard the concept of an unchanging or frictionless world useful, even though it is a pure abstraction. They call it a stationary state or the static state, i.e., a state of balance or a state of rest. This concept helps in theorising about ultimate tendencies of prices, although we must always keep this in mind that any such perfect balance does not exist in the real world. There may be a tendency to it, but it is a tendency very much interfered with by counteracting influences. The disturbing factors are sometimes more obvious that the balancing tendencies.

The economy of a nation is said to be in a state of equilibrium when the effective demand for every commodity and every factor of production is exactly equal to its respective supply. From the point of view of an individual producer, equilibrium position will be attained when he enjoys maximum profit. Similarly, for a consumer equilibrium will be reached at a point when he gets maximum satisfaction from his given income spent on different goods and services. Once, an individual is in equilibrium, he sticks to it because any reallocation of his limited income (resources) will decrease his total utility or satisfaction (profits). Also, an industry will be in equilibrium when there is no tendency for the size of the industry to change, i.e., when no firms want to leave it and no new firms wish to enter into it. If these conditions did not exist, the adjustment would be incomplete and in a competitive system with freedom for price to move, reactions would result tending to correct the situation.

1. George J. Stigler, *The Theory of Price;* p. 26.

We know that so long as production is not correctly adjusted to demand, price discrepancies arise so as to correct the situation (of disequilibrium). When throughout the economic system production is in perfect equilibrium with the demand, there is no further tendency for prices to change unless some new developments, such as, change in consumers' tastes, or a new invention or different production technique were introduced into the situation.[2] Any change of this type will lead to readjustment in the prevailing price structure until new equilibrium takes place in the economy.

In a dynamic economy, the effects on the distribution of resources are so frequent and disturbing elements are so strong that perfect equilibrium is never attained and the system is always in maladjustment. We face frequent changes in prices in response to the changed situations of demand and supply, but there will always be a tendency which will lead to a more balanced adjustment.

It is, however, possible to find general equilibrium prices and the forces which determine the prices of all goods together by mathematical methods, such as, input-output analysis, linear programming and identification, etc. The procedure comprises setting up of a set of simultaneous algebraic equations in which the choices of ultimate consumers, the existing quantities of factor-inputs and the technical requirements of industries for these factor inputs are clearly specified, while the prices of finished products and the factors of production are left unspecified. Econometricians have constructed such equations and demonstrated that an inter dependent system of prices for all commodities can be determined theoretically by such mathematical methods. These equilibrium prices summarize the important determinants of economic activity.

2. CLASSIFICATION OF EQUILIBRIUM

Equilibriums can be classified in several important respects. The main kinds of an economic equilibrium are the following:

(1) Stable, Unstable and Neutral Equilibrium

According to Prof. A.C. Pigou, "A system is in *stable equilibrium* if, when any small disturbance takes place, forces come into play to re-

2. *Ibid.* A stationary eC9nomy or a state of equilibrium may be defined as one in which there are no changes in the three fundamental set of data—Tastes, Resources and Technology.

establish the initial position; it is in *neutral equilibrium* if, when such a disturbance takes place, no reestablishing, but also no further disturbing forces, are evoked, so that the system remains at rest in the position to which it has moved; it is in *unstable equilibrium* if the small disturbances call out further disturbing forces which act in a cumulative manner to drive the system away from its initial position. A ship with a heavy keel is in stable equilibrium; an egg lying on its side in neutral equilibrium; an egg poised on one of its ends in unstable equilibrium."[3]

Similarly, Prof. Scheneider has also explained clearly the distinction between a stable and an unstable economic equilibrium. According to him, "A position of equilibrium corresponding to a given set of data may be said to be stable if a disturbance of the position leads to a revision of economic plans, and therewith to a change in the disposition of the individual economic units which leads the system back again in the course of time to the initial equilibrium position. On the other hand, if the reason of the individual's economic plans, and of the resulting dispositions, does not lead back to the initial equilibrium position, there we may say that the equilibrium is unstable."[4]

Further, in the words of Prof. Schumpeter, "*A stable equilibrium value* is an equilibrium value that, if changed by a small amount, calls into action forces that will tend to reproduce the old value; *a neutral equilibrium value* is an equilibrium value that does not know any such forces; and an *unstable equilibrium value* is an equilibrium value, change in which calls forth forces which tend to move the system farther and farther away from the equilibrium value. The ball that rests at the bottom of a bowl illustrates the first case; a ball that rests on a billiard table, the second case; and a ball that is perched on the top of an inverted bowl, the third case."[5]

We may now illustrate these three cases with the help of Fig. 10.1. In Fig. 10.1, panel (A) shows the case of stable equilibrium where the ball rests at the bottom of the bowl. If its position is disturbed, the ball will again come to its original position. In Fig. 10.1, panel (B) shows the case of an unstable equilibrium where the ball is balanced at the top of the invested bowl. If its position is even slightly disturbed, the ball will roll down and will never return to its original position. In Fig. 10.1, panel (C) shows the case of neutral equilibrium where the ball rests on a billiard

3. A.C. Pigou, *Economics of Welfare,* 1932, pp. 794-95.
4. Eric Scheneider, *Pricing and Equilibrium,* pp. 234-35.
5. Schumpeter, *History of Economic Analysis,* p. 178.

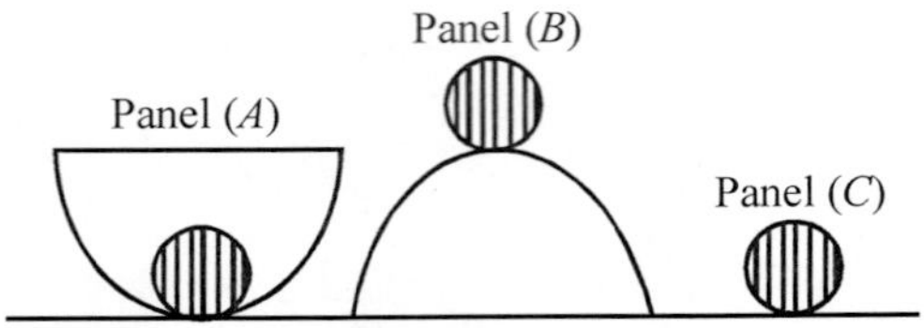

Fig. 10.1

table (or on the flat ground). If its position is disturbed, the ball will move away from its original position and will again rest at some new place. In other words, in the case of neutral equilibrium, if the position is disturbed, it will find a new equilibrium position.

Similarly, we may also illustrate the three cases of equilibrium with the help of a demand and supply model of economic analysis. Under the conditions of perfect competition, the equilibrium price has a tendency to maintain itself so long as the under lying demand and supply conditions remain unaltered.

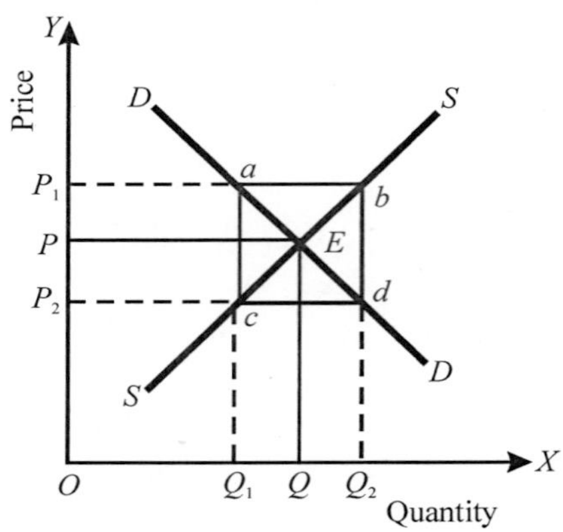

Fig. 10.2

In Fig. 10.2, market demand curve *DD* is negatively sloped while market supply curve *SS* is positively sloped. At point *E,* the demand is equal to the supply and therefore, *OP* is the stable equilibrium price. Any other price will be unstable; because if the equilibrium price *OP* is disturbed, then the forces of demand and supply will again lead price to its original position. For instance, if price rises to OP_1, then at this price, quantity demanded is OQ_1, while quantity supplied is OQ_2. In other words, the quantity supplied (OQ_2) is more than the quantity demanded (OQ_1). This will lead to a reduction in price to the level of *OP* where the quantity demanded is equal to the quantity supplied. In the same way if price falls to OP_2, then the quantity demanded is OQ_2 while the quantity supplied is OQ_1. In this situation quantity demanded is more than quantity supplied. Therefore, it will lead to an increase in the price to the level of *OP,* where again the quantity demanded is equal to the quantity supplied. It illustrates the case of a stable equilibrium.

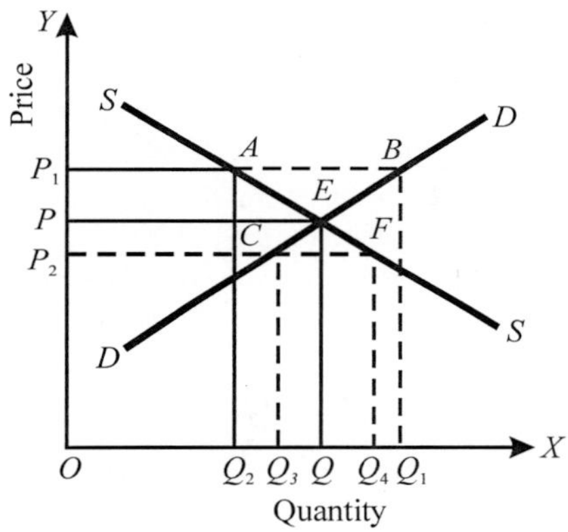

Fig. 10.3

Now, we explain *unstable economic equilibrium.* Here also we take the case of demand and supply model. But in this case, we assume that the demand curve is positively sloped while the supply curve is negatively sloped. This will happen only in the case of a 'Giffen good' where the negative income effect is so strong that it swamps the positive substitution effect of a price change. In normal situations, we do not find such cases. In Fig. 10.3, an increase in price from *OP* to OP_1 leads to excess demand (*AB*), because demand increases from *OQ* to OQ_1 while supply decreases from *OQ* to OQ_2. As a result of this, the price again increases. Similarly, a decrease in price from *OP* to OP_2 will lead to excess supply, because demand decreases from *OQ* to OQ_3 while supply increases from *OQ* to OQ_4. As a result of this, price again falls. In both the situations, price never returns to its original position but moves away and away from the original position. This is the case of an unstable equilibrium.

Now we shall discuss the neutral economic equilibrium. As we know, under this equilibrium, if the initial equilibrium position is disturbed, then the disturbing forces will lead to a new equilibrium position. The neutral equilibrium is classified into two types: (*i*) Static Neutral Equilibrium, and (*ii*) Dynamic Neutral Equilibrium.

Static Neutral equilibrium has been shown in Fig. 10.4 and Dynamic Neutral Equilibrium has been shown in Fig. 10.5.

In Fig. 10.4, the initial equilibrium point is *E,* whereas at *OP* price the demand and supply are equal to *OQ*. If price increases to OP_1, then the new equilibrium point will be *E,* where the quantity demanded and supplied remains the same, i.e., at *OQ*. Thus between the price range *PP,* (or *EE*) the market is in neutral equilibrium.

In Fig. 10.5, an increase in demand will lead to an increase in price from *OP* to OP_1. At this increased price, the producers will have the initiative to produce OQ_1 amount of the commodity. But at this level of output the demand price *OP* is less than the supply price OP_1 and, therefore, the producers will curtail their supply to the extent of *OQ*. But again, at this level demand is more than supply. Thus, it will further lead to an increase in price to the extent of OP_1. In this way, price and quantities will fluctuate along the equilibrium point *E*.

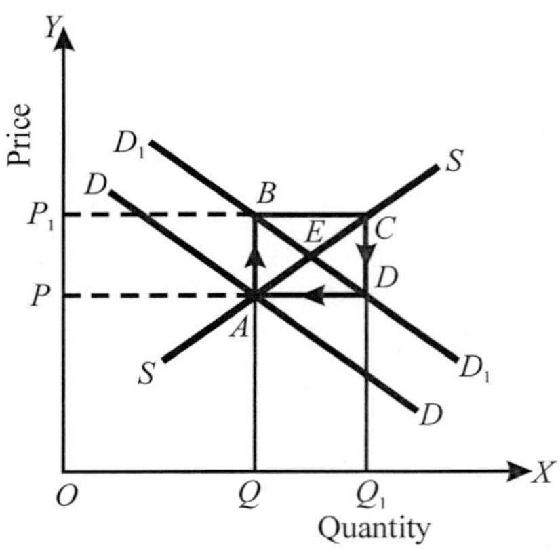

Fig. 10.4

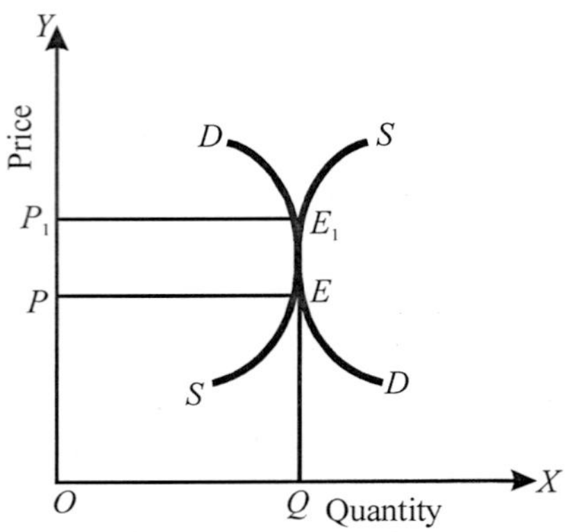

Fig. 10.5

Now, it is important to note that among the three types of equilibrium, it is only the stable equilibrium which is used to analyse the complex economic phenomena by the economists. The unstable and the neutral equilibrium are only of theoretical importance.

Stability Conditions of Equilibrium — Walras *vs.* Marshall

As we have noted above, equilibrium price and quantity are determined by the equality of demand and supply. Equilibrium is characterized by the acquiescence of buyers and sellers in the status quo, i.e., no individual in the market has an incentive to modify his behaviour. However, the existence of an equilibrium point does not guarantee that it will be attained. There is no guarantee that the initital price will happen to be the equilibrium price. Moreover, changes in consumer preference will generally shift the demand curve, and innovations will shift the supply curve. Both these forces will tend to disturb an established equilibrium position. The disturbance (change) may lead to a new equilibrium situation, but there is again no reason to assume that it will be attained. More specifically, an equilibrium is stable, if a disturbance results in a return to initial equilibrium and it is unstable if the disturbance does not lead to the original equilibrium position.[6]

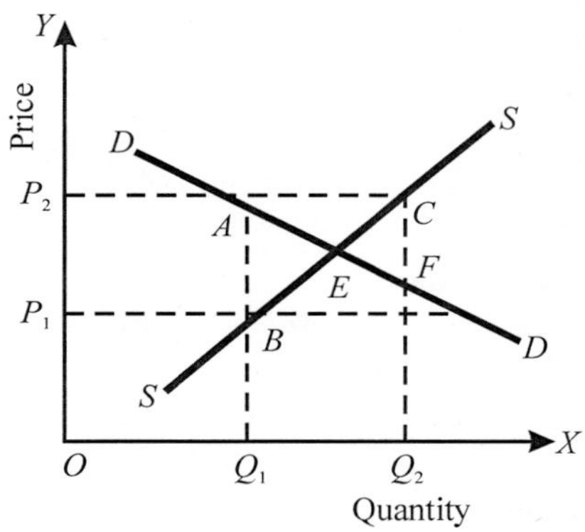

Fig. 10.6

Now, the question is as to what are the stability conditions of equilibrium? In this context, we shall discuss two types of views: The Walrasian View and the Marshallian View, under both the *static stability* and the *dynamic stability* conditions.

---

6. P.A. Samuelson, *Foundations of Economic Analysis,* 1948, pp. 260-62. He states that it is not a rigorous definition of stability and is only one of several alternative definitions.

Static stability conditions. We have already mentioned that a disturbance usually creates an adjustment process in the market. For instance, if the actual price is less than the equilibrium price, the adjustment may consist of some buyers raising their bids (offers) for the commodity. Static analysis abstracts from the time path of the adjustment process and considers only the nature of the change, i.e., whether it is toward, or away from, equilibrium. In Fig. 10.6, the excess demand is positive at the price OP_1, and negative at the price OP_2.

Stability conditions are derived from the assumptions about the market behaviour of buyers and sellers.

The Walrasian stability condition. It is based on the assumption that buyers tend to raise their bids (offers) if excess demand is positive and sellers tend to lower their prices if excess demand is negative. If this assumption holds good, market is stable if a price rise diminishes excess demand. In other words, Walras assumes that it is price that adjusts itself to quantity changes. The excess demand price is defined as the difference between the price that buyers are willing to pay and the price that sellers are charging for a given quantity. In Fig 10.6, there is a positive excess demand price at OQ_1 quantity, (i.e., the demand price at Q_1A is more than the supply price Q_1B, or $Q_1A > Q_1B$, and a negative excess demand price at OQ_2 quantity, i.e., the demand price Q_2F is less than the supply price Q_2C, or $Q_2F < Q_2C$.) Now, according to the Walrasian stability condition, when excess demand is positive, then the buyers will increase the price and if it is negative then the sellers will reduce the price, as a result of which the equilibrium position *E* in Fig. 10.6 is attained.

The Marshallian stability condition, on the other hand, is based on the assumption that producers will tend to raise their output when the excess demand price is positive and lower it when it is negative. In other words, Marshall's analysis is based upon the assumption that quantity adjusts to price changes. If excess demand price is positive, the producer realises that consumers are offering a higher price than he is charging and concludes that he can profitably increase the quantity supplied. Also, if excess demand price is negative, the producer curtails the quantity supplied. As we may notice in Fig. 10.6, when excess-demand price is positive (i.e., $Q_1A > Q_1B$), then it means that consumers are ready to pay more price which the producers want, therefore, producers will increase the supply. When supply increases, it will lead to a decrease in price and that again leads to increased demand; as a result of which equilibrium will be attained at point *E.* Analogous reasoning holds for the converse case.

In this way, both the Walrasian and the Marshallian stability conditions are satisfied if the demand curve is negatively sloped and the supply curve is positively sloped, as shown in Fig. 10.6. The ordinary supply-demand situation is, therefore, stable according to both the Walrasian and Marshallian definitions.

However, if the supply curve is negatively sloped, an equilibrium cannot be stable according to both the definitions.[7] Also, in such a case both the conditions—Walrasian and Marshallian stability conditions—cannot be fulfilled simulta-neously. Both the conditions are applied in opposite directions. If an equilibrium is stable in the Walrasian sense, then the equilibrium will be unstable in the Marshallian sense. The converse is also true. First of all, we will study these stability conditions with the help of straight line demand and supply curves.

The equilibrium is stable in the Walrasian sense if the supply curve is steeper than the demand curve and unstable in the opposite case. Equilibrium is stable in the Marshallian sense if the supply curve is less steep than the demand curve and unstable in the opposite case. These concepts are illustrated in Figs 10.7 and 10.8 respectively.

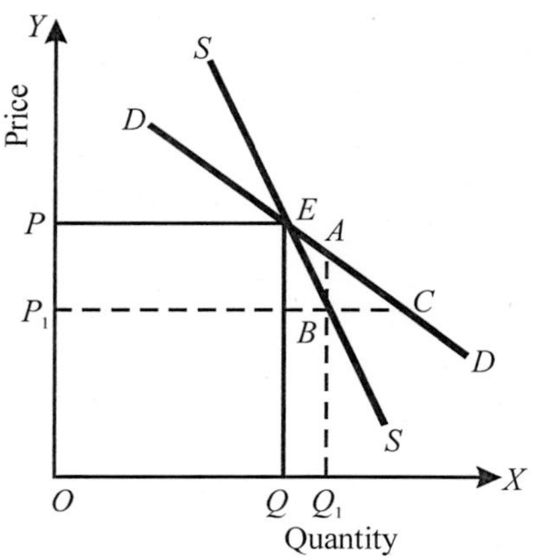

Fig. 10.7

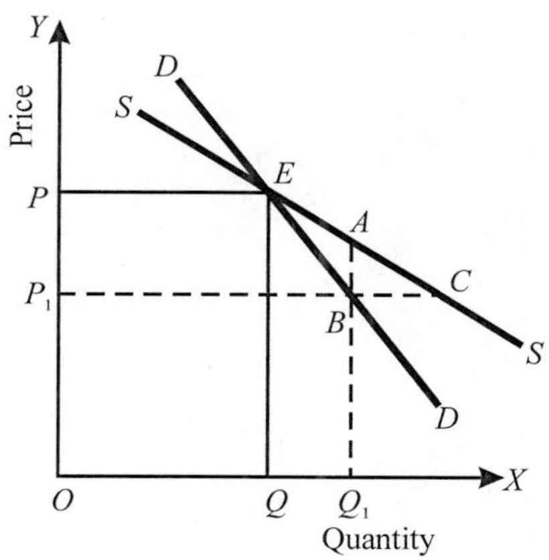

Fig. 10.8

7. The supply curves which may have negative slope are the supply curves for primary inputs, such as, labour and product supply curves in the presence of external economies or diseconomies. Unstable equilibria may occur only in these cases.

Figure 10.7 illustrates the Walrasian stable and Marshallian unstable equilibrium. In Walraslan sense, at price OP_1, the excess demand BC is positive (because demand is more than supply or $P_1C > P_1B$), therefore competition among consumers will tend to raise the price to the extent of OP and excess demand diminishes. Hence the equilibrium is stable at point E in Fig. 10.7. But, in Marshallian sense, at price OP_1, the quantity supplied is OQ_1; the corresponding excess demand price AB is positive (because $Q_1A > Q_1B$). The consumers are ready to pay more price than the actual price. Therefore, the quantity produced will tend to increase, but the excess demand price increases too. Thus, the actual price and quantity move farther away from the equilibrium point E.

Now, Fig. 10.8 illustrates the stable equilibrium in Marshallian sense and unstable equilibrium in Walrasian sense. In Marshallian sense, at price OP_1, the excess demand price AB is negative (because $Q_1B < Q_1A$, i.e., demand price is less them supply price.) It inspires the producers to reduce their supply from OQ_1 to OQ. Price increases and demand decreases, as a result of which the original equilibrium point E is attained. But in Walrasian sense, at price OP_1, the excess demand BC is negative because $P_1B < P_1C$. It will inspire the sellers to make a further reduction in their price. Thus both price and quantity move farther away from the equilibrium point E. Hence, the equilibrium is unstable.

Theoretically, a negatively sloped supply curve may intersect the demand curve at several points. Such a case is illustrated in Fig. 10.9. Each intersection defines an equilibrium position. In Walrasian sense,

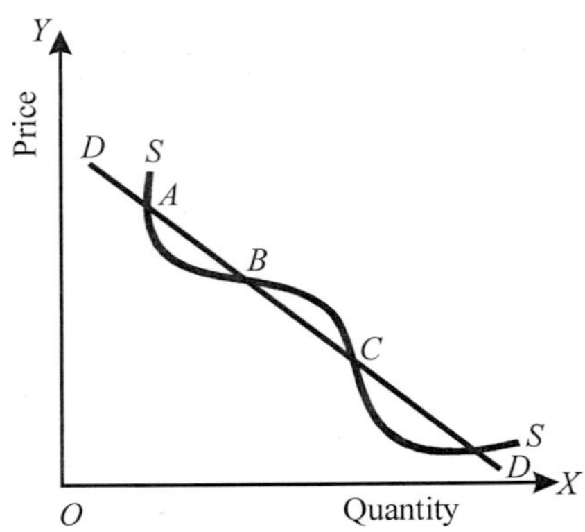

Fig. 10.9

the successive equilibrium points *A, B,* C are alternatively stable and unstable.[8] The supply curve is steeper than the demand curve at point *A,* and therefore, the equilibrium is stable at this point. Similarly, at point *B* the supply curve becomes less steep than the demand curve and, therefore, the equilibrium is unstable at point *B.* By a similar reasoning, point C again represents a stable equilibrium. It is also known as a case of 'multi-equilibrium'.

Thus, the views of Prof. Marshall and Prof. Walras regarding the stability conditions of equilibrium are just opposite to each other. The reason may be that Prof. Marshall and Prof. Walras have developed their ideas about the stability conditions assuming different time periods. Marshall defines his stability conditions in the context of equilibrium in which the adjustment is made by quantity changes. Walras, on the other hand, defines his stability conditions assuming a short-time period in which adjustment is made by changes in price. Therefore, one cannot say a *priori* whether the Walrasian or Marshallian condition is more plausible in reality. In any concrete situation stability of equilibrium can be assessed only after empirical information has been collected, concerning the behaviour patterns of the buyers and sellers in the market.

Dynamic stability conditions. As we have explained, the static stability conditions are stated in terms of change of excess demand with respect to price or the rate of change of excess demand price with respect to quantity. This type of analysis (static) makes no effort to investigate time path of the adjustment process.

We cannot expect instantaneous (immediate) adjustments in the present model of demand and supply. If the initial price is not equal to the equilibrium price, it changes and new equilibrium takes place. If the new price is still different from the equilibrium price, it is again forced to change. This process continues until equilibrium is reached.[9] This is known as the dynamic nature of the model.

Equilibrium is stable in the dynamic sense if the price converges to (or approaches) the equilibrium price over time. It is an unstable equilibrium if the price change is always away from equilibrium. Dynamic

8. The arrangement here is based on the Waliasian behaviour assumption. Analogous arrangement can be given in terms of the Marshallian assumption. In that case the above successive equilibrium points *A, B,* C of Fig. 6.9 will represent alternatively unstable and stable equilibrium positions.
9. The prices which are recorded from period to period are potential, rather than realized prices until equilibrium is reached.

stability may also be defined in terms of the convergence of the quantity supplied to the equilibrium quantity. The former definition corresponds to the Walrasian and the latter to the Marshallian definition of dynamic stability conditions. Both static and dynamic stability depend upon the slopes of the demand and supply curves. But the static and dynamic approaches to stability are fundamentally different. Static stability need not imply dynamic stability, but dynamic stability implies static stability. The reason is that dynamic analysis is a more inclusive tool for investigating the properties of equilibrium. Static analysis concerns itself only with the direction of the adjustment and neglects the magnitude of the adjustment from period to period.

After the development of dynamic economics, the stable and unstable equilib-rium situations are explained with the help of Cobweb theorem.[10]

(2) Short-run and Long-run Equilibrium

An economic equilibrium may also be classified as short-run and long-run equilibrium. Such type of classification was made by Prof. Marshall who for the first time introduced the element of time in the theory of value. In the short-run, individual firms seek to maximize profits or minimize losses. The scale of plant is fixed for each firm. Available techniques of production and input-prices determine the individual firm's costs.[11] Losses are increased by some firms and profits are made by others. No firm operates unless the price of its product exceeds average variable costs. The supply is adjusted to the changes in demand with the existing means of production because the time is too short to vary the means of production or the scale of plant. Such an equilibrium is termed as *short-run equilibrium.*

In the long-run those resources (or costs) that were fixed in the short-run become variable. These are the costs that constitute the plants of individual firms. As they become variable, it becomes possible for individual firms to change scale of plant, for firms to exit from those industries in which losses occur, and for firms to enter those industries which make profits-provided entry or exit of a firm is easy, as it is under conditions of pure and monopolistic competition. Therefore, in the long-run the time available to adjust the supply to change in demand is quite

10. Hendersen and Quandt, *Microeconimic Theory—A Mathematical Approach,* pp. 113-23.
11. In our discussion on the short-run equilibrium, we distinguish between "fixed" costs and "variable" costs. The maximum loss that a firm may accept will not exceed its fixed costs.

adequate. The supply can be adjusted to the changes in demand by varying the means of production (or scale of plant) and the resulting equilibrium is called *long-run equilibrium.*

In other words, long-run equilibrium will be reached when all resources are so allocated that their respective marginal revenue products (*MRP*) are equalized in all alternative uses. No shortage or surpluses occur for any resource; that is, the marginal revenue product of each is equal to its price, i.e., $MRP = P$. When the equilibrium allocation of resources is achieved, each firm will be using resources in the least-cost combination. Firms will adjust their scales of plant in such a way that their long-run marginal cost equals marginal revenue ($LMC = MR$), and will use least-cost resource combinations for the outputs which they produce.[12]

The difference between the two types of equilibrium—short-run and long-run equilibrium—can be illustrated with the help of an example of perfect competition. Here, short-run equilibrium requires that each firm must produce that level of output for which its marginal cost equals marginal revenue ($MC = MR$). On the other hand, long-run equilibrium requires that each firm must produce that level of output for which its $MC = MR = AR = AC$.

Figure 10.10 shows the short-run equilibrium, while Fig. 10.11 shows the long run equilibrium of a perfectly competitive firm. In Fig. 10.10, the equilibrium point *E* indicates that the firm is producing *OX* level of output where its $MC = MR$. It is a profit-maximising output and the firm has no incentive to deviate from this. The firm's total abnormal profits are shown by the area of rectangle (*PEA*).

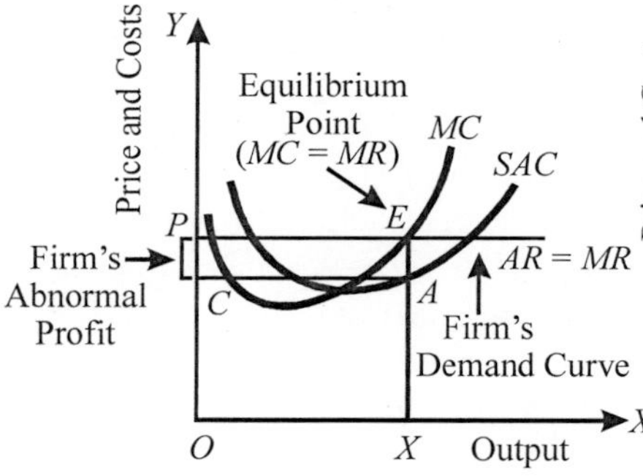

Fig. 10.10

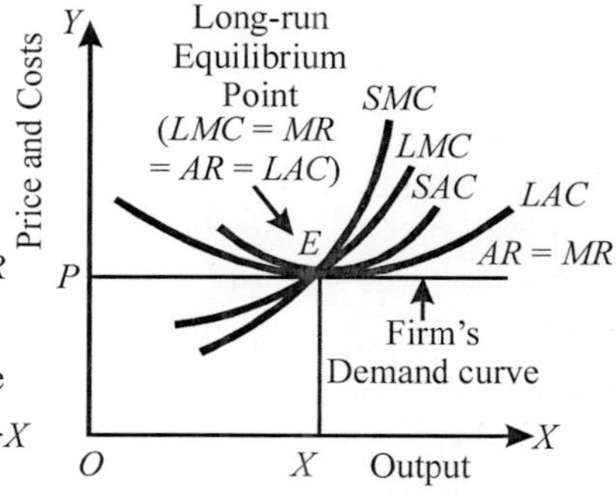

Fig. 10.11

12. It holds only in the case of perfect competition when entry is free.

Figure 10.11 shows the case of long-run equilibrium. Here, the equilibrium point *E* indicates that the firm will produce *OX* level of output where its $MC = MR = AR = AC$. The important point to notice here is that the abnormal profits of the firm disappear due to the entry of new firms in the market. Also for the firm, there is no incentive to increase or decrease the scale of plant or the output. This also means that long-run equilibrium of the firm also requires the short-run equilibrium to exist at the same time. But the converse may not be true; that is short-run equilibrium of the firm (or the industry) can exist even though there is long-run disequilibrium of the firm (or the industry).

(3) Unique and Multiple Equilibrium

According to Prof. Stigler, "Equilibrium may be unique or multiple. A position of unique equilibrium arises if there is a single set of prices and quantities which fulfil the conditions of equilibrium. Multiple positions of equilibrium exist when several different sets of prices and quantities will meet the equilibrium conditions. The study of multiple equilibrium positions is essentially formal; no important empirical cases have yet been advanced to illustrate it. ... In general, a unique position of equilibrium will be treated as the typical case."

In this sense, Fig. 10.6 represents the situation of a single or unique equilibrium which is very common to the real world, while Fig. 10.9 represents the situation of multiple equilibrium which is very rare in the real world.

(4) Static and Dynamic Equilibrium

As we have already explained, static equilibrium represents a stationary state. According to Prof. Mehta, "Static equilibrium which maintains itself outside the period of time under consideration." It is such a gainful situation which every consumer, firm, industry or factor-input wants to achieve and when it comes, nobody would like to leave it. A consumer is in static equilibrium if he gets maximum satisfaction from his limited income to be spent on various goods and services. Deviation from this position will necessarily reduce his total satisfaction. Similarly, a firm is in static equilibrium if she gets maximum profit and will have no initiative to increase her output. In the same way, an industry will be in static equilibrium if no firm has the incentive to enter into it and no firm wants to exit from it. In other words, an industry is in equilibrium if all the firms (which constitute it) are earning only normal profits.

An economic system, on the other hand, may be said to be in a dynamic equilibrium if its total stock changes at a constant rate, and if the rates of production and consumption of all items of the stock increase at the same time. According to Prof. Mehta after a certain time period when the equilibrium position is disturbed, then it is said to be dynamic equilibrium. Today, the concept of dynamic equilibrium is explained with the help of Cobweb theorem. In real world, the concept of dynamic equilibrium is of little importance in interpreting economic change; but the concept of static equilibrium is realistic and is generally used to interpret the economic change.

(5) Partial and General Equilibrium

According to Prof. Stigler, "Equilibrium may be partial or general. A partial equilibrium is one which is based on only a restricted range of data; a standard example is the price of a single product, the prices of all other products being held fixed during the analysis. General equilibrium is ostensibly based on all of the data relevant to the problem which is being studied: the corresponding example would be the prices and outputs of all industries. The method of partial equilibrium analysis is associated with Marshall and the Cambridge School; that of general equilibrium with Walras and the Lausanne School." In simple words, an equilibrium pertaining to a single variable—a single price or a consumer or a firm or an industry—may be called partial or particular equilibrium. More specifically, it studies the movements of particular individuals, firms or industries towards equilibrium on the basis of given economic data. General equilibrium, on the other hand, deals with the economy as a whole.

The economic analysis of Prof. Marshall is related to the study of partial equilibrium. While analysing the behaviour of an individual consumer or a firm or a sector of the economy, it is generally assumed that the changes in these individual units make no effect on the rest of the economy. In other words, micro-economic analysis of economic units is based on the assumption of "ceteris paribus". Thus, all microeconomic studies are concerned with partial or particular equilibria. Generally, partial equilibrium analysis is related to two types of problems:

(1) Problems which are related to a particular aspect of the economic behaviour of an individual consumer, firm or an industry. For example, if the workers of a particular industry go on strike, the effects of such strike are likely to remain confined to that particular industry only.

(2) Problems which are concerned with the *first order* effects of an economic disturbance of any kind. For example, suppose a rearmament

programme increases the demand for steel suddenly and substantially. Partial equilibrium analysis will provide answers to the first-order effects on the steel industry—what happens to its prices, its output, its profits, its demand for resources, resource prices and resource employment levels. However, the first-order effects by no means end the repercussions from the initial disturbance. In other words, it will continue even after the steel industry has attained a new equilibrium position.

Partial or particular equilibrium analysis will be helpful in reviewing the operation of a free enterprise economy. In a free enterprise economy, individual consumers seek to maximise satisfaction. In terms of utility analysis, each consumer will spend his limited income among different goods and services in such a way that the marginal utility of the rupee spent on them must be the same.

A firm will be in equilibrium, if it does not want to make any change in its production. In the short run, its marginal cost equals marginal revenue ($MC = MR$) and in the long run it performs the conditions of complete equilibrium, i.e., $MC = MR = LAC$. Thus, the firm earns only the normal profit and does not want to leave the industry. In the analysis of a firm, the production technique, and prices of goods and factor inputs are given.

Similarly, an industry will be in equilibrium, if all the firms in the industry enjoy normal profit and the number of firms is fixed.

There are two main limitations of the partial equilibrium analysis:

(1) It does not deal with the economy as a whole. It is limited to a particular phenomenon of the economy.

(2) It assumes other things remaining the same; therefore, it cannot be used as a policy guide.

Due to these limitations, the study of general equilibrium is required. The general equilibrium analysis considers all the sectors of an economy simultaneously. It attempts to deal explicitly with inter-relationships between different sectors of the economy. The concept of general equilibrium implies that all economic units—all consumers, firms, industries and factor inputs—are in equilibrium. If some units were in equilibrium and others were not, those in disequilibrium will move toward equilibrium. In other words, general equilibrium for the entire economy could exist only if all economic units were to achieve simultaneous partial equilibrium adjustments, as all economic units are assumed to be inter-dependent.

According to Prof. Leftwich, a line of demarcation between particular equilibrium analysis and general equilibrium analysis is hard to draw. Instead of establishing a dichotomy, it will be preferable to think in terms of moving along a continuum from particular into general equilibrium, or from first-order effects of a disturbance into second-order effect and further of higher-order effects. For instance, in price and output determination under perfect competition, we are concerned first with the (partial) equilibrium of the individual firm. Next, we extend the analysis to an entire industry. Then we observe, how a purely competitive free enterprise economy operates according to consumer tastes and preferences. This shows progressive movement from the application of particular analysis to the application of general equilibrium analysis.

According to Prof. Stigler, the main advantages of general equilibrium analysis are the following:

(1) It provides a demonstration that equilibrium in any particular sector of the economy is not incompatible with equilibrium in other sectors.

(2) It provides an outline of the general structure and the working of the economy as a whole.

(3) It is of great assistance in discovering which data are relevent to any specific problem.

When the impact of an economic disturbance is of sufficient magnitude to have repercussions throughout most of the economy, general equilibrium analysis provides the more relevant answers regarding its ultimate effects.

There are two principal variants of general equilibrium analysis.

(1) *Walras Model* which discusses general equilibrium in mathematical terms. Here the interdependence of economic units is shown through, a system of simultaneous equations relating many economic variables to each other. There are as many variables to be determined as there are equations relating them.

(2) *Leontief's Input-Output Analysis.* It is an empirical descendant of the abstract Walrasian approach. It divides the economy into a number of sector or industries, including households and the government as the sectors of final demand. Here, the inter-dependence of each industry on the others is established, statistical data provide an informative and useful picture of the inter-industry flows of goods, services arid resources.

The Walrasian Model of General Equilibrium

The general equilibrium situation of Prof. Walras is static in which all prices are in equilibrium and demand and supply of the products are equal on equilibrium prices. Walras developed a system of equations to explain the state of general equilibrium. He distinguished between product-markets and factor-markets. In the product-market the goods are supplied by the business firms or industries and the same are demanded by the consumers. In the factor-markets, the households (or consumers) supply factor-inputs, such as, land, labour, capital, etc. to the industries and in return receive incomes from the industries. Therefore, consumers are buyers in the product-markets and sellers in the factor-markets. Similarly, the industries are sellers in the product markets and buyers in the factor-markets.

Assumptions of the Model

The Walrasian model is based on the following assumptions:

(1) The income and tastes of the consumers are given and constant.
(2) There is perfect competition in both the markets—the product market and the factor market.
(3) Factors of production are perfectly mobile.
(4) Constant returns prevail in the economy.
(5) All the units of a product or service are homogeneous.
(6) Production technology is unchanged.
(7) Factors of production are fully employed.

Under these assumptions thy economy is in equilibrium if the demand and the supply of each product or service are equal. The unknown variables in the Walrasian Model are the prices and quantities of the factors of production used in the production of each product. Walras called them technical coefficients. If there are n commodities and m factor-inputs, then there would be n commodity-prices and m factor-prices. It will create $n \times m$ technical coefficients.

Criticisms of the Walrasian Model

The main criticisms of the model are the following:

(1) It is based on a number of unrealistic assumptions. Its assumptions are far from the reality. Perfect competition, which is the basis of this model, is only an imaginary concept.

(2) This model is static in nature. It assumes *ceteris paribus.* But in real world, the tastes and preferences of the consumers are changing. Constant returns to scale are not found in the long run. Further, the cost situations are different for different producers.

(3) The model assumes a set of simultaneous equations which makes it complicated. A non-mathematical student of economics is unable to understand it.

EXERCISES

1. Discuss the significance and the concept of equilibrium in economic theory.
2. What do you understand by the term 'equilibrium'? What are the various types of equilibrium?
3. Distinguish between the conditions for stable and unstable equilibrium.
4. Define stable, unstable and neutral economic equilibrium. Prove with suitable diagrams that equilibrium is actually achieved in the real world from time to time.
5. Write a brief note on the Walrasian Model of General Equilibrium.
6. Distinguish between partial and general equilibrium. What are the advantages and limitations of general equilibrium analysis?
7. Write short notes on the following:
   (*i*) Short-run and Long-run Equilibrium.
   (*ii*) Unique and Multiple Equilibrium.
   (*iii*) Static and Dynamic Economic Equilibrium.
8. Distinguish between static and dynamic equilibrium. Explain your answer with the help of diagrams and equations.
9. Define equilibrium and show with the help of the Cobweb theorem that under given conditions equilibrium can actually be achieved in practice.

Multiple Choice Questions

10. (*i*) Which of the following statement is most closely associated with general equilibrium analysis?
    (*a*) everything depends on everything else
    (*b*) *cateris paribus.*
    (*c*) the equilibrium price of a good or service depends on, the balancing of the forces of demand and supply for that good or service
    (*d*) none of the above [*Ans.* (*a*)]

    (*ii*) The market equilibrium of a commodity determined by
    (*a*) the market demand for the commodity
    (*b*) the market supply of the commodity
    (*c*) the balancing of the forces of demand and supply of the commodity
    (*d*) any of the above [*Ans.* (*c*)]

    (*iii*) The long-run equilibrium of a firm under perfect competition, requires that each firm must produce that level of output for which its
    (*a*) $MC = MR = AR = AC$
    (*b*) $MC = MR$
    (*c*) $AR = AC$
    (*d*) P = NR [*Ans.* (*a*)]

Chapter 11

NATIONAL INCOME : CONCEPT AND MEASUREMENT

1. INTRODUCTION

The national income of a country in a year is the value, expressed in monetary terms, of the net contribution of the factors of production through the production units in the country and abroad in the year. It is thus the monetary expression of the current flow of net final goods and services resulting from the production activities of the normal residents, of a country during the year. Concretely, national income is the net domestic product (or net domestic income) of a country plus net income from abroad.

The significance of national income is that it is the value of the goods and services which can be used up in consumption by the residents of the country without causing, a reduction in the production capacity of the country. It represents that part of the flow of goods and services generated by the production process which is produced in order to satisfy the wants of the people.

If all the national income is in fact consumed then national income consists of consumers goods and services only. If only a part of the national income is, consumed in the year then the part which remains accumulate as stocks of goods or as capital stocks. National income then would consist of consumers goods and services plus increase in stocks of goods, i.e., of consumption plus net investment. Net investment include increase in the "stocks of fixed capital goods and of working capital goods. If, however, people consume more than the national income then it would probably mean that the stock of capital goods has been eaten into or that the people have received gifts from abroad. Eating into stocks of capital means negative net investment because of using up more inventory goods than is produced during the year or because of not replacing depreciation of fixed capital stocks. (While net investment may be negative, gross investment can only be at worst zero, not negative.) Gifts from abroad refer to current transfers from abroad of consumers goods and services. The national income is, thus the goods and services available to the normal residents in a country; as a result of their production efforts in the year, to consume or to invest.

2. DEFINITIONS OF NATIONAL, INCOME

National income or national dividend has been defined in a number of ways. The various definitions of national income can be classified into two categories. The first category includes the traditional definitions given by Marshall, Pigou and, Fisher. While the second category includes the modem, definitions given by Simon Kuznets, V.K.RV. Rao and others.

Marshall's Definition. According to Marshall, "The labour and capital of a country acting on its natural resources produce annually a certain net aggregate of commodities, material and immaterial, including services of all kinds. This is the true net annual income or revenue, of the country or national dividend."[1]

In this definition the word 'net' is used to indicate that net national income can be found only after deducting the depreciation of plant and capital from the gross national income. Further, the net income due on account of foreign investments must, be added to it to find out the true net annual income or revenue of the country.

The, main criticisms of Marshall's definition are the following:

(1) Today, a country produces a number of commodities and services whose correct evaluation, becomes difficult. Thus, we cannot get an accurate estimate of the, national income of a country.

(2) There are some commodities which are used more than once. Thus, there is a possibility that the produce of such commodities may be counted twice. This will give a wrong estimate of the national income.

(3) There are some commodities which do not appear in the market and they are consumed directly by the producers. This normally happens in the case of agricultural commodities. Marshall's definition fails to provide, a measure for such items.

Pigou's Definition. According to Pigou, "National income is that part of the objective income of the community, including of course income derived from abroad, which, can be measured in money:"[2]

---

1. Alfred Marshall, *Principles of Economics,* p. 434.
2. A.C. Pigou, *The Economics of Welfare,* p. 31.

In simple words, Pigou's definition indicates that we must count only those things and services which are objective and which are exchanged for money. This definitions superior to Marshall's definition because it is free from the difficulties implicit under the Marshall's definition. It is a practical definition. In spite of this fact that it is a simple arid comprehensive definition, it is not free from criticisms. The following are the important limitations of this definition:

(1) While calculating national income, Pigou includes only those goods and services which are exchanged for money. Thus, the services which a person renders to himself, and those which he performs for the sake of his family or friends should not be regarded as parts of national dividend. Thus, the definition does not provide a correct picture of the national income of a country.

(2) This definition is applicable only to developed countries of the world where barter system is not found. It cannot be used to calculate the national income of the backward and less developed countries where the barter system still occupies an important place in the economy.

Fisher's Definition. According to Fisher, "The national dividend or income consists solely of services as received by ultimate consumers, whether from their material or from their human environments. Thus, a piano or an overcoat made for me this year is not a part of this year's income, but an addition to capital. Only the services rendered to me during this year by these things are income."[3]

This definition is different from Marshall's definition and Pigou's definition. Here, Fisher assumes consumption as the base of national income, while Marshall and Pigou assume production as the base of national income. According to Fisher, national income of a country is determined by its annual consumption and not by its annual production. For example, if a machine is produced in 1997, then according to Marshall and Pigou, the entire value of machine should be included in the national income of 1997. But according to Fisher the entire value of machine should not be included in the national income of 1997; instead a money value of its actual consumption should be included in the national income of 1997. It will depend upon the life of the machine. Suppose, the life of the machine is 10 year and its present value is Rs. 20,000. Then the money value of the consumption of the machine during 1997 will be Rs. 2,000. Therefore, according to Fisher, only Rs. 2,000 should be included in the

3. J. Fisher, *The Nature of Capital and Income,* p. 104.

national income of 1997, and not Rs. 20,000 as suggested by Marshall's and Pigou's definitions.

This is the reason why Fisher's definition may be considered better and more scientific than the other definitions given by Marshall and Pigou. Moreover, Fisher's definition gives a proper idea of the economic welfare of a country. Economic welfare depends upon consumption and the level of consumption is an index of the standard of living. Besides these advantages, Fisher's definition has a little practical value; because it is very difficult to calculate the money value of the annual consumption of goods and services in a country. The following are the main criticisms of Fisher's definition:

(1) There are a number of consumers of a commodity and they live at different places in a country. Thus it is difficult to calculate the money value of the annual consumption. Further, the number of commodities is very large and each possesses a number of varieties. In such a situation, it is easier to find out the value of production than the value of annual consumption.

(2) Durable commodities have their different periods of life for different consumers. It is difficult to allot a definite 'life' to each and every commodity produced in a country.

(3) A durable consumer good may pass through the hands of a number of persons. Here, it will be difficult to find out the original price and the exact date of manufacture of such commodities.

Modern Definitions. Modern definitions have been given by modern economists. The important definitions are as below:

According to Simon Kuznets, "It is the net output of commodities and services flowing during the year from the country's productive system in the hands of the ultimate consumers."[4]

According to Colin Clark, a British authority on the subject, "The national income for any period consists of the money value of the goods and services becoming available for consumption during that period, reckoned at their current selling prices, plus additions to capital reckoned at the prices actually paid for the new capital goods, minus depreciation and obsolescence of existing capital goods, and adding the net accretion of, or deducting the net drawings upon stocks, also reckoned at current prices. Services provided at non-profit-making basis by the state and local authorities (e.g., postal services, and municipal tramway services) are included on the basis of charges made. Where taxation is levied upon

---

4. Simon Kuznets, article in *Readings in the Theory of Income Distribution,* p. 3.

particular commodities and services, such as, customs and excise duties on commodities or the entertainment tax, such taxes are not included in the selling value."

According to V.K.R.V. Rao, an Indian authority on the subject, "National income may be defined as the money value of the flow of commodities and services, excluding imports becoming available for sale (or capable of being sold) within the period, the value being reckoned at current prices minus the sum of the following items: (*i*) the money value of any diminution in stocks that may have taken place during the period. (*ii*) the money value of the flow of goods and services used up in the course of production; (*iii*) the money value of the flow of goods and services used to maintain intact existing capital equipment (value being reckoned at current prices); (*iv*) receipts of the state from indirect taxation; (*v*) favourable balance of trade including transactions in treasure; (*vi*) net increase in country's foreign indebtedness or the decrease in the holdings of balances and securities abroad whether by individuals or the government of the country."

In simple words, national income is the aggregate factor income (i.e., earning of labour and capital, etc.) which arises from the current production of goods and services by the nation's economy. The nation's economy refers to the factor of production (labour and capital) supplied by the *normal* residents of the *national territory.*

From the above definitions it is clear that the concept of national income has three types of interpretations:

(1) National income represents a receipt total,

(2) National income represents an expenditure total, and

(3) National income represents a total value of production.

This three-fold interpretation takes place because of the fact that every expenditure is at the same time a receipt, and if goods or services bought are valued at their sales prices, we have a three-fold identity that the value received equals the value paid, equals the value of goods and services given in exchange.

3. ELEMENTS OF NATIONAL INCOME

A description of the above definitions brings out three points. *Firstly,* national income refers to the income of a country, say, India. *Secondly,* its measurement refers to a specified period of time, say, a year. *Thirdly,* national income includes all types of goods and services which have an exchange value, counting each one of them *only* once.

When we calculate the national income of a nation, we should remember that no commodity or service should be counted twice; otherwise the results will not be accurate. For example, if raw cotton has been evaluated in agricultural production, it should not be included while calculating the total value of cotton textiles. In the same manner, the value of raw cotton shall have to be kept out while calculating the total value of ready made garments, such as, bush-shirts and trousers made out of cotton textiles.

Generally, two statistical methods are used to avoid *double counting* or *multiple counting* in the calculation of national income: (*i*) final products method, and (*ii*) value-added method. According to the first method, we add up the value of *final* products only. We first take the total value of the *final* consumer goods produced in to country during the year. To this, we add the total value of durable producer goods, such as, machinery and plants, etc. This will provide us the aggregate value of all the *final* goods produced in the country during the year. Collective and government services (evaluated at cost price) are also to be added to this aggregate value of the final goods in order to arrive at the total product of the nation concerned.

According to the value-added method, we do not take into account the value of the *final* goods and services produced in the country. On the contrary, we go on adding the values created at each stage in the manufacture of a commodity. Then all such values accruing at all processes in the manufacture of all commodities are added up together to arrive at the national income of the country.

The value-added method can be explained by means of a simple example. Let us suppose that a ready-made bush-shirt passes through four stages of production. In the first stage, the farmer produces raw cotton from the soil. In the second stage, the raw cotton is converted into cotton cloth in a factory. In the third stage, the cotton cloth is converted into a bush-shirt by the ready-made garments firm. In the fourth stage, the ready-made bush-shirt is sold to a retailer from whom it is finally purchased by the customer. Now money value of all the transactions which take place in the various stages of production of a bush-shirt should not be added up while making an estimate of the national income of the country; otherwise, there will be multiple counting and the result will not be accurate. This can be illustrated with the help of Table 11.1.

Table 11.1: *Increase in Value in the Production of a Multi-Process Commodity*

Stage of Production	*Sale-Value of the Commodity (in Rupees)*	*Increase in Value (in Rupees)*
1. Cotton-growing farmer	30	30
2. Cloth-manufacturing factory	100	70
3. Ready-made garments firm	150	50
4. Retailer	170	20
Total	450	170

When we add values at all the stages of production of the bush-shirt, the aggregate comes to Rs. 450. The customer, however, pays Rs. 170 for the bush-shirt. Therefore, we should add only Rs. 170 to the national income of the country, because this represents the value of the final product, namely, the bush-shirt. Under no circumstances should we add Rs. 450 to the national income of the country. If we do, so, it will give us a wrong picture of the national income of that country. The amount (Rs. 170) represents not only the value of the final product; it is also the aggregate of the values added to the commodity at various stages of production (i.e., Rs. 30 + 70 + 50 + 0 = Rs. 170).

We find that no matter we adopt the first or the second method, the result will be the same. If proper adjustments are made, the 'final products' method will give us the same results as the 'value-added' method. As shown in Table 38.1 the amount to be added to the national income on account of the bush-shirt is Rs. 170, whether we adopt the 'final products' method or the 'value-added' method. It should however, be made clear that the 'final products' method is better than the 'value-added' method because there are less chances of errors in the former than in the latter. Even then, the choice between the two is a question of the relative case or difficulty of collecting the statistical data in each case.

National income or product is, thus, the aggregate money value of all goods and services produced in a country during a year, avoiding double or multiple counting.

In the words of Prof. J.R. Hicks, "The national income consists of a collection of goods and services reduced to a common basis by being measured in terms of money." The producers received payments for the goods they were responsible for producing, paid out of these sums rent, interest, wages and salaries to the factors participating in production, and keeping the balance of profit as their own reward. It is evident, therefore, that the total volume of production and the aggregate of all incomes are one and the same thing. The calculation of the national income can consequently be approached either from the side of the production of goods and services or from the side of income. In other words, there are two methods of calculating the national income of a country: (*i*) *Census of Production Method;* and (*ii*) *Census of Income Method.* In the former, we evaluate in terms of money all the goods and services produced in a country in anyone year. In the latter, we aggregate the incomes of all the income-earning members of the community. If full information were available; either of the two methods should yield the same result.

4. FACTORS DETERMINING NAT'IONAL INCOME

There are a number of influences which determine the size of the national income in a country. It is on account of these influences that one country may have a larger national income than another. Following are the three main influences:

(1) ***Quantity and Quality of Factors of Production.*** The quantity and quality of a country's stock of the factors of production is one of the most important influences on its national income. The quantity and quality of land, the climate, the rainfall etc., determine the quantity and quality of agricultural production, and hence, the size of national income. The quantity of labour has a double influence since labour is at the same time both a factor of production as well as the consumer of what is produced. The quality of labour, depending upon inborn intelligence, education and training, also influences the volume of industrial production. Capital may comprise simple, primitive tools or the most modern type of industrial equipment. The quantity and quality of capital is one of the greatest influences on total output. Likewise, the quantity and quality of entrepreneurial ability is also an important element to reckon with in the determination of the size of national income of a country.

(2) ***The State of Technical Know-how.*** Another influence on output and national income is the state of technical know-how in the country. A country with a poor technical knowledge cannot have a large-sized national income, because it will not be in a position to make the best possible use of its resources.

(3) ***Political Stability.*** Political stability is an essential prerequisite for maintaining production at the highest level. The economic development of several countries, particularly the South American Republics, has been hindered in the past by political instability.

5. CONCEPT OF NATIONAL INCOME OR NATIONAL INCOME ACCOUNTS (SOCIAL ACCOUNTING)

A system of social accounting does for the economy as a whole what private accounting does for the individual business enterprise; it allows us to keep a finger on the economic pulse of the nation. The various types of national income accounts help us to measure the level of production in the economy at some point of time, and explain the immediate causes of that level of performance. Further, by comparing the national income accounts over a period of time, it is possible to pinpoint the long-term trends at work in the nation of economy. Finally, the information obtained from the national income accounts provides a reliable basis for the formulation and application of governmental policies designed to improve the economic health of the nation.

Under the above head, we shall study seven 'totals' relating to national income accounts. They are: (*i*) Gross National Product (*GNP*), (*ii*) Net National Product (*NNP*), (*iii*) National Income (*NI*), or Net National Income at Factor Cost (*NNI* at Factor Cost), (*iv*) Net Domestic Product at Factor Cost (*NDP* at Factor Cost), (*v*) Personal Income (*PI*), (*vi*) Disposable Personal Income (*DPI*), and (*vii*) Real Income (*RI*).

Thus instead of giving a single comprehensive estimate of national income, the economists use different aggregates. There are two reasons for so many different concepts. One is that there is disagreement among the economists over what should and what should not be counted as national income. Instead of passing judgment on this controversy, the statistics department of the government gives some totals leaving it to each user to select the one he prefers. Another reason for this is that a certain total may be most useful for one purpose, and a different total for another purpose. We shall discuss their comparative advantages in the following section.

Gross National Product (GNP)

The gross national product is the basic social accounting measure. It is the most frequently used national income aggregate in economic discussion. It is the nation's total production of goods and services (usually for one year) evaluated in terms of the market prices of goods and services produced. It includes all the economic productions in the economy during one year. *Strictly speaking, then the GNP is the money value of the total national production for any given period.*

Two points must be kept in mind while calculating the *GNP* of a country. *Firstly,* we must take into account the money value of the *final* goods (and services) produced in the economy to avoid double or multiple counting. It should be remembered that *final* goods and services are those which are *finally* consumed by the consumers. Such goods and services do not enter into the manufacture of other, goods. As against this, *intermediate* goods and services are those goods and services which do enter into the production of other goods and services (Bread, for example, is a final good, but flour is an intermediate good). Intermediate products are to be excluded from the *GNP.*

Secondly, we must take into account the money value of only *currently* produced goods and services while estimating the *GNP* of the country. This is due to the fact that the *GNP* is, a measure of the economy's productivity during a particular period of time. Thus, if certain goods and services are produced in 1917, but are not sold till 1998, they would be part of the *GNP* for 1997, and should not be counted as part of the *GNP* of 1998.

The use of the word *gross* should be particularly noted in relation to the term *GNP*. It refers to the *inclusion* in national income of that part of the total output which represents what is called *depreciation* or *replacement.* As is well-known, in producing goods and services, there is some depreciation or wear and tear of fixed assets. This depreciation or replacement is one of the items in the case of production of the commodity. Every year an economy has to bear this loss on account of depreciation or replacement. But in computing the *GNP,* we do not deduct this total depreciation of the fixed assets.

There are *two* methods of estimating the *GNP* of a country. Both the methods lead to the same results. The two methods are: (1) Expenditure or Output Approach to *GNP*, and (2) Income or Allocation Approach to *GNP*.

(1) Expenditure or Output Approach to GNP. The *GNP* can be viewed as the nation's total expenditure on goods and services produced during the year. Each unit of goods and services produced is matched by an expenditure on that unit. Most of the goods and services produced in the country are bought by the consumers. But there are some goods and services which remain unsold. If the unsold goods and services are regarded as having been bought by the producers who hold them as *stocks* or *inventories,* then the monetary value of the total national production would be *equal* to the total national expenditure.

Under the expenditure approach to *GNP*, the total national expenditure can be broken down into the *following four* categories:

(*i*) *Personal Consumption Expenditure.* It includes the consumption expendi-tures made for both durable goods (such as, motor-cars, radio-sets, etc., but not houses) and non-durable goods (such as, food, drinks, clothing, etc.) produced in the country during the year. This sub-head also includes expenditure on services, such as, transport, educational and postal services, etc. Expenditure on the purchase of a house is treated as investment rather than consumption expenditure.

(*ii*) *Gross Domestic Private Investment.* This item includes private investment in 'capital' or 'Producer goods', such as, buildings, machinery, plant, equipment, etc. Such goods are primarily purchased by business firms. Houses are also included in this category of expenditure, because they are so durable that they represent, in fact, capital goods. Three points should be carefully noted here. *Firstly,* this sub-head includes capital or investment goods needed not only to replace the existing depreciated capital goods, but also the capital goods required to increase the society's production of goods and services. *Secondly,* the term 'investment' here means real investment in the Keynesian sense rather than *financial* investment. It means the purchase of real investment goods, such as, buildings, machinery, plant, etc. produced during the year. If a person buys a 5-year old machinery, it is not real investment, though it may be called *financial* investment; because that machinery was included in the *GNP* five years ago when it was manufactured first. *Thirdly,* 'investment' here does not include mere financial transfers, such as, the purchase of *existing* stocks and shares on the Stock Exchange. The purchase of existing stocks and shares does not represent new investment for purposes of the national income accounts, since it does not involve any production.

(*iii*) *Governments' Purchases of Goods and Services.* The governments—central, state and local purchase from the market consumer goods, such as, paper, station-ery, cloth, etc. as well as investment goods, such as, machinery, equipment, plant, etc. for their own enterprises. In addition, the governments also purchase a number of different services—military, police, secretarial etc. Governments do spend large amounts of money on what are called *transfer payments* (e.g., unemployment insurance and social security payments). Since these payments are not payments for currently produced goods and services, the amount spent on transfer payments is not included in the *GNP* of the country.

(*iv*) *Net Foreign Investment.* As is well-known, the entire production of a country is not sold within the country. A part of it is the *GNP* of the country. At the same time, the country imports some finished goods from other countries during the year. To make proper allowance for such exports and imports, the value of imports should be deducted from the value of exports. If the balance is positive, it should be *added* to the other items of expenditure. If it is negative, it should be *subtracted* from the sum of the other expenditure items.

It is, thus, clear that if the entire production of a country is purchased at market prices, the amount so spent will represent the *GNP* of the country. Therefore, to estimate the *GNP,* we have to *add* the above four categories of expenditures.

(2) Income or Allocation Approach to GNP. The *expenditure* incurred on purchasing goods and services produced in a country during the year also becomes the *income* of the various factors which collaborated in the production of those goods and services. We can group these factor-incomes in the following categories: (*i*) wages and salaries of the employees (or compensation to employees), (*ii*) incomes of non-company business, (*iii*) rental incomes of persons, (*iv*) corporate profits, and (*v*) incomes from interest.

The first category, as said above, includes the wages and salaries received by the employees during the year *plus* certain supplements. These supplements are the contributions which the employers make to social security and other provident funds or pension funds of the workers. The second category includes the incomes earned by individual proprietors, partners and self-employer persons. The third category comprises rental income earned by individuals on agricultural and non-agricultural property. The fourth category includes corporate profits earned by, business corporations before the payment of corporate profits taxes or the payment of dividends to the shareholders. Thus, the corporate profits, used in calculating the *GNP,* are *equal* to the sum of corporate profits taxes *plus* dividends paid to the shareholders *plus* undistributed corporate profits. The fifth category contains *net interest* earned by individuals from sources other than the organs of the govern-ment.

An *aggregate* of the above five categories of incomes will not be equal to the *GNP* as estimated by the Expenditure Method. The reason is that a part of the total expenditure incurred by the community *does-not* become available to the factors of production in the form of incomes. There are two such *leakages. First,* indirect taxes levied by the government on goods and services; and *second,* depreciation of machinery, plants and buildings. The expenditure incurred by the households (factors) on goods and services includes the indirect taxes levied by the Government.

The income from these indirect taxes goes to the government and is not available to the households (factor). Likewise, while calculating the *GNP,* we include the depreciation (loss in value suffered by machinery, equipment, buildings etc.). Like the indirect taxes, the payment on account of depreciation does not become available to the households (factors) in the form of income. In other words depreciation is no part of the factor incomes. Therefore, while estimating the *GNP* by the Income Method, we have to add indirect taxes and depreciation charges to the factor incomes. The two approaches (expenditure and income) are illustrated in Table 11.2.

Table 11.2: *Expenditure and Income Approaches to GNP*

Expenditure Approach	*Income Approach*
(*i*) Personal Consumption Expenditure plus	(*i*) Wages and salaries of employees plus
(*ii*) Gross Domestic Private Investment plus	(*ii*) Incomes of non-company businesses plus
(*iii*) Govt. s' Purchases of Goods and Services plus	(*iii*) Rental incomes of persons plus
(*iv*) Net Foreign Investment	(*iv*) Corporate profits plus
Total = GNP	(*v*) Income from net interest plus
	(*vi*) Indirect taxes plus
	(*vii*) Depredation of capital goods
	Total = GNP

GNP is the most frequently used national income concept. It has its own merits and demerits. It is a better index, than any other concept, of the actual conditions of production and employment in a country during a specified period. It is also statistically a simpler concept as it takes no account of depreciation and replacement problems. But at the same time, it is not a *net* measure of the nation's economic performance, for it is; as the term states, a *gross* measure. Just as a business firm's gross profits give only a rough idea of the firm's performance, in the same manner the *GNP* provides us with only a general idea of the economy's accomplishments during the year. Just as to get a true picture of the business firm, it is necessary to find out its net profits, similarly, to get an accurate idea of the achievements of an economy, we have to find out its *net national product.* Nevertheless, *GNP* is a useful concept for analysis over a short period of time when changes in capital are not so important.

Net National Product (NNP)

The second important concept of national income is that of net national product. It is defined as the net production of goods and services in a country during a year: As we know, in the course of a year's production, part of the physical plant that was on hand at the beginning of the year is worn out, or it may depreciate in value as it becomes outdated. Buildings gradually deteriorate, machinery wears out or becomes obsolete, and so on for others. Now sooner or later, if the depreciated capital is not replaced, the income of the nation will decline, and the economy as a whole will become poorer. If we want to measure the level of income that can be sustained, therefore, we must deduct from gross output (*GNP*) the depreciation of capital during the period concerned. What is left after this deduction is the net national product. Thus,

$$NNP = GNP - \text{Depreciation}$$

Net national product is a better concept than gross national product, because it makes proper allowance for the depreciation suffered by the capital goods during the period under consideration. This concept gives a proper idea of the net increase in total production of a country. It is, therefore, used in analysing the long-period problems of maintaining and increasing the supply of capital goods in the country.

In spite of this fact that for some purposes of economic growth *NNP* is much more important than *GNP,* it is more difficult to measure statistically, because we have no accurate record of the amount of depreciation that takes place over periods of time. We do not have appropriate rates of depreciation for various capital goods, such as, buildings, equipments, plants etc. The result is that the deduction that has to be made from *GNP* to arrive at *NNP* is a matter of judgement, rather than of exact measurement. Because of this difficulty, this concept of *NNP* is not fairly used.

Net National Income at Factor Cost (NNI)

National Income at factor cost means the sum of all incomes earned by resource suppliers for their contribution of land, labour, capital and entrepreneurship during the year's net production. In other words, national income at factor cost shows how much it costs society in terms of economic resources to produce that net output. Sometimes, we simply call it as national income.

Both *GNP* and *NNP* measure the values of goods produced in industry at the prices that those goods actually bring in the market. Here the difficulty is that when we buy these goods at market prices, then the prices include the respective taxes on these goods levied by the government. Hence, not all of the payment made for goods goes to the people who produced them. Some part of it goes to the government. It does not constitute a part of the true cost of producing the goods concerned. This violates the basic identity that the value of goods produced is equal to the sum of the money incomes received by the producers. In others words, the *GNP* will exceed the sum of money incomes received by the people of the country (resource suppliers). The excess is explained by the fact that we have included in *GNP* the entire output of government services, but we have also included part of the payments made for these services in the prices of the products (in terms of sales tax). In other words, a part of the cost of government has been counted twice. In order to get rid of this double counting, we may introduce the concept of net national income at factor cost. It is equal to net national product minus indirect tax plus subsidies. To put it differently,

National Income (at Factor Cost)= Net National Product (or National Income at Market Price) – Indirect Taxes + Subsidies

The concept of national income at factor cost occupies an important place in economics. It indicates the nature of distribution of wealth among various factor inputs. This concept is more satisfactory than the concepts of *GNP* and *NNP,* because it eliminates the element of double counting inherent in those two concepts. It accords with the basic principle of economic theory, that the payments received by the factor suppliers equal the value of the goods produced. Further, the components of national income (at factor cost) are very useful in dealing with certain economic problems. Changing relative shares of different elements in the population from time to time have an important bearing on the fluctuations of economic activity, and on the personal inequality of incomes which has much to do with economic welfare.

Net Domestic Product at Factor Cost (NDP)

Net domestic product at factor cost is defined as that national production which is made by the domestic factors of a country during the period of a year. In other words, we can get net domestic product (at factor cost) if we deduct net income received from abroad from the net national product at factor cost. Thus,

NDP at Factor Cost = *NNP* at Factor Cost – Net Income from Abroad

Persoual Income (PI)

Personal income is the sum of all incomes actually received by all individuals or households during a given year. National income (that is, total income earned during a year) is different from personal income (that is, the income actul1y received by households). We know that all which is produced by industry and government must necessarily belong to someone, and hence can be regarded as national income received or accrued by the people (of the country), but not all of the value of this product is paid to them as money income. Part of the net earnings of business firms are taken away from them by government in the form of corporate income taxes excess profits taxes, and the like, before being paid to the owners of the business firms. These are direct taxes that do not enter into the prices of commodities. Further, many firms retain part of their earnings in the business, to make additions to their plants or as a reserve for future emergencies, instead of distributing the entire profits to their shareholders. Therefore, these earnings are not received by the shareholders. Again, the employees of the business firms are not allowed to receive in money all of the salaries or wages that they earn. The government charges a withholding tax which is used to finance social security payments to the aged, the unemployed and certain other persons. Similarly, the government make some other transfer payments to people of the country.

All these things create a difference between the total incomes received by individuals and the total social income produced. We subtract from national income all undistributed corporate profits, corporate income taxes and social security withholding taxes and then add transfer payments from government and business firms directly to persons; the resulting figure win be the personal income Thus,

Personal Income (*PI*) = Net National Income – Undivided Corporate Profits – Corporate Income Taxes – Social Security Contributions + Transfer Payments.

The above concept of personal income is useful for certain special purposes. For example, it shows the ability of people to pay taxes. The personal income data are available on monthly basis whereas is the data for national product and national income are not published so frequently and, therefore, the accurate idea cannot be drawn. This is the reason that personal income data are used for analysing current changes in the economy.

Disposable Income (DI)

The main drawback of personal income data is that they do not tell us how much is actually at the disposal of people for their personal expenditure. For this we use the concept of disposable income. After a good part of personal income is paid to government in the form of personal taxes (such as income tax, property tax etc.), what remains of personal income is called disposable income. Thus,

Disposable Income (DI) = Personal Income – Personal Taxes

Disposable Income data are useful for studying the purchasing power of the consumers. Since disposable income can either be consumed or it can be saved; with its help we may study the amount of consumption and saving that individuals make in the economy.

Real Income (RI)

When the national income is expressed in terms of the base year's price index, it is known as real income. Net National Income is the money value of the goods and services produced during a given year at the current prices. This figure does not indicate the real situation of the economy. Due to an increase in the prices of goods and services, the figure for net national income may be high but real production is not much. The reverse is also possible. To avoid this deficiency we make use of the concept of real income. It is calculated by the following formula:

$$\text{Real Net National Income} = \frac{\text{Net National Income}}{\text{Price Index for that year} \times 100}$$

6. METHODS OF MEASURING NATIONAL INCOME

The national income of a country can be viewed in three ways, namely, in terms of the operations of the producing units, in terms of residents as suppliers of the production and in terms of the spending units (individual factors, families, enterprises, etc.). There are, therefore, three aspects of the national income, namely, as an aggregate of net products, as an aggregate of factor incomes, and as an aggregate of final expenditures. Correspondingly, three ways of measuring national income, namely, the production method, the income method, and the expenditure method respectively.

In each of these methods, national income measurement involves calculating two types of magnitudes. They are in the production method the number of producing units and the values of their net products; in the income method the number of the owners of the factors of production and the incomes earned by them; and in the expenditure method the final goods and services and their market prices.

Production Method

The production method is also known, by such other terms as the value added method, net output method, inventory method, the census of manufacture method or the industry of origin method.

The production method measures national income as the sum of net products produced by the production units in the given period. This totals to the net domestic product or the net domestic income of the economy. Net income from abroad added to net domestic product yields net national product or national income of the country.

The production method involves, therefore, the following steps—(1) Identifying production units and classifying them into industrial sectors. (2) Estimating their gross and then net products. The aggregate of gross products is gross domestic product and of net products is net domestio product. (3) Net income from abroad must be added to the domestic product totals to get national product totals.

Classification of production units into industrial sectors makes calculation of net products more manageable and less costly. Moreover, it focusses attention on inter- industry relationships, the industrial structure of the economy, and so on.

The broadest classification of producing unit into industrial sectors is that between the primary sector include production and the tertiary sector. The primary sector include production units which exploit natural resources to produce material goods. It includes production units engaged in cultivation, animal husbandry, fishery, forestry, mining, etc. The secondary sector, also known as the manufacture sector, includes production units which produce material goods by transforming goods from one form into another. The tertiary sector includes production units which produce services and is, therefore, also known as the services-sector. It includes production units engaged in, for example, trade, transport and communications, administration, banking and finance, lawyers, teachers, entertainers, domestic servants, etc. Each of these three broad sectors may be further sub-divided into industrial sectors. Thus, the industrial classification of the Indian economy (or the measurement of domestic product in India distinguishes between three broad industrial sectors. Each of these broad sub-sector can be further sub-divided into commodity groups or on some other basis.

The next step in the production method is the estimation of the net product of each sector. This involves: (*a*) estimation of gross output of each sector, (*b*) estimation of intermediate consumption by each sector, and (*c*) estimation of depreciation incurred by each sector. The calculation of the net products of the industrial sectors requires information about gross output of the sector, the raw materials and other intermediate goods, and services used by the sector and depreciation of the capital stock in the sector. This follows from the fact that net product equals gross output minus intermediate consumption minus depreciation. The goods and services. Whether intermediate or final are valued at market prices.

The production method yields the net products or the net value added of each industrial sector and thus measures the contribution of each industrial sector to the total net value added or national income in the country.

The production method is beset with several difficulties. For example, whether government services are intermediate or final in nature. This is decided in favour of treating government services as final on the assumption that it is statistically difficult to separate the intermediate and final aspects of government services. Again, housewives services are excluded because of the statistical difficulty of valuing them. Lack of data for the unincorporated enterprises, particularly in underdeveloped countries also creates problems. Then, measurement of depreciation also raises problems.

Income Method

The income method has two variants, namely, the income paid out variant and the income received variant.

In the income paid out variant the units are the factor owners. The other magnitude is the incomes earned by the factor owners.

The first step in the income paid out variant is the classification of the production efforts of people into factor groups. The factors of production are broadly classified into labour and capital. This kind of classification into factor groups is known as functional classification.

However, in many unincorporated enterprises, particularly in the unorganized sectors of the economy, the functional classification of people engaged in the production unit into factors of production is difficult.

The second step is to identify and estimate factor incomes. Two things are to be noted at the outset. *First,* illegal incomes are excluded from national income because of the statistical difficulty of accounting for them. *Secondly,* transfer incomes are also excluded because only incomes earned of current production activities figure in national income of the year. Wages currently paid are an instance of factor incomes while pensions are an instance of transfer incomes. Similarly interest on production borrowing are factor incomes. While interest on consumption borrowing are transfer incomes. (Interest on national debt or government debts are treated by assumption for statistical reasons as on consumption borrowing.)

Labour incomes include wages and salaries including cash bonuses, commission supplements to labour incomes like employers contributions to provident fund and compensations in kind like food and clothing and medical and educational benefits etc.

Non-labour incomes or capital incomes include dividends, undistributed profits of corporations, profit taxes, interest, rent, royalties, profits of unincorporated enterprises and profits or surplus of government enterprises.

Where functional differentiation is not possible as for the self-employed or for unorganised production units in agriculture, etc. then the income generated in a production unit cannot be separated into labour incomes and capital incomes. In this case, a third category is introduced, namely, mixed incomes. These mixed incomes are a composite of labour incomes, rent on own property, interest on own capital and profits. Incomes in kind like farm products consumed on the farm are also included.

The above income paid method measures factor incomes from the point of view of the production units situated in the country. Therefore, the total of factor incomes will add up to net domestic income. To get net national income it will be necessary to add net earned income from abroad. Since national income is being measured terms of factor remuneration, the total will be at factor costs.

$NNP_{FC} = NI =$ Wages + Interest + Rent + Profit + Net earned income from abroad.

In the income received variant, the units are classified into institutional sectors, namely, households, enterprises and government.

Income is measured as the sum of the legal incomes received by the households, enterprises and the government.

The part of the national income accruing to the household sector includes wages, rent, interest and dividends to individuals and payments in kind to individuals. The part of the national income accruing to the household sector is a part of the aggregate 'personal income'. However, personal income also includes transfer incomes.

The part of the national income accruing to the business sector consists of undistributed profits or retained earnings of enterprises before taxes.

The part accruing to the government consists of the surplus or profits of government enterprises and rental income accruing to the government.

Net income from abroad need not be added in the income received method since they are already included. This is because the incomes received include incomes from abroad. In other words, the incomes received method leads directly to national totals (unlike the income paid method which leads first to the domestic totals). In the income received variant, therefore, NI = household sector income (excluding transfer incomes) + business sector income + government sector income.

It can be seen that personal income or the sum of incomes received by individual is not national income for two reasons: (1) personal income includes transfer incomes, and (2) business income and government income does not accrue to the households sector.

Certain cautions should be observed while using the income method. For example, corporate profits include dividends, corporate profits tax and undistributed profits of corporations. If corporate profits are included then, to add its components separately would amount to double counting. Again, if profits or rents are mentioned as such then these should be taken to include profits and rents from all sources, private or government. Again, labour incomes are generally quoted gross of income taxes. Therefore, to add personal income taxes separately would amount to double counting. Similar is the case with rents. Corporations, however, give a breakdown of its profits before tax and after tax.

Expenditure Method

The expenditure method also has two variants, namely, the income disposal variant and the product disposal variant.

In the income disposal variant, national income or product is estimated from the expenditures of the three institutional sectors, namely, household, business and government. These sectors dispose of their incomes either on consumption or on savings. Ex-posts, savings is synonymous with investment or accumulation of capital stocks.

Of the gross expenditures in the economy by the three sectors, only the expenditures on currently produced final goods and services and net foreign investment are taken into account for estimating national income.

Expenditures on domestically transacted financial assets (whether new or old shares and bonds etc.) on goods produced in preceding periods and second hand goods and on intermediate consumption are excluded.

Expenditures of the three sectors on currently produced final goods and services are classified broadly into expenditure on consumers goods and services a consumption expenditure and expenditure on capital goods or investment expenditure. Consumption is broken up into private consumption expenditure by the government sector. Similarly, investment is classified into private investment expenditure and public sector investment expenditure. Private investment includes capital accumulation by the business sector, with the exception of new residential dwellings constructed by the household sector which is regarded as household investment. In fact, residential construction is the only item of household expenditure included under investment. All other household expenditures are included under consumption, including those on consumer durables whether actually consumed in the year or accumulated. (In other words, inventory investment by the household sector is ruled out by assumption.) To sum up: Gross national expenditure consumption expenditure + gross national investment, where gross national investment gross domestic investment + net foreign investment.

And, gross domestic investment = replacement investment or depreciation + net domestic investment.

Hence, net national expenditure = net domestic expenditure = consumption + net domestic investment + net foreign investment:

But, net national expenditure measures the expenditure of residents of the country and net national product or income generated by the residents. If national expenditure exceed national income then it means that the residents have received gifts from abroad in the form of current and capital transfers from abroad. If national expenditure is less than national income then it means that residents have given gifts to abroad (current or capital transfers to abroad). In short:

NNP_{MP} = net national expenditure + net current transfers to abroad + net capital transfers to abroad. Or, NNP_{MP} = private consumption expenditure + public consumption expenditure + net domestic investments + net foreign investment + net current transfer to broad + net capital transfers to abroad.

In the product disposal variant, however, national income or product is measured not from the point of view of income disposed by residents but from the point of view of sales of production units in the country. These domestic production units may sell either to residents or to foreigners (exports or X).

However, residents' expenditures on consumption and investment may be on goods and services produced domestically or on foreign goods and services (imports = M). That is, gross domestic expenditure on goods and services = C + gross domestic investment + M. It follows then that residents' expenditure on the gross domestic product = $C + I - M$. And, therefore, gross domestic product = sales to residents (or $C + I - M$) plus sales to, foreigners or X). Rearranged, Gross domestic product = $C + I + X - M$.

And, gross national product = $C + I + X - M$ + net income from abroad.

Measurement by type of product thus pertains to the product disposal variant the expenditure method. Here, the first step is to classify and quantity products by type and the second step is to find out their market prices. The method increasingly in use today to find out expenditures by type of product is the commodity flow method.

Conclusion. Ideally, the national income of a country should be measured by the three methods separately. This is because each method provides a different view of the economy. The production method provides information about the relative size of the different industrial sectors in the economy and their relative contribution to value added or national income in the economy (i.e., national income by industrial origin). The income method provides information about the factoral distribution of incomes in the economy and also about the institutional distribution of the national income between the household sector, the private business sector and the government sector. The expenditure method provides information about the level of consumption and investment in the economy and their break-up into the private and government sectors and about the role of foreign aid and foreign capital in the economy. Thus, a three-dimensional view of national income gives an all round view of the economy.

Moreover, each method provides a check on the accuracy of the other methods in as much as the national income total by each method should be the same.

The method of national income measurement preferred will depend on the purpose for which data is required. For example, desire for knowledge about the national income by industrial origin would mean preference for the production method, knowledge of income distribution would mean preference for the income method and knowledge of standards of living or role of foreign aid or growth analysis would mean preference for the expenditure method.

Table 11.3: *Methods of Measuring National Income*

Production Method	*Income Method*		*Expenditure Method*	
	Income paid out variant	*Income received variant*	*Income disposal variant*	*Production disposal variant*
I. NNP_{MP} by industrial origin:			Consumption	consumption
Net value added by A		+	+	
+ Net value added by B		Net domestic	Net domestic	
+			investment	investment
⋮	Labour incomes	National incomes	+	+
⋮	+	accruing to: Households	Net foreign	+
⋮	Capital income		investment	Export
⋮	+	+	+	+
⋮	Mixed income	Business	Net transfers	Imports
⋮	+	+	to abroad	+
				Net income from
+ Net value added by N =	+ =	+		abroad
	Business	Government	NNP_{MP}	NNP_{MP}
	Transfer payments	+		
II. Net income from abroad	+			
	Net indirect taxes	Net indirect taxes		
	+			
NNP_{MP}	Net incomes from abroad			
	NNP_{MP}	NNP_{MP}		

Note. If the totals by the three methods do not tally then we need the item "discrepancies". This includes statistical discrepancy and errors and omissions. The item adjusts the production/expenditures results with the income method.

Thus NNP_{MP} by production/expenditure methods exceeds NNP_{MP} by income method then "discrepancies" are to be subtracted from production/expenditure totals.

However, and practice differ. The stage of development of the economy and the state of data availability may force us to depend on one or the other method. For, example, in India national income is measured by a mix of the three methods, the income generated in the different industrial sectors being measured by different methods.

7. MEASUREMENT OF NATIONAL INCOME IN INDIA

The first systematic effort at the Government level to calculate India's national income commenced with the appointment of the National Income Committee (NIC) in 1948. The NIC submitted its first Report in 1951 which contained the estimates for the year 1948-49. Subsequently, the NIC submitted its second Report in 1954 containing the estimates for 1949-50 and 1950-51. Since then the Central Statistical Organisation (CSO) of the Department of Statistics, Ministry of Planning, Government of India, has been entrusted with the task of estimating India's national income for the subsequent years. The CSO followed broadly the same method as the NIC till 1964-65. In 1967 some major changes were effected and a new series of national estimates were prepared. The series which followed strictly the NIC approach is referred to as the 'Conventional-Series'. The new series is entitled as the 'Revised-Series'. The revised series differed from the conventional series in that its methodology was improved, the sectoral division of the economy was changed, more detailed information being available was provided regarding a larger number of sectors and the base year was changed from 1948-49 prices to 1960-61 prices. In 1978, the constant price base was changed to the 1970-71 prices. Further it was changed to 1980-81, 1993-94 & 1999-2000.

The revised series classified the economy into the following sectors:

Primary Sector

1. Agricultural, livestock and ancillary activities
2. Forestry and logging
3. Finishing
4. Mining arid quarrying

Seconday Sector

5. Manufacturing—registered and unregistered
6. Construction
7. Electricity, gas and water supply

Transport, Communications and Trade

8. Transport, storage and communications
9. Trade, hotels and restaurants

Finance and Real Estates

10. Banking and insurance
11. Real estate, ownership of dwellings and business services

Cummunity and Personal Services

12. Public administration and defence
13. Other services

Different methods are used to measure the income generated in the different sectors of the economy. Broadly, the production method is used to estimate income generated in the first five sectors, namely, the four sectors under primary sector and the manufacturing (registered) sector under the secondary sector. In the remaining sectors except construction the income method is used. In the construction sector the expenditure method based on the community flow method is used.

For example in sector 1 (agriculture etc.) the commodities are classified into 68 groups, divided into four broad categories. Estimates of net output of each commodity is prepared first at the state level. This is done by, first estimating average yield per acre on the basis of random sample crop cutting surveys and by obtaining data from the various official and non-official agencies. Second, gross value of output is calculated by multiplying the total physical output by the weighted average of wholesale prices prevailing during the peak marketing period; and third, net value of output is obtained by deducting costs like seeds, manures, repairs and maintenance of fixed assets, feed of livestock, irregular charges, market charges, electricity and allowance for depreciation. They are then aggregated to arrive at the national total. The estimates are prepared at constant prices by revaluing each item of output at 1980-81 prices.

Sector 5A covers all manufacturing and processing establishment (called factories) which are registered under the Indian Factories Act, 1948. The entire sector is divided into 20 industry groups. The estimate of gross and net product of each group is prepared on the basis of data obtained from Annual Survey of Industries (ASI). Adjustments are made for non-reporting units with the help of data on employment in such units after regrouping them into the 20 broad industry groups. Adjustments are also made for those imputed banking services which were not accounted for in the actual banking and insurance charges paid by the manufacturing establishments. Net product at constant prices (1980-81) is arrived at by using the appropriate indices of industrial production.

The measurement of income generated of sector 5B or small scale manufacturing units (i.e., units not registered under the Indian Factories Act, 1948) is by the income method. The sector is divided into: (*i*) Household manufacturing, and (*ii*) non-household manufacturing. The working force in these categories are classified into seven industry groups. Gross product per worker is estimated in each industry group. In this, National Sample Survey reports are the main sources for household industry while for non-household industry the sources are scattered (such as various surveys by different agencies). Allowances for depreciation are then made on the basis of Sample Survey of ASI to arrive at the net value of output.

As said the income method is used in all the tertiary sectors. The sources of data are various. For example, for banking the Reserve Bank of India, for the Life Insurance Corporation of India, etc.

The expenditure method is used to measure income generated in the construction sector. This includes construction, repair and demolition of buildings, highways, streets, etc. Expenditure on urban construction activities are estimated by the commodity flow method while expenditure on rural construction activities are estimated by other methods.

The total of income generated of sectors 1 to 13 is net domestic product. Net factor income from abroad must be added to obtain net national product. Information on this is obtained from the balance of payments data which in turn largely depends on the exchange control data collected by the Reserve Bank of India. Thus, we see that India has been unable to measure national income by each of the three methods separately. The reason for this is partly conceptual and partly statistical.

The conceptual problems arise because India follows the methodology suggested by the United Nations. But this methodology, being influenced by the structure of developed economies, is difficult to apply in under-developed countries with its large non-monetary sectors and unorganised of ten household enterprises. Quite a few of these enterprises produce at subsistence or semi-subsistence levels, are functionally undifferentiated in the sense that they produce agricultural goods in season and manufacture off season and do not keep a proper record of their secondary and factor inputs of production.

Small capital assets like hand tools, primitive agricultural equipment, office furniture, etc. are not included under fixed capital investment in developed countries but they are important as capital for underdeveloped countries. Similarly, it is difficult to estimate the inputed value of owner-occupied dwellings in India's rural areas.

The nature and character of the economy and enterprises results in the statistical problems of paucity and unreliability of data. As a result, the income method can not be used. In fact different methods are applied to collect data from different sectors of the economy.

8. NATIONAL INCOME AND ECONOMIC WELFARE

Increase in national income is generally regarded as art indicator of the level of economic activity in any country. An improvement in the *per capita* income of the country is treated as proof of the increased economic welfare of the people of that country. Likewise, a country with a higher *per capita* income is supposed to enjoy greater economic welfare (or, a higher standard of living) than a country with a lower *per capita* income. Here we shall examine the question: How far is national income a reliable index of economic welfare?

Total welfare is generally divided into two parts: (*i*) economic welfare, and (*ii*) non-economic welfare. The two types of welfare are intertwined and are rather difficult to separate from each other. Nevertheless, Prof. Pigou has distinguished economic welfare (from non-economic welfare) as "that part of social welfare that can be brought directly pr indirectly into relation with the measuring rod of money." Thus, according to Pigou, economic welfare, is that part of total welfare, which can be expressed in monetary terms directly or indirectly. Non-economic welfare, on the contrary, is that part of total welfare which is *not* amendable to money measurement.

As we know economic welfare is a part of total welfare. The question is sometimes raised: Can economic welfare then serve as an index of total welfare? If the economic welfare increases, does it mean that total welfare will also increase? At first sight, it appears that if economic welfare increases, total welfare will also inevitably increase, because the former is a part of the latter. An increase in the size of the part will increase the size of the whole. Thus, an increase in economic welfare will also mean an increase in total welfare. But if we go deep into the matter, we may find that it is not necessarily so. Any cause which increases economic welfare may *not* necessarily increase total welfare. The reason is obvious. That cause, no doubt, increases economic welfare, but at the same time, it *diminishes* non-economic welfare to an equal extent so that the total welfare remains unchanged. It is also possible that that particular cause diminishes the non-economic welfare to an extent *greater* than the increase in economic welfare. In that case, the total welfare may actually go down despite the increase in economic welfare. Economic welfare cannot, therefore, be said to be an *index* or *barometer* of total welfare. An example will serve to illustrate the truth of this statement. In the 19th century Great Britain, the economic welfare of the people, no doubt, increased consequent upon rapid increases in production, but it is not certain whether their total welfare also increased in the same proportion, the reason being that the rapid industrialization of the country had adverse effects on the non-economic welfare of the people consequent upon the loss of spiritual values.

Let us now revert to the question with which we started this section: How far is national income a reliable index of economic welfare within a country over a period of time? Does an increase in the national income of the country always mean a corresponding increase in the economic welfare of the people? The answer to this question is not so easy because several factors have to be taken into account before we arrive at any positive conclusion. The following points have to be borne in mind before arriving at any positive conclusion.

(1) As already emphasised earlier, the national estimates take into account only those transactions which are carried through the medium of money. The nominal value of the national income of a country may increase in one year simply because some activity which was previously carried on without the use of money is now being conducted with the help of money, even though there has been no change in the real supply of goods and services being produced in the economy. For example, if the farmers in a country decide to keep a smaller proportion of their food-output at home for self-consumption (or, decide to bring a larger proportion of it in the market for sale), the nominal value of the national income of the country will increase, though there is no increase in the total output of food in the economy.

(2) Since the national income is generally measured in terms of current monetary values, a rise or fall in the general price-level will cause the national income to rise or fall even though there is no change in the actual production of goods and services in the economy.

(3) The national income total may not reveal the true picture of an economy. A rise in national income does *not* necessarily mean a rise in the living standard (or, the economic welfare) of the people. If the national income of a country increases, but its population increases at a faster

rate, the per capita income will certainly decline, and along with it, the economic welfare of the people will also go down. Per capital income is, therefore, a better index than the national income total of the economic welfare of a community.

(4) Even the per capita income is not a fool-proof index of economic welfare. An increase in per capita income may not necessarily be accompanied by an increase in the economic welfare of the community. Suppose the national income of a country increases and the per capita income also increases. But the increase in the national income may be due more to the production of capital goods than to the output of consumers goods. Though the national income (and also the per capita income) has increased due to the faster output of capital goods, it indicates little or no improve-ment in the economic welfare of the people. (The economic welfare of the people, it should be remembered, is determined *more* by consumer goods than by capital goods.)

(5) An increase in per capita income may not indicate an improvement in the economic welfare of the community for another reason. The national output, no doubt, increases (and consequently, the per capita income also increases), but there may be a change in the composition of national output in favour of *war-goods.* An increase in the production of war-goods, though it may increase the national income (and also per capita income), will not increase the economic welfare of the people. War-goods like arms and ammunitions may increase the fighting capacity of the nation, but they do not increase the economic welfare of the community.

(6) An increase in the total of the national income (or, per capita income) should also be interpreted with reference to the general economic environments in which it has been brought about. Higher national income may have been brought about by employing women and children or by forcing the workers to work for long hours (without holidays) under extremely insanitary conditions, or by resorting to indus-trial conscription and forced direction of labour, In all such cases, the rise in the national income will not indicate a rise in the economic welfare of the people.

(7) To enquire whether the increased national income has increased economic welfare, we have also to take into account the distribution of the increased income. A rise in the national income does not necessarily imply a rise in everyone's income. If the increased national income goes into the pockets of the richer sections, it is possible that the other sections may even be poorer than before. Some people, no doubt, will be better off than before, but the decline in the welfare of the poor may be greater

than the increase in the welfare of the rich. Hence, economic welfare as a whole may be reduced.

(8) Finally, if an increase in the national income is accompanied by a deterioration in the tastes of the people or a decline in public morality, the economic welfare of the people may actually be *reduced* consequent upon the increase in national income. For example, as the national income increases beyond a point, the people of the country may spend their increased, incomes on drinking, gambling and other evil things, which by reducing the non-economic welfare, will ultimately reduce the economic welfare of the people also.

We, therefore, conclude that neither national income nor per capita income of a country can be a true index of economic welfare. We should take into account the above mentioned points before making a prediction about the relationship between national income and economic welfare.

9. DIFFICULTIES IN THE MEASUREMENT OF NATIONAL INCOME

We have to face a number of difficulties in the measurement of national income of a country. The following are the important difficulties of national income analysis:

(1) We know, national income is always measured in terms of money, but there are certain goods and services whose money measurement is not possible; for example, the services performed by the housewife for her family, voluntary services performed with a charitable object, hobby products, etc. Such items are excluded from the national income figures. This leads to an underestimate of the national income.

(2) Income obtained from illegal activities (such as black-marketing) are not included in the national income and their exclusion results in an under valuation of the national income.

(3) It is difficult to obtain accurate statistics. This is the reason that we find big differences between the national income statistics collected by the different institutions.

(4) The calculation of depreciation on capital consumption presents another formidable difficulty. There are no accepted standard rates of depreciation applicable to the various categories of capital goods. Thus, the national income estimate will I not be correct.

(5) Again, there is the difficulty of avoiding double counting in the national income. To avoid this difficulty, final goods and services are to be included in the national income, but it is no more an easy task.

(6) Further, the difficulty of price changes arises in the national income estimate. When general price index increases, the national income will also increase, even if the national output is reduced. Similarly, if general price index decreases, the national income will also decrease, although there may be an increase in national output. Therefore, due to price changes, we may not find an accurate estimate of national income.

(7) The problem of transfer payments also arises in the national income analysis. Interest on public borrowings and unemployment allowances should or should not be counted in the national income; it becomes an acute problem.

(8) Further, the prevalence of non-monetised transactions in under-developed countries like India creates an important problem in the measurement of national income. A considerable part of output does not come into the market at all. In agriculture, a major part of output is consumed at the farm itself. This reduces the national income figure to a great extent.

(9) Due to illiteracy, most of the producers in less developed countries have no Idea of the quantity and value of their output and do not keep regular accounts. This again creates the difficulty in national income analysis.

(10) The application of the consumption-saving method or the expenditure method too is full of difficulties. It is difficult to estimate all personal expenditures as well as investment expenditure.

10. IMPORTANCE OF NATIONAL INCOME ANALYSIS

Today national income statistics are collected by all the countries of the world for a number of reasons. Raising national income is the important goal of all economic activity. Economic welfare of a country depends upon what goods and services are available for the consumption of its individuals. The changes in national income statistics show how the economy is developing and enables the government to lay down the appropriate economic policy necessary under the circumstances. With the help of national income statistics it is possible to chart cyclical movements, find out the inflationary gap, measure economic growth and development, and evaluate the country's material standard of living in comparison with other countries and other time periods. Shoup gives a long list of various objectives for which the national income data can be used. The following are the main uses of national income statistics:

(1) Since income is a flow of wealth, changes in the national income give some indication of economic welfare. The total figure, however,

can be misleading, since account must be taken of the changes in the value of money, and changes in the total production. Per capita income is the best indicator of development. Other things being equal, economic welfare of a country is greater if income per head is greater.

(2) National income per head is used to compare standards of living in different countries.

(3) Economic growth is measured in terms of per capita national income and the national income figures (in real terms) are used to measure the rate of growth of a country.

(4) The national income accounts make possible an analysis of the behaviour of the different sectors of the economy. They provide the details of the changes in consumption and investment spending, in the level of savings, in the output of different branches of industry, in the expenditure of public. authorities, and in the distribution of income among the different income groups. These details are essential in planning development of various sectors.

(5) Inflationary and deflationary pressures can be estimated with the help of national income statistics. The inflationary or deflationary gaps are the "inconsistencies of certain subtotals."

(6) National income statistics can be used to forecast the level of business activity at later dates and to find out trends in other annual data.

(7) The national income figures are useful in providing a correct sense of proportion about the structure of the economy.

(8) In war time the study of the components of national income is of great importance because they show the maximum possible production possibilities of the country.

(9) National income statistics can be used to determine how an international financial burden should be apportioned between different countries. The national income is a possible "tax-base." The quantum of national income measures the ability of a country to pay contributions for international purposes, just as the income of a person measures his ability to pay for the upkeep of his country.

(10) Above all, the national income statistics are used for planned economic development of a country. In the absence of such data, planning will be a leap in the dark.

In the words of Prof. Samuelson, "By means of statistics of national income, we can chart the movements of a country from depression to prosperity, its steady long-term rate of growth and development, and finally, its material standard of living in comparison with other nations."

11. LIMITATIONS OF NATIONAL INCOME ANALYSIS

National income statistics are highly useful for several purposes, but it is necessary to use these statistics with caution. Shoup mentions the following limitations of the national income statistics:

(1) For short periods of two or three years (possibly even a decade), comparisons of income totals are valid for most purposes, but over a longer span of time they can be very misleading. Over a longer period, a number of new products may appear in the economy and a number of old products may disappear from the consumption. For example, if we want to compare the change of income between 1979 and 1980 in money terms, no great error is involved, because the character of goods entering into the income stream in two years so close together does not change enough to matter; but if we make a similar comparison between 1880 and 1980 or even between 1930 and 1980, the content of real income has changed so greatly that the comparison loses much of its meaning.

(2) Another difficulty arises if we want to compare incomes between two different countries with very different types of economic systems. The per capita income of a country whose principal diet is rice and fish (as in Japan) is not comparable with our own, where the diet is so much more varied. Money units do not measure these differences in kind of products consumed.

(3) National income estimates are usually confined to goods and services sold in the market; but in some countries (particularly the underdeveloped countries) most production takes place in the homes of the people. Statistics confined to production for the market would make the per capita income in such, countries look ridiculously small, and very much smaller than it is in fact. The statistics would omit the largest part of the real incomes of such a country. It is possible to make some adjustments for this by putting estimates of the values for household production into the national income totals, but these estimates must necessarily be crude.

(4) Another weakness of national income statistics is that they do not take sufficient account of the changes in the nation's stock of capital equipment. The qualitative aspect is completely ignored. The calculation of depreciation on capital goods is not accurate.

(5) Again, we must take into consideration the way in which the national income is distributed among the people of the country. A large aggregate of goods, divided very unequally, may not represent as wholesome an economic condition as a smaller income, divided more equality.

Unless we know, therefore, what changes there have been in the matter of equality or inequality, we must not draw too hasty conclusions from statistics of total national income.

For all these above mentioned reasons, we must be cautious in our use of national income statistics.

EXERCISES

1. How would you define and measure the National Income of a country?
2. What precautions are to be taken in the calculation of national dividend?
3. Distinguish between the gross national product, net national product and disposable income.
4. Discuss the various methods of calculating national income. Also discuss the meaning and uses of Gross National Product, Net National Product, National Income, Personal Income and Disposable Income.
5. Define national income. Bring out the difficulties involved in national income estimation in underdeveloped countries like India.
6. Critically examine the definitions of national income given by Marshall, Pigou and Fisher.
7. Discuss the concept of economic welfare and its relationship with the national income of a country.

Multiple Choice Questions

8. (*i*) In calculating a country's *GNP* at market prices, one of the following is not included:
   (*a*) wages and salaries before tax
   (*b*) indirect taxes
   (*c*) retirement pensions and depreciation allowances
   (*d*) subsidies [*Ans.* (*d*)]

   (*ii*) National income at market prices plus subsidies, but less indirect taxes is equal to
   (*a*) *GNP*
   (*b*) *NI* at factor cost
   (*c*) Private income before tax
   (*d*) Gross personal income [*Ans.* (*b*)]

   (*iii*) Which of the following equation is wrong?
   (*a*) National Income = Effective Demand
   (*b*) National Income = *GNP*
   (*c*) National Income = C + *I*
   (*d*) National Income = C + S [*Ans.* (*b*)]

Chapter 12

OBJECTIVES OF THE FIRM

1. INTRODUCTION

In every market, the main objective of a firm is to get maximum profit. But sometimes the empirical studies show that the firm has to serve some other objectives such as sales maximisation, output maximisation, utility maximisation, growth maximisation etc. Some of these objectives of the firm may be discussed as below.

2. PROFIT MAXIMISATION

In the traditional theory of the firm, the main objective of a firm is to get maximum profit. Under the assumption of perfect competition, a firm is simply a price taker and quality adjuster. Here a firm goes on production till the price becomes equal to the marginal cost of the product. A firm gets maximum total profit when marginal revenue becomes equal to the marginal cost. Since the price is the same for all levels of output. The marginal revenue equals the price. If a firm goes beyond that point where $MR = MC$, then it has to incur loss from the additional output. Thus the rules for profit maximisation are:

(1) $MC = MR$

(2) MC should cut MR from below.[1]

Its Criticisms

The profit maximisation objective as discussed above has been severly criticized by many economists. Some of the points of criticisms are as follows:

(1) Here it is assumed that the firms are certain about the levels of their maximum profits. But in practice profits are most uncertain. It is not

1. To prove these conditions, please refer to the matter given under short-run equilibrium of the rum under perfect competition and monopolistic competition.

possible for firms to maximise their profits under the condition of uncertainty. If profit becomes certain then everybody would like to enter into the production line. But in fact profit is the reward of risk. Sometimes the firm has to incur losses also when the price of the product is less than the average cost of production.

(2) The aim of profit maximisation has much relevance only under perfect competition when the firm is a price taker. A monopoly firm would be getting supernormal profits more or less automatically.

(3) Profit maximisation objective bears little or no direct relevance to the internal organisation of the firms. For instance, some managers incur expenditures apparently in excess of those that would maximise profits of the owners of the firm.

(4) The objective of profit maximisation assumes that all firms have perfect knowledge not only about their own cost and revenue functions but also of their rivals. But in practice, firms do not possess sufficient knowledge about the conditions under which they operate. They always produce under the conditions of uncertainties. If they find a large demand for their product, they get profits; otherwise, they may have to lose if the estimates about demand are not correct.

(5) The profit-maximisation hypothesis presupposes that producers can calculate marginal cost and marginal revenue of the firm's product so as to equate them. But it is not possible to make correct and accurate calculations about the *MC* and *MR* of the product.

(6) Firms can know about their cost conditions but they cannot estimate the demand in future. Nor the demand for the product can be ensured with the insurance company. Thus the entire risk of demand is to be borne by the producer.

(7) The profit maximisation objective of the firm is always related to the short-run. If we presume that firms do maximise profits, then they do so only in the long-run and not in the short-run.

3. SALES MAXIMISATION

Baumol has exphasised the sales maximisation objective of the firm. According to him, with the separation of ownership and control, managers seek higher salaries by trying to expand company sales even if it is at the cost of profits. Being a consultant to a number of firms, Baumol observes that when asked how their business went last year, the business managers often respond "our sales were up to 10 million dollars or so." It would mean that firm concentrates on sales rather than profits. A firm assigns much importance to the size of its sales and is always concerned when sales decline. But if sales are large, the size of the firm expands, which, in turn, means larger profits. By sales maximisation, Baumol means maximisation of total revenue of the firm. When there is very short-run, the firm's sole objective is sales maximisation and not profit maximisation as such.

Its Criticisms

The main criticisms of sales maximisation objective of the firm are the following:

(1) According to Rosenberg, it is difficult to specify exactly the relevant profit constraints for a firm, and choose the sales maximisation and minimum profit constraint is Baumol's analysis.

(2) If expenditure on advertising is introduced in Baumol's theory, the likelihood of sales maximisation is increased. But this opinion of Baumol is not realistic because the expenditure on advertising increases or decreases with the rise or fall in output.

4. OUTPUT MAXIMISATION

Milton Kafolgis[2] suggests output maximisation as the main objective of a business firm. According to him, "the performance of firm frequently is measured directly in terms of physi6al output with revenue occupying a secondary position." Thus Kafolgis prefers output maximisation both to profit maximisation and revenue maximisation as the objective of a firm. Given a certain minimum profit, a firm always tries to maximise its output. It will spend its money on increasing output rather than on advertising.

Its Criticisms

The above proposition of output maximisation is started by Kafolgis is not a satisfactory explanation of the objective of a firm. If the firm simply aims at output maximisation without sales maximisation, it would not be a situation for long-run survival of the firm. Both the objectives are complementary rather than competitive.

---

2. Milton Z. Kafolgis, 'Output of the Restrained Firm', *AER*, Sept. 1969.

EXERCISES

1. Explain in brief the main objective of a firm. How is it attained?
2. Write a brief note on sales maximisation and profit maximisation objectives of the firm.

Multiple Choice Questions

3. (*i*) A firm gets maximum profit if
   (*a*) $MC = MR$
   (*b*) MC cuts MR from below
   (*c*) both (*a*) and (*b*)
   (*d*) none of the above [*Ans.* (*c*)]

   (*ii*) In the long-run under perfect competition a firm gets
   (*a*) super normal profit
   (*b*) normal profit
   (*c*) price equals its Average Variable Cost
   (*d*) none of the above [*Ans.* (*b*)]

PART 2
CONSUMPTION THEORY

Chapter 13

THE NEO-CLASSICAL UTILITY ANALYSIS OF CONSUMER DEMAND

1. INTRODUCTION

The term 'utility' was employed by the classical economists of the late 18th and 19th centuries. The 20th century version of the concept is the neoclassical. The utility approach was developed in the 1870s with the simultaneous publication of major works by three economists working independently. These were William Stanley Jevons (1835-1882) of England, Karl Menger (1880-1921) of Austria, and Leon Walras (1840-1921) of France. Later on, in 1890, Alfred Marshall made a pioneering effort by bringing the concept of price in line with marginal utility.

2. THE MEANING OF UTILITY

With given constraints, i.e., given prices of goods and services and given income, a consumer makes his purchases according to his tastes or desires or preferences or wants. A consumer may desire a unit of good *X* more than that of a unit of good *Y*, because commodity *X* gives him more utility. Utility means the power to satisfy a want. Any commodity or service which can satisfy a human want is said to have utility. According to Wicksteed, "Utility as an economic concept, means only desireness." It signifies only the fact that a thing is wanted, that it is expected to satisfy a given want. It does not mean usefulness, as is generally assumed. The consumption of a particular commodity may be harmful, illogical or immoral; nevertheless, if it satisfies some want of somebody, it is deemed to possess utility from the economic standpoint. Therefore, we can very well say that utility is subjective, not objective. Utility resides in the mind of the consumer. The consumer knows it by introspection.

The term utility is commonly used as equivalent to satisfaction. But in economics, it has a different meaning. The amount of satisfaction actually obtained from the consumption of a thing is a psychological entity which is incapable of measurement, because it varies according to time, place, and the mental makeup of the individual concerned. The intensity of a person's desire for a commodity depends upon his habits, tastes and various other circumstances. At different times, the intensity of desire may be different. A consumer thinks of utility when he is buying a commodity but he secures satisfaction only after its consumption. To avoid confusion between utility and satisfaction some economists (like Wicksteed) use the term "significance" in place of utility. Wicksteed states that a thing has economic significance if it is scarce in relation to human wants, whatever may be the satisfaction it gives. Some economists use the term "intensity of desire" which seems better. Hence, utility is the measure, not of usefulness, nor of satisfaction, but of the intensity of desire. In fad, the entire theory of consumer behaviour is based on the assumption that utility and satisfaction are synonymous or that the expected satisfaction from a commodity is equal to the realised satisfaction.

3. CARDINAL AND ORDINAL UTILITY

The terms cardinal and ordinal are borrowed nom the vocabulary of mathematics. The numbers 1, 2, 3, 4, 5, etc. are cardinal numbers. The number 2, for example, is twice the size of number 1. In contrast, the numbers 1st, 2nd, 3rd, 4th, 5th, etc. are ordinal numbers. Such ordinal numbers are ordered or ranked, and there is no way of knowing, just from the ranking, what is the size relation of the numbers. The second one might be or might not be twice or thrice as big as the first one. The ordinal numbers 1st, 2nd, 3rd, 4th and 5th could be 50, 100, 150, 200 and 250 or they could be 50, 51, 52, 53 and 70. All we can know of the ordinal numbers is that the second number is greater than the first, the fourth is greater than the fifth, etc.

The concept of cardinal utility assumes that the measurement of utility of different commodities is possible. For example, the consumption of an apple may give 40 units of utility whereas the consumption of an orange may give only 20 units of utility. From this, it is clear that the utility of an apple is just twice the utility of an orange. On the other hand, the concept of ordinal utility permits us to say that the consumer prefers an apple to an orange, or prefers a cup of coffee to a glass of milk. It means that ordinal utility analysis is unable to compare the quantities of the two commodities. The neo-classical (Marshallian) utility approach assumes that utility can be measured. The units of measurement are arbitary; they are called "utils". Thus, under some given conditions, the utility of an apple is 40 utils and that of an orange is 20 utils. This is just another way of saying that one apple has twice as much utility as one orange. Contrarily, the concept of ordinal utility (indifference curve approach) maintains that quantities of utility are inherently immeasurable theoretically and conceptually, as well as practically. These economists argue that the theory of consumer behaviour can be explained without the idea of measurable utility.

4. MEASUREMENT OF UTILITY

There are two views on the question whether utility can be measured. Pareto, Hicks and other economists are of the opinion that utility cannot be measured in quantitative terms. According to them, utility is a subjective concept. The mental attitude on which utility depends differs from person to person. For the same consumer it differs from time to time. Even at a particular moment of time it is impossible to calculate the utility of a commodity in physical terms. All that a consumer can say is whether he prefers a cup of tea to a glass of milk. As such, it is not possible to measure directly the utility of a commodity.

But the 19th century economists (W. Stanley Jevons, Leon Walras, Alfred Marshall, etc.) are of the opinion that it is possible to measure utility indirectly by finding out how much a consumer is prepared to sacrifice in order to get one unit of certain commodity. According to Prof. Marshall, "If we find a man in doubt wit ether to spend a few pence on a cigar, or a cup of tea, or on riding home instead of walking home, then we follow ordinary usage, and say that he expects from them utilities."[1]

Marshall argued that utility is correlative to want or desire. He conceded to the fact that wants cannot be measured directly. However, he developed an indirect measure for it in "the price which a person is willing to pay for the fulfilment or satisfaction of his desire or want". In

1. Marshall, *op. cit.*, p. 15. We have substituted the word "utilities" in place of "pleasures".

other words, Marshall provided a cardinal measurement of utility. Higher the, price paid my a consumer for a commodity higher shall be its utility and vice versa. Price can, thus, be a measure of the utility of a commodity. In this way, a consumer is assumed to be capable of assigning to every commodity a number representing the amount of utility associated with it. The utility numbers could be manipulated in the same fashion as weights. For example, we assume that the utility of Q_1 is 10 units and the utility of Q_2 is 40 units. The consumer would like Q_2 four times as strongly as Q_1. Therefore, difference between utility numbers could be compared.

5. TOTAL UTILITY AND MARGINAL UTILITY

Total utility is the sum of the utilities obtained from each unit consumed. The more of the commodity a consumer consumes per unit of time, the greater will be the total utility or satisfaction from it up to a certain point. At some rate of consumption total utility from the commodity will reach a maximum. The consumer will not, be capable of enjoying any greater satisfaction from it even though more of it were thrust upon him. This is called his *saturation point* for that commodity.[2]

Marginal utility, is defined as the change in total utility resulting from a one unit change in consumption of the commodity per unit of time. In other words, marginal utility is the additional utility which a person derives from a small addition to his stock of the commodity in question. Thus, the marginal utility of n units of commodity X is the difference between the total utility of n units and the total utility of n-1 units of the commodity. Symbolically,

$$MU_n = TU_n - TU_{n-1}$$

where MU_n = Marginal utility of n units

TU_n = Total utility of n units

TU_{n-1} = Total utility of $_{n-1}$ units

The marginal utility of any quantity can also be stated as the slope of the total utility curve for the same quantity.

Since marginal utility defined as an increase in the total utility due to the consumption of an additional unit of a commodity, total utility will increase till the marginal utility remains positive. When marginal utility becomes negative, total utility will decrease. When marginal utility is equal to zero, total utility becomes maximum. Table 13.1 and Fig. 13.1

2. After attaining the saturation point, if the consumer is forced to consume more of the same commodity, it will cause his total utility to decrease. The study of the segment of the total utility curve beyond the saturation point is of no importance for our purposes.

show the relations between total utility and marginal utility. Table 13.1 indicates that the total utility is nothing but the sum of the marginal utilities.

Table 13.1: *Total Utility and Marginal Utility*

Units of Commodity X	*Total Utility (TU)*	*Marginal Utility (MU)*
0	0	—
1	40	40
2	75	35
3	95	20
4	105	10
5	105	0
6	95	–10
7	75	–20

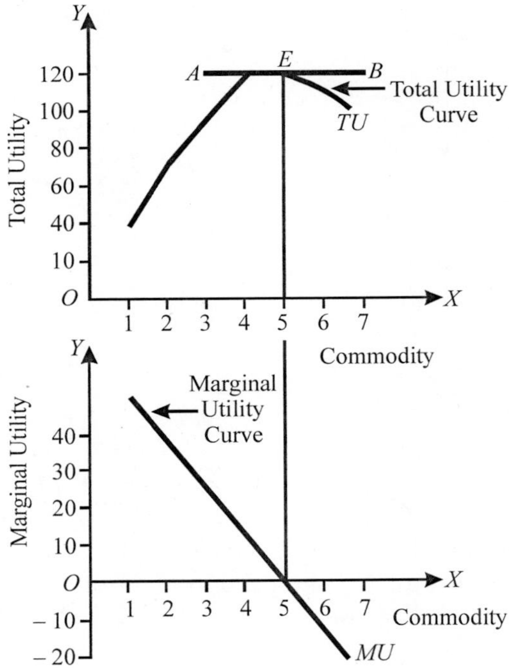

Fig. 13.1

In Fig. 13.1, the upper part shows the total utility curve and the lower part of the figure displays only the increases in total utility, i.e., the marginal utilities of different units of the commodity. The slope of total utility curve at a point is the gain of utility at that point and is equal to the height of the marginal utility curve at the corresponding quantity of the commodity. When the total utility curve reaches the maximum at point *E,* its slope becomes zero as shown by the horizontal line *AB* that is tangent at the maximum point *E.* Marginal utility is zero when total utility is a maximum. Further, when total utility is declining, its increases are negative, which is something as stating that marginal utility is negative.

The economic meaning of zero marginal utility is that the consumer has all that he desires of the commodity. Also, he would not care if he loses a unit of the commodity (whose $MU = O$). In our diagram it is 5th unit that is marginal unit whose marginal utility is zero and therefore, the consumer will buy only 4 units of the commodity. In Fig. 13.1, we have assumed that the units are divisible and therefore, the *TU* curve and the *MU* curve are presented in smooth lines. The important relations are summarized in Table 13.2.

Table 13.2

	Total Utility	*Marginal Utility*
1.	Increasing at an increasing rate	increasing
2.	Increasing at a constant rate	constant
3.	Increasing at a decreasing rate	decreasing
4.	Becomes maximum	zero
5.	Decreasing	negative

Importance of the Concept of Marginal Utility

The concept of marginal utility is of extreme importance in economic theory, particularly in price theory. With the help of this, price of a commodity is determined in the market. Consumers do not pay more price than its marginal utility that they derive from the use of that commodity. As we know that an individual demands a particular commodity because of the satisfaction or utility he receives from consuming it. When he consumes more units of the same, the marginal utility diminishes. Thus the individual will not be ready to pay a price higher than the marginal utility of the commodity. This fact explains why certain prices are higher than other prices. Commodities which provide higher marginal utility can be sold at higher price.

The concept of marginal utility is helpful in explaining the *diamond-water paradox*— water is more useful than diamond but diamond is more costly than water. The price of a commodity is related to its marginal utility. Water being available in plenty commands no price. This is because relative importance of water brings down its marginal utility to zero. While, on the other hand, diamonds being scarce have a very high marginal utility and have a high price.

6. LAW OF DIMINISHING MARGINAL UTILITY

The law of diminishing utility is a generalisation deduced from observations of human nature. As we get more and more of a commodity, the want for that commodity diminishes. The want of a thirsty man for water is very strong, but after he takes one glass of water, his intensity of desire for another glass of water becomes less. This tendency towards diminishing utilities from successive doses of the same commodity is operative in all types of commodities and services. The rate of diminishing utility may be slow for some commodities, or rapid for others, but the tendency is still operative and a point will come when further additions of the commodity would yield no utility at all. This generalisation is known as the law of diminishing marginal utility. This law has been stated by Boulding as follows:

"As a consumer increases the consumption of anyone commodity, keeping constant the consumption of all other commodities, the marginal utility of the variable commodity must eventually decline."[3]

According to Marshall, the law of satiable wants or of diminishing (marginal) utility can be defined in the following words:

".... the additional benefit (marginal utility) which a person derives from a given increase of his stock of a thing, diminishes with every increase in the stock he already has."[4]

Translating the law of diminishing marginal utility in terms of price, Marshall argued that the price a person is willing to pay rather than go without a thing, would also diminish with every increase in its stock. For example, we may assume that a person will be just willing to pay Rs. 20 for one pair of shoes. Then Rs. 20 measures the marginal utility of one pair of shoes to him. The second pair of shoes will give him less satisfaction than the first and hence, he is ready to pay lees price for it, say Rs. 15. Now Rs. 15 measures the marginal utility of the second pair

3. Boulding, K.E., *Economic Analysis,* 1950, p. 616.
4. Marshall, *Principles of Economics.* p. 79.

of shoes. Similarly, for the successive pairs of shoes he will offer lower and lower prices, until a point will come when he will refuse to purchase any more pairs of shoes.

Prof. William J. Baumol expressed the law in another way. According to him, when we have only a little of a particular commodity, we put it to the most urgent use. As we get more and mote of it, we begin to putting it to less urgent uses. It happens so because we give priority to more highly valued uses. If we have only one piece of cake we give it to our child; if we have two we give the second to our wife, a third we keep for ourselves and a fourth we give to our mother-in-law (assuming that mother-in-law lives with family).[5]

Thus, the marginal utility of a commodity diminishes as its quantity increases. But it is possible that, in the first stage of consumption, intensity of our desire may increase. In such a situation marginal utility will increase and as a result, total utility will increase at an increasing rate. But a situation will certainly appear when the law of diminishing marginal utility will become operative.

Fig. 13.2 explains that the consumer gets higher marginal utility from the second unit of the commodity than the first one. The third unit still yields more utility, but thereafter from the fourth unit of the commodity the marginal utility starts declining.

Also, the marginal utility of the eighth unit is zero and no rational consumer would like to consume the commodity after this level, even if

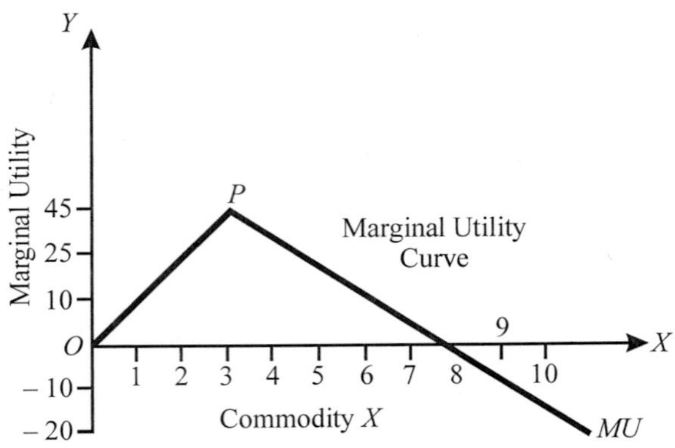

Fig. 13.2

5. William J. Baumol, *Economic Theory and Operations Analysis,* 3rd Edition, p. 205.

the commodity is available tree of cost. As we observe that the 9th and the 10th units of the commodity yield negative marginal utilites, i.e., the total utility will decline from the successive consumption of the commodity. As a practical matter no consumer will reach the saturation point (where total utility is maximum and marginal utility is equal to zero) for any good that commands a price, except by accident. Thus, the negative slope of the marginal utility curve explains the law of diminishing marginal utility. This law is applicable only under certain assumptions.

Assumptions of the Law

The main assumptions of the law of diminishing marginal utility are as follows:

(1) *The units of the commodity must be relevantly defined.* The law of diminishing marginal utility holds only if the units of a commodity are relevantly defined. For example, the law holds for pairs of shoes but not for a single shoe. An unit must be complete for its consumption or use.

(2) *The tastes are given and unchanged.* The law holds for individual commodities wanted by individual consumers with given tastes. If the taste of a consumer changes, so that he likes a commodity more, then the marginal utility of the commodity in question increases.

(3) *The units of the commodity are homogeneous.* All the units of a commodity must be the same in all respects, i.e., in size and quality, etc. If the units are non-homogeneous then the law will not hold.

(4) *There in no time-lag between the consumption of the two units of a commodity.* The law holds only when the process of consumption is continuous without any time-interval. For example, if a consumer drinks three glasses of water at a time. Then the marginal utility of each will decline. But if he drinks the second glass and third glass of water at an interval of two hours, then the marginal utility of these glasses of water will rather increase; thus the law fails.

(5) *The income and prices of the commodity and its substitutes are given.* If the price decreases or income increases, then the consumer will buy more of the commodity. Also, if the price of substitutes falls, the consumer will buy mote quantity of the commodity in question and the law fails.

Hence, for the law of diminishing marginal utility to hold, the above conditions must exist.

Exceptions to the Law of Diminishing Marginal Utility

In fact, there is no real exception to the law of diminishing marginal utility. But some exceptions arise when we misinterpret the law. The following are the important exceptions to the law.

(1) There are certain groups of commodities, the marginal utility of which does not diminish with every increase in the stock of them. In the collection of curios and antiques, stamps, old paintings, coins, etc. the law of diminishing marginal utility does not hold. A person may desire the additional units of the curios articles, or stamps with increasing intensity. But according to Prof. Viner,[6] this is no exception to the law; if we take a complete set as the proper unit of observation. For instance, if there are known to be in existence two pearls of the same type, these two should be taken as one unit. The addition of pearls of the same type to this unit will yield diminishing utility. In other words, a person will not pay higher prices in acquiring the same type of stamps or coins. Therefore, it is not a real exception to the law of diminishing marginal utility.

(2) It is said that the law of diminishing marginal utility does not hold in the consumption of liquor. The additional doses of liquor will yield increasing marginal utility to a drinker. But this argument is not correct because a drinker is not a rational consumer and we do not study his irrational behaviour in economics.

(3) It is said that the law fails when there is a large number of consumers to consume a commodity. The marginal utility of one set of telephone, for example, rises with increasing use of telephones.[7] Similar is the case with fashion or style commodities. But the law still remains true with regard to those commodities that at any given period of time, given the extent of the use of the commodity, the marginal utility of additional units diminishes. For instance, we may imagine a situation when all the families of a city possess telephone facility; then it is certain that an additional set of telephone will yield lessened satisfaction to the same family.

(4) It is also said that the law does not apply to money. A person gets increasing marginal utilities from additional amounts of money. This is particularly true in the case of a miser. But in the long run, the law will also apply to the miser. Moreover, the miser is not assumed to be a rational roan and therefore, his activities are not studied in economics.

The above exceptions are not real and hence the law of diminishing marginal utility is the universal law applicable in all cases of consumption. According to Taussig, "The tendency shows itself so widely and with so

---

6. Viner, "The Utility Concept in Economic Theory", *Journal of Political Economy,* 1925.
7. Chapman, *Outlines of Political Economy,* p. 32.

few exceptions that there is no serious inaccuracy in speaking of it as universal. The law of diminishing marginal utility is of paramount importance, because it is the basis of the law of demand, and provides adequate reason for the negative slope of the demand curve.

Criticisms of the Law of Diminishing Marginal Utility

Like the other laws of economics, the law of diminishing marginal utility is subject to the following limitations:

(1) The law of diminishing marginal utility holds only if "other things remain the same", i.e., the habits, tastes, temperament and income of the consumer do not change. If any of the things change, the law may not be true. In real life, these things are changing.

(2) The law may not operate in the initial stages of consumption, i.e., for very small increments of the commodity. If thirsty person is offered water in teaspoons, the utility he gets from the second teaspoon of water will be greater than that from the first one.

(3) This law assumes no time-gap in the consumption of various units of a commodity. In practical life it is not necessary that all the units of a commodity are consumed at a time.

(4) This law assumes utility measurable in terms of money. Marshall took this assumption for analytical purposes, but modern economists criticise this assumption. According to them, utility is a subjective concept and its quantitative measurement is not possible.

In spite of these limitations, the law of diminishing marginal utility assumes a great theoretical and practical importance.

Importance of the Law of Diminishing Marginal Utility

The law of diminishing marginal utility possesses the following points of importance:

(1) *Basis of the law of demand.* The law of diminishing marginal utility is one of the fundamental laws of economics. The basic law of demand is based on this law. The law of demand states that more amounts of a commodity will be purchased at a relatively lower price. The reason for this is that as more and more units of a commodity are purchased and consumed, its marginal utility to the consumers becomes less and less. And the consumer will be ready to pay the price of a commodity just equal to its marginal utility (or $MU_i = P_i$). Therefore, the additional units of a commodity will be purchased only at a lower price. The law of demand, thus, has been directly based on the law of diminishing marginal utility.

(2) *Basis of the progressive tax-policy.* The government can formulate a progressive tax-policy on the basis of the law of diminishing marginal utility. Adam Smith exphasized the canon of "ability to pay tax" which was later presented in terms of marginal utility of money by Prof. Pigou. They argued that the marginal utility of money or wealth is more for the poor than for the rich. This is the reason why the rich have to pay tax at a progressive rate and the poor at a lower rate.

(3) *Basis of the policy of redistribution of wealth.* The government's public expenditure policy is also based on the law of diminishing marginal utility. The government's tax-cum-expenditure policy helps in transferring the purchasing power from richer to the poorer classes. It leads to an equi-distribution of wealth in the society.

(4) *Determination of optimum level of consumption.* This law helps in the determination of the optimum level of consumption. It is attained at a point where the marginal utility of the commodity equals its price. We shall discuss this concept in the following section of this chapter.

7. THE LAW OF EQUI-MARGINAL UTILITY (THE PROPORTIONALITY RULE)

To solve the problems of a consumer which we have discussed in the beginning of the chapter, Marshall gave his famous Principle of Equi-Marginal Utility. The law of equi-marginal utility is also known as the law of substitution, or the law of economy in expenditure, or the law of maximum satisfaction or the principle of income allocation, etc. Marshall defined this law in the following manner:

"If a person has a thing which he can put to several uses, he will distribute it among these uses in such a way that it has the same marginal utility in all. For, if it had a greater marginal utility in one use than another he would gain by taking away some of it from the second use and applying it to the first."[8]

Thus, a consumer attains maximum total utility from his available resources (income) only when the marginal utilities of all the goods consumed are equal.

Symbolically,

$$MU_1 = MU_2 = MU_3 = \ldots MUn \qquad \ldots(1)$$

where MUi indicates the marginal utility of the ith commodity and $i = 1, 2, \ldots n$.

8. *Alfred Marshall, op. cit.*, p. 98.

Marshall stated that in a barter economy, equalisation of marginal utilities is not possible, because there is no common measurement of value. In a money economy, price becomes a common denominator of value. Hence, the law of equi-marginal utility is useful only in money economy. If the prices of all the commodities are equal, the consumer attains maximum total utility ... when $MU_1 = MU_2 = MU_3 = ... = MUn$. If prices ($Pi$) of various goods are different, then the consumer will attain maximum total utility only when the following condition holds:

$$\frac{MU_1}{P_1} = \frac{MU_2}{P_2} = \frac{MU_3}{P_3} .... = \frac{MUn}{Pn} \qquad ...(2)$$

Assumptions of the Law

The law of equi-marginal utility is based on the following assumptions:

1. Utility is measurable in terms of money.
2. The income of the consumer is limited and remains constant.
3. There is perfect competition in the market. It means that the consumer is unable to change the price of those commodities which he consumes. The consumer has to accept the market prices in the determination of his budget.
4. The marginal utility of money remains constant.
5. The utility schedule of a commodity is independent of the utility schedules of the other commodities.
6. The law of diminishing marginal utility holds.

On the basis of above assumptions, the law of equi-marginal utility can be explained clearly with the help of an example. Suppose that the consumer purchases two commodities—commodity X and commodity Y—the prices of which are P_X and P_Y' respectively. As long as P_X *and* P_Y are fixed or constant, a rupee's worth of X or a rupee's worth of Y represents a certain quantity (utility) of X or of Y. Suppose, that the consumer's marginal utility schedules for X and Y are those of Table 13.3.[9]

Now the question is as to how should the consumer allocate his income between X and Y? Here we suppose that the consumer has an income of

9. Here we assume that the marginal utility schedule of each commodity is independent of the level of consumption of the other commodity. It enables us to allocate our income among the two commodities in such a way that leads to maximum satisfaction. If X and Y were substitutes, the more of X consumed, the lower the marginal utility of Y would be at various consumption levels of Y. If they were complementary, the more of X consumed, the higher the marginal utility of Y would be at various consumption level of Y.

Rs. 10. The consumer will spend his first rupee on commodity *X*, because it gives him 50 units of utility which is the highest in his utility schedule of Table 13.3. Now the consumer also spends his second rupee on commodity *X* which will increase his total utility by 45 units; whereas, if instead he spends it on *Y*, it would increase total utility by 38 units only. Hence, the second rupee will be spent on *X*. Similarly, the third rupee will also be spent on *X*. But the 4th rupee will not be spent on *X*, because it will increase his total utility only by 35 units; whereas if it is spent on *Y*, it will increase total utility by 38 units. Thus, the 4th rupee will be spent on *Y*. The 5th rupee will again be spent on *Y*. The 6th on *X*, the 7th on Y and 8th on *X*; and the 9th and 10th, one each on *X* and *Y*. The order in which he spends his Rs. 10 on *X* and *Y* commodities is shown in brackets in Table 13.3. In this way, when the consumer spends all his income, he should be enjoying six rupees' worth of commodity *X* and four rupees' worth of commodity *Y*. The marginal utilities of the last rupee spent on *X* and of the last rupee spent on *Y* are equal to 25 units. In other words,

Table 13.3

Money Units Spent	*Marginal Utility for Commodity X* (MU_X)	*Marginal Utility for Commodity Y* (MU_Y)
1st Rupee	50 (1)	38 (4)
2nd ,,	45 (2)	36 (5)
3rd ,,	40 (3)	32 (7)
4th ,,	35 (6)	25 (10)
5th ,,	30 (8)	18
6th ,,	25 (9)	15
7th ,,	20	10
8th ,,	15	5
9th ,,	10	2
10th ,,	5	1

$$\frac{MU_X}{P_X} = \frac{MU_Y}{P_Y} = 25$$

It satisfies the consumer's objective of getting maximum total utility. In our example, the total utility of Rs. 10 spent on *X* and *Y* is equal to the total utility derived from the consumption of commodity *X* plus the total utility derived from the consumption of commodity *Y*, i.e.,

$$\begin{aligned} TU_{X+Y} &= TU_X + TU_Y \\ &= [50 + 45 + 40 + 35 + 30 + 25] + [38 + 36 + 32 + 25] \end{aligned}$$

= 225 + 131
= 356 units

If the consumer disturbs this allocation of income, then he would not be able to secure the maximum total utility from his consumption. For instance, if he transfers his 10th rupee from *Y* to *X*. Now giving up a rupee's worth of *Y* will decrease his total utility by 25 units. The additional rupee's worth of *X* will increase his total utility by 20 units. So that, the transfer results in a net loss of 5 units of utility to his total satisfaction. If the transfer were made from *X* to *Y*, the net loss would be equal to 7 units of utility. Hence, no other allocation of consumer's income will yield as much satisfaction as the one set by the law of equi-marginal utility.

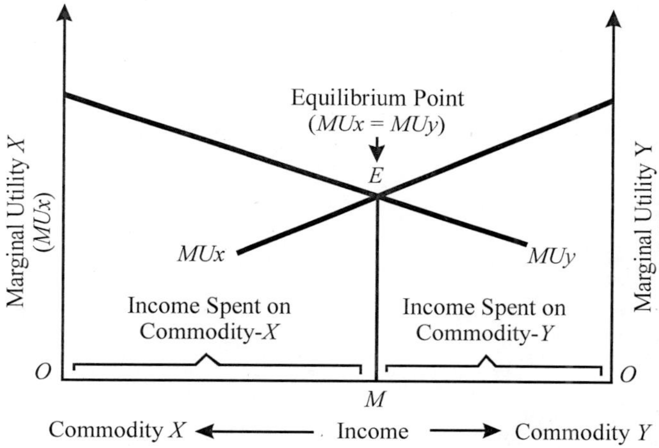

Fig. 13.3.

The above explanation can also be made with the help of a diagram. In Fig. 13.3, the marginal utility curves for *X* and *Y* commodities are MU_X and MU_Y respectively. The equilibrium point is *E* where the marginal utility of *X* is equal to the marginal utility of *Y*. At this equilibrium point the consumer will attain maximum satisfaction by spending *OM* income on commodity *X* and *MO′* income on commodity *Y*. Any other allocation of his limited income *OO′* on these two commodities will not yield him maximum satisfaction.

The principle of equi-marginal utility can be extended to as many goods as confront the consumer and is not limited to the two commodities. The first necessary condition for maximising total utility will be

$$\frac{MU_X}{P_X} = \frac{MU_Y}{P_Y} = \frac{MU_Z}{P_Z} \qquad ...(3)$$

If there are only two commodities under the consumption, then the proportionality condition (3) becomes

$$\frac{MU_X}{P_X} = \frac{MU_Y}{P_Y}$$

or

$$\frac{MU_X}{MU_Y} = \frac{P_X}{P_Y} \qquad ...(4)$$

where $\frac{MU_X}{MU_Y}$ = the ratio of the marginal utilities of the two commodities X and Y

$\frac{P_X}{P_Y}$ = the ratio of the prices of the two commodities X and Y.

Thus, in equilibrium, the ratio of their marginal utilities must be equal to the ratio of their prices.

The above necessary condition does not take into account the income restraint under which the consumer operates. Thus, the second sufficient condition of consumer equilibrium can be written as

$$I = XP_X + YP_Y + ZP_Z + ... + NP_N \qquad ...(5)$$

where I represents consumer's income, $P_X, P_Y, P_Z ... P_N$ are the prices of various commodities and $X, Y, Z, ... N$ are the respective quantities bought.

The original law of equi-marginal utility as developed by Prof. Marshall does not assume the second condition of equilibrium to hold, while the modern interpretation of the law of equi-marginal utility is based on this assumption that under the income constraint a consumer will attain maximum satisfaction only if the equality between the ratio of marginal utilities and the ratio of prices exist. Nevertheless, there is no basic difference between the Marshallian concept and modern interpretation of the law of equi-marginal utility. If the prices of all the goods are assumed to be the same, will get similar conclusions from them. Prof. Boulding has represented this law in terms of "weighted marginal utilities". In his opinion the weighted marginal utility of a commodity indicates the ratio of its marginal utility to its price. It means that the consumer attains maximum satisfaction only when the weighted marginal utilities of all the goods included in the budget of a consumer are equal. In the words of

Prof. Boulding, "The best division of expenditures is that at which the weighted marginal utilities in all lines of expenditure are equal."[10]

Applications or Importance of the Law of Equi-Marginal Utility

The law of equi-marginal utility is of great practical importance in economics. According to Prof. Marshall, the law of equi-marginal utility or returns is a universal law applicable to every branch of economic activity. Some of its important applica-tions are described below.

(1) *Determination of an optimum budget.* As we have already discussed, a consumer has unlimited wants and limited means to fulfil them. All the wants are not fulfilled with his limited means. Now, the question before the consumer is as to which commodities should be included in his budget and how much of them should be purchased. The law of equi-marginal utility provides him the answer. According to this law, he distributes his limited income among various commodities, in such a way that the last rupee spent on each of them gives equal utility. By doing so, he gets maximum satisfaction, i.e., optimises his budget.

(2) *Determination of saving and consumption.* Every consumer has to decide how much of his income should be put for saving (i.e., for future consumption) and how much for consumption. In other words, the economists call it the rate of time preference. According to Prof. Marshall, a rational consumer will distribute his resources between his present needs and future needs in such a way that the marginal utility of the last rupee put in saving equals the marginal utility of the last rupee put in consumption. Thus, the law of equi-marginal utility helps the consumer in solving the problem of the allocation of income between consumption and saving.

(3) *Determination of least cost combination of resources.* According to Marshall, the principle of substitution is also used in the field of production.[11] Like a consumer, an entrepreneur also uses his limited factor inputs in the production process in such a way that the marginal product of each factor input becomes equal. He constantly substitutes one factor of production for another, until the marginal returns from all the factors are equal. The modern economists state that the least cost combination off actors of production will be attained at a point when the ratio of their marginal products is equal to the ratio of their prices. Thus, if there are only two factors of production, say labour (L) and capital (K), then

10. K.E. Boulding, *Economic Analysis,* Vol. I, *Micro Economics,* Fourth Edition, pp. 527-28.
11. Marshall, *op. cit.,* pp. 295-99.

$$\frac{MP_L}{P_L} = \frac{MP_K}{P_K}$$

or
$$\frac{MP_L}{MP_K} = \frac{P_L}{P_K}$$

where MP_L = Marginal product of labour, MP_K = Marginal product of capital, P_L = Price of labour, P_K = Price of capital

(4) *Expenditure of time.* Prof. Boulding relates the Marshall's law of equi-marginal utility to the expenditure of limited time (24 hours). He states that a person should spend his limited time among alternative uses, in such a way that the marginal utility gained from those uses must be equal, i.e., he gets maximum satisfaction. Thus the optimum utilization of time is possible through this law.

(5) *Determination of exchange.*[12] The important part of economic activity deals with exchange among individuals. Exchange will take place only when both the parties gain from it. It is the prospect of gain that causes voluntary exchange to occur. This point can be illustrated with the help of utility analysis. Suppose, there are two consumers, *A* and *B*. Each holds the stocks of two commodities, *X* and *Y*. Now suppose, initially (before exchange) for *A,* 1 unit of *X* equals 2 units of *Y* and for *B,* 1 unit of *X* equals two-third units of *Y*. Now exchange will take place, and *A* will exchange *Y* for *X* and *B* will exchange *X* for *Y*. Exchange will continue till *A* gets more than one-half units of *X* for 1 unit of *Y* and *B* gets more than two-third units of *Y* for 1 unit of *X*. In equilibrium (i.e., at a point where exchange stops),

$$\frac{MU_K}{MU_Y} \text{ for } A = \frac{MU_X}{MU_Y} \text{ for } B$$

In such a situation, both the consumers will attain maximum total satisfaction.

Limitations of the Law of Equi-Marginal Utility

The criticisms of this law are based on the unrealistic assumptions that the law assumes in the beginning. The points of criticisms are the following:

(1) *The measurement of utility is not possible.* The law assumes that the utility of a commodity is measurable in terms of money. As Prof.

12. Leftwich, *The Price System and Resource Allocation,* Fourth Edition, pp. 66-68.

Marshall states that the price a consumer is willing to pay for a commodity is its utility for him. But modern economists argue that when two persons are paying equal price for a given commodity, it would not mean that both are getting the same level of utility. Thus, utility is a subjective concept which cannot be measured in quantitative terms.

(2) *Utilities are inter-dependent.* Marshall's law of equi-marginal utility is based on the assumption that commodities are independent, and, therefore, their marginal utilities are also independent. But in real life, we see that commodities are either substitutes or they are complementary. Their utilities are, therefore, inter-dependent.

(3) *The marginal utility of money is not constant.* The law assumes that the marginal utility of money remains constant. But it is not true. The marginal utility of money increases with every decrease in its available stock. Further, the marginal utility of money for a rich person is less than that for a poor person.

(4) *Indivisibility of goods.*[13] According to Prof. Boulding, this law is applicable only if commodities (or money, time, etc.) are divisible because the weighted marginal utilities of various commodities in terms of money (MU_X / P_X) will be made equal only if the commodities are purchased in small pieces. But there are certain commodities which are not divisible, such as, a house, a car, a cooler, etc. In such cases, the law of equi-marginal utility will not be applicable.

(5) *Indefinite budget period.*[14] According to Prof. Boulding, another difficulty of the law is the indefinite budget period. Normally, one year is assumed to be a budget period. But there are certain commodities under the consumption of a person whose durability (or life) is more than one year. For such commodities, it is difficult to calculate the marginal utility. Thus, the law is not applicable in these situations.

8. MEANING OF DEMAND

In economics the term 'demand' is used in a particular sense. According to Stonier and Hague, "Demand in economics means demand backed up by enough money to pay for the good demanded." In the absence of purchasing power, demand is not effective. For instance, many people would probably like to have a big modernised house, a brand new car, a summer cottage, etc. But they have no effective demand for these things. In order for them to have a demand for these things, they must be *able*

13. Boulding, *op. cit.*, pp. 530-31.
14. Stonier and Hague, *A Textbook of Economic Theory,* 3rd ed., p. 15.

and *willing* to buy them. Hence the use of the term "effective demand" has a particular meaning in economics. Demand then shows us the quantities of goods that people are willing to purchase at different prices. As Benham rightly points out, "The demand for anything, at a given price, is the amount of it which will be bought per unit of time at that price. Demand means always demand at a price, the term has no significance unless a price is stated or implied."

The demand has the following four characteristics:

(1) *Price.* The demand is always at a price. If we say that there is a demand for one thousand motor-cars in the market, this type of statement is meaningless. The person must state the price at which he is prepared to purchase the said quantity of the commodity.

(2) *Time.* Demand must mean demand per unit of time, per month, per week or per day.

(3) *Market.* Demand is always held in the market. Market is a set of points of contact between buyers and sellers. It need not be a definite geographical area.

(4) *Amount.* Demand is always a specific amount which a person is willing to purchase. It is not an approximation, but is to be expressed in numbers.

A demand schedule, as we shall note shortly, shows us how much of some product people will buy at different price. On the other side of the picture, supply tells us the quantities of goods that producers are willing to sell at different prices.

9. THE LAW OF DEMAND

Generally speaking, the amount of a commodity people (consumers) are willing and able to buy varies with the price. The lower the price, the more people tend to buy of a commodity, and the higher price the less people tend to buy. In fact, the 'law of demand' states that the quantity of a product demanded varies inversely with the price. Putting it more concisely, we can say, the lower the price, the greater the effective demand; or, the higher the price, the less the effective demand. It follows from this law that sellers cannot get as high a price for a large quantity as for a lesser quantity. The greater the quantity of a good they are trying to sell, the lower the price must be.

We should note, however, that this law is a generalisation to which there are *some exceptions.* Mainly, there are two, situations in which this law will not hold true, but they are exceptional. If the price of a thing is declining, and it is expected to fall still further, buyers may hold off until they think it has reached the bottom, so as to get, it at the lowest possible price. This is particularly true of dealers and speculators; but it also holds for consumers in certain situations. But when the bottom has been reached, consumers will buy more than they would at a higher price, so that the general principle inherent in the law is valid, even for this case. The other exception runs directly counter to the principle. There are a few commodities (like diamonds) that are bought largely for the prestige that they confer upon the possessor. To display a diamond necklace or a big diamond in a ring confers a distinction upon the wearer as a person of great wealth. If diamonds were to become so inexpensive that even the poor could have plenty of them, they would no longer carry any prestige, and the demand for them might fan off. Not with standing the existence of a great many such goods, for most commodities the law of demand is a valid generalisation.

Alfred Marshall defines the law of demand as follows: "The greater the amount to be sold, the smaller must, be the price at which it is offered in order that it may find purchasers; or, in other words, the amount demanded increases with a fall in price, and diminishes with a rise in price. Marshall understood it as the general law of demand. It will be proper to make it clear that like the other laws of economics, the law of demand holds only when other things remain the same. This assumption is known as the assumption of *ceteris paribus.* We shall explain this condition of the law under demand function.

10. THE DEMAND FUNCTION

In a given market in a given period of time, the demand function for a commodity can be defined as the relationship between the various amounts of the commodity demanded and the determinants of those amounts. Generally, the determinants of the demand for a commodity are the following:

(*i*) The price of the commodity,
(*ii*) The incomes of the consumers,
(*iii*) Tastes of the consumers, and
(*iv*) The price of other commodities.

In general, therefore, the demand function for a commodity can be Written as

$$Dx = f(Px\ P,\ Y,\ T) \qquad \ldots (6)$$

where Dx = Quantity of commodity X demanded per unit of time,

Px = Price of the commodity X,
P = Average price of other commodities,
Y = Income of the consumer,
T = Taste of the consumer.

The accurate or exact form of such a demand function depends on how consumers respond to changes in the value of each of the determinants. If prices of other commodities, income and taste are all assumed to be a constant, the demand function (6) reduces to the simple form,

$$Dx = (Px) \qquad ...(7)$$

The demand function (7) states that the demand for a commodity (X) is a function exclusively of its own price (Px).

But when the other determinants are not held constant or when structural changes occur in the economy over a time period, then a dynamic demand function may be used to allow for all changes. Econometrics is the subject that combines economic and statistical theory for the purpose of measuring actual economic relations. Mathematical models are developed on the basis of economic theory. Statistical methods and techniques are used to estimate the values of the parameters of these mathematical models from the empirical statistics collected for the purpose.

Demand functions are generally homogeneous, of degree zero in prices and income, i.e., if all prices and income change in the same proportion, the quantity demanded remains unchanged.

If income, price of other commodities, tastes and other independent variables are held constant, the demand function takes the simple form $Dx = f(Dx)$. This form of the demand function can vary considerably as long as the demand curve is monotonic (i.e., it always moves in the direction) with quantity varying inversely with price.

Demand Schedule and Demand Curve

Demand Schedule. According to Prof. Alfred Marshall, a demand schedule is a list of prices and quantities. In other words, a demand schedule states the relation between the two variables of price and quantity. In Table 13.4 we have a hypothetical illustration of *A*'s demand schedule for oranges. In this table we see that at a price of Rs. 16 per kg., the consumer *A* buys 1 kg. of oranges; if instead the price were Rs. 15, the quantity demanded would be 2 kg. and so on.

A demand schedule does not say what the price is. It only says that amounts would be bought at different possible prices. The lower the price,

Table 13.4: *A's Demand Schedule for Oranges*

Price per kg. (*in Rupees*)	*Quantity Purchased* (*in kgs.*)
16	1
15	2
14	3
13	4
12	5
11	6

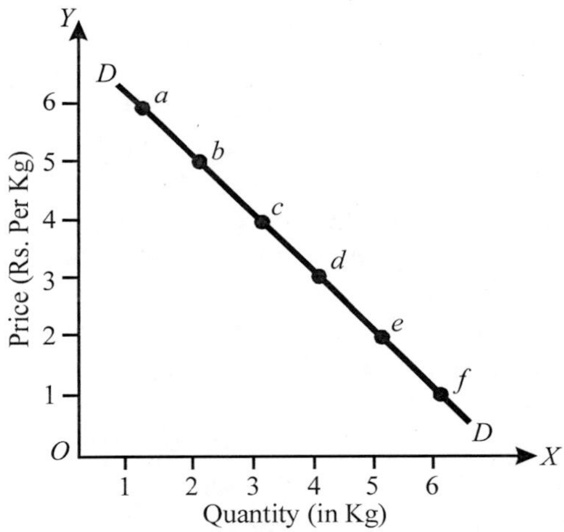

Fig. 13.4

the larger is the quantity that is bought. Similarly, the higher the price, the smaller the quantity. Therefore, Table 13.4 is a "demand schedule", which, in turn, is defined as a list of the quantities of any economic good that will be purchased in a given market at a given time.

Demand Curve. The material in Table 13.4 can be made into a demand curve, as shown in. Fig. 13.4. The vertical axis repre-sents price and the horizontal axis quantity.[15] We proceed by plotting first purchases at Rs. 16. To do this we reach up the vertical axis until we come to Rs. 16 point; then we go across to the right until we come 15. Some mathematical economists reverse the axes on the ground that quantity is

15. Some mathematical economists reverse the axes on the ground that quantity is the dependent variable, which belongs on the *Y*-axis. To put price on the *Y*-axis and quantity on the *X*-asis is a convention established by Prof. Alfred Marshall.

the dependent variable, which belongs on the *Y*-axis. To put price on the *Y-axis* and quantity on the *X-axis* is a convention established by Prof. Alfred Marshall to Rs. 11 on the quantity scale and place a dot there. We do the same thing for the other prices. We then connect these points by drawing a smooth curve through all of them. This is our "demand curve". This demand curve shows the relationship between the two variables of price and quantity—in particular the manner in which quantity is demanded upon price. The demand curve is always so called, even when it happens to be a straight line.

According to Friedman, "A demand curve of a particular group for a particular commodity can be defined as a locus of points, each of which shows the maximum quantity of the commodity that will be purchased by the group per unit time at a particular price. It represents an attempt to relate a rate of flow to a price at an instant of time. For many problems, it is useful to conceive of a demand curve as boundary line separating two spaces, the space to the left of the demand curve representing points that are attainable wider the given conditions of demand, in the sense that demanders would be willing to buy the indicated quantity at the indicated price, and the space to the right of the demand curve representing points that are unattainable in the sense that demanders would not be willing to buy the indicated quantity at the indicated price."[16]

Fig. 13.4 shows the demand curve for one person, and it is downward sloping. With other persons or families it may be different, although it will tend to be a decreasingly downward-sloping curve. It is possible that a higher income person would purchase more oranges at each given price. In such a case the curve would be farther to the right; or, a lower income person might buy less at each price, in which case the curve would be to the left.

Market Demand Curve

Figure 13.4 illustrates the demand curve of an individual consumer, which, in terms of the total number of consumers, constitutes only a small part of the total demand for this particular product. This individual consumer's demand has little influence on the price and quantity of oranges sold, but the total demand for this or any other product does influence the market price and the quantity sold. The market demand curve (or schedule) is the sum of the demand curves (or schedules) of all consumers. As noted above, such schedules are made up of the reactions to prices of many

16. Milton Friedman, *Price Theory-A Provisional Test* (First Indian ed., 1920), pp. 13-14.

consumers, each of whom decides how much of a given commodity it is worth his while to buy. At high prices he buys less, and at low prices he buys more, Also, at certain prices some consumers will purchase very little, some a lot as price increases or decreases, some consumers will vary their purchases very little, some will vary their purchases significantly. Thus, the demand curves for all consumers show different slopes, different positions and different shapes. By adding up the potential purchases of all the consumers at each possible price, we get the demand schedule (curve) for the market.

To give a very simple illustration, suppose there are only three possible buyers of oranges in a given market. We can picture their possible purchases in Table 13.5.

Table 13.5: *Market Demand Schedule*

Price per kg. (in Rs.)	*Effective Demand of Oranges (in kg.)*			*Total Effective Demand of the Market (in kg.)*
	Consumer A	*Consumer B*	*Consumer* C	
16	1	–	–	1
15	2	1	–	3
14	3	2	1	6
13	4	3	2	9
12	5	4	3	12
11	6	5	4	15

The schedule of demand for the market will then be shown in the last column, which is obtained by adding the demands of *A,* Band C horizontally across the table for each price. By plotting this schedule on a graph, we would get the required curve. In Fig. 13.5, the individual demand curves are added to arrive at the market demand curve.

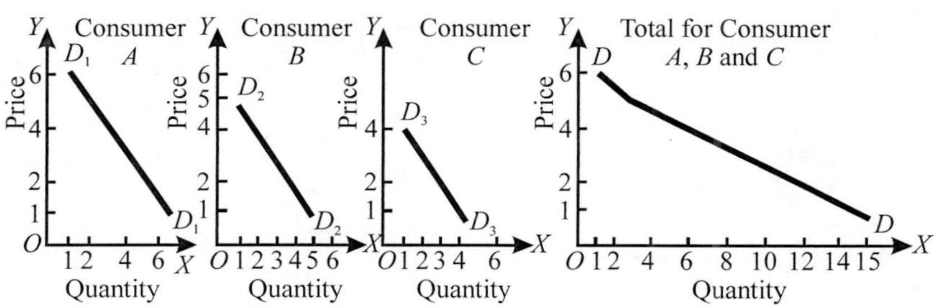

Fig. 13.5

Fig. 13.5 indicates that the demand curve for the market may not be a linear demand curve while the individual consumers may have linear demand curves.

11. TYPES OF DEMAND

We normally study three types of demand: (*i*) Price Demand, (*ii*) Income Demand, and (*iii*) Cross Demand.

As we have already discussed, price demand shows us the quantities of goods that people are willing to purchase at different prices, assuming *ceteris paribus*. It is the price demand that the economists frequently make use of. Figure 13.6 illustrates the case price-demand curve which has a negative slope indicating an inverse relationship between the price and the quantity demanded. Figure 13.6 shows that at price *OP*, the quantity demanded is *OX*; when price increases to OP_1' the quantity demanded reduces to OX_1; also when price falls to OP_2' quantity demanded increases to OX_2.

Similarly, income demand shows us the quantities of goods that people are willing to purchase at different income levels, assuming other things remaining the same. For superior goods or normal goods, the income demand curve will have a positive slope, and for inferior goods, or Giffen goods, the income demand curve will be of a backward-bending type. Figure 13.7 shows the income demand curve for a superior or normal commodity. At *OY* level of income, the consumers buy *OX* quantity of commodity *X*. If income increases to OY_1, then people will demand OX_1 quantity of the commodity and for higher levels of income, more of commodity *X* will be demanded.

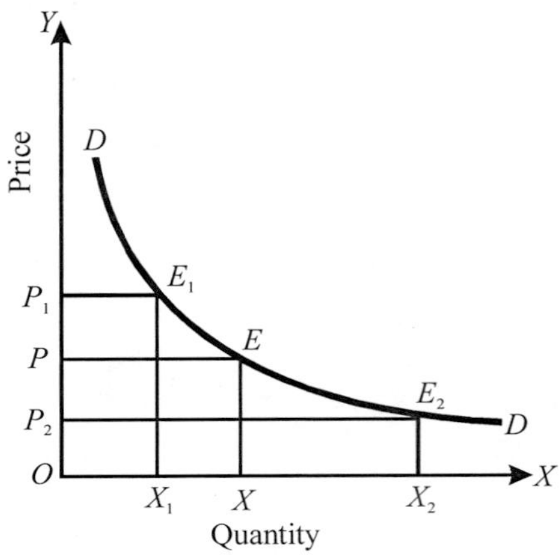

Fig. 13.6

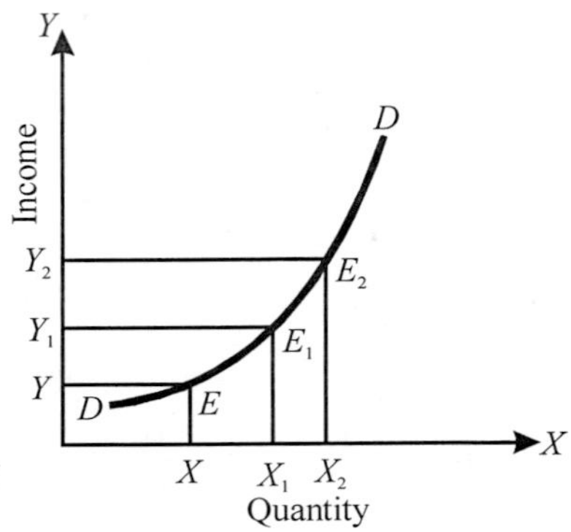

Fig. 13.7

Figure 13.8 indicates the case of an inferior good or a "Giffen good."[17] Here with every rise in income of a consumer above OY level of income will lead to a fall in quantity. At OY level of income, the consumer purchases OX quantity of commodity X. If his income increases to OY_1, then he demands only OX_1 of the commodity.

Now cross demand shows us the quantities of commodity X that people are willing to purchase at different prices of other commodities, say commodity Y (some related commodity), assuming *ceteris paribus*. Here, we may draw two types of demand curves—demand for substitutes and demand for complementary goods.

There are some commodities whose demand decreases as a result of an increase in the price (prices) of other commodity (or commodities), or their demand expands due to a decrease in the price (or prices) of other commodity (or commodities). Such, commodities are known as complementary commodities. The demand curve of these complementary goods has been drawn in Fig. 13.9. This demand curve is very similar to the normal or general demand curve.

In Fig. 13.9, X and Y are complementary goods. If price of Y increases from OP to OP_1, then the demand for X decreases from OX to QX_1.

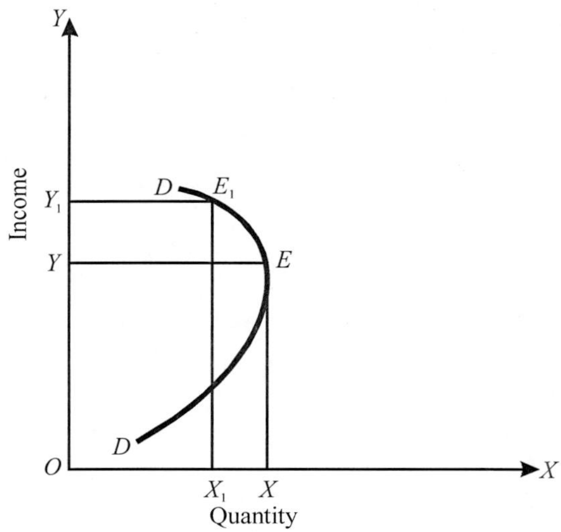

Fig. 13.8

17. Although Giffen good is an inferior good, but every inferior good cannot be a Giffen good. Because in the case of an inferior income effect is negative, but in the case of a Giffen good the negative income effect is strong enough to more than swamp the positive substitution effect of a given price change.

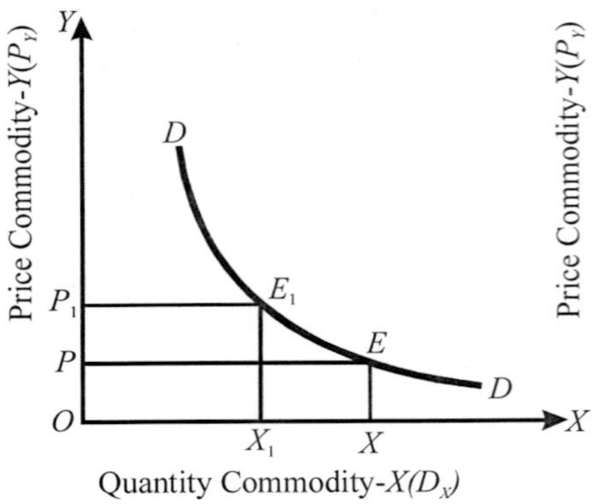

Fig. 13.9

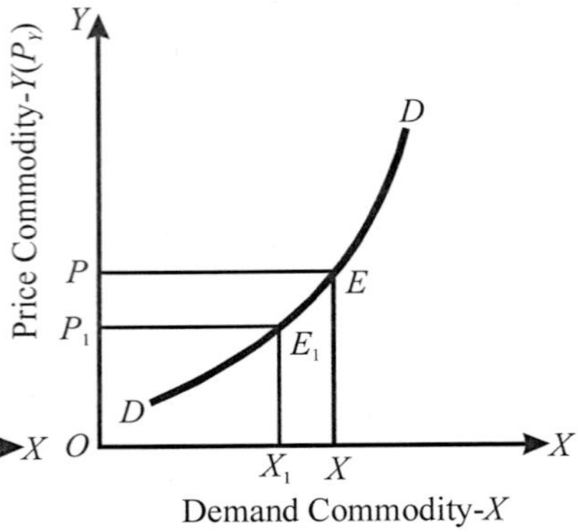

Fig. 13.10

Figure 13.10 shows the demand curve of substitute goods. It has a positive slope, because a decrease (or increase) in the price of *Y* will lead to a decrease (or increase) in the demand for *X*.

The demand for complementary goods is also known as *joint demand.* For example, there is a joint demand for tennis rackets and tennis balls, automobiles and automobile tyres. More generally, the demand for any product is always a joint demand for the resources used to produce it. Also, the demand for any commodity or service may be a *composite demand,* compounded out of the demand for a number of different uses, e.g., demand for leather is a composite demand of the demand for leather for shoes, for pocket books, etc. Of these various types of demand, the one frequently used is the price-demand.

12. THE DETERMINANTS OF THE DEMAND CURVE[18]

As we have already discussed under the demand function that the following fundamental factors will determine the demand for a commodity:

(1) ***Price of the Commodity.*** The first and the most important obvious determinant is the price of the commodity which is being demanded. As the law of demand states, in general, larger quantities of a commodity will be purchased at lower prices. We also observe that a 10 per cent reduction of price will lead to very different percentage increases of

18. George J. Stiglar, *The Theory, of Price,* pp. 86-88.

purchases of various goods; the elasticities of demand for various commodities are most diverse.

(2) ***Urgency of Consumer Needs.*** The other thing that affects elasticity of demand is the urgency of consumers need for the commodity in question. In the case of luxuries, demand is usually pretty elastic. These are items which we can do without; consequently, when they become more expensive, we curtail our purchases of them. Conversely, when they become cheaper, we buy them more freely. The demand for necessities, on the other hand, is usually more or less inelastic. For instance, if the price of bread were doubled, purchases would not decrease very greatly. Consumers would feel that they must have their usual quantity of bread, even at the high price. Rather than be deprived of it, they would go without other things that they considered less essential. Demand is also inelastic in the case of commodities which are very low in price, but for a different reason. Such things as matches, salt, or spool cotton, which cost but a few paise, represent so small a percentage of our total expenditures that we buy all we desire of them without much thought of economy. Lower the price, and very few more will be bought, for everyone has already all that he needs. Raise the price to even double what it was still the amount is so small that consumers will not greatly curtail their purchases. However, if the price were raised ten or a hundred fold, this would no longer be true, and a considerable reduction in consumption (demand) might be made.

(3) ***The Degree of Substitution.*** The degree to which substitutes for a, given commodity are available also has much to do with elasticity of demand. Commodities for which there are good substitutes will have high demand elasticities; commodities for which there are only poor substitutes will have low elasticities.

(4) ***Income of the Consumer.*** Another determinant of the quantity demanded by a consumer is his income. *Ceteris paribus,* there will be some correlation between income and demand elasticities, however, changes in income will be accompanied by changes in the purchases of various goods and services. The income elasticity of demand will assume different values for different goods. Necessities are not much responsive to changes in income while goods are very responsive to changes in income. Generally speaking, the influence of income change upon the demand for commodities will depend upon the value of the marginal propensity to save of the consumers. The lower the marginal propensity to save, the more will be the income elasticity of demand and vice versa.

(5) *Price of Related Goods.* One of the important determinants of demand is the prices of the related goods. In the case of substitute goods, if the price of commodity *Y* falls, then it will lead to a reduction in the demand for commodity *X.* Similarly, if the goods are complementary, then a rise in the price of *X* will lead to a reduction in the demand for *Y,* because *X* and *Y* both are jointly demanded.

(6) *Size of Population.* The demand for a good will also depend upon size of the population in the economy. An increase in population will lead to an increase in the demand for a good and vice versa.

The future expectations about the price of the commodity and the various policies of the government are also some of the determinants of the demand for a commodity. We, generally, assume these determinants of demand to be constants while drawing a demand curve. Any change in any of these other determinants will lead to a shift in the demand curve.

13. CHANGE IN DEMAND AND CHANGE IN QUANTITY DEMANDED

According to Friedman, in the demand analysis, it is necessary to make a clear distinction between "demand" in the *schedule sense* and "demand" in the *sense of quantity demanded.* Here we must be very careful about our use of the words, because the concept of changing demand in everyday speech is beclouded with some confusion, which must be clarified. In this concept the following statements are important: (*i*) "The price went up and therefore demand went down", and (*ii*) "Demand went up and therefore price went up." Each statement separately looks sensible, yet the two are clearly' contradictory if the word "demand" is supposed to have the same meaning in both. Of course, it does not. In the first statement the word demand means quantity demanded, while in the second statement the word demand means demand schedule.

Sometimes, we find that the demand does not change only because of a change in price. Demand can, and does, increase or decrease without any change in price. In such case, when the price remains the same but the demand either increases or decreases, the entire demand curve is shifted either to the right or to the left. It shifts to the right in the case of an increase in demand and to the left in the case of a decrease in demand. This is called change in demand. We refer to these changes as *shifts in the demand curves.* In other words, there has some force at work which has altered the demand situation such that there will be a shift in it. These forces which influence the demand curve are many.

An increase in consumer income may result in a willingness on the, part of consumers to buy a larger quantity of a product at each price. In this case our demand curve will shift to the right (from *DD* to D_1P_1 for example) as shown in Fig. 13.11. If, on the other hand, consumers decide to purchase less of a product at each price, then the demand curve will shift to the left from *DD* to D_2D_2 (for example), as shown in Fig. 13.11. A change in income may bring a change in consumer preference, but other factors, such as technology, may also change preferences and tastes.

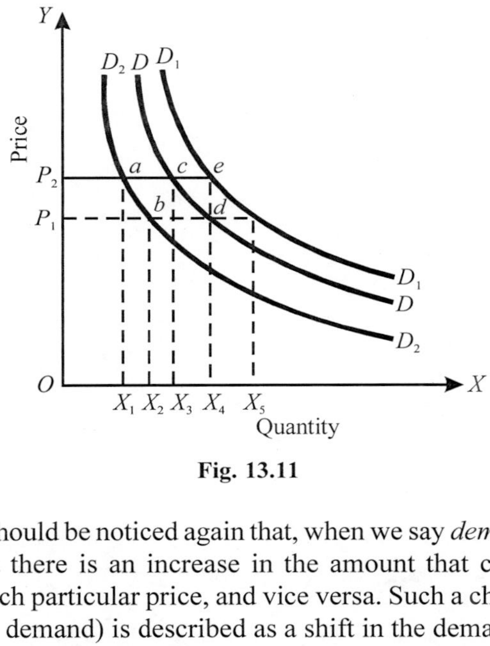

Fig. 13.11

Therefore, it should be noticed again that, when we say *demand increases,* we mean that there is an increase in the amount that consumers will purchase at each particular price, and vice versa. Such a change (increase or decrease in demand) is described as a shift in the demand curve. This is different from a movement along a demand curve.

When we talk about extension (or expansion) of demand and contraction of demand, then we refer to the movement along the same demand curve. Extension of demand means an *increase in the quantity demanded* while contraction of demand means a *decrease in the quantity demanded.* Hence, an increase (or decrease) in demand should not be confused with an increase (or decrease) in the quantity demanded because of a fall (rise) in price. A change in the quantity demanded as a result of the change in the price of a given commodity alone (other factors such as income, technology, etc. remaining unchanged) does not require the draw-ing of a new demand curve as shown in Fig. 13.12.

Figure 13.12 indicates that when price increases from OP to OP_1, quantity demanded reduces from OX to OX_1. Also, if price falls to OP_2, quantity demanded would increase to OX_2. On a particular demand curve, the movement from one point to another represents the law of demand, be cause it indicates the effect of a price change on the quantity demanded assuming *ceteris paribus*.

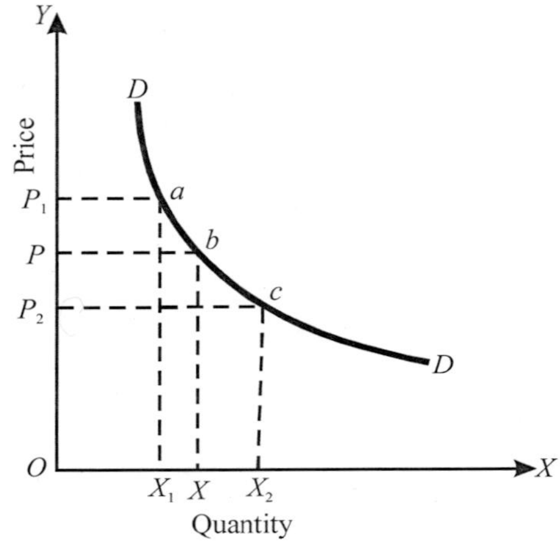

Fig. 13.12

13. REASONS FOR THE NEGATIVE SLOPE OF THE DEMAND CURVE

These are the following reasons for the negative slope of the demand curve or for the operation of the law of demand:

(1) ***The Law of Diminishing Marginal Utility.*** According to the law of diminishing marginal utility, as a consumer consumes more of a given commodity, the marginal utility of the additional units will diminish. Further, the price of a commodity that the consumer is ready to pay will not be greater than the marginal utility of it. Therefore, a consumer will buy more units of a commodity only if its price goes down. Hence, the law of demand holds.

(2) ***Substitution Effect.*** The law of demand states that when the price of a commodity goes down, its demand will rise. The reason is that substitutes of the commodity are available in the market. If the price of a commodity goes down, other things being the same (i.e., the prices of its

substitutes remain unchanged), the consumer would like to substitute this commodity in place of other substitute goods. To what extent the substitution takes place will depend upon the degree of substitutability. This part of a rise in the demand for a good due to a fall in its price is known as substitution effect.

(3) ***Income Effect.*** When the price of a commodity goes down, the real income of the consumer will increase. In other words, if the consumer buys the same basket of goods, he can easily save a part of his money income. This amount can be spent on any commodity, depending upon the desire of the consumer. Since the consumer, buys more of a commodity as its price declines, this means he is spending more on it. This part of increase in consumption is known as the income effect.

The above are some of these important reasons for the negative slope of the demand curve. But we may also find certain exceptions of it which we have already explained.

EXERCISES

1. Explain fully the law of diminishing marginal utility. What is the practical importance of this law? Do you think that the law is universally applicable?
2. Define utility. Explain the relationship between total utility and marginal utility with the help of a diagram.
3. State and explain the law of equi-marginal utility. What are its assumptions and limitations?
4. How does a consumer maximise his total utility function under the utility analysis?
5. Explain the 'law of proportionality' in consumption. Discuss its limitations.
6. Explain the importance of the law of equi-marginal utility. What are its limitations?
7. "The application of the Principle of Substitution extends over almost every field of economic enquiry." (Marshall). Explain this statement.
8. Define utility. Distinguish between marginal utility from total utility. Prove that the total utility of a commodity is maximum only when its marginal utility is zero. Illustrate your answer with the help of a diagram.
9. Why does the demand curve slope downwards to the right? Under what circumstances a demand curve slopes upward to the right?
10. Analyse the circumstances in which a fall in the price of a commodity leads to a fall in its demand.
11. State and explain the assumptions underlying the demand curve in Marshallian analysis.
12. Explain how the demand for a commodity is affected by: (*i*) change in the price of other commodity, and (*ii*) changes in the income of the consumer.

Multiple Choice Questions

13. (*i*) Utility is always related to
    (*a*) Usefulness (*c*) Profit
    (*b*) Want satisfying power (*d*) Maximum returns [*Ans*. (*b*)]

(*ii*) The Cardinal Utility Approach was developed by
    (*a*) Marshall (*c*) Fisher
    (*b*) Hicks (*d*) Samuelson [*Ans*. (*a*)]

(*iii*) Total Utility is maximum when Marginal Utility is
    (*a*) Positive (*c*) Zero
    (*b*) Negative (*d*) Maximum [*Ans*. (*c*)]

(*iv*) Marginal Utility (*MU*) is equal to Average Utility (*AU*) when
    (*a*) *MV* is maximum (*c*) *AU* is minimum
    (*b*) *AU* is maximum (*d*) *MU* is minimum [*Ans*. (*b*)]

(*v*) An individual's demand for goods is
    (*a*) the amount he will buy at any given price
    (*b*) the total amount he is able to buy
    (*c*) his ability to buy a given quantity
    (*d*) the satisfaction he obtains from a given quantity [*Ans*. (*a*)]

(*vi*) In the typical demand schedule, quantity demanded
    (*a*) varies directly with price
    (*b*) varies proportionately with price
    (*c*) varies inversely with price
    (*d*) is independent of price [*Ans*. (*c*)]

(*vii*) A fall in the price of a commodity leads to
    (*a*) a shift in demand
    (*b*) a fall in demand
    (*c*) a rise in the consumer's real income
    (*d*) a fall in the consumer's real income [*Ans*. (*c*)]

(*viii*) In the case of a Giffen good, like bajra, a fall in its price tends to
    (*a*) increase the demand (*c*) change demand in an abnormal way
    (*b*) reduce the demand (*d*) more the demand remain constant
    [*Ans*. (*b*)]

Chapter 14

THE INDIFFERENCE CURVE APPROACH

1. INTRODUCTION

The real elaboration of the indifference curves was made by Hicks and Allen. In 1934, J.R. Hicks and R.G.D. Allen wrote an article, 'A Reconstruction of the Theory of Value' in *Economica* (Feb., May 1934) presenting the indifference curve analysis. A detailed treatment of the new approach is to be found in Hicks' famous work entitled, *Value and Capital* published in 1939. The new analysis or the indifference curve analysis is also known as substitution analysis. Here, the diminishing marginal rate of substitution (*MRS*) is the basic concept.

The great merit of indifference curve analysis is that it leads to ordinal measurement of utility. The consumer needs is not assign specific amount to the utility he derives from the consumption of a good or a combination of goods. He is simply capable of comparing the different utilities or satisfactions in the sense whether one level of satisfaction is equal to or lower than or higher than another. He cannot determine how much one level of satisfaction is higher or lower than the other. For the purpose of explaining the consumer's behaviour, it is quite sufficient to assume that the consumer is able to rank his preference consistently. Thus, the ordinal measurement of utility has a greater element of realism than the cardinal measurement of utility. It is why the indifference curve analysis is now regarded as superior to the old utility analysis.

2. MEANING OF INDIFFERENCE CURVES

A consumer possesses a definite scale of preferences for goods and services. Each scale of preference consists of a number of alternative combinations of two or more goods, which give the consumer the same amount of satisfaction, so that if he chooses any out of many alternative combinations, he is neither better nor worse off. He is, therefore, found indifferent towards these various combinations. Such combinations of commodities as between which an individual is indifferent are called *indifference combinations.*

On the basis of above description one can think of combinations of numerous commodities which yield an equal level of satisfaction to the consumer. For convenience we assume that there are only two commodities under consumption. The points of indifference, at a particular level of satisfaction, when joined together produce a curve which is kown as the indifference curve. In other words, ***an indifference curve is a locus or path indicating different combinations of commodities X and Y which yield an equal level of satisfaction.*** An indifference curve is also known as an isoutility or an iso-satisfaction curve.

For the purpose of drawing an indifference curve, we require an indifference schedule. An indifference schedule may be defined as a schedule of various combinations of the two commodities that will equally be acceptable to the consumer. According to Prof. Watson, "An indifference schedule is a list of combinations of two commodities, the list being so arranged that a consumer is indifferent to the combinations, preferring none of any others."[1]

An imaginary indifference schedule is given in Table 14.1.

Table 14.1: Indifference Schedule

Combinations	*Quantity of X*		*Quantity of Y*		*Total Satisfaction*
I	1 *X*	+	20 *Y*	=	Z
II	2 *X*	+	12 *Y*	=	Z
III	3 *X*	+	7 *Y*	=	Z
IV	4 *X*	+	4 *Y*	=	Z
V	5 *X*	+	3 Y	=	Z

In Table 14.1, five different combinations of *X* and *Y* commodities are given. By definition all these combinations give the consumer the same level of total satisfaction Z. Thus, the consumer is indifferent as to whether he gets the first combination, of 1 unit of *X* + 20 units of *Y,* or the second combination of 2 units of *X* + 12 units of *Y,* or the last fifth combination of 5 units of *X* + 3 units of *Y.* We find from the indifference schedule that, while the quantity of *X* is increasing, that of *Y* is diminishing. This is true because the consumer has to remain at the same level of total

1. D.S. Watson, *Price Theory and Its Uses,* p. 77.

satisfaction. When the consumer is at the second combination, he is less eager to keep commodity Y than when he is lower down on the fifth combination. That is why, he is willing to surrender 8 units of Y for 1 unit of X in the former position and only 1 unit off for 1 unit of X in the latter position. But in all cases he derives the same total satisfaction. We have discussed only one indifference schedule, but there may be a number of indifference schedules of the two commodities. The various indifference schedules may represent different levels of total satisfaction yielded by a consumer.

Now, if the indifference schedule is plotted on a graph and the various points of combinations are joined by a curve, then the resulting curve is the indifference curve [see Fig.14.1 (A)]. Several other indifference curves can be drawn on the same principle. They will represent different levels of total satisfaction. But all points on any indifference curve, must represent the same level of satisfaction. Also, the higher the indifference curve, the more will be the level of satisfaction. It is because of the fact that as the consumer shifts to the right from one indifference curve to another, he gets more of one or both the commodities. For example, in Fig. 14.1 (B) at point C on indifference curve IC_2, he gets the same units of Y as a point f on indifference curve IC_1' but more units of commodity X. Thus, point C is preferred to point f.

From the above description, it is clear that an indifference curve shows nothing about the absolute amount of satisfaction or utility derived by the consumer. It merely shows the various combinations which will give equal satisfaction to the consumer. In fact indifference curve is a curve showing equal satisfaction in different combinations of goods. Every point

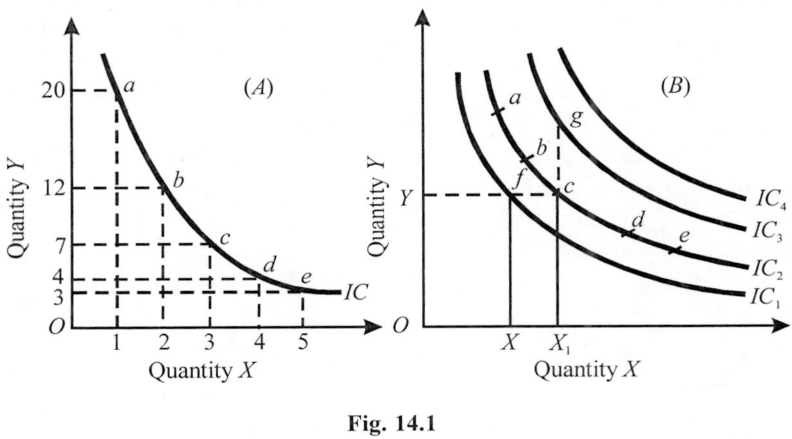

Fig. 14.1

given on indifference curve represents a different combination. It is, therefore, a matter of indifference for the consumer whether he chooses one combination or the other. The consumer is found as indifferent between all such combinations, which represent the same level of satisfaction.

A family of indifference curves is known as *indifference map.* In Fig. 14.1 (B) we represent an indifference map off our indifference curves IC_1, IC_2, IC_3, and IC_4. The indifference curve, labelled higher number is preferred to one labelled lower number. In the words of Stonier and Hague, "An indifference curve is, thus like a counter line on a map which shows all places at the same height above sea level. Instead of representing height, each indifference curve represents a level of satisfaction. It is, however, quite impossible to measure levels of satisfaction in the way that one can measure heights above sea level. There are obviously no units of measurement. One can say whether one indifference curve represents a higher or lower level of satisfaction than another, but one cannot say by how much satisfaction is higher or lower."[2]

Thus, it must be noted that though by definition, every combination of X and Y on indifference curve IC_2 is preferred to every other combination of X and Y on indifference curve IC_1, there may be infinite number of indifference curves in between, and by definition, all of them will also be preferred to IC_1.[3]

3. ASSUMPTIONS OF INDIFFERENCE CURVE ANALYSIS

The indifference curve analysis is based on the following important assumptions:

(1) ***Complete knowledge about the market.*** The consumer possesses full knowledge about all matters pertaining to his consumption decisions. For example, he knows the complete range of goods and services available in the market. He also knows the technical capacity of each commodity to satisfy his want. He possesses the information regarding the prices of various goods and services.

(2) ***Entire income is spent on consumption.*** The budget constraints of a consumer are the given prices of different goods and services and the constant income of the consumer.

---

2. Stonier and Hague, A Textbook *of Economic Theory,* p. 45.
3. In general, an indifference curve can be represented on the basis of (ordinal) utility function as

$$U = f(x, y)$$

where U is a constant. An indifference map is generated by assigning different values to U.

Under the budget constraint, we have assumed that the consumer spends his entire income to attain his objective of maximising satisfaction.

(3) ***Scale of preference can be expressed.*** Every consumer has a scale of ordered preferences which enables him to compare any two combinations of two or more goods and to decide whether or not a given combination of any two goods, say Q_1 and Q_2, is preferred, not preferred or equivalent to any other combination of Q_1 and Q_2. Naturally, he can indicate when between two particular combinations of goods he is *indifferent,* i.e., likes them equally. It must be noted that indifference in this context does not mean indecision. It only implies that the consumer assigns the same rank order to both the combinations of goods.

The taste of the consumer can therefore be described with the ideas of preference and indifference. If he can choose between two goods or combinations of goods, he always prefers one to the other or else he is indifferent. Here we observe that the only assumption is that the consumer prefers or is indifferent. Why he prefers can be left out of it? And so can by how much the consumer prefers. This last is the assumption omitted in the indifference curve analysis and is not needed.

(4) ***Preference towards a combination of goods.*** The indifference curve analysis assumes that the consumer is not interested in any one commodity at a particular time as asserted by the utility analysis, but he is interested in a combination of goods and services. He is able to compare the total satisfaction derived by one particular combination of goods with that given by other.

(5) ***Rational behaviour.*** The indifference curve analysis also assumes that the consumer acts in a rational manner.

(6) ***Falling marginal rate of substitution.*** The marginal rate of substitution of one commodity for another is always falling.

4. MARGINAL RATE OF SUBSTITUTION (MRS)

According to Leftwich, **"The marginal rate of substitution of *X* for *Y* (MRS_{XY}) is defined as the amount of *Y* the consumer is just willing to give up to get an additional unit of *X* (and still remain on the same indifference curve)."**[4]

Table 14.2 explains the concept of diminishing marginal rate of substitution. To get a second unit of *X,* the consumer is ready to give up 8 units of *Y.* For a third unit of *X,* he can give up the consumption of only 5 units of *Y;* for a fourth unit of *X,* he is ready to sacrifice only 3 units of

4. Richard H. Leftwich, *The Price System and Resource Allocation,* 4th edition, p. 72.

Table 14.2

Combinations	*Quantity of X (in units)*		*Quantity of Y (in units)*	*Marginal Rate of Substitution* (MRS_{XY})
I	1 *X*	+	20 *Y*	—
II	2 *X*	+	12 *Y*	1 *X* = 8 *Y*
III	3 *X*	+	7 *Y*	1 *X* = 5 *Y*
IV	4 *X*	+	4 *Y*	1 *X* = 3 *Y*
V	5 *X*	+	3 *Y*	1 *X* = 1 *Y*

Y and for a fifth unit of *X*, he will sacrifice only one unit of *Y*. It means that, as the consumer gets more and more units of *X*, he is willing to surrender fewer and fewer units of *Y* for each additional unit of *X*. This because of the fact that the importance of good *X* in terms of *Y* goes on falling with each addition to his total of the former (good *X*). This feature of the consumer's behaviour is known as the ***principle of diminishing marginal rate of substitution.***

As mentioned above, a consumer gets the same level of satisfaction along a given indifference curve. It means that an increase in the quantity of commodity *X* is always accompanied by a similar decrease in the quantity of commodity *Y* and thus the marginal rate of substitution must be negative. Symbolically,

$$MRS_{XY} = -\frac{\Delta X}{\Delta Y} \qquad \ldots(1)$$

where ΔX represents change in *X* and ΔY represents change in *Y*.

Equation (1) represents the slope of indifference curve at a particular point. Since each addition in *X* leads *Y* to diminish less and less, the numerical value of the slope of indifference curve also goes on falling. This situation has been shown in Fig. 14.2.

In Fig. 14.2, the total satisfaction remains constant between combination point *A, B, C,* and *D* on indifference curve IC_0. However, the composition of commodity *X* and commodity *Y* changes while the consumer moves from point *A* to *B, B* to *C* and *C* to *D*.

Thus, MRS_{XY} is nothing but the slope of an indifference curve. MRS_{XY} measures the ratio of the marginal utility of *Y* to the marginal utility of *X*. This implies that *MRS* and marginal utility are sim-ilar concepts. According to Prof. Hicks, although utility is not measurable, we may still give a precise meaning to the ratio of the marginal utilities, when the quantities of both the commodities are given. In his opinion, this quantity

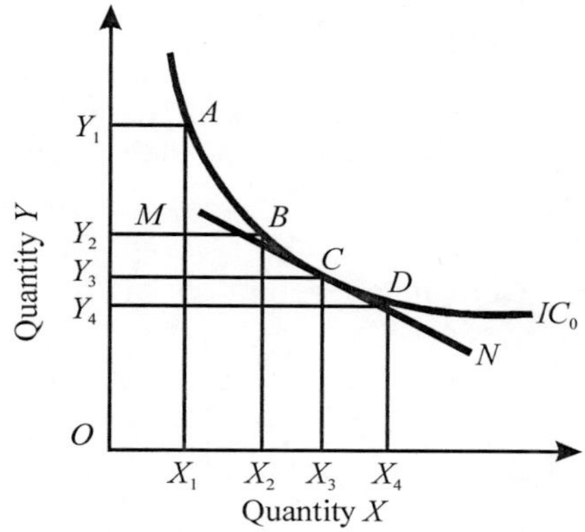

Fig. 14.2

is represented by the slope of an indifference curve; and the slope of indifference curve represents the ratio of the marginal utility.[5]

5. PROPERTIES OR CHARACTERISTICS OF INDIFFERENCE CURVES

There are five basic properties or characteristics of indifference curves:

(1) Indifference curves have a negative slope,

(2) Indifference curves are convex to the origin,

(3) Indifference curves never intersect each other,

(4) Indifference curves need not be parallel to each other, and

(5) A higher indifference curve is always preferred to a lower one.

Now we shall discuss in detail the above properties of indifference curves in the following manner:

(1) ***Indifference curves have a negative slope.*** It means that each indifference curve slopes downward nom left to the right as shown in Fig. 14.3 (a). The negative slope implies that if the consumer is to attain the same level of satisfaction, then for an increase in the stock of one commodity he is required to forgo certain units of the other commodity.

If an indifference curve does not have a negative slope, then the three possible situations may be that: (*i*) it is horizontal to *X* axis, or (*ii*) it is vertical to *X* axis, or (*iii*) it may have a positive slope. These three inconceivable situations are shown in Fig. 14.3 (b), 14.3 (c) and 14.3 (d) respectively. If we are able to disprove these three possibilities, then the

5. J.R. Hicks, *Value and Capital;* pp. 19-20.

only true situation of indifference curve is its downward sloping represented in Fig. 14.3 (a).

Suppose, an indifference curve is a horizontal line as shown in Fig. 14.3(b). As the consumer moves from point *A* to *B* an increase in the quantity of *X* is unaccompanied by any change in the quantity of *Y*, and thus the consumer gets more satisfaction at point *B* than at point *A* on the same indifference curve. But, by definition, this would not be the true situation of indifference curve.

Now suppose an indifference curve is a vertical line as shown in Fig. 14.3 (c). Here also, as the consumer moves from point *A* to *B*, the amount of *X* remaining the same while the amount of *Y* decreases and therefore, the consumer gets more satisfaction at point *A* than at point *B*. In this situation too, total satisfaction (utility) changes with every movement along the curve and hence, by definition, this will not be the true shape of an indifference curve.

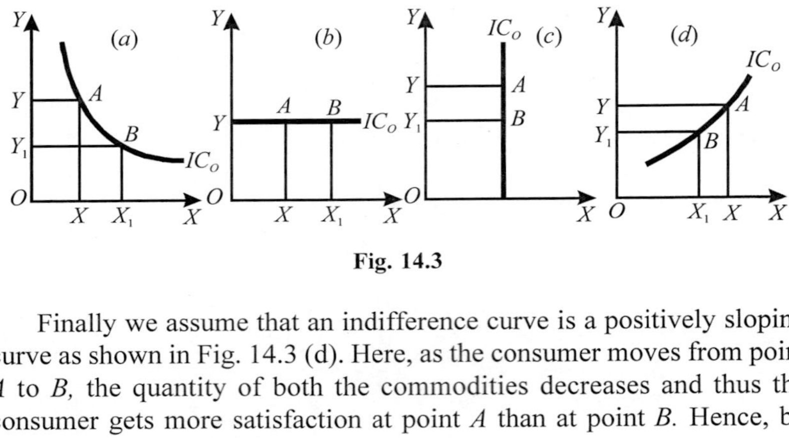

Fig. 14.3

Finally we assume that an indifference curve is a positively sloping curve as shown in Fig. 14.3 (d). Here, as the consumer moves from point *A* to *B*, the quantity of both the commodities decreases and thus the consumer gets more satisfaction at point *A* than at point *B*. Hence, by definition, we also reject this case.

Now, we are also to say that in neither of the three cases (horizontal, vertical and upward sloping curves), the consumer remains *indifferent* between two points and in such cases he is not substituting one commodity for another. But in a true case he must substitute one commodity for another, because his total satisfaction remains the same. Only on a curve that slopes downwards to the right, this requirement is fulfilled. Therefore, indifference curve must slope downward from left to the right.

(2) ***Indifference curves are convex to the origin.*** This is an important property of an indifference curve which can be derived from the *law of*

diminishing marginal rate of substitution. Convexity implies that the consumer is prepared to sacrifice decreasing quantities of *Y* for each given increment in the quantity of *X*. In other words, the greater the number of units of *X* that are acquired, the smaller will be the number of units of *Y* that will be substituted to maintain the given level of satisfaction.

If marginal rate of substitution is constant, the indifference curve would be a straight line and if it is increasing, then the indifference curve would be a concave. In real world, the *MRS* is neither constant nor increasing, but it is diminishing as we move from left to right. Since the principle of diminishing marginal rate of substitution holds in real life, we may explain it with the help of a convex indifference curve as in Fig. 14.4.

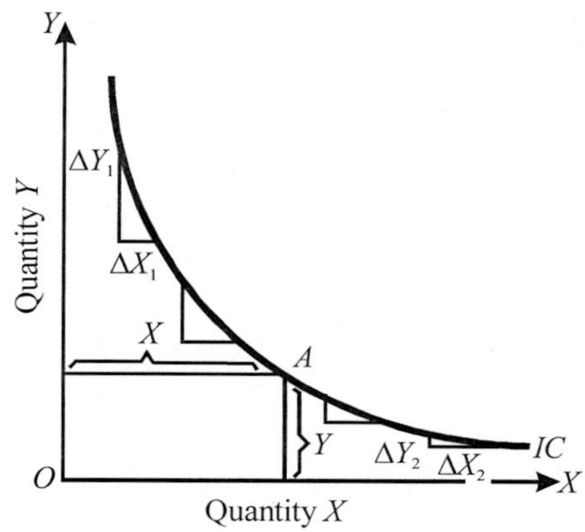

Fig. 14.4

At the top of the curve, the consumer gives up ΔY_1 of *Y* for ΔX_1 of *X* as he slides down the curve. Here the consumer has lots of *Y* and not much of *X*; hence, he is willing to forgo ΔY_1 units of *Y* to get ΔX_1 units of *X*. Thus, the length ΔY_1 is greater than the length ΔX_1—at the top of the curve. But as the consumer moves down to the right of the curve, the relative quantities of *X* and *Y* change. In Fig. 14.4, the distance ΔX is uniform for each time. The lengths of the lines ΔY become shorter and shorter as the consumer moves to the right of the curve *IC*. This signifies that when the consumer has lots of X and not much of *Y*, he will be ready to sacrifice a little of *Y* to get the same number of units of *X*. As we see in Fig. 14.4, how short is the length of ΔY_2 at the bottom of the curve *IC*.

Thus, it proves the principle of diminishing marginal rate of substitution $\left(\frac{\Delta Y}{\Delta X}\right)$, and indifference curve is always convex to the origin. But the degree of convexity of an indifference curve depends upon the ease or difficulty of substitution between the two goods.

(3) ***Indifference curves never intersect.*** We know that each indifference curve represents a particular level of satisfaction and, therefore, it must be different from other indifference curves. To prove the property that two indifference curves never cut each other, let us assume a situation where the two cut each other as shown in Fig. 14.5. In Fig. 14.5 indifference curve IC_1 cuts indifference curve IC_2 at point A. Now we take a point B on IC_1 which gives lower satisfaction than a point C on IC_2. But by definition of indifference curve we may write the following equality:

On IC_1, $\quad A = B$

On IC_2, $\quad A = C$

then $\quad B = C \quad$ ...(2)

Now, mathematically the equality (2) should hold, but as stated above, point B lies on IC_1 while point C lies on IC_2 and, therefore, the two levels

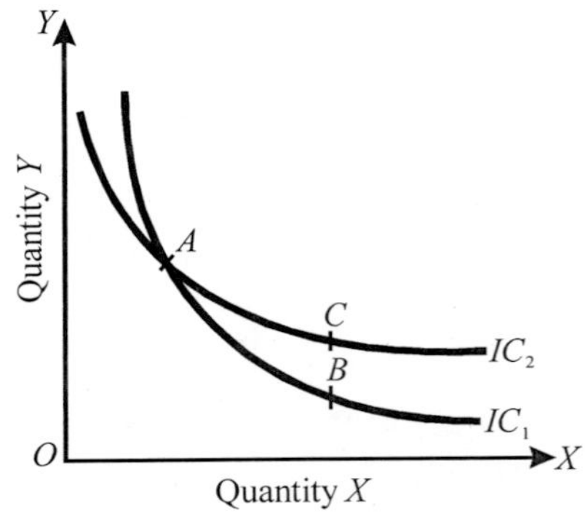

Fig. 14.5

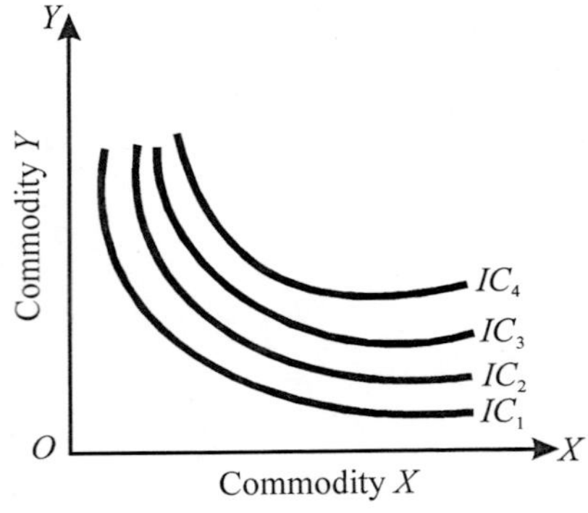

Fig. 14.6

of satisfaction are unequal. The equality (2) is clearly impossible and, therefore, indifference curves can never intersect each other.

(4) ***Indifference curves need not be parallel to each other.*** As we have noted, indifference curves have a negative slope and the marginal rate of substitution between the two commodities need not be the same in

all indifference curves. It depends upon consumer's preference which may change according to his economic position. Thus, it follows that indifference curves may be parallel or may not be parallel as the situation may be Fig. 14.6 indicates that some indifference curves are parallel while some others are not parallel.

(5) ***A higher indifference curve is always preferred to a lower one.*** We have already explained that on higher indifference curves the consumer gets more of one or both the commodities. If marginal utilities of these commodities are positive, then the consumer will certainly get more satisfaction on higher indifference curves. Naturally, a higher indifference curve will always be preferred to a lower one. Mathematically we may write

$$Y = F(U)$$

where $U = f(X, Y)$ and Z is a constant.

Now, total utility (U) along an indifference curve is constant, but Z is an increasing function of U. It means that higher the indifference curve, more will be the level of satisfaction. It also implies that if more units of both the commodities X and Y (or at least one of them) are offered to the consumer, total utility function, U, will go on increasing and as a result, Z will increase.

6. THE BUDGET CONSTRAINT LINE OR THE PRICE LINE

Before we discuss consumer's equilibrium, it is better to understand his budget line. Because, unless we have this information we cannot know how much of the two commodities the consumer will buy. The indifference map helps him only to put various sets of combinations in a certain imaginary order of preference. But, by itself, it does not tell him as to which particular combination to buy. In reality, the consumer is constrained by his money-income and the respective prices of the two commodities in question. If there is no such constraint, the consumer would maximise his total satisfaction by consuming X and Y to that level where the ratio of their marginal utilities becomes zero.

In other words, a consumer would like to go to the highest indifference curve. But this would not be the case in the real world and he has to confine his decision under his given constraints. His budget constraints are referred to as his "opportunity factors" which consist of three factors: (*i*) given money income (I); (*ii*) price of commodity X (P_X); and (*iii*) price of commodity Y (P_Y). If he spends his entire income on X and Y, then the budget equation becomes:

$$I = XP_X + YP_Y \qquad ...(3)$$

where I, P_X, and P_Y are exogenous variables and X and Yare endogenous variables.[6]

If the consumer spends his entire income on commodity X, then his budget, equation becomes:

$$I = X.P_X$$

$$X = \frac{I}{P_X} \qquad ...(4)$$

Similarly, if he spends his entire income on commodity Y, then his budget equation becomes:

$$I = Y.P_Y$$

$$Y = \frac{I}{P_Y} \qquad ...(5)$$

Equations (4) and (5) are the two extremes within which a consumer is able to fix quantities of X and Y to be purchased. There may be a number of combinations of X and Y which can be purchased by the given budget constraint. These combinations are shown by the help of a budget line in Fig. 14.7.

From equation (3) we may derive the equation of a budget line in the following manner:

$$I = X.P_X + Y.P_Y$$

$$Y = \frac{I}{P_Y} - \left(\frac{P_X}{P_Y}\right)X$$

or

$$Y = a - bX \qquad ...(6)$$

where $a = \frac{1}{P_Y}$ constant or intercept $b = \frac{P_X}{P_Y}$ slope of the budget line.

Equation (6) is the equation of a straight line. Here the ordinate intercept a shows the quantity of commodity Y when commodity X is not purchased at all. In Fig. 14.7, *MN* is the price line which is also known as *the consumption possibility curve* or *total outlay curve.*

---

6. Exogenous variables are those variables which are determined from outside and assumed to be constant in the model. Here income of the consumer price of X and Y are given from outside and thus are exogenous variables. Endogenous variables, on the other hand, are the variables which are determined within the model. Here the quantities of X and Y are to be determined and thus the variables X and Y are endogenous.

Let the consumer's money income be Rs. 100 and the price of *X* be Rs. 10 per unit and the price of *Y* be Rs. 5. Then the equation of the budget line will become

$$Y = 20 - 2X$$

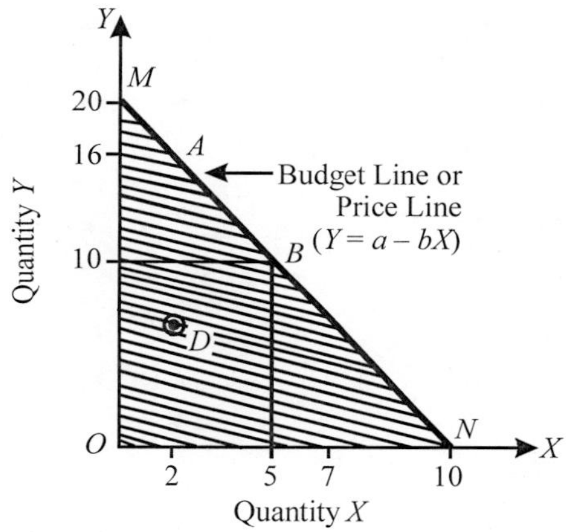

Fig. 14.7

Here, the consumer could buy 10 units of *X* if he spent his entire income on *X*, and he could buy 20 units of *Y* if he spent his entire income on *Y*. A straight line between 10 *X* and 20 *Y* shows every possibility of spending the income on the two commodities at their given prices. If we look at Fig. 14.7, we find that the consumer can buy 20 *Y* and zero of *X* or 16 *Y* and 2*X*, or 10 *Y* and 5*X*, or 6*Y* and 7*X*, etc. These possible combinations are shown by the points *M*, *A*, *B*, *C* and *N* on the price line *MN*.

Further, the consumer can also buy any quantity inside the shaded area under the price line *MN*, such as, combination *R*; but if he does this, he is not spending all of his income. To attain the objective of maximum satisfaction we assume that the consumer spends his entire income on his consumption. Also, the consumer is unable to purchase a combination of *X* and *Y* which lies outside the area of the price line such as point S in Fig. 14.7. The reason is that his constraints do not allow him to go beyond the price line *MN*. Thus, the problem of the consumer is to select a point (combination) on the price line which gives him maximum satisfaction. This will be discussed under the equilibrium of the consumer in the following section.

7. EQUILIBRIUM OF THE CONSUMER

How much of X and Y does the consumer purchase? In order to answer this question, we have to bring together the two earlier diagrams of the consumer's indifference map and the price line. This has been illustrated in Fig. 14.8. The price line MN indicates the various combinations of the two commodities X and Y which the consumer can purchase with the given income and given prices of the two commodities. In Fig. 14.8, the family of indifference curves IC_1, IC_2, IC_3 and IC_4 indicates the liking or preference of the consumer. In the absence of the budget line, the consumer would like to remain on the highest indifference curve IC_4, but with the given money income, the highest attainable level of sat-isfaction for the consumer is IC_2. Indifference curves IC_3 and IC_4 are beyond the approach of the consumer, as their attainment requires larger mon-ey income than what he has in his pocket.

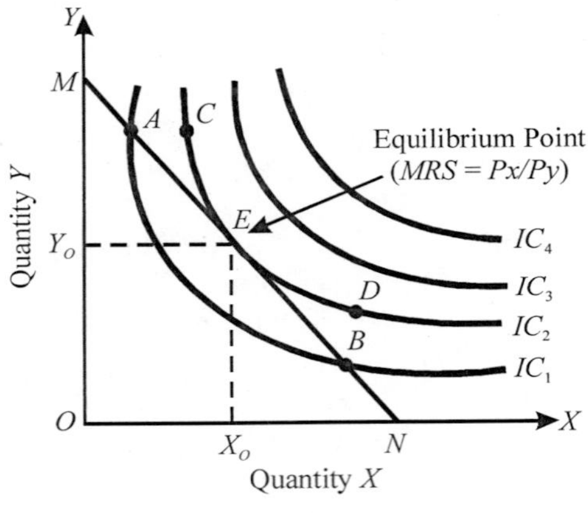

Fig. 14.8

Also, even on the indifference curve IC_2, only one particular combination point E is conceivable to the consumer and other points such as C or D are beyond the consumer's approach, as they lie outside the price line MN.

Thus, point E represents a unique combination of X and Y and it gives maximum satisfaction to the consumer. In other words, point E is the equilibrium point of the consumer where the equilibrium quantities of X and Y are OX_0 and OY_0 respectively. Here, we may notice that the point A and B on IC_1 are fairly attainable by the consumer, since they lie on the price line. But none of them represents the equilibrium point, because in this case the consumer has to remain on a lower indifference curve.

On the basis of above analysis, we may conclude that a consumer maximises his total satisfaction at a point where the indifference curve touches—is tangent to—the price line.

Here, we may observe that the Marshallian utility approach to consumer behaviour also predicted the same conclusion as the indifference curve analysis.

Thus, Marshallian and Hicksian conclusions are similar at the optimisation level. However, their approaches are still different, because Marshall's approach is based on the cardinal measurement of utility while Hicks' approach is based on the ordinal measurement of utility.

8. ABNORMAL INDIFFERENCE CURVES AND CORNER SOLUTION

In certain abnormal cases, the point where the indifference curve is tangent to the price line does not give maximum satisfaction to the consumer. These abnormal situations are the following:

1. When indifference curves are straight lines,
2. When indifference curves are concave to the origin,
3. When indifference curves are convex to the origin, but their slope is either greater or lower than the slope of the price line.

In the first case, the condition of tangency is not fulfilled because the price line and the indifference curve are merged into each other. In such a situation the equilibrium is indeterminate. This case has been illustrated in Fig. 14.9 (a). When the slope of indifference curve IC_0 is everywhere more or less steep than the slope of the price line *MN,* equilibrium will be attained at the corner point where the two curves meet each other. These situations have been shown in Fig. 14.9 (b) and 14.9 (c). The corner solutions are made at points *M* and *N* respectively. Under these situations, however, the consumer buys either *X* or *Y* and certainly not both.

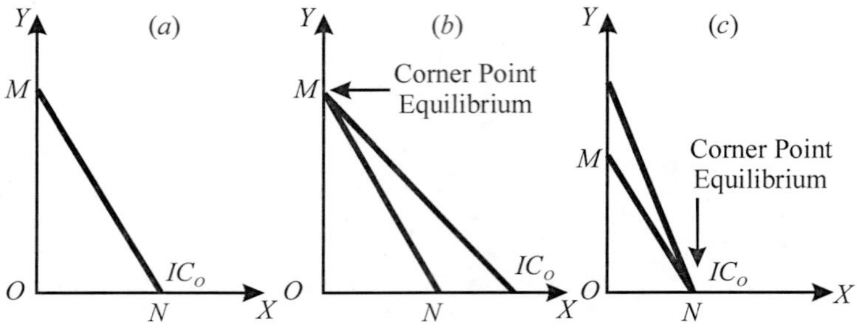

Fig. 14.9

In the second case (Fig. 14.10), when the indifference curves are concave, rather than convex, the MRS_{XY} increases as the consumer moves along the indifference curves. The condition of tangency (or the first order marginality condition) is satisfied at point *S*, $\left(MRS_{XY} = \frac{P_X}{P_Y}\right)$ but this point of tangency does not satisfy the objective of the consumer to attain maximum satisfaction. At point *S*, he remains on a lower indifference curve IC_1. In this situation, the consumer can increase his satisfaction by moving to point *T* which lies on a higher indifference curve IC_3. At point *T*, the consumer will specialise in the consumption of *X* alone. It is also possible that the consumer may specialize in the consumption of *Y* alone. It will depend upon the nature of the slope of indifference curves.

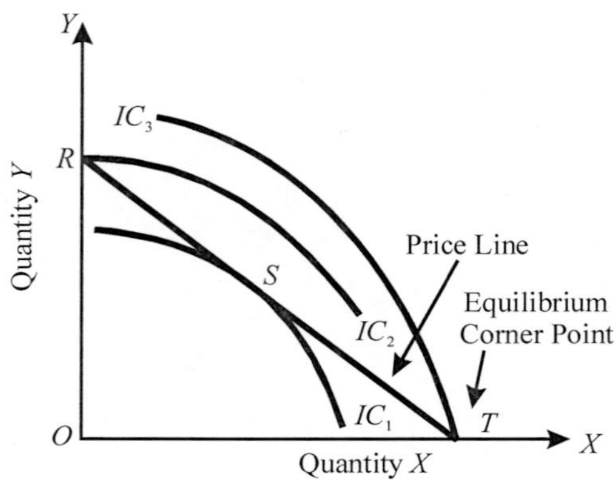

Fig. 14.10

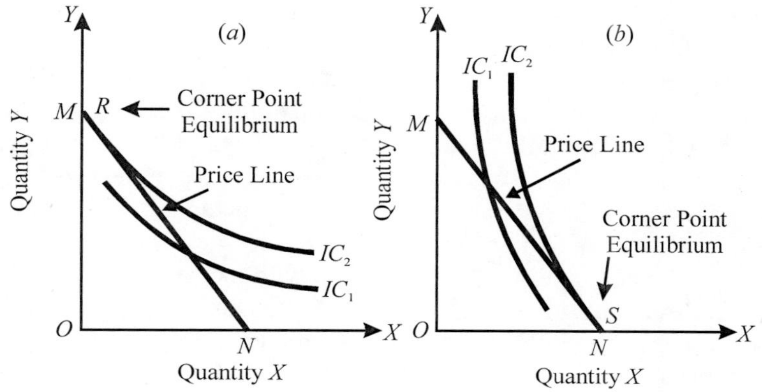

Fig. 14.11

In the third case, Fig. 14.11 (a) and (b), when the indifference curves are convex to the origin, but it does not fulfil the condition of tangency ($MRS_{XY} = P_X / P_Y$); the consumer consumes only one commodity in the optimum situation. If the slope of indifference curve is less steep than the price line i.e., the consumers equilibrium will be attained at the corner point *R* in Fig. 14.11 (a). Here the consumer spends his entire income on commodity *Y* and consumes *OM* units of *Y* only. If, on the other hand, the slope of indifference curve is more steep than the price line, i.e.,

$$MRS_{XY} > \frac{P_X}{P_Y}$$

the consumer's equilibrium will be attained at the corner points in Fig. 14.11 (b). Here the consumer spends his entire income on commodity *X* and consumes *ON* units of *X* only.

These above are the cases of corner equilibria —which do not hold in real life. Normally, consumers buy commodities in groups. They do not purchase a single commodity. Thus, these situations are particular situations where the ordinal utility function of the consumer is transformed as a function of only one commodity.

9. THE INCOME CONSUMPTION CURVE AND THE INCOME EFFECT

As we know that the Marshallian Utility approach is based on the assumption that the marginal utility of money is constant. It means that changes in consumer's money income do not affect the *MRS* between money and any particular commodity. It also implies that the demand for a commodity is independent of consumer's money income. But according to Prof. Hicks, the demand for a commodity is influenced by changes in consumer's income, although the magnitude of the effect depends on the nature of the commodity under consumption and the consumer's preference. It is in this context that the indifference curves analysis helps us to understand as how much the consumer's demand for a commodity changes in response to a given change in the income of the consumer or the price of a commodity. In other words, with the help of indifference analysis we are able to derive consumer's Engel curve (income-quantity) for a commodity or his demand curve (price-quantity relationship) for it.

In this section we shall consider, how the consumer's demand for a commodity will respond to changes in his income, with prices and his tastes remaining constant.

In general, the higher the income of a consumer, the more of a commodity he will buy. If the equation of his constraint is given as:

$$Y = \frac{1}{P_Y} - \frac{P_X}{P_Y} X$$

where $1/P_Y$ is the ordinate intercept and Px/Py is the slope of the budget line. If the money income (I) increases while the price ratio or the slope Px/Py remains the same, the ordinate intercept will increase and the new price line will be parallel to the old price. Thus, an increase in the consumer's income will cause his price line or outlay curve to shift upwards to the right. This new price line is tangent to a higher indifference curve. It means an increase in income puts the consumer on to a higher level of satisfaction. Similarly, a decrease in income will cause his price line to shift downwards to the left and the consumer comes down to a lower indifference curve.

This is shown in Fig. 14.12. The initial equilibrium position is at point E where the indifference curve IC_1 is tangent to the price line MN. If income increases, then the budget line shifts from MN to M_1N_1 and further from M_1N_1 to M_2N_2. The corresponding equilibrium position will also shift from point E to E_1 and further from E_1 to E_2. According to Prof. Hicks, the income consumption curve (*ICC*) is derived by joining these tangency points. The *ICC* shows the way in which consumption varies when income changes but prices of the two commodities remain unchanged. In other words, the *ICC* indicates the income effect of a given change on consumer's money income.

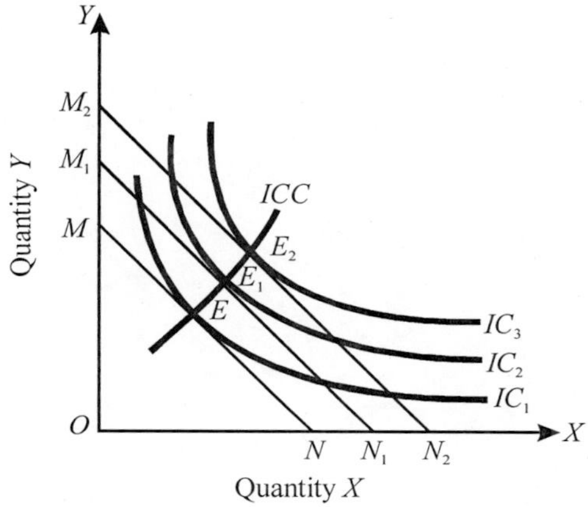

Fig. 14.12

In general (for normal goods), income consumption curves (*ICC*) slope upwards to the right, showing that as the consumer's income increases, his purchases of the two commodities also increase. But this need not be so in all cases.

For instance, in Fig. 14.13, we have three income consumption curves ICC_1, ICC_2 and ICC_3 which show that both the commodities *X* and *Y* are normal goods. Because as the consumer's income increases, he buys more of both. In Fig. 14.13, ICC_2 shows a more or less proportionate increase in expenditure on both the goods; ICC_1 shows the expenditure on commodity *X* is increasing but less than proportionately; and ICC_3 shows that the expenditure on commodity *X* is increasing more than proportionately.

Let us now discuss another case of income consumption curve where the consumer's expenditure on a particular good, instead of increasing, may actually decrease. This happens only when one of the goods is inferior.[7] The consumer consumes this inferior good in large quantities only when he is poor or his income is low. When his income increases he shifts his consumption of inferior good to a superior one. This phenomenon is known as Giffen's Paradox. These cases of inferior goods are shown in Fig. 14.14 (a) and 14.14 (b).

7. In the case of an inferior good, the quantity demanded decreases with increase in income, i.e., income effect is negative, or $\partial X/\partial I$.

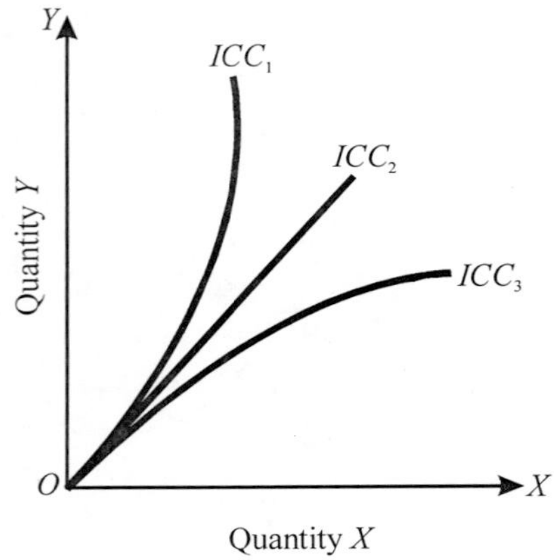

Fig. 14.13

Figure 14.14 (a) shows that after *R,* despite an increase in income, the consumer buys smaller quantity of *X.* In this situation, the *ICC* bends backward and *X* is termed as an inferior good, while *Y* still remains to be a superior good.

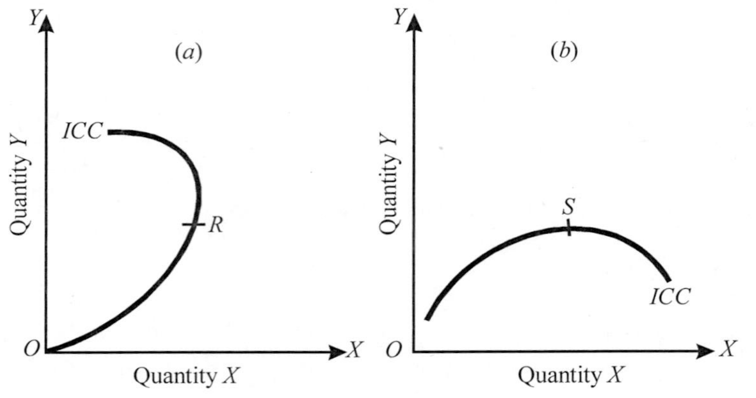

Fig. 14.14

Similarly, Fig. 14.14 (*b*) shows that after point *S*, despite an increase in income, the consumer buys smaller quantity of *Y.* In this case, the *ICC* slopes downward to the left after point *S* and it explains the inferior nature of good *Y.*

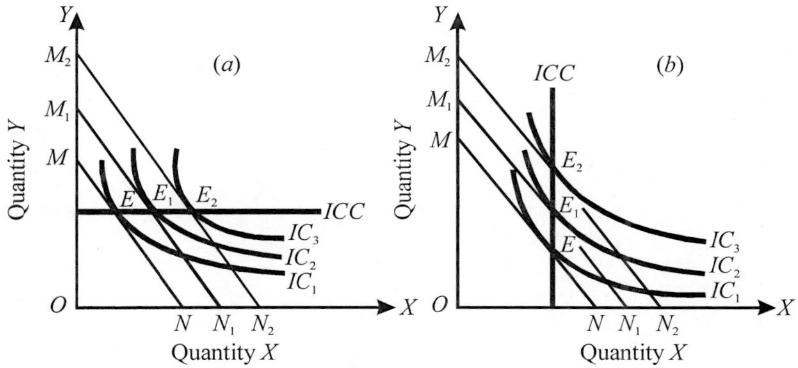

Fig. 14.15

Further, an income consumption curve may be horizontal. In this case, commodity X is a superior good because its consumption increases as income increases and commodity Y is a neutral good because its consumption neither increases nor decreases with an increase in the money income of the consumer. This situation has been illustrated in Fig. 14.15 (a). Similarly, when Y is a superior good and X is a neutral good, the income consumption curve would be a vertical line. This situation has been illustrated in Fig. 14.15 (b). Here, the consumption of Y increases as the money income of the consumer increases while the consumption of X remains unchanged at OX.

Now, on the basis of above discussion, we may sum up the relationship between the income consumption curves and the kind of goods to which they relate in Table 14.3.

Table 14.3

Shape of the Income Consumption Curve (ICC)	*Kind of Goods*	
	X	*Y*
Negative slope (ICC_1)	Superior	Inferior
Horizontal slope (ICC_2)	Superior	Neutral
Positive slope (ICC_3)	Superior	Superior
Vertical slope (ICC_4)	Neutral	Superior
Backward slope (ICC_5)	Inferior	Superior

The five types of *ICC* curves stated in Table 14.3 have been shown in Fig. 14.16. Their respective slopes indicate the nature of the commodities.

ICC_1 slopes negatively. Here after point *E,* the commodity *Y* becomes inferior while commodity *X* is still a superior good.

ICC_2 becomes horizontal after point *E* and thus *X* is a superior commodity while *Y* is a neutral good or necessary commodity; because after further increase in income after point *E,* the consumer does not increase its quantity.

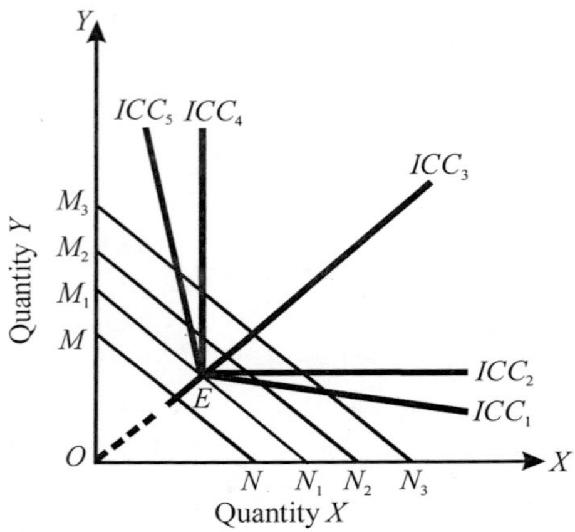

Fig. 14.16

ICC_3 is positively sloped which indicates that the two commodities *X* and *Y* are normal goods.

ICC_4 becomes vertical after point *E* and thus *Y* is a superior commodity and *X* becomes a neutral good or a necessary good.

ICC_5 bends backward after point *E* and thus commodity *X* becomes inferior while *Y* still serves as a superior good.

The above conclusions can also be expressed in terms of Engel Curves. Prof. A. Engel developed the laws of family expenditure on the basis of Engel Curves. This curve represents those quantities of a commodity which a consumer would purchase at different levels of money income assuming the prices and the preferences remaining unchanged.

10. THE SUBSTITUTION EFFECT

According to Stonier and Hague, "A substitution effect occurs when the relative prices of goods change in such a way that the consumer in question is no better or worse off than he was before, but has to re-arrange his purchase in accordance with new relative prices."[8]

Here, it is assumed that when the price of *X* decreases, the price of *Y* would simultaneously increase. It is also assumed that the consumer's mon-ey incomes change in such a way as to compensate for the change in his real income consequent upon a fall in the price of X so that the consumer remains on the same in-difference curve. The substitution effect is shown in Fig. 14.17.

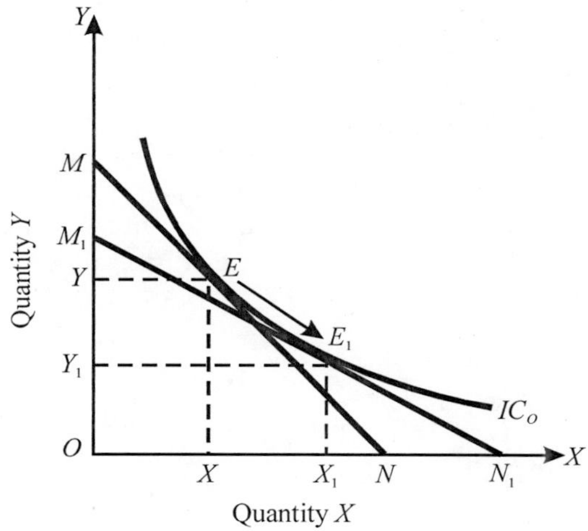

Fig. 14.17

In Fig.14.17, the consumer is in equilibrium at point E on IC_0 buying *OX* units of *X* and *OY* units of *Y*. Suppose the relative prices of the two goods have changed, i.e., the price of *X* falls while the price of *Y* rises. The relative change in the prices takes place in such a manner that then new price line M_1N_1 touch-es the same indifference curve IC_0 at point E_1. It means that the rise in the price of *Y* is compensated by an increase in the income of the consumer in terms of a fall in the price of *X*. Thus the consumer remains on the same indifference curve. He only readjusts his purchases of the two goods at the new equilibrium point E_1. The new combination of the two goods is $OX_1 + OY_1$. It is clear that in the new situation the consumer has more of *X* which is cheaper and less of *Y*

8. Stonier and Hague, *op. cit.,* p. 57.

which is dearer. The movement from equilibrium point E to E_1 indicating the increase of XX_1 quantity of X purchased by the consumer is called the substitution effect of the relative price change.

In the words of Prof. Hicks, it has been a *compensating variation* in the consumer's income in terms of quantity of X to the extent of NN_1, so that the rise in the price of Y is cancelled out. As a result, the consumer remains on the same indifferent curve IC_0 and the movement along this indifference curve nom E to E_1 is due to the substitution effect.

Now we will explain the *substitution effect when the price of only one commodity changes.* Let us assume that the price of commodity X falls while the price of commodity Y remains the same. Now the consumer will substitute X for Y. The substitution occurs even if we assume that the increase in real income (as a result of the fall in the price of X) is not available. Now, the increase in the purchase of commodity X and to a given fall in the price of X after deducting the part which is brought about by the increase in real income is called the substitution effect of a given fall in the price of commodity X alone. Fig. 14.18 illustrates this substitution effect.

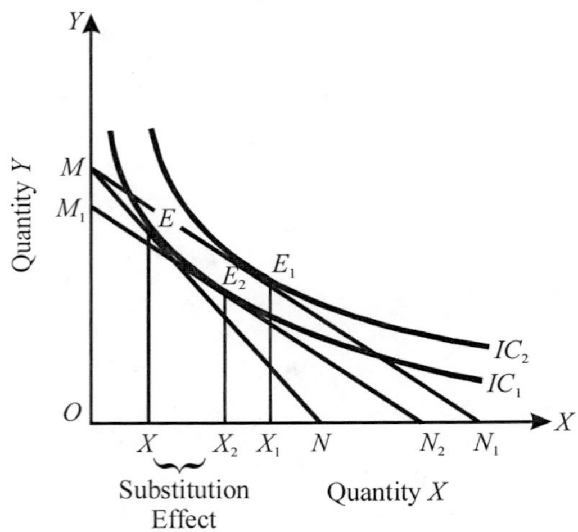

Fig. 14.18

In Fig. 14.18, the original price line is MN and the consumer is in equilibrium at point E where indifference curve IC_1 touches the price line MN. At original equilibrium point E, the consumer consumes OX

quantity of commodity X. Now the price of X falls and a new price line MN_1 takes place. The increase in the real income of the consumer in terms of commodity X is the distance NN_1. The new equilibrium position of the consumer is at point E_1 on the higher indifference curve IC_2. In the new situation, the consumer buys OX_1 quantity of X. We know that the movement from point E_1 on IC_1 to point E on IC_2 is partly due to the income effect and partly due to the substitution effect of a given fall in the price of X. To get the substitution effect we need to eliminate the income effect. For this, we draw a line M_1N_2 parallel to the price line MN_1 in such a way that it is tangent to the old indifference curve IC_1 at point E_2. Thus the movement from E *to* E_2 (i.e., from OX to OX_2 or the distance X_1X_2) is the income effect and the movement from E to E_2 (i.e., from OX to OX_2 or the distance X_1X_2) is the substitution. In other words, if we reduce the money income of the consumer by MM_1, amount (= N_2N_1 amount in terms of commodity X), his real income will remain constant (as in the initial stage) because with his reduced money income he can now get the same level of satisfaction (since both the points E and E_2 lie on the same indifference curve IC_1). Thus, the fall in the price of X results in it net increase of XX_1 in the quantity of X. Of this XX_2 is the substitution effect and X_2X_1 is the income effect. It also shows that the price effect represents the combined operation of income and substitution effects.

11. THE PRICE CONSUMPTION CURVE AND THE PRICE EFFECT

As already explained, a change in the price of a commodity not only induces the consumer to buy more or less because the relative price (P_X/P_T) has altered, but it also affects the demand for a commodity via "income effect" of a change in price. In other words the real income of the consumer is inversely related to the change in price. However, this aspect of consumer demand will be discussed later on. Here we shall discuss the "direct effect" of a change in price assuming that the consumer's income remains constant and the prices of all other commodities remain unchanged. The curve which shows the price effect is known as price-consumption curve (*PCC*). With the help of indifference curve analysis we derive the price consumption curve, and the demand curve for a commodity can directly be derived from the price consumption curve.

Our initial equation of the budget line or price line is

$$Y = \frac{I}{P_Y} - \frac{P_X}{P_Y}X$$

Now, if the price commodity X (P_X) falls, then the intercept (I/P_Y) of the line remains unchanged while the slope (P_X/P_Y) decreases. This has been illustrated in Fig. 14.19 (a) where the original price line is MN and the new price line becomes MN_1. The consumer shifts from his initial equilibrium point E to the new equilibrium point E_1. If we join these two points of equilibrium then the resulting curve is known as price consumption curve (PCC). The shift from E to E_1 is termed as price effect.

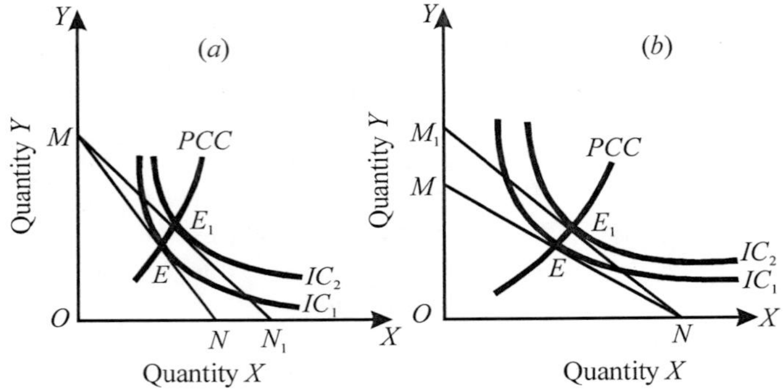

Fig. 14.19

Similarly, if the price of commodity Y (i.e., P_Y) falls, then the ordinate intercept of the price line (P_X/P_Y) will increase and the slope, of price line (P_X/P_Y) will also increase. As result of this, the price line MN shifts to M_1N in Fig. 14.19 (b). In this situation also, the consumer moves from a lower indifference curve IC_1 to a higher indifference curve IC_2. The locus of the equilibrium points E and E_1 is called the price consumption curve and the shift from E to E_1 is called price effect.

Like income consumption curve, the price consumption curve (PCC) may have a negative, positive, zero or infinite slope indicating the nature of the commodities, i.e., whether the commodities are superior, inferior or neutral. In the rare case of a "Giffen Good" it may even be backward bending.

Let us first take the most general type of price consumption curvethe curve which slopes downwards to the right as shown in Fig. 14.20. In this case, commodity X is a superior or normal good, because unless the income effect of a price change (i.e., fall in price) is positive, the PCC cannot have a negative slope. In other words, the income effect here is positive. The original price line is MN where the consumer gets maximum

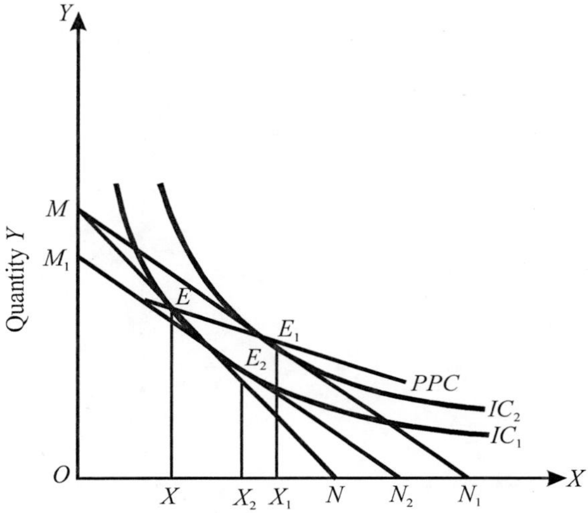

Fig. 14.20

satisfaction, a point E on IC_1. Due to a fall in the price of X, the price line shifts to MN_1 and the new point of equilibrium is E_1. Originally, the consumer was consuming OX units of X_1 but in the new situation his consumption increases to OX_1. The net increase in the consumption of X is equal to XX_1. This is the price effect which is due to the combined operation of the income effect and the substitution effect. If we want to know the income effect, then we need to separate the substitution effect from the income effect. The technique is simple. We draw a line M_1N_2 parallel to the price line MN_1 in such a way that the line M_1N_2 is tangent to IC_1 at point E_2. Now the movement from E *to* E_2 along IC, represents the substitution effect. On commodity X, it is equal to XX_2. If we subtract this from the net increase in the quantity of X (or price effect = XX_1), we get income effect Which is equal *to* X_1X_2. Since this income effect is positive, we conclude that commodity X in this case (Fig. 14.20) is a superior good or a normal good.

The second type of price consumption curve which is horizontal is X-axis whose slope is zero as shown in Fig. 14.21. Here the original equilibrium position is at point E on IC_1. If the price of X falls, then consumer attains a new equilibrium point E_1 on IC_2. The net increase in the quantity demanded of X is XX_1. Of this, the distance XX_2 is due to the substitution effect and the remaining part X_2X_1, is due to income effect

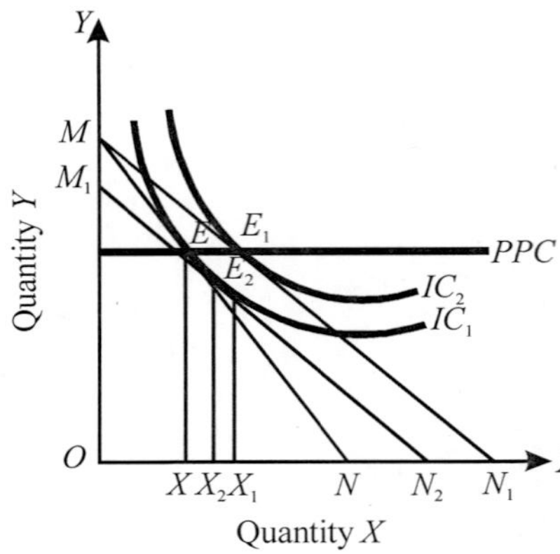

Fig. 14.21

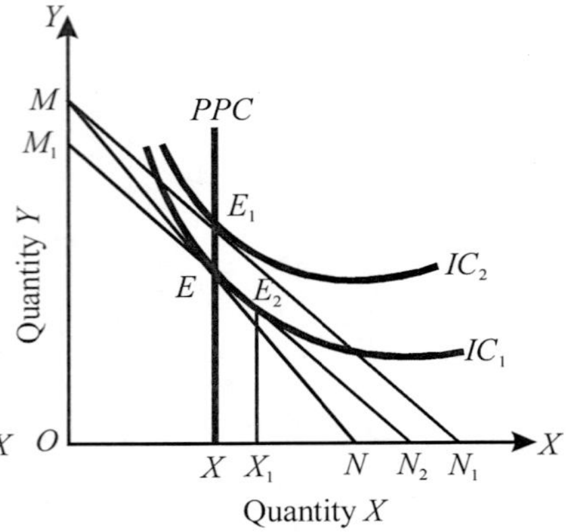

Fig. 14.22

since, here also, income effect is positive, the commodity X is a superior or normal commodity.

The third type of *PCC* is a vertical line with an infinite slope as shown, in Fig. 14.22. Here, if the price of X falls, there will be no increase in the quantity demanded. For instance, in Fig. 14.22, the original equilibrium point is E where the consumer buys OX quantity of X. Now due to a fall in the price of X, the price line shifts nom MN to MN_1 and the new equilibrium point would be E_1. At this new equilibrium position the consumer again buys OX quantity of X. Thus, there is no change in the quantity of X, or price effect is zero. This can happen when the negative income effect just cancels the positive substitution effect which in Fig. 14.22 is represented by XX_1.

The negative income effect shows that the commodity X is an inferior or *sub-normal commodity*.

The fourth type of price consumption curve is a backward bending curve as shown in Fig. 14.23. Here, as a result of a fall in the price of commodity X, the quantity demanded of X, instead of increasing, decreases. For instance, in Fig. 14.23, the original price line is MN where the equilibrium point is E. At point E the consumer buys OX of X. Now, if price of X falls, it will lead to a new price line MN_1. The new equilibrium point is E_1 where the consumer buys only OX quantity of X. Thus, the consumption of H decreases from OX to OX_1. This happens only when the negative income effect is stronger than the positive substitution effect

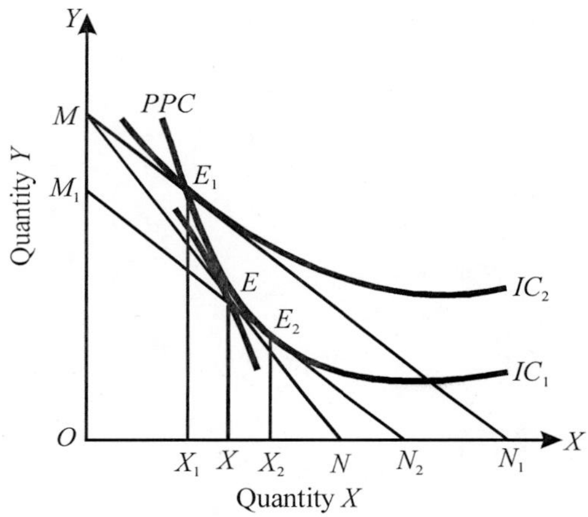

Fig. 14.23

In Fig. 14.23, the negative income effect is equal to X_1X_2 (= $X_1X + XX_2$) while the positive substitution effect is XX_2. Obviously,

$$X_1X_2 > XX_2$$

Thus the commodity X is definitely an inferior commodity. Here, it is a special type of inferior good which in economics is known as the "Giffen Good".

We have discussed above the four important types of price consumption curves. But there may be a number, of other shapes of *PCC.* Thus negatively sloping and horizontal *PCC* show the upper limit while the backward bending and vertical *PCC* show the lower limit. Between these two limits, these is a large range of positively sloping *PCC* where it is difficult to say straightaway whether the goods are superior, inferior or neutral. All that can be said is that the steeper the positive slope of the *PCC,* the greater is the likelihood for X to be an inferior commodity and vice versa. Here we can illustrate the three cases of positively sloping *PCC* with the help of Fig. 14.24 (a), (b) and (c) respectively.

In Fig. 14.24 (a), the net increase in the quantity demanded of X, as a result of a fall in its price, is equal to XX_1. Of this, the substitution effect is equal to XX_2 and income effect is equal to X_2X_1.

Since income effect is positive, the commodity X is a superior or normal commodity.

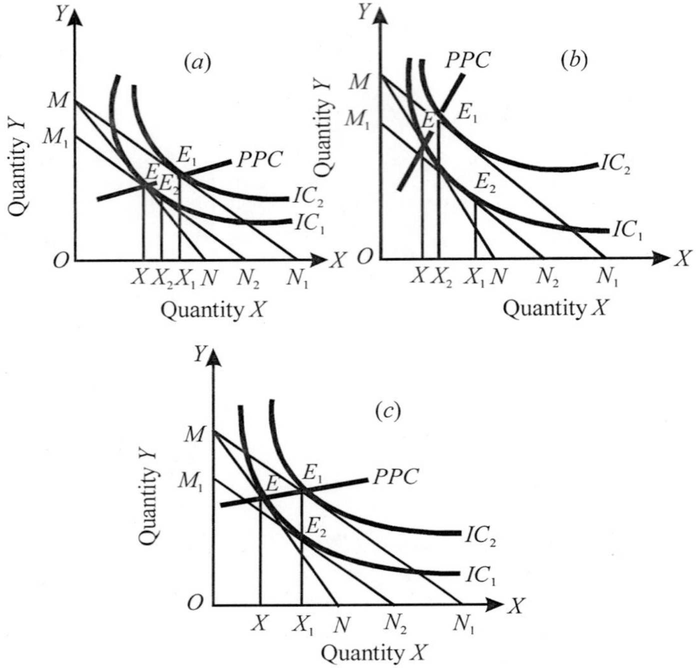

Fig. 14.24

In Fig. 14.24 (b), the net increase in the quantity demanded of *X*, as a result of a fall in its price, is XX_1. This has been calculated by subtracting the negative income effect X_2X_1 from the positive substitution effects XX_2. Thus the negative income effect neutralises a part of the positive substitution effect. But anyhow, since the income effect is negative, the commodity *X* is an inferior or sub-normal commodity.

Also, in Fig. 14.24 (c), as the consequent upon the fall in price of *X*, the net increase in the quantity demanded of *X* is XX_1. Here the income effect is zero and, therefore, the entire increase in *X* is due to the positive substitution effect. Here the commodity *X* is a neutral commodity.

Now we may sum up the above cases of price consumption curves in Table 14.4.

Table 14.4

Shape of the Price Consumption Curve (PCC)	*Nature of the Commodity*
Negatively sloping (PCC_1)	Superior
Horizontal sloping (PCC_2)	Superior
Positively sloping (PCC_3 and PCC_4)	Uncertain (may be superior, inferior or neutral)
Vertical sloping (PCC_5)	Inferior
Backward sloping (PCC_6)	Inferior

The various types of *PCC* curves stated in Table 14.4 are shown in Fig. 14.25. Their respective slopes indicate the nature of commodity *X*.

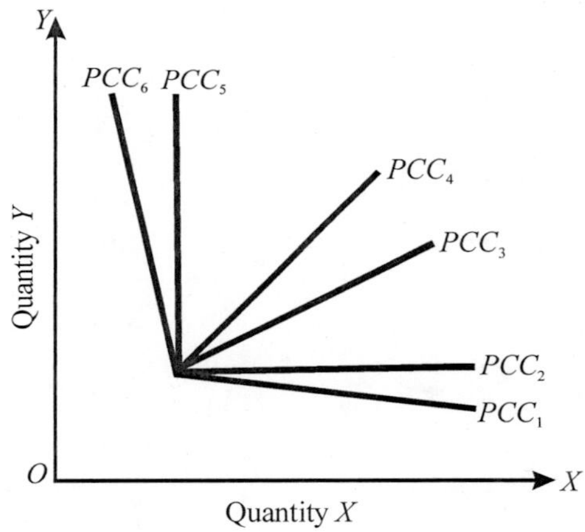

Fig. 14.25

11. SEPARATION OF PRICE EFFECT INTO INCOME AND SUBSTITUTION EFFECTS—SLUTSKY *Vs* HICKS

As we have noted above that a fall in the price of commodity *X* leads to an increase in its quantity demanded. The total increase in the quantity demanded of *X* is, however, the result of the combined action of the substitution and income effect of it given price change. Thus,

Price Effect = Substitution Effect + Income Effect

Here, we are interested to know that of the total price effect (i.e., total increase in the quantity demanded of X) how much is contributed by the substitution effect and how much is contributed by the income effect.

As we know, when the price of commodity *X* falls (the money income of the consumer remaining the same), the real income of the consumer increases. In other words, with the same money income, the consumer can now purchase larger quantities of both the goods *X* and *Y*. Now in order to find out how much of this (total) increase in the quantity demanded of *X* is due to the fall in the price *alone* (or due to substitution effect), it is necessary to keep the real income of the consumer constant. This can be done by reducing the money income of the consumer (through income tax, etc.) to the extent that his real income remains constant.

Two approaches have been developed so far to define the level of constant real income or the income effect.

(1) Slutsky's Approach.

(2) Hicks's Approach.

The first approach has been developed by the well-known Russian economist Prof. Fugen Slutsky. Slutsky states that to keep the real income of the consumer constant, we should reduce his money income to the extent that he should be just able to purchase the original combination of the two commodities (if he desires). This can be done by drawing a line parallel to the new price line which passes through the original combination of the two commodities *X* and *Y*. This approach, however, has been criticised on the ground that here the *apparent real income* remains constant and not the real income of the consumer. Because, this approach enables the consumer to enjoy a higher indifference curve (as he may move to a new point on the drawn price line which lies on a higher indifference curve).

The second approach has been developed by the well-known British economist, J.R. Hicks. According to this approach, in order to keep the real income of the consumer constant, we should reduce his money income to the extent that he is just able to enjoy the original indifference curve. This can also of done by drawing a parallel line to the new price line which at some point touches the original indifference curve.

The difference between the two approaches is clear that the former approach empahsises the attainment of the original combination of the two goods while the latter approach emphasises the attainment of the original level of total satisfaction. Fig. 14.26 illustrates the difference between the Slutsky and Hicks's approaches to income effect.

In Fig. 14.26, MN is the original price line which is tangent to IC_1 at the point E. The original equilibrium point E indicates that the consumer buys OX quantity of commodity X. Now suppose the price of X falls and, therefore, the price line shifts rightward to the new position of MN_1. The new equilibrium point is E_1 where the indifference curve IC_3 touches the price line MN_1. At this new equilibrium point E_1 the consumer buys OX. quantity of X. Thus the net increase in the quantity demanded of X (as a result of the fall in the price of X) is equal to XX_1. This increase of XX_1 is due to the combined contribution of the income and substitution effects.

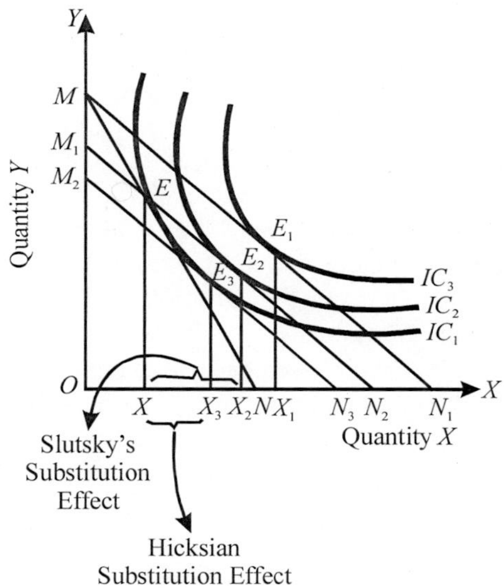

Fig. 14.26

Now we are interested to find out that how much of this total increase in quantity demanded of X $(= XX_1)$ is due to the substitution effect alone. In order to separate the two effects (substitution effect and income effect); we shall apply the techniques separately.

Let us first adopt the Slutsky approach. For this we draw a line M_1N_2 parallel to the new price line MN_1 in such a way that it passes through the original equilibrium (combination) point E. It means that we have reduced the money income of the consumer to the extent of the distance MM_1 (in terms of commodity Y) on axis Y or MM_1 (in terms of commodity X) on axis X. In Slutsky's opinion the line M_1N_2 keeps the consumer's real income constant. Now on the price line M_1N_2, the consumer can buy the original combination of X and Y at the point E, if he so likes. But as a rational consumer, he would not buy the old combination of the two commodities at point E and moves on to the point E_2 which lies on a higher indifference curve IC_2. At this point E_2, the quantity demanded of X increases from OX to OX_2 which is the direct effect (substitution effect) of the price change. In other words under Slutsky's approach, the substitution effect is equal to XX_2. If we subtract this substitution effect (XX_2) from the total effect (XX_1), we get the income effect (X_2X_1). Thus, Income effect (X_2X_1) = Total price effect (XX_1) – Substitution effect (XX_2).

This is the Slutsky approach of separating the price effect into the substitution effect and the income effect.

Now we employ Hicks's approach. According to his approach, to keep the real income constant the money income of the consumer should be reduced to the extent that he is forced to go back to the original indifference curve. For this we draw a line M_2N_3 parallel to the new price line MN_1 in such a way that it touches the original indifference curve IC_1 at point E_3. At point E_3, the consumer's real income remains the same in the sense that he gets the same level of total satisfaction as the original point E, because both the points E and E_2 lie on the same indifference curve IC_1. But at point E, the consumer buys only OX quantity of X while at point E_3, he buys OX_3 quantity of X. Thus the substitution effect is equal to XX_3. From the total increase in the quantity demanded of X due to the fall in its price, i.e., XX_1, if we deduct the substitution effect, XX_3; then the remaining portion X_3X_1 is the income effect, or
income effect (X_2X_1) = Total price effect (XX_1) – Substitution effect (XX_3).

This is Hicks's approach of separating the price effect into the substitution effect and the income effect.

It is now possible for us to sum up the relationship between the total price effect, the substitution effect and the income effect of the two approaches in Table 14.5.

Table 14.5

Method	*Fall in the Price of X*	*Total Price Effect*		*Substitution Effect or Direct Price Effect*		*Income Effect*
1. Slutsky's	$-\Delta P_X$	XX_1	=	XX_2	+	X_2X_1
2. Hicks's	$-\Delta P_X$	XX_1	=	XX_3	+	X_3X_1

Table 14.5 shows that the fall in the price of *X* and the total price effect on the quantity demanded of *X* are the same in the two approaches. But the substitution effect of direct effect is more under the Slutsky's approach than it is under the Hicks's approach because in Fig. 14.26 we observe that.

$$XX_2 > XX_3$$

It means that income effect is less under the Slutsky's approach than under the Hicksian approach, or

$$X_2X_1 < X_3X_1$$

Now as regards to the comparative importance of the two methods, Hicks's method seems to be more scientific than Slutsky's method. Because under Hicks's method, the substitution effect is such that the consumer remains on the same indifference curve due to a fall in the price of *X*. His real income remains the same because he becomes neither better off nor worse off as a result of the substitution effect. While under the Slutsky's approach, the consumer would enjoy a higher indifference curve which gives greater total satisfaction as a result of the substitution effect. Here, one is not able to say that the consumer's real income is constant. Thus, Hicksian approach is more reliable in the interpretation of the substitution effect and the income effect than the Slutsky's approach.

The above analysis clearly indicates the fact that the substitution effect is always positive. Because a cheaper commodity (due to a fall in the price) is always substituted for a dearer commodity.

But we are not sure about the nature of the income effect. In the case of a normal or superior good, the sign of the income effect will be positive. It means that given the prices of the commodities, an increase in the consumer's money income will lead to increase in the quantity demanded of *X*. If on the other hand, the given commodity *X* is an inferior or a sub-normal commodity, then the income effect will be negative. It means that given the prices of the commodities, an increase in the money income of the consumer will lead to decrease in the quantity demanded of *X*. If the commodity is a neutral commodity, the income effect will zero. It means that given the prices of the commodities, an increase in the money income of the consumer will lead to a zero change in the quantity demanded of *X*.

Prof. Slutsky has presented the relationship between the price effect, the substitution effect (direct price effect) and the income effect in an equation which is called the *Slutsky Equation.* The equation can be written in the following manner:

Total Price Effect = Substitution Effect ± Income Effect

13. DERIVATION OF THE DEMAND CURVE FROM THE PRICE CONSUMPTION CURVE

As demonstrated above, the price consumption curve shows the relationship between the change in the price of a commodity and the corresponding changes in the quantity demanded of the commodity by the consumer. The conventional demand curve also indicates the similar relationship that how much quantity of a commodity would be demanded by the consumer at different prices assuming *ceteris paribus.* It may, therefore, be hypothesized that the consumer's demand curve for a commodity must be related in some way to his *PCC* curve. As a matter of fact, the *PCC* as well as the demand curve yield the same information about the demand-price relationship. But in spite of this similarity, there are also some differences between these two curves—The PCC and the deman4 curve of the consumer. The important are the following:

(1) The *PCC* is drawn with the two commodities represented on the two axes-one say *X* on the *X* axis and the other say *Y* on the *Y* axis. On the other hand, the demand curve is drawn with only one commodity, say *X* represented on the *X* axis and its price represented on the *Y* axis.

(2) In the case of *PCC,* the prices of the commodities are not mentioned directly but slope of the price line indicates the ratio of the prices of the two commodities *X* and *Y.* While in the case of the conventional demand curve price of the commodity is directly mentioned on the vertical axis.

(3) The *PCC* clearly brings out separately the income effect and the substitution effect of a change (rise or fall) in the price of a commodity; while the conventional demand curve is unable to separate the two effects.

(4) The *PCC* also indicates the size of the consumer's money income while the conventional demand curve does not provide this information.

The above differences indicate the comparative importance of the two curves—the *PCC* and the demand curve. But if we are given the indifference map of the consumer and the money income of the consumer along with the price of all other goods (labelled as *Y* in our example), we can easily derive the demand curve of an individual consumer from his price-consumption curve. Generally, two different methods are employed to derive the demand curve from the price consumption curve. We shall discuss them separately in the following manner.

Method I

Under this method we shall derive the demand schedule of a consumer from his *PCC.* In Fig. 14.27, the consumer's money income has been represented on *Y* axis and the quantity of commodity *X* has been represented on *X* axis.

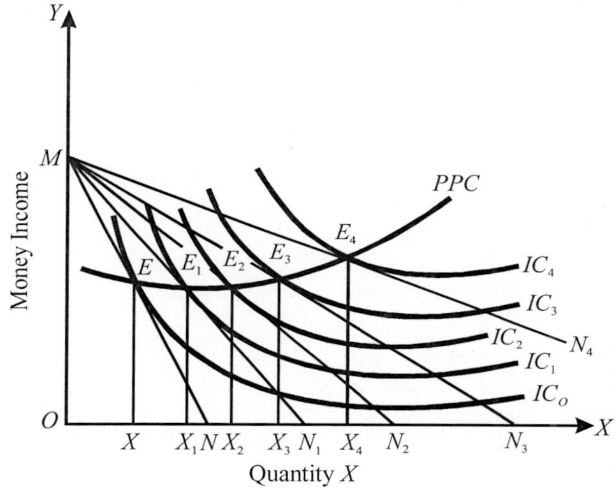

Fig. 14.27

Suppose the line of attainable combinations or the price line is initially *MN.* Now if the price of *X* falls, then the price line *MN* will shift upwards to the right. In Fig. 14.27, we have drawn the different price lines *MN,* MN_1, MN_2, MN_3 and MN_4 showing different prices of commodity *X*, namely *PX,* PX_1, PX_2, PX_3 and PX_4. The consumer's initial equilibrium position is at point *E* where he buys *OX* quantity of *X.* Here the price per unit of *X* is calculated by dividing the total money income of the consumer (*OM*) to the quantity of *X* that can be purchased with the entire money income. So that, the initial price of *X* (i.e., say PX_0) would be equal to the ratio

$$\frac{OM}{ON} = PX_0$$

At this initial price (*OM/ON*), the consumer buys *OX* quantity of *X.* Similarly, on the price line MN_1, the equilibrium position is at point E_1 where the consumer buys OX_1 quantity of *X* at the price OM/ON_1. Likewise, we may easily calculate the various price of commodity *X* and the respective quantities of X purchased by the consumer. This information has been summarised in Table 14.6.

Table 14.6

Price of the Commodity X (PX) (1)	*Quantity Demanded of X (X)* (2)
$PX_0 = \frac{OM}{ON}$	OX
$PX_1 = \frac{OM}{ON_1}$	OX_1
$PX_2 = \frac{OM}{ON_2}$	OX_2
$PX_3 = \frac{OM}{ON_3}$	OX_3
$PX_4 = \frac{OM}{ON_4}$	OX_4

Table 14.6 shows the demand schedule of the consumer. We can now easily construct the conventional demand curve on the basis of the price-quantity information mentioned in Table 14.6. Figure 14.28 indicates the resulting demand curve. Since the denominator of the column 1 of Table 14.6 is increasing, we write,

$$PX_0 > PX_1 > PX_2 > PX_3 > PX_4$$

As the price decreases, the quantity demanded of X increases, i.e.,

$$OX < OX_1 < OX_2 < OX_3 < OX_4$$

In other words, we can say that the law of demand holds. By plotting these various points of the demand schedule we obtain the demand curve DD as in Fig. 14.28.

Method II

Under this method the demand curve is drawn in the same diagram in which price consumption curve is constructed as shown in Fig. 14.29. In Fig. 14.29, horizontal axis measures the quantity of X while the money income is measured on the vertical axis. In this case the trade-off is between the purchase of *X* and the money which would be used for buying other goods (including *Y*). The slope of the price line is now simply the price of *X* (because slope, here, is defined as the ratio of total money income to the maximum attainable quantity of *X* or alternatively, the income spent on *X* divided by the actual quantity purchased which is nothing but the price of X).

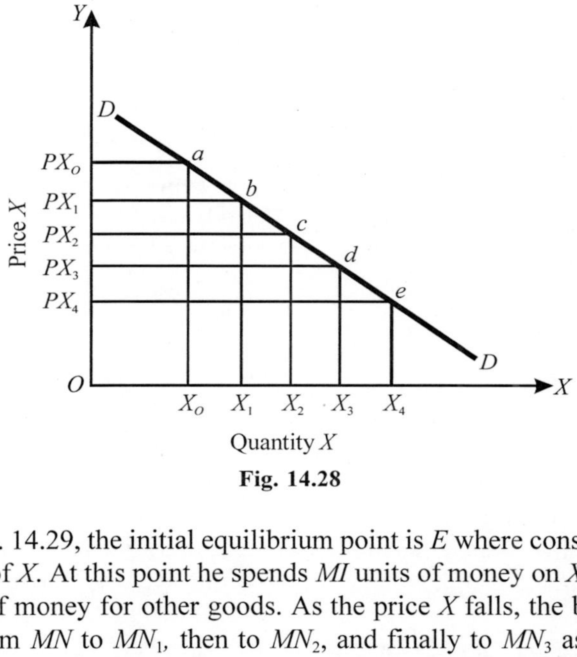

Fig. 14.28

In Fig. 14.29, the initial equilibrium point is *E* where consumer buys *OX* units of *X*. At this point he spends *MI* units of money on *X* and saves *OI* units of money for other goods. As the price *X* falls, the budget line rotates from *MN* to MN_1, then to MN_2, and finally to MN_3 as shown in Fig. 14.29. The equilibrium quantity of *X* bought increases each time the price of *X* falls. First it increases from *OX* to OX_1, then to OX_2 and finally to OX_3. Money income spent on *X* however, decreases from *MI* to MI_1, then to MI_2, and finally to MI_3. Thus a fall in the price of *X* induces the consumers to increase his demand for *X*. This is known as the law of demand.

The *PCC* curve has been usually drawn by joining the various equilibrium points *E*, E_1, E_2, and E_3. Here the price consumption curve tells us the total expenditure that is incurred on *X* at different prices. We, therefore, call the *PCC* as the "Total Outlay Curve" in relation to commodity *X*.

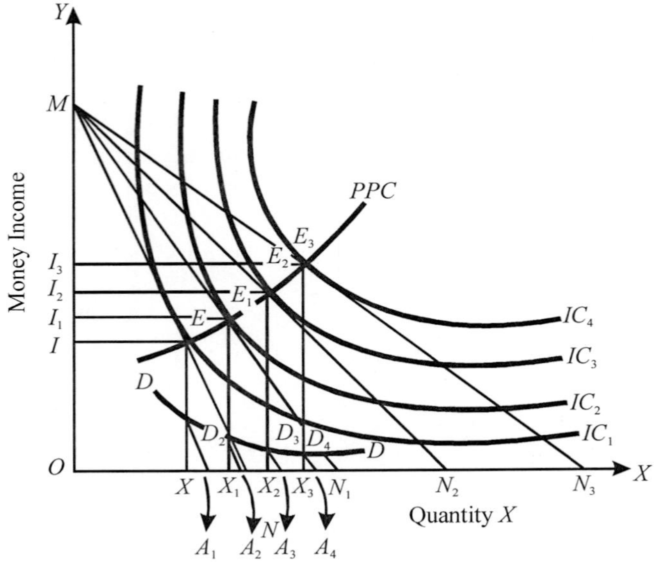

Fig. 14.29

But this curve gives us no information about the price per unit of *X* when different quantities are purchased by the consumer. This information (i.e., the various prices of *X*) can be obtained by dividing the total expenditure incurred on *X* by the number of units of *X* bought by the consumer. If we obtain this information, i.e., the price per unit of *X* when different quantities of it are purchased by the consumer, then it becomes very easy to draw the demand curve of the individual consumer.

The demand curve *DD* in Fig. 14.29 has been derived by establishing price quantity relationship at different levels of price. Thus, at different levels of price, one unit of *X* has been marked off from the equilibrium quantities. For instance, to the right of *EX* along the *X* axis, one unit of *X* (it may be a kilogram, a litre, or a metre as the case may be) is represented by the distance XA_1. We, when draw the line D_1A_1 parallel to the price line *MN*. Since D_1A_1 is parallel to the price line *MN*. It represents the same price (slope of the line) per unit of *X* as *MN*. Since XA_1 represents one unit of *X*, therefore, D_1X represents the price per unit of *X* (because price $= D_1X/XA_1 = D_1X$, since $XA_1 = 1$) when *OX* is purchased by the consumer. Thus D_1 is first point on the consumer's demand curve *DD*. Here price D_1X should be considered equivalent to *OM*/*ON*. Similarly, we mark off one unit of *X* to the right of point X_1 on the *X* axis at an equal distance of X_1A_2 ($=XA_1$) and draw a line D_2A_2 parallel to the price line MN_1. Now since the slope of price MN_1 indicates the price of X when OX_1 units of X are purchased by the consumer, the slope of the line D_2A_2, i.e.,

$\frac{D_2X_1}{X_1A_2}$ also indicates the price per unit of X. Here $X_1A_2 = 1$, therefore the price of X would be equal to D_2X_1. Thus, at price D_2X_1 the consumer purchases OX_1 quantity of X. In this way point D_2 is another point on the consumer's demand curve DD. In a similar manner, we can find out point D_3 and D_4 showing the consumer's demand for commodity X when the price unit is D_3/X_2 and D_4/X_3 respectively. If we join together the points D_1, D_2, D_3 and D_4, we may obtain the consumer's conventional demand curve DD.

14. COMPARATIVE DEMAND CURVES

The conventional demand curve derived above shows that the price and quantity are inversely related. It makes no attempt to explain the change in quantity demanded as a result of the substitution effect distinctly from the one resulting from the income effect of a change (fall or rise) in price. The above analysis is therefore, based on the Marshallian approach. Prof. Hicks and Prof. Slutsky criticised this approach. They hold the opinion that a change in price would lead to an opposite change in the consumer's real income. As already explained the increase in quantity demanded of X due to fall in its price is divided into two parts—one is attributed to the income effect and other remaining part is attributed to the substitution effect (or the direct price effect). Here, both Hicks and Slutsky state that response of quantity demanded to a change (fall) in price should be analysed exclusively on the basis of the substitution effect (or direct price effect), i.e., by ignoring the income effect. In other words, under the derivation of the demand curve the Marshallian approach emphasises the total price effect, i.e., the total change in quantity demanded in the event of a price change while Hicksian and the Slutskian approaches assume the consumer's real income constant and then analyse the effect of a price change on quantity demanded, i.e., exclusively on the basis of substitution effect. To put it differently, Marshallian approach considers the effect of an absolute change in the price of a commodity on quantity demanded in the derivation of the demand curve, while the other two approaches—Hicks and Slutsky—consider the effect of relative price change i.e., $\frac{P_X}{P_Y}$ on the quantity demanded of the commodity.

Again, in spite of this fact that both Hicksian and Slutsky approaches give emphasis to the substitution effect in the derivation of the demand curve, the two are not altogether identical. As we have already noticed, assuming the consumer's real income constant, Prof. Hicks intends the consumer to remain on the same indifference curve and allows him to select a new combination of *X* and *Y* along the original indifference curve; while Slutsky intends the consumer to enjoy the original equilibrium point. It means, to purchase the original combination of *X* and *Y*, Slutsky provides much compensation (negative or positive as the case may be) to the consumer.

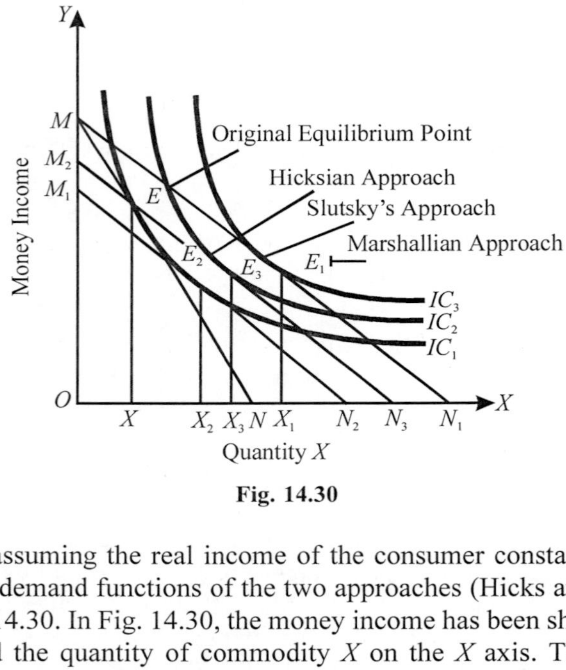

Fig. 14.30

Now assuming the real income of the consumer constant, we may derive the demand functions of the two approaches (Hicks and Slutsky) from Fig. 14.30. In Fig. 14.30, the money income has been shown on the *Y* axis and the quantity of commodity *X* on the *X* axis. The price of commodity *X* is known by the slope of the respective price lines *MN*, MN_1 and MN_2. For example, at the original equilibrium point *E*, the consumer buys *OX* quantity of *X* at the price *OM/ON*. But when the price of *X* falls to OM/ON_1, then the conventional total quantity demanded of *X* would be OX_1, while according to Hicks and Slutsky it would be OX_2 and OX_3 respectively. This information of the three different demand functions—Marshall, Hicks and Slutsky—has been shown in Table 14.7.

Table 14.7

Price of X	*Total Quantity of X purchased*	*Quantity of X purchased according to Hicks*	*Quantity of X purchased according to Slutsky*
$PX_0 = \frac{OM}{ON}$	OX	OX	OX
$PX_1 = \frac{OM}{ON_1}$	OX_1	OX_2	OX_3

The information of Table 14.7 can be represented graphically by the three different demand curves—Marshall; Hicks and Slutsky—as shown in Fig. 14.31. The demand curves in Fig. 14.31 have been drawn under the assumption that a change in the price leads to an opposite change in the quantity demanded. In other words, Fig. 14.31 depicts the demand for a normal good in relation to price. At the original price OPX_0, the quantity demanded was OX. When the price falls from OPX_0 to OPX_1, under the Marshallian approach (i.e., total price effect) the consumer increases the quantity of X to OX_1, but under Slutsky's approach the consumer increases the quantity of X to OX_2, while under Hicksian approach the increase in quantity of X is only equal to OX_2. In other words, the elasticity of demand will be lower if examined under Slutskian approach and still lower if viewed from Hicksian approach. Symbolically,

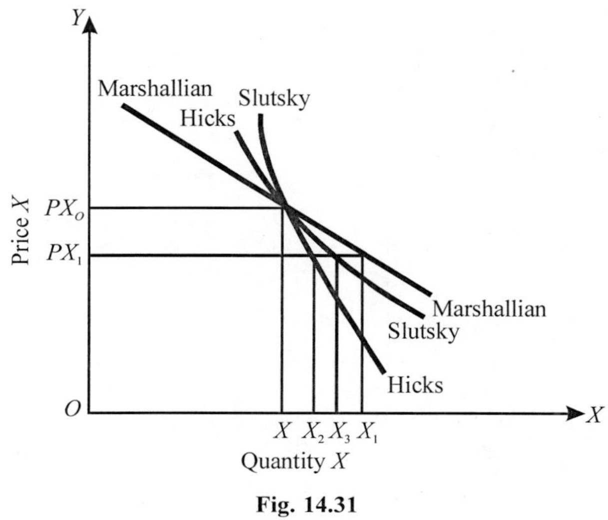

Fig. 14.31

$$Ed \text{ (Marshall)} > Ed \text{ (Slutsky)} > Ed \text{ (Hicks)}$$

In spite of the above differences, the common characteristic to all the three demand curves of Fig. 14.31 is their negative slope. It means that for a normal good, the price and quantity demanded are inversely related in all the three cases of demand curves.

15. DERIVATION OF THE INCOME DEMAND OR ENGEL CURVE

With the help of indifference curve analysis, we may derive the income demand curve or the Engel curve from the income consumption curve (*ICC*). The Engel curve represents the relationship between the income of the consumer and the quantity of *X* demanded by the consumer. It has been shown in Figs. 14.32 and 14.33.

In Fig. 14.32 the income consumption curve slopes positively which indicates that as the money income of the consumer increases, he will buy more of the two goods *X* and *Y*. For instance as income increases, the price line shifts to the right from *MN* to M_1N_1 and then to M_2N_2 respectively. These lines are parallel to each other, because the slope of the price line or price ratio P_X/P_Y remains constant. If *X* and *Y* are normal goods, the increase in income increases the quantity of *X* taken from *OX* to OX_1, then to OX_2 and the amount of *Y* taken from *OY* to OY_1, then to OY_2.

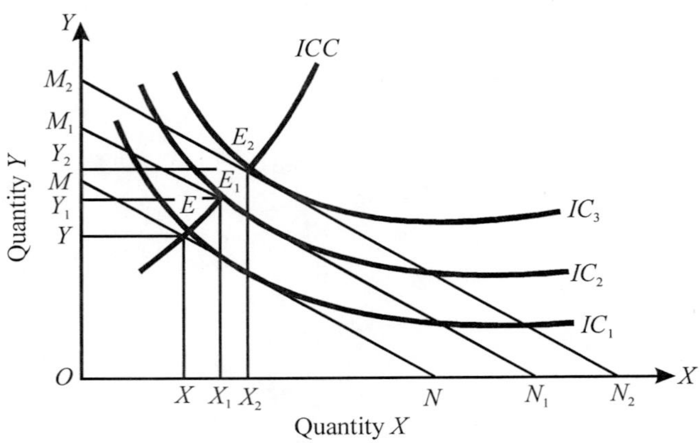

Fig. 14.32

Engel curves or income demand curves for *X* and *Y* can be plotted from the data provided from Fig. 14.32. Here we draw an Engel curve *DD* in Fig. 14.33. Money income of the consumer is measured on the vertical axis while quantities of X are measured on the horizontal axis. Now from Fig. 14.32 we can read that with money income OM the consumer buys OX quantity of X. This is plotted as point A on Fig. 14.33. From Fig. 14.32 we again note that when income increases from OM to OM_1, the consumer will buy OX_1 of X. We plot this as point B on Fig. 14.33. Similarly, from Fig. 14.32 we find that when income rises to OM_2, the consumer buys OX_2 units of X. We plot this as point C on Fig. 14.33. Now if we join these points then the resulting curve is the income demand curve DD. This demand curve slopes upwards rather downwards which shows a positive relationship between the money income of the consumer and the demand for X. The slope of the demand curve will show the respective elasticity of demand for the commodity. In the case of a superior commodity as assumed in our above example, the *ICC* as well as the Engel curve will be positively sloped and the income elasticity of demand will be positive. In the case of an inferior good, the *ICC* will be backward bending, showing a negative relationship between income and consumption changes and, therefore, the income demand curve or the Engel curve will also have a negative slope showing that as income increases, the quantity demanded of X decreases. In this case, the income elasticity of demand will be negative.

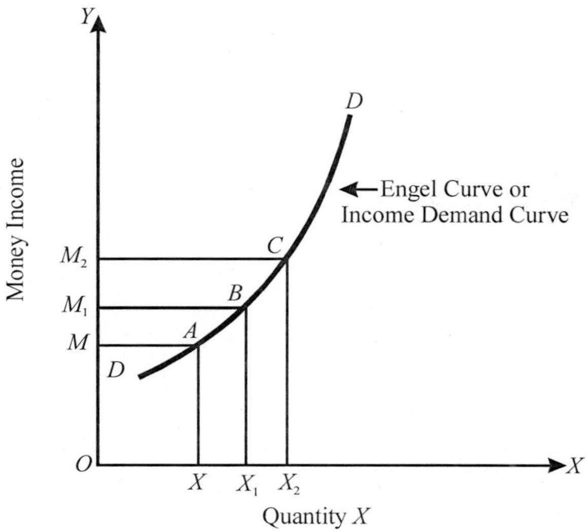

Fig. 14.33

16. ELASTICITY OF DEMAND AND THE PRICE CONSUMPTION CURVE (PCC)

From the price consumption curve (*PCC*) we not only derive the demand curve for a commodity, but the slope of the *PCC* also indicates whether the elasticity of demand for the commodity *X* is unitary, greater than one, or less than one.

In Fig. 14.34 (a), the slope of price consumption curve is zero because it is horizontal to *X* axis. It indicates that the elasticity of demand is unitary, because it states that total expenditure incurred on *X* remains unchanged. In other words, a percentage fall in the price of *X* is equal to the percentage increase in the quantity demanded of *X* and thus leaving the total expenditure incurred on the commodity unchanged. Symbolically,

$$Ed = \frac{\text{Percentage change in the quantity demanded of } X}{\text{Percentage change in the price of } X}$$

$$= \frac{\Delta X / X}{\Delta P_X / P_X} = 1$$

because $\Delta X/X = \Delta P_X/P_X$

In Fig. 14.34 (b), the *PCC* slopes upward which indicates that the elasticity of demand for *X* is inelastic. Because when price of *X* falls, the quantity demanded of *X* increases from OX to OX_1 but the total expen-

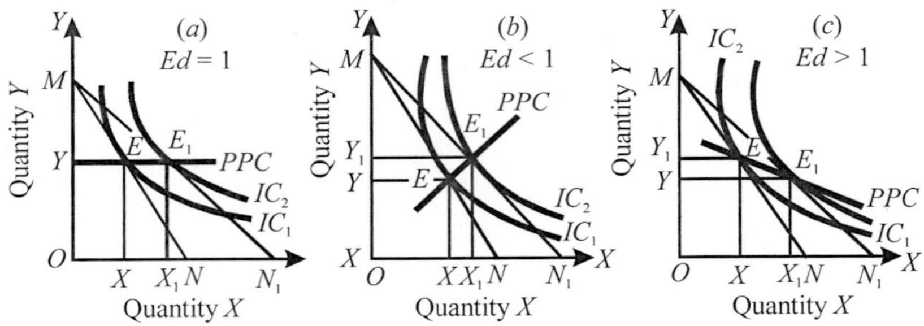

Fig. 14.34

diture (in terms of *Y*) incurred on *X* falls from MY to MY_1. In other words, the percentage increase in the quantity demanded of *X* is less than the percentage fall in its price. Thus the elasticity of demand for *X* is less than one. Symbolically,

$$Ed = \frac{\Delta X / X}{\Delta P_X / P_X} < 1$$

because $\Delta X/X < \Delta P_X/P_X$

In Fig. 14.34 (c), the *PCC* slopes downwards to the right indicating that the elasticity of demand for *X* is elastic. Because when price of *X* falls, the quantity demanded of *X* increases nom *OX* to OX_1, while at the same time the amount of money income (in terms of *Y*) spent on it also increases nom *MY* to MY_1. It means that the percentage in quantity demanded of *X* is greater than the percentage fall in its price. Thus, the price elasticity of demand for *X* is greater than one. Symbolically,

$$Ed = \frac{\Delta X / X}{\Delta P_X / P_X} > 1$$

because $\Delta X/X > \Delta P_X/P_X$

17. APPLICATIONS OF INDIFFERENCE CURVE ANALYSIS

As we have already explained, indifference curve analysis is useful in the derivation of the demand curve of an individual consumer for particular products. However, indifference curve analysis can also be fairly used in the fields of consumption, production, exchange and distribution. It may also be used to explain the impact of various government policies related to rationing, taxation, international trade, etc. Here we shall narrate some of the important uses of indifference curve analysis in the following section:

(1) ***Optimisation in a Barter Economy*** **(*or the Determination of the Rate of Exchange*).** A situation where prices are not expressed in monetary units, is generally called a barter economy. The first application of indifference curve analysis relates to the determination of the rate of exchange between two commodities bartered by two individuals. In 1881, Prof. Edgeworth[9] made the first attempt to show the limit within which exchange could take place between the two individuals. Assuming the scale of preferences of the individual's and the supplies of the commodities given, he laid down the limits of exchange with the help of his famous box diagram and pointed out that it is not possible to ascertain the precise rate at which the two commodities will exchange. The most that can be done is to indicate the limits within which the exchange ratio must lie, its actual position within these limits is determined by the relative abilities

9. Edgeworth, E.N., *Mathematical Physics,* 1881, p. 20.

of the two individuals to bluff, to coerce, to harangue, and the like. This has been illustrated in Fig. 14.35.

Let us assume that the two individuals are *A* and *B;* and the two commodities are *X* and *Y*. In Fig. 14.35, *A*'s family of indifference curves (showing the scale of preference) is IC_1^A, IC_2^A, IC_3^A and IC_4^A and starts with the origin O_A. Likewise, *B*'s family indifference curves (showing his scale of preferences) is IC_1^B, IC_2^B, IC_3^B, and IC_4^B and starts with the origin O_B. The two persons *A* and *B* get maximum satisfaction in exchange where their indifference curves touch each other. In other words, the slope of indifference curves of *A* and *B* must be equal. Since the slope of indifference curve represents the marginal rate to substitution of *X* for *Y* (*MRSxy*), we may write the condition:

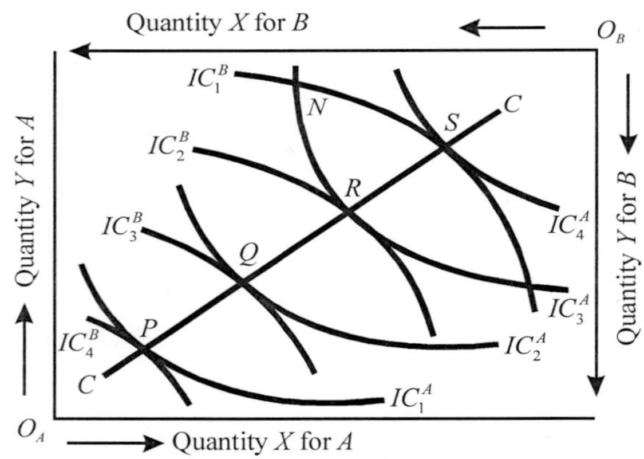

Fig. 14.35

$$MRSxy \text{ for } A = MRSxy \text{ for } B$$

It is clear from Fig. 14.35 that the above marginality condition is satisfied at the points *P, Q, R* and *S*. These points are the equilibrium points of exchange. The locus or path of these points is *CC* which is generally known as the ***Contract Curve.***

To prove that the touching points *P, Q, R,* and *S* are the relevant points for exchange, we assume a new point of exchange *N* where the indifference curves of *A* and *B* cut each other. Now we will see that the total welfare can be increased by moving point *N* to *S* or *R.* In other words, at point *N* only one of the individuals will give his acceptance for exchange and the other will not; thus exchange will not be possible. On the other hand, at point *S* or *R* both will agree for exchange and thus exchange between them will take place. We summarise the positions of *A* and *B* at the point *N*, *R* and *S* in the following manner.

	A	*B*
At point *N*	IC_3	IC_1
At point *R*	IC_3	IC_2
At point *S*	IC_4	IC_1

Now if we compare point *N* and *R*, then we find that *A* gets the same level of satisfaction on both the points as he remains on IC_3, but *B* gets more satisfaction on point *R* (because he enjoys IC_2), then point *N* (lies on IC_1). It means that *B* will give his acceptance on point *R* and *A* will have no objection for this point and thus exchange will take place only on point *R* and not on *N*.

Similarly, if we compare points *N* and *S*, then we find that at point *S* both agree for exchange because *A* shifts to a higher indifference curve IC_4 (from a lower indifference IC_3 at point *N*) while *B* does not lose anything (because at both the points he remains on IC_1). Thus, point *N* will not be the relevant point of exchange while point *S* will be the relevant point of exchange. Now, it is proved the every point on the contract curve represents a position of final contract between the two individuals.

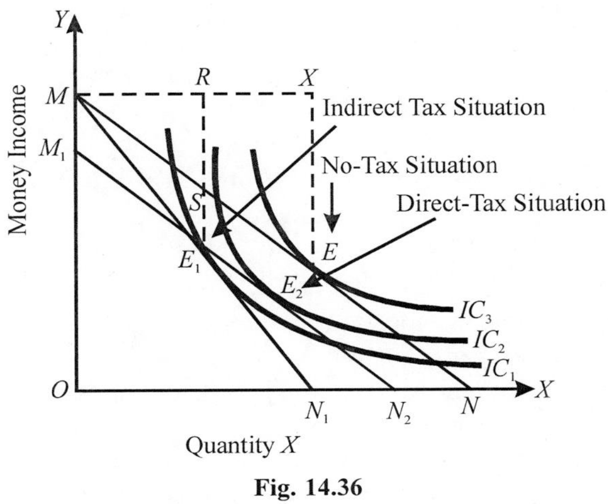

Fig. 14.36

(2) *Determination of Tax Policy.* A second application of indifference curve analysis lies in the determination of a tax policy. With the help of

indifference curves we can show that income-tax (direct tax) is better than an equivalent sales-tax or an excise tax (indirect-tax). This can be proved by means of Fig. 14.36. In this figure *X* axis represents the commodity taxed and *Y* axis the consumer's money income. The consumer's (or tax payer's) money income is equal to *OM.* We now draw the price line *MN,* whose slope is, equal to Px / Py. Since *Py* is equal to unity (the price of Rupee 1 is 1), the slope of the price line *MN* equals *Px.* If there is no tax on the consumer, then the individual will buy *MX* quantity of commodity *X* at a total expenditure of *XE* rupees and will initially enjoy point *E* on IC_3.

If a tax is imposed on commodity *X,* than the price of *X* will rise. The new price line will become MN_1, where the equilibrium point is E_1. At E_1, the consumer buys *MR* quantity of *X* at a total cost of RE_1 of which SE_1 will be taxes.[10] In this situation of indirect tax, the consumer enjoys indifference curve IC_1. If an equal amount of tax is levied on the income of the consumer, his income is reduced to OM_1 (where $MM_1 = SE_1$), but the slope of the price line M_1N_2 retains its former slope since the price of *X* is unaffected. The consumer's equilibrium point will be E_2 which lies on IC_2. It proves that the consumer will be on a higher indifference curve if a certain amount of money is taken from him by a personal income tax than if it is raised by means of a commodity tax.

(3) ***Explaining the Effects of Subsidies.*** Subsidy is generally provided by the government to help consumers (low income groups) in such a way that they are able to purchase goods at a price lower than the market price. Here the question is: whether the benefit to the consumer (s) is more than the cost of the subsidy to the government. This has been illustrated in Fig. 14.37. Suppose, consumer's money income is *OM* and in the absence of any subsidy his price line is *MN.* The consumer was originally optimising the use of his money income at point *E* where he was placed on the indifference curve IC_1. Now if government provides him commodity *X* at (fair) lower prices, then his price line shifts to MN_1. At this new price line, the consumer's equilibrium position is at point E_1 on IC_2 where he buys *OX* quantity of *X* at a total expenditure of MR_1. Originally, the consumer was required to pay a total expenditure of *MR* to purchase same quantity *OX* of commodity *X.* This means that the government provides RR_1 amount of money in terms of subsidy. But the consumer does not get this amount in cash (i.e., in money units). If it could be given in terms of money income, then the amount would be

10. Here we assume that the rise in price of *X* will be just equal to the amount of the tax.

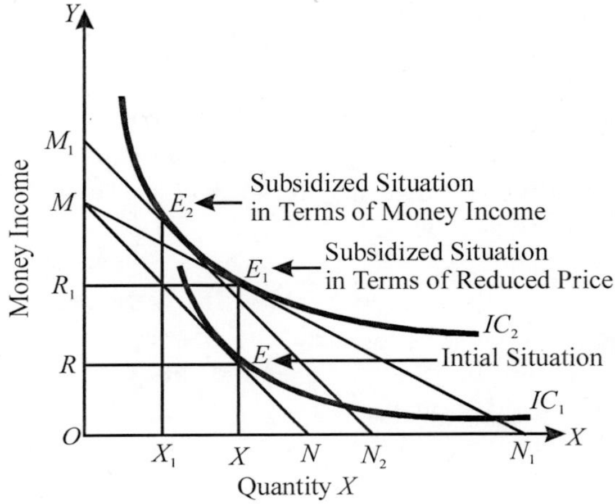

Fig. 14.37

equal to MM_1. Now as far as the individual consumer is concerned, he is equally benefited from both types of transfer payments (i.e., either in cash or in terms of price reduction); because he remains on the same indifference curve IC_2 (where $E_1 = E_2$). But the cost of the subsidy to the government is more when it is given in terms of price reduction than in terms of money (because $RR_1 > MM_1$). Thus, the subsidy should be given in cash terms than in terms of fair prices. Moreover, the consumer purchases lesser amount of X at point E_2 than at point E_1. The government also wants to curtail the consumption and thus cashsubsidy is recommended in place of the other type of subsidy.

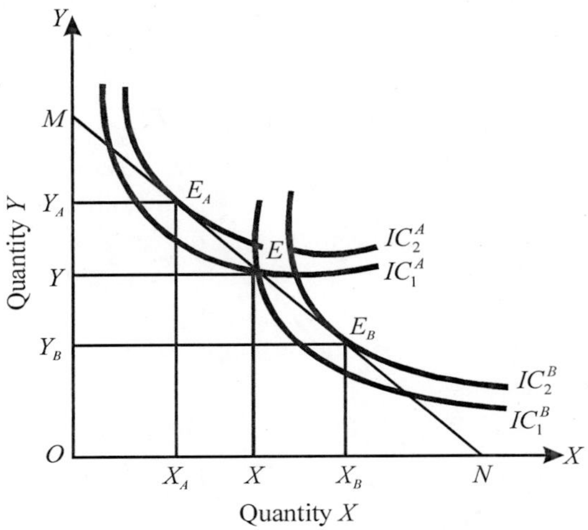

Fig. 14.38

(4) *Explaining the Effects of Rationing.* Indifference curves are also used to explain the effects of rationing. There are different methods of rationing. For example the first method is that each consumer is entitled to a fixed quantity of the commodity. The second method is that the consumer is entitled to get ration according to his taste and preference. Now with the help of indifference curves we can show that the second method of rationing is better than the first method.

We assume that the two consumers, *A* and *B* have the same amount of money income at their disposal. Also, there are two commodities *X* and *Y* where the rationing is imposed. The prices of the two commodities are also given. In Fig. 14.38, *MN* is the price line. The indifference curves (which show their respective tastes) of *A* and *B* are given as IC_1^A, IC_2^A, IC_1^B and IC_2^B respectively to the first method of rationing both *A* and *B* get fixed) quantities of *X* and *Y*, i.e., *OX* of *X* and *OY* of *Y*. The forced equilibrium point for both is *E* where *A* enjoys IC_1^A and *B* enjoys IC_1^B. Now, if the second method of rationing is introduced, then both the consumers will buy *X* and *Y* according to their tastes. In such a situation *A* will enjoy equilibrium point E_A which also lies on a higher indifference curve IC_2^A and *B* will enjoy equilibrium point E_B which also lies on a higher indifference curve IC_2^B. *A*'s combination of the two commodities *X* and *Y* will be $OX_A + OY_B$ and *B*'s combination of the two commodities *X* and *Y* will be $OX_B + OY_B$. Thus under the second scheme both the consumers get higher level of satisfaction. Here we may notice that total quantities of *X* and *Y* sold in the market remain the same, because when *B* buys XX_B more of *X*, then he has to sacrifice the purchase of *Y* to the level of YY_B. Similarly when *A* buys YY_A more of *Y*, then he reduces the purchase of *X* to the level of XX_A. Thus the controlled quantity of commodities *X* and *Y* remaining the same, the distribution according to consumer preferences will lead to higher satisfaction.

(5) ***Derivation of the Supply Curve of Labour.*** Here we consider the attitude of a consumer toward his income. A consumer sells his services (labour) to business firms. The indifference curve analysis can be used to indicate the supply of labour available at different wage rates. The supply curve of labour can easily be derived from the *Wage Offer Curve,* provided the indifference map, of labour and the entire range of wage-rates are known to us. In general, a consumer would like to earn higher incomes and for this he has to work more. In other words, more work means the sacrifice of some leisure.[11] Since leisure is also necessary for life, a

11. Here leisure means the time not spent in remunerative work. i.e., in earning money income.

consumer has to make balance between work and leisure. In other words, the gain in utility from more income has to be balanced against the loss of utility from less leisure. Obviously, there is a direct substitution of income for leisure, and vice versa. The utility function of the consumer can be written as,

$$U = f(L, I) \qquad ...(7)$$

where L indicates leisure and stands for the money income of the consumer. Again the money income of the consumer is a positive function of work (N). Symbolically,

$$I = f(N)$$

or $$I = w.\, N \qquad ...(8)$$

where w is a coefficient or represents wage rate.

also $$w = \frac{1}{N} \qquad ...(9)$$

Now a number of indifference curves may be drawn by assigning different values to the utility function (7) In Fig. 14.39 we have drawn four indifference curves IC_1, IC_2, IC_3 and IC_4 showing various combinations of income and leisure. The vertical axis shows money income in rupees and the horizontal axis shows leisure/work. When we read the horizontal axis from left to right, it shows hours of leisure per week and when we read it from right to left, it shows hours of work per week. Moreover, by definition, along an indifference curve, the total utility obtained from work (or income) and leisure remains constant. For instance,

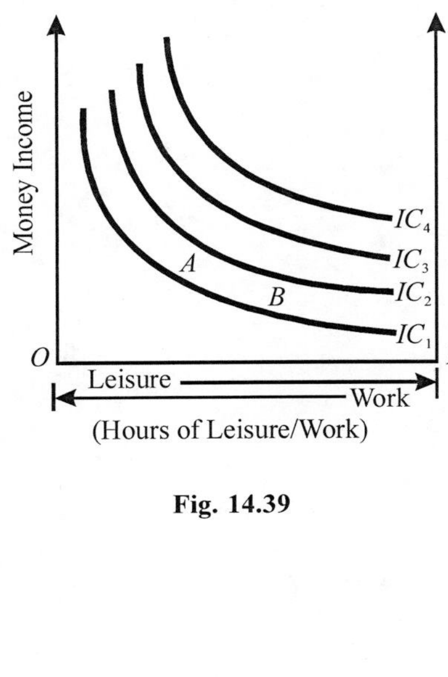

Fig. 14.39

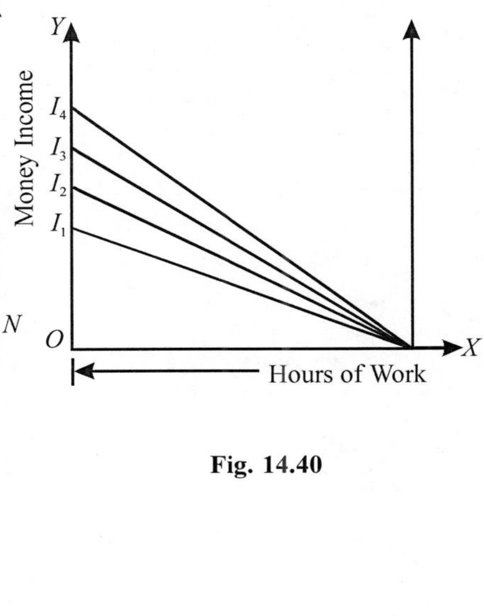

Fig. 14.40

on indifference curve IC_1, if the consumer shifts from combination point A to combination point B, then he sacrifices income but gains enough leisure to compensate, so that he is indifferent between these two combinations.

The slope (or shape) of indifference curve, here, represents the attitudes toward income and leisure.

Now the different hourly payments or wage rates (w) can be represented by the slope of wage lines. In Fig. 14.40, we have drawn four wage lines showing different wage rates.

Now for optimisation, the rational consumer wants to be on the highest reachable indifference curve. Thus, he will select that point where the indifference curve is tangent to the respective wage line. In Fig. 14.41, the wage lines are tangential to the indifference curves IC_1, IC_2, IC_3, IC_4 at points E_1, E_2, E_3, E_4 respectively. Joining these various points of equilibrium, we obtain the wage offer curve. Its meaning is that the wage rate rises, the individual first works more hours and then works fewer hours. The wage-offer curve may take any shape depending upon shapes of the indifference curves. Thus the wage offer curve indicates that at difference wage levels how many hours of work the consumer is ready to

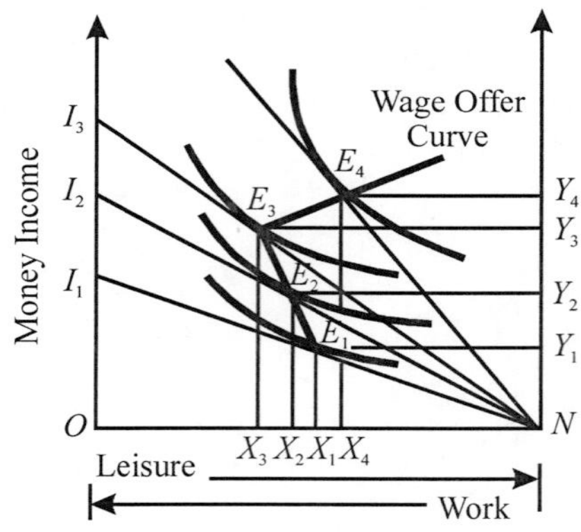

Fig. 14.41

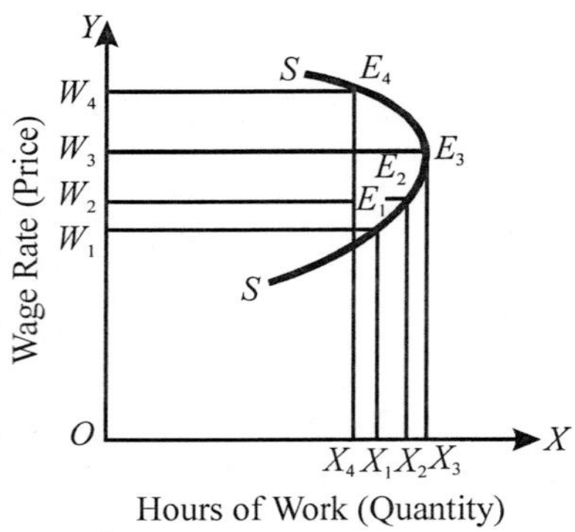

Fig. 14.42

offer. This information can be rearranged and presented in an ordinary price-quantity diagram. This is shown in Fig. 14.42. Here the curve SS is a supply curve of labour showing the relation between wage rates (price) and the number of hours (quantity) worked at each.[12] The backward

12. The wage offer curve in Fig. 14.41 and the supply curve of labour in Fig. 14.42 face in opposite directions. The reason is obvious that Fig. 14.41 measures work from right to left whereas Fig. 14.42 measures work from left to right.

bending supply curve in Fig. 14.42 is the supply curve for an individual labour (consumer). But the same curve can also be made to stand for a group of labourers in a labour market, when the supply curves of different labourers are added.

(6) ***Explaining the Theory of Index Numbers.*** Index number indicates the changes in the level, and thus enables us to compare the standards of living in two different periods or situations. Here we assume that the consumer's preference between the two goods remains the same, i.e., the same indifference curves apply for both the periods.

In Fig. 14.43, we have drawn three indifference curves $IC_{0,}$ IC_1 and IC_2 which represent the consumer's satisfaction from goods X and Y in both the periods. MN represents the price line in the initial period O, and M_1N_1 represents the price line in the current period I. Initially or in the base period the consumer was enjoying point E on IC_0 where he was buying OX_0 units of X and OY_0 units of Y in current year when price of X increases and that of Y decreases, the consumer's new equilibrium point becomes E on IC_1. At point E_1, he buys OX_1 of X and OY_1 of Y. Since E_1 lies on a higher indifference curve than the equilibrium point E attained in the base year, the consumer is better off.

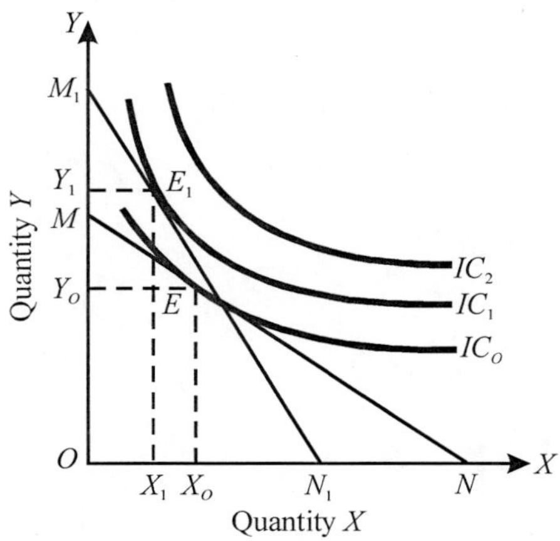

Fig. 14.43

The above analysis can be put in the form of real income index numbers in the following manner:

$$I_0 = \frac{P_{X0}X_0 + P_{Y0}Y_0}{P_{X0}X_0 + P_{Y0}Y_0} \times 100 = 100$$

and $$I_1 = \frac{P_{X1}X_1 + P_{Y1}Y_1}{P_{X0}X_0 + P_{Y0}Y_0} \times 100$$

where I_0 and I_1 are the index numbers in the base year 0, and the current year 1. P_{X0} represents the price of X in the base year, P_{X1} represents the price of X in current year, P_{Y0} is the price of Y in the base year and P_{Y1} is the price of Y in the current year. Similarly X_0, Y_0 represent the quantities of X and Y in the base year and X_1, Y_1 represent the quantities of X and Y in the current year.

If $I_1 > I_0$, it means the consumer is better off because his current year's real income is greater as compared to the base year's real income.

(7) ***Explaining Changes in Tastes and Preferences.*** As we have explained earlier, the slope of an indifference curve explains the relative preferences (or tastes) of the two commodities. If his tastes and preferences remain the same, then the slopes of different indifference curves will also remain identical. In other words, the indifference curves will be parallel to each other in the event of a rise in the money income of the consumer, i.e., he will purchase larger quantities of both the commodities. This case has been illustrated in Fig. 14.44. Initially, the consumer's equilibrium position is at point E where his indifference curve IC_1 is tangent to the original price line MN.

If his money income increases, then the price line shifts from MN to M_1N_1 and the new equilibrium position becomes E_1. At point E_1' IC_2 is tangent to the price line M_1N_1 and it is also parallel to the old indifference

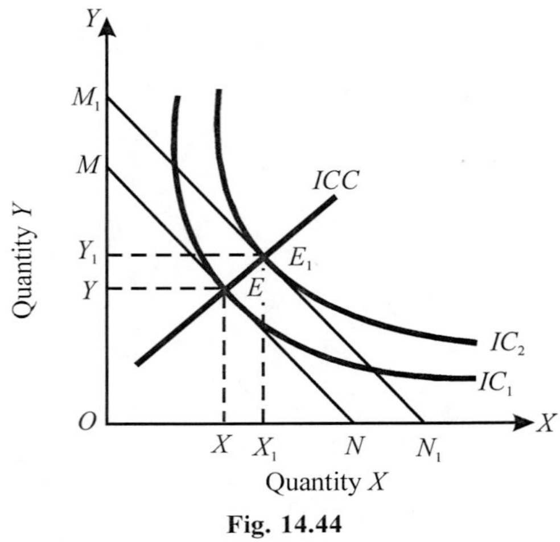

Fig. 14.44

curve IC_1. It indicates that the consumption of both the commodities increases.

Now, let us assume that an increase in income leads to change in his tastes. In such a case the slope of the indifference curves will not be the same. In other words, they would not be parallel to each other. The changing slope will indicate whether he prefers more of X to Y or more of Y to X. In Fig. 14.45, it is clear that if the consumer assigns higher preference to X than before, he will move from point E on IC_1 to point E_1 on IC_2. The slope of IC_2 is higher than the slope of IC_1 which implies that along indifference curve IC_2 the relative marginal utility of X $\left(\frac{MU_X}{MU_Y} = MRS\right)$ is higher than the corresponding marginal utilities along IC_1. Symbolically,

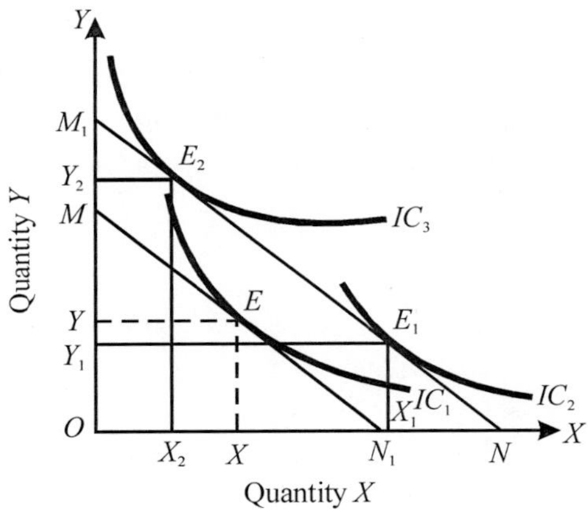

Fig. 14.45

$$MRS_{XY} \text{ of } IC_2 > MRS_{XY} \text{ of } IC_1$$

or
$$\frac{MU_X}{MU_Y} \text{ of } IC_2 > \frac{MU_X}{MU_Y} \text{ of } IC_1$$

It means X is preferred to Y, and thus commodity Y may be termed as an inferior commodity. The quantity of Y decreases from the initial level of OY to OX_1 despite a rise in consumer's money income.

Hence, a change in taste leads to an increase in the quantity of

(X from OX to OX_1) at the cost of Y (because the consumer moves from E to E_1).

On the other hand, if as a result of an increase in consumer's income he assigns higher preference to Y than before, he will move from IC_1 to IC_3. The consumer's new equilibrium position is E_2 where he buys OY_2 of Y and OX_2 of X. Thus, the consumption of Y increases to the extent of YY_2 while that of X decreases to the extent of XX_2. It is so because the slope of IC_3 or the ratio of marginal utilities all along IC_3 is lower than the corresponding slope or the ratio of marginal utilities, all along IC_1. Symbolically,

$$MRS_{XY} \text{ of } IC_3 < MRS_{XY} \text{ of } IC_1$$

or
$$\frac{MU_X}{MU_Y} \text{ of } IC_3 > \frac{MU_X}{MU_Y} \text{ of } IC_1$$

Therefore, commodity Y is more preferable to commodity X, i.e., its utility has increased as a result of an increase in the consumer's money income.

(8) ***Measurement of the Consumer's Surplus.*** Prof. Hicks makes use of indifference curve analysis in the measurement of the consumer's surplus attained by an individual consumer from certain commodity. In

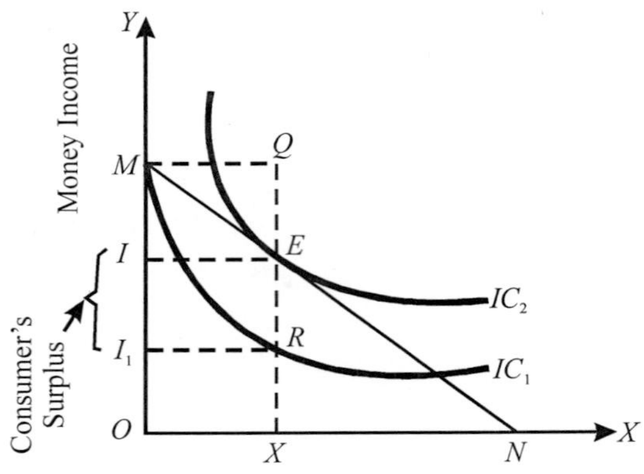

Fig. 14.46

Fig. 14.46, the consumer's imaginary indifference curve is IC_1 which states that the consumer is ready to pay MI_1 money for OX units of X rather than going without it. Also, the consumer is indifferent to point M or R, as both the points lie on the same indifference curve IC_1. In this case, the consumer actually needs to sacrifice MI amount of money (or

EQ) at the equilibrium level of quantity *OX*. Thus, he is able to save II_1 (or *ER*) amount of money which is the measure of his consumer's surplus. Hence, indifference curve analysis is also of much help in the measurement of consumer's surplus which is of paramount importance in various welfare policy determinations.

These above are the important applications of indifference curves. Besides, it is fairly used in the determination of various government policies.

18. COMPARATIVE STUDY OF UTILITY ANALYSIS AND INDIFFERENCE CURVE ANALYSIS

If we compare the two approaches, we find that the indifference curve analysis is an improvement over the old conventional demand analysis which is based on utility concept. In this connection the following points may be noted:

(1) ***The indifference curve analysis is not based on the cardinal measurement of utility, while the utility analysis is based on the cardinal measurement of utility.*** Under indifference curve analysis we take into account merely the preference of the consumer which is found on the basis of comparison between different levels of satisfaction. We do not bother about the measurement of psychological satisfaction, but depend upon choices of the consumers.

(2) ***The utility analysis assumes the price of other goods to be constant while the indifference curve analysis don't have such assumptions.*** The utility analysis does not consider the price of the other commodities and assumes that the prices of other commodities are constant. But in real life the prices of other commodities do not remain the same. Changes in the prices of other goods influence the commodity under consideration. The indifference curve analysis takes into account the changes in the prices and quantity of other commodities.

(3) ***The utility approach is a single commodity approach while the indifference curve analysis is a two commodity model.*** Under utility analysis, Dr. Marshall confines himself to a single commodity model and fails to analyse correctly the imulti commodity models. It is also unable to explain the relationships of substitution and complementary. The indifference curve analysis, on the other hand, successfully, deals with all such cases.

(4) ***Utility analysis assumes that the marginal utility of money is always constant and therefore, it ignores the income effect of price***

change. Thus it fails to distinguish between the two components of price effect. In other words, the utility analysis fails to explain the income effect and the substitution effect of a change in the price of commodity. It indicates that demand rises with a fall in price, but it does not indicate how much of it has gone up due to change in income and how much due to substitution effect.

The indifference curve analysis does not assume the marginal utility of money to be constant; and therefore, it enables us to distinguish between the income effect and substitution effect of a price change.

(5) ***Indifference curve analysis develops the theory of demand.*** The indifference curve approach developes the general theory of demand through the ordinal utility theory which enables us to enunciate the general theorem of demand in the following manner:

(*i*) The demand for a good varies inversely with price when the income elasticity of demand for that good is zero or positive.

(*ii*) The demand for good varies inversely with price when the income effect of a change in price is smaller than the substitution effect.

(*iii*) The demand for a good varies directly with price, when the income elasticity of demand for that good is negative and the income effect of a change in price is larger than the substitution effect.

When either the first or the second condition is fulfilled, the law of demand based on utility analysis holds good; but when the third condition applies we get the Giffen case of positively sloping demand curve. This is the reason that Giffen case is an exception of Marshallian raw of demand. The problem of inferior goods was a paradox to Marshall. Hicks' explanation (or indifference curve analysis) of a Giffen case is that the negative income effect is so powerful that it outweighs the positive substitution effect and hence when the price of a Giffen good falls, its demand also falls, instead of rising.

These above points clearly shows that indifference curve analysis is an improvement over the utility analysis in explaining the consumer's demand.

19. A CRITICAL APPRAISAL OF THE INDIFFERENCE CURVE ANALYSIS

Since the outcome of Prof. J.R. Hicks' book *Value and Capital* in 1939,[13] the indifference curve analysis has been widely accepted by the modern

13. Although, Prof. Hicks did not originate the indifference theory, yet it was his exposition and elaboration of the indifference curve that gave its present position in economics.

economists, and it has been greatly elaborated in various directions. As we know, today indifference curves are used in the explanation of many economic phenomena. The modern economists (Hicks, Allen and others) claim that the indifference curve analysis is superior to marginal utility analysis, in that it avoids the allegedly untenable assumption (implicit in utility approach) that consumers can measure the amounts of utility in the various goods that they buy. The indifference curve analysis assumes only "that the consumer is able to decide whether two combinations of goods are equivalent or whether he prefers one to the other; but it is not assumed that he can tell by how much he prefers one combination to the other."[14]

An indifference curve represents the consumer as being able to tell exactly how many units of commodity *Y* will compensate him for loss of one unit of commodity X (or vice versa); and he is supposed to be able to do this for any two goods or more goods, or for any good as against all the others put together. This would appear to necessitate his measuring the amounts of utility in every economic good. Otherwise, how can he know much more of one exactly balances little less of one (or all) of others? There is just as much measurement implied in the one theory as the other. And both the terminology and the mechanics of the indifference curve analysis are more awkward than the marginal utility explanation.

Another advantage of indifference curve analysis over the cardinal utility analysis is that the former explains the income and substitution effects of a given change in the price of commodity and thus it enables us to derive the *real income costant demand curve* which proves a more general and more inclusive theorem of demand than the Marshallian law of demand.

Beyond this, the indifference curve analysis is open to the same criticisms that we raised against the old utility analysis. It is why some economists argue that it (indifference analysis) is merely the utility analysis put in a new garb. According to Prof. Robertson, the new (indifference curve) analysis is only the old wine put into a new bottle. Instead of the concept of utility, it introduces the term 'preference'. Instead of the cardinal numbers (1, 2, 3, ... etc.), it makes use of the ordinal numbers (first, second, third, etc.) to indicate the consumer's preferences. The concept of marginal utility has been replaced by the concept of marginal rate of substitution. Similarly, the assumption of diminishing marginal

14. George J. Stigler, *The Theory of Price,* p. 76.

utility has been replaced by the new principle of diminishing marginal rate of substitution.

Like the old utility approach, the new indifference curve approach assumes that consumers are entirely rational in spending their money, and they proceed to plan their expenditure by a complicated process of mathematical calculation. Thus neither of the approaches is correct. As a complete and realistic explanation of how consumer purchases are actually determined, both the approaches—the cardinal utility approach and the ordinal indifference curve approach—are faulty.

20. A NOTE ON CONSUMER'S SURPLUS

Thus, consumer's surplus can be defined as the difference between the satisfaction which the consumer derives from the commodity and that which he forgoes in order to procure that commodity. To put it differently, the satisfaction that consumer obtains from the consumption of a commodity may be measured by the price he would pay for it rather than go without it; while the satisfaction he loses in procuring a commodity is measured by the price he actually pays for it. As such, consumer's surplus is defined as the excess of what a consumer would pay over what he actually pays. According to Dr. Marshall, "The excess of the price which he would be willing to pay rather than go without the thing, over that which he actually does pay, is the economic measure of this surplus satisfaction. It may be called *consumer's surplus*."[15]

Two different approaches have been developed to measure the consumer's surplus. The first is the Marshallian approach based on the utility analysis and the second is the Hicksian approach based on the difference curve analysis. We explain the two approaches in the following section.

1. Marshallian Approach

Marshall derives the economic measurement of consumer's surplus from the demand curve (marginal utility curve). In Fig. 14.47, *DD* is the demand curve which shows the set of prices that the consumer is willing to it pay for successive units of a commodity. The demand curve *DD* is based on the marginal utility. Since the price of the commodity is fixed by the market, it is constant for all units for our consumer. In Fig. 14.47, *PP* is the price line which is horizontal to *X*-axis. At this given price, the consumer buys *OX* quantity of the commodity. Thus, the area *ODEX*

15. A. Marshall, *op. cit.*, p. 103.

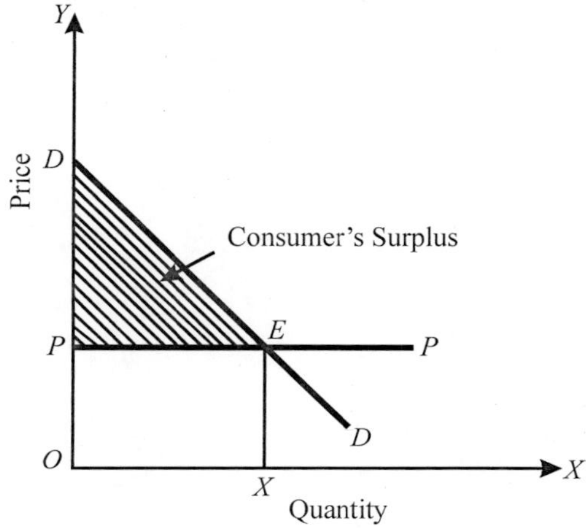

Fig. 14.47

indicates the total amount of money the consumer is willing to pay for *OX* quantity of the commodity. The area *OPEX* indicates the total amount of money that he actually pays for *OX* quantity of the commodity purchased. Thus, the shaded area *PDE* represents the consumer's surplus.

To make it more clear, let us take a numerical example. Suppose, a consumer goes in the market with 120 paise in his pocket with a view to purchasing some oranges. He thinks that the utility of the first orange will be equal to 100, of the second 80, of the third 60, of the fourth 40, of the fifth 20 and of the sixth zero. Now the price per orange in the market is 20 paise. Let us also assume that one unit of utility is equal to one paisa. Now the consumer will purchase the first four oranges without any hitch because the utility of each of them exceeds 20 which he will have to pay per unit (price). He will also buy the fifth orange because he will derive 20 paise worth of utility from it, which is just equal to its price. Now, he will stop his purchases at this point. The consumer's surplus derived by him from the purchase of oranges is shown in Table 14.8.

Table 14.8 states that the total utility derived from 5 units of oranges is equal to 300 paise and the price paid for these five oranges is equal to 100 paise. Thus, the total consumer surplus is 300 – 100 = 200

Table 14.8

(in Paise)

Units of Oranges	*Marginal Utility (Imaginary Price)*	*Actual Price*	*Consumer's Surplus*
1st	100	20	80
2nd	80	20	60
3rd	60	20	40
4th	40	20	20
5th	20	20	0
Total	300	100	200

The consumer's surplus can also be expressed by a mathematical formula as given below:

$$C.S. = TU - (P \times N)$$
$$= \Sigma\, MU - P \times N$$

where TU is the total utility, MU the marginal utility, P is the price of the commodity and N indicates the units of oranges purchased and consumed. Also Σ (sigma) indicates the sum total. If we supplement the necessary information in our above formula from Table 14.8, then we get

$$\text{Consumer Surplus} = 300 - 20 \times 5$$
$$= 300 - 100$$
$$= 200 \text{ paise.}$$

It is obvious that the consumer's surplus derived from some commodities is much greater than that from the other. There are many comforts and luxuries of which the prices are very much below those which many people would pay rather than go entirely without them; and which, therefore, afford very great consumer's surplus. Good examples of such types of commodities are matches, tea, salt, newspaper, and a postage stamp etc.[16]

The above concept of individual consumer's surplus can very well be extended to the society as a whole. According to Marshall, if we assume that interpersonal, differences in income, tastes, fashion, etc. are cancelled out, we can measure the total surplus satisfaction enjoyed by the society as a whole. This can be calculated by the simple process of adding together

16. According to Marshall, this benefit may be called the benefit he derives from his opportunities or from his environment; or to recur to a word that was in common use a few generations ago, from his conjective (the sum total of the technical, economic, social and legal conditions).

the consumer's surpluses enjoyed by all the consumers individually.

Assumptions of Marshallian Approach

The Marshallian concept of consumer's surplus is based on the following important assumptions:

(1) ***Marshall assumes that there is a fixed relationship between utility and satisfaction.*** As we know that utility implies expected satisfaction while satisfaction means actual or realised satisfaction. Utility is measured at the time of purchasing a commodity whereas satisfaction is derived when it is consumed. Thus, utility is different from satisfaction. A commodity may possess more utility, but when consumed the realised satisfaction may not be to that extent. But Marshall assumes that there is a definite relationship between expected satisfaction (utility) and realised satisfaction.

(2) ***Marshall assumes that the marginal utility of money is constant throughout the process of exchange.*** This assumption is very important because no comparison can be made in the absence of this assumption, and it becomes difficult to calculate consumer's surplus.

(3) ***It assumes all the assumptions of the demand analysis.*** The idea of consumer surplus is based on the demand curve or the marginal utility curve (according to Dr. Marshall, the two curves are the same). Thus, the assumptions underlying the demand curve become the assumptions of Marshallian approach to consumer's surplus. It includes *ceteris paribus* conditions.

(4) ***It assumes that the utility of a commodity depends, upon the quantity of that commodity alone.*** In other words, each commodity is an independent commodity. It means, the commodity in question has no substitutes. In the case of substitutes, all substitutes should be grouped as one commodity.

(5) ***Other things remaining the same.*** It assumes that differences in incomes, fashions, and tastes etc. between consumers are to be cancelled out.

The Marshallian approach to consumer's surplus holds only if the above assumptions are accepted.

Criticism of Marshallian Approach

The Marshallian Approach to the measurement of consumer's surplus has been criticised by Ulisse Gobbi, Cannan, Nicholson, Taussig, Hicks, Samuelson and others. According to Prof. Hicks, Marshall's concept of consumer's surplus has been based on certain assumptions which are not tenable in actual life. Thus the concept has been criticised on the basis of its unrealistic assumptions. The important criticisms of Marshall's concept of consumer's surplus are given below:

(1) ***Utility cannot be measured numerically.*** Marshall's approach is based on the assumption that utility is measurable. But utility cannot be measured numerically; it can only be realised. Due to this limitation, Prof. Hicks has explained the concept with the help of indifference curve technique.

(2) ***Marginal utility of money does not remain the same.*** Marshall's approach also assumes that the marginal utility of money is constant throughout the process of exchange. But this is not true; because when the consumer buys some quantity of a commodity, his stock of money is correspondingly reduced with the result that the marginal utility of money increases. The law of diminishing marginal utility also states that the greater the stock of money, the smaller is the marginal utility and vice versa. Thus, Marshall's assumption of constant marginal utility of money does not hold in real life.

(3) ***Utility is interrelated.*** Another assumption of the approach is that the utility of each good depends on the quantity of that good alone. In other words, it assumes that utility of any commodity is independent. The critics have challenged this assumption. The utility of a commodity also depends upon its related goods.

(4) ***Substitutes are available.*** Further, a commodity may possess a number of substitutes and it is neither possible nor feasible to assume the various substitutes of a commodity as one commodity.

(5) ***Assumptions are unrealistic.*** Again Marshall's concept of consumer's surplus is based on the demand curve. Critics point out that it is not possible to know the whole demand schedule of the commodity in question. It is difficult to know that how much price the consumer is willing to pay for each unit of the commodity because complete list of demand prices is not available. Thus, we cannot calculate the accurate estimate of consumer's surplus. Moreover, the assumption of *ceteris paribus* does not hold in real life.

(6) ***Utility and satisfaction are different.*** Marshall assumes that there is a definite relationship between utility and satisfaction. But the facts of experience do not follow the relationship. The satisfaction may not always be proportional to utility. It is possible that in the cases of utility we may obtain some consumer's surplus, but in the case of (realised) satisfaction,

we have to incur losses. Thus, Marshall's assumption that satisfaction is directly proportional to utility is not valid in real life.

(7) ***Other things do not remain the same.*** Again, the critics do not accept Marshall's assumption that the differences in incomes, fashions and tastes etc. are cancelled out in order to measure the consumer's surplus of the society as a whole. This is only an arbitrary assumption. There are large number of purchases in the market with different incomes, fashions and tastes etc. Different people act differently to a particular economic situation. All this will lead to a number of difficulties in the measurement of consumer's surplus of the society as a whole.

These above are the important limitations of Marshall's measurement of the consumer's surplus.

2. Hicksian Approach

Prof. Hicks derives the measurement of consumer's surplus from the indifference curve analysis. It has been shown in Fig. 14.48. In Fig. 14.48, consumer's money income has been measured along *Y*-axis while the *X*-axis measures the quantity of commodity *X*. Let us assume that the consumer has *OM* of income. If he spends his entire income on *X*, he would get *ON* quantity of *X*. Thus, *MN* is the price line which touches the indifference curve IC_2 at point *E*. At point *E*, he gets *OX* quantity of *X*

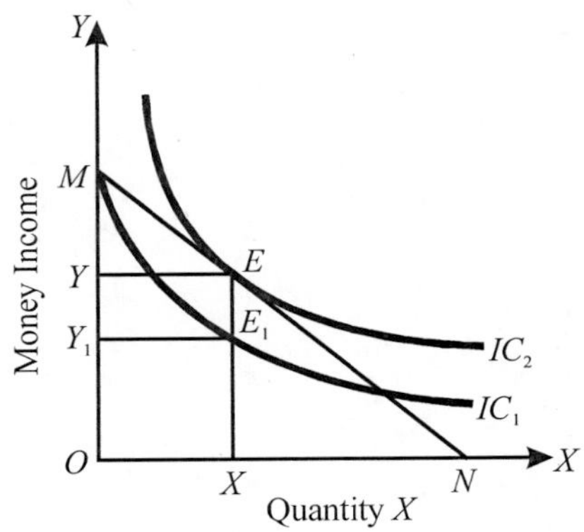

Fig. 14.48

and *OY* amount of money income. In other words, in equilibrium he spends *YM* money for *OX* quantity of *X*. Now, let us assume that the consumer does not know the price of *X*. In the absence of the price line, the imaginary indifference curve IC_1 indicates that for ON quantity of X, consumer is willing to spend MY_1 amount of money income and would like to remain at point E_1 on IC_1. But actually he has to spend MY money income for the same quantity. Thus the difference $(MY_1 - MY_1)$ YY_1 is consumer's surplus. In other words, consumer's surplus is the difference between the imaginary price and the actual price.

Further, we can also the effect of a price change or income change upon consumer's surplus through the indifference curve technique. This has been explained in the following section.

Change in Price and Consumer's Surplus

Here we assume that the price of X falls but the money income of the consumer remains unchanged. Due to a fall in the price of X, the price line MN shifts MN_1 in Fig. 14.49. Originally, the consumer was in equilibrium at point E where he got OX quantity of X and amount of money income. In other words, he was purchasing OX quantity of X with MY of money income. His consumer's surplus at point E was shown by YY_1 $(= EE_1)$. In the new situation when the price of X decreases, it enables the consumer to enjoy equilibrium point E_2 with a combination of OX quantity of X and OY_2 amount of money income. In other words, he needs to spend MY_2 money for the same OX quantity of X. It implies that at point E, his consumer's surplus has increased to Y_2Y_1.

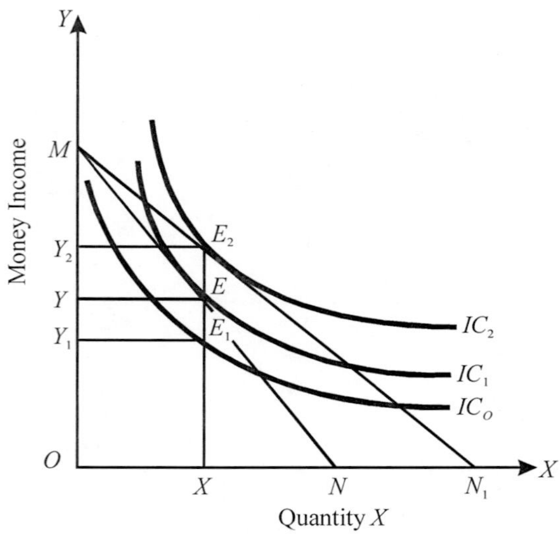

Fig. 14.49

Similarly, the students can also show the effect of arise in price of X on consumer's surplus assuming that money income remains the same.

Change in Income and Consumer's Surplus

This case has been illustrated in Fig. 14.50. Here we assume that the money income of the consumer changes while the price of the commodity remains the same. Let us assume that the money income of the consumer increases. Due to an increase in money income the line shifts nom MN to M_1N_1. Originally, the consumer's price line was MN which touches the indifference curve IC_1 at point E. His original consumer's surplus was YY_1 (= E_1), because the consumer was willing to pay MY_1 amount of money for OX quantity of X. If consumer's income increases from OM to OM_1 his new price line becomes M_1N_1 (assuming that the price of X remains constant). In this new position of increased income the consumer's preference schedule has changed. The original imaginary indifference curve was IC_0 but in the new position the imaginary indifference curve would be IC_2. It indicates that the consumer is now ready to pay M_1Y_2 amount of money for the same OX quantity of X. But he is able to get the same quantity of commodity X by actually paying only M_1Y_3 amount of money (here we may note that $M_1Y_3 = MY_2$ because the price of X and the

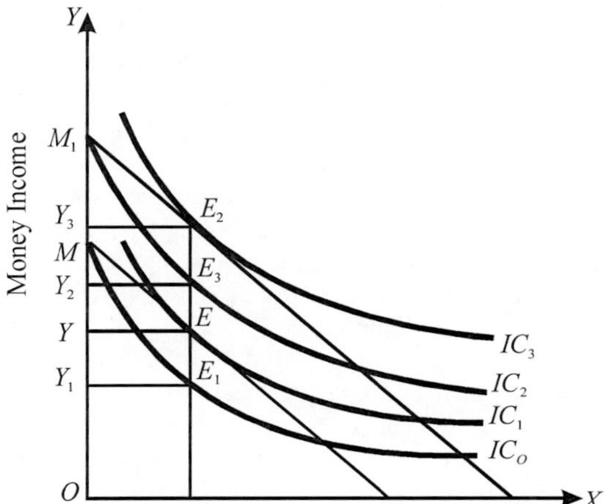

Fig. 14.50

quantity purchased remain the same). Thus, the new consumer's surplus is Y_3Y_2 (= E_2E_3) which may be equal to or more or less than the original consumer's surplus. The amount of consumer's surplus depends upon the slope of imaginary indifference curves IC_0 and IC_2. If the slope of IC_0 and IC_2 is the same, then in both the situations (the initial situation and the increased income situation) the consumer's surplus will be the same.

EXERCISES

1. What are the weaknesses of the Marshallian utility approach? Show how does the indifference curve technique overcome these weaknesses in the law of demand?
2. What are the characteristics of indifference curves? How would you explain a consumer's equilibrium with the help of these curves?
3. Show the effect of a change in income and a change in the price on consumer's demand with the help of indifference curves.
4. What do you understand by indifference curves? Explain fully the uses of indifference curve.
5. State and explain the concept of diminishing marginal rate of substitution (MRS). Whether this law is superior to that of the law of diminishing marginal utility?
6. Explain that the point of tangency between indifference curve and the price line alone is the point of consumer's equilibrium.
7. (*a*) Differentiate between "income effect" and "substitution effect" caused by the change in the price of a commodity.
   (*b*) Under what conditions may the fall in the price of the commodity lead to a reduction in the demand for it?
8. Supposing that utility can be measured. Show that utility analysis and indifference curve analysis give the same conditions of equilibrium of the consumer. Use diagram and/or formula to prove your answer.
9. What is Giffen Paradox? Explain it with the help of indifference curves.
10. What do you mean by a price consumption curve? Is it possible to derive the price-quantity demand curve from the consumption curve?
11. Write short notes on the following:
    (*i*) The Diminishing Marginal Rate of Substitution
    (*ii*) The Budget Line or the Price Line
    (*iii*) Indifference Curves Map
    (*iv*) Abnormal Indifference Curves and Corner Solution
    (*v*) Comparative Demand Curves
    (*vi*) Engel Curves or Income Demand Curves
    (*vii*) Elasticity of Demand and Price Consumption Curve.
12. Explain with the help of a diagram the concept of indifference curves. How far is it an improvement over the utility concept?
13. What do you understand by consumer's surplus. How fat can it be measured?
14. Explain Marshallian Doctrine of Consumer's Surplus. What is the contribution of Hicks towards this doctrine?

Multiple Choice Questions

15. (*i*) An indifference curve indicates, other things remaining the same,
    (*a*) Combinations of goods *X* and *Y* which yield equal level of satisfaction
    (*b*) Combinations of goods *X* and *Y* which a consumer would prefer to any others
    (*c*) A consumer's preference for any two goods
    (*d*) The amount of commodities *X* and *Y* that a consumer will buy at given prices [*Ans.* (*b*)]

(*ii*) An indifference curve
    (*a*) slopes upward from right to left
    (*b*) slopes upward from original point
    (*c*) slopes downward from left to right
    (*d*) is parallel to the *Y* axis [*Ans.* (*c*)]

(*iii*) An indifference curve is always
    (*a*) concave to the origin
    (*b*) convex to the origin
    (*c*) a vertical straight line
    (*d*) a horizontal straight line [*Ans.* (*b*)]

(*iv*) Indifference curve is convex to origin since
    (*a*) MRS_{XY} decreases
    (*b*) MRS_{XY} increases
    (*c*) MRS_{XY} remains the same
    (*d*) Marginal utility of commodity *Y* is decreasing as one increases the consumption of commodity. [*Ans.* (*a*)]

(*v*) The slope of an indifference curve shows
    (*a*) the price ratio
    (*b*) the diminishing *MRS*
    (*c*) factor substitution
    (*d*) level of indifference [*Ans.* (*b*)]

(*vi*) The statement $A = B = 100$ utilities implies
    (*a*) an ordinal measure of utility only
    (*b*) a cordinal measure of utility only
    (*c*) an ordinal and a cardinal measurement of utility
    (*d*) none of the above [*Ans.* (*c*)]

(*vii*) *Which* of the following figures can not be an indifference map?
    (*a*) *B and C*
    (*b*) *C and A*
    (*c*) *A and B*
    (*d*) *A, B and C* [*Ans.* (*a*)]

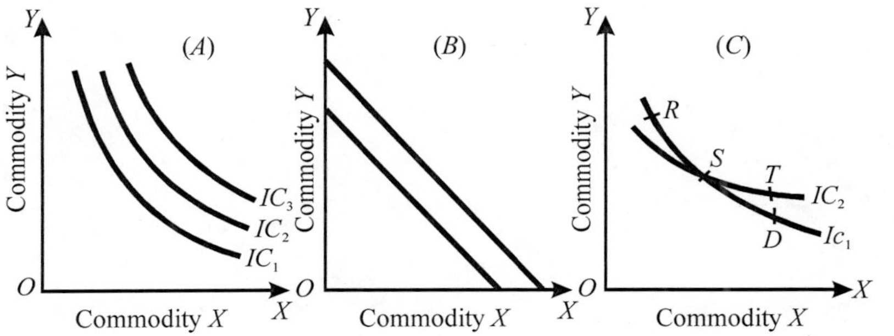

(*vii*) *At equilibrium, the slope of an indifference curve is*
(*a*) equal to the slope of budget line
(*b*) greater than the slope of budget line
(*c*) less than slope of budget line
(*d*) any one of the above [*Ans.* (*a*)]

(*ix*) Consumer's Surplus is described as
(*a*) extra quantity bought
(*b*) low price available
(*c*) difference between imaginary price and actual price
(*d*) none of above [*Ans.* (*c*)]

Chapter *15*

REVEALED PREFERENCE HYPOTHESIS

I. INTRODUCTION

The theory of revealed preference has been developed by Prof. Paul A. Samuelson of America[1]. This theory is different to that of Marshall's utility approach and Hicksian indifference curve approach. As we have noticed that the Marshallian utility approach to consumer behaviour is based on the assumption that utility is measurable and the Hicksian indifference curve approach to consumer behaviour is based on the assumption that the consumer is able to tell his preference among the various alternative combinations of the two commodities. These assumptions are unrealistic assumption. The Samuelson's revealed preference theory of demand is free from such unrealistic assumptions and it seeks to enunciate the demand from observed market behaviour of the consumer. Thus, it is third root of 'the logical theory of demand' and has been called by Hicks as the Direct Consistency Test under strong ordering. The theory is based on the fact that 'choice reveals preference.' In other words, the theorem of revealed preference draws its conclusions about the preferences of the consumer from the reactions of the consumer to price changes that take place in the market.

2. ASSUMPTIONS OF REVEALED PREFERENCE THEORY

Now, before we explain the theory let us understand the assumption on which the theory is based. The important assumptions of the theory are given below:

(1) The tastes and preferences of the consumer are given and they remain unchanged during the period of analysis.

---

1. P.A. Samuelson, *Foundations of Economic Analysis,* 1947, Ch. V-VI and "Consumption Theorems in terms of over compensation rather than indifference comparisons," *Economica,* February 1953.

(2) The consumer prefers more goods to less in any situation.

(3) The consumer chooses only one combination of the two commodities on a given income-price line (or budget line).

(4) The consumer's choice is based on strong ordering.

(5) The consumer's choices are consistent. Here, consistency or transitivity implies that once combination *A* is preferred to *B,* the latter must never be revealed.

(6) Revealed preference will alter only if the price is sufficiently lowered.

(7) The theory is based on the assumption of transitivity. Transitivity, however, refers to three term consistency. If *A* is preferred to *B,* and *B* is to *C*, then the consumer must prefer *A* to C. This assumption is necessary for the revealed preference theory, if the consumer is to make a consistent choice from given alternative situations.

(8) Income elasticity of demand is positive i.e., more good is demanded when income rises, and less when income falls.

3. CHOICE REVEALS PREFERENCE

Prof. Samuelson's theory of demand is based on the revealed preference axiom or hypothesis which states that choice reveals perference. In this context, a consumer buys a combination of two goods, either because he likes it in relation to the other combinations or it may be cheaper as compared to others. The idea of the revealed preference theory of demand has been explained in Fig. 15.1. Given the income of the consumer and the prices of the two commodities, *MN* is the income-price line in Fig.15.1.

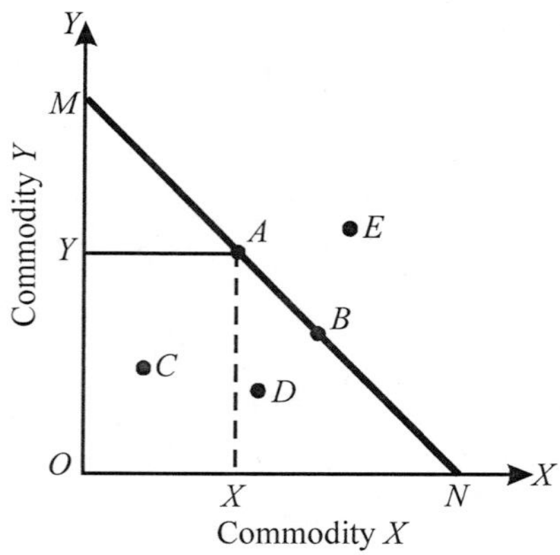

Fig. 15.1

Triangle *OMN* is the area of consumer's selection. The consumer can select any of the combinations *A, B,* C, and *D* with the help of his given constraints under the price line *MN.* Now the consumer will decide to buy some particular combination of the two commodities *X* and *Y* because he likes it more than the others or because it happens to be cheaper. If the consumer chooses to buy combination *A,* then *A* is *revealed preferred* to *B;* and combinations C and *D* are *revealed inferior* to *A.* To put it differently, combinations *A* and *B* both lie on the same price line *MN* and, therefore, are equally costly and equally good. If both are equally costly and also equally good, and even then the consumer buys combination *A,* the conclusion is obvious that the consumer buys A because he likes *A* better. It means that by purchasing combination *A,* the consumer has *Y* revealed his preference for it. On the other hand, combinations *C* and *D* are revealed inferior because they are lying to the left of the price-income line *MN.* Also, in Fig. 15.1, combination *E* lies outside the price-income line which indicates that it is more expensive and the consumer is unable to buy it with his given constraints. Thus, combination' *A* is revealed preferred to all other combinations where the consumer buys *OX* quantity of X and *OY* quantity of *Y.* Therefore, this choice becomes preference and strong ordering *preference hypothesis* is the basis of Prof. Samuelson's revealed preference theory.

The strong ordering preference hypothesis implies that there is a definite ordering of the various combinations of the two commodities in the consumer's scale of preferences. The selection (choice) of a particular combination by the consumer reveals his definite preference for it over all other combinations that are possible. Under the indifference curve approach, the consumer was assumed to be indifferent to the various alternative combinations on an indifference curve, but under the revealed preference approach, the consumer reveals a definite preference for one particular combination of the two commodities. In Fig. 15.1 the consumer chooses combination *A* out of various alternative combinations available to him and there is no possibility of A being indifferent to any other combination (say B) on the same price line under strong ordering hypothesis. But according to Prof. Hicks, strong ordering implies that the chosen combination is preferred to all other combinations below the price-income line but may be indifferent to the combinations on the same price-income. In Prof. Hicks' own words, "The difference between consequences of strong and weak ordering, so interpreted amounts to be more than this, that under strong ordering the chosen position is shown to be preferred to all other positions in and on the triangle, while under weak ordering it is preferred to all positions within the triangle but may be indifferent to other positions on the same boundary as itself."[2]

The assumption of the revealed preference theory also states that the consumer has to choose one and only one particular combination of the available combinations. It implies that he cannot be indifferent between any two combinations on the price-income line. Thus, according to Prof. Samuelson, strong ordering implies a definite preference and there is no question of indifference relationship between the various alternative combinations. To this extent, the revealed preference theory is an improvement over the previous two theories of demand—the Marshallian utility analysis and the Hicksian indifference curve analysis.

Prof. Samuelson's revealed preference approach can also be explained in terms of index numbers. Let us assume that in a given situation, X_1 and X_2 represent the two combinations of various goods and P_0 represents the prevailing price level. If the total cost of combination X_1 at price P_0 is considered to be not greater than the total cost of combination X_2 at price P_0, we may write the consumer's preference function in the following manner:

$$X_1P_0 \leq X_2P \qquad ...(1)$$

The condition (1) implies that the expenditure incurred on combination X_2 would also have adequate to buy combination X_1. In other words, combination X_1 is within the buying range of the consumer when he chooses X_2. X_2 combination is, thus, revealed preferred to X_1. Consistency or transitivity implies that once X_2 is "revealed" preferred to X_1, the latter must never be revealed preferred to X_2.

Here, it should be clearly noted that the condition (1) or the revealed preference will change if the price is lowered sufficiently. In other words, in a changed situation, X_1 can be revealed to be preferred to X_2 if

$$X_2 P_1 \leq X_1P_1 \qquad ...(2)$$

where P_1 is the price level of the changed situation.

The theory of revealed preference is based on the axiom that the condition (2) can never hold if the condition (1) does hold. Also, if (2) holds, then (1) cannot hold. In other words, let us assume that X_1, X_2... X_k are the various combinations of the commodities. Now, if X_2 is revealed to be preferred to X_1, which is revealed to be preferred to X_3 ..., which is revealed to be preferred to X_k; then X_k must never be preferred to X_2. This axiom ensures the strong ordering or the transitivity of revealed preferences.

2. I.R. Hicks, *Revision of Demand Theory* (1956), p. 43.

4. REVEALED PREFERENCE THEORY AND THE DEMAND THEOREM OR THE LAW OF DEMAND

The conventional law of demand states that there is an inverse relationship between the price of a commodity and its demand. Other things being equal, the quantity demanded will increase if the price of the commodity decreases and it will decrease if the price increases. Prof. Samuelson has derived the law of demand from his revealed preference theory assuming that the income elasticity of demand is positive. He recalls the demand theorem as the *fundamental theorem of consumer behaviour* and defines it in the following words: "Any good (simple or composite) that is known always to increase in demand when money-income alone rises must definitely shrink in demand when its price rises." It means that the demand for a good always increases with an increase in income, and obviously, it would always decrease when the price of the good increases. The "fundamental theorem" (demand theorem), therefore, states that positive income elasticity implicity depicts the consumer will increase his purchases of the lower priced good and consequently the demand curve will slope negatively.

We may also illustrate the damand theorem on the basis of revealed preference hypothesis in two stages — (*i*) by assuming a rise in price, and (*ii*) by assuming fall in price.

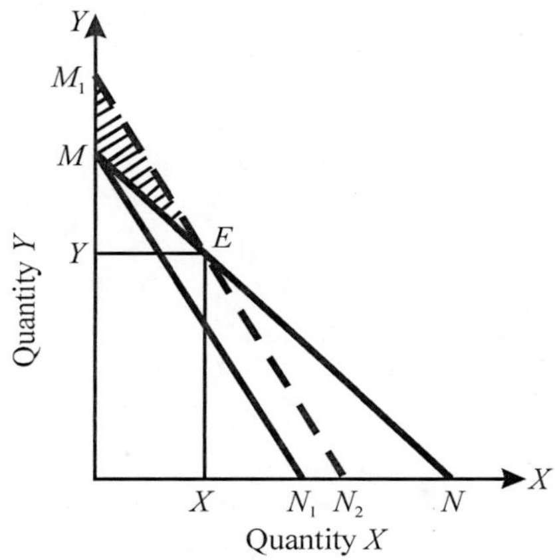

Fig. 15.2

In Fig. 15.2 *MN* is the original price-line (budget line). The area *OMN* represents the area of consumer's choice. Suppose, the consumer chooses combination point *E* where he buys *OX* quantity of commodity and OY quantity of commodity Y. Thus, initially point E reveals his preference. Or, point E is revealed to be preferred to all other combinations on and under the triangle OMN. Now suppose that the price of commodity X increases—the price of commodity Y remains the same—i.e., the new price line (or budget line) becomes MN_1. Here, we have proved that in the new situation the consumer wilt buy less of X, i.e., he will purchase less than OX quantity' of X, because the price of X has increased. The new price line MN_1 indicates that point E will not be possible for the consumer to buy, because it lies beyond the budget line MN_1.

Now let us assume that the consumer is given sufficient extra income which enables him to buy the original combination point E. Due to a sufficient increase in income the price line shifts to M_1N_2 which is parallel to the price line MN_1. The price line M_1N_2 passes through point E. Thus the area of consumer's choice becomes OM_1N_2. Now under the new price line M_1N_2, the consumer can choose point A or any other point on segment M_1E of the new budget line M_1N_2. This is because of the fact that segment M_1E will provide higher quantities of both the commodities to the consumer than the segment ME of the old initial price line MN. Moreover, the choice of the consumer for the remaining part (EN_2) was also available under the initial situation of the price line MN. But the choice on M_1E was not available to the consumer before when the price line was MN. Under the consistency assumption, the consumer will not select any point on the EN_2 segment of the budget line M_1 N_2 except of course point E itself because segment EN_2 lies below segment EN. Therefore, there are two alternatives open to the consumer; either to buy the old combination point E (i.e., OX of X and OY of Y) or to choose any combination on segment M_1E, i.e., above point E which will mean less quantity of X (i.e., less than OX) and more quantity of Y (i.e., less than OY of Y).

Hence, even after the consumer is given sufficient income to compensate the loss of a price increase (in commodity X), the consumer demands either the same quantity of X or a smaller quantity of X at higher price. If somehow the extra income is not given to the consumer, then he will definitely buy a smaller quantity of X at a higher price. Thus the inverse relationship between price and demand is proved.

Further, we can also explain the demand theorem by assuming a fall in the price of X. In Fig. 15.3 MN is the original budget line. At this price line, the consumer chooses point E which is revealed to be preferred to all other available combinations. Here the consumer buys OX of X and OY of Y. Now suppose the price of X falls—assuming the price of Y to be the same—the new price line becomes MN_1, and the area of consumer's choice is OMN_1. Now if some income is taken away from the consumer via taxation (income-tax), i.e., he comes down to a lower price line M_1N_2. Now he can choose either point A or some other point on the segment EN_2. He will not chooses any point on the remaining segment M_1E of the budget line M_2N_2 because it (the segment M_1E) lies to the left of (below) the segment ME of the original price line MN. Thus, the consumer can choose either Point E ($OX + OY$) or some other combination beyond E to the right (or segment EN_2 which is above the segment EN of the original price line MN), which would mean more of X and less of Y. If the consumer's money income remains the same, i.e., remains on the price line M_1N_2, he will always demand a higher quantity of X (provided that the income elasticity of demand for X is positive which has already been assumed by Prof. Samuelson between price and demand is proved.

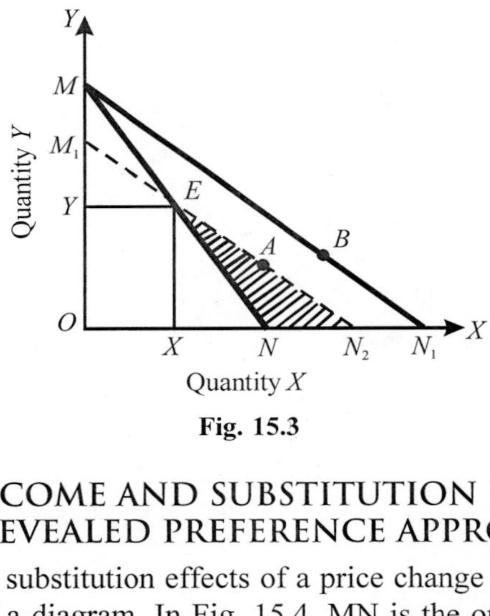

Fig. 15.3

5. PRICE, INCOME AND SUBSTITUTION EFFECTS UNDER REVEALED PREFERENCE APPROACH

The income and substitution effects of a price change can be explained with the help of a diagram. In Fig. 15.4, MN is the original price line. Suppose, the consumer chooses point E, so that it indicates the quantities of the two commodities X and Y which are revealed to be preferred to any other point on MN. Now suppose that the price of commodity X falls while the price of commodity Y is assumed to be constant; the price line becomes MN_1. At this new price line MN_1, the consumer chooses point E_1. The movement from point E to E_1 is due to the price effect and the price effect comprises the substitution effect and income effect. In order to separate these effects, we assume that the consumer's money income is reduced to the extent that he comes do to his original point E; or the price-income line passes M_1N_2 through point E. Now the consumer will choose any point to the right of E on segment EN_2 .Let us assume that this is point E_2, At this point E_2, the consumer buys more of X ($OX_2 > OX$) which is due to substitution effect. If the income of the consumer is not reduced, so that he remains on the price-income line M_1N_2, he will move from E_2 to E_1 purchasing more of X ($=X_2X_1$ units) purely income effect. Thus, as indicated in Fig. 15.4, XX_1 is the price effect which is divided into two parts, the substitution effect (XX_2) and the income effect (X_2X_1). It is to be noted that the Samuelson's explanation of the substitution effect is different from that of indifference curve analysis. In the case of indifference curve analysis, the consumer moves from one combination to another on the same indifference curve and his real income remains constant. But in the revealed preference theory, indifference curves are not assumed and the substitution effect is a movement along the price income line arising from changing relative prices.

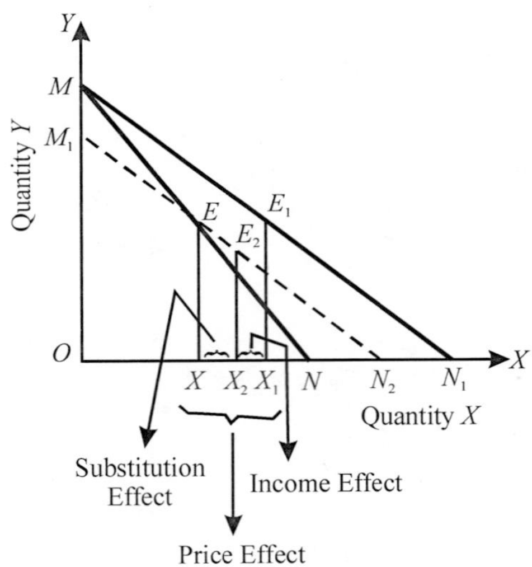

Fig. 15.4

6. DERIVATION OF DEMAND CURVE FROM REVEALED PREFERENCE

We may also derive the demand curve from the revealed preference hypothesis. This can be explained with the help of Fig. 15.5. In panel (A)

of Fig. 15.5 money is measured along the vertical axis while commodity X is measured along the horizontal axis. MN is the original price-income line on which the consumer shows his preference at point E and buys OX of commodity X. Suppose that the price of commodity X falls. As a result of this, the price-income line shifts to MN_1. On this line the consumer may reveal his preference, say at point B, where he buys a larger quantity BX_1 of commodity X which has resulted in his increased demand from OX to OX_1.

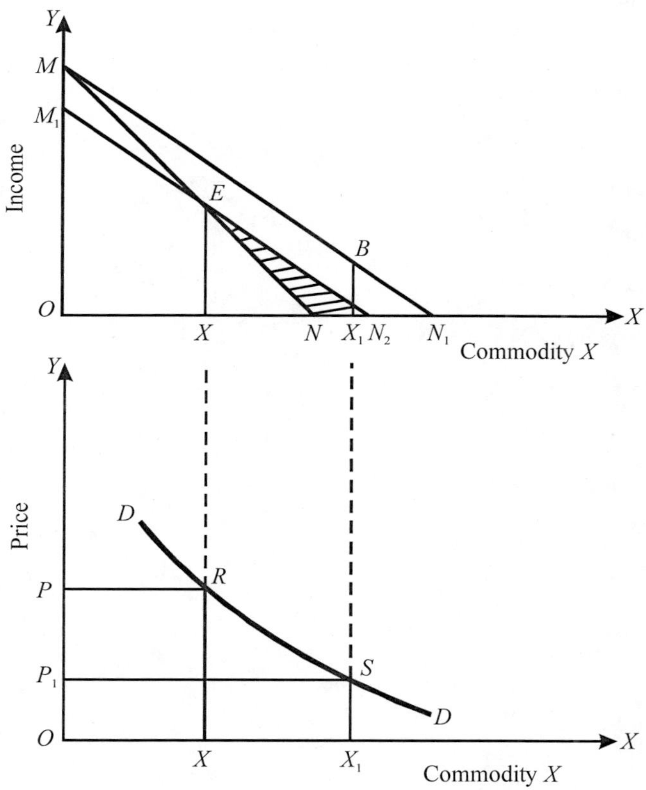

Fig. 15.5

Now if we withdraw the increased real income (as a result of a fall in price) equal to MM_1 then M_1N_2 will become his new price-income line which is drawn parallel to MN_1 and passes through point E, The new triangle OM_1N_2 becomes his area of choice. Since the consumer was showing his original preference at point E on the original price-income line MN, therefore all points above E on the segment EM_1 of the line M_1N_2 are inconsistent with his choice. This is because of the fact that he will not have less quantity of commodity X when price falls. He will therefore reject all combinations above point E and either choose combination E or any other combination in the shaded triangle NEN_2. If the MM_1 amount of money taken from the consumer is returned to him, he will again be at Point B .on the price-income line MN_1 where he buys larger quantity OX_1 of X than before. The shift from point E to point B develops the relevant demand curve. in panel (B) Fig. 15.5.

As we have shown income .on the vertical axis in panel (A), the price of commodity can be calculated by dividing the total money income by the number of units of X purchased. Thus the initial price of X would be OM / ON (= OP in panel B) where the quantity demanded is OX. When the price of X falls to OM/ON_1 (= OP_1 in panel B) then the quantity demanded or purchased would be OX_1. Now in panel (B) we may plot this information and join the points R and S to get the relevant demand curve DD.

7. SUPERIORITY OF REVEALED PREFERENCE THEORY

The above discussed revealed preference approach is superior to the Hicksian ordinal utility approach (indifference curve approach) on the basis of following points:

1. ***Consumer behavioural aspect.*** The revealed preference approach does not involve psychological introspective information about he behaviour of the consumer. Instead it shows a behaviouristic analysis based on observed consumer behaviour in the market. Thus the revealed approach is more realistic than the earlier utility approach developed by Marshall and Hicks.

2. ***Assumption of continuity.*** The revealed preference approach rejects the continuity assumption of the utility and indifference curve approach. An indifference curve is a continuous curve where the consumer may choose any combination of two goods. Samuelson believes that there is discontinuity because the consumer can have only one combination. Once it is selected, the consumer does not talk about the others. Following this argument, later on Hicks in his, *Revision of Demand Theory* does not talk about this assumption and replaced it by the assumption of strong and weak ordering.

3. ***Assumption of rationality.*** Hicks, theory of indifference curve is based on the assumption that the consumer always behaves rationally to maximise his satisfaction from given income and given prices of goods and services. Samuelson's demand theory (revealed preference theory) is superior because it does not talk about rationality or the law of diminishing-marginal utility in his analysis.

4. ***Explanation of substitution effect.*** Samuelson's demand theorem is more realistic as an explanation of consumer behaviour towards the substitution effect than the Hicksian approach. Samuelson permits the Consumer to shift to a higher price-income situation (i.e., price line) in case of a fall in price shift while Hicks puts the consumer an the same indifference curve. This improvement was later also admitted by Hicks when he dropped the compensating variation principle in his revision of demand theory.

8. DEFECTS OF THE REVEALED PREFERENCE THEORY

The Samuelson's theory of vealed preference suffers from a number of limitations. The following are the important defects of the theory:

(1) ***Strong ordering hypothesis is not correct.*** According to Prof. Armstrong, the revealed preference theory ignores the possibility of indifference in the behaviour of the consumer. The strong ordering hypothesis of Prof. Samuelson completely rejects the indifference points on the same price-income line. He states that only and only one point is revealed to be preferred over the other points available to the consumer. But the critics say that if the preference of the consumer is to be made from a number of combinations available to the consumer, then the possibility of indifference in the behaviour of the consumer cannot be overlooked.

(2) ***Behavioural factors have been ignored.*** The theory is based upon the behaviour of the consumer to changes in (market) price-level. But, actually the behaviour of consumers is also affected by other factors which the theory has completely ruled out.

(3) ***Conditional approach.*** The Samuelson's revealed preference theory of demand is conditional and not general. It is based on the fundamental postulate that the income elasticity of demand for the commodity is positive. But if the income elasticity of demand (or income effect) is negative, the theory fails. To put it differently, if income elasticity of demand is negative, the theory is unable to determine accurately the change in demand in response to a change in price.

(4) ***Giffen's paradox has not been explained.*** The theory does not explain Giffen's paradox, because Giffen's paradox is related to the negative income elasticity of demand which the theory does not assume. In the case of a Giffen good, the negative income effect is very strong which overcomes the positive substitution effect. Thus the exclusion of the Giffen's paradox is a great drawback of the new approach. This is the reason why Prof. Hicks' indifference curve theory of demand is more comprehensive than Prof. Samuelson's fundamental theorem of consumption.

(5) ***Welfare purpose has been ignored.*** The revealed preference analysis does not serve that welfare "purpose" of the demand theory. It only serves the economic purpose of the demand theory. Sometimes, it is possible that a consumer has chosen a wrong point, but the revealed preference theory does not permit him to correct the mistake. Thus, it is only an academic exercise and is not based upon the rational behaviour of a consumer in the market.

The above points of criticism indicate that the revealed preference theory of demand is not an improvement over the Hicks-Allen indifference curve analysis. Nevertheless, it can be assumed as an alternative of the old approaches to the consumer behaviour.

EXERCISES

1. Explain the revealed preference theory of consumer behaviour.
2. Write a critical note on the theory of revealed preference.
3. Explain that how Prof. Samuelson has derived the conventional (Marshallian) law of demand from his revealed preference theorem.
4. Illustrate the Fundamental Theorem of Consumption as developed by Prof. Samuelson.
5. "Choice reveals preference." Explain this statement.
6. Bring out the improvements introduced in demand analysis by the theory of revealed preference.
7. Assess the impact of revealed preference on the theory of demand.
8. Derive the demand curve from the theory of revealed preference.
9. Explain the superiority of revealed preference over the utility and indifference curve approach to consumer behaviour. What are the defects of the theory of revealed preference?

Multiple Choice Questions

10. (*i*) Who has developed the revealed preference theory of demand?
    (*a*) Marshall (*c*) Samuelson
    (*b*) Hicks (*d*) Baumol [*Ans.* (*c*)]

    (*ii*) Samuelson's revealed preference theory of demand is based on the assumption:

(*a*) consumer's behaviour is rational
(*b*) income elasticity of demand is positive
(*c*) income elasticity demand is negative
(*d*) all of the above [*Ans.* (*b*)]

(*iii*) Revealed preference approach is superior to the Hicksian ordinary utility approach to consumer behaviour because
(*a*) it does not involve any psychological introspective information about the behaviour of the consumer
(*b*) it admits the assumption of continuity
(*c*) it is based on the assumption that the consumer always behaves rationally to maximise his satisfaction
(*d*) none of the above [*Ans.* (*a*)]

Chapter 16

THE CONCEPT OF ELASTICITY OF DEMAND

1. MEANING OF ELASTICITY OF DEMAND

The elasticity of demand refers to a particular behaviour of a demand curve. It tells us something about how the quantity demanded responds to changes in price. The degree to which quantity demanded responds to a change in price is known as the elasticity of demand. If a small change in price causes a relatively large change in the quantity demanded, we say that demand is elastic. If the change in the quantity demanded is relatively small, then demand is said to be inelastic. It is important to note that we are concerned with *proportionate* change in price and quantity, and not with *absolute* changes. Elasticity will, therefore, be different at each and every price, and it can only be meaningful when related to small changes in price. Elasticity of demand is the relationship between proportionate change in price and the resulting proportionate change in quantity demanded.

The concept of elasticity of demand was mainly developed by Marshall. According to him, "The elasticity (or responsiveness) of demand in a market is great or small, according as the amount demanded increases much or little for a given fall in price, and diminishes much or little for a given rise in price."

In the words of Albert L. Meyers, "The elasticity of demand is a measure of relative change in the amount purchased in response to relative change in price on a given demand curve."

Modern economists, however, define the elasticity concept in a mathematical way. For instance, Prof. R.G. Lipsey states that "Elasticity of demand may be defined as the ratio of the percentage change in the quantity demanded to percentage change in price." Mrs. Joan Robinson defines it more clearly. According to her, "The elasticity 'of demand at any price or at any output, is the proportional change of amount purchased in response to a small change in price, divided by the proportional change of price."

These above definitions analysed only the responsiveness of demand to a given change in price, and thus obliviated the effect of a variation in the prices of other commodities or in the income of the consumer. In their views, demand is a function of price alone, and therefore, they discussed only price elasticity of demand. In the modern analysis of consumer behaviour, however, the following elasticities of demand are considered important, albeit their relative significance may be different in different situations—(1) Price Elasticity of Demand, (2) Cross Elasticity of Demand, (3) Income Elasticity of Demand, (4) Demand Elasticity of Substitution.

Price elasticity is, of course, the most important. among the above elasticities of demand. That is why the concept of price elasticity of demand is popular among the economists. Now we shall discuss these various concepts under the following analysis.

2. PRICE ELASTICITY OF DEMAND

Alfred Marshall was the first economist to give a clear formulation of price elasticity as the ratio of a relative change in quantity to a relative change in price. Let *Ed* stand for price elasticity of demand. Then mathematically, the formula for calculating the price elasticity of demand can be written as:

$$Ed = \frac{\text{Percentage change in quantity demanded}}{\text{Percentage change in price}}$$

$$= \frac{\frac{\Delta X}{X}\times 100}{\frac{\Delta P}{P}\times 100}$$

$$= \frac{\Delta X}{X} / \frac{\Delta P}{P}$$

$$= \frac{\Delta X}{X} \times \frac{P}{\Delta P}$$

or $$Ed = \frac{\Delta X}{\Delta P} \cdot \frac{P}{X}$$

Also $$Ed = \frac{dX}{dP} \cdot \frac{P}{X} \qquad ...(1)$$

Here, X is quantity, P is price, and Δ (delta) is the symbol meaning "a change in". Thus, $\Delta X/X$ is a relative change in quantity, and $\Delta P/P$ is a relative change in price. Generally, a negative sign is put before the term dX/dP. P/X, which simply indicates that quantity demanded and price are inversely related. *Ed* is also called the coefficient of elasticity of demand. It is a pure number, that is, it stands by itself being independent to units of measurement. When numerical estimates are possible, the coefficients of elasticity of different commodities can be directly compared. The value of the coefficient *Ed* will He between O and ∞. If *Ed* equals 1, demand has unit elasticity. If *Ed* is less than 1, but more than zero, demand is inelastic. If the coefficient is zero, demand is said to be perfectly inelastic. If the coefficient is greater than 1, but less than ∞, demand is elastic. If it is ∞, demand is said to be perfectly elastic. Thus, the value of the coefficient *Ed* will tell us the nature of the demand curve. Conveniently, we put the following five categories of the demand curve.

(1) ***Perfectly Elastic Demand.*** It refers to that situation where a small rise in price will cause the quantity demanded to be zero. In such ii situation

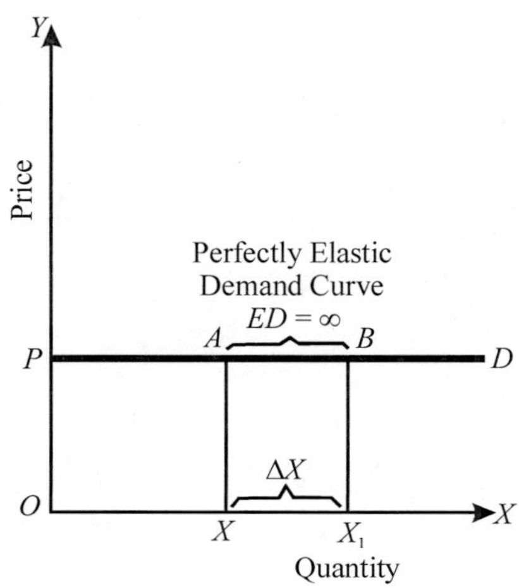

Fig. 16.1

price of a commodity remains constant. In a perfect competitive firm,. the demand curve is perfectly elastic. The numerical value of the coefficient *Ed* will be infinite, or

$$Ed = \frac{dX}{dP} \cdot \frac{P}{X} = \infty \quad \text{because } dP = 0$$

It should, however, be noted that cases of perfectly elastic demand are very rare in actual life and, therefore, only of theoretical importance. Figure 16.1 indicates this situation where the price *OP* is fixed and at this fixed price any quantity of the commodity can be sold. In short, perfectly elastic demand for a commodity refers to those cases in which the quantity demanded is independent of price.

(2) ***Elastic Demand.*** It refers to that situation where the proportionate change in quantity demanded is much greater than the proportionate change in price. In such a case the numerical value of the coefficient *Ed* will take the limit $1 < Ed < \infty$ or normally,

$$Ed = \frac{dX}{dP} \cdot \frac{P}{X} > 1$$

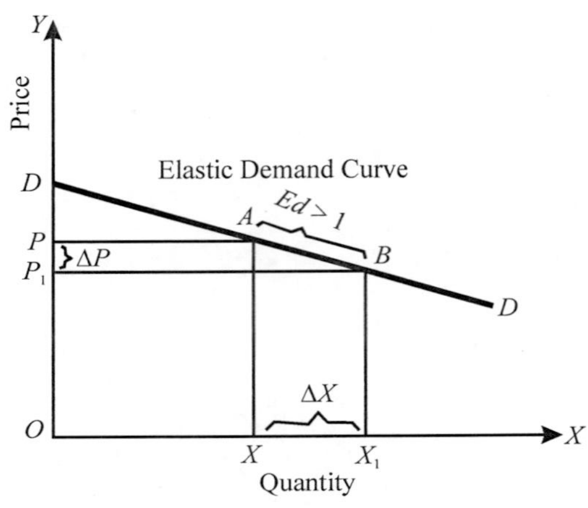

Fig. 16.2

which implies that the relative change in quantity demanded is much greater than the relative change in price, or $\frac{dX}{X} > \frac{dP}{P}$. For example, a 10 per cent change in pirce will lead to a 20 per cent change in quantity. demanded, then

$$Ed = \frac{20 \text{ per cent}}{10 \text{ per cent}} = 2$$

This case has been shown in Fig. 16.2.

(3) ***Unit Elasticity of Demand.*** It refers to that situation where the proportionate change in quantity demanded is equal to the proportionate change in price. In such a case the numerical value of the coefficient *Ed* will be equal to unity, i.e.,

$$Ed = \frac{dX}{dP} \cdot \frac{P}{X} = 1$$

because $\frac{dX}{X} = \frac{dP}{P}$

This case has been shown in Fig. 16.3.

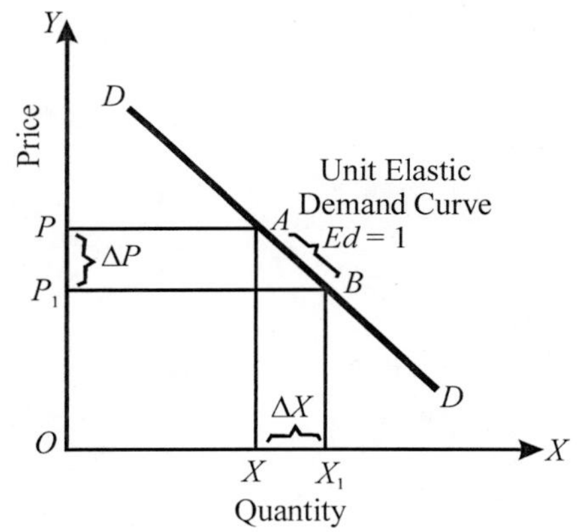

Fig. 16.3

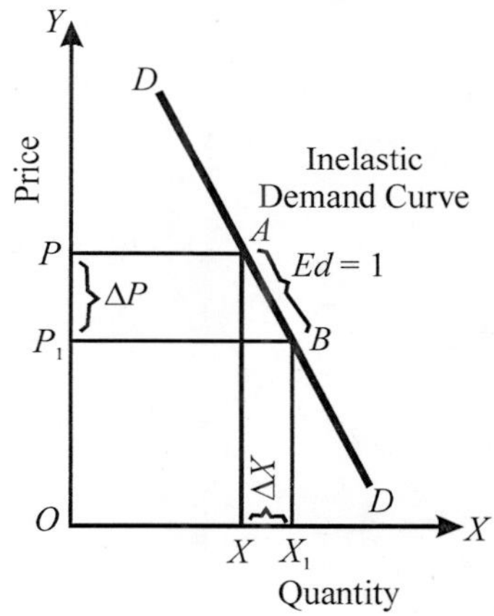

Fig. 16.4

(4) ***Inelastic Demand.*** It refers to that situation where the proportionate change in quantity demanded is less than the proportionate change in price. In such a case the numerical value of the coefficient *Ed* will take the limit, $O < Ed < 1$, or normally,

$$Ed = \frac{dX}{dP} \cdot \frac{P}{X} < 1 \text{ because } \frac{dX}{X} < \frac{dP}{P}$$

For example, a 10 per cent change in price will lead to a 5 per cent change in quantity demanded, then.

$$Ed = \frac{5 \text{ per cent}}{10 \text{ per cent}} = \frac{1}{2} \text{ which is} < 1$$

This case is shown in Fig. 16.4, where the ratio $\frac{\Delta P}{\Delta X}$ or $\frac{dX}{dP} < 1$

(5) ***Perfectly Inelastic Demand.*** It refers to that situation where quantity demanded is perfectly independent of price changes. In such a case the demand is non-responsive and the value of the coefficient *Ed* will be. equal to zero, i.e.,

$$Ed = \frac{dX}{dP} \cdot \frac{P}{X} = 0 \quad \text{because } dX = 0$$

This situation has been shown in Fig. 16.5 where the demand *OX* is fixed. If price increases or decreases, it will be unable to make any change in quantity demanded. This case is rarely found in real life.

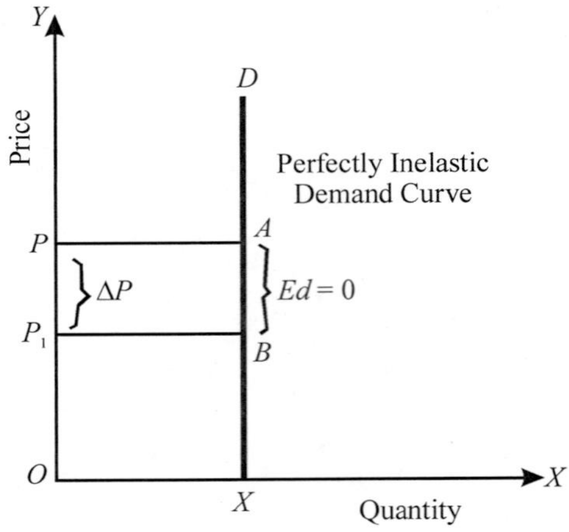

Fig. 16.5

It should, however be noted that the first and the last categories of price elasticity of demand are unrealistic situations. We cannot visualise any situation in which the quantity demanded is independent of price, or where

$$Ed = \infty \text{ and } Ed = 0$$

changes in price do induce changes in the quantity demanded, although the magnitude of such change may be different for different commodities.

Hence, in reality the demand for a commodity may be elastic. unitary elastic or inelastic. More specifically,

$$|Ed| \gtreqless 1$$

Further, it should be remembered that a demand curve does not have the same elasticity throughout its entire length. Therefore, the above classification of the price elasticity of demand applies to the different segments of a demand curve. A demand curve will change its elasticity at different points. But there are three cases of perfectly elastic, perfectly inelastic and unit elastic demand curves, where it possesses only one elasticity throughout its entire length. These are exceptions to the general rule.

Measurement of the Price Elasticity of Demand

The price elasticity of demand can be measured in several alternative ways. We shall discuss the following three methods of measurement—(1) Total Outlay or Expenditure Method, (2) Point Method, and (3) Arc Method.

(1) ***Total Outlay or Expenditure Method.*** This method was devised by Alfred Marshall. Marshall said that the price elasticity of demand can be measured on the basis of change in total outlay (or expenditure) following a change in the price of a commodity. In the words of Marshall, "If the elasticity of demand be equal to unity, any fall (or rise) in price will cause a proportionate rise (or fall) in the amount brought (quantity demanded) and, therefore, it will make no change in the total outlay which purchasers make for the commodity." Therefore, in this method, we consider the change in price and the consequent change in the outlay on the purchase of the commodity. If we multiply the quantity purchased by its price, then we get total outlay incurred on it, i.e.,

Total Expenditure = Quantity Demanded × Price

If with a price increase, total spending also increases, then demand is *inelastic.* If, with a price reduction, total spending declines, the demand is also *inelastic.* If, with a price increase, total spending declines, the demand is *elastic.* If, with a price reduction, total spending increases, demand is elastic. In other words, if total spending changes in the same direction as the change in price, demand is inelastic; if total spending changes in the opposite direction of a change, then demand is elastic. If total spending remains the same as price goes up or down, we have unitary elasticity. Examine the demand schedule of Table 16.1.

Table 16.1: Elastic Demand, Unitary Elasticity and Inelastic Demand

Price (Rs.)	*Quantity Demanded*	*Total Revenue (Rs.)*	*Demand Elasticity*
10	100	1,000	Elastic Demand
9	120	1,080	($Ed > 1$)
8	140	1,120	Unitary Elasticity
7	160	1,120	($Ed = 1$)
6	180	1,080	Inelastic Demand
5	200	1,000	($Ed < 1$)
4	240	960	

From Table 16.1 we draw the following conclusions:

(*i*) If demand is elastic, a given fall in price causes a relativey larger increase in the quantity demanded. From this it follows that a drop (rise) in price causes consumers to make a larger (lesser) money expenditure on a commodity whose demand is elastic.

Table 16.2. Changes in Price, Outlay and Elasticities of Demand

Nature of the Change in Price	*Change in Total Expenditure (Outlay)*	*Value of the Coefficient (Ed)*	*Nature of the Elasticity of Demand*
I. Effect of a fall in price	(*a*) Decrease	$Ed < 1$	Inelastic
	(*b*) Increase	$Ed > 1$	Elastic
	(*c*) Constant (No change)	$Ed = 1$	Unitary Elastic
II. Effect of a rise in price	(*a*) Decrease	$Ed < 1$	Elastic
	(*b*) Increase	$Ed > 1$	Inelastic
	(*c*) Constant (No change)	$Ed = 1$	Unitary Elastic

(*ii*) If demand has unit elasticity, a fall (or rise) in price causes no change in expenditures.

(*iii*) If demand is inelastic, a fall (or rise) in price causes consumers to spend less (more) money on the commodity.

The relations between elasticity and expenditure are stated in more general form in Table 16.2.

These relationships may be illustrated graphically. In Fig. 16.6 the area OP_1AX_1 (total revenue) exceeds the area $OPBX$ and illustrates a situation where demand in this price range (OP to OP_1) is inelastic.

Figure 16.7 shows a situation where demand is elastic in the price range $OP - OP_1$, because here total revenue is greater at lower price (i.e., the area $OP_1BX_1 > OPAX$).

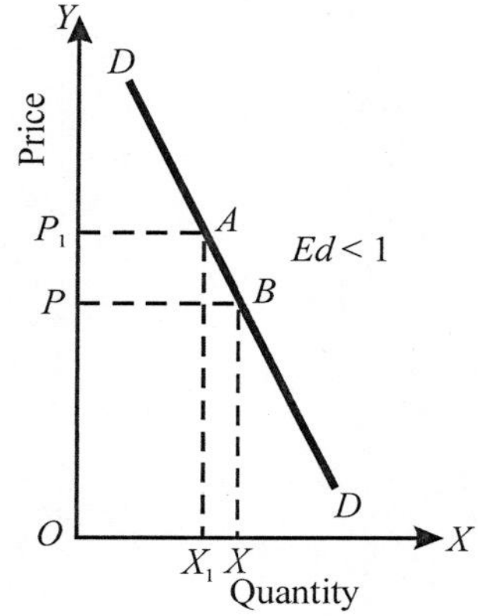

Fig. 16.6

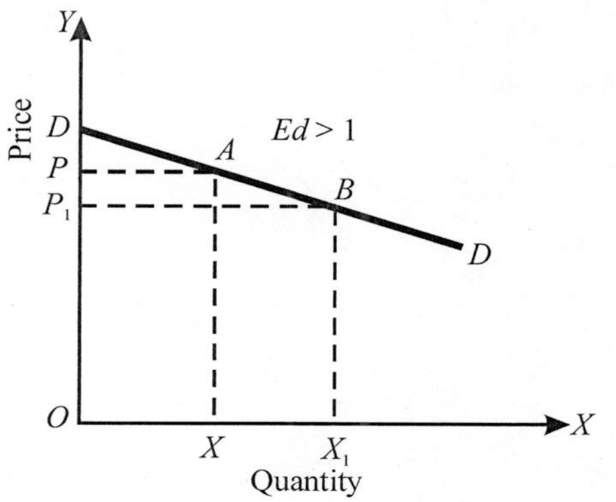

Fig. 16.7

Figure 16.8 illustrates the interesting case where the elasticity of demand is unity and the total revenue will be the same at all prices (i.e., $OPAX = OP_1BX_1$).

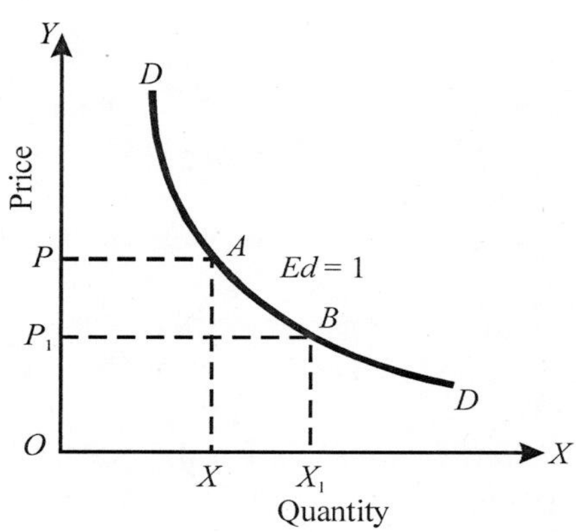

Fig. 16.6

The relationship between the total outlay and price elasticity of demand can also be shown by the help of Fig. 16.9. In Fig. 16.9 we take three different price ranges from OP to OP_1, from OP_1 to OP_2, and below OP_2. If price fall from OP *to* OP_1, total outlay increases and the total outlay curve slopes downward to the right. Also, if price increases from OP *to* OP, the total outlay decreases as shown by the segment *AB* of the curve sloping upward to the left. Thus, over the price range OP to OP_1, elasticity of demand is greater than one or the demand is elastic.

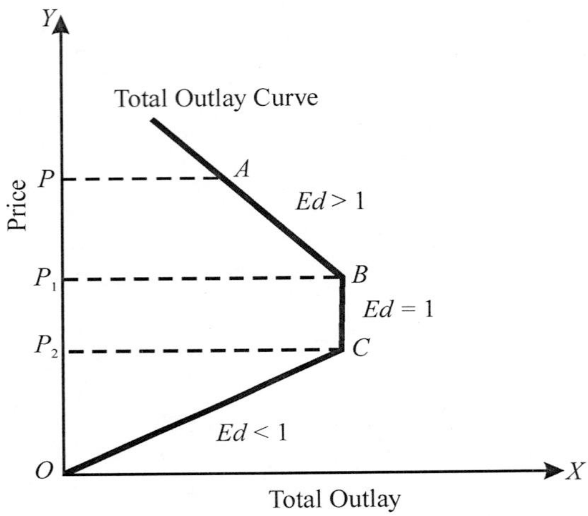

Fig. 16.6

If price falls from OP_1 to OP_2 or it rises from OP_2 to OP_1, total outlay remains the same. Therefore, the elasticity of demand over the price range $OP_1 - OP_2$ will be unitary elastic ($Ed = 1$). Over the price range OP_2, total outlay decreases as price falls; thus the elasticity of demand is inelastic ($Ed < 1$).

The main limitation of the total outlay method is that it simply classifies the price demand into elastic, inelastic and unitary elastic. This method is unable to measure the elasticity in numerical terms, i.e., it does not explain the situation of perfectly elasticity elastic demand ($Ed = \infty$) and the situation of perfectly inelastic demand ($Ed = \infty$).

(2) ***Point Method or Point Elasticity of Demand.*** The point method of measuring price elasticity of demand has also been developed by Prof. Alfred Marshall. Under total outlay method, the terms "elastic" and "inelastic" have been applied to the whole demand for a commodity. This is correct only for some purposes, but not for others, because the

demand for a commodity can be elastic in one price range and inelastic in another. The degree of elasticity or inelasticity—as indicated by the size of the coefficient (*Ed*)—can also vary from one price range to another. Figures 16.10 and 16.11 show two demand curves. We may notice that the demand curve in Fig. 16.10 is elastic at high prices and inelastic at low prices. The demand curve in Fig. 16.11 is just the opposite. Both kinds of demand curves are possible. Hence, by itself, "price range" is not a precise expression. The coefficient of elasticity could vary within some given range, as well as from one price range to another. Thus, precision requires that the elasticity of demand must be measured at a point on a demand curve.

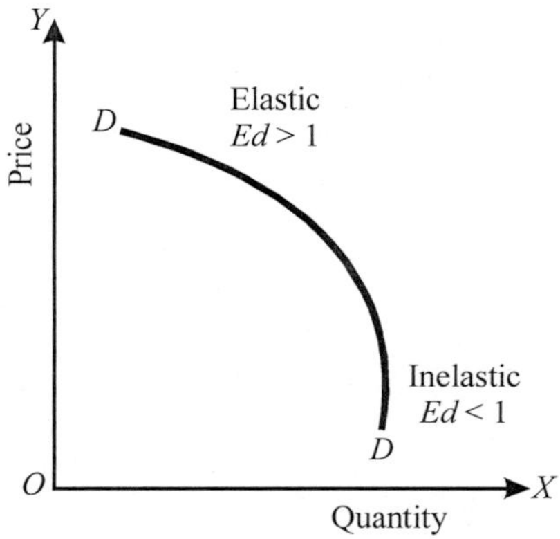

Fig. 16.10

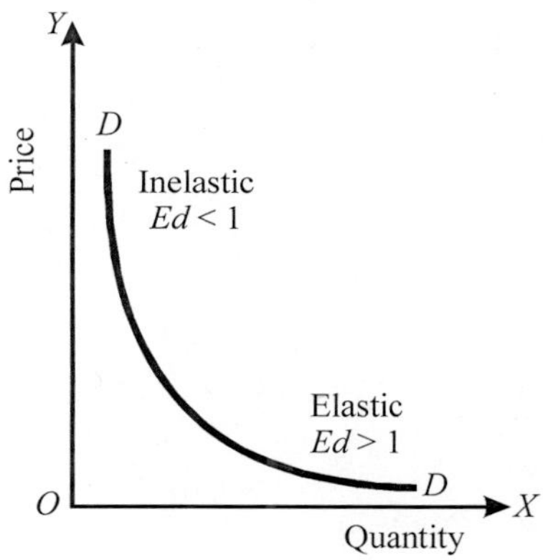

Fig.16.11

Point elasticity of demand is the corresponding concept for each particular point on the demand curve. But, at any such point, there is no change in price or $\Delta P = O$ and also there is no change in quantity, or $\Delta X = O$. We, therefore, define point elasticity in much the same way as the derivative concept used in the beginning, that is, we take the point elasticity to be the limit of the arc elasticity where the arc (a segment of the demand curve) is made smaller and smaller to arrive at the definition:

$$\text{Point elasticity of demand} = \frac{dX}{dP} \cdot \frac{P}{X}$$

Figure 16.12 shows how to find the elasticity at a point *A* on the demand curve *DD*. If price changes from OP_1 to OP_2, then the quantity demanded will increase from OX_1 to OX_2 Now the consumer is at point

A_1 of the same demand curve. Since we want to measure elasticity of demand at a particular point A on the demand curve DD, we therefore draw a straight line MN which is tangent to the demand curve at point A.

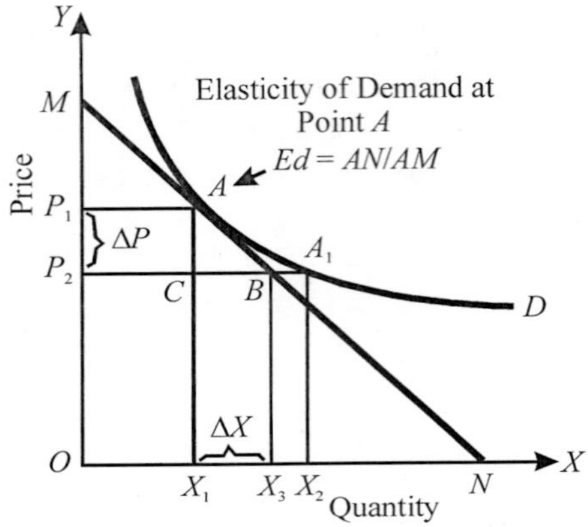

Fig. 16.12

The slope of the line MN is the same throughout. We here assume that point A_1 is very near to point B (as the limiting case) and, therefore, $OX_2 \equiv OX_3$. At point A and B the slope is the same. Now we supplement the information in our above formula of Ed, i.e.,

$$Ed = \frac{\Delta X}{\Delta P} \cdot \frac{P}{X} \qquad \text{... (2)}$$

where ΔX = change in quantity, ΔP = change in price, P = original price, X = original quantity

In Fig. 16.12, $dX = X_1X_3$ and $dP = P_1P_2$.

Similarly, $X = OX_1$ and $P = OP_2$

Substituting these values in (1) we obtain

$$Ed = \frac{X_1X_3}{P_1P_2} \cdot \frac{OP_1}{OX_1} \qquad \text{... (3)}$$

But $$\frac{X_1X_3}{P_1P_2} = \frac{CB}{AC}$$

$$\therefore \quad Ed = \frac{CB}{AC} \cdot \frac{OP_1}{OX_1}$$

Furthermore, by the theorem of similar triangles $\Delta ABC = \Delta AX_1N$; thus

$$\frac{CB}{AC} = \frac{X_1N}{AX_1} = \frac{X_1N}{OP_1} \qquad \text{... (4)}$$

$$\therefore \qquad Ed = \frac{X_1N}{OP} \cdot \frac{OP_1}{OX_1}$$

$$= \frac{X_1N}{OX_1} \qquad \text{... (5)}$$

But $\frac{X_1N}{OX_1} = \frac{AN}{AM}$, hence the coefficient of price elasticity at point A is approximately,

$$Ed = \frac{AN}{AM} \qquad \text{... (6)}$$

Hence, elasticity of demand at point A is equal to AN.

If $AN = AM$ then $Ed = 1$
If $AN > AM$ then $Ed > 1$
If $AN < AM$ then $Ed < 1$
If $AN = 0$, then $Ed = 0$
If $AM = 0$, then $Ed = \infty$

This proves the theorem that elasticity of demand at various points on the same demand curve is different. Equation (5) states that along a linear demand curve as shown in Fig. 16.13, the elasticity coefficient will increase if point A (where $Ed = 1$) approaches M and exactly at point M, $Ed = \infty$. Similarly, the elasticity coefficient Ed will decrease if point A leads to N and exactly at point N, $Ed = 0$.

(3) ***Arc Method or Arc Elasticity of Demand.*** The important limitation of the point method is that it is used only when a demand curve is known, either by assumption or through a statistical calculation based on many observations of prices and quantities. In real life, only scanty data are available, the data being a, few price-quantities observations of purchases of a commodity. In other words, the change in price may not be infinitesi-mal i.e., it may be finite. We do not possess such information about minute changes in price and quantity. We may possess demand schedules in which there are wide gaps in price as well as the quantity demanded. In such a situation, the elasticity of demand cannot be measured

at a point on the demand curve. Instead, the problem is now related to the measurement of elasticity over a certain range of values of price and quantity, or over a certain arc of the demand curve. Thus, there is another methód of price elasticity known as arc elasticity of demand. An arc is a portion or a segment of a demand curve.

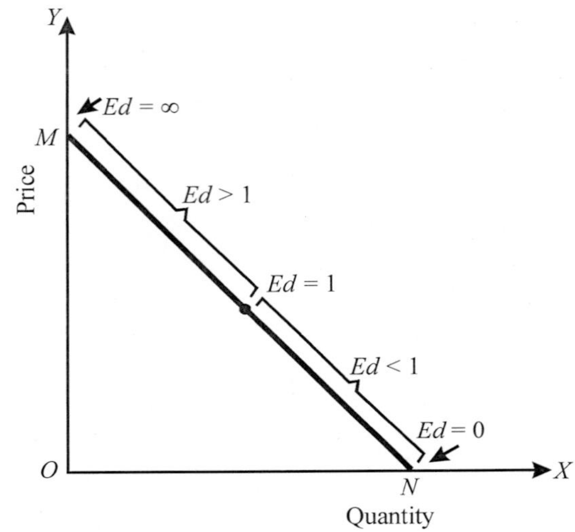

Fig. 16.13

The question now is the appropriate formula for arc elasticity. Differential calculus cannot help us measure the arc elasticity of demand, as the demand curve *DD* in Fig.16.14 hasdifferent slope at points A and *B*.

Arc elasticity is a measure of the average responsiveness to price change exhibited by a demand curve over some finite stretch of the curve as *AB* in Fig. 16.14. In *X* Fig. 16.14, we may very well find, the absolute change in price ($\Delta P = P_1 - P_0$) and the absolute change in quantity demanded ($\Delta X = X_1 - X_0$) But what are the exact values of *X* and *P?* Since a number of values may occur between X_0X_I and. between $P_0\,P_1$, no unique value of these variables (*X* and *P*) is called for by the definition. It is customary for this purpose to use the average of the two end values of *X*, that is, $X = (X_1 + X_0)/2$, and to do the same for $P = (P_1 + P_0)/2$. Hence the arc elasticity of demand is defined by the expressions:

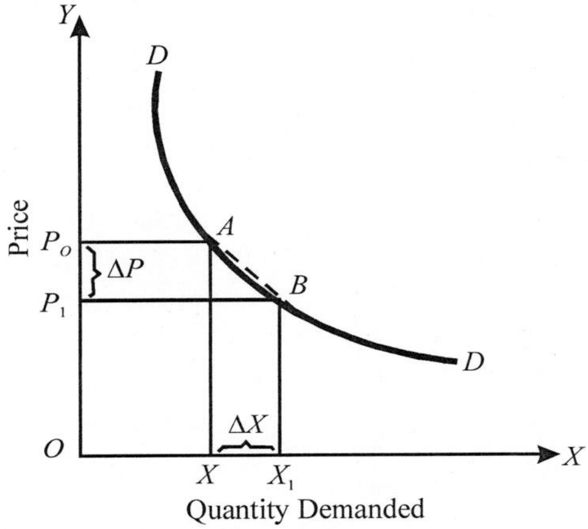

Fig. 16.14

$$Ed = \frac{\Delta X}{\Delta P} \cdot \frac{P}{X}$$

$$= \frac{X_1 - X_0}{P_1 - P_0} \cdot \frac{(P_1 + P_0)/2}{(X_1 + X_0)/2}$$

$$= \frac{X_1 - X_0}{P_1 - P_0} \cdot \frac{P_1 + P_0}{X_1 + X_0}$$

$$= \frac{X_1 - X_0}{X_1 + X_0} \cdot \frac{P_1 + P_0}{P_1 - P_0} \qquad ...(7)$$

where X_0 = Old level of quantity
X_1 = New level of quantity
P_0 = Old price
P_1 = New price

It is, however, to be remembered that the concept of arc elasticity of demand is not as precise as that of point elasticity of demand. But, on the other hand, are elasticity is a real concept which is applicable in real life.

Elasticity and Slope of the Demand Curve

Elasticity of demand must not be confused with the slope of the demand curve. As we have seen, elasticity will be different at every price. The slope of the demand curve may remain constant and yet its elasticity may be different at different points on the same demand curve. In Fig. 16.13, we have a straight line demand curve whose slope is uniform but the elasticity changes throughout the length of the curve. In the middle of the curve at point *A*, elasticity is equal to unity; below the mid-point *A*, it is less than unity; and above the mid-point *A*, it is greater than unity. Hence, the slope and the elasticity are not one and the same thing. The exceptions to this general rule, that elasticity will be different at every price, are:

(1) Where the demand curve is a rectangular hyperbola (slope keeps changing), elasticity is unity at every price.

(2) Where the demand curve is perpendicular to the quantity axis; elasticity of demand, is zero.

(3) Where the demand curve is perpendicular to the price axis; elasticity of demand is infinite.

In conclusion, we may say that no demand curve (except the rectangular hyperbola demand curve, or the vertical or the horizonal straight-line demand curve) will have a single elasticity throughout its length. It will have different elasticity on different points of it.

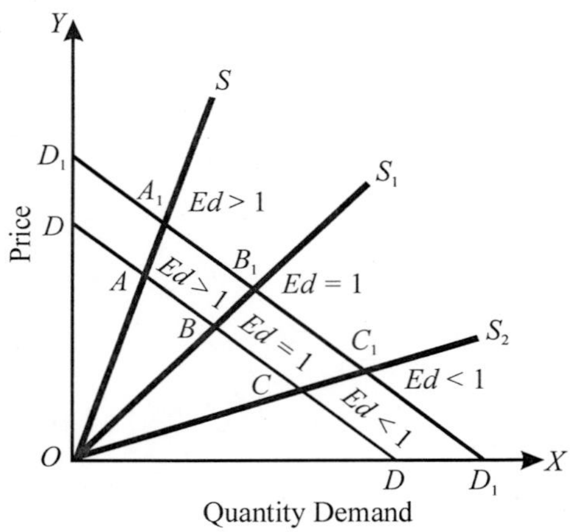

Fig. 16.15

Further, we can also compare elasticity on different points of two demand curves. In. Fig. 16.15, we draw two straight-line demand curves *DD* and D_1D_1 parallel to each other. If we draw a line through the origin point *O*, it cuts the two demand curves at points of equal elasticities. As shown in Fig. 16.15, the straight lines *OS*, OS_1 ' OS_2 cut the demand *curves* *DD* and D_1D_1 at points of equal elasticity. The elasticity of demand on the demand curve *DD* at points *A*, *B*, C is the same as that of the demand curve D_1D_1 at points A_1 B_1 and C_1. The elasticity at points *B* and B_1 is equal to unity, while the elasticity at point *A* and A_1 is more than one and at points *C* and C_1 it is less than one. In brief,

At points *A* and A_1 $Ed > 1$

At points *B* and B_1 $Ed = 1$

At points *C* and C_1 $Ed < 1$.

Now if we draw a line perpendicular to *X*-axis, it will cut the lower demand curve at a point of lower elasticity and the higher demand curve at a point of higher elasticity (see Fig: 16.16). In Fig. 16.16, we have two demand curves—*DD* the lower demand curve and D_1D_1 the higher demand curve. *MN* is the vertical line which cuts the two demand curves *DD* and D_1D_1 at the points *A* and A_1 respectively. Elasticity at point *A* is lower than the elasticity at point A_1.

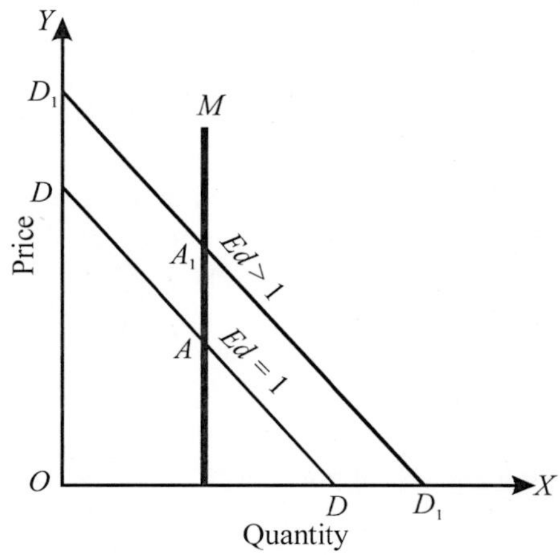

Fig. 16.16

Similarly, if we draw a line perpendicular to the *Y*-axis or horizontal to the *X*-axis, it will cut the lower demand curve at a point of higher elasticity and the higher demand curve at a point of lower elasticity. In Fig. 16.17, *MN* is a horizontal line to *X*-axis. It cuts the demand curve *DD* at point *A* and demand curve D_1D_1 at point A_1 respectively.

Now the elasticity at point *A* is higher than the elasticity at point A_1.

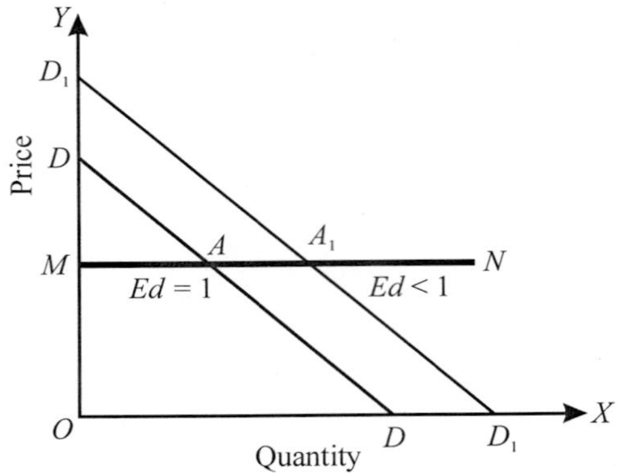

Fig. 16.17

The Determinants of Price Elasticity of Demand

A question normally arises that as to what makes the demand for one commodity elastic and the demand for another inelastic? The determinants of price elasticity of demand for a commodity can be studied under the following headings:

(1) ***The number and closeness of its substitutes.*** The available substitutes for a commodity are the most important determinants of the price elasticity of demand. If a product has many close substitutes in the relevant price range, its demand is almost certain to be highly elastic. If the producer of such a commodity were to raise his price, consumers buy less of the commodity and buy more of its substitutes. If the producer reduces the price, the consumers desert the substitutes and buy the commodity in (relatively) much larger quantities. The more close substitutes the commodity has, the more elastic will be the demand for it. The demand for cigarettes will be inelastic because there are no close substitutes, but the demand for a particular brand of cigarettes will be elastic because there are a number of very effective substitutes in the relevant price range.

(2) ***The importance of the commodity in buyers' budgets.*** The proportion of consumer's income which is spent on the commodity will be an important determinant of the price elasticity of demand. Where this proportion is very small, demand will tend to be inelastic. Matches account for a very small part of our total spending and a relatively large increase in their price would not have any great effect on the quantity demanded. Also, the demands for soap, salt, ink, and for many other similar commodities are highly inelastic, because the typical household spends only a few paise a week on each of them. The percentages of family

budgets devoted to such commodities are exceedingly small. We, however, notice that the demands for such commodities are inelastic and not perfectly inelastic.

(3) ***Degree of necessity.*** It is sometimes held that the demand for necessities is inelastic and the demand for luxuries elastic. The demand for necessities, such as, bread, potatoes, water, and clothing is certainly inelastic, but is this not another aspect of the availability of substitutes? There are no close substitutes for these articles in the relevant price ranges. The demand for luxuries will be elastic, it is argued, because if their prices rise, we can manage without them. But the demands for motorcars, petrol, cigarettes and alcoholic drinks have proved to be extremely inelastic. There are hardly 'necessities' in the strict sense of the word. The use of word as 'luxury' and 'necessity' raises many problems. In an economy where incomes are steadily rising, the luxuries of one generation become necessities for the next.

(4) ***Habit of the consumers.*** It is also an important factor determining the elasticity of demand. Some commodities are habit-forming—tobacco and alcohol are good examples—and the demand for such goods will tend to be inelastic.

(5) ***The number of uses of the commodity.*** Here we may say that the more uses a commodity can be put to, the more elastic its demand. If a commodity has only a few uses, its demand is likely to be inelastic. The various uses of a commodity can be put in the order of their importance. If the price of a commodity is very high, consumers will put the few units they buy only to the most important use of the commodity. At successively lower prices, more of the commodity is purchased, to be devoted to the less important uses.

(6) ***Time and Elasticity.*** The demand for a commodity always exists in some period of time which can be a day, a week, a month, a season, a year or a period of several years. Elasticity of demands varies with the span (length) of time periods. In general, demand is more elastic (or less inelastic), the longer the period of time. The longer the period of time, the greater is the case of substitution for both consumers and producers. If for instance, the price of fuel oil should increase but not the prices of other fuels, it is likely that the consumption of fuel oil in the month after the price increase would diminish very little. The demand for fuel oil in anyone month's period, then, is probably highly inelastic. But the demand over a year is certain to be less inelastic, because a year is long enough for people to change their plans about the kinds of furnaces to install. Over a period of, say, five years or more, the demand for fuel oil is probably highly elastic, because such a period is long enough to permit full substitution. Thus, time is also an important determinant of price elasticity of demand.

Any judgement of the elasticity of demand for a commodity must take all these above determinants into account. They can reinforce one another, or work in opposite directions.

3. CROSS ELASTICITY OF DEMAND

In real problems of demand analysis, commodities stand in more or less definite clusters of substitutes and complements. Under the demand function we have seen that demand for a commodity is not only a function of its on price but also a function of the prices of related goods. Hence, the idea of elasticity of demand can also be applied in a situation where two commodities are related to each other. The concept of cross elasticity of demand is useful in handling inter-commodity relations. Once more, we assume that two commodities *X* and Y are related. i.e., a change in the price of one will certainly affect the demand for the other. The expression of cross elasticity of demand is—

$Ed^* =$

$$\frac{\text{Relative (percentage) change in the quantity demanded of commodity } X}{\text{Relative (percentage) change in the price of commodity } Y}$$

$$= \frac{\Delta X}{X} \bigg/ \frac{\Delta Py}{Py}$$

$$= \frac{\Delta X}{\Delta Y} \cdot \frac{Py}{X} \qquad \text{... (8)}$$

where X = quantity demanded for commodity X, Py = price of commodity Y.

The cross elasticity of demand for commodity *X* may be positive or negative, depending upon the nature of relationship between *X* and *Y* commodities.

The coefficient (*Ed*) is positive if *X* and *Y* are substitutes because the price change and the quantity change are in the same direction. If the price of *Y* goes up, so does the quantity demanded of *X*, and vice versa. But if commodities *X* and *Y* are complements, the coefficient (*Ed*) is negative because changes in the price of one commodity cause opposite changes in the quantity demanded of the other.[1]

1. Such definition that substitutes have positive cross elasticity of demand and complements have negative cross elasticity of demand are valid for commodities bought in the markets, i.e., for the mass behaviour of consumers. For an individual consumer however, mathematical reasoning can show that such definitions might not be correct. It is a question of the income effect.

Let us assume the two commodities are Coca Cola and Gold Spot. If the price of Coca Cola increases, people in large number will drink Gold Spot. The cross elasticity in such a case would therefore be positive, because the change in the demand for Gold Spot and the change in the price of Coca Cola move in the same direction. The closer two commodities are substitutes for each other, the greater is the size of the cross-elasticity coefficient. Close substitutes have high cross elasticity of demand. Two commodities are poor substitutes for each other, if the cross elasticities are low.

If the two goods are complementary products, such as sugar and tea, the cross elasticity will be negative. Because, an increase in the price of sugar would reduce its demand, and simultaneously, the demand for the tea will also fall. Thus, the two variables, the change in the price of sugar and the change in the demand for tea move in opposite directions. Therefore, the cross elasticity of demand for complementary goods will be negative.

Sometimes, it is possible that the two goods *X* and *Y* are neither substitutes nor complements, i.e., they are unrelated or independent goods. In such a situation the cross elasticity of demand for the independent goods will be zero.

The above three situations of cross elasticity of demand can be illustrated diagrammatically in panels (*a*), (*b*) and (*c*) of Fig. 16.18. Panel (*a*) of Fig. 16.18 explains that an increase (decrease) in the price of *Y* will

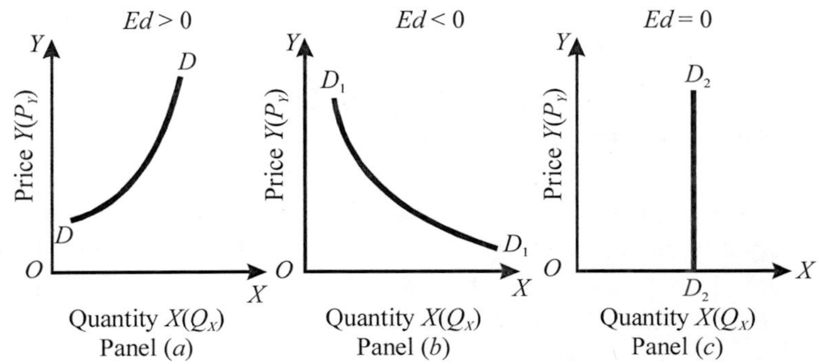

Fig. 16.18

lead to an increase (decrease) in the quantity of *X*. Thus the two goods will be labelled as substitutes and the cross elasticity of demand will be positive ($Ed^* < 0$). Panel (*b*) of Fig. 16.18 explains that an increase (decrease) in the price of *Y* will lead to a decrease (increase) in the quantity of *X*. Thus, the two goods will be labelled as complements and the cross elasticity of demand will be negative ($Ed^* < 0$). Panel (*c*) of Fig. 16.18 explains that an increase or decrease in the price of *Y* will make no effect on the quantity of *X* and, therefore, the cross elasticity of demand will be zero ($Ed^* = 0$).

We can, however, say that for the perfectly substitutable products, the cross elasticity of demand is highly positive and generally tends to be infinity. And, for the perfectly complementary goods, the cross elasticity of demand may assume any value below zero. In brief,

for substitutes, $0 < Ed^* < \infty$

for complements, $-\infty < Ed^* < 0$ ...(9)

4. INCOME ELASTICITY OF DEMAND

Under the demand function, we have seen that consumer's income is one of the determinants of his purchases of a commodity. The income elasticity of demand is defined as the responsiveness of demand, *ceteris paribus* to the change in consumer's money income. In other words, it may be defined as the ratio of the proportionate (percentage) change in the quantity demanded to the proportionate (percentage) change in income. Symbolically,

$$Ey = \frac{\text{Proportionate change in the quantity demanded of } X}{\text{Proportionate change in money income}}$$

$$= \frac{\Delta X}{X} \Big/ \frac{\Delta Y}{Y}$$

$$= \frac{\Delta X}{\Delta Y} \cdot \frac{Y}{X} \qquad \text{... (10)}$$

where X = commodity, and Y = income.

Normally, income elasticity of demand for a commodity is positive, except in the case of inferior goods where the income effect is negative. In the case of an inferior good, the demand varies inversely with income, and, as a result, the income elasticity of demand is negative. The five possible income demand curves are shown in panels (*a*), (*b*), (*c*), (*d*) and (*e*) of Fig. 6.19. The geometrical properties of an income-demand curve are the same as those of a supply curve. Panel (*a*) of Fig. 16.19 explains a *high income elasticity of demand.* Here the value of the coefficient *Ey* is greater than unity. In this case increases in income are accompanied by relatively larger increase in quantity demanded.

The *unitary demand* curve is drawn in panel (*b*) of Fig. 16.19. Here the value of the coefficient (*Ey*) is equal to unity. It explains that the proportionate change in quantity is equal to the proportionate change in money income.

The case of *low income elasticity* of demand is shown in panel (*c*) of Fig. 16.19. Here the relative change in quantity demanded is less than the relative change in money income. The value of the income elasticity coefficient (*Ey*) is less than unity.

The case of *zero income elasticity of demand* is shown in panel (*d*) of Fig. 16.19. It shows that quantity bought is constant regardless of changes in income. The value of the coefficient (*Ey*) is equal to zero.

The case of *negative income elasticity of demand* is shown in panel (*e*) of Fig. 16.19. It explains that less is bought at higher incomes and that more is bought at lower incomes. The value of the coefficient (*Ey*) is less than zero or negative.

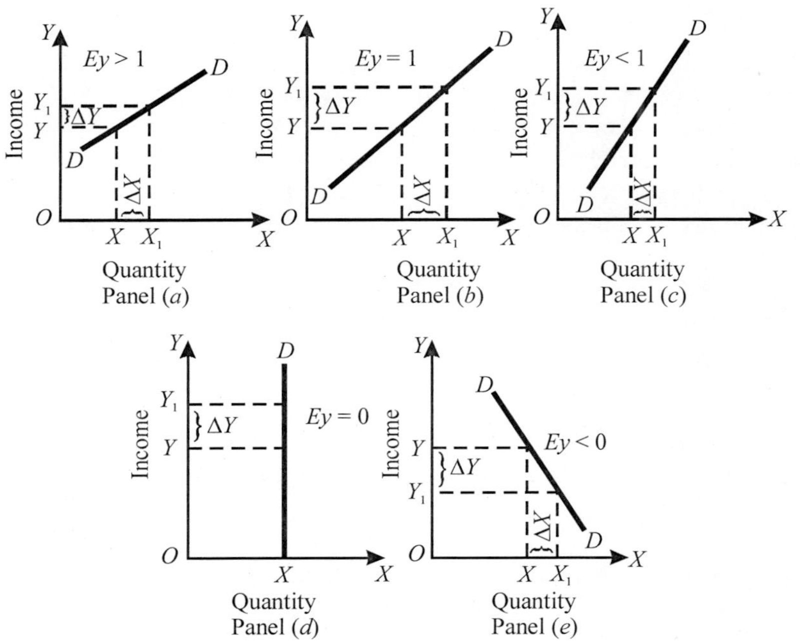

Fig. 16.19

Here, we may notice the important difference between the price elasticity and income elasticity of demand. If the coefficient is greater than one, income elasticity is "high"; if the coefficient is less than one, income elasticity is "low". In contrast, demand is "elastic" if the coefficient of price elasticity is greater than one, and "inelastic" if it is less than one.

Goods differ widely in their income elasticities. Ornaments, jewellery, automobiles, precious stones, etc. are the examples of goods whose income elasticities tend to be high. In contrast, soap, salt, matches, newspapers, etc. are the examples of low income elasticities of demand. The proportion of income spent on a good is a major determinant of its income elasticity of demand. An exception to this definition is probably housing. Housing takes a considerable part of consumer's income; it seems to have an income elasticity equal to unity. But goods that people regard as expensive, as luxuries, generally have high income elasticities. Therefore, the best way to define luxuries is that goods whose income elasticity of demand is high are luxuries. Similarly, necessities can be defined as goods whose income elasticities are low. It is quite possible that for one time a commodity may be necessary one, but for another time it becomes a comfort or luxury.

In modern times, economists have developed another concept, *the concept of income sensitivity* of consumption expenditure, which is very similar to the concept of income elasticity. Income elasticity is concerned with changes in physical units purchased, whereas income sensitivity deals with changes in rupee expenditures; The income sensitivity of a commodity in a period of time is measured by calculating the percentage change in rupee expenditures associated with a one per cent change in disposable income in the same period. Income sensitivity, therefore, also has a coefficient. But these coefficients of income sensitivity are only approximations and rough estimates, because there is still no method developed to disentangle the effects of changes in income nom the effects of changes in prices and tastes.[2]

Income Elasticity of Demand and the Propensity to Consume

We may define income elasticity of demand in terms of the average and

2. See Donald S. Watson, *op. cit.*, p. 109. The American Department of Commerce has found that the following commodities and services have high income sensitivities (coefficients equal to 1.5 or more): telephone service, automobiles, air transportation, television repairs and foreign travel. Commodities and services with low income sensitivities (coefficients less than 0.5) are exemplified by shoes, clothing, local bus transportation and dental care.

marginal propensities to consume. The marginal propensity to consume (*MPC*) may be defined as the ratio of change in consumption expenditure to the change in income, i.e.,

$$MPC = \frac{\Delta C}{\Delta Y}$$

where ΔC = Change in consumption, ΔY = Change in income

The average propensity to consume (*APC*) may be defined as the ratio of aggregate consumption to aggregate income, i.e.,

$$APC = \frac{C}{Y}$$

where C = Total Consumption, Y = Total Income

Now, income elasticity of demand can be defined as the ratio of the proportionate (percentage) change in consumption expenditure to the proportionate (percentage) change in income. Symbolically,

$$Ey = \frac{\text{Proportionate change in consumption expenditure}}{\text{Proportionate change in income}}$$

$$= \frac{\Delta C}{C} / \frac{\Delta Y}{Y}$$

$$= \frac{\Delta C}{\Delta Y} \cdot \frac{Y}{C} \qquad \text{... (11)}$$

where C = Original Consumption, Y = Original Income, ΔC = Change in Consumption Expenditure, ΔY = Change in Income.

Since, $\frac{\Delta C}{\Delta Y} = MPC$ and $\frac{C}{Y} = APC$,

We may write,

$$Ey = \frac{MPC}{APC} \qquad \text{... (12)}$$

Equation (12) states that income elasticity of demand is the ratio of marginal propensity to consume to average propensity to consume.

Income Elasticity of Demand and Engel Curves

According to Christian Lorenz Ernst Engel, a nineteenth century economist, the quantity demand is directly related to the consumer's money income. Prof. Engel's analysis of family revealed that the responsiveness of demand to a change in income is different for different goods. He showed these relationships between the income and the quantity demanded by the help of Engel curves.

According to Ferguson, "An Engel curve is a function relating equilibrium quantity purchased of a commodity to the level of money income." We know that a change in demand as a result of a change in money income will depend on the nature of the commodity in question. Figure 16.20 presents three out of a number of Engel curves, each indicating a different type of demand response to a given change in income.

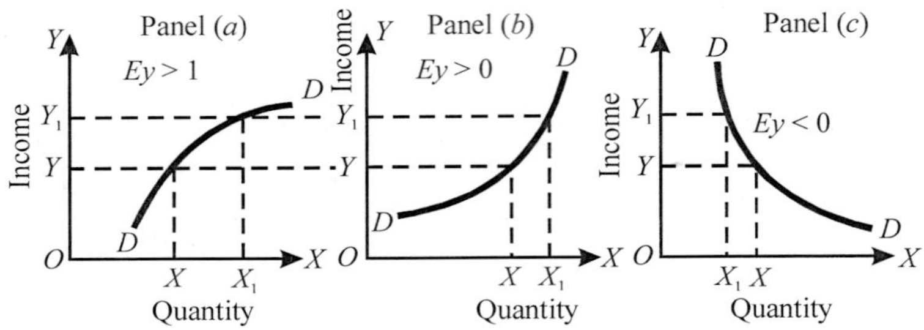

Fig. 16.20

It is very clear from Fig.16.20, that an equal increase in consumer's money income from OY to OY_1, the demand for commodity X increases relatively more in the case of a superior good (see panel (*a*) of Fig. 16.20) as compared to the normal good (see panel (*b*) of Fig. 16.20). Further, in the case of an inferior good, an increase in income from OY to OY_1 will reduce the quantity of X purchased from OX to OX_1 (see panel (*c*) of Fig. 16.20).

We can, therefore, write

for the superior goods, $Ey > 1$

for the normal goods, $Ey > 0$

for the inferior goods, $Ey < 0$

Now, given the indifference curve map and different levels of income, the Engel curve can be easily derived from the slope of the Income Consumption Curve (*ICC*).

5. DEMAND ELASTICITY OF SUBSTITUTION

The concept of elasticity of substitution is of great importance in modem economic analysis. It is the corresponding concept of substitution effect. Elasticity of substitution may be defined as the degree to which one commodity can be substituted for another as a consequence of a given change in their price ratio.

In other words, elasticity of substitution is the proportionate change in the ratios of two goods of the proportionate change in the price-ratio. Symbolically,

$$Es = \frac{\text{Proportionate change in the commodity quantity ratio}}{\text{Proportionate change in the commodity price ratio}}$$

$$= \frac{\Delta\left(\frac{X}{Y}\right) \Big/ \frac{X}{Y}}{\Delta\left(\frac{Px}{Py} \Big/ \frac{Px}{Py}\right)}$$

$$= \frac{\Delta\left(\frac{X}{Y}\right) \Big/ \frac{Px}{Py}}{\Delta\left(\frac{Px}{Py}\right) \frac{X}{Y}}$$

$$= \frac{\Delta\left(\frac{X}{Y}\right)}{\Delta\left(\frac{Px}{Py}\right)} \times \frac{\frac{Px}{Py}}{\frac{X}{Y}} \qquad \text{... (13)}$$

where $\frac{X}{Y}$ = quantity ratio of goods X and Y, $\frac{Px}{Py}$ = ratio of prices of X and Y.

Now, we may draw the following three conclusions: -

(l) If two goods are perfect substitutes for each other, elasticity of substitution will be infinite, or $Es = \infty$.

In this case the rate of substitution between them will be constant or uniform. A fall in the price of commodity X, assuming the price of commodity Y to be a constant will induce a consumer to substitute commodity X completely for commodity Y. But in real life we do not find such cases of infinite elasticity of substitution. In case the two commodities are perfect substitutes, they should be considered as one commodity.

(2) If two commodities are close substitutes for each other, elasticity of substitution will be greater than one, or $Es > 1$.

(3) If there is no possibility of any substitution between them, so that, they are used in fixed proportions, elasticity of substitution will be equal to zero, or $Es = 0$.

In between these two extreme values of the coefficient, $0 \leq Es \leq \infty$, we may have high or low elasticity of substitution depending upon whether the rate of substitution is falling rapidly or slowly. We may also represent these cases diagrammatically with the help of indifference curves. The elasticity of substitution coefficient in terms of indifference curve analysis can be written as,

$$Es = \frac{\text{Proportionate change in the ratio of } X \text{ and } Y}{\text{Proportionate change in the marginal rate of substitution } (MRS) \text{ of } X \text{ in terms of } Y}$$

In other words, elasticity of substitution measures that rate at which the marginal rate of substitution (*MRS*) of *X* for *Y* diminishes when the consumer buys relatively more of *X* and less of *Y*. Thus the slope of indifference curves ($\Delta X/\Delta Y$) explains the relative importance of *X* and *Y* in the measurement of preferences. The more flat the indifference curve, the lesser will be the *MRS* of *X* for *Y*. It means that for an additional unit of *X*, the consumer is ready to sacrifice less and less amount of *Y*. Various combinations of two commodities on an indifference curve are the best substitutes for one another. The substitution elasticities are expressed in terms of substitution effect in panel (*a*) and (*b*) of Fig. 16.21. In panel (*a*) of Fig. 16.21 the original equilibrium point is set where the indifference curve *IC* touches the price line *MN* at point *E*. At point *E*, the consumer consumes *OX* of *X* commodity and *OY* of *Y* commodity. In a new situation of price change, the relevant price line is M_1N_1 and the new equilibrium point is E_1 where the original indifference curve touches the price line M_1N_1, At point E_1 the consumer consumes OX_1 of *X* commodity and OY_1 of *Y* commodity. Therefore, the movement from *E* to E_1 represents the substitution effect. For XX_1 quantity of *X*, the consumer sacrifices YY_1 quantity of *Y*. The slope $\Delta Y / \Delta X$ is less than one; the difference curve is flat; and, therefore, elasticity of substitution is highly elastic.

In contrast, the steeper the indifference curve, the higher will be the marginal rate of substitution (*MRS*). It means that to consume an additional unit of *X*, more units of *Y* are to be sacrificed. In this situation, the elasticity of substitution of *X* for *Y* will be *less elastic.* In panel (*b*) of Fig. 16.21, for attaining an additional quantity XX_1 of commodity *X*, the consumer has to sacrifice YY_1 quantity of *Y* commodity (and $YY_1 > XX_1$), The movement from equilibrium point E to E_1 on the same indifference curve *IC* represents the substitution effect. The ratio $\Delta Y/\Delta X$ is relatively higher which means that the slope of indifference curve is more steep in panel (*b*) of Fig. 16.21.

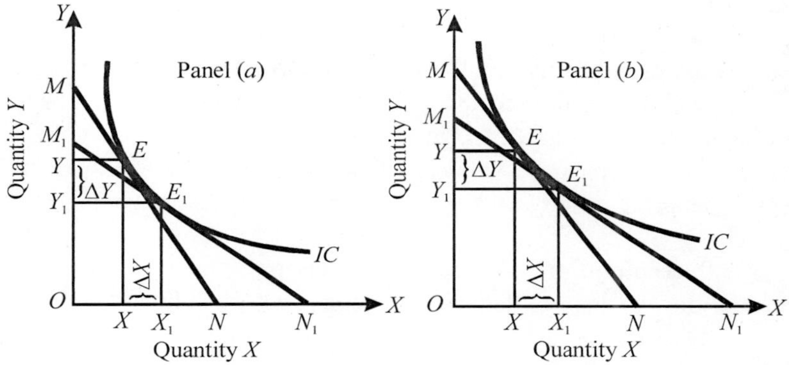

Fig. 16.21

When the two commodities are perfect substitutes, the indifference curve is a straight line, as shown in Fig. 16.22. *X* and *Y* will be deemed as perfect substitutes. Here, the slope of indifference curve is the same throughout, and the marginal rate of substitution between the two commodities remains constant. If the *IC* is a 45° line to *Y*-axis, the two goods are exchanged in fixed ratio (i.e., 1 : 1). If the two goods *X* and *Y* are identical, the marginal rate of substitution between them is infinite. Since indifference curve will never be a straight line, and therefore, phenomena of perfect substitutes are out of the scope of substitution effect.

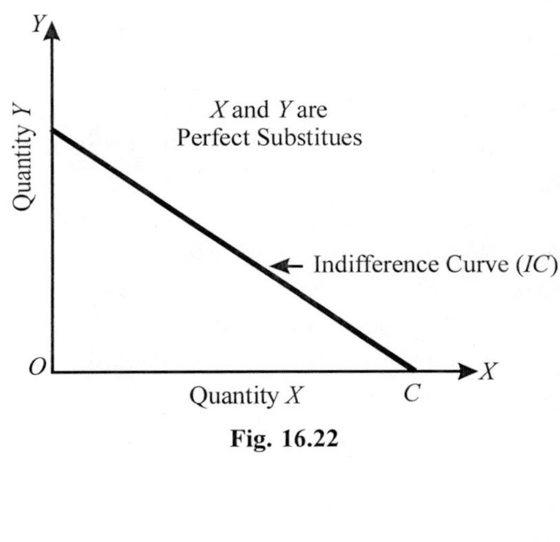

Fig. 16.22

6. SIGNIFICANCE OF THE CONCEPT OF THE ELASTICITY OF DEMAND

The theory of elasticity of demand plays an important role in the solution of economic problems and the determination of various economic policies. Many of the applications of the concept of price elasticity of demand have to do with pricing decision of business firms or government agencies that directly or indirectly regulate price. All too often decisions on prices fail to take elasticity into account, or give it insufficient attention. Changes in costs usually dominate on prices; costs can be calculated, and higher costs usually seem to be valid justification for higher prices. Even if demand and its elasticity cannot always be calculated, they should not be ignored.

(1) Determination of price under monopoly. A monopolist has to consider the elasticity of demand for his product when he determines its price or changes the existing price. If the elasticity of demand for his product is highly elastic, he will maximise his profits by fixing a lower price; because at a lower price he is able to increase his sales. If the elasticity of demand for his product is less elastic or highly inelastic, he is in a position to fix a high price for the commodity. If he fails to study the elasticity of demand for his product, he would not be able to optimise his profits in the market.

(2) Determination of price under discriminating monopoly. The policy of price discrimination can be successfully implemented only on the basis of different elasticities of demand in different markets of the same product. A monopolist will fix a higher price in a less elastic market and a lower price in a more elastic market. By doing so, he will be able to attain maximum total revenue.

(3) Determination of prices of product mix. Some commodities are jointly produced such as wheat and grass, cotton and cotton seeds, etc. It is difficult to find out their separate costs of production. In such a situation, their prices are determined only on the basis of their elasticities of demand. The prices of relatively inelastic goods are higher and prices of relatively more elastic goods are lower.

(4) Determination of the prices of public utilities. The concept of elasticity of demand is also of much importance in the determination of the prices of public utility services. Economic welfare of the society to a very large extent depends upon the cheap availability of the essential products like water, electricity, cooking gas, transportation, etc.

Public utilities possess a public interest and hence it is desirable that those industries for whose products the demand is inelastic must be declared public utilities and they should be controlled by the government. The government will distribute these products at fair prices and therefore, will remove the fear of restricted output and high prices.

(5) Determination of various government policies. The concept of elasticity of demand is helpful in the formulation and determination of various government policies:

(*i*) *Policy of granting protection.* The government provides protection or subsidy to those industries whose demand for their products is elastic. As a result, they are unable to face foreign competition until the prices of their products are reduced through subsidy.

(*ii*) *Explaining the paradox of poverty in the midst of plenty.* The concept of elasticity of demand also explains the paradox of poverty in the midst of plenty. A bumper crop of food-grains, the demand for which is inelastic, might spell economic disaster instead of bringing prosperity among the producers (farmers) because a rich harvest will bring less and not more money to them. Therefore, a protective policy must be framed in favour of the farmers.

(*iii*) *Tax-policy.* The Finance Minister considers the elasticity of demand for a product while imposing a tax on it. It will help the government to make a correct probable estimate of the tax-revenue. Moreover, taxes impose burden upon the final tax-payers (consumers) and this burden should be equally distributed between the different groups of tax-payers. In other words, the equity canon of taxation must be justified. The problem of incidence of taxation depends upon the elasticities of demand and supply of the goods taxed. A proper tax policy will be determined only when the authority has a perfect knowledge about the elasticities of demand and supply.

(6) Determination of international trade policies. The concept of elasticity of demand plays a significant role in solving the problems of international trade, such as, the problem of terms of trade, gains from trade, balance of payments, etc.

(*i*) *Determination of the terms of trade.* The terms of trade are determined by the mutual elasticities of demand of the two countries for each other's goods. The "terms of trade" implies the rate at which one unit of a domestic product will exhange for some units .of a foreign commodity. A country's gains from trade will therefore, depend upon the elasticity of "demand" and the terms of trade. If we export goods whose demand is inelastic and import goods whose demand is elastic, we shall gain from international trade. Because, in such a situation, we may get higher price d our exports and would be ready to pay a lower price for the imports.

(*ii*) *Determination of tariff policy.* We know that export-import duties will increase the internal prices of the commodities. The elasticity of demand for the protected goods depends upon the increase in the domestic prices. If the elasticity of demand for protected goods is elastic, an increase in their prices will lead to fall in their quantity demanded. If, on the other hand, demand is elastic, the burden of increase in price will be borne by the people as a result of the policy of export-import tariffs.

(*iii*) *Determination of the policy of devaluation.* The policy of devaluation will be successful only when the country possesses the perfect knowledge of the elasticities of its exports arid imports. Due to devaluation a country's exports become cheaper and imports dearer. But an increase in exports will take place, only when the elasticity of demand for our exports is elastic. Similarly, our imports will be reduced only when the import elasticity is elastic. In other words, devaluation will be helpful in correcting the disequilibrium of the balance of payment, only the sum of the elasticity of our exports and imports is greater than one.

EXERCISES

1. What do you mean by elasticity of demand? Explain its theoretical and practical importance.
2. Distinguish between point elasticity and arc elasticity of demand.
3. What are the kinds of price elasticity of demand? How would you measure the price elasticity of demand?
4. What is cross elasticity of demand? How will you express the nature of the commodities with the help of this elasticity?
5. Explain the concepts of income, elasticity of demand and substitution elasticity of demand.
6. What are the determinants of elasticity of demand? Why elasticity of demand is always negative?
7. "Elasticity of demand, therefore, depends equally on the shape of the price consumption curve, which depends, in turn, on the nature of income effect and of the substitution effect." Thus, elasticity of demand depends upon two other elasticities. Discuss.
8. Prove that elasticity of demand is different at different points on the same demand curve.
9. Define the term elasticity of demand. What is the relation between elasticity of demand and the slope of the demand curve?
10. Explain the concept of elasticity of demand and distinguish between elastic and inelastic demand with the help of diagrams. What are the factors which explain variations in elasticity?

11. Define elasticity of demand. How are income and cross elasticities of demand for a commodity determined?

Multiple Choice Questions

12. (*i*) Consider a demand curve which takes the form of a straight line cutting both axis. Elasticity at the mid-point of the line would be
    (*a*) 0 (*c*) 1.5
    (*b*) 1.0 (d) 2.0 [*Ans.* (*b*)]

    (*ii*) If the quantity demanded remains unchanged as its price changes, the coefficient of price elasticity of demand is
    (*a*) greater than 1 (*c*) smaller than 1
    (*b*) equal to 1 (*d*) zero [*Ans.* (*d*)]

    (*iii*) Cross elasticity of demand between two perfect substitutes will be
    (*a*) very high (*c*) Zero
    (*b*) very low (d) infinity [*Ans.* (*d*)]

    (*iv*) If the income elasticity of demand is greater than 1, the commodity is
    (*a*) a neccesity (*c*) an inferior good
    (*b*) a luxury (*d*) a non-related good [*Ans.* (*d*)]

PART 3
PRODUCTION THEORY

Chapter 17

FACTORS OF PRODUCTION

1. CLASSIFICATION OF FACTORS OF PRODUCTION

A factor of production may be defined as that good or service which is needed for production. Production is the result of a cooperative work of various resources. To produce a pair of shoes, the cobbler requires tools and leather (besides his own labour). Therefore, we note that a number of factors are required to produce a good. These factors have been called by economists land, labour, capital, organisation and enterprise respectively. These factors are also called inputs and the production is called 'output'.

Sometimes it is not easy to distinguish between man-made resources and natural resources. These have some common features and one is mixed up with the other in such a fashion that it becomes difficult to disentangle them. Some writers like, Karl Marx and J.R. Hicks, therefore, group them under one heading, namely, capital. In this general sense, capital includes natural resources and man-made resources and represents that part of the productive resources on which labour works to produce goods. If we adopt this approach we are left with only two factors of production—Capital and Labour. We shall, however, like to distinguish land from capital. We shall adopt the three fold classification; Land, Labour and Capital.

Some writers have rightly stressed that enterprise is not a factor of production in the sense in which land, labour and capital are, because it is not a part of available resources. It is a quality of human beings and refer to the capacity and willingness to take risk. In the same way organisation is also a quality of skilled labour and can not be regarded as a separate factor. However, we discuss the following factors of production:

1. *Land.* It is a free gift of nature. It stands for natural resources. Land, therefore; refers to all natural resources, and not simply to a piece of land. Land includes, forests, lakes and seas, mountains, climate, weather, air, etc.

2. *Labour.* All types of physical and mental work, undertaken for getting an income is called labour. It includes all types of workers—those who use their brains. (Doctor, Lawyer, Teachers etc.) and those who work with hands (Carpenter, Blacksmith etc.).

3. *Capital.* It means man-made productive assets. Therefore, it refers to all man-made tools and machinery and all types of wealth which are used in production. It is simply a productive means of production.

4. *Organisation.* As stated already, it is a part of labour, but due to complexities of the productive mechanism, we define this as the factor which bring together all the factors of production and make them work harmoniously. But in modern business, everyone from the top managing director to the lowest peon, is paid and hence all may be regarded as labour.

5. *Enterprise.* This is also a part of labour. Modern productive mechanism is so complex and full of uncertainties and risks that, each and every individual cannot dare to take up the responsibility of launching a new enterprise. Therefore the prime function of entrepreneur is to take risk. The entrepreneur's reward for their valuable service is known as profit.

2. RELATIVE IMPORTANCE OF THE FACTORS OF PRODUCTION

The problem of the combination of various factors is solved in different ways in different countries. In some of them (India, China etc.) labour is plentiful, while land and capital are scarce. Productive activities in such countries will naturally have to be so arranged as to make use of more labour, i.e., labour intensive techniques of production. On the other hand, we have countries (USA, Canada) where labour is scarce, but land and capital are plentiful. Such countries will like to depend more on capital and land i.e., capital intensive techniques of the factors of production in a particular economy depends upon their availability.

Taking things in an historical context, we find that land was the most dominant factor of production in the early stages of human existence. At that time man lacked skill as also capital. It was mostly the free gifts of nature which provided the needs of his life. At that time, some crude form of capital such as wooden plough for cultivation or a bamboo for plucking fruits) was used. Land was the most important factor and produced goods with the help of labour. With the passage of time and advance of science and technology, the relative position of the factors of production has changed. In modern production, land is less important and capital plays a dominant role. Labour has become skilled. In this way, we find that with economic growth, the importance of natural resources has declined and that of man-made resources—labour and capital-has gone up. Economic development is, essentially, a man-made process. It is this characteristic of growth which promises bright future for the people of various countries. The decline in the importance of natural resources has, thus, been accomplished through the efforts of man in discovering new technology and methods of production. Modern production has become roundabout and capitalistic. It requires huge capital as also skilled labour.

Today the theory of cost of production also depends upon the combination of factors of production employed in the production process and the prices paid to them. As regards, the cost of production, we may divide the factors of production into two categories—the fixed factors and the variable factors. Fixed factors are those factors whose costs (or quantity) do not change with the change in output such as machinery, land, building etc. Variable factors are those whose quantities and cost change with the changes in output. If output is zero, then variable cost is zero. If output increases then variable cost will increase. Such factors are labour, fuel, raw material etc. So long as the firm is able to get the variable cost of production, it will continue output and go on employing the variable factors of production. In no case a firm would be like to employ variable factors of production or incur variable cost if the price of the output is not sufficient to cover this cost. In such a case a firm's maximum loss will be equal to the cost of fixed factors of production. It happens only in the short period. In the long-period, it must cover the cost of production of both the fixed and the variable factors. Thus the distinction between fixed and variable factors is of much importance for the theory of the firm.

EXERCISES

1. Discuss a broad classification of factors of production. Explain the significance of factors of production in economic analysis.
2. What do you mean by factors of production? How are they classified?

Multiple Choice Questions

3. (*i*) Production is defined as
   (*a*) creation of a new commodity
   (*b*) increase in the utility or creation of utility
   (*c*) physical production of goods
   (*d*) none of the above [*Ans.* (*b*)]

   (*ii*) Capital means
   (*a*) man-made resources
   (*b*) a part of wealth which is used for further production
   (*c*) the process of increasing knowledge, the skills and capabilities of all people in the country
   (*d*) all of the above [*Ans.* (*d*)]

Chapter 18

CHARACTERISTICS OF LAND AND LABOUR

1. MEANING OF LAND

The term land, according to dictionary, means the surface of the ground. In economics, however, it is used in a wider sense to signify all the gifts of nature, the surface of the ground being one of them. In land we include only those resources which are under our ownership and control and give us income. Resources, such as rain and sunshine, which are very useful but not under anybody's control, are excluded. They are resources over which we have no power and which, therefore, we can not economise. As time passes, more and more of the free gifts of nature come under our control and ownership; they become economic resources.

2. CHARACTERISTICS OF LAND

As a factor of production, land possesses certain characteristics which are not common to other factors. Land has features which are common to capital also. At occasions it becomes difficult to disentangle one from the other. It is because of this that some writers regard them as the two species of the same genus. We shall, however, examine here the main features of land, as it is distinguished from capital.

(1) ***Fixity of Supply.*** Since land is Nature's gift, its supply is fixed. Man cannot add even an inch to the existing supply of land. It is true that man can secure for himself more land surface by drying up it lake or a part of the sea. For example, a part of the sea has been dried up and made cultivable in Holland. But it does not mean that there has been an addition to the existing supply of land. The land surface was already there. Only it has been made fit for cultivation.

(2) ***Land* is *a Free Gift of Nature.*** It is not a 'produced' or man-made agent. It follows, therefore, that we have to accept it as it is. No

doubt man tries to improve and modify nature. But he cannot completely master it. A poor soil and a bad climate are great handicaps in the way of agricultural prosperity.

(3) ***Land is Imperishable.*** It is the fertility of land declines or get exhausted, it can be resorted through the application of the chemical fertilizers and through proper crop rotation practices.

(4) ***Land* is *Immobile.*** Unlike other factors, land is not physically mobile. But in the wider sense even land may be said to be mobile in so far as it can be put to several 'alternative uses. From cotton cultivation, it can be shifted to wheat cultivation. This is known as use-mobility of land.

(5) ***Land Differs in Fertility and Situation.*** Some lands are too sandy and some too rocky; some are dry, while others receive ample rainfall. Some have a good climate, while others cannot support human life. In the same manner, all land are not equally well situated. Lands located in the heart of a city enjoy a better situational advantage than the lands located in the suburbs.

(6) ***Passivity.*** Land is a passive factor of production. It does not take an active part in the process of production but is itself acted upon by man and machine. "In production man is the directing, active agent; Nature the obedient passive agency."

There is not the least doubt about the great importance of land in production. It is an indispensable factor of production. In fact, the economic development of a country, in the last resort, depends upon the quality of its land.

3. MEANING OF LABOUR

The term labour is used in a wider sense in economics. According to S.E. Thomas, *"Labour consists of all human efforts of body or of mind which are undertaken in the expectation of reward."* This definition comprises two points: *(i)* Labour can be physical as well as mental. The labour of a worker is physical, while that of a college teacher is mental. *(ii)* Under labour we include only those exertions, physical or mental, which are undertaken in the expectation or a reward. For example, if a teacher attends his own son, his action cannot be called labour. But if he teaches other students to earn money, his exertions would be termed as labour.

4. CHARACTERISTICS OF LABOUR

Labour, as defined above, has certain characteristics. These are as follows:

(1) ***Inseparable from Owner.*** The first important characteristic of labour is its inseparability from the worker. Labour and the labourer go together. The service cannot be separated from the owner. Labourer, the provider of labour, is a human being. Problems of labour, thus, cannot be devoid of human elements. This is a feature peculiar to labour only.

(2) ***Perishable.*** Labour is a highly perishable factor. If we fail to make use of the service of a labourer, it is lost forever. It is a permanent loss to society; it is a waste of a productive resource. As labour is perishable, unemployment of labour is a more serious problem than unemployment of capital and land.

(3) ***Heterogeneous.*** Labour is a highly heterogeneous factor. It includes, on the one hand, the manual worker and, on the other, the most skilled worker. There are unskilled as well as skilled labourers; there are trained as well as untrained labourers. The coollie, the manual worker, the bus driver, the production manager, the engineer and the technician, all are labourers. But they are not alike.

(4) ***Labour has Weaker Bargaining Power.*** The bargaining power of the worker is low compared to that of the employer. *Firstly,* labour is perishable. This accounts for its low bargaining power vis-a-vis the employer. The worker considers it expedient to accept the low wages offered by the employer rahter than go without work. *Secondly,* the economic position of the worker is much weaker than that of the employer. *Thirdly,* there is lack of organisation among workers.

(5) ***Labour is an Active Factor of Production.*** Land and capital are passive factors, but labour is an active factor of production. Neither land nor capital can yield much without labour.

(6) ***The Labourer Sells His Labour But Not Himself.*** A worker does not sell himself; he sells his labour only. In the days of slavery the workers even sold his body to the master but that is no longer true now.

(7) ***Labour is Mobile.*** Labour alone is a factor which is mobile. It can move from one place to another; from one occupation to another.

(8) ***Supply of Labour is Inelastic.*** The supply of labour can neither be increased nor reduced easily and quickly. Hence, there is no rapid adjustment of the supply of labour to its demand.

In view of its inseparability from the owner and its perishability, labour has occupied an important place in economic discussions. Based on these characteristics, we have now developed anew branch in economics called labour economics." There is, however, an element of exaggeration in these peculiarities of labour. Some of these peculiarities are also to be found in other factors. For example, if a machinery (Capital) is not used, it deteriorates. The supply of entrepreneurship is also inelastic like labour.

5. EFFICIENCY OF LABOUR

The term efficiency of labour signifies the capacity of the labour to do more work or better work or both during a given period of time. The term is relative. The efficiency of labourers can be compared when we consider the amount of work done by them in a certain period or when we consider the amount of time taken by them to do a certain work. Thus when we say that an English worker is more efficient than an Indian worker, it means that within an hour an English labourer can do more work than an Indian labourer.

Factors Determining Efficiency of Labour

(1) ***Racial Qualities.*** Racial qualities and hereditary characteristics may be put down as the first important factor which determines efficiency of labour. It is as a result of racial and hereditary qualities that the English are better sailors, the Swiss better watchmakers and the Italians better artists.

(2) ***Climatic Conditions.*** Climate has an important effect upon efficiency of labour. Extremes of climate reduce the capacity of the labourers to work. Hot climate breeds indolence and a dislike for hard work whereas a cool, bracing climate makes the labourers hardworking and is thus conducive to efficiency.

(3) ***General Conditions.*** Efficiency of labour also depends upon the general intelligence of the labourer. If the labourer is intelligent, he will have clearness of thought, accuracy of judgement and speed of action. All these contribute to efficiency.

(4) ***General Education.*** Education stimulates the intelligence of a man and develops his mental and moral qualities. The spread of general education among the people makes them more efficient.

(5) ***Technical Education.*** Technical education has a direct bearing upon the efficiency of labour. It befits a labourer for a particular trade or occupation. A man, who understands the working of the machine he is to work on, is bound to prove a better worker.

(6) ***Standard of Living.*** The efficiency of worker depends to a large

extent on the fact whether he gets sufficient food and clothes and a good house to live in. The adequate supply of all these things paves the way of efficiency.

(7) ***Wages.*** The remuneration received by the worker also affects his efficiency. Quality work cannot be expected from a low-paid worker. Ill-paid workers remain discontented and their efficiency is reduced.

(8) ***Moral Qualities.*** Good moral character is another factor which determines the efficiency of a worker. Virtues of self-reliance and self-respect, honesty and industry, ambition and cheerfulness go a long way in making a worker thoroughly efficient.

(9) ***Prospects of Promotion.*** The prospects of rapid promotion fire the ambition of many a young man. There is nothing like hopefulness to spur the workers on to greater and sustained efforts.

(10) ***Working Conditions.*** Efficiency is also affected by general working conditions. Pleasing and cheerful atmosphere inside a factory increases the efficiency of the workers. Again, improved lighting, ventilation and sanitation in the factories increase the muscular and mental strength of the workers, and thus promote efficiency.

(11) ***Hours of Work.*** The number of working hours is also an important factor. One cannot put in sustained effort for long hours. Long hours sap the energy of workers. If hours of work are short with reasonable rest periods and level, the efficiency of labourers will increase. .

(12) ***Organising Ability of Employers.*** Efficiency of labour also depends, to some extent, on the organising capacity of the employer. If each labourer is given the task for which he is best fitted, if he is supplied with good appliances and if he is inspired to greater efforts in the right manner, his efficiency is bound to increase.

To sum up, efficiency of Iabour depends partly on the employer and partly on the employee, partly on the organisation and partly on individual efforts, partly on the tools, machines etc., with which the worker is supplied and partly on his own skill and industry in making use of them.

6. LABOUR EFFICIENCY IN INDIA

Comparisons made by various writers reveal that Indian labour is less efficient than labour of other countries. In his evidence before the Industrial Commission, Sir Alexander McRobert stated that the English worker was 3.5 or even 4 times as efficient as Indian. Such mathematical comparisons are, however, misleading, as the conditions obtaining in the British factories are riot identical with those prevailing in the Indian mills. The relatively low efficiency of the Indian labourer is not innate or inborn. There are several external factors such as hot climate, low wages and low standard of living, long hours and unsatisfactory working conditions, bad housing, bad machinery and material, lack of education and training etc., which make him what he is. To improve his efficiency the first necessity is general and technical education. Housing facilities should be improved. Wages must be raised to a reasonable level. Better provision should also be made for the proper ventilation of the factory buildings. Introduction of prohibition in the industrial areas is essential. Welfare measures such as provision of recreation, medical aid, maternity benefits and social security must also be adopted.

EXERCISES

1. Define Land. What are its important characteristics?
2. Define labour in economics. What are its important peculiarities? Explain.
3. What do you mean by the term efficiency of labour? What are the important factors on which it depends?

Multiple Choice Questions

4. (*i*) Which of the following is not a characteristic of land?
   (*a*) land is man-made
   (*b*) land is free gift of nature
   (*c*) land is fixed in quantity
   (*d*) none of the above [*Ans.* (*a*)]

   (*ii*) Which work is known as labour in economics?
   (*a*) work of a gardener in the garden
   (*b*) a teacher teaches his son
   (*c*) a doctor treats his wife
   (*d*) all of the above [*Ans.* (*a*)]

   (*iii*) Labour has the following peculiarity:
   (*a*) labour cannot be separated from the labourer
   (*b*) weak bargaining power
   (*c*) inelastic supply of labour
   (d) all of the above [*Ans.* (*d*)]

   (*iv*) Efficiency of labour refers to
   (*a*) the productive capacity of labour
   (*b*) personal qualities of labour
   (*c*) both of the above
   (*d*) none of the above [*Ans.* (*c*)]

Chapter 19

THEORIES OF POPULATION

1. INTRODUCTION

The study of population is important from the point of view of economic welfare. It is particularly important because human beings are not only instruments of production but also ends in themselves. As instruments of production, population (human resources) provide the labour force of the community which helps in the process of production so that the people of a country can live in conditions of comfort and healthy living. It will lead to the welfare of the society. It becomes necessary to study the population in quantitative terms and the rate at which it is growing.

Various attempts have been made to formulate economic principles relating to population. Thomas Robert Malthus was the first to give a systematic account of population principles. Since then the interest has been growing. In the present chapter we shall discuss the following important theories of population:

(1) The Malthusian Theory of Population,

(2) The Optimum Theory of Population,

(3) The Biological Theory of Population, and

(4) The Theory of Demographic Transition.

2. THE MALTHUSIAN THEORY OF POPULATION

The Malthusian theory of population is the most well-known theory of population. Malthus, a clergyman by profession, developed a scientific and systematic thinking on the problem of population. He wrote his essay on "Principles of Population" in 1798 and modified some of his conclusions in the next edition in 1803. The rapidly increasing population of England, encouraged by a misguided Poor Law, distressed him very deeply. He feared that England was heading for a disaster, and he considered it his solemn duty to warn his countrymen. He pointed out that the accelerated increase in population was undesirable and thus the need to keep it in check. His views are collectively known as the Malthusian theory of population. The main conclusions of the theory are explained below in his own words:

(1) According to Malthus, "the power of population is infinitely greater than the power in the earth to produce subsistence for men."

(2) "By nature human food increases in a slow arithmetical ratio; man himself, increases in a quick geometrical ratio unless want and vice stop him."

(3) "The increase in numbers is necessarily limited by the means of subsistence. Population invariably increases when the means of subsistence increase, unless prevented by powerful and obvious checks."

(4) "By the law of our nature which makes food necessary to the life of man, the effects of these two unequal powers must be kept equal."

(5) "This implies a strong and constantly operating check on population from the difficulty of subsistence."

On the basis of the above statements of Prof. Malthus, we may find the following important ingredients or features of the Malthusian theory of population:

(1) The increase in population is more than the increase in food supply. The population of a country, left to itself, increases in geometrical progression, i.e. in the ratio of 1 : 2 : 4 : 8 : 16 : 32 etc., where each subsequent series is a clear multiplication of the previous one. The present level of population will be doubled in 25 years if no population checks take place. On the other hand, the food supply (means of subsistence) increases only in arithmetical progression, i.e. in the ratio of 1 : 2 : 3 : 4 : 5 : 6 : 7 etc., where each subsequent series is merely an addition by one over the previous one. It is because of the fact that the law of diminishing returns prevails in agriculture. The supply of land is fixed and the additional units of labour and capital on the land will yield output at a diminishing rate.

Malthus himself stated that the growth of population would outrun the increase in food production. He thought that man's sexual urge to bear offspring knows no bounds. He seemed to think that there was no limit to the fertility of man. But the power of land to produce food is limited. He thought that the law of diminishing returns operated in the field of agriculture and that the operation of this law prevented food production from increasing in proportion to labour and capital invested in land. In his own words, "Taking the whole earth... the population would tend to increase at a geometric rate' (1, 2, 4, 8, 16, 32, 64, etc.) but food supply would tend to increase at an arithmetic rate (1, 2, 3, 4, 5, 6, 7, etc.). Thus, at the end of two hundred years population would be to the means of subsistence as 259 to 9; in three centuries as 4,096 to 13; and in two thousand years the difference would be incalculable." Therefore, Malthus asserted that population would ultimately out-strip food supply. This leads to disequilibrium and over-population. This has been shown in Fig. 19.1. The arithmetical increase in food supply has been shown along the horizontal axis while the geometrical increase in population has been shown along the vertical axis. The Malthusian population curve is *PP* which indicates the relationship between the increase in food supply and the increase in population. It rises upward at a faster rate.

(2) Population increases in a geometrical series while food supply increases in arithmetical series; and thus it leads to disequilibrium between population and food supply. This situation is also known as the situation

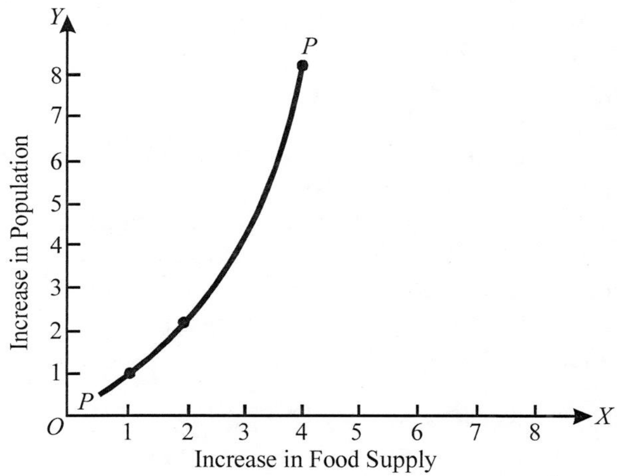

Fig. 19.1

of over-population. According to Malthus, this imbalance is corrected by the operation of two types of checks:

(1) The preventive checks, and

(2) The positive or natural checks.

Preventing checks exercise their influence oil the growth of population by bringing down the birth rate. Preventive checks are those checks which are applied by man. Preventive checks arise from man's reasoning faculties which enable him to see distant consequences. People think that with a large number of children, the standard of living of the family is bound to be lowered. They may not be able to give proper education to their children if they are more in number. Further, they may not like exposing their children to poverty or charity by their inability to provide for them. These considerations may force people to limit the size of their families. Late marriage and self-restraint during married life are the examples of preventive checks applied by man to limit the family. According to Malthus, "The preventive checks include late marriages, chastity (purity of conduct) and other similar measures aimed at checking population growth deliberately including self restraint, moral and prudential."

On the other hand, positive checks exercise their influence on the growth of population by increasing the death rate. They are applied by nature. The positive checks to population are various and include every cause, whether arising from vice or misery, which in any degree contributes to shorten the natural duration of human life. The unwholesome occupation, hard labour, exposure to the seasons, extreme poverty, bad nursing of children, common diseases, wars, plagues and famines are some of the examples of positive checks. They all shorten human life and increase death rate.

Maltnus recommended the use of preventive checks if mankind was to escape from the impending misery. If preventive checks were not effectively used, positive checks like diseases, wars, famines, floods, droughts, and the like natural calamities would come into operation. As a result the population would be reduced to the level which can be sustained by the available quantity of food supply. Thus the balance between population and food supply will be achieved.

Criticisms of Malthusian Theory of Population

The Malthusian theory of population has been a subject of keen controversy. The following are some of the grounds on which it has been criticized:

(1) Malthusian theory of population was correct only at that time when Malthus developed it; but since then the world has considerably changed, and many forces unforeseen by Malthus have come into existence and have rendered his theory inapplicable to modern times. During the time of Malthus, the population of England was increasing and food supply was getting scanty. Food supply could not be increased through international trade. But now, due to the expansion of international trade, England (or any country) can exchange her manufactured products

with the agricultural products of other countries and very well sustain a much larger population than what Malthus could imagine. Thus, in modern times, the theory does not hold.

(2) The critics point out that while formulating his theory, Malthus did not realise the biological fact of life. It is a biological fact that the fecundity of human beings diminishes with advance of civilization. In other words, the power and desire of reproduction progressively diminish with the advance of civilization and culture. If this fact is realised then there will be no fear of excessive growth of population.

(3) The theory also failed to foresee the rapid increase in the production of foodstuffs which the modem nations can command. Malthus did not realise that the law of diminishing returns could be checked by improvements in methods of agriculture. He also did not understand that food supply produced by a nation is not an effective limit to her population; the limit is, in fact, set by the quantity of foodstuffs that a country can command either by herself producing it or by importing it from other countries.

Recent statistics clearly show that agricultural production has increased so tremendously hi advanced countries like USA, France, UK, etc. on account of scientific methods of cultivation that there is absolutely no fear of any shortage of food supply. Here population has not increased so rapidly as the means of subsistence.

(4) The Malthusian theory of population did not realise the influence of standard of living. A general rise in the standard of living of the world. population has decreased birth rate. People produce a smaller number of children in order to maintain their standard of living.

(5) Malthus also failed to give weight to the various social tendencies which today operate against large families. For instance, there is a strong feeling in modem society against a large family which is regarded as a folly, and the old pride in large family has now vanished. Besides, on account of the expansion of female education, the young women of the country become aware of the family planning concept. They do not like to accept the burden of a large family.

(6) Malthlis compared the population growth with the increase in food production alone. He held the opinion that because land was available in fixed quantity, food production could not rise faster than population. But he should have considered all types of production in considering the question of optimum size of population. England did feel the shortage of land and food. If England had been forced to support her population entirely from her domestic food production, there can be little doubt that

England's population would have been checked. But England did not experience such a disaster. It is because England industrialised itself by using her natural resources in various industries. This enabled. her to produce plenty of industrial and manufacturing goods which she then exported in exchange for food stuffs from other countries. There is no food shortage in England. Thus, Malthusian theory of population failed even in the context of England.

(7) Further, the critics pointed out that Malthus gave no proof of his assertion that population increased exactly in geometric progression and food production increased exactly in arithmetic progression. It has been rightly pointed out that population and food supply do not change in accordance with these mathematical series.

(8) According to Prof. Seligman, the problem of population is not merely one of size, but of efficient production and equitable distribution. If with the increase of population, production also increases and the increased national output (income) is equitably distributed, then the increase in population may be fairly justified.

(9) Malthus pointed out that in an overpopulated country if preventive checks were not effective then positive or natural checks would become operative. But, in real world we find that natural calamities do occur even in those countries which are underpopulated.

(10) The Malthusian theory of population is not applicable in European countries. The rate of growth of population has actually gone down in European countries like France, Germany, etc. The population is rather static in these countries.

Malthusian Theory of Population and Underdeveloped Countries

Despite the criticisms of Malthusian theory, the fact cannot be denied that though the theory is not applicable to the western countries, it is applicable to the under-developed countries of Asia and Africa. We may give an example of India. In India population has been increasing at a faster rate than the agricultural output. Her manufacturing industries are also not so much developed that she may get adequate food supplies from other countries in exchange for manufactured goods. The consequences is that population often presses against the limit set by food supplies. In spite of this fact that India imports millions of metric tonnes of food grains from foreign countries, she is not able to provide sufficient food to her increasing population.

Further, the government of India is suggesting to her people to adopt preventive checks to control population. Family planning has been given top priority in five year plans. But the people of the country are illiterate and so blindly wedded to old religious and social customs that they do not practise moral self-restraint. The absence of this restraint is associated with the absence of the practice of artificial methods of birth control because of poverty, illeteracy and conservatism. Naturally, therefore, nature brings into action her own rough and crude methods of exterminating surplus population. Diseases, floods, earthquakes, riots, and other natural calamities take place very often and carry off the surplus population every now and then. Thus the Malthusian theory of population is fully applicable to the under-developed countries like India.

3. THE OPTIMUM THEORY OF POPULATION

Modern economists have rejected the Malthusian theory of maximum population. Instead of the maximum population, the modern economists have substituted the idea of the optimum population. Thus the modern economists such as Sidgwick, Cannan, Dalton and Robbins have propagated the theory of optimum population. It is an attempt to define what would economically be the ideal size of population for a country. The modern theory of optimum population traces the relationship between changes in population and the consequent changes in per capita income.

By optimum population is meant the ideal number of the population that a country should have, considering his resources (national resources, capital, technical knowledge, etc). If we assume that all factors of production are constant but only population can be increased, or decreased, we will find that there is a certain quantity of population which will make income per head maximum. If the quantity of population is less than this, the per capita income will decline and, on the other hand, if the quantity of population is more than this, even then the per capita income will decrease. Thus ***the quantity of population which maximises the per capita income is called the optimum population.*** Various economists have defined the optimum population in different ways.

According to Robbins, "The population which just makes the maximum returns possible is the optimum population or the best possible population."

According to Carr Saunders, "Optimum population is that population which produces maximum economic welfare."

According to Dalton, "Optimum population is that which gives the maximum income per head."

Now, if we study the above definitions, then we say that Dalton's opinion seems to be real and scientific. The optimum population is, thus, the ideal or desirable population of a country. A country should have this particular size of population if it wants to maximise its income per head. If the population of a country is below the optimum, i.e. below what it ought to be, then the country is said to be *under-populated.* The number of the people is sufficient to take the fullest possible advantages of the natural and capital resources of the country. This is what happens in a new country. The resources are plenty and much can be produced; but there are not enough workers to carry on the work of production efficiently. Under such conditons, increase in population will be followed by an increase in per capita income. But this increase cannot go on indefinitely. When the shortage of workers has been made up, the per capita income will reach the maximum, and we shall say that the optimum has been reached.

If, however, the population still goes on increasing and the optimum is exceeded, then we shall have a state of over-population. There will be too many workers on the land. The resources will not be sufficient to provide gainful employment to all. This will lead to a decrease in both the marginal productivity and the average productivity of the workers. In other words, per capita income will diminish and standard of living will fall. This is the situation of *over population.* As Prof. Edwin Cannan stated, "At any given time, increase of labour up to a certain point is attempted by increasing proportionate returns and beyond that point further increase of labour is attended by diminishing proportionate returns."

Assumption of the Theory

The theory of optimum population is based on the following assumptions:

(1) It assumes that the proportion of working population to total population remains constant as the population of a country increases.

(2) It assumes that as the population of a country increases, the natural and capital resources and the technical knowledge remain the same.

Illustration. Let us suppose that the stock of natural resources, capital resources and the state of technology remain fixed in a country. Now assume that population which is initially very small relative to the available resources begins to increase. With the increase in population, the labour force or the number of workers of the country will also increase. As more and more labour is combined with the unchanged amount of the other factors of production, output per capita (average productivity) or real income per head will rise. It is because of the fact that the increase in the quantity of labour will make possible greater degree of specialisation and more efficient use of available resources of the country. The country will take advantage of the economies of large-scale production. As population increases, the market for goods expands, large-scale production becomes possible which adds greatly to the productivity of the economy.

As the population continues to increase, a point will finally be reached when available capital and natural resources are fully utilised and, therefore, output per capita or per capita income will be the highest. The level of population at which per capita real income is maximum is called the optimum population.

If population further increases, then the output per capita will not rise but rather it will decline. It is because of the fact that the available resources are already fully utilised and further increase in population will mean that the given amount of capital and natural resources have to be spared among a larger number of workers with the result that their average productivity will decrease. This will be the situation of over-population.

Thus it is clear that both under-population and over-population will lead to lower per capita income. It is the optimum level of population which assumes the maximum per capita income and which is most desirable for a country to attain.

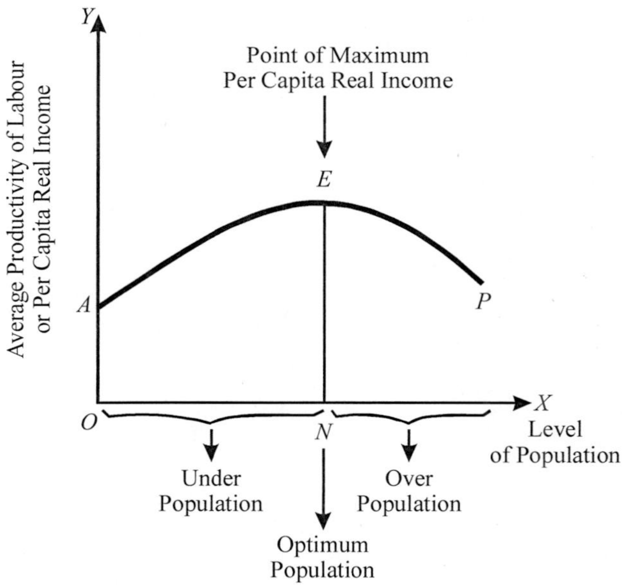

Fig. 19.2

The above concepts of optimum population, under-population and over-population can also be illustrated with the help of a diagram. In, Fig. 19.2 *AP* curve represents the average productivity (of labour) or the per capita real income of a country. It is evident in Fig. 19.2 the in the beginning as population increases output per capita or per capita real income also increases. Output per capita goes on increasing with every increase in population till *ON* level of population is reached. At *ON* level of population, per capita real income becomes maximum and is equal to *ON*. If population increases beyond *ON*, per capita real income will decline. Thus, *ON* is the optimum level of population. If the actual level of population of a country is less than *ON*, it will be under-populated and if the actual level' of population is. more than *ON*, it will be a case of over-population.

It may, however, be remembered that optimum population is not a fixed and rigid number, but it is a moving figure. As we have already explained, optimum population is relative to resources and, technology. Given the amount of natural and capital resources and the state of technology, there will be a definite size of population at which per capita real income is maximum. But the amount of capital and natural resources and the state of technology are subject to changes. When there is a change in these resources, the optimum level of population will also change. This has been shown in Fig. 19.3.

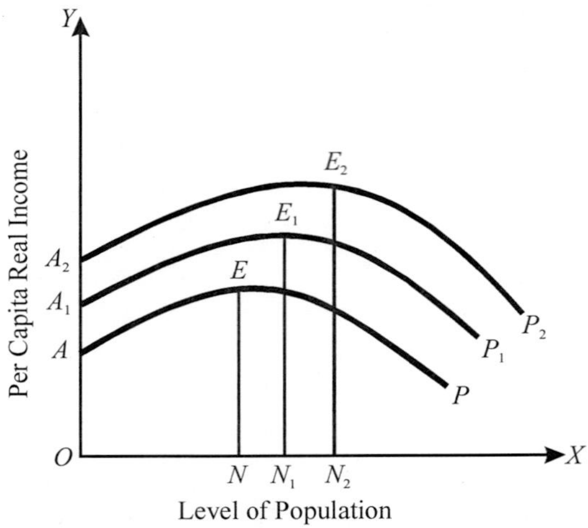

Fig. 19.3

In Fig. 19.3, *AP* is the original average product curve of the labour with *EN* per capita income and *ON* optimum population. With change in resources and technique, this curve shifts to $A_1P_1$and then further to A_2P_2 A higher population, *ON.* and ON_2 respectively, now becomes optimum population. Thus we find that with different resources or different tech-nology, there will be a different level of optimum population.

Dalton has given a formula by which we can judge the extent to which the actual population of a country deviates from the optimum population. The extent of the deviation is called *maladjustment.* The formula seeks to measure the degree of this maladjustment. It is given as below:

$$M = \frac{A-O}{O}$$

where, M = degree of maladjustment
A = actual population
O = optimum population

If M > O{i.e., positive), it is a case of over-population.

If M < O (i.e., negative), the country is under-populated.

If M = O, population is of the optimum size.

For example, let us assume that the actual population of a country is 60 crores and its optimum population is 40 crores, then the country is over-populated to the extent of

$$M = \frac{A-O}{O}$$

$$= \frac{60-40}{40} = \frac{20}{40} = \frac{1}{2}, \text{ i.e. 50 per cent.}$$

Superiority of Optimum Theory over the Malthusian Theory of Population

The optimum theory of population is certainly an improvement over the old Malthusian theory of population. The following are the main differences between the Malthusian theory and the optimum theory of population. These differences will clearly indicate the superiority of optimum theory over the Malthusian theory of population:

(1) Malthusian theory of population relates population to food production only where as the optimum theory of population takes into consideration all the resources and economic development in all its

respects, i.e. all types of production. Thus the optimum theory is superior to the Malthusian theory of population.

(2) Malthus was very much afraid of the operation of the law of diminishing returns in agriculture. He ignored the possibility of increasing returns in food supply and agricultural production. While, on the other hand, the optimum theory of population assumes increasing returns up to a certain point. Diminishing returns take place only after a point. This clears the superiority of optimum theory over the Malthusian theory of population.

(3) According to Malthus every increase in population was harmful. But the modern economists who propagated the optimum theory of population are of the opinion that in the beginning the increase in population is rather desirable because it leads to fuller use of the available resources.

(4) The Malthusian theory of population is applicable only to those countries which suffer from the problem of over-population. Whereas the optimum theory of population is applicable to all the countries of the world, i.e., to over-populated as well as to under-populated countries.

(5) The Malthusian theory of population views man as a consumer and ignores his role as a producer. Where as the optimum theory of population recognises both these roles of man. He is a producer as well as a consumer.

(6) Malthus thought of a maximum number for a country which, if exceeded, would spell misery. According to the optimum theory, there is no rigidly fixed maximum.

(7) According to Malthus, famine, war, diseases and other natural calamities were the signs of over-population. But the optimum theory of population tells us that, even in the absence of such distressing phenomena, there can be over-population, provided it can be shown that per capita income has gone down, or that with a decrease in population, per capita income well go up.

Criticism of the Optimum Theory of Population

In spite of this fact that the optimum theory of population is superior to that of the Malthusian theory of population, it is not free from its criticism. The following are the important limitations of the optimum theory of population:

(1) The theory is based on the assumption that the proportion of working population to the total population remains constant as the

population of a country increases. This assumption does not hold in real world.

(2) It also assumes that as population increases, the available capital and natural resources and the state of technology are unchanged. But in a dynamic world this is also not possible. Things are changing day by day.

(3) The concept of optimum population is a static concept inapplicable and irrelevant to a dynamic world. In Dalton's formula, the value of *O* (the optimum population) depends on the capital resources, the modes of business organisation and the rate of investment. As all these factors are constantly changing, the optimum population is a fluctuating figure. The invention of a labour-saving machinery, for instance, would immediately convert a country with optimum population to over-population. Conversely, the discovery of a new economic resource (a new fine for instance would make the same country under-populated.

(4) The optimum theory of population has no place in state policies. It cannot be a guiding principle to any practical policy. Modern economists, following Keynes, show how employment and income can be increased by a judicious fiscal policy. In the formulation of such fiscal policies the concept of optimum population is of no use.

(5) It is impossible to measure the degree of maladjustment. Because the theory neglects the social and institutional conditions which are more powerful than the economic conditions.

(6) This theory neglects the distributional effect of increase in per capita income which assumes to be more important.

3. THE BIOLOGICAL THEORY OF POPULATION

In modern times biologists and statisticians have made intensive studies of population growth and have developed certain principles regarding it. We may describe these principles in the following section:

(1) ***The Logistic Curve Theory.*** The logistic curve theory was developed by well-known American biologist, Raymond Pearl in his famous book, *The Biology of Population Growth.* According to this theory, the population does not increase at a constant rate but it varies from time to time. It has been found that if population growth is graphically shown, it looks like the S-shaped curve known in mathematics as the *Logistic Curve.* This indicates that population increases first very slowly, then comparatively rapidly and finally becomes either stationary or declines. These phenomena may be explained on the following hypothesis. In a primitive civilisation, there are obstacles to growth like lack of security,

lack of food, unfavourable social customs, etc. Therefore, population increases slowly. With development, these obstacles are removed and population increases rapidly. But as soon as the community reaches an advanced stage of civilisation, the rate of growth becomes steady or declines. This has been shown in Fig. 19.4.

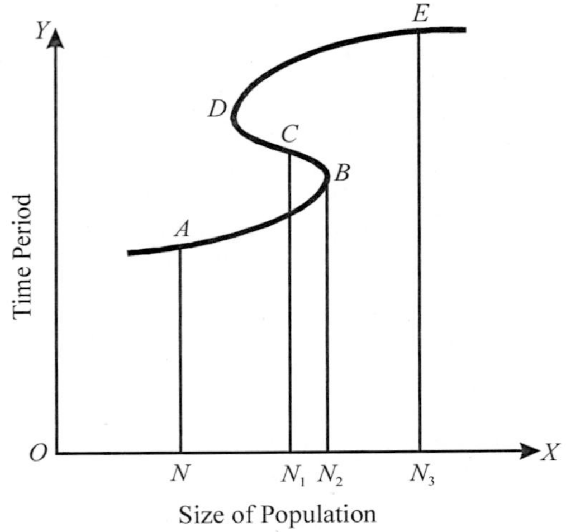

Fig. 19.4

In Fig. 19.4, we represent the size of population along the horizontal X axis and the time period along the vertical axis. Here, at point *A* the population begins to increase and it goes on increasing until point *B* is reached. Now from *ON* to ON_2, the population increases at a faster rate. After point *B,* the population decreases. For example, at point *C*, population decreases from ON_2 to ON_2. This decrease in population continues until point *D* is reached. From point *D,* the population again begins to increase. But now, this increase will continue until point *E* is reached. In other words, the population at point *E* becomes to the level of ON_3. In this way population increases and decreases. But the overall tendency of the population is to increase in a steady manner. The biological theory of population, therefore, confirms the Malthusian theory of population.

Prof. Pearl has studied the history of population growth in France, Germany and USA to confirm his conclusions.

(2) ***Net Reproduction Rate Theory.*** This theory deals with the measurement of population over a period of time. Prof. Kuczynski has

presented this theory in a mathematical way. According to this theory, the growth rate of population in a country does not depend upon the differences between the birth rate and the death rate, but it depends on the number of females of child-bearing age. Thus to find out the rate of growth we need to calculate the number of females of child-bearing age (between 15 to 50 years). Thus the theory states that the net reproduction rate is the rate at which the female population is replacing it self. Mathematically,

$$\text{Net Production Rate} = \frac{\text{Total number of child-bearing women}}{\text{Net number of child-bearing women}}$$

Let us take an example to make it more clear. Suppose the total number of child-bearing women is 2000 and their net number is also 2000; then the net reproduction rate will be equal to unity. It means that the growth rate of population is constant. Now, if the net number of child-bearing women is 1400, then the net reproduction rate would be 0.7 which is less than unity. It would mean that population is decreasing. If, on the other hand, the net reproduction rate is greater than unity, then it implies that population is increasing.

4. THE THEORY OF DEMOGRAPHIC TRANSITION

The theory of demographic transition is the latest theory of population. This theory is more scientific and more convincing than the other theories of population. It postulates a three-stage sequence of birth and death rates as typically associated with economic development. In the first stage, the birth and the death rates are both high. Here, the size of population is more or less stable. In the second stage, the birth rate is high but the death rate declines and consequently population increases at a faster rate. In the third stage, birth rate also declines and becomes equal to the death rate; it results in a decrease in the growth rate of population. Now we shall discuss in detail these three stages of demographic transition.

First Stage of Demographic Transition. In the first stage, the country is a backward and less developed one. Its main occupation is agriculture. During this stage of demographic transition the birth and death rates are very high. The death rate is high on account of poor diets, primitive sanitation and absence of effective medical aid. Birth rate is high on account of widespread prevalence of illiteracy absence of knowledge about family planning techniques, early age of marriage and deep-rooted social beliefs and customs about the size of the family, attitude towards children, etc. Moreover, in a primitive society, there are economic benefits of a large family size. It is believed that larger the number of children in a family, larger will be the earnings of that family, because children instead of being liabilities, will be positive assets for the family. Children start working at an early age and contribute to the family earnings. According to Coale and Hoover, "children contribute at an early age... and are the traditional source of security in the old age of parents. The prevalent high death rates, especially infancy, imply that such security can be attained when many children are born." Thus, in such an agrarian economy, the actual rate of growth of population is not high since the high birth rate is balanced by the high death rate. It is a stage of high growth potential but of low actual growth.

If we look at the population statistics of India, upto 1921 India can be put in the first stage of demographic transition. During the period, both the birth and the death rates were high and the size of population was more or less stationary.

Second Stage of Demographic Transition. During the second stage, some development takes place in the economy. Rise in income levels enables the people of the country to improve their diet. Economic development leads to the improvement in transport facility which makes the supply of food articles regular. These factors tend to reduce the death rate. Thus, in the second stage of demographic transition, birth rate remains high but death rate begins to decline rapidly. This accelerates the growth of population. This stage is, therefore, characterised as the stage of "population explosion." Now the high growth potential of the first stage is realised in the high actual growth in the second stage as a result of decline in death rate. High birth rate and falling death rate lead to increase in the average size of the family. The present situation of India can be placed in the second stage of demographic transition. The birth rate in India continues to increase while death rate falls due to effective medical aid; this leads to an annual increase of 2.4 per cent in India's population.

Third Stage of Demographic Transition. During this stage the country attains sufficient economic development which changes the character of the economy from an agrarian to a partially industrialised one. With the growth of industrialisation, population tends to shift away from rural areas towards industrial growth centres. Increase in urban population and with the development of economic tasks for women outside the home, tends to increase the possibility of economic mobility that can better be achieved with small families. Now children are assumed to be more of a burden and less of an asset. To maintain standard of living, it is necessary to reduce the size of the family. Since the death rate is already low, this is possible only if birth rate falls. Therefore, the main feature of the third stage of demographic transition is low birth rate and low death rate which leads to a low rate of growth of population. The Western countries of the world can be put in the third stage of population growth.

Under the above three stages of demographic transition, the modern economists describe their theory of population. These stages reveal the transformation of a traditional economy of high birth and high death rate to an advanced economy of low birth rate and low death rate. When the economy shifts from the first stage to the second stage, an imbalance or disequilibrium is created, in the economy as a result of falling death rate and relatively' high birth rate. This imbalance requires a period of transition for adjustment.

During the period of transition the demographic factors get out of harmony. Thus in the final stage, birth and death rates are balanced at a lower level. A new equilibrium is now established between birth rate and death rate. Population grows only at a slow and normal rate.

5. POPULATION AND ECONOMIC DEVELOPMENT

The growth of population promotes economic development of capital-abundant countries, on the one hand; on the other hand, it becomes an obstacle to the economic development of labour-abundant countries. Therefore, the role of population in economic development depends upon the circumstances which prevail in a country.

Population has been a contributing factor in the economic development of more developed countries (MDCs). It provided them labour input which was badly needed for productive activities. These countries have accumulated capital resources at a fast rate and with the complementary natural resources being present, increase in labour force has helped in increasing national output. It also offers a big market for their goods and as such, attracts prospective industrialists. It provides the fullest possible use of the available resources. In this way, a growing population may accelerate economic growth of advanced countries.

But, on the other hand, the under-developed countries of today are capital-poor and labour-abundant countries. They do not possess the complementary resources needed to give employment increasing labour force. Thus the growing population of these countries has proved to be the greatest curse and the biggest obstacle in economic growth of such economies. The impact of growing population as a drag on economic resources is felt in a variety of ways.

(1) *Population and Per Capita Income.* The growing population of under-developed countries such as India has adversely affected its per capita income. It has burdened the country with a large unproductive population (e.g., childern) who make no contribution to production. The average expectation of life being low, there is a large number of aged persons who form another set of unproductive consumers. The number of unproductive consumers has been estimated in India at 25 crores nearly. This leads to a sharp reduction in the per capita income of the country. The annual average growth rate of India's national income works out to be 3.3 per cent (compound) and per capita income to be less than 1 per cent.

(2) *Population and Food Supply.* The growing population of India has created a serious food shortage and necessitated the importation of huge quantities of foodgrains. Thus valuable foreign exchange has been squandered. This could have been better used for importing capital goods such as plant, machinery, equipment and other essential raw materials. This would have resulted in rapid economic growth of the country.

(3) *Population and Unemployment.* Rising population is accompanied by a rise in labour force of the economy. It leads to unemployment problem. Disguised unemployment in rural areas (agriculture) and a large-scale unemployment in urban areas (industries) is a common phenomenon in under-developed countries which are over-populated. The problem of unemployment is becoming more and more difficult every day and night.

(4) *Population and Capital Formulation.* The most serious consequence of the fast growing population is that it reduces the country's capacity to save and invest. This is a crucial factor which checks economic growth of a country. For instance in India the present rate of growth of population is 2.5 per cent per annum. To maintain a constant per capita real income (or per capita output), the national income must rise at the rate of 2.5 per cent per annum. To achieve this, capital investment is necessary. The capital output ratio for the Indian economy has been estimated at 4 : 1. It implies that almost 4 units of capital are needed to produce one unit of output. Thus, in order to bring about an increase in national income at the rate of 2.5 per cent capital accumulation of the order of about 10 per cent (2.5×4) is necessary.

According to Planning Commission of India, "In an underdeveloped economy with very little capital per person, a high rate of population growth makes it even more difficult to step up the rate of saving which, in turn, largely determines the possibility of achieving higher productivity and incomes. Moreover, for a given investment, a large proportion will need to be devoted to the production of essential consumer goods at the expense of investment goods industries, thereby still further showing down the potential rate of growth."

All these factors lead to the conclusion that a rapidly increasing population retards the economic development of overpopulated under-developed countries like India.

EXERCISES

1. Write a critical note on the Malthusian theory of population.
2. State and explain the Malthusian theory of population. How far is it valid today?
3. What is meant by over, under and optimum population? In what way is the optimum theory of population an improvement on the Malthusian concept?
4. What is optimum population? Do you consider the size of the Indian population to be optimum?
5. "The optimum theory of population becomes useless in a dynamic state." Discuss.
6. Explain the theory of demographic transition. How far is this theory superior to other theories of population?
7. Explain the biological theory of population. What are its merits?
8. Explain the effects pf the growth of population on economic development.

Multiple Choice Questions

9. (*i*) If the capital output ratio is 3, the savings rate is 5 per cent and the economy is growing at 4 per cent in simple terms and 1.5 per cent in per capita terms, what is the rate of population growth?
   (a) 1.5 per cent (*c*) 3.5 per cent
   (*b*) 2.5 per cent (*d*) 4.5 per cent [*Ans.* (*b*)]

   (*ii*) Which is correct about the Malthusian Theory of Population?
   (*a*) population increases in geometrical progression
   (*b*) food increases in arithmetical progression
   (*c*) imbalance between population growth and food supply leads to over-population
   (*d*) all of the above [*Ans.* (*d*)]

   (*iii*) Optimum population means that level of population at which
   (*a*) average product of labour is maximum
   (*b*) total product of labour is maximum
   (*c*) marginal product of labour is maximum
   (*d*) none of the above is correct [*Ans.* (*a*)]

Chapter 20

DIVISION OF LABOUR

1. MEANING OF DIVISION OF LABOUR

Division of labour refers to the process of splitting production into a number of parts and allocating each part to a group of workers in such a way that these people working separately, co-operate with each other to turn out the complete commodity. When two or more persons work together for a common end by doing different tasks, this type of organisation of work is called division of labour. Adam Smith has beautifully illustrated the advantages of the division of labour by taking an example from the pin making industry. If one man starts making the complete pin from beginning to the end, he can only make 20 pins in a day. But if one man beats the iron, the second draws the wire, the third cuts it, the fourth sharpens the edge, the fifth places the cap and so on the work being divided into 18 distinct processes, they can make something like 48,000 pins in a day. In the words of Watson, "Production by division of labour consists in splitting up the productive process into its component parts." Thus the division of labour means that the main process of production is splitup into many simple parts and each part is taken up by different persons who are specialised in the production of that specific part.

The need for division of labour arose when with the advance of civilisation the human wants multiplied. Now it became impossible for anyone individual to make all the things he needed for consumption. Therefore every one started making those commodities for which he was best fitted. This started the process of division of labour. Further as the work assumed complexity, it was divided in smaller and smaller parts and workers specialised in the production of these smaller parts. This specialisation also spread to the different parts of the country as well as to various countries. Some countries started specialising in agriculture while other concentrated on industry. This country wise specialisation or international division of labour is, in fact the basis of international trade.

2. FORMS OF DIVISION OF LABOUR

The division of labour has been divided into different forms by the economists. which may be explained as below:

(1) ***Simple Division of Labour.*** As we have seen, in the primitive times, each one of the people used to produce all those things which he needed. But with the passage of time and dawn of civilization the wants multiplied at such a fast rate that it became impossible for anyone to satisfy all his wants by his own production. As a result of this, people started engaging themselves in different occupations specialising in such branches as agriculture, industry, trade, transport and services. The weaver, for example, makes the cloth; he spins the cotton, weaves the cloth and also dyes it. Thus he performs all the operations from the beginning to the end. This type of division of labour where work is divided on the basis of complete occupations and where in each occupation every person performs the whole task from the beginning to the end is called a simple division of labour.

(2) ***Complex Division of Labour.*** In each one of the occupations the work is further divided into processes and sub-processes or parts and sub-parts. For example the work of making cloth can be split into picking of cotton from the fields, separating cotton-seeds from cotton, spinning it, weaving it and dying it. All these are different processes. If all these processes are done by separate people this is called complex division of labour.

Complex division of labour can be further divided into two parts:

(*i*) ***Division of Labour into Complete Processes.*** This is that type of division of labour where each one of the complete parts of a certain work is being done by a person, or a group of persons. For example, spinning of cotton is a process which is complete in itself. Similarly weaving is a complete process. When this type of division is there, this is called division of labour into complete processes.

(*ii*) ***Division of Labour into Incomplete Processes.*** When each one of the complete process is further divided into sub-processes and each one of such sub-process is allocated to a group of people, we call it a division of labour into incomplete processes for example, if in case of book binding, one man cuts the card, the other makes holes into it and the third one stiches it, this is division into complete processes. But the division of labour has gone far beyond it. In place of one man making the hole in the card, if two people work on it, one man holds the nail over card and the other strikes it from above and thus make the hole, this is a division of labour into incomplete processes. In the field of production today, it is this type of division of labour which is more common.

(3) ***Territorial or Geographical Division of Labour.*** It is a simple fact that different parts of a country specialise in the production of different goods. In our own country, for example the production of jute comes from the areas in and around Calcutta. Cotton and textile industry is located primarily in Bombay and Ahmedabad. Kanpur is well known for its leather work while Ludhiana has a reputation for its hosiery. Thus all these parts of the country specialise in some fields of production. Similarly wheat is mainly produced in northern India while rice is the main produce of the south. This type of specialisation among various parts of the country or among the various countries which make the things of each other's requirements, is known as territorial or geographical division of labour. If such division is among various countries, it is also called the international division of labour.

3. ADVANTAGES OF DIVISION OF LABOUR

The division of labour has the following advantages:

(1) ***Increase in Production.*** The whole idea of introducing division of labour into the field of production is to increase its quantity. When the work is divided into smaller parts it is done very quickly. As a result the production increases. As we have already mentioned, the example given by Adam Smith shows that while one man making the whole of a pin cannot produce more than twenty pins in a day, after the division into smaller parts, his production would be many times more.

(2) ***Increase in skill.*** It is wellknown saying that practice makes the man perfect. The worker who is continuously working on a small part of a work for a long time becomes the master of it. The work becomes so automatic for him that he does not have even to think about it. Thus there is an increase in his skill and dexterity. In the words of Adam Smith, "The division of labour, by reducing every man's business to some one simple operation, and by making this operation the sole employment of his life, necessarily increases very much the dexterity of the workman."

(3) ***Improvement in Quality of Production.*** By division of labour the quality of production also improves. Since each man becomes perfect in his work by continuous practice, he can give fine finish to the

commodities. Each unit of production comes from the hands of the master craftsman. He would be in a position to take note of even the minute details of production. Hence the quality of production is bound to improve.

(4) ***Increasing Use of Machinery.*** It is impossible to use more and more machinery, when there is division of labour. With the division of labour, work is divided into smaller and smaller parts. Each small part can be easily made with the help of machines. The whole product as such cannot be made by any machine. For example, it may not be possible to make a complete shoe with a machine. But when shoe is divided into heel, sole, flap, laces etc. we can make each one of these parts by some machinery and then combine them to make the complete shoe.

(5) ***Scope for New Inventions.*** With the division of labour, the scope for making new inventions becomes wider. A man who is continuously working on a certain part of work would always try to find out some method by which the work may become easier and quicker. Continuous efforts in this direction would ultimately lead to new inventions and innovations, which would make production larger, quicker and better.

(6) ***Right Man in Right Place.*** With the division of labour each man gets a job according to his taste, capacity and suitability. Every worker cannot be equally good at all processes of production. A worker may, for example, be very good at spinning but not at weaving. Now, if we ask this man to make the complete unit of cloth be would easily spin the yam, but take much time in weaving if we divide the work between different people, those who are good at spinning would come to this job, while those who know weaving well would go there. This would increase the production many times.

(7) ***Less Physical Strain.*** We have seen that with the division of labour, there is increasing use of machinery. The machines would be used for all those processes where work involves a heavy strain. For example, a crane would be used to lift the heavy weight or a conveyer belt would be used to pass raw material and other things from one department to another. This would naturally reduce the strain on human nerves.

(8) ***Saving of Time.*** With the division of labour considerable time is saved which, otherwise, would have been wasted in changing over from one process to another. For example, if a book binder does the whole work by himself, then first of all he will cut the card with scissors. Then to make the holes he will put down scissors and pick up nail and a hammer. And after making holes, he will have to stitch with the needle and thread. Some time is bound to be wasted in changing over these tools and

implements. But if there is division of labour then one man will go on continuously cutting the cards while the others will make holes and stitch them without any time being wasted in changing over from one process to another.

(9) ***Economy in the Use of Tools.*** To make the whole commodity every worker requires all tools to be used in production. But when he is working on one part, all tools except those which are being currently used, lay idle. He would pick some of them in the next process. But then others would remain idle. Thus each one of the workers will have to be supplied with all the tools but most of them would remain idle for most of the time. On the other hand when there is division of labour, each man would be supplied with only those tools which he requires to do that part of work. He would use the tools continuously without keeping them idle. The number of tools supplied to every man would be very small. Thus there is an economy in the use of tools.

(10) ***Saving of Time, Effort and Money in Learning the Trade.*** Under division of labour since each worker is supposed to do only a part of the job, it is not necessary for him to learn the whole trade. He would learn only that part of the job which he is going to take up. This would naturally reduce the training period, save the efforts of the workers and also reduce expenses of learning. Learning of the whole job would involve a longer period of training and the workers will have to put in more of efforts.

(11) ***Diversification of Employment.*** By dividing a work into many parts, more avenues of employment are opened. Women and children can take up easier and lighter jobs. Jobs of all types and tastes may be now available to the workers. Thus it becomes easier for every worker to find out a job of his own taste and preference.

From the above mentioned points, it, becomes clear that division of labour increases efficiency, saves time and improves quality of production. Goods are produced on a large scale and their cost is reduced. Thus better quality of goods become available to the consumers while at the same time their prices become lower. This is a great benefit of the division of labour.

4. DISADVANTAGES OF DIVISION OF LABOUR

The division of labour has certain demerits also which can be explained as below:

(1) ***Monotony of Work.*** The worker under division of labour has to do the same process again and again. Repeating the job continuously

every day makes him feel dull and monotonous. The work becomes a matter of routine which he performs without much interest and. initiative. This sometimes results in mental depression which is very harmful and reduces the efficiency of the worker.

(2) ***Destruction of Creative Instinct.*** Every worker takes pleasure in making a complete commodity. If the goods produced are of high quality, he would take pride in being the man who produced them. And the appreciation of his work would induce him further to improve the quality of his work. But under division of labour every worker makes only a part of the commodity. His work is only a small fraction of the whole thing. Thus that instinct which made him feel proud of making a fine commodity has no role to play. He is working in a team and acts in accordance to the instructions given to him. This kills his creative instinct.

(3) ***Retards Development of Human Personality.*** During the same job again and again narrows down the mental outlook of the worker. He is required to do only a part of the work, and he does not know anything more than that. His imagination, thinking and actions revolve around only that part of the job. This naturally retards the physical development and mental outlook of a person.

(4) ***Loss of Mobility.*** Being specialised only in one part of the work, the labourer cannot leave one job and go to another easily. He can go only if the same type of job is available. But since jobs of the same type are not available every where, it becomes difficult for him to move from one place to another. This reduces the chances of progress and at the same time increases the risk of unemployment. If he leaves the present job it may become difficult to find out a similar job. Thus if he gets unemployed here, he may not be able to find out employment elsewhere easily. On the other hand a man who knows many jobs would find out a suitable work any where and every where.

(5) ***Loss of Responsibility.*** It is well known that a collective responsibility is ultimately no one's responsibility. Under division of labour many people work together on the various processes to make the whole commodity. Therefore any defect in the commodity cannot be attributed to anyone of them. Being the work of the whole group of workers, it may not be possible to hold anyone responsible for the defect. Hence every worker thinks that even if he does not take proper care of the work he is not likely to be held responsible. So every one starts taking the work lightly and stops bothering about it. This results in the growth of irresponsibility among the workers.

(6) ***Employment of Children.*** With the division of labour, many parts of work become very simple and generally children are employed to do it. Employment of children impairs their health and retards their mental development. Mentally retarded and physically depressed children are a threat to the future of the nation.

(7) ***Evils of Factory System.*** Division of labour gives rise to factory system. The evils associated with the factory system are well known. Over-crowdedness, slums, immorality and industrial diseases are the results of factory system. Insanitary conditions and unhygienic atmosphere not only spoil the health of the workers, but also pollute the climate of the whole area. This is a great social cost of division of labour.

(8) ***Loss of Contact between Employer and Worker.*** Under division of labour the number of workers being very large, the personal contact between employer and the worker is lost. The lack of personal contact results in labour unrest, which assumes the form of strikes, lock-outs and other industrial disputes. As a result of such disputes, much of the man hours are wasted, which could have otherwise resulted in the production of larger number of goods. This labour unrest when it becomes widespread, assumes the form of class struggle, a struggle between the rich and the poor. If such a struggle starts, it becomes a threat to the stability of the society itself.

From the above discussion about the division of labour, it is sufficiently clear that although, division of labour is harmful to the workers in certain ways, its advantages to workers, employers and the society as a whole, outweigh the disadvantages. Further, most of the disadvantages are such that they can easily be removed, cured or at least minimised. Sufficient attention is being paid these days to the welfare of the workers. Their conditions of work are being constantly improved. Recreation facilities are being increasingly provided. Measures have been taken regarding improvement in health and sanitation. All these steps have mitigated most of the evils that we have associated with the division of labour and the factory system of production. In fact the division of labour is a precondition for the growth of any economy.

5. LIMITATIONS OF DIVISION OF LABOUR

The division of labour, as we have seen, is advantageous to an economy in many ways. But is it possible to introduce division of labour in all types of industries? If not, then what are the limits to the division of labour? These are some of the questions which naturally arise in connection with the division of labour.

First, there are certain industries where division of labour cannot be introduced to any great extent. Division of labour can be introduced only in those industries, where various processes of production can be carried on simultaneously. But there are may such industries where one process follows the other. All the work is not done at the same time. One such case is that of agriculture. Here first the land is ploughed, the seeds are sown, then the crop grows and thereafter it is harvested. Now it is not possible to divide the work in such a manner that one man goes on ploughing the land, the other is sowing the seeds and the third is harvesting it at the same time. Since every process follows the other, it is natural that every one will perform each process by himself.

Secondly, the division of labour is limited by the extent of the market. When the demand is large, it is possible to introduce the division of labour and produce a larger supply of goods. But when the demand is very small, it would be ineconomical to introduce the division of labour. If in a village only two pairs of shoes are required every day, it would not be wise to introduce division of labour and turn out twenty pairs every day. And if the producers do so, they will incur losses because the workers would remain without work for all those days till the shoes are sold. Thus the division of labour is possible only when the size of the market is large, i.e. there is a larger demand for goods.

Thirdly, division of labour for its introduction requires a large supply of labour. If in a country the labour force is very small, sufficient number of labourers will not be available for doing each one of the processes under the division of labour.

And *finally,* division of labour is possible only where the work can be split up into various processes. But in some cases, as for example in painting, embroidery and other artistic jobs, it is not possible to split work into various parts and give a part to each worker. Thus every worker has to do the complete work by himself.

Therefore it may be concluded that although division of labour is advantageous, its introduction is limited by various factors, some of which are inherent in the nature of production while the others arise from the external factors like the limited supply of labour and disadvantages of division of labour itself.

EXERCISES

1. What do you mean by division of labour? Discuss its advantages and disadvantages.
2. Discuss the meaning and forms of division of labour. What are its merits and demerits?
3. Discuss the advantages and the limitations of the principle of division of labour.

Multilple Choice Questions

4. (*i*) Division of labour leads to
    (*a*) increase in mobility of labour
    (*b*) increase in the efficiency of labour
    (*c*) increase in production
    (*d*) all of the above [*Ans*. (*d*)]

   (*ii*) Division of labour means
    (*a*) division of workers in different occupations
    (*b*) split up the productive process into different parts
    (*c*) specialisation of work
    (*d*) all of the above [*Ans*. (*d*)]

Chapter 21

LOCALISATION OF INDUSTRIES

1. MEANING OF LOCALISATION

The tendency on the part of an industry to be concentrated in an area is known as localisation of industries. Some areas have some natural or acquired advantages and offer special facilities to certain industries. As a result such industries tend to be localised at such places. For example, jute industry is located near Calcutta while the cotton textile industry is more or less localised in Bombay and Ahmedabad. Similarly Switzerland specialises in watches, Brazil in Coffee and India in Tea etc. All such examples are the examples of localisation of industries. Localisation of industries is based on the principle of division of labour and is, therefore, also known as geographical or territorial division of labour. Thus localisation means the concentration of a certain industry in a particular area, locality or region.

2. CAUSES OF LOCALISATION

The following are the important causes which explain why a particular industry establishes itself in anyone locality in preference to others:

(1) ***Natural Advantages.*** Natural advantages exist in the form of suitable climate and desirable physical conditions. The cotton textile industry requires a moist climate so that fine thread may be spun out of cotton. It is thus the climate of Bombay which has made it the centre of the cotton manufacturing industry in India. The climate of Bengal is similarly suited to the cultivation of jute and jute industry is, therefore, localised in Bengal.

(2) ***Nearness to Raw Materials.*** This is another important cause of localisation. The areas where raw materials are available sometimes become the centre of industries. The jute industry of Calcutta and the iron and steel industry of Tatanagar were mainly the result of this cause.

(3) ***Nearness to Sources of Power.*** Power is another important industrial requisite. Coal is one of the most important sources of power and industries tend to be drawn near coal fields. The concentration of iron and steel industry at Jamshedpur is, to a considerable extent, due to the availability of the supplies of coal in the neighbourhood.

(4) ***Nearness to Market.*** Nearness to market is another important factor conducive to the localisation of industries. The factories near the consuming centres have a great advantage over those situated at a distance. Cotton textile mills are being set up in the northern parts of India due to this reason. In this way transport charges are saved by the manufacturers.

(5) ***Availability of Labour.*** Availability of trained labour is another great facility. If somebody wants to start a hosiery industry, it will be advantageous for him to start it at Ludhiana. There he will not find it difficult to obtain adequate supply of specialized labour.

(6) ***Availability of Capital.*** This is another important attraction. Industrialists flock to centres where financial facilities are available. Bombay and Calcutta are centres of industry because they are centres of finance.

(7) ***Royal Patronage.*** In earlier times court patronage also led to localisation of certain industries. Gold and silver thread industry, for example, flourished in Delhi due to the patronage of Moghul courts.

(8) ***Momentum of an Early Start.*** Sometimes a place where an industry gets an early start begins to enjoy so many advantages in respect of that industry. Ultimately that industry gets localised there. The hoisery industry of Ludhiana is a good example.

Thus, there are numerous causes which account for the localisation of industries. "The main reason," in the words of Benham, "why different districts specialise in the different products is that factors of production are distributed in unequal proportion over the surface of the earth."

3. ADVANTAGES OF LOCALISATION

The following are the advantages of localisation:

(1) ***Reputation.*** A localised product acquires a commercial reputation and it becomes easier to market it. Sheffield cutlery is famous all the world over.

(2) ***Skilled Labour.*** It encourages the growth of specialised labour. Industrial skill is preserved and passed on from father to son.

(3) ***Development of Transport.*** It leads to the development of the means of communication and transport.

(4) ***Development of Financial Facilities.*** It leads to the development of financial facilities. Banks and financial houses are established at such places.

(5) ***Research Centres.*** Common economic problems can be better solved by mutual consultation. Research laboratories can be setup and facilities for the training of labour can be easily provided.

(6) ***Subsidiary Industries.*** It leads to the establishment of several subsidiary and other industries. The tin-plate and barbed wire industries as subsidiaries to Tata Iron and Steel Works are good instances.

(7) ***Solution of Common Problems.*** Localisation finally facilitates organization of both workers and industrialists.

4. DISADVANTAGES OF LOCALISATION

The following are the disadvantages of localisation:

(1) ***Dependence.*** Dependence on one industry might cause misery if there is a depression in it. It leads to economic dependence of one locality on another which may be dangerous in times of war.

(2) ***Limited Employment.*** It provides employment only to one type of skill.

(3) ***Lack of Labour Mobility.*** Specialised labour loses mobility.

(4) ***Social Problems.*** Congestion and over-crowding are a necessary concomitant of localisation. This raises rents and prices and makes the standard of living costly.

(5) ***Danger of War.*** Localisation also provides an easy target for enemy air attacks.

5. DECENTRALISATION OF INDUSTRIES

Of late there has been a tendency towards decentralisation. Factories are spreading out and main efforts at present are towards dispersal of already localised units. Several factors are responsible for this development, most important of which are:

(1) ***Development of the Means of Transport.*** It is now possible to procure raw materials from far off places and to transport finished articles to the consumers at a much lower cost. This obviates the necessity of factories being localised near the sources of supply or the market.

(2) ***Advent of Electricity.*** Electricity can be carried over long distances. Industries are, therefore, moving out to places where they find other facilities.

(3) ***Higher Costs in Urban Areas.*** Great rise in urban rents, high land prices, high municipal taxation, etc., are also driving out industries to rural areas. This also avoids evils like congestion and over-crowding which characterise modern factory life.

(4) ***Fear of Bombardment and Destruction during War.*** Finally, decentralisation also avoids the danger of industries being destroyed during war.

EXERCISES

1. Explain the meaning of localisation of industries. What are its causes and consequences?
2. What factors determine localisation of industries? Explain the reasons which have prompted governments to follow the policy of dispersal of industries.
3. What are main advantages and disadvantages of localisation of industries?
4. Write a brief note on decentralisation of industries.

Multiple Choice Questions

5. (*i*) Localisation means
   (*a*) territorial division of labour
   (*b*) concentration of a certain industry in a particular area
   (*c*) specialisation by areas or regions
   (*d*) all of the above [*Ans.(d)*]

   (*ii*) The following is the main cause of localisation of industries:
   (*a*) fear of war
   (*b*) climatic conditions
   (*c*) equal development of an areas
   (*d*) all of the above [*Ans. (b)*]

   (*iii*) Which is not a disadvantage of localisation of industries?
   (*a*) Dependence
   (*b*) Limited Employment
   (*c*) Regional Imbalance
   (*d*) Reputation. [*Ans.(d)*]

Chapter 22

ENTERPRISE AND ORGANISATION

1. MEANING OF ENTERPRISE

The entrepreneur is assumed to be one of the most important factors of production in modern times. The present system of production has become very complex. It needs the co-ordination of a variety of factors of production. The different factors of production lie scattered. Land, labour and capital are not found at one place but at different places. Thus a person or group of persons are needed to bring all these factors together in order to organise a business. The entrepreneur is the person who organises the business as also undertakes the risks of the business. He is the person who decides the various questions regarding the actual working of the business, e.g., questions about the place of the business, the quantity and the quality of production and the combination of the different factors of production. In Short, *the entrepreneur is the initiator, the organiser, 'the controller and the riskbearer of a business.* In the words of Benham, "the term entrepreneur means the person or a group of persons controlling the policy of a firm." According to Frank H. Knight, "an entrepreneur is a person who performs the duel functions of risk taking and control."

2. FUNCTIONS OF THE ENTREPRENEUR

The main work of the entrepreneur consists of taking risk but according to the principle 'where the risk lies, there the control lies', the organisation of industry itself has become an important function of the entrepreneur. It has been aptly remarked that "management of business has it self bcome a business." Important functions of entrepreneur ate discussed as below:

(1) ***Planning and Starting of the Business.*** The entrepreneur chalks out the plan of a business and gives it practical shape. It is due to the efforts of entrepreneur that the business comes into existence. Thus he plans and initiates the business.

(2) ***Policy Making.*** The entrepreneur determines the policy of the business. He decides the quantity and the quality of production, the scale of production and takes similar other decisions concerning the business.

(3) ***Co-ordination.*** Production needs the co-operation of the different factors. The entrepreneur brings about the necessary co-ordination among these factors. He combines them in a suitable proportion so that there may be maximum production at the minimum-cost.

(4) ***Supervision and Direction.*** The entrepreneur surpervises the activities of all working under him and directs every minor detail of the business. He keeps a watch on the punctuality of his employees, discourages fraudulent practices and ensures execution of his instructions.

(5) ***Advertisement and Marketing.*** The entrepreneur works for pushing up his sales. He organises an advertisement campaign, engages travelling agents. sales agents, sales managers etc., for increasing his sales and expanding his business.

(6) ***Control.*** As the failure or success of the business affects the organiser directly, he keeps the control of the business in his own hands. He may keep certain assistants to help him in this work but he does not leave the final control to anybody else.

(7) ***Distribution of Rewards to the Different Factors of Production.*** The entrepreneur serves as the agency for the distribution of the national dividend. All the sale proceeds come to him and it is he who pays rent to the landlord wages to the labourers and interest to the capitalist. What is left over after paying due rewards to the above three factors is pocketed by the entrepreneur.

(8) ***Risk-taking.*** The modern system of production is very complex. The whole production is carried on in anticipation of demand. If the estimate of the expected demand goes wrong, the entrepreneur has to suffer a loss. Thus he has to shoulder the entire risk of the business. Risk taking, or more precisely the bearing of uncertainties, as a matter of fact, is the most important function of an entrepreneur and it is this function which distinguishes him from the other factors of production.

(9) ***Innovation.*** The entrepreneur has to adopt innovations to his business. He makes all arrangements for introducing innovations which help in the increase of production on the one hand and reducing costs on the other. Innovations may take the form of the adoption of new techniques and new methods in the process of production.

(10) ***Quality of Production.*** The entrepreneur determines the quality as well as the quantity of the product to be produced. How much and

what type of goods are to be produced would be main decision to be taken by the entrepreneur himself.

The role that the entrepreneur plays in the modem business organisation is thus of very great importance. In the absence of the entrepreneur production would come almost to a standstill, or it would become negligible and most inadequate to meet the needs of modem society. Little wonder the entrepreneur has been described as the 'captain of industry'.

3. DIFFERENCE BETWEEN ORGANISATION AND ENTERPRISE

In old times, production was carried on small scale and there was no difference between organisation and enterprise. The person who used to undertake production had to perform both the functions of an organiser and an entrepreneur. He had to manage his business and also to bear the risk of profit and loss. But now production is carried at a large scale and the work of organising and risk taking is performed by different persons. In fact the emergence of joint stock companies to undertake the large scale production has separated the organisation and the enterprise. In fact stock companies, shareholders are responsible for profit and loss of the business. So that the risk-bearing activities are undertaken by the shareholders. The actual work of organisation and management is carried out by the paid managers and directors of the company.

4. DIFFERENCE BETWEEN CAPITALIST AND ENTREPRENEUR

The main differences between a capitalist and an entrepreneur are the following:

(1) A capitalist only invests his capital and gets interest on it, whereas an entrepreneur manages the investment and bears the entire risk of business.

(2) A capitalist possesses capital, whereas an entrepreneur possesses particular skill and invests capital.

(3) The income of the capitalist is predetermined in terms of interest on capital while the income of the entrepreneur is always uncertain.

(4) A capitalist bears no risk where an entrepreneur always bears risk. He may get profit and also incur losses.

EXERCISES

1. Explain the important functions of an entrepreneur.
2. Explain the role of an entrepreneur in a capitalist economy. Why is he known as Captain of Industry'?
3. What is the difference between a capitalist and an entrepreneur? Discuss the main functions of an entrepreneur.

Multiple Choice Questions

4. (*i*) In modern system of production, the main function of an entrepreneur is
   (*a*) to get profit of the industry
   (*b*) to bear the risk of the industry
   (*c*) to manage the work of the industry
   (*d*) to get interest on the capital invested [*Ans. (b)*]

   (*ii*) Innovation means
   (*a*) increase in production
   (*b*) increase in profits
   (*c*) new methods and techniques of production
   (*d*) all of the above. [*Ans. (e)*]

Chapter 23

TYPES OF BUSINESS UNITS

There are various types of business units or business organisations. Some of the important types of business organisations found in the world are as follows:

1. Sole or Individual Proprietorship
2. Partnership
3. Joint Stock Company
4. Cooperative Societies
5. Public or State Enterprises.

We shall discuss these types of business organisations one by one.

1. INDIVIDUAL PROPRIETORSHIP

Organisation of a business refers to the making of various decisions regarding the establishment, management, control and the directions of a business enterprise. It involves the regulation of the various aspects of business, may it be the production and sale of the output produced or the purchase of materials and other things necessary for production. If all such decisions regarding the promotion of business, its management and control are taken by one man, this form of business organization is known as sole proprietorship or one man business. And when the ownership of a business is vested in a large number of shareholders, the business assumes the form of a joint stock company or a corporation.

The one man business or the sole proprietorship, is historically the oldest form of business organisation which, even today, is most popular and widely prevalent in all the free economies of the world. In such a business, the owner is all in all. He looks after all the aspects of business. Of course, he may acquire the services of other people to assist him. But all the important business decisions are taken by him, and therefore, he is himself responsible for all the profits or the losses which may arise from the business activity.

The sole proprietorship has no separate legal existence apart from the person who owns it. From the legal point of view, there is no distinction between the personal assets and liabilities of the owner and the assets and liabilities of his business. Therefore, he can be called upon to meet his business obligations even from the assets which he may own for his personal use. Since there is no difference between his personal and business property, the creditors can legally claim his personal property for the repayment of liabilities which arise in connection with his business. This is known as the principle of 'Unlimited Liability'.

Merits of Sole Proprietorship

Sole proprietorship being one man business has certain advantages which make it most widely prevalent form of business organisation. Some of these advantages are discussed here.

(1) *Easy Formation.* The individual business or the sole proprietorship is most simple form of business organisation which can be established without any legal formalities. This type of business comes into existence whenever an ,individual decides to start it. No time need to be wasted in consultations with others. No persuation is required to enlist partners in the business. It is primarily because of this case of formation that sole proprietorship is so numerous and most popular form of business organisation.

(2) *Quick Decisions.* The individual proprietor, being the sole owner of his business, can take decisions regarding various business problems without consulting other people. He has not to seek anybody's approval or counter any outside interference. He can introduce all those changes which he thinks necessary in his business interest. He can also reverse these decisions whenever he likes. This quickness in making decisions avoids the delays in business and prevents confusion.

(3) *Personal Attention.* The owner in the one man business pays his full and personal attention to all the details of business. Since the profits belong to the sole owner, he would spare no effort to maximise profits by minimising the cost of production. For this he would personally look after the different departments in order to minimise the wastage of resources. He would conduct his transactions in most prudential and economic manner.

(4) *Cordial Relations.* The sole proprietorship being a small business the relations between the employer and the employees are generally most cordial. Since the employer knows each one of the workers personally, he can understand their problems and difficulties. The workers, being in

close touch with employer, would try their best to satisfy him by hard and sincere work. Similarly, the owner of the small business knows his customers individually. Thus he tries to pay personal attention to them and satisfy them to the utmost. This contributes to the success of the business.

(5) *Safe Business Secrets.* The whole business being entirely in the hands of one man, he can keep his business secrets very safe. Business secrets are perhaps one of the most valuable assets of a business. These secrets relate the methods of production or sale or the financial position of the concern. If the number of owners is more than one, such trade secrets are likely to leak out. This would endanger the position of the entire business.

(6) *Quick Adjustments.* The owner of the business is in direct touch with the market requirements. Production and sale being his sole responsibility, he would fully acquaint himself with the market trends and fluctuations. Thus quick adjustment in business activity in close conformity with the market conditions would render flexibility and add to the profits of the business.

(7) *Small Capital Requirements.* The sole proprietorship form of business organisation being generally a small business, requires only a small amount of capital to start. Those people who own a small amount of money can undertake such business without much difficult. The problem of raising larger loans from the market do not generally arise in the case of individual business.

(8) *Easy to Wind-up.* As the individual proprietorship is very easy to form, it is also very easy to wind-up such a business. The decision to close down a business has to be taken entirely by the owner of the business. He has not to go into any legal formalities regarding the closure of the business. He would simply payoff his liabilities, dismiss his workers and thus close down the business. The large number of legal problems which arise in connection with the breaking of partnership business or closing a joint stock company are absent in the case of sole proprietorship.

Demerits of Sole Proprietorship

Sole proprietorship has the following demerits:

(1) *Limited Resources.* The financial resources at the command of the owner of sole proprietorship form of business organisation are very limited. For carrying on his business, he has to depend generally upon his own resources. Thus. the financial resources being very small, he cannot expand his business to any large extent.

(2) *Highly Risky.* The individual proprietorship being based upon the principle of 'Unlimited Liability', makes this type of business very risky. In case the business liabilities exceed the business assets he will have to meet them even from his personal property. This naturally prevents him from undertaking any big risk and restricts the scale of his business.

(3) *Low Credit-worthiness.* The assets of the sole proprietor being not very large, he faces a difficulty in securing loans from banks and other financial institutions, because he cannot provide sufficient security against them. The banks and money-lenders prefer to lend to partnerships, joint stock companies and co-operative organisations, because of their larger assets. Thus the low credit-worthiness of the individual proprietor puts a limit on the size of his business.

(4) *Limited Managerial Ability.* The ability of the individual proprietor being essentially limited, it becomes difficult for him to look after all the details of the business. If he is wise and intelligent, his business would flourish. But if he is unsound and makes wrong decision, the whole business would suffer. Further his limited ability also puts a limit to the expansion of his business.

(5) *Temporary Existence.* The one man business has generally a short life. Since the whole business depends upon the owner, it would cease to exist at the time of his death. This business comes to a close even when the owner goes mad or becomes insolvent. It is, thus, lack of continuous existence which makes such business unfit for those industries which are to run for a long time.

Conclusion

The easy formation, absolute control, complete independence to take decisions and the possibility of making quick adjustment, combined with the smaller amount of capital requirement, have made the sole proprietorship a most popular form of business organisation. In all lines of production and distribution, this is the most common type of business which one comes across in his daily life. But because of some inherent factors like limited financial resources, unlimited liability and the limited managerial capability, this form of business organisation is not suited to the requirements of large-scale industries. Since many of the projects yield profits only in the long run, the individual proprietors, guided by their immediate profit motive, may not like to undertake such investments. Therefore this type of business does not find favour in those lines of production which are of long term nature. However, this form of business organisation is most popular in small business like shoe-making, tailoring, hair dressing etc. In brief, in all those lines of production where business is of a simple nature and requires less capital, individual proprietorship is most common.

2. PARTNERSHIP

When two or more persons enter into an agreement to carry on some business jointly and share the profit or loss resulting from it, this is known as the 'partnership' form of business organisation. The agreement between the partners relates to amount of capital to be invested, the method of sharing profits or losses and the other matters relating to the entry of a new member, dissolution of the business form etc. It is not necessary that each member of the partnership should contribute equal amount of capital. Some partners may put in more capital while the others may contribute less. Some members may not contribute and yet become the partners by undertaking to contribute to the business in some other capacity. All the partners are equally responsible so far as the liabilities of the business are concerned.

The minimum number of members who can form a partnership business is two. The maximum number of partners, according to the Indian Partnership Act, can be twenty in a non-banking business and ten is a banking business. Each member of the partnership business is individually known as a 'partner' and the business is known as a 'firm'. Each one of the partners has the right to enter into dealings with others on behalf of the firm of which he is a partner. And such dealings made by the individual partners are binding, upon the others as well.

Partners are generally of two types, active partners and sleeping partners. Active partners are those who take an active interest in the business. They are concerned with making of day to day decisions' relating to the business and perform the managerial duties. Such partners are generally paid a greater share of the profit, a part of it being the reward for the function of management, and the rest being the reward for their capital. Sometimes, such partners are also paid the salaries for the duties that they perform in connection with the organisation and management of the business.

Sleeping partners are those who contribute their capital to the business but do not take any active part in the running of the business. They do not interfere into the normal working of the firm and therefore remain away from the problems related to the management and control. Such partners are generally paid a lower share of the profits. These profits simply represent a reward on the capital invested.

Merits of Partnership

The following are the merits of Partnership:

(1) *Larger Financial Resources.* In the partnership form of business organisation the number ofn1~mbers being larger, the capital of the firm is also quite large. Not only that the partners contribute more capital, but the mere association of so many people in a business raises its' credit-worthiness in the market. Therefore, as far as the raising of capital is concerned, partnership has certain superiority over the sole proprietorship.

(2) *Diverse Capabilities.* Every one of the partners is likely to have some special ability and business skill and certain specialised field of business interest. Selection of right partnership, thus, makes a team of experts in various branches of business. Each one of the partners may decide to look after some particular aspect of the business. This type of division of labour, within the management, would contribute greatly to the success of the business.

(3) *Better Decisions.* The decisions made by the partnership firm may be better and well thought out, because they are made by the partners after thorough examination of the various aspects of the business. To arrive at a decision, the partners would discuss the problem among themselves and hence benefit from each others experience. These decisions are also flexible and prompt, and take full account of the changing market conditions.

(4) *High Efficiency.* Having more resources, a partnership firm can expand the business and thus secure the advantages of large scale production. At the same time, the personal and direct contact between management and workers would lead to greater efficiency. Smooth relations between labour and capital avoid labour disputes and the industrial unrest.

(5) *Greater Care.* The principle of unlimited liability makes the partners extremely careful about the business. They take great interest in the business and work with great caution. Unlimited liability prevents them from undertaking risky and speculative enterprises.

(6) *Easy Formation.* Partnership business is comparatively easy to form. Only a few legal formalities have to be performed and the agreement to be signed by the' partners. The time which is wasted in the formation of joint stock company is generally saved in the case of partnership business.

Demerits of Partnership

The following are the demerits of Partnership:

(1) *Unlimited Liability.* The principle of unlimited liability is a double edged weapon. Its advantage is that it makes the partners responsible. But its greatest disadvantage is that it prevents a man with more wealth to enter into partnership with men of less wealth. Nor the partners are prepared to undertake any larger business because it involves larger risk. Thus the size of partnership business remains essentially small.

(2) *Lack of Permanent Existence.* Partnership lacks permanent existence. It comes to an end whenever a partner dies, goes mad or is declared insolvent. Further the shares of partnership business are non-transferable. Hence whenever, one of the partner decides to leave the business, the partnership comes to an end.

(3) *Internal Differences.* Disagreement and lack of faith among the partners leads to internal conflicts among the partners which may ultimately lead to its dissolution.

(4) *Lack of Resources.* The partnership business has got a larger amount of resources as compared to the sole proprietorship. But its resources are not enough to meet the requirements of a very large business. To increase the resources, more members may have to be admitted to the partnership. But the maximum number of partners to join a business is limited by law. Further the larger the number of active partners, larger are the chances of quarrels among them.

(5) *Money Gets Locked-up.* Since a partner cannot transfer his share without the consent of the others, no one likes to block his money in the partnership. It is difficult to get the unanimous consent of all the partners. This discourages many people to join the partnership form of business organisation.

(6) *General Lack of Interest.* In a partnership everybody tries to shirk his responsibility. Since in the partnership the money goes from the common pool, it may lead to reckless and unwise spending by some of the partners. Irrational or irresponsible behaviour of some partners will have to be borne by all of them. The corrupted partners may achieve their selfish motives at the expense of the partnership.

Conclusion

The partnership tries to combine the good features of a small business, viz. direct control and personal supervision, with those of the larger business, viz. larger capital and economies of large scale production. But partnership suffers from some serious handicaps. Because of its temporary existence and the lack of financial resources to meet the requirements of a big business, partnership form of business organisation does not suit the large scale industries in modern times.

3. JOINT STOCK COMPANY

The joint stock company or the corporate form of business organisation is by far the most important and most suitable method of organising the large scale business in the modern economies. The stock or capital of the company is contributed by a large number of shareholders. The actual management of the company is entrusted to the paid managers who work under the direct supervision of a board of directors elected by the shareholders. The ultimate ownership of the company is vested in the shareholders (those who have subscribed to the stock of the company). However the ownership of the company is collective and not individual. It belongs to the body of shareholders as a whole, and not to anyone of them individually. In USA joint stock company is known as corporation.

Formation of a Joint Stock Company

The minimum number of people required to promote a joint stock company is seven. Thus, anyone man who wants to float a company has to find six more persons who are willing to join business with him. These seven persons who decide to form a joint stock company are known as 'promoters of the company. The promoters then draw up two documents which they submit to the Registrar of Joint Stock Companies. These documents are:

(1) *Memorandum of Association.* This contains the name of the company, office and the information regarding its aims and objects, its capital structure, and the declaration that the liability of the shareholders is limited.

(2) *Articles of Association.* This document contains information regarding the rules and regulations formulated by the company. They set out the laws and bye-laws for day to day functioning of the company.

After verifying these documents, if the Registrar is satisfied that the company fulfils all the legal requirements, he issues the certificate of incorporation. which bears his consent for the formation of the company. The promoters then announce the incorporation of the company and issue the shares for raising the capital required for running the company.

Features of Joint Stock Company

In the eyes of ' law a joint stock company is an artificial person created by an association of people for carrying on a joint business. According to C.J. Marshall, "A corporation is an artificial being, invisible, intangible and existing only in contemplation of the law. Being a mere creation of law it possesses only the properties which the charter of its creation confers upon it expressly, or incidental to its very existence." In a more comprehensive manner a joint stock company can be defined as an artificial person recognised by law, with a distinctive name, a common seal and having an uninterrupted succession. The main features of a corporation form of business organisation are given below:

(1) *Separate Legal Entity.* A joint stock company is a legal entity, its existence being recognised by law as quite distinct from the people who form it. Being an artificial person created by law, a joint stock company can sue other people and can be sued by them in its own name, without involving any law suit against the persons who form the company. No shareholder can be held liable for the acts of the company, although he may own the majority of the shares. Further, being a separate legal entity, the company has the right to own or transfer property.

(2) *Limited Liability.* The liability of the shareholders of a joint stock company in meeting the obligations is limited to the extent of value of shares that an individual holds. If a shareholder has purchased a share of the value of Rs. 100, and has already paid Rs. 70, then his liability is only Rs. 30, which is the balance remaining with him. If he has already paid the full value of the share, he does not owe any more money to the company. Thus, even if the financial obligations of the company are very large, no shareholder can be called upon to pay more than the value of the shares that he has purchased.

(3) *Continuous Existence.* The existence of a company is perpetual or continuous and is not affected by the death, insolvency or exit of some shareholders. Shareholders may leave the company by selling its shares, yet the company would continue. The shares of the company in fact change hundreds of hands, without in any way affecting the existence of the company. This feature of the joint stock company lends it a longer life and greater stability when compared with the other forms of business organisation.

(4) *Common Seal.* A company, being only an artificial person created by law, cannot sign document for itself. Therefore, a common seal on which the name of the company is engraved is used as a substitute for

signatures. The seal is kept in a safe custody of the secretary of the company and is used only in accordance with the directions of the Board of Directors. After being affixed on the documents it has to be witnessed by two directors of the company.

(5) *Separation of Ownership from Management.* As has already been pointed out, the shareholders own the company but do not manage it. The management of the company is done by the Board of Directors and the executives appointed by them for the implementation of various policies. Thus, while the capital comes from the shareholders, the management of the company rests with the people who have ability and experience of carrying on the business. This has led to a greater popularity of this business in modern times.

(6) *Capital Structure.* The total capital of the company is divided into shares of smaller denominations. These shares are then issued to the public for being subscribed. The shares are generally of two types, preferential shares and ordinary or equity shares. The holders of preferential shares get a preference in the matter of payment of dividend and also in repayment of the share capital if the company is to be wound up preferential shares are again of two types, viz. non cumulative or ordinary preferential hares and cumulative preferential shares. If there are no profits during any given year, the holders of cumulative preferential shares will have to be paid dividend in the coming years not only for those years but also for the years for which dividend have not been paid. But the holders of non-cumulative or ordinary preferential shares do not get any such advantage. Of course the holders of such shares arc paid their dividend before anyone else is paid.

Equity shares or ordinary shares are those which are not given any kind of pre-ferential treatment. The dividend on these shares is paid only after the dividend on preferential shares has been paid. The rate of dividend to be paid on such shares depends upon the amount of profits made by the company during a given year. If the company is liquidated the amount of equity shares will be repayable only when every other claim, including that of preferential shareholders has been met.

Apart from the issue of shares, the company also raises capital by the issue of debentures or bonds. The holders of debentures only get a fixed interest on their capital, irrespective of profits or losses occurring to the company. Issue of debentures represent a borrowed capital and therefore the debentureholders are not the proprietors of the company. They do not play any role in the management or control of the company. In the case the company is to be wound-up, the holders of bonds or debentures will get a preference over the shareholders in repayment of capital.

The total amount of capital which the company is permitted to raise from the market by issue of shares is called authorised capital. The value of actual number of shares issued by the company at any time is known as issued capital. The number of shares which the people have purchased represents the subscribed capital of the company. It is not necessary that one who purchases a share is asked to pay the full value of the share immediately. In fact, generally he is asked to pay a certain amount at the time of purchasing the share and the balance at some future date, whenever the company requires it. The amount of money which the people have thus actually paid to the company is called paid up capital. Paid up capital represents the actual amount of capital at the disposal of the company.

Management of Joint Stock Company

A joint stock company is owned by the sharehoders but it is not managed by them. This is a contrast to the sole proprietorship or partnership form of business organisation where the management of the company is entrusted with those who own it. Joint stock companies are managed on democratic basis. The shareholders usually meet once a year and elect the director of the company. These elected representatives of the shareholder (directors) carry on the actual management. If the company in accordance with the policy approved by them. The Board of Directors is the top administrative body in a joint stock company. But all the directors are not whole time officials of the company. Some of them may be associated with a number of other companies. Thus the directors only formulate the policies and programmes, and for their implementation hand them over to the chief executives, the General Manager and the other officers controlling various departments. These executives of company receive constant instructions and guidance from the board of directors and also acquaint them with the problems concerning the execution of various policies.

Merits of Joint Stock Company

The following are the important merits of joint stock company:

(1) *Large Resources.* In a joint stock company, there is generally no limit to the number of shareholders. Therefore, a large amount of capital can be collected by the issue of shares. The shares being generally of smaller denominations, even those people who have only small amount of money at their disposal can purchase them.

In case of a partnership, such large funds cannot be collected because the number of partners is limited by law.

(2) *Large Scale Business.* With such a large amount of resources at its disposal the company can carry on business on a large scale and thus benefit from the economies arising out of the bigger business. Production on a large scale would be cheaper and more economical due to the economies of scale. This would reduce the average cost of production and raise the level of profits.

(3) *Scope for Expansion.* Since a joint stock company generally makes a very high amount of profits it is always in a position to accumulate larger capital reserves. The accumulation of such reserve funds of capital enables the company to further expand its business. The availability of larger finances and superior managerial ability ensures a continuous expansion of business activity. In a partnership business, on the other hand, the managerial ability being limited and capital stock being lower, not much expansion of business activity is possible.

(4) *Shares are Transferable.* The shareholders in a joint stock company can transfer their shares to anyone else without having to take the consent of other members in the company. The shares are bought and sold in the stock exchange by the individual shareholders without consulting the management of the company. This facility to transfer the shares of business, which a joint stock company provides to the members, has encouraged the people to invest their money in this form of business organisation. The shares of a partnership being non-transferable, many people are hot willing to become members of such a business.

(5) *Limited Liability.* The liability of a member in a joint stock company is limited to the extent of the value of shares that he holds. Even if the company incurs very big losses, the shareholder cannot be asked to pay an amount more than the value of his shares. This has encouraged people to purchase the shares of such companies, thereby minimising the risk of business. In a partnership, on the other hand, the principle of unlimited liability, discourages the people from joining the business.

(6) *Diffusion of Risk.* The number of shareholders in a joint stock company being very large, the risk of the business is widely diffused. Risk is spread over a larger number of people so that each shareholder bears a very small amount of it. In a partnership, however, each one of the partner runs a great risk because he can be asked to make good all the losses undergone by the business.

(7) *Stability.* The joint stock company is a stable form of business organisation. Its shares being transferable, it is not affected by the death of anyone of its members. Even if some members leave the business, the company continues in an uninterrup-ted manner. But, in a partnership, if anyone of the partner dies or leaves the company, the firm has to close down.

(8) *Bolder Programmes.* One of the greatest advantages of a joint stock company is that it can undertake bigger risks. Since the management of the company is separate from the ownership, the managers can undertake business involving heavy risks. The establishment of new industries which do not guarantee any profits would have been difficult, in the absence of the corporate form of business organisation.

(9) *Democratic Management.* The management of the joint stock company is done in a democratic way. The Board of Directors, which guides the whole business consists of the members who have been elected by the shareholders as their representatives. The directors are responsible to the of shareholders for their acts of commission and omission. Those directors whose work is not found to be satisfactory can be removed by the body of shareholders.

Demerits of Joint Stock Company

The following are the important demerits of joint stock company:

(1) *Diffculties in Formation.* The process of formation of a joint stock company is full of a number of formalities. A large number of legal requirements have to be met, a large number of people to be approached and a large sum of money to be spent upon numerous legal and other formalities. As against this the formation of a part-nership is easy' and requires lesser wastage of time and money.

(2) *Dishonest Management.* Very often the management of the company gets into the hands of dishonest people. In many cases innocent investors are cheated by the unsprupious directors who indulge in fraudulent practices and financial embez-zlements.

(3) *Lack of Motivation.* In a joint stock company, there is a separation of management from ownership. The company is managed by the directors or managers while the ownership of the company rests with the shareholders. These paid officials cannot be expected to watch the interest of the company. Sometimes the management may undertake reckless investment in hazardous business thereby endangering the interest of the investors.

(4) *Growth of Monopolies.* The growth of joint stock companies has resulted in the establishment of huge factories which control a major part of supply in the market. This has given rise to monopolies in various sectors of economy. The monopolistic companies exploit both the workers and the consumers and pose a dangerous threat to the whole society.

(5) *Concentration of Economic Power.* Since the organisation of business on the joint stock principles has led to the emergence of big monopolies which control economic activity in various sectors, it has resulted in the concentration of economic power in a few hands. A few at the rich capitalists by purchasing a majority of shares in a large number of firms control the majority of the industrial units in the country. Thus they exercise a considerable influence on the economy which may prove dangerous to the society as a whole.

(6) *Oligarchic Management.* Although in theory joint stock companies are managed in a democratic manner, in practice, however, management is oligarchic (concentrated in the hands of only a few persons). The shareholders know nothing about the affair of the company. The entire management is done by a small number of persons who invariably ignore the interest of the shareholders.

(7) *Conflict of Interests.* In a joint stock company the interests of different groups of people often clash with each other. There is a clash between the interests of workers and the management which often takes the form of industrial disputes and result in a tremendous waste of economic resources. Similarly, there is a clash of interest between different categories of shareholders and there is a conflict between the shareholders and the directors. Such conflicts are economically wasteful, politically dangerous and socially undesirable.

(8) *Delay in Decisions.* A joint stock company does not enjoy the same amount of flexibility and promptness in arriving a decision as is enjoyed by partnership or sole-proprietorship. Decisions get delayed because the directors meet only after certain intervals of time, or because there may be a difference of opinion among the directors themselves and, therefore, some time is required to resolve these differences.

(9) *Political Corruption.* Since the joint stock companies control a major part of economic activity, some of the powerful companies often influence the legislators in various ways such as contributing to the party funds or supporting some candidate in elections. The whole idea behind such actions is to get the laws passed in accordance with their own requirements. The civil servants and the junior staff in government

departments often becomes corrupt under the influence of business community who get their things done by bribing these officials.

(10) *Encouragement of Speculation.* The joint stock companies have encouraged speculation in shares at the stock exchange. The value of the share depends upon the dividends declared by a company and the reputation of the company. Changing expectations with regard to he future dividends often lead to reckless speculation. When carried to its example, speculation tends to become an antisocial activity.

Conclusion

From an analysis of the various merits and drawbacks associated with the joint stock companies it can be safely concluded that the merits of this type of business organisation outweigh its weaknesses and drawbacks. Most of the evils discussed above emerge from the mismanagement or misuse of power by unscrupulous people. There is nothing wrong with the principles of the joint stock business. In those lines of production where huge investment is needed or where superior business ability is required no other form of business organisation can be a substitute for a joint stock company.

4. CO-OPERATIVE SOCIETIES

According to International Labour Office, "A co-operative society is an association of economically weak, who voluntarily associating on the basis of equal rights and equal responsibility transfer to and undertake one or several of their economic needs which are common to them all, but which each of them is unable to satisfy fully by his own individual efforts, and manage and use such undertaking in mutual collaboration to their common material advantages." The whole idea underlying the co-operative form of business organisation is to replace competition and private profit motive by the principles of co-operation, self-help and service.

Characteristics of the Co-operative Society

The important features of co-operative form of business organisation are given below:

(1) *Voluntary Association.* A co-operative society is generally defined as a voluntary association of workers. Any person irrespective of his caste, creed or status in the society can join a co-operative society, and also leave it whenever he likes. A co-operative society neither denies

membership to anyone nor compels any one to become member. The shares of a co-operative society are non-transferable.

(2) *Equality.* All the members of a co-operative society enjoy an equal status. Every member has only a single vote irrespective of the amount of capital that he has contributed to the society. Hence no member can acquire a position of influence in a co-operative society merely because he has contributed more capital.

(3) *Democratic Management.* The management of a co-operative society is democratic. At a meeting, the members of the co-operative society elect a managing committee which is entrusted with carrying out the policy and programmes decided by the members. Since each member has one vote, he gets an equal right in the management of the society.

(4) *Service Motive.* The object behind the formation of a co-operative society is to render maximum service to its members. Profit is given only a secondary consideration. Of course, it does not mean that co-operative societies do not make any profits. They do make profits, which are distributed among the members or which are used for further expansion of co-operative activities.

(5) *State Control.* The co-operative societies, although they are purely voluntary organisations, the yare subject to the supervision and control of the government in the event of their getting registered with the government. On being registered, a co-operative society attains the corporate status (the status of a company) and becomes entitled to certain privileges. The liability of the members of a co-operative society may be limited or unlimited, depending upon the rules and regulations framed by these companies. Generally the liability is unlimited in smaller societies, but it is limited in the case of bigger ones.

Forms of Co-operative Societies

A co-operative society, being a voluntary association of workers, can be formed in all walks of life—economic, social or political. But since here we are concerned only with the co-operative societies as a form of business organisation, we should take up only those societies which undertake some economic business. The important types of co-operative societies are discussed below:

(1) *Consumer's Co-operative Societies.* The consumer co-operative societies are generally formed by the consumers with a view to obtaining their daily requirements of consumer goods at cheaper rates. The societies organise consumer's co-operative stores, where goods ate bought directly from the producers, wholesalers, or distributors at lower rates and then

sold at the market prices to the members as well as non-members. A profit is thus earned by the society is divided among the members in proportion to the purchases made by each one of them. The bonus received by the consumers on their purchase represents the profits which would have otherwise gone to the shopkeepers and middle-men. Thus the idea behind the, formation of a consumer's co-operative society is to eliminate the profits going to the middle-men and secure cheaper goods to its members.

(2) *Producer's Co-operatives.* A producer's co-operative society is a form of industrial organisation where labourers contribute their own capital, thus eliminating the capitalist class from the system of production. The workers pool their financial resources and invest them in some business. The business is controlled and managed by the elected representatives of the workers on the basis of equal voting rights. Thus the foreman, the manager, the supervisor and all other officials are the people elected by the workers from among themselves. The profits arising out of the business are distributed among the workers. The capitalist class, which is charged with exploiting the workers, is thus eliminated. The profits, instead of enriching a few, are enjoyed by the actual workers.

(3) *Credit Co-operatives.* The co-operative credit societies are formed with the object of giving financial assistance to the members at reasonably, low rates of interest. The members create a fund out of their financial contributions in the form of share purchased by them and advance loans from this fund to those who are in need. The shares, are generally of low denominations so that even people with small means cart purchase them and become the members of the society. The loans are given generally for productive purposes and the rate of interest is kept very low. Whatever interest is charged, a part of it is generally distributed among the members as dividend.

(4) *Other Forms of Co-operatives.* Apart from the above mentioned societies, a number of such societies have been formed in other fields *I* economic activity. Important among them are co-operative farming societies and co-operative marketing societies.

(*i*) *Co-operative Farming Societies.* Carry on cultivation tm a joint basis. The co-operative society decides about which crops are to be produced and allocates work to its various, members. Crops are produced and sold jointly and the receipts are divided among the members.

(*ii*) *Co-operative Marketing Societies.* These societies are organised with a view to selling goods directly to the dealers, thus eliminating a long chain of middle-men. Such societies play an important role in marketing of agricultural output. The innocent and ignorent farmers usually get a very low price for their output because the middle-men swallow a good part of it as their commission. Co-operative societies are also formed in such activities as house-building, motor, transport, etc.

5. PUBLIC OR STATE ENTERPRISES

In the nineteenth century the State followed the policy of *laissez faire,* i.e. non-intervention in economic matters. But this apathy of the State led to so many economic evils, viz. maldistribution of wealth, exploitation of toe workers and consumers and so on. The State could no more remain an indifferent spectator to all these economic ills, to all these miseries and sufferings. The idea of Police State is now replaced by the concept of Welfare State. In the present century, thus, with the growth of socialistic ideas, the State has begun to interfere more and more in economic matters.

The days of *laissez faire* have long departed. The State has not only pledged itself to spend large sums of money annually on the social services, but in recent years it has interfered with and regulated economic affairs to an extent that would have been thought impossible in 1914. A large majority of people now agree that it is duty of the State to maintain a reasonable standard of living for its workers; to provide social security for all citizens; to reduce social and economic inequalities and to maintain full employment.

State or municipal enterprise is becoming increasingly popular day by day. Today we find that the government runs the railways, post and telegraphs, motor buses and manages and controls various key industries. In socialist countries like the USSR, State enterprise is the only type of business organisation. Even in capitalist countries of the world this tendency is on the increase, due to certain advantages which it possesses.

Merits of State Enterprises

The chief advantages of State Enterprises are the following:

(1) *End of Industrial Profits.* The more force behind a State enterprise is not profit but service. Public utility services like post and telegraph system, railways, supply of electricity, gas and water, etc., can be best organised by the government. More-over, there are certain enterprises which are not profitable or are not expected to yield profit for a considerably long period of time but are very important for the community; e.g. the construction of bridges, roads; canal, etc. These are generally neglected by private capitalists and are taken up by State.

(2) *Public Welfare.* Profits, if any, are not pocketed by private individuals but go to swell the revenues of the State which uses them for the welfare of the public. Thus public welfare is promoted.

(3) *Easy Credit.* The government-can take up huge undertakings as it can borrow large funds at low rates of interest. People consider investments in government securities and concerns to be safe. Hence large funds at low rates are made available to the government. State enterprises can also attract superior talent because of attractive service conditions and the security of service which no private enterprise can ensure.

(4) *Able Employees.* The best business mind is attracted by the government service. The government can secure the services of talented persons who are abler than the personnel in the service of private businessmen. It leads to better organisation of the business.

(5) *Quality Products.* State managed concerns supply goods of genuine quality. The consumers are safeguarded against the supply of adulterated goods.

(6) *Democratic Control.* State enterprise is more amenable to popular control. People have enough control over the business through the elected representatives.

Demerits of State Enterprises

State enterprise suffers from certain serious drawbacks. The main disadvantages of the State enterprise are:

(1) *Red Tapism.* Government enterprise suffers seriously from the defects of bureaucratic machinery. There is too much red-tapism which makes quick decision impossible. This is detrimental to the success of the business.

(2) *Lack of Incentive.* Government business is all routine and there is little possibility of any initiative being displayed by any officer. There is, in fact, no such urge to display any initiative.

(3) *Inefficiency of Workers.* Government business' cannot work with the same efficiency with which the private business works. A government servant is not so much interested in his work as a private individual is. He does not take much pains, because he knows that his pay is certain and his promotion depends on seniority.

(4) *Corruption.* Corruption, favouritism, nepotism and bribery are generally associated with State enterprise. Scandals are not uncommon. The experience of rationing and controls in India has not been very happy. Black-marketing and other allied evils are still fresh in our memory.

(5) *Frequent and Sudden Transfers.* Transfers of government officials are very frequent. This is harmful to the success of the enterprise. The valuable experience which the government officials gain during the course of their service is lost to the business due to their transfers.

(6) *Wasteful Expenditure.* Government servants do not bother whether the enterprise is running at profit or loss. If there is any loss, it can easily be shifted to the tax-payers who have to bear the burden in the shape of increased or new taxes.

Thus government undertakings suffer from certain serious defects. State enterprise should, therefore, be extended only to those businesses which are of a strictly routine character. The State should also take up the public utility services where the aim is not to earn profits but to promote public welfare.

EXERCISES

1. Discuss the main features of individual proprietorship. What are its merits and demerits?
2. What is partnership business? Explain its merits and demerits.
3. What is joint stock company? How is it formed? Discuss its various features.

Multiple Choice Questions

7. (*i*) The liabilities of a partner in the partnership form of organisation is
   (*a*) limited (*b*) unlimited
   (*c*) no liability (*d*) fixed liability [*Ans.* (*b*)]

   (*ii*) Under joint stock company, the maximum loss is born by the
   (*a*) Preference Shareholders (*b*) Ordinary Shareholders
   (*c*) Debentureholders (*d*) Promoters [*Ans.* (*b*)]

   (*iii*) A joint stock company has, the following feature:
   (*a*) Legal Existence (*b*) Limited Liability
   (*c*) Democratic Management (*d*) All of the above [*Ans.* (*d*)]

Chapter 24

SCALE OF PRODUCTION

1. MEANING OF SCALE OF PRODUCTION

The scale of production is related to the amount of factors of production and the techniques of production adopted by a producer. As production of a commodity increases with the increase in the quantity of factors of production, the scale of production expands. Thus production may be carried on a small scale or on a large scale by a firm. When a firm uses a small quantity off actors of production, the scale of production is said to be small. On the other hand, if it makes a use of a larger quantity of factors of production, it is said to be operating at a large scale of production. Thus a firm may produce goods at small scale or at a large scale depending upon the quantity of factors being applied to production process. When the number of firms increases in an industry, it would mean that the industry expands its scale of production. Similarly, when the number of firms is reduced or the sizes of the firms are curtalied, it would mean that the industry is operating at a small scale. Now we shall discuss the advantages and disadvantages of large scale production as well as small scale production in the following section.

2. LARGE SCALE PRODUCTION

Large scale production is the most outstanding feature of the modern industrial system. It refers to the production of a commodity on a large scale. It involves the employment of costly machines worked by a large number of organised labourers under the same management. Small scale production is being replaced by large scale production because large scale production enjoys several economies.

Advantages of Large Scale Production

Important advantages of large scale production are the following:

(1) *Benefits of Division of Labour.* Benefits of division of labour can be more easily secured. There is scope for specialisation of labour. Expert personnel can be employed by offering better remuneration.

(2) *Commercial Advantages.* There are commercial advantages of buying and selling wholesale. Raw materials can be bought cheaper. A big concern also commands a wide market and it can obtain better prices for its products.

(3) *Advantages of Specialised Machinery.* A large scale producer can acquire and instal up-to-date and costly machinery. He can also have his own reparing arrangements and has not to depend on inexperienced *mistries.*

(4) *Economies in Overhead Expenses.* There are economies in rent and other supplementary costs. Overhead charges like costs of management come to much less per unit when there is large scale production.

(5) *Utilisation of By-products.* Waste products and by-products can be utilised. In big mineral oil factories, lubricating oil is made of the material which was previously thrown away as waste. A small firm may not find is profitable to utilise its small amounts of waste products.

(6) *Research and Experiments.* A large scale producer can employ experts to carry on research which more than repays its cost in the long run. A small concern will not find it possible to undertake research on its own account.

(7) *Extensive Publicity and Advertisement.* A big concern can give proper publicity to its products by spending vast amounts on advertisement and salesmanship. This helps in pushing up the sales.

(8) *Cheap Credit.* A large scale producer as against a small scale producer has greater credit in the capital market and can thus raise loans at a low rate of interest. Small firms generally do not have such opportunities.

(9) *Greater Stability.* A large concern is capable of facing hard times. It possesses greater stability as compared with a small scale enterprise. It can easily withstand minor shocks which often overwhelm a small concern.

Disadvantages of Large Scale Production

Large scale production, however, has its disadvantages. The main disadvantages are the following:

(1) *Individual Taste go Unheeded.* A large scale producer cannot cater to individual requirements. He can only produce standardised goods.

The individual tastes of the consumers cannot be taken into consideration by a large scale producer.

(2) *No Direct Contact between Employers and Employees.* In a large business, there is little direct contact between the employers and the employees. This often results in lack of understanding between the two and there are strikes and lock-outs.

(3) *Wasteful Competition.* Big businesses start a bitter struggle against one another. They generally indulge in cut throat competition to divert customers from other producers. It is a great national waste.

(4) *Over-production.* Large scale production sometimes leads to over-production. Over-production means depression and unemployment. The danger is very real in society in which economic life is unplanned.

(5) *International Complications and Wars.* Large scale producers are always on the look-out to capture foreign markets. This gives rise to international complications and often results in untimely wars.

(6) *Lack of Adaptability.* A large business finds it very difficult to adapt itself changes in demand. In case the product of a large scale producer goes out of demand the business suffers and the entrepreneur is ruined.

(7) *Factory System with all its Evils.* Large scale production involves factory system with all its evils. Overcrowded slums, immorality, foul atmosphere etc., are some of the evils of the factory system of production.

On balance, the advantages of large scale production outweigh its disadvantages. That accounts for the tendency in the modem times to increase the scale of production in most industrial concerns. All the industrially advanced countries of the world have organised their production on a very large scale.

Economies of Scale

A large scale-producer enjoys economies which may be grouped under two Heads—(1) Internal economies, and (2) External economies.

(1) *Internal Economies.* Internal economies are special to a particular business unit. They are the secrets of a business firm and are not shared by its rivals. They may be due to early start, better managerial ability or trade name. Or they may be the outcome of specialised methods of production, control and sale. These economies are thus the result of efficiency of management in any particular firm and are mainly due to the superior administrative ability of the entrepreneur, his commercial foresight and technical efficiency. They depend upon the size of the individual firm and are independent of the general growth of the industry.

(2) *External Economies.* External economies depend on the growth of the industry as a whole. They are known to and are enjoyed by all units engaged in the production of anyone article. They do not depend on the expansion of the size of a single firm. They depend on the growth of an industry. A typical example is the decrease in the cost of machinery as machinery is produced in large quantities. External economies are mostly advantageous arising out of localisation of industries. Specialised means of communication and transport, credit institutions, technical training facilities, technical journals and subsidiary occupations etc., are some of the external economies. These economies are known as external economies because they are external to firms even though they are internal to the industry.

Limitations of Large Scale Production

Although large scale industries enjoy many economies, they are subject to the following limitations:

(1) The business may become unwieldy. The problem of supervision and management becomes more and more intractable as the firm grows larger. This is a serious obstacle to the growth in the size of firms.

(2) It is also sometimes not easy for a firm to raise large sum of money or the interest may be very high. A businessman may feel reluctant to saddle him self with high interest charges.

(3) Demand for the product may be subject to considerable fluctuations. In such a case, a large scale producer will not find it easy to adapt production to the changed conditions of demand.

(4) Costs of growth may also impede expansion. Large expenditure in sales organisation, marketing etc, may render further growth unprofitable.

(5) Expansion of a business enterprise may also be limited by the existence of imperfect markets and the inertia of the buyers. We don't have perfect competition. Consumers have their own preference, real or imaginary, and a firm may have its own protected customers.

(6) The entrepreneur's own inclination also is responsible for the existence of small firms. There are people who prefer to run a small business of their own rather than be a subordinate at a higher rate of pay.

Optimum Size of the Firm

In every business there is a certain size which may be considered the ideal or the right size of the business. The firm of such a size is called the *optimum firm.* Such an optimum-sized firm realises the economies of scale to the maximum possible extent and has the lowest cost. If the size of the firm is smaller than the optimum the economies of scale are not fully tapped. If the size is a little larger than the optimum the diseconomies of scale exceed the economies. In either case the average costs are higher than the absolute minimum.

The optimum represents the ideal scale of enterprise. If there were no diseconomies of large scale production a firm would go on expanding indefinitely. It is because the diseconomies of scale gradually grow till they exceed the economies of scale that the optimum point is reached long before output is adequate to meet the entire market demand. *There is thus scope for the existence of a number of optimum firms.*

The optimum firm differs from Marshall's representative firm. The representative firm of Marshall is an average firm but the optimum firm is a least-cost firm. The optimum firm is also different from Pigou's equilibrium. The latter is a mere hypothetical concept while *the optimum firm refers to the size towards which all firms must be tending under conditions of perfect competition.*

3. SMALL SCALE PRODUCTION

Inspite of the substantial gain from large scale production, we find that in actual life many small firms exist in an industry. It appears paradoxical but it is due to several reason. There are limitations on large scale production and limits to which gains can accrue from extension in the scale of production. There are also certain advantages peculiar to small business concerns.

Advantages of Small Scale Production

The main advantages of small scale production areas follows:

(1) *Close Supervision.* In small scale production, there can be close supervision of the business. The producer can himself supervise the smallest detail of the business. There is no waste of labour or material. Employees cannot cheat the employer. Any defects in an employee's work or any mishandling of machinery can easily catch the eye of the master. The result is reduction in the cost of production.

(2) *Economy in Management.* When the proprietor himself supervises the work, much of the red-tapism is avoided. No unnecessary hand is employed. No superfluous account-keeping is necessary. It makes for prompt decisions in the business. Moreover, much expenditure is not incurred on maintaining a top heavy administrative machinery. Thus economy is effected in the management of the work.

(3) *Close Contact with the Customers.* The small scale producer can pay personal attention to his customers. If there is any grievance the proprietor himself attends to it and gets it promptly redressed. He can understand the actual demand of the customers and is able to send every one of them fully satisfied.

(4) *Personal Touch with the Employees.* In a small scale business, there is a direct contact between the employer and the workers. If the workers have any grievance, they can directly approach their employer and bring their difficulties to his notice. The employer can deal with the matter sympathetically and settle the differences, if any. Thus the number of industrial disputes in a small scale business is very small. The chances of strikes and lock-outs are reduced to a great extent.

(5) *Independence.* The small scale producer is his own boss. He is not subservient to anybody. This economic independence develops in him the qualities of self reliance and initiative. He is happy with his position and does not like to work as a subordinate. He works with great enthusiasm because there is nobody to exploit him.

(6) *Great Adaptability to Changes.* The small scale producer can adapt himself easily to the changing conditions of trade. He can take decisions more promptly and also execute them more expeditiously.

Causes of the Survival of Small Industries

Apart from these advantages which small scale production enjoys, there are some special circumstances in which small scale production is the most suitable. Such circumstances are the following:

(1) *Limited Demand for the Commodity.* Where demand is limited or is of a fluctuating nature. Under such circumstances a small scale producer has an advantage over a large scale producer. If the demand is fluctuating, it is not wise to produce more while production on a large scale is unnecessary when the demand is small.

(2) *Indivisibility.* Where the nature of the industry does not admit of division of labour on any good scale. Agriculture, tailoring and repairing concerns provide examples. There is a very limited scope for division of labour in agriculture. Tailoring business cannot he organised on a large scale as the tailor has to meet the varying tastes of the individual customers. In repairing concerns also individual attention is needed and they cannot, therefore, be organised on a large scale.

(3) *Personal Ability.* Where personal care, judgment and skill of the workers is required. In jewellery work, embroidery work and production of other artistic wares, small scale production is the only possibility.

(4) *Nature of Business*. Where business cannot be reduced to a routine. Agriculture again is an example. The operations of agriculture are spread over a large area and are not easily subjected to a fixed routine. The result is that agriculture has nowhere shown a tendency to enlargement of the scale of production.

Besides the exclusive fields for small scale production, there are some facilities of recent origin which help the small scale producer. Owing to the advent of electricity, it is no longer necessary for a small scale producer to install a power-house of his own. He can conveniently obtain electrical energy as much as he desires. Further, external economies which are mainly the advantages of localisation of industries are as much available to the small scale producers as to big business concerns. There is also a tendency nowadays to disseminate technical knowledge as and when it is available. The small scale producer does also benefit from it.

EXERCISES

1. What do you understand by scale of production? Discuss the limit of large scale production.
2. Discuss the advantages and disadvantages of large scale production.
3. Explain the term Internal and External Economies of scale. What are the merits and demerits of small scale industries?
4. What are the causes for the survival of small scale industries in an economy?

Multiple Choice Questions

5. (*i*) The scale of production refers to
    (*a*) the amount of factors used
    (*b*) the quantities of products produced
    (*c*) the techniques of production adopted
    (*d*) all of the above [Ans. *(d)*]

   (*ii*) Internal economies are those economies which
    (*a*) are open to a single firm-independently of the actions of other firms
    (*b*) are acquired by a firm due to the actions of other firms in the market
    (*c*) are the result of innovation
    (*d*) all of the above [Ans. *(a)*]

   (*iii*) External economies are those economies which
    (*a*) are shared by a number of firms or industries when the scale of production increases.
    (*b*) are acquired by the firm within its own system
    (*c*) cannot be shared by any other firm in the market
    (*d*) are acquired by the firm because of its peculiar position in the industry [*Ans.* (*a*)]

   (*iv*) Which one of the following is the cause for the survival of small industries in an economy?
    (*a*) Limited demand in the market (*b*) Artistic goods
    (*c*) Subsidiary industries (*d*) All of the above [*Ans. (d)*]

Chapter 25

CAPITAL AND CAPITAL FORMATION

1. MEANING OF CAPITAL

The term capital has been used in a variety of senses. In fact, even today there is no uniform or one opinion with regard to the meaning and contents of capital. The earlier economists had some entirely different notions of capital. Adam Smith regarded capital as a stock of consumption goods necessary to feed the workers for the period between the beginning of production and the sale of final goods. Karl Marx held a different concept of capital. In his view capital consisted of durable goods such as machines and factories, all of which were the product of labour. Thus, in his view, capital represented the stored up labour. Now a days, the term capital is used to denote that part of man's wealth, other than land, which yields him an income through further production. It consists of cash, raw materials, unfinished and semi-finished goods and the durable goods like machines, plants and factories. Capital has been defined by Bohm Bawerk as "the produced means of production". It is production with the help of land and labour, which are called the primary factors of production. But when more capital has been produced, it is used for further production. Thus capital is a means of production, but is different from land which is a gift of nature. While land is a free gift of nature, capital is produced by, man working with the nature. Capital, in the words of Prof. Thomas, "is that wealth of individuals and communities other than land which is used to assist in the production of further wealth."

(1) *Wealth and Capital.* Capital is that part of wealth which is meant for further production of wealth. Wealth consists of all types of goods whether consumer or producer goods. Wealth includes landed property, ornaments and jewellery, farms and factories, cars and trucks and so many more things. From all this wealth we exclude those things which are the free gift of nature. Under this comes the land, which is a form of wealth. Further, from the man-made wealth, we exclude those goods which are

meant for, personal satisfaction, like motor car or residential bungalow. The rest of the wealth, which consists of truks, factories, machines and the cash to be invested, is called capital. Thus capital is only a part of the total wealth. All capital is, therefore, wealth but all wealth is not capital.

(2) *Income and Capital.* As we have seen, capital consists of income yielding assets. Thus while capital is the total stock of such goods which are to be used for further production, income is the flow which these goods yield by way of return. The house given on rent is capital but the rent that is received annually is the income. Income thus flows from the capital goods and the level of income in a community depends upon the stock of capital in the country.

(3) *Land and Capital.* Capital has been defined as consisting of all goods which are man-made and which yield an income. But land, although it gives an income, is not capital, because it is a gift of nature. Further, while the stock of capital can be increased by human efforts, the amount of land available is fixed by nature. Man can neither create nor destroy land. Thus, while the stock of capital can be adjusted to the requirements of the community, the amount of land cannot be altered according to our needs.

(4) *Money and Capital.* In the common language, money and capital are used interchangeably. A man who is rich is also sometimes called as a capitalist. But in economics money is not the same thing as capital. Whether money can be called capital or not, depends upon the use which money is being put to. If money is used for purchase of machines, plants, and factories or other capital goods, then this part of money is called capital. If money is used for the purchase of consumer goods, or for hoarding, then this is not capital.

2. CHARACTERISTICS OF CAPITAL

Capital possess certain peculiarities which distinguish it from other factors of production. Some of the important characteristics of capital may be described as below:

(1) *Man Produces Capital.* Capital is the result of human labour. Every type of capital such as roads, machines, equipments, buildings, industries etc. are all produced by men and are not the free gift of nature.

(2) *Capital is a Passive Factor of Production.* Without the help of labour, capital cannot make production. Labour is an active factor of production while capital is passive in nature. It will always be utilised by labour. In the absence of labour, it will be lying idle.

(3) *Capital is a Produced Means of Production.* Supply of capital is not automatic, but it is created by the joint efforts of labour and land. Hence, capital is a produced means of production.

(4) *Capital is Variable.* The supply of capital can be varied as and when required while the supply of land is fixed. If the people of the country save more and invest more, then the supply of capital can be increased.

(5) *Capital is More Mobile than other Factors of Production.* As compared to land and labour, capital is more mobile in the sense that it can be transferred very quickly from one place to another through cheques, drafts, T.T. etc.

(6) *Capital Depreciates.* As we go on using a capital good, its value will depreciate. It has some life. We cannot go on using the same capital good for an unlimited time.

(7) *Capital is Stored up Labour.* When a person performs labour, he gets some income. Now the part of this income or wealth which is used for further production, becomes capital. Hence capital is the result of accumulation of savings of man.

3. IMPORTANCE OF CAPITAL

Capital plays a vital role in the process of production these days. Production without machines is hard to be imagined. In the old times, when people used to work primarily with their awn physical efforts, without people using any sophisticated tools and implements, the output they produced was too small in quantity and too poor in quality. These days, not much of the work is done by hand. An important feature of the modern economies is the extensive use of capital in the field of production. Capital goods, like machines, factories, plants, tools and implements are, these days, indispensable to the process of production. With the use of machinery the volume of production has tremendously increased. The quality of production has also improved because machines can take note of even those details which the human beings cannot. Even the primitive man in the simplest economy used capital in the farm of bows and arrows far hunting or same simple tools for cultivation of land. But the technological advancement of the past two centuries have made the use of capital wider and deeper. Today, we use huge complicated and automatic type of machines. Every economy these days invests large part of its resources far making of capital goods. Those countries which produce larger, amaunt of capital goods are in fact the richest countries of world This is so because the machines add to the productive capacity of the notion. The larger is the number of machines, factories and plants in the country the greater would be the flaw of goods a out of them. The greater productivity in the advanced economies like USA, UK and Japan is the result of extensive use of capital in production in these countries.

Because the strategic role of capital in raising the productivity the process of capital formation has assumed a vital place in the process of economic development. Large scale investment in capital projects like factories, plants, dams, roads and bridges is made in those economies which have initiated the programme of economic development. It would not be possible for an economy to grow if sufficient amount of capital is not available. That is why, so much stress is laid upon the savings and capital formation in all the developing economies. The rate of capital formation must be kept sufficiently high if development is to proceed smoothly, thereby raising the level of output, income and employment in a country.

4. MEANING OF CAPITAL FORMATION

The term "capital formation" implies an increase in the stack of capital goods in an economy. Accumulation of capital is nothing but an increase in the stocks of real capital goods like machines, tools, factories, plants, ships, railways and other transport equipment, and making of roads, canal, dams etc. all of which are used for further production of goods. But in order to make more of such goods, the economy has to produce less of consumer goods, thus saving some of the resources which are to be used for capital goods production. In other words, to have more of capital goods, people in that economy will have to make a sacrifice in terms of consumers goods. In the words of Prof. Regnar Nurkse "the meaning of Capital Formation is that society does not apply the whole of its current productive activity to the needs and desires of immediate consumption, but directs part of it to the making of capital, goods, tools and instruments, machines and transport facilities, plant and equipment—all the various forms of capital that can so greatly increase the efficiency of productive effort. The essence of the process then, is the diversion of a part of society's currently available resources to the purpose of increasing the stock of capital goods so as to make possible an expansion of consumable output in the future."

From the above definition it is clear that if a community wishes to increase the stock of her capital equipment, she will have to make some sacrifice in her current consumption. The larger the extent to which the people are prepared to sacrifice their current consumption the greater is the amount of resources which the economy can devote to the production of real capital. If the community decides to consume all its current output, it will not have anything for the production of capital goods. In such a case the community's stock of capital will keep on declining through the process of depreciation and non-replacement of worn out machinery. This would impair the productive capacity of the nation and reduce the flow of consumer goods in some future date. A sacrifice of consumer goods at present would result in their production in larger quantities in future. The machines that would be made now with the help of resources released by the lower production of consumer goods would start turning out much greater quantities of consumer goods in the times to come. But to sacrifice the present consumption in order to have much greater amount of consumer goods in future requires a certain degree of foresightedness and the spirit to make sacrifice.

5. PROCESS OF CAPITAL FORMATION

It is evident from the definition of capital formation that saving is an essential pre-condition for capital formation. But the saving itself should not be confused to be the same thing as capital. It would become capital only when it is invested in some real capital-goods like plants and machinery. It is not necessary that all those people who save money must also be making the investment. In the modem economies, the function of savings and investment are in fact performed by the different sets of people. Thus, it is necessary that savings must be mobilised and made available to those persons who are willing to invest it. Thus the process of capital formation requires three things:

(l) Formation or accumulation of savings,
(2) Mobilisation of savings,
(3) Investment of savings in capital goods.

Formation or Accumulation of Savings

The growth of savings in a country depend upon quite a large number of factors, some of which involve social, economic and political considerations. Savings as we know is the difference between income and consumption expenditure of individuals and households. In the ultimate analysis the savings depend upon the individuals (*I*) power to save and (*II*) willingness to save.

Power to save. The power to save of the community depends upon the following:

(*a*) *Surplus of income and Over Expenditure.* The power to save of an individual depends upon the level of his income and his consumption expenditure. If the income is more than the expenditure then the individual is said to have the capacity to save. Thus the excess of income over expenditure represents the saving potential of an. individual. As with the individuals, similarly with the countries, the power to save depends upon the surplus of income over expenditure of the community as a whole. Those countries which have higher per capita incomes are in a position to save. That is why the rate of savings in the advanced countries of Western Europe and Northern America is much higher as compared to the poor and underdeveloped countries of Eastern Europe, Asia and Africa.

(*b*) *Distribution of National Income.* The level of savings in a community also depends upon the pattern of income distribution in the country. In a community, where there is an unequal distribution of income, where some people are very rich and the others are poor, more savings is likely to occur. This is because, in such an economy, the rich people who enjoy a very high level of income, would be left over with considerable surplus, after they have met their expenses. Thus, savings would be automatic for them. Those who are poor would be somehow making their both ends meet and, thus, having no savings. On the whole there will be some savings in the economy. But if there is an equal distribution of income, no one is very rich and no one is poor, there savings may not occur. With the reduction in inequalities, those who were rich earlier and could make some savings, are now not in a position to save. Those who were poor, and have now become a little better off, would spend all the additional income in fulfilling those wants which they could not satisfy earlier. Thus no savings would come from any group of people. Hence the over all savings in the country would decline. Thus uneven distribution of income in a community is helpful to savings and capital formation while equal or even distribution is harmful for it.

Willingness to Save. Even if the income of a person is higher than his expenditure, he would not be making any savings until he has the willingness to do so. The willingness to save a part of the income depends upon a number off actors some of which are influenced by personal, family or national considerations. Below are mentioned some of the considerations which influence an individual desire or willingness to save:

(*a*) *Foresight.* People some time save money in order to insure themselves against some uncertain or unforseen emergencies that may arise in future. Unemployment, sickness or accident are such risks which affect every one of us, Thus all those people who are foresighted, they are likely to save for the rainy day. Wise and foresighted people also save for such purposes as the education of children, the marriage of the daughter or for some unforeseen expenses which are likely to occur in future.

(*b*) *Social Consideration.* In the present society, the wealth gives political power and social system. A man who is rich is respected every where. A man without money is not well treated by this world. Thus anybody who wants to become socially more popular and win some respect in society must save some money.

(*c*) *Political Consideration.* The political consideration and the political climate plays a very important role in promotion of savings. Firstly, money is the stepping stone to political power and a man has a to save sufficient money is gain some political authority. Secondly, the political circumstances themselves may have a direct effect upon the willingness to save. A national emergency, by awakening the patriotic spirit of the people, may lead to a much larger volume of savings in the country.

(*d*) *Economic considerations.* There are a number of economic considerations which have a direct bearing upon the individual's willingness to save money. Some of these considerations are as follows:

(*i*) *Rate of interest.* Some of the people are prepared to save more money if they can get a high rate of interest" by lending it. A high rate of interest is a positive, inducement to save more. If the rate of interest is low, then people may not bother about savings because the reward for savings is not sufficiently attractive.

(*ii*) *Level of taxation.* If the profits, income and savings are being fixed at a high rate in the country, then people would not be interested in making any substantial savings. If tax rates are low and sufficiently reasonable, more savings may be made in the country.

(*iii*) *Money stability.* Stability in the value of money is an essential condition for making any great savings in the country. If the prices are fairly stable and therefore the purchasing power of money is also stable, then people may like to save money. But if they expect some violent changes in the value of money, for example, if they expect the prices to rise sufficiently high in the near future then they would not he prepared to Save money, because they know that money would lose much of its value in future.

(*iv*) *Banking system.* If there is a sufficiently large number of banks in a country and if these banks have branches spread allover the country, then there might be more savings. This is because of the fact that banks provide two attractions to the savers. Firstly, the banks provide a safe custody to the savings of a person and secondly, they also pay a certain rate of interest to those who save. Thus the spread of banking facilities may make many of the people willing to save and thus increase the volume of savings in the country.

(*e*) *Temperamental Consideration.* There are some people who have a natural habit of saving. Thus, in their case, the saving is a part of their nature. They do not require any special efforts/facilities to make savings. What is true of the individuals, is also true of nations. Some nations are known for their thrifty people. England, for example, is a country where people are generally saving minded, while the French people are known for their extravagance.

(*f*) *Security of Life and Property.* Any country where the law and order conditions are good, where there is security of life and property, people may be willing to save more money. But in those countries or in those parts of a country where there is general lawlessness where robberies and thefls are common, savings are risky because they might be lost. They may put the life of the saver also into some risk. Thus, no one could be prepared to save under such conditions.

(*g*) *Policy of the Government.* The amount of savings which are made in a country, to some extent depend upon the policy of the Government. If the Government is following a policy of nationalisation and Government control of business and property, people may not be prepared to save. Anyone who saves some money would like to enjoy it in future. But if he known that the Government is going to confiscate his savings and property, he would not save much money.

(h) Political Stability. Not only the policy of the Government should be very clear and helpful, if the savings are to be made, but also the government itself should be of a stable nature. If the governments change quite frequently or if there are frequent revolutions and counter revolutions in the country, it would shake the faith of the people in the government. Thus they may not be prepared to save much under such circumstances.

2. Mobilisation of Savings

Simple saving of money does not lead to capital formation in the country. Capital would be formed when these savings are invested in the real life capital goods like tools, machines, buildings and transport equipment to further produce more of goods and services. But it is not necessary that all those people who have saved money, must be prepared to invest it. Investment involves certain risks, and every one may not like to undertake the risks of business. Thus these savings must be moved from those people who have made the savings and made available to those who do not have money, but who are prepared to invest and undertake the risk of the business. This process of moving the saving from those who have it but do not want to invest, to those who do not have it but are prepared to invest, is known as mobilisation of savings. For mobilisation of savings, the essential requirement is the existence of a well developed capital market in the country. Capital market consists of those institutions who receive money from one group of people in the form of deposits etc. and give it as loads and advances to the others for investment. Thus all the banks, finance houses and insurance companies are the members of the capital market. If the capital market is well developed and well organised, that is, if there is a fairly large number of banks and other financial institutions, then the investors would be in a position to borrow money easily. Thus there would be more capital formation. One of the factors which led to the economic development in Britain in the 18th and 19th centuries was the existence of a well developed and well organised capital market in that country.

3. Investment of Savings

Savings, when they become available to the people who are prepared to invest them, would lead to, the capital formation in the country only when they are invested in the purchase of capital goods. A man would be prepared to undertake an investement when it is profitable to do so. Thus, for a large scale capital formation there should be a sufficiently large number of avenues which are fairly attractive for investment. Otherwise money may be invested in some unproductive channels like purchase of gold or purchase of landed property, which do not in any way increase the productive capacity of the nation. The profitability of investment depends upon the expected receipts from the sale of the product and its cost of production. Since not mach can be done about the demand and price of the commodities, investment can be encouraged if the cost is reduced. It is here where the government can do a lot. It can provide loans at a low cost. It can build up social and economic overheads like rods, railways and provide transport facilities. It can open up training centres and thus impart technical knowledge. All these would be very useful to the individual producers and .reduce their cost of production. Since these projects involve a lot of expenditure, no one of the producers may be willing to undertake them at his own cost. But once such facilities are provided, many producers may find it worthwhile to undertake investment in certain lines of production. This would lead to the construction and purchase of more capital goods and thus lead to capital formation.

6. ROLE OF GOVERNMENT IN CAPITAL FORMATION

In the advanced capitalist countries, the level of per capita income being sufficiently high some amount of savings is likely to occur with the individuals and households, even after meeting all those expenses which are required for maintaining a decent standard of living. Thus the voluntary savings of the people are sufficient to acquire the machinery and other capital goods required for production. But in a backward, country the level of voluntary saving is very low because of an extremely low per capita income. While in the advanced countries the level of voluntary savings comes to about 15 to 20 per cent of national income, it is around 5 to 8 per cent in most of the backward countries. Not only the level of savings is very low, but whatever savings are made, are not properly mobilised and made available to the people who want to invest. Besides, the profitability from investment is also very low. Thus not much of the savings which have been made are properly invested. Much of the investment takes place in the unproductive channels like purchase of ornaments and landed property.

Since the volume of voluntary capital formation is very low in the backward countries the government is called upon to play an important role in the process of capital formation. First of all the government has to step-up level of savings by some compulsory methods. These methods include the raising of the level of taxation and introduction of compulsory saving schemes. If the level of domestic savings is not sufficient, the government might borrow from the foreign countries or even resort to deficit financing, i.e. creation of new money and' purchasing capital goods with that newly created money. Further, the government can build up social and economic overheads like roads, railways, training institutions etc. so that the cost of production may become low for the private producers. This might induce them to undertake new investment. If the private people are not willing to undertake new investment, the government may itself take the place of the entrepreneur and undertake direct investment. Thus, the government cap initiate and promote the process of capital formation in the underdeveloped countries.

EXERCISES

1. Define capital. How is it different from wealth, land and income?
2. Discuss the meaning of capital and its important characteristics.
3. What do you understand by the term "capital formation"? Explain how an economy accumulates capital?
4. Explain the role of government in capital formation in an economy.

Multiple Choice Questions

5. (*i*) Capital can be defined as
    (*a*) wealth
    (*b*) a part of wealth which yields income
    (*c*) accumulated labour
    (*d*) an active factor of production [*Ans.* (*b*)]

    (*ii*) Which of the following is a characteristic of capital as a factor of production?
    (*a*) It is a passive factor of production
    (*b*) It is a active factor of production
    (*c*) It is fixed in supply
    (*d*) It never depreciates [*Ans.* (*a*)]

    (*iii*) The process of capital formation involves
    (*a*) increase in the volume of real savings
    (*b*) mobilisation of savings
    (*c*) investment of savings
    (*d*) all of the above [*Ans.* (*d*)]

Chapter 26

LAWS OF RETURNS : THE TRADITIONAL APPROACH

1. INTRODUCTION

A firm combines factors of production in order to produce one or more products and then offers this product (or products) for sale to consumers. There are two important theories in this process: (*i*) the theory of production; and (*ii*) the theory of costs. The theory of production analyses the physical relationship between inputs and outputs, while theory of costs 'presents the relationship between the levels of output and the levels of costs (the outlay incurred on different inputs used in producing a given output), production functions, which embody the technical and technological conditions of production, are in a sense more basic than cost functions. If factor prices are given, then cost functions can be derived from production functions.

This chapter deals with production theory in the traditional manner while the modern approach in terms of the isoquant-isocost analysis ,is explained in the next chapter.

2. THE PRODUCTION FUNCTION

A production function is a precise way to represent a technology involved in the process of production. An entrepreneur transforms his inputs into outputs, subject to technical rules specified by his production function. The production function tells us how much output we can hope if we have so much of labour and so much of capital and so much of land, etc.

A production function is a mathematical expression to the relationship between the quantities of inputs employed and the quantity of output produced.

The concept is perfectly general. Any specific production function may be given by: (*i*) a single point, (*ii*) a single continuous or discontinuous function, and (*iii*) a system of equations.

Though we are mainly concerned with the second category which is most general also; we shall give brief attention to the first and third categories also. Briefly, we can say that the basic relationship between physical inputs and physical outputs is referred to as a production function. A production function is a technical or engineering relation between input and output. Since money prices do not appear in it, it merely depicts the physical relationship between the output and the inputs. Algebraically, such a basic relationship between the inputs and the output may be expressed as:

$$X = f(L, K, N, ...)$$

where X = output of a commodity per unit of time; L = labour; K = capital; N = land and other natural resources.

The above equation shows that the quantity of output produced (X) depends upon the quantities be different factors (L, K, N,...) available to the firm. The above function shows that there exists some relationship between output X and the quantities of inputs L, K, N, etc; but it does not tell us the specific form which this relationship is assumed to have. This unspecified relationship is denoted by the letter, If the form of the function f is given, that is, if the right hand of the equation is given in a specific mathematical form, we can then fully find out by the use of mathematical methods the nature of the relationship.

In the simplest case, where here are assumed to be only two inputs, labour (L) and capital (K) and one output (X), the production function becomes,

$$X = f(L, K)$$

And the maximum production that a firm can produce from various combinations of L and K can be presented by a two-way table as in Table 26.1.

In Table 26.1 along the left side we have taken various labour units, going from 1 unit to 10 units of labour. Similarly, along the top right hand side, amount of capital has been taken, going from 1 unit to 10units of capital. If we are interested in knowing exactly what output there will be when 5 units of capital and 2 units of labour are available, then our answer will be that given this amount of input the producer will be able to produce 30 units of X. Similar answers will be given to other combinations of labour and capital units. Thus for any combination of labour and capital, the production function tells us how much product we shall have (using, of course, the best methods as decided by the technical engineer).

Table 26.1. The Physical Production Schedule

Units of Labour (*L*) ↓	Capital (*K*) →	*1K*	*2K*	*3K*	*4K*	*5K*	*6K*	*7K*	*8K*	*9K*	*10K*
1*L*		12	14	16	16	14	13	12	11	10	9
2*L*		20	24	26	28	30	32	33	32	31	30
3*L*		24	32	36	38	40	42	44	46	48	50
4*L*		24	40	44	48	50	52	54	56	58	60
5*L*		22	44	52	56	60	62	64	66	68	70
6*L*		20	48	60	64	70	72	74	76	78	80
7*L*		18	48	64	72	78	82	84	86	88	90
8*L*		16	48	68	80	44	88	92	96	98	100
9*L*		14	46	72	82	90	96	100	104	108	112
10*L*		12	44	76	84	96	104	108	112	118	120

Table 26.1 shows not only the output levels obtained from different combinations of *L* and *K* but also states the relative changes in inputs and the output. If we move vertically, then we assume capital (*K*) to be constant and try to analyse the responsiveness of output (*X*) to various levels of labour (*L*) units. On the other hand, if we more horizontally, then we assume labour (*L*) to be constant and try to analyse the reponsiveness of output (*X*) to various levels of, capital (*K*) units. If both are variable, we move diagonally and try to find out their responsiveness on output levels.

Two things must be noted in respect of production function:

(1) Production function, like the demand function, must be specified with reference to a particular period of time. Thus, production function expresses a flow of inputs resulting in a flow of output in a specific period of time.

(2) Production function of a firm is determined by the state of technology. When the technology advances, the production function changes with the result that the new production can yield greater flow of output from the given quantities of inputs, or smaller quantities of inputs can be used for producing a given quantity of output.

Short-Run Production Function and Long-Run Production Function

In economic theory, we are interesed in two types of input-output relations or production functions:

(1) *Short-Run Production Function.* Here we study the production when the quantities of some inputs yelield constant and the quantity of

input (or quantities of few inputs) are varied. This kind of input-output relation forms the subject matter of the law of variable proportions.

When one input is in, creased while other inputs are kept constant, the resulting output, as we have shown in Table 26.1 increases first at an increasing rate, then at a constant rate and then at a decreasing rate. These three different situations lead to the formation of three different laws of returns. When the percentage increase in output is more than the percentage increase in a single input, the situation is of law of increasing returns. When the percentage increase in output is equal to percentage increase in input, then it will be a situation of law of constant returns. When percentage increase in output is less than the percentage increase in input, then the situation is of law of diminishing returns. The first two laws hold only temporarily, and therefore, the law of diminishing returns will take place in the economy.

(2) *Long-Run Production Function.* Here we study the input-output relation by varying all inputs. This forms the subject matter of the laws of returns to scale.

As we have three types of laws of returns, similarly, we also have three types of laws of returns to scale. But in the case of returns to scale, we examine the relationship between all inputs and the resulting output. In other words, all inputs vary in the same proportion under the case of returns to scale. *In the case of returns to scale, the production is homogeneous.* The degree may vary between zero and infinity. Thus, if all the inputs in a production function are increased by a constant (λ), the degree of the function (n) will be measured by the magnitude of the change in the value of the function. If the change in output is equi-proportional with A, the production function is linearly homogeneous of degree one. In this situation, the firm is operating under constant returns to scale.

If the production function is homogeneous of degree 2 (non-linear-homogeneous), then following an increase in all inputs by a constant λ, the output will increase to a level equivalent to λ^2. In such a situation (when the production function is of degree greater than one) the firm operates under increasing returns to scale.

If the production function is homogeneous of degree less than one (non-linear homogeneous) then a firm operates under diminishing returns to scale, that is, output increases less than proportionately with a given increase in the level of all inputs.

Nature of Production Function

The nature of a production function may take the following forms:

(1) Homogeneous Production Function
(2) Non-Homogeneous Production Function
(3) Linear-Homogeneous Production Function
(4) Linear-Non-Homogeneous Production Function
(5) Non-Linear-Homogeneous Production Function
(6) Non-Linear-Non-Homogeneous Production Function.

In the case of homogeneous production function, all inputs are changed in the same proportion or in other words, factor proportions are held constant over time. It refers to the situation of returns to scale.

In the case of non-homogeneous production function, only one input changes and others are kept constant. Therefore, it refers to the situation of laws of returns.

In the case of linear homogeneous production, the firm operates under constant returns to scale.

In the case of linear non-homogeneous production function, the firm operates under law of constant returns.

In the case of non-linear-homogeneous production function, the firm operates under either increasing returns to scale or diminishing returns to scale.

In the case of non-linear non-homogeneous production functions, the firm operates under either increasing returns or diminishing returns.

Types of Production Functions

In economic theory, we normally discuss two types of input output relations or production functions:

(1) Firstly, we study the production function when the quantities of some inputs are held constant and the quantities of one input (or quantities of few inputs) are varied. This kind of input-output relation forms the subject matter of the law, of variable proportions.

(2) Secondly, we study the input-output relation by varying all inputs. This forms the subject matter of the laws of returns to scale.

A number of economists studied actual production functions and have used statistical methods to find out relations between changes in physical inputs and physical outputs. A most popular and empirical production function is the Cobb-Douglas production function. Originally, the Cobb-Douglas production function was applied not only to the production process of an individual firm but to the whole of the manufacturing production. In Cobb-Douglas production function, there are two inputs, labour and capital. In its general exponential form it is stated as:

$$Q = \alpha\,[K^{\beta} L^{1-\beta}]$$

where Q stands for the quantity of output, L and K stand for labour and capital inputs respectively and α and β are the positive parameters. In logarithmic form it can fie written as:

$$\log Q = \log \alpha + \beta \log K + (1 - \beta) \log L.$$

This function is known as log linear production function.

3. THE LAWS OF PRODUCTION

The laws of production explain the characteristics of the production function. The laws of production are necessarily the generalisations which contain no precise quantitative results, and in fact their usefulness in economic theory turns on their applicability to all important forms of productive activity. The quantitative relationships between the factors of production and the output are, therefore, expressed in ordinal terms, such as, increasing or greater than, rather than cardinal terms, such as an increase of 15 per cent or so.

The productive factors land, labour, capital and the entrepreneur, combine to form units of production. It is important to look at the question of the proportions in which they are combined, or should be combined, to perform different tasks. These proportions vary widely from industry to industry. The production of commodity, such as, wheat requires a combination of a large amount of land with relatively small amounts of labour and capital, whereas the production of steel requires very large amount of capital, but small amounts of land and labour.

Normally, the laws of production are divided into two parts: The first branch known as the *law of variable proportions,* is concerned with the behaviour of the total product (*TP*) when only one productive factor input (say labour, *L*) is varied in quantity. The second branch, known as the *law of returns to scale of plant,* is concerned with the behaviour of the total product when all the productive factor-inputs are varied in the same quantity. These two branches of the laws of production are discussed in the following section.

4. THE LAW OF VARIABLE PROPORITIONS OR THE LAW OF DIMINISHING RETURNS

This law is usually associated with the early 19th century economist, David Ricardo. Ricardo developed the relationship with land treated as the fixed input. Later economists demonstrated that the law holds whether the fixed input is land, labour, capital or organisation. Towards the end of the 19th century, Alfred Marshall indicated that "an increase in the capital and labour applied in the cultivation of (fixed land causes in general a less than proportionate increase in the amount of produce raised, unless it happens to coincide with an improvement in the art of agriculture".

Marshall stated that a tendency to diminishing returns holds due to the following conditions:

(*a*) that labour and capital are used in a fixed proportion and for higher levels of output, incremental units of both the inputs are to be used;

(*b*) that land is fully utilised; and

(*c*) that methods of production (i.e., the state of arts In agriculture) do not change.

In simple words, the law of diminishing returns defines a relationship between inputs (resources) and outputs (goods and services), *with a given level of technology.* It states that, as an increasing number of units of one factor-input are applied to a fixed number of units of other factor-inputs, output first increases at an increasing rate, then at a diminishing rate, and eventually decreases absolutely. That point in the application of the variable input beyond which output increases at a diminishing rate is known as the point of diminishing returns.

The assumption of a fixed technology is an essential part of the law of diminishing returns. The law does not deny that progress in the technical arts may delay indefinitely the tendency to diminishing returns. However, at a given moment of time, the production place of the firm must be constructed with the use of specific techniques of production. Once the plan is in operation, it cannot be revoked overnight; the plant, building and machines cannot be revised every day. Thus the importance of the diminishing returns cannot be destroyed by the assumption of a fixed technology. If we consider a situation where the law does not apply, we find no economic problem in the world. The world's food problem can be solved by increasing the "doses" of labour and capital to a few plots of ground. Similarly, the total supply of any commodity can be increased by simply adding larger and larger quantities of labour and capital to one plant

Illustration of the Law

Let us assume that we have a fixed area of land on which we are to grow a given crop, say, wheat. We shall also assume that the amount of capital equipment which is to be used is also fixed in supply. We can now vary the number of workers (L) who are put to work on this land (with the fixed supply of capital). The results which might be obtained from such an experiment are set out in Table 46.2. If we put 3 men then the total product from the land would be 270 units. If instead we put 4 men, the total product would be 300 units, and so on. The basic data in the first two columns are the production function. The third and fourth columns are derived from the first two.

Table 26.2: Diminishing Returns Illustrated

(in physical units)

Number of Men (1)	*Total Product* (2)	*Average Product* (3)	*Marginal Product* (4)
1	100	100	100
2	220	110	120
3	270	90	50
4	300	75	30
5	320	64	20
6	330	55	10
7	330	47	0
8	320	40	– 10

Column 3 shows the average product per worker employed and is obtained from the formula:

$$\frac{\text{Total Product}}{\text{Number of Men Employed}} = \text{Average Product or } \frac{TP}{L} = AP$$

Column 4 shows the increase in the total product (i.e., the marginal product) which can be obtained from the employment of one more man. The addition of the sixth man adds ten units to the total product, while the employment of a fifth man adds twenty units to the total product. As farm (land) hands, the men are assumed to have equal efficiencies, so that there is nothing peculiar about the sixth man that causes his marginal product to be less than that of the fifth. The marginal product of any quantity of the variable input depends on the state of technology and on the amounts and. quantities of the fixed inputs.

Table 26.2 also illustrates that both the average and the marginal. products increase at first, and then decline. The marginal product declines faster than the average. When 6 men are employed, total product is r11aximum. No more is produced with 7 men; i.e., the marginal product of the 7 men is zero ($MP_L = 0$) and the marginal product of 8 men is minus 10 units (i.e., $MP_L < 0$)

The point of diminishing marginal product should not be confused with the point of diminishing total product. Total product will increase so long as marginal product is positive. But, the maximisation of total product would not be the optimum point of the product. In other words, as a matter of fact, we shall find that the optimum rate of use of the variable factor usually lies beyond the point of diminishing (marginal) returns but short of the point of diminishing total product.

The above idea can be more clearly illustrated with the help of a diagram as in Fig. 26.1

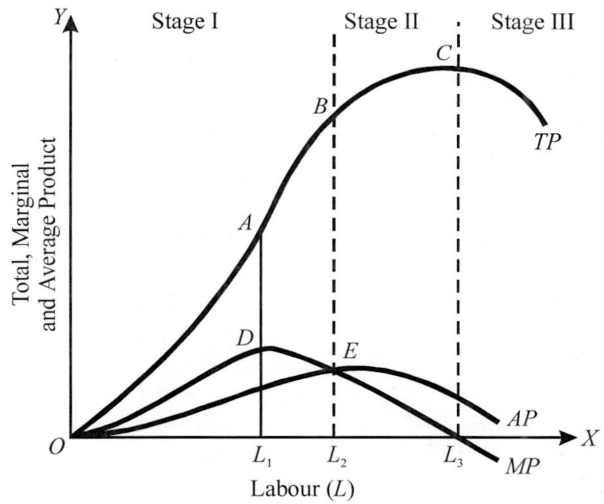

Fig. 26.1

Figure 26.1 shows the relationship between the product (output) of the firm and the number of units of labour (the variable input) employed by the firm. The units of labour are assumed to be of equal quality and to be used in conjunction with a fixed plant, i.e., in conjunction with a given-size "bundle" of land, capital and entrepreneurship. Inspection of the graph shows that the total output of the firm (*TP*) increases as the amount of labour hired increases, until the addition of a marginal labour causes total output to decrease. The total output curve is continuous because it is assumed that the units of the variable input can be made as small as desired. As the Figure suggests, the total product will usually first increase at an increasing rate, then at a decreasing rate until it reaches an absolute maximum and finally. Decreases to zero. The average product curve represents the total product of any given number of units of labour divided by the number; the marginal product curve represents the rate of increase the total product (i.e., the slope of the *TP-curve*). Thus, both of these curves may be derived geometrically from the total product curve. With these concepts in mind, it is possible to distinguish three stages of the law of proportion-ality. The summary has been given in Table 26.3.

Three Stages of Production

When one input is variable and others are held constant, the relations between the input and the product are conventionally divided into three "Stages" These three stages have been marked on Fig. 26.1 and described, in Table 26.3.

Stage I. The first stage goes from the origin to the point where the average product curve reaches a maximum and where marginal and average products are equal. The marginal product first increases and then decreases in this region.

Stage II. The second stage begins from the point where the average product curve reaches a maximum and ends at the point where the marginal product becomes zero. The marginal product becomes zero when the total product reaches a maximum.

Table 26.3. Properties of Total Product, Marginal Product and Average Product Curves and the Three Stages of Production

Total Product	*Marginal Product*	*Average Product*
Stage I		
first increases at increasing rate then increases at diminishing rate	increases reaches amaximum, and begins to diminish	increases continues to increase and becomes maximum
Stage II		
continues to increase at diminishing rate and becomes maximum	continues to diminish and becomes equal to zero	becomes equal to *MP* and then begins to diminish
Stage III		
diminishes	becomes negative	continues to diminish but will always be greater than zero

Stage III. The third stage begins from the point where the marginal product becomes zero, and ends at the point, where the total product (and hence the average product) becomes zero. In other Words, stage *III* of the variable input usage is that range over which marginal product is negative ($MP_L < 0$) or in which increasing use of labour yields smaller total product.

Clearly no firm would deliberately and voluntarily push its hiring of labour into stage *III.* Now the question is that where should the firm stop production? What number of men should it employ? No precise answers can be given to these questions on the basis of the present available information. For the precise answer we need to know the wages, which the firm would have to pay for each additional worker hired and the value of marginal product that the firm expects. Lacking this information, all that we can say is that the firm will try to balance extra revenues against extra cost in trying to determine the right size of employment. We can, of course, say that if the variable input is free, the entrepreneur will go to the end of the second stage. If, on the other hand, the fixed input is free, the entrepreneur will maximise the return per unit of variable input; that is, he will operate at the beginning of the second stage. The second stage where the marginal product is less than the average product but still positive, is the only economically significant region. Thus, to get the most out of the combination of all of the inputs used, the firm will normally be compelled to operate with a labour force and total output that places it somewhere in stage *II.*

In our above example, we have assumed labour as the variable input. But it does not mean that labour is always the variable input and that land, capital and entrepreneurship are always the fixed inputs. On the contrary, labour may be assumed as the fixed input, and land, capital or management or some combination of the three may be taken as the variable input. The law holds whatever the variable and whatever the fixed inputs. The law of diminishing returns applies when 'other things remain unchanged.' Improvements in techniques and equipment can offset the effects of the law.

6. THE LAWS OF RETURNS TO SCALE

To get the maximum efficiency in production, we must ensure that the proportions in which the factors are combined are as near the optimum as possible. The most economic use of inputs means that we are getting the greatest possible output per unit of input. But there is a further law of production to be observed. This law is concerned, not with the proportions between the factors of production, but with the scale of production. The scale of production of the firm is determined by those factor inputs which it cannot change in the short period. The fixed factor inputs set the upper limit to the rate of output. In our above example, land was fixed and it was combined with the increasing units of the variable input, labour. The fixity of land determined the limits to the maximum output capacity of the firm. Within these limits the rate of output can be varied by changing the units of the variable input in the short run. But in the long period, the scale itself can be varied. Thus, in the long run, the previous assumption that some inputs are fixed amount can be avoided. The firm, therefore, can expand production by using more of all inputs-more labour, more capital and more land, etc.

In other words, the law of variable proportions explains the behaviour of output when changes are made in factor proportions, but the concept of returns to scale explains the behaviour of output when changes are made in the scale of production. To put it differently, in the case of law of variable proportions, some of the inputs are held constant while in the case of returns to scale all the inputs are changed in the same proportion. Here, we must also remember that factor-proportions do not change when the scale of production changes under the case of returns to scale.

Let us take a simple case when a firm is increasing all its inputs by 10 per cent at a time. As a result of this the total product will increase. In the first stage, total product will increase by more than 10 per cent, and in the second stage by 10 per cent and in the third stage by less than 10 per cent. Now, if the increase-in output is more than proportional to the increase in the quantities of the inputs, the returns to scale are said to be increasing. If instead, the increase in total output is proportional to the increase in the quantities of inputs, the returns to scale are said to be constant. And if the increase in total output is less than proportional, returns to scale are said to be decreasing.

Table 26.4 shows the manner in which total product might change as the scale of production increases. Up to the point where 40 men are employed on 50 units of land, output per man rises as the size of firm increases. The firm is experiencing increasing returns to scale. We use the words "to scale" to emphasise the fact that the proportions between the factor inputs are not being changed. The increasing returns arise from the growth in the size of the productive unit. In simple words, doubling the capacity of a firm might lead to more than double the previous output. In Table 26.4 as the size of the business unit increases from 8 men and 10 units of land to 16 men and 20 units of land (an increase of 100 percent), total product changes from 130 units to 270 units (an increase of 108 per

Table 26.4. Situation of Returns to Scale

Units of Labour	*Units of Land*	*Total Product*	*Marginal Product*	*Average Product*
			(*Output* per *man*)	
8	10	130	16.25	16.25
16	20	270	17.50	16.88
24	30	430	20.00	17.92
32	40	610	22.50	19.06
40	50	770	20.00	19.25
48	60	910	17.50	18.90
56	70	1,040	16.25	18.57
64	80	1,140	12.50	17.81
72	90	1,230	11.25	17.08

cent approx). As the firm increases in size, it is able to take advantage of certain economies of scale. But Table 26.4 also indicates the fact that as the size of the firm increases beyond the employment of 40 men and 50 units of land, the returns to scale are diminishing. This is because of the fact that beyond a certain size, the efficiency begins to diminish.

Now we shall discuss the causes of increasing returns to scale, constant returns to scale and diminishing returns to scale in the following sections.

Causes of Increasing Returns to Scale or the Economies of Scale

(1) ***Economies of Increased Specialisation.*** As the unit of production (firm) increases in size, it becomes possible to employ the principle of the division of labour to an increasing extent. The larger the firm, the greater are the opportunities for the specialisation of men and machines. According to Adam Smith, the cause of increasing returns to scale comes from higher degrees of specialisation. In a small industry, each labour has to perform a number of tasks and consequently, the efficiency of the work will be less. But when the industry increases its size, specialisation will take place. With more labour, the industry can subdivide tasks, with gains in the efficiency of labour. Similarly, with more machinery, the firm can buy special types and also assign special jobs even to standardised kinds of machinery. Thus, the economies of increased specialisation lead to increasing returns to scale.

(2) ***Economies of Indivisibility of Plant.*** A closely related cause of increasing returns to scale is indivisibility of the plant. In general, indivisibility means that equipment is available only minimum sizes or in definite ranges of sizes. As a firm's scale of operations increases, it can use the minimum sizes and then the larger sizes of more efficient equipment. But indivisibility is a matter of degree. Though there cannot be half Ii typewriter, a typewriter can be rented halftime. Similarly, there can-not be half an accountant, yet part-time accounting services can be employed. Indivisibility therefore, quickly exhausts itself as a cause of increasing returns to scale.

To put it differently, a large output of a standard product makes possible the continuous use of specialized machines. Some types of capital equipment can only be employed efficiently in units of a minimum sire, and this minimum may well be too large for the small firm. There is a lower limit to the size of a blast furnace, a rolling mill, a car assembly line and a power press. This lower limit is often a technical limit; a smaller version of the equipment is impracticable. More generally, the lower limit is an economic one, smaller versions of the equipment could be made but their usefulness would not justify their cost. Such indivisibility of plant means that small enterprises with mall outputs cannot make use of large specialised plant and machinery. With a limited output it means that such plant would not be fully utilised, and would be standing idle for most of the time. The cost of using such equipment would be disproportionately high. Let us assume that a shoe-making machine available in the minimum size operates with of following cost structure.

Fixed costs	Rs. 2,000 per day
Variable costs	Rs. 10 per pair of shoes produced

(*i*) With a daily output of 1,000 pairs of shoes, the cost per pair attributed to this machine would be:

Fixed costs	Rs. 2,000
Variable costs	Rs.10,000
Total costs	Rs. 12,000

Average cost per pair = 12,000/1,000 = Rs. 12

(*ii*) With a daily output of 100 pairs, the costs will be:

Fixed costs	Rs.2,000
Variable costs	Rs.1,000
Total costs	Rs.3,000

Average cost per pair = 3,000/100 = Rs. 30

This leads to the general conclusion that as the output is increased, the machinery comes to be utilised more intensively and consequently the cost of production per unit declines. This advantage of machinery and plant to produce large quantities at lower costs is referred to as *technical economies of production.*

(3) ***Economies of Increased Dimensions.*** We know that costs do not always increase proportionately with size. For example, a double-decker bus does not cost twice as much as a single-decker, nor does it use twice as much petrol. It only requires the same staff to operate it as does a single-decker. Similarly, if we double the dimensions of a ship we increase is capacity by eight times. A very large modern oil tanker of 80,000 tons is only twice the size of a 10,000 ton tanker in terms of its length, width and height. Also, if the diameter of a pipe is doubled, the flow through it is more than doubled. A wooden box that is a 3-foot cube can contain 27 times as much as a box that is a 1-foot cube, but only 9 times as much wood is needed for the larger box. Similarly, if the labour and materials in a motor car are doubled, its horsepower is more than doubled. All this states that as the size of a capital good increases, its total output capacity will increase at a rate greater than the costs involved in increasing its size.

This particular economy of scale accounts for the tendency of industries which use tanks, vats and furnaces, to operate larger and larger units.

(4) ***Marketing Economies.*** Larger firms can buy their (raw) materials and sell their products more cheaply than small firms. Normally, a larger firm is able to buy its requirements in large quantities. Bulk buying enables them to obtain preferential terms; it will normally obtain its goods at lower prices than the small firm, and will be able to dictate its requirement with regard to quality and delivery much more effectively. Large firms will be able to employ marketing experts, whereas in the small firm marketing will be a function of an employee who will require to perform a number of other tasks.

Further, the selling, advertising and packaging costs per unit win be very much lower for a large firm. This indicates that the larger is the size of the firm, lesser will be the (per unit) cost of production, i.e., more will be the returns.

(5) ***Financial Economies.*** The large firm has several financial advantages. This is fact that a large firm being well known will be able to borrow money more easily and more cheaply than the small firms. Its

larger assets and greater selling potential provide the banks with greater security and make it possible for them to provide loans at lower rates of interest than would be charged to the smaller firms. Further, the large firms find it easy to raise funds through the sale of shares or bonds. This source of capital is only available to the large public company, and is only economic when large sums of money are required.

(6) ***Risk-Bearing Economies.*** Large firms are much better equipped to meet the risk of trading than are small firms. The larger the firm, the greater is the share of the total market under its control. A firm which has a large share of the total market is able to judge much accurately than the small firm the shifts which are taking place in the demand for the product and hence is able to adjust its production schedules accordingly. The small firms are not able to face such situation of risk.

The principle of averages operates to the benefit of the large firms. The large firms are able to reduce the risks of trading by means of a policy diversification. The large firms produce a variety of products. All their eggs are not in one basket. This variety of products means that a fall in the demand for anyone of them does not mean serious trouble for them; it may well be offset by a rise in the demand for one of the other products.

Causes of Constant Returns to Scale

The situation of increasing returns to scale cannot go on indefinitely. The firm then enters the phase of constant returns to scale. In other words, a stage comes when a given increase in all the inputs is followed by a proportionate increase in total output. In this situation *internal and external economies* are neutralised by *internal and external diseconomies.*

The situation of constant returns to scale can be brief, before decreasing returns to scale set in. When internal and external economies are more powerful than the internal and external diseconomies, the result is increasing returns to scale. When internal and external economies are exactly balanced with internal and external diseconomies; the result is constant returns to scale. And when the economies are less than the diseconomies, this will lead to diminishing returns to scale.

The concept of constant returns to scale occupies an important place in economics. It introduces a welcome simplification of theoretical analysis. Economists often use the language of mathematics in defining the constant returns to scale. A production function exhibiting constant returns to scale is said to be "linearly homogeneous or "homogeneous of the first degree". The Cobb-Douglas production function, as we have already discussed in the previous chapter, is linearly homogeneous production function of degree one.

Causes of Decreasing Returns to Scale or the Diseconomies of Scale

When a firm continues to increase its size, even beyond the point of constant returns to scale, a stage will come when diminishing returns to scale set in. Increasing size brings many advantages, but it can bring disadvantages too. As a firm expands, it encounters growing diseconomies, which ultimatlely, more than cancel out the economies of large scale production and will cause average costs of production to start rising. Now the question is that why should costs begin to rise? What causes are at work to offset the economies of scale?

Most of the economists hold the view that the diseconomies or diminishing returns to scale occur primarily because of increasing marginal difficulties or the difficulties of co-ordination and control. As the firm continues to expand, the tasks of organisation and co-ordination become more and more difficult. Essentially, management consists of two basic activities, the taking of decisions and seeing that the decisions are carried. In the small firm, the entrepreneur can both decide and supervise. He is able to exercise all the functions of the management. He has to take all the key decisions and does not have to refer matters to anyone else. There is no 'communication problem.' But as the size of the firm grows, it is impossible for one man to carry out all the activities of management. The only solution is to subdivide the duties and responsibilities of control. It becomes necessary to create specialist departments, such as, production control, sales, purchasing, accounts and personnel departments. Now the lines of communication increase. A hierarchy of authority becomes established (managing director, director, head of the department, manager of section and foreman, etc.) and the decision making becomes all the more difficult. The managers, with whom the power to take decisions lies, are not very close to the actual level of production and must inevitably depend upon others for information. Thus, the reports move from the lowest level to the top and decisions are conveyed from the top to the levels below. This leads to unnecessary delays and untimely decisions. Efficiency suffers unavoidably. Hence, the economies of large scale production are swamped by the diseconomies of large scale management and that ultimately leads to decreasing returns to scale.

To put it differently, we may say that decreasing returns to scale will become operative when management becomes a problem. It is generally recognised that the problems of management are particularly serious agriculture. Uncertainties over which man has hardly any control make it difficult for an agricultural undertaking being managed and run on a large scale. But in manufacturing industries scientific techniques of management can be more easily adopted. Many of the managerial problems are being solved these days with the help of electronic computers. Thus, the problems of management depend upon the nature of the industry. It becomes complicated as the size of the industry expands. But there is no such thing as the law of increasing, constant or decreasing returns to scale. The firms may remain in any of these situations.

EXERCISES

1. What is meant by a production function? What is the difference between short-run and a long-run production function?
2. Explain clearly the concept of production function.
3. Discuss the law of variable proportions and explain the, conditions of its applicability.
4. "As we add more and more of a variable input to a fixed input, the amount of extra products will fall off"—Samuelson. Explain the conditions under which this law operates and discuss if it will also operate with several variable inputs.
5. Show in diagram the three stages of normal total product curve of a factor of production. How does the marginal product behave in each stage and why? Distinguish between increasing returns and increasing returns to scale.
6. Explain the various economies and diseconomies of scale.
7. State and explain the modern version of Law of Diminishing Returns and point out clearly the conditions under which it applies.
8. "As the proportion of one factor in combination of other factors is increased, after a point, the marginal and average product of the factor will diminish." Discuss the statement.
9. State and explain the law of returns to scale.

Multiple Choice Questions

10. (*i*) In general most of the production functions measure:
    (*a*) the productivity of factors of production
    (*b*) the relation between the factors of production
    (*c*) the economies of scale
    (d) the relation between changes in physical inputs and physical outputs [*Ans.* (*d*)]

    (*ii*) Marginal product is
    (*a*) what is produced when all factors of production are employed at optimum efficiency
    (*b*) the extra output obtained from employing an additional unit of a factor
    (*c*) what is left to the entrepreneur after he has paid all his expenses
    (*d*) annual output of the most efficient firm in an industry [*Ans.* (*b*)]

(*iii*) Production is a function of
(*a*) profits (*b*) factors
(c) price (d)costs [*Ans.* (*b*)]

(*iv*) When average product is falling, it is
(*a*) less than the marginal product (*c*) greater than the marginal product
(*b*) equal to the marginal product (*d*) none of the above [*Ans.* (*c*)]

(*v*) When the marginal product is zero, total product is
(*a*) zero (*c*) minimum
(*b*) maximum. (*d*) falling. [*Ans.* (*b*)]

(*vi*) When the average product increases, the marginal product is
(*a*) less than the average product (*c*) more than the average product
(*b*) equal to the average product (*d*) none of the above [*Ans.* (*c*)]

(*vii*) If we have constant returns to stale and we increase the quantity of inputs by 10 per cent, output will
(*a*) increase by 10 per cent
(*b*) decrease by 10 per cent
(*c*) increase by less than 10 per cent
(*d*) decrease by less, than 10 per cent [*Ans.* (*a*)]

(*viii*) The law of diminishing returns depends on the assumption that
(*a*) land is a factor kept constant
(*b*) the state of technical knowledge is unchanged
(*c*) total output is constant
(*d*) average output declines faster than marginal output. [*Ans.* (*b*)]

Chapter 27

LAWS OF RETURNS : ISOQUANT-ISOCOST APPROACH

1. INTRODUCTION

This chapter presents a more general case of a production function with two variable inputs. It is assumed that the two inputs used for producing a good are labour and capital and that they are substituted for each other. The problem facing the firm is that using factor inputs, capital (*K*) and labour (*L*) in such production or in such a ratio that whatever the output produced, the cost outlay made for capital and labour will be as small as possible for that particular output. To put it differently, the firm should use the combination of capital and labour that will produce the greatest amount of product for a given outlay.

The production faced by the firm is very similar to the problem faced by the consumer in maximising satisfaction with a given income. Thus the technique that is being used here is very similar to that indifference curve used in consumption analysis.

2. ISOQUANTS OR ISOPRODUCT CURVES

A production function with two variable inputs can be represented by a family of isoquants. The word "isoquants" simply means equal quantities. They are also known as equal product curves or isoproduct curves. In other words, an isoquant is the firm's counterpart of the consumer's indifference curve. It is defined as the locus or path indicating different combinations of the two input labour (*L*) and capital (*K*) which yield a specified level of output:

Let us take an example. Suppose that a firm can produce a given level of output of a 10 units of a good by employing anyone of the alternative combinations of the two inputs, labour and capital as shown in Table 27.1.

Table 27.1: Isoquant Schedule

Combination	*Units of Labour*		*Units of Capital*	*Total Product (in units)*
I	1*L*	+	20*K*	100
II	2*L*	+	15*K*	100
III	3*L*	+	11*K*	100
IV	4*L*	+	8*K*	100

Table 27.1 indicates that an output of 100 units of a good can be produced either by one unit of labour and 10 units of capital or 2 units of labour and 15 units of capital or by any of the four combinations mentioned in the table. All combinations are equally likely because all of them produce the same level of output. Now, if we plot these combinations on a diagram and join the points of various combinations of *L* and *K,* we can get a curve. This curve is known as an isoquant. In Fig. 27.1, we measure the units of labour along the horizontal axis and the units of capital along the vertical axis. The four combinations are shown as *a, b, c,* and *d.* After joining these points, we get the iso-product *Iq.* Here, we assume that technical production conditions are constant. Thus, an isoquant shows various combinations of the two inputs in the existing state of technology which produce the same level of output.

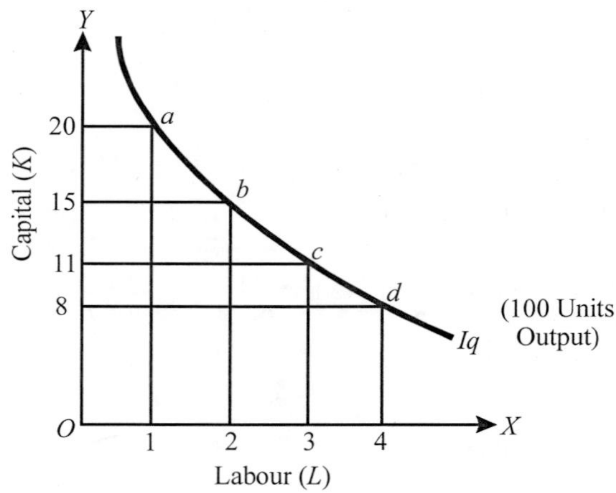

Fig. 27.1

Isoquants *vs.* Indifference Curves

The isoquant or the equal product curve *Iq* in Fig. 27.1 is similar to an indifference curve. It shows all those combinations of factor inputs which yield a given quantity of product, just as an indifference curve shows all those combinations of goods which provide a given level of satisfaction. Thus, the equal product curve is also known as the producer's indifference curve. However, there are some important differences between equal product and indifference curves, which we must note:

(1) An indifference curve indicates a level of satisfaction which cannot be measured in physical units. While an equal product curve measures output in physical units.

(2) We may very well say that a higher indifference curve will yield more satisfaction than a lower indifference curve, but we are unable to say that how much satisfaction is greater (lower) on a higher (lower) indifference curve. But in the case of equal product curves, it is easy to say by how much production is greater or less on one equal product curve than on another.

(3) Since satisfaction on indifference curves is not measured in physical units, we have to label them with such non-committal numbers as IC_1, C_2, IC_3, etc. While we can label equal product curves in units of output.

Equal Product Map or Isoquant Map

Figure 27.2 shows a family of isoqiuants which is generally known as an isoquant 'map'. Each isoquant in this map indicates a different level of output. The distance of an isoquant from the origin depicts the relative level of output. The farther the isoquant from the origin the greater will be the level of output along it. It may be noted, however, that the distance between two equal product curves does not measure the absolute difference in the volume of output. For example, the second isoquant (Iq_2) in Fig. 27.2 indicates that output is 200 units—100 units greater than on the first isoquant (Iq_1). Similarly, the third isoquant (Iq_3) represents an output 100 units greater than on the second isoquant 300 units instead of 200 units and so on.

The reason behind it is that as we go further from the origin more units of *L* and *K* (or at least more of one of them) are used; and therefore, the output on a higher isoquant will be greater than that on a lower isoquant.

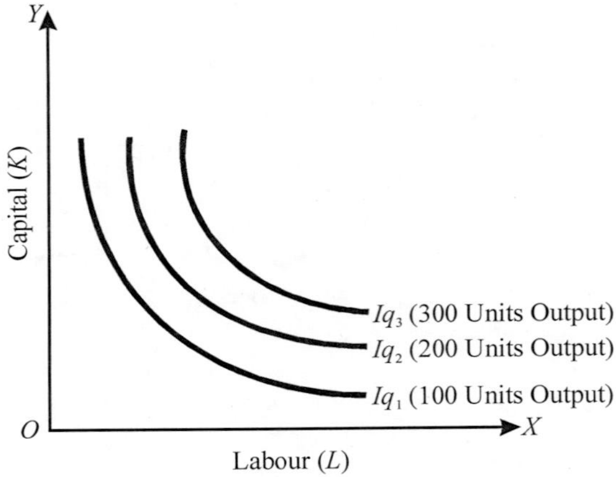

Fig. 27.2

Properties of Equal Product Curves

The following are the important properties or characteristics of isoquants:

(1) ***The slope of an isoquant is negative.*** Like indifference curves, the slope of isoquants is always negative. The reasons are the same. If the isoquant does not possess a negative slope, then the other probable

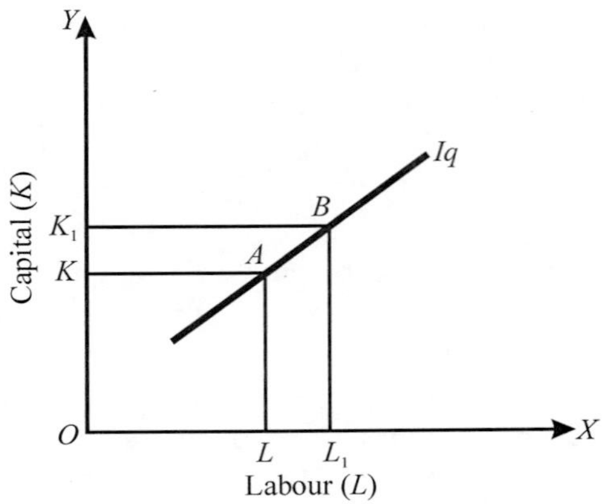

Fig. 27.3

shapes may be positively sloped, horizontal or vertical. If the isoquant slopes upward, it explains that a given level of output can be produced with less or more of both the factors of production. Under the assumption of constant technology and rationality in the behaviour of a producer such a situation seems to be highly implausible. Output cannot be the same when more or less of both the factor inputs are used. This situation has been shown in Fig. 27.3. The diagram shows that the amount of capital and labour used at point *A* is less than the amount of capital and labour used at point *B* and, therefore, the two points *A* and *B* will not yield the same level of output. In other words, the output at point *B* will be more than the output at point *A*. Thus the isoquant will never slope upward.

Likewise, it can be demonstrated that a horizontal or a vertical isoquant is also inconceivable as it would indicate that output remains constant despite an increase (or decrease) in the application of one input. Fig. 27.4 indicates that if we go from point *A* to point *B* on the same isoquant then we are increasing the amount of labour while he amount of capital remains the same; the resulting output must increase. According to the definition of an isoquant they must produce the same level of output and, therefore, isoquants cannot be horizontal.

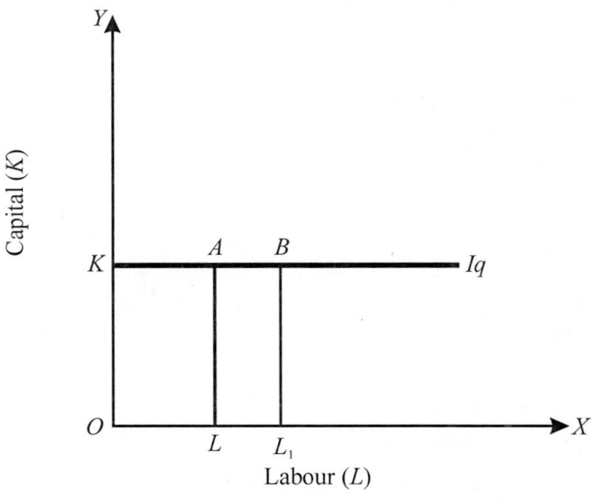

Fig. 27.4

In Fig. 27.5, we show a case when the isoquant is vertical. Here, the quantity of labour is fixed while the quantity of capital may change to any extent but the output remains the same. This would not be the situation, because as we move from point *A* to point *B*, the quantity of capital input increases with the same quantity of labour and, therefore, output must increase.

Thus isoquants cannot lie vertical.

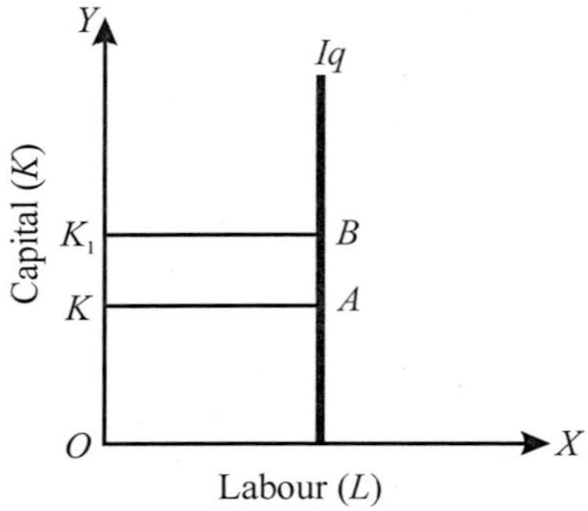

Fig. 27.5

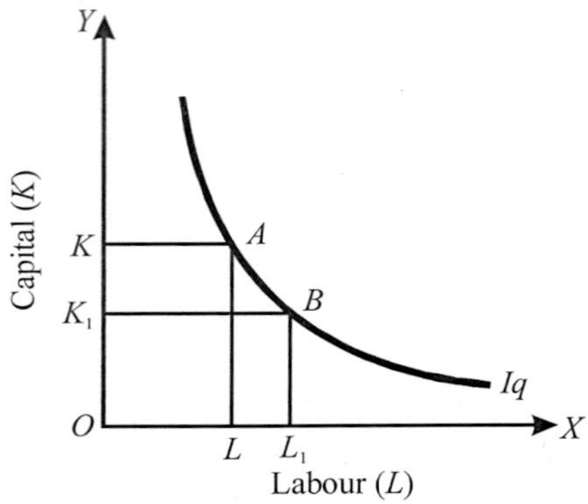

Fig. 27.6

Now, we have proved that the isoquant can neither slope upwards to the right nor it can be horizontal or vertical. It is, therefore, clear that they must slope downwards to the right. This is so because as the firm employs more units of labour, it has to give up some units of capital as the total outlay to be spent on two inputs is constant. A negatively sloping isoquant indicates all combinations of the two factors, labour and capital which will yield the same level of output. This has been shown in Fig. 27.6. At point *A,* the firm employs *OL* units of labour and *OK* units of capital to produce a certain level of output which can also be produced by OK_1 units of capital and OL_1 units of labour at point *B.* This means that as we increase the units of labour, we decrease the employment of capital. At both the points the output remains the same.

The shape of the isoquants displays the substitutability of the two inputs. If the inputs are perfect substitutes, the isoquants would be straight lines. If they are good substitutes, the isoquants are slightly convex, as in Fig. 27.6. If the inputs are poor substitutes, the isoquants would be highly convex. If the inputs can be used only In a fixed ratio, then the isoquants are right angles.[1]

1. Sometimes equal product curves 'are drawn so as to be bent around like hairpins. Toward the *Y*-axis, such isoquants curl up and away from the axis; and at the other end, they curl up and away from the *X*-axis.

(2) ***Isoquants need not be parallel to each*** **other.** 1t so happens because the rate of substitution in different. isoquant schedules need not be necessarily equal. Usually they are found different and, therefore, isoquants may not be parallel as shown in Fig. 27.7. We may note that the isoquants Iq_1 and Iq_2 are parallel but the isoquants Iq_3 and Iq_4 are not parallel to each other.

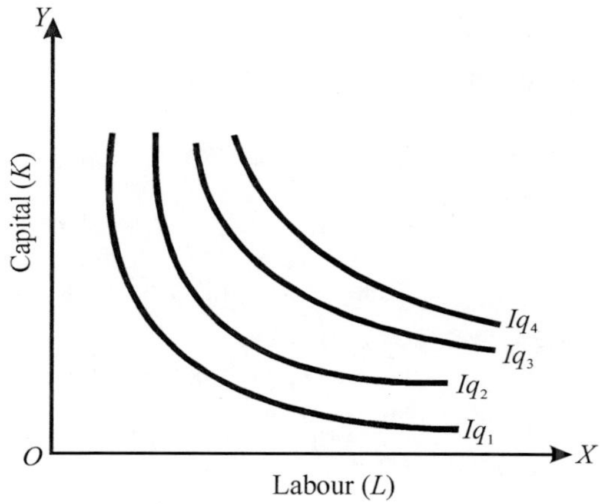

Fig. 27.7

(3) ***Isoquants never cut each other.*** Like indifference curves, isoquants can never cut each other. If they did, there would be a logical contradiction. This can be illustrated with the help of a diagram as in Fig. 27.8.

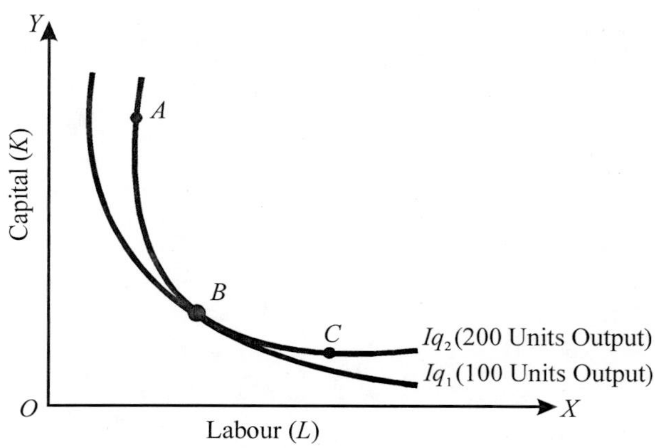

Fig. 27.7

Figure 27.8 indicates that isoquant Iq_1 cuts isoquant Iq_2 at point *B*. Now by definition we may write the following results:

On Iq_1 we have $A = B$

On Iq_2 we have $B = C$

Therefore, $A = C$

But *A* lies on a lower isoquant Iq_1 while C lies on a higher isoquant Iq_2. Thus combination *C* must yield a greater level of output (200 units) than the combination *A* yields (100 units of output). Thus by the definition of an isoquant *A* cannot be equal to *C* and, therefore, the two isoquants will never cut each other.

(4) ***Isoquants are convex to the origin.*** Like indifference curves, isoquaitts are convex to the origin. To prove' this property we have to understand the concept of diminishing marginal rate of technical substitution (*MRTS*), because convexity of an isoquant implies that the *MRPT* diminishes along the isoquant. The marginal rate of technical substitution between *Land K* is defined as the quantity of *K* which can be given up in exchange for an additional unit of *L*. It can also be defined as the slope of an isoquant. Symbolically,

$$MRPT_{LK} = \frac{\Delta K}{\Delta L} \quad \text{... (1)}$$

where ΔK is the change in capital and ΔL is the change in labour.

Equation (1) states that for an increase in the use of labour, fewer units of capital will be used. In other words, a declining *MRPT* refers to the falling marginal product of labour in relation to capital. To put it differently, as more units of labour are used, and as certain units of capital are given up, the marginal productivity of labour in relation to capital will decline.

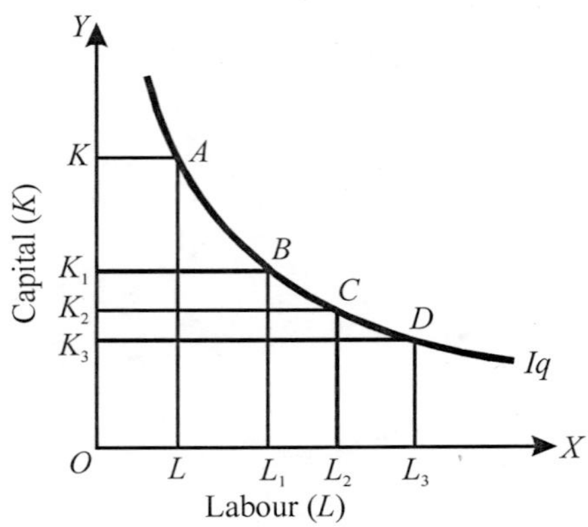

Fig. 27.9

This fact can also be illustrated in Fig. 27.9. As we move from point *A* to *B,* from *B* to *C* and from C to *D* along an isoquant, the marginal rate of technical substitution (*MRTS*) of capital for labour diminishes. Every time we are increasing labour units by an equal amount (ΔL) but the corresponding decrease in the units of capital (ΔK) decreases.

Thus it may be observed that due to falling *MRTS,* the isoquant is. Always convex to the origin.

(5) ***No isoquant can touch either axis.*** If an isoquant touches *X*-axis then it would mean that without using any capital the firm can produce output with the help of labour alone. But this is wrong because the firm can produce nothing with the *OL* units of labour alone. Similarly, without the use of labour the *OK* units of capital can produce nothing. Thus, the isoquants as shown in Fig. 27.10 will never exist in real life.

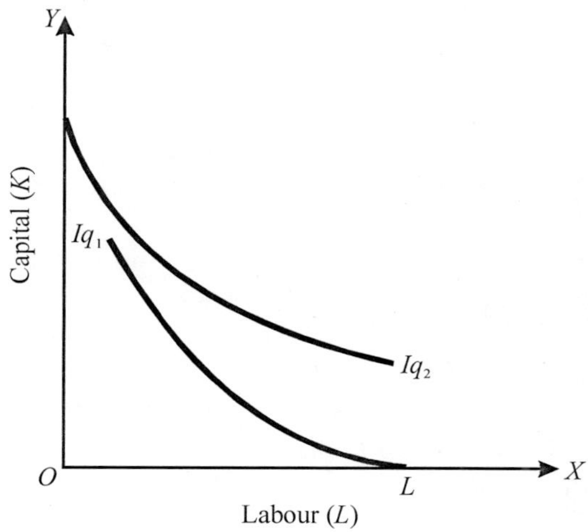

Fig. 27.10

(6) ***Each isoquant* is *oval-shaped.*** (Construction of Ridge Lines and Economic Region of Production). It is elliptical which means that at some point it bends backward with positively sloped segments at both the ends. It indicates the fact that if the producer goes on employing more of capital or labour or both, a point will come when total product will decrease. Thus, the firm will continue production only to that part of isoquants which is convex to the origin and which lies between the ridge lines. The area between the ridge lines is known as the economic region of production. This fact has been explained in Fig. 27.11.

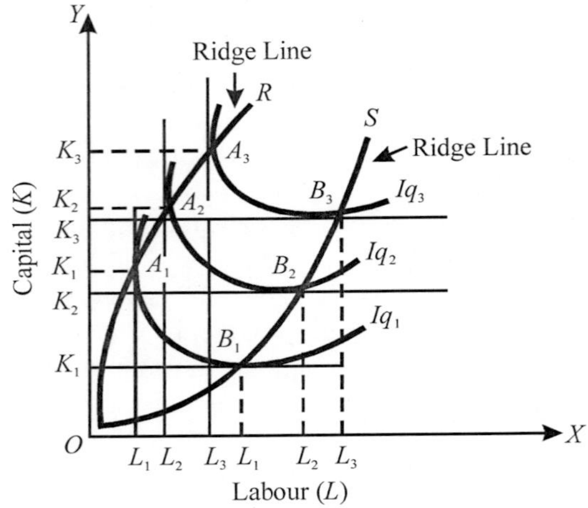

Fig. 27.11

Fig. 27.11 shows a family of three isoquants Iq_1, Iq_2 *and* Iq_3. All of the them bend back upon themselves with positively sloped segments at both ends. Iq_1 assumes a positive slope at points A_1 and B_1. Similarly, Iq_2 assumes a positive slope at point A_2 and B_2; and Iq_3 assumes a positive slope at points A_3 and B_3 respectively. At point A_1 the firm is using OK_1 units of capital and at this level of output (Iq_1) the minimum amount of labour to be used is OL_1. Also, OK_1, will be the maximum amount of capital which a rational producer can use in order to produce a level of output represented by Iq_1. We may note that at point A_1 the slope of the isoquant (Iq_1) is infinite.

It means that at point A_1, the marginal product of capital is zero. If more capital is used beyond OK_1 then the marginal product of capital will become negative.

Thus the part of isoquimt Iq_1 beyond point A_1 will not be economic for the firm. Similarly, for the output levels shown by Iq_2 and Iq_3 points A_2 and A_3 represent the intensive margins for capital input. Beyond these points, the use of capital will not be economic. Now, if we join these points A_1, A_2 and A_3, then the resulting curve is known as *Ridge Line.* It represents the boundary line for the economic region of production. In other words, beyond this ridge line *OR,* the marginal product of capital is negative and no rational firm would use capital input in this range. It may also be seen in Fig. 27.11, that beyond the ridge line *OR,* the isoquants bend back upon themselves and assume a positive slope.

Similarly, we may draw another ridge line *OS* which is the locus or path of all intensive margins for labour input. Beyond this ridge line *OS,* the marginal product of labour is negative and no rational firm would use labour input. It in this range. For example, the maximum amount of labour used to produce a level of output re-presented by Iq_1 is OL_1. At point B_1 the slope of the isoquants Iq_1 becomes zero. Now, the use of labour beyond this point B_1 will not be economic in the sense that the marginal product of labour will become negative.

Similarly, points B_2 and B_3 represent the intensive margins for labour input for producing the levels of output (x) represented by Iq_2 and Iq_3 respectively. Now if we join the points B_1, B_2 and B_3 then the resulting line *as* is another ridge line. It indicates all the points of intensive margins for labour. Beyond this ridge line os, the isoquants bend back on themselves. In other words, beyond this line, the marginal productivity of labour becomes negative.

Thus the area between the two ridge lines *OR* and *OS* represents the economic region of production. The area beyond these ridge lines is the area of uneconomic production.

3. THE PRINCIPLE OF DIMINISHING MARGINAL RATE OF TECHNICAL SUBSTITUTION (MRTS)

As we have already explained that the downward slope of isoquants from left to right stems from the technical substitutability of factor inputs for one another, that is, upon the ability of one input to substitute for the, other in the productive process. Generally, the combinations of factor inputs necessary to produce a given amount of product can be changed by substituting quantities of one input for another. Labour can be substituted for capital and vice versa. When factor inputs are technical substitutes, if less of one is used, more of the other must be used to compensate for its loss if total product is to remain constant. Now, the rate at which one factor input can be substituted for another keeping the total output constant is termed as the marginal rate of technical substitution or *MRTS*.

But we should remember the fact that while different factor inputs may be technical substitutes for each other, they are not perfect substitutes. Within limits they can be substituted for each other. For example, consider two factor inputs, labour and capital which are used to produce output *X*.

Now the more labour and less capital used to produce the same output X, the more difficult it becomes to substitute additional units of labour for capital. This is called the principle of diminishing marginal rate of technical substitution of labour for capita. In other words, the principle indicates the marginal significance of one factor input (*L*) in terms of another factor input (*K*). Table 27.2 illustrates this concept.

Table 27.2

Factor-Input Combinations	*Units of Labour*		*Units of Capital*		*Units of Output*	*MRTS of Labour for Capital*
A	1*L*	+	10*K*	=	100	—
B	9*L*	+	7*K*	=	100	1 : 3
C	3*L*	+	5*K*	=	100	1 : 2
D	4*L*	+	4*K*	=	100	1 : 1

In Table 27.2, we have indicated four situations *A, B,* C, and *D* which produce the same quantity of output, i.e., 100 units. They are all iso-product combinations of two factor inputs, labour and capital. In the initial situation, *A,* one unit of labour and ten units of capital are being used to produce 100 units of output. Now, if the output is to be kept constant while one unit of labour is added to the factor combination already being used, a certain quantity of capital must be dispensed with. Otherwise the total output would increase. Thus combination *B* indicates that 3 units of capital are to be given up for one additional unit of labour. In this situation, the marginal significance of labour in terms of capital or the marginal rate of technical substitution between labour and capital would be 1*L* = 3*K.* If, further, one more unit of labour is used, then the producer cannot give up 3 units of capital to produce the same level of output, because the marginal significance of labour for capital has reduced. In other words, the more the units of labour are used, the lesser will be the marginal productivity of labour and the smaller the amount of capital used, the higher will be its marginal productivity. Thus, in the new situation of combination *C*, the producer gives up the use of only two units of capital for one unit of labour. It means that *MRTS* between labour and capital now is 1*L* = 2*K.* Similarly, in the fourth situation of combination *D,* it becomes 1*L* = 1*K.* It follows that the *MRTS* is diminishing.

The concept of *MRTS* can also be explained with the help of a diagram as in Fig. 27.12. Here, as the firm moves from point *A* to *D* along the isoquant *Iq,* the quantity of capital used decreases while the quantity of labour used increases. The increase in the quantity of labour is the same at each time but the corresponding decrease in the quantity of capital diminishes. For instance, if the firm moves from *A* to *B*, she employs one more unit of labour, but she has to reduce 3 units of capital. At point *C*, a further increase in the quantity of labour by one unit is accompanied by a reduction in the quantity of capital to the extent of two units. It is, thus, evident that every additional unit of labour is being substituted for a diminishing quantity of capital.

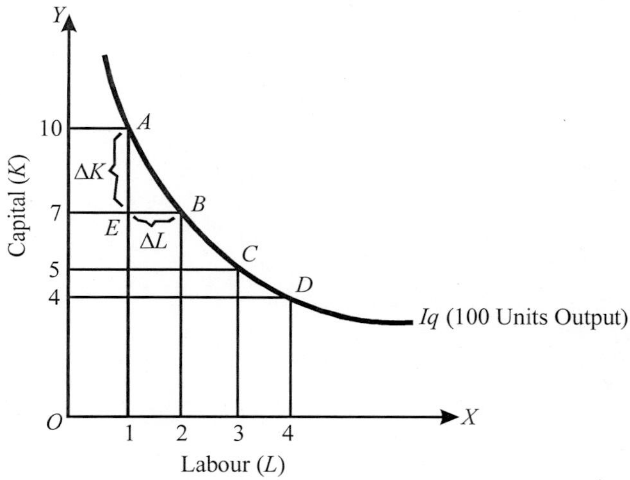

Fig. 27.12

To put it differently, the marginal rate of technical substitution (*MRTS*) of labour for capital is measured at any point on an isoquant by the slope of the isoquant at that point. It is the loss of certain units of capital which will just be compensated for by additional units of labour at that point. Thus

$$MRTS = \text{Slope of Isoquant}$$

$$= \frac{\Delta K}{\Delta L}$$

In Fig. 27.12, the marginal rate of technical substitution at point *B* on isoquant *Iq* can be written as,

$$MRTS = \frac{\Delta K}{\Delta L}$$

$$= \frac{AE}{EB}$$

where AE are the units or capital that the firm gives up for EB units of labour.

The marginal rate of technical substitution of labour for capital can also be thought of as the ratio of marginal physical product of labour to the marginal physical product of capital. Thus

$$MRTS_{LK} = \frac{MPP_L}{MPP_K}$$

or $$MRTS_{LK} = \frac{\Delta K}{\Delta L} = \frac{MPP_L}{MPP_K}$$

or $$\Delta K \times MPP_K = \Delta L \times MRTS_L$$

where $$\Delta L \times MPP_K = \text{Loss in output}$$

$$\Delta L \times MPP_L = \text{Gains in output}$$

$$\text{Since Loss in output} = \text{Gains in output}$$

$$\therefore \quad \frac{\Delta K}{\Delta C} = \frac{MPP_L}{MPP_K}$$

i.e., $$MRTS_{LK} = \frac{MPP_L}{MPP_L} \quad ...(2)$$

Limitations of the Concept of Diminishing Marginal Rate of Technical Substitution

There are two important limitations (exceptions) to the principle of diminishing *MRTS*: (1) When the substitutability between labour and capital is not at all possible, and (2) When they are perfect substitute of each other.

(1) ***Use of factor inputs in fixed proportions.*** When the two factor inputs labour and capital are complements, then the *MRTS* between them will not diminish. Figure 27.13 indicates that labour and capital are used in fixed proportions. At point *A,* 5 units of capital and 1 unit of labour will be employed to produce 100 units of output. If the firm wants to double the output then she has to double the employment of both labour and capital. This means that at point *B,* the firm produces 200 units with the help of 10 units of capital and 2 units of labour. Here the isoquants will take the shape of the English letter '*L*' where a proportionate increase

in both the inputs is required to make an increase in the total output. In such a case, the factor inputs are complementary and they cannot at all be substituted. The vertical portion of the isoquants indicates that the rate substitutability of labour for capital is zero, because the isoquants have no slope; while the horizontal part of the isoquants indicates an infinite marginal rate of technical substitutability.

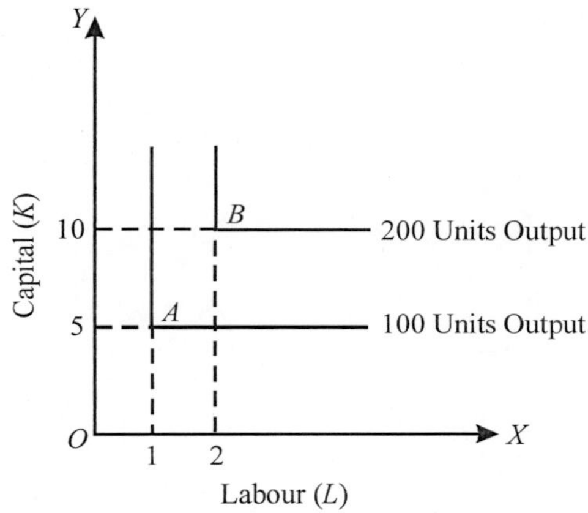

Fig. 27.13

(2) ***Factor inputs are perfect substitutes.*** Figure 27.14 indicates a situation when the two factor inputs labour and capital are perfect substitutes. The two isoquants Iq_1 and Iq_2 represent 100 units and 200 units of output respectively. On Iq_1 100 units of output can be produced either by 10 units of capital and zero unit of labour or by 10 units of labour and zero unit of capital. Similarly, Iq_2 indicates that 200 units of output can either be produced by 20 units of capital and zero unit of labour or by 20 units of labour and zero unit of capital. Thus, at all points of the isoquants the *MRTS* of labour for capital is constant (which is neither zero nor infinite). This situation is not a real situation because labour and capital are not the same factor inputs and thus they cannot be perfect substitutes.

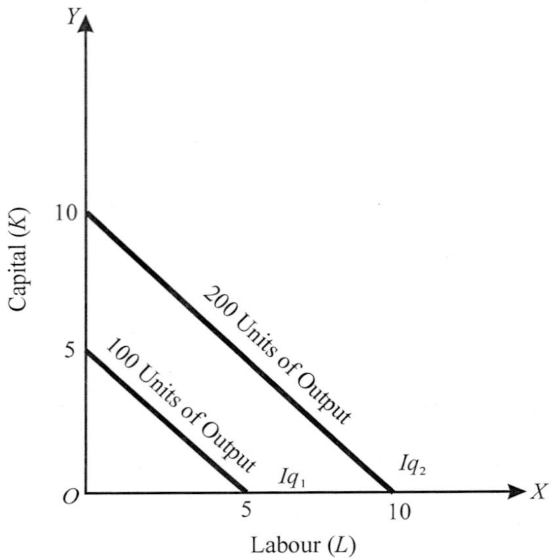

Fig. 27.14

Optimum Combination of Inputs

The economic objective of the firm can be specified as the maximisation of output from the given cost outlay too be spent on labour and capital, or the minimisation of the cost of producing a given level of output. The graphical solution of this problem is very similar to the indifference curve solution to that of an individual consumer who maximises the satisfaction from his limited income. The theory of isoquants enables the producer to choose a input combination which produces maximum output at the minimum cost. This input combination is known as optimum input-combination.

A firm's equilibrium will be attained at a point where the isoquant touches the isocost line. We have already explained the isoquant map and now we need to explain the isocost line.

The isocost line is the counterpart of the budget line or price line. It show all the combinations of the two inputs, labour and capital that the firm can purchase with a given total outlay and at given input prices. To make it more clear let us take an example. In Fig. 27.15, we assume that the price of capital is twice the price of abour. The price of capital is Rs. 10 pet unit and the price of abour is Rs. 5 per unit. Now the line *MN* is an isocost line, representing a constant expenditure of Rs. 1,000 on various combinations of the two inputs, labour and capital. In other words, the firm can purchase either 100 units of capital and zero unit of Iabour or 200 units of labour and zero unit of capital or any combination of the two inputs in between these extremes as shown by the *MN* isocost line. The isocost line will shift to the right if the firm's total outlay increases while the input prices remaining the same. Thus the isocost lines of Fig. 27. 15 refer to the costs of production inputs purchased on the market. So long as we assume that the market prices of factors (inputs) of production are unaffected by the amounts of the inputs that are purchased by the particular firm, the expenditure (outlay) incurred by the firm in purchasing different combinations of the two inputs can be represented graphically by a straight line (like *MN* in Fig. 27.15), the slope of the line being determined by the relative prices of the two factor-inputs. The isocost line M_1N_1 in Fig. 27.15 represents a constant total outlay (expenditure) of Rs. 1,500 on the combination of the two factor inputs, labour and capital, purchased on the market, and the isocost line M_2N_2 an expenditure of Rs. 2,000. All the three isocost lines *MN*, M_1N_1 and M_2N_2 in Fig. 27.15 are parallel to each other which indicate the fact that prices of labour and capital remain the same despite a successive increase in the firm's total outlay to be spent on labour and capital.

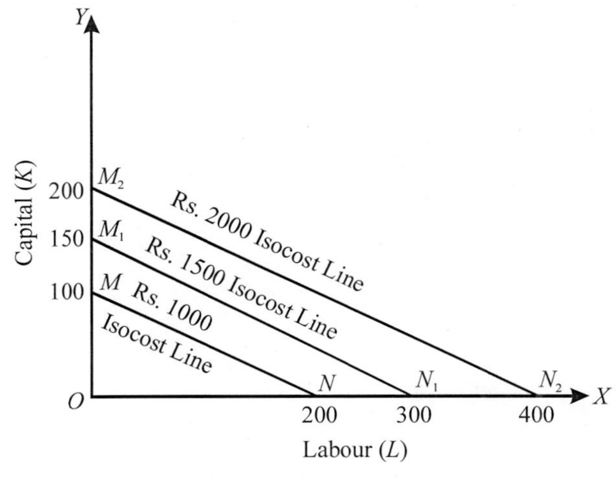

Fig. 27.15

Now we may solve the problem of the firm. The problem faced by the firm is that of getting on the highest possible isoquant that its given isocost curve will allow. To put it differently, it is that of getting the highest amount of output from the given cost outlay. This has been illustrated in Fig. 27.16.

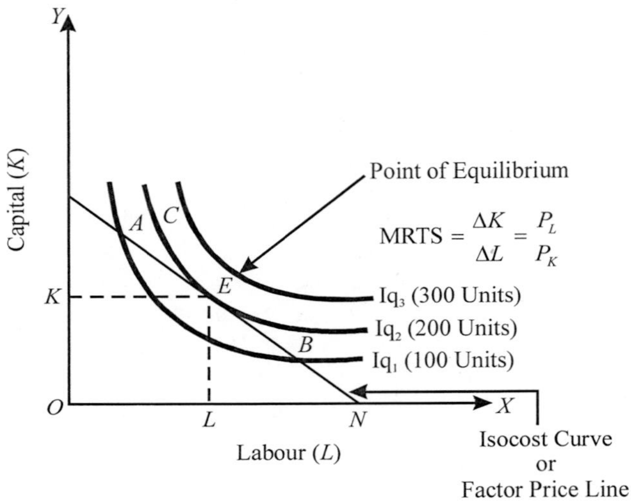

Fig. 27.16

Suppose the firm's isocost line is *MN*. The curves Iq_1, Iq_2 and Iq_3 are the lines of equal physical product or isoproduct lines (isoquants); Iq_2 referring to a greater quantity of output (200 units) than Iq_1 (100 units), and Iq_3 to a still greater quantity (300 units). In other words,

$$Iq_3 > Iq_2 > Iq_1$$

Since the isocost line *MN* reaches to its highest iso-product curve at point *E,* where it is tangential to the iso-product curve Iq_2, the position *E* indicates the best combination of labour and capital. The firm will get maximum output (200 units) when it buys *OL* units of labour and *OK* units of capital.

Here, we should also note that the points *A* and *B* cannot be the equilibrium points although they satisfy the condition that the slope of isoquant equals the slope of isocost curve or factor price line and they also lie within the approach of the firm. But the fact is that at these points the firm remains at a lower isoquant Iq_1 which yields a lesser amount of product than that on Iq_2. Thus the optimum factor combination will be attained at point *E*.

Also point *C* lies on Iq_2 and that yields the same units of output as point *E*, but to reach point *C* the firm has to incur more expenditure and that lies outside his constraint line *MN*. Thus the only point which can be the equilibrium point is the point *E* where the isoquant Iq_2 touches the isocost curve *MN*.

The equilibrium position of the firm can also be explained in terms of the equality between *MRTS* arid the factor price ratio. As we have already explained the slope of an isoquant indicates the marginal rate of technical substitution (*MRTS*) and the slope of the isocost line indicates the factor price ratio. The optimum input combination will be indicated by the point where the slopes of the two curves coincide with each other; or

$$MRTS = \frac{P_L}{P_K}$$

$$\text{But } MRTS = \text{Slope of Isoquant} = \frac{\Delta K}{\Delta L} = \frac{MPP_L}{MPP_K}$$

$$\text{Thus } \frac{P_L}{P_K} = \frac{MPP_L}{MPP_K} \qquad \ldots (3)$$

where MPP_1 is the marginal physical product of labour and MPP_K is the marginal physical product of capital.

Changes in Outlay and Expansion Path

Until now, while determining the equilibrium point, we have assumed firm's resources or total outlay to be constant. But if there is a change in its total outlay, the firm has to establish a new equilibrium point. The firm may produce a higher level of output if the total outlay has increased (assuming input prices to be constant). Since the marginal productivities of factor input are always not constant and not equal, change in outlay may reflect in varying degree of change in the use of different inputs.

The isocost line or the factor price lines will make a parallel shift following every change in the cost outlay, as the ratio of input prices has been assumed to be constant. As cost outlay increases, the firm would be able to purchase more of labour and more of capital. Figure 27.17 indicates a family of three isocost lines *MN*, M_1N_1 and M_2N_2. Now every increase in cost outlay will enable the firm to raise the level of employment of both the inputs and thus produce higher levels of output. The equilibrium points of input combinations will be E, E_1 and E_2. If we join these equilibrium points with the help of a curve, then this curve is known as the *expansion path* of a firm. Hence, an expansion path indicates different points of least cost combinations of labour and capital required to produce different levels of out- put. In other words, the expansion path curve (or scale line) shows the various *input-optima* as the firm expands the size of the output.

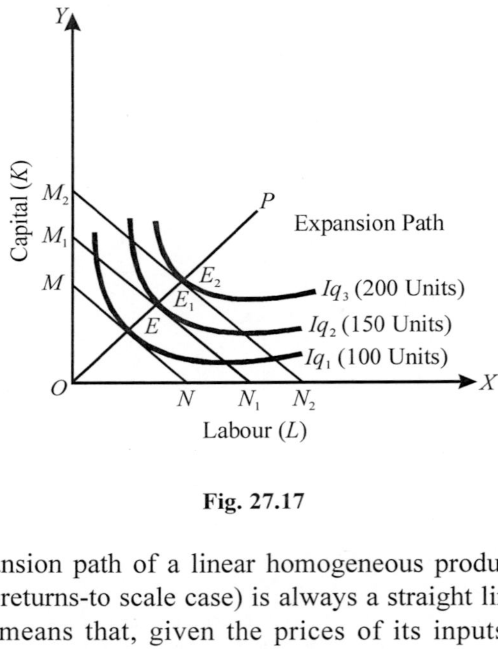

Fig. 27.17

The expansion path of a linear homogeneous production function (the constant-returns-to scale case) is always a straight line through the origin. This means that, given the prices of its inputs, the optimal proportion of the inputs of the firm will not change with the size of the firm's input budget (cost outlay). This expansion path which is also known as an *isocline* has been shown in Fig. 27.17. In such a particular case, the businessman does not have further input-proportion decision problems, as long as input prices do not change.

The expansion path of a general production function (where constant returns are absent) will not be a straight line; in that case an increase in the total outlay will be followed by varying proportions of capital and labour. It means that an increase in total cost outlay does not necessarily result in an equivalent increase in the use of both the inputs. In fact, the relative responsiveness of the use of an input will depend ,upon the value of *outlay elasticity* with respect to labour or capital as the case may be. The outlay elasticity will tell us the nature of the input. In the case of normal inputs, the outlay elasticity will be unity ($h = 1$). In the case of superior input, the outlay elasticity will be greater than one ($n > 1$). In case of inferior inputs, the outlay elasticity will be less than unity ($n < 1$).

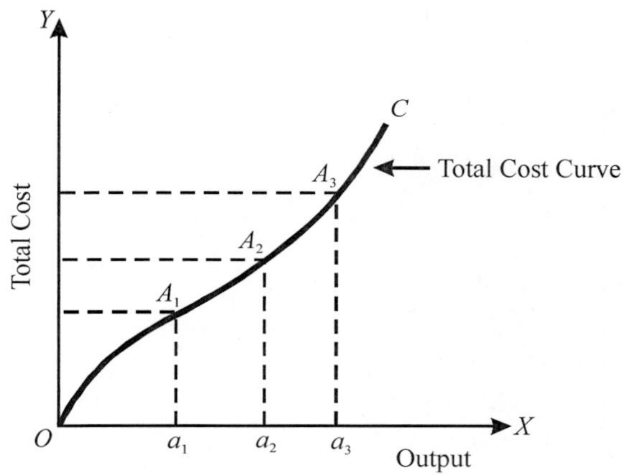

Fig. 27.18

An expansion path may also be termed as the *long-run expenditure curve* of a firm, as it relates various levels of output to different levels of total outlay. Also, from the firm's expansion path it is fairly easy to find the firm's total and average cost curves. As we know the *total cost curve* (*TC*-curve) is defined as a curve which shows how total cost outlays of a firm vary with firm's level of production. The average and marginal cost curves can easily be calculated by the total cost curve. In Fig. 27.17, isocost line *MN* represents a cost outlay *C* and its tangency point (equilibrium point) *E* tells us the maximum output obtainable, i.e., q_1 (100 units). This information is represented by point A_1 in Fig. 27.18. Similarly, point A_2 in Fig. 27.18 tells us that it will cost C_2 to produce output level q_2, and so on.

The curve *OC* in Fig. 27.18 which is the locus of all points like A_1, A_2

and A_3 is the total cost curve of the firm.[2] Once the *TC* curve is obtained, we can also draw the firm's *AC* curve and *MC* curve from its *TC* curve.

Changes in Input Prices

Figure 27.19 analyses the effect of a change in the relative prices of the two factors of production. The line *MN* in this figure is the original isocost curve. On this isocost curve, point *E* is the equilibrium point because the highest possible isoproduct curve Iq_1 touches this curve at this point *E*. It indicates that the firm purchases *OK* units of capital and *OL* units of labour. Now let us suppose that the prices of the two factor inputs labour

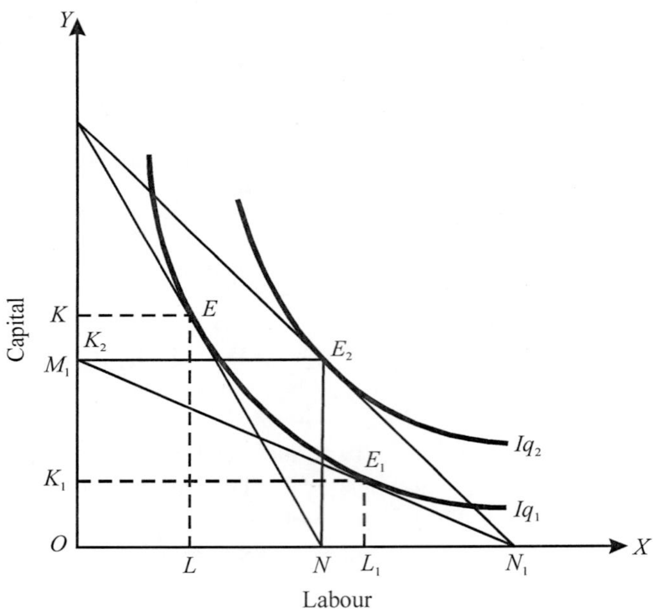

Fig. 27.19

2. Here we must remember that if all the information of points A_1, A_2 and A_3 of Fig. 27.18 has been taken from Fig. 27.17, then our resulting *TC*-curve will be a straight line like *OP* expansion path of Fig. 27.17. But here we have assumed that for all the time constant returns to scale (Linear Homogeneous Production Function) is not prevailing in the production process of the firm. Hence the *TC*-curve will be like that of Fig. 27.18. Likewise, the expansion path of Fig. 27.17 will turn to the shape of TC-curve in Fig. 27.18.

and capital are reversed, so that the price of labour becomes the price of capital and price *of* capital becomes the price of labour. Now the new isocost line M_1N_1 represents the same cost outlay devoted to various combinations of the two inputs. Since in the figure the iso-product lines are symmetrical, the new isocost line M_1N_1 is tangential to the same isoproduct curve as the isocost curve MN, i.e., the isoquant Lq_1; but the point of tangency will be E_1 instead of E. With the new prices, the firm in equilibrium will purchase OK_1 amount of capital and OL_1 amount of labour. It means, as a change in the relative prices of factor inputs, the firm substitutes the cheaper factor input for the dearer, i.e., LL_1 of labour is substituted for KK_1 of capital.

It is quite possible that price of capital remaining the same while the price of labour declines. It means nom the same cost outlay we may get more amount of labour (ON_1) or the same amount of capital (OM). The line MN_1 will be the new isocost line. This line is tangential to its highest isoproduct line at point E_2 on the curve Iq_2. Whereas on isocost line MN the optimum quantity of labour was OL and of capital was OK, the optimum quantities now (at MN_1 isocost curve) become OL_2 of labour and OK_2 of capital. An amount of LL_2 of labour is substituted for KK_2 amount of capital. Also, the new optimum position at point E_2, is on a higher iso-product line, Iq_2, so that total output is increased. Thus, here we find that a lower price for a factor of production gives the producer an advantage that he can get also nom a greater cost outlay.

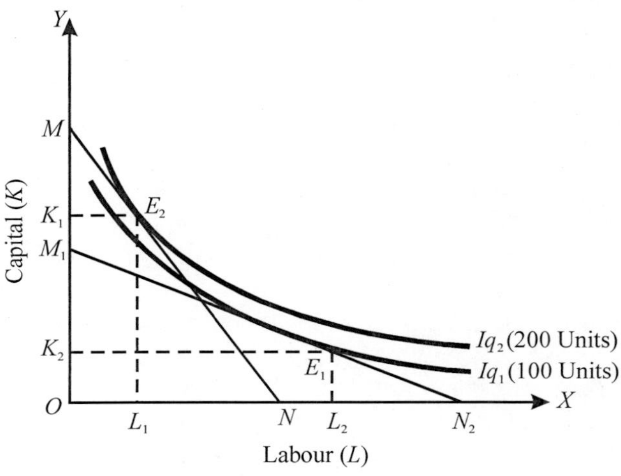

Fig. 27.20

In actual life, it is very unlikely that a set of isocost curves will be symmetrical, as in Figure 27.19. Figure 27.20 illustrates a situation in which the isoproduct curves are asymmetrical. The lines *MN* and M_1N_1 in this figure may be supposed to refer to a constant (or same) expenditure (outlay) on factors *L* and *K*. In spite of the same cost outlay, it will be noticed that *MN* and M_1 N_1 are tangential to different isoproduct lines, *MN* to the higher iso-product line Iq_2 at *E* and M_1N_1 to the lower iso-product line Iq_1 at E_1. The relative change in factor prices causes substitution of the factor input that has become cheaper for that which is relatively dearer; L_1L_2 of labour being substituted for K_1K_2 of capital. Also total production declines, the isoproduct line Iq_2 representing a smaller physical output (100 units) than the iso-quant Iq_2 (200 units).

Output and Substitution Effect of a Fall in the Price of one Input (Labour). We know that a fall in the price of labour will lead to an increase in the quantity of labour used, assuming that it is a normal factor of production. As a fall in the price of labour while the price of capital remain the same, the resulting output will be greater than the previous level. Like a change in the price of a commodity, a change in the price of an input affects the demand for it via the substitution effect and the output (income) effect. Figure 27.21 illustrates the effect of a fall in the price of labour. In Fig. 27.21, the original isocost line or factor price line is *MN*. If the price of labour falls (while price of capital remains constant), then tire factor price line MN_1 will indicate the new price ratio of capital and labour. The original equilibrium position is indicated by point E_1 on isoquant Iq_1, and OL_1 amount of labour is used by the firm. It is also evident that a fall in the price of labour enables the firm to move to a higher isoquant and the new equilibrium position is shown by point E_2 on the higher isoquant Iq_2.The new equilibrium point indicates that the firm uses OL_2 units of labour. A lower price of labour, therefore, has increased the use of labour from OL_1 to OL_2 —i.e., an increase of L_1L_2 units of labour. This may be called *as the price effect* on the use of labour.

This price effect is partly due to the substitution effect—the cheaper input, labour is substituted for relatively costlier input capital—and partly due to output effect, i.e., a greater use of input as more output being used. Thus

Total Price Effect = Substitution Effect + Output Effect.

In Fig. 27.21, the change in labour input resulting exclusively from a given change in the ratio of input prices is shown by L_1L_3. Since labour is now relatively cheaper, the firm uses more labour by reducing the level of capital input from OK_1 to OK_3 in order to produce the same level of output. This is the substitution effect. The factor price line M_1N_2 is parallel to the new isocost line MN_1 and thus reflects the (same) new input price ratio $\left[\frac{OM}{ON_1} = \frac{OM_1}{ON_2}\right]$. However, the firm is capable of employing more units of capital and labour and thus produce a higher level of output (at point E_2). As a result, the firm further increases the use of labour by L_3L_2 and increases the amount of capital from OK_3 to OK_2, and produces a level of output represented by Iq_2 (150 units). This (L_3L_2) is the output effect of a fall in the price of labour.

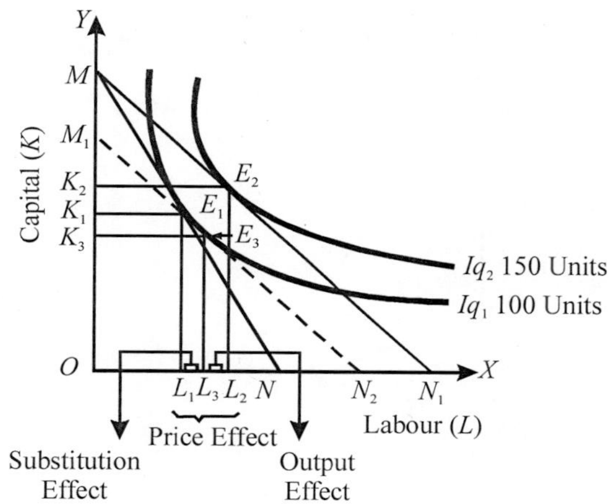

Fig. 27.21

To put it differently, as a fall in the price of labour, the firm increases its level of output from Iq_1 (100 units) to Iq_2 (150 units) by moving from equilibrium point E_1 to a new equilibrium point E_2. However, the movement from E_1 to E_3 is the substitution effect, and from E_3 to E_1 we have the output effect of a change in the ratio of input prices. In a summary form, we have

Total Price Effect = Substitution Effect + Output Effect

or $$L_1L_2 = L_1L_3 + L_3L_2$$

In a similar way we may also demonstrate the price effect, substitution effect and output effect of a rise in the price of labour.

Optimum Combination of Outputs

In the above analysis we have discussed a case of two inputs and one output where the firm's problem was to get the optimum combination of factor inputs. This was achieved by the help of isoquant and isocost lines. Now, we shall discuss the problem that how a firm can maximise its revenue by producing an optimum combination of its outputs. Assume that the firm produces only two outputs *X* and *Y*. It is also assumed that the firm is working with fixed input quantity (fixed resources) within the framework of a given technology.

The production possibility curve shows different points of combinations of outputs *X* and *Y* that the firm can produce with the fixed resources. This curve is also known as production transformation curve. In Fig. 27.22, the production possibility curve *MN* indicates that with the fixed resources, the firm can produce either *OM* quantity of product *Y* and zero quantity of product *X*, or *ON* quantity of product *X* and zero quantity of product *Y*, or any combination between these two extremes, such as *A*, *B*, *C* and *D*.

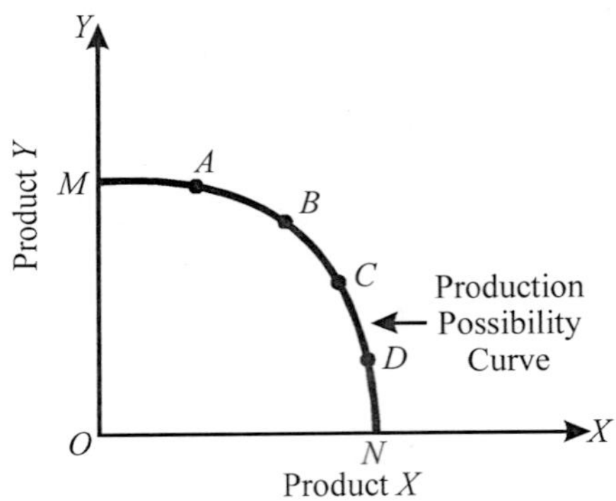

Fig. 27.22

The production possibility curve is concave which indicates that for every additional unit of product *X* produced, the sacrifice of produce *Y* goes on increasing. This curve is also referred to as Product Transformations Curve, because when the firm moves from one point to another on the same curve, it trans-forms one product into another product through the transference of physical resources.

The slope of this curve is termed as marginal rate of product transformation (*MRPT*). *MRPT* is the rate at which one output is transformed into another output assuming the same production resources.

Symbolically, $$\text{MRPT} = \frac{-\Delta Y}{+\Delta X} \qquad \ldots (4)$$

where ΔY is the change in output Y and ΔX is the change in output X.

The production possibility curve is concave to the origin point because of the law of increasing cost. To put it differently, the *MRPT* goes on increasing as the firm produces more of X and less of Y, and this is the increasing *MRPT* that is responsible for the concavity of the curve. The slope of this curve (*MRPT*) is always negative, because to increase the quantity of one output the firm has to sacrifice the production of other output; since the factor-inputs remain the same.

We may also draw a map of production possibility curves according to the level of fixed resources. If the resources of the firm are increased, it is able to produce more of both the product. Figure 27.23 shows the three production possibility curves, MN, M_1N_1, and M_2N_2 which represent successive increments in productive resources of the firm.

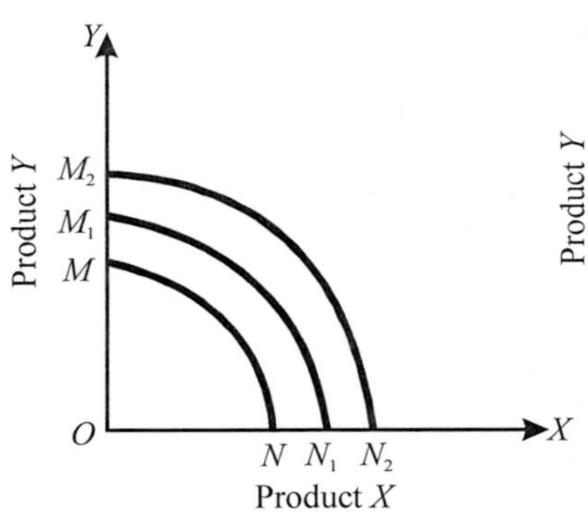

Fig. 27.23

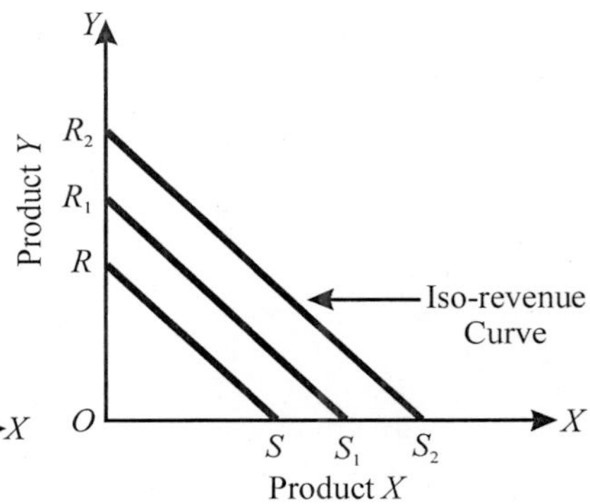

Fig. 27.24

Now, our problem is to find out the optimum combination of products from a number of available combinations such as *A, B, C, D* in Fig. 27.22. It requires a further explanation of the *Iso-revenue curves.* An iso-revenue curve can be defined as a straight line curve indicating different combinations of two outputs X and Y which yield the same amount of revenue to the firm. There may be a series of iso-revenue curves representing different levels of revenues. In Fig. 27.24, we have drawn three iso-revenue curves, RS, R_1S_2 and R_2 S_2 indicating different levels of revenues. The higher the iso-revenue curve, the more will be the revenue and vice versa. The iso-revenue curves are parallel to each other, indicating that the prices of the two products *X* and *Y* are fixed. The slope of the iso-revenue curve indicates the price-ratio. Thus

$$\frac{P_X}{P_Y} = \text{Slope of the iso-revenue curve} \quad \text{... (5)}$$

Now to get equilibrium point of the firm (where she will be able to get maximum revenue), we have to combine the two diagrams of the production possibility curve and the iso-revenue curves.

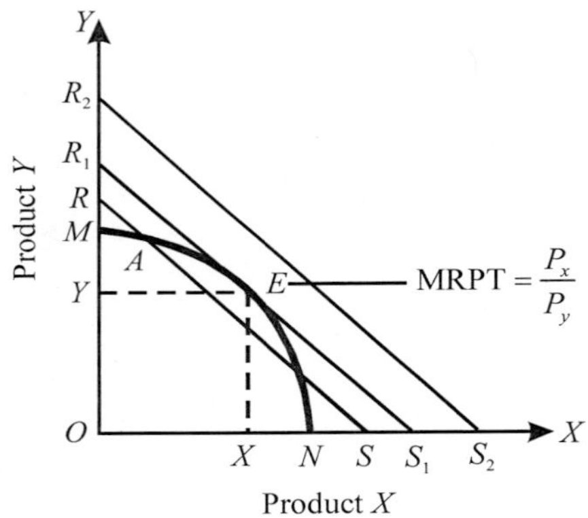

Fig. 27.25

In Fig. 27.25, point *E* is the equilibrium point, because yield the highest possible maximum represented by the iso-revenue curve R_1S_1. At this point *E*, the production possibility curve *MN* touches the iso-revenue line R_1S_1. At the other points on the *PP* curve, say *A* and *B*, the firm will not be able to get maximum revenue because they lie on a lower iso-revenue curve *RS*. Thus, with the given resources, point *E* represents an optimum combination of two outputs *X* and *Y*. Here, the firm produces *OX* amount of *X* and *OY* amount of *Y*. Also, the optimum combination point indicates that the slope of the production possibility curve is equal to the slope of the iso-revenue line, or

$$MRPT = \frac{\Delta Y}{\Delta X} = \frac{P_X}{P_Y} \quad \text{...(6)}$$

Isoquants and Returns to Scale

Before we discuss the use of isoquants, we must understand that under the isoquants we can show the use of only two factors of production while in real situation, there are three or four factors of production. Thus, here we shall confine our discussion to two factors only which can easily be extended to situations with. more than two factor inputs.

We are interested to explain the laws of production and we may look at the problem in two ways. In this section, we shall consider returns to two factors of production where both can vary—returns with two variable factors. In the next section, we shall discuss returns to two factors where one can vary and the other is fixed, i.e., returns with one variable factor (or the law of variable proportions or the law of returns or the law of diminishing returns). Here, our main assumption is that there is perfect competition, i.e., all price lines are straight line curves.

From the isoquants map and the corresponding isocost lines (or factor price lines), we may derive the *scale line.* Here, we shall continue to assume that the firm wishes to produce each output as cheaply as possible. The amounts of factor inputs employed will depend on the relative prices of these factors as well as on the technical conditions shown in Fig. 27.26. In this diagram, we have shown the isoquants map consisting of three isoquants Iq_1 (100 units), Iq_2 (150 units) and Iq_3 (700 units) and the corresponding isocost lines MN, M_1N_1, and M_2N_2. In the existing situation the price of factor input labour divided by the price of factor input capital, i.e., the price ratio is equal to

$$\frac{OM}{ON} = \frac{OM_1}{ON_1} = \frac{OM_2}{ON_2}$$

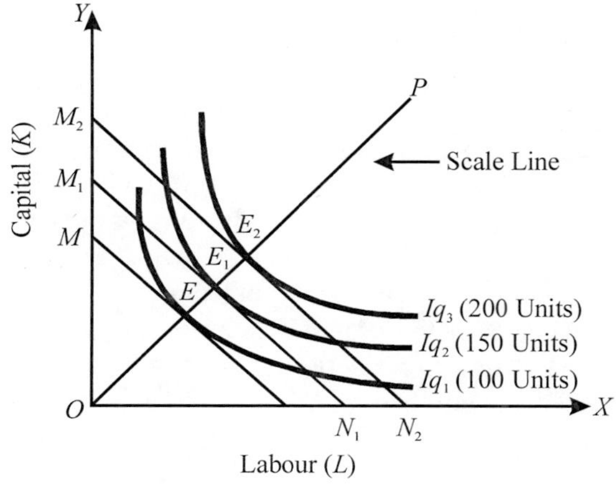

Fig. 27.26

Now, if the firm wishes to, produce 100 units of output, it will be in equilibrium at the point *E* on the isoquant Iq_1 (100 units). At this point *E,* the isocost curve *MN* is tangential to the isoquant Iq_1. Only at point *E,* the firm will be producing the 100 units of output as cheaply as possible. To reach any point other than *E,* on the equal product curve Iq_1 representing 100 units of output, the firm will have to spend more than *ON* in terms of labour or *OM* in terms of capital, for appropriate combinations of factors. Similarly, if the firm wishes to produce 150 units of output, it will be in equilibrium only at point E_1. ON_1 in terms of *L* (labour), or OM_1 in terms of *K* (capital), represents the lowest cost at which 150 units of output can be produced. Likewise, the firm shall be in equilibrium at the point E_2 if it wishes to produce 200 units of output. It will be noted that at all points such as *E,* E_1 and E_2 the marginal significance of labour input in terms of capital input is equal to the relative money prices of the two factors labour and capital, or

$$MRTS_{LK} = \frac{P_L}{P_K} \qquad \text{... (7)}$$

The above condition is shown by the fact that each isoquant is tangential to the relevant price line. If we join the various points of equilibria, such as *E,* E_1 and E_2 we get a curve which is known as the *Scale Line.* In Fig. 27.26, *OP* represents the scale line. It is analogous to the income-consumption curve in the theory of indifference curve analysis. The scale line shows, different amounts of the input produced at the minimum cost of production when the two factor inputs are variable and their relative prices (i.e., price ratio) are fixed. In other words, the scale line shows the way in which the firm adjusts the scale of its operation with given relative factor prices. It shows the cheapest way of producing each output in these circumstances (i.e., given the factor price ratio and the two factors are variable inputs). The scale line is also referred to as the expansion path of the firm. The shape of the scale line will depend both on the relative prices of the factors concerned (i.e., the factor price ratio) and on the shape of the isoquants. Now, having obtained the scale line corresponding to any particular factor price ratio, we can find out whether, as the factors are varied, total output to them increases at an increasing rate, or constant rate or diminishing rate.

(*i*) *Increasing Returns to Scale.* As the factors of production are increased or the scale of production is increased, the returns to outlay will be increasing in the beginning, because as output rises there are economies of scale to be repeated. It is likely, for instance, that where one of the factors is labour, the division of labour will increase output as the number of men employed rises. There are likely to be increasing returns to outlay in some parts of an equal product map, whether or not the scale lines are straight lines. This has been illustrated in Fig. 27.27.

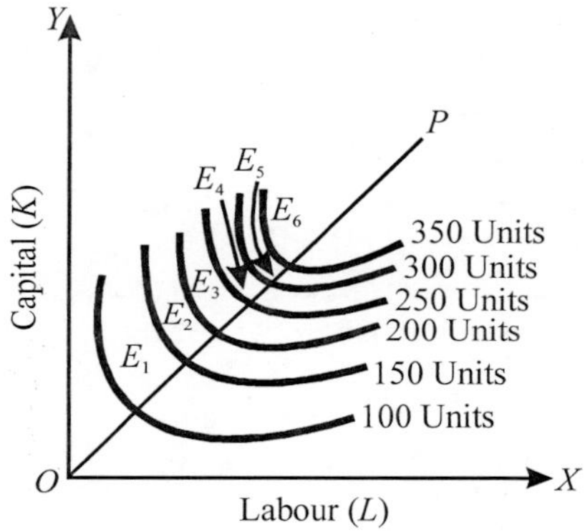

Fig. 27.27

In Fig. 27.27, *OP* is the scale line which is a straight line purely to simplify the construction of the diagram. It indicates how different quantities of output could be produced at the minimum cost with the two factor inputs labour and capital. Along this scale line *OP,* as the output increases, the returns to outlay increase. The increasing returns to outlay are indi-cated by the gradual decrease in the distance between the isoquants.

For example,

$E_1E_2 > E_2E_3 > E_3E_4 > E_4E_5 > E_5E_6$

In other words, for a given increase in output from say 100 units to 150 units or from 150 units to 200 units, etc. cost outlay on capital and labour increases, but the increase in cost outlay is proportionately less than the increase in output. Therefore, Fig. 27.27 represents the situation of increasing returns to scale.

(*ii*) *Constant Returns to Scale.* It is possible sometime that returns to scale are, constant. It implies that when the factors of production are changed in a certain proportion and the output also changes exactly in the same proportion, then the returns to scale are constant. This situation has been shown in Fig. 27.28.

In Figure 27.28, *OP* represents the scale line. It shows the different levels of output represented by various isoquants. The constant returns to, outlay are indicated by the equal distances between the isoquants. In other words, if output is doubled from 100 units to 200 units then the quantity of factor inputs is to be doubled. This means,

$$OE_1 = E_1E_2 = E_2E_3 = E_3E_4$$

Thus, Fig. 27.28 illustrates the situation of constant returns to scale.

(*iii*) *Diminishing Returns to Scale.* We know that as the factors of production are increased, the returns to scale may be increasing in the first instance, but ultimately it will have to decrease. In the situation of diminishing returns to scale, the economies of scale which are responsible for increasing returns to scale will give place to diseconomies of scale. Diminishing returns to scale implies that for a given increase in output, a larger increase in quantities of factors of production is required. In other words, the proportionate increase in factor inputs will be more than the proportionate increase in output. This has been illustrated in Fig. 27.29.

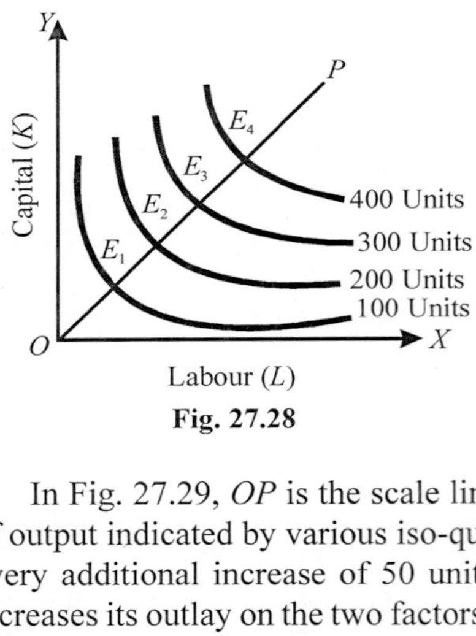

Fig. 27.28

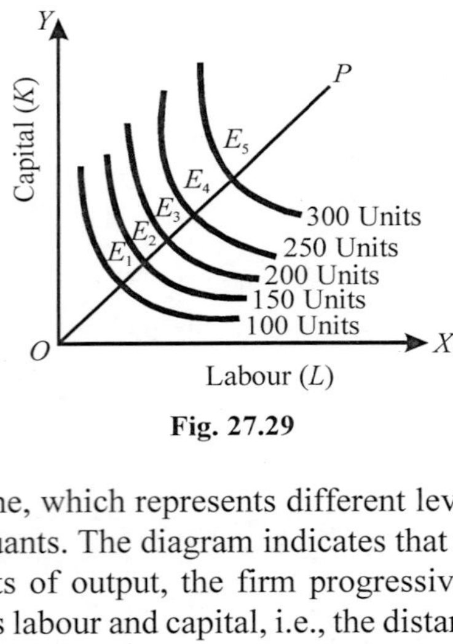

Fig. 27.29

In Fig. 27.29, *OP* is the scale line, which represents different levels of output indicated by various iso-quants. The diagram indicates that for every additional increase of 50 units of output, the firm progressively increases its outlay on the two factors labour and capital, i.e., the distance between the isoquants increases as the firm produces higher levels of output. This means,

$$E_1E_2 < E_2E_3 < E_3E_4 > E_4E_5$$

Thus, Figure 27.29 shows the situation of diminishing returns to scale.

4. ISOQUANTS AND LAWS OF RETURNS OR RETURNS TO A VARIABLE INPUT

In the above section, we have discussed the various situations of returns to scale when the two factor inputs labour and capital were variable. This kind of analysis is of limited use in economics because we do not find such situations of returns to scale in real world. In practice, at least one factor of production (say entrepreneurship) is usually fixed in amount. Thus a more realistic analysis is of laws of returns. Here, we shall assume that one of the factors of production used by the firm is fixed while the other is variable. In Fig. 27.30, we assume that capital (*K*) is fixed and labour (*L*) is a variable input. *OM* amount of the fixed factor capital is used in conjunction with varying amounts of the variable input labour. The way in which returns to labour (*L*) change as the amounts of labour vary can be found by studying what happens along the horizontal line *MN* in Fig. 27.30.

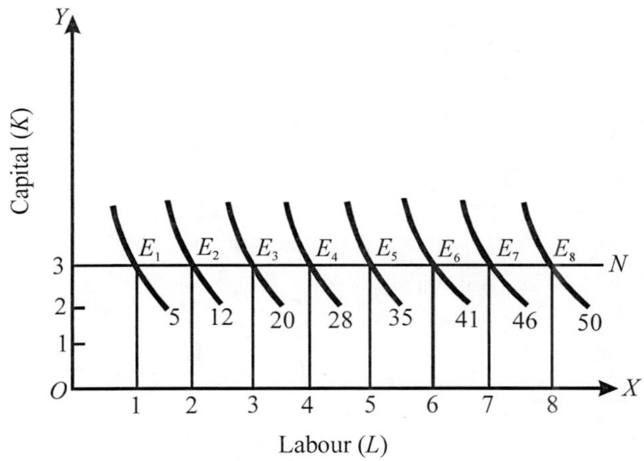

Fig 27.30

At each point on the line *MN,* a fixed amount (OM = 3 units) of capital is being used in conjunction with a different amount of the variable input labour. We may show the physical returns to the variable factor in several ways. Just as we can represent costs and revenues by total, average and marginal cost curves, we can also represent the physical productivity of it variable factor of production (labour) by drawing total product curve, average product curve or marginal product curve. In the present section we shall draw the marginal physical productivity curve (or *MPP* curve) for labour.

It is assumed that the level of capital input is held constant at 3 units of capital and the firm adds one unit of labour input per unit of time. The isoquant map given in Fig. 27.30 presents a family of isoquants, each labelled with a numerical value signifying the level of output produced along it. Since the level of variable input (labour) increases by one unit each time, we can easily discover the marginal physical productivity of labour from the isoquant map. It (MPP_1) will be the difference between the numerical values between two isoquants. For instance, as employment increases from 1 unit of labour to 2 units of labour, total production rises from 5 units to 12 units. The marginal physical productivity of labour is therefore 7 units (12 units—5 units) of output. Similarly, the third unit of labour adds 8 units of output, the fourth unit of labour adds 8 units of output and so on.

The derivation of marginal physical productivity curve of labour has been illustrated in Fig. 27.31. The upper part of Fig. 27.31 indicates that total output increases at an increasing rate until 3 units of labour are used. If the labour is employed beyond 4 units, output increases at a decreasing rate. For this reason, the marginal physical productivity curve of labour as shown in the lower part of Fig. 27.31 first shows a positive slope and then it falls downwards to the right. It is also possible to draw an average physical productivity curve, or (*APP* curve derived from the isoquants map by dividing total output at each level of employment by number of units of labour employed). This bears the usual average-marginal relationship to the marginal physical productivity curve and can, of course, be derived from the MPP_L curve itself. The total physical productivity curve of labour (TPP_L curve) can also be derived from the isoquant map or from the MP_L curve or $AIPP_L$ curve.

The phase of diminishing marginal physical productivity occupies an important place in economics. In the old time, it has usually been known as the *law of diminishing returns,* or more recently, the *law of variable proportions.* In this sense, the law of diminishing turns can be defined as "an increase in the amount of a variable factor added to a fixed factor causes, in the end, a less than propOrtionate increase in the amount of product given technical condition."[3]

Thus, the law of diminishing returns in modern times is not defined in terms of diminishing marginal physical productivity, but it is couched in terms of propol1ionality.

---

3. Alfred Marshall, *OP. cit.,* 150.

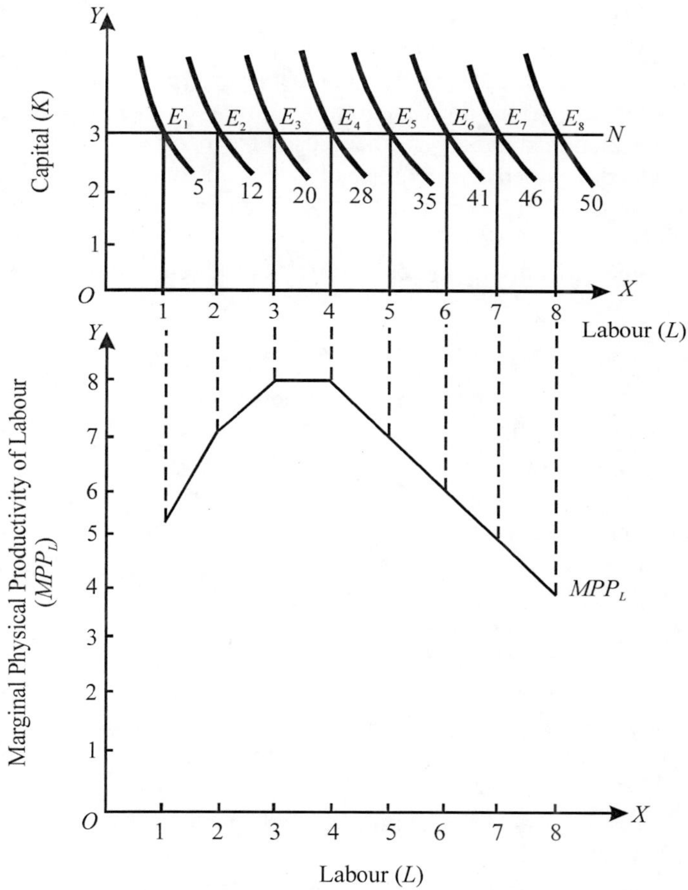

Fig. 27.31

5. THE COBB-DOUGLAS PRODUCTION FUNCTION

The statistical investigations into the laws of production by C.W. Cobb and P.H. Douglas[4] are of great importance in the field of economics. Their production function is used as a fairly universal law of production.

---

4. C.W. Cobb and P.H. Douglas, "A Theory of Production", *American Economic Review* (Supplement), 1928.

They have estimated it in numerous samples of manufacturing industries throughout the world. This exponential type of production function ($X = AL^{\alpha} K^{\beta} U$) has no more claim to general validity as a description of technology than other mathematical functions. Moreover, it possesses certain interesting properties which make it a very convenient choice of a researcher. Even before the research of Cobb and Douglas, the similar type of production function had been used by many economists. But it was clearly developed and empirically verified by these two persons, Cobb and Douglas. It is why this function is almost always referred to as the *Cobb-Douglas Production Function.*

The general form of the Cobb-Douglas production function is

$$X = AL^{\alpha} K^{\beta} U \quad \text{... (8)}$$

where X = output, L = labour input, K = capital input, U = random disturbance term, A = a constant (may be treated as an efficiency parameter), and α and β = positive parameters

Also $L > 0$ and $K > 0$, $\alpha > 0$, $\beta > 0$.

The sum of exponents ($\alpha + \beta$) represents the degree of homogeneity (or returns to scale) of this function which it assumes to be equal to one.

In this production function the output (X) is a function of two output L and K or symbolically,

$$X = f(L, K,) \text{ such that,}$$

$$f(\lambda L, \lambda K) = (\lambda L)^{\alpha} (\lambda K)^{\beta}$$

$$= \lambda^{\alpha+\beta} K^{\beta} L^{\alpha}$$

$$= \lambda^{\alpha+\beta} f(L, K)$$

Thus, if $\alpha + \beta = 1$, the firm would be operating under the constant returns to scale and the production function is homogeneous of degree one;

if $\alpha + \beta < 1$, it will have diminishing returns to scale;

if $\alpha + \beta > 1$, it will operate under increasing returns to scale.

Although the Cobb-Douglas production function in equation (8) *is non-linear, it can be transformed into a linear function* by converting all variables into logarithms. It is why this function is known as a log linear function. Thus, taking the log of equation (8) on both the sides, we have,

$$\log K = \log A + \alpha \log L + \beta \log K + \log U \quad \text{... (9)}$$

Properties of Cobb-Douglas Production Function

(1) *Constant Returns to scale prevails in the economy.* As we have seen that Cobb-Douglas production function assumes that ($\alpha + \beta$) = 1 which means constant returns to scale prevails in the economy. In other words, it proves the validity of *Euler's theorem.* Euler's theorem states that if

factors of production are paid according to their marginal product then total product will just exhaust.

In other words, if factors are rewarded according to their marginal products, the combined share of the factors is equal to total output (X).

Since this condition is satisfied by production functions of degree one; the Cobb-Douglas production function which was used to attempt an empirical verification of the marginal productivity theory of distribution, statisfies Euler's theorem.

In short ($\alpha + \beta$) is the degree of homogeneity of the Cobb-Douglas production function. Suppose that labour and capital have increased by 10 per cent then the Cobb-Douglas function becomes,

$$X = AL^{\alpha} K^{\beta} U$$

Now $$X = A\,(1.10\,L)^{\alpha}\,(1.10\,K)^{\beta}\,U$$

$$= A(1.10)^{\alpha+\beta}\,L^{\alpha}\,K^{\beta}U$$

Thus output would increase by ($1.10^{\alpha+\beta}$) and if $(\alpha + \beta) < 1$, output would increase by less than 10 per cent, if $\alpha + \beta > 1$, output will increase by more than 10 per cent and if $\alpha + \beta = 1$, output will increase by exactly 10 per cent. In Cobb-Douglas production function, returns to scale are, therefore, characterised by the following:

$\alpha + \beta < 1 \rightarrow$ Diseconomies of scale,

$\alpha + \beta = 1 \rightarrow$ Constant returns to scale,

$\alpha + \beta > 1 \rightarrow$ Economies of scale.

Since the Cobb-Douglas production function can characterise any degree of returns to scale, it has been commonly used by many economists.

(2) *Elasticity of substitution is equal to one.* The elasticity of substitution of the Cobb-Douglas production function (where constant returns to scale holds) is equal to unity everywhere and that it is the only function which satisfies this property.

(3) *Expansion path generated by the Cobb-Douglas production function is linear and passes through the orgin.*

(4) α *and* β *represents the labour share and capital share of the output respectively.*

(5) α *and* β *are the elasticities of output with respect to labour and capital respectively.* In the case of Cobb-Douglas production function, a is defined as the partial elasticity of production (x) with respect to labour (L). It denotes the percentage change in labour input, *keeping capital input constant.* Similarly, (β is defined as the partial elasticity of production (X) with respect to capital input (K), *keeping labour input constant.*

Since α and β represent individually the per cent change in output given per cent changes in labour and capital respectively, the two coefficients taken together measure the total per cent change in output for a given per cent change in labour and capital.

(6) *If one of the inputs is zero, output will also be zero.* The Cobb-Douglas production function assumes constant returns to scale under which all the inputs are changed in equal proportions. If one of the inputs is zero, naturally other inputs are also held to be zero and the consequent output will also be zero.

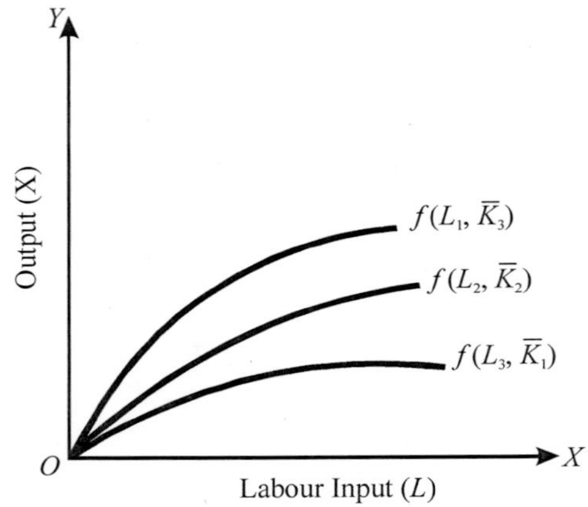

Fig. 27.32

Moreover, we have seen that the Cobb-Douglas function has constant elasticities of output variation with respect to labour or capital input. The relation-ship between output and input is non-linear (though we may convert it into a log-linear type of relationship). For constant levels of capital, the outputlabour input relation is shown as the series of curved lines in the Figure 27.32.

If either input is zero ($L = 0$ or $K = 0$), output is zero ($X = 0$). Thus both the inputs are necessary to the production process to take place. The curvature is such that marginal productivity falls as input grows. There is no asymptotic level of output (or ceiling) beyond which production can not grow, but the rate of increase in output decreases as higher levels of input are employed in the production process.

Importance of Cobb-Douglas Production Function

As we have noticed earlier that Cobb-Douglas production function is most commonly used function in the field of economics. It graduates data on output and input well. Many economists used it independently under the name of "Cobb-Douglas Production Function." Hence there are a number of varieties of the Cobb-Douglas form which yield variable elasticities of production and substitution. We can quote three examples of this kind, as:

$$X = C^{1-\alpha} N^{\alpha} e^{\beta N} \quad \rightarrow \text{ Ferguson and Pfoubs}$$

$$X = AC^{\alpha}N^{\beta}e^{\beta \log N \log e} \quad \rightarrow \text{ Newmann and Read}$$

$$X = AC^{\alpha}N^{\beta}e^{\gamma G}e^{\alpha N} \quad \rightarrow \text{ Heady and Dillon}$$

The Cobb-Douglas function is convenient in international or inter-industry comparisons. Since α and β are elasticity coefficients, they are pure number and easily be compared among different samples using varied units of measurement.

In a sense, one is able to capture the flavour of essential non-linearities of the production process and yet benefits from the simplifications of calculation from linear relationship by transforming to logarithms. The logarithmic function is linear in the 'parameters, which is an essential point to the statistician or to the economists.

Other functions may give a similar type of curvature and keep linearity in parameters. For example, we may write parabolic functions as,

$$X = \alpha_0 + \alpha_1 L + \alpha_2 K + \alpha_3 L^2 + \alpha_4 K^2 + \alpha_5\ LK + L$$

However, this type of equation (parabolic) uses many more parameters than does the Cobb-Douglas yet the later (Cobb-Douglas) is economical in the use of degrees of freedom, or parameters and yet gives us non-linearity. The parameters of the Cobb-Douglas function, in addition to being elasticities, possess other attributes important in economic analyses. For example, the sum of the exponents (α + β) shows he degree of "returns to scale" in production process.

Cobb-Douglas's research has been a test of the marginal productivity theory of wages (or theory of distribution) as well as descriptions of production technology.

In six cross section samples, Douglas found the average labour exponent (α) to be 0.63 and the average capital exponent (β) to be 0.34. In Australian studies, the average components in nine cross-section samples (1912–1937) are 0.60 for labour (α) and 0.37 for capital (β). In this way various comparisons were made between different states.

In this Cobb-Douglas type of production function the elasticity of substitution (σ) between labour (*L*) and capital (*K*) is compelled to take on a value of unity, whether or not the empirical, situation so dictates. However, a less restricative and much more fruitful approach would be to allow the elasticity of substitution (σ) to vary in accordance with the empirical requirements under consideration.

Criticisms of Cobb-Douglas Production Function

Although Douglas as been a great pioneer and proponent of research into the laws of production, he has not overlooked the points at which his analysis is open to criticism. The main critics of the Cobb-Douglas function are K.J. Arrow, H.B. Chenery, B.S. Minhas and R.M. Solow. The critics have pointed out the following points of criticisms of the Cobb-Douglas production function.

(1) *The Cobb-Douglas function includes only two factor inputs—* Capital and labour, but other factors are equally important in the production process. Moreover, the studies of the Cobb-Douglas function were often made for the manufacturing sector alone, raw materials do not conceal as intermediate goods produced and used within the same sector. Even for an economy as a whole, imported raw materials are significant factor inputs to be taken into account on the same footing as labour and capital inputs. In various countries of the world, we find open economies where raw material imports are of great significance in the production process.

(2) *The function assumes constant returns to scale can not be possible.* There are certain inputs of production which can not be increased in equal proportion, for example, entrepreneurship. Moreover, constant returns, may take place only in the short-run. But in the long run we can not hope the same situation.

(3) As far as the measurement of labour-input is concerned we may count it in number or in man-hours, but it is very *difficult to measure capital input* due to its depreciation over time. Therefore, the whole problem of aggregation has been overlooked.

(4) Again, the *output measure is usually a form of aggregate value* added. This means that raw materials are not treated as a separate factor of production, but as an automatic subtraction from the total value of output. Raw materials, especially of the fuel variety, may not have the fixed relation to output (as is assumed under constant returns to scale) that is implied by the use of the value added concept.

(5) At different levels of productive operation there may be economies (increasing returns) or dis-economies (diminishing returns) in the use of materials (or factor inputs). It has been overlook by the functions.

Here we may argue that the true underlying curve of production follows the usual S-shape as shown in Fig. 27.33.

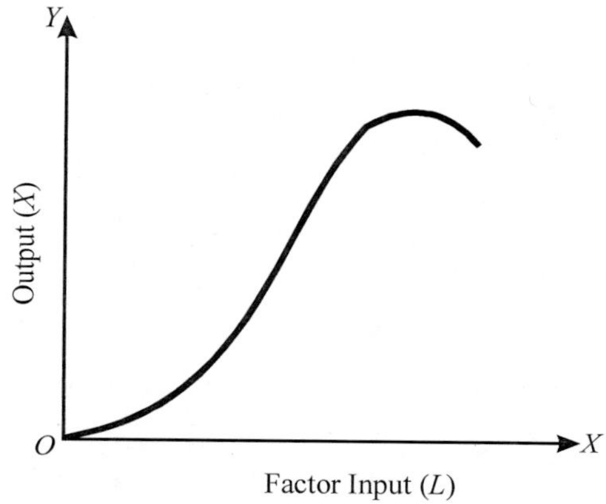

Fig. 27.33

Figure 27.33 shows that in an input-output relation there are phases of increasing, constant, and decreasing *marginal* returns. A sample of data usually approximates some portion of this curve and, there fore, form a limited number of observations, it is not possible of estimate the entire curve. It's quite possible that a sample heavily dominated by depression period may produce a portion of the curve showing in-creasing returns. Now if there are increasing returns to scale, we can not have factor shares equal to corresponding exponents (α and β) of the function because the sum of the exponents will exceed unity ($\alpha + \beta > 1$).

(6) *The function assumes that there is perfect competition* in the market and that is why the equalities between the shares and the exponents (α and β) exist. But if there is monopoly and monopolistic competition, the above relationship fails to hold in the economy.

(7) In Cobb-Douglas production function, *all labour units are considered as a homogeneous* input which is a great drawback of the function.

(8) We know that *Multicolinearity* is frequently encountered in economic time-series analysis. It is quite possible that there may be high inter-correlation between capital and labour in the estimation of a production function. Inter-correlation or multicolinearity is not necessarily a problem unless it is high relative to the over-all degree of multiple correlation among all variables simultaneously. In the case of Cobb-Douglas type of research, we have to face this problem of multicolinearity.

In spite of the above criticisms, the Cobb-Douglas production function is widely used in an economic research.

EXERCISES

1. What is an isoquant? Explain its main properties.
2. What do you understand by Ridge Lines? How can you find out the economic region with the help of these ridge lines?
3. Explain the principle of diminishing marginal rate of technical substitution. What are its limitations?
4. Explain the producer's equilibrium position with the help of isoquants.
5. How does a firm succeed in securing the least-cost combination of the factors of production?
6. "Iso-product curves are the lines connecting all the points which yield the same product"— Boulding. Discuss.
7. Explain the concept of 'returns to scale', with the help of isoquants.
8. Discuss the law of variable proportions with the help of iso-product curves.
9. "The isoquant-isocost approach to production theory, like the traditional approach, explains the principles which underline costs, resource pricing and employment, resource allocation and product distribution." Explain the above statement with the help of diagrams.
10. Write brief notes on the following:
    (*i*) Production Possibility Curve,
    (*ii*) Expansion Path,
    (*iii*) Marginal Rate of Technical Substitution, and
    (*iv*) Marginal Rate of Product Transformation.
11. Explain output and substitution effects of a fall in the price of one input.
12. How does a firm get an optimum combination of two outputs? Illustrate your answer with the help of suitable diagrams.
13. Distinguish between returns to factor and return to scale. What will be the return to a factor if the returns to scale are increasing, constant and diminishing?
14. What is homogeneous production function? Discuss the properties of any such function.
15. Explain the Cobb-Douglas production function.

Multiple Choice Questions

16. (*i*) Normally the isoquants slope
    (*a*) upwards from left to right
    (*b*) upwards from right to left
    (*c*) downwards from left to right
    (*d*) backwards from left to right [*Ans.* (*c*)]

    (*ii*) An individual's production possibility boundary line
    (*a*) contains all efficient combinations of productions
    (*b*) forms boundary of the production possibility set
    (*c*) indicates the marginal cost of an additional unit of either goods
    (d) all of the above. [*Ans.* (*d*)]

    (*iii*) On a production-possibilities curve, the amount of *Y* foregone to produce another unit of *X* has been given a special name, what is it?

(*a*) substitute goods (*c*) opportunity cost
(*b*) production rate (*d*) price of production

(*iv*) Imagine a firm employs the four factors of production namely *L, K, N* and *E*. The least cost combination of *L, K, N* and *E* will generally be the point at which

(*a*) $\frac{P_L}{P_K} = \frac{P_N}{P_E}$

(*b*) $\frac{MP_L}{P_L} = \frac{MP_K}{P_K} = \frac{MP_N}{P_N} = \frac{MP_E}{P_E}$

(*c*) $P_L = P_K = P_N = P_E$
(*d*) $MP_L = MP_K = MP_N = MP_E$ [*Ans.*(*b*)]

(*v*) Stage II of production function begins where AP_L begins to decline
(a) ways (*c*) sometimes
(*b*) never (d) often [*Ans.*(*a*)]

(*vi*) Within the relevant range, isoquants
(*a*) are negatively slopped (*c*) can not cross
(*b*) are convex to origin (*d*) all of the above [*Ans.*(*d*)]

(*vii*) If we plot capital on the vertical axis and labour on the horizontal axis, the slope of a straight line isocost curve drawn on such a graph is
(*a*) P_L / P_K (*c*) $-P_L / P_K$
(*b*) P_K / P_L (*d*) $-P_K / P_L$ [*Ans.* (*c*)]

(*viii*) At the point of producer's equilibrium
(*a*) the isoquant is tangent to the isocost curve
(*b*) $MRTS_{LK} = P_L / P_K$
(*c*) $MP_L / P_L = MP_K / P_K$
(*d*) all of the above [*Ans.* (*d*)]

(*ix*) The expansion path of production theory is analogous in consumption theory to the
(*a*) price consumption curve (*c*) income-consumption curve
(*b*) Engel curve (*d*) budget-constraint line
[*Ans.* (*c*)]

PART 4
PRODUCT PRICING

Chapter 28

THE NATURE OF COSTS

1. INTRODUCTION

Until now we were discussing the physical relationships between inputs and the output. These relationships have been summarised in the law of non-proportional outputs. Thus, the physical side of production can be translated into money costs of production by assigning prices to the resources (inputs) used. In this chapter we will look at production from the stand-point of a single business firm.

2. THE CONCEPT OF COSTS

Generally, the costs of production are assumed to be the money expenditure incurred by the business firm for the resources used to produce its product output. In other words, the ordinary accounting statements of costs cover only the money costs incurred in production, such as, the payments made for buying raw materials, rent for building, wage for labour, hiring of transportation and payments made for taxes, etc. Such accounting statements do not present a real picture of total costs of production. The firm's actual expenditures on resources constitute only a part, of total cost. That in economics the word 'cost' is given a special meaning, which is much broader than the sense in which a firm or the accounting authority uses it. Prof. Alfred Marshall made a distinction between the cost of production and the expenses (expenditures) of production by saying that "All the efforts and sacrifices made by the producer is the real costs of production while the money paid (to other factors of production) for these efforts is termed as the expenses of production."[1]

In general, what is called a cost is a payment made, or a sacrifice incurred, in order that a benefit may be secured. Regarded from the viewpoint of the entire society, costs fall into two categories: (*i*) Factors of production are called into use, excluding any benefit which might arise from non-use. Thus workers enjoy leisure when not working. (*ii*) Factors of production are withdrawan from productive uses, so that society loses their alternative products. Costs to individual producer or the business firm can be regarded in the same two ways. Either they can be looked upon as resources that are called into use, excluding benefits from non-use, or else they are assessed in terms of forgone alternative products.

In this context, we shall discuss the following two doctrines of economic costs: (1) The Opportunity Cost or Alternative Cost Doctrine; and (2) Explicit and Implicit Costs.

1. The Opportunity Cost or Alternative Cost Doctrine

Practically, every factor of production has many possible uses. Since it is scarce, it is impossible to employ it fully in all of them. To use it for anyone purpose means to forgo the opportunity of applying it to other purposes. Its use, therefore, costs whatever it might have been worth if it had been put to its possible alternative uses. An enterpriser in one industry must, then; pay for his factors of production as much as his competitors in other industries (or, for that matter, in his own industry) are willing to pay. The combined bidding of all the competitors for the limited supply of the factors of production thus establishes prices for them which, as we know, constitute the costs of production. This is known as the doctrine of opportunity cost. It may be stated as follows: The use of any factor in production involves a cost which is equal to the prices offered for that factor in its possible alternative uses.

Thus economists define the cost of production of a particular product as the value of the forgone alternative products that resources used in its production could have produced. The costs of resources to a firm are their values in their best alternative uses. For example, a certain fixed amount of labour can be used in the production of either washing machines or refrigerators. Now the cost of the labour in the manufacture of washing machines is the value of refrigerators that the labour could have produced. Unless the manufacturer of washing machines pays that amount for the

1. Alfred Marshall, *Principles of Economics* (Eighth Edition), pp. 282-83.

labour, it will go into or remain in refrigerator production. The principle of opportunity costs is very significant in the decision making of the productive firms.

In business management, frequently there are two or more opportunities for utilising factors of production, whether these are supplied by the enterpriser himself or procured from others. Choices are made whenever the enterpriser is confronted by alternative uses. At the time a worker is hired, the entrepreneur has a choice between hiring and not hiring. The opportunity cost of the labour at this time is the money outlay necessary to secure the worker's services. Once the labour has been hired, for the period of his contracted service the contracted wage no longer represents a practical alternative for the entrepreneur. The opportunities for utilising the labour's services, now open to the entrepreneur, are the various employments which he has available for the labour, or the possibility of paying the worker to stand idle. The entrepreneur who aims at maximising his profit or minimising his loss will make his calculations on this basis. For instance, a building contractor may have an employee for whose services he has a year's contract, at a wage of Rs. 500 a month. During a slack season the contractor may have no employment for this labour. A local park service offers to pay the contractor Rs. 300 a month for the labour's service. Now Rs. 300 is a real alternative; but not the Rs. 500 since the employer's contract with the worker requires Rs. 500 to be paid regardless of how the labour is used. Thus the doctrine of opportunity cost is very important in the decision making of the enterprisers.

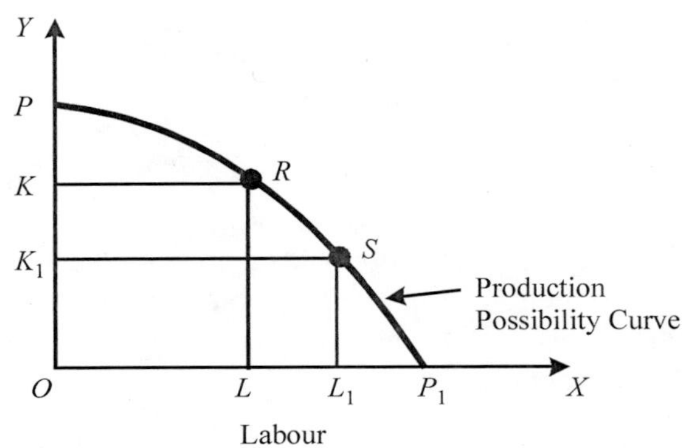

Fig. 28.1

The concept of opportunity cost can also be explained diagrammetically as in Fig. 28.1. In Figure 28.1, PP_1 is the production possibility curve which indicates the different combinations of labour and capital necessary to produce a given level of output. At point *R,* the producer employs *OL* units of labour and *OK* units of capital to produce a certain level of output. Now if he goes to point *S* then he employs more of labour and less of capital to produce the same level of output. Thus at point *S*, he employs LL_1 more of labour and forgoes $K K_1$ units of capital. Thus the opportunity cost of LL_1 quantity of labour is KK_1 quantity of capital.

Significance of Opportunity Cost Concept

The concept of opportunity cost is widely used in solving economic problems. Some of the points may be mentioned as follows:

(*i*) The concept of opportunity cost is applied in the determination of factor prices, i.e., rent, wages and interest, etc.

(*ii*) It is applied to explain the theory of comparative costs in the field of inter national trade.

(*iii*) It explains the consumer's surplus as well as the producer's surplus.

(*iv*) The Government makes use of it in the determination of various policies such as the policies related to expenditure and taxation, etc.

(*v*) It is also applied in the determination of consumer's equilibrium where the consumer wants to maximise his total utility function.

Limitations of Opportunity Cost Concept

The concept of opportunity cost has got the following limitations also:

(*i*) It can not be applied to those factors of production whose supply is fixed, i.e., in the case of specific factors of production which have no alternatives at their disposal and in such cases the opportunity cost becomes zero.

(*ii*) If the factors of production are immobile because of one reason or the other, then the concept of opportunity cost can not be applied. Sometimes the factors of production are prevented going abroad or entering into some field then this concept may not be applied, because their prices do not reflect the opportunity cost.

(*iii*) When the forgone alternative is not ascertainable then the concept of oppor-tunity cost can not be applied.

(*iv*) This concept is based on the assumption of perfect competition which is not found in practical life.

2. Explicit and Implicit Costs

The modern economists divide the costs of production into two parts: (*i*) Explicit costs (overhead costs or money costs), and (*ii*) Implicit costs (or imputed costs). Explicit costs refer to the expenses incurred by a firm on buying the productive services owned by other factors of production. In other words, explicit costs are the contractual money payments that a firm makes to the factor owners. It hires workers and pays them wages. Similarly, the payments of interest for the capitalist, rent for the land owner, etc. are the contractual payments made by the firm. Besides, it spends money on raw materials, fuels, power, transportation and advertising. It also pays a number of taxes to the government. All these payments are termed as explicit costs of production. The ordinary accounting statements usually cover the *explicit or the money costs of production.* Alfred Marshall called them the expenses of production.

Implicit costs (or non-expenditure costs) on the other hand, do not involve any contractual payment made by the firm to any outsider. These may be the evaluation of the firm's own efforts and sacrifices incurred in production. More specifically, the *imlicit costs* or the *imputed costs* refer to the reward which the firm would realise for self-owned, self-employed resources. According to Leftwich, the entrepreneur's salary as a cost can be easily explained. In accordance with the alternative cost doctrine the cost of single producer's services in producing his product is the forgone alternative product which would have been produced had he worked for someone else in a similar capacity. We consider as a part of the firm's costs, then, a salary for the entrepreneur equal to the value of his sevices in his best alternative employment. The other important implicit costs are depreciation of capital goods and a normal return on money capital invested by the firm. As far as the depreciation charges are concerned, some economists assume it as implicit costs because they are not contractual and accrue to the firm itself. But other economists, including Leftwich, consider the depreciation charges as explicit costs because according to them a cost accounting authority counts them as the firm's operating expenses. In fact, implicit costs include the normal return on his (entrepreneur's) investment, and the opportunity cost (alternative earnings) of his own labour.

Thus, for microeconomic analysis a more realistic approach of costs of production is to add both the explicit costs and the implicit or imputed costs of production. To make the approach still more realistic, the modern economists prefer to add 'normal profit' to the implicit and the explicit costs of production. According to Prof. Boulding, in economic analysis the concept of cost includes a normal profit because it is only after profit's inclusion in cost that an entrepreneur can show his incentive to combine different factors of production and offer certain quantity of the product for sale. Thus, total cost of production of a commodity is the sum total of: (*i*) explicit costs, (*ii*) implicit costs, and (*iii*) normal profit.[2]

3. BEHAVIOUR OF COSTS OVER TIME

As already mentioned, a cost function is defined as the relationship between costs and output. The production function of a firm and the prices it pays for its factor inputs determine the firm's cost function. As a production function may take different forms (with either one or some or all of the inputs variable), likewise a cost function may also take different forms. The two important cost functions are the short-run cost function and the long-run cost function.

Short-run is defined as that period of time in which some inputs are fixed in amount and the firm can expand or contract its output only by varying the amounts of other (variable) inputs. In the short-run, the firm attempts to minimise the cost of variable inputs. In other words, it tries to obtain the least cost combination of inputs. Output can range from zero, where the firm has to bear a maximum loss of the fixed inputs. Thus, in the short-run the firm's decision making rests in the minimization of the costs of variable inputs. In the long run, all inputs are variable in amount, a firm's output can range from zero to an infinitely large quantity. In other words, in the long-run the firm is capable of identifying the most efficient scales of its operation.

Now we shall explain the nature of short-run and long-run cost curves under the following section.

4. SHORT-RUN COST CURVES

Since in the short-run firm has fixed as well as variable inputs, short-run costs of the firm are also divided into fixed costs and variable costs.

Symbolically, $TC = TFC + TVC$

Fixed Costs (*TFC*) are, by definition, "fixed", that is whose total amount remains constant over a range of output. Having been incurred, it is sunk or remains unalterable with respect to a particular output range. In other words, total fixed costs exist no matter how much the firm

---

2. K.E. Boulditig, *Economic Analysis Vol. 1: Microeconomics,* p. 250.

produces. They consist of overhead expenses such as interest charges, depreciation of machinery and the plant, maintenance, and similar items.

Variable Costs (*TVC*) are those costs whose total amount changes with output. As the firm increases its level of production, it must purchase greater amounts of raw materials, hire more labour, use more fuel, etc. As output increases, these costs increase and vice versa. The variable costs will shrink to zero if operations are suspended, because then no materials need be purchased and none but the irreducible maximum of maintenance workers need be hired.

In fact, there is no sharp dividing line between fixed and variable costs. The one shades off into the other, so that the difference is one of degree, rather than of kind. For instance, interest on bonds will not change at all during the life of the bonds, but depreciation and executive staff are likely to vary a little as output is changed; fuel will vary considerably, but is hardly likely to increase or decrease as much as output; while raw materials and manual labour must change in very close correspondence with variations in the product. Here, then, are four different degrees of fixity and variability. In the long-run, all costs are variable, given time for old plant to wear out and new plant to be constructed, the size of the plant will be adjusted to the demand, involving greater or less costs for interest, taxes, etc., as the case may be. For the present, we are concerned with shorter periods, in which the plant is a fixed factor for the time being.

Thus, in the short-run, total cost is the sum of total fixed costs and total variable costs. These are indicated in Table 28.1 and in Fig. 28.2. It is important to note the trend of *TVC* (Total Variable Cost) curve in Fig. 28.2. The curve rises rapidly at first, then its slope becomes less and then rises rapidly again—why is this? Since in the short-run period different quantities of variable factors are combined with a given scale of plant, law of variable proportions comes into play. As variable factor inputs are increased, physical marginal returns to the same increase in the first phase, are constant for a while and then begin to decline. Consequently, as the total output increases from zero to upwards, the total variable inputs and hence costs increase at a falling rate to begin with, at a constant rate for a while and finally at an increasing rate. Thus, up to five units of output in Table 28.1, and Fig. 28.2, the successive increases in total variable cost (*TVC*) are smaller and smaller. For fifth and sixth units the successive increases in *TVC* are constant. Beyond six units of output the successive increases become larger and larger. It is because of this behaviour that in

Table 28.1

(in Rs.)

Quantity of X	*Total Fixed Cost (TFC)*	*Total Variable Cost (TVC)*	*Total Cost (TC = TFC + TVC)*
0	500	—	500
1	500	200	700
2	500	240	740
3	500	270	770
4	500	298	798
5	500	324	824
6	500	350	850
7	500	386	886
8	500	430	930
9	500	480	980
10	500	576	1,076
11	500	736	1,236
12	500	966	1,466

Fig. 28.2, the *TVC* curve is concave to the *X*-axis in the early stage and after a certain level of output it becomes convex to the *X*-axis. The *TC* (Total Cost) curve is nothing but the *TVC* curve and the *TFC* curve added

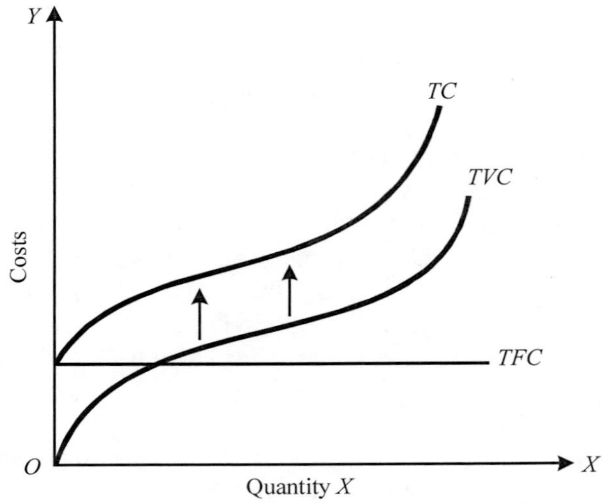

Fig. 28.2

vertically at each point. The vertical distance between *TC* and *TVC*, therefore, is constant throughout arid is equal to *TFC*.[3]

Per Unit Cost Curves

Per unit cost curves are used fairly for the determination of output and price. The per unit cost curves are of following types:

(*i*) Average Fixed Cost *(AFC)* curve,
(*ii*) Average Variable Cost *(AVC)* curve,
(*iii*) Average Cost (*AC*) curve, and
(*iv*) Marginal Cost (*MC*) curve.

(*i*) *Average Fixed Costs.* Average fixed costs are obtained by dividing total fixed costs by the level of output, or

$$AFC = \frac{TFC}{X}$$

In Table 28.2, the average fixed cost column is computed by dividing the total fixed cost column by the different quantities of *X*. As the rate of output increases, total fixed cost remaining the same, the average fixed cost will become smaller and smaller. The corresponding *AFC* curve, as shown in Fig. 28.3, is downward sloping to the right throughout its entire length.

As the quantity of *X* increases, it approaches but never reaches the quantity axis. Thue, a firm can reduce substantially its fixed costs per unit by producing larger quantities of output *X*. In other words, the *AFC* curve is a rectangular hyperbola asymptotic to the axis, i.e., the curve approaches the vertical and the horizontal at each end. For very small outputs, *AFC* per unit is high, and for larger outputs it is low. The *AFC* is a rectangular hyperbola because *AC* multiplied by output is always exactly the same amount.[4]

(*ii*) *Average Variable Costs.* Like average fixed costs, average variable costs are obtined by dividing the total variable costs by the respective level of output *X*. Thus,

$$AVC = \frac{TVC}{X}$$

In the Table 28.2, we have computed the average cost column from the total variable cost column by using the above formula. Average

3. The short-run total cost function can be defined in mathematical terms as below:

$$C = a + f(X)$$

where C = Total cost, a = Total fixed cost, $f(X)$ = Total variable cost.

4. Donald S. Watson, *Price Theory and Its Uses,* Second Edition, p. 195.

Table 28.2

Quantity of X (1)	*TFC* (2)	*AFC* (3)	*TVC* (4)	*AVC* (5)	*TC* (6)	*AC* (7)	*MC* (8)
1	500	500	200	200	700	700	—
2	500	250	240	120	740	370	40
3	500	167	270	90	770	257	30
4	500	125	298	75	798	200	28
5	500	100	324	65	824	165	26
6	500	83	350	58	850	142	26
7	500	71	386	55	886	127	36
8	500	63	430	54	930	116	44
9	500	56	480	53	980	109	50
10	500	50	576	58	1,070	107	96
11	500	45	736	67	1,236	112	160
12	500	42	966	80	1,466	122	230

variable costs behave in a different manner. Since in beginning total variable cost increases at a diminishing rate, average variable cost falls. Then, for some level of output, total variable cost increases at a constant rate, thus average variable cost becomes minimum and constant. Further, for higher levels of output, total variable cost increases at an increasing rate, and therefore, the average variable cost moves up for higher quantities of *X*. This has been clearly shown in Fig. 28.2. The *AVC* curve usually will have a *U* shape. It means that the *AVC* curve first falls, reaches a minimum and then begins to rise. In other words, it explains the three laws, of production or cost.

(*iii*) *Average Costs.* Another cost which will be useful to us is average cost or average total cost per unit of output. It is simply total cost divided by quantity (see Table 28.2). Thus,

$$AC = \frac{TC}{X} = \frac{TVC + TFC}{X} = \frac{TVC}{X} + \frac{TFC}{X}$$

where *AC* is average variable cost, *TC* is total cost, *TVC* is total variable cost, *TFC* is total fixed cost and *X* is the quantity of output. In Fig. 28.3 we have shown the *AC*-curve. It is the vertical summation of the *AFC* curve and the *AVC* curve. In Fig. 28.3, we note that it starts out at a very high point, then falls rapidly and finally rises again. Thus the average cost curve, too, is usually thought to be a. *U*-shaped curve. Its *U*-shape depends upon the efficiency with which both fixed and variable inputs are used. Given the scale of plant (quantity of fixed inputs), the greater the output of the firm, the greater the efficiency of the fixed inputs, i.e., the smaller the average fixed cost becomes. In other words, with increased production, fixed costs are spread over a larger number of units of *X; AFC* will fall and *AC* will fall with it. On the other hand, as production of *X* continues to increase, diminishing returns set in, inefficiencies occur and variable cost increases. It happens then, as in Fig. 28.3, that, as production increases, *AFC* move towards zero, but *AVC* rise and become a larger part of *AC* (since $AC = AFC + AVC$). This is illustrated as the *AC* and *AVC* curves come closer and closer together. With increasing quantity of *X,* fixed cost is spread over more units, and *AFC* has a declining influence in *AC.* At the same time however, *AVC* increases and causes *AC* to rise. The net effect of all this is that the *AC* curve is *U*-shaped. We must remember that the minimum point of the *AVC* curve must be to the right of the minimum point of the *AVC* curve. This is to say that the minimum point on the *AVC* curve lies at a lower output level than does the minimum point on the *AC* curve.

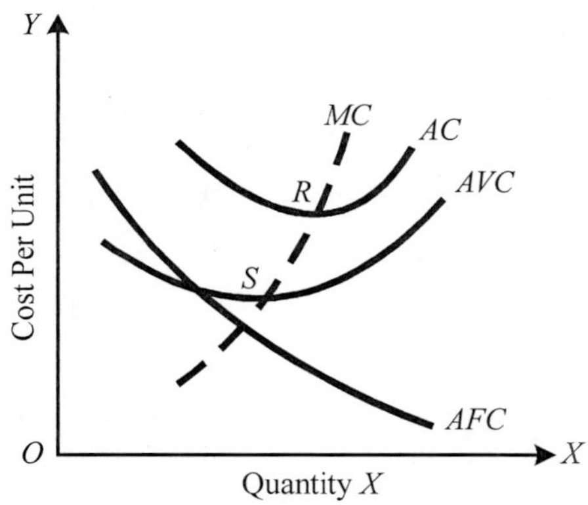

Fig. 28.3

(*iv*) *Marginal Cost.* Another cost in which the economists and businessmen are interested is the marginal cost (*MC*). It is defined as the extra cost of producing an additional unit. It can also be defined as the change in total cost resulting from a one unit change in output. Since a change in total cost is caused only by a change in total variable cost, marginal cost may also be defined as the increase in total variable cost resulting from a one-unit increase in output. Marginal cost depends in no way upon fixed cost. Marginal cost can either be computed from the total variable cost or from the total cost column (see Table 28.2). Thus, mathematically,

$$\begin{aligned} MC_n &= TC_n - TC_{n-1} \\ &= [TVC_n + TFC] - [TVC_{n-1} + TFC] \\ &= TVC_n - TVC_{n-1} \end{aligned}$$

where n stands for any volume of output.

It, therefore, is clear that marginal cost is independent of the fixed cost. It makes no difference what the fixed cost is. The derivation marginal cost curve has been shown in Fig. 28.4.

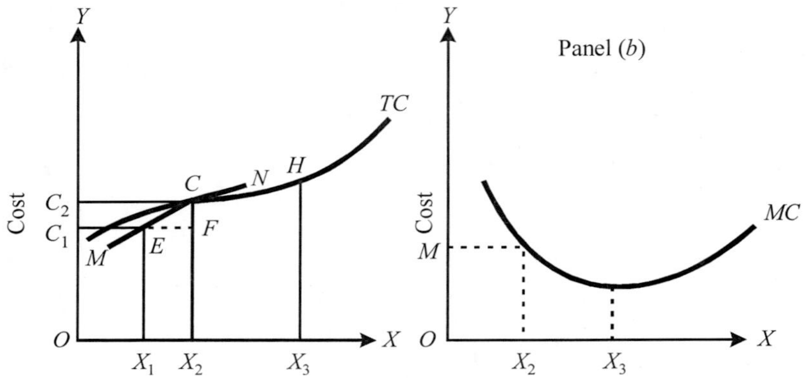

Fig. 28.4

The *MC* curve in Panel (*b*) of Fig. 28.4 has been drawn simply by taking the slopes of different tangents (first derivatives) on the *TC*-curve [Panel (*a*) of Fig. 28.4]. As output increases from OX_1 *to* OX_2, we move from point *E to G* along the *TC*-curve and total cost increases from OC_1 *to* OC_2 Therefore, at OX_2 level of output, the marginal cost will be C_1 C_2. The marginal cost of a unit of output at any level of output can be found in the same way. These information can be represented by the marginal cost curve as shown in Panel (*b*) of Fig. 28.4. Thus, at OX_2 level of output the marginal cost is *OM*, which is the same amount as C_1C_2.

The marginal cost curve usually is *U*-shaped and its shape comes from that of *TC*-curve. Upto OX_3 level of output, the *TC*-curve is concave to *X*-axis, which implies that each one unit increases in output upto that point (*H*) will increase total cost by a smaller amount than did the preceding one. Hence, marginal cost is decreasing as output is increased to OX_3 level. Point *H* on *TC* curve is the *point of inflection.* At output level OX_3, at which the point of inflection occurs, marginal cost takes on its minimum value. At outputs greater than OX_3, the total cost curve is convex to the horizontal axis which means that each one-unit increase in output increases total cost by more than the preceding one. Therefore, marginal cost will be increasing for outputs beyond OX_3. Thus marginal cost first decreases and then increases as output increases.

Relationship of MC to AC and to AVC

In Fig. 28.2, it may be observed that the *MC* curve intersects the *AVC* and *AC* curves at their minimum points. Also, when *AVC* and *AC* decline, *MC* is less than *AVC* and *AC*. When *AVC* and *AC* rise, *MC* is greater than *AVC* and *AC*. Furthermore, it may be observed in Fig. 28.3 that the *MC* curve intersects the *AVC* (at the latter's minimum level) at a smaller level of output than the level where it (the *MC* curve) intersects the *AC* curve. As already explained, this is due to the fact that *AC* comprises *AFC* and *AVC*.

5. LONG-RUN COST CURVES

In the above section, it has been assumed that each firm is working within the limits of an established plant whose capacity is fixed. Associated with this plant are certain fixed costs that remain the same regardless of the output produced. In the short-run nearly all firms find themselves in this kind of position. Over a longer period, a firm can change the size of its plant, and it will do so if its situation seems to require it. The existing plant can be allowed to wear out, and be abandoned: or perhaps it can be sold to another firm and converted to some other use. Thus, in the long-run the firm can build any desired scale of plant. All resources are variable and there will be no average fixed cost-curve. Thus, the firm would choose that size of operation (plant) at which it can maximise its profits, or where it can produce at the minimum cost.

When the firm plans to expand the scale of its operation, it may expect to have a different set of cost curves associated with each plant. In other words, we can think of the long-run as a series of alternative short-run situation into anyone of which the firm can move. Now we shall derive the long-run cost curves from the short-run cost curves.

Long-run Average Cost (LAC)

We may find that there is an optimum size of the firm which is more efficient than any other. A firm any smaller than the optimum will not be able to take full advantage of the economies of large-scale production, and it will not be able to get its costs down to as low a point as if it were larger. Beyond a certain point, however there is no further advantage to be gained from increasing size (of the plant), and some diseconomies are even likely to result which interfere with efficiency, because as a firm gets larger, the difficulties of management become greater. Anyway, this characteristic of production costs to fall as we approach to the optimum size of firm, and to rise thereafter, is shown graphically in Fig. 28.5.

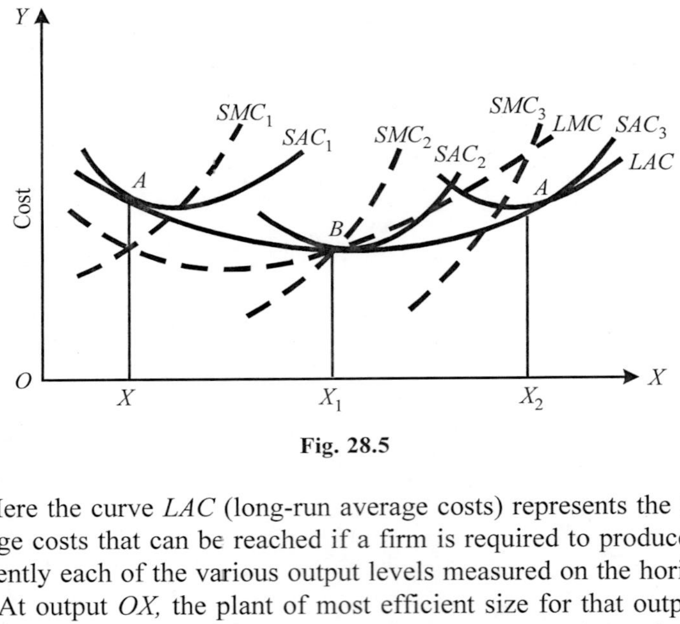

Fig. 28.5

Here the curve *LAC* (long-run average costs) represents the lowest average costs that can be reached if a firm is required to produce most efficiently each of the various output levels measured on the horizontal axis. At output *OX,* the plant of most efficient size for that output can produce at a minimum average cost of *XA.* A plant of the size most appropriate for output of OX_1 can produce more cheaply. Its minimum average cost would be X_1B. A firm, which produces still larger output as OX_2, will be less economical, and its per unit costs cannot be less than X_3C.

In formulating its policy, a firm will plan to build the plant most efficient for the volume of business it expects to do. The *LAC* curve indicates the best possibilities available for it. This is the reason why the *LAC* is sometimes known as a *planning curve.* Once the decision for the future has been made and the plant considered most appropriate has been constructed, it is not likely that it will always be possible to operate this plant at its most economical output. Changes in demand for the produce may force the firm to operate above or below its optimum size. The costs of production will, therefore, vary along the *SAC* curves. The reaction of *SAC* curves to the *LAC* curve is shown in Fig. 28.5. SAC_1 is the short-run average cost curve for the plant most appropriate to the output *OX*; and SAC_2 and SAC_3 are the corresponding short-run average cost curves for outputs OX_1 and OX_2 Now if a firm has a plant suited to the output *OX,* but is producing more or less (depending upon the demand for its product) than that in fact, its average costs will move to the left or right of *A* on SAC_1 and will deviate from *XA* accordingly. This, the level of output actually produced will depend upon the changes in demand for the product.

In Fig. 28.5, we have drawn *LAC* curve in such a way, that it is tangent to the *SAC* curves. Since the *LAC* curve so envelopes the *SAC* curves, it is also known as an *envelope curve.* Actually, there is a large number of short-run average cost curves tangent to the long-run average cost curve, but for the simplicity, we have shown only three *SAC* curves. It is interesting to note that SAC_2 curve is tangent to *LAC* curve at the former's lowest point. But we cannot generalise this statement with other *SAC* curves. Rather, it is the only one of the *SAC* curves of which this is true. The *LAC* curve does not touch the minimum points of any of the other curves. By definition, the *LAC* curve represents the lowest possible cost for each possible output. It means that, although the plant represented by SAC_1 is the most efficient plant that can be designed for output *OX*, that plant could operate even more efficiently at a somewhat greater output. It may be, for example, that this plant uses machinery that reduces its costs, but it cannot utilise this machine to its fullest capacity, i.e., the plant is underutilised. Yet it is the best plant possible for *OX* level of output. In contrast with this situation, the plant represented by SAC_3 is a bit over-utilised, yet even so, it constitutes the most efficient way of producing the output level OX_2. This proves the fact that *LAC* curve will hot pass through the minimum point of all *SAC* curves, but it must be drawn as shown in Fig. 28.5.

The actual shape of the average cost curve in the long-run-will depend on the assumptions we lay down. One assumption can be regarding the price of the factors of production. We can presume factor prices constant. Secondly, we have to lay down assumptions regarding the divisibility of factors. *If we assume that all factors are infinitely divisible and no economies can be reaped from the division labour, then the long-run average cost curve will be a horizontal straight line*. But in real life, it is difficult to find all the factors perfectly divisible. Usually we find that some factors are also indivisible even in the long-run. Management and entrepreneur are factors which are not perfectly divisible during the long period also. An entrepreneur will not be able to produce twice a given output as efficiently as he produces a given output. Therefore, it is rightly possible that a firm will produce more cheaply at some scales of output than at others, even in the long-run. This means that, in real life, the short-run average cost curves of a firm will have different minimum points.

Long-run Marginal Cost (LMC)

There is also long-run marginal cost curve shown in Fig. 28.5—the dashed *LMC.* It indicates the extra costs entailed in enlarging production facilities so as toget greater quantities of output. It bears precisely the same relationship to the *LAC* curve that the *SMC* curve bears to its *SAC* curve.

The Optimum Scale of Plant

The optimum scale of plant means the most efficient scale plant that the firm can build. It is that plant where the short-run average cost curve forms the minimum point of the long-run average cost curve. In Fig. 28.4, this situation takes place at points where SAC_2 curve is tangent to *LAC* curve at the minimum point *B* of both. The optimum level of output is OX_1. Normally, firms will not operate at this level of output they will do so in the situation of perfect competition in the long-run. Economic believe that the tendency of competition is to force firms to that position; other wise they could not remain in business. In the long-run, then, we must expect competition to bring the price down to X_1B. This idea will be more fully explained in the chatpter that deals with pricing and output under perfect competition.

EXERCISES

1. Distinguish between fixed costs and variable costs as the terms are used by the economists.
2. Distinguish between the accounting costs and economic costs. Explain the importance of economic costs in economic analysis.
3. Distinguish between short-run cost curves and long-run cost curves. Why must the average cost curve be *U*-shaped? What does this shape precisely signify?
4. Define marginal cost. Indicate at what point the marginal cost curve cuts the average variable cost curve and the average cost curve and why it must cut them at these points.
5. Why is the long-run average cost curve known as a planning curve?
6. Define the terms "optimum size" and "normal capacity" and state which of the following costs will, be at a minimum when a firm of optimum size is operating at normal capacity: *AC*, *AVC*, *AFC*, *MC*.

7. Discuss the nature of the short-run and long-run average cost curves. Why is the long-run cost curve flatter than the short-run cost curve?
8. How do economies and diseconomies of scale affect the *LAC* curve?

Multiple Choice Questions

9. (*i*) Opportunity costs are also known as
   (*a*) overhead costs (*c*) alternative costs
   (*b*) money cost (*d*) social costs [*Ans*. (*c*)]

   (*ii*) The opportunity cost of a factor of production is
   (*a*) what it is earning in its present use
   (*b*) what it can earn in the long period
   (*c*) what it can earn in some other use
   (*d*) what has to be paid to retain it in its present use [*Ans*. (*d*)]

   (*iii*) All money costs can be regarded as
   (*a*) implicit costs (*c*) opportunity costs
   (*b*) explicit costs (*d*) social costs [*Ans*. (*b*)]

   (*iv*) Implicit costs are the costs
   (*a*) which are not incurred by the firm, and may accrue to the company
   (*b*) of resources owned by the firm
   (*c*) of resources supplied by the households
   (*d*) all of the above [*Ans*. (*b*)]

   (*v*) The fixed costs of a firm
   (1) are fixed only in the short period
   (2) when expressed as an average, do not change with output
   (3) do not reflect diminishing marginal returns
   (*a*) (*i*) and (2) only (*c*) (2) only (*e*) all of them
   (*b*) (1) and (3) only (*d*) (2) and (3) only [*Ans*. (*b*)]

   (*vi*) Average fixed costs
   (*a*) remain the same whatever the level of output
   (*b*) increases as output increases
   (*c*) diminishes as output increases
   (*d*) show no pattern [*Ans*. (*c*)]

   (vii) Fixed costs are known as
   (*a*) special cost (*c*) prime cost
   (*b*) direct cost (d) overhead cost [*Ans*. (*c*)]

   (*viii*) In a short period, when production increases, the *AFC*
   (*a*) increases (*c*) remain constant
   (*b*) decreases (*d*) none of the above [*Ans*. (*b*)]

   (*ix*) A firm's *TC* curve
   (*a*) lies below its *TVC* curve
   (*b*) rises more steeply than its *TVC* curve because *TC* includes fixed as well as variable costs
   (*c*) is a horizontal curve
   (*d*) is identical in shape to its *TVC* curve, but higher in position [*Ans*. (*d*)]

   (*x*) All of the following curves are *U*-shaped except
   (*a*) the *AVC* curve (*c*) the *AC* curve
   (*b*) the *AFC* curve (*d*) the *MC* curve [*Ans*. (*b*)]

Chapter 29

CONCEPT OF REVENUE

1. INTRODUCTION

In modern economics, the equilibrium of a firm is discussed in terms of cost and revenue. The profits of the firm are also calculated by the costs and the revenues of the firm. In the previous chapter we have explained the costs of production and now in the present chapter we shall describe the concept of revenue.

2. TOTAL, AVERAGE AND MARGINAL REVENUE

The revenue of a firm consists of price times the number of units the firm can sell. Mathematically,

$$R = PX$$

where, R = Total revenue, P = Price, X = Quantity sold

Since the demand schedule of a firm tells us how much the firm can sell at each price, we can calculate the total revenue from it merely by multiplying price times quantity. In other words, the demand curve provides information to the firm about the total revenue it can get from its sales. In Table 29.1 we can see what total revenue would be at different price levels.

The information given in Table 29.1 can also be shown by a demand curve as in Fig. 29.1. We may see that the total revenue is maximum at price Rs. 8 where 8 units of X are sold. If price increases nom Rs. 8, then total revenue will decline and if price decreases, total revenue will also decline. This fact can also be seen in Fig. 29.1. Since total revenue is PX, it can be represented by a rectangle underneath the demand curve. At price Rs. 8, total revenue is shown by the area of shaded rectangle. At a price higher than Rs. 8, total revenue will decrease, because the return per unit is higher but the gain in revenue due to higher price is not sufficient to offset the loss in revenue due to reduced sales—the demand at this level is elastic (*Ed* > 1), i.e., the percentage increase in price is less than percentage decrease in quantity sold. At a price lower than Rs. 8, more

Table 29.1

Quantity (Units) X	*Price or Average Revenue (Rs.)* P	*Total Revenue (Rs.)* $R = PX$	*Marginal Revenue (Rs.)* MR
1	15	15	—
2	14	28	13
3	13	39	11
4	12	48	9
5	11	55	7
6	10	60	5
7	9	63	3
8	8	64	+ 1
9	7	63	– 1
10	6	60	– 3
11	5	55	– 5
12	4	48	– 7

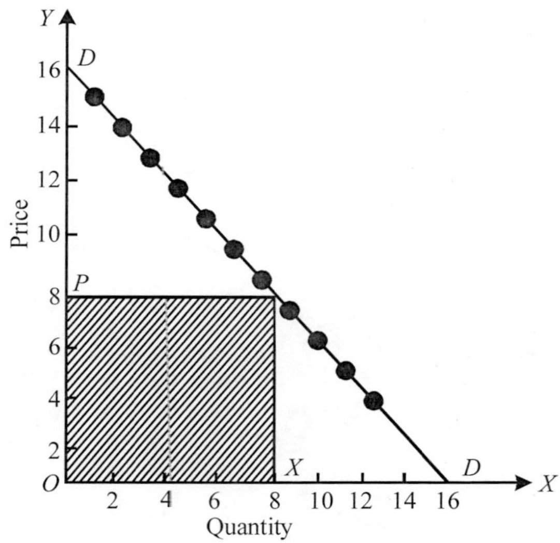

Fig. 29.1

units will be sold but total revenue will decrease because demand is inelastic (*Ed* < 1, i.e., the percentage change in price is greater than percentage change in quantity demanded). Thus any other rectangle under the demand curve of the firm will be of a smaller area than the one shown in Fig. 29.1. Thus, it is interesting to note that although the price Rs. 8 is not the highest price, yet the (total) revenue of the firm is maximum. But in the following chapters we shall note that the maximisation of revenue is not the objective of the firm—it is maximisation of profit. Revenue does not give us the facts about profit. It requires a simultaneous information about the costs of the firm. We shall discuss this problem of equilibrium in the following chapters.

While discussing the revenue of the firm. We use three concepts: Total Revenue, Average Revenue and Marginal Revenue.

As we have already explained, total revenue is the total receipts of the firm through its sales, i.e., it is calculated by price per unit of the commodity multiplied by the total number of units sold.

Average revenue is the revenue per unit of the commodity sold. It is found by dividing total revenue by the number of units sold. Thus, average revenue means price. It is revenue for the seller and price for the consumer. Symbolically,

$$AR = \frac{TR}{X}$$

where, AR = Average revenue, TR = Total revenue, X= Number of units of the commodity sold.

Now, average revenue curve is the same thing as demand curve. As the consumer's demand curve is the graphic relation between price and quantity demanded, it also represents the average revenue or price at which the various quantities of a commodity are sold, since price offered by buyers is the revenue from the seller's point of view. Therefore, average revenue curve of the firm is really the same thing as demand curve of the consumers.

Marginal revenue (*MR*), on the other hand, is defined as the extra revenue secured from the scale of an additional unit of the commodity. It then the revenue derived from the last unit sold. Since our demand curve (*AR*-curve) is downward sloping, the last unit can only be sold at a lower price. To calculate *MR*, we subtract total revenue of the sale of a unit or several units at some particular price from total revenue derived from the sale of the next. Algebraically, it is the addition to total revenue earned by selling units of the commodity instead of (n–1) units. Thus,

$$MRn = TRn - TR_{n-1}$$

where, MRn = Marginal Revenue of the nth unit, TRn = Total Revenue of n units, TR_{n-1} = Total Revenue of $n - 1$ units, n = Any given number of units sold.

In Table 29.1, we have calculated the *MR* column with the help of the above formula. For example, marginal revenue when two units are sold would be Rs. 13 (i.e. Rs. 28 – Rs. 15); when three units are sold, Rs. 11 (Rs. 39 – Rs. 28) and so on. Here we should note that *MR* is not the same as price (or *AR*) because, in order to sell the third unit, it was necessary to reduce the price of the first two units to the selling price of the third, Rs. 13. In other words, two units can be sold for Rs. 14, but in order to sell three units, it is necessary to reduce the price to Rs. 13. We suffer loss on all the units sold at the old price. Thus the decrease in *MR* will be higher than the decrease in *AR*.

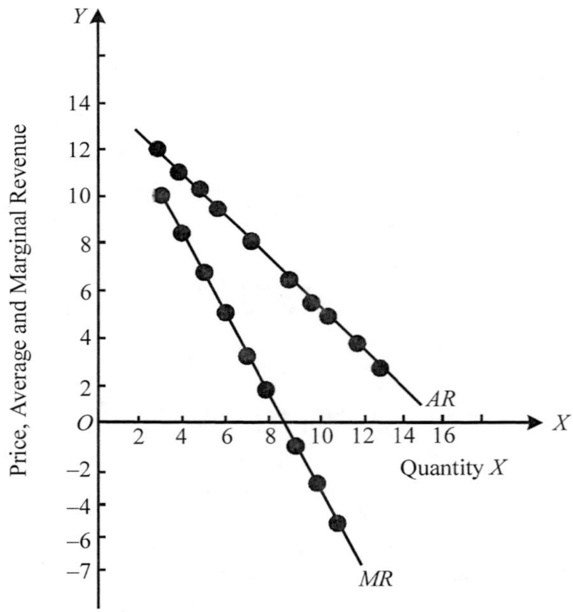

Fig. 29.2

Now, in Fig. 29.2, we draw the average revenue (demand) and the marginal revenue curves on the basis of the data provided in Table 29.1, and see that *MR* will be less than *AR* (or price) at all levels. Notice that when nine units are sold, *MR* becomes negative: as price is lowered from Rs. 8 to Rs. 7. *TR* decreases from Rs. 64 to Rs. 63.

Generally speaking, marginal revenue is less than average revenue (or price) as indicated by the Fig. 29.2. But in perfect competition, when a firm has to sell any quantity at the ruling market price, marginal revenue is equal to average revenue, because there is no loss incurred on the previous units.

3. REVENUE CURVES FOR A PERFECTLY COMPETITIVE FIRM

Perfect competition is the term applied to a situation in which the individual buyer or seller (firm) represents such a small share of the total business transacted in the market that he exerts no perceptible influence on the price of commodity in which he deals. Thus in perfect competition an individual firm is a price taker, because the price is determined by the collective force of market demand and market supply which are not influenced by the individual. When price is the same for all units of a commodity, naturally average revenue (price) will be equal to marginal revenue (*AR* = *MR*).

Table 29.2. Demand and Revenue Schedule of a Competitive Firm

Quantity of X (in units)	*Price (P) or Average Revenue (AR)*	*Total Revenue (TR)*	*Marginal Revenue (MR)*
1	200	200	200
2	200	400	200
3	200	600	200
4	200	800	200
5	200	1,000	200

This can also be illustrated with the help of an imaginary revenue schedule as in Table 29.2. It indicates that price of Rs. 200 is given to the individual firm which is determined by the industry. As the firm sells more and more at the given price, its total revenue will increase but the rate of increase in total revenue is constant because *AR* = *MR*.

The total revenue, marginal revenue and average revenue curves are also drawn in Fig, 29.3. It clearly shows that *OP* price is fixed by the industry and at this given price the firm can sell any quantity of the commodity. Its demand curve is horizontal and *AR* is equal to *MR*. The price of the commodity coincides with the sum received by the seller, per unit of sales, that is to say, with the seller's average revenue. It stands at the same amount, regardless of the sales volume, as in this case it stands at Rs. 200 a unit. Marginal revenue is the additional sum that the firm 'receives from an additional unit of the commodity that it sells. It also coincides with the price, Rs. 200 in this example, since every additional unit sold brings this amount.

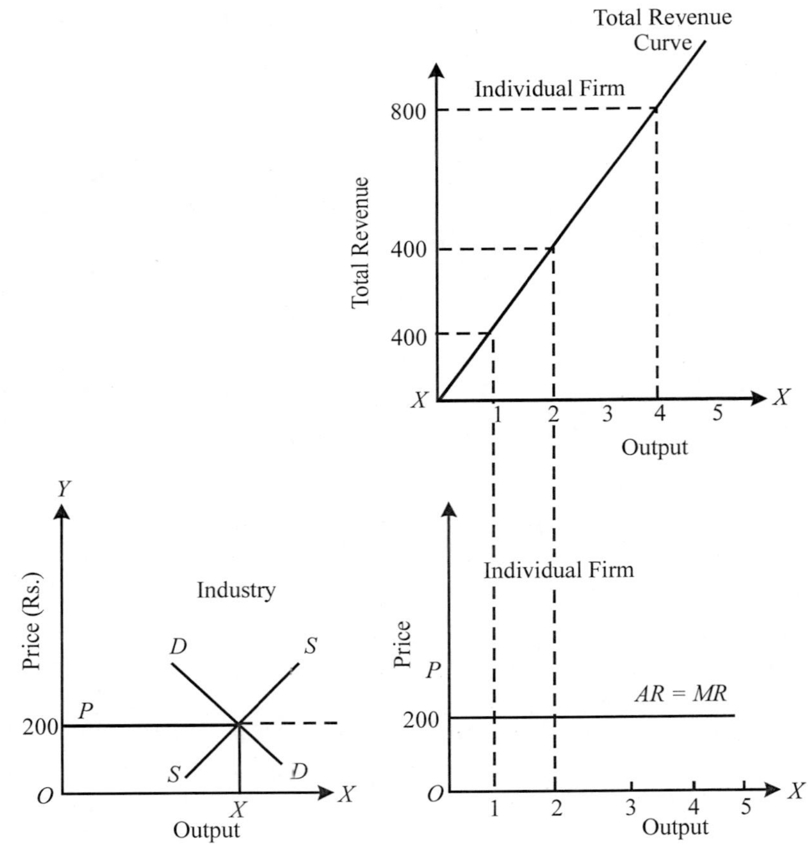

Fig. 29.3

4. REVENUE CURVES FOR A FIRM UNDER MONOPOLY OR IMPERFECT COMPETITION

When a firm is working under conditions of monopoly or imperfect competition, its demand curve (or *AR*-curve) is less than perfectly elastic, the exact degree of elasticity being different in different market situations, depending upon the number of sellers and the nature of the product. In other words, the demand (*AR*) curve has a negative slope and the *MR*-curve lies below it, This is because the monopolist seller ordinarily has to accept a lower price for his product, as he increases his sales. In the situation of monopoloy, he is the only seller, and he is faced by a situation that is generalised with respect to final goods by the law of demand: the market will absorb an additional quantity only at a lower price. Exceptionally, there may be situations where the market will absorb a larger quantity at the same or even a higher price, but they are uncommon and can be neglected here. If it is granted that the monopoly firm has to accept a lower price for her product, in order to sell a greater quantity, it is obvious that the *AR*-curve will be falling and the *MR* must always be less than *AR,* because a falling price must mean some loss on the sale of additional supply.

To make it more clear, let us construct an imaginary demand and revenue schedule for a monopoly firm. The first two columns of Table 29.3 give us the demand curve of the monopolist. It shows that price per unit and average revenue are one and the same. The quantity demanded will increase only when the price (*AR*) falls. Now to derive the column 4 of marginal revenue, we first calculate the total revenue column which is simply the product of price multiplied by the quantity sold. Now marginal revenue column can be derived from the total revenue column. As already explained, it (*MR*) is the net addition to the total revenue from the

Table 29.3. Demand and Revenue Schedule of a Monopoly Firm

Quantity of X (*in units*) (1)	*Price* (*P*) *or Average Revenue* (*AR*) (2)	*Total Revenue* (*TR*) (3)	*Marginal Revenue* (*MR*) (4)
1	100	100	100
2	90	180	80
3	80	240	60
4	70	280	40
5	60	300	20

additional unit of commodity sold. Thus, in going from one to two units, the marginal revenue is Rs. 80 and this is found subtracting Rs. 100 from Rs. 180 and so on for the other unit.

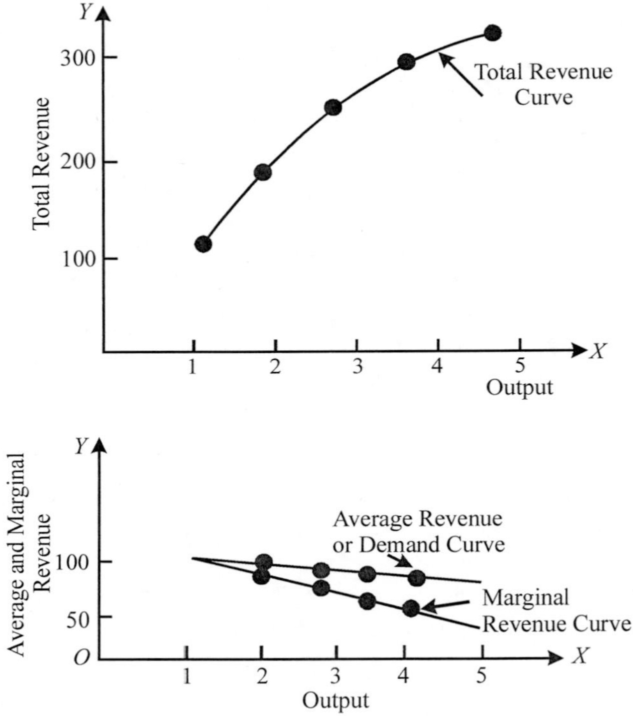

Fig. 29.4

These facts can also be explained in Fig. 29.4. It should be clear that the demand curve is sloping downward to show that more can be sold only at lower prices. The corresponding marginal revenue curve is below the *AR*-curve. From Table 29.3, it may be noted that where *AR* falls by Rs. 10, the *MR* falls by Rs. 20, i.e., the *MR* falls by double the rate the fall in *AR*.

5. RELATIONSHIP BETWEEN AVERAGE AND MARGINAL REVENUE CURVES

In most of the following analysis of price theory, we shall be concerned only with average and marginal revenue curves, so that we can ignore total revenue curves. There are geometrical relationships between an average revenue curve and the corresponding marginal revenue curve. We have already explained some of the relationships between them. In this section, we shall discuss the main relationships between the average revenue curve and the marginal revenue curve with the help of Fig. 29.5.

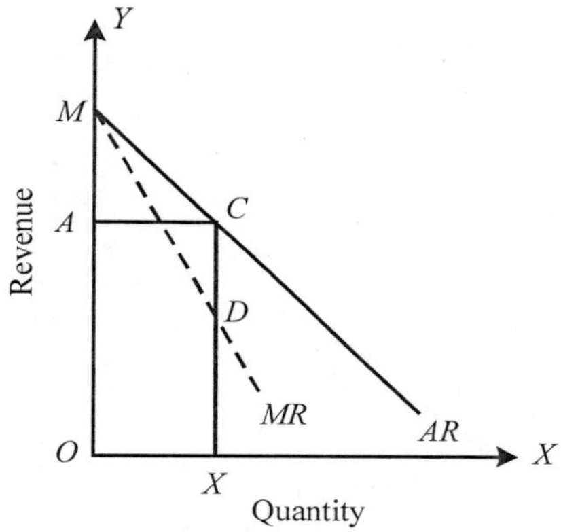

Fig. 29.5

So long as the average revenue curve is falling, marginal revenue must be less than average revenue. The marginal revenue curve itself may be rising, falling or horizontal according to the market situations or circumstances, but normally it falls downward. If we consider straight *AR* and *MR* curves as shown in Fig. 29.5, marginal revenue curve falls twice as much as the fall of average revenue curve. In other words, in such a situation, the marginal revenue curve will cut any line perpendicular to the *Y*-axis half-way to the average revenue curve. In Fig. 29.5, $AB = BC$. Now to prove this, let us consider the following steps:

Area $ACXO$ = Area $MDXO$

where, $ACXO$ = Area of total revenue under demand curve at point C and $MDXO$ = Area of total revenue under marginal revenue curve.

Also $\quad ACXO = ABDXO + \Delta BCD$

and $\quad MDXO = ABDXO + \Delta AMB$

$\therefore \quad ABDXO + \Delta\, BCD = ABDXO + \Delta\, AMB$

or $\quad \Delta\, BCD = \Delta\, AMB$

Since $\Delta\, BCD$ and $\Delta\, AMB$ are congruent triangles, thus

$$AB = BC$$

Hence, it is proved that marginal revenue will cut any line perpendicular to the *Y*-axis half-way to the average revenue curve. But this happens only in the situation when the average and marginal revenue curves are straight lines.

When the average revenue curve is *concave upwards* or convex downward, as in Fig. 29.6 (*a*), the marginal revenue curve cuts any perpendicular less than half-way from the *Y*-axis to the average revenue curve. If the average revenue curve is concave downwards or convex upward as shown in Fig. 29.6 (*b*), the marginal revenue curve cuts any perpendicular more than half-way from the *Y-axis* to the average revenue curve.

Thus, in Fig. 29.6 (*a*), $AB < BC$ and
in Fig. 29.6 (*b*), $AB > BC$

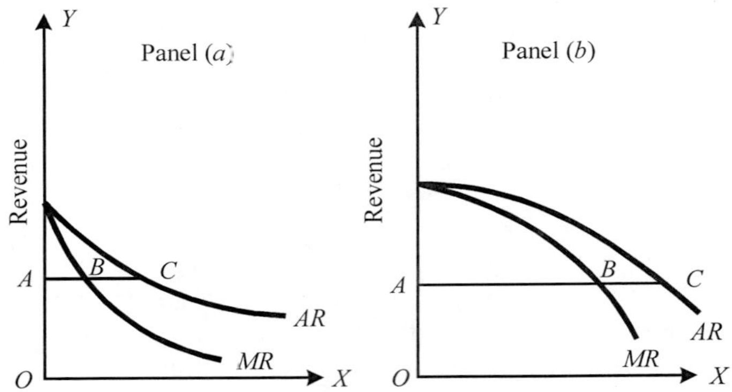

Fig. 29.6

So far we have discussed the relationship between the average and marginal revenue along a perpendicular to the *Y*-axis. Now, we shall discuss the relationships between average revenue and marginal revenue curves along a perpendicular to *X*-axis. In other words, we shall explain the relationship between marginal and average revenue at any level of output (which is measured along the X-axis). This type of relationship will assume a greater importance in economic analysis. This can be done in terms of elasticity of demand. Because, it is clear that the average revenue curve of a firm is really the same thing at the demand curve of consumers for the firms product.

6. AVERAGE REVENUE, MARGINAL REVENUE AND ELASTICITY OF DEMAND

As we have already explained, the demandcurve for the firm's product is the same thing as the average revenue curve of the firm. Thus, we shall measure the elasticity of demand on a firm's average revenue curve and then explain the relationship between *AR, MR,* and the elasticity of demand. It is also true that all average revenue curves (or for that matter demand curves) will not be straight lines. We, therefore, measure elasticity of demand on the average revenue curve which is really a curve.

In Fig. 29.7, the elasticity of demand at point *A* on the *AR* curve is equal to *NA/AM.* This can be proved in the following manner. As we know that elasticity of demand can be defined as:

$$Ed = \frac{\text{Percentage change in the quantity demanded for } X}{\text{Percentage change in the price of } X}$$

or $$Ed = \frac{\frac{\Delta X}{X} \times 100}{\frac{\Delta P_X}{P_X}} \times 100$$

or $$Ed = \frac{\Delta X}{\Delta P_X} \cdot \frac{P_X}{X}$$

where, Ed = Elasticity of demand; ΔX = Change in quantity demanded for X; ΔP_X = Change in the price of X; X = Original amount demanded for X; and P_X = Original price of X.

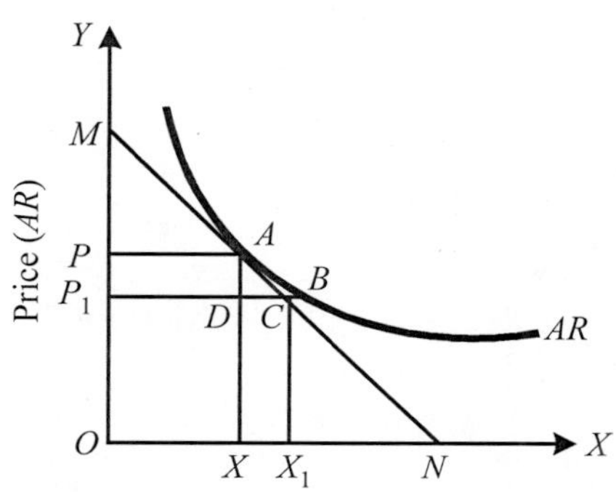

Fig. 29.7

Now, to measure elasticity at a particular point A on AR curve, it is necessary to draw a tangent (MN) to the curve at point R. The slope of the line MN is the same throughout its length. Thus, instead of measuring the elasticity of demand between points A and B on AR curve, we measure it between A and C. Since it is a case of point elasticity of demand; we assume that point C is very near to point B. Also, the slope of points A and C is the same and thus as a limiting case the distance AC is very small. If we supplement the required information from Fig. 29.7 to the above formula of elasticity of demanded, we get

$$Ed = \frac{XX_1}{PP_1} \cdot \frac{OP}{OX}$$

$$= \frac{DC}{AD} \cdot \frac{OP}{OX}$$

where $XX_1 = DC$; and $PP_1 = AD$.

But since by a mathematical theorem, triangles ADC and AXN are similar, we can write $\frac{DC}{AD}$ as $\frac{AX}{XN}$. Thus

$$Ed = \frac{AX}{XN} \cdot \frac{OP}{OX}$$

$$= \frac{AX}{OP} \cdot \frac{OP}{OX} \quad \text{where } XN = OP$$

$$= \frac{AX}{OX}$$

But, since triangles XNA and PAM are similar, $\frac{AX}{OX} = \frac{NA}{AM}$. Thus, point elasticity of demand at point A is

$$Ed = \frac{AX}{OX} = \frac{NA}{AM}.$$

It means, numerical point-elasticity of demand is given by dividing the length of the portion of the tangent above point A (AM) into the portion below point A (AN). With this measure of point elasticity of demand we can study the relationships between average and marginal revenue curves along any perpendicular on the X-axis.

For instance, in Fig. 29.8, the elasticity of demand at point A on AR

curve is *AN/AM.* The two triangles *PMA* and *XAN* have equal angles. Therefore, *AN/AM* can be alternatively written as *AX/MP*. Now, we draw a line from *M* which cuts the perpendicular *PA* at *C* and then passes through point *B*. This straight line *MS* is marginal to the tangent *MN* because it cuts the perpendicular *PA* at its mid-point, *C*.

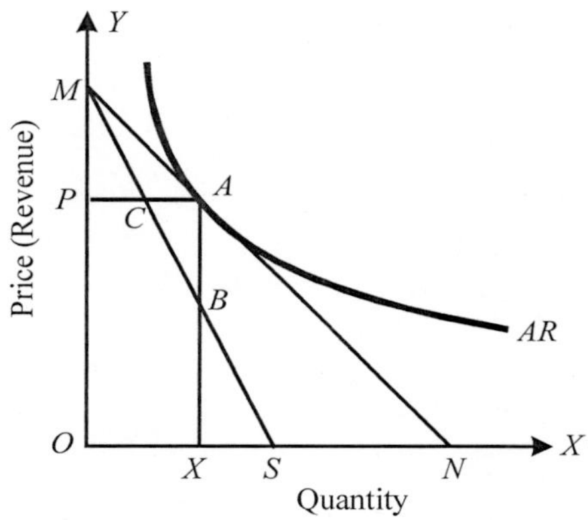

Fig. 29.8

Therefore, $PC = CA$

Also, angle *PAM*= angle *ACB* (being vertically opposite)

and, angle MPC = angle CAB (being *M* right angles)

$\therefore$ $\Delta\, PMC = \Delta\, BCA$ (in all respects)

In other words, the triangles *PMC* and *BCA* are the congruent triangles.

Thus,

$MP = BA$

Now, instead of explaining elasticity point *A* as $\frac{AN}{AM} = \frac{AX}{MP}$, we can write it as:

$$Ed = \frac{AX}{AB}$$

or

$$Ed = \frac{AX}{AX - BX}$$

Ed = Elasticity of demand at the output OX

$$AX = \text{Average Revenue}$$

and, $$BX = \text{Marginal Revenue}$$

Thus, the above formula of elasticity of demand can be written as:

$$Ed = \frac{\text{Average Revenue}}{\text{Average Revenue} - \text{Marginal Revenue}}$$

$$= \frac{A}{A-M}$$

$$Ed\,(A - M) = A$$

$$EdA - EdM = A$$

or $$m = \frac{EdA - A}{Ed}$$

or $$M = A - \left(1 - \frac{1}{Ed}\right)$$

where, M= Marginal revenue, A = Average revenue, and Ed = Value of elasticity of demand.

Now, on the basis of above formula, can we find out the relationship between MR and AR at various point elasticities of demand.

If $Ed = 1$, then $MR = 0$

If $Ed = 2$, then MR equals half the AR

If $Ed > 1$, then $MR > 0$

If $Ed < 1$, then MR is negative

These situations can also be illustrated with the help of a diagram as in Fig. 29.9.

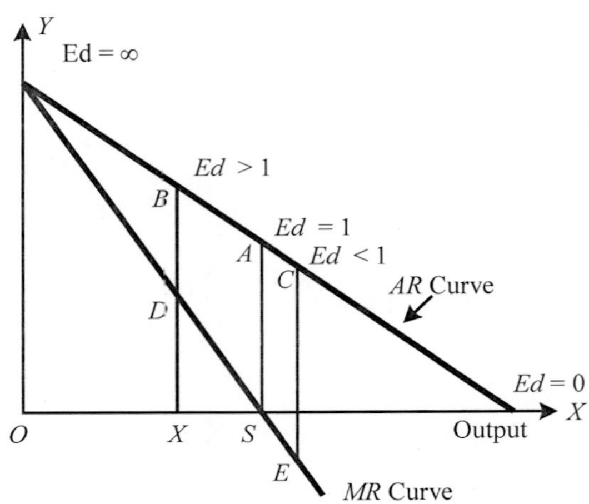

Fig. 29.9

Figure 29.9 indicates that at point *A*,

$Ed = \dfrac{AN}{AM}$ and since $AN = AM$, therefore, $Ed = 1$. At this level of output *OS*, marginal revenue is zero. If elasticity of demand is greater than unity, marginal revenue will always be positive. In Fig. 29.9, this will be the case at any point between the range *A* and *M*. If elasticity of demand is less than one, then marginal revenue is negative. In Fig. 29.9, this will happen at any point between *A* and *N*.

7. OTHER SPECIAL CASES OF REVENUE CURVES

Mrs. Joan Robinson has mentioned many special cases of average and marginal revenue curves. Here we shall mention only the two types of special cases of average and marginal revenue curves.

(1) As we have already mentioned, if the elasticity of demand is unity throughout the length of *AR* curve, marginal revenue will be zero throughout. Thus, the resulting marginal revenue curve will coincide with the horizontal *X*-axis. This case has been shown in Fig. 29.10.

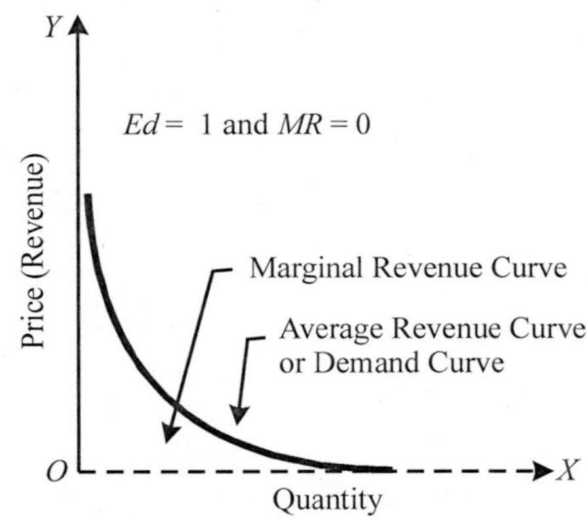

Fig. 29.10

In Fig. 29.10, the demand curve of the firm's product or the *AR* curve is a rectangular hyperbola, having unitary elasticity throughout its length, or $Ed = 1$.

If $Ed = 1$ and putting this value in the formula $M = A\left(1 - \dfrac{1}{Ed}\right)$, we get the value of marginal a; revenue as:

$$M = A\left(1 - \frac{1}{1}\right)$$
$$= 0$$

Therefore, when the elasticity of demand at all points on the *AR*-curve (or demand curve) is equal to one, the marginal revenue will be zero throughout its length and in Fig. 29.10, the *MR* curve is nothing but the *X*-axis.

(2) *In oligopoly situation,* a firm has to face a kinked demand curve or average revenue curve. It is shown in Fig. 29.11. Here, there is a kink at point *P*. This indicates that more or less the price is fixed for an oligopoly firm. The firm does not normally like to change the price, because it expects its competitors to follow price decreases but not increases. Thus, if the firm in question increases its price above existing level (i.e., *XP* in Fig. 29.11), its sales will decline rapidly because other firms in the market do not increase their prices. Similarly, if the firm reduces its price below the existing price, *XP,* then the other firms reduce their prices to a greater extent. This will again reduce the sales of the firm in question. Thus, it is in the interest of the firm to accept the existing price level.

Now, when there is kink in the average revenue curve, the marginal revenue is discontinuous at the point of the kink, as shown in Fig. 29.11. The discontinuous portion or gap in the marginal revenue curve can easily be drawn in a graph. In Fig. 29.11, it is clear that there are two parts of

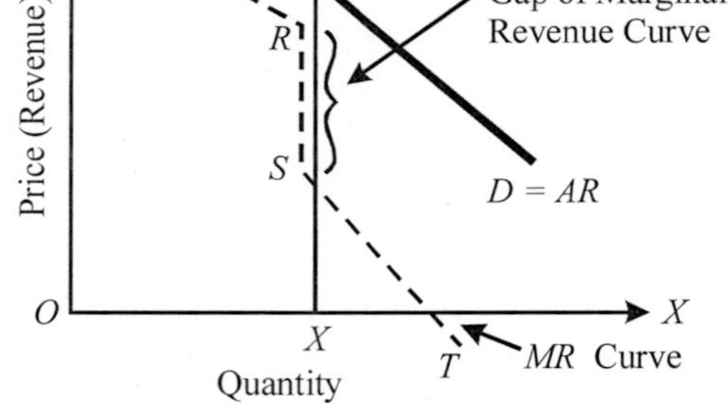

Fig. 29.11

the demand curve, *AP* and *PD;* and therefore, the marginal revenue curves for these two parts of the *AR*-curve will be different. First draw the *MR*-curve corresponding to the demand curve *AP*. This *MR* curve is *AR* in Fig. 29.11. Then draw the *MR*-curve for the second part of the demand curve *PD*. This *MR*-curve is *ST*. Thus *RS* represents the discontinuous portion of the marginal revenue curve in Fig. 29.11.

EXERCISES

1. Explain the relationship between average revenue, marginal revenue and total revenue curves.
2. Show that an individual firm in perfect competition faces a perfectly elastic demand curve.
3. Explain the relationship between average revenue, marginal revenue and elasticity of demand.
4. Write a short note on the kinky demand curve of an oligopoly firm.
5. Prove that: Elasticity of Demand = $\frac{\text{Average Revenue}}{\text{Average Revenue} - \text{Marginal Revenue}}$
6. Explain the relationship between *AR* and *MR* curves of a firm under perfect competition and imperfect competition.

Multiple Choice Questions

7. (*i*) By Marginal Revenue (*MR*), we mean
   (*a*) the revenue of a firm earns when it has increased its output by one unit
   (*b*) the increase in costs a firm incurs when it increases its output by one unit
   (*c*) the change in revenue a firm earns when it increases its output by one unit
   (*d*) the change in fixed revenue but not the variable revenue due to a one unit change in sales [*Ans.* (*c*)]

   (*ii*) When *MR* = 0, elasticity of demand will be equal to
   (*a*) zero (*c*) infinity
   (*b*) unity (*d*) none of the above [*Ans.* (*b*)]

   (*iii*) When *MR* > 0 elasticity of demand will be
   (*a*) greater than unity (*c*) less than unity
   (*b*) equal to unity (*d*) equal to zero [*Ans.* (*a*)]

Chapter 30

LAW OF SUPPLY AND ELASTICITY OF SUPPLY

1. INTRODUCTION

The theory of supply is as much necessary as the theory of demand for the analysis of prices. In everyday use people often do not distinguish between the supply of a product and its quantity produced. However, the economists make a distinction between the two terms and they are not to be used interchangeably. Supply refers to the quantity to a good that is offered for sale in the market per period of time. Thus the supply of a commodity is different from its stock of a point of time. The stock of a commodity refers to its total available quantity while the supply relates to only that quantity which is brought to the market for sale. It is noteworthy that the supply of a commodity differs at different prices. Hence supply can be considered meaningfully only when it is seen in relation to some price. The concept of supply thus explained above suffers from the defect that it fails to relate supply to price. Keeping this fact in view that a more scientific definition must overcome the limitation we may define supply of a commodity as the quantity that will be available for sale in the market at a certain price per period of time. This definition of supply clearly suggests that it would be wrong to consider total stock of a commodity to be as supply. Indian mines are full of iron ore, but till such time iron ore is not extracted from the mines and is not offered for sale at a price. We cannot include it in the country's supply of iron ore. In the words of Meyers, "We may define supply as a schedule of the amount of good that would be offered for sale at all possible prices of anyone instant of time or during anyone period of time, for example a day or a week and so on in which the conditions of supply remain constant."

2. THE LAW OF SUPPLY

Supply of a commodity refers to the various quantities of it which a seller is willing and able to sell at a given price, in a given market and in a given period of time, other things remaining the same. It is the amount that is actually offered for sale at a given price, in a given market and in given period of time. Other tings remaining the same, at any point of time a change in the price of a commodity itself results in a change in its supply. As a matter of fact the is a direct relationship between the price of a commodity and its supply. This implies that a rise in the price will induce producers to supply a larger quantity of the product while a fall in the price will result in is diminished supply. The behaviour of supply in response to changes in the price of the commodity is known as the law of supply. We may state that *ceteris paribus,* the quantity produced and offered for sale in a market varies directly with the changes in the price.

3. FACTORS DETERMINING SUPPLY

The important factors which determine the supply of a commodity are as follows:

(1) the price of the commodity in question;
(2) the prices or related commodities;
(3) the prices of the factors of production;
(4) the state of technology; and
(5) the goals of producers.

(1) *Price of the Commodity.* The supply of a commodity depends upon the price of that commodity. Other things being equal, sellers of a commodity are normally willing to sell more of it if its price is high than if it is low.

(2) *Prices of Related Goods.* The supply of a commodity depends upon the prices of all other commodities. Generally arise in the prices of other commodities will make production of the commodity whose price does not rise relatively less attractive than it was before. We thus expect, other things remaining the same, that the supply of the commodity will fall as the price of other commodities increase.

(3) *Prices of Factors of Production.* The supply of a commodity depends upon the prices of factors of production. An increase in the price of one agent of production may lead to a larger increase in the costs of making those commodities that use a great deal of that agent of production and only a small rise in the costs of producing those commodities that use a small amount of that factor of production. Thus a change in the

price of one agent of production may cause changes in the relative profitability of different producers and this may cause producers to shift from one line of production to another and to cause changes in the supplies of different commodities.

(4) *State of Technology.* The supply of a commodity depends upon the state of technology. The tremendous results which have occurred in production, in national income, in per capita income and in the standard of living of the people and so on is very largely due 10 the improved methods of production. At any time, what is. produced and how it is produced depend upon what is known. Overtime, knowledge changes and so do the supplies of individual commodities.

(5) *Goals of Producers.* The supply of commodity depends upon the goals of the firms. If producers of some commodity want to sell as much as possible even if it costs them some profits to do so, more will be sold of that commodity than if they wanted to make maximum profits. If producers are not prepared to take risks, we would expect smaller production of any commodity the production of which was risky.

4. SUPPLY FUNCTION

The supply of a commodity is a function of the price of that commodity, the prices of all other commodities, the prices of the factors of production, technology and the goals of the producers. The statement may be expressed in symbols by writing down what is called a supply function, as follows:

$$Sx = f(Px, Py, R, T, G)$$

where Sx is the quantity of commodity X supplied;

Px is the price of commodity X;

Py is the price of all other related commodities;

R is the price of factors of production;

T is the state of technology; and

G is the goals of the producers.

This is a very complicated functional relationship and we shall not succeed in developing a simple law of supply if we consider what happens to supply of a commodity when these things, i.e., prices of all other related commodities, prices of factors of production, changes in technology and the tastes of the producers—all change at once. For a simple theory of price we want to know how the quantity supplied of a commodity varies with its own price. There is a functional relationship between price and amount supplied of a commodity. The functional relationship can alternatively be written as:

$$Sx = f(Px).$$

where Sx is the amount of commodity X supplied

Px is the price of the commodity X.

5. SUPPLY SCHEDULE AND SUPPLY CURVE

Supply Schedule. A supply schedule is a relation between prices and quantities for a given commodity in a given market and in a given period of time. The quantity supplied of a commodity varies directly with the price. When the price falls supply will contract and when the price rises supply will extend. To illustrate the relation between the amount of a commodity supplied and its price, we shall take imaginary data for the prices and quantities of wheat.

Table 30.1. Supply Schedule

Price of Wheat (*Rs.*)	*Quantity Supplied (kgs.)*
10	500
9	450
8	400
7	300
6	150
5	50

It is clear from the schedule in Table 30.1 that if the price of wheat increases, sellers will supply more wheat, on the contrary, if the price of wheat falls sellers will offer lower quantity of wheat for sale.

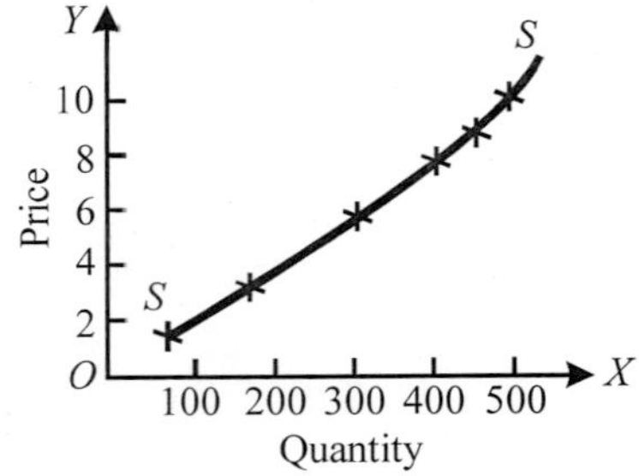

Fig. 30.1

The Supply Curve. We can plot the data from the schedule on a graph with price on the vertical axis and quantity supplied on the horizontal axis. In the Fig. 30.1 we have shown such a graph. It gives the supply curve *SS*. It indicates the relation between the price and the quantity of that commodity.

6. CHANGE IN SUPPLY AND CHANGE IN QUANTITY SUPPLIED

Under change in supply, we talk about increase in supply and decrease in supply while under change in quantity supplied we talk about extension of supply and contraction of supply: All these terms are explained as follows:

Increase in Supply. When more units of a commodity are supplied at the same price or the same units are supplied a lower price, it is an increase in supply with an increase in the supply of a commodity, the supply curve will get shifted to the right. This is shown in Fig. 30.2 when an increase in supply of a commodity occurs, supply curve also shifts from *SS* to *S'S'*. It can be seen from Fig. 30.2 that at the same price *OP* now OX_1'units (instead of *OX)* of the commodity are supplied, i.e., an increase in supply or the same units *OX* are now supply at a lower price OP_1.

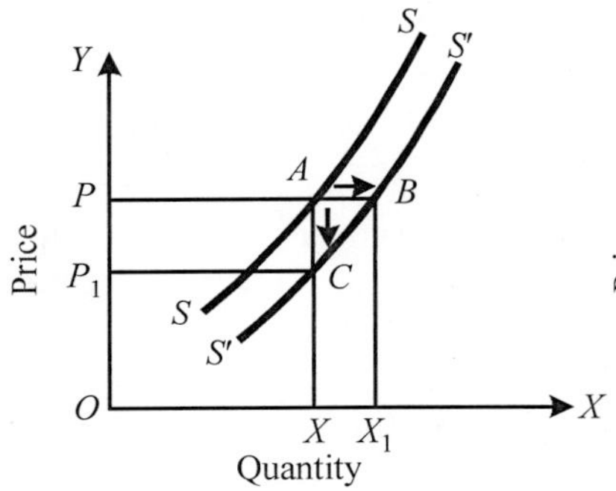

Fig. 30.2

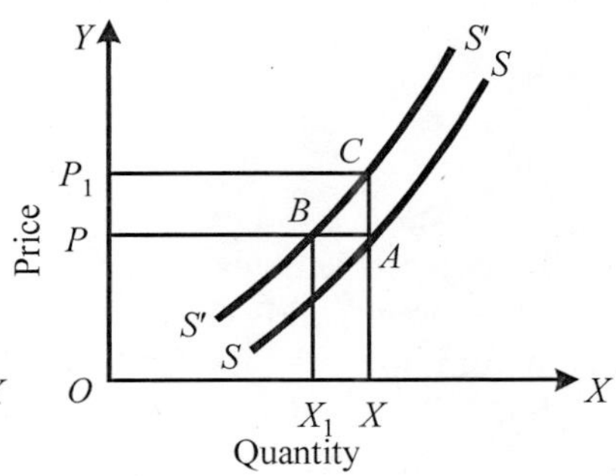

Fig. 30.3

Decrease in Supply. Decrease in supply means the same units of a commodity will be supplied at a higher price or at the same price less units of a commodity will be offered for sale. With a decrease in supply of a commodity the supply curve win get shifted to the left. This is shown in Fig. 30.3.When there is a decrease in the supply of a commodity, the supply curve shifts to *S'S'*. At price *OP, OX* units of the commodity are offered for sale. When there is a decrease in supply of a commodity the same amount of the commodity (OX) is offered for sale at a higher price OP_1 or at the same price (OP) less quantity, i.e., OX_1 units are supplied.

Extension of Supply. When more units of a commodity are supplied at a higher price it is called the extension of supply. The extension of supply is shown in Fig. 30.4. Here at OP price OX units of commodity are supplied by the sellers. At price OP_1, the firm supplies OX_1 units of the commodity. At a still higher price OP_2, OX_2 units of commodity are supplied. Higher the price the larger will be the quantity supplied of a commodity.

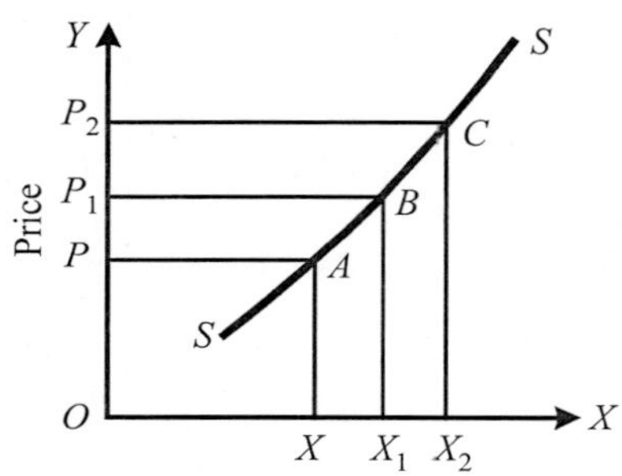

Fig. 30.4

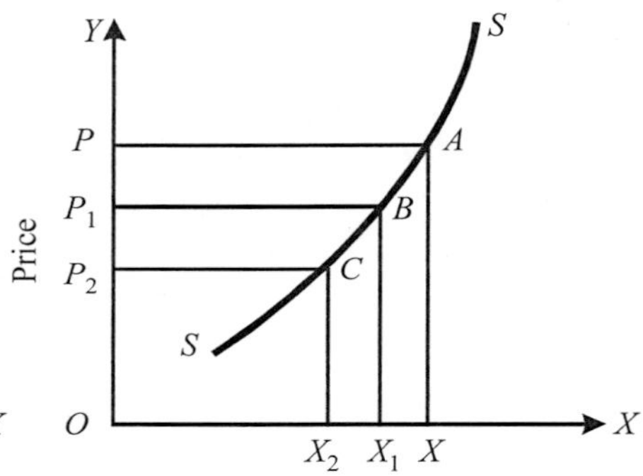

Fig. 30.5

Contraction of Supply. Contraction of supply means lower the price, smaller will be the quantity supplied of a commodity. The contraction of supply is shown in Fig. 30.5. At the price OP the firm supplies OX units of the commodity. At a lower price OP_1 the units of the commodity supplied will be reduced from OX to OX_1. At a still lower price OP_2 the units of commodity supplied will come down to OX_2. A movement along a supply curve indicates that a different quantity is being supplied because the price has changed.

7. ELASTICITY OF SUPPLY

The relationship between the proportionate (percentage) change in the quantity supplied and the proportionate (percentage) change in price is known as the Elasticity of Supply. The formula for the elasticity of supply is similar to that for the elasticity of demand.

$$\text{Elasticity of supply} = \frac{\text{Percent change in quantity supplied}}{\text{Percent change in price}}$$

$$Es = \frac{\Delta X}{\Delta P} \cdot \frac{P}{X}$$

or

where

X = Original quantity supplied

P = Original price

ΔP = Absolute change in price

ΔX = Absolute change in quantity supplied

If this ratio $Es > 1$, supply is said to be elastic.

If this ratio $Es < 1$, supply is said to be inelastic.

If this ratio $Es = 1$, supply is said to have unit elasticity.

When the supply curve is perpendicular to the quantity axis, the elasticity of supply is zero ($Es = 0$).

When the supply curve is perpendicular to the price axis, the elasticity of supply is infinite ($Es = \infty$).

In fact, the steepness of supply curves varies with the commodity; certain supply curves tend to be elastic, others inelastic, anti so on. This follows from the fact that an increase or decrease in price may bring about very little or a great change in the quantity producers are willing to supply. We see then that, when the percentage change in quantity is greater than the percentage change in price, supply is elastic [see panel (*a*) of Fig. 30.6], and when the proportionate change in quantity is less than the proportionate change in price, supply is inelastic [see panel (*b*) of Fig. 30.6]. In panel (*c*) of Fig. 30.6 we have the interesting case of supply having an elasticity of unity—the proportionate changes in price and quantity being equal. Panel (*d*) of Fig. 30.6 illustrates a situation of a completely inelastic supply curve—the vertical line *SS.* This is obviously the most extreme case of an inelastic supply in which a change in price results in absolutely no change in the production of the commodity, and its quantity is fixed. If we were to use our formula for determining elasticity, we would see that elasticity in this case is zero. Zero (which would be the percentage change in quantity divided by any number (the percentage change in price) is zero. The supply curve *SS* in panel (*e*) of Fig. 30.6 illustrates the other extreme case of perfectly elastic or infinitely elastic supply. In this case a small change in price results in an infinite increase in quantity. In instances such as this, or when the supply moves in the direction of horizontal line, we say that the elasticity of supply is infinite, or moves towards infinity.

The degree to which supply is elastic depends upon the flexibility of the productive resources. If production, with existing capacity, can be expanded easily and quickly in response to changes in demand, then supply will be elastic. An increase in the demand for many manufactured products could be met by employing more men, bringing into use stand by equipment, and by working overtime. This would no doubt be true in the case of products such as footwear, hosiery and razor blades.

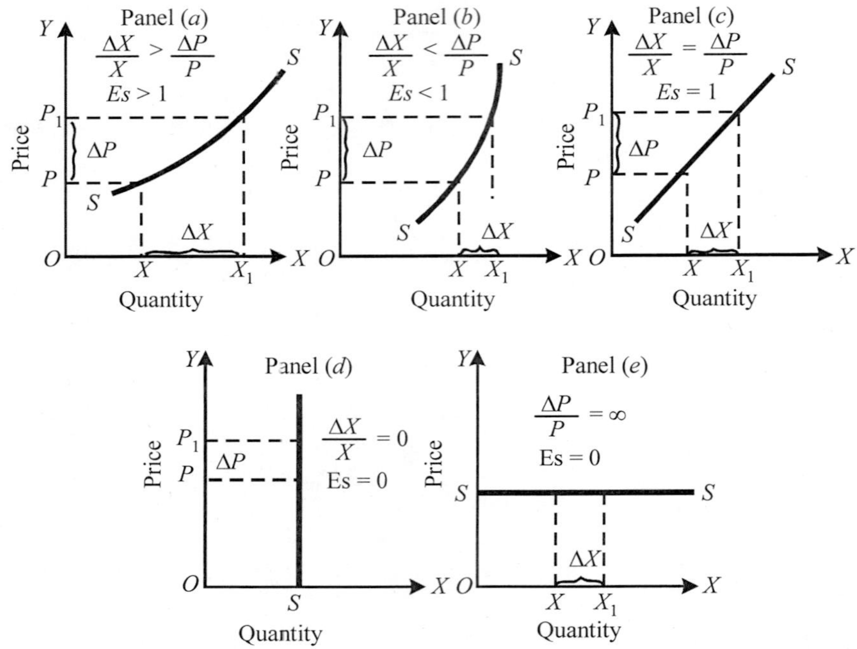

Fig. 30.6

On the other hand, the supply of agricultural products must be fairly inelastic, because the quantity supplied in anyone year is governed by acreage planted in the sowing season. Some natural raw materials and some foodstuffs have supply curves which are extremely inelastic; rubber trees take five to seven years to reach maturity, and a significant increase in the size of dairy and beef herds would take several years. Hence, the element of time exercises an important influence on elasticity of supply. The longer the period of time, the more elastic is the supply likely to be.

8. MEASUREMENT OF ELASTICITY OF SUPPLY

Elasticity of supply can be measured with the help of Fig. 30.7. The supply curve is *SS'* and *NM* is tangent to the supply curve between *R* and R_1 (*R* and R_1 should be close to each other). The rise in price is PP_1 or R_2, R_1; the increase in the quantity supplied is QQ_1 or RR_2

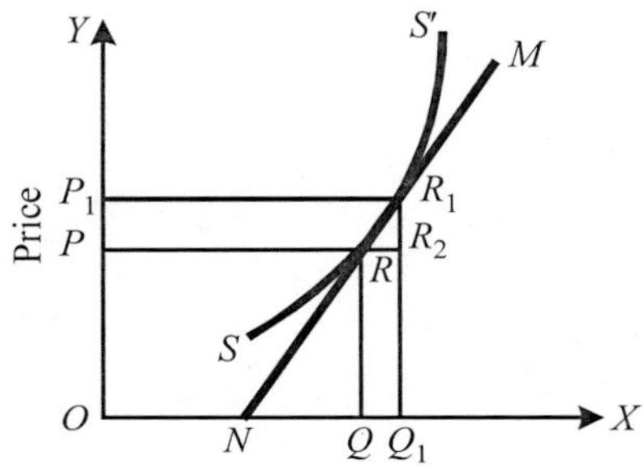

Fig. 30.6

Now the elasticity of supply formula is:

$$Es = \frac{\text{Percentage change in supply}}{\text{Percentage change in price}}$$

This formula of elasticity of supply is the same as elasticity of demand. It can be formulated as follows:

$$Es = \frac{\dfrac{\text{Change in supply}}{\text{Original supply}}\times 100}{\dfrac{\text{Change in price}}{\text{Original price}}\times 100}$$

$$= \frac{\text{Change in supply}}{\text{Original supply}}\times\frac{\text{Original price}}{\text{Change in price}}$$

(Reorganising the above equation we get)

$$= \frac{\text{Change in supply}}{\text{Change in price}}\times\frac{\text{Original price}}{\text{Original supply}}$$

Substituting the required information from the Fig. 30.7, we get

$$Es = \frac{RR_2}{R_1R_2}\times\frac{RQ}{OQ}$$

ΔRR_1R_2 and ΔNRQ are similar, therefore, the ratio of their sides is equal.

This implies that $\dfrac{RR_2}{R_1R_2}\times\dfrac{NQ}{RQ}$

$$\therefore \quad Es = \frac{NQ}{RQ} \times \frac{RQ}{OQ} \quad \text{[}RQ\text{ may be cancelled from both sides]}$$

$$\therefore \quad Es = \frac{NQ}{OQ}$$

This is how we measure elasticity of supply with the help of a diagram. It may be observed that in Fig. 30.7 *NQ* is less than *OQ* and therefore, elasticity of supply in this case will be less than one. On the other hand, if *N* coincides with the origin of the axis, *NQ* and *OQ* will be equal, consequently elasticity of supply will be equal to 1 or unity. If, finally, *N* happens to be beyond O, the elasticity of supply will be more than unity.

9. SUPPLY CURVE UNDER PERFECT COMPETITION

The basis of the demand curve lies in the marginal utility of a commodity, while the basis of the supply curve lies in the costs of production. In considering how much of a commodity firm is willing to supply, it is evident that its cost of production will be the major determinant.[1] We have already discussed the various types of costs in an earlier chapter; the most important types to be studied in relation to supply, are marginal cost and average cost.[2] As we know, marginal cost represents the cost of producing one more the addition to total cost resulting from the expansion of supply of output by one unit. The firm will continue to expand her output as long as the receipts from the sales of extra units exceed the cost of producing them. Here we assume that the firm always attempts to get maximum profits (or maximum loss). Maximum profits will be attained at that level of output where marginal cost is equal to marginal revenue *(MC = MR)*. As we know, marginal revenue represents the change in total revenue which results from the sales of one more unit. If price does

10. THE SHORT-RUN SUPPLY CURVE OF THE FIRM

As we have already explained, a firm is unable to change the sale of plant

1. If the costs of production are raised, the supply curve will be pushed upwards; if cost of production are reduced, the supply curve will be pushed down. Thus, the cost is the vital determinant of supply. Yet, the supply will also depend upon its price and the technological progress.
2. In the short-run the firm will consider the average variable cost and not the average cost as the determinant of supply. In the long-run, average variable and average cost are one and the same thing not change as the number of units sold increases, then marginal revenue must be equal to the price *(MR = P)*.

in the short period. Thus, there are some fixed factors of production in the short-run and firm can increase production only by increasing the quantities of variable inputs. The marginal and average cost of the individual firm are assumed to behave in the manner as shown in Fig. 30.8.

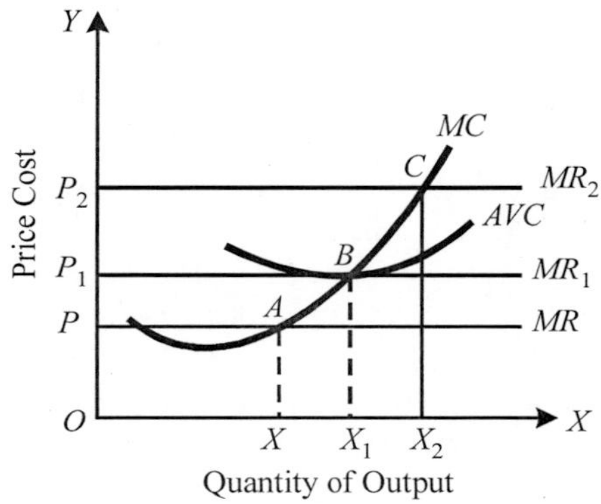

Fig. 30.8

Figure 30.8 presents the firm's *MC* and *AVC* curves and the three exogeneously determined price levels.[3] *OP*, OP_1 and OP_2 are given prices and *OX*, OX_1 and OX_2 are the respective quantities of output where Price = Marginal Cost. Since we are assuming that the price remains constant over the range of output, price will be equal to marginal revenue ($P = MR$) each additional unit sold will add to the total revenue a sum of money which is equal to its price. Therefore, the equilibrium condition of the competitive firm can be written as:

Price = Marginal Revenue = Marginal Cost

Now our question is, what will be the level of supply? At a price of OP_2, the firm is willing to supply OX_2 quantity of output. At any level of output smaller than OX_2 the firm's profits (or losses) will not be maximised (minimised) because additions to costs will be smaller than additions to revenue (or $MC < MR$), and the firm will gain by expanding her output to the extent of OX_2. Also, at higher levels of output than OX_2, the additions to costs will be greater than additions to revenue (or $MC > MR$), and it

3. Since it is the situation of perfect competition, the price of the commodity will be determined by the industry and not by the individual firm. The firm is a price-taker. Therefore, it (price) will be an exogeneous variable for the firm.

would pay the firm to reduce her output. Thus, at OP_2 price, the firm will maximise her profits (or minimise her losses) only at OX_2 level of output (where at point *C*, its $MC = MR$).

Further, at price OP_1, the firm will produce OX_1 quantity of output because at point *B*, $P = MR = MC$. In this particular case, price is also equal to average variable cost. It means that the revenue (price) only just covers the variable costs and there is a loss of fixed costs. But the loss of fixed costs is to be incurred even if the firm produces nothing. Thus at price OP_1, the firm is willing to supply only OX_1 quantity of output.

But at any price below OP_1, the firm will produce nothing. In Fig. 30.8 at *OP* price, firm's (first order) profit maximising condition is satisfied at *OX* level of output. The equilibrium point is *A* where $P = MR = MC$. But at this level of output *(OX),* however, price is below average variable cost (or $P < AVC$). In such a situation production could only be carried on at a loss of available costs and no rational firm would like to bear it. Thus, at price *OP,* the firm would not produce at all. The minimum price acceptable by the firm is OP_1, and the corresponding (minimum) level of output would be OX_1.

Now we are able to answer the question, what quantities would a firm like to supply at any given price? The answer lies in the marginal cost curve; but only that part of marginal cost curve may be regarded as the supply which lies above the average variable cost curve. If we choose any price above OP_1, then the quantity supplied at the chosen price is determined by the intersection or the price line ($P = MR$) and the marginal cost curve.

Therefore there is a "relevant range" of *MC* curve over which it assumes the from of a firm's short-run supply curve. In Fig. 30.8, this range is shown beyond the point *B* at which the *AVC* is minimum and is equal to the *MC.*

11. THE SHORT-RUN SUPPLY CURVE OF THE INDUSTRY

The total (market) supply curve or the industry supply curve for the product can be obtained by adding the supply curve of the individual firms. Figure 30.9 illustrates the construction of the industry supply curve from the firms' marginal cost (supply), curves. For simplicity, let us assume that there are only two firms in the industry. In Fig. 30.9. Panels, (*a*) and (*b*) present the marginal cost curves of two firms in their relevant ranges where they face the situations as

$$P > \text{min. } AVC$$

because only then there can be assumed a positive supply.

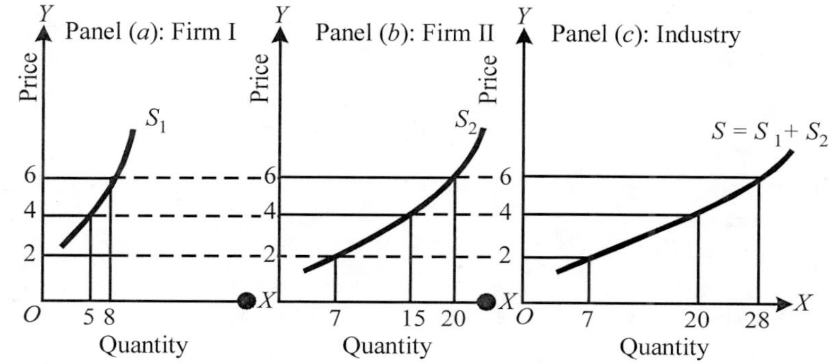

Fig. 30.9

Panel (c) in Fig. 30.9 shows the industry (market) supply curve SS which has been derived by taking the horizontal summation of the individual supply (MC) curves of the firms. The market supply curve is positively sloped which implies that each firm supplies a larger quantity of output at successively higher prices. In Fig. 30.9, it is clear that at price of Rs. 2, firm I will produce nothing because this price is below the -minimum of its AVC, while firm II will produce 7 units of output; thus the total supply of the industry will be equal to 7 units. At price of Rs. 4, firm I produces 5 units of output and firm II produces 15 units of output; thus the total supply of the industry at price of Rs. 4 is equal to 20 units (5 units + 15 units). When price is Rs. 6, firm I is willing to supply 8 units and firm II is willing to supply 20 units; thus the total supply of the industry becomes 28 units (8 units + 20 units) at price of Rs. 6. Hence, the industry supply curve of the output is the horizontal summation of the individual firm's supply (marginal cost) curves.

12. THE LONG-RUN SUPPLY CURVE OF THE FIRM AND THE INDUSTRY

Like the short-run supply curves of the firm and the industry, we may also derive the long-run supply curves of the firm and the industry. As we know, in the long-run, there are no fixed costs, thus the average variable cost curve of the short-run now becomes the average cost of the long-run. In the long-run, the minimum price acceptable by the firm for her product must be equal to the minimum of its average cost. Therefore, in the long-run, the supply of the firm will be determined by the equality of marginal revenue (price) and marginal cost *(MR = MC),* subject to the condition that the long-run price of the product must cover the average cost of production. The reason is that, in the long-run, no firm would like to bear the loss, how little it may be. In a situation when price is just equal to the average cost, i.e., there is no profit, no loss to the firm it would like to produce that level of output at which its *MR* = *MC.* Because, although the firm is not getting any abnormal profit, yet she is gaining normal profits which the economist includes in his average cost of production. Normal profit is defined as that level of profit which makes it just worthwhile for the firm to stay in its present line of business. Since this minimum level of profit is needed to keep the firm in production, it is legitimate to regard these profits as a cost of production.

At that level of output where price is below average cost, productions could only be carried on at a loss and we must assume that the firm would not, in the long-run, produce at this price. Although, in such a situation, our rule of profit maximisation *(MR* = *MC)* may be satisfied, yet, in such a case "maximum profits" must be read as "minimum losses". Hence, the minimum condition necessary for a firm to produce in the long-run is that the price must be equal to the average cost of production. If this condition is satisfied, then the firm will determine its exact supply of the product at a point where its marginal revenue (price) is equal to its marginal cost. The part of marginal cost curve of the firm which is above the minimum point of average cost curve is the supply curve of the firm in long-run. This has been illustrated in Fig. 30.10. Here, the part of *LMC* curve which is above point *A* is the supply curve of the firm.

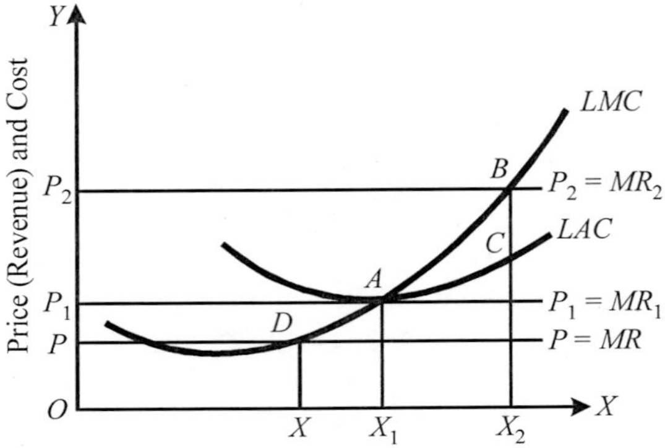

Fig. 30.10

If the price is OP_2, the firm is willing to supply OX_2 units of output; because this is the level of output at which she gets maximum profit. At OX_2 level of output, the firm's per unit profit is equal to *BC*. If the firm produces a smaller amount than OX_2, its profit per unit will be reduced arid if it produces more than OX_2 level of output, the addition to total cost (i.e., *MC*) is higher than the price (i.e., *MR*). Thus, at OP_2 long-run price the firm's long-run supply will be OX_2. The minimum price acceptable by the firm is equal to OP_1 at which the firm would like to produce OX_1 quantity of output. This price is just equal to its minimum long-run average cost. If price is below this level, then she will produce no output. For instance, at *OP* price, although firm's profit and output determination rule ($MC = MR$) is fulfilled at point *D*, where she requires to produce *OX* quantity of output. But this situation does not satisfy the other minimum long-run condition, that is, the price must be equal to the average cost. Hence, at *OP* price, the firm would like to no output and will change the line of business.

Now, the long-run supply curve of the industry can be obtained by the horizontal summation of the long-run supply (*MC*) curves of all the individual firms, the diagram will be the same as in Fig. 30.9. The shape of industry supply curve will depend upon the shape of marginal cost curves of the individual firms. Normally, the supply curve of the industry slopes upwards from left to right, indicating that more is supplied at higher price.

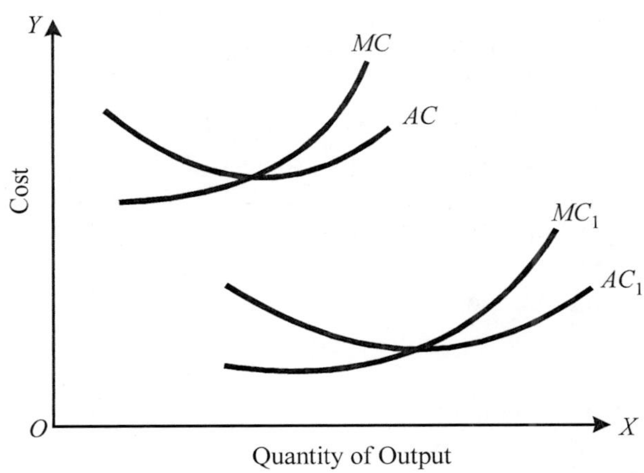

Fig. 30.11

Changes in Supply. Changes in supply are made by changes in the scale of plant or the introduction of new techniques and methods of production. In each case the changes will mean that the costs of production have altered. An increase in scale or an improvement in the methods of production will mean a lowering of costs and new cost curves become applicable. Figure 30.11 shows the effects of a firm expanding and modernising its production processes. The original average and marginal cost curves are represented by *AC* and *MC*. An increase in the scale of plant and new techniques of productions result in greater efficiency and a lowering of its cost, curves. Their new average and marginal cost curves are represented by AC_1 and MC_1 respectively. The supply curves of the firm are shown by heavier-lined sections of the marginal cost curves. Here, we may note that the increased efficiency of the firm shifts its supply curve to the right downward.

13. LAWS OF RETURNS AND THE LONG-RUN SUPPLY CURVE OF AN INDUSTRY

The Laws of Returns have an important bearing on the shape of the long period supply curve of an industry under perfect competition. The long period supply curve of the perfectly competitive industry will have different shapes depending upon the fact whether the industry is subject to constant returns, diminishing returns or increasing returns. The long period industry supply curve will be horizontal, if the industry in question is subject to the Constant Returns. It will slope upwards to the right if the industry is subject to Diminishing Returns. It will slope upwards to the left if the industry is subject to the Increasing Returns.

Industry Supply Curve under Constant Returns or Constant Costs

The cost of an industry subject to constant returns remain unchanged if the output of the industry is expanded through the application of additional doses of inputs. As the industry expands, the external economies resulting from it get cancelled with the external diseconomies flowing from it. The result is that the production costs remain constant. No doubt, the new firms will enter into industry in the long period but their costs will remain constant owing to the operation of the Law of Constant Returns.

This has been shown in Fig. 30.12 where the firm has achieved its equilibrium at the point *E*. At this point the *LMC* and *LAC* curves of the firm intersect each other. The firm is in equilibrium at the point *E* producing *OX* output at *OP* price. In the long period, the firm, expands

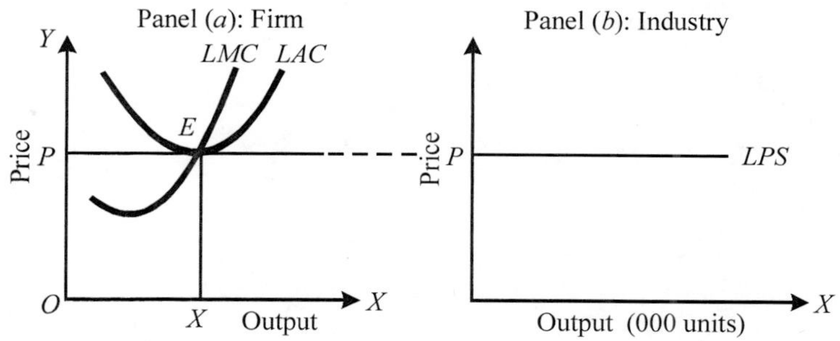

Fig. 30.12

its output but the costs remain constant. So the firm achieves its new equilibrium at the same point *E* without any rise in the average and the marginal costs of production. This applies to the new firms also which enter into the industry. Their costs do behave in the same manner as the cost of the firm in question. The result is that the long-run supply curve of the industry assumes a horizontal shape as shown in Fig. 30.12. It may be noted that for the purpose of this discussion, we assume all the firms to be indentical.

Industry Supply Curve under Diminishing Returns or Increasing Costs

The costs of an industry subject to Diminishing Returns go on increasing if the output of the industry is expanded through the application of additional doses of inputs. As the industry expands, the external diseconomies resulting from it outweigh the economies flowing from it. The result is that the cost of production per unit goes on increasing with the expansion of output of the industry. In the long period, the new firms enter into the industry, there is increased pressure on the existing factors of production which now become scarce as a result of an increase in their demand. So the production costs start rising up with every expansion of the industry. This has been shown in Fig. 30.13. The firm is in initial equilibrium at the point *E* where the *LMC* and *LAC* curves intersect each other.

At this point, the price = *MC* = *AC*. The firm is in equilibrium producing *OX* output at *OP* price. With the expansion of industry production, the factors get scarced and the costs start mounting up. The firm now achieves equilibrium at the point E_1 where its LAC_1 and LMC_1

curves intersect each other. The firm, no doubt produces less output OX_1, but this output is achieved with higher costs. Since the number of firms is increasing and even if the individual firm's output is less but the output of the industry increases. As Fig. 30.13 shows, the firm achieves its new equilibrium at a higher costs and at higher prices. Since the production costs of all the firms register an increase, the industry will be able to supply increased quantities of the product only at a higher price. At the old OP price; the industry was supplying OR quantity of the commodity. At the new price OP_1 which is higher that the original price OP; the industry supply has increased to OR_1. This shows that the industry supply increases with every increase in the price of the commodity. It is for this reason that the LPS curve of the industry slopes upwards to the right.

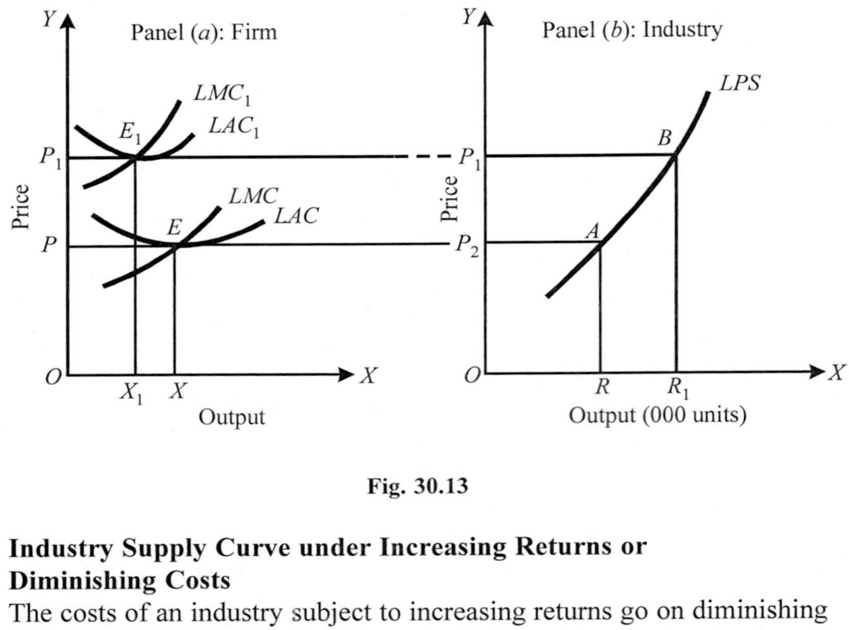

Fig. 30.13

Industry Supply Curve under Increasing Returns or Diminishing Costs

The costs of an industry subject to increasing returns go on diminishing as the output of the industry is expanded through the application of additional doses of inputs. As the industry expands the external economies resulting from it outweigh the external diseconomies flowing from it. The result is that the cost of production per unit goes on diminishing with every expansion of the output. In the long period, as the firm expands and the new firms enter into the industry, the production costs start declining with every expansion of the industry. This has been shown in

Fig. 30.14. The firm is in initial equilibrium at the point E when the price $= MC = AC$. The firm is in equilibrium at the point E producing OX output at OP price. Then the firm in question starts expanding in production. It achieves the new equilibrium at the point E_1 where the LAC_1 and LMC_1 curves intersect each other. At this point, the firm produces the increased output OX_1 at the lower price OP_1. The Fig. 30.14 clearly shows the firm has achieved its new equilibrium at a lower cost and also at a lower price on account of the operation of the law of increasing returns or diminishing costs. The new firms which enter into the industry in the long period will also achieve equilibrium at lower costs and also at lower prices. Since the production cost of all the firms register a decline, the industry will be able to supply increased quantities of the product at lower prices. At this old OP price, the industry was supplying OR quantity of the commodify. At the new price OP_1 which is lower than the original price OP, the industry supplies increased output namely OR_1. This shows that the additional supplies from the industry are forthcoming at lower prices. It is for this reason that the LPS curve of the industry slopes downwards to the right.

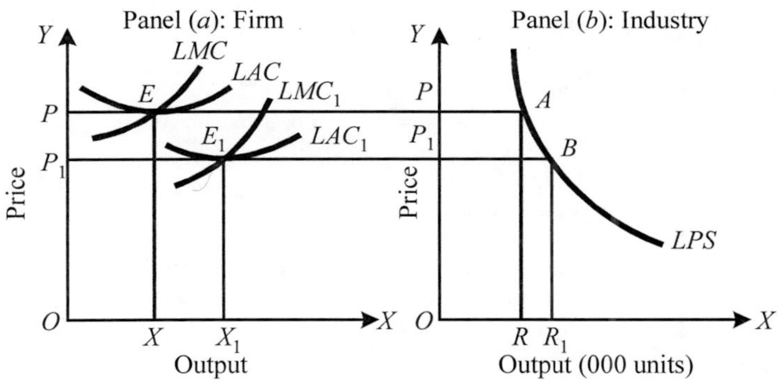

Fig. 30.14

14. SUPPLY CURVE UNDER MONOPOLY OR IMPERFECT COMPETITION

We do not have a unique supply curve under imperfect competition or monopoly. It is because of the fact that price is simultaneously determined along with the quantity of the commodity produced unlike perfect competition, the price is not given to a firm under monopoly or monopolistic competition. Here the firm is a price-maker for her product. Thus the firm fixes a price where it gets maximum profit. The supply of the commodity is determined by the market demand for its product. It is therefore impossible to talk of a supply curve under monopoly or monopolistic competition. The output supplied by the producer under such monopolistic situation will depend upon the market demand conditions for his product and no unique supply curve (as well as the supply schedule) can be drawn.

EXERCISES

1. Derive the short-run supply curve of a firm under perfect competition. How would you obtain the industry supply schedule?
2. Derive the long-run supply curve of the firm and the industry under perfect competition.
3. Explain the conditions under which the supply curve slopes downward.
4. Discuss why does the supply curve of the firm and the industry slope upward to the right in the short-run?
5. Explain the fact that the shape of the long-run supply curve depends on the laws of production.
6. "There is no unique supply curve under monopoly." Explain the statement.
7. State the law of supply and explain the elasticity of supply. How will you measure the elasticity of supply?
8. Distinguish between change in supply and change in quantity supplied.

Multiple Choice Questions

9. (*i*) Other things being equal, a rise in supply can be caused by
   (*a*) a rise in the price of the commodity
   (*b*) a rise in the income of the consumer
   (*c*) an increase in the income of the seller
   (*d*) all of the above [*Ans.* (*a*)]

   (*ii*) Given the supply of a commodity in the market period, the price of the commodity is determined by
   (*a*) the market demand curve alone
   (*b*) the market supply curve alone
   (*c*) the market demand curve and the market supply curve
   (*d*) hone of the above [*Ans.* (*a*)]

   (*iii*) At the shut-down point
   (*a*) $TR = TVC$
   (*b*) $P = AVC$
   (*c*) the total losses of the firm equal *TFC*
   (*d*) all of the above [*Ans.* (*b*)]

   (*iv*) The short-run supply curve of the perfectly competitive firm is given by
   (*a*) the rising portion of its *MC* curve over and above the shut-down point
   (*b*) the rising portion of its *MC* curve over and above the break-even-point
   (*c*) the rising portion of its *MC* curve over and above the *AC* curve
   (*d*) the rising portion of its *MC* curve [*Ans.* (*a*)]

(*v*) An increase in output in a perfectly competitive constant cost industry which is in long-run equilibrium will come
(*a*) entirely from new firm.
(*b*) entirely from existing firm
(*c*) either (*a*) or (*b*)
(d) partly from new firm and partly from existing firm [*Ans. (a)*]

Chapter 31

EQUILIBRIUM OF THE FIRM AND THE INDUSTRY

1. INTRODUCTION

As we have already explained, equilibrium indicates a situation in which there is a complete adjustment of the various forces operating there and there is no inducement to change. It is an ideal stage. In Part Two of this book, we have analysed the behaviour of a consumer. A consumer is said to be in equilibrium when he is deriving maximum satisfaction. In Part Three of this book, we have analysed the behaviour of a rational producer (firm). He tries to minimise the cost of producing a given level of output or maximise his revenue (output) for given level of resource use. Thus, in the case of a producer, equilibrium is attained when he gets maximum output with the least cost-combination of different inputs.

In the present chapter, we shall discuss the equilibrium of the firm and the industry. A firm is said to be in equilibrium when it has no incentive either to expand or to contract its output. A firm would not like to change its level of output only when it is earning maximum profits. Hence, the firm attempts to maximise its profits, or to minimize its losses. Maximisation of profits or minimisation of losses (in case losses are met with) is a condition of a firm's equilibrium. Similarly, an industry is said to be in equilibrium when the market demand and the market supply are perfectly equal and changes in demand and supply are absent.

2. EQUILIBRIUM OF THE FIRM UNDER PERFECT COMPETITION

the equilibrium of the firm can be discussed in terms of marginal cost and marginal revenue as well as in terms of total cost and total revenue. Many firms, nowadays, use a device known as a *break-even chart* for determining what output of their product would be most profitable in the market situation that confronts them. This kind of chart is based on a comparison of total costs for differel1t outputs with the total receipts that it is anticipated can be derived from sales. It means that every firm intends to obtain the greatest return on its investment, or to maximise the difference between total revenue (receipts) and total cost. Suppose, a perfect competitive firm has to face with the costs and revenues as given in Table 31.1. Price for the firm has been assumed to remain constant. The fixed costs are assumed to be Rs. 40. The sum of the fixed and variable costs for different outputs amounts to the figures shown in

Table 31.1. Revenue, Cost and Profit for a Hypothetical Firm Under Perfect Competition

Quantity of Output Cost	*Total Fixed Cost*	*Total Variable*	*Total Cost*	*Marginal Cost*	*Price*	*Total Revenue*	*Marginal Revenue Loss*	*Profit or*
1	2	3	4	5	6	7	8	9
0	40	—	40	—	—	—	—	– 40
1	40	13	53	—	20	20	20	– 33
2	40	24	64	11	20	40	20	– 24
3	40	33	73	9	20	60	20	– 13
4	40	40	80	7	20	80	20	0
5	40	48	88	8	20	100	20	+ 12
6	40	57	97	9	20	120	20	+ 20
7	40	77	117	20	20	140	20	+ 23
8	40	100	140	23	20	160	20	+ 20
9	40	140	180	40	20	180	20	0
10	40	183	223	43	20	200	20	– 23

Column 4. The total costs are plotted in the wavelike curve of Fig. 31.1. Table 31.1 also states that the price, Rs. 20 per unit is fixed for the firm's output. The total revenue (receipts) from sales for various quantities sold will then be as shown in column 7 of the table. The figures of total revenue are also plotted on the diagram which gives us the diagonal straight line marked "Total Revenue Curve." The profit or loss resulting from sales for each unit is shown in the last column of the Table 31.1. It can be observed from Table 31.1 and from Fig. 31.1 that the entrepreneur maximses his profit where the difference between total cost and total revenue is maximum. In equilibrium, he will produce seven units of output for maximisation of profit. We notice that for small outputs, the total costs exceed the total receipts obtained. This is because the fixed costs

are not distributed over a large enough number of units to bring the cost per unit down below the selling price. But if more is produced, the losses shrink until a break-even point is reached (at 4 units of output), where the total revenue is just equal to total cost (Rs. 80). This is shown in Fig. 31.1 at point *A* where the total cost curve cuts the total revenue curve. From

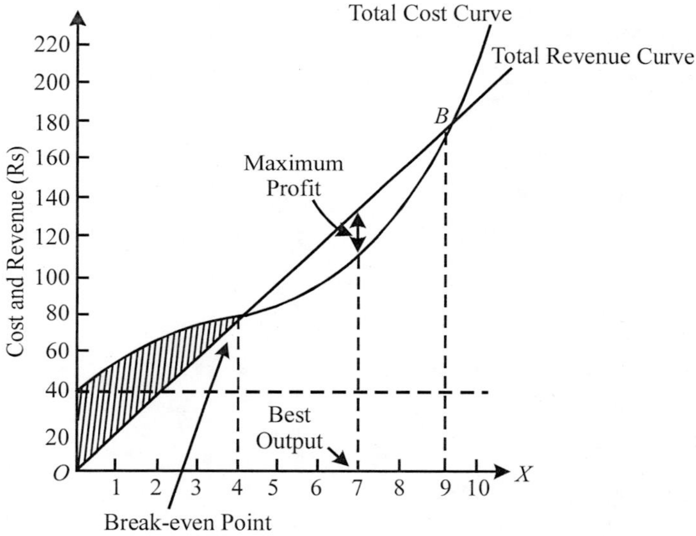

Fig. 31.1

point *A,* the total revenue exceeds the total costs, and results in a profit to the firm. The profits become larger with greater output, but after some point they will decline again as the maximum capacity of the plant is approached. Costs then creep up on the selling price until profits reduce to zero. In Fig. 31.1, point *B* shows that at nine units of output, profit becomes zero. Beyond this point *B,* losses would again be incurred. Thus, firm will always produce a level of output which is above the break-even point. It will try to increase its sales to that point where it gets maximum profit (7 units in our example).

The equilibrium of the firm can also be analysed in terms of marginal revenue and marginal cost. The firm will maximise its profits only at that level of output at which $MC = MR$. It may be observed from Table 31.1 that the firm maximises her profits at 7 units of output where $MC = MR =$

Rs. 20. Beyond 7 units of output, marginal cost exceeds marginal revenue and, therefore, on each additional unit produced beyond this level, the firm incurs a loss. This means a reduction in total profits. This situation has been illustrated in Fig. 31.2. Panel (*a*) of Fig. 31.2 shows that profit

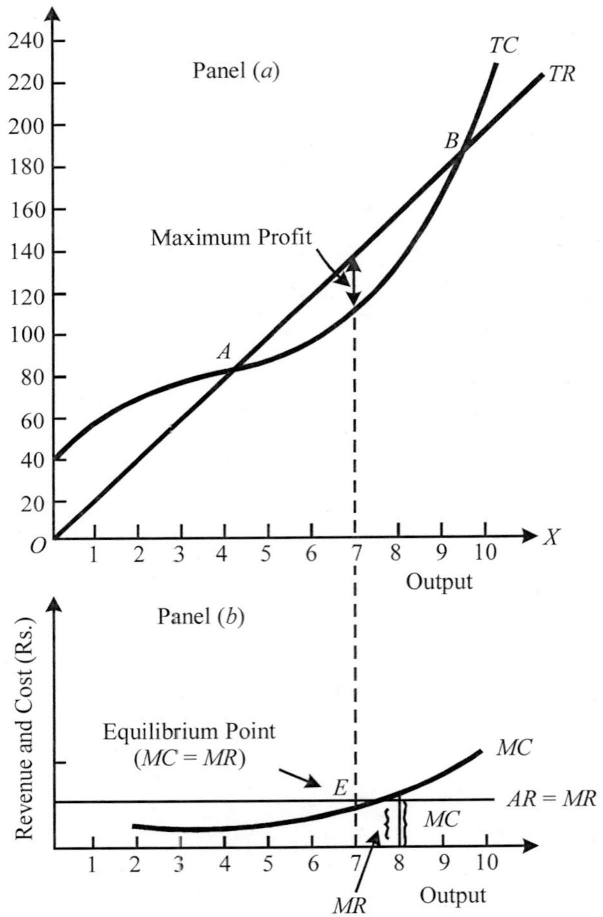

Fig. 31.2

is the vertical difference between *TR* curve and the *TC* curve. It indicates that profit is maximum when the firm produces 7 units of output. This is confirmed by Panel (*b*) of Fig. 31.1 in which the *MC* curve cuts the *MR* curve exactly at this level of output (7 units). The *MR* curve is horizontal to *X*-axis and is similar to the *AR* curve. The reason is that the price of the output is fixed for all units sold by the firm. If the firm produces more than 7 units of output, then the marginal cost will be greater than marginal revenue and the firm has to incur a loss. Thus, the best output is the one indicated by he equality of marginal revenue and marginal cost. If the firm produces this output, it is in equilibrium since there is no tendency for it to produce more or less than this output.

3. EQUILIBRIUM OF THE FIRM UNDER MONOPOLY

The monopoly firm also tries to maximise her profits, and profits will be maximumat that level of output where the difference between total revenue and total cost is maximum or where the marginal cost is equal to marginal revenue.

Under perfect competition we assume that price is given to the firm and thus its *AR*-curve will be horizontal to *X*-axis. The *MR*-curve of the firm under perfect competition is the same as the *AR*-curve. Since under perfect competition, the price remains constant regardless of the level of output or sales, the total revenue would be a straight line. But under monopoly, the firm has to face a negatively sloping demand curve (or *AR* curve) and the marginal revenue curve. The reason is that if at all she wants to sell more output, she has to reduce the price of her output. The consequent *TR*-curve for monopoly firm will not be a straight line but it will be as shown in Fig. 31.3. Now, for profit maximisation the same rules will be applied as we have discussed under the perfect competitive firm. Figure 31.3 indicates that profits will be maximum at that level of output at which the vertical difference between the *TR*-curve and the *TC*-curve is maximum. It is also observed that exactly at this level of output *MC*-curve cuts the *MR*-curve. Point *E* is the equilibrium point where the firm produces *OX* level of output and attains maximum profit. The second order condition is also satisfied, as if the firm produces beyond *OX* output, its *MR* will be less than its *MC*. Thus, the monopoly will always try to produce *OX* level of output. At this equilibrium level of output, the equilibrium price will be equal to *PX* (it is also the average revenue of the firm).

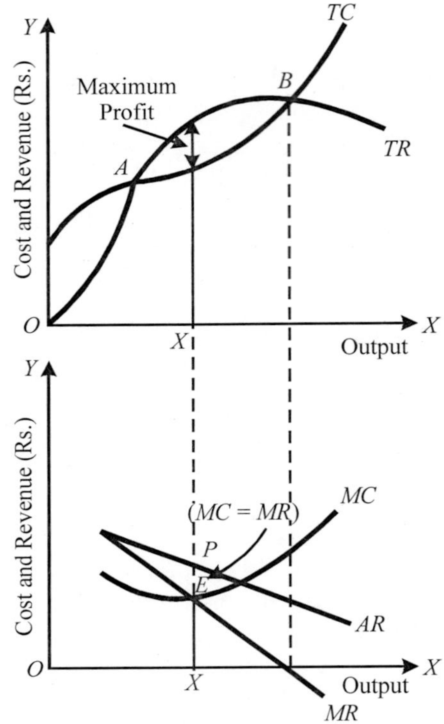

Fig. 31.3

4. EQUILIBRIUM OF THE INDUSTRY

Under perfect competition, an industry consists of a number of firms producing identical or homogeneous output. The industry is said to be in equilibrium when the industry's demand and the industry's supply of the product are equal. In other words, the equilibrium price is given by the intersection of the demand and supply curves of the industry as shown in Fig. 31.4.

In Fig. 31.4, the equilibrium price is OP_2, for only at this price are the quantities demanded and supplied equal. At prices higher than the market price (for example, OP_3), the quantity supplied (OX_3), exceeds the quantity demanded (OX_1), and this excess supply (AB) will mean that firms will be obliged to lower prices in order to dispose of their output; a situation sometimes referred to as a *buyers' market.* At lower prices (for example, OP_1), the quantity demanded will exceed the quantity supplied and competition between buyers will force up the price giving rise to conditions known as a *sellers' market.* Only at a price of *OP* are there no forces at work which are tending to change the price. Thus, in Fig. 31.4, OP_2 is the equilibrium price and OX_2 is the equilibrium quantity demanded and supplied.

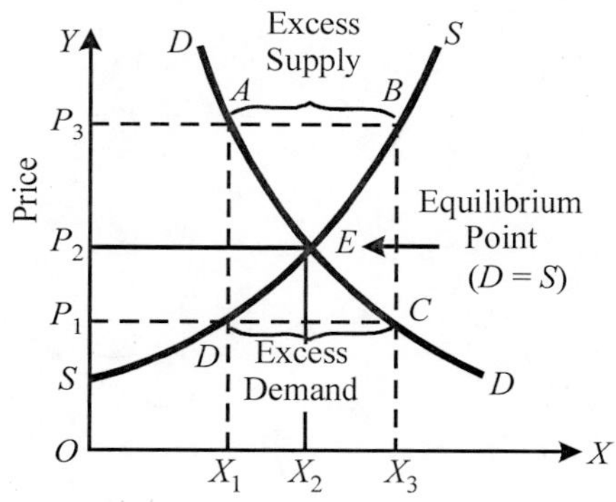

Fig. 31.4

5. RESOURCE ALLOCATON UNDER PERFECT COMPETITION

There are two ways to deal with the problem of resource allocation under perfect competition:

(1) Resource Allocation under Partial Equilibrium,

(2) Resource Allocation under General Equilibrium.

(1) *Resource Allocation under Partial Equilibrium.* Under perfect competition in the long-run every firm builds the least cost plant and operates it at its optimal level of output, i.e., the per unit cost becomes minimum. Since each firm operates the plant at full capacity, so that the resources of the economy are allocated in the most efficient way within and between industries. This tendency will lead to full employment of resources within the economy. All the firms get normal profit and that leads to the following equilibrium condition to hold in the economy:

$$LMC = MR = P = AR = LAC \qquad ...(1)$$

Under the above condition (1), the aggregate consumer satisfaction is also maximum as the goods are distributed among them according to their demands at the minimum per unit cost because price equals the marginal cost of the product. Given the above conditions under equation (1), we may explain below the optimal allocation of resources. In perfect competition, firms are simply price-takers and quantity-adjusters. Every firm has to accept the price determined by the industry demand and supply. In panel (*a*) of Fig. 31.5, price *OP* is fixed by the industry. It is given to every firm. Thus the demand curve for the firm's output is perfectly elastic where $AR = MR = P$. In panel (*b*) of Fig. 3 1.5, firm's profit maximisation output is *OX* where firm's $LMC = MR$ and also $MR = AR = P$.

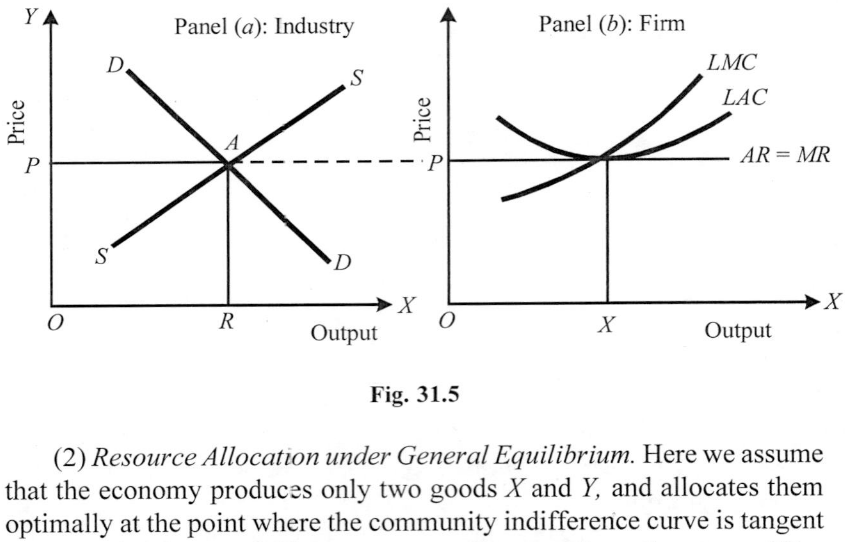

Fig. 31.5

(2) *Resource Allocation under General Equilibrium.* Here we assume that the economy produces only two goods *X* and *Y,* and allocates them optimally at the point where the community indifference curve is tangent to the production possibility curve or product transformation curve. Here it is assumed that there is perfect competition where the prices are given to all individual units both in the product market as well as in the factor market. Tastes and technology remain unchanged, i.e., we deal with only one production possibility curve only. The resources of the economy are fully employed. Under these assumptions, the optimal allocation of resources is shown in Fig. 31.6.

In Fig. 31.6, IC_1, IC_2 and IC_3 are the community indifference curves showing various possible combinations of goods *X* and *Y* available to the society for consumption. The slope of indifference curve is the marginal rate of substitution (*MRS*) between *X* and *Y*. Curve PP_1 is the production

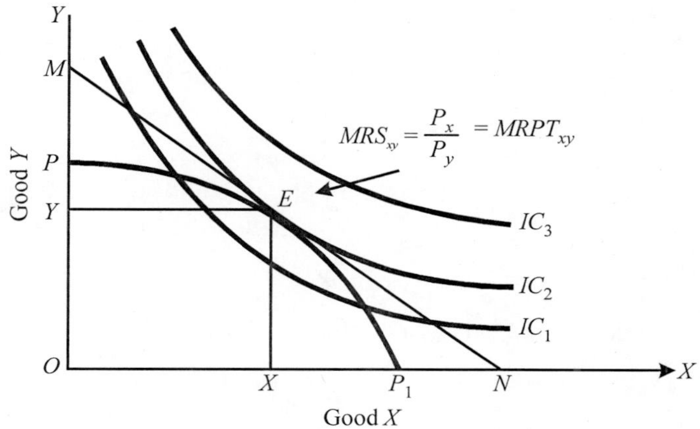

Fig. 31.6

possibility curve which shows the various possible output combinations that the economy may produce under the given resources and technology. The slope of the PP_1 curve is the marginal rate of product transformation (*MRPT*) between *X* and *Y*. The *MRPT* measures the ratio of marginal social cost (*MSC*) of *X* to that of *Y*. In Fig. 31.6, *MN* is the price line or the constraint line whose slope shows the price ratio *Px Py*. Now the society attains the optimal allocation of resources at point *E* where the slope of price line equals the slope PP_1-curve and the slope of the community indifference curve. It is the point where the product transformation curve touches the highest possible community-indifference curve IC_2. At this point the society produces and consumes exactly *OX* quantity of *X* and *OY* quantity of *Y*. Here, there is neither the situations over production nor the situations of under production but it is the situation of optimal production. From demand side, equilibrium is established at point *E* where the price line *MN* is tangent to the indifference curve IC_2. Thus at point *E*,

$$MRSxy = \frac{Px}{Py} \qquad ...(2)$$

From the supply side, the competitive equilibrium requires that the slope of the price line *MN* must be equal to the slope of PP_1-curve. Thus at point *E*,

$$\frac{Px}{Py} = MRSxy \qquad ...(3)$$

$$\text{Since} = MRPTxy = \frac{MCx}{MCy} = \frac{MSCx}{MSCy}$$

∴ from equation (2) and (3), we have

$$MRSxy = \frac{Px}{Py} = MRSTxy \qquad ...(4)$$

It follows that the resources are optimally allocated under perfect competition.

EXERCISES

1. Explain with the help of a diagram the firm's equilibrium under perfect competition.
2. Explain with the help of a diagram the equilibrium of the firm under monopoly.
3. How does the competitive industry attain its equilibrium position? Illustrate the answer with the help of a diagram.
4. Explain the equilibrium of a firm under monopoly.
5. State and show in diagrams the conditions of equilibrium of the firm and industry under perfect competition.
6. Explain how resources are optimally allocated under perfect competition.
7. "No firm can be in equilibrium unless its marginal revenue and marginal cost are equal. Comment on this statement.

Multiple Choice Questions

8. (*i*) When the perfectly competitive firm and industry both are in long-run equilibrium
   (*a*) $P = MR = SMC = LMC$
   (*b*) $P = MR = SAC = LAC$
   (*c*) $P = MR =$ lowest on the *LAC* curve
   (*d*) all of the above [*Ans.* (*d*)]

   (*ii*) When the perfectly competitive firm but not the industry is in long-run equilibrium
   (*a*) $P = MR = SMC = SAC$
   (*b*) $P = MR = LMC = LAC$
   (*c*) $P = MR = SMC = LMC \neq SAC = LAC$
   (d) $P = MR = SMC = LMC \neq SAC =$ lowest point on the *LAC* curve [*Ans.* (*c*)]

   (*iii*) Under perfect competition the economy attains general equilibrium when the resources are allocated in such a manner that
   (*a*) $MRSxy = \frac{Px}{Py}$ (*b*) $MRPTxy = \frac{Px}{Py}$
   (*c*) $MRPTxy = \frac{MCx}{MCy} = \frac{MSCx}{MSCy}$ (*d*) $MRSxy = \frac{Px}{Py}$ $MRPTxy$ [*Ans.* (*d*)]

Chapter 32

PRICING AND OUTPUT UNDER PERFECT COMPETITION

1. INTRODUCTION

We have so for been discussing the basic tools of analysis which we shall now use in the process of price and output determination under various market situations, such as, perfect competition, monopoly and imperfect competition. The analysis which will be carried out in the following chapters of Part IV, we shall assume that there is perfect competition between consumers. What we shall study is the difference in the kind of competition between firms.

In the present chapter, we assume that monopolistic elements are absent and proceed to consider how a price is arrived at under conditions of perfect competition. We shall look first at the conditions necessary for the existence of perfect competition and then at the process of price and output determination in various time per ods.

2. CHARACTERISTICS OF PERFECT COMPETITION

An industry (market) is said to be operating under perfect competition when the following requirements are met:

(1) Large number of buyers and sellers.

(2) Homogeneity of the products.

(3) Free entry or exit.

(4) Perfect mobility off actors of production.

(5) Absence of transport cost.

(6) Perfect knowledge of the economy.

(1) ***Large Number of Buyers and Sellers.*** There must be many buyers and many sellers, so that the behaviour of any one seller, or anyone buyer will have no influence on the market price. Each buyer comprises such a small part of the total (market) demand for the product, and each seller

such a small part of the total (market) supply that any change in their plans will have no influence on the market price. In other words, the price of the product is determined by the collective forces of industry demand and industry supply. The individual firm and the buyer must take the price of the product as given. The firm is a 'price taker'. As we have already explained in the previous chapters that demand curve of the firm in perfect competition is perfectly elastic. Each firm has to adjust her output or sale according to the prevailing market price.

(2) ***Homogeneity of the Products.*** In perfectly competitive industry, the product of any one firm is identical to the products of all other firms. This means, all the firms in an industry produce perfectly identical or homogeneous products. Not only this, but all units of the commodity must be homogeneous (i.e., one unit is exactly like another). If this is so, then buyers will be completely indifferent as to the firm (seller) they approach, and the sellers will be indifferent as to the buyer to whom they sell. It does not make any difference to a consumer whether he buys the product from firm *A* or firm *B* or any other in the industry because the shape, packing, colour, weight, and other attributes of one product are identical to the products offered by other firms. As a consequence, a single price will rule over other entire industry. Since all the products are perfect substitutes, the elasticity of demand for the product will be perfectly elastic and the numerical value of the elasticity coefficient will be infinity. This will lead to the conclusion that the average revenue and marginal revenue of the perfect competitive firm will be the same.

(3) ***Free Entry or Exit.*** The third important feature of perfect competition is that there should be complete freedom for the firms to enter into the industry or to leave the industry. New firms must be permitted to set themselves up in the industry if they find it often an attractive opportunity—otherwise competition would be restricted and hence it would not be perfect competition. This is not always listed as a separate condition, because it is considered to be implicit in the second. That is, if producers (firms) in an industry are many and small, acting independently of each other, there is not likely to be any bar to the entry of new firms. If profits are incurred in the short run, new firms can enter the industry and/or the existing firms can expand the scale of their plants. The entry of new firms wilt shift the industry supply curve to the right and will tend to reduce the equilibrium price. After sometime this will lead to zero profits.

Similarly, if the firms are incurring losses in the industry in the short run, a few firms may exit from the industry. This will reduce the supply of the industry and will raise the equilibrium price to the level of the long-run average cost. Again, this will mean that only normal profits (which are included in *LAC*) will be attained by the competitive firms and the industry in the long-run. Thus, in perfect competition, due to free entry or exit, each firm will be of optimum size in the long run.

(4) ***Perfect Mobility of Factors of Production.*** Another assumption of perfect competition is that there must be perfect mobility of factors of production. It means, the factors of production (such as labour and capital) are mobile, not only geographically, but also among different jobs. Workers will move from one employer to another and entrepreneurs from one industry to another and by doing so, they can increase their returns or satisfaction. Thus, perfect mobility also implies that each firm is optimising the use of each factor input. While each factor owner gets its opportunity cost in a competitive market, each firm minimises the cost incurred on a particular factor use.

(5) ***Absence of Transport Cost.*** In perfect competition price is the same. It is possible only when we assume that transport cost does not exist in a perfect competitive market. This assumption (ignoring the cost of transportation) will lead to price equalisation of product and factor inputs geographically and also among all the alternative uses.

(6) ***Perfect Knowledge of the Economy.*** In a perfectly competitive market, all the buyers and sellers must possess a perfect knowledge about the market activities. Every buyer or seller knows the price of the product. In the absence of perfect knowledge, it is possible that some buyers may buy the commodity at higher prices when the same product is available at a lower price. Thus, in the situation of the absence of perfect knowledge, there will be different prices for the same product. Also, due to the perfect knowledge of buyers, it would not pay a firm to reduce the price. Because the reduction in price will be known immediately and the buyers will buy at the lowest prices. This forces sellers charging higher prices to lower their prices immediately. Conversely, the firm will lose all its sales if it increases the price. At the same time, advertisement and publicity would prove futile in a competitive market as all the products are homogeneous. Thus, the fact is that only a single price will prevail in the market for any particular product (or factor-input).

Sometimes, economists distinguish 'pure competition' from 'perfect competition.' The difference between, them is one of degree. For pure competition, the first five assumptions mentioned above are normally considered necessary. For competition to be perfect, the additional requirement is that all economic units (consumers, producers, and resource owners) must possess complete knowledge of the economy. In perfect competition, at all times, there must be one single ruling price for a particular product in the entire market. Given the price of the product, the individual firms take decisions independently. They have to decide, how much output should be produced at the given price. This is the reason that the examples of perfect competition are very rare.

When a situation of perfect competition exists, it means that one price, and only one price for the commodity will be established. Perfect knowledge ensures that buyers will not pay different prices. Perfect mobility ensures that consumers and factors of production will move to equalise any price differentials which may take place. Homogeneity of product ensures that preferences will not arise which might be converted into price differentials. Similarly, non-existence of transport cost ensures that price will be the same at all places it is sold. All of this means that an equilibrium price will be established which is due entirely to forces of supply and demand which cannot be influenced by individual buyers or sellers, and there will be no associations of buyers or sellers which might, by their actions, affect the market conditions. The only difference of degree between pure and perfect competition can be explained as: under conditions of perfect competition adjustments of the economy to disturbances in the conditions of demand and supply will be instantaneous; while under condition of pure competition, it will take longer for adjustment to occur because of incomplete knowledge on the part of buyers and sellers. We will, however, use the term perfect competition in our discussion of price and output determination.

3. IMPORTANCE OF TIME ELEMENT IN THE THEORY OF VALUE (MARSHALL'S TIME ANALYSIS OF VALUE)

We know that price is determined by the forces of demand and supply, but the relative influence exerted by them on price varies with the period of time under consideration. Dr. Alfred Marshall was the first economist who recognised the influence of time on the determination of price. When demand for a commodity changes, its supply will also change. But changes in demand and supply are not instantaneous. For instance, an increase in demand will lead to an increase in supply, but the increase in supply will be made only after sometime. Thus supply takes time to adjust itself to a change in demand. Further, the cost functions which are the basis of, supply of a product also vary over time. In short period of time, the cost of production will be higher because there is not enough time to change the scale of plant. While in the long period, a firm is able to produce at a lower cost, because she can change the scale of plant to any extent she wishes. Hence, the element of time is very important in the determination of the price of a product. Marshall showed that there are four fundamental time periods in valuation: (*i*) The Market-Period or Very Short-Period, (*ii*) The Short-Period, (*iii*) The Long-Period, and (*iv*) the Very Long-Period or the Secular Period. For the purposes of price determination, we shall consider only the first three types of time period. We shall include the secular period in the long period. Here it is important to note that Marshall did not classify the time periods in terms of calendar time but in terms of operational period (time) required for economic forces to work. Marshall divided the time periods on the basis of forces of supply and ignored the forces of demand. When the period is too short to change the supply of a product, it is referred to as market period or very Short-period. When the supply of a product can be changed with in the limits set by the given scale of plant, the period is said to be a short-period. When the supply takes a longtime to adjust themselves to changes in demand, i.e., there can be any change in the supply of a product, the period is known as long-period.

We shall now discuss these time periods in the following section.

(1) ***The Market Period or the Very Short-Period.*** The market period or very short-period is defined as the period in which the supply of a commodity is more or less fixed. For example, fish which has come to the market on a certain day and must be sold. Similarly, after the harvest is over, the amount of wheat coming to the market is absolutely fixed and it can not be increased until the next harvest. Thus, the market period for wheat is approximately one year, while for vegetables it may be a week or a month or so. The market period for different commodities will be different. The main characteristic of this period is that supply of the product is absolutely fixed and therefore, the supply curve of each firm will be a vertical line. The market supply curve is simply the horizontal summation of all individual firms' supply curves. Thus, in such cases, price is determined primarily by demand. The equilibrium price is that price at which the entire supply is sold. If the demand is high, the price will be high; if the demand is low, the price will be low. The equilibrium price in the very short period is called the *market price.*

(2) ***The Short-Period.*** The short-period is defined as the period in which the firm is free to vary its output but does not have time to change its scale of plant. The number of firms in the industry will be fixed because

new firms do not have sufficient time to enter into the industry, nor the existing firms will have time to leave the industry. Any changes in supply must come from the plant capacity of the existing firms. If the demand for a commodity increases, the individual firms will increase their output by intensive working of its existing capital equipment (plant or machine). Increase of supply with the existing equipment generally means increased marginal costs because ordinarily all firms operate their plants at the level where cost is minimum. The short-period supply curve of most commodities is, therefore, a line moving upwards. The point of equilibrium is the point at which the demand and supply curves intersect.

If, in the short-period, demand is low and the price is less than the average cost, firms will incur losses. But, by definition, the short-period is too short to change the scale of a plant, a producer (firm) will continue production even in the situation of loss. The reason is that if the stops production, the maximum loss will be equal to the fixed costs. For a time, therefore the firms may carry on production if their variable costs are covered. In the long-run, however, the price most be high enough to cover both the variable costs and the fixed costs, otherwise production will be stopped. The equilibrium price in the short-period is called the *short-period normal price* which is determined by the intersection of the short-period normal supply and the short-period normal demand. The short-period normal demand will be nearly the same as market demand and the short-period normal supply curve will be less steep than the market supply curve.

(3) ***The Long-Period.*** The long-period is defined as the period long enough to enable the industry to adjust its supply of output completely to changes in demand. During this period of time, new firms may enter into the industry and the existing firms may leave the industry. Thus, the possibilities of output variation in a purely competitive industry are much greater in the long-period than in the short-period. In the long-period, the existing firms can vary output through increases or decreases in the utilisation of available plant-capacity as is the possibility in the short-period. But they can vary output more than this via changing their scales of plants to any extent. All the factors of production are the variable factors. There is no question of fixed cost. The minimum price of the product cannot be less than the average cost of production. Thus, there will be no loss to the firm. Also, during this period of time, complete adjustment of supply to demand is possible as all factors on which supply depends can be changed. The shape of the supply curve in the long period depends on the law of returns applicable to the production conditions of

the commodity in question. It rises upwards under diminishing returns, slopes downwards under increasing returns and moves horizontally under constant returns. In all the situations, the point of equilibrium is the point at which the demand for the commodity and the supply of the commodity are equal. The equilibrium price in the long-period is called the *long-period normal price.* Market equilibrium price and output will oscillate round the long-period equilibrium price and output.

(4) *The Secular Period.* for the sake of completeness, Marshall also talked of a secular period or very long-period. The secular period will include all the changes in demand and supply which require a long-period of time, such as the changes in the size of population, supplies of raw materials, supply of capital, etc. These are the structural changes that we shall study in theories of growth. In other words, the very long-period is essentially a historical category.

4. PRICE DETERMINATION BY THE INDUSTRY UNDER PERFECT COMPETITION

As we have already discussed that the price of a commodity will be determined at that point where industry demand for a product is equal to its supply. We have also seen in the previous chapters that market or industry demand is the sum total of all the quantities demanded by consumers at a given price and the market (industry) demand curve can be derived by the horizontal sum of all the individual demand curves. Similarly, the industry supply curve can be derived by aggregating the marginal cost functions of different firms in their relevant ranges. From the above discussion, it is also clear that time is an important factor to influence the industry price via supply variations. We shall now explain the equilibrium of the industry under three periods of time: the market period, the short-period, and the long-period.

Price Determination in the Market Period

In the market period the supply of the commodity is fixed and, therefore, price will depend upon the variation in demand. It does not mean that supply plays no role in the determination of price. The role of supply will depend upon the nature of the commodity. If a commodity is perishable, such as vegetables, fruits, fish, etc. such a commodity con not stay fresh for some time and thus its entire supply must be sold at the same (market) time. The same is the case with the goods of purely seasonal interest like calendars and greeting cards. These goods deteriorate economically, but not physically; there will be no demand for them after a particular season is over. In all these cases, the supply curve of the commodity is a vertical line as shown in Fig. 32.1.

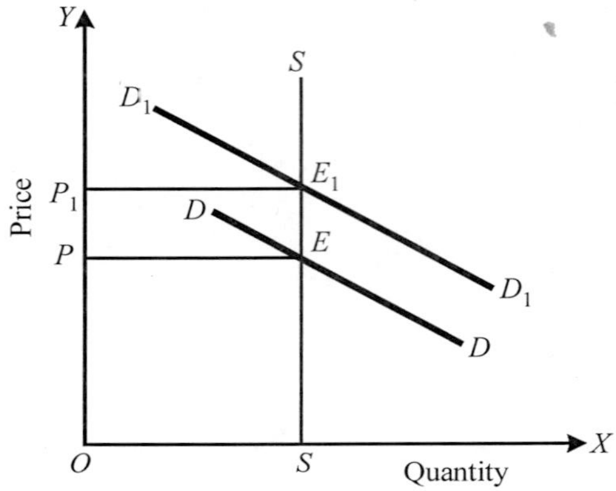

Fig. 32.1

Here, the costs of production do not come in the picture at all. The vertical shape of the supply curve indicates that whatever the price is, the fixed supply is to1te sold in the market. Now, the price will entirely be dependent upon the demand curve. Higher the demand, the more will be the price and the lower the demand, the lesser will be the price. In Fig. 32.1, if demand curve is *DD,* then the equilibrium price will be *OP.* If demand increases, and supply remains the some, price will increase. Let us assume that demand increases to D_1D_1, the price will become OP_1. Thus, in such a case, supply is fixed and demand exerts its full influence on the price of the product.

If, on the other hand, the commodity under consideration is a durable good, it can be stored. A firm selling such a commodity has a reservation price below which it will not like to sell it. The reservation price is influenced by the cost of production. In the market period, all costs are fixed costs and we know that fixed costs do not govern price. Thus, in the market period price will depend upon the variation in demand, but according to Marshall both demand and supply are equally needed for price determination. Now if demand for such (durable) goods is so low that the consumers offer a price less than the firm's reservation price, it will sell no output. This case has been illustrated in Fig. 32.2. The supply curve is *SS* which indicates that the firm will refuse to sell anything below the os price. The quantity supplied increases up to the market price OP_1 but above this price, supply is the same (OX_1), however high the demand may be. The reason is that in the market period supply is fixed which cannot be adjusted to the variation (increase) in demand. Thus, even if a high price is offered by the buyers, the sellers are unable to supply accordingly. Thus, in Fig. 32.2, after point E_1, the supply takes the vertical shape. This type of behaviour takes place for durable and semi-durable goods.

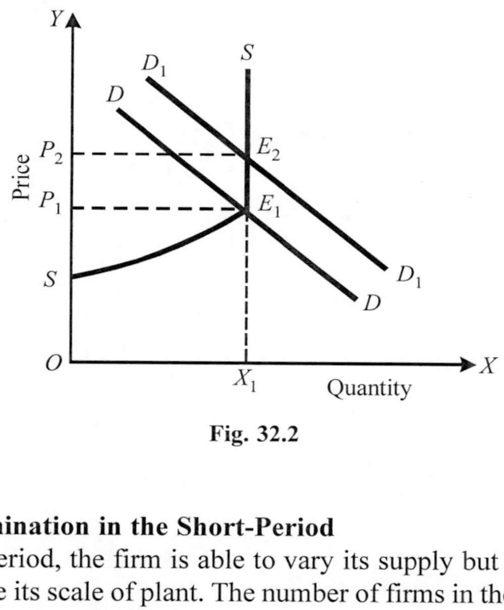

Fig. 32.2

Price Determination in the Short-Period

In the short period, the firm is able to vary its supply but does not have time to change its scale of plant. The number of firms in the industry will be fixed because new firms will not have time to enter into the industry and the existing firms have no time to leave the industry. Thus, the supply of the industry can be changed only within the limits set by the plant capacity of the existing firms. In other words, the supply curve will be upwards sloping and there will be no shift in the industry supply curve.

The short-period normal price is determined by the interaction of short-period supply and short-period demand curves. It has been illustrated in Fig. 32.3. *DD* is demand curve and *SS* is the supply curve. The equilibrium price is *OP* where the demand is equal to the supply of the product. Now, suppose that the demand increases from *DD* to D_1D_1, the supply curve remaining the same and the price will increase from *OP* to

OP_1, At this OP_1 price, the quantity increases from OX to OX_1. This increase in quantity is made by an intensive use of the scale of plant. Similarly, if demand curve shifts from DD to D_2D_2, then the short-run equilibrium point will be E_2, where the quantity supplied is equal quantity demanded. It is reduced from OX to OX_2. This reduction supply is made by a smaller use of the existing plant. It means, given the short-period supply curve (*SS*), a higher or lower price will be determined on the basis of the shift in demand. If demand increases, price will increase and if demand decreases, price will decrease.

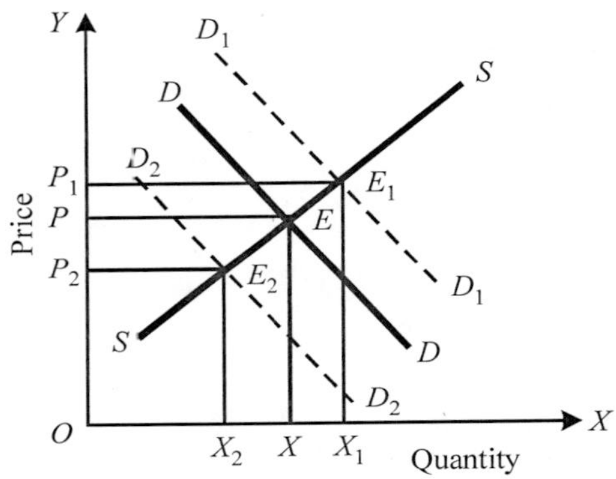

Fig. 32.2

Relation between Market Period and Short-Period Price Determination

As we have explained, the equilibrium (market) price in the market period is determined at a point where the demand curve intersects the fixed (vertical) supply curve. While in the case of short-period, equilibrium price is determined at a point where the demand curve intersects the positively sloping supply curve. This means that in the short-period some adjustments in supply to demand are made by making a smaller or intensive use of the scale of plant. At any particular time, the market price may be more or less than the short-period equilibrium price, but all the time, it will tend to equate the latter.

Fig. 32.4 illustrates the relationship between the market period price and the shortperiod price. The supply curve in the market period is shown by a vertical straight line *MPS,* while the short-period supply curve is *SPS.* Sup-pose, *DD* is the initial demand curve. The initial equilibrium point is *E,* where the demand curve cuts the market period supply curve *MPS.* The market period is *OP* and quantity sold by the firms taken together is *OX.* If it is also assumed to be a short-period, then the short-run supply curve *SPS* also cuts the demand curve *DD* at point *E* and, therefore, at price *OP,* the industry (all the firms together) offers OX units of quantity for sale in the market period also. This is why *DD, MPS* and *SPS* have a common point of intersection *E.* But it is clear that market period supply curve *MPS* is perfectly inelastic, showing that there is no possibility to change the level of output offered for sale. Shift in demand

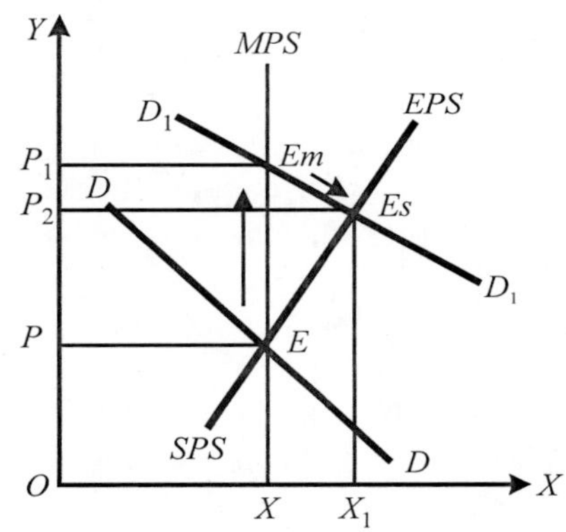

Fig. 32.4

curve, therefore, makes no effect on quantity supplied. While in the case of short-period the supply curve *SPS* is elastic, showing that there may be some adjustment in supply to demand for the commodity. For instance, if demand curve shifts from *DC* to D_1D_1; in the new demand conditions the new market equilibrium will be set at point *EM* where the market price increases from *OP* to OP_1 (subject to the condition that output remains the same). The short-period supply curve *SPS* shows that, in the short-period, the increased (variable) resources available allow supply to adapt itself in some degree to the changed demand conditions. In other words, if this increase in demand promises to last for some time (short-period), the existing firms in the industry begin to use their existing plant and equipment more intensively. As a result a new short-run equilibrium is established at point *Es* where the short-period supply curve *SPS* intersects the demand curve D_1D_1. We may note here that the short-run normal price will be OP_2 and quantity will be OX_2. This new short-run equilibrium price OP_2 is higher than the initial market-period price OP, but not so high as the second market period price OP_1. The short-run supply has also increased from OX to OX_1. Thus in the short-period more quantity is sold and price is not quite so high as in the market period (when the demand conditions are changed as shown by D_1D_1 curve in Fig. 32.4.

Price Determination in the Long-Period

In the long-period, the normal price of a commodity is determined by the long-period demand and long-period supply of the industry. The long-period demand curve represents the various levels of collective demand of the buyers over a long-period of time. The long-period supply curve represents the various levels of collective supply of the firms which are placed on the market at different prices over a long period of time.

In the long-period the shift in demand will be met by greater output adjustments, and smaller price adjustments than those that occurred in the short-period. There is ample time for the existing firms to leave the industry in the situation of loss and there is ample time for the new firms to enter into the industry in the situation of profit. As such, the supply of the commodity win be adjusted fully to the changed demand. Suppose that the demand for the commodity in question increases. This is assumed to be a once-for-all increase and no further change will take place during the process of adjustment. The new long-run price may be more than, equal to, or less than the initial price. It depends on whether the industry operates under increasing cost, constant cost or decreasing cost conditions. But it is sure that in the short run due to an increase in demand, the price will increase. Now to make a complete adjustment in supply to demand, the scale of plant will be varied and the resulting long-run normal price will depend upon the prevailing law of return in the industry. In the case of increasing cost (or decreasing returns), the new long-run equilibrium price will be higher than the old one. In the case of constant cost (or constant returns), (long-period) price, after a short-run increase will settle down at the old level. While in the case of decreasing cost (or increasing returns), new equilibrium long-period normal price after rising in the short-period will be actually lower than the initial price. Now, the determination of long-period normal price under the various cost conditions will be discussed in the following section.

Increasing Cost Industry

Here we assume that the industry is operating under increasing cost conditions. In this situation, the long-period supply curve of the industry rises upwards to the right as output increases. In other words, it has a positive slope. In Fig. 32.5, *LPS* is the long-run supply curve which slopes upward to the right. How can we get this supply curve? For this let us assume that the initial equilibrium point is *E* where the, industry demand curve *DD* intersects the short-period supply curve *SPS* and the market supply curve *MS.* At this point the industry is supplying *OX* output at *OP* equilibrium price. Now suppose, demand curve shifts upward to D_1D_1. The short-run effect of this increase in demand is that the industry is able to supply only OX_1 output at OP_1 price. But in the long-run, the industry can fully adjust the supply to increase in demand. The existing firms can increase their plant capacities and the new firms can enter into the industry. Thus, the long-run in crease in a supply will not be only OX_1, but it will be OX_2, because short-run supply curve also shifts to the right as SPS_1. The new equilibrium is established at point *E.* where price is OP_1 and output is OX_2 Now if we join points *E* and E_1, we get the long-period supply curve of the industry. The long-run equilibrium price (OP_2) is more than the initial price (*OP*). The extent to which the long-period price will differ from the original price will depend on the ease with which extra output can be produced in the long-run.

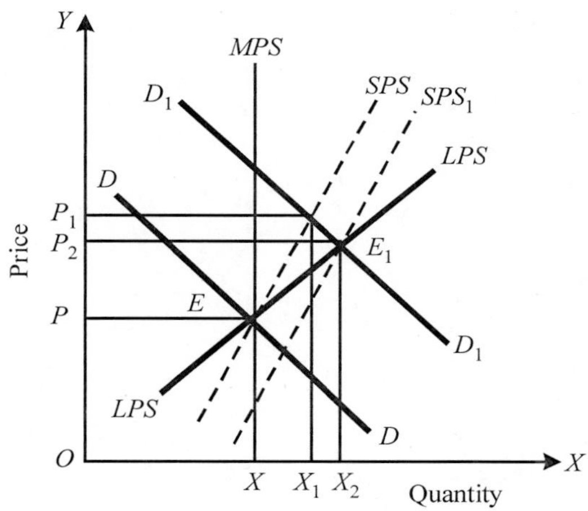

Fig. 32.5

Constant Cost Industry

Here we assume that the industry is operating under constant conditions. In this situation, the long-period supply of the industry is horizontal to X-axis as shown in Fig. 32.6 by the *LPS* straight line. Although the short-period price will increase as a result of increased demand, yet the price will fall again to the initial level in the long-run when the supply is fully adjusted to the changed demand conditions. For instance, let us assume that the initial equilibrium point is *E* in Fig. 32.6 where the equilibrium price is *OP* and quantity is *OX*. Now, if demand curve shifts from *DD* to D_1D_1 the short-run price will increase for *OP* to OP_1 and at this short-period price the industry is able to make OX_1 supply of the output. Since, in the long-period, there is enough time to increase the scale of plant, the short-period supply curve *SPS* shifts to the right as SPS_1. This leads to a new long-period equilibrium point E_1 where the long-period price is *OP* and long-period equilibrium quantity is OX_2. If we join the two points *E* and E_1, we get the long-period supply curve, *LPS* which is horizontal. This indicates that under conditions of constant cost, the long-period normal price is the same as the initial price while the output has increased.

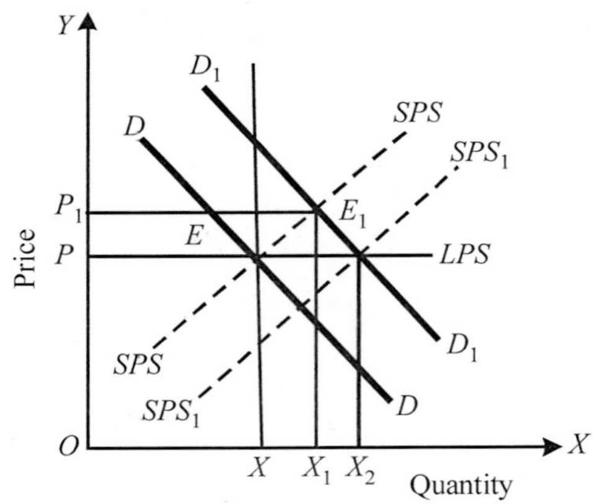

Fig. 32.6

Decreasing Cost Industry

Here we assume that the industry is operating under decreasing cost conditions. This situation is common. It is found only in the presence of external economies. As the Industry expands in the long run, external economies take place. These external economies lead to the firms' cost curves shift downwards. In such a case the long-period supply curve of the industry slopes downwards. Although the short-period price will increase as a result of increased demand, yet the long-period price will be less than the initial price.

This case has been illustrated in Fig. 32.7. The initial equilibrium point is *E* where the price is *OP* and the output is *OX*. If demand increases from *DD* to D_1D_1, the short-period price will increase from *OP* to OP_1 land the short-period quantity increases from *OX* to OX_1. But in the long-period, the firms are able to increase their scales of plant. Thus the short-period supply curve *SPS* shifts to SPS_1. New equilibrium will take place at point E_1 where the price is OP_2 and quantity demanded and supplied is OX_2. If we join the equilibrium points *E* and E_1, then the resulting curve is the long-period supply curve *LPS*. This curve *LPS* is falling. In fig. 32.7, it is also clear that the long-period normal price OP_2 is less than the initial price *OP*. Also in the long-period the quantity demanded and supplied increases from *OX* to OX_2.

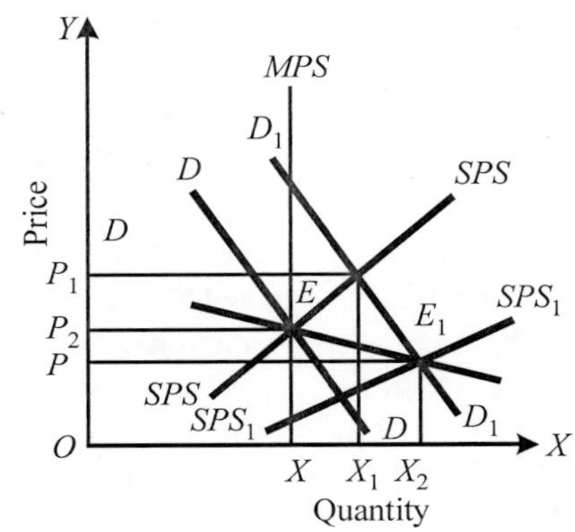

Fig. 32.7

Therefore, it is clear that the long-period normal price can be higher, lower or the same as the initial (original) market price, depending on supply (cost) conditions in the industry in question. It depends on whether or not there are internal and external economies or diseconomies of scale and how much they are. However, it is certain that the short-period normal price will invariably be higher than the long-period normal price.

5. OUTPUT DETERMINATION BY THE FIRM UNDER PERFECT COMPETITION

Under conditions of perfect competition, the individual firm supplies but a tiny fraction of the total supply. It is powerless to exert any influence on the price of the commodity. The price of the product is determined by the industry. A firm, in perfect competition has to accept the price given by the industry. In other words, the industry is a price-maker, while the firm is a price-taker. Thus the only decision the firm has to take is how much to be produced at the given price? In the present section we shall show how the price affects the behaviour of the competitive firms. The demand curve for the products of such a firm must be a horizontal line, or more precisely, the demand curve is perfectly elastic. No matter how many units the firm sells, it cannot change the price. It can sell its entire output at the ruling market price. If it tries to sell at any higher price, there will be no demand for its products, and there is no incentive to sell at any lower price. This is true that firms will attempt to maximise profits at the point where marginal revenue (*MR*) equals marginal cost (*MC*), no matter what the degree of competition in the market. Also, for profit maximisation, it is necessary that before the point where $MR = MC$, the marginal cost must be less than the marginal revenue and after the equilibrium point the marginal cost must be greater than the marginal revenue. This means that the *MC* curve must cut the *MR* curve from below and after the equilibrium point, it (*MC*) must lie above the *MR* curve. In perfect competition, the firm's *MR* curve is the same as its *AR* curve and the *MR* curve is horizontal to *X*-axis. Thus, the firm will be in equilibrium when the following condition is satisfied:

$$MC = MR = AR \text{ (price)}$$

By taking the help of the above fundamental rule, the firm will determine its equilibrium level of output. We shall discuss the firm's equilibrium under the three market periods: the market period, the short-period and the long-period.

Equilibrium of the Firm in the Market Period

In the market period, time is too short to change the supply of the product both for the firm and the industry. The price of the product is determined by the industry and at that price the firm sells its entire output. In Fig. 32.8 we have illustrated this case. In the industry, the supply curve is a straight vertical line and, therefore, demand plays a dominant role in determining the equilibrium price. The industry demand curve *DD* cuts the industry supply *MS* at point *E* and, therefore, the equilibrium price is *OP*. This price is given to the firm. At this given price *OP*, the firm can sell any level of output. In other words, the firm's demand curve is a horizontal line. Since, it is a case of market period, the firm will sell its entire output (inventory) at this given price. Here, we may very well introduce the concept of reservation price[1] which the firm assumes in the case of a durable product. For such a product, the firm will sell its output if reservation price is less than or equal to the market price (*OP*) given to it. If the market price is lower than the reservation price, the firm will not sell its output.

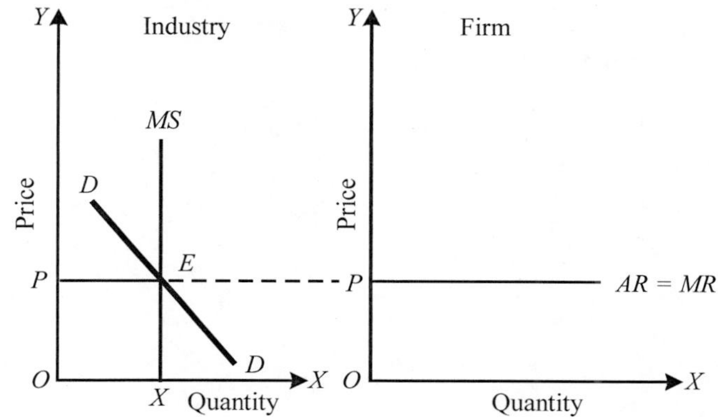

Fig. 32.8

Equilibrium of the Firm in the Short-Period

We have already explained how price is determined by the industry in the short-period. The price so determined by the short-period industry demand and industry supply is given to the individual firm. Now the firm adjusts its output accordingly. In other words, the firm has to decide whether to produce or not to produce. Also, if she is to produce, then how much should it produce? For this the firm has to see its costs of production. It is also clear to us that the purpose of the firm, in short-

1. The *reservation price* of the firm refers to the price below which the firm will not sell its output. This reservation price will depend upon many factors, such as the nature of the commodity, future expectations about the product price, the cost of storage, and the cost of production, etc.

period, is either to maximise its profits or to maximise its losses. Its objective will be attained if it produces that level of output at which its marginal revenue is equal to its marginal cost. In other words, the firm will be in short-run equilibrium when it holds the condition $MR = MC$. Now we shall discuss the two situations of the firm in the following manner.

Profit Maximisation. Figure 32.9 shows that the equilibrium price *OP* is determined by the industry at point *E* where the industry demand is equal to industry supply. The price so determined by the industry is passed on to the firm. This is shown by the horizontal demand curve of the firm. This line is also known as the price line. Since competition is perfect, the average revenue (demand) curve of the firm is also the marginal revenue curve of the firm. The firm's short-period average cost curve and short-period marginal cost curve are shown by *SAC* and *SMC* respectively in Fig. 32.9. The profits of the firm are maximum at the output at which marginal cost equals marginal revenue, that is, at output *OX* where $SMC = MR$. At any output less than *OX*, marginal revenue exceeds marginal

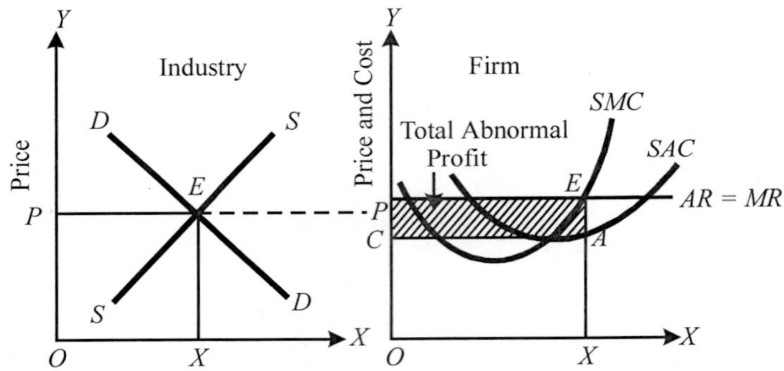

Fig. 32.9

cost, which would mean that if the firm produces more, its profits will increase. Also, at any output more than *OX*, marginal revenue becomes less than marginal cost, which would mean a loss if the firm exceeds output level *OX*. Thus, *OX* is the output of maximum profits. Total abnormal profits of the firm are equal to the shaded area. At the equilibrium point *E*, price is equal to *EX*, while average cost per unit equals *AX*. Abnormal profit per unit must be equal to *EA* (*CP*) and total abnormal profits will be equal to *PEAC*. Here we may note that at output *OX*, profit per unit is not maximised (for instance, the last unit of the output sold adds zero profit to the total profit), nor the firm is concerned with this. This objective of the firm is to maximise total profits and not the rate at which they are increasing.

Loss Minimisation. As has been explained, the determination of price is not a jurisdiction of an individual firm—it can only determine its own output level on the basis of given price. If this price is too low and does not cover the average cost, the firm would be incurring losses. If on the other hand, the price is higher than the average cost, the firm would make abnormal profits. We have explained above the situation of profit maximisation and now we shall discuss the situation of loss minimisation. Although, the situation of short run losses (or profits) would be wiped out in the long run as in the long run (industry) demand and supply both adjust themselves in such a fashion as to yield only the normal profits to the firm.

In Fig. 32.10 the firm's *AC* curve is above the price line (given by the industry'. Its *MN* curve cuts the *MR* curve at point *E* and, therefore, point *E* is the equilibrium point where *MR* = *MC*. With the help of this point, the firm determines its equilibrium level of output *OX*. At this level of output the cost per unit is *OC*, while the price is *OP*. Therefore, the loss per unit will be equal to *PC*. The total loss of the firm is shown

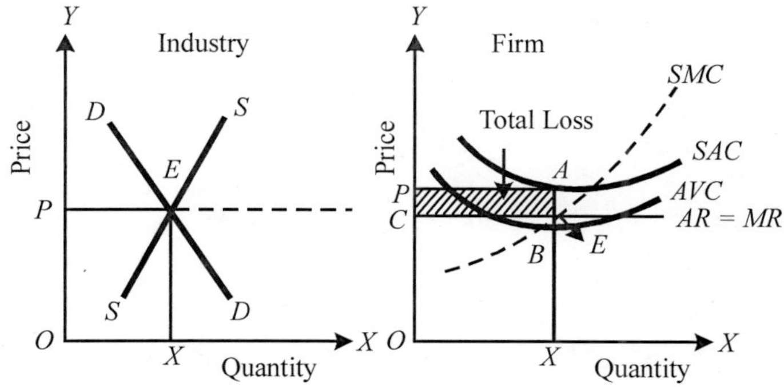

Fig. 32.10

by the shaded area (*CAEP*). If the output level is less than or greater than *OX*, the firm's total loss would be more than at the level of optimisation. The maximum loss that a firm can bear would be equal to its fixed cost which is the difference between *AC* and *AVC*. At *OX* level of output, the firm's average variable cost is *XB*. The firm's average receipt (*AR*) is *XA*. The excess of *AR* (or price) over *AVC* is equal to *AB*. In other words, *AB* is the fixed cost per unit. Now at *OX* level of output, the firm is minimising its loss to *AE* per unit, because the maximum loss per unit that it could bear is *AB*. Hence, if the firm produces *OX* level of output, it covers *BE* part of its per unit fixed costs. If the price is less than the firm's average variable cost, *XB* (= *OV*) losses will be minimised by stopping production altogether, i.e., leaving losses equal to the total fixed costs.

Effect of a Tax on the Short-Run Equilibrium

A tax on commodity generally changes the optimum level of the individual firm. When a tax, such as sales tax, is imposed on a commodity, it has the same economic effect as an increase in the costs of production. Due to the imposition of sales tax, the marginal cost function will shift upward and as a consequence, the whole industry supply curve moves upwards and to the left. The cost of bringing the commodity to the market is now increased by the amount of tax being levied. Thus the equilibrium price will be higher than before.

In Panel (*a*) of Fig. 32.11, the original industry supply curve is *SS* which shifts to S_1S_1 due to the imposition of tax. The distance between the two supply curves will depend upon the amount of tax levied on the commodity. As a consequence, price has risen from *OP* to OP_1, and the quantity supplied by the industry has fallen from as to as. It is also clear that the price has not increased by the full extent of the tax. The tax is equal to the amount *AC*, but the price has risen by the amount *AB* (= the increase in price, PP_1) and the producers or the firms are obliged to bear the amount *BC*.

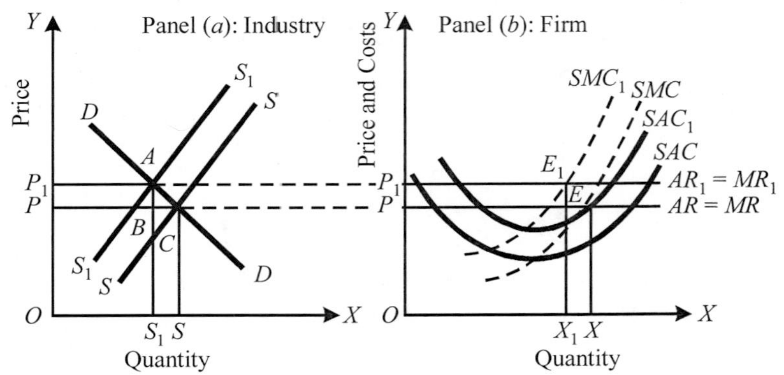

Fig. 32.11

Although the new price of the commodity is OP_1 (=AS_1), the industry (firm) only receives CS_1 while the government takes AC in taxation. In other words, the burden of tax on the industry depends upon the nature of the demand and supply curves.

In Panel (*b*) of Fig. 32.11, the effect of tax on the individual firm has been shown. Due to the composition of tax, its cost curves shift upwards as shown by SAC_1 and SMC_1. *At OP* price, the firm's equilibrium level of output is *OX*; while at the new increased price, its equilibrium level of output is OX_1. It shows that taxation on commodity reduces the optimum level of firm's output from *OX* to OX_1.

Equilibrium of the Firm in the Long-Period

We have seen that in the short-run a firm can adjust its output within the limits set by the fixed factors of production. But in the long-run, the firm can adjust its output to any extent because it can vary all factors of production. Thus, it is certain that the firm will not incur losses in the long-run. Also in the long-run, the free entry of the new firms into the industry will wipe out the short-run abnormal profits of the firm. Hence in the long-run, the firm will be of optimum size where there is no (abnormal) profit-no loss. The firm gets only the normal profits which are included in the long-run average cost. In other words, under perfect competition the individual firm is in equilibrium, earning normal profits when

$$AR = MR = LAC = LMC$$

This point of equilibrium will be established at which the firm's horizontal *MR*-curve touches its *LAC* curve at the latter's minimum point. It is at this point also that *LMC* = *LAC*. This position has been illustrated in Fig. 32.12. The long-run equilibrium of the firm requires that short-run equilibrium exists at the same time. But the converse is not true. This means that short-run equilibrium of the firm can exist even though there is long-run disequilibrium of the firm. In Fig. 32.12, it is clear that to produce *OX* quantity of output at the minimum unit cost, the firm builds a plant associated with the short-run average cost curve, *SAC* whose minimum point is the same as that of the long-run average cost, *LAC*. Also *SMC* must intersect *SAC* at latter's minimum point. Thus, when a firm is in long-run equilibrium, the following condition will exist:

$$P = MR = LMC = LAC = SAC = SMC$$

The above long-run condition is applicable to all the firms in the industry. In other words, in the long-run, price must be equal to the minimum average cost of each firm. This is the situation, when no new firm will like to enter the industry and no old firm would like to leave the industry. The number of firms in the industry is fixed.

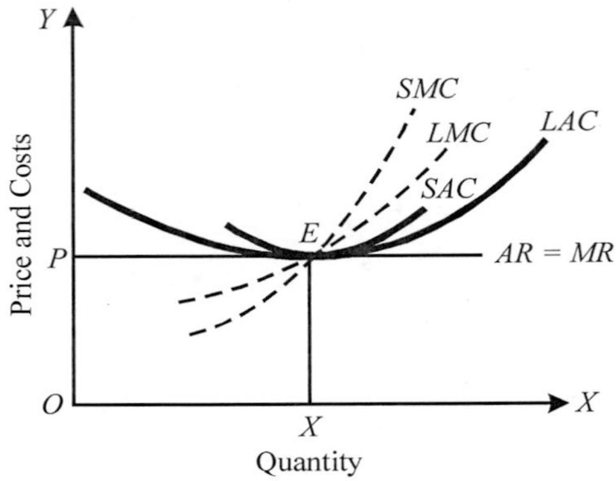

Fig. 32.12

So far we have introduced the concept of long-period equilibrium of the firm in a perfect competitive industry. But it does not describe a complete analysis of the long-period adjustments within the industry that occur as a result of some disturbing force. Usually, cost changes as well as price changes will takes place as new firms, attracted by profits, enter the industry. The nature of the cost adjustments, if any, will depend upon whether the industry (or the firm) is operating under increasing costs, constant costs, or decreasing costs.

Increasing Costs. We have already explained the equilibrium of the industry under the increasing costs condition. Here we shall explain the long-run equilibrium diagrams for the industry and for a representative firm of the industry. The case of increasing costs has been shown in Fig. 32.13. Initially, the industry demand curve is *DD* and the industry supply curve is *SS*. The original price is *OP* where *DD* cuts SS at point *E*. This price is initially given to the firm. Now suppose, that at this price *OP*, the firm's short-run average cost, *SAC* and long-run average cost, *LAC* touch at point *A*. Since at point *A* the *SAC* is minimum, therefore the *SMC* curve will cut the *SAC* at point *A*. Point *A* is the initial equilibrium point of the firm where *P* = *SMC* = *SAC* = *LAC*. The long-run marginal cost curve is omitted, because it is not essential for the present analysis and unnecessarily complicates the diagram.[2] Thus, initially, firm's equilibrium output is OX while industry output is OX which is the summation of individual firm's outputs at price OP. Here, the firm is using the optimum scale of plant at the optimum rate of output because there is no profit no loss.

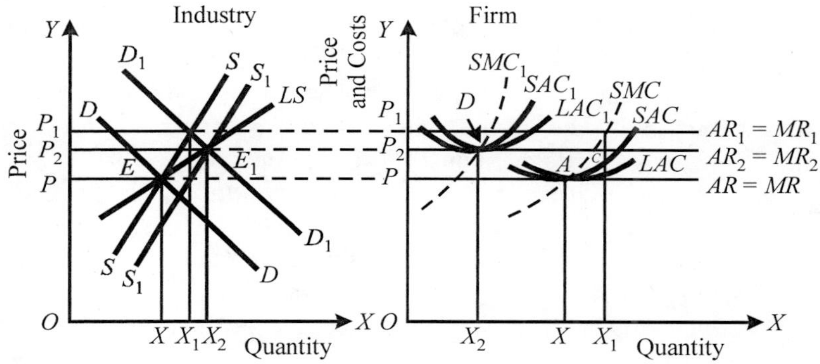

Fig. 32.13

Now, suppose, industry demand increases to D_1D_1 but at the same time supply cannot be adjusted according to demand. This means that such a shift in demand will raise the price to OP_1 in the short-run. Since in the short-run, the firm is not able to increase the size of the plant, it can make an intensive use of it by producing OX_1 output at price OP_1. This is the output (OX_1) at which SMC equals the new marginal revenue (MR_1). This allows the firm to make short-run profits equal to BC per unit. Thus the short-run effects of the increase in demand are: (*i*) price has increased, (*ii*) output has increased to the extent that the existing plant-capacity is worked with greater intensity, and (*iii*) profits are attained by the existing firms.

But in the long-run, these short-run advantages of the firm will disappear. The existence of profits in the industry will attract new firms to enter into the industry in the long-run. As new firms enter the industry, the short-period supply curve (SS) of the industry will shift to the right as S_1S_1. The increase in supply will reduce the price from OP_1 to OP_2, An

2. Here it is obvious that, when LAC is minimum at point A, it will also be equal to LMC. In other words, at point A, we shall have the condition

$$P = MR = SMC = SAC = LMC = LAC.$$

this price the firm will reduce output from OX_1 to OX_2. This is because the prices of factors of production, which were fixed in the short run, have risen more than those of the other inputs. In other words, all inputs have become variable inputs and in order to economise inputs which are relatively more expensive, the firm builds a smaller plant.[3] In such a case, the total output of old firms will actually be less than that of initial situation. But since the total industry output has increased to OX_2 the increase in output by the new firms is more than the decrease in output by the old (existing) firms. Here, the conclusion is that in the long run, the firm again establishes its equilibrium where there is no profit no loss to the firm. The firm as well as the industry is of optimum size.

The long run industry supply curve is *LS* in Fig. 32.13. It joins all the points of long run equilibrium for the industry such as, *E* and E_1. It demonstrates the fact that under increasing cost conditions, increased demand can be satisfied by the industry only at a higher supply price.

Constant Costs. In the case of constant costs, the firms in the industry can expand their scale of operations without causing any increase in factor prices. In other words, the entire industry (all firms) was only a small

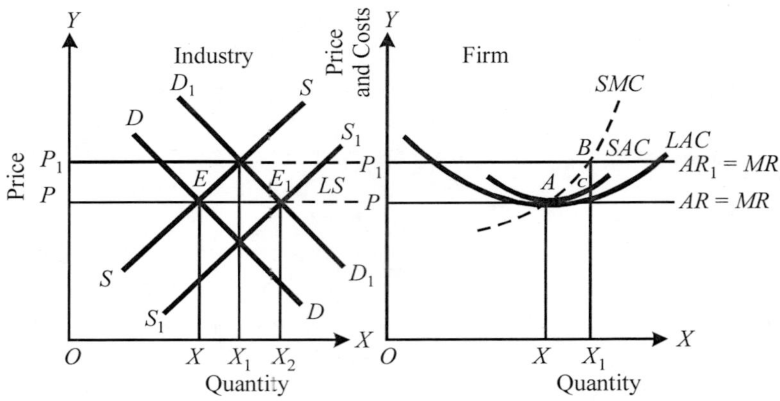

Fig. 23.14

3. If all factor prices rise in the same proportion, the firm's cost curves would shift straight up and equilibrium output of the individual in the would be the same as before (in the initial situation). In such a case the entire increase in the industry output would be the result of the new firms. If, on the other hand factor prices (which were fixed previously) rise less than the prices of other inputs, it would be cheaper to operate on a higher scale plant. In such a, case, the increase in the industry output is partly due to the increase in the size of plants of the old firms and partly due to the output of new firms.

part of the total supplies of various factors of production of the economy, so that its expansion or contraction will not affect the factor prices. As a result, the individual firm's cost curves will not be disturbed at all. The procedure of determining price and output is the same as that under increasing costs. This has been illustrated in Fig. 32.14. The initial equilibrium was at the price *OP* and each firm in the industry was producing *OX* quantity of the product. Now, suppose demand for the product increases and as a result, there is a shift in the industry demand curve from *DD* to D_1D_1. Since in the short-period, industry supply curve can not be shifted accordingly, thus price rises to OP_1. At price OP_1 each firm produces OX_1 quantity of the product. The existing firms are enjoying abnormal profits at this increased price. Now, in the long-run new firms are attracted by this profit and they enter into the industry. This leads the industry supply curve to shift to the right. Entry of new firms, and the corresponding shift in the industry supply curve will continue until the original price *OP* is restored, at which the individual firm produces *OX* quantity of the product and earns only the normal profit. We must remember that the cost curves of the industry will not shift in the changed conditions because the entry of new firms does not cause any increase in factor prices.[4] Also, the existing firms produce the same initial level of output. Thus, the increase in industry output (from *OX* to OX_1) will absolutely be the result of the output of new firms. This is the reason that the shift in industry supply curve is equivalent to the shift in demand curve. As a result, the long-run supply curve of the industry is *LS* and it is horizontal at the level of minim urn long-period average costs. In such a situation the optimum size of the firm remains the same.

Decreasing Costs. In the case of decreasing costs, the firms in the industry meet the increased demand for the product at a lower price than the initial price. This case is not, in general, found in real life. It is possible only when the firms are unable to obtain external economies, such as cheap transportation, cheap power, technical information, etc. These external economies will lead to reduce the costs of production as they produce more. This has been illustrated in Fig. 32.15. The process of adjustment is the same as we have discussed under increasing or constant costs. The initial price is *OP* where the industry equilibrium output is *OX*

4. In a constant cost industry the entry of new firms does not increase market demand for resources sufficiently to cause their prices to increase. Of the total supply of resources necessary for the production of the commodity, this industry takes a small enough part so that on influence is exerted on their prices by the new films coming in. This means that the cost curves will remain the same.

and firm's output is OX. At this level of output the firm is getting no profit no loss. If industry demand curve shifts from DD to D_1D_1, the short-period price increases from OP to OP_1. At this price OP_1, the firm is getting abnormal profit to the extent of BC per unit at OX_1 level of output. In the long-run, new firms will enter into the industry and in the situation of decreasing costs, it will result input prices to decrease. The supply curve of the industry shifts from SS to S_1S_1. The increase (shift) in supply is more than the increase (shift) in demand. Consequently, the long-run supply price falls to OP_2.

On the other hand, as new firms enter into the industry, external economies take place and it will cause resource prices to fall. Consequently, the cost curves of the firm shift downwards. Both price, of the product and costs of production are decreasing. Thus the profits, attained by the firm in the short-run disappear. At price OP_2, the firm produces OX_2 quantity of output, at which $P = MR = SMC = LMC = SAC = LAC$. The new industry output is OX_2 and the long run supply curve of the industry is LS which is downward-sloping to the right. According to Ferguson, the decreasing supply curve is inconsistent with the assumptions of perfect competition. It is possible only in the situation of monopoly.

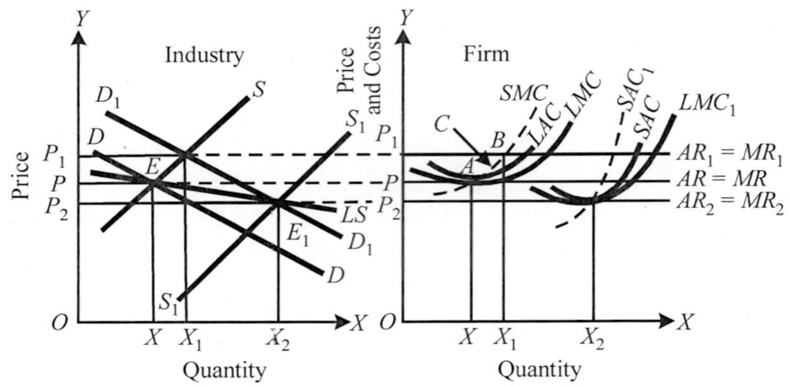

Fig. 32.15

EXERCISES

1. Explain the effect of a shift in demand curve on the industry equilibrium in the short-run under perfect competition.
2. Show the effect of a change in price on the short-run equilibrium of the individual firm under perfect competition.

3. Explain and illustrate diagrammatically the short-run and long-run equilibrium of the firm and the industry under the conditions of perfect competition.
4. What are the main characteristics of perfect competition? Distinguish between pure competition and perfect competition.
5. Explain the importance of time element in the theory of value.
6. Illustrate diagrammatically the long-run equilibrium of the firm and the industry under perfect competition assuming that increasing costs prevail in the industry.
7. Explain the market period equilibrium of the industry under perfect competition.
8. How is price of a commodity determined under perfect competition?
9. Discuss the conditions of short-run and long-run equilibrium of the industry under perfect competition.
10. Do you think that under perfect competition, in the short-run a firm may continue its production even in the situation of loss?
11. Write short notes on the following:
    (*i*) Effect of a tax on the short-run equilibrium under perfect competition.
    (*ii*) Long-run equilibrium of a perfect competitive firm and industry under increasing constant and diminishing cost conditions.
12. Explain with the help of a diagram how price is determined in a perfectly competitive market.
13. Explain Marshall's three-period analysis on pricing of products in a competitive market. Illustrate with the help of diagrams.
14. Discuss the importance of time element in the theory of value.

Multiple Choice Questions

15. (*i*) Under perfect competition, the demand curve for an individual firm is
    (*a*) perfectly elastic (*c*) less elastic
    (*b*) more elastic (*d*) perfectly inelastic [*Ans,* (*a*)]

    (*ii*) The best level of output for a perfectly competitive firm is given by the point where
    (*a*) *MR* = *AC* (*c*) *MR* exceeds *MC* by the greatest amount
    (*b*) *MR* = *MC* (*d*) *MR*=*MC* and *MC* is rising [*Ans.* (*b*)]

    (*iii*) At the best short period level of output, the firm will be
    (*a*) maximising total profits
    (*b*) minimising total losses
    (*c*) either maximising total profits or minimising total losses
    (*d*) maximising profits per unit [*Ans.* (*c*)]

    (*iv*) If price exceeds *AVC* but is smaller than *AC* at the best level of output, the firm is
    (*a*) making a profit
    (*b*) incurring a loss but should continue to produce in the short-run
    (*c*) incurring a loss and should stop production immediately
    (*d*) breaking even [*Ans.* (*b*)]

    (*v*) Which of the following the main characteristic of perfect competition market?
    (*a*) Homogeneity of the product
    (*b*) Free entry and free exit of the firm into the industry
    (*c*) Perfect knowledge of the economy
    (*d*) all of the above [*Ans.* (*d*)]

(*vi*) In the very short period, the supply curve of the industry is
(*a*) perfectly elastic (*c*) more elastic
(*b*) perfectly inelastic (*d*) less elastic [*Ans.* (*b*)]

(*vii*) In the very short period, under perfect competition the prices of vanishable items are determined by
(*a*) demand only
(*b*) supply only
(*c*) demand and supply
(*d*) partially demand and partially supply of the commodity [*Ans.* (*a*)]

(*viii*) In the short period a firm will continue output if the following condition is satisfied
(*a*) $MC = MR = AC$ (*c*) Price < AVC
(*b*) Price > AVC (*d*) *Price*=*MC*=*MR* [*Ans.* (*b*)]

Chapter 33

MONOPOLY

1. INTRODUCTION

Monopoly may be defined as that market form in which a single firmcontrols the whole supply of a single commodity which has no close substitutes. Thus, by definition, monopoly firm and industry refer to one and the same thing; a single firm constitutes the industry. It follows that the definition remains valid so long as no other firm is able to, or is allowed to, enter into the industry. Thus, the cases of monopoly in this sense of a single firm are rare as those of perfect competition. We may find certain examples of public utilities, such as water supply, gas, electricity, telephone, railways, etc. which are in the hands of (state) monopolies.

The term "monopoly" has been used by various economists in different ways. Some economists call it "pure" monopoly which implies that there is one and only one producer of the particular product in the market. According to John D. Summer, pure monopoly implies a perfectly inelastic demand in contrast to the perfectly elastic demand of perfect competitive firm. Piero Sraffa uses the word "absolute" monopoly which implies one firm controlling the supply of all goods in existence.

In technical language, we may define monopoly as a single firm/ industry where the cross-elasticity of demand between the product of the monopolist and. the product of the closest rival must be very row (near to zero), i.e., the product of a rival cannot take the place of the monopolised product.

2. SOURCES AND TYPES OF MONOPOLY

There are different types of monopolies as described below:

(1) *Natural Monopoly.* If the supply of a commodity is localised in a single place, then the monopoly is known as natural monopoly. For example, Bangladesh possesses the monopoly of raw jute and India possesses the monopoly of manganese.

(2) *Legal Monopoly*. When a firm is given the legal right to produce a unique commodity, it is known as legal monopoly. For example, the right of note issue has been given by law to the Reserve Bank of India only, thus it is legal monopoly.

(3) *Public Monopoly*. When a monopoly is created for the interest of the public, it is known as public monopoly. For example, the various public utility services, such as water supply, electricity, telephones, railways, etc., are the public monopolies.They provide their services to the public at reasonable prices. Some economists prefer to call them welfare monopolies.

(4) *Private Monopoly*. It is owned and operated by the private individuals or organisations for the purpose of getting maximum profits. Profit maximisation is the primary objective of private monopoly. Such monopoly is established by liquidating the competitors. This may also be classified into simple and discriminating monopoly. A simple private monopoly charges a single price for his product from all the consumers. While, on the other hand, a discriminating monopoly charges more than one price for the same product from different consumers.

3. EMERGENCE AND ASSUMPTIONS OF MONOPOLY

A monopolist has no control over the demand for the product, but he can control the supply of the product. A monopolist has the power to determine either: (*a*) the price of the product, or (*b*) the quantity to be sold in the market. He cannot determine both because he cannot control the demand. Thus, the main assumption of the monopoly firm is that its demand curve slopes downward; to sell more he must cut his price. Also when the demand curve (*AR*-curve) slopes downwards from left to right, marginal revenue in no longer equal to price. It will lie below *AR-curve.* While in the case of perfect competition, demand curve of the firm is a horizontal line. Thus, when the monopolist decides on the price at which he is prepared to sell, then the demand curve will determine the quantity sold at this price. If the is determined to market a given quantity per month, then the demand curve will decide the price at which this quantity can be disposed of. If the monopolist produces a large quantity, the price will be low and profits would be low. If he produces a comparatively small quantity, the price will be high but the sales will be low. and total profits will be low. The monopolist will, therefore, not follow either of these policies. He will fix his output in such a way as to secure the maximum revenue net revenue or net profits.

The monopolist's power to influence price depends upon two factors:

(1) The availability of close substitutes, and

(2) The power to restrict the entry of new firms.

If a number of close substitutes are available in the market, then the monopolist will not be able to change his prices upwards to any significant extent, and his monopoly power will not be very high. In such a situation (when close substitutes are available), an increase in the price of the product will lead to heavy losses.

Again, if in some way, the entry of new firms is restricted, then the monopoly firm will continue to enjoy its privileged position even in the long-run. We have seen, that due to "free entry" in perfect competition, an individual firm enjoys only normal profits (which are included in long-run average costs) in the long-run. The monopolist can, on the other hand, protect his abnormal profits, even in the long-run, by preventing the entry of prospective competitors in, the market. Thus, monopoly power can be defined, as the ability to earn long-run abnormal profits without attracting competition.

Thus, the more effective the restrictions on the emergence of new competitors, and the fewer the close substitutes for his (monopolist's) product, the greater will be the power of the monopolist to charge higher prices. According to Prof. Robinson, "a monopoly firm can exist only so long as it is able to bar the entry of its potential competitors or rivals." Therefore, the essence of monopoly is the ability to 'restrict entry'. The following are the important measures which are used to debar the potential competitors from that particular industry by the monopoly firm.

(1) *Control Over the Raw Materials.* We know that geographical distribution of natural and mineral resources is very uneven, and the known deposits of some minerals are concentrated into very small regions. In such a situation, there is a great incentive for producers to form a monopoly, in order to control the market, by manipulating the supply. When the monopoly firm can own all the deposits of some minerals, and if there are no other deposits, it has to face no direct competitors. Thus, monopoly may emerge due to one single firm's control of raw materials, specially those the supply of which depends on nature.

(2) *Technical Barriers.* In modern capitalist states, there are a number of industries which are now dominated by a few giant firms. This is essentially true of the science-based industries where firms have been able to get very great technical economies of scale. For instance, tyre manufacturing, oil processing, chemicals and the motor-car industry may

be cited as typical examples of the (monopoly) firms which are getting large technical economies of scale. They are operating on a large scale and making use of expensive capital goods. In such cases, the entry of new firms is almost impossible. The small new firms cannot compete with the existing large firms because the former will have a greater average cost of production. Firms already operating are in a protected position and this is always an inducement to form a monopoly.

(3) *Legal Bariers.* This is the most important factor to restrict the new entry into the industry. Here the law confers the monopoly right and prevents the entry of the potential competitors. In other words, monopoly may emerge as a result of some statutory regulations of the government. The government may issue licences to only some firm who can sell particular products. The rivals of these monopoly firms cannot enter into the market. For instance, a marketing society maybe given an exclusive right to sell fertilizers in a group of villages or a fair price shop (*FPS*) is given the exclusive right to sell some essential products within its jurisdiction. Such monopolies are made due to. specific policies of the state.

The granting of patent rights in a further example of competition being limited by law. The firm holding the patent rights is protected from the threat of competition from new firms (or existing) making identical products, at least for the period of time for which the patent has been given to the firm by the government.

More recently, we have the example of the nationalised industries where the controlling boards have complete control over the supply of the goods and services produced by these industries.

(4) *Transport Costs and Tariffs.* Transport costs and tariffs are also the important factors which determine the monopoly power of a firm. Although two (or more) firms may be operating at similar costs, it is possible for one (or more of the firms) to enjoy local monopoly (monopolies). For example, firm *A* will be able to sell more cheaply, in its own locality, than firm *B,* if firm *B* is producing in a location which is far from the local market of firm *A.* Therefore, firm *A* is able to raise its price in its local market by the amount of the transport costs which firm *B* has to incur if at all it wants to sell in firm. *A's* local market.

Similarly, import tariffs are imposed to protect the domestic firm against the competition of foreign firms. The domestic firm can raise the price by the extent of any differential between its own costs of production and the artificially high price (due to the imposition of import tariffs) of the foreign good.

The above are some of the important ways by which a firm occupies monopoly power in the market. But we must remember that the above measures are more or less temporary in nature. They cannot be made permanent. It is only in the case of social monopoly or public utility, that we may find a tendency to continue as monopoly. This is also socially desirable.

4. PRICE AND OUTPUT DETERMINATION UNDER MONOPOLY

As we have explained in the previous chapter that under perfect competition, the price of a product is determined by the interaction of market demand and market (industry) supply. Under monopoly conditions, too, there is bound to be interaction between the forces of demand and supply. But there is a difference between the two market situations. Under perfect competition the supply can completely be adjusted to demand in the long-run while under monopoly the supply is not free (because the entry of new firm is blocked) to adjust itself to demand. It is under the control of the monopolist. A monopolist is the sole producer of his product which has no close substitutes. He can easily influence the price by changing his supply. In fact, he sets the price. While in the case of perfect competition, an individual has nothing to do with the price. He is simply a price-taker.

Again, the demand curve for the product of the monopoly firm is the same as the demand curve of the industry. It is negatively sloped. This demand curve (or *AR*-curve) will show that it can sell more only by cutting down its price. As we have already explained earlier, the corresponding marginal revenue curve of the monopoly firm will lie below the average revenue curve. If average revenue curve or the demand curve is a straight line negatively sloping curve, the *MR*-curve will also be a straight line and its slope will be double that of the demand curve. This has further been illustrated in Fig. 33.1. In the case of perfect competition, the demand curve of the industry is slopping downward but the demand curve of the firm is a horizontal straight line. This would mean that *AR* and *MR* will be the same for a competitive firm.

The cost curves of a monopoly firm are generally the same as that of a perfectly competitive firm. The only difference, that we can say, is that a firm under perfect competition can purchase any quantity of resources (factors of production) at constant prices while a monopoly firm has to pay higher prices as it expands its output and needs more quantity of resources. As a result, the *MC*-curve of a monopoly firm will have an additional reason for rising at an increasing rate with the additional increase in the output.

Now, the aim of the monopolist is to make maximum profit. Hence he fixes the price of his commodity in such a way that he might earn maximum profit. According to Alfred Marshall, "The *prima facie* interest of the owner of a monopoly is clearly to adjust the supply to the demand... in such a way as to afford him the greatest possible net revenue."

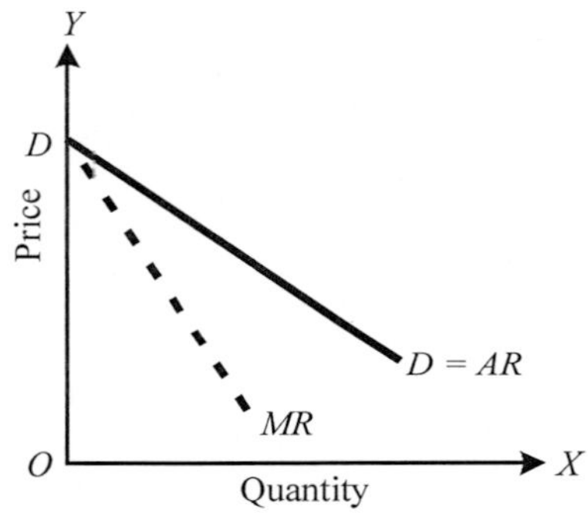

Fig. 33.1

In the case of perfect competition, the long-run equilibrium price will be equal to the (average) cost of production. Price cannot rise above the cost, for owing to the competition of several new firms anxious to secure extra profit, the supply of that product will increase, and the price will fall. Due to similar reason, the price cannot fall below the (average) cost of production. But in the case of monopoly, the cost or production sets only the *minimum limit* below which price would not fall. The price of the product may rise above cost and it will be the efforts of the monopoly firm to raise it as far as possible, so that it will be able to attain maximum monopoly profit. Cost of production, therefore, affects price under monopoly in a different way.

Under the given conditions of demand and supply (cost), the monopoly firm will always try to fix such a price of the product that gives him the maximum net revenue or profits. We also know that neither very high price nor a very low price will bring him the largest profit. If the keeps the price high his sales will be less; and if the keeps the price low, he would be able to increase his sales. Which particular price will yield maximum profit, cannot be predicted. It depends upon the nature of the commodity. Thus, he must pay attention to both the demand schedule and the supply schedule of the commodity. If the demand for a commodity is highly elastic (such as comforts and luxuries), the monopolist can earn maximum profit by keeping the price at a low level. Because, in such cases, a low price will result in large sales and a smaller profit per unit but a large sale will then perhaps give them more (net) revenue than a larger profit per unit with reduced sales. Thus, for highly elastic goods, he will fix his price at a low level. If, however, the demand is inelastic (i.e., the article is of daily use), a lower price would not stimulate sales very much, but a higher price will make greater profits. Similarly, if the supply is restricted, the price would rise very high. In such a case; a larger profit per unit on a small sale will yield maximum profit to the monopolist. He will, then fix the price at a high level.

To determine a long-run price, the monopolist should also study the conditions of supply (cost). If the production of the commodity is subject to the law of constant returns, his cost per unit would remain the same, whatever the volume of the output. In such a situation, he will, fix the price according to the nature of the demand for the product and will allow the volume of output change with demand. If the production of the commodity is subject to the law of increasing returns (or the law of diminishing cost), i.e., every increase in output will lead to a decrease in costs per unit. In such a situation, the monopolist will put a larger output in the market. He will specially be induced to do so, if the demand for the commodity is elastic. Here he adopts the principle of smaller profit per unit on a larger output. If, on the other hand, the production of the commodity is subject to the law of diminishing returns (or the law of increasing cost), it will be in his interest to reduce output and thereby to reduce cost per unit. In such a situation he will fix a higher price. But if the demand for the commodity is highly elastic (i.e., a slight fall in price will lead to a larger increase in quantity demanded), it will be in his interest to reduce the price. The reason is that even though the cost per unit increases as output increases, yet the increase in cost per unit is less than the increase in profit per unit.

The above explanation clears that neither a high price nor a low price would serve the objective of the monopolist. For this he should carefully study the conditions of demand and supply (cost) of the commodity and fix his price at a level that will bring him the maximum profits possible. He will go on producing so long as additional units add more to revenue than to cost. He will stop at that point beyond which additional units of production add more to cost than to revenue.

In other words; the monopolist will be in equilibrium position at that level of output at which marginal revenue equals marginal, cost.

The monopolist will continue expanding output so long as marginal revenue exceeds marginal cost. He will do so because profits will go on increasing as long as marginal revenue exceeds marginal cost. At the point, where marginal revenue is equal to marginal cost, the profits will be maximised. If the production is carried beyond this point, profits will begin to decrease.

Now we shall discuss the price-output equilibrium of the monopolist in different time periods.

Price and Output Equilibrium of Monopoly in the Market Period

The total costs of the, monopoly firm are fixed in the market period as those of a perfect competitive firm. Thus, by definition, these fixed costs do not affect the pricing policy of the monopolist during the market period. We have defined the market period as that period in which the supply of a product is absolutely fixed and shows no response to any price change. Therefore, in the market period, the monopolist possesses a certain quantity of a given commodity which he must dispose of. The price that he can charge for it entirely depends on the demand conditions. Costs do not come in the picture and this is a time of production without costs.

Let the monopolist have a fixed stock of the product shown by *OX* in Fig. 33.2 Panel (*b*). In Fig. 33.2 Panel (*b*), the demand curve facing the monopolist is linear and is represented by *AD* (which is the same as the *AR*-curve of the monopolist). The corresponding marginal revenue curve is represented by *MR*. Now, if the monopolist wants to sell its entire output *OX*, he has to keep his price at *OP*. But if he. does so, marginal revenue (*MR*) will be negative and his total revenue (*TR*) will be less than the maximum level shown by point *E*. Now, in the market period, however, the monopolist would like to maximise his total revenue as the costs of producing the present level of output *OX* have already been incurred by him. Moreover, instead of getting a negative return from the last unit (i.e., negative marginal revenue), he would always like not to sell it. Thus the best thing for him is to sell only OX_1 quantity of output at price OP_1. At OX_1 level of output, he will maximise his total revenue where $MR = O$.

When he sells OX_1 quantity out of the *OX* quantity, he remains with X_1X quantity in inventory. Even if the product is perishable, he would like to destroy it rather than to place it on the market. Because, placing it on the market reduces his total revenue. If, on the other hand, the product is not perishable, the monopolist will keep it with him for the next period. Also if the firm sells less than OX_1 quantity of output, his total revenue will not be maximum and he has to destroy a larger amount of the product (than X_1X). Thus, only at OX_1 level of output, the monopolist will maximise his receipts. Since he has no costs to consider, it will also maximise his profits. At point *R,* the average revenue curve (demand curve) will have an elasticity equal to one and the monopolist's total receipts (*TR*) will be at a maximum. Marginal revenue will be zero, as it always is when elasticity of demand is equal to unity. It will equal marginal cost, because marginal cost cannot be negative and the least it may be zero. This analysis also clears that a monopolist's equilibrium position will always be where the elasticity of demand for his product is greater than (or equal to in a special case of market period) one.

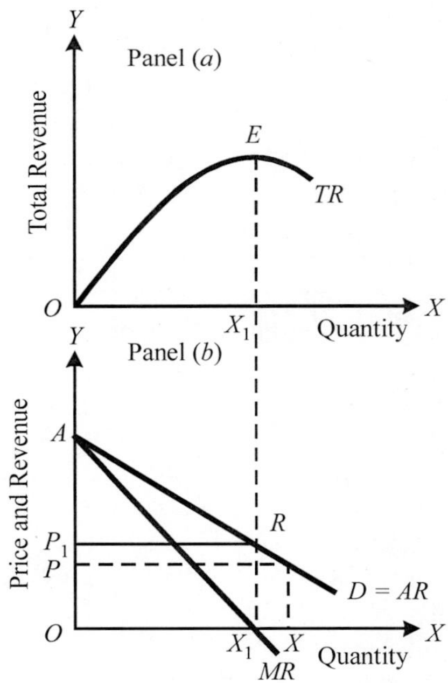

Fig. 33.2

Price and Output Equilibrium of Monopoly in the Short-Period

As we know, in the short-period the scale of plant is fixed and the firm is unable to change it. Thus, like a purely competitive firm, the monopolist operates with a given plant during the short-period. If the monopolist desires to produce more, he can make, an intensive use of the available plant. In other words, the monopolist will increase the supply of the product by increasing the variable factors (the fixed factors being fixed). Similarly, if the monopolist desires to reduce the supply, he can make a less intensive use of the fixed factors (such as machinery or plant etc.) by decreasing the amount of variable factor inputs. The main thing is that the monopolist would like to maximise his profits (or to minimise his losses if at all he has to incur). For this, the equilibrium condition is the same as we have explained under perfect competition. The monopolist will produce that level of output at which his marginal revenue is equal to his marginal cost.

Since the monopolist has to incur fixed costs in the short-run, the minimum price acceptable by him must be equal to his average variable cost. Thus the monopoly price may be greater than, equal to, or less than the average costs in the short-run. It will depend upon the conditions of demand. If price is greater than average cost, the monopolist will earn abnormal profits. If price is equal to the average cost the monopolist will earn only the normal profits which are included in his average cost. If price is less than the average cost, the monopolist will incur losses. Anyway, the maximum loss that the monopolist would accept will be equal to his fixed costs. If the monopolist is to incur losses greater than the fixed costs, it will stop production. But in the short-period, he will continue production even in the situation of loss, if the is able to minimise the loss of his fixed costs. The minimisation of loss will be made at that level of output at which $MR = MC$. These three possible situations in the short-run are explained in the following section.

Profit Maximisation in the Short-Period. Profits of a monopolist are maximised at the output at which his short-period marginal cost (*SMC*) equals his marginal revenue (*MR*). This case has been illustrated in Fig. 33.3. Here, the monopolist's *SMC* curve cuts the *MR* curve at point *E* where the monopolist produces *OX* quantity of output. At *OX* level of output, the monopolist can charge *OP* price per unit because price is determined by the demand curve or the *AR*-curve. At *OX* level of output, the average cost is *OC*. Thus, the monopolist's per unit abnormal profit is equal to *CP* which is the difference between the price (*OP*) and the corresponding average cost of production (*OC*). The shaded area, *CPAB* in Fig. 33.3 represents the total monopoly profit. The total profits of the monopolist will be maximum only at *OX* level of output. At output smaller than *OX*, *MR* is greater than *SMC*; thus larger outputs upto *OX* add more to total receipts than to total costs and increase profits. At output beyond OX_1, *MR* is less than *SMC*; hence larger outputs beyond *OX* add more to total costs than to total receipts and cause profits to decrease. To sum up, the monopolist attains maximum profit at *OX* level of output where *SMC* = *MR* and at this level of output the second order condition of profit maximisation is also satisfied.

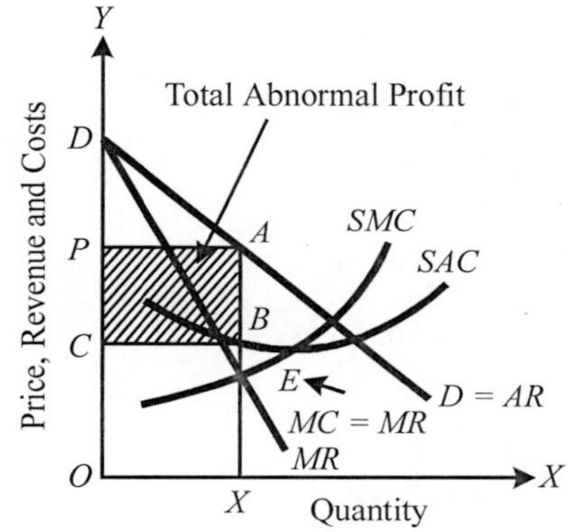

Fig. 33.3

Loss Minimisation in the Short Period. Generally, we find a misconception that a monopolist always makes profits. Whether the monopolist gets profits or not, depends upon the conditions of demand costs. It is not necessary that the monopolist should always operate at a (abnormal) profit. It is possible that his entire short-run average cost curve lies above the demand curve or *AR*-curve. In such a case, he has to incur losses. Sometimes, in the short-period, it is in his interest to operate even in the situation of loss, if the price of his product is high enough to cover his average variable cost. The situation of loss has been illustrated in Fig. 33.4. Here the monopolist's costs are so high and his market is so small that at no output will price (*AR*) cover average costs. In other words, his *SAC* curve lies above the *AR*-curve. Now his losses are maximised at output *OX,* at which *SMC* equals *MR.* At this level of output, price is *OP* while cost per unit is *OC.* Thus the monopolist has to incur losses to the extent of *CP* per unit. But the maximum loss that he is ready to bear in the short-run at *OX* level of output is *VC* per unit (which is equal to the fixed cost per unit). Since the average variable cost at *OX* output is *OV*, it is less than the price *OP*; thus a part of the maximum loss is covered by price. The total loss to be incurred by monopolist is. shown in Fig. 33.4 by the shaded area *PCAB*. This is the minimum loss that the monopolist would incur in the short-period. If the level of output is less than *OX* or greater than *OX*, the total amount of loss would be greater than area *PCAB*.

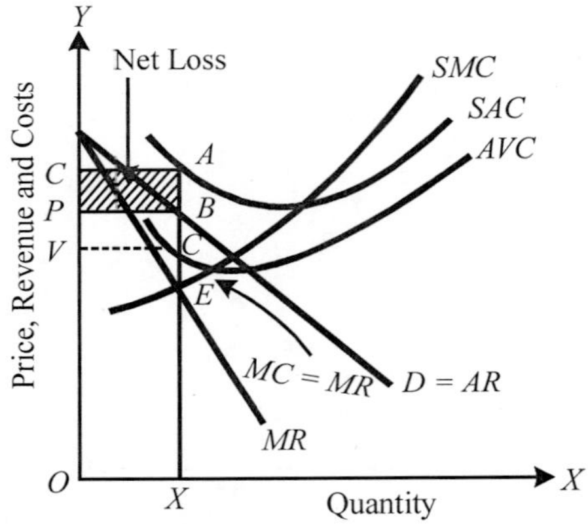

Fig. 33.4

Normal Profits in the Short-Period. In the short-period, it is possible that the monopolist neither makes abnormal profits nor incurs losses, but earns only normal profits. This happens only when the average cost curve of the monopolist is tangent to his average revenue curve and at the same time his marginal revenue curve cuts his marginal cost curve. In such a situation the monopolist must be producing at less than optimum size. This case has been illustrated in Fig. 33.5.

In Fig. 33.5, the monopolist is in equilibrium at *OX* level of output because at this level of output his marginal cost curve (*SMC*) cuts the marginal revenue curve (*MR*) at point *E* from below. Also, at the same level of output (*OX*), the monopolist's *AC*-curve touches his *AR*-curve at point *A*. Thus, *OP* (=*XA*) is the monopoly price which is also equal to the cost per unit. Thus, the monopolist earns only normal profits—his average revenue (price) being equal to his average cost; and the normal profit is included in the average cost of production.

From the above analysis of the short-period price and output equilibrium, it may be contended that profit maximisation or loss minimisation or the attainment of normal profit will be accomplished only at that level of output at which the marginal cost equals the marginal revenue.

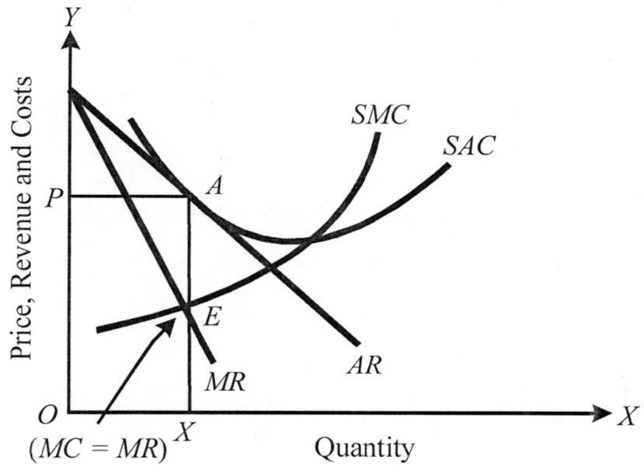

Fig. 33.5

Price and Output Equilibrium of Monopoly in the Long Period

Under perfect competition in the long period a firm gets only normal profits because of the free entry or exit of the firm into the industry. But under monopoly, entry of the new firms is not possible and therefore, the monopolist can easily protect his short-period abnormal profits in the long-run. The magnitude of the long-run profits will depend upon the cost conditions under which he has to operate production and the demand curve he has to face in the long-run. His long-period profits may be higher than or less than that of the short-period profits. But this is true that the monopolist, like a perfect competitive firm, will not accept any loss in the long period. The minimum price acceptable by the monopolist for his product must equal the long-run average cost. Under perfect competition we have seen that in the long-run every firm would be of optimum size where its long-period average cost (*LAC*) is minimum. But in the case of monopoly, the equilibrium level of output (where *LMC*=*MR*) may or may not have the lowest long-run average cost. The monopolist will build the optimum plant only if his *MR* cuts his *LAC* at its lowest point. If *MR* passes through *LAC* before its (*LAC*) minimum point, the monopolist will build a smaller than optimum plant and operate it at a less than optimum rate. On the other hand, if *MR* cuts *LAC* beyond its (*LAC*) minimum point, the monopolist will build a plant greater than the optimum plant and operate it at a more than optimum rate.

Now we can say that since entry into the industry (market) is blocked, the monopolist adjusts his long-run output by means of scale of plant adjustments and there are three possibilities to exist: (*i*) the relation between his *MR* (or demand, *AR*) and his long-run average costs (*LAC*) may be such that he will build a less than optimum scale of plant, (*ii*) the relation between *MR* (or demand, *AR*) and *LAC* is such that he will build an optimum scale of plant, and (*iii*) the relation between *MR* (or demand, *AR*) is such that he will build a greater than optimum scale of plant. These three possible situations may be described in the following manner.

Less than Optimum Scale of Plant and the Law of Increasing Returns or Decreasing Costs. Here we assume that the monopolist has to operate under the conditions of diminishing costs which mean that as he produces more, his per unit cost of production decreases. But his market is so small that his marginal revenue curve cuts his long-run marginal

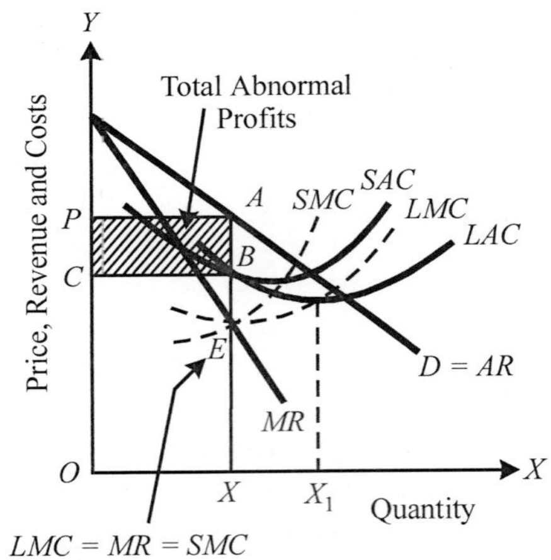

Fig. 33.6

cost curve to the left of *LAC's* minimum point. Thus, he is to produce only that level of output where his *MR* = *LMC*. Only at this level of output he maximises his prof its. In other words, larger output cannot be produced if the demand is low. This case has been illustrated in Fig. 33.6. The long-run equilibrium point is *E* where *LMC* = *MR*. Here, the output will be *OX* and price will be *OP*. The monopolist should build the scale of plant that will produce output *OX* at the least possible average cost. The monopolist's *SAC* (short-run average cost) curve should be tangent to *LAC* curve at output *OX*. If *SAC* is tangent to *LAC* at output level *OX*, *SMC* is necessarily equal to *LMC* at that output. This indicates that the long-run equilibrium of the monopolist is also the short-run equilibrium of the monopolist; because *SMC* = *LMC* = *MR*. At *OX* level of output, the monopolist obtains maximum profits shown by the are a *PABC*. This level of output is less than optimum level of output. The optimum level of output is that where the *LAC* is the minimum. In Fig. 33.6, the optimum level of output will be OX_1 but the monopolist will not produce more than *OX* quantity (and $OX < OX_1$), because he has no inducement to expand the existing plant size beyond *OX* as he is already getting maximum profits.

Optimum Scale of Plant and the Law of Constant Returns or Constant Costs. Here we assume that the monopolist has to operate under the conditions of constant returns or constant costs. In such a case the monopolist will build the optimum scale of plant only if his *MR* cuts *LMC* at the minimum point of *LAC*. This is shown in Fig. 33.7. Here point *E* is the equilibrium point at which *MR* = *LMC* = *LAC* = *SMC* = *SAC*. The optimum level of equilibrium output is *OX*. The monopolist is in both short-period and long-period equilibrium. His price of the product at *OX* level of output is *OP* and cost per unit is *OC*. Thus the maximum abnormal profit per unit is *CP*. The shaded area *PAEC* represents his total minimum profits.

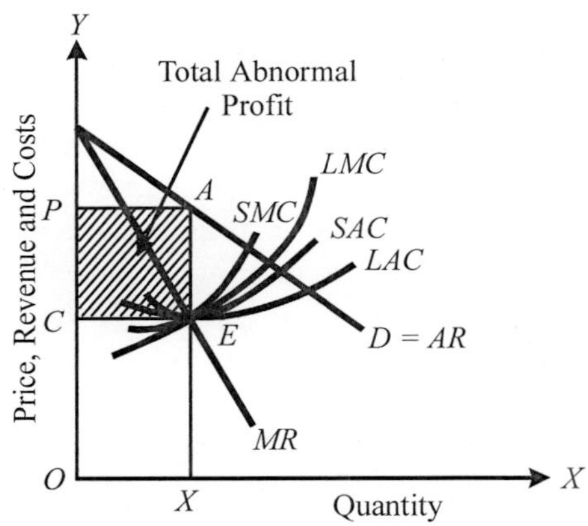

Fig. 33.7

Greater than Optimum Scale of Plant and the Law of Diminishing Returns or Increasing Costs. Here we assume that the monopolist has to operate under the conditions of increasing costs which means that as he produces more, his costs per unit of production will increase. In such a case the monopolist will try to reduce output and increase price. But his market is large enough for his marginal revenue to cut his *LAC* curve to the right of its (*LAC*) minimum point. In other words, the *MR* curve cuts the *LMC* curve beyond the minimum point of the *LAC* curve. This case has been illustrated in Fig. 33.8. Here the equilibrium point is *E* where *MR* = *LMC* = *SMC*. Thus the profit maximising output level will be *OX*. The proper scale of plant to be used is *SAC* which is tangent to *LAC* at

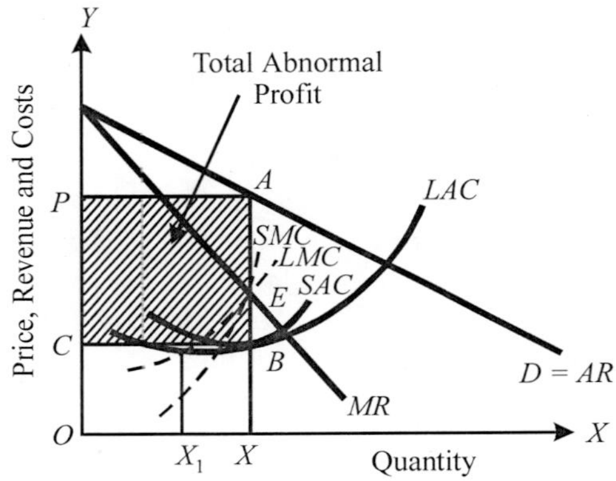

Fig. 33.8

output level *OX*. In this situation, the monopolist builds a greater than optimum scale of plant and produces *OX* quantity of output which is more than the optimum level of output (as shown by OX_1 quantity of output in Fig. 33.8). At *OX* level of output, price is *OP*, cost per unit is *OC* and profit per unit is *CP*. The total maximum profits are shown by the shaded area *PABC*. In such a situation, his scale of plant is so large that diseconomies of scale occur (because per unit cost is more than the minimum of *LAC*), but a reduction of output would mean lower profits. Thus he has no incentive to contract the plant size, as this would reduce his profits. Only at *OX* level of output, he is able to attain maximum profits.

5. MONOPOLY *VS*. PERFECT COMPETITION (WELFARE EFFECTS OF MONOPOLY)

It can easily be demonstrated that a perfect competitive market is superior to monopoly as the latter has some adverse effects on the welfare of consumers.

We know that in a perfect competitive market price and output are determined at the point where the industry-supply curve (or the aggregate marginal cost curve) intersects the industry-demand curve. Now, we will see that a profit maximising monopoly will sell a smaller quantity of output at a higher price than a competitive industry faced with the same demand and cost situation. Fig. 33.9 compares the competitive and monopoly situations. We may assume here, that the monopolist has the same number of plants as the competitive industry, that costs are identical for both and that the industry absorbs only a small fraction of each input.

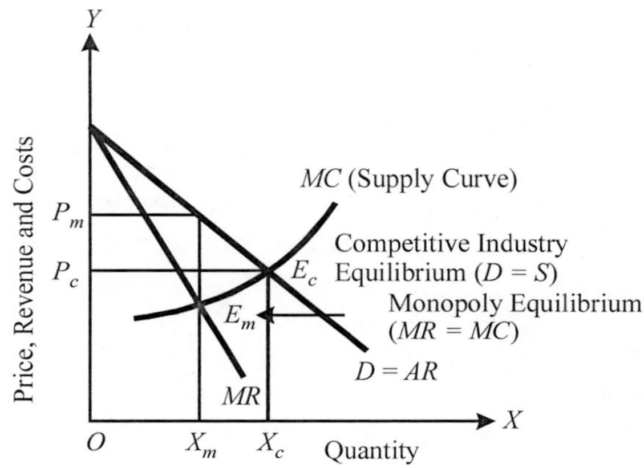

Fig. 33.9

Fig. 33.9 indicates that E_c is the equilibrium point of the competitive industry where the industry demand and the industry supply of the product are equal. At this equilibrium point E_c, the industry price would be *OPc* and output would be OX_c. In Fig. 33.9, point E_m is the equilibrium point of the monopolist where $MR = MC$. Therefore, the monopolist will produce OX_m quantity of output and will charge OP_m price. Now, we may conclude that under monopoly the consumers will enjoy OX_m quantity at OP_m price while under perfect competition, they will enjoy OX_c quantity at *OPc* price. The output available in perfect competition is more than the output available in monopoly. Also the price charged by the monopolist will be higher than the price charged by the firms in perfect competition. In other words, introduction of monopoly in place of perfect competition will mean a loss of consumer's surplus to the consumers.

6. CONTROL AND REGULATION OF MONOPOLY (MONOPOLY PRICING WITH THREAT OF ENTRY)

In this section we shall discuss some of the economic measures that can be used to prevent the monopolist from using his monopoly power to the full extent. The two important methods generally used by the state to control the operation of a monopoly firm are the following:

(1) Direct Regulation of Monopoly Price, and

(2) Regulation through Taxation.

Regulation of Monopoly Price

This method is generally used in the case of natural monopolies. Natural monopolies are very necessary to be controlled. If they are put in the hands of private entrepreneurs, and are free to work, it would lead to the exploitation of the people. Thus the government should regulate them. This can be done either to control prices or to control output or control both price and output. The government appoints Price Tribunals or State Regulatory Commissions to govern the rates or prices charged by the public utility monopolies, such as gas and electric power companies, railways etc. These commissions have to face a number of economic problems. The main economic problem involved, is the determination of the price that will induce the monopolist to produce the greatest amount of the commodity consistent with his costs and with consumer demand. In other words, the price should be such that the monopolist should produce greater quantity of output to maximise his profits and at that price the consumers should also be ready to purchase greater amounts of the output. If price is fixed at a very low level, the market demand for the product will increase tremendously but at that price the monopolist will produce a smaller level of output which satisfies the rule $MC = MR$ (price). This will lead to black-marketing where the monopolist may charge a very high price for his product. Thus, a very small price would give rise to excess demand and unless price regulation is coupled with rationing, it would result in black-marketing by the monopolist. Therefore, the price commission must take care to fix a fair price for the product. This case has been illustrated in Fig. 33.10. In the absence of any restriction by the state authority, the monopolist maximises profits at that level of output 'where marginal cost equals marginal revenue. In such a free situation, the price he wants to charge is *OP* and the output he wants to produce is *OX*. At *OX* level of output his maximum profit per unit is *CP* (which is the difference between the price, *OP* and the cost per unit, *OC*).

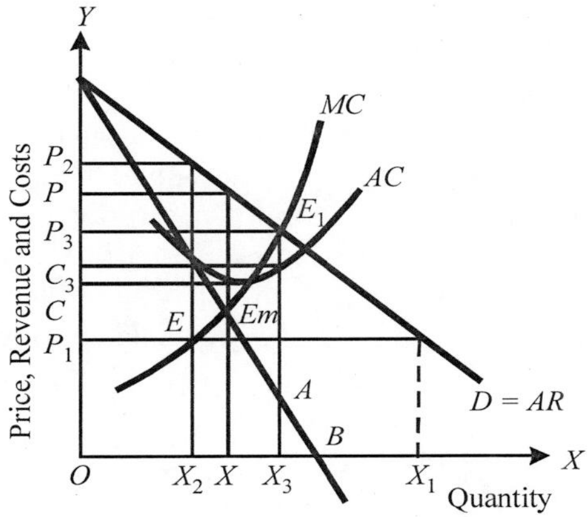

Fig. 33.10

Now first suppose that the government authority (or the price tribunal) fixes a very lower price of the product as OP_1. It may be seen that at this price consumers demand OX_1 quantity of the product; but the monopolist produces OX_2 quantity of the product, because only at OX_2 output he is able to maximise his profits (whereas at point *E,* his *MC* equals the given price or marginal revenue). It is obvious that at OP_1 price, there will be an excess demand to the extent of X_2X_1. Now, at OX_1 level of output, the black-marketing price would be very high, OP_2. Thus such a lower price will result in black-marketing by the monopolist.

Now, suppose that instead of fixing a very low price (OP_1), the regulatory commission fixes a maximum price OP_3 at which the monopolist's marginal cost curve cuts the demand curve at point E_1. In such a situation, the demand curve faced by the monopolist becomes P_2E_1D. It indicates that upto OX_3 level of output, the monopolist can charge OP_3 price but if at all he desires to sell more than OX_3 quantity of the output, he has to reduce the price below OP_3. Now the new demand curve P_3E_1D faced by the monopolist also changes his marginal revenue curve. Upto OX_3 the demand curve is perfectly inelastic as the demand curve faced by a perfect competitive firm and therefore marginal revenue will equal OP_3 Beyond output OX_3, the market demand curve and the original marginal revenue curve become relevant. At OP_3 price fixed by the commission, the monopolist's marginal revenue curve takes the shape as P_3E_1AB.

In this controlled situation, the monopolist will maximise his profits by producing OX_3 quantity of the output, because only at this level of output his marginal cost equals marginal revenue (price) at point E_1. At OX_3 output, his maximum profit per unit is C_3P_2. Thus at OP_3 price, the monopolist acts as a perfect competitive firm because only in a perfectly competitive market $MR = P$ to an individual firm. Here, the price regulatory commission succeeds not only in lowering the monopoly price, but also in forcing the monopolist to sell larger quantity at this price as compared to the pre-control situation. This is all possible only when the commission is able to make the necessary calculations regarding the costs and price structure of the monopoly.

Regulation through Taxation

The second important method of regulation is taxation. Here we shall consider two types of taxes which the government can impose on the monopolist: (*i*) A Specific Tax which is a tax per unit on the monopolist's output, and (*ii*) A Lump-sum Tax which is a fixed amount of tax levied without regard to the monopolist's output level. The specific tax may be treated as a fixed cost. Now we shall explain the effects of these taxes on the monopolist's equilibrium with the help of diagrams in the following manner.

A Specific Tax. In Fig. 33.11, the original average cost and marginal cost curves of the monopolist are AC and MC respectively. His original equilibrium position is established at point E where $MC = MR$. The original price and output are OP and OX respectively. The original maximum profit per unit is CP (which is the difference between the price and the cost per unit). Now, suppose that a specific tax is levied on his output. This will lead to an increase in both the AC and MC of the monopolist. Thus, the imposition of a specific tax shifts the AC and MC curves upwards as AC_1 and MC respectively. The MC curve also shifts upwards because this tax is a variable cost. The new mar-ginal cost curve (MC_1) intersects the MR at point E_1 which lies to the left of the previous equilibrium point E. As a result, the profit maximising level of output is reduced from OX to OX_1, whereas the monopoly price rises from OP to OP_1. The per unit cost at output OX_1 increases from OC to OC_1. This reduces the monopolist's profits per unit from CP to C_1P_1; because the rise in price is less than the rise in costs. The monopolist's total profits fall from $PABC$ to $P_1A_1B_1C_1$.

However, the proportion of such a tax borne by the monopolist out of his profits will depend largely on the elasticity of demand for his product. Here we can say that the higher the elasticity of demand, the larger will be the proportion of the tax borne by the monopolist and vice versa.

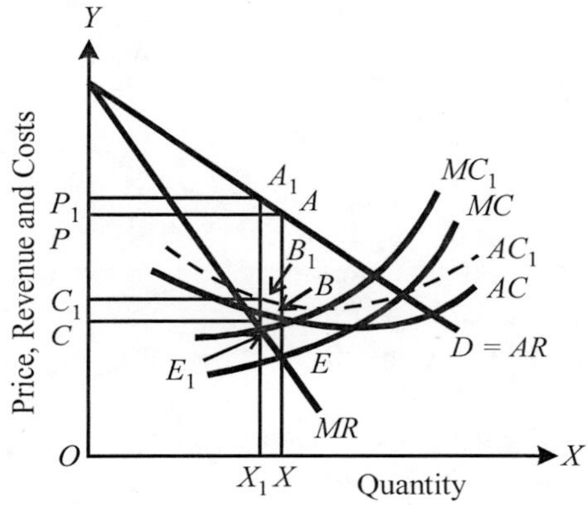

Fig. 33.11

A Lump-sum Tax. In Fig. 33.12, we show the effects of a lump-sum tax on the monopolist. The original profit maximising output and price are *OX* and or respectively. Originally, the monopolist earns *CP* profit

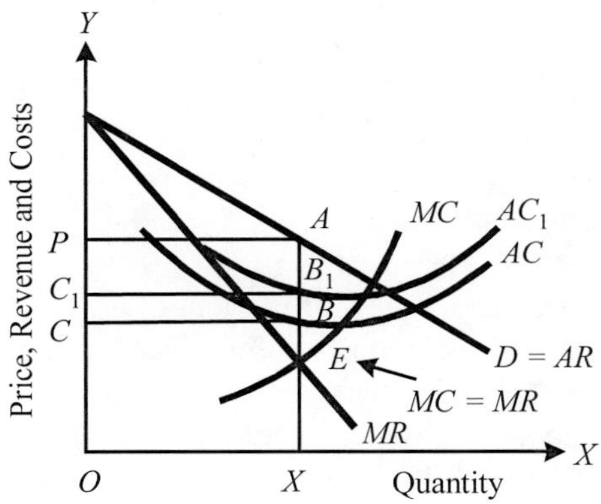

Fig. 33.12

per unit. Now, suppose that a lump-sum tax is levied on the monopolist. It is a fixed cost to the monopolist. Thus, it only shifts the average cost curve *AC* to AC_1, and makes no effect on the original marginal cost curve

MC. Consequently, the profit maximising price and output remain at the original level as *OP* and *OX* respectively. The entire amount of the tax is paid by the monopolist from his profits. Thus, his profits fall from *PC* per unit to PC_1. In other words, the total profits fall from *PABC* to PAB_1C_1. From consumers' point of view this method is the best method. Through this method all of the monopolist's profits may be taxed away with no effect on output and price.

7. RESOURCE ALLOCATION UNDER MONOPOLY

The comparison between a perfectly competitive firm and a monopoly firm may clearly point out that monopoly leads to malallocation of sources. For this one has to compare price, output and profits under both the situations. Under perfect competition in the long-run every firm satisfies the condition: Price = *AR* = *MR* = *LMC*= *LAC* at its minimum. This means that under perfect competition every firm gets only the normal profit which is included in the cost. Here the firms are of the optimum size and producing to their full capacity. But under monopoly, in the long-run, we have *P* > *LMC* = *MR.* Also the minimum point of the *LAC* curve is to the right of the equilibrium point (*LMC* = *MR*). It indicates the fact that the monopoly firm is of less than optimum size and does not produce to its full capacity and earns abnormal profit. Since, the monopoly firm has excess capacity, there is under allocation of resources to the monopoly firm and a misallocation of resources in the economy. It is also cleared in Fig. 33.9 (monopoly *vs.* perfect competition), that the monopoly price is higher than the competitive price and monopoly output is less than competitive output. Thus the consumers are worse off under monopoly because they are supposed to pay more and get a smaller output than that under perfect competition. This is a net loss to consumers' welfare in the society.

Having examined the effects of monopoly on welfare of consumers and resource owners one would naturally be tempted to infer that monopoly is an evil and that every effort to introduce competition in a monopoly situation would increase social welfare. Yet there might be situations in which introduction of competition may do more harm than, good. Particular situation may be explained when due to large plant capacity, the cost of production can be covered only if output is undertaken at a relatively sufficient scale. Thus in Fig. 33.13, if there is only one firm in the market, it would produce *OXm* output at *OPm* price where his *MR* (i.e., D_1) and *MC* are equal at point E_m. It however another firm is allowed in the market (i.e., competition is being created in the market) then the demand curve now becomes D_1 (instead of D) and the corresponding marginal revenue curve becomes MR_1. Each firm now produces OX quantity at OP price. In this new situation, price has fallen to consumers from OP_m to OP, but each firm produces at a very small scale and incurs a loss of $PCTS$. Thus in such a situation where market is small, an entry of second firm would imply unused capacity as well as net loss for both the firms in the market and this situation becomes more worse as more and more firms enter into the market. Hence monopoly may be desired instead of competition.

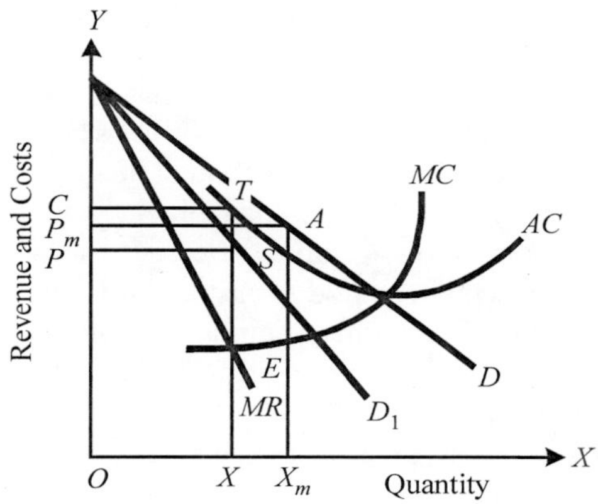

Fig. 33.13

Further, monopoly may also be desired in the areas of public utility such as supply of water, electricity or the distribution of scarce goods through fair price shops.

8. PRICE DISCRIMINATION

Price discrimination means charging different prices from different buyers of the same product of service. This cannot be done under perfect competition where the individual firm is unable to influence the market-supply of the product. This can be done only under monopoly or it has some monopoly power. A monopolist need not always charge a single price to all his consumers. Since he is the only producer in the market, he has a control over the supply of the product. He can charge different prices to different consumers or in the different markets. In the preceding chapter it was contended that a monopolist may not derive any benefit from a price rise as every increase in price is likely to induce consumers to buy smaller quantity of the product. He may, however, increase his profits by adopting price discrimination. *Discriminating Monopoly* or *Price Discrimination* occurs when a monopolist charges different prices for different units of a product, even though these units are identical in their physical characteristics. In general, price discrimination means that a firm charges two or more prices for the same thing at the same time.

Types of Price Discrimination

Price discrimination may take place in many forms. We shall discuss only the important forms of price discrimination which are practised to increase the profits of the monopolist.

(1) *Personal Discrimination.* Personal discrimination occurs when different prices are charged to the different consumers in accordance with the intensity of either desire or according to their incomes. The monopolist can charge higher prices from the persons who are more eager to buy or whose ability to pay is more. A higher price is generally charged from the rich than the poor. This type of discrimination is not always possible, for it may arouse violent resentment among the consumers. It is usually possible only in a disguised manner and will not be made openly. This type of price discrimination is applied to railway passengers, and cinema tickets. People traveling in upper classes always pay more than the cost of providing the extra conveniences. Similarly, people purchasing balcony tickets or going to box always pay more than the cost of providing the extra comforts.

(2) *Local Discrimination.* In this situation different prices are charged from different localities. The monopolist charges a lower price at one place and a higher price at other places. 'Dumping' is the best example of local discrimination. In the case of dumping, the monopolist sells his output at a lower price in a foreign market and at a higher price in the domestic market.

(3) *Trade Discrimination.* It is also known as use discrimination. In this situation, the monopolist charges different prices for different uses. In other words, trade discrimination take place when the monopolist charges a lower price to one trade than to another. For example, electric current may be sold at low price to industrial concerns, at a higher price for the purpose of domestic cooking, and at a still higher price for domestic lighting.

Conditions for Price Discrimination

Price discrimination is profitable only if the following conditions are satisfied.

1. *Two or More Separate Markets.* There must be two (or more than two), separate markets; otherwise, his product will be purchased in the market with the lower price and resold in the market, with the higher price. This will iron out the price differential that the monopolist attempts to establish. Thus, the different markets must be such that no buyer of one market may enter the other market and vice versa.

2. *Differences in Elasticity of Demand.* The elasticities of demand in each market must be different. It means that if one market is less elastic, then the other should be more elastic. This condition is vital. If the demand elasticities in the different markets are equal, there will be no scope for price discrimination. If, on the other hand, elasticities are different, the monopolist will gain by selling his product at different prices indifferent markets.

Hence, the pre-requisites of price discrimination are the (two) separate markets and the differences of elasticity of demand between the markets. An old example is the monopoly that charges a high price of its product in the domestic market and a low price in foreign market. The two markets are kept separate by tariff wall; domestic buyers cannot buy goods at lower foreign price by importing them. The price is lower in the foreign market, because demand for the product is highly elastic (the product has to face competition from similar products); while price is higher in domestic market, because the monopolist is the only producer of it and the demand is inelastic. At the same time it is not necessary that the markets should be separated geographically. There are many other ways by which the markets can be separated. For instance, the markets of box seats, balcony seats and the first class seats in theatres are segregated by tickets, and ushers. Similarly, electric power companies use metres and other devices to separate the markets for electrical energy for lighting, cooking and other commercial and industrial uses. But price discrimination will take place only when the above two conditions—separate markets and the different elasticity of demand in the market—are satisfied.

Degrees of Price Discrimination

Here, the question is how far a monopolist goes in charging different prices for his product? The extent to which price discrimination is possible will depend on the circumstances. Prof. A.C. Pigou, the English economist, created the idea of degrees of price discrimination and imperfect discrimination. Pigou speaks of the following three degrees of price discrimination.

(1) ***Discrimination of the First Degree or Perfect Discrimination.*** In discrimination of the first degree, the monopolist knows the maximum amount of money each consumer will pay for any quantity. He will set the prices accordingly and take from each consumer the entire amount of his consumer's surplus. In other words, in the first degree of price discrimination, the price charged by the monopolist will be different for every individual unit of a homogeneous commodity. The monopolist tries to charge the highest price from each consumer that he will be ready to pay for each unit rather than go without it. Mrs. Robinson calls this situation as 'perfectly discriminating monopoly', because it is perfect only from the point of view of the monopolist.

Such discrimination is possible only if the consumers buy one unit each from the monopolist. The monopolist will charge different prices from different consumers, depending upon their willingness to buy it. If all of his consumers have different tastes, the monopolist has a different price for each one. In such a case his minimum price will be determined by his costs. In a situation when the consumer buys more than one unit of the monopolist's product, then he will do so only at lower prices. The monopolist will now adjust his sales accordingly.

For example, in Fig. 33.14 the monopolist will sell one unit at OP_1 price, a second unit at OP_2 price, a third unit at OP_3 price and so on. Now assuming that the marginal unity of money is constant to the consumer;

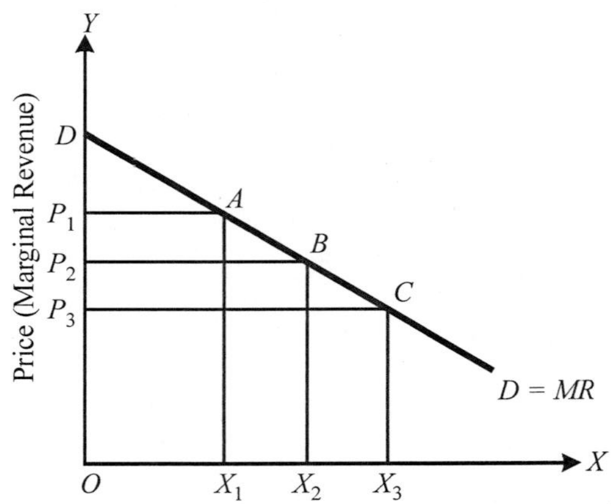

Fig. 33.14

OP_1, OP_2, OP_3 can also be assumed as the prices which the consumer will pay for OX_1. OX_2 and OX_3 quantity of the product. Therefore, the demand curve DD will become the marginal revenue curve. If the monopolist sells OX_3 units of his product, his total revenue will not be equal to the rectangle $OP_3 CX_3$ but will be equal to the total area under the (marginal revenue) curve, i.e., ODP_3X_3. Thus, assuming the marginal utility is equal to price, the area under the demand curve represents the total utility to the consumers. This indicates that under the first degree of price discrimination,

$$TU = TR$$

where TU = Total Utility (in terms of money or price)

TR = Total Revenue

It also means that under the above situation, the monopolist takes away the entire utility obtained by the consumers in terms of the different prices charged by him and leaves no consumer's surplus with the consumers.

Price discrimination of the first degree is the limiting or extreme case. It can occur only rarely where a monopolist has only a few buyers of his product and where he is clever enough to judge the maximum prices that the consumers are willing to pay for his product. Thus its technical feasibility would be limited because the monopolist usually does not possess a perfect knowledge of the demand of the consumers. It would be most unusual to find a single consumer being offered a number of units of an identical good, each at different prices. Discrimination between buyers is more usual than the discrimination between the units of a homogeneous product.

(2) ***Discrimination of the Second Degree.*** In discrimination of the second degree, the monopolist is able to get a part of consumer's surplus but not the entire consumer's surplus of the consumers. In other words, the monopolist changes different prices from different consumers and different prices for different units of the same product, but not the maximum possible prices that the consumers could pay for it. He will be able to charge a lesser price than the maximum imaginary price of the consumers; leaving a certain amount of consumer's surplus with the consume. The monopolist will sell the consumer several units at a lower price and another several units at a lower price, etc. Mrs. Joan Robinson meant it 'imperfect discriminating monopoly.' This has been illustrated in Fig. 33.15.

In Fig. 33.15, DD is the demand curve of the consumers for the monopolist's product. It indicates that the monopolist charges a high price

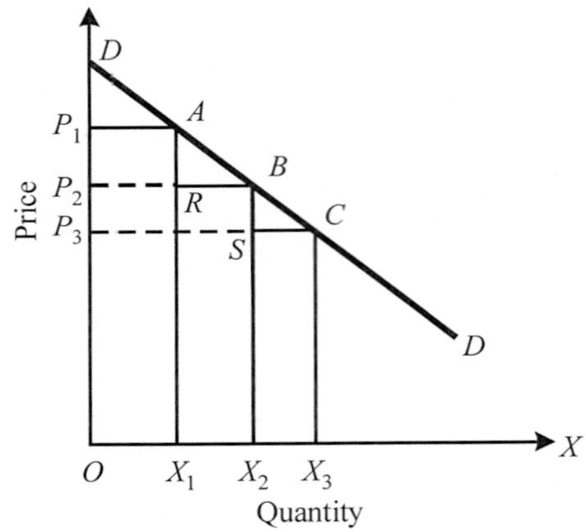

Fig. 33.15

for a low level of output and for additional levels of output he charges lower prices. For instance, OX_1 output is sold at price OP_1, X_1X_2 (additional units) out put is sold at OP_2 price and further X_2X_3 output is sold at OP_3 price. The demand curve shows that the consumers will consume these various output levels at the said prices. Now the total revenue of the monopolist will be equal to the total area under the demand curve upto point C and nor it will be equal to the rectangle OP_2CX_3 if the monopolist sells OX_2 quantity of output. But in this situation, the total revenue of the monopolist will be equal to the area $OP_1AX_1 + X_1RBX_2 + X_2SCX_3$. If the monoplist charges a single price OP_2 for his entire output sold, OC; his total revenue will be equal to the area OP_3CX_3 which would be smaller than the revenue derived under the second degree of price discrimination. Thus with the three prices, the total revenue is the sum of the three rectangles. The monopolist in this way snatches a part of the consumer's surplus. The part which the monopolist leaves with the consumers is equal to the sum of the areas of the three little triangles as $\Delta\, DP_1A + \Delta\, ARB + \Delta\, BSC$.

This type of second degree price discrimination is normally practised in such markets where there are a number of buyers of the product. Since tastes and incomes of the consumers differ, the monopolist is able to seize some part of their consumer's surplus depending upon their (different groups of consumers) desire to buy the commodity.

(3) ***Discrimination of the Third Degree.*** In discrimination of the third degree, the monopolist divides his consumers into two or more

classes or groups or markets and charges different prices from different markets. This type of discrimination is most common in practice. The simplest form of this kind of price discrimination is that when the monopolist sells his output, already produced, in two separate markets. Since he has some given amount to sell, his costs of production can be ignored. When he sells his output only in the two markets, he adjusts the amount in each market such that the marginal revenue derived from the first market becomes equal to the marginal revenue derived from the second market.

Though the marginal revenues are equal in the two markets, prices are unequal due to different elasticities of demand in the two markets. Thus, discrimination of the third degree will occur only if the markets are separate and their respective elasticities of demand are different. In the following section we shall discuss the determination of price and output under the third degree of price discrimination which is the most common form of price discrimination.

Determination of Price Under Discrimination

Let us assume that the monopolist has a given output already produced and merely wants to distribute it in the most profitable way between the two markets. As we have already mentioned, for price discrimination it is necessary that elasticities of demand must be different in the two distinct markets. Let us suppose that market *I* is less elastic and market *II* is more elastic. The respective marginal revenues of these markets *I* and *II* will also be different. Now, in order to maximise profits (revenues because costs are ignored here), the monopolist should distribute his given output among the markets in such a way that marginal revenue in each market is equal to the marginal revenue in the other market. If marginal revenue of market *I* is greater than that of market *II,* he will sell the additional unit of sales in market *I.* This type of substitution will go on until the marginal revenues in each market are made equal. Once marginal revenue in the two markets is equal, he will stop switching sales from one market to the other. He will gain nothing in switching a marginal unit of output and will actually lose if he continues the process because marginal revenue in the market with low elasticity of demand will eventually become less than marginal revenue in the other. Thus, the equality between marginal revenues will bring him (monopolist) the greatest total receipts from a given output. We can illustrate this case with the help of a diagram. In Fig. 33.16, AR_1 and AR_2 are the average revenue or demand curves of the two markets *I* and II respectively. Their corresponding marginal revenue

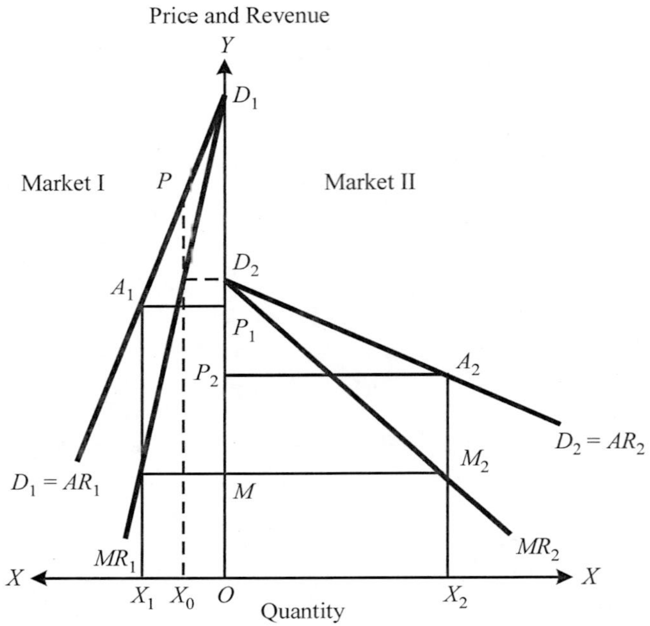

Fig. 33.16

curves are MR_1 and MR_2. Now, if the given amount of output is below OX_o, the monopolist should sell the entire amount in market *I* because upto this level of output the marginal revenue of the *I* market is higher than the marginal revenue of the *II* market. If his total output is equal to X_1X_2 ($= OX_1 + OX_2$), he should sell OX_1 output in market *I* and OX_2 output in market *II*, so that marginal revenue in market *I* equals marginal revenue in market *II*. The level of marginal revenue in both the markets will be equal to OM ($= X_1M_1 = X_2M_2$); or

$$MR_1 = MR_2$$

where MR_1 = Marginal Revenue of Market *I*

MR_2 = Marginal Revenue of Market *II*

This is the fundamental rule of output distribution when the costs are ignored. At this point the monopolist will be in equilibrium and his total revenue from the given output will be maximum. With this distribution of output, the price in market *I* will be OP_1 and the price in market *II* will be OP_2. It clears that the price in market *I* is higher than the price in market *II*. Also, output is more in market *II* than in market *I*. In other words, we can say that in equilibrium marginal revenue in the markets will be the same but prices will be different. Price will be higher in the market with the less elastic demand curve and vice versa.

Determination of Price and Output Under (Third Degree) Discriminating Monopoly

The problem of the monopolist is to maximise his total profits. For this he must take account of his costs and revenues. He will maximise his profits when the marginal revenues in each of the two markets are equal and at the same time they are also equal to the marginal costs of the monopolist's entire output.

Suppose, in Fig. 33.17, the monopolist has two markets *I* and *II*. The average revenue curves or demand curves in the two markets are AR_1 and AR_2 respectively. The corresponding marginal revenue curves in the two markets are MR_1 and MR_2 respectively. These markets have different elasticities of demand at each price. Now the monopolist has to determine

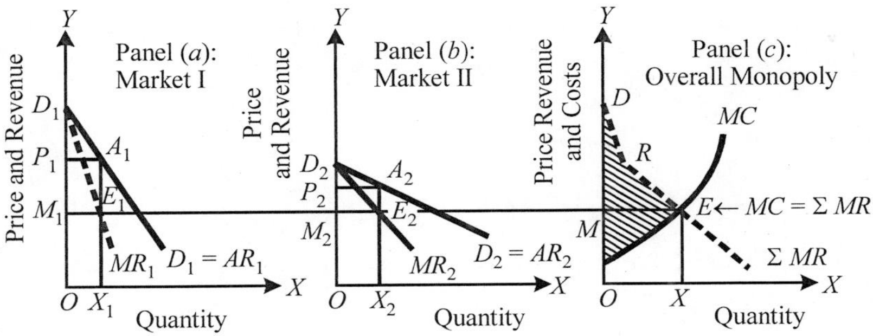

Fig. 33.17

his entire output regardless of how it is distributed. For this he has to follow the profit maximising rule $MR = MC$. The total (combined) marginal revenue curve (ΣMR) and the marginal cost curve (MC) for the monopolist's whole output are shown in Panel (*c*) of Fig. 33.17. The marginal revenue for the entire output (ΣMR) is the horizontal summation of the two separate marginal revenues MR_1 and MR_2 of the individual markets. Now the monopolist will establish his equilibrium point at E where $MC = \Sigma MR$. His equilibrium level of output is OX. Now the problem before the monopolist is how to distribute the output OX between the two markets *I* and *II*. For this he will follow the rule $MR_1 = MR_2 = MC = \Sigma MR$. Following this principle, the discriminating monopolist will sell OX_1 output in market *I* and OX_2 output in market *II*. With this distribution of total output, marginal revenue in market *I* (OM_1) is equal to marginal revenue in market *II* (OM_2). The equilibrium points of market *I* and *II* are E_1 and E_2 respectively. The prices charged by the monopolist from market *I* and *II* are OP_1 and OP_2 respectively. The total maximum profit of the monopolist is equal to the shaded area *DRES* shown in Panel (*c*) of Fig. 33.17.

This same solution can also be shown by combining the above three panels of Fig. 33.17 in a single diagram as in Fig. 33.18. The marginal and average cost curves of the monopolist are represented by *MC* and *AC*, respectively. The combined marginal revenue curve $\Sigma\, MR$ is derived by taking the horizontal summation of the marginal revenue curves of the two markets—market *I* starts from point D_1 while market *II* starts from point D_2. Thus up to point *A*, the marginal revenue curve of market *I* will be relevant and thereafter we add the marginal revenue of market *II* to market *I* and get the total marginal revenue curve $\Sigma\, MR$ of the monopolist. The equilibrium level of output of the monopolist is *OX* which if distributed properly (by following the rule $MR_1 = MR_2 = \Sigma\, MR = MC$) in the two markets, then the profits in Market *I* will be equal to the area $CP_1\, TS$ and profit in market *II* will be equal to the area $CP_2\, NR$. Total profit of the monopolist will be equal to the profits of market *I* plus the profits of market *II*.

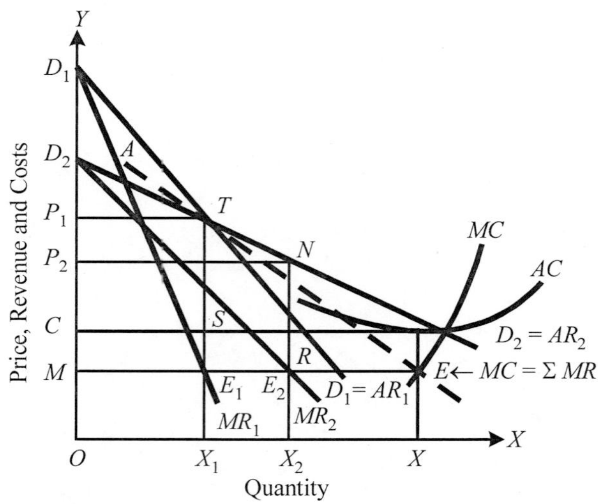

Fig. 33.18

Dumping

Dumping means charging a higher price in the domestic market and a lower price in the foreign market for the same product. Under the above forms of price discriminations both the markets were assumed to be imperfect; but under dumping, we assume that perfect competition exists in the foreign market while the monopolist enjoys monopoly power in the home (domestic) market. In other words, in the foreign market, the elasticity of demand for his product is infinite while in the home market, elasticity of demand for his product is very low. Thus the monopolist has to face a horizontal straight line demand curve or average revenue for the foreign market. In the home market, the average revenue curve or the demand curve slopes downwards and the marginal revenue curve for the home market will be below it.

In Fig. 33.19, AR_d and MR_d are the average and marginal revenue curves for the domestic market which are one and the same. AR_f and MR_f are the average and marginal revenue curves for the foreign market. *MC* represents the marginal cost curve of the monopolist's total output. Now the problem of the monopolist is how much quantity of the output is to be

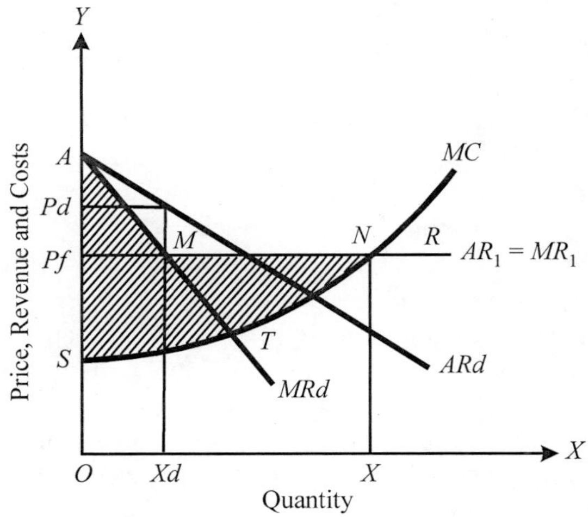

Fig. 33.19

produced? For this, he has to find out the equilibrium point where his marginal cost equals the combined marginal revenue. The combined marginal revenue curve is *AMNR*. On this curve, marginal revenue in the foreign market is added horizontally to the marginal revenue in the domestic market. The intersection of the monopolist's marginal cost curve with the combined marginal revenue at point N gives a total output of OX as that which maximises profits. The total output must now be distributed between the two markets—the foreign market and the domestic market. Following the fundamental rule of distribution ($MR_1 = MR_2 = MC$), the monopolist sells OX output in the domestic market at a price of OP_d and a marginal revenue of MX_d. This leaves $X_d X$ ($= OX - OX_d$) to be sold in the foreign market at a price of OP_f and with a marginal revenue NX (= OP_f).

It is clear from Fig. 33.19, that the marginal revenue of domestic market, MX_d, is the same as the marginal revenue of the foreign market NX; but price in the domestic market (OP_d) is higher than the price in the foreign market (OP). The monopolist's total profits are shown by the shaded area $AMNS$. These profits of the monopolist are at a maximum and are contributed to by both the markets. It is important to note that point T does not indicate the equilibrium of the domestic market because at this point the marginal revenue of the domestic market is less than the marginal revenue of the foreign market. Moreover, point T does not lie on the combined marginal revenue curve of the monopolist. Thus, point Twill not be the relevant point for the output determination by the monopolist. For this, he has to follow the fundamental principle, $MC = MR_1 = MR_2 = \sum MR$.

Justification of Price Discrimination

In modern times, the theory of price discrimination has a number of applications of varied kinds. But in the ideal economy of the welfare theorists, there would be no price discrimination. The welfare theorists assume perfect competition throughout their economic analysis under which price discrimination is impossible any way. The natural monopolies in the ideal economy would set their prices equal to their marginal costs. Price differences between products would exactly equal differences in marginal costs, which is another way of expressing the absence of price discrimination. It means that the consumers pay the same prices at the same time for the same products is one of the marginal conditions for maximum economic welfare.

But it does not mean that for all the time price dicrimination is not desirable in the context of a partial welfare analysis, price-discrimination may assume a great importance. Partial welfare means the economic welfare flowing from one commodity or industry, considered by itself, and without regard to or for possible cross effects with other commodities or industries. Sometimes, the demand cost relations of a monopolist are such that without discrimination he would not like to produce any quantity of the output. Also where the government regulates prices of the products, it may allow or even encourage price discrimination if it increases the welfare of the consumers and to the society as a whole.

There are many services, such as, rail transportation, or services of the doctors etc. which cannot be provided profitably unless price discrimination is allowed to take place, because a single price for such services will mean low incomes to the entrepreneurs.

Another reason to justify price discrimination by the government is that it will reduce the inequalities of personal real incomes. Normally, the reduced price or low price is meant for the poor class while the higher price is meant for the rich class. Here the equity criterion pushes aside the efficiency criterion. Tenants in public-housing projects, who must have incomes below specified levels pay rents that are in general fairly below the full costs.

Now, we can say that whether price-discrimination is economically justified or not will depend upon the question whether it is advantageous or disadvantageous to the welfare of the society. Anyway, the classification of buyers or of markets for charging different prices must satisfy legal tests of 'reasonableness'. Price differences must also be 'reasonable', which usually means that they must conform to demonstrable differences in costs as measured by accounting standards. In fact, differences in elasticities of demand are hardly ever put on an equal footing with differences in costs. The recognition given to elasticities of demand is oblique or implicit. A monopoly regulated by the government may be allowed to charge a lower price for its product where it has to face tough competition as we have seen under dumping. Sometimes, the discriminating monopolist resorts to price discrimination with the selfish motive of destroying his rivals and keeping his own monopoly power in the bargain. He adopts this policy both in the domestic market as well as the foreign market. Thus, if price discrimination leads to larger outputs of the society, it must be justified because larger output implies greater economic welfare. If, on the other hand, it leads to smaller output than that of simple monopoly, it must not be justified.

EXERCISES

1. Describe the main assumptions of monopoly. How does monopoly emerge in real world?
2. How is price determined under monopoly?

3. Explain and illustrate diagrammatically the price and output determination of monopoly in the market period.
4. "The prima facie interest of the owner of a monopoly is clearly to adjust the supply to the demand, not in such a way that the price at which he can sell his commodity shall just cover its expenses of production, but in such a way as to afford him the greatest possible net revenue." — Marshall. Discuss the' above statement.
5. How does a monopolist determine the price and output of his product in the short-run? Would the monopolist like to continue his production in the situation of loss in the short-run?
6. Explain the price and output equilibrium of monopoly in the long-run.
7. Discuss in brief the welfare effects of monopoly.
8. How does the state control the operations of a monopoly firm?
9. How does a monopolist fix price of his product? Is it inevitable that the monopoly price is higher than the competitive price?
10. How far is it possible for the state to induce the monopolist through price regulation, to furnish the greater amount of product consistent with his costs and consumer demand?
11. How are resources allocated under monopoly?
12. Explain the emergence and assumptions of monopoly.
13. What do you understand by price discrimination? Explain the conditions for price discrimination.
14. How far a monopolist goes in charging different prices for his product?
15. "A discriminating monopolist adjusts his sales in such a way that the marginal revenue obtained from selling an additional unit in anyone market is the same for all the markets." Explain the statement.
16. Explain discriminatory pricing under monopoly. Is price discrimination economically justifiable?
17. (*a*) What conditions must be present for 'price discrimination' to be possible under monopoly? Under what circumstances might price discrimination be possible, but not profitable?
    (*b*) How far is it possible for the state to induce the monopolist through price regulation to furnish the greatest amount or product consistent with his costs and consumer demand?
18. State the conditions under which monopolistic price discrimination is possible. How will a discriminating monopolist determine his output and the output to be sold in each market? Will the price be higher in the more elastic market?
19. "The main aim of the monopolist is to sell in such a manner that he may get maximum monopoly profit." Discuss.
20. Explain price and output determination under discriminating monopoly.
21. What do you understand by dumping? How are price and output determined under dumping?

Multiple Choice Questions

22. (*i*) Monopoly means
    (*a*) a single producer of a particular product in the world
    (*b*) a single producer of a particular product in India
    (*c*) a single producer of a particular product in a particular town or city

(*d*) a single producer of a particular product in a single market. [*Ans.* (*d*)]

(*ii*) The demand for the product of a monopoly firm is
(*a*) inelastic
(*b*) elastic
(*c*) unitary elastic
(*d*) impossible to know without knowledge of the market demand elasticity for the product [*Ans.* (*d*)]

(*iii*) If P = Rs. 10 at the point on the demand curve where $ed = 0.5$, MR is
(*a*) Rs. 5
(*b*) Rs. 0
(*c*) Rs. 1
(*d*) Rs. 10 [*Ans.* (*d*)]

(*iv*) The best level of output for the pure monopolist occurs at the point where
(*a*) TC is minimum
(*b*) $TR = TC$
(*c*) TR and TC curves are parallel
(*d*) TR is maximum [*Ans* (*c*)]

(*v*) At the best level of output for the pure monopolist
(*a*) $MR = SMC$
(*b*) $p = SMC$
(*c*) P = lowest SAC
(*d*) P is highest. [*Ans.* (*a*)]

(*vi*) In the short-period, the monopolist
(*a*) breaks even
(*b*) incurs a loss
(*c*) makes a profit
(*d*) any of the above [*Ans* (*d*)]

(*vii*) Which form of monopoly regulation is most advantageous for the consumer?
(*a*) price control
(*b*) lump-sum tax
(*c*) per unit tex
(*d*) all of the above [*Ans.* (*a*)]

(*viii*) Pursuing a policy of price discrimination will increase the profits of a monopolist who sells in two sub-markets
(*a*) only if he sells more than one product
(*b*) if the price elasticity of demand for his output differs in two markets
(*c*) if buyers in either sub-market can easily resell his output to buyers in the other sub-market.
(*d*) only during the short-run when capital stock is fixed [*Ans.* (*d*)]

(*ix*) Price discrimination will always lead to
(*a*) increase in output
(*b*) increase in output
(*c*) no change in output
(*d*) none [*Ans.* (*c*)]

(*x*) Discriminating monopoly is possible if two markets have
(*a*) rising cost curves
(*b*) rising and declining cost curves
(*c*) different erasticities of demand
(*d*) equal elasticities of demand [*Ans.* (*c*)]

(*xi*) Which of the following statements is not true? A discriminating monopolist
(*a*) operates in more than one market
(*b*) makes more profit because he discriminates
(*c*) maximises his profits in each market
(*d*) charges same prices in different markets [*Ans.* (*d*)]

(*xii*) Under price discrimination, the equilibrium condition of a monopoly firm is
(*a*) $MR_1 = MR_2$
(*b*) $MC = MR$
(*c*) $MR_1 = MR_2 = MR$
(*d*) $MR_1 = MR_2 = MR = MC$ [*Ans.* (*d*)]

Chapter 34

MONOPSONY AND BILATERAL MONOPOLY

1. INTRODUCTION

Monopsony refers to a market situation when there is a single buyer of a commodity or service. According to Prof. Liebhafsky, "Monopsony can be formally defined as a case of a single buyer who is not in competition with any other buyers for the output which he seeks to purchase, and as a situation in which entry to the market by other buyers is impossible." Such a situation may arise when the consumers of a certain commodity are organised or when a certain individual happens to have a taste for some commodity which no one else requires. It may also happen when a single big factory in an isolated locality is the sole buyer of some commodity from different firms.

A bilateral monopoly on the other hand is a market situation in which a single seller faces a single buyer. As we have studied earlier, a monopolist is the single seller of a product (or a factor) in the market. When he faces a single buyer, or the monopsonist, this situation is termed as a bilateral monopoly. Since both the firms are capable of exercising their respective strength, there will be bargaining and the stronger of the two will have a better bargain by having the more favourable terms than the other fellow.

2. PRICING AND OUTPUT UNDER MONOPSONY

The process of monopsony price determination is very similar to that under monopoly. The monopsonist aims at the maximisation of his surplus while the monopolist tries to maximise his profit. For profit maximisation, the monopolist applies the condition $MC = MR$. The monopsonist tries to make his purchases in such a way that $MC = MU$. It is only at this point that the monopsonist gets maximum consumer's surplus.

Fig. 34.1 explains the process of price determination by a monopsonist. The *AC* curve of the monopsonist is the supply curve of the industry or of the market. It is from the industry that he buys the product. In Fig. 34.1, *AC* and *MC* curves are the average and marginal cost curves respectively. *MU* is the marginal utility curve of the monopsonist. The equilibrium point is *E* where the *MC* curve cuts the *MU* curve. Thus the monopsonist purchases *OX* quantity at *EX* price, which is the supply price for that output. The surplus obtained by the monopsonist is the area, *CPER.* This is the difference between what he is prepared to pay *(ODEX)* and what he actually pays *(OCRX).*

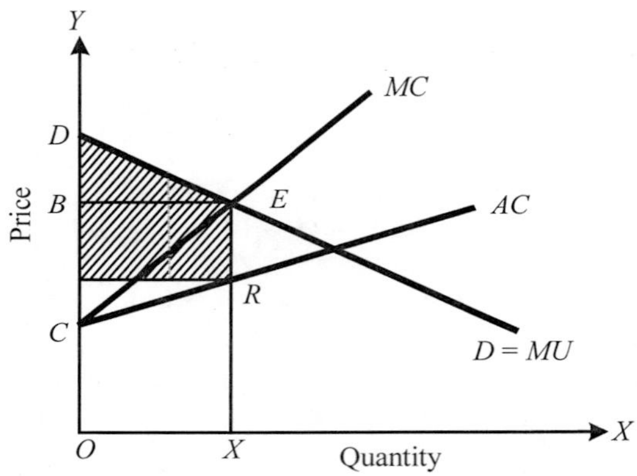

Fig. 34.1

3. COMPARISON BETWEEN MONOPSONY AND PERFECT COMPETITION

(1) *Constant Cost Case.* In Fig. 34.2, the supply price is constant, and therefore the *AC* and *MC* curves will coincide. Here *E* is the equilibrium point where *OX* quantity of the output is purchased at *EX* (= *OP)* price. The *OX* quantity bought at *EX* price under monopsony is the same as under perfect competition because *MC* curve will cut the horizontal *AR* = *MR* curve from below under perfect competition at the equilibrium point *E.*

(2) *Increasing Cost Case.* Under increasing cost situation, *AC* and *MC* curves are rising, the monopsonist will pay less price than that under perfect competition, and he will buy a little more than half the competitive amount. This case is presented in Fig. 34.3. Here monopsonist equilibrium

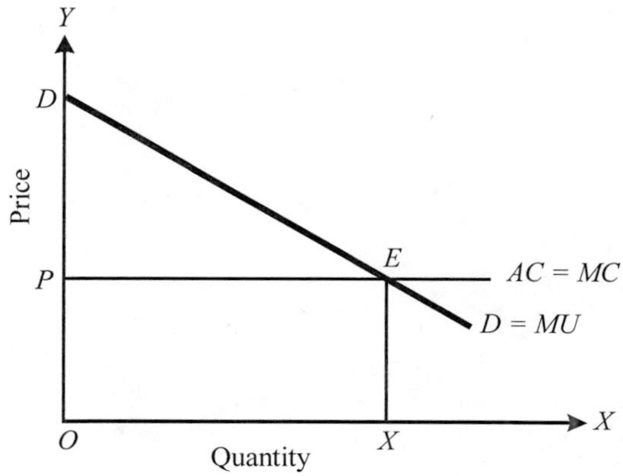

Fig. 34.2

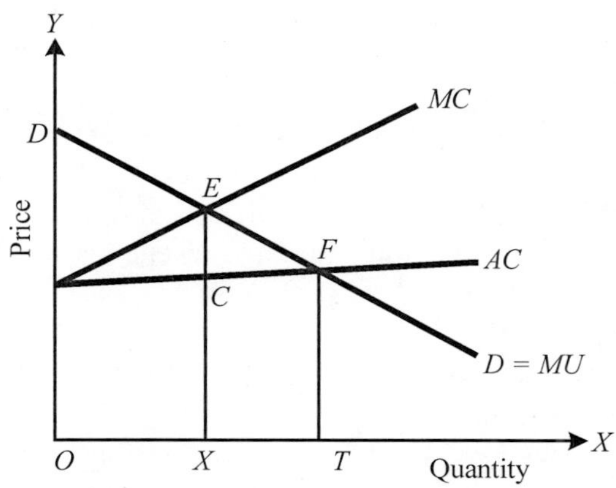

Fig. 34.3

point is *E* while the perfect competitive buyer's equilibrium point will be *R*. Thus the monop-sonist's price is *CX* which is less than the competitive price *RT*. Also, the quantity purchased by the monopsonist is *OX* which is less than competitive quantity *OT*.

(3) *Diminishing Cost Case.* It is shown in Fig. 34.4. Here *AC* and *MC* curves slope downwards. In such a situation the monopsonist buys

more than that under perfect competition. Here monopsonist's equilibrium point is E where he buys OX quantity at RX price. Under perfect competition, the equilibrium point is B where the price is. BT and quantity is OT. Hence it is clear that $OX > OT$ and price $BT > RX$.

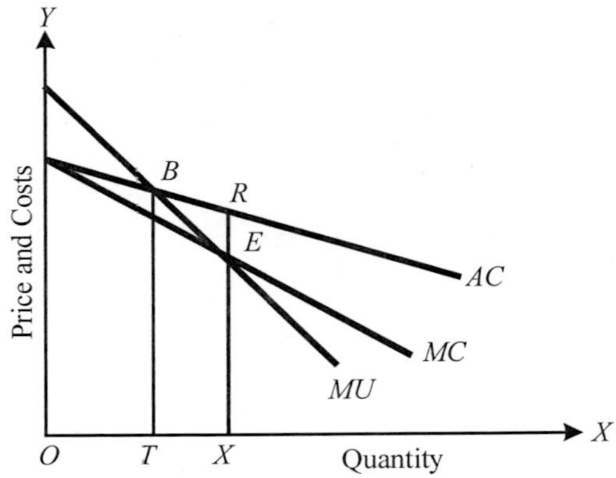

Fig. 34.3

4. PRICING AND OUTPUT UNDER BILATERAL MONOPOLY

In Fig. 34.5, the monopsonist consumer's demand for the product is shown by DD or AR; the corresponding marginal revenue is shown as MR. The monopolist's marginal cost of production is shown by MC. If the monopolist alone were to exercise his monopoly power, he would maximise his profits by producing OX_1 where $MC = MR$. On the other hand, if the monopsonist alone were to set price, subject to the cost conditions of the supplier, then he would regard MC as the seller's supply curve. Thus, MC represents the schedule of the average supply price of the product. The corresponding marginal supply cost (MSC) curve it would, therefore, be MSC. The monopsonist would prefer to buy that quantity at which the seller's MSC would be equal to the price he is willing to pay, but assuming that he can exercise his monopolistic power, he would offer only OP_2 rupees per unit for OX_2 units. At what price the two "giants" agree to trade the particular product will depend on their relative strength. This price will, however, lie between OP_1 and OP_2 which are the highest and lowest price levels acceptable to the monopsonist buyer and the monopolist seller respectively.

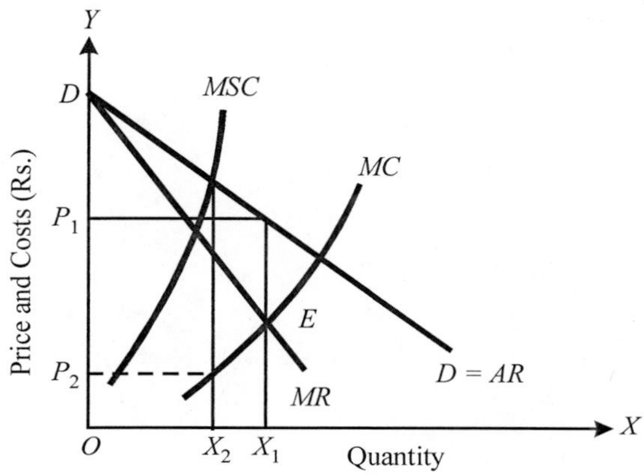

Fig. 34.4

EXERCISES

1. What do you understand by the tenn monopsony? How is monopsony price determined?
2. Distinguish between monopsony pricing and perfect competitive pricing under different cost conditions.
3. Explain pricing under bilateral monopoly.

Multiple Choice Questions

4. (*i*) When there is a single buyer of a commodity in the market, it is known as
    (*a*) monopoly (*b*) monopsony
    (*c*) bilateral monopoly (*d*) none of the above [*Ans*. (*b*)]

   (*ii*) Bilateral monopoly refers to a market situation in which
    (*a*) a single producer (monopolist) of a product faces a single buyer (monopsonist) of that product.
    (*b*) there is only one seller in the market
    (*c*) there are two sellers in the market
    (*d*) there are two buyers in the market [*Ans*. (*a*)]

Chapter 35

MONOPOLISTIC COMPETITION

1. INTRODUCTION

In the preceding chapters we have examined the polar extremes of perfect competition and monopoly. In real life, competition is rarely perfect. In the majority of cases, there is neither a single individual who controls the total supply, nor are there many sellers so that their individual shares are negligible in relation to the total supply of the market. Thus, the real situation is of imperfect competition where there is neither perfect competition nor absolute monopoly. This market situation is also known as monopolistic competition.

The classical economists and the neo-classical economists (of the late 19th century, such as, Marshall and Pigou) assumed competition and monopoly as mutually exclusive and always emphasised the competitive market situation as it would always increase material welfare. Imperfect competition as a market situation was given no importance. It was only after 1926, that the modern economists felt that absolute monopoly and perfect competition were unrealistic market situations. The Cambridge economists, Piero Sraffa, H. Hotelling and Zeuthen, etc. were of the opinion that the models of perfect competition and monopoly do not depict the real market situations. Further in 1933, the simultaneous publication of *The Economics of Imperfect Competition* by Mrs. Joan Robinson of England and *The Theory of Monopolistic Competition* by Prof. E.H. Chamberlin of America, revolt against the traditional theories related to perfect competition and Joan monopoly. According to Mrs. Joan Robinson, even in the presence of a large number of firms producing a particular product, a buyer may prefer to buy from a seller of his choice and may also be willing to pay a relatively higher price. It means price will not be the same in the market and it will never be a situation of perfect competition. Mrs. Robinson calls it the situation of imperfect competition.

On the other hand, Prof. Chamberlin introduces competitive forces in a monopoly market. He does not assume the presence of large number of firms producing identical products but concentrates on the individual firm whose product is a close substitute of the other firms products. According to him, in real world we do not find an absolute monopoly. Product differentiation exists in the market and that limits the monopoly power of the firm. Thus, due to the availability of substitutes, a firm enjoys, "limited monopoly". Prof. Chamberlin calls it the situation of monopolistic.

Thus, the terms imperfect competition or monopolistic competition[1] are used to describe the market situations found in modern capitalist states, the basic features being a large number of firms selling differentiated products. Sometimes the term monopolistic competition is also referred to as *Group Equilibrium*.

2. MAIN FEATURES OF MONOPOLISTIC COMPETITION

According to Prof. Chamberlin, the main features or characteristics of monopolistic competition are the following:

(1) ***Relatively Small Number of Firms.*** Under perfect competition, we assume that there are a number of firms which produce identical products. It means no individual firm can influence the market price which is determined by the industry demand and industry supply. In monopolistic competition, the number of firms is less than that under perfect competition. Due to this reason that a firm enjoys some monopoly power. Since the firms under monopolistic competition sell differentiated products, they are able to charge different prices for their products.

(2) ***Product Differentiation.*** Product differentiation is the main feature of monop-olistic competition. According to Prof. Chamberlin monopolistic competition is a market situation in which there are many firms of a particular product, but the product of each firm is in some way differentiated from the product of every other firm in the market. Product differentiation may take the form of brand names, trade-marks, etc. This means that the product of a firm may find close substitutes and its cross-elasticity of demand is very high.

1. Imperfect competition is a much wider and more comprehensive term than monopolistic competition. In fact, monopolistic competition is only one of the many sub-categories of imperfect competition. In the present chapter we shall discuss the theory of monopolistic competition which was developed by Prof. E.H. Chamberlin.

This is the reason that Chamberlin's analysis of monoplisstic competition deals largely with the individual firm and does not refer directly to the industry. The commodities produced by any industry are not homogeneous; the technique of branding differentiates the product of any one firm from the products of other firms in the same industry. Thus, each firm has an independent demand schedule, but at the same time, each demand schedule reflects the competitive nature of the market. According to Prof. Chamberlin, the concept of industry equilibrium has no relevance in the context of product differentiation. Although we can talk about the equilibrium of the group of firms producing similar products, yet it is difficult to make an effective combination of all firms producing similar products into a product group, as the degree of product substitutability is not well defined. For this reason the case of monopolistic competition differs from that of monopoly only in the degree of competition that is present. No monopolist is entirely free from competition. If a monopolist charges an exorbitant price for his product, there are usually other products of close substitutes, that can be used in its place. These possibilities of substitution give some elasticity to the demand curve, and this limits the price. If the substitutes are not close, the demand may be rather inelastic and the, monopoly power will be great, but if good substitutes are available, the demand will be more elastic and the monopoly power will be less. This last is usually the case with product differentiation or monopolistic competition.

(3) ***Freedom of Entry of New Firms.*** Under monopolistic competition, the individual firm has a monopoly of its own product, but it faces keen competition from firms making very similar products, and it does not have the power to restrict the entry of new firms:

(4) ***Competitive Advertisement.*** Product differentiation is also, emphasised by the practice of competitive advertising. In fact, the practice of competitive advertising is the more striking feature of monopolistic competition. Advertising is employed to heighten, in the mind of the consumer, the differences between Brand *A* and Brand *B.* It is important to realise that we are concerned with the differentiation of goods in the economic sense and not in the technical sense. Two branded products may be almost identical in their technical features or chemical composition, but if advertising and other selling practices have created different images in the consumers mind, then these products are different from our point of view, because the consumers will be prepared to pay different prices for them. Thus, advertisement or sales promotion technique is the important feature of monopolistic competition.

(5) ***More Elastic Demand.*** the shape of the demand curve faced by the firm under monopolistic competition comes from product differentiation. In the absence of product differentiation, the demand curve of the firm will be perfectly elastic like the demand curve of a perfectly competitive firm. But due to a differentiated product, the individual firm possesses some monopoly power and therefore its demand curve will be more elastic. In other words, under monopolistic competition, each producer is a monopolist and the demand curve for his product will slope downwards, but the availability of close substitutes will mean that the demand curve for his product will be more elastic. Thus, diagrammatically, the demand curve of a firm under monopolistic competition will be less steep as compared to that of monopoly firm. This means that a small decrease in the price of the product will lead to a large increase in the demand for her product assuming the prices of other firms remain the same.

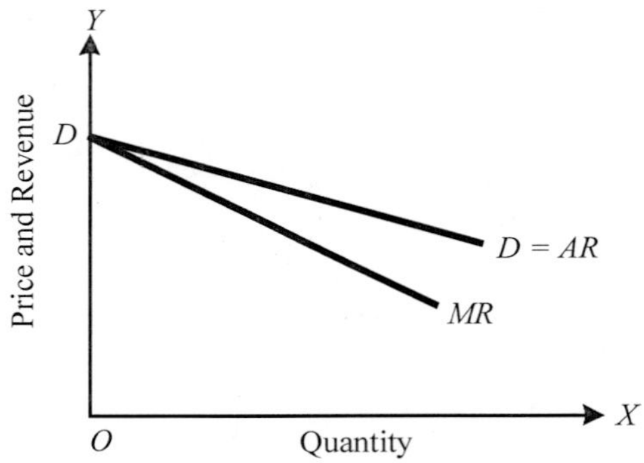

Fig. 35.1

It has been illustrated in Fig. 35.1. *DD* is the demand curve or average revenue curve of the firm under monopolistic compedtition. It is more elastic and not perfectly elastic. The corresponding marginal revenue curve lies below the demand curve. These curves are drawn on the assumption that the prices of other firms remain the same in response to the changes by a particular firm.[2] The slope of these curves will depend upon two factors: (*i*) the importance of the individual firm in the market, and (*ii*) the extent of product differentiation or product homogeneity. Product

2. This is an important assumption, especially when price changes are of the nature of price cutting.

differentiation leads some consumers to prefer the products of particular sellers over those of other sellers. Consequently, the demand curve faced by an individual firm has some downward slope to it and enables the firm to exercise a small degree of control over her price. Ordinarily, the demand curve faced by the firm will be very elastic within its relevant range of prices because of the numerous good substitutes available for its product. Here, the firm may expect a substantial expansion in sales by contemplating a price-cut. This also implies that the demand for the firm's product is highly elastic. Therefore, each firm seeks to maximise her profits only by varying the price of her product.

3. MONOPOLY INDEX

We have seen that in monopolistic competition, a firm has monopoly as well as competition. The more close substitutes of its product are, the less will be the monopoly power of the firm and vice versa. The output of the firm under monopolistic competition must be smaller, and its unit cost and price higher than it would be under pure competition. Here the question is that how can we measure this monopoly power of a firm? The following formula (which is known as a monopoly index) may be used to calculate the monopoly power of a firm.

$$M = P\left(1 - \frac{1}{|e|}\right)$$

where M = Marginal revenue, P = Price, $|e|$ = Elasticity of demand

Given the value of the coefficient e (elasticity of demand), one can find out the relation between price and marginal revenue.

In perfect competition, elasticity of demand of a firm is infinite ($e = \infty$), then price will be equal to the marginal revenue ($P = M$).

In monopoly, the demand curve is more inelastic, so that the coefficient 'e' has a smaller value, say $e = 2$.

then, $$M = P\left(1 - \frac{1}{2}\right)$$

or $$M = \frac{1}{2}P$$

or $$P = 2M$$

which means price will be twice the MR or price is 100 per cent higher than marginal revenue.

In monopolistic competition, the demand curve of the firm is more elastic, i.e., the coefficient 'e' has a larger value, say $e = 20$, then $$M = P\left(1 - \frac{1}{20}\right)$$

$$= \frac{19}{20}P$$

or $$OM = 19P$$

This means that price is nearly 5 per cent more than the marginal revenue. In other words, the firm has a monopoly power to increase price by 5 per cent more than the price in perfect competition (where $P = MR$).

Hence, above formula explains the monopoly power of a firm.

4. PRICE AND OUTPUT DETERMINATION UNDER MONOPOLISTIC COMPETITION

As we have already explained, under monopolistic competition due to product differentiation, it is rather impossible to present the analysis of the industry in graphic terms. In the case of perfect competition, where the product differentiation is absent, we can draw industry demand and industry supply curves to determine the equilibrium price and output of the industry. But under monopolistic competition, construction of industry (market) curves is a rather unsatisfactory practice. Unless the differentiated products are converted in terms of a common denominator, it will be difficult to measure the quantity of the industry along the horizontal axis. Further, no single price prevails for differentiated products of the industry and that creates another difficulty of presenting the industry analysis in graphic terms. Therefore, under monopolistic competition, we shall confine our diagrammatic analysis to the individual firm. The market as a whole is there, but we shall discuss it only in terms of theoretical analysis.

Here our main assumption is that each firm in this market situation operates with an impression that its action would go unnoticed by its rivals in the market. The firm will attempt to maximise her profits only by varying the price of her product. Prof. Chamberlin also assumes that demand and cost functions are uniform throughout the product group. The equilibrium of the firm under monopolistic competition involves the usual conditions as discussed under other market situations. Now we shall discuss the equilibrium position of the firm and the group under the following section.

Short-Period, Equilibrium of the Firm under Monopolistic Competition

Short-period equilibrium of a monopolistically competitive firm is very similar to that of a monopolist. Here the firm produces a differentiated product and attains some degree of monopoly power. In short-period, the firm does not have time to change its scale of plant and no new firms will enter the industry. Now, in order to maximise its profits, the monopolistically competitive firm will produce that level of output at which its marginal cost equals marginal revenue. This case has been illustrated in Fig. 35.2. The firm's demand curve is represented by *AR,* which is negatively sloped. The corresponding marginal revenue (*MR*) curve lies below it. The firm's short-run average cost and marginal cost curves are *SAC* and *SMC* respectively. The *SMC* curve cuts the *MR* curve at point *E.* Thus the equilibrium level of output is *OX*, price is *OP* and cost per unit, is *OC.* At *OX* level of output, the firm enjoys *PC* abnormal profit per unit. The total maximum profit of the firm is represented by the shaded area *CPAB.*

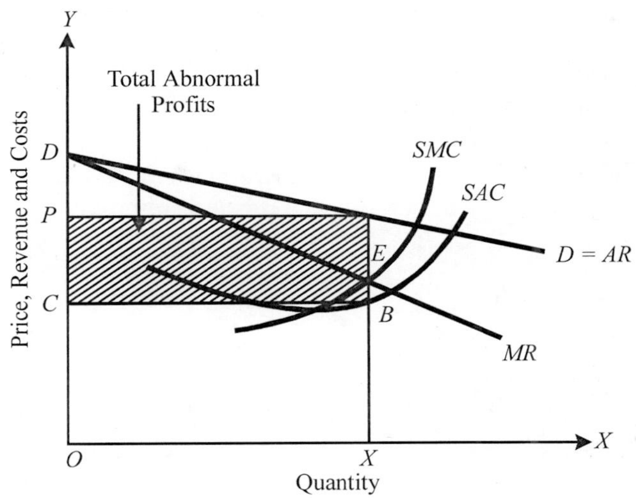

Fig. 35.2

The short-period equilibrium does not mean that all the firms charge the same price. In fact the firms charge different prices for their differentiated products. Each firm seeks its own profit maximising position. Figure 35.2 indicates the equilibriurn of a representative firm under monopolistic competition. The other firms also attempt to maximise their individual profits in the same manner. We must, however, remember that it is not necessary that under monopolistic competition all the firms will attain abnormal profits in the short-period. It is possible that some firms may take abnormal profits while at the same time others may incur losses or make normal profits only. Like other market situations, the firm under monopolistic competition has to incur certain fixed costs in the short-run which are not related to the volume of output. Thus, the minimum price acceptable by the firm in the short-run will be equal to its average variable cost. When the price of a firm's product is equal to its *AVC,* the firm's maximum loss will be equal to its entire fixed costs. If price is higher than the *AVC,* but less than the *AC*, the firm's short-run objective will be the minimisation of its loss. Thus, the two other possible situations of the short-period equilibrium (i.e., the situation of normal profits and the situation of losses) are shown in Fig. 35.3.

Panel (*a*) of Fig. 35.3 illustrates the situation when the firm gets only the normal profits which are included in the costs. The equilibrium level of output is *OX.* At *OX* output the price is *OP* which is also equal to its cost per unit. Thus the firm's abnormal profit is zero. In Panel (*b*) of Fig. 35.3, we have shown a case when the firm is minimising its losses. The equilibrium level of output is *OX* where the firm could bear *VC* amount of loss per unit (equal to fixed cost per unit). But since at *OX* output, price is *OP* and, cost per unit is *OC*, the firm has to in cut only *PC* amount of loss per unit (*PC* < *VC*). Therefore, the firm is minimising its losses by producing *OX* quantity of output in short-run equilibrium.

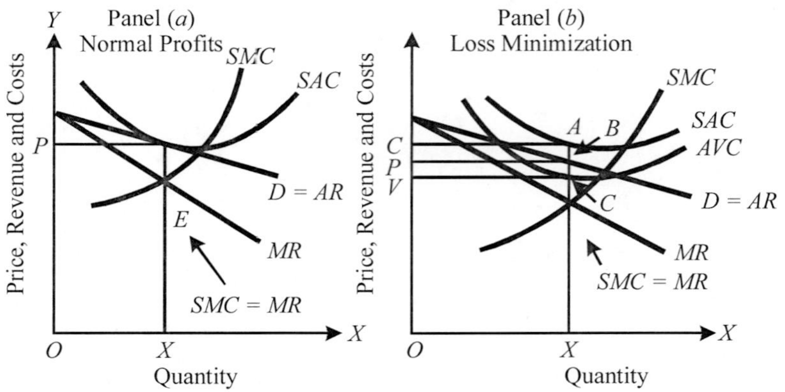

Fig. 35.3

Long-Period Equilibrium of the Firm under Monopolistic Competition

In the long-period, all factors of production used by the firm are variable and therefore, the firm can change its scale of plant to any extent. The firm will always try to build the scale of plant which makes the per unit cost minimum. As we have mentioned, the monopolistic competitive firm in the long-period can increase its sales by introducing a policy of price-cut for his own product. Here the firm assumes that its actions (i.e., price-cuts) will not be reacted by its rivals in the market. Thus it will be able to get the full benefits of its economies of scale. For sometime the entry of the new firms will be blocked, but when the firms enjoy high level of short-run profits, it will induce the entry of new firms into the industry. Thus, the long-period equilibrium of the firm under monopolistic competition can be discussed in two ways: (*i*) when entry of new firms is blocked, and (*ii*) when entry of new firms is free.

Long-Period Equilibrium of the Firms when Entry of New Firms is *Blocked.* Under monopolistic competition, the case of blocked entry into an industry will not be the usual case. But for sometime it may happen. In such a situation, the industry has an optimal number of firms; each

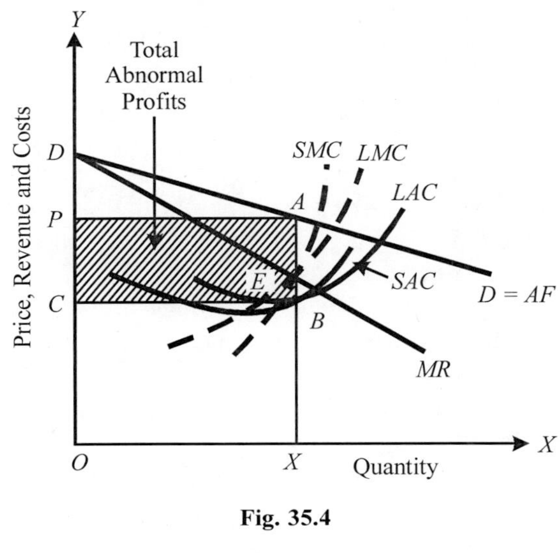

Fig. 35.4

would attempt to adjust its scale of plant to the size required for long-period profit maximisation. The firm under monopolistic competition adopts the policy of price-cut to increase its sales. Thus, it will go on reducing its price until it produces that level of output at which its cost per unit becomes minimum possible and the profit maximising conditions are satisfied. This case has been depicted in Fig. 35.4. The demand curve faced by the firm is *DD* and the marginal revenue curve is *MR*. The respective long-period average cost curve and marginal cost curve are *LAC* and *LMC*. Profits will be maximised at output *OX*, at which long-period marginal cost equals marginal revenue at point *E*. The equilibrium price is *OP*. Now to produce output *OX*, at the least possible cost per unit, the firm should build the scale of plant which has its short-period average cost curve tangent to the long-period cost curve at that output. In Fig. 35.4, *SAC* is tangent to *LAC* at output *OX* and at the same time *SMC* = *LMC* = *MR*. Thus, cost per unit is *OC* at output *OX*. The firm gets the maximum abnormal profits *CP* per unit. The total profits are shown by the shaded area *CPAB*.

Now, the firm has no incentive to cut its price below *OP* and to increase its sales beyond *OX* because the cost of producing an additional unit of output will be more than the revenue it gets from it (i.e., *MC* > *MR*) and, therefore, its profits would decline. Nor the firm would like to produce less than *OX* quantity of output, because in that case (when *MR* > *LMC*) it would not be able to maximise its profits. Therefore, in the long-period when the entry of new firms into the industry is blocked, the firm will produce that level of output at which two conditions are satisfied: (*i*) *SMC* = *LMC* = *MR*, and (*ii*) *SAC* = *LAC*.

Long-Period Equilibrium of the Firm when Entry of New Firm is Open. When the existing firms in the monopolistic competition are earning abnormal profits, there will be a tendency in the long-period for new firms to enter the industry. As new firms enter, they encroach upon the markets of existing firms, causing the demand curve and the marginal revenue curve faced by each firm to shift downward. In other words, the entry of new firms into the industry creates larger output without any significant increase in the total sales of all the firms. The increase in supply (and in the number of suppliers) pushes the whole cluster of price ranges for individual firms downward. Thus the firms will reduce their prices to check the decline in their individual sales as a result of the wholesale entry of new firms into the market.

On the other hand, the entry of new firms into the industry will also affect the costs of production for the existing firms. If the industry (i.e., all the existing firms) is operating under increasing cost conditions, the entry of new firms would cause factor-prices to rise which would shift the cost curves of existing firms upward. If it is operating under constant costs, the entry of new firms would have no effects upon factor-prices and upon the cost curves of individual firms. In an unusual case of decreasing costs, the entry of new firms would cause resource prices to decrease and cost-curves of the firms to shift downward. Here, we shall illustrate the case of increasing costs only.

Thus the effects of the entry of new firms into the industry will be: (*i*) to shift the demand curves faced by the individual firms downward, and (*ii*) to shift the cost curves of the existing firms upward. These two simultaneous effects will cause profits of the existing firm to decrease. But the new firms will continue to enter so long as profit possibilities remain. Thus in the long-run when entry is open, abnormal profits will be squeezed and the firms will get only the normal profits.[3] This means, in the long-run, price or average revenue is just, equal to average cost. The same argument can be given when there are losses in the short-run and the exit of firms will lead to eliminate the losses in the long-period. Therefore, the basic difference between monopoly and monopplistic competition is that in the long-period profits are possible in monopoly simply because new firms are not allowed to enter the industry while such profits are impossible in monopolistic competition, simply because new firms are allowed to enter the industry.

This situation has been illustrated in Fig. 35.5. The relevant demand (or average revenue) and marginal revenue curves are *AR* and *MR* respectively; and the long-period average cost and marginal cost curves are *LAC* and *LMC* respectively.[4] Since we want to show the final long-run position of the adjustments in the scale of plant, the tangency between the firm's *LAC* and *AR* curves is the fundamental condition. Now the firm will get normal profits only at the situation where *LAC* = *AR* at that point at which *LMC* = *MR.* Thus the firm's equilibrium output is *OX* at which *SMC* = *LMC* = *MR* and *LAC* = *AR.* Any deviation from *OX* level of output with 'scale of plant *SAC* will cause losses to be incurred. The industry as a whole will be in equilibrium since the firms are operating at no profit-no loss. In such a situation the number of firms in the industry is fixed because there is no incentive for the firms to enter into or exit from the industry. This is usual position that occurs in the long-period.

3. Thus the long-period equilibrium of the firm under monopolistic competition when the entry is open is very much similar to that of a perfect competitive firm.
4. The demand and marginal revenue curves are shifted downward as compared to the initial situation which has been discussed in Fig. 35.4. Similarly the *LAC* and *LMC* curves are shifted upward as compared to the initial position of Fig. 35.4. This is all due to the present assumption that entry of new firms into the industry is open.

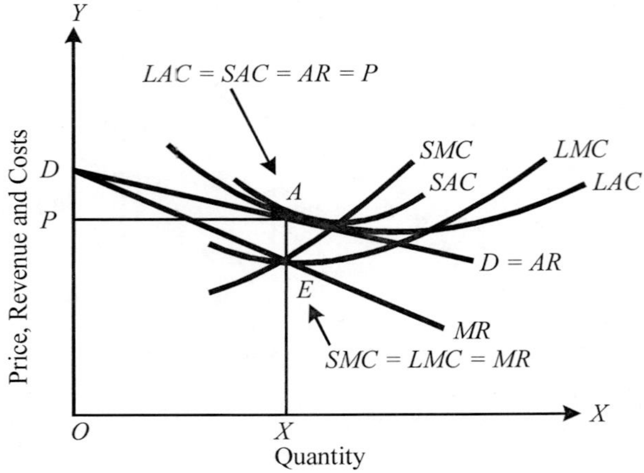

Fig. 35.5

5. CHAMBERLIN'S ANALYSIS OF GROUP EQUILIBRIUM

Prof. Chamberlin calls the several firms whose markets are closely interwoven as "group" An industry can consist of two or more groups of closely competing firms. Since the firms in a particular group produce goods which possess a greater degree of homogeneity and, therefore, within any group, close competition exists. But competition between the groups is not keen. The Chamberlin's group is vague because it is very difficult to draw sharp lines between groups. Moreover, the firms in a group are producing differentiated products and they will have their different revenue and cost curves. The prices charged by the firms in a group are also different. All this enables us to draw a group revenue curve or a group cost curve under monopolistic competition. While under perfect competition, it is possible to draw the supply curve of the industry and the revenue and cost curves of the individual firms.

Chamberlin tries to overcome these difficulties by making simple assumption with the basic objective of ignoring the diverse conditions surrounding each firm. His assumptions are:

(*i*) All the firms in the group are producing more or less identical product.

(*ii*) All firms have equal share of the market which means that all of them have similar demand curves (similar in elasticity and position).

(*iii*) All firms have equal efficiency in production, and therefore, have similar cost curves.

(*iv*) The number of firms in the group is so large that each firm regards itself independent, i.e., one firm's action regarding price and output will have a negligible effect upon the numerous competitiors.

The first three assumptions are known as the "uniformity assumptions" and the last one is known as the "symmetry assumption". Given these assumptions, it is possible to explain group equilibrium in the long-run. Existence of super normal (or abnormal) profits in the short-run and the anticipation of the same in the long-run will attract new firms to enter the industry or induce the existing firms to expand: On the other hand, existence of losses in the short-run and the anticipation of the same in the long-run will induce existing firms to leave the industry.

If the new firms are set up or existing firms expand there will be a tendency for prices to decline and equal the average cost. New firms in the industry will mean large production but will not mean a significant increase in the total sales. The existing market will now have to be shared between a large number of sellers. In the long-run there comes a situation when every firm will tend to be a no profit-no loss firm and will reap only normal profit.

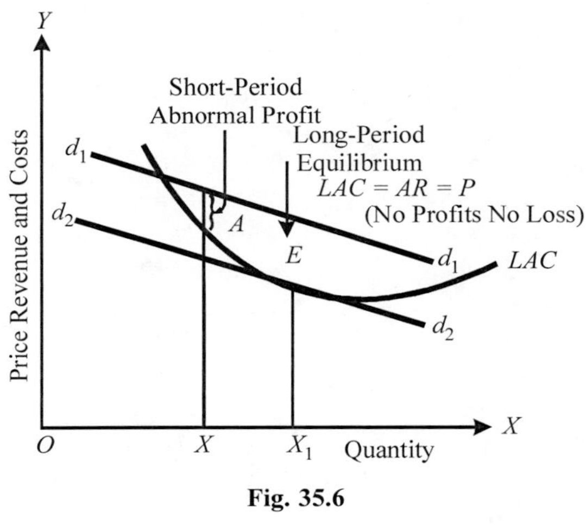

Fig. 35.6

Thus, under monopolistic competition, the behaviour of a group must be reflected in the behaviour of one firm. For this Prof. Chamberlin calls his heroic assumption, namely, that each firm has identical demand and cost curves. If the demand curves are the same, it would mean that the firms in a group have equal shares of the market (of the commodity). If there are 100 firms in a group, then each firm has one per cent of total sales of the group. Now keeping this assumption in mind, we can illus-trate both the individual equilibrium and the group equilibrium with the help of a diagram.

Suppose, in Fig. 35.6, each firm's demand curve is d_1d_2 and the long-run averag, cost curve is *LAC*. Initially, in the short-period, each firm can make large abnorma profits. In Fig. 35.6, we have not drawn the marginal cost curve and marginal revenu curve and, therefore, we have not shown the shortperiod abnormal profits of each firm. It can be easily visualised in the imagination. Since all firms are assumed to be identical and, therefore, the total abnormal profits of the whole group will, be high enough. The distance between the demand curve and the average cost curve will show the profits of each firm at some level of output (determined by the rule $MC = MR$). But we are in the long-period in which new firms can enter and put new products on this market. As a result of the entrance of new firms in the group, the demand curve (d_1d_1) of each firm shifts to the left as d_2d_2 The reason is that the new products reduce the sales of the existing firms. Now the firms are forced to reduce their prices in order to check the constant decline in their sales. The process of price-cutting will go on so long as profits of the group (or each firm) are present. The process, stops when the demand curve, d_2d_2 slides far enough left to become, tangent to the long-period average cost curve *LAC*. Here we must remember that due to the assumption of constant costs, *LAC* will remain the same. Now the tangency point *E* will become the long-period equilibrium point of the group. This implies that price (*AR*) equals average cost and there is no profit-no loss in the group. With tangency, the firm can neither raise nor lower its price without suffering losses. This is the point where the number of firms in the group is fixed, that is, no firm has the incentive to enter the group or to exit from the group. Hence the group is in equilibrium.

6. SELLING COSTS AND THEIR IMPLICATIONS ON EQUILIBRIUM UNDER MONOPOLISTIC COMPETITION

Unlike a perfect competitive firm or a monopoly, a monopolistically competitive firm has to incur certain costs on advertisement or publicity. In perfect competition, all products in the industry are homogeneous and, therefore, the price is the same. In monopoly, no substitution is generally possible for the monopolist's product. For this reason, the firm in perfect competition or monopoly need not advertise the attributes or special features of its product. But in the case of monopolistic competition, each firm sells a differentiated product and for this reason, advertise-ment or selling costs would be crucial. According to Prof. Chamberlin, "Selling costs are those costs which are to be incurred in order to alter the position or shape of the demand curve for a product." Therefore, the "expenditures on advertising do increase the demand for a product, ail other things—price, quality, incomes of the consumers. etc.—being equal.

According to Prof. Baumol, the decision as to how far to carry advertising cost will depend upon the firm's objective-whether it wants to maximise its sales or to maximise its profits. He says that total revenue increases with increasing advertising expenditures, but it will not always be the case. After a point diminishing returns will take place. Thus, the level of advertising outlay at which the differences between total revenue and total costs is maximurn must be incurred for profit maximisation.

Prof. Buchanan, on the other hand, is of the opinion that advertising cost is a fixed cost and, therefore, it has no relationship with the volume of output. The average selling cost or advertising cost will decline as output increases. According to him, net returns to advertising expenditures depict the difference between the increased total revenue emanating from selling costs and the increased total costs (costs of production plus costs of advertising).

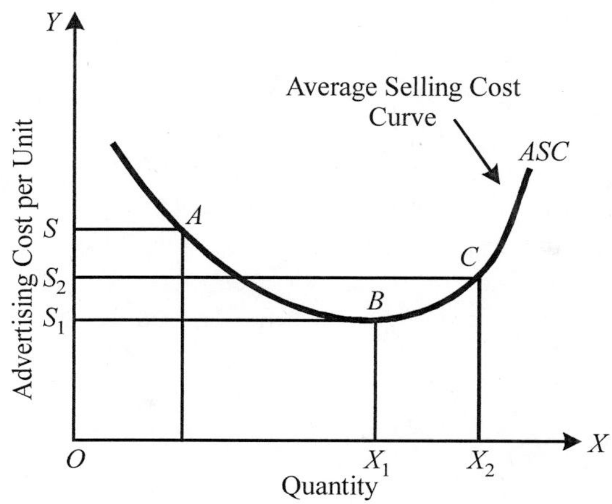

Fig. 35.7

The task now is to set up a relationship between the advertising expenditures of a firm and the unit sales of its product. The relationship can be shown by the selling cost curve. This is another contribution of Chamberlin to economic theory. Figure 35.7 presents the average selling cost curve, *ASC*. This is a *U*-shaped cost curve. It shows that as output increas-es, selling costs per unit will decrease, but after a certain point an increase in output will lead to an increase in selling costs per unit of output. At *OX* level of output, the advertising cost per unit is *OS*. The minimum advertising cost is OS_1 when the firm sells OX_1 quantity of output. If the firm wants to sell more than OX_1 quantity of its product, then the per unit cost of advertising will increase. For instance, at OX_1 units of sales, the per unit cost of advertising is OS_2. Thus, the curve *ASC* first declines, because of initial economies of scale in advertising; advertising expenses that are too small are said to be wasteful. After reaching a minimum level, the curve rises indicating the diseconomies of scale in advertising. In all likelihood, the curve *ASC* finally becomes vertical when the sales have reached the "saturation point". The vertical part of the curve will indicate that any flirt her increase in advertisement expenditure will make no increase in the sales of the firm. Selling costs or advertising expenditures may be very high or very low. No generalisation is possible. The shape and position of the selling cost curve will depend upon a number of factors, such as, the price of the product, availability of substitutes and the degree of substitution, the quality of the product and the qualities of its substitutes, the incomes of the consumers and their tastes, etc. A change in any of these factors will vary the shape and the position of the curve.

Now the question is how much should a firm spend on advertising? The profit-maximising firm spends an amount on advertisement such that the combined marginal cost of production and of advertising is equal to the price (or average revenue) the firm gets for its product. The last unit sold is just worth the cost of producing and selling it. Figure. 35.8 explains this situation. The price of the product is *OP*. The horizontal line from *P* can be viewed as if it were a marginal revenue curve because by advertising, the firm can sell more without having to lower its price. In Fig. 35.8, the average production cost is *APC*. The average total cost is the summation of the average production cost and average selling cost which is shown by *APC* + *ASC*. The *MC* curve gives the marginal cost associated with the average total cost. The equilibrium or optimum level of output sold is *OX*, because at this level of output $MC = D = MR$. At *OX* output, the firm's advertising expenditure, *AB*, per unit is optimum because here profits are maximised. Any level advertising expenditure than this will reduce the profits of the firm.

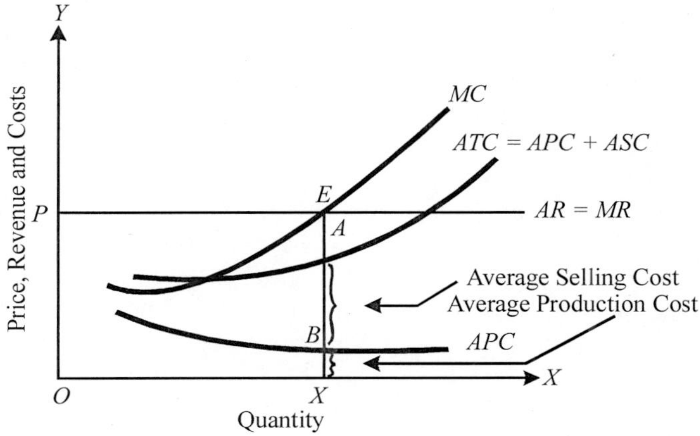

Fig. 35.8

7. WASTE OF MONOPOLISTIC COMPETITION
(Problem of Resource Allocation under Monopolistic Competition)

As we know, under perfect competition and monopoly, then is no need of advertisement by the individual firms and as such there will be no waste in the economy. Under monopolistic competition, the firm in the market has to incur a lot of expenditure to increase its sales. This expenditure is a waste of the economy because it adds nothing to the total output of the economy. When there are profits in the industry, this waste further increases. New firms enter into the industry and increase the supply of the industry. Since the total demand of the industry more or less remains the same, the surplus production becomes a waste of the economy. Again, the waste will be more when the consumer's preferences are changed.

Prof. Rothschild has pointed out five kinds of wastes of monopolistic competition. These are: (1) Unemployment, (2) Excess Capacity, (3) Cross Transport, (4) Failure to Specialise, and (5) Competitive Advertising.

1. *Unemployment.* There are certain types of unemployment which will be found under all conditions. In imperfect competitive situation, the problem of unemploy-ment is aggravated by various reasons. For one thing, part of the productive capacity may remain unused. Cyclical unemployment may be intensified through price maintenance in place of production maintenance. Finally, monopolistic factors may increase the

share of profits in national income which will reduce property to consume without creating a comparable increase in the desire to invest.

2. *Excess Capacity.* Under monopolistic competition, firms will not produce optimum output at the lowest average cost point. Since competition is not perfect, the demand curve for a firm is not perfectly elastic and, therefore, is not equal to the lowest average cost point. This is the well known fact of excess capacity or unused capacity with its corollary of non-minimum production costs and price above marginal cost. Excess capacity is regarded as a waste of monopolistic competition.

3. *Cross Transport.* The waste of cross transport arises when under monopolistic and oligopoly situations, markets are not clearly divided between different producers in different regions. Cloth sold in Kanpur may be sold in Delhi, and cloth produced in Delhi may be sold in Kanpur. The cost of cloth to the consumer is necessarily increased to include transport charges. If the market for cloth is conveniently divided so that the Delhi market is served by the Delhi mills and Kanpur market and northern regions are served by Kanpur mills, transport costs can be reduced. The wasteful use of transport facilities is the direct result of product differentiation and as such is similar in nature to the problem of excess capacity.

4. *Failure to Specialise.* Another disadvantage of monopolistic competition is the sufficient specialisation. The cost advantages arising out of specialisation cannot be escaped under monopolistic competition because the sales of the firm cannot be expanded without reducing the prices. To some extent, the failure to specialise and the costly maintenance of several lines of production is also owing to a desire to reduce the risks which are involved in too great a dependence on the demand for one a few products. In such a case, this waste is due to the ul1certainty of competition.

5. *Advertising.* The waste of advertising is the outcome of the absence of perfect competitive conditions. Marshall in his book, *Industry and Trade* distinguished between constructive and comparative advertisements. Constructive advertisement is to spread information of a product and this is compatible with pure competition where knowledge of the product is not perfect. It may be remembered that perfect competitive system with perfect knowledge' is an impossibility and therefore, this type of advertisement cannot be regarded as a waste. But the bulk of the advertisement is of the combative type, connected with the boosting up of differentiated products. Such advertisement is clearly wasteful for it leads to unnecessary competition among rivals and high cost to the

consumers. Some may argue that advertisements increase consumer's satisfactions by adding to the prestige, the glamour and the desirability of the advertised goods to the buyers. But against this argument, Rothschild states that the dissatisfaction created by advertisements in people who cannot buy the advertised goods may amount to much more-this is psychological waste arising out of advertising.

Thus imperfect or monopolistic competition involves many inherent defects or wastes. These defects are mainly due to the preferences of consumers for different varieties; or there are imaginary differences which have been increased by competitive advertisement. It is the interest of the community, if there is a reduction in the number of varieties of a product, reduction in the number of firms, elimination of cross transport and advertisement expenditures.

Figure 35.9 illustrates the waste of the economy under monopolistic competition. Here the demand for the firm's product is d_1d_1. Assume that the consumers have perfect information about the product, i.e., about the

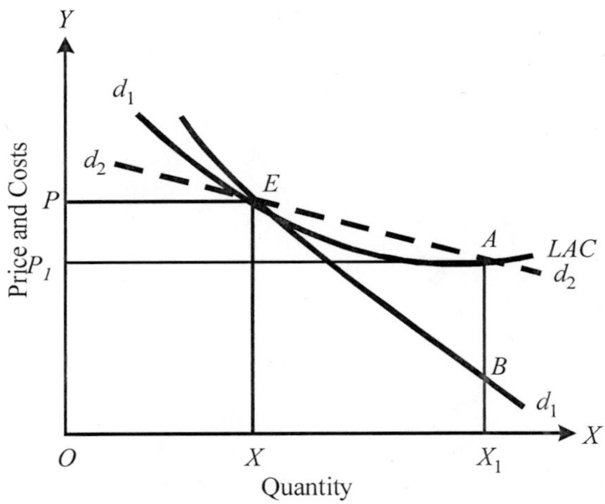

Fig. 35.9

quality and about the prices and qualities of all other available substitutes. The long-period equilibrium of the firm will be established at point E where the long-period average cost curve touches the demand curve d_1d_1. At this tangency point it is implied that $MR = MC$ (which are, not shown in the diagram). At this equilibrium point E, the consumers buy OX quantity at OP price. The most efficient output level to be produced by the firm is. OX_1 where the average total cost of production is minimum, i.e., AX_1 per unit. At OX_1 output, the minimum long-period price acceptable by the firm must be equal to the average cost. This means that the firm will produce the most efficient level of output OX_1 only if the price is OP_1. But the consumers' demand curve for the product (d_1d_1) shows that they are unwilling to pay X_1B price for OX_1 quantity. They are ready to pay only BX_1 price for OX_1 quantity. At this low price the firm will not like to produce any amount of the product because it has to incur a great loss. The consumers could prefer to pay a higher price for a smaller quantity. If their demand curve were d_2d_2, which it is not, the consumers would be indifferent between the two choices; that is, they would be ready to purchase OX quantity at OP price or OX_1 quantity at OP_1 price. Since the actual demand curve faced by the firm is not d_2d_2 but d_1d_1, the firm will never produce the most efficient output OX_1 but accept to produce OX output where he gets only the long-period normal profits. Therefore, it is the net loss of efficiency of the firm as well as of the economy. It is also known as the excess capacity of the firm under monopolistic competition. It is the excess of what a firm can produce with its given plant size over what it actually produces in order to maximise its profit.

In perfect competition, all the firms in the industry produce at optimum level, i.e., at that level where the long-period average cost is minimum. But it is possible only when the demand curve for the product is horizontal. When the demand curve is negatively sloped, as in the case of monopolistic competition and monopoly, demand curve cannot be tangent to *LAC* curve, and the profit maximising level of output is, therefore, less than optimum in the long-run.

This situation of excess capacity or unused capacity leads to unemployment in the economy. Further, the over-abundant multiplication of small firms, each producing a differentiated product, leads to a faulty distribution of factors of production. Monopoly or oligopoly (where the industry consists of a few firms) may probably lead to a better resource-use than monopolistic competition.

In spite of the above wastes or disadvantages of monopolistic competition, it possesses some ethical values also. It provides consumers a wide range of types, styles and brands of particular products. It provides the opportunity to choose a product which the consumer likes most According to Prof. Chamberlin, although a firm fails to produce the "sort of ideal" level of output, firms may tacitly agree to avoid any type of price competition. Moreover, the theory of monopolistic competition presents the actual situation of the market. The economists and the policy makers should try to remove the shortcomings of this realistic situation.

EXERCISES

1. Define monopolistic competition. Why does it tend to be a multi-price market form? Examine the performance of a monopolistically competitive industry from the point of view of economic efficiency.
2. What are the main characteristics of monopolistic competition. Explain the equilibrium of the firm in the short- and long-run under monopolistic competition.
3. Explain the differences between perfect competition, monopolistic competition and monopoly. Show with the help of a diagram, how price is determined under monopolistic competition.
4. Explain the concept of group equilibrium under monopolistic competition.
5. What are the selling costs? Explain the equilibrium of monopolistic competitive firm under selling costs.
6. State and show in diagrams the conditions of equilibrium of the firm and the industry under perfect competition and monopolistic competition (with open entry). Bring out the main differences between these two equilibrium positions.
7. What do you understand by product variation? How does a firm reach equilibrium with product variation?
8. Is it true that under monopolistic competition firms possess much "excess capacity" and yet remain "undersized"?

Multiple Choice Questions

9. (*i*) A monopolistically competitive market is distinguished from a perfectly competitive market by the fact that
   (*a*) it contains few buyers
   (*b*) it contains few sellers
   (*c*) it deals **in** a differentiated products
   (*d*) all of the above [*Ans.* (*c*)]

   (*ii*) Under imperfect competition degree of monopoly power depends upon difference between
   (*a*) *MR* and MC (*c*) *AC* and MC
   (*b*) *MR* and *AC* (*d*) none of the above [*Ans.* (*d*)]

   (*iii*) When entry into the industry is open (the usual case) and the industry is in long-run equilibrium, the monopolistic competition will produce at the lowest point on its *LAC* curve
   (*a*) always (*c*) sometimes
   (*b*) never (*d*) can not say [*Ans.* (*b*)]

Chapter 36

DUOPOLY AND OLIGOPOLY

1. DUOPOLY

Meaning of Duopoly

Duopoly refers to that market situation in which there are two sellers of the product. There is no basic difference between the theory of duopoly and the theory of oligopoly. In fact, duopoly is a limiting form of oligopoly. According to Cohen and Cyret, "When there are exactly two sellers in the market, this is a special case of oligopoly called duopoly." Like oligopoly, duopoly can be with or without product differentiation.

As there are only two duopolists in the market, each is fully aware of this fact that whatever he does will affect his rival's price-output policies, in the same way as he would react according to what his rival does. In this case, each duopolist tries to make a correct estimate (guess) of his rival's motives and actions. It is possible that the two duopolists may agree to form a tacit cartel after experiencing that competition between them is harmful to both. It is also possible that they may agree to charge a single price and free otherwise, i.e., competition is restricted to advertisement only. Anyway, it is very difficult to generalise as to which situation the duopolists would like to adopt. The older classical models of duopoly assume that the firms are of equal size and sell homogeneous product. It is also assumed that the costs of each firm are the same, or at any rate not very different. The unit costs of the forms are constant over any range of output that would come into question. Further, the total demand in the market they share is linear. Both the producers behave in the same way and want to maximise their individual profits.

In the context of the above assumptions of older classical models, we shall discuss the Cournot Solution, the Edgeworth Solution, the Bertrand Model, the Stakleberg Model, the Hotelling Model and the Chamberlin Solution of duopoly problem in the following section. The Cournot solution does not assume the interdependence of the firms in the industry. According to him, the firms do not conspire; they do not agree even tacitly. Each one sees what the other is doing, assumes he will continue to do the same thing, and then acts accordingly. According to them, the duopolists adjust their outputs, not their prices. The Chamberlin Solution, on the other hand, assumes the presence of interdependence between the firms in the industry. Prof. Edgeworth is of the opinion that each seller assumes the price of his rival constant.

All those models are classical models of duopoly because they are based on classical assumptions and do not deal with the current economic problems.

2. THE COURNOT MODEL

Augustin Cournot, a 19th century French economist was the first person who introduced the theory of duopoly in 1838. He was of the opinion that there is some independence in the decision making of the competing firms (duopolists). The main assumption of his model is that each seller assumes the supply of his rival constant. Cournot takes the example of two mineral springs situated side by side and owned by two persons (duopolists) *A* and *B*. The persons have to incur no costs of producing Water and each expects that his rival will never change the level of his output. This case has been illustrated in Fig. 36.1.

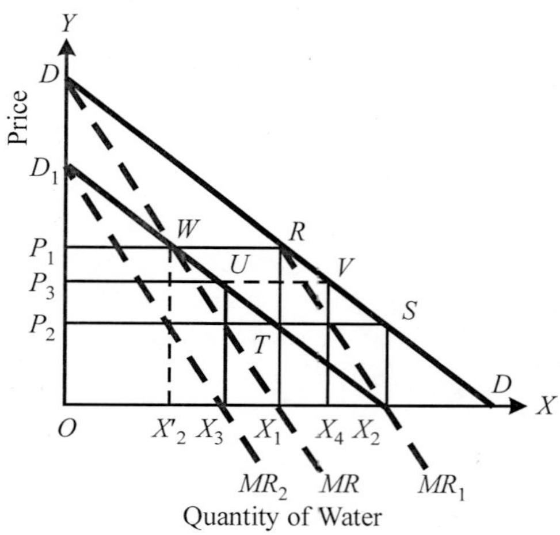

Fig. 36.1

In Fig. 36.1, *DD* is the market demand curve for water and the corresponding marginal revenue curve is *MR*. Suppose, initially firm *A* exists in the market. According to Cournot, for profit maximisation, *A* will sell OX_1 quantity of water as at this level $MR = MC = 0$. If *A* produces more than OX_1 quantity, then his marginal revenue becomes negative. Therefore, he would like to produce only OX_1 quantity and charge a price OP_1 for this quantity. His total profits will be equal to area OP_1AX_1.

Now suppose, firm B enters into the market with the assumption that A will not change his level of output, i.e., he (A) will continue to sell OX_1 quantity. If it is so, then B has to consider the segment RD (the remaining portion of the market demand curve DD) as his individual demand for water. Now the corresponding marginal revenue curve for B becomes MR_1. Given this demand curve and marginal revenue curve for B, he would like to sell X_1X_2 quantity of water as at this level his $MR = MC = 0$. For this output level, B charges a price OP_2 ($= X_1T$) and expects to get a profit equivalent to the, area $X_1\ TSX_2$.

Now, since the product is homogeneous and therefore, A has to accept the price OP_2 fixed by B. This will reduce A's profits from OP_1RX_1 to OP_2TX_1. Further, A assumes that B will always produce and sell X_1X_2 quantity of water (which is equal to X_2D). It means, still X_2 demand for water remains unsatisfied because

$$X_2D = OD - OX_1 + X_1X_2$$

OD = total market demand for water

OX_1 = quantity sold by A

X_1X_2 = quantity sold by B

In other words, A thinks that only a quarter of the total demand for water is sold by B and therefore, assumes that his market demand will not be equal to OX_1 but now he is able to sell OX_2 quantity of water. In other words, A may visualise his new demand and marginal revenue curves to be as D_1X_2 and MR_2 respectively. These curves are linear straight lines and are parallel to the original, demand and marginal revenue curves. Now assuming these new demand and marginal revenue curves, A would like to sell OX_3 quantity at OP_3 price; because at OX_3 output his $MR = MC = 0$. At OX_3 output, A's profits will be equal to the area OP_3UX_3. Here we notice in Fig. 36.1 that OX_3 output is just half the distance OX_2.

Now, B will observe that the market situation has changed and in this new situation the demand for his output left is X_3D ($= OD - OX_3$. Thus, he again assumes his straight line demand and marginal revenue curves and would like to produce half of the X_3D quantity as he follows the profit maximising rule ($MR = MC = 0$).[1]

In this way, every time each duopolist in the market will adjust his price and output assuming other's output to be constant. Changes in price and quantity sold by A and B will occur until the two have sold out equal

1. Actually, we have not drawn these new demand and marginal revenue curves for B, but it is always implied due to the linear nature of the curves.

quantities. In Fig. 36.1, the final quantity sold by *A* will be OX_3 and by *B* will be X_3X_4 and the market price would be fixed at OP_3. The equilibrium total profits of *A* and *B* will be equal to the area, OP_3UX_3 and the area X_3UVX_4 (= OP_3UX_3) respectively.

The above Cournot model can also be extended even to more than two firms. As more and more firms enter into the oligopoly industry, the equilibrium output and price of the industry will lead to perfectly competitive output *OD* and zero price.

The Cournot Model in Terms of Reaction Curves

Some economists have used the reaction curves to explain Cournot's duopoly model. The reaction curves may be output reaction curves or price reaction curves depending upon whether it is the output or the price which is the adjustment variable. Since in Cournot model, it is the output which is subject to the adjusting variation, output reaction curves are relevant. It should be carefully notified that these reaction curves do not indicate the reactions which a seller expects will be forthcoming from his rivals but to the sellers' own reactions to the moves of his rival. In Fig. 36.2, output reaction curves of producers *A* and *B* are drawn as *MN* and *ST* respectively. *A*'s output reaction curve *MN* explains how *A* will react to any change in output of *B*, that is, *A*'s output reaction curve shows how much output *A* will determine to produce for each output level of

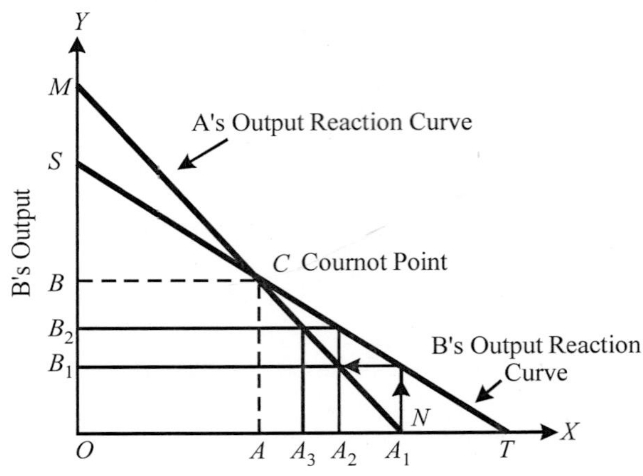

Fig. 36.2

producer *B*. In other words, it indicates, the most profitable output for *A* for each given output level of *B*. Similarly, *B*'s output reaction curve *ST* explains how much output *B* will determine to produce for each output level of producer *A*. For example, if *B* produces output OB_1, *A*'s output reaction curve *MN* shows that *A* will produce output OA_2 in response to *B*'s output OB_1. Likewise, for all other output levels the reaction can be explained. On the other hand if *A* produces OA_2, *B's* output reaction curve shows that *B* will produce OB_2 and so forth for all other levels of output. This reaction in the output of one to the other's output will continue till both reach the Cournot point *C* where both *A* and *B* produce the same output. *A*'s output *OA* equals *B*'s output *OB*. The same conclusion follows if we move from lower right to upper left. Thus the reaction curve analysis also provides us with a unique and stable equilibrium in terms of the Cournot model.

It will be noted from Fig 36.2 that output reaction curves have been drawn to be straight lines. This is due to the assumption that the marginal costs of production of both *A* and *B* are constant (at zero). It should be noted that output *ON* is the monopoly output since producer *A* will produce *ON* if producer *B*'s output is zero. In other words, producer *A* will produce and sell *ON* if he were the monopolist. On the other hand output is the output which *B* must produce in order to force the producer *A* to produce zero output. Given the marginal costs, as zero, producer *A* will be forced to produce zero output when the price has fallen to zero, and therefore production is no longer profitable. Output *OM* will be produced under conditions of pure competition since at output *OM* the price will be zero and therefore equal to marginal cost which is assumed to be zero in the present case. Thus while *ON* is the monopoly output, *OM* is the purely competitive output. We assume the two producers *A* and *B* to be completely identical, therefore, *OS* will be equal to *ON,* and *OT* will be equal to *OM.*

Output reaction curves, as explained above, can be used to explain Cournot's duopoly solution. Each producer, as before, assumes that his rival will continue producing the same amount of output regardless of what he might himself decide to produce. To begin with, suppose producer *A* goes into trade first and is, therefore, initially a monopolist. Thus *A* produces output *ON.* Suppose now *B* also enters into trade. *B* will assume that *A* will keep his output constant to *ON.* *B*'s output reaction curve *ST* reveals that for output *ON* of *A,* he will produce OB_1. But when *A* sees that *B* is producing OB_1, he will reconsider his previous decision. Assuming that *B* will produce OB_1, *A* will produce OA_2 in reaction to

OB_1, Now when B observes that A is producing OA_2, then he will react and will produce OB_2 in reaction to OA_2 of producer A. But when A observes that B is producing OB_2, he will again react and produce OA_3. This process of adjustments and readjustments will continue until the point is reached where the two reaction curves intersect each other at point C when both A and B are producing OA and OB output respectively. Here the duopolists attain stable equilibrium when they will not make any readjustment. This will be the most profitable output for both of them.

3. THE BERTRAND MODEL

In 1883, Joseph Bertrand, a French mathematician, criticised Cournot's duopoly solution on its assumption that the supply of the rival duopolist is constant. Instead, he presented his own model based on the assumption that each producer believes the price of his rival would remain constant and keeping all other assumptions of the Cournot model the same. It means that under Bertrand model, the producers first set the price of the product and then produce the output which is dependent at that price and not output (as is the case under Cournot model).

Let there be two producers A and B. Suppose that A goes into business first. Now since A is the only producer in the market at present, he sets the price at monopoly level, which is the most profitable for him. Then B enters the market on the assumption that A will continue to charge his monopoly price and sell the same quantity of output. B, therefore, reduces the price of his product. Consequently B takes away some of the customers of A. Now A thinks that B will continue to charge this price and therefore he reduces his price to a lower level than B, thereby taking away some of B's customers. In this way, they will indulge in price war till both reach the perfectly competitive level of output and price in the long-run. Once the price reaches the competitive level, neither of the two duopolists A and B would like to lower or raise the price further. If any of the duopolist reduces his price below the competitive level, he would be incurring losses. On the other hand if one of them increases the price above the competitive level, then he is likely to lose his entire sales to his rival on the presumption that the latter would continue to charge the competitive prices. Hence, here the stable equilibrium is reached at the competitive price where the total output is equally divided between the two duopolists.

The above analysis of Bertrand model can also be explained with the help of Fig. 36.3. In Fig. 36.3, OY is the price axis of both A and B. YA and YB are their demand curves respectively. The maximum quantity of output that A can produce is OA and that B can produce is OB. Thus the total competitive output is $OA + OB$. If they happen to share the market jointly, they sell $\frac{1}{2}(OA + OB) = OA_1 + OB_1$ at the price OP.

Let us suppose that there is no collusion between A and B. Also suppose that A is already selling OA_1 output at OP price. Now B assumes that A will not change his price, so he fixes a lower price OP_1 where he is able to sell OB_2 quantity. Now A finds his sales being reduced (because of B's action), he reduces his price to OP_2 (lower than B's price OP_1) and sells OA_2 output by attracting some of B's customers. Now it is B's turn to react and he fixes a still lower price OP_3 and sells a larger quantity OB_2. This type of pricewar (action and reaction) will continue on the part of both A and B till both sell their entire output OA and OB at the zero competitive price. This is stable equilibrium in Bertrand model.

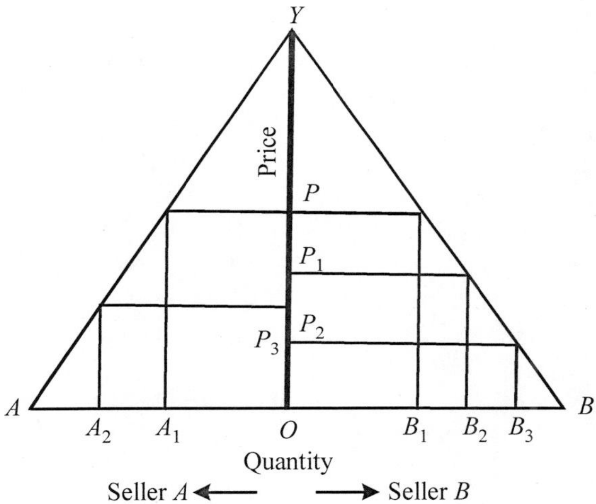

Fig. 36.3

It is clear from the above analysis of the Cournot and Bertrand models of duopoly that the fundamental assumption about the behaviour of the duopolists in the two models is the same. The assumption of zero cost of production is unrealistic because no firm will be prepared to sell its product at zero competitive price. They are also closed models which do not allow entry of firms. Further the assumption that each duopolist can act without any price-reaction from the other is unrealistic. Further these models are static models which do not explain the time period involved in the action and reaction process of price moves by the duopolists.

4. THE EDGEWORTH'S MODEL

In 1897, Prof. F.Y. Edgeworth developed another classical model of duopoly. This model is based on the same classical assumptions as were taken by Cournot's model, except one that it assumes that each seller takes the price of his rival as constant, instead of assuming the supply of his rival to be constant Prof. Edgeworth has presented his solution of duopoly problem with the help of Fig. 36.4. Here, it is assumed that there are only two firms in the industry (*A* and *B*) selling homogeneous product and incurring zero marginal cost ($MC = 0$). It is assumed that the market is shared equally by both the duopolists. In Fig. 36.4, DD_A is the demand curve for *A* and DD_B is the demand curve for *B*. OA_1 ($= A_1D_A$) and OB_1 ($= B_1D_B$) are the maximum probable outputs (where $OA_2 = OB_2$) at which the marginal revenue (MR) = marginal cost (MC) = 0. If both the duopolists have got some sort of tacit agreement then they will sell OA_1 and OB_1 quantities respectively at OP_1 price. In other words, under collusion, they will act as a monopoly.

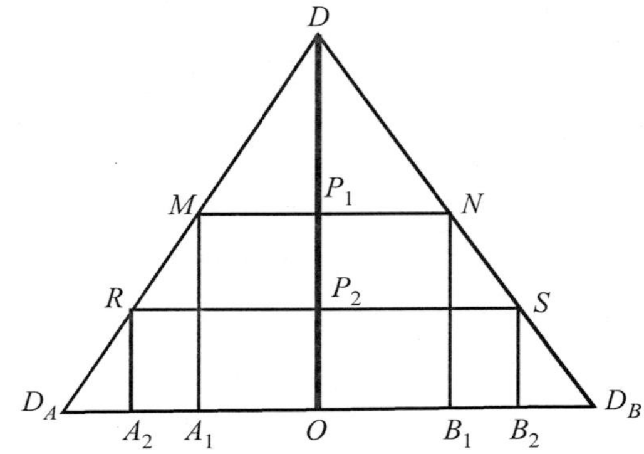

Fig. 36.4

But suppose there is no collusion of any type between the two firms in the industry and also assume that initially firm *A* exists in the market. Being a single seller in the market, *A*'s behaviour is very similar to that of a monopolist. In equilibrium, *A* would like to sell OA_1 quantity at OP_1 price and his total profit at this level will be equal to the area A_1MP_1O.

Now, *B* enters into the market and sets a lower price than OP_1 with the assumption that *A* will keep his priceconstant at OP_1. By doing this he (*B*) will be able to increase his sales sufficiently. But, on the other hand, when *A* observes this new situation, he fixes a price lower than *B*'s price assuming that *B* will keep his price constant. *A* will now sell more than before and will be able to catch a large part of B's market. This will be followed by reappraisal of the market situation by Band he will again fix a price lower than the new price set by A, assuming that A will keep his price constant.

In this way, a situation of price-war will take place in the market. The price-war will continue until the price comes to be OP_2.At this price both the firms will sell OA_2 and OB_2 quantities of their products respectively. In other words, the firms will reach their maximum capacity. But according to Edgeworth, OP_2 price will not be understood as the equilibrium price, because at this price OP_2, the firms' total sales will be equal to A_2B_2 and still D_AA_2 and D_BB_2 consumers will not be satisfied by the firms. Thus these consumers would be ready to purchase the quantity at any price below OD. Therefore, let us assume that A begins to raise his price with the assumption that B has already placed his entire capacity on the market and he will keep his price constant. But, on the other hand, at the same time B has a similar strategy to increase the price and get advantage of the remaining market. It means that the market price starts rising until it again reaches OP_1. This is the maximum limit of price-increase. After this, the only possibility remains is to start reducing the same and the same process of price-war starts which we have already discussed. Thus, price-war is the main feature of duopoly situation. According to Edgeworth, price will always oscillate between OP_1 and OP_2. In other words, price is indeterminate in Edgeworth's Model of Duopoly.

The Edgeworth model is, however, an improvement upon the Cournot model in that price rather than output is used as the decision variable, though it leads to indeterminacy.

5. THE STACKLEBERG MODEL

A German economist, Heinrich von Stackeberg provided an interesting solution to the duopoly problem. It is based on the assumption that each seller recognises the interdependence of other's actions. Each duopolist either regards himself a leader or a follower. Each duopolist determines the maximum profits he can get both by being a leader and a follower. He will then choose to play whatever role brings him greater profits.

Let us assume that A and B are the two sellers and that each desires to play the role of a leader, leaving the other fellow to act as a follower. A's maximum profit from followership is determined by substituting B's optimum leadership output level in A's reaction Junction. Each seller can determine his maximum profit from leadership on the assumption that his rival obeys his reaction function and acts as a follower. To put it differently, each duopolist determines his maximum profits levels from both leadership and followership and desires to play the role which yields the *larger maximum.* Four outcomes are possible: (1) *A* desires to be a leader and *B* a follower, (2) *B* desires to be a leader and *A* as follower, (3) both desire to be leaders, and (4) both desire to be followers. Outcome (1) results in consistent behaviour and therefore a determinate solution. *A* assumes that *B* will act as a follower, and he does, *B* assumes that *A* will act as a leader, and he does. Likewise outcome (2) also results in a determinate solution. But if outcomes (3) and (4) are obtained, the expectations of *A* and *B* are not realised, as under (3) each assumes that the other will act as a follower which he does not, while under (4) each assumes that the other will act as a leader which he does not. In the latter case neither of the reaction functions is obeyed and we have a Stackleberg disequilibrium.

The above cases can be explained with the help of reaction curves as follows:

(1) *Seller A desires to be a leader, and B a follower.* It is presented in Fig. 36.5 where the "variable" is interpreted as price. In this case, each seller will raise his price, if the rival's price increases. If *A* acting as the leader raises his price from L_B upward, *B* follows him by raising his price from L_A upward, so that both finally reach the equilibrium point *E*. Thus here the model is determinate.

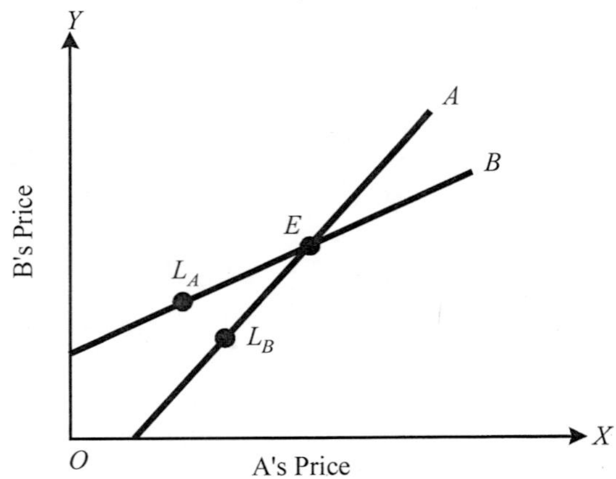

Fig. 36.5

(2) *If B desires to be a leader and A as a follower.* Here also the solution is determinate because both follow consistent behaviour patterns. In Fig. 36.5 when *B* as a leader raises his price from L_A upward, *A* follows him by raising his price from L_B upward, till both reach the equilibrium point *E*. Thus the model is determinate.

(3) *If both A and B desire to leaders.* Here each assumes that the behaviour of the other is governed by his reaction function but in fact, neither follows the reaction function of the other. Thus there is no equilibrium situation. This is known as the "Stackelberg disequilibrium." It is shown in Fig. 36.6 where the variable is interpreted as the quantity of output. Each seller suffers from the rise in the output of his rival. The profit maximisation output of one seller falls when his rival's output increases. If *B* acts as the leader and increases r is output from L_A onward, the reaction on *A* would be to reduce his output from L_B downward. But *A* does not follow *B* because he also considers himself a leader and so does not reduce his output from L_B downward. So there is no possibility of equilibrium at point *E*. This is the Stackelberg disequilibrium.

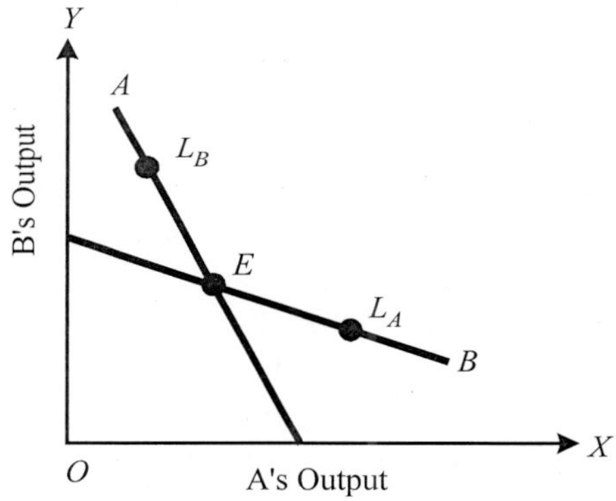

Fig. 36.5

(4) *If both A and B desire to be follower.* Fig. 36.5 above seller *B* thinks that seller *A* has raised the price of his product, so *B* will follow him by raising the price of his product. Now it is *A*'s turn to follow *B* in raising the price of his product. Then *B* will follow him and so on till both reach equilibriumpoint *E*. Thus the followership solution is determinate.

6. THE HOTELLING MODEL

In 1929 Harold Hotelling presented an empirical analysis of the market behaviour and constructed a model which is generally known as the Hotelling's stable solution.

Once again, we find *A* and *B* as the two entrepreneurs who produce a homogeneous product at zero marginal cost. However, the two products appear differentiated to the consumers due to differences in the locations of the two sellers. In Hotelling's view, markets are commonly sub-divided into regions within each of which a seller enjoys a quasi-monopolistic position. As shown in Fig. 36.7, buyers are uniformly distributed along a line of length *L,* which may be the main street. *A* and *B* are initially located at points *A* and *B* in this market.

Every buyer must go to the vending point and transport his purchases home at a cost per unit distance (say kilometre) carried. Thus a buyer located X kilometres distance from A must pay a transportation cost of CX for each unit of product he buys.

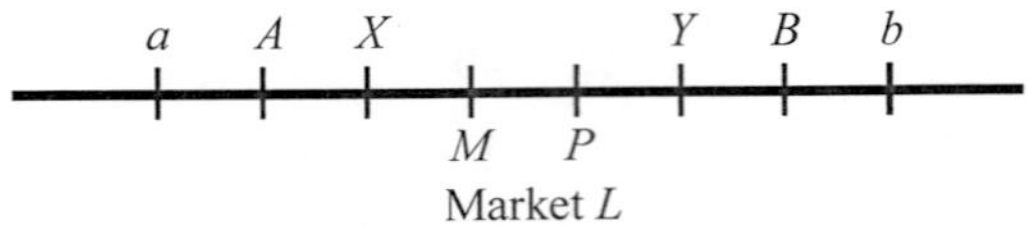

Fig. 36.6

Hotelling then assumes that there are a buyers situated to the left of A and b buyers situated to the right of B. Assuming that each buyer purchases only one unit of the product, A and B will have protected or sheltered markets in respect of a and b buyers located to their left and right respectively. The total sales of A and B will be $L = a + x + y + b$.

A and B both have some leeway in setting their price, although neither will set a price so high that buyer in his sheltered market find it less expensive to buy from his rival. Since the products differ only in transportation cost, delivered price must be equal. In other words, if price charged by A and B are assumed to be P_A and P_B, together with transportation costs we should have $P_A + cx = P_B + cy$. A's total profit will be $P_A\ (a + x)$ while B's profit will be $P_B\ (b + y)$. In the initial stages P_A may be different from P_B, but eventually they are equalised.

Hotelling believes that in the long-run both A and B attempt to expand their respective "sheltered" markets. As a result, A starts moving to the right, B moves to his left and ultimately both are located at M, selling the product at the same price. The incentive which different sellers have to conglomerate in the central part of a city or in the down-town areas is but a reflection of the market behaviour of different sellers highlighted by Hotelling.

Hotelling provided a stable and determinate solution to the oligopoly problem and argued that in the long-run both A and B charge the same price and sell the same quantity.[2]

7. THE CHAMBERLIN'S MODEL (SMALL GROUP MODEL)

Prof. Chamberlin's model of duopoly gives a result quite different from those of the older classical models—the Cournot's model and the

2. See C.E. Ferguson. *Microeconomic Theory*. pp. 311-12 for a mathematical proof.

Edgeworth's model, etc. Although, the Chainberlin's model is based on the same assumptions of classical models, yet it recognises the mutual dependence between the price and output of the duopolists in the market. Here, the firms are assumed to have full and far-sighted recognition of their interdependence and its consequences. The Cournot model and the Edgeworth model assume the firms to be independent, i.e., do not give recognition to the interdependence between the firms. This is the main point of difference between the Chamberlin's model and the other classical models of duopoly.

Chamberlin's model can be understood by both: (*i*) the output adjustment, and (*ii*) the price adjustment. First we discuss the output adjustment. For this we go back to Fig. 36.1 to understand the model. In Fig. 36.1 Cournot has represented his model assuming the non-existence of interdependence between *A* and *B*. With the same Fig. 36.1, we may understand the Chamberlin's model by adding the assumption that on *B's* entry in the market *A* recognises their mutual interdependence.

In Fig. 36.1, we observe that initially *A* was selling OX_1 quantity of his product at OP_1 price. Being a single seller of the product, he behaved like a monopolist. Thus, *A*'s initial total profits were equal to the area OP_1RX_1.

Now, *B* enters the market and intends to sell X_1X_2 quantity at OP_2 price. Now the moment *B* enters the market, Prof. Chamberlin assumes that interdependence between *A* and *B* arises. Under this assumption of mutual interdependence, *A* will not expect that *B* will keep his price and output constant but he (*A*) realises that *B* will always try to maximise his profits. Thus he (*A*) reduces his supply to X_1X_2 (= OX_2^1). Thus the total supply of the industry will be $OX_2^1 + X_1X_2 = \frac{1}{2}$ (*OD*). In this way at OP_1 price the total supply OX_1 [= $\frac{1}{2}$ (*OD*)] is equally divided between *A* and *B* (i.e., $OX_1 = OX_2^1 + X_2^1X_1$). Here, *A* and *B* will also share the monopoly profits of the market (OP_1RX_1) equally. *A*'s $X_2^1WRX_1$ profits will be equal to the area $OP_1WX_2^1$; and *B*'s profits will be equal to the area (= $OP_1WX_2^1$). Thus, the total profits of the industry would be $OP_1RX_1 = OP_1WX_2^1 + X_2^1WRX_1$. Therefore, OP_1 will be a stable equilibrium price. No duopolist would like to vary output at this price. If one attempts to do so, it leads to a harmful situation to both of them.

Now, under the second method of price adjustment (instead of output adjustment as discussed above) also, we shall be getting the same result. Here we shall take help of Fig. 36.4 which represents the Chamberlin's model. Let us now assume that some price takes place between OP_1 and OP_2. If A increases his price to OP_1. for maximising his profits, then B will also do the same immediately. In this way B also increases his price to OP_1 for attaining maximum profits. Once OP_2 price is fixed, no duopolist would like to reduce it because each duopolist knows that by doing so he would be reducing his total profits. Thus, at OP_1 price, the equilibrium becomes stable and joint profits are at a maximum.

The equilibrium in Chamberlin's model is stable, stable as granite, because each firm is looking to its ultimate interest never gives a moment's thought to any other possible course of action. In this model there is no collusion in any meaningful sense. Each firm acts independently, while it recognised the mutual dependence of all the firms in the industry. This recognition of mutual dependence leads to a stable equilibrium or a sort of monopolistic equilibrium in duopoly (or oligopoly).

8. OLIGOPOLY

Meaning of Oligopoly

The term "Oligopoly" is developed from two Greek words, "Oligoi" meaning a few and "pollein" meaning to sell. Oligopoly refers to that market situation in which there are a few enough sellers of a particular product (or differentiated products) for the activities of one to be of importance to the others. Oligopoly differs from monopoly where there is only one seller, and from perfect and monopolistic competition where there are many sellers. In oligopoly, a single seller occupies a position of sufficient importance in the commodity market for changes in his market activities to have repercussions on the others. Other sellers react to the market activities of the one and their reactions in turns have repercussions on him. The individual seller is aware of this and in changing his price, output sales promotional activity or quality of his product, he must take into account the reactions of others. Hence, the oligopoly situation has one important feature which distinguishes it from other forms of market situations. This is the interdependence in the decision making of the various firms, an interdependence which is recognised by all of them. Every seller in such a situation knows that at least some of his rivals' decisions depend on his own behaviour, and he must take this fact into account in his own decision making.

The reason is that changes in the output and price of one firm will affect the amounts which other firms can sell and the prices which they can charge. Hence other firms will react in one way or another to price output changes on the part of one. Individual firms are, therefore, not independent as they are under perfect competition or under monopoly.

This feature has made the formulation of a systematic analysis of oligopoly very difficult. The analysis of pricing and output under oligopoly lacks the neatness and precision of the theory of perfect competition and the theory of monopoly. This is partly because of oligopolistic uncertainty (in many cases an oligopolistic cannot be sure what his rivals' reaction will be to various kinds of activities on his part) and partly because oligopoly covers such a wide range of cases, each with its own unique characteristics. This is why we cannot find a general theory of oligopoly. As a result, the literature of oligopoly is full of different models.

Before we define different models of oligopoly, let us clear one more point. An oligopoly situation invites collusion among the firms in an industry because of three reasons: (*i*) by reducing the degree of competition the collusion may enable the firms, to act monopolistically and thereby increase their profits; (*ii*) a collusion may reduce oligopolistic uncertainty; and (*iii*) a collusion may restrict the new firms from entering into the industry. Once a collusion is made, only a high profit incentive may initiate a firm to leave the collusion and to act independently.

Collusion and Blocked Entry

The kind of pricing that is likely to develop in the conditions of oligopoly depends mainly on the degree of collusion among the several firms and the extent to which free entry is possible into the industry concerned. Collusion is more likely to prevail if the number of firms is few than if there are many, and it is most effective if it can be put in the form of a formal agreement. However, where (as in the case of United States) the anti-trust laws make any combination or agreement in restraint of trade illegal, formal agreements may be replaced by some kind of tacit understanding. A spirit of 'live and let live, among the rival firms may come to prevail, because each knows that he has most to gain by refraining from active competition, especially pricecutting. Each is conscious of the price policies pursued by the others, and fears retaliation on their part if he becomes too aggressive. Or, tacit understanding can be fostered by occasional informal meetings, trade conferences, and like. But collusion of this kind is naturally precarious, and this gives an element of instability to oligopoly pricing. The greater the number of firms in the industry, the more likely is the competition to prevail; because it is difficult to make the contacts for concerted policy among a great many concerns (firms), and where each one is small in relation to the total output of the industry, a firm is less conscious of the effects of its policies on the market (industry) as a whole.

Furthermore, collusion requires some kind of a pooling arrangement for giving each party a satisfactory share of the market. This must take into consideration the capacity of each plant, its costs, geographical location, the quality and variety of its products, etc. All this is more difficult to work out if there are many firms. Even where cartels[3] are legal (as in Europe), these factors have made them rather easily broken up. The presence of numerous firms, however, need not be an insuperable bar to collusion if, one of them is so much larger than the rest that it can assume a position of price leadership[4].

How effectively oligopolies can exploit their position will depend also on the difficulty or ease with which new firms can come into the industry or market. If entry is easy, high prices will soon attract competitors, and they will force the price down. This may deter the present oligopolists from pursuing too greedy a policy, and induce them to keep their prices moderate. But, if entry into the industry or market is difficult, the position of the oligopolists is more secure, and hence they are likely to set their prices higher. Entry may be difficult if the industry is a manufacturing one in which the economies of large scale production are great. Here large firms already established may be able to produce so much more cheaply than new firms, that no newcomer can hope to compete successfully. Again, when the oligopoly industry is based on some natural resources found in only a few areas, other new firms cannot enter the industry. Further, patents are often a means of blocking entry into an industry. These are the basis of oligopolistic situations in the manufacture of electric pumps, cameras, radios, pastes and many other products.

Thus the effectiveness of oligopoly depends upon the degree of collusion among the firms and the Bower to restrict new firms to enter into the industry.

---

3. A cartal is a combinations of firms in an industry where competition is restrained by an agreement among them concerning prices, the share of the market to be allotted to each, the interchange of patent rights, or the matters of similar kind.

4 In the case of price leadership, the leader sets a price high enough to assure a reasonable profit for all, and the small firms (or followers) accept the price without attempting to alter it.

Classification of Oligopoly

Oligopoly situation can be classified on different bases:

(1) ***Basis of Product Differentiation.*** On the basis of product differentiation, oligopoly may be classified as Pure or Perfect Oligopoly and Imperfect or Differentiated Oligopoly. In the case of pure oligopoly, the product of different firms in the industry is identical or homogeneous while in the case of differentiated oligopoly, the products of different firms are not identical but rather differentiated products. Thus, differentiated oligopoly will exist where the competing firms produce products which are close substitutes but not perfect substitutes.

The distinction between pure oligopoly and differentiated oligopoly does not play a significant role in the analysis. In real situation, firms in most oligopolistic industries produce differentiated products. But theoretically we may determine price and output in both kinds of oligopoly.

(2) ***Basis of Entry of Firms.*** On the basis of the possibility of entry of new firms into the industry, oligopoly may be classified as Open Oligopoly and Closed Oligopoly. An open oligopoly provides full freedom to new firms to enter into the industry. In the situation of open oligopoly there is no restriction of any kind for the desiring firms to enter into the market. A closed oligopoly, on the other hand, refers to that market situation where only the few firms control the entire market and new firms are not allowed to enter the industry.

(3) ***Basis of Price Leadership.*** On the basis of presence or absence of price leadership, oligopoly may be classified as Partial Oligopoly and Full Oligopoly. Partial oligopoly refers to that market situation where the industry is dominated by one large firm (known as the leader) and the other firms (known as the followers) of the industry follow the price policy determined by their leader. Full oligopoly, on the other hand, refers to that market situation where there is no leader and no followers.

(4) ***Basis of Agreement.*** On the basis of agreement, oligopoly is classified as Collusive Oligopoly and Non-collusive Oligopoly. A collusive oligopoly refers to that market situation where the firms of the industry follow a common policy of pricing. In other words, they combine together to avoid competition among them selves regarding .the price and output of the industry. A non-collusive oligopoly refers to that market situation where there is no agreement among the firms regarding the price and output of the entire market. In other words, the firms under non-collusive oligopoly act independently.

Characteristics of Oligopoly

In order to distinguish oligopoly from other market situations, such as, perfect competition, monopoly and monopolistic competition, etc. it is necessary to understand the characteristics or assumptions or features of oligopoly situation. The main characteristics of oligopoly are the following:

(1) ***Very Few Sellers of the Product.*** The important feature of oligopoly situation is that the number of sellers dealing in a homogeneous or differentiated product is very small. It means that the pricing and output policy of an individual seller in the market can influence the industry price and output. Each firm controls a large share of the markets and therefore, it is able to make a noticeable effect on the market activities by changing his output.

(2) ***Interdependence.*** Under perfect competition, no individual can influence the market demand, supply and price. The firms are simply price-takers in perfect competition and they take their output decisions independently. No firm is worried about the actions or reactions of the other firms in the perfect competitive industry. Similar is the ease under monopoly. The monopoly firm takes its decision independently. Although, the monopolist has to see the market elasticity of demand for his product while determining the price of the product, yet he does not bother about the pricing decisions of other firms.

It is only under oligopoly, that a firm has to take into consideration the actions and reactions of other firms while determining its price and the level of output. As we have already mentioned, there are only a few firms in oligopoly market, each producing a homogeneous or a slightly differentiated product (close substitute). Since a firm controls a large share of the market, it is able to make a significant influence on the price and output of the oligopoly market. Thus the firms in oligopoly are independent and each has to take into account the actions and reactions of the others. The cross-elasticity of demand for their products is very high because of the availability of close substitutes. This is the reason that no firm would normally like to change its existing price. Only in some abnormal cases they may dare to take independent decisions.

(3) ***Presence of Monopoly Power.*** As we have said that the number of firms in oligopoly market is very small and, therefore, collusion among them is possible. Under collusion, the firms act as monopoly and they may charge higher prices for their products. Also, different firms sell differentiated products and to that extent each may charge a high price. The element of monopoly becomes still more conspicuous when the

consumers become habitual of consuming particular products.

(4) ***Existence of Price Rigidity.*** In oligopoly situation, each firm has to stick to its price. If any firm tries to reduce its price, the rival firms will retaliate by a higher reduction in their prices. This will lead to a situation of price war which benefits none. On the other hand, if any firm increase, its price with a view to increase its profits, the other rival firms will not follow the same. Hence, no firm would like to reduce the price or to increase the price. The price rigidity will take place.

(5) ***Excessive Expenditure on Advertisement.*** As we have seen that the firms under oligopoly produce close substitutes and they are interdependent. Each firm has to stick to its prevailing price. Now the only way to increase the sales is the advertisement and the improvement (or variation) in the design and quality of the product. Each firm spends a lot on advertisement. It plays an important role in determining the demand function of the firm's product.

Thus the primary purpose of advertising is to shift to the right the demand curve faced by the firm, and also to make it less elastic. This will enable the firm to sell a larger volume of output at the same price or probably at higher price without the risk of price-war. Each firm tries to encroach upon the markets of others through advertising instead of through price-cutting.

Under oligopoly, the products of various firms can be differentiated effectively only by advertising. Each firm tries to attract consumers to its particular brand name by advertising; although basically the product of each firm may be the same as that of other firms in the industry. Variations in quality and design of particular products are usually used along with advertising to differentiate the product of one firm from another.

The object of quality variation is the same as that of advertising. The primary object is to shift the demand curve to the right and to make it less elastic. In addition to it, quality variation may also be used to extend the market vertically—different qualities to appeal to different classes of the consumers. In both, advertising and quality variation, retaliation by the rivals will take place. Individual firms may succeed in increasing their market shares temporarily, but if a permanent increase is to be obtained, such firms must be able to keep ahead of their rival firms.

Cost Curves and Demand (Revenue) Curves of Oligopolistic Firm

Here we assume that the oligopolistic firm buys its resources from a perfect competitive factor market and, therefore, its cost curves are like those of the purely competitive firm or those of the pure monopolist.

It is the demand side that distinguishes oligopoly from other market situations. Mutual interdependence of firms creates an atmosphere of uncertainty for all the firms under oligopoly market. It is very difficult for a firm to visualiseits price-output policy with any degree of certainty. What one firm is able to do in attempting to make its profits as large as possible is conditioned by the ways in which other firms react to the market activities of the one. The extent of oligopolistic uncertainty is highly variable from case to case. As such, the demand or average revenue curve of the oligopolistic firm cannot be definite or determinate, because the firm in question cannot correctly estimate the reactions of its rivals to its price-output policy.

We have, therefore, two observations to make regarding the shape of the demand curve of an oligopoly firm: (*i*) The demand curve can be definite, certain and determinate only if the reactions of the rivals are predictable or known, and (*ii*) The oligopolistic firm has only series of conjectures regarding the probable reactions of its rivals.

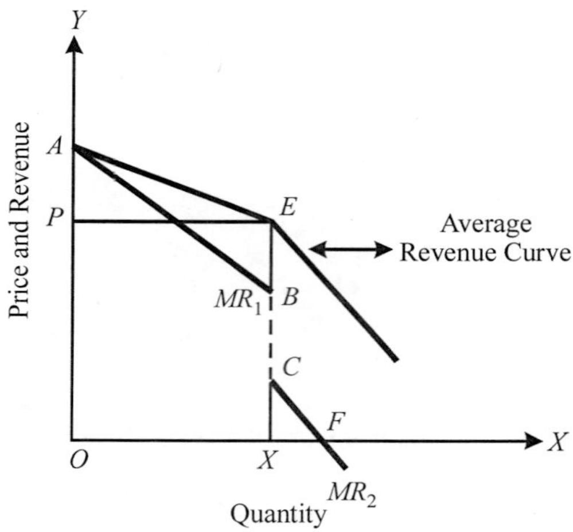

Fig. 36.8

The 'kinked' demand curve does provide a simple way of conceiving an average revenue curve for the oligopolistic firm which helps us to understand oligopoly pricing problems. It explains the oligopolistic price regidity. The case of kinked demand curve occurs only if certain assumptions are fulfilled. Figure 36.8 assumes that there is a small group of firms each producing the same product. It also assumes that a price *OP* has been accepted by all the firms in the industry. At this price *OX* our particular firm sells *OX* quantity of its product; other firms may sell more or less than *OX,* depending on the relative popularity of their particular products and the extent to which they are being advertised. In Fig. 36.8, the demand curve *AED* (which is also the average revenue curve of the firm) has a kink at point *E.* It divides the demand curve into two parts' *AE* and *ED* respectively. *AE* part of the demand curve is more elastic while *ED* part of the demand curve is less elastic. The reason of the kink at point *E* is as follows. We assume that if this particular firm raises its price, none of its rivals follow, because they feel that a higher price would lead to lower sales. Since price-increase is not followed by the rivals, a small increase in the price of this particular firm's product will lead to a very large fall in its sales; demand is very elastic if one firm alone increases its price. On the other hand, if this particular firm cuts its price, its rivals will react and cut their prices to exactly the same extent. Although a general price cut will be unprofitable to all, yet it takes place to maintain the old market share of each firm. Consequently, the kinked point *E,* the average revenue curve slopes downwards very steeply. Since all firms are assumed to be charging the same price, anyone of them gains extra sales only to the extent that the sales of the whole oligopoly group can be expanded through the general price-cut. Therefore, the demand curve of the oligopoly firm can be drawn only under certain assumptions such that a single price or a cluster of prices has been established in the industry and a price-increase by one firm is not followed by its rivals while a price-decrease by one firm is followed by its rivals. In Fig. 36.8 the demand curve faced by the firm for price increases is *AE* and at each possible price it will have a considerably greater elasticity than the market demand curve. Also, for price decreases, the demand curve faced by the firm is *ED* and it will have about the same elasticity at different prices as the market demand curve.

The kinked demand curve *AED* has important implications for the, marginal revenue curve of the oligopolistic firm. The marginal revenue curve is discontinuous at *OX* output, that is, it has a gap which is shown by the dashed line *BC* in Fig. 36.8. It (gap) comes from the abrupt change from the more elastic to the less elastic parts of the demand curve.

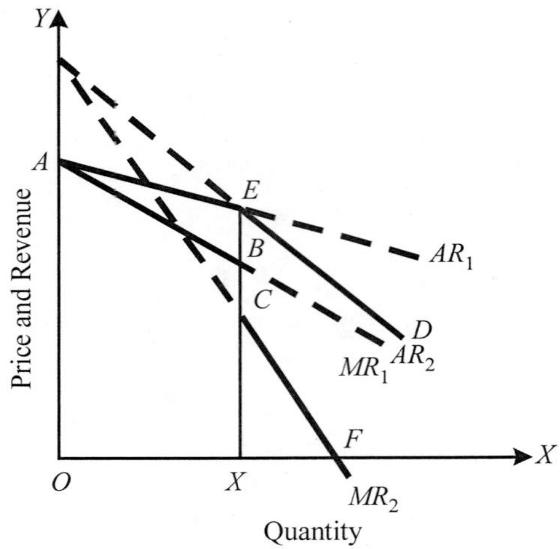

Fig. 36.9

We can draw such a marginal revenue curve by assuming two separate demand curves and their respective marginal revenue curves. In Fig. 36.9, this case has been illustrated. The *AE* portion of the demand curve and its dashed extension gives one demand curve while the *ED* portion and the demand curve and its dashed extension upto the price axis gives another demand curve. Now we draw the appropriate marginal revenue curve MR_1 and MR_2 for the respective smooth demand curves AR_1 and AR_2 Since the dashed parts of the distinct demand curves do not exist, their respective portions of the marginal revenue curves will become irrelevant for our purposes. In other words, *AB* portion of MR_1 and *CF* portion of MR_2 will be relevant for the given portions of the firm's demand curve. The same conclusion can be drawn in terms of elasticity of demand. If the demand curve were a continuous curve, elasticity would be changing continuously as we move from higher to lower prices. Since $MR = (1- 1/e)$, the marginal revenue curve would also be continuous as we move down the demand curve. However, at point *E* the demand curve breaks. Elasticity at an output infinitesimally below *OX* is substantially greater than elasticity at an output infinitesimally above *OX*. Thus, marginal revenue must drop sharply at output *OX*. Hence, it is proved that in the case of a kinked demand curve or average revenue curve, the marginal revenue curve will have a gap in it at the kinked point of the demand curve.

9. PRICE AND OUTPUT DETERMINATION UNDER OLIGOPOLY

As we have mentioned above, the interdependence of the demand curves of the firms in oligopoly poses serious difficulties in establishing a theory of the determination of prices and outputs. No firm, under such conditions, is sure of the price and output combination which would maximise its profits or revenues (sales). According to William J. Baumol there are three possible approaches to the oligopoly problem[5] A firm may adopt anyone of the following alternative approaches:

(1) *Ignoring Interdependence.* The very simple approach is to ignore the interdependence and take independent decision. The firm may follow its own independent line of action, on the assumption that its competitors will also do in their own interests. In such a situation the entire theory becomes the simple theory of monopoly where firm attempts to maximise its profits in the conventional manner, i.e., it produces that level of output at which, its $MR = MC$.

(2) *Estimating the Competitors' Countermoves.* The second approach is that the oligopoly firm attempts to estimate or anticipate the nature of competitive reactions on the basis of past experience. For example, the firm estimates that his competitors will follow (or react) its' price changes within a few days, so that, the firm will adopt such a strategy which is optimal in terms of this assumption.

(3) *Preparing against Optimal Moves by the Competitors.* Unlike the second approach, the firm in this case does not guess at its competitors' reactions, but it calculates the optimal moves of its opposition (his competitors' best possible strategies) and prepares its own defences and counter-moves accordingly. Therefore, the approach is associated with the theory of games.

Now we shall discuss the determination of price and output under oligopoly situation in the following manner—Equilibrium under Independent Action, and Equilibrium under Collusion,

10. EQUILIBRIUM UNDER INDEPENDENT ACTION

(The Sweezy Model of Kinked Demand Curve)

Cases of independent action are just what the name implies. Here we assume a single firm, operating without overt collusion, but aware of the fact that what it does will be closely watched by the other oligopolists in

5. William J. Baumol, Economic Theory and Operations Analysis. Third Edition. pp. 353-54.

the industry, and will very likely be met by some competitive retaliation on their part. Thus, independent action often touches off price wars when the reactions of rivals to actions of one are retaliatory in nature.

Under independent action an oligopoly firm faces a kinked demand curve. Therefore, the solution of oligopoly problem under independent action is also known as the Kinked Demand Curve Solution. The kinked demand curve was first used by Prof. Paul M. Sweezy to explain price rigidity under oligopoly. The kinked demand curve represents the behaviour of an oligopoly firm which has no incentive either to increase or to decrease its price. Each firm in the oligopoly industry has learned by experience what the reactions of rivals will be to actions on her part and may voluntarily avoid any activity that will lead to the situation of price war. It is also possible that each firm is reasonably well satisfied with present prices, outputs and profits and is content to let things continue as they are, rather than chance starting a chain reaction. Hence, firms usually do not change their price-quantity combinations in response to small shifts in their cost curves.

The most significant aspect of Sweezy Solution is the existence of a 'kink' in the demand curve of an oligopoly firm. At this kink, the firms sticks to its price. It does not raise it for the fear of being disobeyed by its rivals. On the other hand, it does not cut its price as all the rivals will follow. Therefore, there is a rigidity in price at the kink point of the demand curve, and under normal conditions, the firm will not move in either direction from this point. Sweezy argued that at this kinked point we have finite discontinuity in the *MR*-curve of the firm. It is because of the fact that price is rigidly fixed at this point.

This case has been illustrated in Fig. 36.10. The price prevailing for the moment is assumed to be *OP*, and sales for this oligopoly firm are *OX*. This price may be the aftermath of prior competition, in which the firms have come to a common price.

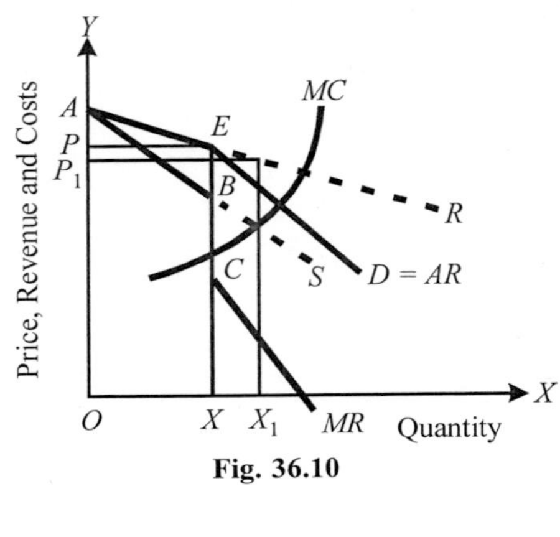

Fig. 36.10

Now if the firm raises its price and its competitors do not, many of its customers will shift their patronage to others, so that its sales will decline sharply. This gives the demand curve for this firm a nearly horizontal slope (such as *AE* portion of demand curve) for prices higher than *OP*. If the product of this firm is identical with that of its rivals, the curve will actually be horizontal, and it will make no sales at all at higher prices; but if it has a differential advantage (however slight) in the eyes of at least some of its consumers the curve will be as shown (highly elastic demand curve). Under these circumstances so long as the prevailing price is yielding a reasonable profit, there is little or nothing to be gained by raising it.

Now suppose this oligopoly firm reduces its price with a view that it will be able to increase its sales at the expense of its competitors. If this firm could be sure that its rivals would not follow the price cut, it could assume that its demand curve would continue along the slope *AE* to *R*, and the marginal revenue curve would extend on from *AB* and *S*. With marginal costs or *MC*, the most profitable output would then be OX_1 where its marginal cost (*MC*) is equal to its marginal revenue (*MR*). The firm could reach this optimum output (OX_1) and maximise its profits by cutting the price to OP_1. But in fact, if this firm cuts its price from *OP* to OP_1 it is probable that its rival s would cut their prices too, and some of them might cut below OP_1. This would cause some consumers to shift to the other firms, so that the demand curve would dip downward at *E* to *D*, instead of going out along *ER*. Thus the demand curve of the firm under individual action will be a kinked demand curve and the resulting marginal, revenue curve will have a gap at the kink point.

This type of situation tends to give oligopoly prices a sort of rigidity or stability. It means that each oligopolist in the market hesitates to disturb the existing price even if his cost curves shift upward or downward. But the price-rigidity takes place only within the limits determined by the gap of marginal revenue curve. That is, the firm would not like to change the price so long as the cost curves shift between the discontinuous part of the marginal revenue curve. In a situation when the cost curves shift beyond this limit, the firm has the incentive to change the price accordingly. But it happens only when all the firms of the oligopoly industry realise the same situation. For instance, if costs have been rising and profits declining for all the firms, a boost in the price may be indicated, yet each one fears to quote a higher price. Now if one has the courage to do so, all the rest will follow suit, and each will occupy the same relative position with respect to the others as before. On the other hand, if costs are falling and profits are so high that there is the danger of entering new firms into the industry, a price-cut by one firm may merely be the signal for others to cut their prices to the same level. A new position of stability will then be reached without a price war with the relative positions of the oligopoly firms remaining the same.

11. EQUILIBRIUM UNDER COLLUSION

Most of the modern economists are of the opinion that independent price determi-nation cannot exist for long in oligopoly. It leads to a sense of antagonism uncertainty and insecurity and to overcome them there is a tendency among oligopolists to act collectively by tacit collusion. In addition, the firms can gain the economies of production. All the firms in oligopoly tend to enlarge their size and lower their costs of production per unit and capture as large a share of the market as possible.

Literally, collusion means the "act of playing together". In common parlance, collusion is used with the idea of deceit or fraud or trickery. But in economics, collusion means the act of agreeing on a common live-and-let-live policy by legally independent and potentially competitive firms or organised groups of resource owners or a combination of firms and resource owners. The collusion may be legal or illegal, depending upon the laws of the country concerned. In this section we shall deal with the collusion among the oligopolistic firms. We can distinguish among cases of perfect collusion and cases of imperfect collusion.

Perfect Collusion in Oligopoly

Cases of perfect collusion consist primarily of cartel arrangements. A cartel is an explicit agreement, usually formal, among independent firms on prices, output, and often on other matters such as division of sales territories. In other words, a cartel is a formal organisation of the firms within a given industry. Cartels are often short-lived. Firms do have the desire for large joint profits; this desire gives the impulse to form cartels. Firms are likely, however, to quarrel over the division of joint profits; this propensity is the leading cause of the break-up of cartel arrangements. Here we shall discuss oligopoly pricing under two types of cartel arrangements—(1) Pricing under the centralised cartel, and (2) Pricing under the market-sharing cartel.

In the centralised cartel, we shall assume that decision making with regard to pricing, output, sales and distribution of profits is possessed by the central association. The market sharing cartel, on the other hand, is a somewhat lower form of organisation. Here, we assume that firms forming the cartel agree on market shares with or without an understanding regarding prices. Under the market-sharing cartel, member firms perform their own marketing activities, but they are careful to observe the cartel agreement made by them.

(1) ***Pricing under the Centralised Cartel (Joint Profit Maximisation Perfect Cartel).*** A centralised cartel or a perfect cartel is an agreement among the firms in an industry that results in the maximisation of the joint profits of the member firms. Thus, the cartel can act as a single monopolist. It is assumed that the constituent firms of the cartel produce a homogeneous product. The market demand for the product now becomes the cartel's demand. It is assumed that the board of control, established by the cartel, has full knowledge of the demand for the product of the industry at each possible price. Therefore, the board of control can calculate marginal revenue for the industry. The board of control also knows the marginal costs of all of the firms and can easily find out the marginal cost of each volume of output of the industry.

For simplicity we assume that the demand curve or average revenue curve of the cartel is linear and, consequently, the marginal revenue curve will also be linear. This case has, been illustrated in Fig. 36.11. Here it is assumed that we have five firms *A, B, C, D* and *E*; each with differing capacities and somewhat different cost schedules. The curve *MC* represents the sum of the marginal costs for all these firms combined, that is,

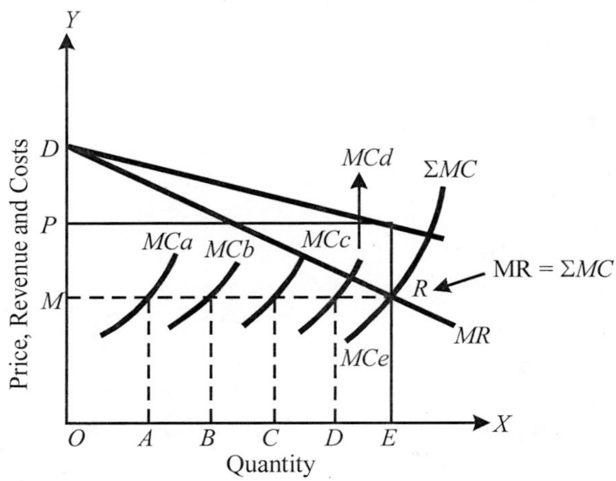

Fig. 36.11

$$\Sigma MC = MC_a + MC_b + MC_c + MC_d + MC_e.$$

The demand curve for the product of the industry is shown by *DD* and *MR* is the marginal revenue curve derived from it. As in pure monopoly, the most profitable output is where the *MC* curve cuts the *MR* curve. Hence, the equilibrium point is *R* where *MC* = *MR*. The optimum output level of the cartel is *OE* and the equilibrium price is *OP*. At this price *OP*, the output shares of firms *A*, *B*, *C*, *D* and *E* are *OA*, *AB*, *BC*, *CD* and *DE* respectively. This is really a case of pure monopoly, and, therefore, it permits of a determinate solution.

Allocation of output will be done on the basis of efficiency of firms. If there are a number of firms, the inefficient firms may be asked to close down either temporarily or permanently. In a few extreme cases, member firms of a cartel may agree to share the market equally. It is possible only if the firms have identical cost curves. But this is not true in practice.

Now profits can be calculated on a firm-by-firm basis and then summed for the industry. It is also true that the larger the number of firms forming the cartel, the harder it will be to hold the cartel together, particularly if the individual firms shares of the industry profits are small. There exists a strong incentive for individual firms to leave the cartel and operate independently.

(2) *Pricing under the Market-Sharing Cartel.* In this case the firms of the industry produce a homogeneous product and agree upon the share of the market that each is to receive at each possible price. Homogeneity of the product will establish the rule of a single price in the product market. In other words, each firm is to limit its sales to the given districts, states or regions. One common price will prevail in the entire market. Such a system can, however, function only when the cost functions of different firms are the same.

To simplify the cost of market sharing cartel, let us assume that there are only two firms in the industry. The two firms have identical cost functions and agree to share the market half and half. If the context of the above assumptions, the two firms will charge similar prices for their products and will sell equal shares of the sales of the market.

In Fig. 36.12, *DD* is the demand curve of the industry and for each firm the relevant demand curve is *dd.* Since cost functions of the two firms are identical, *AC* and *MC* may be assumed as the respective average cost and marginal cost curves of the two firms. The marginal revenue curve faced by each firm is *MR* (because it is common to both). The profit-maximising output for each firm will be *OX* at which *MC* is equal to *MR*. Each firm will charge *OP* price and will sell *OX* output. If firm *I*

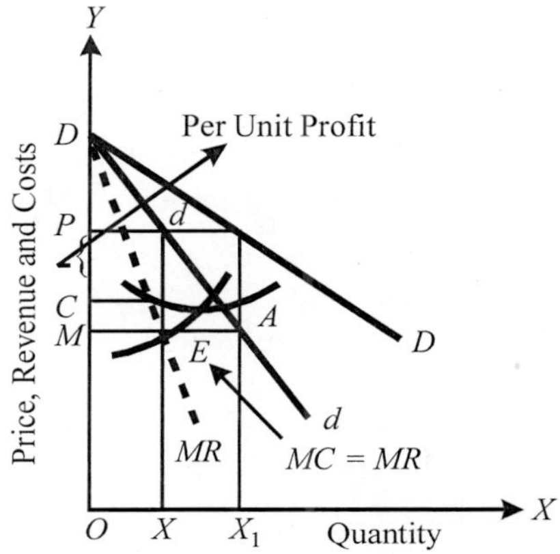

Fig. 36.12

sells OX output, the other firm will sell XX_1 output (= $OX_1 - OX$). The total output of the industry at price OP is equal to OX. The output of each firm will be the same (i.e., $OX = XX_1$) only if the individual firm's demand curve dd lies halfway between the market demand curve and the vertical axis. In this situation, per unit profit of each firm will equal CP.

In the above case we have assumed that the firms in the industry agree to share the market half and half; but it is possible that they may agree on different market shares. It will depend upon their individual capacities. High-capacity firms may receive larger market shares than low capacity firms. Even in this situation the process of equilibrium will be the same. The total marginal cost curve can be obtained by the horizontal summation of the individual firm's marginal cost curves. Applying the rule of profit maximisation ($MR = \Sigma\ MC$), we may find out the industry output and the common price to be charged by the firms in the industry. Now the output distribution will be made according to the agreement between the firms of the industry.

Market-sharing case is possible only when the cost functions of the member firms are identical. In fact, costs of production for the individual firms are likely to differ rather than being identical. Thus, the differences in costs and the degree of independent action will make pricing and output problems much more uncertain than they have been discussed in the above oligopoly model. In case, it exists, it has a very short life.

Imperfect Collusion in Oligopoly

As we have mentioned above, the cases of perfect collusion (centralised cartel and Market-Sharing cartel) do not exist in real world. The case of a perfect collusion stands as a polar extreme where the maximisation of joint profits is emphasised. But mutual distrust among member firms and their unwillingness to give up all of their sovereignty make it most unlikely that cases of perfect collusion could long endure. The better and more lasting cases than that of perfect collusion are the cases of imperfect collusion. In fact, collusion is always imperfect. The cases of imperfect collusion also try to raise prices and profits, but they never assume the position of monopoly. We may find a number of cases of imperfect collusion, but in the present section, we shall discuss the important case of price leadership. Price leadership is said to exist when the price at which most or all ofthe firms in the industry offer to sell is determined by the leader (one of the firms of the industry). This method was devised by the German economist, Prof. Heinrichvon Stackelberg. This device is also known as Leadership Solution or Followership Solution.

In the words of Prof. Arthur Burns, "If changes are usually or always inaugurated by the same firm and usually or always followed with similar price changes by other sellers, price competition may be said to involve price leadership." In real world, there are many types of price leadership. But among them, the two important types of price leadership are the following—(1) Price Leadership by a Low-Cost Firm, and (2) Price Leadership by a Dominant Firm.

(1) *Pricing under Price Leadership by a Low-Cost Firm.* Here we take a simple case of two firms industry. Suppose, the first firm is a high-cost firm while the second firm is a low-cost firm. In Fig. 36.13, the average cost and marginal cost curves of the high-cost firm are AC_1 and MC_1 respectively, while those of the low-cost firm are AC_2 and MC_2 respectively. The industry demand curve is *DD*, and each firm has an equal share of the market. Therefore, *dd* is the demand curve for each firm. The corresponding marginal revenue curve for each firm is *MR*. Now given the demand curves and cost curves, each firm will like to fix that level of output and price at which it will get the maximum profits. Thus, the first firm will like to produce OX_1 output and charge OP_1 price, while the second firm would like to produce OX_2 output and charge OP_2 price.

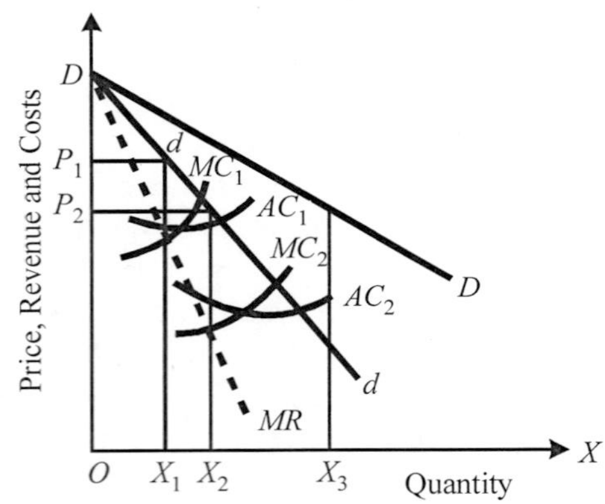

Fig. 36.13

Now, if we assume that the two firms are producing a homogeneous product, then the only price possible in the market is OP_2. Since the low-cost firm can afford to sell at a lower price than can the high-cost firm the latter will have no alternative than to sell at the price (OP_2) fixed by the low-cost firm. Therefore, in such a situation the low-cost firm (second firm) becomes the price leader and the high-cost firm (or firms) will become the follower. If, in this situation, the high-cost firm does not want to become follower, then the low-cost firm can drive out the high-cost firm from the market by fixing a price lower than the average cost of the (first) high-cost firm. In such a situation the entire output (OX_3) will be sold at OP_2 price.

(2) *Pricing under Price Leadership by a Dominant Firm.* Generally, in an oligopolistic industry, one or more large firms are found, together with a number of small firms. In the present analysis, we assume that the industry comprises a large dominant firm and a number of small firms. A dominant firm, if it so desires, can drive out all its rivals by a price war. Now, to avoid large-scale price cutting, tacit collusion may occur in the form of price leadership by the dominant firm. In this situation the dominant firm fixes the price for the industry and allows the small firms to sell all they desire to sell at that price. Thus, the small firms of the industry are simply the price-takers. The residual of the industry demand at this price (set by the dominant firm) will be supplied by the dominant firm. This type of price-leadership is also called as partial monopoly. The partial monopoly is more than just a price leader, because he wields more or less monopoly power.

Under this situation, each small firm of the industry behaves like a perfect competitive firm. The price of the product is set by the dominant firm and this price is given to all the small firms. In other words, the demand curve for the small firm is perfectly elastic or it is horizontal to X-axis. The marginal revenue curve of the small firm coincides with the demand curve; therefore, $AR = MR$. Now to maximise profits the small firm produces that level of output at which its marginal cost is equal to its marginal revenue. The combined supply curve for all the small firms can be obtained by summing horizontally the individual marginal cost curves of all the small firms. This combined supply curve shows how much all firms together will supply at each possible price. In Fig. 36.14, this combined supply curve of the small firms is indicated by ΣMC.

In Fig. 36.14, the industry demand curve is *DD* which shows different combinations of price and output that the consumers a would like to purchase. The ΣMC curve shows how much the small firms combined will sell at each possible price. The horizontal differences between the two curves—*DD* and ΣMC—at all possible prices show how much the dominant firm can sell at those prices. Thus, the demand curve faced by the dominant firm is P_1D_d; which is obtained by subtracting horizontally the Σ *MC* curve from the *DD* curve.

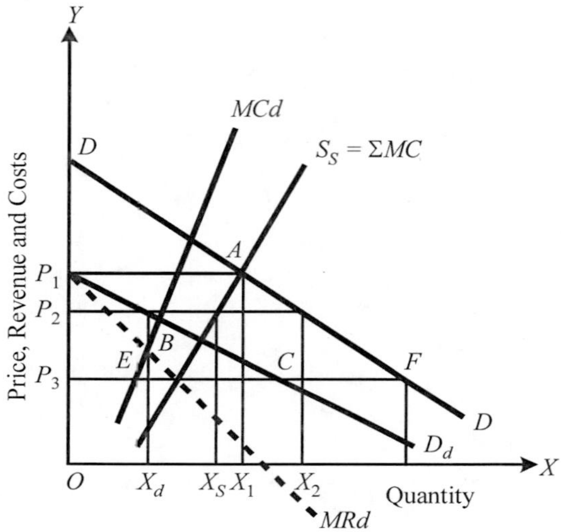

Fig. 36.14

To show in detail how the demand curve of the dominant firm is obtained, the following analysis is relevant. As we have mentioned, the dominant firm sets the price for the industry and allows the small firms to sell whatever they want to sell. The residual of the market demand will be filled up by the dominant firm. Now, suppose the dominant firm sets the price at OP_1 where the total market demand for the product is OX_1. At this price OP_1, the entire market demand will be met by the small firms as their supply curve Σ *MC* cuts the market demand curve *DD* at point *A*. At this price, there will be zero demand for the dominant firm's product. If the dominant firm reduces price from OP_1 to say OP_2; then the market demand increases from OX_1 to OX_2. Now, at this new lower price OP_2, the small firms would like to supply only OX_s quantity and the rest OK_d, (i.e., $OX_2 - OX_s = X_s X_2$ or which is equal to OX_d) will be met by the dominant firm. Now suppose, the dominant firm sets the price at OP_3, then the market demand will be P_3F. From this the small firms will sell only $P_3 B$ amount of the product and rest *BF* (which is equal to

P_3C) will be met by the dominant firm. In this way we get the demand curve of the dominant firm (P_1D_d) from the market demand curve (DD) and the aggregate supply curve of the small firms (ΣMC).

Now, once the demand curve of the dominant firm is obtained, it is very easy to draw the marginal revenue curve of it. In Fig. 36.14 MR_d is the marginal revenue curve of the dominant firm corresponding to its derived demand curve P_1D_d. The marginal cost curve of the dominant firm is MC_d. In this situation, the dominant firm will fix that price at which its profits become maximum. For profit maximisation, the dominant firm takes the help of the fundamental rule, $MC = MR$. Thus profits are maximum for the dominant firm at an output level of OX_d at which MC_d is equal to MR_d. The equilibrium price fixed by the dominant firm is OP_2. Each small firm maximises profits by producing the output at which its marginal cost is equal to its marginal revenue, and here marginal revenue for each small firm is equal to the price OP_2. Total output for the small firms combined is OX_s, where $\Sigma MC = MR$ (Price). Thus, the profit maximising quantity and price for the dominant firm would be OX_d and OP_2 respectively. At this price, total market demand is OX_2, out of which small firms supply OX_s quantity and the rest X_sX_2 (= OX_d) is supplied by the dominant firm.

12. WELFARE EFFECTS OF OLIGOPOLY

(Resource Allocation under Oligopoly)

We can draw certain conclusions regarding the welfare effects of oligopoly market situation as compared with other market situations in the following manner.

Competition versus Collusion

It appears likely that some output restriction and increase in prices will occur in oligopolistic market as compared with purely competitive markets. Generally, this final result of a collusive agreement is that all the firms in the agreement end up operating so far short of their normal capacities; and with such high cost per unit (average cost) that all profits disappear. This outcome, in a sense, resembles that reached through pure competition in the long-run where the long-run abnormal profits become zero. The social results, however, are very much less satisfactory under oligopolistic situations. In perfect competition, in the long-run, all the firms of the industry are operating at normal (optimum) capacity and selling relatively large quantities at prices just covering the minimum average total costs. On the other hand, in collusion (oligopoly situation), a larger number of firms would be operating at below capacity and providing consumers with smaller quantities at a higher price. Thus the excess capacity and the excess management tied up in these operations of oligopoly represent a waste of valuable resources. Moreover, the reduced employment increases job applications in other and more competitive industries and drives wages there to lower levels than would otherwise prevail. Therefore, collusive practice reduces the national income and increases the inequalities in its distribution.

Panel (*a*) and Panel (*b*) of Fig. 36.15 illustrate the difference in the end results (long-run outcomes) of these two no-profit situations—one under pure competition and the other under oligopoly or collusive agreement. Panel (*a*) of Fig. 36.15 states that under perfect competition, consumers would get a larger quantity of the product at price *OP* from all the firms in the industry operating at their most efficient scales, and each firm supplies *OX* units of the product. Whereas Panel (*b*) of Fig. 36.15 states that under the collusive agreement consumers get a smaller quantity at the higher price *OP*, a larger number of firms, each producing *OX*' units of the product and operating at high cost and inefficient plant (*SAC*) at point *A*'. Therefore, an oligopolistic firm will produce less than a perfect competitive firm and would charge higher price than the latter. This would be so because an oligopoly firm has to face a negatively sloped demand curve.

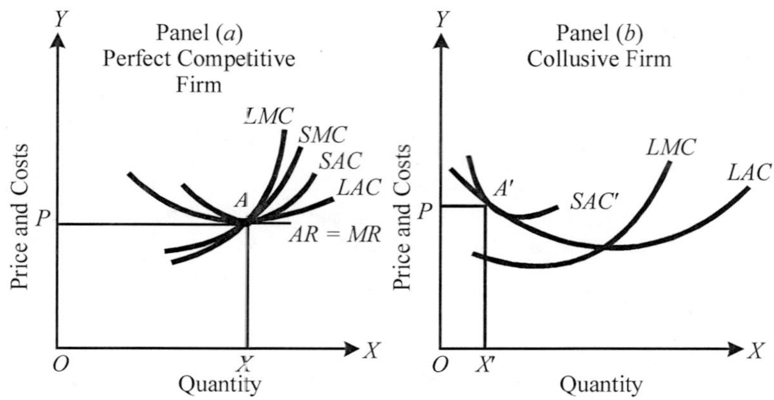

Fig. 36.15

Monopoly versus Collusion

We know that both the monopoly firm and the collusive firm have to face a negatively sloped demand curve, yet the monopoly solution may be preferable from the social point of view. The monopolist would control production capacity and see to it that this capacity was effectively utilised. The wastes involved in indefinitely tying up excess capacity and excess management (which is always a scarce and very valuable resource in any society) would be avoided. To the, extent that the competition of substitutes did not protect the consumer, government regulation or government ownership would be necessary. Either of these solutions would be preferable to overt government encouragement of collusion.

Moreover, under oligopoly, the non-price competition through advertising and introduction of variations in quality and design involve some cost which has to be borne by the consumers of the society. Although advertising enables the consumers to make a choice between a wide range of commodities available in the market. yet too much expenditure on non-price competition may not be socially desirable. This non-price competition involves a heavy social cost.

Collusion and Factoral Rewards

Monopolistic practices under oligopoly tend to depress the rewards going to resource owners. If the resource owners have zero reservation prices for their services, i.e., if they accept any reward offered, rather than allow their resources to go idle, the economy will operate at the full employment level and the factor-prices (wages, interest, rent, etc.) going to factor-owners will be determined by their marginal productivity in the competitive sector of the economy. Firms operating in the non-competitive sector (oligopoly firms) will be obliged to pay only enough to secure from the competitive sector the resources required for their operations, and the scale of their operations will be determined by the considerations discussed in the preceding section. The firms operating in the competitive sector (perfect competitive firms) will operate at zero profits and the owners of the resources will receive in wages, interests, and rents the equivalent of the value output from this sector of the economy. Then will be persistent profits in the non-competitive sector, yet these profits will not, in and of themselves, induce expansion. They will go to the owners of the equity capital and, if expected to persist, they will become capitalised by the process of capital formation. Thus, how adversely the long-run interests of the society are affected by monopolistic practices of oligopoly will depend upon the relative size of the non-competitive sector, the spending and investing habits of the profit earners and the capital requirement of the society. For instance, on balance the US economy has gained from the monopolistic practices of the 19th century.

Moreover, oligopoly provides consumers with a broader range of products among which they can make the choice than does either pure competition or pure monopoly. It also possesses the advantage of promoting research and development in the society, because it gives emphasis on variations of quality and design of the products. It is indication of dynamism in the society.

EXERCISES

1. Define duopoly. How is price determined under duopoly?
2. Show why price is indeterminate under duopoly conditions and point out how this difficulty can be overcome?
3. Write short notes on the following:
   (*i*) Cournot's Model of Duopoly Problem
   (*ii*) Edgeworth's Model of Duopoly Problem
   (*iii*) Chamberlm's Model of Duopoly Problem
4. Explain the characteristic features of the Cournot model of duopoly.
5. Discuss the Stackleberg solution to the duopoly problem.
6. Explain the Bertrand solution of duopoly problem. How does it Cournot solution?
7. Define oligopoly and show how price is determined under it: (*i*) with product differentiation and (*ii*) without product differentiation.
8. Why there is a kink in the demand curve of an oligopoly firm? How do you draw the marginal revenue curve of the oligopoly firm?
9. What are the main characteristics of oligopoly? Is it correct to say that pricing under oligoply is indeterminate?
10. Define collusion. Describe the conditions on the side of supply and of demand that favour collusive practices. Show why collusion tends to breakdown unless it is legalised and enforced by government.
11. Explain the kinky demand curve solution under independent action.
12. What are the main types of collusion? Explain briefly the pricing problem of oligopoly under the centralised cartel and under market sharing cartel.
13. What do you understand by price-leadership? Explain the pricing process under price leadership by a low-cost firm and by a dominant firm.
14. Write a short note on the welfare effects of oligopoly.
15. Does the kinky demand curve solution offer a satisfactory explanation of price-output decision under oligopoly?

Multiple Choice Questions

16. (*i*) With reference to the Cournot model, determine which of the following statements is false?
    (*a*) The duopolists do not recognise their interdependence

(*b*) Each duopolist assumes the other will keep its quantity constant
(*c*) Each duopolist assumes the other will keep its price constant
(*d*) The solution is stable [*Ans.* (*c*)]

(*ii*) With reference to the Edgeworth model, determine which of the following statement is correct?
(*a*) The duopolists recognise their interdependence
(*b*) It explains price regidity
(*c*) Each duopolist assumes the other keeps its price constant
(*d*) Each duopolist assumes the other keeps its quantity constant
[*Ans.* (*e*)]

(*iii*) If there is a market structure in which there are only two buyers for a commodity, it is called
(*a*) Duopoly (*b*) Duopsony
(*c*) Discrimination market (*d*) None of the above [*Ans.* (*b*)]

(*iv*) Oligopoly describes
(*a*) a kind of monopolistic competition in which each seller is aware of the influence of his actions on the other sellers
(*b*) an industry engaging in more competition than a monopoly but less than perfect competition
(*c*) an industry with more than one firm
(*d*) none of the above [*Ans.* (*a*)]

(*v*) An oligopolistic firm
(*a*) is a price-taker
(*b*) sells a product for which there are no good substitutes
(*c*) does not influence the actions of the other firms
(*d*) none of the above [*Ans.* (*d*)]

(*vi*) Which of the following most closely approximates our definition of oligopoly
(*a*) the cigarette industry
(*b*) the barber shops in a city
(*c*) the gasoline stations in a city
(*d*) wheat farmers in the midwest [*Ans.* (*a*)]

Chapter 37

FULL-COST PRICING THEORY AND SALES MAXIMISATION

1. INTRODUCTION

"In the previous chapters we have explained those theories of price and output determination under oligopoly which are based on profit maximisation assumption. After the marginalist revolution, profit maximisation by the firm is generally explained by the marginal analysis, that is, by the use of marginal revenue and marginal cost concepts. An important alternative approach to profit maximisation and marginal analysis based upon it is the full-cost pricing theory which does not assume that rational firms seek to maximise profits. It may be pointed out in the beginning that full-cost theory has been given several names. Full-cost pricing theory is also known as *average-cost pricing* theory, since in this theory price of a product is fixed on the basis of average cost. It is also called *cost-plus pricing,* or *mark-up pricing* theory, since this theory visualises that in order to fix price businessmen add a mark-up to their average cost of production.

2. FULL-COST PRICING THEORY

Two Oxford economists, Hall and Hitch, found empirically in 1939 that instead of equating marginal cost with marginal revenue, many firms engage in *full cost pricing.* To quote them, "The way in which businessmen decide what price to charge for their products and what output to produce, casts doubt on the general applicability of conventional analysis of price and output policy in terms of marginal cost and marginal revenue and suggest a mode of entrepreneurial behaviour which current economic doctrine tends to ignore." They suggest that after the sellers have worked out their total cost in respect of the level of output expected for the next period of time, they would add to this a *satisfactory* profit margin. The price would be equal to *full cost* including an acceptable profit margin. They contended that the firms' main pre-occupation is price and not the output as implied by the traditional theory.

However, in order to arrive at such an acceptable profit margin the rival firms must have some sort of mutual understanding, tacit collusion, moral conviction of fairness, consideration for long run cost and demand. Generally oligopolistic firms keep their prices rigidly fixed. It was also discovered by Hall and Hitch that marginal costs and marginal revenue are very difficult to work out, hence firms emphasise on full-cost pricing.

Hall and Hitch's findings may be summarised as follows: Firstly, unlike the classical and neo-classical belief, the firms do not behave atomistically. The behaviour of interdependent oligopolistic firms, as Hall and Hitch put it, could not be dealt with within the framework of the traditional theory. They found that firms do not attempt to maximise their profit by applying the marginalistic rules, but normally attempt to $(MC = MR)$ set their price on the *average-cost principle* or as they put it, on the lines of *full-cost* pricing. That is,

$$P = AVC + AFC + \text{Normal profit margin}$$

Hall and Hitch gave two reasons for the breakdown of marginalistic rules: *(a)* Firms do not know the tastes and preferences of consumers and so are not aware of their demand function, nor their marginal costs, hence the application of the marginalist rule $(MC = MR)$ becomes impossible. *(b)* Firms believe that the full cost price is the "right" price as it covered normal profit over the cost of production when the plant was normally utilised. However, if a firm wanted to secure a big order, it may not insist on the average-cost pricing, or if it thought that such pricing may damage its goodwill or endanger its future position.

Finally, it was found by Hall and Hitch that prices of manufacturers were fairly sticky, despite changes in demand and costs. Traditional theory predicted a change in price and output in the event of changing costs and/or demand. In the real world, however, this was not observed. Referring to the apparatus of the kinked demand curve, they argued that normally businessmen set the price equivalent to average cost ($AVC + AFC$ + Profit margin) and the kink would occur at that price. It was reported by most firms that they did not have any collusive agreement with their rivals for raising the price, as they had a fear of potential entrants who may endanger the position of established firms. Likewise, firms did not think that collusive reduction in the price would be profitable to the 'group.' Furthermore, in the firms' view, frequent changes in price were disliked by their customers.

In 1948, R.A. Gordon also endorsed these views. He contended that the real industrial world is extremely complex and the determinants of demand and costs vary so frequently and so continuously that a firm can not extrapolate their past and have a realistic set of marginal cost and demand functions. In short, due to uncertainty prevailing in the modern industrial/business world, marginalist behaviour (i.e., maximisation profit by the rule $MC = MR$) has lost its relevance.

Full-Cost Pricing and Kinked Demand Curve

Hall and Hitch combine full-cost pricing with kinked demand curve analysis. Current price is fixed on the basis of full-cost (as defined above), and a kink in the demand curve is formed at this price. Full-cost pricing together with the kinked demand curve analysis is illustrated in Fig. 37.1. Here let us assume that the firm decides to produce *OX* output. This output is fixed on the basis of expected sales. At *OX* level of output the average cost is equal to *KX* which includes the direct cost and the normal profit. Thus the firm will fix a price *OP* which is equal to its average cost.

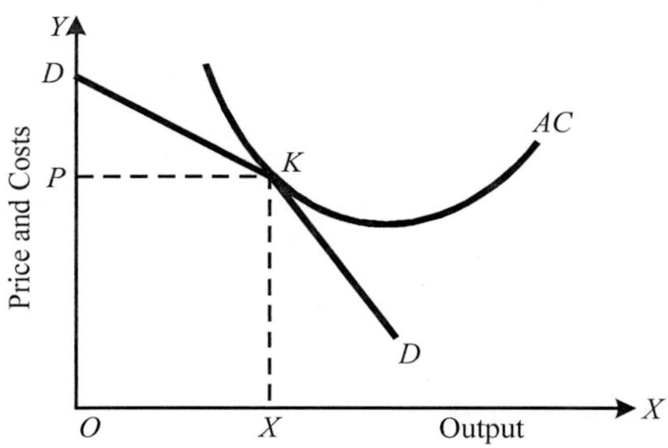

Fig. 37.1

Kinked demand curve analysis as used by Hall and Hitch along with his full-cost pricing theory provides an explanation for the stability or rigidity of prices under oligopoly in the short run. Increases or decreases in demand will usually shift the kink to the right or left but will leave the price unchanged. But Hall and Hitch have mentioned the following two exceptions to this general rule in which case price of the product changes:

(1) If the demand remains at a low level for some time, there is every likelihood that price will be reduced so as to maintain output. According

to Hall and Hitch the explanation for this reduction in price in the context of depressed demand is that one entrepreneur may become panicky and his irrational behaviour forces the others to cut prices.

(2) If the *AC* curves of all firms shift by similar amounts on account of changes in factor prices or technology, then this is "likely to lead to a revaluation of the full cost" price. However, Hall and Hitch point out that "there will be no tendency for prices to fall or rise more than the wage and raw material costs".

It should be noted that, given that the average cost curve falls for quite a large range of output, the full-cost pricing suggests that price of the products will vary inversely with output; smaller levels of output will involve higher cost per unit and therefore higher prices will be fixed. But, according to Hall and Hitch, the oligopolists will not produce small outputs and therefore will not charge higher prices. This is because oligopolists: (1) prefer price stability, (2) are prevented by the kink to raise price, and (3) they have propensity to produce larger levels of output or in the words of Hall and Hitch, they desire to "keep plant running as full as possible. giving rise to a general feeling in favour of price concessions".

Full-Cost Pricing and Andrews' Version

As we have noted that the kinky demand curve analysis has created some compli-cations in the explanation of full-cost pricing, Prof. Andrews has developed a modified version of the full-cost pricing. His analysis is similar to that of Hall and Hitch, but there are some differences between the two. An important difference between the two lies in the use of the concept of *costing-margin* by Andrews. The costing-margin is conceived by Andrews as an addition to *constant* average direct cost and "will normally tend to cover the costs of the indirect factors of production and provide a normal level of net profit." Thus, like the analysis of Hall and Hitch, addition of costing margin to the average variable cost for fixation of price of the product goes against the price fixation on the basis of profit-maximisation principle of the traditional theory of value. Thus the concept of costing margin of Andrews is similar to the mark-up of Hall and Hitch, but there is a difference in that whereas Hall and Hitch visualise a *constant or inflexible* mark-up or a margin for overhead cost and normal profit, Andrews discusses at length the circumstances in which there might be some *flexibility* in the costing margin in response to competitive and market forces. As shall be brought out later, on the introduction of flexibility in the costing margin brings Andrews' full-cost price theory closer to the price theory based on profit maximisation principle. Another difference between Andrews and Hall and Hitch's versions of full-cost pricing theory is that while the latter use kinked demand curve along with full cost pricing, the former does not make use of the kinked demand curve hypothesis in his full cost theory. Still another important difference between the two is that whereas Hall and Hitch consider that average cost varies with output and average cost curve is *U*-shaped, Andrews visualises that for a large relevant range of output, average direct (variable) cost remains constant.

The usual formula for costing-margin (or mark-up) is,

$$M = \frac{P - AVC}{AVC}$$

$$\therefore \quad P = AVC\,(1 + M)$$

where

M = Mark-up

P = Price

AVC = Average Variable Cost

Suppose that firm's AVC = Rs. 1000, and the firm sets $M = 0.20$ (or 20 per cent). They would fix price P = Rs. 1000 (1 + 0.20) = Rs. 1200. Once this price is fixed by the firm, the costing-margin-will remain constant, given its organisation, whatever the level of its output. But it will change with any general permanent changes in the prices of the indirect factors of production.

The theory of full-cost pricing as put forward by Andrews is illustrated in Fig. 37.2. In Figure 37.2 *AC* represents the average direct cost (i.e., average variable cost). It will be seen that average direct cost curve *AC* is saucer-shaped, that is, it first falls, then remains constant for quite a large increase in output and then eventually rises. Corresponding to this, *MC* is the marginal cost curve; *MC* curve falls in the beginning and lies below *AC*, then it coincides with *AC* curve and eventually *MC* lies above *AC*. In order to proceed to fix the price, besides average direct cost, a business firm has to calculate the total indirect costs (i.e., fixed costs) and also the amount of profits it wishes to earn. The total indirect costs plus the amount of profits planned will yield a *fixed sum of money* which will remain constant for fixation of price in the short-run. The 'costing-margin', according to Andrews, is obtained from this fixed sum of money by dividing it by "some chosen output".

This chosen output used for the purpose of estimating costing margin can be determined in several ways. Firstly, it may be fixed on the basis of *capacity output* with the given plant when by the capacity output is meant the maximum output that can be produced with the given plant. Output can be fixed by a business firm as some percentage of this capacity output: Secondly, the chosen output can be fixed on the basis of *sales of product made in the preceding production period,* or average or sales achieved over a number of previous production periods. Thirdly, the output may be determined on the basis of *expected sales in a future period* for which output is being produced.

If a new firm has to set the price of its product, or if the firm has introduced a new product for which it has to set the price, then the above mentioned second way of choosing the output for estimating the costing-margin is ruled out and in these circumstances only the first and third methods become relevant. In fact, when the firm is a new one or where an existing firm is introducing a new product, then the first add third methods of choosing output amount to the same thing. This is because the designed capacity of the plant will be determined by the expected sales of the product in the future periods.

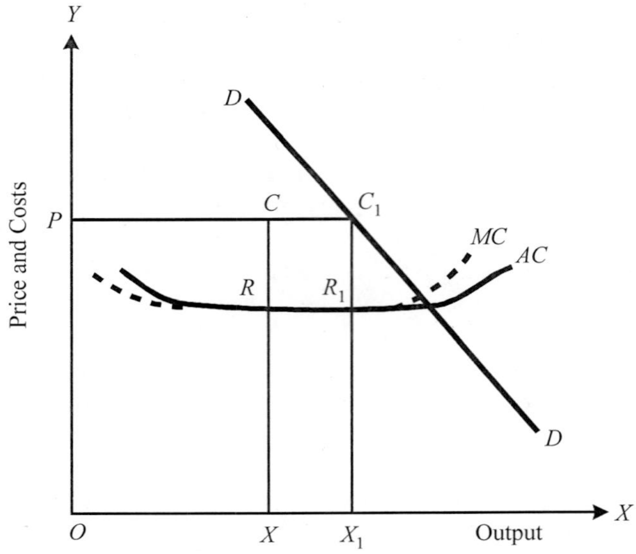

Fig. 37.2

In Figure. 37.2, let us assume that the firm has chosen output *OX* for estimating, costing margin and for fixing price of the product. Further, suppose that if the given fixed sum of money, representing the total overhead (indirect) costs and the normal level of profits is divided by the chosen output *OX* it yields *RC* amount which will be the costing margin to be added to the average direct cost for determining the price of the product. It will be seen in Fig. 37.2 that at *OX* level of output, average direct cost is *RX.* If we add costing margin *CR* to *RX,* we get full-cost equal to *CX.* Thus, the price *OP* will be fixed equal to full-cost *CX.* It should be noted that *price OP fixed on the basis of full cost CX will remain unchanged* whatever the amount *demanded and the actual output produced in the given period.* Now, if the demand for the product is given by the curve *DD*, then it will be seen from the figure that at *OP* price, *OX* quantity of the product will be demanded and therefore produced.[1] Now, even if the *demand for the product increases or decreases, the price will remain unaltered at OP, provided the amount demanded lies within the range of constant average direct cost, that is, within its horizontal straight line portion;* and further provided that costing margin remains unaltered. Thus, we see that according to Andrews' version of full-cost theory also, price will change as a result of the changes in direct and indirect costs of production and not as a result of alteration in demand. Thus, according to full-cost theory "The price will not be altered in response to changes in demand, but only in response to changes in the prices of the direct and indirect factors."

Limitations of Full-Cost Pricing Theory

The theory of full-cost pricing is adopted on the assumption that a firm does not have the information required about demand conditions, nature and degree of competition, technology used, etc. Further, modem business conditions are extremely uncertain. Besides, a firm may be producing or selling a number of varieties of goods and to calculate prices on the basis of profit maximisation may be almost impossible. The cost-plus method is convenient since the firms have only to add some standard mark-up to their cost. Over a period of time, through trial and error, they can find out the proper mark-up. It is argued that this is what happens in practice. It is difficult to assess whether fixing price on the basis of a particular mark-

1. It should be noted that output *OX* must lie within the maximum capacity output of the firm if the given 'demand is to be fully met. However if *OX* exceeds the maximum capacity and the firm has accumulated stock of the product from the previous periods, then it can draw upon the stocks to meet the demand.

up and changing the mark-up according to changing market conditions will result in actually maximising profit. This will, in fact, depend upon the ability of the management of a firm.

Another weakness of the full-cost pricing theory is its assertion that firms do not maximise their profits. In the opinion of most economists, profit maximisation is always the major and often the only objective of firms, though there can be other supplementary aims also, such as security. Besides, empirical studies of firms by Hall and Hitch and many others do not really invalidate profit maximisation assumption because businessmen and industrialists do often contradict themselves when they have to explain their views on profits, pricing, etc. Many of them speak about their social responsibilities and hide their real motive of profit maximisation.

Although full-cost pricing theory was formulated as fm alternative to marginal principle, there is no contradiction between the two approaches; in fact, the marginal principle is consistent with the full-cost pricing theory. It is pointed out that even under the full-cost pricing theory, firms attempt to calculate the mark-up on the basis of profit maximisation assumption, i.e., the mark-up is the maximum percentage which a firm thinks it can charge under the given circumstances. Besides, firms do change the mark-up according to changes in the demand and cost conditions and this implies that they are following profit maximisation approach while fixing prices and output on the basis of full cost.

Further it is difficult to fix a satisfactory profit margin in full-cost pricing, yet it would be possible for firms to get some idea of profit margin over a period of time. The normal or conventional profit margin will enable a firm to find out the prices it should charge. In general, therefore, the full cost pricing will roughly give us the some conclusion as the marginal cost analysis.

The full-cost pricing is also criticised on the ground that there is no clear motivation in choosing a price on the basis of full cost or fixing a particular mark-up. Under the marginal analysis the basic motive of every firm is to maximise its profits. Such a motivation is absent in the full-cost pricing theory. Naturally, it is difficult to predict how a firm fixes a particular mark-up or how a firm changes its price when demand and cost conditions change. But this criticism is not well founded since under the full-cost principle, firms do have some motivation or objective, i.e., they aim at a *reasonable* or *satisfactory* level of profit. But this concept of *reasonable* or *satisfactory* level of profit is much less precise than the concept of *maximisation of profit.* Moreover, the motive of reasonable and satisfactory level of profit comes under suspicion when firms raise their mark-up during business booms. If a firm is satisfied with a reasonable level of profit, why should it raise. its mark-up during a business boom when making more profit is relatively easy?[2] The full-cost pricing principle has obviously no answer to such a question.

The theory of full-cost pricing attempts to explain price determination on the basis of full-costs of every firm. But a real problem arises when the industry is composed of a number of firms of different sizes and efficiencies producing a similar product. In fixing prices each firm will have to consider, not only its cost of production but also the cost of production of others. In practice, it may not be possible to find out the cost of other firms. But there will always be some one firm whose price (based on its average cost) will serve as the standard price for the other firms. Such a firm will be the price leader and all other firms will become price-followers. Full-cost pricing without reference to price leadership does not, therefore, explain price determination in modern business realistically.

Merits of Cost-Plus Pricing

Despite these limitations, full-cost pricing principle attempts to explain the practice of price determination by manufacturing firms on the basis of their cost production. It offers a realistic explanation to the common business practice of maintaining prices for a long-period despite changes in demand. It is safer to set price on the basis of cost which is more stable. Besides, under conditions of competition, when prices are more or less the same, fixing price on the basis of full-cost and maintaining it will avoid price-wars and assure price stability.

Joel Dean argues that full-cost pricing is quite safe in pricing a new product. If the prevailing price in the market is such that it will not cover the estimated cost of the new product, the firm can as well not produce and market the product and thus avoid the loss.

---

2. Sometimes a firm may not raise its price to the maximum level possible eyen when the demand for its product exceeds its supply and thus there is scope for raising price. This may be because the firm does not want to give the impression that it is exploiting the consumers. Or the boom conditions may be short lived and, therefore, price may have to be lowered later. In general goodwill of consumers and profit maximisation in the long-run may induce firms to forgo short-run profit maximisation.

3. BAUMOL'S SALES MAXIMISATION MODEL

William J. Baumol[3] has presented a managerial theory of the firm based on the sales maximisation. According to this principle, the objective of a business firm is *sales maximisation* rather than *profit-maximisation.* (Let it be remembered that in terms of the traditional marginalist principle the objective of a firm is to maximise its profit or the firm is looked upon as the maximiser of profits.) But, according to this new principle, the ultimate objective of a firm is not to maximise its profit, but to maximise its sales. According to Baumol, every modern business firm wishes to maximise its sales revenue (i.e., price multiplied by quantity) rather than its profit. In other words, it desires to capture as large a portion of the market as possible, though in doing so it may not succeed in earning the maximum profit for itself. Why? The reason is to be found in changes that have taken place in the constitution and structure of the modern business corporation in recent years. As is well-known, ownership and control do not vest in the same hands in a modern business firm. The ownership lies in the hands of shareholders while the actual control and management vest in the hands of professional managers. The shareholders are, undoubtedly, interested in maximum profits, but the professional managers are not. The latter are more interested in maximising the sales revenue rather than in maximising the profits. The reason is that the remuneration of the professional managers is very often related to the sales revenue rather than to the profits of the firm. Further, maximisation of sales revenue also adds to the prestige, reputation and standing of the firm in question. Hence, profit-maximisation is no longer the sole or even the major objective of a modern business firm. This, however, does not imply that Baumol has ignored completely the profit-motive or profit-considerations in the pricing policy of a business firm. According to him, the firm should fix a price which not only covers the cost of production, but also yields adequate profit for the shareholders. After all, the satisfaction of the shareholders is of primary concern for the professional managers.

If the sales maximising output does not bring adequate profit to the shareholders, the firm will have to select another level of output which will yield sufficient profit, even though it may not maximise the sales of the firm. In Baumol's words, 'The typical oligopolist's objective can usually be characterised approximately as sales maximi-sation subject to profit constraint."

---

3. Baumol, W.J., *Business Behaviour,* Value and Growth (1959).

Baumol's sales maximisation principle can be illustrated with the aid of Fig. 37.3. In Fig. 37.3, we have compared two equilibria of the firm; the first equilibrium is the equilibrium) of the firm when its objective is sales or revenue maximisation while the second equilibrium represents the equilibrium of the firm when the objective is profit-maximisation.

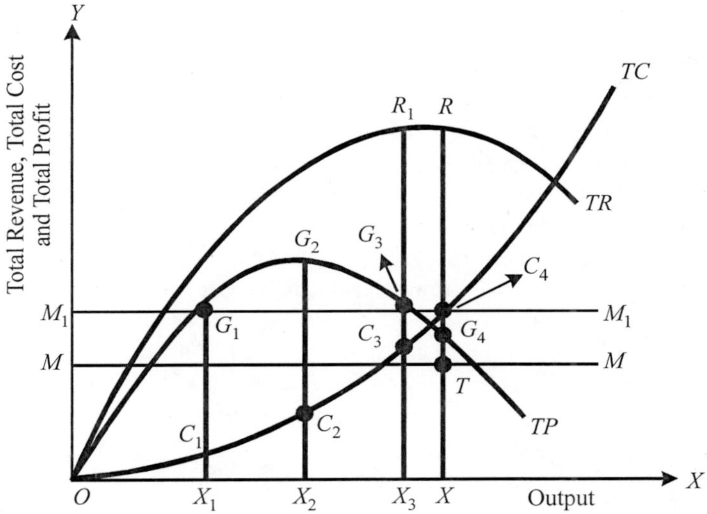

Fig. 37.3

We have shown three curves in the Fig. 37.3—*TR* (Total Revenue), *TC* (Total Cost) and *TP* (Total Profit) curves. The *TP* curve represents the difference between *TR* and *TC*. The *TP* curve reaches its peak at G_2 and G_2X_2 is the highest or maximum profit. OX_2 is the profit-maximising output in the diagram. If the objective of the firm is to maximise its profit, then it shall produce OX_2 output. Likewise, the *TR* curve reaches its peak at *R,* and *RX* is the maximum sales revenue of the firm. *OX* is the sales revenue maximising output. If sales maximisation is the objective of the firm, it will produce *OX* output. [It should be observed that the sales-maximisation output *(OX)* is larger than the profit maximising output *(*OX_2*).*] Now let us suppose that the sales maximisation objective of the firm is subject to the *minimum profit constraint.* In other words, the firm is required to earn a minimum amount of profit to satisfy the shareholders. Suppose, the minimum profit constraint is repre-sented in the diagram by the line

MM. Now the minimum profit constraint *OM* (or *TX*) is smaller than the actual profit (G_4X) being earned by the firm when it produces the sales-maximising output of *OX.* So the firm in question will go ahead by producing the sales-maximising output of *OX* as shown in the diagram. Now suppose that the minimum profit constraint is *OX* instead of being *OM.* The line M_1M_1 indicates the newly-risen minimum profit constraint. The sales-maximising output OM_1 now does not yield the minimum profit represented by the line M_1M_1. The firm will now give up its sales-maximising objective and retreat backwards to produce OX_3 output. This output does not bring maximum sales revenue to the firm, but it does assure the minimum profit of OM_1 (or, G_3X_3) to the shareholders. In other words, the firm waters down the sales maximisation objective to assure minimum profit to its shareholders. It may be pointed out that the minimum profit constraint line M_1M_1 intersects the Total Profit curve *(TP)* at the point G_1 as well. This implies that the firm can, if it likes, produce OX_2 output also. But, in actual practice, the firm will not opt for this output because at this output the total sales revenue is much less that what it is at the output OX_2. The firm will, thus, go in for OX_2 output because it assures larger sales revenue to it. Thus, the output is much larger under the sales maximisation objective (with minimum profit constraint) than under the objective of profit maximisation.

The main advantage of Baumol's sales maximisation hypothesis lies in the fact that it provides still another motive to the modern business firm for its operations, namely, the motive of sales maximisation in addition to the motive of maximum profit. Baumol's hypothesis also furnishes a more realistic explanation of the behaviour of an oligopolistic firm. The oligopolistic firm, as is well-known, is influenced more by the sales-maximisation motive than by the consideration of profit-maximisation. Baumol's hypothesis also explains, why an oligopoly firm resorts to non-price competition (i.e., advertising, publicity, product differentiation, quality improvement, etc.) in relation to the other oligopolistic firms. In other words, the oligopoly firm in question does not adopt price-cutting as a method to compete with other firms in the market. The reason is obvious. The effect of price-cutting by the firm on its sales-revenue is uncertain. Price-cutting by the firm will be followed by price-cutting by other firms as well. The result is that there shall be little or no improvement in the sales-revenue of the firm in question. Price-cutting may not, thus, bring about any increase in the sales revenue of the firm concerned. But expenditure on advertisement, publicity, product differentiation, etc, is bound to increase the sales of the firm. It is on account of this that an oligopoly firm keeps the price of its product fixed but competes with its rivals through increased expenditure on advertisement, etc.

The main drawback of Baumol's hypothesis is that it has not been able to divest itself completely of the profit-motive. Though Baumol emphasises sales-maximisation as the objective of the firm, yet he does not rule out the profit-motive altogether. He stresses the importance of earning adequate profit by the firm to satisfy the shareholder. He goes so far as to say that a firm should select that level of output which yields adequate profit to the shareholders, even though it may not lead to sales-maximisation. In other words, he is prepared to sacrifice the objective of sales-maximisation to ensure adequate profit to the shareholders of the firm.

Effect of Changes in Overhead Costs on Price and Output

Baumol's sales maximisation hypothesis also gives rise to an important conclusion with regard to the influence of changes in overhead or fixed costs on the price and output of a commodity produced by a firm. The traditional price theory (based on the assumption of maximisation of profit) held the position that a change in overhead or fixed costs did not influence the equilibrium output of the firm, because the equilibrium output was determined as per the marginalist principle by the equality of *MR* and *MC*, and the *MC*, in its turn, was not affected by changes in overhead costs. Hence, changes in overhead costs had no effect on the equilibrium level of output. Nor did changes in the overhead costs affect the price in the short period. Thus, the conclusion of the traditional price theory was that changes in overhead costs produced no effect on the output or price of the commodity in the short period. Baumol, however, challenged this assertion of the traditional price theory with his sales maximisation hypothesis, and pointed out that changes in fixed costs do affect prices and outputs of the firm even in the short period. Baumol's argument can be illustrated with the help of Fig. 37.4.

In Fig. 37.4, *TP* is the total profit curve in the initial situation. The minimum profit required to be earned by the firm is indicated by *OM* and *MM* line is the minimum profit constraint line for the firm. If the objective of the firm is profit-maximisation, then it shall produce *OX* output, because at this output *GX* profit is the maximum. Butif the objective of the firm is sales maximisation subject to the minimum profit constraint, it shall produce OX_2 output. Now let us suppose that the government levies a lump-sum levy on a the profit of the firm to the extent of IT_1. This means

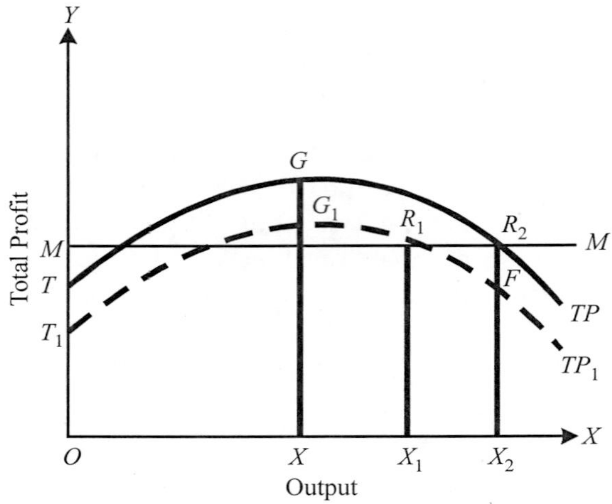

Fig. 37.4

that the overhead or fixed cost of the firm will rise by this amount, or in other words, the profit of the firm will be reduced by this amount the reduced profit of the firm is indicated in the diagram by the dotted curve TP_1. In other words, the total profit curve descends downwards on account of the increased fixed costs consequent upon the imposition of the levy. The new profit curve TP_1 (dotted curve) runs parallel to the original curve *TP*. Despite the increase in fixed costs, the profit-maximising output remains constant at the old *OX* level, confirming the conclusion of the traditional price theory, namely that the changes in fixed costs do not change the output and price in the short period. But as pointed out earlier, according to Baumol's sales maximisation hypothesis changes in fixed costs do influence outputs and prices in the short period. Before the imposition of the governmental levy, the firm was producing an output of OX_2, and was earning a profit of R_2X_2 at this output. But after the imposition of the levy, the firm's profit at this level of output is reduced to FX_2. Now this FX_2 profits is less' than the minimum profit constraint of *OM* (or, R_2X_2. Obviously, the firm shall not stick to this output of OX_2. It will reduce its output to OX_1, because this output enables it to earn the minimum profit of R_1X_1 indicated by the line *OM*. Due to the reduction in the output, the firm will also raise the price of the product. Thus, according to Baumol's hypothesis, the firm will change the output and price of the commodity even in the short period in response to changes in fixed costs.

Baumol has also applied his hypothesis to explain the incidence of corporation tax levied by the government on the profit of the firm. According to the traditional price theory (based upon the profit maximisation assumption), the entire money burden of the corporation tax will fall on the firm. The tax will, undoubtedly, increase the fixed costs (or, lower down the profit) of the firm as explained in the above diagram. But the firm shall not be able either to lower down its output or to raise the price to be charged from the consumers, meaning thereby that the entire burden will fall on the firm itself. But according to Baumol's hypothesis, 'the imposition of the corporation tax will reduce the total profit of the firm and compel it to cut down its output and raise the price of the product. Thus, a part of the money-burden of the corporation tax will be passed on to the shoulders of the customers, according to Baumol's sales maximisation hypothesis.

EXERCISES

1. Explain the sales maximisation model of Baumol. What are its important assumptions and limitations?
2. Discuss the full cost pricing theory. Mention its merits and demerits.

Multiple Choice Questions

3. (*i*) The managerial approach has been analysed and developed by
   (*a*) W.J. Baumol (*b*) Oliver E. Williamson
   (*c*) R.L. Marris (*d*) All of the above [*Ans.* (*d*)]

   (*ii*) According to W.J. Baumol, the typical oligopolist's objective is
   (*a*) sales maximisation subject to minimum profit constraint
   (*b*) to attain maximum profit
   (*c*) to incur minimum cost
   (*d*) to get maximum output with minimum cost [*Ans. (a)*]

   (*iii*) What is full-cost?
   (*a*) Average Direct Costs (*b*) Average Overhead Costs
   (*c*) Normal Margin for Profit (*d*) All above taken together
   [*Ans.* (*d*)]

   (*iv*) According to Hall and Hitch, business firms under oligopoly and monopolistic competition do not determine price and output by comparing *MC* and *MR* but fix prices on the basis of
   (*a*) full average cost of production
   (*b*) full fixed cost of production
   (*c*) satisfactory margin of profit
   (*d*) none of the above [*Ans. (a)*]

   (*v*) Under oligopoly, the price of the product is fixed at the point
   (*a*) of kink in the demand curve
   (*b*) where $MC = MR$
   (*c*) where $AC = MC$
   (*d*) where $AC = MR$ [Ans. (*a*)]

Chapter 38

INTERDEPENDENT PRICES[1]

1. INTRODUCTION

In the preceding chapters of pricing and output, we confined ourselves to the partial equilibrium analysis. The price of a single commodity was assumed to be determined by its demand and supply. When the price of a commodity is said to be determined by the conditions of demand and supply pertaining to it, it may seem as though this price is an isolated phenomenon, standing more or less apart from the prices of other goods; but this is an erroneous impression. We must always bear in mind that the prices of various commodities are rarely determined in isolation. They are, in fact, a system in which each is related to all the rest in greater or lesser degree. In other words, the price of a commodity is not the result of isolated factors of demand and supply for it alone, but of a multitude of interrelated factors in which the prices of many other goods are involved. Therefore, the entire price system comes under the analysis of general equilibrium.

Each price is related to every other price, for the simple reason that the money incomes (or purchasing powers) of consumers are limited, as are also the means (factors) of production. In simple words, the interdependence of all prices goes back to the fundamental fact of scarcity, which underlines all things economic. If a person spends a portion of his income for commodity *X*, he is unable to spend it for commodity *Y*; for the simple reason that he cannot eat his bread and have the money too. Every consumer has to decide how to spend his limited income or which commodities are to be purchased and how much of them is to be purchased. These decisions will affect the price of all the commodities the consumers buy. If the consumers decide that they need more amusement, and they spend more on theatres or on travel than they previously did, they must

1. This analysis is also known as the Pricing of Related Goods.

reduce their purchases of other commodities. By doing so, they add to the demand for theatres and such other commodities and thus tend to raise their prices. While on the other hand, the consumers reduce the demand for those goods which come under the second group, such as, clothing, furniture, etc.; and therefore, tend to depress their prices. It means that a change in the consumption pattern may shift the direction of demand so as to affect strongly the prices of various goods produced in the economy.

Similarly, the principle of opportunity costs on the supply side will reinforce these observations. According to this principle of opportunity costs, any factor of production can be used in one industry only on the condition that firms in that industry will pay a price for it equal to what it would be what in other industries. This, establishes a price connection between all commodities in so far as they draw on the same basic resources of land, labour and capital.

Hence, we find that the prices are not isolated, but are interrelated in an elaborate, coherent whole. This complex of prices is known as the price system. In the following section we shall examine some specific types of relations that are specially close, i.e., relations between the prices of related goods.

2. SUBSTITUTES AND COMPLEMENTS

The two important types of related commodities are substitutes and complements. Some goods are fairly good substitutes for each other. The examples of such goods are cane sugar and beet sugar, aluminium and magnesium, television and movies, tea and coffee, etc. The degree of substitutability varies from the cases in which one commodity is an almost perfect substitute for another, to cases of only poor substitutability. Beet sugar is an almost perfect substitute for cane sugar, but vegetables are very poor substitutes for meat. Similarly, tea and coffee are assumed to be very close substitutes but bread and fruits are not close substitutes to each other. Thus, where the possibilities for substitution are good, changes in the price of one commodity will result in similar changes in the price of its substitute. For example, if the price of sugar increases, people will switch to the cheaper gur, then the increased demand for gur will cause its price to increase along with that of sugar, although not necessarily to the same degree. On the other hand, if sugar becomes cheaper, people will buy more sugar and less gur, resulting in the price of gur to go down and the fall ‘ in the price of gur is not necessarily the same.

The other type of goods are complements rather than substitutes. Complement goods are those goods which are jointly used. The examples of such complements are: ink and paper, tennis rackets and tennis balls, scooter (automobile) and petrol, window frames and window glass, etc. Here again, changes in the demand for, or price of, one of the complementary commodities will cause responsive changes in the demand for, or price of the other; but in this case the change will be in the opposite direction. For example, if tennis rackets become expensive (or the price of tennis rackets increases), people would play less tennis and this would lead to a reduction in the demand for tennis balls and finally resulting in the prices of both the complementary goods (here tennis rackets and tennis balls) to go down.

The extent of the changes in the demand and price of the related commodities can be measured by the cross-elasticity of demand. In simple words, cross-elasticity of demand states the extent to which the demand for one commodity responds to changes in the price of the other commodity. Mathematically, the formula of cross-elasticity can be written as below:

$$\text{Cross-elasticity of demand between } X \text{ and } Y \text{ commodities} = \frac{\text{Percentage change in the quantity of } Y \text{ bought}}{\text{Percentage change in the price of } X}$$

When commodities X and Y are good substitutes for each other the cross-elasticity will be positive and the magnitude will be high. If the substitutes are perfect or nearly so, the value of cross-elasticity will approach infinity.

When commodities X and Y are complementary, the cross-elasticity will be negative. And the absolute magnitude of this elasticity coefficient will indicate the degree of complementarity between the two commodities.

The degree of substitutability is very important for the distinction between perfect competition, imperfect competition, product differentiation and pure monopoly. Where the products of different firms are perfect substitutes for each other, we have only one homogeneous commodity, then it will be a situation of pure competition. Where the products of different firms are fairly good but not perfect substitutes, i.e., the products are slightly different; then it will be a situation of product differentiation or monopolistic competition. Where the products of different firms are very poor substitutes, then each firm will act as pure monopoly.

But, for the present discussion of interdependent prices or mutually related prices, we assume that perfect competition prevails in commodity markets. There are four different ways in which the problem of interdependent prices may arise:

(*i*) Pricing under Joint Demand,
(*ii*) Pricing under Composite Demand,
(*iii*) Pricing under Joint Supply, and
(*iv*) Pricing under Composite Supply.

Now we shall discuss these different ways one by one in the following manner.

3. PRICING UNDER JOINT DEMAND

Joint demand exists when two goods are closely complementary. Two goods will be complementary in the sense that the use of one implies the use of the other. For instance, the demand for petrol is associated with the demand for motor cars, the demand for tennis balls is linked to the demand for tennis rackets, etc. An increase (or decrease) in the demand for one of these goods will be accompanied by an increase (or decrease) in the demand for the other. An increase in the demand for tea might well cause an increase in the price of sugar.

Joint demand is often associated with derived demand. This occurs in the building of a house, where there is a derived, joint demand for lumber, stone, plaster, cement, and other materials. In the production of most commodities, we find a similar situation. However, joint demand should not be confused with derived demand. Derived demand arises from the fact that goods at more or less remote stages of production are needed for the final use. It (derived demand) refers to the successive stages of production. Where joint demand refers to the situation in which a number of articles (goods) may be demanded simultaneously at anyone stage or by the consumer himself for the final use. This distinction between derived demand and joint demand rests in the difference between succession and simultaneity.

Thus the case of Joint demand may arise in both for factors of production and for the goods of final use. The valuation of complementary goods (goods demanded jointly) is complicated by the fact that the demand schedules of such goods are interrelated. The demand for motor cars will be seriously affected if petrol becomes scarce. We can draw a separate demand curve for motor cars only on the assumption that there would be no change in the supply conditions of petrol (or of any other product required for using a motor car). It is to be noted that Marshall's statement of the Law of Demand (and his concept of the Demand Curve) assumes "other things remaining the same." Therefore. the problem of pricing under joint demand is a complex one. It can be discussed under the following two situations: (*i*) Situation of Varied Proportions; and (*ii*) Situation of Fixed Proportions.

In the situation of varied proportion, the purchaser of several commodities (or factor inputs) that are to be used jointly, can vary the proportions in which they are to be combined. In such a situation, it is possible to estimate the importance of each commodity, independently of the others. The method of *marginal analysis* is used to find out the importance of each commodity or factor input as the case may be. For example, a farmer wants to grow wheat. For this he demands several inputs together such as seeds, fertilisers, water, etc. Although, these factor inputs are used jointly, yet it is possible for the farmer to change the proportion in which they can be used to produce a given quantity of wheat. By doing so he is able to find out the individual demand schedules for these inputs. Suppose, he wants to find out the worth, or importance of fertilisers in the production of wheat. He will try a number of combinations of seeds, fertilisers, water, etc. by varying the proportion of fertilisers and keeping the quantities of other inputs constant. The different contributions of factor inputs applied to the production of wheat will result in different levels of output. In this way he can determine what the fertilisers are worth to him. Thus, it is possible to construct a separate demand schedule (or demand curve) for fertiliser, in spite of the fact that it is used in combination with other inputs.

In such circumstances, we really have a case of simple derived demand and not a true case of joint demand at all. It is, therefore, possible to treat it as a problem of isolated price, by comparing separate demand and cost schedules, as we have used in the previous chapters on pricing and output under various market situations.[2]

The real problem of pricing under joint demand arises when the proportions in which complementary goods are employed are fixed by technical considerations which permit no variation. In such a situation it is impossible to separate the demand for one of the goods from that of the

---

2. The price is determined by applying the rule, $MC = MR$. Since marginal cost (MC) is given and marginal revenue (MR) is calculated by the above method of marginal analysis it, becomes very ,simple to determine the price.

other. For example, in the making of eyeglasses, there is a joint demand for lenses and frames in a fixed proportion. Similarly, in the product of number of other commodities, the factors of production are jointly demanded in the fixed proportion. The problem of price determination in such a case of fixed proportion can be solved by means of demand and supply curves not greatly different from those we have already discussed. Here, we have to set a single demand curve for eyeglasses (final output) against the two different supply (cost) curves for. frames (the first factor input) and lenses (the second factor input) in such a way as to find the separate equilibrium prices for frames (first factor input) and lenses (second factor input). This case is illustrated in Panel (*a*) and (*b*) of Fig. 38.1. Here, we assume the situation of perfect competition. In Panel (*a*) of Fig. 38.1, S_f S_f curve represents the marginal costs of producing the frames. In Panel (*b*) of Fig. 38.1, S_LS_L represents the marginal costs of producing the lenses. Since two lenses (glasses) are used with each frame, the unit quantities shown on the horizontal axis indicate pairs of lenses and the prices shown on the vertical axis indicate the prices per pair of lenses.

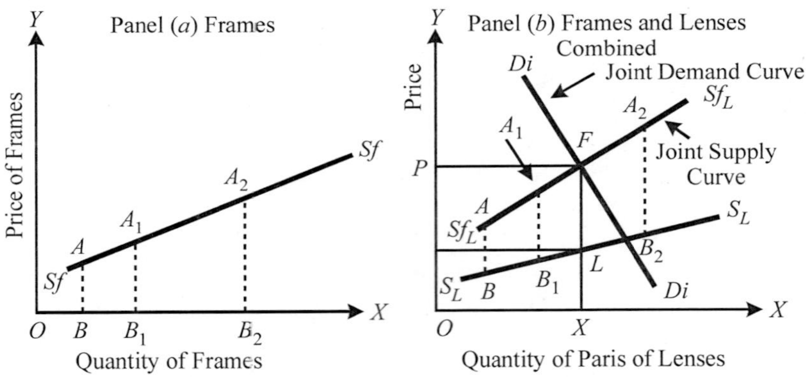

Fig. 38.1

Now, we combine the curves, S_fS_f and S_LS_L in order to obtain the combined cost of two factor inputs (frame and lenses) in the finished product (eyeglasses or finished glasses). We do this by superimposing the curve S_fS_f upon the curve S_LS_L in Panel (*b*) of Fig. 38.1. Thus S $S_{fL}S_{fL}$ curve is drawn by adding vertically the S_f S_f curve of Panel (*a*) into the S_LS_L curve of Panel (*b*). Therefore, the distances AB, A_1B_1 and A_2B_2 in Panel (*b*) will be exactly the same as the corresponding distances in Panel (*a*) Therefore, $S_{fL}S_{fL}$ is the combined cost (supply) curve for the two constituents (factorinput) of the finished glasses (eyeglasses). Now let us assume that D_jD_j is the joint demand curve for the two products in the finished glasses. It (D_jD_j) intersects the supply (cost) curve ($S_{fL}S_{fL}$) at point *E*. Therefore, at price *OP*, demand and supply are in equilibrium. In other words, the equilibrium price for eyeglasses is *OP*. At this level, the price for lenses (first factor input) should be equal to *XL* and the price for frames (second factor input) should be equal to *LF*. Hence, under joint demand, we may determine the separate equilibrium prices for the complementary products.

In the above analysis, we have discussed the price determination under joint demand, i.e., the determination of the prices of two complementary goods. Now we shall try to examine the relationship between the prices of two jointly demanded commodities. As we have already mentioned, changes in the price of one of the complementary commodities will cause an opposite change in the price of the other commodity.

This is illustrated with the help of Panel (*a*) and Panel (*b*) of Fig. 38.2. Panel (*a*) and Panel (*b*) of Fig. 38.2, explain the positions of demand, supply and price of the two complementary commodities, bread and butter respectively. Suppose, the price of bread increases (from *OP* to OP_1) due to some restrictions (tax) imposed by the government. Thus, the supply

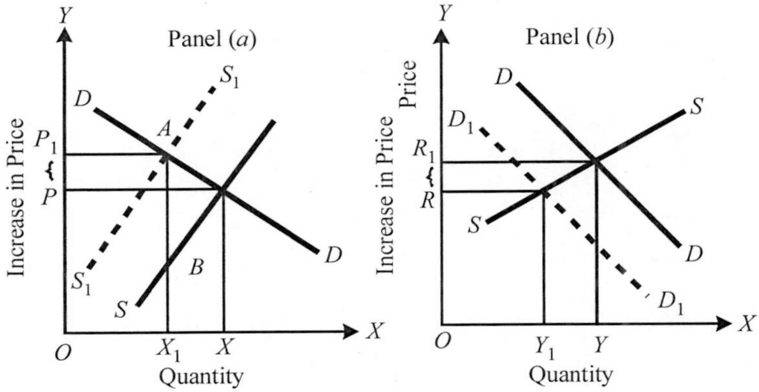

Fig. 38.2

curve of bread has moved up (from *SS* to S_1S_1) by the extent of the tax (*AB*). Now at the higher price (OP_1), the demand for bread falls (from *OX to* OX_1). Now since the demand for bread has been reduced, there will be a similar reduction in the demand for butter. In other words, the demand curve, for butter in Panel (*b*) shifts from, *DD* to D_1D_1, As a result of this, the price of butter goes down from *OR* to OR_1. Here, we may see that the increase in the price of bread is more than the increase in the price of butter. The reverse will happen, if the price of bread falls instead of rising.

4. PRICING UNDER COMPOSITE DEMAND

When a commodity is demanded for more than one use, it is said to be in composite demand. The demand for such goods is the aggregate of the demand of the various users. For example, wool will be demanded by the textile industry, carpet manufacturers, blanket manufacturers, hosiery manufacturers, and many others. An increase in the demand for anyone use, say clothing, will raise the price of wool and affect the prices of all other commodities made from wool. Another good illustration of a commodity for which the demand is a composite of many separate demands would be electricity. It is demanded for light, heat and also for various production purposes. The same is true for the factors of production-skilled and unskilled labour, land, and capital.

The determination of price of a commodity having composite demand is not a complex task. Like other commodities, the price of such a commodity is also determined by its demand and supply curves.

Where the demand for a good is composite, its total demand schedule (or demand curve) will be the sum of the demand schedules (curves) for it in all the different uses to which it is put. For example, at each price on demand schedule for wool, a certain quantity of it will be bought by the textile industry, a certain additional quantity will be bought by carpet manufacturers, a certain additional quantity will be demanded by blanket producers and hosiery manufacturers and so on. The sum of these quantities constitutes the total effective demand at each price. This will give us a demand curve of the usual type, i.e., it will be a negatively sloping curve. The supply (or cost) curve for wool is given. Now it will become a simple price problem. The equilibrium price will be attained at that point where the total effective demand, so computed, equals the total effective supply. Under perfect competition, in the long-run, the equilibrium price will tend to equal the optimum cost of production.

In the case of composite demand, because the total demand for the commodity is made up of many separate demands, a change in anyone of the component demand schedules will have only a slight (negligible) effect on the price. For instance, an increase in the demand for socks or mufflers will have very little effect upon the price of wool, because only an infinitesimally small portion of the total demand for wool is derived from that for socks or mufflers. On the other hand, a change in the conditions of supply (cost) for a commodity whose demand is composite may affect greatly the prices of all the products in which it is used.

5. PRICING UNDER JOINT SUPPLY OR JOINT COSTS

An interesting relationship, and one which gives rise to a number of economic problems, is that of joint supply. Joint supply exists when two or more products are automatically produced together. In such a case, joint costs arise; the cost of producing one of the commodities cannot be clearly separated from the cost of producing the other. In mining ore, the production of both silver and copper results in a joint cost. The production of coal gas entails the production of coke. The production of petrol leads to the production of benzene and fuel oil. Similarly, from the ginning of cotton there results, not only the cotton-fibre, but also the seed, from which a valuable oil can be extracted. Also in a meat-packing industry, hams, bacon, hides, blood, bone, hair, glue, fats, gut, and other useful raw materials are produced more or less together. All Cases of so-called by-products fall in the same category. In these cases of joint supply, we have just the opposite of joint demand. Instead of several articles derived from separate sources being combined in use, and therefore, demanded jointly, we have several articles which are separately demanded but which are combined in production and, therefore, supplied jointly. Thus, *joint supply can be defined as that relation where two or more products are obtained at the same time, in a single production process.* It is also called joint costs, because, where two or more commodities are produced together, their costs of production cannot be entirely separated. We cannot produce beef unless we also produce hides. Similarly, when copper and silver found in the same ore, how can one say what part of the cost of mining the ore is the cost of producing copper and what part of the cost of producing silver?

Therefore, in the case of joint products, the problem is, how to find the marginal cost of each of the products. If the marginal cost is found, we can apply the theory of value and say that the price of each of the joint products will tend to equal its marginal cost (assuming perfect competition in the market). For pricing under joint supply, we divide joint products into two categories:

(*i*) Joint products whose relative proportions can be varied, and

(*ii*) Joint products whose relative proportions are fixed.

In the case of the first type of joint products, it is possible to calculate the marginal cost of each of the products with the help of marginal analysis. Suppose, for example, 10 units of gas and 8 units of coke can be obtained by incurring a cost of Rs. 200. Also, suppose that with a new production process it is possible to get 11 units of gas and 1 unit of coke with a cost outlay of Rs. 220. Then the marginal cost of gas is Rs. 20 per unit. With variable proportions, the conditions of equilibrium are:

(*a*) in the situation of long-run perfect competition, $MC = P = MR$.

(*b*) in the situation of imperfect competition, $MC = MR$.

The real problem of pricing arises when the relative proportion of joint products is fixed. For example, the proportion between cotton-fibre and cotton-seeds is more or less fixed. To get more fibre, we have to increase the quantity of cotton. The problem here is to find out the separate marginal costs of the two products, i.e., their prices can be determined separately. The solution to this problem is the same as is worked out under the joint demand (Fig 38.1). Now, Panel (*a*) and Panel (*b*) of Fig. 38.3 illustrate this case in Panel (*a*) of Fig. 38.3, d_fd_f curve shows the separate demand curve for cotton-fibres while in Panel (*b*) of Fig. 38.3, d_s d_s shows the separate demand curve for cotton-seeds. The combined demand curve for the fibres and seeds can be shown by superimposing d_f d_f and d_sd_s curves, using the latter (i.e., d_sd_s curve) as its base line. Therefore, in Panel (*b*) of Fig. 38.3. $D_{fs}P_{fs}$ indicates the combined demand curve for the two joint products (fibres and seeds). The construction of this curve ($D_{fs}D_{fs}$) is such that any distance between it and d_sd_s, such as A_1B_1, A_2B_2, or A_3B_3, exactly equal to the corresponding distances between d_fd_f and the horizontal axis in Panel (*a*) of Fig 38.3. In Panel (*b*) of Fig. 38.3, C_jC_j represents the marginal cost of producing the two commodities (cotton-fibres and seeds) jointly. We must remember that each unit space along the horizontal axis of Panel (*b*) indicates the combined unit of the two products (i.e., each unit may indicate, say, two bales of cotton and one ton of seeds). Similarly, along the vertical axis of Panel (*b*) we measure prices per two bales in the case of cotton-fibre and per ton in the case of cotton-seeds. Now equilibrium is reached at that point where the combined or effective demand curve $D_{fs}D_{fs}$ intersects the combined or effective supply (cost) curve C_jC_j. This point is *F* in Panel (*b*) of fig. 38.3, where the equilibrium quantity of cotton-fibres and cotton-seeds is equal to *OX*. The equilibrium price of the seeds will, therefore, be SX (= OP_3) per ton, and the price of the cotton-fibres will be SF (= P_3P) per two bales. Here, we observe that the costs are divided between the two products in proportion to their marginal demand prices.

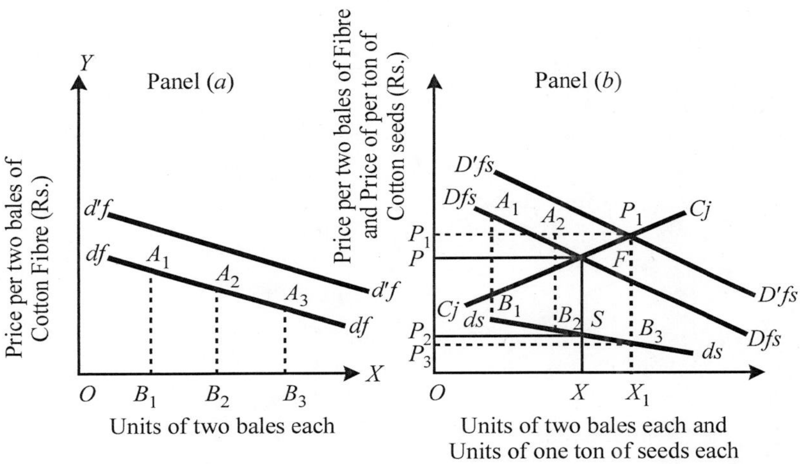

Fig. 38.3

Further, since the joint costs are apportioned between the two joint products according to the relative demand for them, the product, for which the demand is greater, will bear the larger part of the costs and consequently, it will be sold at a higher price than the price at which the other product would be sold. In the above diagram, the demand price of cotton-fibre is higher than that of cotton-seeds; therefore, cotton-fibre will be sold at a higher price than cotton-seeds. In Fig. 38.3, it is clear that the demand curve $d_f d_f$ or cotton-fibre [see Panel (*a*)] is higher than the demand curve $d_s d_s$ for cotton-seeds [see Panel (*b*)]. Consequently, the price *FS* of cotton-fibre is higher than the price *SX* of cotton-seeds.

Now, in case the demand schedule for anyone of the two (or more) joint products increases, its price will rise. and the price (s) of the other commodity (s) produced jointly with it may be expected to fall. For example, suppose, the demand schedule or demand curve for cotton-fibres in Panel (*a*) of Fig. 38.3 increases from $d_f d_f$ to $d'_f d'_f$; assuming the demand schedule (curve) for cotton-seeds remaining the same. Superimposing the new curve on $d_s d_s$, as before, we get the new combined demand curve $D'_{fs} D'_{fs}$ in Panel (*b*) of Fig. 38.3. This new combined demand curve $D'_{fs} D'_{fs}$ intersects the cost (supply) curve $C_j C_j$ at point F_1. Thus, point F_1 becomes the new equilibrium point. At this point, the output of both cotton-seeds and cotton-fibres increased from OX to OX_1. The increased demand for cotton-fibre has resulted in an increased supply of cotton-fibre. The price of cotton-fibre has increased from FS to F_1S_1 on account of rise in its demand. But the price of cotton-seeds has fallen from SX to S_1X_1, because its output has automatically increased with the increase in the production of cotton-fibre, though there is no increase in the demand for cotton-seeds. The increased supply of cotton-seeds can be disposed of only by reducing its price. Cotton-fibre now bears a larger portion of the joint costs, cotton-seeds a smaller portion, than was formerly the case. Similarly, a decrease in the demand schedule of cotton-fibre will make the opposite effect.

6. PRICING UNDER COMPOSITE SUPPLY

Composite supply refers to that case where two or more goods are perfect substitutes. This case is the opposite of composite demand. In composite demand, we have one product used for two or more purposes. In composite supply; we have two or more goods used for one purpose. In other words, different commodities satisfying the same want are said to be in composite supply. Composite supply commodities are substitutes of one another; e.g., tea and coffee, roadways and railways transport, butter and margarine, beet-sugar and cane-sugar, etc.[3]

Perfect cases of composite supply are rare, for it is not often that one commodity is a perfect substitute for another. Usually, there are slight differences which make one of them better adapted to certain uses than its competitor. In some cases, however, the differences are negligible; for instance, beet-sugar and cane-sugar are so close that an average consumer cannot find the difference between them.

The price of substitutes (composite supply goods) move in the same direction. If the price of tea falls, some people will use tea for coffee. The demand for coffee will fall and its price will fall. Goods which are substitutable for one another are also called *competiting goods.*

The price of commodities that are in composite supply will be determined by the cost of producing them and by their marginal utilities or marginal net products. In case the products (or factor inputs) are nearly perfect substitutes (such as beet-sugar and cane-sugar), they can be combined into one supply schedule, showing several quantities of each

3. The factors of production may also constitute a case of composite supply. For example, labour and capital, so far as the one can be substituted for the other, may be said to constitute a case of composite supply.

of the two substitutes that will be offered at each of a series of corresponding prices. That is, at one particular price, a certain quantity of beet--sugar and a certain quantity of cane-sugar will be produced; the sum of these constitutes the effective (combined) supply at that price, and so on for every possible price. Thus, we are able to draw the combined supply schedule of the close substitutes. The separate demand schedules for each are already known to us. Thus the pricing problem of composite supply becomes very simple. Production of the two substitute commodities will be carried to the point where their marginal costs are the same, and the price (same for both) will be fixed at that level where the marginal demand-price equals its marginal cost.[4]

In conclusion, we can say that the problem of interdependent prices discussed above under the four main headings is of paramount importance. It touches almost every branch of production. The demand and supply of most of the commodities and resources are closely interconnected with each other. And the value of a thing may depend on the remote influences affecting the 'value of a thing. The price of petrol, for example, depends on the fare tables of the tramway company. For if the tram fare is reduced, more people would ride in them in preference to buses. The buses would be making smaller journeys in that case, and the demand for petrol would fall. Hence the prices of most commodities are interconnected with each other.

EXERCISES

1. Explain the problem of interdependent prices. How are the prices of commodities determined when they are produced jointly under perfect competition?
2. Write short notes on the following:
   (*i*) Joint Demand
   (*ii*) Composite Demand
   (*iii*) Joint Supply
   (*iv*) Composite Supply
3. Explain the pricing problem under joint demand and under joint supply (or joint costs).
4. Distinguish between substitutes and complements. How can you measure the degree of substitutability and complementarity?

4. This case of composite supply has not been represented with the help of a diagram, but if so desired, it can easily be shown diagrammatically. Any change in the price of one of the substitute commodities will result in a similar change in the price of the other.

Multiple Choice Questions

5. (*i*) Which of the following pairs of commodities is an example of substitutes
   (*a*) Coffee and milk (*c*) Pen and ink
   (*b*) Diamond and cow (*d*) Mustard oil and coconut oil
   [*Ans*. (*d*)]

   (*ii*) For most consumers apples and oranges are substitute goods. Therefore, we would expect a rise in the price of apples to lead to
   (*a*) a fall in the price of oranges
   (*b*) an upward change in the demand curve of oranges
   (*c*) a leftward shift in the supply curve of apples
   (*d*) a rightward shift in the supply curve of oranges [*Ans*. (*b*)]

   (*iii*) A fall in the relative price for fruit would
   (*a*) lead to a fall in the demand for fruits
   (*b*) have no effect on the demand for potatoes
   (*c*) increase the quantity of sweets demanded
   (*d*) none of the above is correct [*Ans*. (*b*)]

   (*iv*) If two goods are complements, this means that a rise in the price of one commodity will induce
   (*a*) an upward shift in demand for the other commodity
   (*b*) a rise in the price of the other commodity
   (*c*) a downward shift in demand for the other commodity
   (*d*) no shift in demand for the other commodity [*Ans*. (*c*)]

Chapter 39

LINEAR PROGRAMMING

1. INTRODUCTION

The technique of linear programming was developed in 1947 by the American mathematician, George B. Dantzig, for the purpose of scheduling the complicated procurement activities of the US Air Force. Actually, it was however, the Russian mathematician L.V. Kantorovich, who first formulated the technique of linear programming. Several other economists have made important contributions to this technique. Notable among these are T.C. Koopmans, R. Dorfaman, and W.W. Cooper. But we must undoubtedly award the honour to mathematician George Dantzig, inventor of the first succesful (and still one of the most efficient) general computational techniques, the *simplex method.* Since 1947, the technique of linear programming has made considerable advances both in theory as well as in its applications to practical problems in industry. The post-war development of computers has greatly contributed to the growth of linear programming as a device to solve the business problems of individual firms. Linear programming means the systematic planning or decision making which is made by the firm in relation to production. In the absence of this technique, the mechanics of making all the calculations of all the possible combinations of the productive inputs would pose a difficulty, if not an impossible task of the firm. Under the technique of linear programming the variables are put into equations and the equations are generally solved through the use of high-speed computers.

2. MEANING OF LINEAR PROGRAMMING

According to Prof. Leftwich, "Linear programming is the simplest and most widely used of the mathematical programming techniques that have come into vogue since World War II. It is a teehnique for solving maximisation and minimisation problems confronting decision making agencies subject to certain side conditions or constraints that limit what the agencies are able to do." This definition of linear programming states that linear programming is entirely a mathematical technique. Like the calculus of any branch of mathematics, it can only help us to find out the implications of the economic information which we are willing to assume. Thus, linear programming is a mathematical tool for the analysis of optimum decisions subject to constraints in the form of linear inequalities. Mathematically speaking, it applies to those problems which require the solution of maximisation or minimisation problems subject to a system of linear inequalities in terms of certain variables. In real sense, linear programming problems are concerned with the efficient (optimum) use or allocation of limited resources to fulfil desired objectives.

Now we shall discuss the assumptions of linear programming problems.

3. CHARACTERISTICS OR ASSUMPTIONS OF LINEAR PROGRAMMING

(1) *The Constraints.* In linear programming problems, the firm[1] is assumed to face a number of limitations within which it has to operate. For example, there may be quantity limitations on particular kinds of inputs or facilities used by the firm. The firm is also assumed to have limited number of alternative productior processes. Here a production process is defined in terms of a constant ratio of input. Therefore, production carried on with a given production process can be increased or decreased until input quantity limitations are reached.

(2) *Constant Price.* In linear programming problems, it is also assumed that all input and output prices are constant. It means that linear programming techniques follow the purely competitive approach to prices. Perfect competition prevails in both the markets— the commodity market and the factor market. As a result, prices are exogenously given to the individual firm.

(3) *Linearity.* In linear programming problems, it is assumed that the firm's input-output, output-output and input-input relations are linear. This assumption implies that the input-output coefficients are fixed in respect of all the available inputs and the number of products to be produced. In other words, a firm purchasing an input at a constant price

1. For simplicity, we discuss the case of a firm, but linear programming techniques can be and are used by agencies other than firms, for example, military procurement units, or governments, etc.

faces a linear *TC*-function for that input. Similarly, *TR*-function will also be linear when the product is sold at a constant price. Linearity of the input-output relations would also mean a constant *MRTS* and the resultant linear isoquant in respect of each item to be produced. Although, an isoquant is ordinarily a non-linear constant product curve for two resources, the linear-programming counterpart is a series of connected linear relations. Similarly, actual production functions may very well show non-linear relations between input and output. In linear programming problems they are assumed to be homogeneous of degree one.

4. MAXIMISATION PROBLEMS

Here, we shall consider two maximisation problems:

(1) One Output-Two Inputs Case,

(2) Multiple Outputs-Multiple Inputs Case.

1. One Output-Two Inputs Case

In can be considered in two ways—(a) Cost-outlay constraints, and (*b*) Input quantity constraints.

(*a*) *Cost Outlay Constraints.* Here we assume that a firm, producing one output *X* and using two inputs L and *K* seeks to maximise output subject to a given cost outlay. This problem is simple and similar to the previous theory of production. In our previous analysis we assumed the possibilities of continuous substitution between *L* and *K* but now we drop this assumption and instead suppose that there are only four processes (possible ratios of *K* to *L*) by which the firm can produce the product (*X*). By assumption, the firm faces constant input and output process.

Figure 39.1 illustrates that the four processes for the firm are the *A, B,* C, and *D.* They are linear production rays. On each process the ratio of inputs is constant. Say, process *A* requires 3 units of *K* and 1 unit of *L* to produce 20 units of *X.* Now if we want to double the output level, then 6 units of *K* and 2 units of *L* will be needed, i.e., the ratio remains the same (3 : 1). Similar will be the case for other production processes. The points on the various production rays showing any given level of output (*X*) can be joined by a series of straight lines and the resulting kinked curve is known as an isoquant. Also, the higher the output level, the farther from the origin the isoquant lies. The linear segment of an isoquant between two production processes will always be parallel to the corresponding linear segment of any other isoquant.

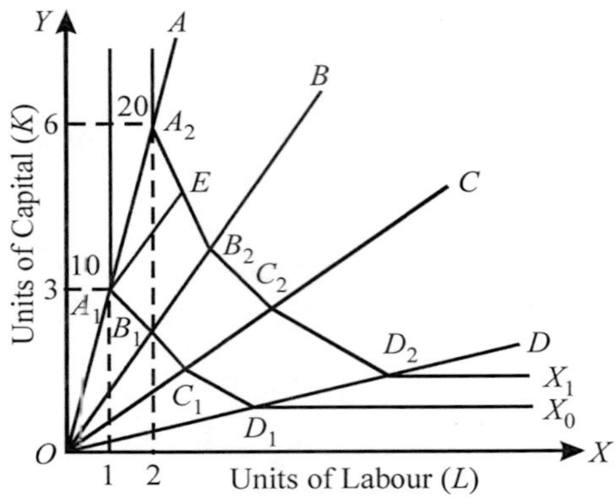

Fig. 39.1

Further, any point such as E on isoquant X_1 in Fig. 39.1 represents the simultaneous use by the firm of two processes to produce a given level of output (X_1), In. this case the firm is using processes A and B. Now at point E, quantity OA_1 of X is produced by process A and the remaining quantity of X ($A_1E = B_1B_2$) is produced by process B.

Now the cost outlay constraints of a firm can be repre-sented by an isocost curve. An isocost curve is also known as the budget line or the factor price line. In Fig. 39.2, the cost outlay of the firm has been represented by *MN* isocost curve which shows various points of the combinations of L and K available to the firm with the given cost outlay. Therefore, the isocost curve and production processes *OA* and *OD* tell the limits within which the firm is able to produce output. Any point on or within the triangles *ORS* is a possible combination of inputs L and K and lies on some isoquant of the firm. The area bounded by *ORS* is called *the area of feasible solutions* to the firm's problem. No production possibilities outside this area are open to the firm so far as input prices and cost outlay are constant.

From the feasible solutions to the firm's solution, *the optimal solution* must be found. The optimal solution will be one that maximises the firm's output subject to the cost outlay constraints. The optimal solution, here will occur at point C_2 at which the isocost curve touches the highest possible isoquant X_1. Therefore, to produce output level X_1, the firm will use process C. No other process than this C, will produce output level as high as X_1.

Further, a change in the cost outlay with the prices of factor inputs remaining the same, will not affect the process used, but will certainly affect the level of output. If cost outlay is reduced, i.e., the isocost curve takes the shape M_1N_1 in Fig. 39.2. Now *the area of feasible solutions* is *OGH.* The firm maximises output at point C_1 by using the same process *C*. The maximum output is X_0.

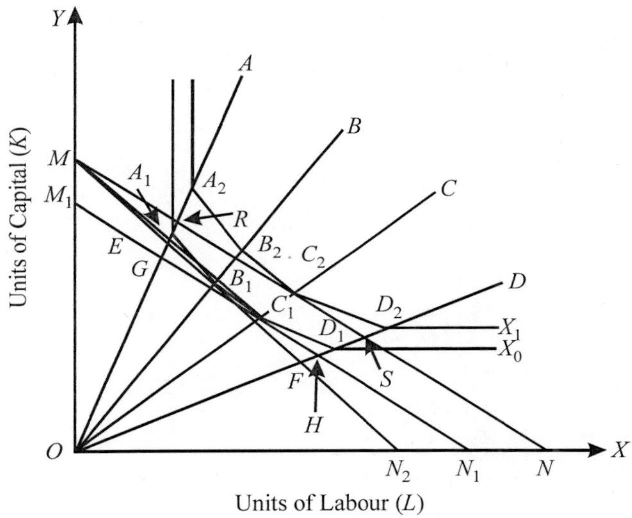

Fig. 39.2

Further, an increase in the prices of input (*L*) while price of *K* and cost outlay remaining the same, will shift the isocost position as MN_2 and the *area of feasible solutions* becomes *OEF.* Here, *the optimal solution* will be at point B_1 where the firm produces output X_o by using production process *B*.

(*b*) *Input Quantity Constraints.* Here, first we assume that one of the inputs is limited and the other input is abundant. In Fig. 39.3 only K_o of input *K* is available to the firm and input *L* is available in an unlimited quantity. In such a situation, *the area of feasible solutions* will be the triangle ORD_1. On this feasible solution, *the optimal solution* will be at point D_1 where the isoquant X_1 represents the highest output level available 'with quantity K_o of *K*. Process *D* used at level OD_1 will maximise the firm's output.

On the other hand, if input L is limited to L_o where input K is available in an unlimited quantity, the area of feasible solutions will be OA_3T and on which the optimal solution will be at point A_3. The relevant isoquant is X_3 and the maximum output level OA_3 will be produced by process A.

Now, *if both the inputs are limited* in quantity as input L is limited to L_o and input K is limited to K_o in Fig. 39.3. Subject to these limitations, *the area of feasible solutions* is *ORET*. *The optimal solution* lies at point *E*. The maximum output of the firm X_o which will be produced by process *B* and process *C*. Output *OM* will be produced by process *B* and the remaining output *ME* (= *NG*) will be produced by process *C*.

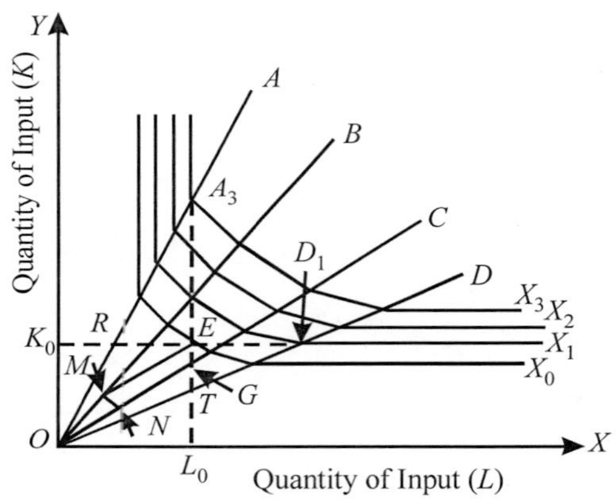

FIg. 39.3

2. Multiple Outputs-Multiple Inputs Case (Maximising Revenue)

Here we assume that the firm is producing two different outputs, *X* and *Y*. Also, the firm possesses four kinds of facilities (or the constraints), each of which is fixed in capacity. These facilities are shown in Fig. 39.4 as *M, N, R,* and *S*. These facilities could be such things as the assembling, painting, packaging and transport departments of the firm. These departments have limited capacities. The firm's attempt to produce the maximum output is limited by these constraints.

Profit (or rent) derived per unit of *X* and per unit of *Y* will depend upon the prices received for each of the outputs and the average variable cost (*AVC*) of each. The *AVC* is constant because the fixed units of variable inputs are needed per unit of *X* and *Y* regardless of the amount of *X* and *Y*. Profit (or rent) per unit of the output is equal to the price of the product minus its AVC, and thus will be a constant amount. The profits per unit of X and Y may be denoted by π_X and π_Y respectively.

Now the *objective function* can be established as below which the firm wants to maximise within the given constraints.

$$\pi_X X + \pi_Y Y = \pi \qquad ...(1)$$

where π = total profits (total rent)

$\pi_X X$ = profit (rent) of product X

$\pi_Y Y$ = profit (rent) of output Y

The objective equation (1) is the equation for a family of isorent curves (for different values of π).

In Fig. 39.4, we illustrate how the firm will maximise its profits (π) from two outputs X and Y. The production of these com-modities X and Y is subject to the constraints M, N, R, and S. Constraint M limits the production of Y; no more than OY_1 of Y can be produced. Constraint R limits the production of X; no more than OX_1 of X can be produced. The rectangle formed by act the lines Y_1M and X_1R indicates the combined effects of the two constraints M and R. However, constraints N and S limit the production of both X and Y.

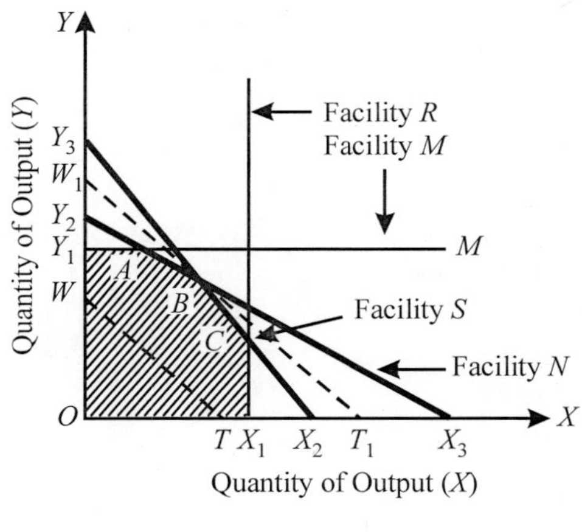

Fig. 39.4

The shaded area in the Fig. 39.4 represents *the area of feasible solutions.* In other words, Y_1A, AB, BC, and CX_1 constitute the linear-segmented production possibility curve. Now, the point of *optimal solution* on this area of feasible solution will depend upon the relevant isorent curve. In Fig. 39.4, WT is the isorent (or isorevenue) curve. Since, the optimal solution consists of the maximum revenue and, therefore, the isorevenue line W_1T_1 (which has the same slope as WT) hits the area of feasible solutions at point B. At this point B, the firm produces more of Y than of X. If there is some disturbance in the relative prices of X and Y, other things being the same, will also disturb the slope of isorevenue curve and thereby the point of optimal solution as well.

5. GRAPHICAL TREATMENT OF THE LINEAR PROGRAMMING PROBLEM

Linear Programming Solution: Revenue Maximisation

For simplicity we take *a case of two outputs and two inputs.* First, we must see how an inequality Y is represented graphically. Consider the inequality $2X + Y = 5$. Here, if only Y is produced (i.e., $X = 0$), the maximum output of Y will be equal to 5 units (= OM in Fig. 39.5). Similarly, if only X is produced (i.e., $Y = 0$), then the maximum of X will be equal to $2X + 0 = 5$ or $X = 2.5$ units (= ON units in Fig. 39.5).

Now, if we join these two extreme points M and N, with the help of a straight line, then it will tell us the various possible combinations of X and Y to be produced under full capacity.

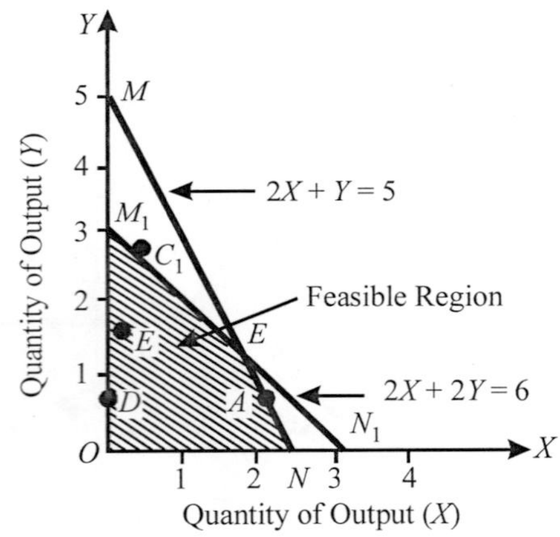

Fig. 39.5

In Fig. 39.5 any point such as A on the line MN which represents the equation $2X + Y = 5$ (and represents full use of capacity) clearly satisfies the inequality. But point such as B and C, or D which lies before the line MN also satisfies the inequality because it involves values of X and Y smaller than those which completely use up the capacity. Therefore, we observe that while a two-variable equation is represented by a line, a two-variable inequality is represented by a region.

We shall also see that the variables must also satisfy a second inequality, say $2X + 2Y \leq 6$ which is represented by a straight line M_1N_1 in Fig. 39.5. Now all the points which satisfy both inequalities must lie below both the lines *MN* and M_1N_1. i.e., below the area OM_1EN. It also satisfies $X \geq 0$ and $Y \geq 0$. This area is known as the *feasible region* to the linear programming problem.

Now we can represent the following problem diagrammatically in Fig. 39.6.

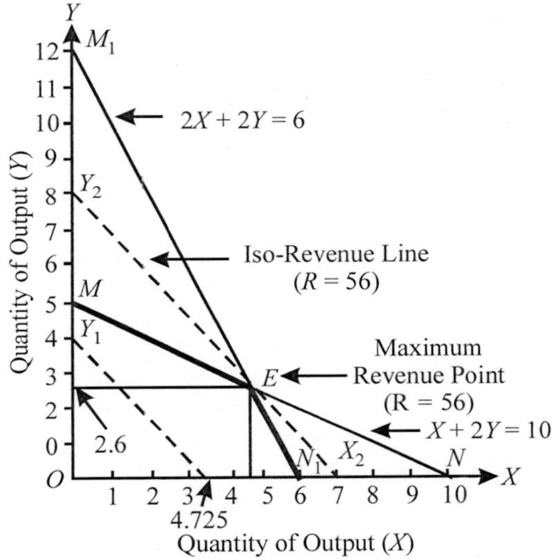

Fig. 39.6

$$\text{Maximise} \quad R = 8X + 7X$$
$$\text{Subject to} \quad X + 2Y \leq 10$$
$$(X \geq 0 \text{ and } Y \geq O)$$
$$2X + Y \leq 12$$

where R = Total Revenue which is constant

X and Y are two outputs

From revenue function, it is clear that price of X is equal to 8 (or $P_X = 8$) and price Y is equal to 7 (or $P_Y = 7$) because $R = P_X X. + P_Y Y.$

Now, the constraints are represented by the line *MN* ($X + 2Y = 10$) and M_1N_1 ($2X + Y = 12$) respectively. These two lines (or constraints) produce the area of feasible solutions which is $OMEN_1$ in Fig. 39.6. Now the solution to our above linear programming problem will lie either on or within the *feasible region* $OMEN_1$. For this we have to include our given objective function into our Fig. 39.6. It can be represented by the isorevenue curves. We convert our objective function in term of the isorevenue equation as,

$$Y = \frac{1}{7}R - \frac{8}{7}X$$

We may find a set of such equations (or lines) by assigning different values to *R*. Taking the partial derivative of *Y* w.r.t. *X* we get,

$$\frac{\partial Y}{\partial X} = \frac{8}{7}$$

or $$-\frac{\partial Y}{\partial X} = \frac{8}{7}$$

Since in equilibrium, $MRTS = \dfrac{P_X}{P_Y}$

∴ $$-\frac{\partial Y}{\partial X} = MRTS = \frac{P_X}{P_Y} = \frac{8}{7} = \text{slope of lisorevenue curve.}$$

The isorevenue curve can be represented by Y_1X_1 line in Fig. 39.6. To get the opti-mal solution we go on increasing the value of R, i.e., shifting our iso-reuenuecurve to the right (having the same slope because output prices are held constant) till we reach point *E* on our feasible region. At this point *E* we will obtain maximum possible revenue ($R = 56$). At this point, the firm produces 2.6 units of output *Y* and 4.725 units of output *X*. Therefore, the basic feasible solution or the optimal solution consists of,

$$R = 56$$
$$X = 4.725 \text{ units}$$
$$X = 2.6 \text{ units.}$$

Linear Programming Solution: Cost Minimisation

Cost minimisation is known as the dual problem of linear programming when the primal problem is of maximisation. Here, under the linear inequalities[2] (constraints), we must consider the fact that the value of all inputs used (input prices) to produce one unit of X_1 must be at least equal to the price of output or average revenue. Likewise, the value of all inputs

2. The positive constraints are imposed in order to emphasise that the imputed values of "shadow-prices" of inputs cannot be negative.

used in producing one unit of X_2 must be at least equal to its price (price of X_2).

Let us assume that the firm's objective function and constraints are given as follows:

Minimise, $C = 3X_1 + 5X_2$

Subject to $5X_1 + 2X_2 \geq 10$

$X_2 + X_2 \geq 4$

$X_1 + 3X_1 \geq 6$

where C = Total cost, X_1 and X_2 are the two inputs.

The above problem can be represented diagrammatically in Fig. 39.7. The three inequalitie (constraints) have been represented by MN, M_1N_1, and M_2N_2 respectively. The lower boundary of the feasible region has been shown by $MABN_2$.

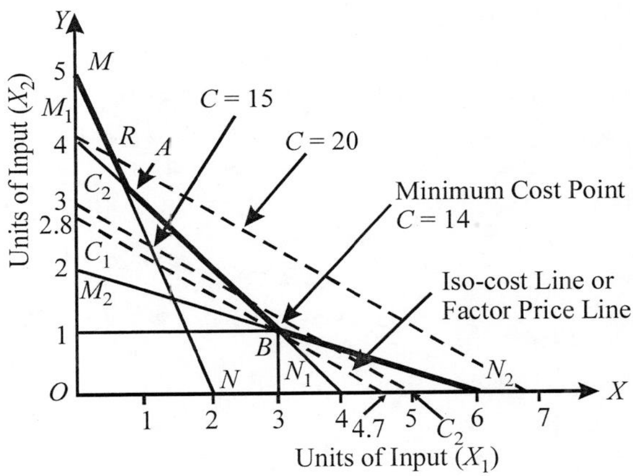

Fig. 39.7

Now, from the objective function we get the isocost equation as,

$$C = 3X_1 + 5X_2$$

or $$X_2 = \frac{1}{5}C - \frac{3}{5}X_1 \text{ (Isocost equation)}$$

∴ $$\frac{\partial Y_2}{\partial X_1} = -\frac{3}{5}$$

or $$-\frac{\partial Y_2}{\partial X_1} = \frac{3}{5} = \frac{PX_1}{PX_2} \text{ (In perfect competitive condition)}$$

where PX_1 =Price of input X_1, and PX_2 = Price of input X_2.

If we give different values to C (input prices remaining the same), we may get a family of isocost curves and we will choose that which minimises the objective function. We draw the isocost equation in Fig. 39.7 as C_1C_1 which touches our feasible region $MABN_2$ at point B. Therefore, point B will be the minimum cost (C) point. No other point than Bin our feasible region will be minimum cost point. For example, at point R, the firm has to incur $C = 20$. Therefore, the optimal solution will be at point B which will consist of,

$$C = 14$$
$$\text{Input } X_1 = 3\text{units}$$
$$\text{Input } X_2 = 1 \text{ unit}$$

6. APPLICATIONS OF LINEAR PROGRAMMING IN INDIAN ECONOMY

We know that in a developing country like India, the factors of production such as skilled labour, capital and raw material, etc. are very scarce. The econometrician is, therefore, faced with the problem of scarce resource allocation to meet the competing demands and conflicting objectives. The traditional methods of hunch are losing their importance in the present time economy. Therefore, the Indian planners are constantly in search of objective and result-oriented techniques for decision making at all levels of planning. The decisions may be of two types: (*i*) Non-programmed decisions, and (*ii*) Programmed decisions.

Non-programmed decisions consist of capacity expansion, plan location, product line diversification, etc. These are one time decisions. On the other hand, programmed decisions consist of budgeting, replacement, purchasing, transportations, maintenance, etc. Those decisions are changing decisions over time and, therefore, repetitive in nature. They require the cooperation of different departments holding different responsibilities.

In moden times, a number of new methods, techniques and tools have been developed by world econometricians. All these findings come under the science known as operations research. Some of these operations research techniques have been successfully applied in Indian situations, such as, business forecasting, inventory models and linear programming, etc.

Linear programming approach enables the Indian entrepreneurs to arrange for that combination of inputs which optimises the cost of production or the production profit or any other given objective function.

The *LP*-approach is also used to a class of problems where the limited resources are to be allocated in an optimum manner to the different competing facilities. There are not enough resources (or inputs) to perform all activities (or facilities) in an efficient manner.

Specifically, such problems are the following:

(*a*) How to minimise the use of scarce factor inputs, such as, imported raw materials, skilled labour, foreign capital, etc. in order to get maximum profit?

(*b*) What should be the best combination of products or product mix to be produced in order to reach the maximum profits.

(*c*) How many salesmen should a company have, such as, its cost is minimised?

(*d*) How to allocate the scarce resources of the country into different sectors of the economy?

The main applications of the linear programming are the following:

(1) We know that at the national level, well known *Mahalanobis Four Sector Model* was used to fix the objective of the *Second Five-Year Plan.* Therefore, in the formulation of the country's Five-Year Plans, the *linear programming approach* and *econometric-models* are being used in various areas, such as, foodgrain storage, transportation, multi-level planning (national, state and district levels) and urban system.

(2) Again, Indian Railways have applied linear programming in a number of areas. For instance, the location of Rajendra Bridge over the Ganges linking South Bihar with North Bihar at Mokamal in preference to other sites has been done with the help of linear programming approach. For other decisions, such as routing, transportation of various goods, etc., *LP*-approach is being tried. In order to facilitate this, a senior officer in charge of application of operations research techniques is appointed at Rail Bhavan at New Delhi.

(3) Again, linear programming approach is being used in agriculture also. It has been tried on a limited scale for crop rotation mix of cash crops and food crops, and fertiliser mix.

(4) Again, the national airlines are also using linear programming in the selection of routes and allocation of aircrafts to various routes. This has been facilitated by the computer system located in the headquarters. The officials found it most suitable and appropriate tool in solving their problems. Their decisions are totally based on the results of these computers.

(5) Again, the commercial institutions as well as the individual traders are also using linear programming techniques for cost reduction and profit

maximisation. The oil refineries are using *LP*-technique for blending decisions and for the improvement of finished products.

(6) Again, the paint industry decisions pertaining to the selection of the product mix and location of warehouse for distribution are taken with the help of *LP*-techniques. TELCO uses *LP*-approach for deciding what casting and forgings to make in their own shops and what should be bought from outside suppliers.

(7) Again, the steel-plants are using linear programming techniques for determining the combination of the final product such as billets, rounds, bars, plates and sheets.

(8) Again, the organisation like Hindustan Lever uses *LP*-approach for the distribution of consumers goods throughout the country. *LP*-approach is also used for capital budgeting decisions like the selection of one project from a number of different projects.

Hence, the linear programming approach can be applied to a variety of decisionmaking problems in planning which seeks to optimize a goal (or objective) from the total system's point of view, such as, resource allocations, product-mix, transportation, aircrafts routing, etc.

7. LIMITATIONS OF LINEAR PROGRAMMING APPROACH

(l) Linear programming technique assumes linearity between input-output, or output-output or input-input relations. Since, most of such relations are non-linear, this approach can be used for a limited number of cases.

(2) Linear programming technique also assumes that inputs are used in different production lines (different facilities) which are additive. This means that the sum total of input-use is less than or equal to the available input quantity. The problems where additivity of different activities is not possible, it cannot be solved by this technique (*LP*) of operations research. For example, the machine time needed for producing X_1 and X_2 cannot be added because some time is requited in converting the machine to its different uses.

(3) This approach is based on the assumption of constant returns in the economy which is not realistic.

(4) This approach again assumes input prices and output prices as parameters. In other words, there must be perfect competition in both the markets—the product market and the factor market. In real world, the situation of perfect competition cannot be seen.

(5) Sometimes, the inequalities define the constraints of a *LP*-problem. For simplicity, we use stack variables to remove there inequalities of the

constraints. But, in such cases, a firm has to move accordingly. In fact, the firm is helpless to accept these changes partly due to its (input) indivisibility and partly due to non-availability of scarce inputs. Therefore, we may of course, get optimal solution from *LP*-approach; however, it is not of much help to the firm in question.

EXERCISES

1. What do you understand by linear programming? Explain its important assumptions.
2. Explain the linear programming approach to the theory of production.
3. What are the chief applications of linear programming? Explain briefly the limitations of linear programming.
4. Solve the following linear programming problem by the diagrammatical method.

Maximise $R = X + 4Y$

Subject to $2X + 3Y \leq 4$

$3X + Y \leq 3$

$(X \geq 0 \text{ and } Y \geq 0)$

Where R is total revenue and X and Y are the two respective outputs.

Multiple Choice Questions

5. (*i*) Linear Programming is a technique to solve the problem of
   (*a*) maximisation (b) minimisation
   (*c*) any one of the above (*d*) none of the above [*Ans*. (*c*)]

   (*ii*) Linear Programming can be defined as a method to decide
   (*a*) the optimum combination of factors to produce a given output
   (*b*) the optimum combination of products to be produced by a given plant and equipment
   (*c*) between a variety of techniques to produce a commodity
   (*d*) anyone of the above [*Ans*. (*d*)]

PART 5
FACTOR PRICING

Chapter 40

THEORIES OF DISTRIBUTION

1. THE PROBLEM OF DISTRIBUTION

The economies of distribution deals with the distribution of the total product (or the total income) of the country among the various sections of the community. The division of the national income may be analysed with reference to the factors of production or with reference to the individuals composing the nation. The first type of analysis is known as *Functional Distribution;* while the second type of analysis is known as *Personal Distribution.*

Functional Distribution is a study of factor incomes, i.e., how much is earned by each factor of production. (land, labour, capital and organisation). The income of a factor of production is equal to the price that it can get for its services. For instance, wages and salaries are paid for labour, interest and dividends for capital and rent for land, etc. Thus, Functional Distribution can also be described as the "Pricing of the Factors of Production".

Personal Distribution is the study of individual incomes, i.e., how much is earned by the individuals of the nation. Personal distribution is a complicated task, because it is very difficult to determine the incomes of the individuals accurately. The income of an individual depends not only on the value of his services but also on the prevailing rules of the government, the social set-up and the distribution of political power. This is the reason why economists generally confine themselves to the study of relative incomes of the individuals, i.e., the inequalities of income and wealth of the individuals.

It should be noted that the economics of distribution does not discuss the problem of personal distribution, i.e., how the income of each individual is determined; but it deals with functional distribution, i.e., how the share of each factor is determined. Thus, two main issues are involved in the problem of distribution.

(1) What is to be distributed?

(2) How distribution takes place among the various factors of production?

The first issue deals with the nature and the amount of national income or national dividend. The second issue is concerned with the marginal productivity theory of distribution. The second issue will be discussed in the next chapters.

2. MARGINAL PRODUCTIVITY THEORY OF DISTRIBUTION

The marginal productivity theory of distribution attempts to provide a general explanation of how the income of each factor of production is determined. The theory was developed by J.B. Clark, Wicksteed and others during the last quarter of the 19th century. In the words of J.B. Clark, "The distribution of income of society is controlled by a natural law and that this law, if it worked without friction, would give to every agent of production the amount of wealth which that agent creates."[1]

In simple words, the marginal productivity theory states that the income of each factor of production tends to equal its marginal product. This situation is brought about through the forces of competition and the principle of substitution. The entrepreneurs rationally follow their own interests. As we know, it is possible for an entrepreneur to vary the combination of factors that he employs, in production. A farmer can cultivate his lands extensively, with much land and little labour and capital, or intensively, with much labour and capital and little land. A manufacturer can use hand methods, using much labour and relatively little machinery (capital), or he can use a highly mechanised process, in which were is a large amount of capital (investment in machinery) with relatively less labour employed. In deciding what combination of factors to employ, the entrepreneur will be governed by considerations of cost. He will try to economise on the dearer factors by using processes that require less of them. He will substitute as much as possible of the cheap factor for the

1. J.B. Clark, *The Distribution of Wealth* (1899).

dear factor. The enterprisers will employ all the units of a factor whose costs are less in, money than the addition that the respective input units make to the money value of the product. Also, no input units will get employment whose costs is estimated to be more in money than the money value that they add to the product. A profit maximising entrepreneur will employ variable factor input to that point at which its last unit adds as much to revenue as to costs. This is true of all firms—perfect competitive firm or monopoly firm.

Thus, the maximum price that the entrepreneur will be prepared to pay for a unit of factor of production (i.e., the price of that factor unit) will depend upon its marginal productivity. The greater the productivity of a factor, the higher will be its price or remuneration. If all factor units are homogeneous, then the maximum remuneration of each factor unit will be equal to the productivity of the marginal factor unit. The marginal productivity theory further states that under certain conditions, the remuneration of a factor unit will not only be equal to its marginal product, but also to its average product. Here we must understand two important points.

First, the price (remuneration) which a factor of production receives is income for that factor of production, but it is a factor of production. The remuneration or price of each factor (labour, capital, land and entrepreneurship) is designated differently as wages, interest, rent and profit. In the case of perfect competition where all the factor units are homogeneous, the remuneration which an employer will have to pay will be the same for all units of factor. This means that the supply curve of factor input will be a horizontal line indicating that average factor cost (*AFC*) and marginal factor cost (*MFC*) are the same to the producer.

Secondly, the productivity of a factor of production can be expressed in two different ways: (*i*) physical productivity, and (*ii*) revenue productivity. Physical productivity of a factor refers to the amount of a commodity in terms of physical units such as kilos, metres, etc. Revenue productivity, on the other hand, refers to the money value of the physical productivity. Since factors of production are paid in terms of money, we are concerned with revenue productivity and not with physical productivity of a factor of production.

Revenue productivity can again be divided into average revenue productivity (*ARP*) and marginal revenue productivity (*MRP*). Average revenue productivity of a factor of production can be calculated by dividing the total revenue by the total number off actor units which produce it. Marginal revenue productivity, on the other hand, refers to the contribution made to the total revenue productivity by the employment of an additional unit of a factor of production.

We know that average and marginal products (and consequently, revenue products too) follow the law of variable returns. It means that they will first rise, reach a maximum and then fall. Now the marginal productivity theory of distribution states that in a freely competitive market in the long run, the price (remuneration) paid to the factor units will be equal to the average and marginal products of that factor. This is illustrated in Fig. 40.1. In Fig. 40.1, *ARP* and *MRP* are the respective average revenue productivity and marginal revenue productivity curves. *SS* is the supply curve of factor of production which is horizontal. It indicates that the price that the employer will have to pay for any of the factors is fixed for him by the rate (transfer earning) that the factor units have earned when employed by another entrepreneur, or in another industry. With the price of factor units thus given, the employer will continue employing the various factor units to that point at which the price he has to pay for each unit of factor will just be equal to its marginal revenue product. Thus the equilibrium point is *E* where the marginal revenue product is equal to the factor price. The factor price is also equal to average revenue product. In other words, at the highest point of the average revenue productivity curve, the average factor cost equals the average revenue product of the factor which equals the marginal revenue product of the factor. Therefore, the marginal productivity theory states that in equilibrium under the conditions of perfect competition in the long-run, the remuneration paid to the factor input will be equal to both the average and the marginal revenue productivities of that factor.

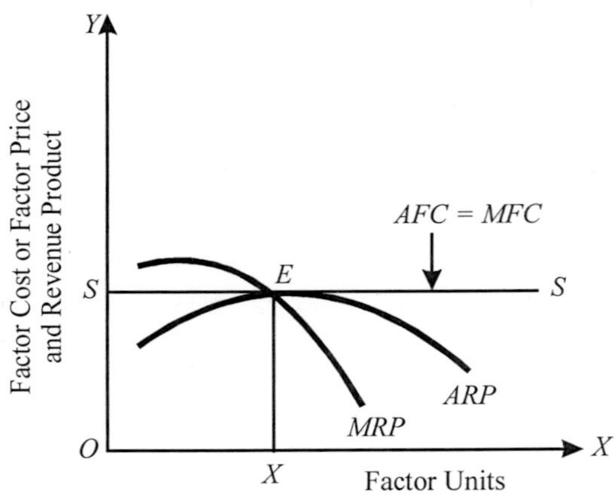

Fig. 40.1

In case the price of factor units is less than the marginal productivity, they would change their use or shift from those uses where the reward is less to those where the reward is high. Due to this mobility of factor units in the long-run, a given amount of a factor of production gets distributed between different uses in such a way that its marginal productivity in each of the different uses is equal. Similarly, entrepreneurs will continue substituting one factor for another so long as they gain by such substitution. They will get maximum gain at a point when the marginal productivity of each factor of production is equal to that of every other factor of production and also the price of factor of production is equal to the value of its marginal product. Thus, in equilibrium, the share of each factor will be determined by its marginal productivity.

Assumptions of the Marginal Productivity Theory

The marginal productivity theory of distribution rests upon the following assumptions:

(1) It assumes that all the units of a factor of production are homogeneous and perfectly substitutable for one another.

(2) It assumes that the law of variable proportions is in general, operative.

(3) It assumes that the entrepreneurs are rational and they always try to maximize their profits.

(4) It assumes that payment to each factor according to its marginal product, completely exhausts the total product.[2]

(5) The theory is based upon the assumption of perfect competition.

(6) This theory is applicable only in the long-period. In the short-run the remuneration paid to a factor of production may be more or less than its marginal product.

(7) The theory assumes that alternate uses of factor units are available in the economy.

Criticisms of the Marginal Productivity Theory

The marginal productivity theory of distribution is true only under certain assumptions which make the theory unrealistic. This theory is not applicable to actual conditions. It, therefore, fails to explain the actual rewards earned by the factors of production. The following are the main criticisms of the theory:

2. The proposition can be proved mathematically by the use of the Euler's Theorem.

(1) The theory assumes that all the units of a factor are homogeneous. This is not actually the case. All labour units are not alike, they are of varying efficiency. Similarly, all units of land are not similar; some may be more fertile than others. Thus, we cannot generalise the marginal productivity theory of distribution.

(2) The theory assumes that different factors of production are capable of being substituted for one another; so that at the margin, it is possible to use a little more land or a little more labour or capital, etc. In actual life, it is not always possible to substitute labour for capital and vice versa. In such a situation, marginal productivities of the various factors may remain unequal. Different factors of production are not close substitutes for one another.

(3) It is assumed that the amount of particular factor can be continuously varied. In other words, the theory assumes that it is possible to use a little more or a little less of the same factor, because then and only then its marginal productivity will become equal to its price. For some factors of production, this may not be true and the theory fails.

(4) The theory assumes that factor units are mobile between alternative uses. But actually, all factors of production are not perfect mobile. For example, land lacks mobility and labour and capital are not perfect mobile. In such a situation, the marginal productivity in various uses may remain unequal.

(5) According to the marginal productivity theory, marginal productivity determines the remuneration of a factor of production. It means that the two are independent. But actually, this is not the case. One affects the other. The marginal productivity of a factor also depends on the remuneration it gets.

(6) A most common criticism of this theory is that advocated by Taussig, Davenport and Adriance. In their opinion, every product is a joint product, and cannot be separately ascribed to either capital, or labour, or land. It is impossible to isolate and measure the 'specific' product of each of the factors. As Carver puts it, "You cannot unscramble the eggs." The product is the inextricable mixture of the different factors. But this misconceives the use of the marginal productivity theory. When we say that the marginal net product of a factor is this, we do not mean thereby that this net product is due solely to that factor. We merely impute that product to that factor. There is no other way, except this, of measuring the contributions of factors used jointly in production. It is merely a case of joint demand.

(7) Another criticism of the theory has been made by Wieser and Hobson. According to them, the marginal net product cannot afford a good measure of the contributions of a factor, because when one unit is withdrawn from production, that would so disorganise the whole business that the productivity of the other agents will be considerably diminished. Hence the amount by which the total output will diminish, when the marginal unit is withdrawn will be much greater than what can be imputed to that unit alone. This follows the paradox that the sum of the marginal net products of all the factors, as determined separately according to the theory, will be greater than the actual total product.

This criticism is also due to the wrong application of the theory. The attention is fixed on a small business organisation and large units of factors. But generally the actual size of the business is so large, and the ordinary units of the factors are so small that the withdrawal of one unit of a factor will not affect the productivity of other factors appreciably.

(8) Another important criticism of the theory is that it assumes the supply of the factors as given and then explains why they are demanded. The factors are demanded because of their marginal contributions to the entrepreneurs. Thus this theory approaches the problem from the side of demand only. But demand cannot explain the value of anything, much less of a factor of production. The supply of the factors is not fixed, but it is elastic to a considerable degree, being dependent, for example, on the remuneration paid to them. Thus the marginal productivity theory is a onesided explanation.

(9) The theory is valid only under the assumption of perfect competition. In real life, since competition is not perfect, actual rewards paid to the factors of production do not conform to their marginal productivity.

(10) The theoryassumes that entrepreneurial behaviour is always guided by the objective of profit-maximisation. In actual life we find entrepreneurs guided by a number of other objectives.

In conclusion, we can say that the marginal productivity theory is not a complete theory. It takes no account of the forces which influence the supply of the factors of production. As Prof. Samuelson states, "It is simply a theory of one aspect of the demand for productive services by the finrt."[3]

---

3. Samuelson, *Economics—An Introductory Analysis.*

3. MODERN THEORY OF DISTRIBUTION: DEMAND AND SUPPLY THEORY

We have explained above the marginal productivity theory of distribution which only tells us how many factor units will an entrepreneur employ at a given factor price in order to maximise his profits. The theory fails to explain the influence of supply of factor units and thus does not tell how the factor price is determined. In other words, the marginal productivity theory approaches the problem of the determination of the remuneration off actors of production from the side of demand only and it completely ignores the supply side. It is, therefore, not an adequate explanation of the determination of the factor prices.

The modern theory of factor pricing provides a satisfactory explanation to the problem of distribution. It is known as the demand and supply theory of distribution. According to this theory, as the price of a product is determined by its demand and supply, similarly the price of a factor of production is also determined by the demand for and the supply of that particular factor. This theory is superior to the marginal productivity theory, because it takes into account both the forces of demand and supply in the determination of factor price.

Demand for a Factor of Production

We first consider the demand side. We know that the demand for a factor of production is not a direct demand, but it is an indirect demand. It is derived demand. It is derived from the demand for the final products that the factor produces. As the demand for goods and services increases, the demand for the factors which are used in their production will also increase. Also, if the demand for final goods is elastic or inelastic, in the same way the demand for factors of production too will be elastic or inelastic.

The demand for a factor of production will also depend upon its marginal productivity. The more units of a factor of production are employed, the lower will be its marginal productivity and consequently the lower will be its demand price. The industry (or market) demand curve for a factor of production is the sum-total of the demand curves of the various firms in the industry (or market). The demand of the firm for a factor depends on its marginal revenue productivity (or marginal productivity) and the quantity of the factor that a firm will employ will depend on the prevailing factor price. It means that more units of a factor will be employed if factor prices are low and less will be employed if factor prices are high. Figure 40.2 illustrates the demand for a factor. When the factor price is *OR*, the firm is in equilibrium at point *E* where it demands *OX* units of the factor of production. If factor price is OR_1, its equilibrium point will be E_1) where it demands OX_1) units of the factor input. Similarly, at OR_1 factor-price, the demand would be OX_2 units. The *MRP* (Marginal Revenue Productivity) will be the demand curve for a factor of production by an individual firm. But for determining the price of a factor, we require the total demand of the market. The total demand of the market is the sum-total of the demands of all the firms in the market. This can be derived by summing the *MRP* curves of all the firms. In Panel (*b*) of Fig. 40.2 *DD* is the market demand curve. It can be seen that in both the Panels (*a*) and (*b*) of Fig. 40.2, *Y*-axes measure the same scale while *X*-axes are drawn on different scales. We may assume that there are thousands of firms in the market. At *OR* factor price, the demand for the individual firm is *OX* units, but the demand of the entire market at the same factor price *OR* is equal to *OM*. In the same way, we may find out the market demand for the factor at different factor prices. In Panel (*b*) of Fig. 40.2, the market demand curve *DD* slopes downward to the right. The reason is that *MRP* curve whose summation is represented by *DD* slopes downward to the right.

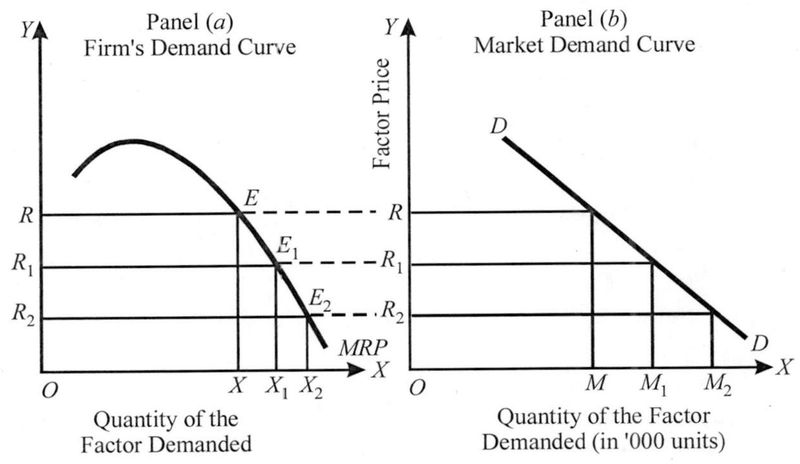

Fig. 40.2

Supply of a Factor of Production

Now we discuss the supply side. The supply curve of a factor of production depends on the various conditions of its supply.

In the case of commodities, we find that if price of a particular commodity increases, its supply will also increase. This, however, does not necessarily hold good in the case of some factors of production. For example, take the case of labour, if after a certain level wage (the price of labour) goes up, labour may be able to satisfy its wants by working for less time than before. They may prefer leisure to work. In this case, after a certain point the supply curve will become backward bending. Similarly, for the economy as a whole, the supply of labour also depends upon the size and composition of population, its occupational and geographical distribution, its efficiency etc. Similar reasoning can be given with other factors of production. But the least we can say is that if the price of a factor increases, its supply will also generally increase, and vice versa. Thus the supply curve of a factor of production will generally rise from left to right upwards. This is shown in Fig. 40.3.

Interaction of Demand and Supply Curves

To determine the price of a factor of production we need both the demand curve and the supply curve of the factor of product ion. In Fig. 40.3 *DD* is the demand curve and *SS* is the supply curve of the factor of production. Now the equilibrium price of the factor of production will be determined at the point of intersection of the demand and supply curves. In Fig. 40.3 at point *E* the two curves intersect each other and therefore the equilibrium price of the factor of production is *OR*. If price is higher than *OR* (say OR_1), then demand for the factor will be less than its supply. In this case the competition among the sellers of factor will tend to reduce the price to *OR*. On the other hand, if price is lower than *OR* (say OR_2), then the demand for the factor will be greater than the supply of it, the compe-tition. among the buyers of the factor will tend to increase the price to *OR* at which the demand and supply of the factor of production will be equal. This is all about the modem theory of distribution or the demand and supply theory of distribution. This theory is an im-provement

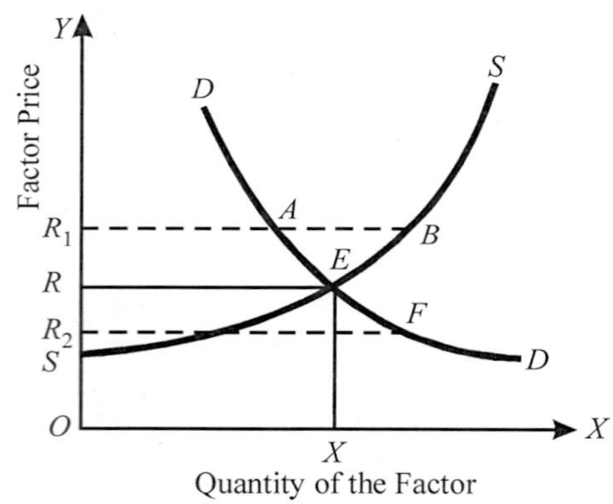

Fig. 40.3

over the marginal pro-ductivity theory of distribution, Fig. 40.3 because it deals with both the sides of the factor of production—i.e., the demand side as well as the supply side.

Some modern economists also make use of the concept of transfer earnings or opportunity costs in order to explain the remunerations or the prices of the different factors of production. The amount of money which any particular factor unit can earn in its next best-paid alternative use is called its transfer earnings or its opportunity costs. The transfer earnings are, therefore, the minimum prices which must be paid to the factors of production to induce them to remain in their present job. In this case the supply curve of the factor of production will start from above the original point. In Fig. 40.3 *OS* is the transfer earnings of the factors of production.

4. FACTOR PRICING UNDER PERFECT COMPETITION

According to the modern theory of pricing of factors of production, under conditions of perfect competition, it is the forces of demand and supply of factors which determine their prices. It is, therefore, essential to understand first the nature of demand for factors of production. The demand for a factor input is a derived demand which is derived from the demand for the product that it helps to produce. Thus the demand for a factor ultimately depends upon the demands for goods it helps to produce. The greater the demand for goods a particular type of factor helps to make, the greater the demand for that type of factor. Just as demand for a good depends upon its utility, the demand for a factor depends upon the *MRP* of the factor. In fact the *MRP* curve of the factor is the demand curve for that factor.

We shall first explain firm's equilibrium with regard to the employment of factors under conditions of perfect competition and then we shall talk about the equilibrium of the industry.

When there is perfect competition in the product market, a firm's $AR = MR =$ price of the product. Thus the value of marginal product (*VMP*) of the factor service is arrived at by multiplying its *MPP* by its price, so that

$$VMP = MPP \times \text{Price of the Product.}$$

Also, under perfect competition $MRP = VMP$.

When there is perfect competition in the factor market, the firm can not affect the price of the factor by varying its level of factor employment. An individual firm's demand for the factor can not affect the market demand for the factor and, therefore, the factor price. The firm can employ as many number of factor units as it wishes at the prevailing factor price in the market. Therefore, the supply curve of the factor for an individual firm under perfect competition in the factor market will be perfectly elastic. Here the marginal factor cost (*MFC*) is equal to the price of the factor (P_f). Also under perfect competition for an individual firm in the factor market, its *AFC* = *MFC*. They are horizontal to *X*-axis and coincide to each other.

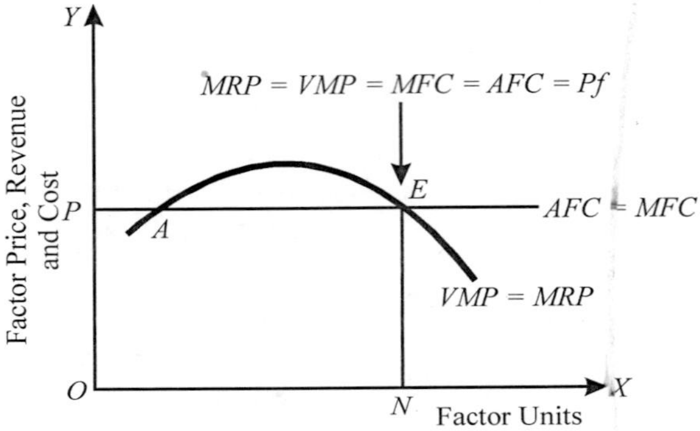

Fig. 40.4

Given the demand and supply conditions of the factor input as enumerated above, the firm's equilibrium position can be shown in Fig. 40.4. In Fig. 40.4, the prevailing price of the factor in the market is *OP* which the firm has to accept as given and constant. *VMP* = *MRP* is the demand curve and *AFC* = *MFC* is the supply curve of the factor input for the firm. The firm's equilibrium point is *E* where *VMP* = *MFC* and also the *VMP* curve cuts the *MFC* curve from above. Here the firm employs *ON* units of the factor at *OP* factor price. At point *E,* firm fulfils the equilibrium condition:

$$MRP = VMP = MFC = AFC = \text{Factor Price.}$$

Thus we conclude that under perfect competition in the both the markets, a factor of production will get the price equal to the value of its marginal product.

Further to show whether a firm is getting profit or no profit, we have to explain the firm's short-run equilibrium and long-run equilibrium situations.

Short-Period Equilibrium of the Firm

In the short-period under perfect competition, a firm may get profit or loss depending upon the situation of average revenue productivity of a factor input. In order to explain the possible cases on a diagram, we have to draw the average revenue product (*ARP*) curve along with the *MRP*-curve.

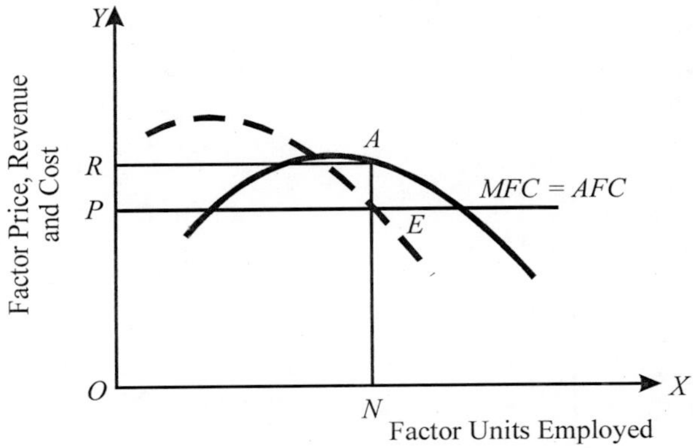

Fig. 40.5

Profit Situation. It is shown in Fig. 40.5. It can be seen in the figure that when the firm is in equilibrium at point *E,* it employs *ON* units of the factor at *OP* factorprice. At *ON* units of factor employed, the average revenue product is *OR*. Thus *P R* is the per unit profit. Total profit of the firm is represented by the rectangle *PRAE.*

Loss Situation. It is shown in Fig. 40.6. Here at *ON* level of factor employment, average factor cost (or factor price) is *OP* while the average revenue product is *OM.* Since *ARP* < *AFC,* the firm gets a loss. Its per unit loss is *MP* while the total loss is represented by the area *PEAM.*

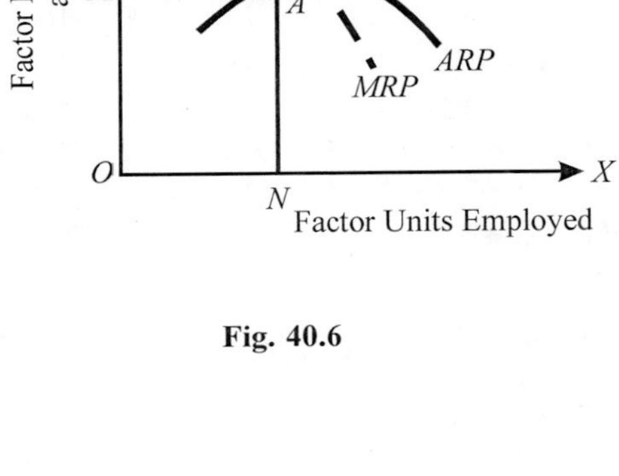

Fig. 40.6

No-Profit Situation or Normal Profit Situation. It is shown in Fig. 40.7. Here at *ON* level of factor employment, average factor cost (or factor price) is *OP* which is just equal to average revenue product and therefore the abnormal profit of the firm becomes zero.

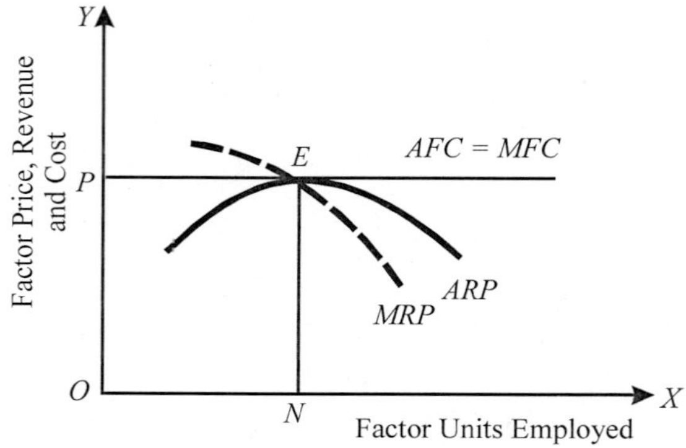

Fig. 40.7

Long-run Equilibrium of the Firm

When there is perfect competition in the product as well as in the factor market, a firm gets no profit-no loss in the long-period. It is because of free entry and free exit of firms into and from the industry and perfect mobility of factors of production. When there is super normal profit in the industry, new firms will enter into it. As a result of the entry of new firms in the industry, the demand for the factor will rise. The increased demand for the factor will increase its price and thus the *AFC*-curve will shift upward. With the entry of

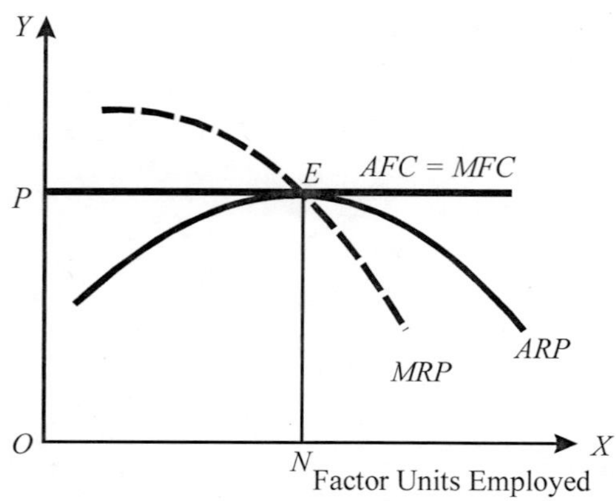

Fig. 40.8

firms, the output of the product will also rise which will lead to a fall in the price of the product, so that the *ARP* and *MRP* curves will shift downward. Thus *AFC* or *MFC* curves will shift upward while *ARP* and *MRP* curves will shift downward and in the long-run they become tangent to each other. In Fig. 40.8, the long-run equilibrium point is *E* where the firm employs *ON* units of the factor at *OP* price.

Similarly, if there is loss in the short-period, then it will also disappear in the longrun because of exit of old firms from the industry. In the long-run, equilibrium point of the firm is established at the highest point of the *ARP* curve.

Equilibrium of the Industry

Under perfect competition, like the price of products, the prices of factors, of production are also determined by the demand and supply of the factors of production. Modern theory of factor pricing is the same as the Marshall-Hicks version of marginal productivity theory of distribution. Marshall and Hicks are of the opinion that the price of a factor of production is determined by both the demand for and supply of the factor, but would be equal to the marginal revenue product of the factor.

At different factor prices, every firm determines its demand for the factor by adopting the rule *MRP* = *MFC*. The industry demand would be the sum of the demands of individual firms. The industry demand curve for the factor will also be a negatively sloping curve as the *MRP* of the individual firm. Similarly the supply curve of the factor in the market will be a positively sloping curve indicating the fact that higher the price of the factor, more will be its supply by the owners of the factor and vice versa. The equilibrium price of a factor is determined by the intersection of these demand and supply curves of the factor. In other words, given the demand and supply curves of a factor, the price of the factor will adjust to the level at which the amount of the factor supplied is equal to the amount demanded. This is shown in Fig. 40.9, where *DD* is demand curve and *SS* is the supply curve of the factor. Only at *OP* price, quantity demanded for the factor is equal to the quantity supplied of the factor. At any other price the demand and supply will not be the same. At a lower price OP_1 the competition among the producers or entrepreneurs demanding the factor of production will push up the price to the *OP* level. Similarly at a higher price OP_2, the competition among the owners of the factor will force down the price to the level *OP* where quantity supplied is equal to the quantity demanded. We should also remember that though price of a factor is determined by demand for and supply of the factor, yet it is always equal to *MRP* of the factor as we have already seen in the case of anindividual firm.

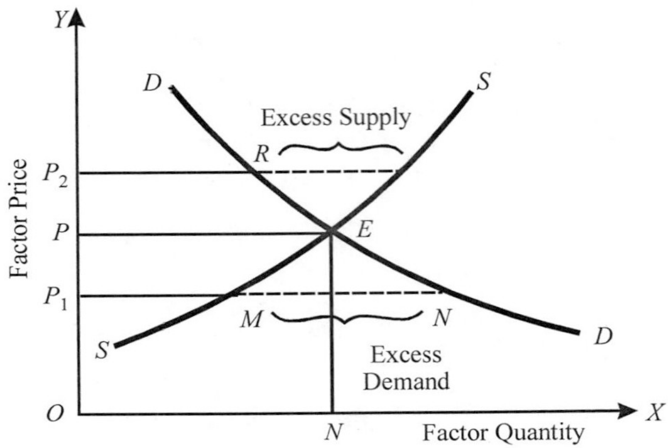

Fig. 40.9

5. FACTOR PRICING UNDER IMPERFECT COMPETITION

1. Factor Market Perfectly Competitive and Product Market Imperfectly Competitive or Monopolistic Competitive

Under perfect competition, the factor price is given to the firm and the firm has to determine only the level of employment. Also the *MRP* and *VMP* of the factor were assumed to be the same. But when there is imperfect competition (i.e., monopoly, oligopoly and monopolistic competition) in the product market, marginal revenue (*MR*) is different from the price of the product, rather *MR* < Price of the product. This affects the demand for a factor and the price it will get under conditions of imperfect competition in the product market.

Since perfect competition is assumed to be prevailing in the factor market, price of the factor will be determined by demand for and supply of factor of production. The supply curve or the cost curve is horizontal to the *X*-axis (*AFC* = *MFC*). But because there is imperfect competition or monopoly in the product market, the *MRP* curve will lie below the *VMP* curve. Symbolically, *MRP* < *VMP* since *MR* < *P* (under imperfect composition or monopoly both *AR* and *MR* curves slope downwards). In such a situation the firm will be in equilibrium where *MRP* = *MFC*. This is presented in Fig. 40.10. In Fig. 40.10, point *E* is the equilibrium point where the firm employs *ON* quantity of factor at *OP* price (or factor cost). Here the marginal revenue product of employing *ON* quantity is *EN* which is less than *RN* (the value of marginal product). Thus under imperfect competition in the factor market, the factor of production gets less than the value of its marginal product by *RE* amount.

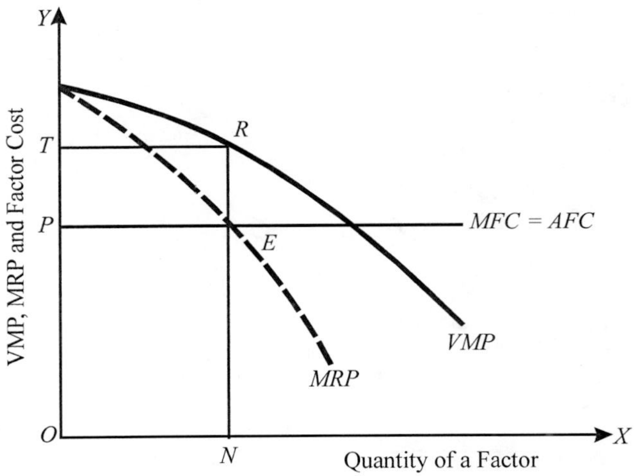

Fig. 40.10

2. Monopsony in the Factor Market and Perfect Competition in the Product Market

A monopsony in the factor market means that there is only one firm which buys the factor units. Just as a monopolist in the product market faces a downward sloping demand curve and can influence the price of the product by changing the level of his output, similarly a monopsonist in the factor market faces an upward sloping supply curve of the factor and can affect the price of the factor by changing the level of its employment. By reducing employment, it can lower the price of the factor. And if he wants to buy more amount of the factor, he will have to pay a higher price for the factor. Therefore, the supply curve of the factor or *AFC*-curve to the monopsonist will be rising upward to the right. As the *AFC*-curve is rising, *MFC*-curve will lie above it. *MRP*-curve and *ARP*-curve will have their usual shape. Since we assume that there is perfect competition in the product market, *MRP* = *YMP*. In other words *VMP* and *MRP* will coincide in one, and the same curve. These curves have been drawn in Fig. 40.11. The firm is in equilibrium at point *E* where the *MRP* (or *VMP*) curve cuts the *MFC*-curve from above. The firm employs *ON* quantity of the factor at *OP* price. Since there is monopsony in the factor market, it gets super-normal profits equivalent to the area *PRST*. In other words, the factor is being paid *NT* (= *OP*) price, while its marginal revenue product is *SN*. The difference *TS* between them is called monopsonic exploitation per unit of the factor of production. It is the monopsony power of the firm.

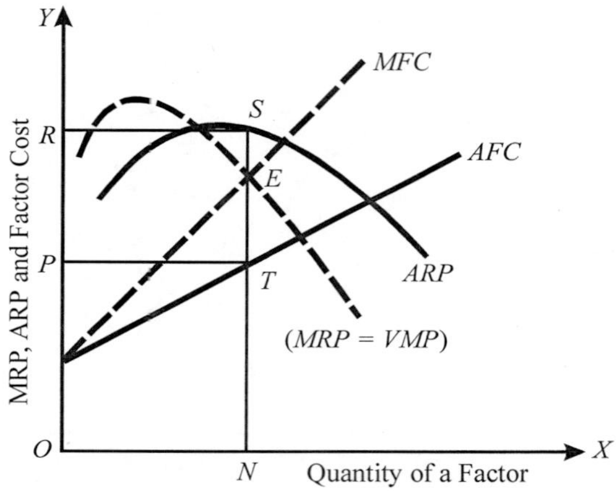

Fig. 40.11

3. Monopsony in the Factor Market and Monopoly in the Product Market

It is clear from the above analysis that when there is monopsony in the factor market and monopoly in the product market, the *MRP* < *VMP* and the *MFC* > *AFC*. Under these conditions, the equilibrium point will hold the following equation:

$$VMP > MRP = MFC > \text{Price of the Factor}$$

This is shown in Fig. 40.12[4] Here the equilibrium point is *E* where the *MRP* curve cuts the *MFC* curve from above and equals it. The firm

---

4. To avoid complications, *ARP* curve is not drawn in the diagram. Further, the gap between *VMP* and *MRP* will be increasing as the factor employment is increasing since the difference between *AR* and *MR* increases as output increases.

employs *ON* units of the factor at *OP* (= *TN*) price which is less than *NE* (the marginal revenue product of the factor). The gap *ET* is due to the existence of monopsony in the factor market and is therefore called monopsonistic exploitation of the factor. The gap *SE* between *VMP* and *MRP* is due to the existence of monopoly in the product market and is, therefore, called the monopolistic exploitation of the factor. Thus the total exploitation is *ST* (= *RP*). Here we may conclude that in the case of monopsony in the factor market and monopoly in the product market, the factor employed in production by the firm is exploited from both the sides.

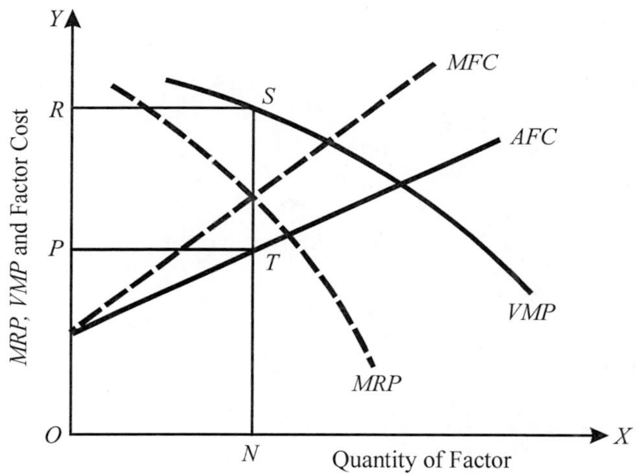

Fig. 40.12

6. DISTRIBUTION OF SHARES: THE PRODUCT EXHAUST THEOREM (THE ADDING UP PROBLEM)

Meaning and Solution

The adding-up problem shows that under perfect competition in me factor market, every factor of production is paid a price equal to the value of its marginal product. In such a situation, the payments to the factors of production would just exhaust total value of the product. When there are only two factors of production it can be written as:

$$X = MP_L.L + MP_K.K \quad \dots (1)$$

where X = Total Output

MP_L = Marginal Product of Labour

MP_K = Marginal Product of Capital

L = Quantity of Labour Employed
K = Quantity of Capital Employed

To find out the value of output, we have to multiply the physical quantity of output by its price (P_x). Thus:

$$Px - X = (MP_L.P_X).L + (MP_K.P_X).K = VMP_L.L + VMP_K.K \quad ...(2)$$

where $VMP_L = MP_L.P_X$ and $VMP_K = MP_K.P_X$

Also VMP_L is the value of marginal product of labour and VMP_K is the value of marginal product of capital.

Diagrammatic Representation of Euler's Theorem

The analysis of Euler's theorem is represented diagrammatically in Fig. 40.13. We represent labour along the horizontal axis and total product along the vertical axis. The curve OP is the total product curve which represents the production function $X = f(L,K)$. The tangent R on the OP curve at point E represents constant returns to scale. The slope at point E is equal to $EB/AB = EB/OL$ (OL = AB).

As we know, the equation of Euler's theorem is

$$X = \frac{\partial X}{\partial L} \cdot L + \frac{\partial X}{\partial K} \cdot K \quad ...(3)$$

Now in Fig. 40.13 at point E, we have

$$\frac{\partial X}{\partial L} \cdot L = \frac{EB}{OL} \cdot OL = EB \quad ...(4)$$

where $\partial X/\partial L$ = marginal product of labour which is the slope of production function and equal to EB/OL. Also the quantity of labour (L) at point E is OL. The share of labour $\left(\frac{\partial X}{\partial K} \cdot L\right)$ in the total product is represented by EB in the Fig. 40.13.

Also from equation (3) we have

$$\frac{\partial X}{\partial K} \cdot K = \text{Total product } (X) - \frac{\partial X}{\partial K} \cdot L$$
$$= \text{Total product } (X) - EB$$
$$= BL \text{ (in Fig. 40.13).}$$

This is the share of capital in the total product (X). Thus we may write

$$X = \frac{\partial X}{\partial K} \cdot L + \frac{\partial X}{\partial K} \cdot K$$

or

$$EL = EB + BL$$

Hence the total product (in Fig. 40.13) *EL* is fully exhausted or distributed between the two factors labour (*L*) and capital (*K*) respectively in the manner shown in Fig. 40.13.

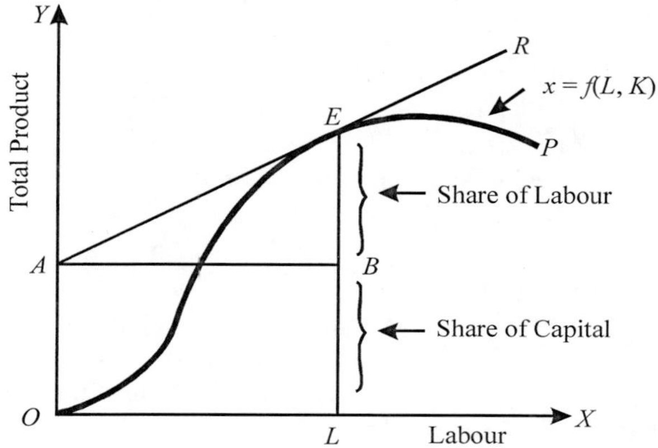

Fig. 40.13.

Assumptions of Euler's Theorem

The above stated Euler's theorem is based on the following assumptions:

(1) The production function is homogeneous of degree one which indicates constant returns to scale.

(2) Factors of production are perfectly divisible.

(3) The relative shares of factors of production are constant and independent of the level of the product.

(4) There is a stationary, riskless economy where there are no abnormal profits.

(5) Perfect competition is prevailing in the economy.

(6) The theorem is applicable only in the long-run.

Clark's Production Exhaustion Theorem

J.B. Clark in his book The *Distribution* of *Wealth* (1899) has explained the production exhaustion theorem diagrammatically. He assumes that there are only two factors of production labour and capital. Let *L* stands for labour and *K* for Capital. It should be noted that marginal product of a factor can be known when it is varied, holding the other factors fixed. The reward of a variable factor can be shown as equivalent to marginal product when a certain quantity of the variable factor is used or employed in the production process. The reward for the fixed factor can be shown as surplus or residual income of the total product over the marginally determined reward of the variable factor.

Let us first assume that labour is the variable factor and capital is assumed to be fixed. In such it situation the marginal product curve of labour (*MPL*) has been drawn in Fig. 40.14. Let us assume that *OL* is the equilibrium quantity of labour employed, then the marginal product of labour is *AL* and the wage rate determined accordingly is *OW*. The total wage bill, so that the share of labour is represented by the area equal to *OWAL*. The total product is the sum total of marginal product, that is the whole area under the marginal productivity curve of labour which is shown by the area *OSAL*. Now the residual income after marginally determined wage share of labour (*OWAL*) will go to capital as interest. Thus the total interest (share of capital) on capital will be equal to *OSAL–DWAL* = *SWA*. It is clear that with *OWAL* wage share and *SWA* as residual income to capital paid, the total product *OSAL* will be exhausted. But here under product exhaustion theorem we have to prove that the residual income as paid to capital is also equal to the marginal product of capital used multiplied by the quantity of capital employed. It is shown in Fig. 40.15. Here we treat capital as a variable factor and labour as a fixed factor. Let us assume that in Fig. 40.15, the equilibrium amount of capital employed is *OK* and its marginal product is equal to *TK*. The rate of interest paid to capital is equal to *OR* (=*TK*). Thus the area *ORTK* is the marginally determined interest income which is paid to capital as interest share. Now the residual income will go to the fixed factor labour as wage-share. Thus in Fig. 40.15, the area *MRT* is the wage-share which is determined as residual income (*OMTK* – *ORTK* = *MRT*).

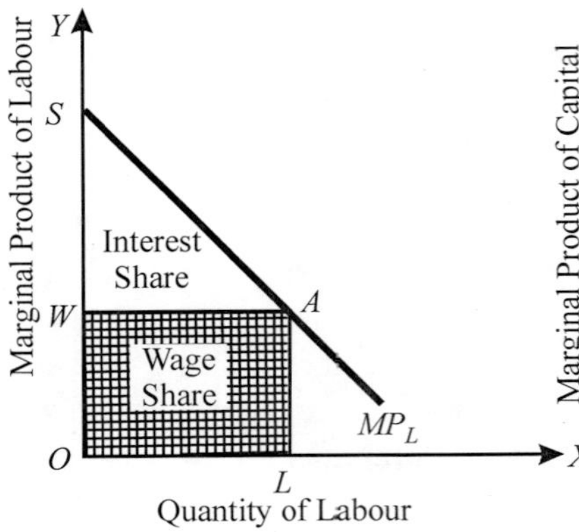

Fig. 40.14

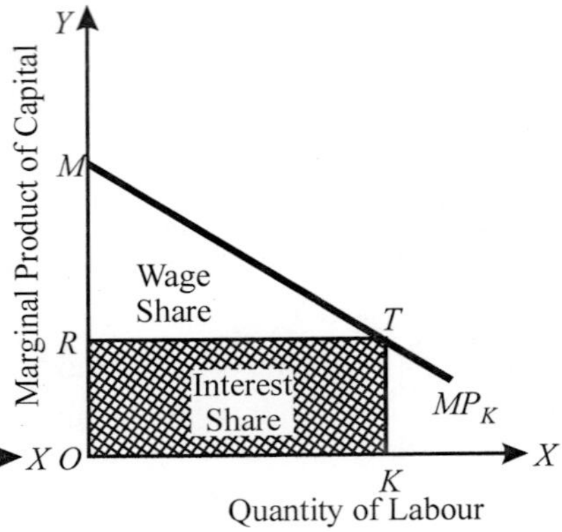

Fig. 40.15

EXERCISES

1. Explain the marginal productivity theory of distribution. What are its assumptions and criticisms?
2. How would you explain the factor pricing in terms of the marginal productivity theory of distribution under the conditions of perfect competition?
3. Explain the modern theory of distribution. Is it an improvement over the marginal productivity theory of distribution?
4. Explain demand and supply theory of factor price determination.
5. Explain the product-exhaustion theorem.
6. "In equilibrium all factors of production receive a payment just equal to the value of their marginal product." Explain.
7. Explain diagrammatically the Euler's Theorem.
8. How is the problem of distribution solved with the help of Euler's Theorem? Explain it fully.
9. Write notes on:
   (*i*) Adding-up Problem
   (*ii*) Clark's Product Exhaustion Theorem
   (*iii*) Euler's Theorem
10. How is price of a factor determined:
    (*a*) when the firm is a monopolist in product market and monopsonist in the factor market;
    (*b*) when there is perfect competition in the product market and monopsony in the factor market; and
    (*c*) when there is monopoly in the product market and perfect competition in the factor market.
11. "In equilibrium all factors get a payment equal to the value of their marginal product." Explain.
12. How is price of a factor determined when there is perfect competition in both the product and the factor markets?
13. Distinguish between the following:
    (*a*) Value of the Marginal Product (*VMP*) and Marginal Revenue Product (*MRP*)
    (*b*) Average Factor Cost and Marginal Factor Cost.
14. Explain diagrammatically the process of factor pricing under imperfect competition.

Multiple Choice Questions

15. (*i*) Which of the following is the most acceptable statement?
    (*a*) an employer will continue to hire units of a variable factor until *MRP* = Money Wages
    (*b*) an employer hires a variable factor input upto the point where diminishing returns operate
    (*c*) an employer hires a variable factor input until its *MRP* becomes zero
    (*d*) variable factors are employed until their *MRPs* become equal.
    [*Ans.* (*a*)]

    (*ii*) Under perfect competition, a factor will be demanded upto the point:
    (*a*) where its *MRP* equals its price
    (*b*) where its *MRP* is more than its price
    (*c*) where its *ARP* equals its price
    (*d*) where *MRP* increases and price falls [*Ans.* (*a*)]

(*iii*) The *MRP* of any factor of production is the product of
(*a*) its *MP P* × the price of per unit of the factor
(*b*) the price per unit of output × *MPP* of the factor concerned
(*c*) the *ARP* × the number of units of the factor used
(*d*) the total value of the product × the physical product of the factor
[*Ans.* (*b*)]

(*iv*) The adding-up problem shows that under perfect competition in the factor market, every factor of production is paid a price equal to
(*a*) the value of its average product
(*b*) the value of its marginal product
(*c*) the value of its total product
(*d*) the value of its product price [*Ans.* (*b*)]

(*v*) Euler's theorem is based on the assumption that
(*a*) the production function is homogeneous of degree zero
(*b*) the production function is homogeneous of degree one
(*c*) the production function is non-linear homogeneous
(*d*) the production function is non-linear non-homogeneous [*Ans.* (*b*)]

(*vi*) According to Wicksteed, in the distribution of total output, product will exhaust if and only if the production function is
(*a*) linearly homogeneous (*b*) linearly non-homogeneous
(*c*) non-linear homogeneous (*d*) non-linear non-homogeneous
[*Ans.* (*a*)]

(*vii*) Under perfect competition, a factor will be demanded upto the point:
(*a*) where its *MRP* is more than its price
(*b*) where its *MRP* equals its price
(*c*) where its *MRP* increases and price falls
(*d*) where its *ARP* equals its price [*Ans.* (*b*)]

(*viii*) An imperfectly competitive seller's resource demand curve slopes downward because
(*a*) marginal product diminishes and product price falls as output increases
(*b*) marginal product increases and product price falls as output increase
(*c*) marginal product decreases and product price rises as output increases
(*d*) marginal product remains constant and product price falls as output increases [*Ans.* (*a*)]

(*ix*) Other things being equal, more of a factor will be supplied to an industry at
(*a*) a lower reward than at a higher reward
(*b*) a higher reward than at a lower reward
(*c*) lower taxes than at higher taxes
(*d*) higher taxes than at lower taxes [*Ans.* (*b*)]

(*x*) The shape of the demand curve for a factor of production is generally the same as that of
(*a*) the total revenue curve
(*b*) the marginal revenue product curve
(c) the total cost curve
(d) the average variable cost curve [*Ans.* (*b*)]

Chapter 41

RENT

1. INTRODUCTION

In the previous chapter, we explained the theory of distribution in general terms. We now turn to apply it in succession to the various factors of production. We shall start with land and in the present chapter we shall explain theories which determine rent.

2. MEANING OF RENT

It was said in the previous chapter that the share of the national dividend accruing to the landlord is called rent. Rent may, therefore, be defined as the income which accrues to the landlord from the ownership of any natural factor, such as, land, mines, water-power etc. According to Marshall, the income derived from the ownership of land and other free gifts of nature is commonly called rent.[1] From the point of view of the entrepreneur (uses of land), rent may be said to be the payment for the use of land.[2]

According to Ricardo, "Rent is that portion of the produce of the earth which is paid to the landlord for the use of the original and indestructible powers of the soil." In this sense, rent is a payment by the tenant to the landlord for the services of land in production. It, however, refers to the payment made for the original and indestructible power of land, i.e., pure land. It excludes any payment for improvements made in land through the use of capital etc. As such, Ricardo's definition of rent

1. Alfred Marshall, *Economics of Theory*, p. 52.
2. In some cases, capital invested on land cannot be distinguished from it and obeys the economic laws concerning land. It means that the capital invested is considered to be a part of land and income from it is known as rent. Thus, rent may be defined as the payment which is made for the use of the primary factor in all production land or natural resources including any capital which may have been so sunk in the soil as to obey the economic laws concerning land and to be no longer distinguishable as capital.—Thomas, *Elements of Economics,* p. 243.

is too narrow. It has been criticised by the modern economists. They state that there are some properties of the soil which are not original but which are not distinguishable from land. Capital sunk in the land after pretty long time becomes indistinguishable from land and obeys the same economic laws which land obeys. The income from such acquired power or property is rightly regarded as rent.[3]

The scientific meaning of the term "rent" should be distinguished from its popular sense. In the popular sense the term is applied to the periodical payment for the use of a house including the ground on which it stands, a farm or an estate, or of a forest, a fishery, or a mine. According to this definition, rent includes not only payment for the use of land, but also interest on capital invested in buildings and elsewhere, depreciation of fixed capital, and profit. For example, the payment which a tenant makes to his landlord for the use of his house includes not only rent in the economic sense (used by Ricardo and other classical economists) but also interest on the capital spent in the construction of the building, its annual depreciation, and remuneration for the risk or enterprise.

We must remember that in economics the term rent is not used in its popular sense but it is concerned with its scientific sense. The modern economists have broadened the meaning of the term rent. According to them, it is no more confined only to land; but it is now defined in terms of the difference between actual earnings and transfer earnings of a factor of production whose supply is inelastic. Rent is that part of payment for any factor of production which is above the minimum necessary to keep it in its present use.

3. CONTRACT RENT AND ECONOMIC RENT

Economists divide rent in its scientific sense, into Contract Rent and Economic Rent. We should, therefore, carefully distinguish between contract rent and economic rent.

The rent which is actually paid by the tenant to the landlord for the use of land (or as a hiring charge) is known as Contract Rent. It is called contract rent, because it is determined by a contract between the tenant and the landlord. Contract rent of a land may be equal to, or greater than, or less than, its economic rent. If competition among landlords is comparatively greater than that among the tenants, contract rent may be less than the economic rent. On the other hand, if tenants compete more

3. See the details in Clay, *Economics for the General Reader,* pp. 351-52.

freely among themselves than landlords, contract rent may be greater than economic rent.

The classical economists, defined the term economic rent as that part of the total payment which is made for use of land only as distinguished from the payment made for the capital invested therein. Suppose, a tenant is paying annually Rs. 1,000 to his landlord. This amount is contract rent. If out of this sum, Rs. 800 represents interest on capital, say, in the tube well (or total cost of the improvements made on the land), the remaining amount of Rs. 200, being only for the use of land, is economic rent.

Modern economists make use of the concept of transfer earnings[4] in explaining economic rent. If a factor of production is earning over and above its transfer earnings or transfer price, the surplus or excess earnings is economic rent. Therefore, in the modern sense, economic rent means surplus or excess over transfer earnings. This sort of surplus or economic rent is not peculiar to land, it may be found in all factors of production.

4. THE RICARDIAN THEORY OF RENT OR THE CLASSICAL THEORY OF RENT

The classical theory of rent is associated with the name of David Ricardo (1773-1823), one of the most distinguished of the English classical economists. This theory was applied specifically to land. Ricardo said that rent was the payment for the 'original and indestructible powers of the soil.'

Now, in order to understand Ricardo's theory of rent, we should first understand certain assumptions of the theory:

(1) Land differs in fertility. Some lands are more fertile than others, i.e., the application of equal doses of labour and capital results in a higher yield in some cases and less in others. It is this difference in fertility, combined with variations in locality which gives rise to a surplus or differential gain on the super marginal lands. This surplus is economic rent.

(2) The cultivation of land is subject to the law of diminishing returns. The return due to the application of particular dose of labour and capital is less than that due to the preceding dose. As such, all the intramarginal doses of labour and capital enjoy surplus or differential gain over the marginal dose or final dose of labour and capital.

---

4. We have already explained that the transfer earnings represent the amount which a factor of production can earn in its next best-paid alternative use.

(3) Rent depends upon two main qualities of the land-fertility and location. The more fertile a land, other things being the same, the higher will be its rent. The location of the land has similar influence on rent.

(4) It assumes perfect competition. Since under perfect competition the product price is given, economic rent is that surplus which accrues over and above the cost of production.

(5) This theory assumes that rent is not a part of the cost of production and, therefore, rent does not enter into the product price.

Now Ricardo explained the emergence of rent with the help of an illustration. He started with the supposition of a vast tract of a virgin land just colonised by a small number of persons. Since the land is abundant and idle, no payment need be made for its use. Rent will not arise at this stage. Given the choice and knowledge, people will first cultivate the most fertile land and will be able to meet their needs.

With the passage of time, population of the island will increase either through immigration or births, or both. Consequently, the demand for agricultural produce will increase and inferior land will have to be brought under plough. Now the application of an equal number of doses of labour and capital will yield more on the superior land and smaller output on the inferior land. The surplus yield of the superior land over the inferior land is the economic rent. The inferior land (marginal land) is unable to pay rent, because its expenditures of production are just equal to the price of agricultural produce. It is therefore, no-rent land. Again, if population increases still further, the third grade land (more inferior than the second grad land) will be cultivated and consequently rent on *A* grade land will increase while that on *B* grade land will begin to appear. In short, rising population and increasing demand for food is the basic cause of increasing rent on superior types of Iand. According to Ricardo, higher prices of yield are not an outcome of higher rent, but rent increases because yield prices are rising. Thus, increase in rent does not reflect in higher prices of yield, but increasing and rising burden of population on land pushes up the produce-prices which would in turn, compel people to cultivate inferior lands and rents on intramarginal lands will consequently increase. The differential nature of rent can be explained both in extensive as well as intensive cultivation.

Rent in Extensive Cultivation

To illustrate the emergence of rent in extensive cultivation, let us suppose that the newly discovered island possesses four grades of land—denoted by *A, B, C* and *D* respectively. Grade *A* land is the most fertile and grade

D land is the least fertile. The first grade land *A* is cultivated in the first instance and let us suppose that for a certain outlay of labour and capital the yield per hectare on *A* grade land is 50 quintals. After some time (when population on the island increases), the second grade land *B* is also brought under cultivation. For the same outlay of labour and capital, its return is, say, 35 quintals per hectare. A surplus of 15 quintals per hectare appears on *A* grade land. This is the economic rent of *A* grade land.

Now, after sometime, the population further increases and consequently, even the third grade land *C* is brought under cultivation. Suppose, for the same outlay, its yield per hectare is 25 quintals. Thus, surplus produce of *A* grade land is now raised to (50 – 25) = 25 quintals; while *B* grade land also begins to show a surplus of (35 – 25) = 10 quintals which is its economic rent.

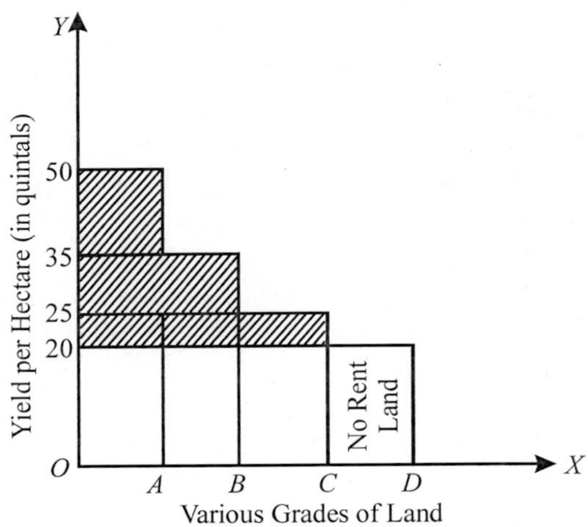

Fig. 41.1

In course of time (due to a further increase in population), *D* grade land will also come under cultivation. Suppose, its yield per hectare is 20 quintals only. It will raise the surplus or economic rent of *A* grade land to (50 – 20) = 30 quintals; of *B* grade land to (35 – 20) = 15 quintals; and on *C* grade land rent will begin to appear to the extent of (25 – 20) = 5 quintals.

In Fig. 41.1, we have shown the grades of land along *X*-axis and their yield along *Y*-axis. *OA, AB, BC* and *CD* are the *A* grade, *B* grade, *C* grade and *D* grade lands respectively. The application of an equal outlay on each of them gives an yield represented by the rectangles standing just above the respective bases. *D* grade land is the no-rent land and does not yield any rent as its expenses of production are just equal to the price of its produce. All the other intramarginal lands yield economic rent equal to the shaded portion of their respective rectangles. Here, it is clear that the marginal (final) land plays an important role in the determination of the economic rent.

Rent in Intensive Cultivation

In the above discussion, we have exposed the classical theory of rent as applied to land cultivated extensively. The theory is also applicable to the land cultivated intensively. When the land is intensively cultivated, the yield due to successive doses of labour and capital goes on diminishing till a stage is reached when the cost of the final dose (marginal dose of labour and capital) is just equal to the price of the yield it gives rise to. This is the marginal or no-rent dose. The produce due to all other intramarginal doses exceeds that of the marginal dose. The surplus or the differential advantage thus appearing is the economic rent. With the help of Fig. 42.1, we may also illustrate rent in intensive cultivation. Here instead of showing various grades of land along *X*-axis, we show the different doses of capital arid the labour employed on. a given price of land. If four doses of capital and labour are employed, then the last dose becomes the marginal dose which produces no rent and the rent in the case of first three doses is 30 quintals, 15 quintals and 5 quintals respectively.

Situational Rent

An important point that arises from the above discussion is that rent will arise even if all the land was of uniform quality. Situation is also a factor in the determination of rent. As Ricardo stated, "The most fertile and the most favourable situated land will be cultivated first. If all lands are equally fertile, rent will not arise unless a particular land enjoys the advantage of situation." For example, suppose all lands to be equally fertile, but some are situated near the market, while others are situated at a distance from the market. The yield from all lands per hectare is 50 quintals. If the price of the produce is Rs. 1000 per quintal, the distant lands will not be cultivated. For, in addition to the expenses due to labour and capital applied in cultivation which are the same on all lands, there is some additional expenditure incurred in sending the produce from the distant land to the market. So the costs will be higher on these lands. As the supply from the distant lands falls off, the price, therefore, rises, and must be such as to meet the additional expenditures of transportation. The better situated lands, therefore, yield rent.

Criticisms of the Ricardian Theory of Rent

Ricardian theory of rent has been criticised on many grounds. The following are the main points of criticism:

(1) Ricardo states that rent is paid for the use of the original and indestructible powers of the soil. This expression is not very much accurate. It is pointed out by the critics that there are no inherent and indestructible powers of the soil. The powers of the soil, for which rent is paid, are not always original; in some cases they are acquired. Fertility of the soil is destructible. Good lands, after a few years of cultivation lose their fertility because the chemical composition on which fertility depends is exhausted after a few years of continuous cultivations.[5]

(2) According to Ricardo, the best land is first put under cultivation and later on land is brought under cultivation on the merit of its goodness. This point has been criticised by Carey and Roscher. They point out that in new countries the best lands are not invariably cultivated first. Those lands situated nearby the human habitation are first cultivated whether they are good or not. Thus, the order of cultivation laid down by Ricardo is wrong.

(3) Again, the assumption of perfect competition, on which the theory is based, is unrealistic. It does not exist in practical life. It makes the theory unrealistic too.

(4) The concept of marginal land is said to be imaginary, theoretical and not realistic.

(5) If Ricardo's definition is followed, the marginal land will possess no original powers of fertility. But, as a matter of fact, each price of land, by its very nature, must possess some original or indestructible Powers of fertility. It is not possible to think of any land which is completely deprived of such natural qualities. Land of all kinds, whether it produces rent or not, possesses some original quality and fertility.

(6) According to the German Historical School, the supply of land is limited in comparison to the demand for it, and, therefore, rent will arise on all kinds of land, superior or inferior. In other words, according to the

5. Some economists defend Ricardo by stating that except fertility, other qualities of land like climate, extent and conformation are certainly indestructible. This statement is correct, but it does not take away the force of the criticism.

critics, the reward for land (rent) arises because of its scarcity rather than the differences in the fertility.

(7) Modern economists are of the opinion that rent no more confines to land, but can also be traced to other factors of production.

(8) It is argued that the (original) qualities of land do not exist separately from the capital invested in it, and are, therefore, indistinguishable. This creates the difficulty in the implementation of the Ricardian theory of rent.

(9) According to Ricardo, rent does not enter into cost of production; and, therefore, it does not affect price. But, in fact, it is itself determined by price. Rent will be greater if price of the produce is high and it will be lower if price is less. This relationship between rent and price, 'the critics point out, is not always true. According to the modem writers, sometimes rent enters into the cost of production and thus affects the price of the produce. For instance, for an individual farmer (who cultivates the land), the entire rent paid by him to the landlord is an item of cost and influences the price of the produce.

5. THE MODERN THEORY OF RENT OR DEMAND AND SUPPLY THEORY OF RENT

As we have already explained that the term 'rent' is used in two senses: (1) rent as a payment for the use of land only, (2) rent as a surplus over the transfer earnings of a factor of production. We shall state the modern theory of rent in respect of these two meanings of rent.

1. Rent as a Payment for the Use of Land (or Scarcity Theory of Rent)

According to the modern economists, rent does not arise due to differential fertility of land as pointed out by Ricardo, but it arises due to the relative scarcity of land in relation to its demand. The higher the demand for land in relation to its supply, the greater will be its rent (or price). Therefore, rent of the land is determined by the interaction of the forces of demand and supply of it. This is the reason that the modem theory of rent is also known as the demand and supply theory of rent.

Demand for Land. Like other factors of production, the demand for land is a derived demand. It is derived from the demand of the products of land. If the demand for these products rises or falls, the demand for the use of land will correspondingly rise or fall leading to increase or decrease of rents. For instance, if the population of a country increases, the demand for food will increase, resulting in increased demand for land and a rise in its rent and vice versa.

We have already mentioned that the demand for a factor of production depends on its marginal revenue productivity (or in short, marginal productivity). The marginal revenue productivity is subject to the law of diminishing productivity. This is the reason that the demand curve for land slopes downwards from the left to the right.

Supply of Land. The supply of land is fixed for the economy as a whole, but individuals can increase their own supply by acquiring more land from others or decrease its supply by parting with land. In spite of reclamation projects (the effect of which on the total supply is negligible), the supply of land remains practically fixed. In other words, the supply curve of land is perfectly inelastic. It means, whatever the rent, the supply of land remains the same. This is the reason that land has no supply price.

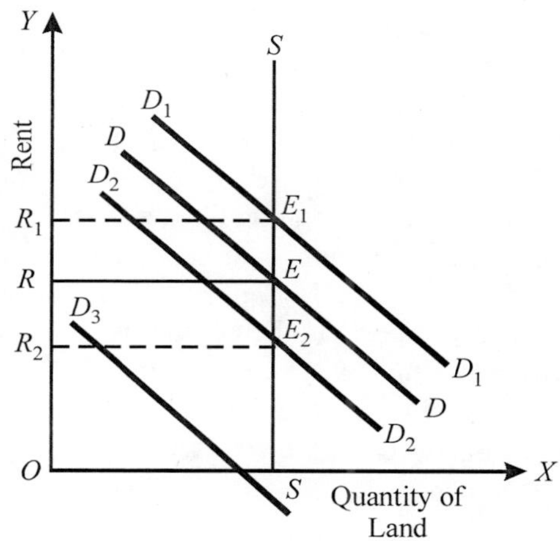

Fig. 41.2

Interaction of Demand and Supply. In Fig. 41.2, *DD* is the total demand curve for land and *SS* is the supply curve which is a vertical straight line. These two curves intersect at point *E*. In this equilibrium position *OR* is the rent. If rent is less (i.e., OR_1), the demand for land will increase; but the supply is fixed, hence rent will again rise to *OR*. Suppose, rent is more than *OR* (i.e., OR_2), then the demand for land will decrease and will again reduce the rent to the initial equilibrium level *OR*. Suppose now that, on account of an increase in population or otherwise, the demand for land has increased from *DD* to D_1D_1. The supply curve is still the same as *SS*. The new point of equilibrium will be E_1 where the rent will be OR_1. If, on the other hand, demand falls to D_2D_2 and supply curve remaining the same, the new equilibrium point will be E_2 where the rent will be OR_2. If demand for land is only D_3D_3 (because the country is entirely new where abundant land is available), then there will be no rent.

In the above discussion, we have assumed that land is homogeneous or it is of one quality only. But in actual life, there may be different qualities of land. In that situation, each quality will have a separate demand curve and they will command different rates. Therefore, the modern theory of rent also explains the concept of differential rent.

In conclusion, we can say that according to the modern theory, the rent of land, like the remunerations of other factors of production, is determined by its demand and supply.

Rent in a Particular Use. We have analysed above the total demand and total supply of land for the commodity as a whole. Now we shall analyse the demand and supply of land for a particular industry (firm) or for a particular use. Like the economy as a whole, demand curve of land for a particular individual unit will also have a negative slope, but the supply curve of land cannot be assumed as a horizontal curve. In other words, by offering more rent, the individual unit can increase the supply of land, and by reducing the amount of rent, the supply of land for it will decrease. The supply curve is therefore, elastic and will rise upwards from left to right. In Fig. 41.3, *SS* is the supply curve which is positively sloped. Suppose, in the beginning *DD* is the demand curve. The demand curve *DD* intersects the supply curve at point *E*. Hence, *E* is the equilibrium point where *OR* is rent and *OX* is the land used. Now, suppose demand increases to D_1D_1 which intersects the supply curve *SS* at point E_1.

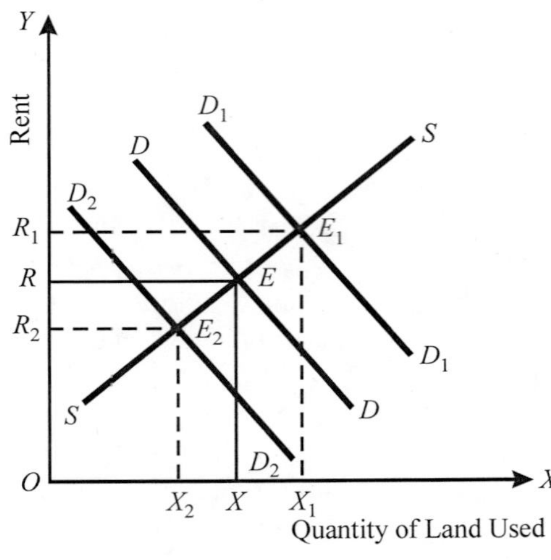

Fig. 41.3

At point E_1, the rent will be OR_1 and the land used will be OX_1. This means that since for this particular use, the rent of land has gone up, XX_1 land has been withdrawn from other uses (other economic units) and put to this use. Similarly, if demand for land decreases to D_2D_2, the rent will be reduced to OR_2 and the quantity of land used will also be reduced to OX_2.

According to modern economists, what is true of land is equally true of other factors of production. The rewards of other factors of production (i.e., interest for capital, wages for labour and profits for entrepreneurs) are also determined in the same manner as rent for the land. According to Mrs. Joan Robinson, "Rent arises on account of the scarcity of a, factor of production (not necessarily land) in relation to its demand. Any factor of production will yield rent if its supply is inelastic in relation to its demand."[6]

2. Rent as a Surplus over the Transfer Earnings of a Factor of Production

As we have already mentioned, rent can also be defined as a surplus over the transfer earnings of a factor of production. Transfer earnings (or opportunity cost) means the amount of money which any particular unit could earn in its next best alternative use.

Rent in the sense of surplus arises only when the supply of any factor of production (it may be land or any other factor input) is less than perfectly elastic. As far as the elasticity of supply is concerned, there are three possibilities:

(1) The supply of a factor of production may be perfectly elastic in which case rent will be zero.

(2) The supply of a factor of production may be perfectly inelastic in which case the entire price of the factor will be assumed as rent.

(3) There may be a situation in between these two extremes (i.e., elasticity of supply is elastic but not perfectly elastic) where the rent will arise.

In these three conditions, rent as a surplus over the transfer earnings will be different.

If the supply curve of a factor of production is perfectly inelastic as shown in Fig. 41.4, then its transfer earnings will be zero. It will be the case for specific factors of population which cannot be transferred to any other use. The supply of such a factor is absolutely fixed and it has only

6. Mrs. Joan Robinson, *The Economics of Imperfect Competition.*

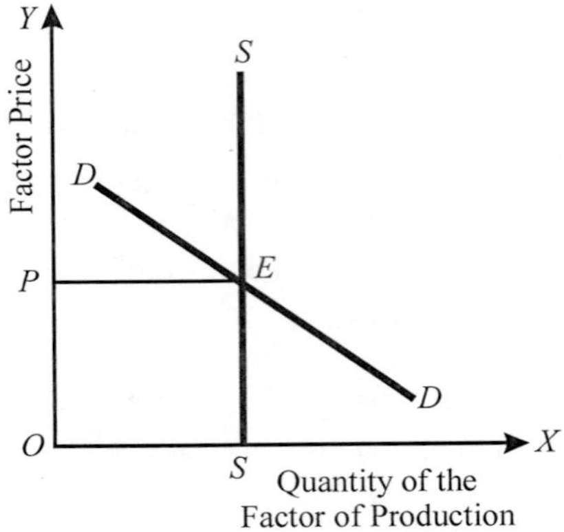

Fig. 41.4

one use, whether it is used or not. The minimum supply price can be zero. The actual price of such a factor will be determined by its demand. In Fig. 41.4, the demand curve *DD* intersects the supply curve *SS* at point *E;* therefore, the price of the factor is *OP*. This price or the entire income is the surplus and hence rent.

Now, if the supply curve of a factor of production is perfectly elastic as shown in Fig. 41.5, then the actual earnings will be equal to its transfer earnings, because the price of the factor is fixed. For example, under perfect competition the supply of a factor of production for an individual firm is perfectly elastic. In this case the demand curve will determine the equilibrium quantity of the factor used. Here the rent will be zero, because the factor will receive no surplus over its transfer earnings. In real life, no factor has a perfectly elastic supply.

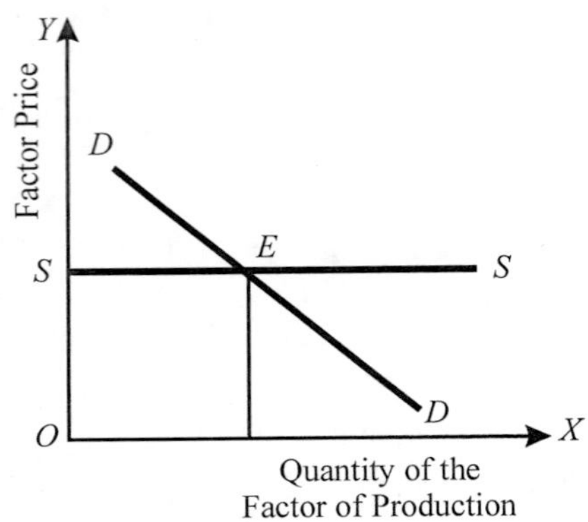

Fig. 41.5

Now, suppose that the supply curve of a factor of production is elastic but not perfectly elastic, then a part of the income (price) of the factor is rent. According to Mrs. Joan Robinson, rent is a surplus over the minimum supply price of the factor of production. She states, "The essence of the concept of rent is the concept of a surplus earned by a particular part of a factor of production over and above the minimum earnings necessary to induce it to do its work." Here the minimum supply price of a factor is the price below which that factor will not be willing to offer its services. In other words, the minimum supply price represents the transfer earnings of the factor of production. But due to its scarce supply, a factor of production gets a reward which is more than its transfer earnings or its minimum supply price. This surplus over the transfer earnings represents the rent of the factor. For non-specific factors of production, the supply curve is positively sloped or it is elastic. It states that if the factor is not paid the minimum supply price, then it will leave the present use and will enter into its next best paid alternative use. This case has been shown in Fig. 41.6. *SS* is the supply curve which is elastic. It cuts the demand curve *DD* at point *E*. Therefore, *OX* will be the equilibrium quantity of the factor used and the factor price will be equal to *OR*. The supply curve starts from point *S* on the vertical axis; which indicates that the minimum supply price to be paid will be *OS* and, thereafter, the supply price will increase for the other factor units. If in equilibrium *OX* units of the factor are employed, then the price paid to the last unit of the factor is just equal to its transfer earnings. But the intramarginal units will produce a surplus over their transfer earnings. In Fig. 41.6, the total earnings of the factor are equal to the area *OREX* while the transfer earnings are equal to the area *OSEX*. Thus, the surplus or rent will be equal to the shaded area *SRE* (= *OREX* – *OSEX*).

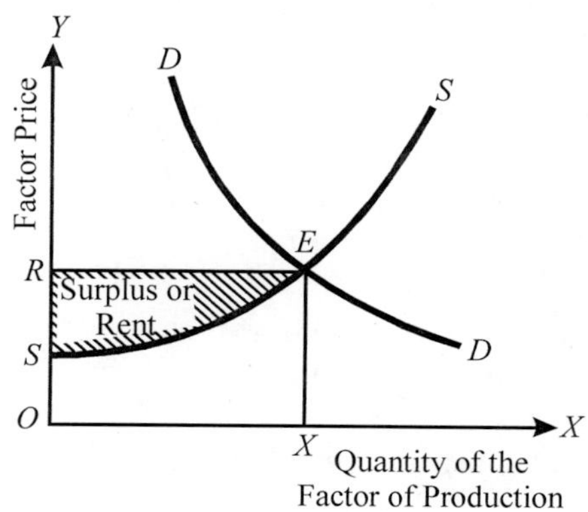

Fig. 41.6

6. MARSHALLIAN CONCEPT OF QUASI-RENT

The concept of quasi-rent was first introduced in economic theory by Marshall. It is an extension of the Ricardian concept of rent to the short-period earnings of capital equipments (such as machinery, buildings etc.) whose supply is inelastic in the short-run; i.e., it (supply) cannot be increased in the short-period. According to Marshall, "Quasi-rent is income derived from machines and other appliances made by man." The supply of some factors of production remains fixed in the short-period, but it can be changed to a considerable extent in the long-run. We have already seen that income from any agent (factor) of production which is permanently fixed in supply (e.g., land) is to be regarded as rent. Marshall also regarded the income from those factors which are permanently fixed in supply as rent; but income from those factors which are not fixed in supply permanently should be regarded as quasi-rent. Quasi-rent is, therefore, a payment which is almost rent but is not exactly economic rent.

To put it differently, we can say that in the short-period, factors of production can be divided into two categories:

1. Fixed factors of production, such as, machinery, plant, technology, etc.
2. Variable factors of production, such as, raw materials, labour, power, fuel, etc.

Fixed factors represent the fixed costs which have to be incurred even if production is stopped; while the variable factors of production represent the variable costs. In the short-run, the minimum price acceptable by the firm will be equal to its average variable cost *(AVC)*. If the short-run price is less than its *AVC,* then it will stop production. In other words, the maximum loss that the firm can bear in the short- run will be equal to its fixed costs. In case, the forces of (market) demand and (market), supply fix a price which is in excess of its variable cost, quasi-rent will emerge. The excess of price over the (average) variable cost (or prime cost) can be described as the returns of the fixed factors of production. This is also known as quasi-rent. Therefore, quasi-rent can be equal to the fixed costs or more than the fixed costs or it may be less than the fixed costs. It can be calculated by the following formula:

$$\text{Quasi-rent} = \text{Price} - AVC$$

If price = *AVC,* then the quasi-rent will be zero. Quasi-rent can never be negative because in case price becomes less than *AVC,* the firm will stop production.

Figure 41.7 shows the determination of quasi-rent. Here we assume that there is perfect competition and therefore, the price of the product is given to the firm exogenously. Price is equal to the marginal revenue. Now, let us assume that initial price is OP_1. Since the marginal cost curve (*MC*) of the firm intersects the marginal revenue curve (or price line) at a level where even the variable costs are not covered by the prevailing price, thus the firm would not produce anything at OP_1 price. The relevant range of marginal cost curve starts at point *S* (from which the supply curve of the firm takes place), where the product price just covers the average variable cost. At price OP_2, the firm produces OX_2 units (because at this level of output, firm's marginal cost equals its marginal revenue). At this level of output OX_2, the firm's quasi-rent will be zero, because entire total revenue obtained by the firm is paid to the variable factors of production and there will be no returns to the fixed factors of production.

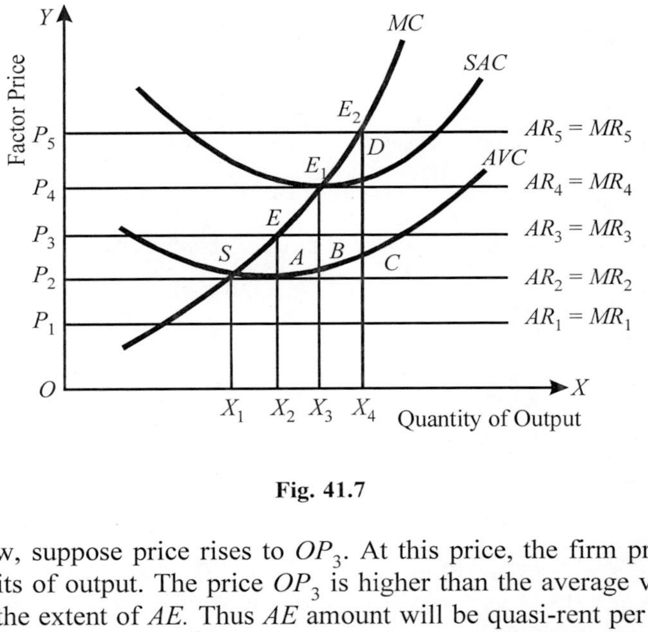

Fig. 41.7

Now, suppose price rises to OP_3. At this price, the firm produces OX_3 units of output. The price OP_3 is higher than the average variable cost to the extent of *AE*. Thus *AE* amount will be quasi-rent per unit of the output. Although at OP_3, the firm is incurring pure losses as its price is still less than the average cost, yet the firm will continue production because it will be able to cover a part of its fixed costs incurred by it on the output level OX_3.

If price further rises to OP_4, then the firm gets only the normal profits arid the amount of quasi-rent will be just equal to its fixed cost. In

Fig. 41.7, at OP_4 price and OX_4 level of output, the amount of quasi-rent (equal to fixed costs) is BE_1 per unit of output.

Finally at OX_5 price, the firm produces OX_5 units of output and earns a quasi-rent equivalent to CE_2 per unit of output. Out of this CE_2 quasi-rent, DE_2 is the pure (abnormal) profit per unit, because quasi-rent is greater than the fixed costs of the firm. Hence, pure profit is a part of quasi-rent.

However, in the long-run, the quasi-rent disappears. The reason is that all costs become the variable costs and the price must necessarily be equal to the average cost of the firm. Under the conditions of perfect competition, in the long-run, there is neither quasi-rent nor a pure profit to the firm.

EXERCISES

1. "Rent is paid for the original and indestructible powers of the soil." Explain the above statement.
2. How does the rent of land arise? Will there be any rent if all plots of land were equally fertile and equally favourably situated?
3. Explain the theory of rent and discuss whether there is any rent element in wages interest and profits.
4. Explain the concept of opportunity cost what effect, if any, does it exert on rent?
5. Distinguish between rent and quasi-rent. Show how the two are related to transfer earnings.
6. State and explain the Ricardian theory of rent Illustrate it diagrammatically.
7. "Rent can arise only if the supply of a factor is less than perfectly elastic." Explain.
8. Distinguish between differential rent and scarcity rent.
9. "Rent is price-determined and not price-determining." Explain.
10. Distinguish between economic rent and contract rent. Explain diagrammatically the Ricardian theory of rent.
11. "Corn is high not because rent is paid but rent is paid because corn in high." (Ricardo). Explain this statement in the light of the modem concept of rent.

Multiple Choice Questions

12. *(i)* The economic rent earned by any factor will be highest if its elasticity of supply is

    (a) zero　　*(c)* equal to one

    (b) between zero and one　　*(d)* infinite　　[*Ans. (a)*]

    (ii) If the supply of a factor can not be increased in the short-period and demand for it increases, it will

    (a) earn an economic rent

    (c) earn a windfall profit

    (b) earn a quasi-rent

    (d) increase its transfer earnings (cost)　　[*Ans. (b)*]

(iii) Economic rent is earned by a factor when its

(a) supply is inelastic

(b) supply is perfectly elastic

(c) supply is more than its demand

(*d*) demand is less than its supply

[*Ans. (a)*]

(iv) Economic rent is

(a) a surplus not a cost

(b) neither surplus nor a cost

(c) a cost not a surplus

(*d*) none of the above is correct

[*Ans. (a)*]

(*v*) In economics "Marginal Land" means, that land on which

(a) no rent is charged

(b) nominal rent is charged

(c) high rent is charged

(*d*) none of the above

[*Ans. (a)*]

Chapter 42

WAGES

1. INTRODUCTION

In this chapter we shall be concerned with the share of income that is assigned to labour in the pricing process. That share is called wages. According to J.R. Turner, "A wage is a price; it is the price paid by the employer to the worker on account of labour performed."[1] In simple words, it may be defined as the price paid by an entrepreneur to the workers employed for productive purposes. Thus, it is the share of the national dividend which accrues to labour in the broad sense of the term, including all kinds of workers whether they receive salaries, pays, or wages; whether they are paid daily, weekly, monthly or annually; whether they are skilled of unskilled labourers; whether their work is manual (physical) or mental.

Wage-payment is a reward for the labour. Sometimes, a distinction is made between nominal (money) wage and real wage. Money wage represents the money income of the labourer while real wage represents his command over goods and services which he can have with the help of his money wage. Real wage also includes the facilities which the labourer can get in his employment, such as, medical treatment, tree or subsidised housing etc. Thus, by real wages, we mean the total benefits, whether in cash or in kind, that a worker enjoys by working at a certain job. Real wage will incorporate even such factors as prospects of promotion, working hours, regularity of employment, nature of job, etc. Thus, in its wider sense real wage cannot be qualified and is beyond the purview of wage theory. Consequently, in studying the wage analysis, the term real wage is given a narrow meaning. In this sense, it represents the purchasing power of money wage of the worker.

Here our main purpose is to bring out the forces which determine wage rate. Since wage is a price paid for the services of labour, the theory

1. J.R. Turner, *Introduction to Economics,* p. 440.

of wage determination is simply a special case of the general theory of value. Like other prices, the price of labour, or wage is determined by its market demand and market supply. But unlike other commodities and factors of production, labour has certain peculiarities. Hence a separate theory for determining the reward of labour is required. The main peculiarities of labour are the following:

(1) The demand for a commodity depends on its utility to the buyer, but the demand for labour depends not on its utility to the employer but on its productivity. In other words, like other factors of production, the demand for labour is a derived demand.

(2) Labour cannot be separated from the labourer. Unlike other factors of production, the labourer has to present himself at the place where labour is required. This is not the case with other commodities and factors of production. Land can be separated from the landlord; capital from the capitalist, commodities from the trader. Due to the inseparability of labourers from labour, various personal factors affecting the former have to be considered when discussing the theory of wage determination. For example, labour is not so mobile as, say, capital because its mobility will depend upon the mobility of the worker which is hindered by a long list of personal considerations. These personal obstacles are absent in the case of other factors of production.

(3) Labour is a commodity, the labourer is not, and he is not bought and sold like machinery and other factors of production. The worker sells his work, but retains property in himself. In other words, commodities are produced for some specific ends, whereas human beings are ends in themselves.

(4) Labour power is the most perishable commodity. If a trader does not sell his commodity today, he hopes to be able to sell it tomorrow. But if a labourer does not work on any particular day, the labour power of that day perishes for ever and cannot be regained. Due to this peculiarity of labour, workers prefer to sell their labour power at any price rather than wait and let it perish irrevocably. As a result of this, the wages are generally less than what they should be. The labourer is always at a disadvantage in bargaining with the capitalist.

(5) The supply of labour increases and decreases very slowly. If the demand for an ordinary commodity increases, its price rises and it will be produced in increasing quantity. This is not the case with labour. If the demand for labour increases, its supply can increase only after a sufficient period of time. The same is true of a decrease in its supply. In other words, the supply of labour cannot adjust immediately to changes in

demand for it. Population and labour supply are dependent primarily upon factors other than wage rates and no functional relationship between the wage rates and population can be formed.

A number of theories have been developed from time to time to explain how wages are determined. We briefly refer below to some old classical theories and explain in detail the Marginal Productivity Theory and the Modern Theory of Wages.

2. THE SUBSISTENCE THEORY OF WAGES OR THE IRON LAW OF WAGES

The subsistence theory of wages owes its origin to the Physiocratic School of France, which flourished during the 18th century. Adam Smith also subscribed to this theory. The German economist, Lassalle named it as the *Iron Law of Wages.* It is also known as the *Brazen Law of Wages.* This is a rather simple theory, the crux of which is that in the long-run, wages would tend to equal just enough of food, clothing and shelter to maintain existence. This theory was based on the Malthusian Theory of Population. The two main assumptions of the theory are: (*i*) the operation of the law of diminishing returns in production, according to which there were definite limits to a continued high rate of expansion of food production, and (*ii*) population in the absence of checks would increase at a faster rate than the rate at which food supply would increase.

In the context of the above two assumptions, the theory states that wages are settled by a bargain between employers and labourers. The employers being few in number can combine and dictate wages, while labourers having no reserve (because labour being most perishable commodity) have to accept whatever wages they are paid. But wages cannot fall below the subsistence level— the subsistence level being the level which just maintains the labourers and their families. If wage rate falls below the subsistence level, the labourers will not be able to marry and to maintain families. After a generation the high death rate would reduce the number of labourers. Thus the supply of labour will fall short of demand and the wages would go up to the subsistence level. If on the other hand, wages are higher than the labourers will marry early and the number of workers will increase. The supply of labour being greater than the demand for it, wages will again fall to the subsistence level.

Criticisms of the Subsistence Theory of Wages

This theory has been criticised on the following grounds:

(1) The theory assumes that an increase in wages will always lead to an increase in population. But this is contrary to the facts.

(2) The theory is only one-sided. It attempts to explain wages from the supply conditions of labour and pays no attention to the reasons why labour is demanded.

(3) The theory is applicable only in the long-run.

It explains adjustment of wages over a generation and does not explain fluctuation from year to year.

(4) The theory ignores the influence of Trade Unions on wages. Trade Unions, today, play an important role in the determination of wages. Sometimes it can increase wages much beyond the level of subsistence.

(5) The theory fails to explain why wages are unequal in various occupations, regions and between different persons.

3. THE STANDARD OF LIVING THEORY OF WAGES

This theory is a modification of the subsistence theory of wages. The subsistence theory was abandoned towards the second half of the 19th century and in its place the standard of living theory was substituted. Here, it was realised that it was not mere subsistence but the standard of living which determined wages. It means that the labourers must not get only that amount of wages which is sufficient to maintain the labourers and their families, but the wages must be such as to keep the labourers in that standard to which they are accustomed. Thus, standard bf living means much more than mere subsistence level. It is defined as the amount of necessaries, comforts and luxuries to which a class of persons is habituated.

This theory is superior to the previous theory of wages be times it takes into consideration the efficiency of labour and also his productivity It is pointed out that wages which are equal to standard of living promote the efficiency of the labourers and labourers deserve because of their higher productivity.

Criticisms of the Standard of Living Theory of Wages

This theory has been criticised on the following grounds:

(1) According to the critics, the standard of living is one of the factors determining wages, but the other factors are more important which the theory fails to explain. Moreover, labourers do not possess a fixed standard of living. Thus, it is very difficult to measure the standard of living of various categories of persons.

(2) The theory states that wages should be determined according to the standard of living. But standard of living, on the other hand, is itself determined by wages. Thus, it is difficult to find out which is the cause and which is the effect.

(3) This theory assumes that wages depend upon standard of living which is fixed for sometime. Wages, however, change frequently in real life. Therefore, the theory is not true.

4. THE WAGE FUND THEORY OF WAGES

This theory was developed by J.S. Mill on the ideas of Adam Smith. According to Mill, "wages depend upon the demand and supply of labour; or as it is often expressed, on the proportion between population and labour. By population is here meant the number only of the labouring classes, or rather of those who work for hire; and by capital, only circulating capital, and not even the whole of that, but the part which is expended in the direct purchase of labour." The wage fund, or the part of capital spent in the direct hire of capital was fixed, being the result of saving or accumulation in the past period. This wage fund constituted the demand for labour, and the average rate of wages was determined by dividing the wage-fund by the number of workers.

It means that the general rate of wages will increase only if the wage fund increases or the supply of labour diminishes. Since the increase in wage fund is a slow process, because savings increase slowly; if the labourers want to increase their standard of living via increased wages, they must restrict the number of their children. Wage fund being more or less fixed, if any group of labourers gets higher wages, the only result will be that the other labourers would get less.

This theory is applicable to the underdeveloped countries of today where the population is increasing at a faster rate than the rate of saving (ware-fund).

Criticisms of the Wage Fund Theory of Wages

This theory has been criticised on the following grounds:

(1) According to the critics like Longe and Thornton, the theory does not explain, how the wage fund arises and why it remains fixed.

(2) The size of the wage-fund is not fixed independently of the quantity and quality of the labourers. Employers will increase the proportion of capital on hiring labour if such amount is warranted by the

greater relative efficiency of workers. Thus the total amount of capital paid in wages (i.e., wage fund) which he will assume to be given is not fixed but depends upon the number of labourers and the efficiency of labourers.

(3) The theory does not explain the differences in wages in different occupations.

(4) In real life, wages do not correspond to the total amount of capital available. In some countries, wages are high even though capital is scarce, e.g., in new countries. High wages are explained because of the smaller number of worker as compared to the demand for them and the higher productivity of these workers.

(5) This theory is not a scientific theory because it first assumes wage-fund to be given and then determines the wage rate. In fact, we should find first, the wage rate and then with the help of this wage rate, the wage fund can be calculated.

5. THE RESIDUAL CLAIMANT THEORY OF WAGES

The residual claimant theory replaced the wages-fund theory. According to this theory, the labourer is the residual claimant of the product of industry. In the words of Walker, the total product of industry is to be divided into four parts-rent, interest, profits and wages. The labourer gets out of the (total) product what remains after land, capital and entrepreneur have been paid their rewards. Thus wages are determined only after rent, interest and profits have been deducted from the total produce.

Criticisms of the Residual Claimant Theory of Wages

This theory has been criticised on the following grounds:

(1) In real life, it is found that at times of inflation, all rent, interest, profits and wages increase.

(2) According to this theory it is the labour who is the residual claimant, but in real practice, it is entrepreneur and not the labour who is the residual claimant. The entrepreneur bears the risk of the business while other factors of production, including labour, get fixed prices.

(3) It does not explain how trade unions are effective to increase the rate of wages.

(4) It ignores the influence of supply of labour in the determination of wages.

6. THE MARGINAL PRODUCTIVITY THEORY OF WAGES

While explaining the general theory of distribution in chapter 39, we have mentioned a detailed discussion of the marginal productivity theory. This theory states that under conditions of perfect competition every labourer will receive a wage equal to the value of its marginal product. This theory is analogous to the marginal utility theory of value. Just as the value of a commodity tends to equal its marginal utility to the individual, so given the supply of labour, its wages will tend to equal the marginal productivity of one unit of labour to the employer.

The marginal product of one unit of labour is determined by adding to, or by withdrawing one unit of labour from a business, provided the supply of other factors of production is kept fixed. Assuming the supply of other factors of production constant and the price of the product remaining the same, the employment of more and more units of labour in a firm will increase the total product at a diminishing rate. The entrepreneur will go on adding more and more units of labour; the marginal productivity diminishes, until a point will come where the increase in product due to the employment of the additional unit of labour is equal to the wages paid to the worker. That unit of labour is the marginal unit; and since all labour units are homogeneous, they will be paid the same wage rate equal to the marginal product or the value of the marginal product of labour. If the wages are greater than the value of marginal product of labour (VMP_L), the employers will reduce the employment they offer to labour. Similarly, if the wages are below the VMP_L, the employers will employ more labour units. Thus, in equilibrium, the following condition is maintained.

$$VMP_L = W$$

where VMP_L = Value of Marginal Product of Labour

W = Wage Rate

The above equilibrium condition can be shown with the help of a diagram as in Fig.42.1. Here WS_L is the supply curve of labour which is horizontal because all labour units are homogeneous and there is perfect competition in the market. D_LD_L is the VMP_L (value of marginal product of labour) curve which represents the demand curve for labour. The slope of the VMP_L curve is negative because of diminishing marginal productivity of labour. Point E is the equilibrium point where $VMP_L = W$. At this equilibrium point, the firm employs OL units of labour and pays OW wages of them.

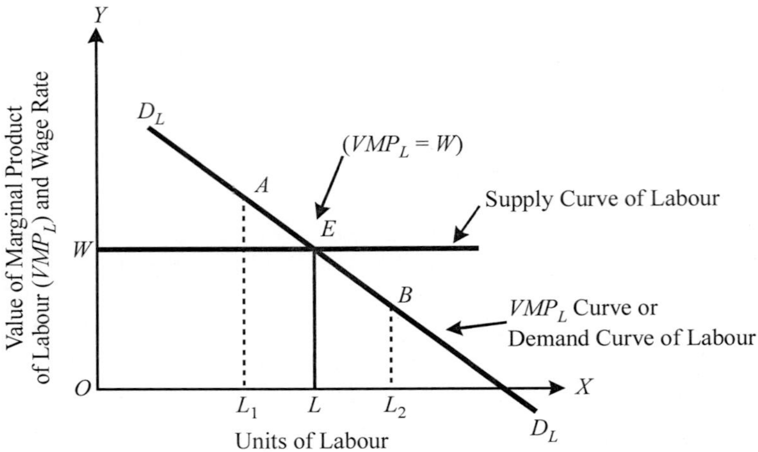

Fig. 42.1

At point A we find that

$$VMP_L > W$$

which means that the firm will still get profits if it employs more units of labour; although the rate of increase in profits will be diminishing, if the total profits will be increasing. Thus point A will not be an equilibrium point.

Also, at point B, we have

$$VMP_L < W$$

which means that the firm is getting a loss as it employs more than it requires. Thus, it will benefit by reducing the employment. So that, in equilibrium, the condition $VMP_L = W$ must hold.

It should be clearly understood that the marginal labourer is not necessarily the least efficient labourer. He is a "worker of normal efficiency whose additional output repays the employer with normal profits (of course after paying wages), and no more." He is marginal in the sense that the addition of him to the labour force equals the supply of labourers upto the number which the employer considers worth employing at the current wage rate.

Criticisms of the Marginal Productivity Theory of Wages

This theory has been criticised on the following grounds:

(1) The theory fails to account for the influences on the supply side. The marginal revenue product of labour determines the demand for labour, but it cannot by itself determine the equilibrium rate of wages.

(2) The theory is true only under certain assumptions, such as, perfect competition, perfect mobility of labour from employment to employment, homogeneous character of all labour and given prices of the product, etc. It means that marginal productivity theory is a static theory. But in actual world, things are dynamic. All the factors assumed to be constant are in fact constantly changing. Competition is never perfect; mobility of labour is restricted for various reasons; all labour is not of the same grade and prices of the products of labour vary. All these changes modify the theory when applied to actual conditions.

(3) This theory fails to explain the wage differentials. Wages differ from place to place, from person to person and from employment to employment.

(4) The market for goods is in general characterised by imperfect competition. This also unsettles the theory.

(5) The productivity of labourers is also dependent on factors, such as, the quality of capital and efficiency of management. These factors are outside the control of labourers. Thus, it is difficult to have a correct measurement of the marginal (revenue) productivity of labourers.

(6) According to Dobb, the demand for labour does not depend on productivity but on the willingness of the capitalists to save which depends on previous profits and on previous wage bargains.

(7) Prof. Taussig also rejects the marginal productivity theory of wages. He says, "Wages are determined by the discounted marginal product of labour." In his opinion, there is no specific product ascribable either to labour or to capital. There is a ''joint product"—the fruit of the co-operation of labour and capital. From this joint product, it is impossible to isolate the separate contributions of each of the two factors. He further believes that capital is not a separate factor of production, but it is the embodiment of past labour. These fruits of past labour, the capital goods—are owned by capitalists or employers. Capital is thus recognized as previous labour. Though organisation is a separate factor, its rewards are best regarded as simply a form of wages. Hence, the same principle would determine the rewards of past as well as present labour, hired as well as independent labour.

Now, labour past and present produce a joint output on the marginal land, i.e., land on which no rent is paid. Since marginal land makes no contribution to the output, this output he calls the marginal output of labour of all kinds. But the labourers cannot get the full amount of the marginal product. For, production takes time. Labour is a future good in the sense that by employing labour one cannot get the final product immediately, but after a period of time. In the meantime the labourers must be supported. It is the function of the (capitalist) employers to support the labourers by giving them advances. They cannot therefore hand over the full amount of the output to the labourers. They would deduct a certain percentage from the final output, on account of the advances they have made, and hand over the rest to labour. This deduction, or discount takes place at the current rate of interest. Thus, wages are equal to the discounted marginal product of labour.

7. THE MODERN THEORY OF WAGES OR THE DEMAND AND SUPPLY THEORY OF WAGES

The modern theory of wages is substantially the same as the theory of value, subject to certain reservations necessitated by the peculiar characteristics of labour discussed in the beginning of this chapter. According to this theory wages are determined by the intersection of the forces of the demand for labour and its supply. The equilibrium wage rate would be that which would just clear the market. A wage rate above the equilibrium rate would produce a "surplus" of workers; a rate below the equilibrium rate would produce a "shortage" of workers. Neither shortages nor surpluses could exist if the wage-rate were free to seek the equilibrium, or market-clearing level.

Now, we shall discuss the modern theory of wages under perfect competition as well as under imperfect competition.

Wages Determination under Perfect Competition

Demand for Labour. The demand for labour is a derived demand. It is derived from the demand for the goods and services produced with the use of laboul. The demand for labour by an employer (firm) at a given moment of time is determined: (*a*) by what labour contributes to the output of the firm, that is, by its productivity, and (*b*) by what the firm receives for its output in the market. Since in perfect competition the price of the product is fixed for the individual firm, the demand for labour will depend upon the marginal productivity of labour. Further, the productivity of labour applied to a given amount of capital, land, and management, obeys the law of diminishing marginal productivity and, therefore, the demand for labour by anyone firm usually shows an inverse relationship between wage rates and the number of workers hired. The higher the wage, the fewer workers hired, and vice versa.

The marginal productivity of labour can also be expressed as the marginal revenue productivity. If the marginal (physical) productivity of labour (MPP_L) is multiplied by the price of the product, it becomes marginal revenue productivity (MRP_L) or the value of marginal product of labour (VMP_L). Thus,

$$MRP_L = MPP_L.P_X$$

where MRP_L = Marginal Revenue Productivity of Labour

MPP_L = Marginal Physical Productivity of Labour

P_X = Price of the Product

Since price of the product remains the same throughout, the MRP_L or VMP_L curve will also be negatively sloped. This curve will represent the demand curve for labour for the individual firm. In order to obtain the demand curve for the whole industry, we have to add up the demand schedules of the individual firms. But one more factor enters into the picture. As the industry's output increases, the price of the commodity falls. This reinforces the tendency for the demand price for labour to decrease as the number of labourers to be employed increases. The industry's *MRP* declines more markedly. Generally, in short-period, the demand curve for labour is less elastic than in the long-run.

Supply of Labour. By the supply of labour, we mean the different amounts of hours or days of a given type of labour which would be offered for hire at different wage rates. Normally, the higher the wage offered, the greater will be the amount of labour supplied. For the economy as a whole, the supply of labour will be determined by the number of potential workers in the economy and by the decisions those people would make regarding the number of hours they would be willing to work at each of a series of wage rates over a given period of time. The last decision would be determined by the psychology of the individual, i.e., his attitude towards work and leisure, and as between possible employments and places, etc.

Under perfect competition, the supply of labour may be considered from two viewpoints:

(1) Supply of labour to the entire economy; and

(2) Supply of labour to the individual firm.

The market supply curve of labour tends to be positively inclined over a very wide range of wage rates. More labour hours will be offered at a higher wage than at a lower wage. But sometimes the market supply curve may be a backward bending curve. The backward bending supply curve as illustrated in Panel (*a*) of Fig. 42.2, shows that the amount of labour offered first increases as the wage is increased from a low level; then, as the wage approaches and passes that needed to bring the level of living upto the maximum or desired standard of living, further increases in wage rates lead to decreases in the amount of labour offered.

Another type of market supply curve of labour is illustrated in Panel (*b*) of Fig. 42.2. It shows that the amount of labour offered increases with increases in wage rate throughout the relevant range of wages.

The supply of labour to the individual firm operating in a competitive market is illustrated in Panel (*c*) of Fig. 42.2. It shows that the firm can hire as many or as few workers as it wishes without producing any finite change in the prevailing wage rate.

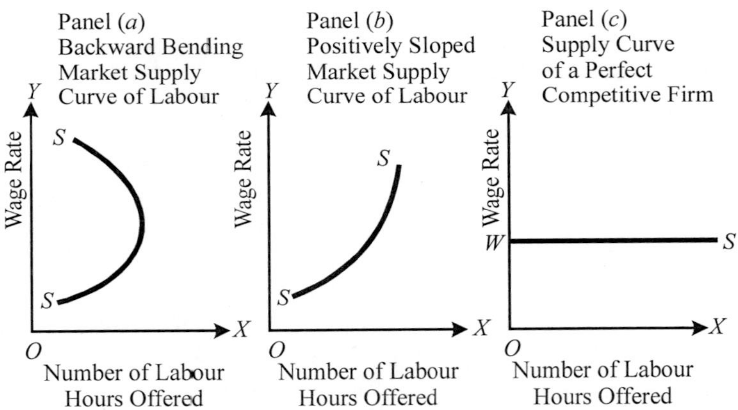

Fig. 42.2

Thus, under perfect competition, the supply of labour to a given firm is infinitely elastic; while for the industry (economy) as a whole, the supply curve of labour is generally elastic. It slopes upwards from the left to the right.

Interaction of Demand and Supply Curves. In perfect competition, equilibrium wage will be determined at that level where the demand for labour of a particular type is equal to the supply of that labour. This wage rate is just equal to the marginal productivity or labour measured in terms

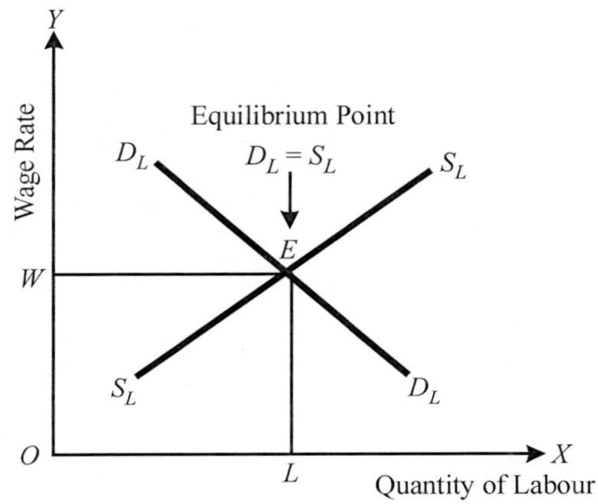

Fig. 42.3

of money (i.e., the *MRP*). Because the combination of the demands for labour from all of the firms (i.e., their *MRP* curves) in the market represents the market de-mand for labour. All labourers would get this rate. This is shown in Fig. 42.3. In this diagram, the curve *SS* represents the supply curve of labour to the economy (industry) as a whole. *DD* is the demand curve for labour of the economy (industry). Demand and supply curves intersect at point *E*. Therefore, *OW* wage rate (which is equal to *EL*) will be established. At this wage rate, *OL* quantity of labour will be employed. The equilibrium wage rate will change if the demand and supply conditions change.

Once the wage rate is determined for the entire industry, each competitive firm accepts that wage rate as given fur it. This is the reason that the supply curve of labour for the individual firm under perfect competition is perfectly elastic. The firm can purchase any quantity of labour it wishes to buy in the labour market without raising the wage rate. In Fig. 42.4, the supply curve of labour for the competitive firm is shown by the horizontal wage line *WW*. It is also shown in Fig. 42.4 that under the competitive conditions, wage rate in the long-run will be equal to both the marginal revenue product and the average revenue product. If the wage rate is less than the average revenue product, the firms would be getting super-normal profits in the short-run. As a result, new firms wilt enter into the industry (market) and the demand for labour will increase, which will push up the wage rate so as to be equal to the average revenue product.

If, on the other hand, wage rate is more than the average revenue product, the firms will be suffering losses in the short-run. As a result, some firms will leave the industry and demand for labour will increase which will lead to a decrease in the wage rate. Panel (*b*) of Fig. 42.4 shows the long-run equilibrium of the firm under perfect competition. The long-run equilibrium wage rate is *OW* where the firm is employing *OL* units of labour. The wage rate *OW* is equal to the marginal revenue product (*MRP*) and the average revenue product at point *A*. This point *A* is the equilibrium position of the firm in the long-run.

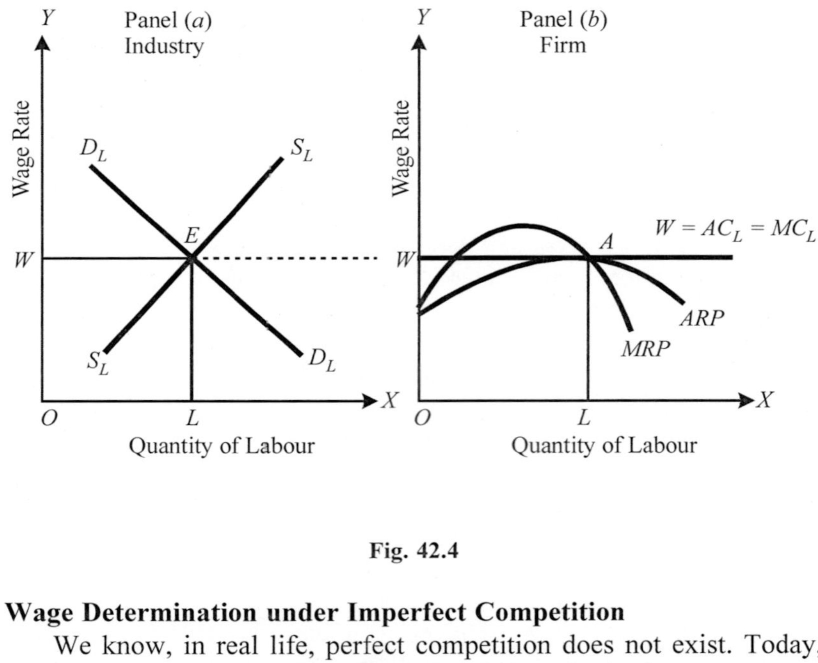

Fig. 42.4

Wage Determination under Imperfect Competition

We know, in real life, perfect competition does not exist. Today, employers as well as labourers are highly organised. There are strong labour unions and employers' associations in every important industry and trade. There are many types of imperfectly competitive situations found in both the labour market and the product market. We shall discuss the following important market situations:

(1) *Wage Determination under the Conditions of Monopoly (Element) in the Product Market.* We know that if product market is perfectly

competitive, demand for labour will be directly determined by the value of the marginal product of labour (VMP_L) or by the marginal revenue productivity of labour (MRP_L). Now, if there is monopoly or monopolistic competition in the product market, then the situation of demand for labour will be different. As we know this fact that except in the perfect competitive market, the demand curve for a firm's product is negatively sloped, and consequently the marginal revenue curve will lie below it. There, the nature of firm's demand curve (i.e., whether it is perfectly horizontal or negatively sloped) has no effect on the marginal physical product of labour (MPP_L); yet, the monopoly firm can no longer accept the VMP curve as its demand curve for labour because every additional unit of the product produced by the increased quantity of labour would bring a lower price than before. This is the reason that the (monopoly) firm's decision variable is now marginal revenue rather than price (of the product). In other words, the monopoly firm will take the decision about the demand for labour on the basis of its MRP_L rather than the VMP_L. In monopoly these two terms will have different meanings.

The MRP_L'[2] here, is defined as the amount of revenue which is added by the marginal product to the total revenue. It can be defined as a change in total revenue by the sale of the output attributable to the additional unit of labour. Mathematically,

$$MRP_L = \frac{\Delta TR}{\Delta L} \qquad \text{...(1)}$$

where ΔTR = Change in total revenue

ΔL = Change in the amount of labour employed

But, ΔTR is the marginal revenue which is defined as below:

$$MR = \frac{\Delta TR}{\Delta X} \qquad \text{...(2)}$$

or

$$\Delta TR = MR.\Delta X \qquad \text{... (3)}$$

where X is the total output, or $X = TP_L$; therefore, ΔX is the marginal physical product (MPP_L) attributable to the additional unit of labour. Thus, MPP_L can be defined as

$$MPP_L = \frac{\Delta X}{\Delta L} = \frac{\Delta TP_L}{\Delta L} \qquad \text{...(4)}$$

or

$$\Delta L = \frac{\Delta X}{MPP_L} \qquad \text{...(5)}$$

2. In perfect competition, $MRP_L = MPP_L.P_X = VMP_L$.

Now substituting the values of ΔTR and ΔL from (3) and (5) into the equation (1), we get

$$MPP_L = \frac{MR}{\Delta X} \cdot \frac{\Delta X}{MPP_L} MR.MPP_L \quad ...(6)$$

Now in perfect competition, we know that $MR = P$ and therefore $MRP_L = VMP_L$. But in monopoly, $MR < P$ and, therefore, for a given amount of labour, $MRP_L < VMP_L$. Once, this difference is noted, the employment of labour by the monopoly firm can be determined in the same manner as under perfect competition. Thus, we can say that wages for a given number of labourers will be lower under monopoly than under perfect competition (because $MRP_L < VMP_L$). In other words, in monopoly situation, MRP_L declines faster and equals the wage rate at employment of smaller number of labourers. In Fig. 42.5, we have drawn the VMP_L (which is the demand curve for labour for the competition firm and equals the MRP_L), and MRP_L (the demand curve of the monopoly firm) curves.

Since, perfect competition prevails in the labour market, the supply curve of labour for the monopoly firm will be a horizontal line as shown by *WW* in Fig. 42.5. As discussed above, even though the marginal physical product of labour remains the same, the introduction of monopoly element in the product market will mean that the additional revenue (*MR*) will decrease for each unit of increased production. Thus, point *Ec* will be the equilibrium point of the competitive firm where it employs *OLc* units of labour at *OW* wage rate. Point *Em* will be the equilibrium point of the mono-poly firm where it employs *OLm* units of labour at the same *OW* wage rate.

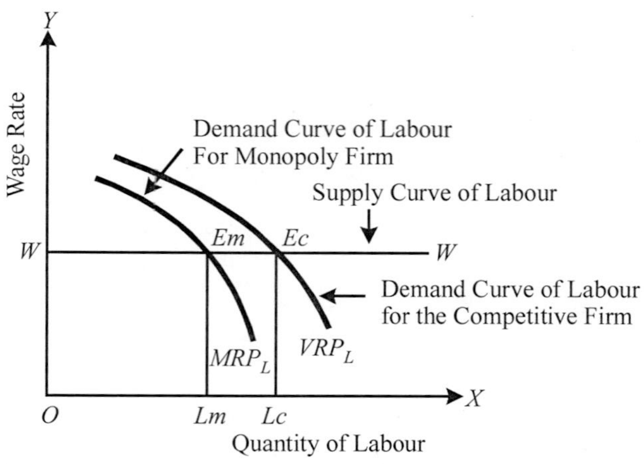

Fig. 42.5

In conclusion, we can say that the introduction of monopoly element in the product market will reduce the level of labour employment, even though wage rate remains the same.

(2) *Wage Determination under the Conditions of Monopoly in the Labour Market.* In our above discussion, we have assumed that there is monopoly or monopolistic competition in the product market, but there is perfect competition in the labour market. Now, we assume a labour-market situation in which there is a single buyer of labour. This situation is called one of the monopsony. Since the firm and the market are the same, the supply curve of labour for the firm is the same as the supply curve of labour for the market. The monopolist cannot purchase an unlimited amount of labour at a uniform price or wage rate; therefore, he has to offer successively higher wages to the new labourers. This means that ordinarily the monopolist faces an upward-sloping supply curve for labour. Contrast this with the supply curve of labour faced by the firm that buys labour under conditions of perfect competition. Under perfect competition, the firm can get as many units of the labour per unit of time as it desires at the going market price or wage rate; hence, it is faced with a horizontal or perfectly elastic supply curve of labour, even though the market supply curve may be upward-sloping to the right or less than perfectly elastic.

The upward slope of labour supply curve faced by the monopolist gives monopsony the characteristics that distinguishes it from pure competition to obtain larger quantities of labour per unit of time, the monopolist must pay higher wages.[3] Hiring of additional workers, therefore, means a sharp rises in the cost of labour as a whole. In other words, the marginal cost rises by more than the amount of the additional wage rate for a single labour. This is shown in Fig. 42.6. Here the curve *SS* indicates the schedule of supply for workers. i.e., the average cost of labour. It has an upward slope indicating that if higher wages are offered, more and more labourers will apply for jobs. MC_L represents the marginal cost (i.e., addition to total costs) of hiring successively greater number of labourers. Now, under conditions of perfect competition among

3. It means, if the monopolist needs more labour, he may have to offer more money to get them. But if he offers higher wages to those newly taken on, he must pay a like amount to those already in his employment, because different rates of wages in the market for labour of the same grade working in the same plant would cause him serious trouble.

employers, the wage would be established at the equilibrium point *P*, which corresponds to *OW* wage rate. But if employer is a monopolist, he will seek to exploit his command over the labour market to the maximum by equating his demand curve (*MRP* curve) with marginal cost curve. The point of intersection of these two curves (at *E*) tells us the number of labourers that it will be most profitable to hire. In this case, *OL* units of labour will be employed. Our supply curve (average cost curve) tells us

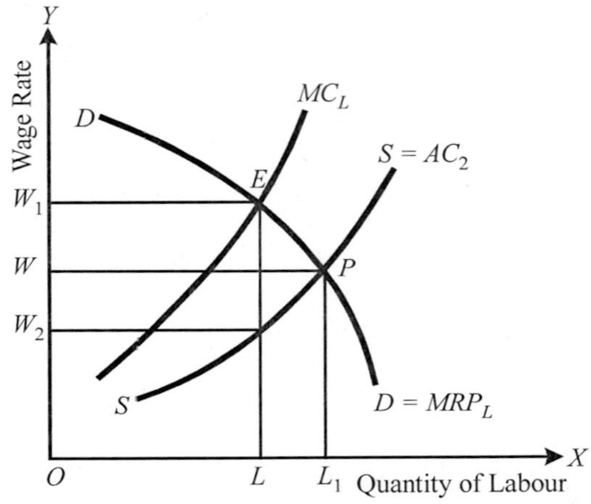

Fig. 42.6

that this number of workers can be obtained by paying OW_2 wage rate; therefore, this is the wage that the monopolist will presumably offer. So he employs fewer labourers, and pays a considerably lower wage, than he would if he were in competition with other employers.

Thus the monopolist differs from the competitive buyer of labour with respect to the price paid for the labour at the profit maximising level of employment. For *OL* quantity of labour, it is necessary for the monopolist to pay a price of OW_L only, although the marginal revenue product of labour (MRP_L) at that level of employment is equal to OW_1 (= *EL*). Should the monopolist employ that quantity of labour at which its *MRP* is equal to its price, i.e., wage as does the competitive firm—he would make less profit to maximise his profits—he restricts the quantity of labour used and pays it a wage rate less than its marginal revenue product.

(3) *Wage Determination under the Bilateral Monopoly or under the Combined Situation of Monopoly and Monopsony.* In the above analysis we have discussed the price-determination separately under monopoly and under monopsony. Now we shall discuss the situation in which the same firm holds monopoly power in the product market and the monopsony power in the labour market. This has been illustrated in Fig. 42.7. If there is perfect competition in the prbduct market as well as in the labour market, wage rate would be equal to the value of marginal product of labour (i.e., $W = VMP_L$). This has been shown by the equilibrium point *Ec* where *OLc* quantity of labour is employed at *OWc* wage rate. Now, if there is monopoly in the product market and perfect competition in the labour market; then the MRP_L curve will represent the market demand curve of labour (which is the sum of the individual firms' MRP_L curves) while the market supply curve will be the *SS* curve (or the *ACL* curve). In this situation, equilibrium will be established at point *Em* where *OLm* quantity of labour will be employed at *OWm* wage rate. Thus, in the case of perfect competition in both the markets, the quantity of labour employed (*OLc*) as well as the wage rate (*OWc*) will be relatively higher than that of the situation where there is monopoly in the product market and perfect competition exists in the labour market.

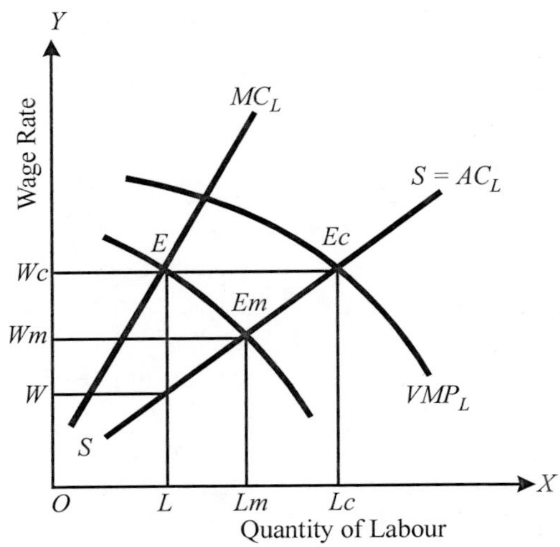

Fig. 42.7

Now if the same firm which occupies monopoly in the product market, also occupies a monopsony power in the labour market, the relevant supply curve will be the MC_L curve and the demand curve will be the MRP_L curve. The equilibrium point will be established at *E* where *OL* quantity of labour will be employed at *OW* wage rate. Therefore, in this case, the wages and quantity of labour employed are further reduced. The total exploitation will be the difference between the wage rate which labourers get in perfect competitive conditions (in both the markets) and the one they get when both the markets are controlled by the same firm. In Fig. 42.7 the amount of total exploitation is equal to *WWc* (= *OWc* – *OW*). Of this total exploitation, *WcWm* is attributable to monopoly element in the product market and *WmW* is attributable to monopsony element in the labour market.

8. ECONOMIC EFFECTS OF TRADE UNIONS

Under the characteristics of labour, we have seen that the bargaining capacity of an individual labour is very week. They can successfully compete with employers only if they combine together and bargain collectively. With this aim, the labourers organise themselves into labour or trade unions. Sydney and Beatrice Webb, authorities on trade unionism, define a trade union as "a continuous association of wage-earners for the purpose of maintaining or improving the conditions of their employment". Trade unions try to curb exploitation of labour by the employer (who assumes a monopoly power in the product-market and a monopsony power in the labour-market). Generally, a trade union forces or compels the monopolist (or imperfectly competitive firms) to pay the competitive wage rates to the workers. It may also aspire to get maximum possible employment to labourers by forcing the government and employers to adopt labour-intensive techniques. Now, the extent to which trade unions succeed in getting their objectives—i.e., acquiring a "fair wage" and "a maximum possible level of employment"—will largely depend in part on the elasticity of labour supply curve and in part on the slope of the MRP_L curve (i.e., the demand curve for labour).

Figure 42.8 clears the economic effect of trade unions. Here suppose that the initial equilibrium point is *E*, where the wage rate is OW_1 and the level of employment is OL_1. At OW_1 wage rate, the total exploitation of labourers will be equal to W_1W_2 (= OW_2 – OW_3), i.e., the difference between the competitive wage rate OW_2 and the actual wage rate OW_1.

Now suppose trade union emerges. It has got three options: (*i*) to increase the wage rate, or (*ii*) to increase employment and provide a competitive wage rate, or (*iii*) to retain the present level of employment and insist on getting the maximum possible hike in the wage rate. We can analyse three types of effects in the following manner:

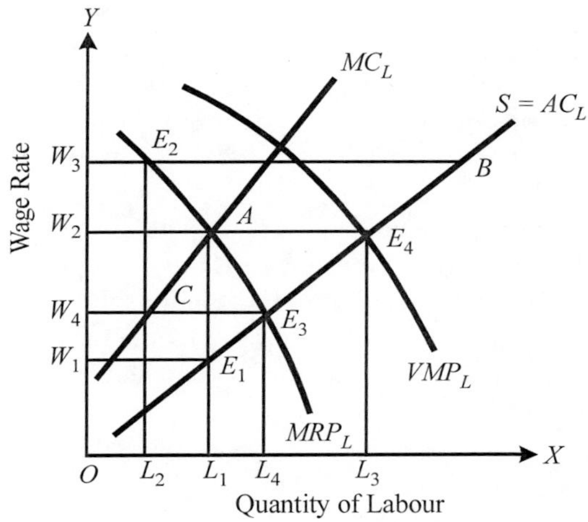

Fig. 42.8

In the first situation, suppose trade union demands a high wage rate, say OW_3. In this case, the labour supply curve will become $W_3 BS$ which is cut by the monopolist's demand curve for labour at point E_2. At this point of forced equilibrium, the employers will employ OL_2 quantity of labour at OW_3 wage rate. This results in a decrease in the level of employment from OL_1 to OL_2.

In the second situation, suppose trade union forces the firm to employ that much number of labourers and pay them that wage which would be admissible in a perfectly competitive labour (i.e., $W = MRP_L$) market. In this case, the equilibrium point will be E_3 where the labourers would get OW_4 wage rate and the firm will employ OL_4 units of labour. This means that the trade union will be able in acquiring high wage rate and high level of employment as compared to the initial equilibrium situation, but it would not be able to increase the wage rate as much as it would be if the first alternative is adopted.

In the third situation, the trade union would like to retain the initial level of employment (OL_1) and insist to increase the wage rate upto the competitive level, i.e., OW_2. In this case, the labour supply curve becomes W_2E_4S. This supply curve states that the monopolist can buy as much as OL_3 units of labour by paying OW_2 wage rate. In other words, the W_2E_4 part of the labour supply curve W_2E_4S is perfectly elastic. The monopolist's demand curve for labour, i.e., the MRP_L curve intersects the supply curve of labour at point A. Therefore, the trade union succeeds in retaining the initial level of employment (OL_1) at a substantial high wage rate (OW_2). This is the real objective of the trade unions all over the world that they always fight for their members to get the maximum possible wage rate from the employers.

The above discussion concludes that trade unions, generally affect the supply curve of labour. To this extent the monopolistic exploitation can be removed by trade unions. But trade unions fail to remove a part of monopolistic exploitation which is enjoyed by the monopolistic firm due to its monopoly power in the product market which is represented by the vertical distance between the MRP_L curve and the VMP_L curve.

9. CAUSES OF WAGE DIFFERENCES

We know that consumers generally pay the same price for a standard commodity regardless of the firm which supplies it. If labour had been like any other commodity, it would also have been sold in the market at the same rate. But, as we have described in the beginning of the chapter that labour possesses its peculiar characteristics. Labourers differ in efficiency. They are less mobile than the other commodities and factors of production. Their supply can be changed only after a sufficient time period. For these peculiarities, wage-differentials exist in the economy. Some of the important causes of wage differences may be described in the following manner:

(1) *Difference in the demand conditions of labour.* As we know, the demand for any type of labour is derived from the demand for the product it helps to produce. In the real world, we find differences in the demands for various commodities. Some products may have greater demand while the other products may possess lower demand. This means that those labour units which are used in the production of goods which are much in demand will command a higher price (wage).

(2) *Elasticity of labour supply differs from person to person.* Different types of labourers respond differently to a given change in wage rate. It

is due to the fact that elasticity of labour supply differs from person to person. Different persons have different transfer earnings. Some persons may not like to work at a wage rate that is lower than their transfer earnings. Further, after a certain point the supply curve of some labourers bends backward, which indicates that a further rise in wage rate will induce these workers to work less; because they now prefer leisure to work.

(3) *Absence of perfect competition and free mobility of labour.* Perfectly competitive conditions do not prevail in the labour market. Trade unions and employers' associations affect considerably the tree play of economic forces, particularly the market supply curve of labour. A strong trade union may force the employer to pay high wages.

(4) *Labour immobility.* Labour is not perfectly mobile as the other factors of production and commodities. The lesser the mobility of particular type of labour, the lesser will be its bargaining power to get high wages and vice versa.

(5) *Differences in efficiency.* Investment of capital into labour increases the efficiency of some labourers. This will result in differences between skilled labour and unskilled labour and hence wage-differences.

(6) *Steadiness of employment.* In the time of a season, the wages are higher than those in a regular period.

(7) *Government regulations.* Sometimes the government fixes minimum wages in particular trades, thus reducing differences between these and other business.

(8) *Non-competing groups.* Society is generally divided into a number of working groups which are non-competing. Caste system has created such groups in India. As a result, a child born to a carpenter will most likely be a carpenter. Thus, inheritance environment, training and sex etc. are some of the factors which create non-competing groups in the country. Labourers belonging to different groups are paid at different wage rates. Thus, the presence of a number of non-competing groups leads to differences in wages.

EXERCISES

1. Compare the process of wage determination under perfect competition witl1 the under imperfect competition.
2. Define 'monopolistic exploitation' and discuss the conditions under which it can happen.
3. (*a*) Give the meaning of wages and distinguish between nominal wages and real wages.
   (*b*) Explain the marginal productivity theory of wages.

4. Discuss briefly the following theories of wages:
   (*a*) The Subsistence Theory of Wages or The Iron Law of Wages
   (*b*) The Standard of Living Theory of Wages
   (*c*) The Wages Funa Theory of Wages
   (*d*) The Residual Claimant Theory of Wages
5. What do you mean by marginal productivity of labour? Explain the marginal productivity theory of wages. What are its main assumptions and criticisms?
6. "Wages under perfect competition are equal to both the marginal and the average produce of labour." Explain.
7. State the modern theory of wages. How far is it true to say that the theory of wages is an application of the general theory of value?
8. Discuss the effects of trade unions in the determination of wages. What are the cause of differences in wages?

Multiple Choice Questions

9. (*i*) Wages Fund Theory was formulated by
   (*a*) J.S. Mill (*c*) Marshall
   (*b*) Walker (*d*) Physiocrats [*Ans.* (*a*)]

   (*ii*) Under perfect competition *MRP* of labour is measured as:
   (*a*) *MP* of labour × Price of the product
   (*b*) *MP* of labour × Total price
   (*c*) *MP* of labour × Marginal revenue
   (*d*) *MP* of labour × Price of labour [*Ans.* (*a*)]

   (*iii*) In a perfect market, under perfect competitive conditions, wage will be determine at tile point where
   (*a*) MP_L = Price of the Product (*c*) Demand for Labour = Supply of Labour
   (*b*) MP_L = Total Revenue (*d*) All of the above [*Ans.* (*c*)]

   (*iv*) Under perfectly competitive conditions, labour will be demanded upto a point when its marginal productivity is
   (*a*) zero (*b*) equal to wages paid
   (*c*) all of the above (*d*) none of the above [*Ans.* (*b*)]

Chapter 43

INTEREST

1. INTRODUCTION

Interest is the "price" paid for the use of money or capital. When a person lends money to a borrower, he ordinarily expects, not only that it will be returned at the expiration of the loan period, but that he will also receive a payment of interest. This interest is usually paid as a percentage of principal sum, payable annually. For example, if the rate of interest is 10 per cent, a seven-year mortgage loan of Rs. 10,000 on a piece of real estate should yield Rs. 1,000 per year, in addition to a repayment of Rs. 10,000 at the end of that period.

Until the end of sixteenth century social philosophers were opposed to the idea of charging-interest on capital funds. The Greek philosophers; Plato, Aristotle and Cicero and the great Kautilya had condemned usury. The Bible was the source of inspiration to the Greek philosophers and the ancient Romans. According to these writers, people used to borrow money to meet their consumption needs and, therefore, from moral point of view they should not be required to pay interest. Further, they assumed that savings were barren, because they could not think that the borrowed funds at all be used for productive purposes. According to Aristotle, "Money is barren, it cannot breed money." The Islamic religion also prohibited interest strictly. Therefore, the old sixteenth century writers did not like the idea of paying and charging interest on borrowed capital.

Later, physiocrats recognised the importance of loans in the production process. Quesnay and Mirabeau stated that whenever a real increase of wealth (production) resulted from the use of capital, the payment of interest might be justified. Adam Smith, the founder of the classical school, justified interest as it was paid by the borrower to the lender for the profits of the former that could arise by the use of money. In modern times, interest regulates the flow of business and industrial activity in economy by influencing the demand and supply of capital.

2. DEFINITION OF INTEREST

In an ordinary sense, interest is the price that is paid for the use of capital. In economics, the term "interest" refers to the payment for the use of capital, when there are no risks of non-payment and no additional work consequent on the loan. In other words, in economics, interest does not refer to the total amount paid by a borrower, but to that of this payment which can be attributed to the use of capital only and for nothing else. The term "interest" has been defined by different economists in different ways. Some of the definitions are the following:

According to T.N. Carver, "Interest is the income which goes to the owner of the capital."

According to J.S. Mill, "Interest is the remuneration for mere abstinence."

According to Knut Wicksell, "Interest 'is a payment made by the borrower of capital by virtue of its productivity, as a reward for his (capitalist) abstinence."

According to Alfred Marshall, "Interest is the price paid for the use of capital in any market. ..."

According to Keynes, "Interest is a premium which is offered to wealthholders to induce them to part with their cash."

On the basis of the above definitions we may conclude that interest is a payment made or received for the use of a sum of money (capital) over a period of time.

3. NET INTEREST AND GROSS INTEREST

As we have seen, economic interest is the price paid for use of capital only. It is called by economists net (pure) interest. It is also sometimes called *time discount*. It is the net payment made to lenders for parting with their money, without any extra compensation for possible risk of loss, expense of collecting payment of interest and principal, or allowance for depreciation in the value of money loaned, and without any monopoly profit.

But, the sum that is usually paid by the borrower includes, besides interest proper (i.e., net interest), payments to cover the risks, payments on account of the troubles and inconveniences to which the lender is put and other types of allowances. This is commonly referred to as gross interest. Therefore, gross interest will be somewhat above the net interest. Here we are concerned with the net interest and not the gross interest. Gross interest comprises the following elements:

(1) *Insurance against Risk.* When money is lent by the lender, he has to bear some risks. Marshall divides these risks into two parts, business risks and personal risks. The former includes the risks related to price and demand while the latter arise from the fact that the borrowers may be dishonest or incapable of returning the money. The lender, therefore, expects a reward in proportion to the degree of risk involved.

(2) *Reward for Management.* Besides running risks, every loan involves some amount of work in keeping records of payments of small instalments, etc. The lender has to keep reminding his debtors by post and through personal visits. He desires some reward for this kind of work. Therefore, gross interest includes, besides other things, remuneration for management.

(3) *Payment for Inconvenience.* The lender will charge a high rate of interest if he is not sure that the interest and principal will be paid in time. For he may not be able to reap the gains of favourable time. The greater the inconvenience involved, the higher will be the gross interest.

(4) *Net Interest.* When we deduct the above items from the gross interest, the remaining part is net interest, It is due to the use of capital.

Hence, gross interest may be very high while net interest may be very low. The net rate of interest will be the same for all because the force of competition will fix one single rate for the whole economy. But the rates of gross interest will differ from place to place and person to person. When we talk about differences in interest, we generally mean differences in gross interest due to a number of factors discussed above. We may also find differences in net interest but it exist only in the absence of perfect mobility of capital.

Now we shall explain the theories of interest. The various theories of interest can be classified under the following two categories:

(*a*) Theories which explain why interest is paid; and

(*b*) Theories which explain how the rate of interest is determined.

4. WHY INTEREST IS PAID?

In the following analysis, we shall describe the various theories which answer the question why interest is paid.

Productivity Theory of Interest

This theory was initially developed by Bohm Bawerk.[1] in 1884. Later, the modern economists have elaborated this theory. According to this

1. Bohm-Bawerk, *The Positive Theory of Capital,* written in German in 1889 and translated in English in 1891.

theory interest arises on account of the productivity of capital. The amount that labour produces with the help of capital is generally greater than the amount it can produce when he works without capital. Thus capital adds the income of those who use it. This is the reason that capital is demanded by entrepreneurs. But the use of capital in production is subject to the law of diminishing returns. Thus, an employer will go on employing the additional units of capital, until the price he has to pay for each unit of capital becomes equal to its productivity. Thus the rate of interest tends to equal the marginal productivity of capital. The maximum price or interest that a producer can pay will be equal to its marginal productivity. According to critics, it is not the productivity which explains interest, but it is the scarcity which explains interest. They argue that if capital were tree, no interest will be paid in spite of its productivity.

(1) *Abstinence or Waiting Theory of Interest.* The productivity theory explains why capital is demanded but ignores the supply side. The abstinence theory explains the supply side of capital. According to Senior, the supply of capital depends on the willingness of the consumers to abstain from consumption in order that resources might be freed to produce capital goods. Interest is viewed as a reward for abstinence come economists (particularly Marshall) use the word waiting in place of abstinence. According to them, saving connotes waiting. When an individual-saves a part of his income he does not thereby refrain from consumption eternally. He only defers his consumption for a certain period, i.e., till the fruits of his saving come in an increasing flow. Meanwhile, he must wait, and as a rule people do not like to wait. Thus, a reward is necessary for the waiting. This reward is known as interest.

This theory has been criticised on the ground that it explains only the supply side and ignores completely the demand side. It does not explain the demand for waiting.

(2) *Austrian or Agio Theory of Interest.* This theory was developed by Bohm-Bawerk. It states that present goods possess an agio over future goods, owing to the fact that people prefer a present satisfaction to future satisfaction of an equal amount and of equal certainty. This preference, according to Bohm-Bawerk, is due to three circumstances: (*a*) The future is less clearly perceived than the present This is called "the perspective underestimate of the future." (*b*) Present wants are felt more strongly than the future wants; the demand for the present goods is relatively greater than that for the future goods. Hence there is relative scarcity if present goods as compared with future goods (i.e., scarcity in relation to demand). (*c*) The more roundabout are the processes of production, the greater is

the final output. Hence, owing to greater productiveness of the time-consuming, or indirect methods of production, present goods possess a 'technical superiority over future goods.' Thus, interest is paid to equate future satisfaction to the present satisfaction.

(3) *Time Preference Theory.* This theory is very much similar to the agio theory of interest. It was developed by Fisher. According to this theory, interest is the price for time preference. The time preference depends on the size of a man's income, the distribution of income over time, the degree of certainty regarding its enjoyment in the future and the temperament and character of the individual. For example, rich people will be able to satisfy their present wants more fully and will, therefore, discount future at a lower rate. Similarly, if the individual is of a spendthrift character, the degree of his impatience to spend would be higher. In this way, we may determine the rates of time preference for different persons. After they are determined, they tend to become equal to the rate of interest. When the rate of time preference of an individual is higher than the market rate of interest, he will borrow and apply the sum to satisfy his more pressing wants just as he would buy additional units of a commodity when the marginal utility of the additional unit to him is higher than the price. Similarly, when his rate of time preference is lower than the rate of interest, he will lend to the market and gain thereby. In this way the individual will vary his income -stream, by borrowing or lending until his rate of time preference is equal to the rate of interest.

(4) *Liquidity Preference and Rate of Interest.* According to Keynes, interest is not a reward for waiting, nor it is payment for time preference; but it is reward for parting with liquidity. Interest is it result of two actions: (*a*) we have to decide as how much of income to spend now and how much to save; (*b*) we have to decide in what form we shall keep our saving. If we save and keep our saving in the form of cash, we cannot get interest. To earn it, we have to convert saving into other less liquid assets, such as, loans and securities. In so doing, we part with liquidity. Interest is paid for this act of parting with liquidity and not for the act of saving.

This theory not only explains why interest is paid, it also explains how the interest rate is determined. We shall discuss this theory in detail under the theories of interest rate determination.

5. THEORIES OF INTEREST-RATE DETERMINATION

We have discussed the question why interest is paid. Now we shall explain how the rate of interest is determined. Here we shall discuss the following theories of interest rate determination.

(1) *The Classical Theory of Interest* which explains interest as determined by the demand and supply of capital.

(2) *The Neo-Classical Theory of Interest or the Loanable Funds Theory of Interest* which explains interest as determined by the demand and supply of loanable funds.

(3) *The Liquidity Preference Theory of Interest* which explains interest as determined by the demand for and supply of money.

(4) *The Modern Theory of Interest or The Neo-Keynesian Theory of Interest* which is a combination of the classical and the Keynesian theories of interest.

We shall now take them up one by one.

1. The Classical Theory of Interest or the Saving-Investment Theory of Interest

This theory is also known as the demand and supply theory of interest because it deals with the demand side as well as with the supply side. This theory was originally developed by the old classical economists. Later, it was refined by Marshall, Pigou, Walras, Taussig and Knight. According to this theory interest is the price paid to the use of capital. This theory states that like the prices of other commodities, the price of capital, i.e., the rate of interest is determined by the deman dand supply of capital. Since the demand for capital is determined by investment and supply of capital is determined by savings, the theory is also known as investment-saving theory of interest. Here the terms savings and investments are used in real sense.[2] Therefore, this theory is also referred to as the real non-monetary theory of interest. The market rate of interest will be determined at a point where demand for capital (investment) is equal to supply of capital (savings).

Demand for Capital (*Investment Schedule*). As we have already explained, the demand for capital arises because of its productivity. But productivity goes on diminishing as more and more capital is employed in the production. The individual firm has to compare the prevailing rate of interest (because it is fixed for the firm) with the marginal productivity of capital. We know that higher the rate of interest, the lesser will be the employment of capital, because marginal productivity of capital goes on

2. Real savings refer to those goods and services which instead of being consumed are employed in the production process Real investment, on the other hand, refers to the net increase in capital stocks in the form of machines, buildings, factories, etc.

diminishing. Thus demand curve for labour will slope downwards nom the left to the right. This is true not only of the individual firm but of the commodity (market) as a whole. This has been shown in Fig. 43.1 by the *II* curve.

Supply of Capital (*Saving Schedule*). The supply of capital depends upon the saving which in itself depends upon a number of factors, such as, the level of income, standard of living, farsightedness, etc. The most important factor which determines the supply of savings is the rate of interest. The higher the rate of interest, other things being the same, the more will be the supply of savings and vice versa. Thus, the supply curve of capital will be positively sloped. The aggregate supply curve of capital is indicated by *SS* in Fig. 43.1. It shows that a larger fund of saving is available at higher rates of interest.

Interaction between Demand and Supply Curves of Capital. The rate of interest is determined by the interaction of the forces of demand for capital (or investment) and the supply of capital (or savings). In Fig. 43.1, *SS* is the supply curve of capital and *II* is the demand curve for capital. These two curves intersect at point *E*. Thus *Or* will be the equilibrium rate of interest. If the rate of interest is greater than *Or,* the supply of capital will exceed the de-mand for capital and competition in the market will lead to the establishment of the equilibrium rate of interest. If, on the other hand, the rate of interest is lower than *Or,* the demand for capital will exceed the supply of capital and competition among the investors will again lead to the establishment of the equilibrium rate of interest *Or*. Hence *Or* is the equilibrium rate of interest which will come to stay in the market. If any change in the demand for investment and/or supply of savings comes about, the curves will shift accordingly and, therefore, the equilibrium rate of interest will also change.

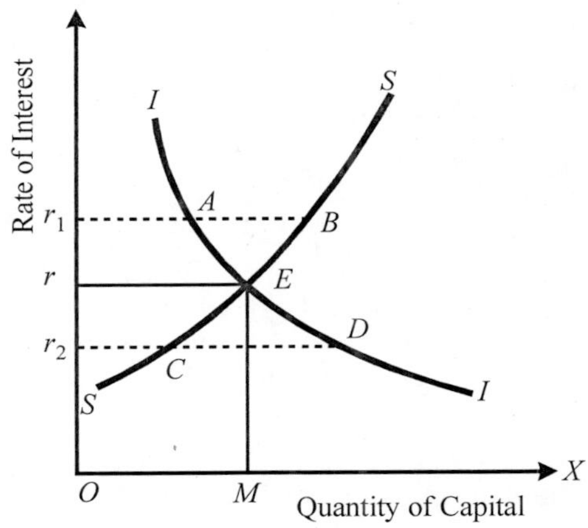

Fig. 43.1

Criticisms of the Classical Theory of Interest

The classical theory of interest has been criticised by the modern economists including Prof. J.M. Keynes on the following grounds:

(1) This theory is based on the assumption of full employment. But in real life we do not find full employment. If all resources are fully employed, payment in the form of interest must be made to induce people to forgo present consumption. But if unemployed resources are present, there is no necessity for this payment. Thus, in an underemployed economy, interest is not necessary to induce savings.

(2) The theory explains that aggregate investment and aggregate savings are brought into equilibrium through changes in the rate of interest. Although, there may be some relationship between the rate of interest and investment and savings; this should not amount to saying that the two are always equated through the rate of interest. The classical economists completely ignored the role of income 'changes in their analysis. According to Keynes, the equilibrium between saving and investment is not made through the variation in the interest rate but through the changes in the levels of income.

(3) The classical theory assumes that investment and savings are interest elastic, but various empirical studies have shown that investment is not so highly elastic as the classical theory assumes. In fact, investment is more influenced by the marginal efficiency of capital (*MEC*) than the rate of interest. Even at a high rate of interest people may demand more investment if the *MEC* is higher than the rate of interest. Further, at low levels of income, savings will no more be interest elastic. In other words, a high rate of interest will not increase the savings of a poor community.

(4) The classical theory ignores the role played by credit money in the determination of the rate of interest. In modern times, the role of credit money is very important the determination of the rate of interest.

(5) The supply schedule of capital is not independent of the investment demand and schedule. If investment varies, income will also vary and therefore, the supply of savings will also change. According to Keynes, to find a new saving schedule the rate of interest must first be determined on the basis of liquidity preference and the supply of money.

(6) The explanation of interest must be sought nom monetary factors and not nom any real factor as the theory assumes.

2. The Loanable Funds Theory of Interest or The Neo-Classical Theory of Interest

This theory was first formulated by Wickwell, the famous Swedish economist. Then the same has been developed by Robertson, Heberlor,

Ohlin, Machlup, etc. According to this theory, the rate of interest is determined by the demand and supply of loanable funds. The term "loanable fund" means the total amount of money which is demanded and supplied in the money market. The supply of loanable funds comes from: (*i*) current savings, (*ii*) funds released nom embodiment in fixed or working capital, (*iii*) reduction in hoardings, (*iv*) net additional bank loans, etc.

The demand for loanable funds on the other hand, comprises: (*i*) requirements for new investments, and (*ii*) increase, if any, in cash balances or hoardings. The rate of interest is positively related to the supply of loanable funds and negatively related to the demand for loanable funds. When the rate of interest increases, the supply of loanable funds will also increase and vice versa. In equilibrium, the rate of interest will be fixed at that point at which the demand for loanable funds equals the supply of loanable funds.

Wicksell who originally formulated this theory, argued that the total supply of loanable funds does not consist of only real savings as was explained by the classical theory, but it also constitutes the amount of bank credit made available by the banking system. Thus, to get the aggregate supply function of the loanable funds to the economy, the classical saving schedule must be added to the schedule of credit money.

The composite schedule. of saving and credit money will represent the schedule of total loanable funds on the supply side which together with the investment demand schedule on the demand side will determine the rate of interest. Further, Wicksell believed that the expansion or contraction of bank credit was not affected by the changes in the interest rate. Thus, the supply of bank credit was regarded as interest inelastic. In such a case the supply curve of credit money will be a vertical line.

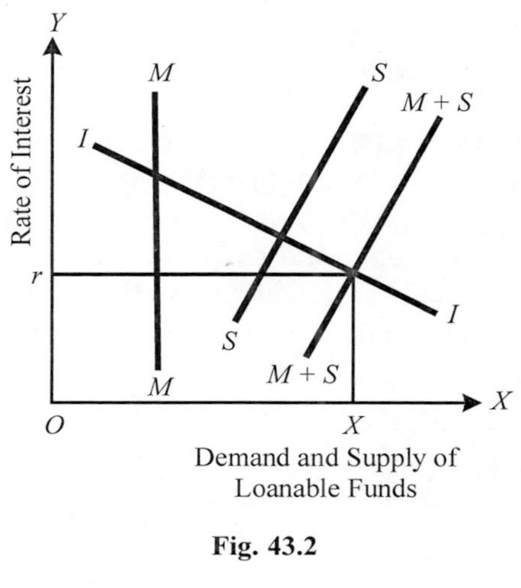

Fig. 43.2

This theory has been explained in Fig. 43.2. The demand and supply of loanable funds are shown along the *X*-axis and the rate of interest is shown along the *Y*-axis. *MM* is the supply curve of credit money and *SS* is the supply curve of savings which is positively sloping curve. Thus, the aggregate supply curve is represented by $M + S$ curve which is derived by adding horizontally the SS curve and the *MM* curve. *II* curve represents the investment demand, i.e., the demand for doanable funds. The equilibrium rate of interest is obtained at a point where the $M + S$ curve intersects the *II* curve. This point is *E* where the rate of interest is *OR* and the equilibrium quantity of loanable funds demanded and supplied is equal to *OX*.

Criticisms of the Loanable Funds Theory of Interest

In spite of an improvement over the classical theory of interest, the loanable funds theory of interest suffers from the following criticisms:

(1) It assumes that the supply of bank credit is interest-inelastic. But this is far from the reality.

(2) The theory assumes that the level of investment has no effect on the incomelevel of the commodity. But it is wrong, because when the volume of investment increases consequent upon a fall in the rate of interest, the level of income in the society will also increase by a certain multiplier times.

(3) According to Hansen, this theory is indeterminate, because it is very difficult to calculate the demand and supply of loanable funds. The loanable funds are not only the functions of the rate of interest but they are also the functions of a number of other monetary factors which have been ignored by this theory.

3. The Liquidity Preference Theory of Interest

This theory was propounded by Keynes in his famous book, *The General Theory of Employment, Interest and Money*. Keynes points out that interest is purely a monetary phenomenon. The rate of interest is the payment for parting with liquidity. Liquidity means the convenience of holding cash. According to this theory, the rate of interest is not the price which brings into equilibrium the demand for capital (investment) and the supply of capital (savings), but it is the price which equilibrates the desire to hold wealth in the form of cash. Of all assets, such as money, securities and real assets, it is the money which is the most liquid. Therefore, people want to hold a part of their total assets (savings) in liquid form—in the form of money. They have a preference for liquidity. Interest is the reward offered to them for surrendering their liquidity or cash-balances. In other words, it implies that if the rate of interest were lower, the aggregate amount of cash which the people would like to hold would exceed the available supply and if the rate of interest were raised, there would be a surplus of cash which no one would be willing to hold. The actual rate of interest will be determined by the equality between the demand for money and the supply of money.

Demand for Money. Money may be demanded to satisfy a number of motives. The following are the important motives:

(*i*) *Transactions motive.* People get income periodically. They want to keep some money with them till they receive income next. It is necessary to carry out the day-to-day transactions.

(*ii*) *Precautionary motive.* People want to keep some amount of their income in cash in order to face the future uncertainties (unforeseen situations and emergen-cies).

(*iii*) *Speculative motive.* This is the important motive. The speculators want to keep sufficient amount of their assets in liquid form, i.e., they may be able to get profits of the favourable situations through their speculative activities.

Money demanded for all these above mentioned motives constitutes demand for money, or liquidity preference. There is an inverse relationship between the demand for money and the rate of interest. The higher the rate of interest, the lower will be the demand for money and vice versa. This is the reason that the demand curve for money slopes downward nom the left to the right. The total, demand for money (L) is the composite of the precautionary demand and the transactions demand for money (L_1) and the speculative demand of for money (L_2). The total demand curve for money is shown by *DD* curve in Fig. 43.3.

Supply of Money. The supply of money is autonomously determined by the monetary authority. Keynes assumes the supply of money to be fixed which has got no relation with the rate of interest. In Fig. 43.3, the supply of money is represented by the vertical lines. The supply of money is determined by the policies of the Government and the Central Bank of the country. It includes coins, notes and demand deposits with the banks.

Interaction between Demand and Supply Curves. In Fig. 43.3, the total demand for money curve is denoted by *DD*. It shows the amounts of money which are demanded at different rates of interest. *MM* is the supply curve of money. They intersect each other at point E where Or rate of interest is fixed. When supply of money increases from OM to OM_1, the position of liquidity preference curve (demand curve) remaining the same, the rate of interest falls from Or to Or_1. If, on the other hand, supply of money decreases from OM to OM_2; the demand curve for money remaining the same, the equilibrium rate of interest increases from Or to Or_2.

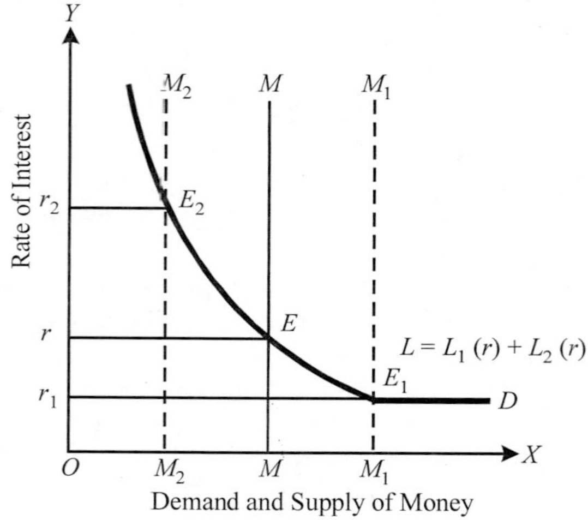

Fig. 43.3

Criticisms of the Liquidity Preference Theory of Interest

The liquidity preference theory of interest has been criticised on the following grounds:

(1) Keynes assumes that the level of income is given, the rate of interest will determine the liquidity preference (demand for money). But liquidity preference is determined by the level of income (supply of money) and, therefore, it cannot be known unless the income level is known.

(2) Keynes assumes that the rate of interest is independent of the demand for investment funds, but it is far from the reality. The cash balances of various persons are significantly influenced by their demand for capital for purposes of investment. The demand for capital being dependent upon the marginal productivity of capital, the rate of interest is not determined independently of the marginal efficiency of capital.

(3) This theory is applicable only in the short-run, because it explains only those factors which are important in the short-run.

(4) This theory is only one-sided theory. It assumes supply of money to be given by the monetary authority. But in real life, it depends upon a number of factors which are assumed to be constant by this theory. Hence, it fails to explain the complex phenomenon of interest rate.

(5) According to the critics, interest is not the reward for parting with liquidity but it is the reward paid to the lender fur the productivity of capital.

(6) Keynesian theory states that rate of interest can be reduced by increasing the supply of money. But if the liquidity preference of the people also increases in the same proportion, then the rate of interest will remain the same.

(7) Keynes considered interest to be a purely monetary phenomenon and ignored the real factors, such as, productivity and time preference which are assumed to be more important.

The above are the main criticisms of the Keynesian theory of interest.

4. The Modern Theory of Interest or Neo-Keynesian Theory of Interest

The modern theory of interest is superior to the other theories of interest, because it includes all the four factors—saving, investment, the demand for money and the supply of money—in the determination of rate of interest. The classical theory and the neo-classical theory include the first two factors, i.e., the demand for capital (investment) and the supply of capital (saving) in the determination of the rate of interest; white the Keynesian theory includes supply of money and the demand for money in the determination of the rate of interest. The modern theory of interest is, the combination of the classical and Keynesian theories of interest. It considers both the monetary and non-monetary sectors (i.e., real sector) of the economy while determining the rate of interest.

To determine the rate of interest, the modern theory develops two curves-the *IS* curve and the *LM* curve—the former shows the equilibrium between the flow variables in the real sector while the latter shows the equilibrium between the stock-variables in the monetary sector. The point of intersection of these two curves establishes the equilibrium rate of interest at which both the real and the monetary sectors of the economy are simultaneously in equilibrium. In other words, at this point of equili-brium, total investment equals the total savings and total demand for money equals total supply of money.

We shall now explain the construction of these two curves. This *IS* curve shows the various combinations of income (Y) and the rate of interest (r) at which the aggregate savings and aggregate investment are in equilibrium. Mathematically, the classical model states that

$$I = S$$
$$I = f(r)$$
$$S = g(r, Y)$$

where I, S, r and Y denote investment, savings, rate of interest and aggregate income respectively, and f and g are the signs of the functions.

Further, we know that investment. (I) is a decreasing function of the rate of interest.

It means, when the rate of interest rises, investment demand decreases and vice versa. In other words, the investment demand function will slope downwards from left to right.

We also know that i saving (S) is an increasing function of the level of income (Y). It means, saving increases as income increases. Thus the saving-function will be positively sloping in relation to the level of income.

Now, we need to find out those combinations of the rate of interest and aggregate (money) income corresponding to which the aggregate investment is equal to the aggregate savings ($I = S$). The curve representing these combinations is the IS curve. This has been illustrated in Fig. 43.4. In Panel (a) of Fig. 43.4, we have shown a 45 per cent identity line $r = r$. In Panel (b) of Fig. 43.4, we have drawn the investment demand function

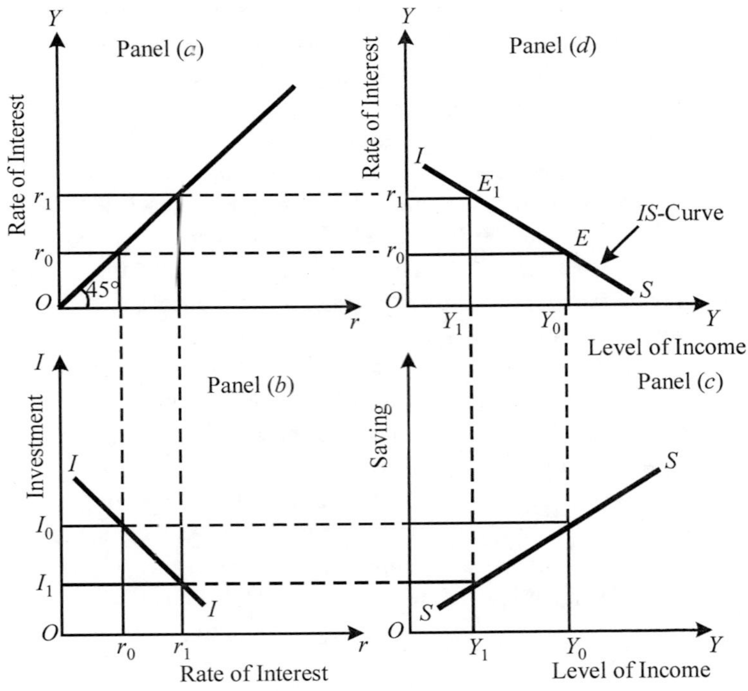

Fig. 43.4

II. It indicates an inverse relationship between rate of interest and the level of investment; the higher the rate of interest, the lower will be the level of investment and vice versa. Suppose initially the rate of interest to Or_0, then the level of investment will be OI_0. If the rate of interest increases to Or_0 then the level of investment will be reduced to OI_1. In Panel (*c*) of Fig. 43.4, we have drawn the saving-function which is positively sloped. At OY_0 level of income, the savings will be equal to OS_0 (= OI_0. If the level of income decreases to OY_1, then the level of savings will also decrease to OS (= CI).

Now Panels (*b*) and (*c*) indicate that at Or_0 rate of interest $OI_0 = OS_0$ and at Or_1 rate of interest $OI_1 = OS_1$. These two equilibrium points have been plotted in Panel (*d*) of Fig. 43.4 as E and E_1. If we join these points then the resulting curve is the *IS* curve. At each point along the *IS* curve, the volume of saving is equal to the volume of investment.

The LM Function

The *LM* curve shows the equilibrium situation in the money-sector. It indicates those combinations of income (Y) and the rate of interest (r) at which the supply of money is equal to the demand for money. Mathematically, the Keynesian model states that

$$L = M$$
$$L = L(r, Y)$$
$$M = M$$

where L and M denote the demand for money and supply of money respectively. M stands for the fixed supply of money. The construction of *LM* curve has been illustrated in Fig. 43.5. Panel (*a*) of Fig. 43.5 shows the speculative demand for money (L_2). Panel (*b*)shows the equality between the total demand for money ($L = L_1 + L_2$) and the total supply of money (M). Panel (*c*) shows the transaction demand for money (L_1); while Panel (*d*) shows the *LM* curve. Let us suppose that in Panel (*a*) of Fig. 43.5, the rate of interest is Or_0, then the speculative demand for money (L_2) will be equal to OA_0. This leads to equilibrium point C in Panel (*b*) where the speculative demand for money is OA_0 and the transactions demand for money (L_1) is equal to OB_0. This leads to equilibrium point in Panel (*c*) where at OY_0 level of income the transactions demand is OB_0. From this point, we get the equilibrium point E in Panel (*d*). In the same way the point E_1 is obtained in the final diagram of Panel (*d*). After joining these equilibrium points we get the relevant *LM* curve. Each point on this curve denotes equilibrium in the monetary sector where the demand for money is equal to the supply of money ($L = M$).

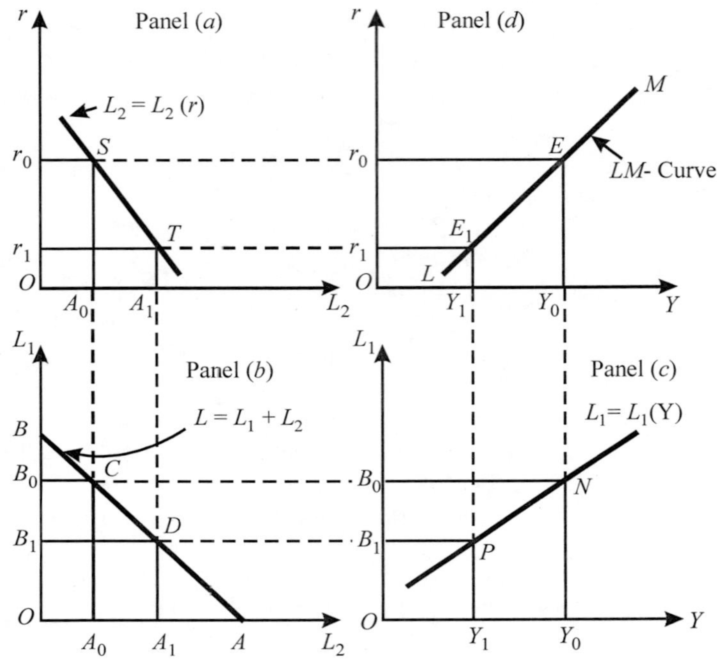

Fig. 43.5

Determination of the Rate of Interest

The equilibrium rate of interest will be determined by intersection point of the *IS* curve and *LM* curve. This has been illustrated in Fig. 43.6. The money income has been shown on the *X*-axis and the rate of interest has been shown on the *Y*-axis. The *IS* and *LM* curves intersect each other at point *E* which satisfies the double conditions of equilibrium, i.e., the equilibrium between savings and investment is the real sector of the economy and the equilibrium between demand for money and supply of money in the monetary sector of the economy. At point *E*, the equilibrium rate of interest is *Or* and the level of income is *OY*. At any other combination of income and the rate of interest, either the real sector or the monetary sector of the economy will be in disequilibrium. This disequilibrium will lead to equilibrium via changes in money income and the rate of interest. This is all about the modern theory of interest.

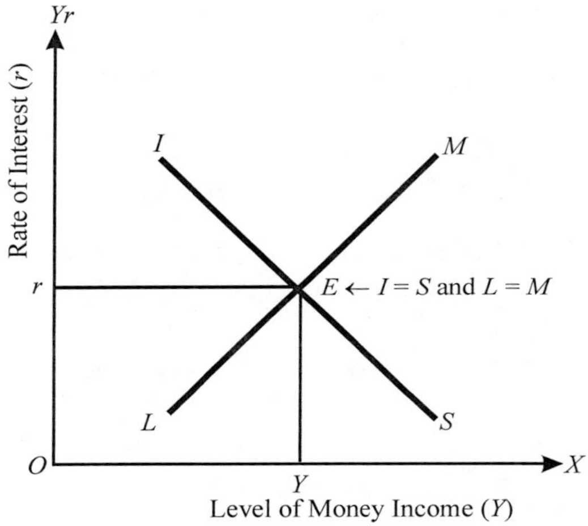

Fig. 43.6

EXERCISES

1. Define interest. Distinguish between gross interest and net interest.
2. Why is interest paid? In this connection discuss the significance of time preference and liquidity preference.
3. Explain how the rate of interest is determined.
4. "Interest balances the supply of capital savings and capital investment," Discuss.
5. What do you understand by loanable funds? Show that the rate of interest is determined by the supply of and demand for loanable funds.
6. Explain fully the Keynes' Theory of Liquidity Preference.
7. Compare and contrast the classical and neo-classical theories of interest.
8. Distinguish between the 'stock' and 'flow' approaches to the determination of the rate of interest. What different pieces of information do we need to propound a complete and satisfactory theory of the rate of interest.
9. "At the equilibrium rate of interest there must be equality between the supply and demand for money, but also between saving and investment." Explain with the help of a diagram, the theory which attempts to satisfy both the conditions.
10. Critically examine the loanable funds theory of interest.

Multiple Choice Questions

11. (*i*) Which is not the characteristic feature of capital as a means of production?
    (*a*) man made factor (*b*) mobility
    (*c*) fixed supply (*d*) all of the above [*Ans.* (*c*)]

    (*ii*) Liquidity preference means
    (*a*) refraining from consumption
    (*b*) desire of the public to hold cash
    (*c*) showing a preference to hold assets like bonds and securities which are liquid
    (*d*) showing a preference to hold money which is liquid than to hold bonds and securities [*Ans.* (*d*)]

    (*iii*) Which of the following is not the element of gross interest?
    (*a*) insurance against risk (*c*) payment for inconvenience
    (*b*) reward for management (*d*) none of the above [*Ans.* (*d*)]

    (*iv*) According to Keynes, the supply curve of money is
    (*a*) perfectly elastic (*c*) unitary elastic
    (*b*) more elastic (*d*) perfectly inelastic [*Ans.* (*b*)]

    (*v*) Austrian or Agio Theory of Interest was developed by
    (*a*) Bohm-Bawerk (*c*) Keynes
    (*b*) Senior (*d*) Fisher [*Ans.* (*a*)]

Chapter 44

PROFIT

1. INTRODUCTION

The share of income that goes to business enterprises in the process of distribution is known as profits. Different persons use the word profit in different senses. A common way of defining profit is that of a percentage return on turnover. In this sense, profit is calculated as a percentage of the total revenue. Some people define profit as the rate of return on the capital employed. In this sense, profit is expressed as a percentage yield on the value of capital employed in the business. But it is very important to know the particular definition of profit which is used in economic sense. It is possible that a firm is making a very small profit on each unit sold, but is having a large turn-over. Similarly, the other firm may be making a large profit on each unit, but having a smaller turnover. In economics, we are concerned with profit as an income and not as a percentage differential on individual transactions. In other words, we are interested in the profit earned overtime, as a flow of income and hence it is the rate of profit on capital employed. It (profit) may be defined as the net income of a business after all the other costs—rent, wages, and interest-have beendeducted from the total income. Profits are, therefore, uncertain and vary from person to person and firm to firm. They may become zero when costs are equal to income and if costs are higher than the income, then profits may be negative.

Therefore, before we proceed to discuss the pricing of entrepreneurship as a factor of production, it is better to understand the main features of entrepreneurship: (*i*) The entrepreneur hires the other factors of production and puts them into the production process. Without his efforts, the other factors of production will remain unutilised. (*ii*) The remunerations of other factors of production are fixed and are determined in advance. The reward of the entrepreneur, on the other hand, is highly uncertain. He has to bear the entire risk of the business. This is the reason that the reward of other factors of production is always positive while the reward of the entrepreneur, i.e., profit can sometimes be negative when he suffers losses. The income of the entrepreneur is less than the costs he has to incur in the production.

2. MEANING OF PROFIT

The term profit has been defined in different ways by different economists. In 1826, *V* on Thunen defined profit as the residue after deduction of interest, insurance for risk, and wages of management. The entrepreneur anticipates the probable future demand and the price of goods he contemplates to produce. On the basis of his estimate, he enters into separate contracts with capitalists, landlords and labourers; and production is commenced. The entrepreneur makes payments to the various agents of production according to the rates agreed upon. If something is left from his income after payments are made to the agents concerned, it is his profit. If, on the other hand, his income falls short of the payments he makes, he incurs a loss. Profit is only a residual share of the produce of industry. There is no other law which governs the determination of profit. The classical economists recognised that the share of capitalist has three elements: (*i*) a payment for the bare use of his capital; (*ii*) payment for his managerial efforts; and (*iii*) reward for bearing the risks of the enterprise. The earlier writers were not clear about the exact role of the entrepreneur and, therefore, they lumped together under profit all that accrued to the entrepreneur for his various roles. As J.S. Mill points out, "Profit connotes the aggregate remuneration of the capitalist entrepreneur." Marshall also defined profit as the supply price of business power. Here, he included all the above mentioned elements of profits.

The economists of the 19th century fail to distinguish between profits from interest and from income of management because the typical entrepreneur of the 19th century was also the owner of the capital of his firm. They have confused the returns which the entrepreneur received. They did not realise that the rate of interest is a reward for waiting and the receipt is a reward for taking the risk of the business. In simple words, they failed to distinguish between gross profit and net profit.

The modern business has changed fundamentally. In the modern joint stock company, those who supply capital are different from those who take decisions. Thus, the risk-bearing and decision-taking functions of the entrepreneurs are separated. Therefore, to get an accurate meaning of profit, it appears necessary to distinguish between gross profit and net profit, and between normal profit and super-normal profit.

3. GROSS PROFIT AND NET PROFIT

Gross profit is the total return to the entrepreneur after paying rent and interest for the land and capital hired and wages for the labourers employed. In other words, it is, equal to the excess of the receipts of a business over the actual expenses (explicit expenditure) incurred by the entrepreneur. In the popular sense, the word profit is used in the sense of gross profit.

Net profit is not so expensive a term as gross profit. A reward accruing to the entrepreneur for hisrisk-taking function and his bargaining skill is known as net profit.

Gross profit is made of various constituents of which net profit is one. It is, therefore, instructive and interesting to find out the constituents of gross profit. They are given below:

(1) *Reward for the Factors of Production Supplied by the Entrepreneur Himself.* Generally, the entrepreneur supplies a number of factors of production of his own; for example, his hand, his capital, his business services and his family members, etc., all are engaged in the production process. He is not required to make any payment in respect of them to any outsider; nor does he himself receive any reward separately. This payment is usually merged in the gross profit. In estimating net profit, we should deduct from gross profits the rewards to the factors of production supplied by the entrepreneur himself. The costs of his own factors of production are known as implicit costs.

(2) *Charges of Maintenance.* It includes two types of charges: (*a*) *Depreciation charges—Some* provision has to be made for the maintenance of the capital, or its replacement, as it is gradually used up or becomes obsolete due to better inventions. This provision is known as depreciation. Depreciation charges must be deducted from gross profit in order to arrive at net profit, as depreciation charges are the expenses of the business. (*b*) *Insurance charges*— The premiums paid by the firm on insurance of firm's property such as building, machinery, plant, etc., are also a part of firm's expenses. Such charges are to be deducted from gross profits in order to get the net profit.

(3) *Extra Personal Gains.* The entrepreneur gets some extra gains which are not due to his efficiency and ability. They are of two types:

(*i*) *Monopoly' gains.* It is possible that the entrepreneur may possess certain monopoly power. He may have an effective control over the supply of the produce he deals in. In such a case, his profits will increase but his own efficiency is not responsible for this increment. Therefore, it has to be deducted from the gross profit while calculating net profits.

(*ii*) *Conjunctural or Chance Gains.* The occurrence of certain unforeseen circumstances may enable the entrepreneur to get additional gains. For instance, due to the outbreak of war, the price of his product may increase and consequently he earns a huge profit. Such profit is called chance profit which must be deducted from gross profit to arrive at net profit.

(4) *Net Profit.* When all the above deductions have been made from the gross profit, the remaining amount is the net profit or pure profit. It is the reward for two main functions of the entrepreneur.

(*i*) *Reward for risk-taking.* An entrepreneur takes risk on his estimate of future price and the extent of the demand. He has to pay a fixed price for the other factors of production. If his income is higher than the price he has to pay for the hired factors of production, he will get large profits. If the price realised (income) falls short of his expenditure, he incurs a loss. Thus, (net) profit is the reward of risk.

(*ii*) *Reward for bargaining skill.* While employing various factors of production, the entrepreneur tries to bargain, as far as possible. The degree of his success depends upon his bargaining skill. Moreover, he may organise new production techniques and bring out altogether new products; thus gets huge profits for himself.

This amount will be included in his net profits. The various constituents of gross profits can be tabulated in the following manner:

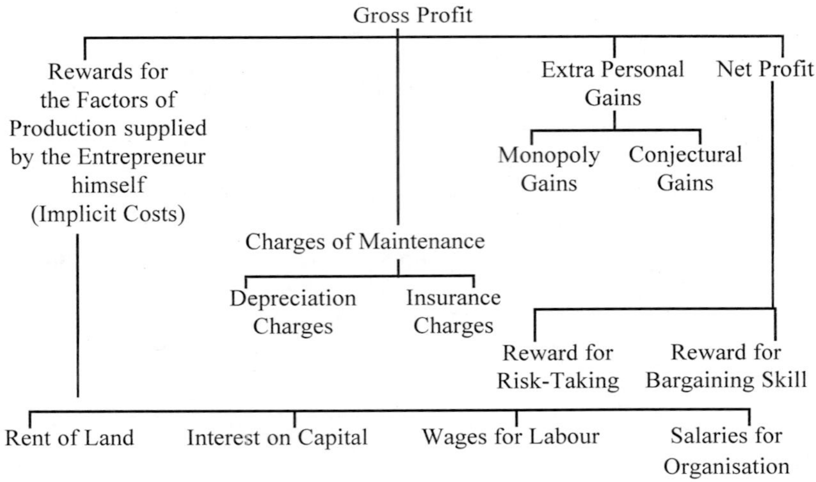

Here we should understand that while discussing the various theories of profits, we shall deal with net profits and not with gross profits.

3. NORMAL PROFIT AND SUPERNORMAL PROFIT

Some economists distinguish between normal profits and supernormal profits. According to them, normal profit is the minimum to induce the entrepreneur to remain in the business in the long-run. If the entrepreneur is not getting this much of minimum return, he will not find it worthwhile to remain in the present business. Under perfect competition, in the long-run each firm gets the normal profit which is included in the costs of production. It is possible that the entrepreneur may not get normal profit in the short run, and may have to sell his product at a loss; but in the long run every entrepreneur must get at least the "normal profit. It is assumed to be a part of the price. In the words of Mrs. Joan Robinson, normal profit is that profit which neither attracts a new firm to enter into the industry nor obligates the existing firms to go out of the industry."

Supernormal profit, on the other hand, is defined as the surplus over the normal profit. It is attained by the super-marginal firms. The marginal firm gets only the normal profit, but determines the supernormal profit of the intramarginal firms. Unlike normal profit, the existence of supernormal profit, is not a prerequisite for the existence of a firm because so long as the firm gets normal profit, it would remain in the industry.

4. DETERMINATION OF PROFIT

Economists are not agreed as to how profits are determined. Different opinions have been put forward by different economists. There is no one theory of profit which is accepted by all the economists. A number of theories of profit have been developed by the economists, but they are all unsatisfactory. None of them provides a comprehensive explanation of the determination of profit. We shall discuss the following theories of profit:

1. Rent Theory of Profit

The rent theory of profit was propounded by the American economist, F.A. Walker. This theory was based on the ideas of Mill and Senior. According to Senior, "Rent was applied to all peculiar advantages of extraordinary qualities of body and mind.". J.S. Mill[2] repeated Senior's ideas of similarity between profit and rent. According to him, "the extra gains which any producer obtains through superior talents for business or superior business arrangements are very much of a kind similar to

1. Nassau William Senior, *An Outline of the Science of Political Economy,* 1836.
2. John Stuart Mill, *Principles of Political Economy.*

rent." Based on these ideas, the Walker's rent theory of profit states that profit is the rent of the superior ability which one entrepreneur commands over the marginal or least efficient entrepreneur in the field of production. Just as there are different grades of land, there are different grades of entrepreneurs. The least efficient entrepreneur who must remain in the field of production to meet the current demand, just recovers his cost of production and nothing besides. Above him are entrepreneurs of entrepreneurs ability. As rent arises because of the differential advantage enjoyed by superior land over the marginal land, similarly profit also is the reward for differential ability of the entrepreneur over the marginal entrepreneur or the no-profit entrepreneur.

Profits are thus like rent and like rent, they do not enter into price of the product. It should be noted that according to Walker, the wages of management, i.e., the amount which the entrepreneur could have earned as a salaried manager in a competitive market, should not be included in profits. Profits not in excess of wages we have agreed to consider no profits at all. The marginal employer only earns the wages of management and no more. With a slight decrease in price or increase in cost, he (the marginal entrepreneur) will prefer to work as an employee rather than as an employer. Thus wages of management must be paid to keep up the given supply of entrepreneurs. Such wages thus enter into price.

Criticisms of the Rent Theory of Profit

This theory has been criticised on the following grounds:

(1) The theory may provide a measure of profit, but it does not provide an explanation of the nature of profit.

(2) According to the cirtics the theory assumes a perfect similarity between rent and profit; but it is far from the reality. The two cannot be identical. Rent is generally positive; only in rare cases, it may be zero, but it never becomes negative. While profit, on the other hand, can be negative when the entrepreneur continues production in the situation of loss. It is usually happens in the short-run.

(3) Again, profit is not always the reward of entrepreneur's business ability, it is a function of a number of other factors, such as the monopoly power of the firm, favourable chances available to the entrepreneur etc. This theory ignores the contribution of those other factors which playa significant role in the determination of the profit of the entrepreneur.

(4) This theory states that like no-rent land, there is no-profit entrepreneur. But in actual practice we do not find a no-profit entrepreneur. If an entrepreneur gets no profit, he will no more remain in the industry.

To remain in the industry, there must be a minimum normal profit to the entrepreneur.

(5) The theory assumes that profit does not enter into the price of the commodity. This may happen only in the short-run; but in the long-run, profit must enter into price.

(6) The theory fails to explain the profit of the ordinary shareholder of joint stock companies.

2. Wage Theory of Profit

The wage theory of profit was propounded by the American economist Taussig. According to Taussig, "Profits are best regarded simply as a form of wages." The businessman's income is extremely irregular, and is a surplus that remains after meeting the expenditures of production. Yet it is not due to chance. Continued success is due to the possession of some qualities-skill and ability in the organisation, and shrewdness in meeting risks. The rewards for these qualities of the entrepreneur are profits which can be known as wages. Because the activity of the entrepreneur is a form of labour-skilled labour. Thus profits may be regarded as wages.

Criticisms of the Wage Theory of Profit

This theory has been criticised on the following grounds:

(1) The theory overlooks the real distinction between wages and profits. Wages are fixed and stipulated income, while profits are uncertain income.

(2) A slight change in the price of the product will affect the profits of the entrepreneur while it would respond to wages in the same degree. For example, a fall in the price may sometime lead to a loss to the entrepreneur but wages can never fall below a minimum level. This theory overlooks this difference.

(3) It is the entrepreneur who takes the risk of the business while the wage-earneris free from such risks.

Owing to these reasons, we may say that profits are not like wages. The wage theory of profit is not a scientific theory at all.

3. Risk Theory of Profit

This theory was developed by the American economist, Prof. Hawley in 1907. According to this theory, the entrepreneur earns profits because he undertakes 'risks'. Hawley points out that the most essential function of the entrepreneur is risk-taking. Risks are inherent in all types of production.

Risks are assumed to be unpleasant and irksome. Therefore, no one would like to bear the risks unless he expects a reward for it. Hence, profit is the reward of risk. The higher the risk, the greater will be the expected reward and vice versa.

In the words of Hawley, "...the profit of an undertaking, or residue of product after the claims of the land, labour, capital are satisfied, is not the reward of management or coordination, but of the risk and the responsibilities that the undertaker takes. ..."

In simple words, Hawley has cleared that it is the risk-taking function of the entrepreneur which is the basis of profit. The real producer of the output is the entrepreneur and not the other factors of production; as the other factors-land, labour and capital—are paid the fixed remunerations. They are mere 'means of production'. In the absence of the entrepreneur, they remain unutilised. Thus, a reward must be given to the entrepreneur for his taking risk. The reward is called profit.

Criticisms of the Risk Theory of Profit

This theory has been criticised on the following grounds:

(1) Critics point out that the earnings of an entrepreneur are not entirely due to risk-taking. Some part of the earnings (profits) is due to his superior organisational ability, his monopoly power and due to some chance factor: The other elements have been entirely ignored by the risk theory of profit.

(2) According to Knight, profit is not due to all types of risks. There are some risks which can be measured and can be guarded by insurance, such as fire, accident etc. It is due to those risks which cannot be insured, such as the risk related to demand and price estimates.

(3) According to Carver profits are earned because risks are avoided, not because risks are, undertaken. In actual life, every entrepreneur always tries to reduce his risks in various ways. The lesser the risk, the more the income (profit) that he receives and vice versa.

(4) According to Willet, it is the capitalist and not the entrepreneur who runs the, risk of the business. He tells that profit is the surplus above price determining costs while risk is an element in the cost of production. He says that profit is a temporary gain which disappears in the long-run due to perfect competition. It arises due to abnormal dynamic conditions, and there is no uniform-empirical relation between profit and risk-taking.

4. Uncertainty-Bearing Theory of Profit

This theory was developed by the American economist, Prof. Knight in

1921. He criticises Prof. Hawley's Theory and the other classical theories of profit on the ground that it is not all types of risks (also changes) which lead to profits, but it is unforeseeable risks which lead to profits. According to him, a known risk is no risk at all: it becomes a part of cost. At the same time he accepts that profit is a result of a unique kind of risk which is not susceptible of measurement. He calls them "uncertainty". An entrepreneur acts upon estimates, opinions, judgement or intuition, based on imperfect knowledge of the data and the environment in which he works. Again, an estimate is similar to a probability judgement. A true uncertainty of Prof. Knight implies estimates only. Such estimates are liable to go wrong. Knight states that it is this true uncertainty that accounts for the peculiar income of the entrepreneur.

In other words, Prof. Knight divides business risks into two parts- insurable and non-insurable. Those risks which can be calculated statistically and can, therefore, be insured with an insurance company do not generate profits. Their premiums are included in the costs. Thus, the second type of risks, i.e. non-insurable risks which are unforeseeable become the basis of profits. These risks are the following:

(1) Competition risks which arise from the possibility of the new firms entering the industry;

(2) Technical risks which arise if the new techniques of production might come into vogue, or some new machine might be evolved. The old firms may not be in a position to adopt them and thus suffer a great loss.

(3) Risk of Government intervention arises when the government fixes the maximum prices of the products. This will lead to a reduction in the profits of the firms in the market.

(4) Business cycle risks which may reduce the effective demand for the product.

These above risks are unforeseeable and cannot be insured with any insurance company and are, therefore, borne by the entrepreneur himself. These non-insurable risks are called "uncertainties" by Knight. Profit is said to arise for undertaking these uncertainties of business.

Criticisms of Uncertainty-Bearing Theory of Profit

This theory has been criticised on the following grounds:

(1) According to critics, uncertainty is not the only factor that causes profit; but it is determined by a number of other factors, such as the ability of the entrepreneur, non-availability of substitutes, etc. which are ignored by this theory.

(2) The theory assumes uncertainty-bearing as an independent factor of production. But according to critics, it depends upon the business ability of the entrepreneur. The more efficient is the entrepreneur, the lesser will be the uncertainty and vice versa.

(3) Uncertainty-bearing is a psychological concept (like abstinence or waiting) which can be considered a part of the real cost of production. The supply of a factor of production does not depend on real opportunity costs. Hence, uncertainty-bearing does not determine the supply price of business ability.

In spite of the above limitations, the uncertainty-bearing theory of profit is an improvement upon the other old theories of profit.

5. Dynamic Theory of Profit

This theory has been developed by the American economist, J.B. Clark. He defines profit as the excess of price of goods over their costs. He makes a distinction between static and dynamic economy. In a static economy, profits either do not arise or if they arise, they are just frictional. But in a dynamic economy, profits arise because of the dynamic changes in the society. In the real world, changes are constantly taking place. Clark points out five important changes which are constanty taking place: (*i*) changes in the size of population; (*ii*) changes in the supply of capital; (*iii*) changes in production techniques; (*iv*) changes in the form of business organisation; (*v*) changes in human wants. He says that profit arises in a dynamic society on account of these changes. These changes affect the market demand and supply of commodities and thus lead to the emergence of profits. These above changes are general dynamic changes. The entrepreneur always tries to introduce many other deliberate changes. They lead to reduce his cost of production and increase his profits.

In static society, neither demand nor supply changes, or they change at a known rate. In such a case, the price of goods as well as wages and interest stand at their natural or normal level. Natural or normal price of a commodity is one which just covers the (average) cost production; i.e. wages and interest at their natural rate. It means; there will be no profit for the entrepreneur. If the price of a commodity increases, then competition will force it down to the natural level and profits will disappear. But competition is not perfect and the forces of competition take some time to have their full impact. Thus, for a short-period, the entrepreneur may get profits. Such profits are known as *frictional profits.* Now, profits other than the frictional are the result of dynamic changes mentioned above. These changes increase the difference between the price of the product and the average cost of production, i.e. lead to increase in profits of the entrepreneur. For example, suppose a firm introduces a new technique of production which results in high productivity with the same costs of production (i.e., wages and interest paid by the entrepreneur remain the same). This increases the difference between receipts and payments. Consequently, the entrepreneur earns a profit. As time passes, the technique comes to be widely known and used. The fruits of this technique are widely diffused. Productivity improves all round. All the firms in the industry get benefit from it. But the natural rates of interest and wages and price also change such that the profit disappears. Thus, according to Clark, profits are the result of the changes which take place in a dynamic society. A particular change creates profit only for a short period of time. But one change is followed by the other and, therefore, changes take place in a continuous manner. Profits arise because of these continuous changes in the society.

Criticisms of the Dynamic Theory of Profit

This theory has been criticised on the following grounds:

(1) According to Prof. Knight, not all types of dynamic changes lead to profit. It is only those changes which cannot be foreseen, gives rise to profits.

(2) The theory takes no account of the fact that business ability like any other factor of production has a supply price.

(3) According to Prof. Taussig, the dynamic theory makes an artificial distinction between profit and the earnings of management. "Even the routine conduct of established industries calls for judgement and administrative capacity, and for the exercise of the same faculties that are more conspicuously and more profitably exercised under conditions of rapid progress." In the static society, the entrepreneur gets wages of management. The reward for risk taking would disappear if risks are non-existent in such a (static) state. The major part of risks would not of course exist, but a certain number of risks; for example, the risks of loss by fire, by the negligence of producers, etc. would remain, and a reward must be given for them.

6. Innovation Theory of Profit

This theory was developed by Prof. Joseph Schumpeter. This theory is very much similar to that of the dynamic theory of Clark. Like Clark, Schumpeter also attributes profit to dynamic changes but instead of five "genetic changes" of Clark, he resorts to innovations to explain the emergence of profits. He states that profit is the reward for innovations.

Innovations may take the form of introduction of new machine, enlargement of the size of the undertaking, exploitation of a new source of raw material, change in the quality of commodity, discovery of new markets, etc. Whenever such innovation is introduced, it reduces the cost of production below the existing price and results in profit to emerge.

It should be noticed that a successful innovation will result in the emergence of profit only for a temporary period. When the new process of production or any other type of innovation is known to other firms in the industry, it ceases to yield profit. However, while one source of innovational profit is disappearing, some new innovation may be born. Hence, innovational profits have a tendency to appear, disappear and reappear.

Criticisms of Innovation Theory of Profit

This theory has been criticised on the following grounds:

(1) Like Clark, Schumpeter also fails to take account of uncertainty which is the essential dynamic element in the economic system. If the innovator can foresee the consequences of his innovation, then what he gets is simply a higher value imputed to his superior ability.

(2) This theory also ignores the role of risk-bearing in the determination of profit. According to Schumpeter, "The entrepreneur is never the risk-taker. The one who gives credit comes to grief if the undertaking fails." He pointed out that it was the capitalist, not the entrepreneur who had to undertake the risk. This is far from the reality.

(3) The theory attributes profits only to innovations and ignores the other factors which are responsible for the profit of the entrepreneur.

7. Marginal Productivity Theory of Profit

As we have already discussed in an earlier chapter, the marginal productivity theory states that like the remuneration of other factors of production, the remuner-ation of the entrepreneur, i.e. profit, will be determined by the marginal revenue productivity of the entrepreneur.

As we know, the marginal revenue productivity (*MRP*) curve of any factor of production represents the demand curve for the same. In the case of entrepreneur, the *MRP* curve of entrepreneurship will become its demand curve. The supply of entrepreneurs, on the other hand, will depend upon the earnings of the entrepreneurs. If perfect competition exists in the market, the supply curve of entrepreneurs will be perfectly elastic.

Now, it is difficult to draw the *MRP* curve of entrepreneurship, because it is not possible to calculate the marginal revenue productivity of entrepreneurship for a single firm. There is only one entrepreneur in the firm and the marginal analysis cannot be applied to him. But, we may

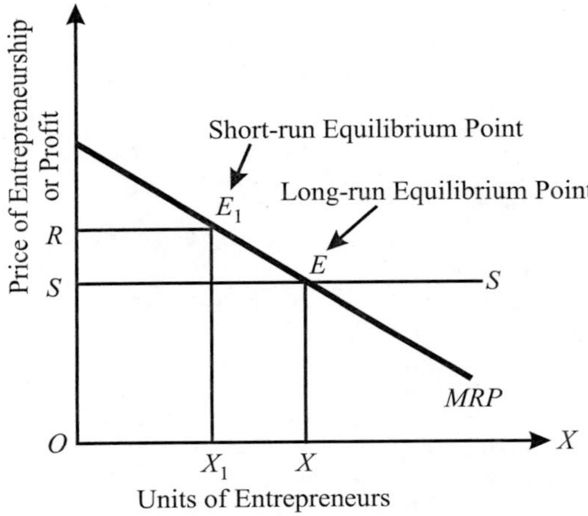

Fig. 44.1

very well calculate the marginal revenue productivity of entrepreneurship in the industry where the number of firms can be varied. As more and, more firms enter into the industry, the marginal revenue productivity of the entrepreneurship decreases. Thus, the slope of *MRP* curve will be negative as shown in Fig. 44.1. *SS* is the supply curve of entrepreneurs in the industry which indicates that all entrepreneurs being homogeneous must get the same price (profit) represented by *OS*. The price *OS* also represents the transfer earnings (opportunity costs) of the entrepreneurs. If the actual price is less than the minimum *OS*, the entrepreneurs will leave the present industry and will enter into a new industry where they can get, this level (*OS*) of price. This means, *OS* is the supply price of the entrepreneurs.

The *MRP* curve (i.e., demand curve of entrepreneurs) and the supply curve *SS* intersect each other at point *E*. Thus, *E* becomes the long-run equilibrium points where *OX* units of entrepreneurs will enter into the industry and get normal profits equal to *OS* (=*EX*). In the short-run, however, the entrepreneurs may earn supernormal profits. Suppose, in the short-run OX_1 units of, entrepreneurs work in the industry. Now, price will be equal to their marginal revenue productivity, which at OX_1 level is *OR*. Out of this price *OR*, the amount *RS* represents abnormal profit of the firm. But in the long run, new firms will join the industry because of this abnormal profit. After some time, this will disappear and all firms in the industry will get only the normal profits.

The marginal productivity theory of profit, as discussed above, is not a satisfactory theory of profit, because it is difficult to calculate the marginal revenue productivity of entrepreneurship. Moreover, it has been criticised on a number of grounds that we have already explained in an earlier chapter.

EXERCISES

1. Explain the meaning and nature of profits and distinguish between gross profits and net profits.
2. Do you agree with the view that profits cannot exist in a stationary state?
3. Explain in brief the important theories of profits.
4. Distinguish between rent and profit and show how profit is determined.
5. "Profits are surplus of the intramarginal over the marginal producers." "Profits are a constituent element of the normal price." Are these two views reconcilable?
6. Explain the risk-bearing and uncertainty-bearing theories of profit.
7. Write short note on the Schumpeter's innovation theory of profit, and the marginal productivity theory of profit.

Multiple Choice Questions

8. (*i*) Which of the following is the main constituent of gross profit?
   (*a*) Rewards for the factors of production supplied by the entrepreneur himself
   (*b*) Charges of maintenance
   (*c*) Extra Personal Gains
   (*d*) All of the above [*Ans.* (*d*)]

   (*ii*) The costs of the factors of production supplied by the entrepreneur himself are known as:
   (*a*) Implicit Costs (*c*) Fixed Costs
   (*b*) Explicit Costs (*d*) Variable Costs [*Ans.* (*a*)]

   (*iii*) Net profit is the reward for which of the function of the entrepreneur?
   (*a*) Risk Taking Function (*c*) Both of the above
   (*b*) Bargaining Skill (*d*) None of the above [*Ans.* (*c*)]

   (*iv*) Innovation Theory of Profit was developed by:
   (*a*) Joseph Schumpeter (*c*) Hawley
   (*b*) J.B. Clark (*d*) Knight [*Ans.* (*a*)]

   (*v*) Uncertainty Bearing Theory of Profit is associated with the name of
   (*a*) American economist Knight
   (*b*) American economist J.B. Clark
   (*c*) American economist Hawley
   (*d*) None of the above [*Ans.* (*a*)]

Chapter 45

INEQUALITY OF INCOME

1. INTRODUCTION

In the last few chapters we have discussed the mechanism of factor pricing. In the present chapter we shall examine the pattern of personal incomes that emerges from the price payments that are made to factor suppliers. This is not just a matter of prices. It depends on who supplies the factors for which prices are paid, and what the suppliers do with the incomes to which their control of factors gives them a chain. In other words, the personal distribution of incomes has an institutional, as well as price aspect. The former has a very significant bearing on the problem of inequality of incomes which is the object of our present study.

In a society where human slavery prevails, the share of income allocated to labour by the pricing process would go, not to the slaves, but to their owners. The slaves would get only a bare subsistence. In a capitalistic society, where most of the capital used in industry is privately owned, the price received for the use of land and equipment goes to the capitalists who own such property. This means that the incomes of wealthy property owners consist largely of interest, rents and in many cases profits. These usually comprise only a small part of the incomes of the wage-earners. The important role played by entrepreneurs in the capitalistic system is another institutional feature that affects the division of income; for it enables the entrepreneurs to make profits which are partly diverted from incomes that would probably go to others. Thus, inequality of income is an important feature of capitalist economies.

2. CAUSES OF INEQUALITIES

Inequality of incomes in an economy arises due to following reasons:

(1) *The System of Inheritance.* The accumulations of rich persons pass to their heirs by the system of inheritance. The heirs are able to

enjoy an income without doing any work. Thus, inheritance has largely been responsible for the emergence of a leisure class whose members live in idleness and luxury without contributing any productive service to the nation.

(2) *The System of Private Property.* Under the system of private property, an individual is free to earn, save and own property. When he knows that he is the owner of his property, he always tries to multiply it. The large funds of an individual breed further capital. If the system of private property is absent, no individual will have the incentive to work more and to save more. Thus, private property is the main cause of inequality of incomes. First, the individual earns income and then his property starts earning. This is the reason that some earn less and others more. The gap between haves and have-nots increases.

(3) *Differences in Ability.* People have different natural qualities and talent. Some are more gifted than others. Persons who are endowed by nature with special qualities, better physique and greater capacities for hard work earn more than the others. This is also, one, of the reasons of inequality of incomes.

(4) *Differences in Economic Functions Opportunities.* Different persons perform different types of jobs. They get different salaries and wages. Generally, the wages of labour-class are less than the salaries of skilled labourers. The environment is an important factor in which people are born. They are offered unequal advantages by environment in which they are placed. Those born in well-to-do families get a favourable start in life through good education, better training and social contact. But those who are unfortunate enough to be born in poor families may not have these advantages. Thus, it is inequality of opportunities which creates great inequalities of incomes. There is a vicious circle in which economic inequalities lead to inequality of opportunity which in turn gives rise to still further inequalities in economic status and economic functions. According to Prof. Tawney[1], "Wealth in modem society is distributed according to opportunity and while opportunity depends partly upon talent and energy, it depends still m1re upon birth and social position, access to education and inherited wealth, in a word, upon property. For talent and energy can create opportunity. But property need not wait for it." The son of a poor man may create opportunity through talents and energy but the son of a rich person has opportunity thrust upon him.

1. Tawney, *Acquisitive Society.*

3. MEASUREMENT OF INEQUALITY OF INCOMES

Several mathematical and statistical measures have been developed to measure the dispersion and inequalities of (personal) income distribution.

(1) ***Coefficient of Variance.*** The most important measure is the coefficient of standard deviation and/or the coefficient of variance. Thus,

$$\text{The Coefficient of Standard Deviation} = \frac{\sigma}{X} \qquad \ldots(1)$$

$$\text{and the Coefficient of Variance} = \frac{\sigma}{X} \times 100 \qquad \ldots(2)$$

where σ = Standard Deviation

$$= \sqrt{\sum_{i=1}^{n}(X_i - \bar{X})^2/N} \qquad \textit{for individual series}$$

also

$$\sigma = \sqrt{\sum_{i=1}^{n} f_1 (X_i - \bar{X})^2/\Sigma f} \qquad \textit{for discrete series}$$

and X_1 is the actual income of the ith individual, $\bar{X}$ is the average of personal incomes of the society, N is the total number of individuals of the society. Σ (sigma) denotes the sum total. f_i indicates the frequency of the ith value.

Equation (1) and (2) state that larger the value of σ, more will be the dispersion of personal income around the mean. If we compare the two situations or the two series of data, we may say that the distribution of personal income will be more unequal in that situation whose coefficient of variance is relatively high; and less unequal for relatively low coefficient of variance.

(2) ***Lorenz Curve.*** The Lorenz curve is a graphic method for measuring the inequalities in the distribution of income (wealth). It was devised by the Dr. Lorenz. This method can be applied with equal advantage for comparing the distribution of profits amongst different groups of business firms and such other things. It is a cumulative percentage curve. In this method the percentage of items are combined with the percentage of such things as income, wealth, profits, etc.

This method of drawing a Lorenz curve is simple. First of all, the various groups of each variable should be reduced to percentages. Thus, if it is desired to show the distribution of income amongst the various groups pf population of a country, the various groups of population should be reduced in the form of percentages of total population; so also, the incomes derived by these groups in terms of the total income of the country. After this, the two sets of the percentages obtained; they should be cumulated and cumulative percentages thus' determined. Finally, they should be plotted on a two-dimensional diagram. The scale along the axis of *Y* begins from zero at the point of intersection and goes upward to 100, while the scale along the axis of *X* begins with 100 at the point of intersection and goes upto zero towards the right. The points 100, 100 along the *Y* axis and the points 0, 0 along the *X* axis should be joined in a straight line. The line so obtained is called the line of equidistribution, and serves as the basis of the determination of the extent to which the actual distribution deviates from the ideal distribution given by this line.

Example. The following table gives the population and earnings of two countries *A* and *B*. Represent the data graphically so as to bring out the inequality of the following earnings.

Country A		*Country B*	
Persons	*Earnings*	*Persons*	*Earnings*
200	150	100	160
200	200	140	240
200	300	60	120
200	450	50	280
200	650	200	400
200	750	90	400
200	900	60	280
200	1,200	160	920
200	1,700	40	240
200	3,700	100	960
2,000	10,000	1,000	4,000

Figure 45.1 shows the Lorenz curves for country *A* and for country *B*. These two Lorenz curves show significant deviation from the line of perfectly equal distribution of personal income. It is very clear in the diagram that country *A* has more inequality than country *B*.

Solution.

Population and Incomes of Two Countries A and B

Country A				*Country B*			
Persons		*Earnings*		*Persons*		*Earnings*	
Comulative Total	*Comulative Percentage*	*Comulative Total*	*Comulative Percentage*	*Comulative Total*	*Comulative Percentage*	*Comulative Total*	*Comulative Percentage*
200	10	130	1.5	100	10	160	4
400	20	350	3.5	240	24	400	10
600	30	470	6.5	300	30	520	13
800	40	1,100	11	350	35	800	20
1,000	50	1,750	17.5	550	55	1,200	30
1,200	60	2,500	25	640	64	1,600	40
1,400	70	3,400	34	700	70	1,880	47
1,600	80	4,600	46	860	86	2,800	70
1,800	90	6,300	63	900	90	3,040	76
2,000	100	10,000	100	1,000	100	4,000	100

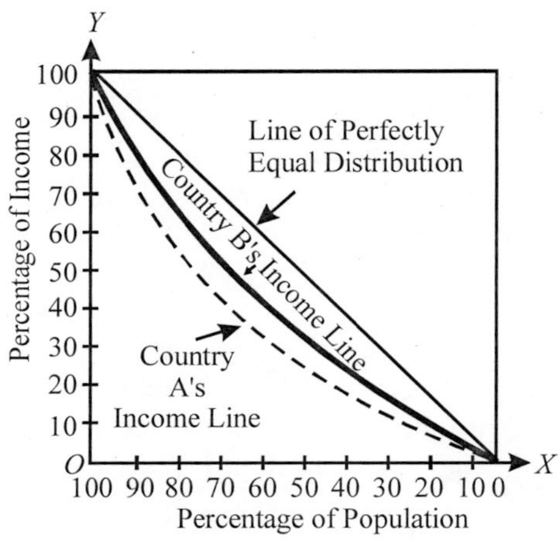

Fig. 45.1

Because the higher the area above, the Lorenz curve, larger will be the share of national output accompanied by a small number of persons.

4. ARGUMENTS IN FAVOUR OF INEQUALITY OF INCOMES

(1) *Economic Incentive.* The primary argument made in favour of income inequality is of the economic incentive. Increases in income are the rewards for producing more goods or producing them more efficiently, for working harder or longer hours, for undergoing long and expensive years of training for particular job. From the individual's point of view, income differentials thus serve as necessary payments for differences in effort. skill, training and ability.

From society's point of view also, the differences are equally important. In the absence of monetary inducements total productivity of the economy would decrease and real income would fall as people in the society reduce their efforts. Consequently, the social welfare will be reduced.

(2) *Proper Allocation of Resources.* A free price economy requires income differentials as a means of allocating resources properly. We know that an income to a labour is a price for his service. Different services can command different prices in the market, because buyers place different values on the services. If the price of a dentist's service is higher than that of a plumber's, the differential would indicate that more men should study dentistry and fewer plumbing. If the difference persists, such a shift over the long-run is likely to occur. Conversely, a higher income going to plumbers would indicate that the society places a higher value on these services, and in the long-run the higher price would attract more men into learning this particular trade. In the absence of differences in the prices paid for various services, there is no indication of how much in demand each service is, no mechanism through which the demand for the service and its supply are equated, and no long-run shift in supply in accordance with price offered. Hence, inequalities of incomes provide alternative schemes for resource allocation.

(3) *Promotes Capital Formation.* Some economists argue that inequalities of income promote capital formation in the country. Since saving varies directly with income, it is the high income group that provides the economy with most of the funds to finance investment. The greater the volume of investment, the greater the productivity and income of the economy as a whole. It would seem to be necessary, therefore, to have a wealthy class to provide the necessary savings for economic growth.

5. ARGUMENTS AGAINST INEQUALITY OF INCOMES

(1) *Class-Conflict.* Some economists have argued that inequality of incomes has created two sections in the society—the haves and the have-nots—which are always on the war path. This has resulted in instability in the economy.

(2) *Prevents the Maximisation of Consumer Welfare.* Inequality of incomes prevents the maximisation of consumer welfare, or total utility. The total utility of a consumer increases with consumption of each additional good, or from each additional rupee part for goods and services. But the marginal utility declines as more and more rupees are spent for consumption. The high income family is in a position to spend money not only on the high priority goods but on the less important, lower utility items. On the other hand, the very low income family must stop buying while the utility of another rupee's worth of goods would be extremely high. Hence, a transfer of a rupee from the rich to the flow income family would increase total utility; that is, it would increase the poor's utility by more than it would decrease the wealthy's utility. In fact, it might be argued that society's total utility is maximised only when income is distributed perfectly evenly.

(3) *Political Domination.* In the presence of inequality of incomes the rich dominate the political machinery and they use it to promote their own exclusive interests. This results in corruption and social injustice.

(4) *Creation of Monopolies.* Inequality of incomes promotes monopolies in the society. These powerful monopolies and big industries charge unfair prices from the consumers and push the small firms out of the market.

(5) *Economically Wasteful.* Extreme inequality is economically wasteful, because the surplus incomes of the very rich persons are responsible for much idleness, unhappiness and demoralisation. Rich persons spend too much of their time in extravagant leisure, clubs, parties, travel, and the like—consuming without producing. Thousands of labourers and many variable resources are employed in providing them with luxuries of little intrinsic worth, dissipating the social product to trifling ends. Further, the influence of poverty is no less disastrous. Undernourished, poorly clothed, improperly housed workmen cannot be efficient. Out of poverty grow disease, dissipation, vice and crime. Here again is loss of productive power.

Inequality of income has, therefore, led to economic insecurity for the middle and working classes. An important consequence of economic inequality is the concentration of economic and political power in the hands of the rich few who dominate the country, direct its policy and exploit the poor to promote their own ends. Inequality of incomes, therefore, has been regarded as one of the most important evils of capitalism. It should have to be removed or at least reduced somehow.

6. METHODS OF REDUCING INEQUALITY OF INCOMES

Perfect equality of incomes for all the members of society is hardly to be recommended, because the needs of different individuals and their capacities for enjoyment are not the same. Neither would equality make for economy in the use of our scarce resources, because it would destroy the incentive to productive efficiency that inequality of incomes can promote. To lessen the extremes of inequality that now prevail is one thing, but to reduce all incomes to exactly the same level is quite another.

The communist programme for social reform sets forth distribution according to needs as its ultimate goal. Ethically, this is a high ideal. It, would greatly lessen the inequality now existing, but it would not result in cent per cent equality of incomes, because of differences in human needs. This principle would give to each person the amount and kind of income that would provide the fullest opportunity for the perfect development of his capacities.

The following are some of the measures which can be suggested to reduce inequality of incomes:

(1) *Principle of Fixing Minimum Wage.* It states that the basic requirements for all should be met before luxuries are allowed to any. The fulfilment of this principle would in itself abolish poverty. The justification for it rests partly in humanitarian impulses, and partly in practical considerations. We do not like to see people suffer, and it seems only merciful to provide each with a sufficient livelihood to maintain a decent level of existence before we allow others to enjoy superfluous luxuries.

In India in 1948, the Minimum Wages Act was passed in pursuance of which minimum wages are being fixed for agricultural labour and labour in what are called the "sweatest trades." This is a step which will level up the incomes from below and remove poverty from the economy.

(2) *The Principle of Incentive.* The principle of a guaranteed minimum assures to each person only a very modest level of existence; beyond that it is important to apply another principle, which will stimulate each person to better his position by making his reward commensurate with what he does to earn it. This principle states that the rewards should vary with the socially useful productive accomplishment of the individual. It only means that extra rewards must be given to those whose activities are socially useful.

(3) *The Principle of Equality of Opportunity.* Here the government should set up some sort of machinery which may provide equal opportunities to all rich and poor in getting employment or getting a start in trade and industry of all types. The objective here is to eliminate the family influence in the matter of choice of a profession. For example, the government should provide scholarships, so that even the poorest in the land can acquire the highest education and technical skill. The recruitment to all jobs may be made by an impartial Selection Board or Public Service

Commission. Similarly, to give a start in trade and industry, the government may give financial aid or loans at very reasonable rate repayable in easy instalments to all those who wish to enter trade and industry in the economy.

(4) *Principle of Progressive Taxation.* We know that the effect of a progressive tax is to reduce income inequality; the effect of a regressive tax is to decrease income equality. The more heavily governments rely on progressive taxes (such as the present type of personal income tax) and the less frequent the use of regressive type taxes (such as sales tax), the greater the redistributive effect of the tax structure. The income tax sharply reduces the higher incomes, without taking any part of the lowest incomes.

In addition to taxation, the government has in recent years effected income distribution by the enactment of important social legislation. The growing significance of transfer payment may be an example of this social security legislation. The most important transfer payments retirement benefits, unemployment compensation, workmen's compensation for accidents on the job.

These are some of the measures that can be adopted to reduce inequality of incomes. As we have already pointed out, inequalities can be reduced; they cannot be eliminated altogether. In fact, absolute equality is not desirable.

EXERCISES

1. What are the measures necessary for bringing about a more equalitarian distribution of income?
2. What are the causes of economic inequality? Explain the arguments for and against it.
3. Why does inequality of income arise? How can it be removed?
4. How will you measure the inequality of incomes? To what extent is it desirable?

Multiple Choice Questions

5. (*i*) Inequality of incomes in an economy arises due to
   (*a*) the system of inheritance (*b*) the system of private property
   (*c*) differences in ability (*d*) all of the above [*Ans.* (*d*)]

   (*ii*) Inequality of income distribution can be measured by
   (*a*) the coefficient of variance (*b*) Lorenz curve
   (*c*) any of the above (*d*) none of the above [*Ans.* (*c*)]

   (*iii*) Inequalities of income distribution can be reduced by applying
   (*a*) Progressive Taxation (*b*) Regressive Taxation
   (*c*) Proportional Taxation (*d*) Degressive Taxation [*Ans.* (*a*)]

   (*iv*) Inequalities of income distribution leads to
   (*a*) class-conflict (*b*) monopolies
   (*c*) political domination (*d*) all of the above [*Ans.* (*a*)]

PART 6
WELFARE ANALYSIS

Chapter 46

PARETO CRITERION AND OPTIMALITY

1. INTRODUCTION

Vilfredo Pareto was the first great economist who provided a positive criterion for increase or decrease in social welfare. His formulation was accepted by Cambridge economists. His concept was a landmark in the history of subjective welfare economics. This theory known as 'A Priori Welfare Theory' is principally concerned with allocations of resources by individual consumers, producers and other participants in the exchange transactions. Pareto differed from the earlier economists on two important points: (*i*) he rejected the notion of cardinal utility and additive utility functions, and (*ii*) he restricted himself to welfare conclusions that are independent of interpersonal comparisons whatever. His formulation shows that the economic welfare of a society will be maximised if only resources are allocated efficiently and simultaneously in consumption, production and exchange. It also states that co-competition enables society to reach an optimum welfare position, regardless of the distribution of income, and even if utilities of different individuals are not considered to be comparable.

2. PARETO OPTIMALITY

Pareto Optimality (often called Economic Efficiency) is defined as a position from which it is not possible, by any reallocation of inputs or outputs to make anyone better off without causing at least one person worse off. In other words, the distribution of consumer goods among consumers is efficient if every possible reallocation of goods among consumers results in the reduction of the satisfaction of at least one. Production is efficient if every feasible reallocation of inputs among (within) firms diminishes the output level of at least one firm (commodity). It means that a Pareto Optimality is a position from which it is impossible to increase anyone's welfare, in the sense of moving him to a position that he refers by transforming goods and services through production or exchange, without impairing someone else's welfare. Conversely, an allocation (or a situation) can be defined as Pareto non-optimality, if the economic welfare of one or more individuals can be increased without harming anyone else.

The Pareto optimality provides us with a criterion, often referred to as *Pareto's Unanimity Rule,* for making welfare judgements. Pareto did not give much attention to the problem of income distribution. He said that within a given framework of distribution a reorganisation of production and exchange will be looked upon as welfare increasing (or decreasing) if it improves (or worsens) the position of at least one person without affecting adversely the position of others. Pareto's Unanimity Rule does not rely on interpersonal comparisons of utility at all. It is based on a fairly broad critical judgement, namely, that it is a good thing to make all person better off without making any person or persons worse off. Pareto does not talk about a policy which benefits some and harms others because to evaluate such cases, the problem of interpersonal comparisons of utility will arise which Pareto's criterion has tactfully avoided. The Paretian concept of social optimum is essentially the same as the Cambridge concept (or Baumol's concept) of ideal output. Pareto, of course, has not given us any mathematical proof that competition leads to the desired social optimum; nor he has derived the marginal conditions which must conform to this position of maximum social welfare. He has only given a definition of society's maximum satisfaction. The derivation of the marginal conditions of welfare in modern form is due mainly to Prof. Hicks and Prof. Reder.[1]

Nevertheless, Pareto provided three marginal conditions to explain the attainment of optimal situation in consumption, production and exchange. These marginal conditions for the General Optimum are based on the following important assumptions:

1. Each individual has his own ordinal utility function and is provided with definite amounts of each product and each other.

---

1. M.W. Reder, *Studies in the Theory of Welfare Economics,* Ch. 2.

2. The production function of each firm (producer) is given by the state of technology.

3. All goods are highly divisible.

4. Each individual buys some of all the goods.

5. All factors are used in the production of each of the goods.

Given these assumptions, the static marginal (or first order) conditions for Paretian general optimum can be derived as follows:

(l) *The Consuming Sector.* The first marginal condition ensures the optimum allocation of goods among the consumers. This condition states that for each consumer in the society, the marginal rate of substitution (*MRS*) between any two goods must be the same.[2]

If the *MRS* between any two goods is not the same for any two consumers, they can enter into an exchange which would increase the satisfaction of both or of one without reducing the satisfaction (welfare) of other. It is known as a *mutually profitable trade* between the two consumers. In order to understand this marginal condition, it seems imperative to introduce the Edgeworth Box diagram.[3]

In Fig. 46.1, the horizontal and vertical axes of the rectangle measure the total available quantities of Q_1 and Q_2 in a pure exchange economy. Any point in the box denotes a particular distribution of the commodities between two consumers *A* and *B*.

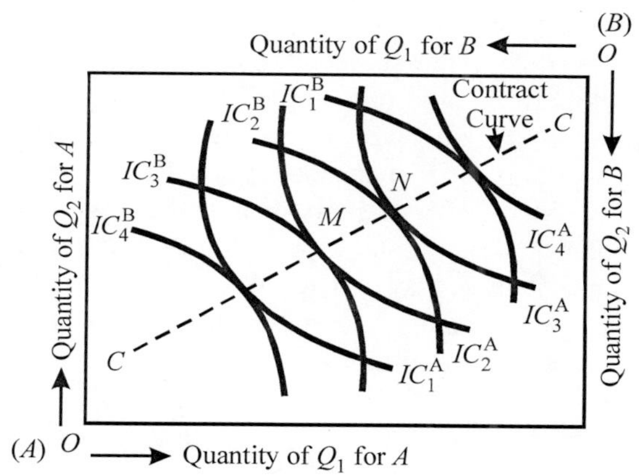

Fig. 46.1

The Fig. 46.1 shows the indifference maps of two individuals *A* and *B* and their levels of satisfaction from various combinations Q_1 and Q_2 The

2. The *MRS* between two goods is the amount of one good necessary to compensate for the loss of a marginal of another to maintain a given level of welfare (satisfaction).

3. Such Edgeworth Box diagrams are equally relevant to understand the problem of optimum factor use and hence will be used in production sector also.

indifference map of A is drawn, using O as the origin, and the indifference map of B is drawn, using O' as the origin. In this two person-two commodity case, equilibrium of exchange will be attained where the indifference curves of the, two consumers are tangent to one another. In other words, the locus of the points of tangency of the two sets of indifference curves is *the contract curve CC*.

Again, we know that the slope of an indifference curve is termed as the marginal rate of substitution of Q_1 for Q_2 (MRS_{Q1Q2}). Since at the tangency points (or equilibrium points of exchange) the slope of indifference curves of the two individuals is the same, the *MRS* for each will be the same. Each point along a contract curve is Pareto optimal and any point of the contract curve represents a non-optimum position, because at such a point one will lose (in the sense that he enjoys a lower indifference curve) while the other does not gain (in the sense that he remains on the same indifference curve). Following Pareto's criterion, a move from a non-optimum point R to any point (M or N) on contract curve CC will benefit one without harming the other, For instance, if the individuals are initially at R, they can move to M, whereby B will attain a higher indifference curve and A will remain on the original curve. This means a net gain for the society. Thus, when the society moves from a non-optimum point to one on the contract curve, social welfare becomes the maximum. However, a movement along the contract curve in either direction cannot make both parties better off; a move of this like will always benefit one individual at the cost of another. Thus while each point on the contract curve denotes optimum social welfare in Paretian sense, it is not easy to determine which of such points is the real optimum.

To evaluate all these positions, one must make an interpersonal comparison of utilities which, however, requires an explicit ethical belief in one's ability to make such comparisons. These utility measurements are purely arbitrary so far as interpersonal utility comparisons are concerned. These utility levels (or numbers) are based on their individual judgements and such comparisons my not be correct. This is the main weakness of Pareto criterion which Pareto wanted to avoid at all costs.

(2) *The Producing Sector*. Pareto optimality in the producing sector involves the fulfilment of three marginal conditions: (*i*) Optimum allocation off actor inputs, (*ii*) Optimisation of output of each firm, (*iii*) Optimum factor-product relationship.

(*i*) *Optimum allocation of factor inputs*. The first marginal condition is very smaller to that of consuming sector. It requires that the marginal rate of technical substitution (*RTS*) between any pair of factors be the same for any two firms using both the factors to produce a given product. Once this condition is satisfied, it is not possible to produce any more of a good without producing less of some other goods. Otherwise, there is some possibility of increasing the total product by shifting each factor marginal) from one product to the other.

We know that the slope of an isoquant is known as the marginal rate of technical substitution between two factors of production. 'Assuming that Q_1 and Q_2 are the only two goods that are produced in the economy (society) and there exist fixed, non-augmentable endowments of the two inputs, labour (L) and capital (K); the Pareto optimality can be explained through the Edgeworth box diagram as given in Fig. 46.2. Here, the locus of mutual tangencies of the two sets of isoquants is referred to as the locus of efficient points, or sometimes as the *production contract curve.* Any point on CC shows the equality of RTS between the factors for each producer, while any point off the CC curve (say P) indicates the inequality of RTS. Therefore, Pareto optimality condition will hold if the producers are at any point on CC.

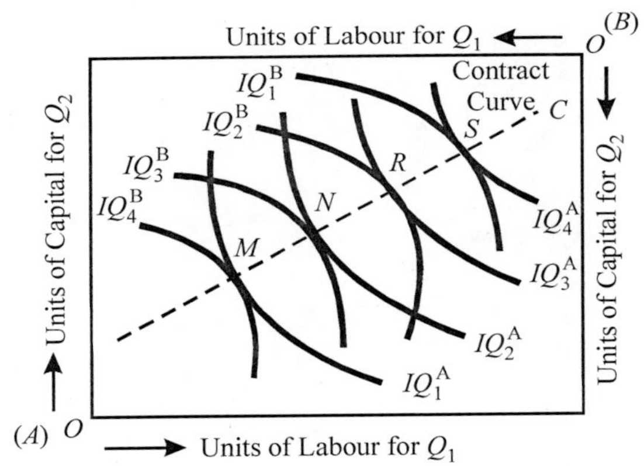

Fig. 46.2

(*ii*) *Optimisation of output of each firm.* The second marginal condition in the producing sector determines the optimum output of each product to be produced by each firm. This condition is satisfied when the marginal rate of product transformation ($MRPT$) between any two goods is the same for any two firms, (producers) which produce both of them. We know that $MRPT$ between two goods is the rate at which one good must be sacrificed to obtain more of the other without varying (increasing) the input used. If the *MRPT* between two goods is not the same for any pair of two producers, it will always be possible to increase the combined (society's) out-put of both the goods, or to increase the output of one good without decreasing the output of the other.

It means that given the total supply of labour and capital, the society has to trade off between the two producers. If the society chooses to produce more units of Q_2, (or Q_2) it will have to cut the production of Q_2, (or Q_1). This can be explained by the production possibility curve or product transformation curve. Fig. 46.3 represents the product-transformation curve. Given the factor endowments and input-output coefficients, we may draw the curve within which the economy can produce Q_1 or Q_2 or both the products. We have already noted that more units of Q_1 can be produced if and only if more resources are transferred from Q_2 to Q_1. This means that the marginal rate of Q_2's transformation into Q_1 must be negative ($dQ_2/dQ_1. < 0$). Here, we should also remember that the marginal rate of one product's transformation into another (*MRPT*) is also equal to the ratio between the marginal costs of Q_1 and Q_2.

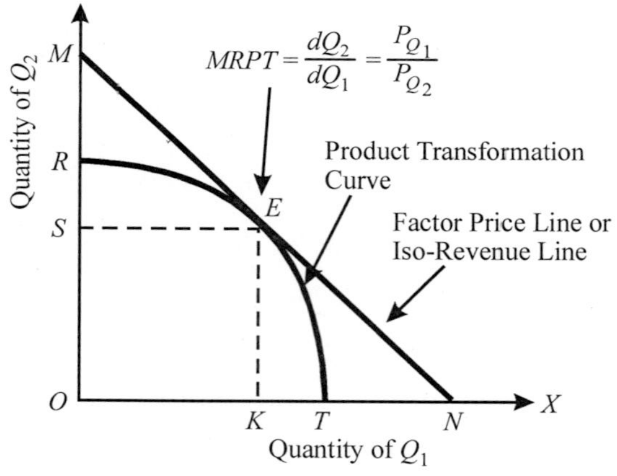

Fig. 46.3

Further, we find in Fig. 46.3 that the increasing quantity of Q_2 must be foregone to achieve a given increase in the quantity of Q_1. Now the limit of this transformation will depend upon the relative prices of two goods. Because we know that under the perfect competitive conditions, for equilibrium output level, the marginal cost (*MC*) must be equid to the marginal revenue (*MR*) or price ($P = MR$). Hence, for any pair of two goods, the ratio of their marginal costS must be equal to the ratio of their prices. In Fig. 46.3 this condition is satisfied at point *E* where the slope of product transformation curve (*MRPT*) is equal to the slope of the iso-revenue line (P_{Q1} / P_{Q2}).

(*iii*) *Optimum factor-product relationship.* This condition states that the marginal rate of transformation (*MRT*) between any factor and any product must be identical in any two firms using the factor and producing the output. A firm can be said to be operating efficiency if and only if it is capable to produce certain product at the lowest possible per unit cost. Until such least-cost combination of capital input (*K*) and labour input (*L*) is arrived at, the firm will substitute the relatively costlier inputs for the one which is (relatively) cheaper. Eventually, a firm's (micro-level) least-cost combination of inputs is attained where the ratio between marginal physical products of labour (MPP_L) and capital (MPP_K) is equal to the factor price ratio (P_L/P_K).

In other words, if the marginal productivity (*MP*) of any factor for a given product is not the same for two firms, the total product can be increased by transferring the factor from the low to the high productivity firm. If this marginal condition is not met, a switching around of inputs can give us something for nothing—it can increase one or both outputs without any increase in input use.

The fulfilment of these three marginal conditions would mean that RTS_s, $MRPT_s$, and MPP_s are the same for all the firms in the economy. In such a situation, Pareto optimality is reached by the producing sector. Now, a further reallocation of inputs among firms can increase the output of one firm only by decreasing the output of some other firm or firms; and a further reallocation of inputs among uses within the firms can increase the quantity of one product by decreasing the quantity of some other product.

(3) *General Pareto Optimality.* Optimality or efficiency in the consuming and producing sectors implies that the allocation of resources is Pareto optimal throughout the society. This general condition is of great significance because it relates the technical conditions of production with the state of consumer preferences.

This proposition requires that the *subjective* rate of substitution (*MRS*), common to all individuals (consumers), must be equal to the *objective* rate of transformation (*MRTP*) for all pairs of goods in the economy. The consuming sector satisfies the optimal condition as:

$$MR_S = \frac{P_{Q1}}{P_{Q2}} \qquad ...(1)$$

Again, the producing sector satisfies the optimal condition as:

$$MRPT = \frac{P_{Q1}}{P_{Q2}} \qquad ... (2)$$

where P_{Q1} is the price of the $Q_1{}^{th}$ product and P_{Q2} is the price of the $Q_2{}^{th}$ product.

Now from (1) and (2) we get,

$$MRS_s = MRPT_s \qquad ...(3)$$

Therefore, equation (3) is true for all consumers, firms and commodities. The equality of the various rates of substitution and transformation ensures Paretooptimality throughout the economy.

This general condition can also be shown diagrammatically in Fig. 46.4.

In Fig. 46.4, *RT* is the community transformation curve between the two goods Q_1 and Q_2. The slope at any point on the transformation curve shows the maximum additional Q_1 that can be produced by the community if it gives up the production of Q_2 by a small amount, keeping the factor supplies and the production of other goods constant. We have further

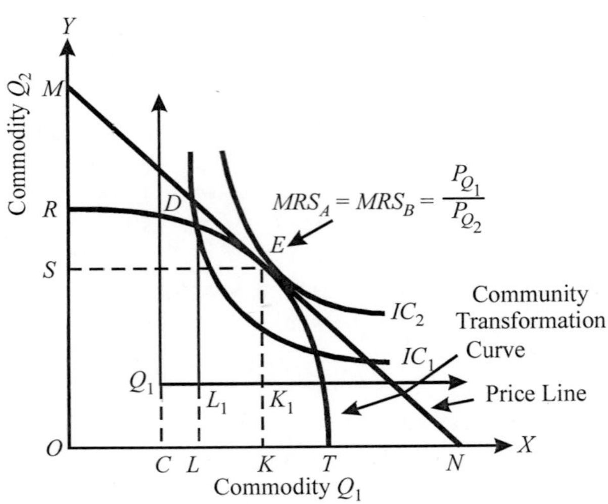

Fig. 46.4

drawn an indifference curves map of one consumer of these two goods. Q_1 and Q_2 consisting of two indifference curves IC_1 and IC_2. Suppose the consumer is at point *D* where the community produces *OL* of Q_1 and *DL* of Q_2 and the consumer consumes Q_1L_1 (= *CL*) of Q_1 and DL_1 of Q_2; it is clear that at point *D*, the community's marginal rate of transformation is not equal to the consumer's marginal rate of substitution; because the transformation curve *RT* cuts the indifference curve IC_1 at point *D*. Hence *D* does not represent an optimum position, because it is technically possible to make the consumer better off without making anyone else worse off, if simply a move from *D* to *E* takes place. *At point E where the community transformation of curve is tangent to a higher private indifference curve* IC_2, the higher subjective rate of transformation (*MRS*) becomes equal to the objective rate (*RPT*) at that point, the consumer is raised to a higher indifference curve having a higher welfare level, which he can leave, as before, *OC* of Q_1 and LL_1 of Q_2 for the other consumers.

Prof. Samuelson has summed up all these marginal conditions necessary for a Pareto optimum in one brief and easily understood rule: "Between any two variables, the marginal rates of substitution must be (subjectively) equal for all individuals, and (technically) equal for all alternative processes, with the common technical and subjective ratios being equivalent, otherwise there exists a physically attainable position that makes everyone off."

3. PARETO OPTIMALITY OF PERFECT COMPETITION

We know that in perfect competition, all inputs and, outputs have fixed prices which remain unaffected by the activities of, any individual buyers or sellers. All the buyers and sellers in the market are assumed to be price-takers. Further, any firm can start or leave the production of any commodity at the given price. Under such conditions of perfect competition, free from all external effects, anyone consumer seeking maximum satisfaction makes the *MRS* between any two goods equal to the ratio of their prices. Since, under competition prices are the same for all consumers, the MRS_s between goods must be the same for all consumers. Hence,

$$MRS = \frac{P_{Q1}}{P_{Q2}} \qquad \ldots(4)$$

where P_{Q1} is the price of Q_1 and P_{Q2} is the price of Q_2.

Similarly, if there is perfect competition among producers in commodity and factor markets then we get,

$$\left.\begin{aligned} P_{Q1} &= \frac{P_{Q1}}{P_{Q2}} \\ \text{and} \qquad P_{Q2} &= \frac{P_L}{MP_{Q2}} \end{aligned}\right\} \qquad \ldots(5)$$

where P_L is the price of labour input (L) and MP_{Q1} and MP_{Q2} are its marginal products in producing Q_1 and Q_2. Since P_L / MP is the marginal cost of output (MC), we obtain an optimum condition $P_Q = MC$ for every commodity. Therefore,

$$MRS = \frac{P_{Q1}}{P_{Q2}} = \frac{P_L}{P_L} \bigg/ \frac{MP_{Q1}}{MP_{Q2}}$$

$$= \frac{\text{Marginal Cost of } Q_1 \text{ in Terms of Labour Input}}{\text{Marginal Cost of } Q_2 \text{ in Terms of Labour Input}}$$

$$= MRPT \qquad \ldots(6)$$

Thus perfect competition ensures Pareto optimality.

4. NON-ATTAINMENT OF OPTIMUM WELFARE UNDER MONOPOLISTIC COMPETITION

The condition for Pareto optimality fails to be realised in a world characterised by monopolistic competition. The efficiency criterion that price must be equal to marginal cost ($P = MC$) is fulfilled only in perfect competition. We know that in the presence of monopolies, oligopolies, monopsonies, etc. the average revenue curve (or the demand curve for the product) of a firm being downward sloping, the marginal revenue of the selling output will be lets than price. Since every firm seeks to maximise its profits, it will produce that level of output where marginal cost equals marginal revenue ($MC = MR$). It would mean that price will be greater than marginal cost and, therefore, factor input is not being paid equal to the value of its marginal product.

The presence of a monopolistic firm ($MC = MR < P$) shows that we may find a situation where not all the consumers and firms are maximising satisfaction. It leads factor price to diverge from the value of its marginal product and that causes misallocation of resources. In such a situation where there is monopolistic element in some firms together with competition in some others, it makes production not in conformity with consumers' preferences; because resources allocation is distorted in such a way that too little resources are used in monopolistic firms where their marginal value productivities MVP_s are higher, and too much in the competitive firms being lower MVP_s

In other words, those goods on which consumers place higher values are produced in smaller amounts, while those goods on which they place lower values are produced in larger amounts.

The existence of monopolistic element in the consumption sector distorts the optimum exchange condition. Consumers are no longer able to buy as much of a commodity, as they want without affecting its price. A consumer requires to pay a higher price as he increases his purchases. He will be in equilibrium when his marginal rate of substitution (*MRS*) equals the ratio of the marginal costs of acquiring additional units of any pair of goods, not the ratio of their prices. But in such a monopolistic situation marginal costs are not equal to product prices. It follows that the marginal condition of consumption-sector for welfare optimum is not satisfied.

Similarly, the existence of monopolistic elements in the production sector leads to misallocation of resources. In such a situation, the price of each input will increase as it is demanded more and more. Here, each firm will be in equilibrium when its marginal rate of product transformation (*MRPT*) is equal to the ratio of the marginal costs of buying additional units of inputs and not the ratio of their prices. The ratios of these marginal costs will not be the same for each firm and this would mean that their respective RTS_s will not be equal. Therefore, the firms are not on their production contract curve. Thus, society's production is not Pareto optimal. An appropriate reallocation of inputs among firms can now increase one firm's output without reducing any other firm's production.

From the above discussion, we may conclude that Pareto optimal allocation of resources is not possible in the absence of perfect competition because of the following reasons:

(1) When there is monopolistic competition among consumers, their corresponding MRS_s are not necessarily equal.

(2) When there is monopolistic competition among producers in factor markets, their corresponding RST_s are not necessarily equal.

(3) When there is monopolistic competition among producers in product markets, their corresponding MRS_s are not necessarily equal.

We know that the necessary condition for Pareto optimality is *MRPT* = *MRS* but it is not a sufficient condition. The sufficient condition for

Pareto optimality is $\frac{MR_{Q1}}{MR_{Q2}} = \frac{PQ_1}{PQ_2}$.

It means the elasticity of demand for Q_1 equals the elasticity of demand for Q_2 because $MR = P[1 - 1/e)]$.

This is intuitively clear from the fact that price exceeds *MC* in the absence of perfect competition. *MC* is a measure of the cost to society of using factor inputs in the production of an additional unit of commodity *Q*, its price is a measure of the benefit of society from producing an additional unit of *Q*. The net benefit to the society can be increased as long as $P > MC$, and imperfect competition violates the principle of efficiency (Pareto optimality) by not producing sufficiently large quantities of commodities. If follows that monopolistic competition does not ensure optimal distribution of resources as well as of commodities in the society.

5. EXTERNAL EFFECTS AND PARETO OPTIMALITY

Until now we have assumed that there are no external effects in consumption and production. In other words, the utility function of a consumer does not depend upon the consumption levels of others and similarly, the total cost of a producer does not depend upon the output levels of others. In such a situation the private marginal utility of a commodity will coincide with its social marginal utility and its private marginal cost with its social marginal cost. If there are external effects in consumption and production, Pareto optimality may not be realised even under the conditions of perfect competition.

External effects are simply *external economies and external diseconomies* in production as well as in consumption sectors. External effects in production arise when a firm's production function depends in some way on the amounts of inputs and outputs of other firms. Similarly, external effects in consumption arise when the shape or position of a consumer's indifference map depends on the consumption levels of others.

External Economies and Diseconomies of Production

External economies of production are different from internal economies. Internal economies are the benefits of the firm's expansion enjoyed. internally by the firm itself; while external economies of production arise when an increase in the firm's production leads to (falls against) favourable repercussions on others. These external economies of production cause marginal social, benefits to diverge from marginal private benefits[4]. For external economies resulting from any particular firm's expansion makes it cheaper for other firms in the industry to operate; but under the prevailing price system the expanding firm gets no payment for the benefits which it has given to other firms.

Similarly, an expanding firm can also have adverse repercussions on other firms. These are known as external diseconomies of large scale production; or more specifically, these are technological diseconomies of production. These external diseconomies cause marginal social costs to diverge from marginal private cost.[5] As the expanding firm is not charged for the harm, it confers on others, the social marginal cost of the product is higher than its private marginal costs.

Such externalities (economies and diseconomies) may imply that due to the nature of the present economic and social institutions, benefits are best owned on others for which no payment is received, or costs are imposed on others which do not have to be paid for. For this reason, externalities are also known as *untraded interdependencies*. It is this general nature of externalities which makes them incompatible with perfect competition.

Hence externalities may be said to exist when there is a difference between marginal social cost arid marginal social benefit. Under perfect competitive situation, marginal private cost is also equal to marginal social cost. Alternatively, it also implies that price equals marginal cost ($P = MC$). If an individual firm benefits from the cost incurred by another individual firm, there exists a divergence between his (private) benefit and marginal social benefit. Conversely, the individual firm may be called upon to bear certain cost for the benefit accruing to someone else. Thus, externalities may also exist when there is a divergence between marginal social cost and marginal social benefit on the one hand and between marginal private cost and the marginal private benefit on the other.

In order to find optimum welfare in the production sector, it is necessary to equate price with marginal cost for all commodities ($P = MC$). The equality of price and marginal cost for all commodities and

---

4. Marginal social benefit can be defined as the addition to national income resulting from die use of an additional unit of input and marginal private benefit can be defined as the addition to the firm's revenue due to the use of the same input unit.
5. The marginal social cost can be distinguished from marginal private cost. The former is the opportunity to society of using a marginal amount of input in one way rather than in another; the latter is the firm's cost of using the same.

firms implies that the corresponding $MRPT_s$ of different firms are the same. The *MRPT* (or the slope of the transformation curve) measures the opportunity cost, for it shows the cost of producing a unit of any given product in terms of opportunities forgone. When there are no external effects in production, this opportunity cost, and hence the firm's private *MRPT* is the same as the social opportunity cost, and hence the social *MRPT*. In this case maximisation of welfare, both from the private as well as social point of view, is carried out simply by equating price with private marginal cost; .and the consumers' *MRS* between any two goods, then, becomes equal to individual firms' $MRPT_s$, the latter being the ratio of the private marginal cost of the two goods. However, in the presence of external effects, an individual firm's total costs depend on the output levels of other firms.

In this case, social marginal costs differ from private marginal costs. Individual maximisation may be carried out by equating price with private marginal cost; but this will not ensure Pareto optimality. Rather, such individual maximisation lead to a misallocation of resources; too much will be produced by firms causing external economies. Therefore, in the presence of external effects, a firm's individual maximisation is not the same as social maximisation.

In the existence of external effects, welfare maximisation from society's poin to view requires that price equals not the private marginal cost but the social marginal cost of each firm ($P = SMC$), and that social marginal cost be rising. It implies that consumers' MRS_s should be equated not with the firms' private $MRPT_s$, but with society $MRPT_s$ which is the ratio of social marginal costs.

External Economies and Diseconomies of Consumption

Here the utility level of one consumer depends upon the consumption of another. External economies of consumption arise when a person's consumption has a direct favourable effect on others. For example, the satisfaction of a person having a telephone increases with an increase in the number of telephone owners. Similarly, a person who maintains a garden provides satisfaction not only for himself but also for passers by. Hence in all such cases, the social marginal utilities of goods exceed their, private marginal utilities; these extra utilities are derived without the intermediary of the market and cannot be measured in pricing terms. In other words, we can say that the market prices in such external economies underestimate the marginal utilities of goods. Contrarily, external diseconomies of consumption arise when a person's consumption level has an undesirable repercussion of other consumes. For example, a person who buys a radio provides satisfaction for himself but often disturbs the peace of his neighbours. Here, the private marginal benefits exceed the social marginal benefits and the market prices overestimate the marginal utilities of goods.

In the presence of externalities in consumption, the condition for optimum exchange is violated. Even under perfect competition, society may fail to reach the level of optimum welfare. Because under these situations, the equality of the MRS_s does not necessarily lead to Pareto optimality. The problem has been analysed diagrammatically by Profs. Henderson and Quandt.

They state that in the presence of external effects, Pareto optimality cannot be achieved. They consider a society consisting of two consumers *I* and *II*. Panels (*a*) and (*b*) of Fig 46.5 show the indifference maps of consumers *I* and *II* respectively. Let consumer *I* be initially at *R* enjoying

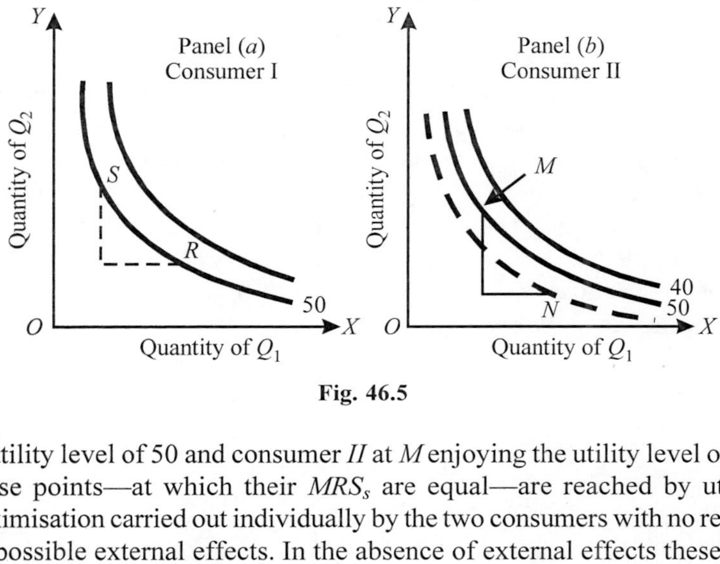

Fig. 46.5

an utility level of 50 and consumer *II* at *M* enjoying the utility level of 40. These points—at which their MRS_s are equal—are reached by utility maximisation carried out individually by the two consumers with no regard for possible external effects. In the absence of external effects these two points correspond to maximisation of social welfare also. However, in the presence of external effects, these of points of individual maximisation do not ensure social maximisation. Let us now assume that *I*'s consumption is not affected by *II's*, but *II's* utility level is reduced by *I's* consumption of Q_1 (but not of Q_2). In this case, welfare maximisation requires that the distribution of commodities is to be altered, so that *I* consumer now moves to *S*, and consumer *II* moves to *N*. As a result, *I*'s level of satisfaction remains unchanged, but the reduction of *I*'s consumption of Q_1 raises the utility level of *II* who consumes more of Q_1. Its utility level rises from 40 to 45; thus showing that his utility can be increased without harming *I*. In the presence of external effects in consumption, therefore, the equality of the MRS_s of the two consumers (as at *R* and *M*) is (course, compatible with individual maximisation, but is not necessarily so wit welfare maximisation. In our example, social maximisation requires that should move to *N*, that is, the *MRS* of *II* (who is affected by external effects) must be small for an optimal distribution than it would be in the absence of external effects.

Hence external effect may affect the allocation of resources in both the sectors— the consuming sector and the producing sector. Too much will be produced b firms subject to external diseconomies, while there will be a less than optimum output in those firms generating external economies. Similar is the case in the consuming sector. These deviations from Pareto optimality can however be corrected by adopting properly devised tax-cum-bounty measures.

Public Good Externalities

Recently, the theory of public expenditure has become very important. Here Paul A. Samuelson has introduced the concept of public goods.[6] Let us again assume a two-person two-good case. We also assume that Q_1 is available in amount $\bar{Q}_1$ .It means that Q_1 is said to be a public good if both consumers *I* and *II* may each consume $\bar{Q}_1$ units of Q_1. Therefore, we cannot say that total quantity $\bar{Q}_1$ is share by *I* and *II* consumers; in the case of public good we would say that consumer *I* (or *II*) would consume without making any loss of $\bar{Q}_1$ on consumer *II* (or *I*). Therefore, by the definition of a public good,

$$\bar{Q}_1 = Q_{11}$$

and

$$\bar{Q}_1 = Q_{21}$$

where Q_{11} is the consumption of Q_1 by consumer *I* and Q_{21} is the consumption of Q_1 by consumer *II*.

Hence consumption of a public good is a violation of the Pareto optimality which states that consumer *I* or *II* can consume some or more units of a good (say Q_1) only at the cost of reducing its availability to the other consumer or consumers.

6. Paul A. Samuelson defines a pure public good as the one whose consumption leads to no subtraction from any other individual's consumption of that good. Please see, Paul A. Samuelson, "Diagrammatic Exposition of a Pure Theory of Public Expenditure", *Review of Economics and Statistics* (November, 1955).

Perfect competition leads to equality of MRS_s in respect of any two goods. In the case of public goods where *I's* consumption Q_1 does not affect the level of the consumption by *II*, the *MRPT* of Q_1 into Q_2 should equal the sum of the two marginal rates of substitution.

$$MRPT = LMRS_s \qquad \ldots(7)$$

It means that if there is a public good in the society, then a Pareto optimum can be reached only when the above equation (7) is satisfied. Thus, externalities (public good externalities) would place a definite constraint on the scope of free market mechanism. The growing state regulation of industry, trade or modes of transportation, even those operating in the private sector also expose the inability of (free) market mechanism to maximise society's welfare.

EXERCISES

1. Two consumers *A* and *B* are sharing and exchanging a fixed supply of two goods *X* and *Y*. Show in a box diagram why they must go on exchanging until they reach the contract curve. Is consumer welfare maximised on the curve? What determines their positions on the contract curve?
2. State and 'discuss the marginal conditions of general Pareto optimality.
3. Explain how the external effects lead to the non-attainment of optimum welfare in the society.
4. Explain the Pareto optimality of perfect competition and the non-attainment of optimum welfare under monopolistic competition.
5. Do you agree with the view that welfare economics involves certain adjustments between families and families, firms and firms, and families and firms? How is this notion related to Pareto optimality condition?
6. How does allocation of resources under perfect competition help in the attainment of maximum social welfare?

Multiple Choice Questions

7. (*i*) Pareto optimality condition will hold if
   (*a*) the producers are at any point on the contract curve
   (*b*) the consumers are at any point on the contract curve
   (*c*) *MRS* = *MRPT*
   (*d*) all of the above [*Ans.* (*d*)]

   (*ii*) The condition of Pareto optimality holds correct under
   (*a*) perfect competition (*c*) oligopoly
   (*b*) monopolistic competition (*d*) all of the above [*Ans.* (*a*)]

   (*iii*) General Pareto optimality requires
   (*a*) equality of various rates of substitution and transformation
   (*b*) the subjective rate of substitution common to all individuals must be equal to the objective rate of transformation for all pairs of goods in the society
   (*c*) any of the above
   (*d*) none of the above [*Ans.* (*c*)]

PART 7
THEORY OF INTERNATIONAL TRADE

Chapter 47

THE PRINCIPLE OF COMPARATIVE ADVANTAGE

1. INTRODUCTION

While studying International Trade, two obvious questions may be asked: *First,* why does international trade take place? and *second,* what are the conditions under which trade is possible? The classical economists (Adam Smith, Ricardo, etc.) were of the opinion that international trade takes place due to differences in the costs. Adam Smith emphasised absolute cost differences, whereas David Ricardo showed that for international trade to take place, even a comparative cost advantage will lead to the exchange of goods between two countries. Both Adam Smith and Ricardo based their theorems on the labour theory of value. The later economists of the so called Marginal School (particularly G. Haberler) developed opportunity cost theorem in place of labour cost theorem. The marginalists argued that labour was not the only factor of production, but other factors were equally important. In modern times, Swedish economists criticised this theorem of opportunity cost and developed a new version of international trade which is generally known as the Heckscher-Ohlin version of comparative cost.

2. THE CLASSICAL DOCTRINE OF COMPARATIVE COST

Adam Smith's Theory of Absolute Cost Advantage

Adam Smith developed the *law of absolute cost advantage* for international trade, according to which trade between countries occurs if one of them has an *absolute* (cost) advantage in producing one commodity while the other has an absolute (cost) advantage in producing the other commodity.

According to the *Absolute Cost Advantage* doctrine of Smith, each country produce, those goods for the production of which it is specially suited on account of its climate, fertility of its land and of its natural resources, and acquired capacities of its people, such as, plants, buildings, means of transport, education, health, etc. It will concentrate on the production of such commodities, producing more than its requirement, getting the surplus exchanged with goods and commodities from other countries what it requires and for which it is ill-suited to produce.

Adam Smith, had assumed that labour was the only factor of production. Hence, exchange between goods was determined by the relative amounts of labour embodied in them. To make his argument clear, he gave the following example: "If among the nation of hunters, it usually costs twice the labour to kill a beaver which it does to kill a deer, one beaver should naturally exchange for or be worth two deer. If we assume this ratio to alter, say one beaver for three deer, then more people will concentrate on killing a larger number of beavers to take advantage of this altered ratio. This will increase the, supply of beavers and reduce that of deer, causing a shift in the exchange ratio against beavers and in favour of deer, till once again the original ratio of exchange prevailed.

There are two main assumptions underlying his doctrine: (*a*) labour is the only factor of production, and (*b*) labour is mobile within the country but immobile between the countries. Given these assumptions, an exchange of goods will occur (assuming a two-country two-commodity case), if each of the two countries can produce one commodity at an absolutely lower labour cost of production than the other.

Example, Let us take a two-country two-commodities case. The following information regarding the labour cost per unit of commodity is given:

Table 47.1: Labour Cost Structure

Countries	*Commodity A*	*Commodity B*
Country I	10	20
Country II	20	10

The above example shows that Country *I* will confine itself to the production of commodity *A* since it has an absolute cost advantage in producing it. Through specialisation it will produce commodity *A* in a larger quantity than its home requirement, getting the surplus exchanged with commodity *B* from Country *II.* As noted above, Country *I*, is ill-suited for the production of commodity *B*. Similarly, Country *II* will specialislise in the production of commodity *B* and, will exchange it with commodity *A* from Country *I.* Thus, through specialisation, or international division of labour and the ensuing international exchange of goods will benefit both the countries.

But such gains derived from absolute cost advantage are rare since every country produces some amount of all the commodities it reuires. In Smith's view trade between two countries can occur if only each has an absolute cost advantage in producing one product such that different countries specialise in the production, of different goods. In other words, *a country having no absolute cost advantage in the production of any commodity cannot expect to gain from international trade.* However, the doctrine of absolute cost advantage is of little practical importance because a backward country is capable of producing all commodities at higher absolute costs. Adam Smith's doctrine of absolute cost advantage is incapable of dealing with this kind of situation.

Ricardo's Doctrine of Relative or Comparative Cost Advantage

The doctrine of comparative cost was developed by David Ricardo. He followed Adam Smith and said that even in the absence of absolute cost advantage, international trade was possible. He perceived that only a comparative advantage and not an absolute advantage was needed to justify the international division of labour. He also postulated that even where one country had an absolute cost advantage in the production of both the commodities as compared to another country, both the countries would get the advantage, if the first country concentrated only on the production of the most advantageous commodity, leaving the second country to produce the other commodity. This theorem is known as the doctrine of comparative cost or relative cost advantage.

Before explaining his doctrine of comparative cost advantage it seems appropriate to understand the basis of this doctrine. Like Smith, Ricardo also based his analysis on the labour cost theory of value. This theory is based on the following assumptions:

(1) Labour is the only productive factor and as such value of a commodity reflects the cost of labour involved in its production.

(2) Since the quantity of labour used in the production of different commodities may be different, the value of different commodities will also be different.

(3) All the units of labour used in the process of production are homogeneous.

(4) Labour is freely mobile within the country but it is immobile across the country.

(5) Perfect competition prevails in the labour market, and therefore, the price of this factor is uniform all over the country.

Now we shall discuss Ricardian doctrine of comparative cost advantage.

Like Adam Smith, Ricardo agreed with Smith that if one country has an advantage over the other country in one line of production and the other country has an absolute advantage over the first country in a second line of production, both countries can gain by trading. However, he added that even if one country is more productive than the other country, both can specialise and can gain by international trade. Ricardo also takes a two-country two-commodity case. The two countries are England and Portugal and the two commodities are wine and cloth. In his example, Portugal has an absolute advantage in the production of both the commodities in the sense that its per unit labour cost of production of both the commodities is lower than England. But this advantage is comparatively more in the production of wine than cloth. This situation can be seen in the following Table by looking at the cost ratios. In England a unit of cloth costs 100 hours and a unit of wine 120 hours of labour; in Portugal a unit of cloth costs 90 hours and a unit of wine 80 hours of labour. If such a cost constellation were to exist between two districts within a country, all goods would be produced only in that district where costs were lower. But in international trade it is usually not possible for factors of production to move from one country to another. This great achievement of the classical economists was to prove that nevertheless an international division of labour would take place.

Table 47.2: Per Unit Labour Cost of Production

Countries	*Per unit labour cost of Production*		*Exchang ratio in each country (or, domestic terms of trade)*
	Wine	*Cloth*	
Portugal	80	90	80 : 90 (or 0.89 : 1)
England	120	100	120 : 100 (or 1.20 : 1)
Cost ratio in terms of Portugal (international terms of trade)	80/120 = 0.67	90/100 = 0.90	

Looking at the cost ratios in Table 47.2 we find that for every one unit of labour required to produce cloth in England, Portugal requires only 0.90 units of labour. Similarly, for everyone unit of labour required to produce wine in England/Portugal requires only 0.89 units of labour. This indicates that Portugal has an absolute cost advantage over England for both the commodities.

The other important fact which we notice in Table 47.2 is that Portugal can produce wine at a lower cost than cloth. In other words, Portugal has a comparative advantage over England in wine relatively to cloth.

Reviewing the domestic terms of trade, we find that in England one unit of wine will exchange for 1.2 units of cloth. Conversely, in Portugal one unit of wine will exchange for 0.89 units of cloth. If England could import I unit of wine at a price less than 1.2 units of cloth she would gain by doing so. On the other hand, trade to Portugal will be advantageous if she obtains more than 0.89 units of cloth in exchange for one unit of wine.

Thus, Portugal will be specialised in the production of wine. She will export wine to England and import cloth from the latter. England will, on the other hand, produce only cloth, and will export it against the import of wine. Using little mathematics we can understand it more clearly in the following manner.

Assuming that the two commodities are X and Y, we may develop the following notations: .

X_1 = The labour cost of commodity X in Country *I*

X_2 = The labour cost of commodity X in Country *II*

Y_1 = The labour cost of commodity Y in Country *I*

Y_2 = The labour cost of commodity Y in Country *II*

If $\frac{X_1}{X_2} < 1$ means commodity X is cheaper in Country *I*, but it is produced at a higher cast in Country *II*.

If $\frac{Y_1}{Y_2} > 1$ means commodity Y is cheaper in Country *II*, but it is produced at a higher cost in Country *I*.

If $\frac{X_1}{X_2} < \frac{Y_1}{Y_2} < 1$ This means that country *I* has an absolute advantage in the production of both the commodities X and Y, but it has a relatively more advantage in the production of X than that of Y.

In conclusion, we can say that the doctrine of comparative cost marks a real advance over Adam Smith's doctrine of absolute cost advantage as the basis of international trade. The comparative cost advantage theorem is more general and explains situations not covered by Smith's work.

If England produces and consumes in isolation she would have to give up 120 hours of labour for every unit of wine she wanted, whereas with trade she only needs to give up 100 hours. With each 20 hours left over she can produce more cloth and enjoy a high level of consumption, or the English workers can enjoy more leisure with no change in their level of consumption.

Similarly, if Portugal produces and consumes in isolation she would have to give up 90 hours of labour to get one unit of cloth. With international trade, however, she can make one unit of wine with the effort of 80 hours of lahour and exchange this unit of wine for one unit of cloth. Thus, for each unit of wine produced she can save 10 hours of labour which may be used to produce more wine or else for providing more leisure to the Portuguese workers.

Yet the theory is incomplete in the sense that it left the actual international terms of trade undetermined.

Criticisms of Classical Doctrine of Comparative Cost

(1) This theorem assumes labour as the only factor of production. But in the production of any commodity we require land, capital and other factor inputs also. It also assumes homogeneity in labour units and assumes that the real wages should be the same for all workers. These assumptions are not valid and the theory based on these assumptions, too, does not yield correct results.

(2) Another important assumption of the doctrine of comparative cost advantage is that labour is perfectly mobile within a country but immobile between the countries. But it is generally seen that in developing countries, a worker would not like to leave his native place even if he were offered a higher wage. In these countries, social and psychological rather than economic factors motivate a worker not to move even within the same country. On the other hand, in view of the increasing international co-operation, factors of production can be exchanged between countries also. India invites experts from advanced countries of the world and also sends its own experts to other developing countries.

(3) In the classical theory of international trade no allowance is given for State intervention in the operations of market mechanism. But today

State control on trade is important. Thus, the classical theory does not depict the real situation prevailing in international trade.

(4) The classical labour theory of value fails to account for time (element of storage) which gives rise to interest. Thus, the very basis of classical theory of international trade appears to be unrealistic.

(5) The classical doctrine of absolute or even the comparative cost advantage assumes constant returns to scale in the economy. In other words, it assumes a linear cost function. In reality, firms may be working under increasing or decreasing cost conditions. In the long run, external economies and diseconomies too may change the shape of firm's cost function and may thus disturb the entire classical theory of international trade.

(6) The classical theory ignores the cost of transport, but in real life such costs also affect the flow of goods from one country to the other. In fact, cost of transport is very important in the determination of cost ratios.

(7) The classical doctrine is based only on two country two-commodity case. In the real world, international trade takes place in a multi-commodity and multi-directional space. Thus, the classical theory does not really depict the exchange of goods among different countries and becomes restrictive in its scope.

(8) The classical economists were more interested in showing the gains from international trade than in explaining its mechanism.

(9) While explaining the doctrine of comparative cost advantage, Ricardo appeared to have assumed that the nature of production functions in the trading countries would not change. In the face of fast changing technology such an assumption does not hold true, as in the modern dynamic setting calculation of comparative costs is a very difficult job.

(10) If out of the two trading partners one country is very big and the other is very small, specialisation by each would not help as the small country cannot meet the needs of big country, nor can the former absorb the entire surplus output of the latter country. Thus, the doctrine of comparative cost advantage holds good if only the two trading nations are of the same size and have about the same population.

(11) The classical theory of international trade is also based on an implicit assumption that the imports and exports of the two trading countries will be balanced out, and there will be no deficit or surplus in the balance of payment. Thus, it ignores the important issues of international flow of capital, etc. which have drawn the attention of all the countries of the world-big and small alike.

(12) According to the theory of comparative advantage gains from trade accrue to the country as a whole. Sodersten, however, points out

that gains from trade to a country does not necessarily imply that all the citizens living in it share such gains. It is quite likely that some citizens become better off through international trade whereas others do not benefit at all.

3. OPPORTUNITY COST DOCTRINE

Haberler's Theory of Comparative Cost

The doctrine or theorem was developed by Prof. Haberler. It shows how much of one commodity must be given up in order to exchange it for another. We have seen above that *exchange ratio between two commodities will depend upon their cost structure.* Let us make it clear by considering the quantities of both the commodities which a country is capable to produce. Generally, as revealed by the price theory, the best output combination of two commodities lies at that point where the slope of isocost line equals the slope of producer's production possibility curve.

A production possibility curve shows different combinations of the two commodities which a country can produce with the given factor endowment and technology. By 'factor endowment' we mean the amounts of factors of production possessed by a country. In the classical sense, factor endowment would refer to the total amount of labour available in the country. Technology in this context refers to the input-output coefficients for the two commodities under consideration.

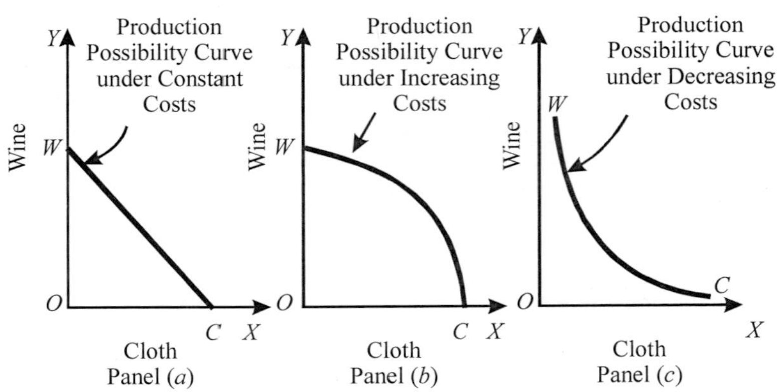

Fig. 47.1

The ratio of the quantity of Y forgone in order to have a given increase in the quantity of $X\left(-\frac{\Delta X}{\Delta X}\right)$ is known as the marginal rate of product transformation (*MRPT*).

The production possibility of a country may be a straight line, concave to the origin or convex to it, depending on whether a country is producing under constant, increasing or decreasing costs. The three situations in respect of wine and cloth have been depicted in Fig. 47.1. The *MRPT* in all the three is $-\frac{\Delta \text{ Wine}}{\Delta \text{ Cloth}}$ showing that for increasing the output of cloth, the country has to forgo wine at a constant rate (panel *a*), increasing rate (Panel *b*) or at a decreasing rate (Panel *c*).

Constant Opportunity Cost and the Production Possibility Curve

If we assume constant costs (or, constant returns), as shown in Panel *a* (Fig. 47.1) the production possibility curve will be a straight line. Let us take a two-country two-commodity case. The two countries are UK and Portugal. The two commodities are steel and cloth. The following Table shows a constant proportionality of output to input over any desired range for each country.

Table 47.3

	Output in Units			
Input Units	*United Kingdom*		*Portugal*	
	Steel	*Cloth*	*Steel*	*Cloth*
200			200	300
100	300	300	100	150
80	240	240	80	120
60	180	180i	60	90
40	120	120	40	60
20	60	60	20	30

These facts have been expressed in Fig. 47.2. Various production possibility curves show the different output levels at different input levels.

In Fig. 47.2 the labour input units are assumed to be implicitly related to output. Since the input-output coefficient remains unchanged throughout the range, the production possibility curves are linear.

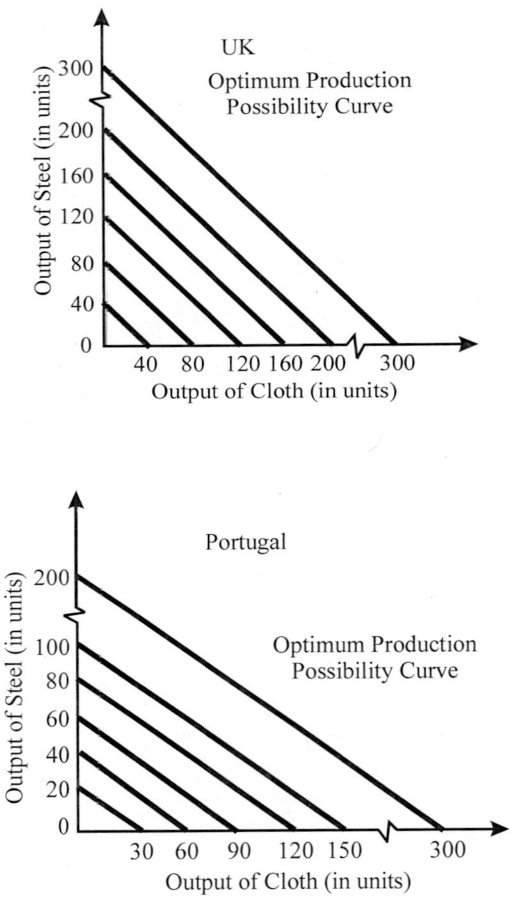

Fig. 47.2

Let us assume that UK possess only 100 units of labour and Portugal possess 200 units of labour. If UK's labour force is fully employed, it can produce either 300 units of steel or 300 units of cloth or a combination of the two. If, on the other hand, Portugal's labour force is fully employed, it can produce either 200 units of steel or 300 units of cloth or some combination of the two. In the case of, constant costs, normally we shall have optimum production possibility curves for both the products. These curves depict the combinations of the two products in UK and Portugal under an assumption that factors of production are fully employed. The *MRPT* for UK $\left(\frac{-\Delta \text{ Steel}}{\Delta \text{ Cloth}}\right)$ will be $\left(\frac{-1}{1}\right)$ whereas for Portugal it will be $\left(\frac{-2}{3}\right)$. Since *MRPT* in this case is constant, the two production possibility curves are linear. A straight commodities where their production possibility curves are tangent to their respective community are indifference curves.[1]

Suppose these points are *U* for UK and *P* for Portugal as shown in Fig. 47.3 (Panel *A* and Panel *B*).

Domestically UK is producing 150 units of steel and 150 units of cloth under the assumption of full employment of labour force. Similarly, Portugal is producing 100 units of steel and 150 units of cloth. If somehow, UK's demand for cloth increases, i.e., UK's community indifference curve

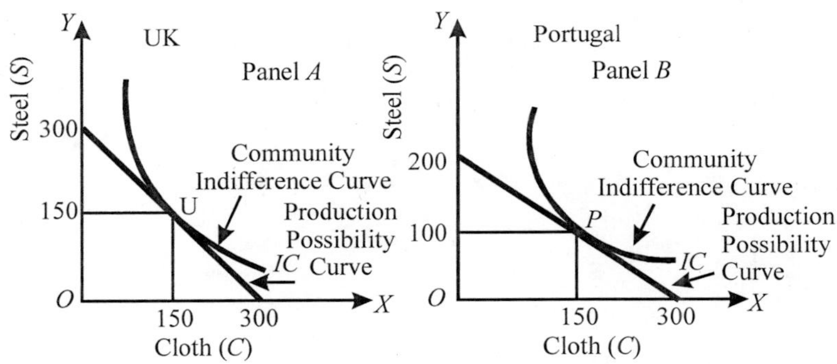

Fig. 47.3

touches at some other point of production possibility curve) then UK will produce more cloth and less of steel at the constant rate of substitution. Similar type of substitution can also occur in Portugal. However, with given community consumption function and also with the given factor

1. As explained above, the slope of Commodity Indifference Curve shows the taste of the people living in the country, or the internal demand for the two commodities.

endowment, any movement from the equilibrium point U or P will imply a lower level of satisfaction for either of the two communities.

Until now we had assumed that labour is the only factor of production. We can conveniently drop this assumption without affecting our analysis for constant opportunity cost or for constant returns to scale.[2] As we had noted above, the marginal rate of product transformation (*MRPT*) is constant in this case. If UK produces more of cloth, then the quantity of steel forgone is defined as the opportunity cost of obtaining the additional quantity of cloth. Since it is a case of constant cost (when the production possibility curve is linear) the opportunity cost (*MRPT*) of either commodity will be constant. In the case of UK, the $MRPT = \frac{-1 \text{ unit of steel}}{1 \text{ unit of cloth}}$. In Portugal, it is $= \frac{-2 \text{ units of steel}}{3 \text{ units of cloth}}$. These rates can also be deemed as the *domestic exchange ratio* for the two goods.

International Trade under Conditions of Constant Costs

As noted above, the domestic price ratios or domestic exchange ratios in each country are shown by the slopes of their respective production possibility curves. These are 1 S : 1 C in UK and 1 S : 1.5 C in Portugal.

We also know that UK has a comparative advantage in steel and, therefore, when international trade takes place between the two countries, UK will specialize completely in the production of steel only. Portugal, on the other hand, will specialise in the production of cloth.

Now international trade will take place only when both the countries are to benefit from it. So that for UK the terms of trade should be better than 1 : 1 (which is its domestic terms of trade)

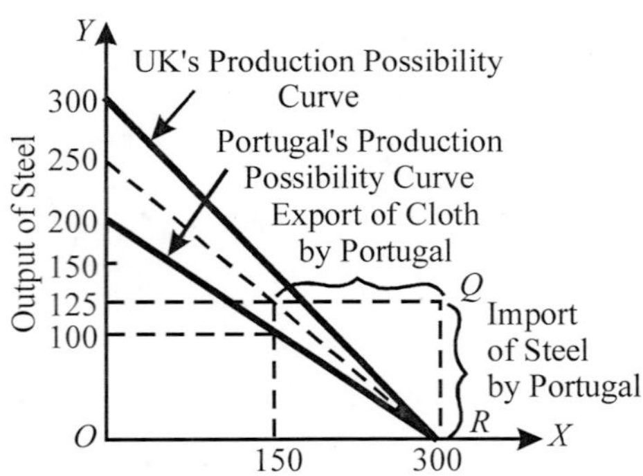

Fig. 47.4

2. In the case of constant returns to scale, all the inputs, such as, land, labour, capital, etc., vary in fixed proportions.

and for Portugal the terms of trade should be better than 1: 1.5. To show the exact position of international trade, we draw the production possibility curves of the two countries in a single diagram (Fig.47.4). As a choice, UK would prefer most the terms of trade that prevail in Portugal and Portugal would prefer most those terms of trade which prevail in UK. Hence, the lines with slopes of 200 : 300 and 300 : 300 indicate the limits to the terms of international trade. The actual international price, or interna-tional exchange ratio or the

terms of trade can be settled anywhere between these limits depending upon the reciprocal demand for the two commodities. Let us assume that it settles at 25 S =30 C (5 : 6 or 1 : 1.2). Let us also, assume that before international trade, Portugal was producing in equilibrium 100 units of steel and 150 units of cloth (according to the domestic or internal requirements). After trade she will specialise in the production of cloth only because she has a comparative cost advantage in terms of cloth. She, therefore, produces 300 units of cloth only and no steel. Out of this quantity she consumes 150 units and exchanges the other 150 units for steel with UK. This enables her to receive in return 125 units of steel from UK, such that she will export *TQ* of cloth in exchange for *QR* of steel. It can be seen once again that because of specialisation, Portugal is better off than she was before the international trade. Prior to international trade for consuming 150 units of cloth she had only 100 units of steel (see point *P*), but after trade she is able to consume 150 units of cloth and 125 units of steel.

A careful study will indicate that UK will also *gain from international trade* becuase she gets more cloth for steel relatively to that quantity which would have been exchanged in the domestic market. Without trade she could have consumed 150 units of cloth only in combination with 150 units of steel. After specialising in the production of steel and exporting only 125 units of steel, the UK is able to obtain 150 units of cloth from Portugal. Thus, international trade leaves 25 units of surplus steel with UK.

Increasing Opportunity Costs or Decreasing Returns and the Production Possibility Curve

Thus far we had assumed constant costs where the efficiency of the resources used remains unchanged. But it is quite possible that in the production of some goods say fruits and vegetables, land as an input is particularly important, though it must be used in collaboration with other factors, such as, labour, capital and fertilisers. In, such cases output will riot increase proportionately with every increase in the inputs used. Rather the production increases at a decreasing rate. This also happens due to imperfect substitutability among the factors of production in different lines of production. Due to diminishing returns, the cost of production increases at an increasing rate. In other words, under this situation, the marginal cost of production increases with increasing level of production. For this reason, the production possibility curve becomes concave to the origin, as shown in Fig. 47.5. Taking again a two commodity case and measuring the units of steel along *OY*-axis and the units of cloth along *OX*-axis, we find that if all the resources are employed' into the production of steel, then *OM* quantity can be produced. On the other hand, if all the resources are directed into the production of cloth, then *ON* can be produced. The production possibility curve *MN* is concave, in Fig. 47.5, depicting that as the production of cloth is increased the *MRPT* or the opportunity cost $\left(\frac{-\Delta \text{ Steel}}{\Delta \text{ Cloth}}\right)$ increases.

As can be seen in Fig. 47.5, in the case of increasing cost conditions the limiting points of production possibility curve *M* and *N*, cannot be joined by a straight line. Here an additional unit of cloth can be produced only with an increasing sacrifice of steel. In other words, the opportunity

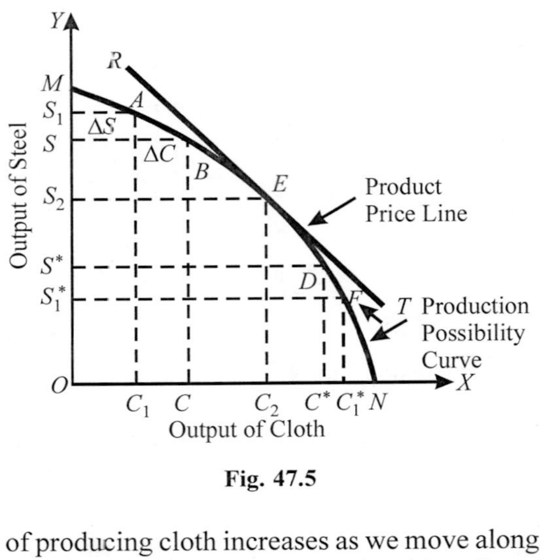

Fig. 47.5

cost (*MRPT*) of producing cloth increases as we move along a production possibility curve. This movement may be in either direction. Suppose that in Fig. 47.5, the initial equilibrium point is *B* where *OS* units of steel and *DC* units of cloth are being produced. If the quantity of steel is to be increased from *SO* to OS_1 then the output of cloth will decline from *OC* to OC_1. Now it can be clearly seen that the increase in steel (ΔS) SS_1 is less than the decrease in cloth (ΔC) which is CC_1. A similar proof can be made to right point *D*. Say initially, at equilibrium OS^* of steel and OC^* of cloth are produced. Now if the quantity of cloth is to be increased from OC^* to $OC_1{}^*$, then the output of steel will decline from OS^* to $OS_1{}^*$. And now it can be seen that an increase in cloth is less than the decrease in the quantity of steel. Thus, for every given increase in the production of either steel or cloth, the opportunity cost in terms of the other commodity will go on rising.

A question arises, at this point, *what will be the domestic level of production?* In the absence of a price indicator, we can not answer the question. Therefore, we have to introduce the price line which is *RT* in the above Fig. 47.5. As explained above, the tangency of this price line *RT* to the production possibility curve *MN* at point *E* determines the equilibrium output of steel and cloth at OS_2 and OC_2 respectively. To sum up, in the absence of international trade, the country will optimise the use of its resources by producing that combination of goods at which the *MRPT* equals the product price ratio.

International Trade under Conditions of Increasing Costs

Suppose now that we open up the possibility of international trade. As has been stated above, trade can benefit both the countries if only specialisation restored to by both the countries. Which commodity country *I* (say Portugal) will export and import depends on the international terms of trade that are established. Let us suppose that Portugal has a comparative advantage in the production of cloth and that the new terms of trade established under trade, shift the price line from its original position of *RT* to R_1T_1. It is evident from Fig. 47.6 that at the original equilibrium *A*, the country was obtaining an optimum product-mix of OC_2 units of cloth and OS_2 units of steel, and the community was maximising the level of satisfaction along the community indifference curve I_1. With specialisation, Portugal now produces OC_3 units of cloth and OS_3 units of steel and optimises the use of resources at *B*. However, the internal demand for steel continues to be OS_2. Thus, Portugal exports C_4C_3 units of cloth ($C_4C_3 = Ec$) to UK and in return imports ($S_2S_3 = Ms$). Thus, international trade makes Portugal better off and the community is placed at a higher indifference curve I_2. Point *C* is the community's new equilibrium position which it attains in correspondel1ce to the new product price ratio (shown by R_1T_1). It is also evident from Fig. 47.6 that Portugal saves C_2C_4 units of cloth in this process of international trade and specialisation. At price ratio other than the one shown by R_1T_1, she can consume more of both the commodities. Thus, by opening the possibility of trade the country can attain a higher level of satisfaction and, at the same time, optimise the use of available resources.

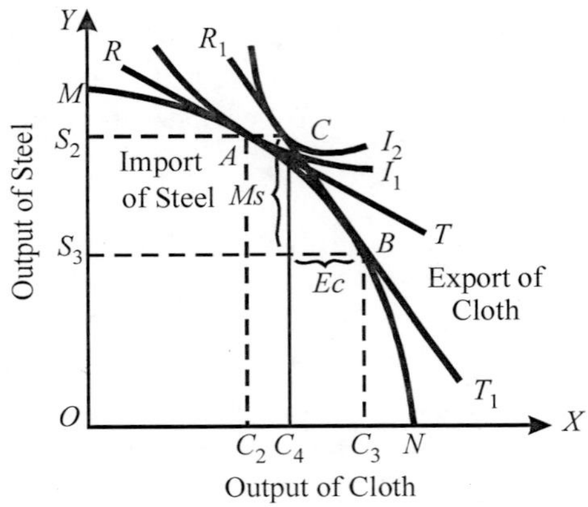

Fig. 47.6

Partial Specialisation

As we had noted above, in the case of constant costs, international trade would lead to complete specialisation by both the countries. But this is not true in respect of increasing costs or decreasing returns (see Fig. 47.6). Here the country continues to devote some part of its resources to domestic production of imported goods. That is some production can still compete witl1 imports, since their relative costs are no longer higher than the international exchange ratio. This is the reason why we have not shown a complete specialisation of cloth by Portugal after trade has taken place. As is evident from Fig. 47.6, Portugal produces, large quantity of cloth due to comparative costs advantage, yet she produces OS_3 units of steel domestically and imports some steel in order to meet the international demand.

Proportional Costs

If the cost structure of both the countries is proportional, then no foreign trade would take place. The costs may be considered proportional only when the superiority of one country over another is the same in both the commodities or in all the lines of production. For example, India takes 200 and 180 labour units to produce per unit of steel and cloth respectively, while China takes 100 and 90 labour units to produce the same. If the factor endowments in both the countries are identical; the slope of their production possibility curves will also be identical with only one difference that the production possibility curve for India will travel at half the distance in relation to the production possibility curve of China. However, the opportunity cost or ratio of internal exchange for both the countries, India and China, will be identical. In such an exceptional case, no exchange of goods is likely to take place between the two countries. Figure 47.7 illustrates this situation where the distance between the production possibility curves of India (MN) and China (M_1N_1) is the same throughout.

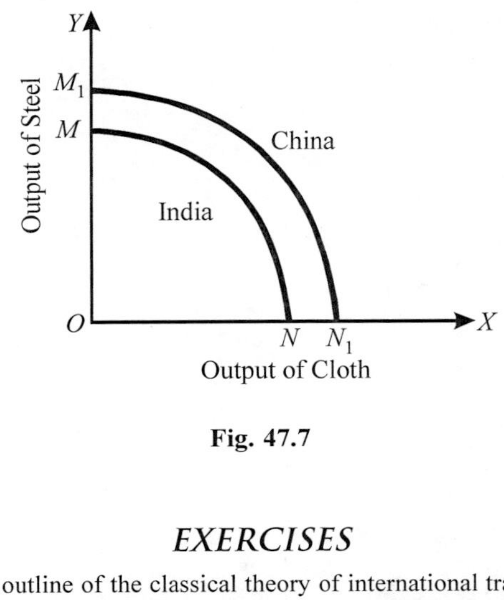

Fig. 47.7

EXERCISES

1. Give an outline of the classical theory of international trade and discuss how far do you consider it adequate to explain international trade in the modern world?
2. Critically examine the classical theory of International Trade. How far is it applicable to the developing countries?
3. State the classical theory of International Trade. What are the main criticisms advanced against this theory?
4. To what extent is the validity of Ricardian theory of comparative costs dependent upon the assumptions that: (*a*) labour is the only factor of production, and (*b*) costs of production within each country are constant?
5. Discuss the classical theory of international trade as propounded by Adam Smith. What modifications have been made in this theory by modern writers?
6. Explain clearly the opportunity cost theory of international trade.

Multiple Choice Questions

7. (*i*) The commodity in which a country has the least absolute disadvantage represents its area of

   (*a*) comparative advantage (*b*) comparative disadvantage

   (*c*) absolute advantage (*d*) none of the above [*Ans.* (*a*)]

   (*ii*) Ricardo's doctrine of comparative cost advantage is based on

   (*a*) the opportunity cost theory

   (*b*) the labour theory of value

   (*c*) the law of diminishing returns

   (*d*) all of the above [*Ans.* (*b*)]

   (*iii*) The opportunity cost theory assumes that

   (*a*) labour is the only factor of production

   (*b*) labour is homogeneous.

   (*c*) cost of production is measured in terms off labour

   (*d*) none of the above [*Ans.* (*d*)]

   (*iv*) If in the absence of trade, the internal equilibrium *Pc/Pw* is lower in India than in USA, then

   (*a*) India has a comparative advantage in cloth (*C*) with respect to the USA

   (*b*) India has a comparative disadvantage in what (*W*)

   (*c*) Both (*a*) and (*b*)

   (*d*) none of the above [*Ans.* (*c*)]

Chapter 48

MODERN THEORY OF INTERNATIONAL TRADE

1. INTRODUCTION

The classical theory of comparative cost was mainly concerned with differences in the productivity of labour, As has been explained in Chapter 47, this theory of international trade has several limitations. In recent years the traditional theory of comparative cost advantage has been replaced by what is commonly known as the *factor-price equalisation theorem* or the Heckscher-Ohlin Theorem of international trade.

Ohlin's Approach to International Trade

Ohlin regards international trade "as a special case of inter-regional trade". Therefore, international values are determined in the same way as the prices of goods and services are determined in internal trade. The basis of determination of prices in internal trade is the general equilibrium of demand and supply which is also applicable to international trade. The main cause of trade between regions is the difference in prices of commodities.

Heckscher's Approach to International Trade[1]

Long before the publication of Ohlin's book, Eli Heckscher had written an article in 1919 explaining the effect of international trade, especially on the distribution of income between land, capital and labour. Heckscher first attempted to explain the reason for differences in comparative costs among different countries. If two countries have the same relative scarcity of factors of production, the relative factor prices in both the countries

1. Eli Heckscher, "The Effect of Foreign Trade on the Distribution of Income," reprinted in American Economic Association's *Reading in the Theory of International Trade* (1950).

will also be identical and "foreign trade between them will be impossible." Heckscher summarises the pre-requisites for initiating international trade as follows: (*i*) Different relative scarcity, i.e., different relative prices of the factors of production in the exchanging conditions, and (*ii*) different proportion between the factors of production used in different commodities. It was also assumed by Heckscher that these proportions (generally termed as input- output coefficients) remain unchanged.

Heckscher argues that foreign trade creates, on the one hand, an increased scarcity of those factors of production which would have otherwise been used to produce importable commodities. Obviously, he contends, the question before us is whether the increases and decreases in scarcity of factors, taken together, results in an equilibrium is arrived at. However, he provides an example to demonstrate that foreign trade always results in a new equilibrium and redistribution of income.

2. HECKSCHER-OHLIN (H-O) THEOREM

Bertil Ohlin focusses on a multi-market theory of value. Eli Heckscher emphasises the relative scarcity of factor of production which lead to differences in relative factor prices and hence to differences in comparative costs which is the main cause of foreign trade. The Heckscher-Ohlin theorem combines these views. The theorem is based on the premise that foreign trade essentially results from the condition that different countries have different factor endowments. Some countries have much capital, others have much labour. The H-O theory now states that countries that are rich in capital will export capital-intensive goods, and countries that have much labour will export labour-intensive goods.

Assumptions of the H-O Theory

The H-O theory considers a two-commodity, two-factor and two-country model for analysing the causes and implications of international trade. The theory is based on the' following assumptions:

(1) The product and factor markets in both the countries are perfectly competitive. This implicitly means that the product and factor prices are so designed as to ensure full employment of resources in both the countries.

(2) Factors of production are freely mobile within their respective countries but not mobile between the two countries.

(3) The relative endowments of the two factors are disproportionate in the two countries; country *A* having too much capital, whereas country

B has abundance of labour. However, qualitatively factors of production in the two countries are homogeneous.

(4) The production function are such that the two commodities show different factor intensities—one commodity is labour-intensive, while the other is capital-intensive. However, production functions for each commodity are the same in both the countries, albeit production functions for different commodities are different.

(5) The input-output coefficient in the respective production functions remain unchanged. In other words; technology of producing the two commodities in both the countries must remain unchanged.

(6) There are no transport costs or other impediments to trade. Thus product prices are determined exclusively by the factor costs.

(7) All production. functions are linearly homogeneous. In other words, in both the countries production of the two commodities is subject to constant returns to scale. The degree of factor substitution must be limited.

(8) The consumer preferences and therefore the demand functions for different goods are identical in' the two countries.

(9) The theory analyses a two-factor and two-commodity case, but that is only for analytical convenience. In the most generalised case, this model will be equally relevant for a, larger number of factors and a larger number of commodities. However, the theory assumes that in any case, number of actors and the number of commodities must be equal.

As stated above, the most important assumption of the H-O theory is; related to different factor endowments in the two countries. If, country *A* has abundance of capital, it will specialise in and export the capital-intensive goods. Conversely, the labour-rich country will export the labour-intensive goods. It, therefore, appears appropriate to define factor abundance, and then have a more detailed analysis of the H-O theory of international trade.

Factor Abundance Defined in Physical Terms

If the relative factor abundance is expressed in terms of the ratio of two factors, say capital (*K*) and labour (*L*), country *A* will be deemed to be capital-rich if $K_A / L_A > K_B / L_B$. In this statement *K* arid *L* are the total amounts of capital and labour available, whereas the subscripts *A* and *B* refer to the respective two countries. At the same time the relative scarcity of labour in country *A* can be explained by $L_A / K_A < L_B / <: L_B$. This latter statement implies that country *B* is (relatively) rich in labour force.

Given the above condition regarding the relative abundance or the relative scarcity of a factor, it can conveniently be demonstrated that country *A* has a bias. in favour of producing the capital-intensive commodity, whereas country *B* has an explicit bias for producing the labour-intensive commodity.

It is assumed in Fig. 48.1 that steel is the capital-intensive commodity and cloth is labour-intensive commodity. If both the countries were to produce steel and cloth in the same proportion, say along the ray *OR*, country *A* would be producing at E_1 whereas country *B* would be producing at E_2 along their respective production possibility curves. The slope of country *A's* production possibility curve at E_1 is steeper than the slope of country *B's* production possibility curve at E_2. This implies that the relative marginal cost of producing cloth in country *A* is higher than the marginal cost of producing cloth in country *B*. In short, if production in the two countries is undertaken at E_1 and E_2 respectively, steel will be produced more cheaply in country *A* whereas cloth will be produced more cheaply in country *B*.

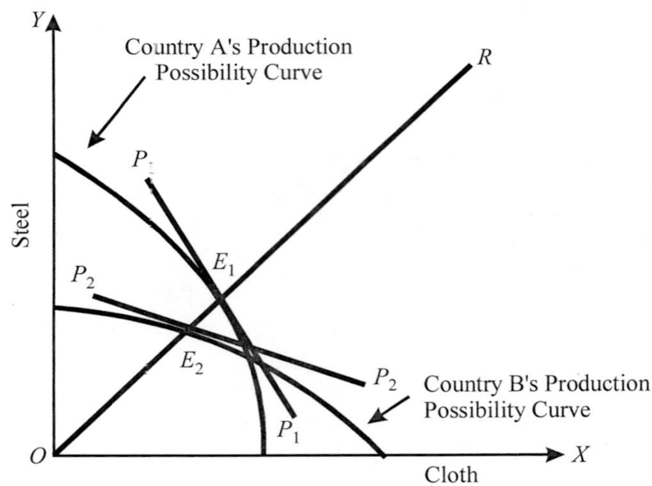

Fig. 48.1

The same facts maybe explained by looking at the slopes of the respective iso-revenue lines (P_1P_1 in country *A* and P_2P_2 in country *B*). P_1P_1 is steeper than P_2P_2 implying that the opportunity cost of expanding production of steel is lower in country *A* than in country *B* and vice versa for cloth. This explains that country *A*, the capital-rich country, has a bias in favour of steel which is a capital-intensive commodity. Conversely, country *B,* being a labour-rich country has a bias in favour of cloth which is a labour-intensive commodity.

In order to show that *A*, the capital-rich country, will export the labour-intensive commodity, i.e., cloth, whereas the labour-rich country (*B*) will export the capital-intensive commodity, i.e., steel, we have introduced in Fig. 48.2 two sets of community indifference curves I_0, I_1, I_1 etc. for country *A* and I'_1, I'_1, I'_2 etc. for country *B,* whereas in country *A* production is biased for steel and production in country *B* is biased for cloth, their demand functions too are biased for the same commodities. If production and consumption are undertaken in the two countries in isolation (without permitting international trade), steel is relatively more expensive in country *A* than in country *B.* This is evident from the fact that the iso-revenue line for country *B* is steeper than for country *A.*

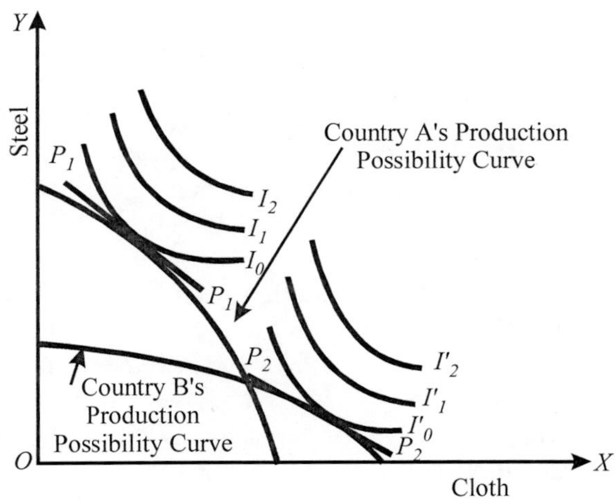

Fig. 47.2

$$\left\{\frac{P/\text{cloth}}{P/\text{steel}} \text{ in } A < \frac{P/\text{cloth}}{P/\text{steel}} \text{ in } B\right\}$$

After international trade is opened up between the two countries, country *A* will export cloth and country *B* will export steel. In short, due to foreign trade a capital-rich country exports the labour-intensive commodity, whereas a labour-rich country exports the capital-intensive commodity. Thus the H-O theory of international trade is capable of explaining that bias in production can be largely offset by demand factors. However, a generalised form of the H-O trade model only explains that the capital-rich country exports only capital-intensive commodity whereas a country having abundant supply of labour would export labour-intensive commodity. This will be demonstrated in the following section.

Factor Abundance Defined by Factor Prices

It is assumed in this sub-section that factor-abundance implies a relatively low price for the factor in question. If country *A* is capital-rich as compared to country *B*, it will mean that capital is cheaper in country *A* and costlier in country *B*. Conversely, labour will be relatively cheaper in country *B* than in country *A*. It may be recalled that in preceding section factor abundance was defined on the basis of capital-labour (or labour-capital) ratio.

Ohlin defines factor endowment on the basis of factor prices. According to him, country *A* has abundance of capital if $P_{AK}/P_{AL} < P_{AK}/P_{BL}$, i.e., the interest-wage ratio in country *A* is less than the corresponding ratio in country *B*. It may be noted that price of labour (wage) is denoted by P_L. The subscripts *A* and *B* refer to the two countries under review.

In order to demonstrate that the capital-rich country (*A*) will export the capital intensive good and the labour-rich country (*B*) will export the labour-intensive good, we have taken two isoquants, *SS* and *CC* in Fig. 48.3. As was noted above, the H-O theory of trade assumes that the production functions in both countries are identical. The two isoquants, *SS* and *CC* are the same in both countries and have been drawn in such a manner that cloth (denoted by *CC*) is the labour--intensive good whereas steel (denoted by *SS*) is a capital-intensive good. Relative factor prices in country *A*, the capital-rich country are given by the line P_0P_0.

Let us now assume that each isoquant represents 1 unit of cloth along *CC* and 1 unit of steel along *SS*. Then, with the given factor price ratio, one unit of steel will be produced with *Ols* units of labour and *Oks* units of capital. The corresponding units to produce one unit of cloth will be *Olc* of labour and *Okc* of capital respectively. However capital and labour are substitutable in a ratio shown by the factor price line P_0P_0. Therefore, *Ols* units of labour is worth $P_1\bar{K}$ units of capital, and *Oks* units of capital is worth I_sL units of labour.

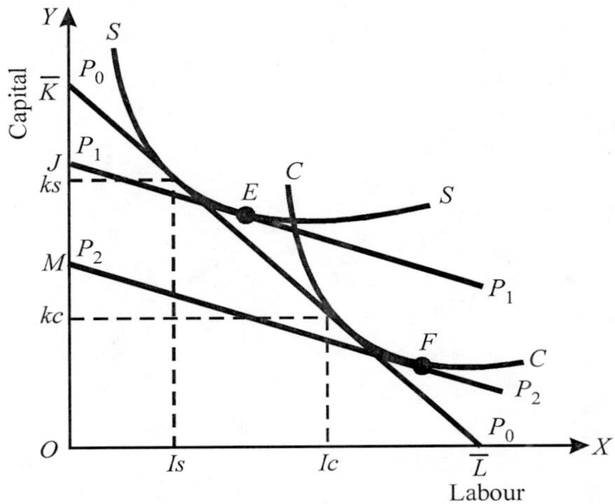

Fig. 48.3

In Fig. 48.3 $\overline{KL}$ line may also be termed as the cost line, explaining that one unit of steel or cloth can be produced either by $O\overline{K}$ units of capital, or *OL* units of labour or a combination of labour and capital along $\overline{KL}$. This, however, applies to both countries because by assumption, both countries have identical production functions.

We have assumed that country *A* is a capital-rich country whereas labour is relatively abundant in country *B*. This implies that in country *B* capital is relatively more expensive and labour is relatively cheaper as compared to the corresponding prices of capital and labour in country *A*. Obviously, the slope of the line representing factor price-ratio in country *B* will be less steep than the slope of P_0P_0.

One probable factor-price line can be P_1P_1. It is tangent to the isoquant *SS* at *E*. A parallel factor-price line is P_2P_2 which is tangent to the isoquant *CC* at *F*. It follows that the cost of producing one unit of steel in country *B* is *OJ* measured in capital whereas it is *OM* (measured in capital) for one unit of cloth. Thus in country *B* it is more expensive to produce a given unit of steel than it is to produce the same amount of cloth.

If production costs in the two countries are compared, we find that it is relatively cheap to produce cloth in country *B*, and relatively cheap to produce steel in country *A*. From this it follows that the capital-rich country will specialise in the capital-intensive good, i.e., steel and that the labour-rich country will specialise in the labour-intensive good, i.e., cloth. Obviously, country *A* will produce more steel and export it, whereas country *B* (the labour-rich country) will export cloth. This establishes the H-O theorem that the country abundant in capital will export the capital-intensive good and the country abundant in labour will export the labour-intensive good.

A Comparison of Ricardian Theory of Comparative Advantage and the Heckscher-Ohlin Theory of International Trade

According to the Ricardian theory, a country specialises in and exports that commodity in which it has got comparative advantage. However, the Heckscher-Ohlin theory makes relative factor abundance as the basis of international trade. As has been explained above, the H-O theory takes a two-factor, two-commodity and two country model whereas the Ricardian theory considers labour as the only productive factor. We have noted above that according to the H-O theory; a labour-rich country exports the labour-intensive product whereas a capital-rich country exports the capital-intensive product.

The H-O theorem explains nothing about the comparative advantage. It however, assumes that for the two commodities in question the production functions in both the countries are identical. Whereas in the Ricardian model, goods produced in the two-countries are ranked according to the amount of labour it took to produce one unit of each good in each country, in the two-factor model of Heckscher and Ohlin, ranking of goods is done according to their factor intensities. Thus if country *A* has abundance of capital and country *B* has abundance of labour, then in order to show comparative advantage in their production, as goods in country *A* can be ranked according to capital intensity used in production. According to H-O theorem, country *A* will first export the most capital-intensive good and then go to the second most capital-intensive good. Likewise, ranking in production and export can be done in respect of labour-intensive goods in country *B*. In this sense, the Ricardian theory of trade appears to be, a completely static type of theory in comparison to the H-O theory.

Criticisms of H-O Theory

(1) The H-O theory is an improvement over the Ricardian doctrine of comparative advantage. However, it also presents an over-simplified

version of trade. This theory cannot explain the phenomenon of production and trade if the number of countries, number of factors and the number of products are increased.

(2) It is unrealistic to argue that the relative abundance of a factor determines its relative price, as it ignores the demand side for a given factor. Its demands more Important, a capital-rich country may also gain in exporting a labour-intensive product. It is quite likely that due to high pressure of demand for capital even in a capital-rich country P_K/P_L may be higher than the corresponding ratio in a labour-rich country. This is generally considered as *Leontief Paradox;* according to which the USA exports more of labour-intensive goods and imports the capital-intensive goods.

(3) The H-O theory also pays little attention to differences in consumers preferences and demand for goods in the two countries. Merely factor-price ratio can riot serve as a basis of trade because demand function or any change therein would also reflect in the product prices.

(4) The assumption on which H-O theorem of trade is based also appears to be unrealistic. Thus, the H-O theorem does not depict the phenomenon of inter- national trade in the present context.

EXERCISES

1. Elucidate the proposition that a country's exports use intensively its abundant factor and lay down the conditions of its validity.
2. Explain and comment on Heckscher-Ohlin theory that a country specialises in the production of goods which are intensive in its relatively abundant factors. In your answer bring out the important assumptions on which this theory is based.
3. Can the composition of trade be predicted by comparisons of the national factor endowments?
4. Discuss critically the modern theory of international trade.

Multiple Choice Questions

5. (*i*) If a nation gains from trade, its consumption point is
   (*a*) on its production possibility frontier
   (*b*) inside its production possibility frontier
   (*c*) above its production possibility frontier
   (*d*) any of the above [*Ans.* (*c*)]

   (*ii*) With trade, specialisation in production is likely to be
   (*a*) complete with increasing costs and incomplete with constant costs
   (*b*) complete with constant costs and incomplete with increasing costs
   (*c*) complete with constant and increasing costs
   (*d*) incomplete with both constant and increasing costs [*Ans.* (*b*)]

Chapter 49

TERMS OF TRADE

1. INTRODUCTION

The price at which goods are cleared in international trade, is known as the Internal Exchange Ratio or Terms of Trade. This price is different from the market price determined in the domestic market. The problem of terms of trade essentially involves an examination of demand-supply schedules.

We have already explained in previous chapters the position at which the international exchange ratio will take place but the analysis does not provide us with the exact equilibrium position.

The concept of terms of trade was developed by John Stuart Mill in the form of the Equation of International Demand. It is also known as the Doctrine of Reciprocal Demand. The Mill's doctrine was further improved by numerous economists such as by Prof. Marshall and Prof. Viner. They introduced the concept of *factoral terms of trade.* The modern approach to the derivation of terms of trade is the foreign trade multiplier theory embodying the price and income effects.

2. TYPES OF TERMS OF TRADE

Mill's Doctrine of Terms of Trade

J.S. Mill developed his *doctrine of barter terms of trade.* According to him, barter terms of trade refers to the quantity an imported commodity trades evenly for some quantity of an exported commodity. Again he states that barter terms of trade is simply the reciprocal of the price-relation. For example, if

P_1 = Price of Commodity *I*

P_2 = Price of Commodity *II*

q_1 = Quantity of Commodity *I*

q_2 = Quantity of Commodity *II*

then the equation of international value may be written as

$$P_1q_1 = P_2q_2$$

or
$$\frac{P_1}{P_2} = \frac{q_2}{q_1}$$

This means equilibrium will be established at that ratio of exchange between the two commodities, at which the quantities demanded by each country of the goods (reciprocal demand) which it imports from the other will be exactly sufficient to pay one another.

The barter terms of trade of a country will improve only when the price received for each unit of her export becomes higher than the price paid for each unit of her import. In other words, this type of exchange would lead to a larger quantity of imports being received for the same quantity of exports. Mathematically,

$$\frac{q_2}{q_1} = \frac{P_1}{P_2} > 1 \text{ if country } A \text{ exports commodity and } I$$

imports commodity *II*

or
$$\frac{q_2}{q_1} > 1$$

This analysis of John Stuart Mill was not in money price but rather in commodity prices (that is price of one commodity in terms of the other).

Here, it should be observed that Mill has not only neglected the money values from his analysis but many other problems of financial equilibrium and income-price relationships which are of great importance in international trade.

Marshallian Doctrine of Terms of Trade (Marshall's Offer Curves and Net Barter Terms of Trade)

According to Marshall the terms of trade will be "governed by international demand and supply. He refused the theory of terms of trade given by J.S. Mill. He believed that the relationship between wage levels in different countries should be taken into account. Hence, he incorporated money costs into the terms of trade argument. The two important points of his generalisation are:

(1) The amount demanded and supplied at any given terms of trade (interna-tional price) will depend upon the capacity of each nation to consume and to produce.

(2) Again, the terms of trade will also depend upon the elasticity of demand and supply of each product.

It is not easy to find a simple way of explaining the demand and supply of each nation, since the basket of goods in each country cannot be assumed to be constant. This will change with the level of wages. It is why Marshall assumed a common denominator to measure all the export goods and import goods of a country. (That is, it should be interpreted as the product of a constant quantity of labour in a given country.) After undergoing a process of trial and error, that exchange ratio (or terms of trade) will prevail at which the demand and supply of the two countries under consideration coincide.

This can be explained in Fig. 49.1 with the help of Marshall's offer curves. An offer curve shows different combinations of demand and supply of each product of a country. An offer is also known as a *demand-supply curve.* We take a two-country two-commodity case. We also assume that the two countries are America and India and the two products are steel and cloth. America exports steel (supply of steel) and imports cloth (demand for cloth). Similarly, India exports cloth (supply of cloth) and imports steel (demand for steel). In Fig. 49.1, along the *OX*-axis we measure the supply of steel (that is the export of steel by America or import of steel by India) by America and long *OY*-axis the corresponding demand of cloth by America (that is the import of cloth by America or export of cloth by India). We plot the various possible identities (demand and supply) of two countries and that results two offer curves—*OA* curve

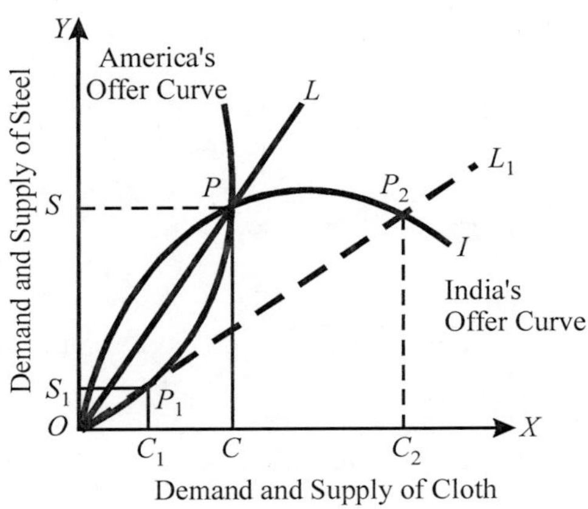

Fig. 49.1

for America and *OI* curve for India. The offer curve *OA* is convex to *OX*-axis, because higher quantities of steel can be sold by America to India only at an increasingly lowered price (that is more of steel has to be sacrificed for less of. cloth or for same unit of cloth). Similarly, *OI* curve is convex to *OY*-axis due to similar reasons.

Now given the offer curves *OA* and *OI*, their intersection at point *P* determines the equilibrium terms of trade.

The equilibrium quantity demanded and supplied is OC_1 of cloth and *OS* of steel. If *P* is not the point of equilibrium and say, it is P_1, at this new level OS_1 of steel can be exchanged against *OC* of cloth. The exchange ratio is $\frac{C_1P_1}{OC_1}$. But at this exchange ratio, it is possible for India to sell OC_2 cloth to America, but at this exchange ratio America is ready to supply only C_2P_2 of. steel to India.[1] It will lead to an unfavourable balance of payments for India. If perfect competition and the presel1ce of a gold standard is assumed, then the monetary mechanism will lead prices and wages down in India and raise them to the same amount in America. This will change the cost structure in the two countries. In this situation India's product (cloth) will become cheaper and there by America will be induced to consume more of India's product (doth). In other words, America will be ready to supply more of steel for doth. This will increase the distance P_1C_1 and reduce the, distance OC_2 to the left. Equilibrium will again be restored at the old point *P* where the exchange ratio between India and America is fixed to $\frac{PC}{OC}$. It is represented by the line *OL*.

The second point of generalisation is that the terms of trade will also depend upon the elasticities of demand and supply of each product. It is due to the fact that the shape of the offer curves depends on the demand and supply elasticities. But the concept of elasticity is not of much importance. This is because, the concept of reciprocal demand leads to an ultimate balance between exports and imports.

The terms of trade can, therefore, be expressed either as a price or the quantity ratio. But in the world of more than two countries and more than two commodities (except in the accounting sense), imports and exports are not always balanced, nor is there constancy in the prices.

1. This is because of the fact that at point P_1 the exchange rate is $\frac{C_1P_1}{OC_1}$ which is equal to $\frac{P_2C_2}{OC_2}$ at point P_2.

This calls forth the concept of *partial terms of trade.*

The ratio of export prices to import prices in any two periods is called the net barter terms of trades or the commodity terms of trade, Mathematically,

$$\frac{PX_1 / PM_1}{PX_0 / PM_0}$$

$$= \frac{PX_1}{PM_1} \cdot \frac{PM_0}{PX_0}$$

where

PX_1 = Price of exports in current year
PX_0 = Price of exports in base year
PM_1 = Current year price of imports
PM_0 = Base year price of imports

i.e., subscript '0' indicates the base year and subscript '1' indicates the current year.

Suppose the export price index has increased from 100 (base year index) to 300 (current year index). And import price index has increased from 100 (base year) to 150 only. Then the new terms of trade are:

$$\frac{300}{150} \times \frac{100}{100} = \frac{2}{1} \text{ or } 2 : 1$$

It shows an improvement in the terms of trade. In other words, a rise in export prices relative to import prices represents a favourable change in the terms of trade. Also a rise in import prices relative to export prices will represent an unfavourable movement in the terms of trade of a country.

Taussig's Doctrine of Terms of Trade

The net barter terms or trade concept developed by Marshall enables to explain the behaviour of the balance of payment position. It does not include the quantities of exports and imports into its account. It includes only the prices of export and import which do not explain the volume of trade. Here, Prof. Taussig devised the concept of Gross Barter terms of Trade[2] and defines it as "the ratio of comparison between real export quantities to real import quantities in any two consecutive periods."

2. F. Taussig, *International Trade* (1927), pp. 113-118. Here Taussig points out the situations under which commodity terms of trade would be a misleading index.

Mathematically,

$$\frac{\dfrac{OX_1}{PX_1} \bigg/ \dfrac{QM}{PM_1}}{\dfrac{QM_0}{PM_0} \bigg/ \dfrac{QX_0}{PX_0}}$$

or $$\frac{QX_1}{QM_1} \cdot \frac{PM_1}{PX_1} \quad \frac{QM_0}{QX_0} \cdot \frac{PX_0}{PM_0}$$

PX_1 = Current year price of exports
QX_1 = Current year quantity of exports
PM_1 = Current year price of imports
QM_1 = Current year quantity of imports
$P\,X_0$ = Base year price of exports
QX_0 = Base year quantity of exports
PM_0 = Base year price of imports
QM_0 = Base year quantity of imports

Viner's Doctrine of Terms of Trade (Single-factoral Terms of Trade)

In the words of Prof. Viner, "If it were possible to construct an index of the cost of production in terms of the average technical coefficients of production of the export commodities and if the commodity terms of trade index was multiplied by the reciprocal of the export commodity technical coefficients index, the resultant index would provide a better guide to the trend of gains from trade than the net barter terms of trade or the commodity terms of trade index by itself." He called it as the single factoral terms of trade. Mathematically,

$$\text{Single Factoral Terms of Trade} = \frac{PX_1 / PX_0}{PM_1 / PM_0} \cdot \frac{FX_0}{FX_1}$$

$$= \frac{PX_1}{PM_1} \cdot \frac{PM_0}{PX_0} \cdot \frac{FX_0}{FX_0}$$

$$= TC \cdot f$$

where $\dfrac{FX_0}{FX_1}$ = Reciprocal of the index of cost in terms of quantity of factors of production used per unit of export.

$$TC = \text{Commodity Terms of Trade} = \frac{PX_1}{PM_1} \cdot \frac{PM_0}{PX_0}$$

$$f = \frac{FX_0}{FX_1}$$

Double Factoral Terms of Trade

Technical coefficient of productivity not only affects the export but also the imports of a country. If we include imports also then we get a double factoral terms of trade. Mathematically,

$$\text{Double Factoral Terms of Trade} = \frac{PX_1 / PX_0}{PM_1 / PM_0} \cdot \frac{FM_1 / FM_0}{FX_1 / FX_0}$$

$$= \frac{PX_1}{PM_1} \frac{PM_0}{PX_0} \frac{FM_1}{FX_1} \frac{FX_0}{FM_0}$$

$$= TC \cdot f^*$$

where $\frac{FM_1}{FM_0}$ = The reciprocal of the index of costs in terms of quantity of factors of production employed per unit of imports, (or Technical coefficient of imports) and f^* = Technical coefficient of export-import.

Robertson has also defined the single and double factoral terms of trade in the same manner as Viner defined them. But this type of measurement is valid only in theory because it is very difficult to measure the factors of productivity (or technical coefficients of exports and imports).

Income Terms of Trade

It is a modern concept to terms of trade which has been developed by mainly A.H. Imlah and G.S. Dorrance. They define income terms of trade as the capacity to import. For this, let us assume an equilibrium position in the balance of payment of a country, i.e.,

$$PX.\ QX = PM.\ QM$$

or $$QM = \frac{PX \cdot QX}{PM}$$

or $$QM = f(PX, QX, PM)$$

where QM = Capacity to import which is a function of three variables PX

(price of export), *QX* (quantity of export) and *PM* (price of imports). Now if there is any change in these variables or any of them, there will be a corresponding change in *QM*. Thus, *QM* will be greater if

(*i*) $PX \uparrow$ (price of export increases)
(*ii*) $QX \uparrow$ (and/or quantity of export increases)
(*iii*) $PM \downarrow$ (and/or price of import falls)

3. TERMS OF TRADE AND ECONOMIC DEVELOPMENT

The study of terms of trade is very important, since it plays a key role in the theory of economic development. It may be seen that low income countries can have more rapid development if their terms of trade are advantageous. A favourable terms of trade encourages the developing countries to import more, increase the availability of resources and hence have rapid growth. But Jevons criticises the terms of trade as an index of the gains from trade. He argues that the terms of trade relates the utility from the marginal unit of imports with the disutility from the marginal unit of exports whereas the gains from trade is measured by the difference between the total utility from imports and total disutility from exports. It is possible that the total gains from trade may increase even with deterioration in the terms of trade. We know that in equilibrium conditions, the gains from trade will be maximum only when $MU_M = MU_X$ (Marginal Utility of Imports equals the Marginal Utility of Exports). It indicates that the marginal unit of trade itself yields no gain.

Causes of Deterioration in the Terms of Trade of Underdeveloped Countries

(*i*) *Lack of Technology.* In underdeveloped countries like India, productivity is lower and costs of production are higher as compared to the advanced countries of the world. Since coefficient of technology is an important factor in the determination of terms of trade, underdeveloped countries possess unfavourable terms of trade while in industrial advanced countries, the use of technology has reduced the costs of production and hence they possess a favourable terms of trade.

(*ii*) *Growth of Population.* Population is growing faster in UDCs than in MDCs (More Developed Countries). It creates a heavy domestic demand and reduces the exportable surplus. It would result a deterioration in the terms of trade of the country .

(*iii*) *Law of Diminishing Returns.* We know that the main occupation of under-developed countries is agriculture where the diminishing return prevails. On the other hand, in the production of industrial goods, the law of increasing returns is applied. The latter is found in advanced countries and that is why the terms of trade are favourable to MDCs than to LDCs (Less Developed Countries).

(*iv*) *Mobility of Factors of Production.* When world prices of certain products are falling, manufacturing countries shift to the production of those goods whose prices are not falling because these countries work with advanced machines that can be used to produce other commodities. This is not possible in primary goods producing countries because their economies are very rigid and lack adaptability. It explains why UDCs suffer from deterioration in their terms of trade when the world prices of such products (primary products) decline.

(*v*) *Unavailability of Substitutes.* We find that underdeveloped countries depend on more developed countries for their requirements while the developed countries do not perfectly depend on them. It is due to the fact that advanced countries possess close substitutes for their needs. This is also one of the important factors why the developing countries have to accept an unfavourable terms of trade.

These above are the important causes of deterioration in the terms of trade of underdeveloped countries.

EXERCISES

1. What is meant by terms of trade? Explain the factors that influence its determinations.
2. What do you understand by commodity terms of trade and income terms of trade? What is the significance of these concepts?
3. Explain clearly the different concepts of terms of trade.
4. Discuss various concepts of terms of trade? Do you think that determination in terms of trade necessarily means loss of economic welfare?
5. Distinguish between (*a*) commodity terms of trade and factoral terms of trade; and (*b*) gross barter terms of trade and net barter terms of trade. Which of these would you rely upon as an indicator of gains from trade?

Multiple Choice Questions

6. (*i*) The offer curve of a country bends toward the axis that measures its
   (*a*) export commodity (*b*) import commodity
   (*c*) export or import commodity (*d*) non-traded commodity
   [*Ans.* (*a*)]

   (*ii*) If a nation's terms of trade is 2, its trade partner's terms of trade is
   (*a*) 4 (*c*) 1
   (*b*) 2 (*d*) $\frac{1}{2}$ [*Ans.* (*d*)]

(*iii*) If the cost of transporting a good between two countries exceeds the pre-trade price difference for the good between the two countries, then trade in that good is

(*a*) possible

(*b*) impossible

(*c*) reversed

(*d*) can not say anything [*Ans.* (*b*)]

Chapter 50

THE GAINS FROM TRADE

1. INTRODUCTION

So far we have been able to concentrate on the reasons for the emergence of international trade. In this chapter let us open the economy to trade and consider the gains from international trade.[1]

We know that the foundations upon which international trade and specialisation rest is the relative endowment of different countries with the productive factors and their different methods—capital intensive and labour intensive, etc. A country would specialise upon those products which are best suited to its factor endowments. Further, for most of its exports, there would be competitors in foreign markets; either from countries with comparatively better factor endowments or from countries using different production techniques. Hence, all products, which are producible at relatively low costs, would be exported and all her products would be imported. In fact, a country will have no incentive for international trade if it does not gain from it.

According to Mercantilists, a country would enrich itself by having constant export surplus vis-a-vis other countries. Nations trade with each other because they benefit from each other. International trade is simply the extension of trade beyond the boundaries of a nation. It, therefore, extends the range of specialisation and the gains from trade. As local trade enables advantage to be taken of the special aptitude of individuals, so international trade makes it possible for each country to draw upon the special aptitudes of other countries and to utilise its own resources more efficiently.

The classical economists dealt the question of gains from trade in

1. Among the many excellent general discussion on this topic are L.A. Metzler, *The Theory of International Trade,* T.C. Schelling, *International Economics* and C.P. Kindleberger, *International Economics.*

different methods: (*i*) comparative cost method, where aggregate real cost of obtaining a given amount of real income is the main criterion, (*ii*) increase in income as a measure of gain, and (*iii*) terms of trade as an index of gain.

According to Adam Smith, "Between whatever places foreign trade is carried on, they all derive two important gains from it. It carries out that surplus for which there is no demand among them, and brings back in return from it something else for which there is a demand. It gives values to their superfluities, by exchanging from something else, which may satisfy a part of their wants and increase their enjoyments. By means of it, the narrowness of domestic market does not retard the division of labour in any particular branch of manufacture. By opening a more extensive market for whatever part of the produce of their labour may exceed the home consumption, it encourages them to improve its productive powers, and to increase its annual produce to the utmost and thereby to increase the real income of the nation."[2]

Therefore, through international trade the consumers of both the trading countries would be able to increase their satisfaction, because they can possibly consume a wide range of commodities at the minimum costs.

Further, those factors which cannot be used efficiently in domestic use, can be transferred to more efficient uses where their marginal returns are higher.

2. MEANING OF GAINS FROM TRADE

According to Malthus, "The gain from trade consists of the value which results from exchanging what is wanted less for what is wanted more, and international trade, by giving us commodities much better suited to our wants and tastes than those which had been sent away, has decidedly increased exchangeable value of our possession and our means of enjoyment."[3] Value here refers to purchasing power over labour.

But Prof. Viner[4] says that to measure gain by increase in labour command without reference to the terms on which labour can be commanded is a misleading procedure. According to Ricardo[5], it does

2. Adam Smith, *An Inquiry into the Nature and Causes of the Wealth of Nations,* Vol. I, p. 413.
3. Malthus, *Principles of Political Economy,* pp. 461-62.
4. Jacob Viner, *Studies in the Theory of International Trade.*
5. David Ricardo, *Principles of Political Economy,* pp. 82-84.

not immediately increase the amount of value but contributes: (*a*) increase in mass of commodities, and (*b*) thereby an increase in sum of enjoyments. Viner says that both these tastes involve serious practical or logical difficulties: (*i*) the sum of enjoyments is not directly measurable, (*ii*) the use of mass of commodities may involve use of index numbers inviting several problems. However, Ricardo does emphasise the existence of gains from trade.

According to Prof. Taussig, the gains occuring from international trade depend on two factors: (*i*) terms of trade, and (*ii*) efficiency of labour producing export goods.

Terms of trade refers to the rate at which the commodities produced in the two countries exchange with each other. As already discussed, the rate of exchange between the two countries depends. upon the reciprocal intensity of demand for each other's goods. The terms of trade keep on changing according to the intensity of the demand for the products. That country gains the most out of international trade, the foreign demand for whose products is the highest and whose demand for other countries' products is comparatively low. That country gains the least out of international trade, whose demand for the products of other countries is the highest.

The second factor affecting the size of the gain arising out of international trade is the *level of efficiency of the workers producing export goods.* In reality, the main reason for the differences in the production costs of the two countries is the difference in the level of labour efficiency in those countries. The difference in comparative costs increases with the increase in the level of labour efficiency in a country. This difference in comparative costs advantage widens the field of international trade. The demand for the exports of a country will be high if the level of efficiency of the labourers in that country is also high. Such a country will gain more from international trade because by stepping up its exports it may obtain more goods and services from other countries.

Further, the gain from trade to a country inevitably influences its money income. The money income of a country will be high if the foreign demand for its product is high. Therefore, the increase in national income of a country is dependent to a very large extent on the gains accruing from international trade.

J.S. Mill calls these benefits as *direct gains* from trade, while the present economists refer to them as static gains from trade.

According to Prof. Myint, international trade improves the division of labour by widening the extent of market. It then raises the general level of productivity in a country and the national income as well. Such gains are "indirect gains" from trade and are also known as "dynamic gains" from trade.

3. MEASUREMENT AND DISTRIBUTION OF GAINS FROM TRADE

A method widely used to estimate not the total gain from trade at any moment, but the trend or direction of the movement of that gains from trade, measures changes in barter or commodity terms of trade. These measure the relation between the prices of a country gets for its exports and the prices it pays for its imports. If, as compared with this relation in a given (base) year, its export prices rise or import, prices fall, its commodity terms of trade are said to have improved. Therefore, an improvement in the terms of trade is an index of the international distribution of and trend in the gains from trade. If, on the other hand, the prices of its exports decline or the prices of its imports rise, its terms of trade are said to have worsened.

To make such comparisons, index numbers are used. For the base year, an average of a country's exports prices are computed, with each commodity in the average weighted according to its importance in trade. For a later year, if similar changes are computed it will reflect the average in export prices. The same procedure is followed for imports. The change in the country's terms of trade can be measured by obtaining a ratio of the change in export prices to the change in import prices, i.e.,

$$T_c = \frac{P_{x1}}{P_{x0}} \div \frac{P_{m1}}{P_{m0}}$$

where T_c = Commodity terms of trade.

P_{x1} = Price of exports in current year.

P_{x0} = Price of exports in base year.

P_{m1} = Price of imports in current year.

P_{m0} = Price of imports in base year.

Suppose the following statistics are given:

Year	*Export Value (X)*	*Import Value (M)*
1990	100	100
1998	339	385

Then $$T_c = \frac{339}{100} \div \frac{385}{100} = 0.88$$

This means that the terms of trade have deteriorated by 12 per cent. Although changes in the commodity terms of trade by themselves indicate the direction of movements of the gain from trade, their implications may be seriously modified by accompanying changes of other kinds. There are three offsetting elements:

(1) *Changes in the character and statistical data.* Because changes in the quality and the composition of exports are constantly taking place the conventional conclusions from index of commodity terms of trade must be limited to short periods.

(2) *Changes in the volume of trade.* With increased exports at lower prices, country's capacity to import may remain the same or may even increase. Such changes can be taken into account by an index of the income terms of trade, which is simply the commodity or barter terms of trade multiplied by the index of change in export volume:

$$T_y = T_c \left(\frac{Q_{x1}}{Q_{xo}} \right) \text{ where } T_y = \text{Income terms of trade}$$

(3) *Changes in productivity.* If due to increase in efficiency, goods are produced and exported at 10 per cent lower, average price, terms of trade can be deemed as deteriorated by 10 per cent. But the real costs of imports in terms of exports remain unchanged. To take account of productivity changes, we should multiply T_c by the index of change in physical productivity of export industries.

Marshall's Measure of Net Benefit from Trade

It is the sum of the excesses of the unit prices at which the country would have purchased successive quantities of imports over the equilibrium 'rate of inter-change' established in trade. In Figure 50.1, *OG* is *UK*'s reciprocal demand curve and under equilibrium *OH* units of UK's commodity are exchanged for *OB* units of India's commodity.

Take any point *P* on *OG* and draw up OPP_1 to cut *BR* in P_1; next *MP* to P_2; so that M_1 being the point at which it cuts *HA*; M_1P_2 being equal to AP_1, UK is willing to pay for *OMth* commodity of India at the rate of *PM* commodity of UK, i.e., UK is willing to trade at the rate *L* of P_1B commodity of UK for *OB* commodity of India. UK thus obtains a surplus on *OMth* commodity of India at the rate which, if applied to *OB* commodity of India, would make an aggregate surplus AP_1 commodity of UK, M_1P_2 or which is equal to M_1P_2 commodity of UK. UK's surplus on that *OMth* commodity of India amounts to *OB*. If *P*, starting point from *O*, is made to move along *OG*, P_2 will start from *U*, the foot of the perpendicular drawn from R on OY and it will trace out a curve UP_2A ending at A. Then UK's aggregate surplus of net benefit from trade will be a *OBth* part of the aggregate lines M_1P_2 as P_2 passes from U to A; i.e., it will be a *OBth* part of area *UHA*. *VW* is drawn parallel to *OX*, so that the rectangle *VHAW* is equal to the area *UHA*. The $VHAW/OB = VH$ will be country UK's net benefit from trade measured in UK's commodity.

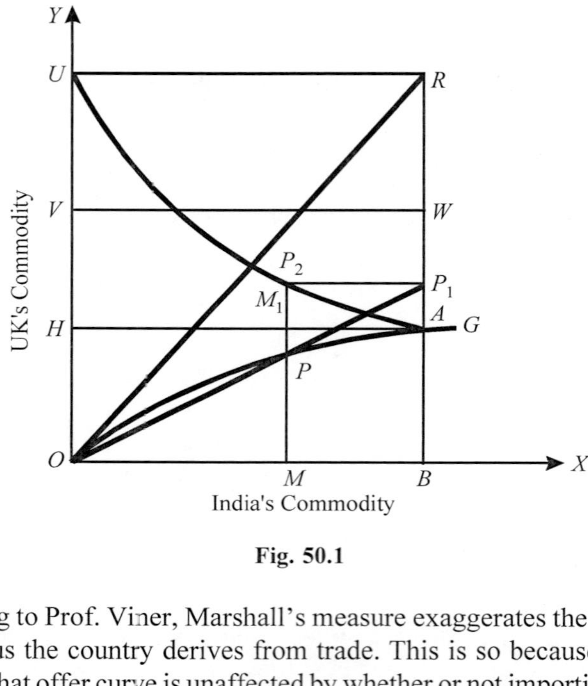

Fig. 50.1

According to Prof. Viner, Marshall's measure exaggerates the amount of the surplus the country derives from trade. This is so because Marshall assumes that offer curve is unaffected by whether or not importing country pays the equilibrium price or the maximum price it is willing to pay for intra marginal increments in imports, which in turn implies constancy of marginal utilities of exportables.

But Viner suggests that marginal utility of exportables is increasing, and therefore, the price the country would pay for a marginal increase of imports is less. Marshall's neglect of this fact leads to an exaggeration of the amount of surplus. In Viner's view, Marshall's measure gives improbable or meaningless magnitudes of the surplus.

In place of Marshall's measure, Viner suggests *going behind the offer curve* to the country's utility function. He derives from it the offer curve which shows the maximum price which the country is willing to pay for each successive unit, and measures the country's benefit from trade as the sum of excesses of the prices shown on this curve for successive quantities of imports over equilibrium price established in internal trade. This measure is the true Marshallian consumer's surplus as contrasted with the exaggerated measure of it obtained by considering the area under the demand curve.

Samuelson's Analysis of the Gains from Trade

In 1939, Professor Paul Samuelson wrote his celebrated paper "The Gains From International Trade"[6] which shows how international trade makes a society potentially better off than it would be if restricted to autarky. Samuelson recognises that free trade may harm some people, but the harm which free trade inflicts upon one factor of production is necessarily less than the gain it confers on the other. In other words, it is always possible to bribe the suffering factors by subsidy or other redistributive methods so as to make all factors better off as a result of trade. Here Samuelson concluded in his article that "If a unanimous decision were required in order for trade to be permitted, it would always be possible for those who desired trade to buy off those opposed to trade, with the result that all could be better off." This follows from the fact that as a result of trade huge (or equal) amounts of every commodity can be obtained with smaller (or equal) amount of every productive service.

The main assumptions, on which the Samuelson's theorem of gains from trade is based, are the following:

(*i*) Perfect competition prevails in the economy.
(*ii*) Production function remains unchanged.
(*iii*) Constant returns to scale prevail in the economy.
(*iv*) Supply of inputs is a function of prices.
(*v*) It assumes that ordinal preference scale, prices and optimum output of goods that an individual selects are given.
(*vi*) The country, whose gains from trade are being considered, is very small, and cannot influence world prices.

Proof of the Theorem. Let us imagine that the economy under autarky has reached a position of competitive equilibrium. Then to this equilibrium, it must correspond a set of commodities and factor prices. It also follows that at these equilibrium prices, resulting optimal quantities of commodities and productive services maximise for the economy as a whole the algebraic difference between total value of output and factor

6. *The Canadian Journal of Economics and Political Science,* May 1939.

costs as compared to any other commodity and factor combinations satisfying the transformation function of the economy.

Suppose. $P_1, P_2, P_3 \ldots P_n$ and $w_1, w_2, w_3 \ldots w_s$ are the set of commodity prices and factor prices prevailing in competitive equilibrium under autarky. And $X_1, X_2, X_3 \ldots X_n$ and $a_1, a_2, a_3, \ldots, a_s$ are optimal set of commodities produced and productive services used.

Then, the total value of commodities produced is given by

$$P_1 X_1 + P_2 X_2 + \ldots + P_n X_n \quad \ldots (1)$$

and total costs are given by

$$w_1 a_1 + w_2 a_2 + \ldots + w_s a_s \quad \ldots (2)$$

Then the above proposition can be stated as:

$$[P_1 X_1 + P_2 X_2 + \ldots + P_n X_n] - [w_1 a_1 + w_2 a_2 + \ldots w_s a_s]$$

$$\geq [P_1 \bar{X}_1 + P_2 \bar{X}_2 + \ldots + P_n \bar{X}_n] - [w_1 \bar{a}_1 + w_2 \bar{a}_2 + \ldots + w_s \bar{a}_s \quad \ldots (3)$$

Where the barred X's and a's indicate any other point satisfying the transformation function of the economy. The inequality can also be written as:

$$[\Sigma PX - \Sigma wa] \geq [\Sigma P \bar{X} - \Sigma w \bar{a}] \quad \ldots (4)$$

Thus no condition other than (4) would give maximum profits.

Let us now introduce the possibility of trade. Such trade will emerge if the country encounters outside (relative) prices differing from its domestic prices in isolation. At these foreign prices the country can buy or sell various commodities without changing these quoted prices. After trade is established, these fixed outside prices will prevail in the country supplanting old set of prices and a new competitive equilibrium will be reached where $P'_1, P'_2, P'_3 \ldots P'_n$ and $w'_1, w'_2, w'_3 \ldots w'_s$ form the new set of commodity and factor prices. Then the quantities will be $X'_1, X'_2, X'_3, \ldots X'_n$ and $a'_1, a'_2, a'_3 \ldots a'_s$.

Since the production inequality (4) will always hold under competitive conditions, we must always have

$$[\Sigma P'X' - \Sigma w'a']_1 \geq [\Sigma P'X - \Sigma w'a] \quad \ldots (5)$$

It means that at the prevailing outside prices, the autarkic set of commodities and factor quantities could have been chosen. Yet, the fact, that international trade takes place, indicates that at the new (after trade) prices, the autarkic set would have yielded a smaller profit, in the sense of inequality proposition stated above. It, therefore, follows that the after trade set of commodity and factor quantitity is superior, in ordinal sense, to the autarkic set. It also follows that if each individual has the same ordinal preference scale and factor endowments, then all individuals of the economy are better off with trade. In case of heterogeneous preferences, trade cannot be expected always to better each and every individual; it may leave some persons to face increased prices for all of their staple consumption items, thus making them worse off than before. But even then, the truth of the modem theorem holds. For ideal co-operation, after the introduction of trade, those who have suffered thereby could be compensated so as to make them as well off as before, without taxing away all the gains of the people who have benefitted.

According to famous *compensation criteria* laid down by Kaldor, Hicks and Scitovsky, the test of increased efficiency is that the gainers from a change can gain more than compensate the losers. There are, however, two objections to this simple test.

(1) It ignores the problem of distribution and base such recommendations on efficiency considerations alone. But since all economic changes affect both the efficiency of the economic system and the distribution of welfare, some economists think that all such changes should be judged by standards both of efficiency and of equity.

(2) The test does not require that persons injured by some economic changes must. actually be compensated from those who have actually gained from it. In the absence of actual compensation, the said change may make the rich richer and the poor yet poorer.

The Samuelson theorem that *trade is poten1ially better than no trade* is established so long as we are willing to accept compensation criteria. What would happen if after trade distribution of income becomes more adverse than the autarkic distribution? In the absence of actual redistribution, trade may well contribute to a worsening of the situation.

The theorem, of late, has been generalised to show that even if it is possible for a country to influence its terms of trade, it can be made potentially better off by trade in the sense that there is a way of reallocating the enlarged total of goods so as to make everyone better off.

The said reallocation after trade is to be carried out by *ideal lump-sum transfers* so that marginal equivalences are not disturbed. If this is done, trade can be shown to be not simply a potential boom but an actual one. But such ideal lump-sum redistribution may not be really available. The only feasible redistributions that are available, cause harmful substitution and other effects. If redistributions that are of this type, Samuelson admits, the highest social welfare obtainable from free trade might be lower than the other obtainable under autarky. In other words, for a given country autarky cannot be optimal if ideal transfers are possible. *Some trade* is better than no trade in the sense of making the nation better off with a farther out consumption-possibility frontier and farther out utility possibility frontier.

Haberler's Views on Gains from Trade

Using Samuelson's proof given in 1939, Prof. Haberler has recently provided a simple geometrical analysis to show how tree trade increases national income and economic welfare.

In Fig. 50.2, *A'A* is a country's production possibility possibility. *H* shows the situation of production and consumption before trade. The slope of *PP* between two goods, *X* and *Y*.

Trade enables the country to reach *T* production point and *H'* consumption point. (At *H'*, the country exports *H'L* of *X* and *LT* of *Y*). It is evident that the country is better off at point *H'* than *H*. Superiority of *H'* over *H* can be shown by community indifference curve. But Haberler is not willing to use this argument, since a shift in production from *H* to *T* is usually accompanied by a redistribution of income, an uncritical application of such curve is not possible.

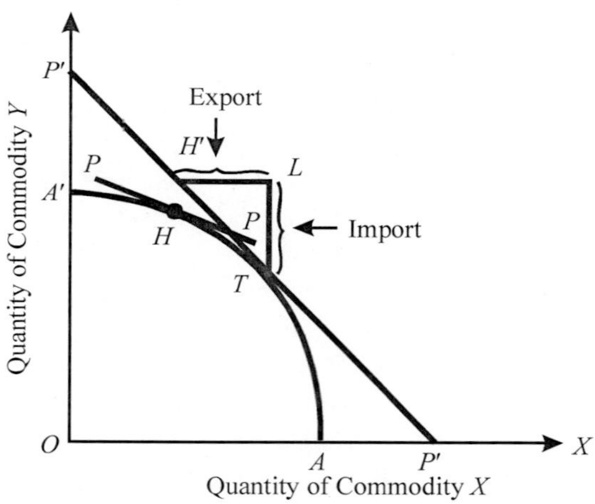

Fig. 50.2

However, superiority of *H'* can be demonstrated even otherwise. If *H'* is above and to the right of *H*, *a* larger quantity of both *X* and *Y* is available after trade. But if it were above and to the left, more of *Y* and less of *X* could be consumed. But still *H'* is better than *H* in the sense that if income were appropriately redistributed, everyone could be made better off than before. For, it is not possible to so distribute the actual bundle of goods under free trade as to make at least one person better off while leaving others worse off, as with the actual bundle in the preceding 'no trade' situation. It is sufficient that everyone could be better off at *H'* than *H.* In other words, what is implied is that the, utility possibility curve corresponding to tree trade policy will be uniformly outside (though it may touch) the utility possibility curve corresponding to the autarky policy.

Kemp's Analysis of the Gains from Trade

Prof. Murray C. Kemp has offered a more generalised and sophisticated analysis of the original Samuelson's theorem. He has extended it to show that for countries of any size whatsoever, not only is *"compensated free trade better than no trade, but compensated restricted trade" is also better than no trade,* provided the restriction is non-prohibitive.

Here, Prof. Kemp increases the generality of Samuelson's theorem by dropping the assumption that the country is too small to affect the terms of trade and shows that the theorem is valid for any country of any size. He retains, however, all other assumptions of Samuelson's analysis discussed above.

4. GAINS FROM TRADE A SIMPLE DIAGRAMMATIC EXPOSITION

The ideas of Samuelson and Kemp can be used to offer a simple diagrammatic exposition of the gains from trade. In Fig. 50.3, only two goods *X* and *Y* are produced in the economy. *PQ* is the production possibility curve or transformation curve of the country. It is concave to the origin. In the absence of trade, the locus of consumption and production are identical, that is, given some domestic price ratio, under autarky, the country's equilibrium production as well as equilibrium consumption will be denoted by the same Point on the production locus *PQ*. Here, *PQ* is country's autarky frontier.

With tree trade, the price ratio between *X* and *Y* will be determined by the prevailing world price ratio, indicated by the slope of *MN* line. The post-trade production equilibrium is held at point *A*. From here to the consumption point the country would move along *MN* line. The latter is thus a budget restraint line or consumption possibility frontier in Samuelson's terminology.

Since frontier *MN* lies everywhere of autarky frontier *PQ*, the country can have more of both the goods. Thus if some distribution of income could bring the country under autarky to point *A* rather than to some other point on *PQ*; opening of trade would at that point, in fact, be followed

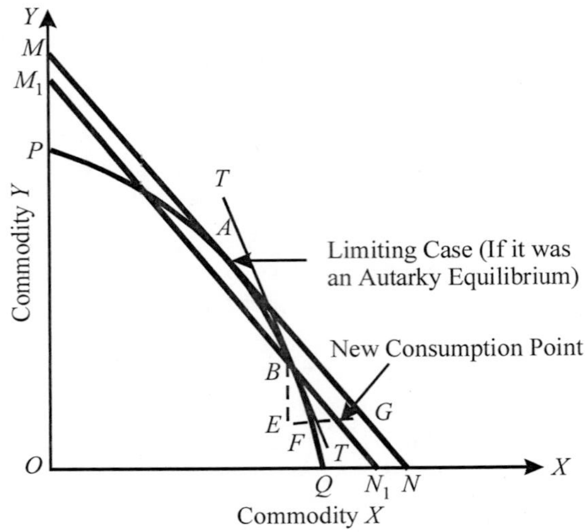

Fig. 50.3

by no international transactions, and hence would represent in limiting case where trade neither benefits nor hurts the country. It is in this context, that the trade makes the country potentially better off.

Further, suppose that the country imports commodity *X*. With an advalorem tariff on commodity *X*, the domestic price ratio between *X* and *Y* goods will change. The new ratio is denoted by the slope of *TT* line in Fig. 50.3. The country's production equilibrium will be at point B rather than point *A*. The country would produce more of *X* and less of *Y*, than before tariff. Now assuming that the world, price ratio (*MN* line) remains Unchanged even in the post-tariff situation, the country exchanges its exports of *Y* for imports of *X* from abroad at price denoted by M_1N_1 (parallel to *MN*). Thus the country's consumption possibility frontier is now M_1N_1 (Let the new consumption point be *G* on the line M_1N_1, the country exchanges *BE* units of *Y* for *EG* units *X*; *EF* units of *X* being received directly by the consumers through the exchange transaction and *FG* being the government revenue. The new frontier M_1N_1 lies everywhere within the area bounded by *MN* line, the free trade frontier. Hence whatever the actual consumption point on M_1N_1, with free trade more of both goods is attained than at that point. Assuming ideal transfers which do not involve a deadweight loss of allocative efficiency, the conclusion is reached that *free trade leads to a higher level of welfare than would be achieved with restricted trade.*

EXERCISES

1. What are the gains from trade? How can we measure them?
2. Discuss digrammatically the Marshall's measure of net benefit from trade.
3. Define Samuelson's theorem of 'gains from trade'.
4. Write short notes on:

   (*i*) Haberler's Views on Gains from Trade,

   (*ii*) Kemp's Analysis of the Gains from Trader.

Multiple Choice Questions

5. (*i*) Gains from trade can be measured by

   (*a*) differences in comparative costs

   (*b*) increase in the level of national income

   (*c*) terms of trade

   (*d*) all of the above [*Ans.* (*d*)]

   (*ii*) A favourable terms of trade always mean a gain from trade

   (*a*) True (*b*) False

   (*c*) Uncertain [*Ans.* (*c*)]

Chapter 51

INTERNATIONAL TRADE AND FACTOR PRICES

1. FACTOR PRICE EQUALISATION

Heckscher-Ohlin Method

On the basis of an earlier work of Heckscher, Prof. Ohlin gave two conclusions: (*i*) Free mobility of commodities in international trade can serve as a substitute for factor mobility, and (*ii*) It will lead to factor price equalisation.

Ohlin argues that international trade takes place if only relative prices used in production inputs differ between countries. Foreign trade continues until these relative factor-price differentials have been eliminated.

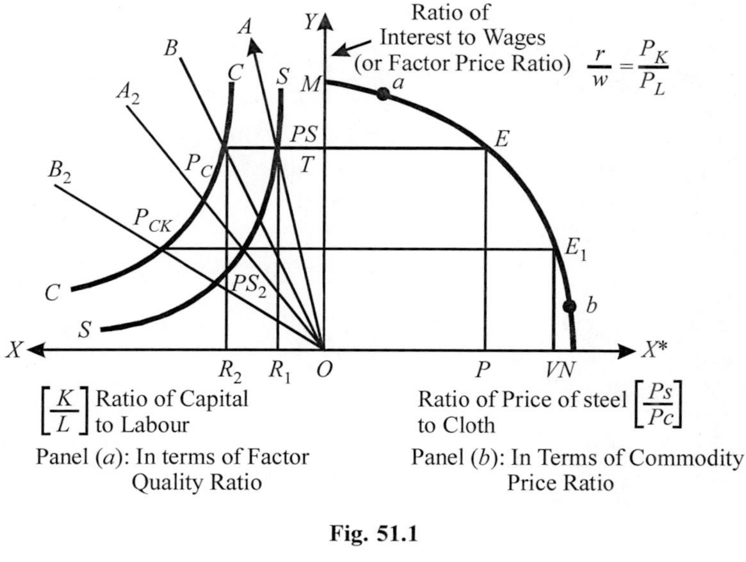

Panel (*a*): In terms of Factor Quality Ratio

Panel (*b*): In Terms of Commodity Price Ratio

Fig. 51.1

Therefore, in a more round about way it may be seen that trade would tend to bring about the equalisation of factor prices. The geometric proof of the theorem is given in Fig. 51.1. On the or axis in Fig. 51.1 we have measured the factor price ratio in terms of their receipts: interest and wages. On the *OX* axis we have measured the ratio of capital to labour (*K/L*) and on the *OX** axis we have measured the ratio of prices of steel and cloth $\left(\frac{Ps}{Pc}\right)$ or the product-price ratio.

In Panel (*a*), SS and *CC* indicate the production isoquants of steel and cloth respectively. (That is the fixed amount of steel and cloth produced by various combinations of capital-labour ratio and factor price-ratio.) Here we have assumed fixity in factor proportions necessary to produce either of, the two commodities. In Panel (*b*) the concave *MN* indicates the phenomenon of diminishing returns. It may be noted that increased supply of either commodity beyond *a* and *b* in Panel (*b*) can be disposed if only prices are reduced. If we assume in Panel (*b*) that *OP* is the market price ratio of steel to cloth, then the vertical line from *P* cuts the *MN* curve at *E.* If from *E* a line is drawn horizontally to *X*-axis, then it cuts the production isoquants at *Ps* and *Pc* respectively. If *Ps* and *Pc* are joined to the origin *O*, then we get the production paths (production rays) *OA* and *OB.* The distance *OPs* and *OPc* represent the quantities of steel and cloth that are likely to be produced and demanded at price ratio $OP\left(\text{i.e. } \frac{Ps}{Pc}\right)$. Given this demand, the respective combinations of factors required in production can be found out by dropping vertical lines from *Ps* and *Pc* to the base *OX.* The corresponding capital labour ratios are OR_2 for steel and OR_2 for cloth in Panel (*a*). The sum of the distances

$$OR_1 + OR_2 = R = \frac{K}{L}$$ should exhaust the supply of capital and labour. At this point what will be the share of capital and labour in the total product has been indicated by the values given along the *OY* axis. The line *OPc* cuts *OY* axis at *T.* The height or *T* from origin *O* indicates whether the factor-price ratio is less than or greater than one. If $\frac{r}{w} > 1$, it indicates that the rate of return to capital is more than that the price paid to labour,

or wage rate, whereas a condition that $\frac{r}{w} < 1$, it indicates that the rate of return to capital or interest is relatively less than that the price paid to labour, or wages.

However, for simplicity it is assumed that at point *R*, the ratio $\frac{r}{w} = 1$.

This was our original position. Now let us introduce a change. Suppose that the demand for steel increases as compared to that of cloth. This will tend to cause a rise in the price of steel, and hence a shift in the product price ratio *Ps/Pc* to position *OV*. When the product price ratio is *OV*, the curve *MN* is cut at E_1, by drawing a perpendicular from *V*. If from point E_1, a horizontal line is drawn, it intersects the production isoquants *SS* and *CC* at Pc_2 and Pc_2 respectively. If Ps_2 and Pc_2 are joined to the origin *O*, then we can get the OB_2 and OA_2 rays of production paths. The distances OPs_2 and OPc_2 represent the new quantity of steel and cloth produced. It can be seen that the quantity of steel produced has declined since $OPs_2 < OPs$. On the other hand, the quantity of cloth produced has increased since $OPc_2 > OPc$. The decline in output of steel is to be explained by the relatively higher cost of labour in the steel producing country. In other, words, the cheapness of capital will induce more of its use relative to labour. This will make all the products employing capital cheaper. Hence, countries with abundance of capital will benefit.

In Fig. 51.2 we have drawn two Edgeworth-Bowley boxes representing the different factor endowments and linear homogeneous production functions of UK and Portugal in steel and cloth. The production functions are assumed to be identical. They are given on a commoon origin in cloth at *O*. The different factor endowments result in two separate origins for steel, *Y* in Portugal and *Y'* for UK.

Given the origins, the maximum efficiency loci may be fitted in as *OY* for Portugal and *OY'* for UK. Before international trade, both countries are assumed to be producing and consuming domestically at points *S* and *T* respectively. On the maximum efficiency loci (on the basis of given demand conditions), when international trade takes place, it is assumed that prices of the two commodities are fully equalised in the two countries because of the absence of transport costs. Now the returns to factor inputs namely to capital and labour must necessarily be equal. This can take place only when trade results in production at either of the points *R* and *U*. At points *R* and *U*, the equality of factor proportions is demonstrated

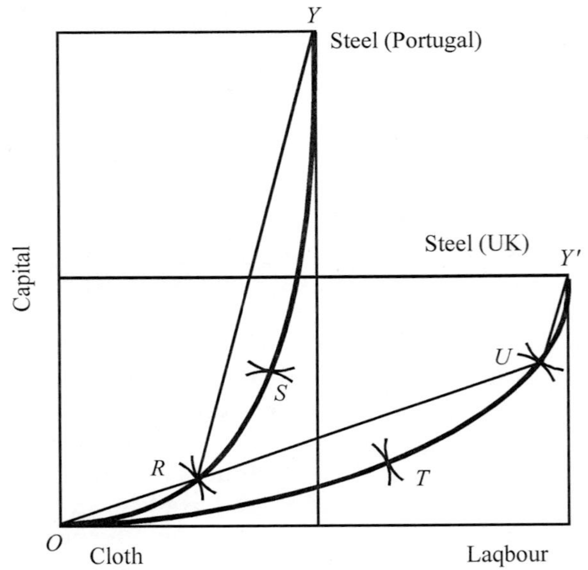

Fig. 51.2

by the fact that *R* lies on the straight line *OU* whereas *U* lies *UY'*, which is parallel to *RY*.

Kindleberger argues that on several grounds it may be, demonstrated that two such points as *R* and *U* may not exist. After trade, one or both countries may be completely specialised, UK producing cloth at *OY*, or Portugal producing steel at *OY'*. Demand conditions in Portugal and UK may be so sharply different that results, in production in Portugal from *S* toward *Y* rather than toward *O*, so that it exports labour-intensive goods despite its abundance of capital.

A.P. Lerner's Method

The second method of illustrating factor-price equalisation has been presented by A.P. Lerner. He picks isoquants for the two commodities which represent their relative prices or the quantities in which they are exchanged after trade between UK and Portugal has started. In Fig. 51.3 these isoquants for steel and cloth have been given. We may assign any values to these two isoquants, say 30 metres of cloth and 2 tons of steel, or 300 metres of cloth and 20 tons of steel. Since the production functions are linearly homogeneous, the shape of successive isoquants representing larger quantities is always the same—thus giving us a straight line expansion path as shown in Fig. 51.3. Since the units chosen reflect product prices which are the same in the two countries after trade (assuming absence of transport cost and prevalence of perfect condition). Figure 51.3 will be identical in both UK and Portugal. But Kindleberger feels that this model breaks down if the isoquants cross more than once because it will imply that there is a wide range of factor substitution possibility in at least one of the commodities.

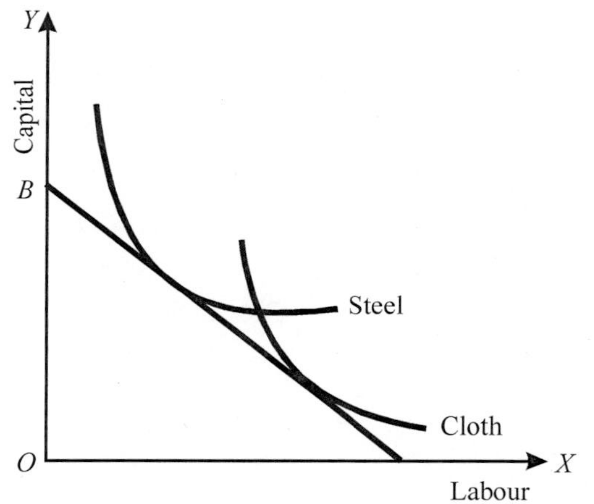

Fig. 51.3

Factor Proportion Method

The third method of illustrating factor-price equalisation is based on factor proportions, factor prices and product prices on the same diagram. The upper half of Fig. 51.4 shows the relations between capital labour ratios and wage rates whereas the relationship between wages and product prices has been shown in the lower half. The central horizontal line is wage-interest rates which rises as it moves to the right.

In the upper half of Fig. 51.4 capital labour ratios for cloth and steel are shown rising as wage-interest ratios increase: the higher the wages, the more incentive there is for producers to substitute capital for labour. It may be noted that cloth is more labour-intensive i.e., capital-intensive than steel at each wage-interest ratio, since the *X–X* schedule for cloth lies everywhere below the *Y–Y* schedule for steel.

The relation between product prices and factor prices has been shown in the bottom part of Fig. 51.4. Here relative product prices are measured in reverse order i.e., downward. The higher the wage-interest ratio, the higher will be the relative price of cloth which is a labour-intensive product.

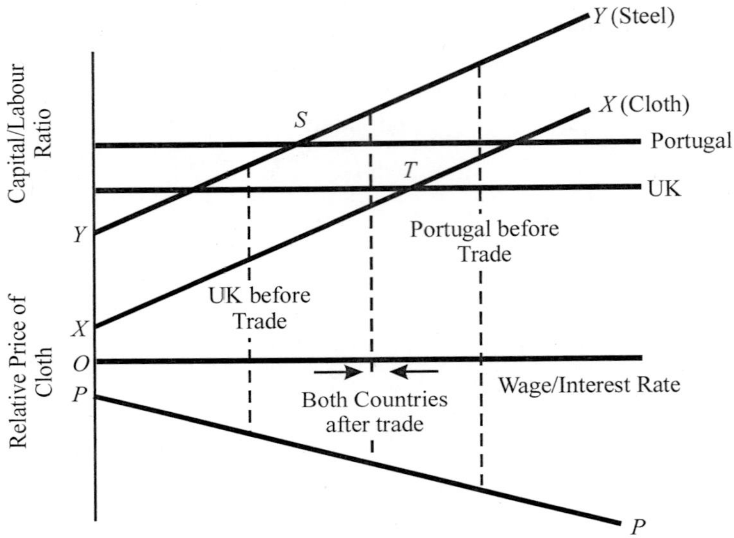

Fig. 51.4

It is evident from the upper half of this figure that Portugal is relatively capital-rich whereas UK is relatively labour-rich. Before trade production in the two countries is determined by the demand condition. However, even before trade, as shown in Fig. 51.4, price of cloth (labour-intensive good) is lower in UK than in Portugal and the wage-rate (relatively) is lower. Conversely, in UK the interest rate and the price of steel is higher than in Portugal. When trade is opened up, product prices have to move together, and under the conditions drawn, the relative wage becomes identical which is, in fact, factor-price equalisation.

EXERCISES

1. Discuss the various methods of factor price equalisation under international trade.
2. Discuss to what extent free movement of goods can bring about equalisation of international factor prices.
3. Prove the factor price equalisation theorem in the case of two factors and two commodities.

Multiple Choice Questions

4. (*i*) Factor price equalisation in international trade is the result of
   (*a*) free mobility of commodities in international trade
   (*b*) internal factor price equalisation
   (*c*) perfect competition in the factor market
   (*d*) none of the above [*Ans.* (*a*)]

   (*ii*) Who developed factor price equalisation theorem?
   (*a*) Heckscher Ohlin (*b*) Kindleberger
   (*c*) A.P. Lerner (*d*) All of the above [*Ans.* (*d*)]

Chapter 52

THE OPTIMUM TARIFF

I. INTRODUCTION

Under the appropriate circumstances a tariff will enable the country to obtain its imports cheaper when a foreigner pays the duty for the most part of it.

When tariff is levied, price goes up in importing country. It is generally believed that the imposition of an import duty raises the price of the imported goods by the full amount of duty. This conception, however, is not very correct. In fact, the price of the commodity may rise by more than, less than or equal to the amount of the duty, or remain unchanged. The price will remain unchanged if the entire duty is borne by the foreigners. It will be possible only when the foreign producer (exporter) can earn larger profits by reducing the sale price by the amount of duty and keeping sales unchanged than those which he can earn from reduced sales at the unchanged sale price.

The price in the importing country will rise by the full amount of duty if the production is subject to the law of constant costs. The praise extent of the rise in price in the importing country and that of the decline in price of the exporting country will depend mainly upon the volume and the elasticity of demand and supply in the importing and exporting countries.

The larger and more elastic the demand in the exporting country, the smaller will be the decline in price in the exporting country and correspondingly larger the rise in price in the importing country. A small decline in price will considerably expand the domestic demand which will compete for a large part of the loss of foreign market caused by the imposition of duty in the importing country. Thus the decline in price in exporting country will be small. Decline in exports will be far larger than the decline in the total output. The importing country will have to step up domestic production considerably to meet the demand which was previously being met with imports. This will considerably raise the cost of production and hence price in the importing country. In contrast, if the demand in the importing country is large and more elastic, the rise in price in the importing country will be comparatively small and the decline in the price in the exporting country correspondingly large.

The larger and more elastic the supply in the exporting country, the smaller will be the decline in price in the exporting country and correspondingly larger the rise in price in the importing country.

Sometimes the price may rise by more than the tariff. It is due to the middlemen who participate in the trade activity and finally supply the articles to the consumers.

A similar discussion may be made more completely with Marshallian offer curves. Figure 52.1 shows a pair of offer curves of UK and India, *OB* and *OA* respectively, which intersect at *P*. This gives a price *OP* between the two commodities, wheat and cloth. A tariff imposed by UK on wheat from India may be represented by a new offer curve *OB′*.

Before tariff, for *OW* of wheat, UK used to offer *WV* of cloth but now (after tariff) offers only WP_1, collecting *P′ V* in taxes. In other words,

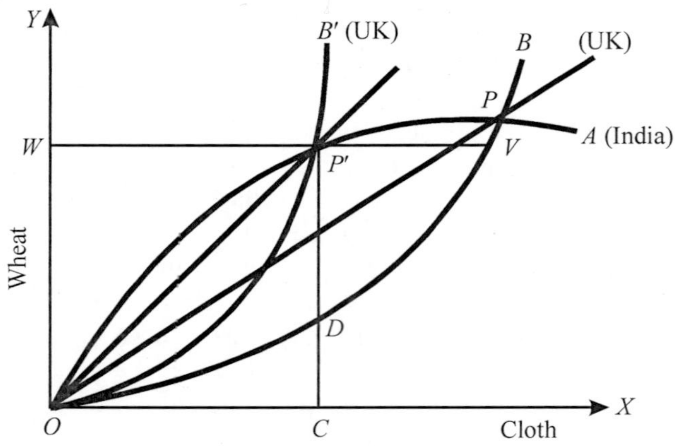

Fig. 52.1

UK, before tariff, used to be prepared to offer *OL OC* cloth for *DC* of wheat, whereas now (after tariff) it requires *P′ C* in wheat, collecting *P′D* as tariff. The shift of the offer curve from *B* to B_1 changes the terms of trade from *OP* to OP_1. This is an improvement in UK's terms of trade.

The improvement in the terms of trade mayor may not make the country as a whole better off. In retailing, profit per item can be very high, but if sales fall way off, total profit is less than if the rate of profit had been more modest. The original UK's gain will accrue only in the absence of retaliation. But if both parties retaliate, both almost certainly lose. Fig. 52.2 shows such a case in which tariffs imposed by UK and India in retaliatory sequence B, B_1'B_2, and A, A_1, A_2, and so on, leave the terms of trade unchanged at the end but greatly reduce the volume of trade. Each country would have been willing to buy and sell much more at these terms of trade if the price relationship in domestic trade were the same. The imposition of tariffs to improve the terms of trade, followed by relation, ensures that both countries lose. The reciprocal removal of tariffs, on the other hand, will enable both countries to gain. *This is an explanation or a rationalisation*, of the reciprocal nature of the Trade Agreement progress in USA and the GATT.

The Competitive Effect

The competitive effect of a tariff is really an anti-competitive effect; competition is stimulated by tariff removal. The competitive effect has been important both historically and currently.

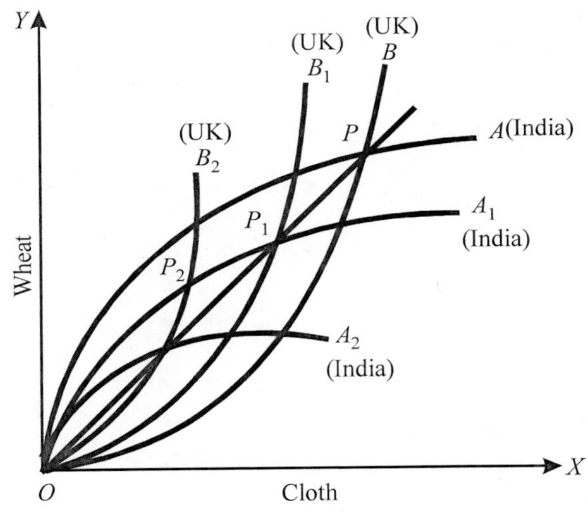

Fig. 52.2

Formation of ECM is said to have enlarged markets and economies of scale, some say that its most significant result was breaking up monopolies (France). Before ECM one or two large companies in France kept high prices over some inefficient firms since competition was limited. When tariff came down, small firms merged with larger one (efficient).

Big firms could have reduced prices to destroy small firms. But this is against national benefits.

Kindleberger's Formula of Optimum Tariff

Prof. Kindleberger has developed a formula to measure the rate of optimum tariff. It can be explained as below:

$$T = 1/e{-}1$$

where T = Optimum tariff rate

e = Point elasticity of the offer curve of the other country

In the case of a straight line offer curve when the elasticity is infinitive, the optimum tariff is

$$T = 1/\infty - 1 = 0$$

Thus the higer the elasticity of the offer curve of the other country, the lower will be the level of the optimum tariff of a country and vice versa.

EXERCISES

1. What do you understand by the term optimum tariff ? Under what conditions is the optimum tariff likely to be (*a*) high and (*b*) zero?
2. Explain tariff retaliation.
3. Explain the terms of trade effect of tariffs.

Multiple Choice Questions

4. (*i*) The tariff that maximises a country's welfare is known as
   (*a*) Optimum Tariff (*b*) Minimum Tariff
   (*c*) Maximum Tariff (*d*) Zero Tariff [*Ans.* (*a*)]

PART 8
TAXATION

Chapter 53

TAX: A SOURCE OF PUBLIC REVENUE

1. INTRODUCTION

Generally, the revenue of the State is taken to mean the income raised by the government through taxes from the public. But tax is not the only source of public revenue. There are various other sources also like fees, price, special assessment, fines and penalties, gifts and government enterprises. It is of no use to blend all these sources into one name 'Taxation' because all these sources have fundamental difference of one kind or another from each other. Their relative comparison itself is of some significance for the purpose of the study of public revenue, The difference between these various resources may also be of the amount which is raised by any one of them. But this has no such significance for the purpose of study as the fundamental difference of their nature, method of raising them and their respective effects on the persons from whom these are collected. Here we are giving the brief account of the nature and form of the various sources of public revenue.

(1) *Taxes.* Taxes are the most important source of revenue of the modern governments. In every country, the greatest part of the public revenue is raised through taxation. Taxes may be imposed on persons or wealth, they may be direct or indirect, and they may be of different rates and nature. But it has some peculiarities which distinguish it from other sources of revenue. In the words of Dalton: "A tax is a compulsory contribution imposed by a public authority, irrespective of the exact amount of service to the tax-payer in return and not imposed as a penalty for any legal offence." This nature of a tax makes it quite distinct from

other sources of revenue.

(2) *Fees.* Sometimes government provides certain special services to the public of the country and in payment of these services charges fees. In the words of Prof. Taylor: "They are characterised by more or less free choice on the part of the payer as to whether or not he will pay more or less direct benefit conferred upon him." According to Seligman, "Fee is a payment to defray the cost of each recurring service undertaken by the government, primarily in the public interest, by conferring a measurable special advantage to the tax-payer." Thus fees is that revenue which is paid to the government for the special services rendered by it. The tax is also a payment to the government and we pay taxes with the initiative that the government provides us many facilities but, the both can clearly be distinguished as under:

(*a*) A tax-payer does not receive any service as a direct return of the tax nor does the government guarantee any specified benefit to be conferredupon him in return of any particular tax paid by him whereas fees in the direct payment of the services rendered to the payer and the government guarantees the services of the person who pays fees.

(*b*) Tax is a compulsory contribution. It has nothing to do whether you enjoy any service given by the government or not. You will have to pay taxes for the purpose of building a lunatic asylum even if there are all sane persons in your family, but a fee payer is free to choose whether he will pay it or not. If he enjoys the service he would pay the fee, if not he will not pay it.

(*c*) The tax may render some services in its return to the tax-payer but the amount of tax and that of service rendered have no relation with each other, while, the more services you want to enjoy you will have to pay more fees in case of the services which are subject to payment of fees.

Licence is one of the form of fees though some people have tried to make it different from fess. Lutz writes, "A licence fee is paid in those instances is which the government authority is invoked simply to confer a permission or a privilege rather than to perform a service of a more tangible and definite sort." Thus when licence fee is realised no direct service is rendered but permission is granted for certain things. The motive of levying licence fee is to impose regulation or control over various types of activities. While in case of fees you are entitled to enjoy certain services rendered by the state by payment of licence fee you are entitled to do certain things which you cannot do otherwise.

(3) *Price.* The government sells some of its services, and goods and receives price in payment for them. In this manner, government acts like

a businessman and the public like its customer; the former sells the goods and services the latter buys them and pay prices to the former. These businesses of the government for which it receives prices may either be services like transport, light, post and telegraph etc., or they may be goods, i.e., the production of the government enterprise.

The differences between tax and price is obvious. Tax is a compulsory contribution to be paid by every citizen in the manner levied, whereas price is to be paid by the persons who purchase services or goods produced by the government. Tax has no guarantee of benefit as to amount and nature while prices are the direct payment for goods and services purchased. The payment made by tax is used in the public interest without particular regard to the payer whereas saleable services are given only to those persons who pay price.

There are also differences between fees and price. The price is the full payment, while fee does not necessarily cover the cost of services. Similarly fees are utilised for interest whereas price is the payment for services and goods to that person who buys them.

(4) *Special Assessment.* Hunter while giving the explanation of social assessment, has observed, "A special assessment is a compulsory levy against-property proportion to which have increased, to it because of some service undertaken for the public good." The essence is this that sometimes the government performs certain services as a result of which the property or wealth of a particular group of persons is increased. A levy in proportion to this increase in wealth is referred as special assessment. The rent or price of houses in a certain locality may increase due to the fact that the government has made it accessible for trains, aeroplanes. The govern-ment may charge special assessment from the house owners of that locality in the proportion of the increase in the price of the houses. This may be termed as special tax but it is not the same as tax since it is levied after the benefit has been conferred upon the payers while tax has no guarantee of benefit. But this also not termed as fees. Fees are the payment for certain services rendered by the government while the special assessment is the levy for increase in one's wealth resulting from some particular services of the government.

(5) *Fines and Penalties.* The aim of these sources of revenue is not the collection of revenue but administration of justice and maintenance of order. Fines and penal-ties are the payments made for the contravention of law.

(6) *Gifts.* A small portion of the revenue of the government is also derived from the gifts by individual, organisations or foreign governments. But this is not a certain and fixed source of revenue and is also out of the control of state. Its significance has been gradually declining.

2. CHARACTERISTICS OF A GOOD TAX-SYSTEM

The tax-system must contain the qualities of equality, certainty, convenience, economy, productivity, elasticity, diversity and simplicity. But it is almost impossible to perceive of a tax-system which is free of all flaws; which consists of only good taxes and has none of bad taxes. Moreover, it is almost impossible to raise sufficient revenue for the state's expenditure and at the same time to please all the taxpayers, Famous philosopher, Edmund Burke has rightly observed, "It is difficult to tax and to please as it is to love and to be wise." We need not enter into the investigation of the details of Burke's simile but the first part of his observation, which is our concern, is undoubtedly true. No tax system may be perfect in all respects and one or the other loopholes are to be found here and there. There may be some taxes which pinch the taxpayers. Similarly, the taxes may not be sufficient to procure considerable revenue to finance the public expenditure and sometimes there may be such taxes which obstruct people's incentive to work and thereby hamper the production. Thus we see that the tax system of a country cannot be expected to fulfil all the canons of taxation.

What we mean by a good tax system is not the perfect tax system; a system which consists of all the taxes which fulfil all the canons of taxation, which procure sufficient revenue for the public services and at the same time leaves the taxpayers as they are found and even better their position. What we mean by a good tax system is simply the predominance of goods taxes; taxes which fulfil the most of the canons of taxation, taxes which procure sufficient revenue, taxes which affect the economic position of the people to the least extent and taxes which least obstruct the incentives for production. For such a system to exist, the following principles must be observed:

(1) *Taxes should be levied on the basis of fundamental principles of taxation.* That is to say the allocation of taxes between different groups of persons is according to the principles of least sacrifice, cost and benefit and above all ability to pay. The last principle is always to be emphasised.

(2) *Taxes observe all the canons.* The taxes should be so imposed that they are equitable, convenient to pay, economical, certain, productive and elastic. All these canons may not be found in all the taxes. But the essence of the argument is that majority of the taxes should observe most of these canons.

(3) *Tax system should be balance.* What we mean by a balanced tax system is simply that there should exist not one kind of tax but of all the kinds of them in a pro-per balance. We know that direct taxes have may

advantages over indirect ones but only direct taxes are not sufficient to earn all the required revenue. Moreover, the indirect taxes also have their own merits such as they are convenient to pay and have wide coverage. So there must be both direct and indirect taxes but not in an arbitrary way but in a properly conceived balance. On the other hand, a tax system cannot possess either progressive or proportional taxes alone at the same time be a good one. Both kinds of tax system have their advantages and disadvantages and it is required of a good tax system to have both kinds of taxes in a proper balance.

(4) *Tax system should ensure maximum social advantage.* The imposition of the taxes should be on the basis of this fundamental principle of Public Finance. To ensure maximum social advantage or least aggregate sacrifice is not the task of one tax, but it is from the combination of all the taxes, i.e., the tax system taken as whole that we examine the advantages rendered by the tax system to the society.

The advantages which the society receives from a tax system are not from the taxes as such taxes can only give pain and disadvantages to the taxpayer. The advantages result from the effects which the taxes produce. The effects fall on production and distribution of wealth in a society and what is supposed of a good tax system is that it must have majority of such taxes which produce good effects on production and equitable results in distribution.

EXERCISES

1. Give the various sources of public revenue.
2. Define a tax. Discuss the characteristics of a good tax system.
3. Distinguish between a tax and a price.

Multiple Choice Questions

4. (*i*) The main characteristics of a tax is the following:
   (*a*) A tax is a compulsory contribution imposed by a public authority
   (*b*) A tax is a payment in return for which no direct specific *quid pro quo* is rendered to the payer
   (*c*) There is no direct give-and-take relationship between a taxpayer and the tax levying authority
   (*d*) All of the above [*Ans.* (*d*)

   (*ii*) Which one of the following is a compulsory payment to the government?
   (*a*) Tax
   (*b*) Fees
   (*c*) Price
   (*d*) All of the above [*Ans.* (*a*)]

Chapter 54

DIRECT AND INDIRECT TAXES

1. MEANING OF DIRECT AND INDIRECT TAXES

According to Dalton, "A direct tax is really paid by the person on whom it is legally imposed, while an indirect tax is imposed on one person, but paid partly or wholly by another, owing to a consequential change in the terms of some contract or bargain between them." Thus income and property taxes are direct taxes, while customs and excise duties are indirect taxes. In the case of direct taxes the impact or immediate money burden and the incidence or the ultimate money burden are on one and the same person. The person upon whom the tax is imposed bears the impact; while the incidence is upon the person who utlimately pays it. If, on the other hand, the impact and the incidence are on different persons, the tax is an indirect tax. The impact of the sugar excise is on the producer, but he may raise the price by the amount of the tax and realise the tax from the consumer. Hence it is an indirect tax. Similarly, the importer of goods pays the import duty to the state, but he may raise the price by the amount of the duty and thus realise the tax from the purchaser, who bears the ultimate money burden of the duty. Here the impact of the import duty is on the importer but the incidence is on the purchaser. The import duty is, therefore, an indirect tax. Thus a direct tax is one which cannot be passed on, but an indirect tax is one which can be shifted or passed on. An income-tax is generally considered a direct tax; but in 1868, the supreme court of the United States held it to be indirect. Inheritance and property taxes are generally considered direct taxes. While taxes on commodities and transactions are regarded as indirect. But the only difference between commodities and property is that the former are less durable than the latter. According to Nicholas Kalder, "The distinction between direct and indirect taxes broadly corresponds to a division between taxes which are levied on persons and corporations and taxes levied on transactions. Thus all taxes on income or the ownership of property would be direct taxes, and taxes on the purchase or sale of property like stamp duties would be indirect taxes."

J.S. Mill defined a direct tax as: "Demanded from the very persons who, it is intended or desired, should pay it and an indirect tax as one demanded from one person in the expectation and intention that he shall indemnify himself at the expense of another." According to the definition of Mill, this tax would be indirect, but it is really direct. Thus, the intention of the legislator is not sufficient to distinguish between direct and indirect taxes. According to Hadley, the distinction between direct and indirect taxes should be based on the immediate and not on the ultimate incidence. Taxes which are legally shifted and those which are not shifted at all are direct, but those which are shifted quickly through commercial competition between consumers are indirect. According to Bastable, taxes levied on permanent and recurring occasions are direct but those levied on occasional and particular events are indirect. Death duties are considered as direct taxes, but according to Bastable's definition they would come under the category of indirect taxes.

Tax systems contain both direct and indirect taxes. Direct taxes are imposed on income, house property, land and state passing at death, while taxes on commodities, i.e., consumption taxes and excise and customs duties are indirect taxes.

2. MERITS AND DEMERITS OF DIRECT TAXES

Merits of Direct Taxes. Following are the merits of direct taxes:

(1) *Equitable.* Direct taxes are equitable because they are charged according to the ability of the taxpayer.

(2) *Elastic.* The yield from direct taxes increases automatically with an increase in wealth and population in a country. Direct taxes permit of an adjustment between the income and expenditure of public authorities.

(3) *Economical.* Direct taxes are economical. The cost of collection of these taxes is very little and, therefore, they are most economical.

(4) *Certainty.* Direct taxes are certain because the tax-payer knows in advance when he has to pay the tax and at which rate. The authority imposing the tax also knows the probable income it is likely to get from the tax.

(5) *Educative Value.* Direct taxes have an educative value. Direct taxes raise consciousness among the people and, therefore, they try to find out whether the money collected by the State is being spent properly or not.

Demerits of Direct Taxes. Following are the demerits of direct taxes:

(1) *Unpopular.* Direct taxes are unpopular because the tax-payer has the knowledge that he is paying the sum. It involves some psychic pain to him.

(2) *Possibility of Evasion.* The possibility of evasion of a direct tax is greater. Dishonest persons are at advantage while honest persons suffer. Therefore, dishonesty is encouraged.

(3) *Inequality.* Is difficult in practice to frame a just basis of assessment for all classes of people. The inequalities and incongruities can be avoided through care and experience. Even then the tax system is likely to be arbitrary to a certain extent, but this would apply to any of tax system.

(4) *Narrowness of Scope.* Direct taxes are levied only on certain groups of persons and, therefore, due to narrowness of their scope they do not raise any civic sense in all the groups. Moreover in poor and backward countries government gets very little revenue from these taxes.

3. MERITS AND DEMERITS OF INDIRECT TAXES

Merits of Indirect Taxes. Following are the merits of indirect taxes:

(1) *Convenient.* Indirect taxes are very convenient to pay; you purchase a packet of cigarette paying the price asked for by the shopkeeper and you never know that 5 paise were paid by you in the form of tax. Moreover, nobody presses you to pay them. If you have money to buy goods, it means that you have to pay for taxes also because taxes are included in price.

(2) *Evasion of tax not possible.* The possibility of tax evasion is not there. You pay the tax if you have to pay the price and enjoy the consumption of goods.

(3) *Equitable.* Indirect taxes can be made equitable by imposing on the luxury goods.

(4) *Social benefit.* Indirect taxes can be used to curtail the consumption of harmful, drugs. They perform a useful social service and produce revenue at the same time.

(5) *Educative value.* They are paid by almost all the groups of society. Thus they are considered as exercising a wholesome influence on people. They can thus have the educative value and raise civic sense in all the sections of society.

(6) *Productive.* Indirect taxes are more productive as compared to direct taxes.

Such taxes bring revenue to government from different sources and naturally the income from these taxes is more.

Demerits of Indirect Taxes. Following are demerits of indirect taxes:

(1) *Inequitable.* Indirect taxes are inequitable. The burden of these taxes falls more heavily on the poor since they are charged at a proportional rate.

(2) *Uneconomical.* Indirect taxes are uneconomical. The collection of these taxes involves many stages and thus the cost of collecting them becomes greater.

(3) *Encourage dishonesty.* Indirect taxes give chance for cheating. Levy of a small amount of tax on a particular goods gives the retailers an opportunity to raise more than for the compensation of the tax. The old stock which was not taxed, is also sold at a price including taxes.

(4) *Damaging for the consumers.* Such taxes are damaging for consumers. The shopkeepers charge the tax from them several times but do not pay it to government. Moreover, they often charge more money from the consumers in the form of tax.

4. COMPARISON BETWEEN DIRECT AND INDIRECT TAXES

"According to Gladstone, direct and indirect taxes were like the 'two attractive sisters' between whom he was perfectly impartial without one being superior to the other. The main issue in the comparison of direct and indirect taxes, however, relates, to the issue as to which one of these two taxes is less burdensome for the taxpayer. Mrs. Ursula K. Hicks and other economists have maintained the superiority of direct taxes over indirect taxes by showing that the taxpayers suffer a smaller amount of sacrifice in terms of satisfaction in the case of direct taxes than in indirect taxes. According to them, if a certain amount of money (revenue) is collected from the community through indirect taxes the burden will be greater than if the same amount of money (revenue) was collected by levying direct tax. Thus, on welfare criterion direct taxes are considered superior. This has been illustrated with the help of indifference curves technique in Fig. 54.1.

Figure 54.1 represents the case of a single consumer whose money income has been measured on the vertical axis while the quantity of commodity has been measured on the horizontal axis. Let us assume that the money income of the consumer taxpayer is *OM.* If he spends his entire income on the commodity, he may buy *ON* quantity of the commodity. Thus; *MN* is the price or budget-line. On this price-line he enjoys certain amount of satisfaction shown by IC_3 indifference curve and his equilibrium position is shown by point *A*. Suppose that an indirect tax is imposed on the commodity making it costlier by the full amount of the tax. Since as result of the higher price of the commodity the consumer can now buy only *OL* quantity of the commodity, the new price-line after the indirect tax levy is *ML*. Consequently, the consumer is forced to move on to a lower equilibrium position shown by point *B* which is situated on the lower indifference curve IC_1 in the diagram. The consumer can now buy only *MG* quantity instead of *MH* quantity of the commodity and he spends *GB* amount of money income to buy it. Of the total amount of money *EB* which is spent by the consumer on the purchase of commodity, *DB* amount goes to the government by way of the payment of excise duty which is an indirect tax.

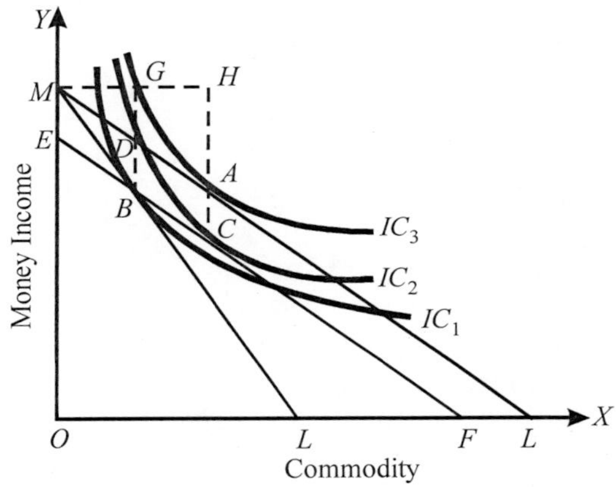

Fig. 54.1

Let us suppose that the taxed amount of money *DB* is taken away by the government by way of direct tax, i.e., through personal income-tax. As a result of this, the personal income of the consumer is reduced by *ME* amount. Since the price of the commodity remains unaffected by the imposition of a direct tax, the new price line *EF* will be parallel to the original price-line *MN*. In other words, the slopes of the old price-line *MN* and the new price-line *EF* will be identical. In the changed situation, the consumer's equilibrium point will be *C*, which lies on a higher indifference curve IC_2 compared with the lower indifference curve IC_1 on which he was forced to move as result of the imposition of indirect tax. This clearly shows that a direct tax (income tax) of equal amount (*DB* = *AC*) is preferable to an indirect (commodity) tax from the consumers' welfare point of view.

The above discussed Joseph-Hicks approach has been criticised by several economists. Milton Friedman has challenged this approach by pointing out that this treatment is related to a single taxpayer and it does not apply to the whole community of taxpayers. Consequently, the Joseph-Hicks approach ignores the expenditure side of the budget and the production possibilities in the economy.

5. COMPLEMENTARITY BETWEEN DIRECT AND INDIRECT TAXES

It is not always the question of direct taxes versus indirect taxes which is important. In fact, either of these two taxes can be made use of depending on its suitability and efficiency in particular circumstances. Under certain situations, it is better to impose indirect taxes rather than direct taxes, while under certain other circumstances direct taxes would be a better device to use. For instance, beyond a certain stage direct taxes may not be suitable for raising the required tax revenue as these may meet with greater taxpayer resistance. In such situations, indirect taxes are obviously a better choice. However, in order to reduce the inequalities of income and wealth, direct taxation should be adopted because indirect taxes are not amenable to fine graduations. Thus, the two kinds of taxes are mutually complementary and not competitive. It is desirable to appraise and to tax all categories and all parts of national income as equally as possible and this can be best done by judiciously dividing the fiscal obligation of every individual between direct and indirect taxes.

The state must strike a proper balance between the direct and indirect taxes. The idea of keeping a balance between these two taxes was stressed by Gladstone who as the British Chancellor of the Exchequer observed that it was "not only allowable, but even an act of duty, to pay my addresses to them both".

EXERCISES

1. Discuss the relative advantages and disadvantages of direct and indirect taxes.
2. Distinguish between direct and indirect taxes. How do they differ in their equity effects?

Multiple Choice Questions

3. (*i*) Which of the following tax involves shifting?
   (*a*) Direct tax
   (*b*) Indirect tax
   (*c*) Both of the above
   (*d*) None of the above [*Ans.* (*a*)]

   (*ii*) Which one of the following is an example of direct taxes?
   (*a*) Sales Tax
   (*b*) Income Tax
   (*c*) Excise Duty
   (*d*) Custom Duty [*Ans.* (*b*)]

Chapter 55

INCIDENCE AND EFFECTS OF TAXES

1. INTRODUCTION

The burden of a tax does not always lie on the person from whom it is collected. In many cases, it may be borne by the same person who hands over the tax to the tax collector but there are not few cases in which it is borne by other people, partially or wholly. It is necessary to know not only who bears the immediate burden of tax but also to know who bears the ultimate burden of the tax. Here we come to know the difference between the two terms—(1) the impact of taxation, and (2) the incidence of taxation.

Impact of a Tax

Impact of a tax is the immediate money burden. The impact of a tax is on the man on whom the tax is imposed. The man who pays the tax to the government, bears its impact.

For example, a tax might be levied on the producer of tobacco. He is said to bear the impact of the tax. The producer; however, raises the price of his products in the attempt to pass the whole or a part of the tax on the consumers of tobacco. If he is able to raise the price he shifts the tax to the consumers of tobacco. The incidence is said to be on the consumers. But the impact is only on the producer. He is responsible for paying taxes to the government. Thus the impact of a tax is on the person who has to find the money and deposit it in the state treasury. It may be noted here that initially he is always subjected to the burden of the tax, though ultimately he may be in a position to pass on the burden of the tax, partially or wholly, to someone else.

Incidence a Tax

Incidence of tax, on the other hand, is the burden of paying taxes ultimately, In the words of Pigou, "Out of whose pocket did the money come which went into the public treasury, or in whose pocket would the money have remained, if it had not been taken by the government? Our study of incidence, thus is concerned with the causes and extent of tax shifting. The incidence of tax, is on the person who cannot shift it to anybody else. According to other eminent scholar, "By incidence of taxes is meant the final resting point of their payment." Thus if there is no shifting of tax the incidence of the tax is on the same person on whom the impact of it falls, i.e., the immediate and ultimate burden of the tax is borne by the same person. But in burden there may be monetary as well as non-monetary burdens, so we speak of money burden when we speak of incidence of a tax since the estimation of non-monetary burden is impossible. Again the difficulty is that a money burden may be indirect or direct. Indirect money burden may come in process of shifting tax, or as a result of the process of shifting tax, but it is only to the direct money burden to which we allude when we talk of the incidence of a tax. Dalton has aptly remarked, "We may say that the incidence is upon those who bear the direct money burden of the tax." Thus, the incidence of a tax is the direct ultimate money burden.

Since we have spoken above of the "direct" money burdens as being called incidence of a tax, we should clarify what indirect money burdens are. They have sometimes been referred as "other effects". The imposition of a tax may set in motion a whole series of effects and adjustment to those effects. A tax is imposed upon the person who becomes a subject of the tax because he owns taxed property, buys taxed goods or for other reasons and it is from his income that the tax is paid. The subject of the tax may bear the burden himself, but the assumption of the burden will reduce the amount of his income available for purchase in various lines, causing a decline in demand for products in those times. On the other hand, the subject of the tax may be able to transfer the burden (partially or wholly) to someone else, who may be able to transfer a part of it further on. In the process of transfer many ancillary effects may be noted.

Mrs. U. Hicks has described about two kinds of incidence—(*i*) formal incidence, and *(ii)* effective incidence. Her formal incidence is akin to Dalton's direct money burden. She has defined the formal incidence in the following words, "We are concerned in economic with two concepts of the falling of taxes on taxpayers, or as it is called the incidence of taxes. In the first place there is the statistical calculation of the way in which the revenue collected from any particular tax over a given period (usually one year), namely the difference between the factor cost and the market price of the product on which the tax is assessed, is distributed between the citizens (for convenience grouped according to their income levels): or alternatively, the proportion of people's income which goes, not to provide the incomes of those who furnish them with goods and services, but is paid over to the governing body to finance collective satisfactions. The result of this calculation may be called the Formal Incidence of the tax. The effective incidence indicates the wider effects of various taxes.

2. SHIFTING OF TAXATION

The process of transferring the burden of the tax from one person to another is known as *tax-shifting.* The incidence of a tax is upon that person who cannot shift it further. Thus all possible tax shifting is completed before its incidence is determined and the incidence of the tax is upon that person who finally bears its burden. But we must distinguish between the burden of incidence and two other kinds of burdens: those created in the process of shifting the tax and those following from the fact of incidence itself. To take an example, suppose that tax is imposed upon a certain commodity. The seller pays the tax to the government and thereby bears the impact of the tax, but then proceeds to shift its burden to the buyer by adding the amount of the tax to the price of the commodity. If it is not shifted further the incidence of the tax is imposed upon the buyer. In addition to the obvious effect the incidence which we have noted clearly, there are also two other effects which are involved in the process of shifting. The first type of effect is produced from the fact that the seller will raise the price of his commodity and it is anticipated that the sales of the product will decline somewhat. This implies that his net income from the sales will decline and or the income of the factors of production the goods would decline. Clearly the process of shifting has created the burden other than incidence. These burdens are sometimes referred to as "those created in the process of shifting the tax". The second type of effect results from the fact that the money burden of the tax which falls on the person who bears the incidence of the tax, would reduce his purchasing power. He would be able to buy reduced quantity of other goods and consequently the demand for the factors producing those goods would decline. These are referred to as burdens "following from the fact of incidence itself".

Thus there must be drawn clear distinction between the incidence and other effects. While talking of incidence we shall be interested to know out of whose pocket did the money come which went into the public treasury, i.e., who actually makes the payment of taxes. Separation of incidence from the other effects of taxation is not the denial of other effects as being real burdens, but it is only an analytical tool.

Processes of Tax Shifting

(1) *Shifting through Price.* If a tax is levied on a commodity which is sold and purchased, what the subject of the tax, the seller who bears the impact of tax has to raise the price of the commodity in order to shift the tax further to the buyer. If he can reimburse himself only partially the incidence of the tax will be divided between him and others. The shifting process, however, may occur only in the case of price transactions. For in our economy there is on vehicle for reimbursement other than prices. By price, of course, we mean prices of all goods and services in broader sense, i.e., including payments to the means of production also. Thus if tax is shifted, some price will be altered to include the tax, i.e., it would be different from what it would have been if the tax had not been imposed. This change in price, however, can be accomplished by a change in quality; the quality of goods may be altered while the price may remain the same as before. Sometimes deliberate efforts are made to make the shifting of taxes public in order to disclose those "hidden" taxes which are really shiftable. The aim behind such attempts to make the taxpayer conscious of his contribution to the government and to remove from the seller the onus of responsibility for price increase due to taxes.

(2) *Forward and Backward Shifting of Taxes.* The shifting of a tax involves the change in the price of the goods and services. When the tax is shifted forward the price which constitutes the vehicle of shifting will increase. If completely shifted the price would be, higher than what it would have been without taxes, by the amount of tax. If partially shifted it would not be higher than the price without taxes, by less than the amount of tax. When the price of the goods and services rises by the amount of the tax, the incidence of tax is borne by the consumers. This is called forward shifting. Forward shifting may be well illustrated by the example of any commodity which is taxed.

When a tax is shifted backward the price which constitute the vehicle for shifting will decrease as compared with what it would have been. When producer reduces the price of the raw material or cuts down the wages of the employees, the wage-earners. This is called backward shifting of tax. There are some circumstances in which the buyer of product upon which the taxes will be levied at a subsequent stage can shift a part of it backward to the seller in the form of lower prices. There is distinction between real backward shifting and seller's inability to shift the tax forward. The distinction rests on the fact who originally was the subject of tax. If originally imposed upon the seller the tax is shifted forward though partially due to seller's inability to shift it wholly and if the tax is imposed on the buyer, the tax is shifted backward. An example of the backward shifting is the payment by the employer, of contribution to the Employees' State Insurance Fund. Some part of the payment is shifted forward in the form of high price of the product but a typically larger part is shifted backward to the employee in the form of lower wages than would otherwise be paid. Here is a tussle between the forward and backward shifting. If the market conditions, are brisk and when labour's bargaining power is strong the tendency would be to shift substantially the whole tax forward to buyer in form of higher prices. But if demand for the product is not strong and the bargaining power of the labour is weak, there will be a strong tendency to shift substantially the whole tax backward to the labour.

(3) *Tax Capitalisation.* Tax capitalisation is a special type of backward shifting. It occurs in cases where the goods are durable one and thus are subject to a series of successive annual taxes during their life time. If the whole series of future taxes is to be shifted backward at time of purchase the future taxes must be capitalised and deducted in the lump sum in the price offered. The shifting, however, may be done partially or wholly owing to different conditions. For example, if a person is going to purchase a house which will be taxed annually during its life time, he would ask the seller to deduct the sum of the taxes to be paid from the price. The whole of taxes to be imposed may not be deducted owing to higher demand for houses.

Tax Evasion and Tax Shifting

A word, however, must be said about the evasion of taxes as making it distinctly different from the shifting of taxes. Though there are not much possibility of this confusion if taken with a little care yet they had been often confused by the students and public alike. Tax shifting is mostly so intended by the government and most of the indirect taxes are levied with the intention that the taxpayer would reimburse himself the taxes by making the prices of his goods higher. But tax evasion is, on the contrary, a legal offence. In shifting of tax there is no loss of revenue to the government while in tax evasion there is certainly a huge loss to government. The evasion of tax may be attempted by the people by showing themselves not in possession of goods or services to be taxed or that can also be attempted after the tax has been levied on his possession.

3. MODERN THEORY OF INCIDENCE OF TAXATION

The modern economists believe that tax is a part of cost of production and it is paid to the government in the same way as other factors of production are paid for. Thus, tax is necessarily included in the price of the commodities. We generally notice that whenever fresh taxes are levied the prices of the commodities switch over. If the prices remain stationary, it implies that sellers were charging excess price. So if the normal price was being charged, the price of the commodity would certainly increase to the extent of fresh taxation. However, if the prices increase but not to the extent of taxes levied, it implies that some burden of tax is being borne by the sellers and some by the buyers. Now an important problem arises as to how the tax burden should be divided between the sellers and buyers. The modern economists are of the view that the incidence of taxation is divided between the sellers and buyers according to their relative elasticities of demand and supply.

Elasticity of Supply. In this connection Dalton writes, "Other things being equal, the more elastic the supply of the object of taxation, the more will the incidence of the tax be upon buyer." Therefore, if the elasticity of supply is greater than the elasticity of demand, the major part of tax burden shall be borne by the buyers as changes in the cost of production due to fresh taxation would affect to a great extent the elastic supply-commodities. In other words, due to fresh taxation the cost of production will go up and the producers who are on the margin of production will have to stop their production. Similarly, other producers will also cut down their production with the fear that they will not be able to dispose of the entire quantity of their product at the enhanced price. The effect of all this is that the supply is reduced and the price is increased. Thus the producers are able to pass on the burden on the consumers. But the amount of tax which the producers will be able to shift on the consumers will depend on the extent upon which they are able to reduce their supply. That is to say, the elasticity of supply would determine the extent upon which the tax can be shifted to the consumers.

Elasticity of Demand. In the words of Dalton, "Other things being equal, the more elastic the demand for the object of taxation, the more will the incidence of the tax be upon the seller." Therefore, if the elasticity of demand is greater than the elasticity of supply, the major part of the tax burden shall be borne by the sellers as the demand for commodity would be more sensitive to the price variations. On the other hand, if the sellers try to pass on the whole burden of fresh taxation on buyers by raising the price of the commodity, the demand will go down considerably and they will not be able to dispose of large stock of their commodity. Thus we see that along with elasticity of supply, the shifting tax is also influenced by the elasticity of demand.

The above discussion makes it clear that the seller try to shift the burden of tax on the buyers by reducing the supply and the buyers in turn try to throw it back by reducing the demand. The shifting of tax therefore, depends on the bargaining powers of the sellers and buyers. Now let us examine as to who of the two will be able to shift the burden of tax on the other and how much of tax burden can be shifted on to the other. If we minutely go through the problem of incidence we may come to the conclusion that the stronger party of the two will succeed in shifting the burden on the other and the extent of shifting will depend on the intensity of the strength. In this connection, Dalton has rightly observed, "The direct money burden of a tax imposed on any object is divided between the buyers and sellers in the proportion of the elasticity of supply of the object taxed to the elasticity of demand for it." In perfect competition the burden of tax is divided between the sellers and buyers in accordance with their bargaining power.

Principle of Elasticity

Supply and demand conditions determine the burden of taxation to a great extent. Other things remaining the same, the greater the elasticity of demand, the greater will be the burden of taxes on the sellers. If the demand is inelastic, accordingly, the burden will fall on the buyers. The argument is like this: if the demand is elastic, any rise in price due to taxes would reduce demands and thereby making the seller unable to shift the tax to the buyer. On the other hand if the demand is inelastic, the buyers would not demand less even at higher prices and the sellers would be able to shift the burden of taxes to the buyer. In case of supply, the case is just the reverse. That is to say, other things remaining the same, the greater the elasticity of supply, the greater will be the burden of taxes on the buyers. If the supply of the commodity taxes is elastic, the producers would lower the production with the levy of a tax thereby creating scarcity and raising prices. Thus they will be able to shift their burden of taxes on the buyers: If the supply is higher prices being resented by the buyers in the form of flower demand, he will prefer to sell at lower prices thus bearing the burden of tax himself.

In Fig. 55.1 the demand curve *DD* intersects the supply curve SS at the point E. OP is the price of the commodity and OX the quantity of the commodity. Suppose the curve SS is the new supply curve and OP_1 is the new price, after the tax has been imposed on the commodity. OX_1 is the quantity which will now be sold. E_1N is the tax per unit of commodity.

Now price will be higher by OX_1 and the sales lower by OX_1. The result which follows is that the EN quantity of tax is equally shared by the buyer and the seller.

It means the E_1M burden of tax will be borne by the seller while MN will be borne by the buyer. The quantities of burden will change with changes in the relative elasticity of demand and supply. If the demand is more elastic the greater burden would fall on the seller and if it is inelastic the greater burden of tax will fall on the seller.

In Fig. 55.2 we have assumed of a situation where the demand is perfectly elastic. As shown in the figure in perfectly elastic demand condition there is no change in price. Therefore, the whole burden of the tax falls on seller although the sales have gone down from OX to OX_1.

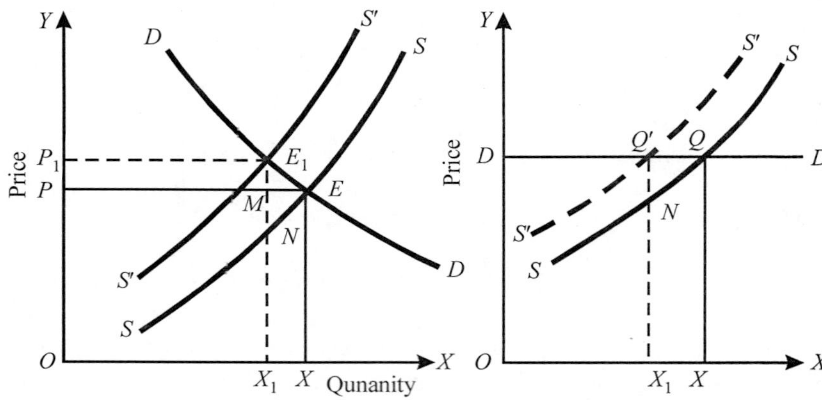

Fig. 55.1 **Fig. 55.2**

Similarly, when the demand is perfectly inelastic the whole burden of tax would be shifted by the seller on buyer as shown in Fig. 55.3.

The curve DD shows the perfectly inelastic demand. By imposing tax the price of the commodity has risen by the full amount of tax EE_1 and thus the whole burden of tax has fallen on the buyer.

Similarly the situation with perfectly elastic supply has been depicted in Fig. 55.4. As the price increases with the imposition of tax, the supply will also decrease and the rise in price would just compensate the tax-

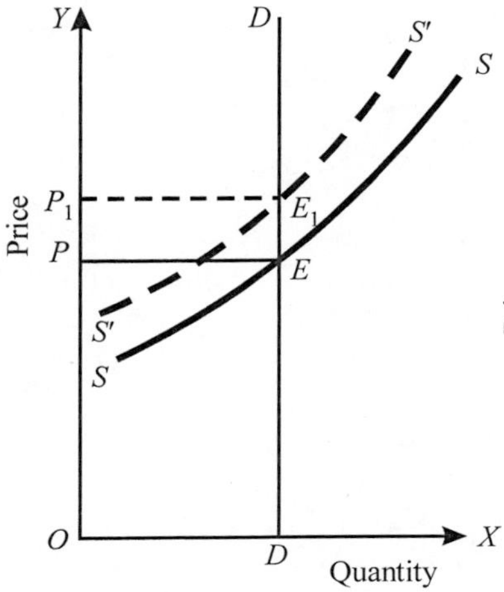

Fig. 55.3

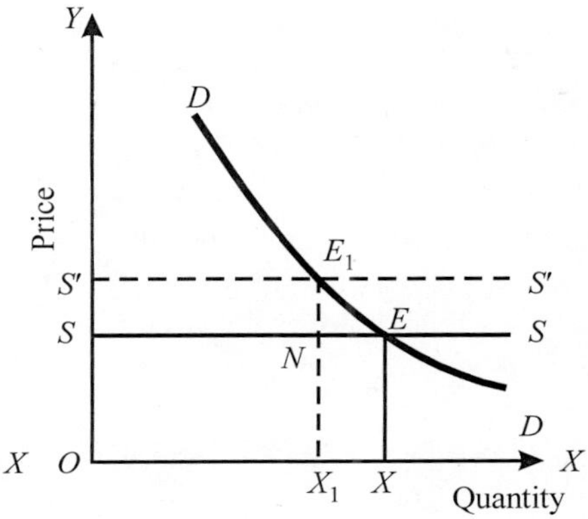

Fig. 55.4

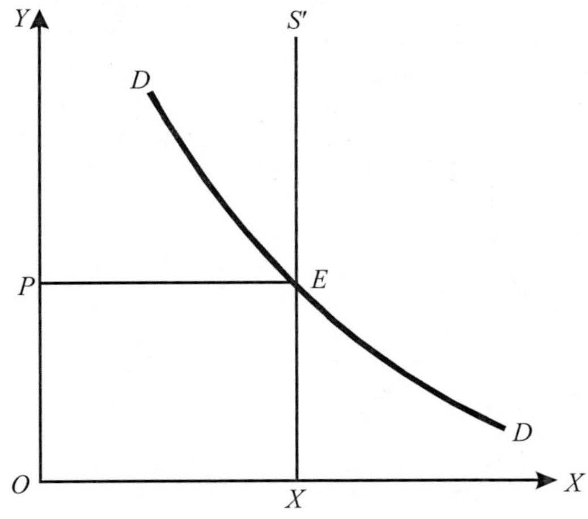

Fig. 55.5

payment. Therefore, the whole burden of tax will be borne by the buyer.

At last the picture can be depicted of a situation with perfectly inelastic supply, as shown in, Fig. 55.5. There is no rise in price due to the imposition of tax and, therefore, the whole burden of tax will be borne by the seller. He will not be able to shift the burden to the buyer, due to his inability to adjust the supply with demand thereby raising price.

Effect of the Laws of Returns on Incidence of Taxation

The different circumstances of production, i.e., increasing, diminishing or constant returns or decreasing, increasing or constant costs differently affect the incidence of taxes. Here we are discussing the effects of the Laws of Returns on the Incidence.

Shifting of tax under the conditions of diminishing returns or increasing costs. If a commodity being produced at the increasing cost conditions is taxed, the, rise in prices is not by the amount of tax, i.e., it is less than, that which implies that the incidence of tax does not fall wholly on the buyers but it is distributed among the buyers and sellers. Since the cost is already high, an increase in price due to tax would reduce the demand. Therefore, he scales his production down to some extent thus shifting a part of tax to the buyer while bearing the rest of the burden himself. How much of the tax burden would be shifted depends on the degree of elasticity of demand of the commodity and also of its supply. If demand is elastic, the greater part of the burden will be borne by the seller while if demand is inelastic the greater part of the burden would be shifted to the buyer. But the burden would not be borne by one party wholly. We can explain this with the help of Fig. 55.6.

In Fig. 55.6, *DD* is the demand curve and *CC* cost curve. Before the levy of tax the competitive price is *OX*. After the levy of tax *C′C′* is the

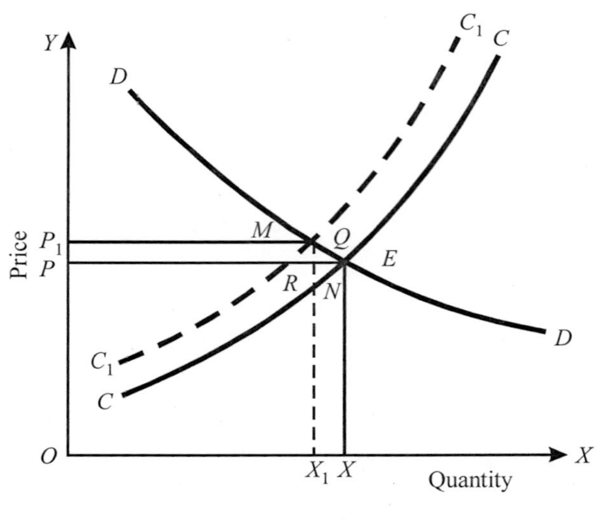

Fig. 55.6

new cost curve, X_1M or OP_1 is the new price *MN* is the amount of tax. But the price does not increase wholly by *MN* amount. *MR* is borne by the seller and *RN* by the buyer, the amount by which price rises.

(2) *Shifting of tax under the conditions of increasing return or decreasing costs:* If a commodity, being produced under such conditions is taxed, the rise in the price of the commodity would be by a amount higher than the amount of tax since every successive unit is being produced with less cost. Thus, not only the whole amount of tax is shifted to the buyer but the seller also earns profit.

(3) *Shifting of tax under constant returns or decreasing costs.* Similarly, if a commodity is being produced under the conditions of constant costs, the increase in price occurs just by the amount of tax. This means the seller is able to shift just the whole amount of tax to the buyer. By imposing a tax the price of the commodity would rise which reduces the demand for it. But since the production is being carried on under the conditions of constant costs, the enterpreneur, is able to make a little contraction in his scale of production. In this way he adjusts the supply with the demand and by raising price by the amount of tax shifts the whole of its burden to the buyer.

Incidence of Tax under Monopoly Conditions

A monopolist fixes a price at which his monopoly profits are the highest. He is not deterred by competition and fixes a price which gives him the highest net profits. He may even charge discriminating price to maximise his profits.

Monopoly is that conditions in which there is only one person/ institution producing/selling the entire quantity of a commodity and thereby having full control over the supply of that commodity. In monopoly there is no competition at all and the monopolist has full liberty to fix such a price of his commodity at which he is capable of getting maximum monopoly profits. Thus at the very outset it may be thought that a monopolist can pass on the entire burden of taxation on the consumers. But this is not correct. Although he has full control over the supply, even then he cannot charge the price arbitrarily as by doing so his object of getting the maximum profits may be defeated. Hence a monopolist always produces that much quantity and so fixes the price of his commodity that he is capable of securing maximum monopoly revenue. A monopolist can well secure the maximum monopoly revenue by fixing the price of his commodity at a point where the marginal cost is just equal to, marginal revenue. That is why, while shifting the burden of tax on consumers/buyers he always keeps in his mind that his maximum revenue is not reduced. Here the shifting of tax depends on the nature of tax imposed on the monopolist. A tax on a monopolist may be a lump sum tax such as licence fee or a tax proportionate to output or a tax proportionate to total sales or total revenue. We are discussing here the incidence of these taxes under monopoly.

Lump sum tax on the monopolist. If a lump sum tax or a, fixed amount of tax is levied on a monopolist, it becomes a part of his fixed cost. In other words, it does not in any way affect his marginal cost of production and it remains the same. A monopolist cannot pass on the lump sum tax on the consumers and the burden of such a tax is borne by him. However, if he tries to pass on the burden of such a tax by increasing the price or reducing the supply, his monopoly revenue will be reduced considerably as his marginal cost will not remain just equal to his marginal revenue. Taylor has aptly remarked, "This being the case, a tax which increases fixed costs will not change marginal costs. Thus, we see that such a tax, since it changes neither marginal costs nor marginal revenue does not change the quantity sold or the price at which it is sold, and the tax is not shifted forward." Although it is a fact that the levy of such a tax reduces the total revenue of a monopolist to some extent; but if he tries to shift the burden of tax on the consumers the fall in his total monopoly revenue will be even more. Thus he cannot pass on a lump sum tax on the consumers and he bears incidence of such a tax.

Tax proportionate to output. If a monopolist is required to pay a tax in proportion to his output, his marginal cost is raised and it becomes unprofitable, for him to sell his product at the old price. Therefore, he produces his production and sells his product at an increased price so as to keep his total monopoly revenue at the maximum. In this connection, Taylor has rightly remarked, "Taxes of the second category (taxes whose total amount varies with the quantity of production or sale, but are constant additions to variable cost per unit) are generally shifted forward. For marginal cost is increased by a constant amount throughout the whole schedule, creating a new intersection of marginal revenue and marginal cost and thus a new price and quantity." Thus we see that a tax proportionate to output can be shifted on to the consumers. But here again it may not be arbitrary. The shifting of tax will be affected by the relative elasticities of demand and supply.

Tax proportionate to total sales or total profits. If a tax is imposed in proportion to total sales or total profits of a monopolist, the burden of such a tax cannot be shifted on to the consumers as the amount of tax cannot be determined before-hand. It can be determined only after the monopolist has obtained his total revenue or he has disposed of his entire product. Thus a monopolist bears the incidence of such a tax.

4. EFFECTS OF TAXATION

We may study the economic effects of taxation under the following three headings.

1. Effects of taxation on production and growth.
2. Effects of taxation on distribution.
3. Other effects of taxation.

1. Effects of taxation on production and Growth

The effects of taxation on production and growth in the economy may be analysed under the following three heads:

1. Effects of taxation on peoples' ability to work save and invest.
2. Effects of taxation on peoples' will to work, save and invest.
3. Effects of taxation on allocation of resources between different trades and regions.

1. *Effects of Taxation on Ability to Work,* Save *and Invest.* When a tax is imposed on the consumer, it immediately reduces his purchasing power of net income because a part of his income is paid to the government as taxes. Consequently, the consumer is compelled to purchase a smaller bundle of commodities and services than before. This effect of tax is similar to the effect of inflation or high prices. The standard of living of consumers (taxpayers), therefore, falls unless the tax payment is accompanied by an increase in their income by the amount of tax. It means that the imposition of a tax reduces the ability of the taxpayer to work, save and invest.

If the tax burden falls on the poor people, it would curb the consumption of essential-to-life goods and services and would certainly reduce their standard of living and ability to work. Conversely, if the tax burden falls on the rich people, it would not curb the consumption, at the most it may reduce the consumption of only luxury goods as result of which their ability to work would not suffer impairment although it is certain that their ability to save would be reduced. In other words, a progressive tax system would reduce the ability to save. But sometimes a tax may prove helpful in increasing the efficiency to work of the taxpayers. For instance, if taxes are levied on those commodities which are harmful for health and efficiency as result of tax the, consumption of such goods would fall and it will have a healthy effect on peoples' efficiency to work.

The effect on ability to work may assume a cumulative form. Reduction in the purchasing power due to taxation would lower the standard of living which in turn would result in low efficiency. Lower efficiency would lead to lower income which would further lead to low efficiency. Similarly, if the tax reduces peoples' ability to save, it will lead to low capital formation because people would consume a major part of their income as a result of higher taxation on goods and services consumed by them. It will reduce their savings. Due to low savings capital formation will be low. The fall in capital formation will lead to low production and low level of income. This would further reduce the ability of people to save. Thus, the effect of taxation will assume a cumulative form.

The ability to invest is related with the ability to save although the two are not identical. As individual economic unit may be able to save but it may not be able to invest for numerous reasons. Similarly, an economic unit may not be able to save but it may be able to invest. Thus, for an individual economic saving may not be essential for investment. It might even borrow from financial institutions to finance its investment activities. However, for the economy as a whole investment is not possible unless savings are made. Given the fact that there exist financial institutions and a mechanism for collecting the community savings and bringing these savings to the investors, the level and pattern of investment will be greatly influenced by the structure, of taxation in the country.

If a tax is imposed on the consumers and if as a result of this the savings are reduced, smaller amount of savings will be available to the investors for productive ventures. Consequently, the overall level of investment in the country will fall. Similarly, the total capacity to invest is likely to decrease as retained profits of the business firms are taxed by the government.

It must, however, be mentioned that these harmful effects of taxation may, to a certain extent, be compensated or neutralised by the pattern of government expenditure. Reduction in investment which has resulted from people's low ability to save due to higher taxation may be partly or wholly offset by increasing the incomes of the people as a result of state expenditure. Similarly, the standard of living and the capacity to work of the taxpayers may not fall due to taxation if the various amenities are provided by the government in greater amount.

2. *Effects of Taxation on Will to Work, Save and Invest.* The effects of taxation on peoples' willingness to work, save and invest are partly due to monetary burden of the tax and partly due to the psychological state of the taxpayers. If an individual happens to secure a huge income suddenly from an unexpected source (for instance, if a person gets a windfall income on the death of a relative) and the government imposes

tax on such income this will produce no adverse effects on person's will to work, save and invest. The reason for this is that the person concerned has not made any endeavour to earn the income himself.

The income elasticity of demand can also influence the will of a person to work, save and invest. Since the income which the taxpayer earns by one kind of work or another is taken away by the government in the form of taxes, he loses incentive for work to earn further income. If the income demand of an individual is inelastic or if he happens to have a large family to support, he will work more consequent upon the imposition of the tax. In such a situation, tax acts as a spur to work harder. The reason for this is that he will have to earn more income in order to meet the requirements of his family. On the contrary, if the income demand of the individual is elastic or if he has only a small family to support, then his will to work may not be affected as a result of the imposition of the tax.

Likewise, the form of the tax may also affect the will to work and invest. It is universally recognised that direct taxes, particularly income-tax, have far greater adverse effect on incentives to work and invest. On the other hand, commodity taxation generally does not have any direct effect on these incentives of the individuals. This is so because in the case of direct tax, the taxpayer has to pay a certain amount of income directly to the government and obviously he will not be willing to work more and to invest more because a part of such efforts will have to be paid out to the government. On the other hand, indirect taxes are hidden in the prices of goods and services. Consequently, the average taxpayer is not fully aware of their burden and existence.

Although the taxpayer can pay some moderate rates of income and other direct taxes without much murmur, but high rates of direct taxes (which at certain stage may take away nearly 80 to 90 per cent of individuals' additional income) will certainly influence the willingness of individuals to work and save. Such high tax rates will not create incentive among the people to work more and invest more, rather these will induce people to evade and avoid the tax imposed by the government.

Again, a high rate of taxation on business profits will induce the business community to increase its business expenditure and reduce the corporate profitability. Earnings from investments, however, are usually taxed unevenly. The result is that differential taxation can bring about several influences on the types of invest-ment. For instance, if the investment in real estate—house building-is taxed lightly compared with profits from business, investment in housing will be encouraged. Similarly, industries which are allowed a high rate of depreciation allowance will find their net profitability higher and consequently will attract investment in preference to others. If some industries are exempted from taxation, then investment will be directed towards such industries. Thus, by imposing lower taxes on capital goods industries, their growth can be encouraged. It contributes to the capital formation and economic growth of the country.

If differential taxation is adopted in the context of certain chosen location of industries, then the industries will tend to shift to lower taxation regions. Thus, the government may to a great extent use its tax policy as an instrument to reduce the regional inequalities and imbalances in the economy.

3. *Effects of Taxation on Allocation of Resources between Different Trades and Regions.* The government may use its tax policy to divert the scarce resources of the country in the desired productive activities. Thus, taxation can influence not only size of production but also the pattern of production in the economy. The diversion of resource between different occupations and regions as a result of taxation may be favourable or unfavourable. High taxation on harmful drugs and commodities will raise the price of such products so much that the demand for these products will be curtailed considerably. Consequently, production of such products will be discouraged and resources engaged in their production will be gradually shifted to other industries which are useful for economic growth of the country. This is, a favourable effect of taxation on the location of resources. Similarly, tax concessions and exemptions on goods produced .in backward areas can help divert economic resources from economy's over-crowded areas to backward areas. This will, apart from promoting balanced regional economic development, lead to an equal distribution of wealth and reduce regional inequalities in the economy.

Conversely, if taxes are imposed on useful products which are not necessaries, there is the possibility of curtailment of the consumption and production of these products. Consequently, the demand and production will be shifted to less useful items. Such misallocation of resources will certainly not be in the interest of the community.

2. Effects of Taxation on Distribution

In modern times, taxes are frequently used as an effective instrument for reducing the inequalities of income and wealth in the country. In almost all countries, efforts are made to reduce economic inequalities through the imposition of progressive taxation. The greater the degree of progression in taxation, the easier it will be to reduce economic inequalities in the society. On the contrary, the greater the regressiveness in taxation, more glaring shall become the existing economic inequalities in the society. It is on account of this that the modern governments have rejected regressive taxation and have increasingly introduced progression in taxation. Income-tax, estate duty, wealth tax, expenditure tax, excess profit tax are of such a nature that they fetch revenue from rich sections of the community and thus help a great deal in bringing about the much needed reduction in the glaring existing, inequalities of income and wealth in the country.

Different taxes affect the distribution of income and wealth differently in the country. Wealth tax is helpful in reducing the inequalities of income as its rates can be made substantially progressive. Incometax and inheritance tax also reduce the inequalities of wealth as both these taxes can be made progressive. Similarly, poll tax, taxes on necessaries and commodities of wide use, etc. are not worth levying taxes as all such regressive taxes do not reduce the inequalities of income and wealth in the country. These taxes are, however, imposed for considerations other than their income and wealth distributional aspect.

Although commodity taxes, such as excise duties and sales tax, are generally regressive in nature and fall equally on the rich and the poor, yet, it is possible to select those goods which are generally consumed by the rich sections of the community for special taxation. High excise duties and sales tax levied on the luxury goods are based on this principle.

The superior brands of a commodity, say cigarettes, may be heavily taxed while the inferior or popular brand of the commodity may be exempted from impost. Similarly, different rates of sales tax may be levied on different commodities; a higher, rate of sales tax rate may be levied on deluxe goods consumed by the rich and lower sales tax rate may be prescribed for standard varieties. But the main difficulty here is that different rates of sales tax will result in complications in tax revenue collection. Thus, indirect taxes or commodity taxes do not generally have favourable distribu-tional effects.

3. Other Effects of Taxation

The other important effects of taxation can be discussed as under:

1. *Effects of Taxation on Employment.* According to some economists, taxation causes reduction in the employment opportunities and, consequently, contributes to high unemployment figures in the society. If the government does not impose heavy taxation on industries and trades, they can plough back their savings for industrial expansion thereby

providing the increasing employment' opportunities to the people in the country. But this argument is, in reality, not tenable because the revenue collected by the government through taxation is not wasted. On the other hand, it is invested in the developmental projects which increase employment in the economy. For example, the massive developmental expenditure incurred by the government of India under the five-year plans has significantly contributed to the creation of new employment opportunities in the country.

2. *Effects o/Taxation on Welfare.* Taxation has unfavourable effects on national welfare in as much as it leads to a decrease in the present and future expenditure. But the proceeds of taxation go to the public authorities which use these for public purposes. Heavy taxation may reduce production, particularly in the private sector of the economy. It may check capital formation and investment in industries. But taxation also produces some favourable effects. The purpose of some taxes is to reduce the consumption of harmful drugs. In the pre-prohibition days in India, heavy excise duties levied on liquor consumption were intended to reduce the consumption of liquor so that the health and efficiency of the people might improve.

In short, taxation creates favourable and unfavourable effects on national welfare. Government's tax policy should be framed as to reduce the unfavourable effects of taxation to the maximum and to produce the maximum revenue for the state with the minimum sacrifice to the taxpayer.

EXERCISES

1. What do you understand by incidence of tax? Differentiate between incidence and impact of taxation.
2. What do you mean by shifting of a tax? What are the important methods of shifting of a tax?
3. How do taxes affect production and distribution in an economy? Discuss.

Multiple Choice Questions

4. (*i*) By incidence of taxes is meant
   (*a*) the final resting point of the tax payment
   (*b*) shifting of taxation
   (*c*) impact of taxes
   (*d*) all of the above [*Ans.* (*a*)]

   (*ii*) The process of transferring the burden of the tax from one person to another is known as
   (*a*) impact of taxation
   (*b*) incidence of taxation
   (*c*) shifting of taxation
   (*d*) all of the above [*Ans.* (*c*)]

SELECT BIBLIOGRAPHY

Albert, L. Meyers, *Elements of Modern Economics,* Fourth edition.
Alfred Marshall, *Principles of Economics,* Eighth edition.
Allen, R.G.D., *Mathematical Analysis for Economist,* 1938.
—, *Mathematical Economics,* 1973.
Andrews, P.W.S., *Manufacturing Business,* 1949.
Arrow, K.J., *Social Choice and Individual Values,* 2nd edition, 1963.
Arrow, K.J. and Scitovsky, T. (eds.), *Readings in Welfare Economics,* 1952.
Asumakopulos, A., *Microeconomics,* 1978.
Bain, J.S. *Pricing, Distribution and Employment,* 1953.
Baumol, W.S., *Economic Theory and Operations Analysis,* 4th edition, 1977.
—, *Business Behaviour, Value and Growth,* 1959.
—, *Welfare Economics and the Theory of State,* 2nd edition, 1965.
Beeker, G.S., *Economic Theory,* 1971.
Bell, P.W. and Todaro, M.P., *Economic Theory,* 1971.
Bilas, Richard A, *Microeconomic Theory: A .Graphical Analysis,* 2nd edition, 1971.
Boulding, K.E., *Economic Analysis,* 1966.
Boulding, K.E. and Spivey, A, *Linear Programming and the Theory of the Firm,* 1960. Bowen, H.R., *Toward Socialist Economy,* 1948.
Briet, W.L. and Hochman, H.M., *Readings in Microeconomics,* 2nd edition, 1971.
Bruce, N. and Boadway, R., *Welfare Economics,* 1984.
Buchler Alfred G., *Public Finance,* 1948.
Calvo, P. and Waugh, G., *Microeconomics,* 1977.
Chamberlin, E.W., *Theory of Monopolistic Competition,* 7th edition, 1959.
Chenery, H.B. and Clark, P.G., *Interindustry Economics,* 1959.
Chiang, Alpha e., *Fundamental Methods of Mathematical Economics,* 1967.
Cohen, KJ. and Cyert, R.M., *Theory of the Firm,* 1965.
Cohen, KJ. and March, J.C., *A Behavioural Theory of the Firm,* 1963.
Dalton, *Public Finance,* 4th edition.
Dean, J., *Managerial Economics,* 1951.
Dobb, *Theories of Value and Distribution,* 1973.
Douglas Paul, H., *The Theory of Wages,* 1934.
Ellis. H.S., *A Survey o/Contemporary Economics,* 1948.
Ellsworth, PT, *International Economics,* 4th edition.
Fellner, W., *Modern Economic Analyses,* 1960.

Ferguson, C.E., *Microeconomic Theory,* Fifth edition, 1969.
Fleming, M., *Introduction to Economic Analysis;* 1967.
Friedman, M., *Essays* in *Positive Economics,* 1953.
—, *Price Theory,* 1962.
Gass, S.I., *Linear Programming,* 1958.
Gide Charles and Rist Charles, *A History of Economic Doctrine,* 1948.
Graaf, 1. de V., *Theoretical Welfare Economics,* 1957.
Gravel, H. arid Rees, R., *Microeconomics,* 1981.
Haley, B.F., *A Survey of Contemporary Economics.* 1952.
Handerson and Quandt, *Microeconomic Theory-A Mathematical Approche.* Third edition.
Hawkins, C.J., *Theory of the Firm,* 1973.
Hicks, 1.R., *Value and Capital,* 2/e, 1946.
—, *A Revision of Demand Theory,* 1956.
Hicks Ursula K., *Public Finance,* 1955.
Hirschleifer, J., *Price Theory and Its Applications,* 1975.
John F. Due, *Public Finance,* Fourth edition.
Johnston, J., *Statistical Cost Analysis,* 1960.
—, *Econometric Methods,* 3rd edition.
Kamerschen, D.R., *Readings in Microeconomics,* 1967.
Kirzner, I.M., *The Economic Point of View,* 1960.
Kindleberger, *International Economics,* Fourth edition.
Knight, F.H.,. *Risk, Uncertainty and Profit,* 1957.
Koutsoyiannis, A., *Modern Microeconomics,* 2/e, 1979.
Leftwich, R.H., *The Price System and Resource Allocation,* 1976.
Leibhafsky, H.H., *The Nature of Price Theory,* 1968.
Lerner, A.P., *The Economy of Control,* 1944.
Leontief, W.W., *The Structure of American Economy,* 1951.
Lewis, W.A., *The Theory of Economic Growth.*
Lipsey, R.G., *An Introduction to Positive Economics,* 5/e, 1972.
Little, I.M.D., *A Critique of Welfare Economics,* 2/e, 1957.
Lloyd, c., *Microeconomic Analysis,* 1967.
Machlup, F., *The Economics of Seller's Competition,* 1952.
Marris, R. T., *The Economic Theory of Managerial Capitalism,* 1964.
Marshall, A., *Principles of Economics,* 8/e, 1920.
Mansfield, E., *Microeconomics,* 3/e, 1979.
—, *Microeconomics: Selected Readings,* 3/e, 1979.
Mehta, J.K., *Public Finance,* 1965.
Miller, R.L., *Intermediate Microeconomics,* 1978.
Mill, J.S., *Principles of Political Economy,* Book V.
Mier & Baldwin, *Economic Development,* Fifth edition.
Mishan, E.J., *Welfare Economics,* 1964.
Musgrave, *Public Finance.* Third edition, 1959.
Myint, H., *Theories of Welfare Economics,* 1948.

Nath. S.K., *A Reappraisal of Welfare Economics.* 1969.
Neumann, J.V. and Morgenstern, O., *Theory of Games and Economic Behaviour. 2/e.* 1947 Newman Harber E., *An In Introduction to Public Finance,* 1968.
Nicholson, W., *Intermediate Microeconomics and Its Applications.* 1975.
Norris, R.T., *The Theory of Consumer's Demand.* Rev. ed., 1952.
Penrose, E.T., *The Theory of Growth of the Firm,* 1959.
Pen, J., *Income Distribution,* 1971.
Pigou, A.C., *The Economics of Welfare,* 4/e, 1932.
Prest, *Public Finance,* 1961,
Quirk, J, and Saposnick, *Introduction to General Equilibrium and Welfare Economics,* 1968, Reder, M,W., *Studies in the Welfare Economics,* 1947.
Robertson, D.H., *Utility and All That,* 1952,
Robbins, L, *An Essay on the Nature and Significance of Economic Science,* 2/e, 1935. Robinson, J., *The Economics of Imperfect Competition,* 1933,
Ryan, W.J.L. and Pearce, D.W., *Price Theory,* 1977.
Salvatore, M., *Microeconomic Theory,* 1976.
Samuelson, P.A., *Foundations of Economic Analysis,* 1947.
Samuelson, P.A, The Pure Theory of Public Expenditure, *Review of Economics and Statistics,* Nov. 1954.
Schubuk, M., *Strategy and Market Structure,* 1959.
Schumpeter, *The Theory of Economic Development,* 1955.
Scitovsky, T., *Welfare and Competition,* Rev. ed., 1971,
Shapiro, E., *Macroeconomic Analysis,* Fifth Edition, 1982.
Shepherd, R.W., *Cost and Production Functions,* 1953.
Shirras Findley, *The Science ofPublic Finance,* 1925.
Stigler, G.J. and Boulding, K.E. (eds.), *Readings in Price Theory,* 1952.
Stigler, G.J., *The Theory of Price,* 3/e, 1966.
Stonier, AW. and Hague, D.C., *A Textbook of Economic Theory,* 4/e, 1972.
Taylor, *The Economics of Public Finance,* macmillan, 1957.
Townsend, H. (ed.), *Price Theory,* 1971,
Triffin, R., *Monopolistic Competition and General Equilibrium Theory,* 1949.
Varian, H., *Microeconomic Analysis,* 1978.
Von Stackelberg, H., *The Theory 0/ the Market Economy,* 1952.
Watson, D.S., *Price Theory and Its Uses,2/e,* 1968.
Weintraub S., *Intermediate Price Theory,* 1964.
Winch, D.M., *Analytical Welfare Economics,* 1971,
Winfrey, John C., *Public Finance,* 1973.
Wiu, S.Y. and Pontney, *An Introduction to Modern Demand Theory,* 1967.
Zeuthen, F., *Economic Theory and Method,* 1955.